Understanding American Government

14E

Understanding American Government

SUSAN WELCH
The Pennsylvania State University

JOHN GRUHL
University of Nebraska—Lincoln

SUE THOMAS
Pacific Institute for Research and Evaluation

MARYANNE BORRELLI
Connecticut College

WADSWORTH
CENGAGE Learning

Australia • Brazil • Japan • Korea • Mexico • Singapore • Spain • United Kingdom • United States

**Understanding American Government,
14th Edition**
Susan Welch, John Gruhl, Sue Thomas,
MaryAnne Borrelli

Executive Editor: Carolyn Merrill

Development Editor: Ohlinger Publishing Services

Assistant Editor: Patrick Roach

Media Editor: Laura Hildebrand

Brand Manager: Lydia LeStar

Market Development Manager:
Kyle Zimmerman

Sr. Art Director: Linda May

Manufacturing Planner: Fola Orekoya

Sr. Rights Acquisition Specialist: Jennifer
Meyer-Dare

Production Service: Cenveo Publisher Services

Cover and Interior Designer: Rokusek Design

Cover Image: ©Shutterstock

Compositor: Cenveo Publisher Services

For product information and technology assistance, contact us at
Cengage Learning Customer & Sales Support, 1-800-354-9706
For permission to use material from this text or product,
submit all requests online at **www.cengage.com/permissions.**
Further permissions questions can be emailed to
permissionrequest@cengage.com.

Library of Congress Control Number: 2012954113

Student Edition:

ISBN-13: 978-1-133-95574-0

ISBN-10: 1-133-95574-6

Wadsworth
20 Channel Center Street
Boston, MA 02210
USA

Cengage Learning is a leading provider of customized learning solutions
with office locations around the globe, including Singapore, the United
Kingdom, Australia, Mexico, Brazil and Japan. Locate your local office at
international.cengage.com/region

Cengage Learning products are represented in Canada by Nelson Education, Ltd.

For your course and learning solutions, visit **www.cengage.com.**

Purchase any of our products at your local college store or at our
preferred online store **www.cengagebrain.com.**

Instructors: Please visit **login.cengage.com** and log in to access
instructor-specific resources.

Printed in the United States of America
1 2 3 4 5 6 7 21 20 19 18 17

Brief Contents

Winner's Electoral College Vote %	Winner's Popular Vote %	Congress	House		Senate	
			Majority Party	Minority Party	Majority Party	Minority Party
**	No popular	1st	38 Admin†	26 Opp	17 Admin	9 Opp
	vote	2nd	37 Fed††	33 Dem-R	16 Fed	13 Dem-R
**	No popular	3rd	57 Dem-R	48 Fed	17 Fed	13 Dem-R
	vote	4th	54 Fed	52 Dem-R	19 Fed	13 Dem-R
**	No popular	5th	58 Fed	48 Dem-R	20 Fed	12 Dem-R
	vote	6th	64 Fed	42 Dem-R	19 Fed	13 Dem-R
HR**	No popular	7th	69 Dem-R	36 Fed	18 Dem-R	13 Fed
	vote	8th	402 Dem-R	39 Fed	25 Dem-R	9 Fed
92.0	No popular	9th	116 Dem-R	25 Fed	27 Dem-R	7 Fed
	vote	10th	118 Dem-R	24 Fed	28 Dem-R	6 Fed
69.7	No popular	11th	94 Dem-R	48 Fed	28 Dem-R	6 Fed
	vote	12th	108 Dem-R	36 Fed	30 Dem-R	6 Fed
59.0	No popular	13th	112 Dem-R	68 Fed	27 Dem-R	9 Fed
	vote	14th	117 Dem-R	65 Fed	25 Dem-R	11 Fed
84.3	No popular	15th	141 Dem-R	42 Fed	34 Dem-R	10 Fed
	vote	16th	156 Dem-R	27 Fed	35 Dem-R	7 Fed
99.5	No popular	17th	158 Dem-R	25 Fed	44 Dem-R	4 Fed
	vote	18th	187 Dem-R	26 Fed	44 Dem-R	4 Fed
HR	39.1†††	19th	105 Admin	97 Dem-J	26 Admin	20 Dem-J
		20th	119 Dem-J	94 Admin	28 Dem-J	20 Admin
68.2	56.0	21st	139 Dem	74 Nat R	26 Dem	22 Nat R
		22nd	141 Dem	58 Nat R	25 Dem	21 Nat R
76.6	54.5	23rd	147 Dem	53 AntiMas	20 Dem	20 Nat R
		24th	145 Dem	98 Whig	27 Dem	25 Whig
57.8	50.9	25th	108 Dem	107 Whig	30 Dem	18 Whig
		26th	124 Dem	118 Whig	28 Dem	22 Whig
79.6	52.9					
–	52.9	27th	133 Whig	102 Dem	28 Whig	22 Dem
		28th	142 Dem	79 Whig	28 Whig	25 Dem
61.8	49.6	29th	143 Dem	77 Whig	31 Dem	25 Whig
		30th	115 Whig	108 Dem	36 Dem	21 Whig
56.2	47.3	31st	112 Dem	109 Whig	35 Dem	25 Whig
–	–	32nd	140 Dem	88 Whig	35 Dem	24 Whig
85.8	50.9	33rd	159 Dem	71 Whig	38 Dem	22 Whig
		34th	108 Rep	83 Dem	40 Dem	15 Rep
58.8	45.6	35th	118 Dem	92 Rep	36 Dem	20 Rep
		36th	114 Rep	92 Dem	36 Dem	26 Rep
59.4	39.8	37th	105 Rep	43 Dem	31 Rep	10 Dem
		38th	102 Rep	75 Dem	36 Rep	9 Dem
91.0	55.2					
–	–	39th	149 Union	42 Dem	42 Union	10 Dem
		40th	143 Rep	49 Dem	42 Rep	11 Dem
72.8	52.7	41st	149 Rep	63 Dem	56 Rep	11 Dem
		42nd	134 Rep	104 Dem	52 Rep	17 Dem
81.9	55.6	43rd	194 Rep	92 Dem	49 Rep	19 Dem
		44th	169 Rep	109 Dem	45 Rep	29 Dem
50.1	47.9†††	45th	153 Dem	140 Rep	39 Rep	36 Dem
		46th	149 Dem	130 Rep	42 Dem	33 Rep
58.0	48.3	47th	147 Rep	135 Dem	37 Rep	37 Dem
–	–	48th	197 Dem	118 Rep	38 Rep	36 Dem
54.6	48.5	49th	183 Dem	140 Rep	43 Rep	34 Dem
		50th	169 Dem	152 Rep	39 Rep	37 Dem

Source for election data: Svend Peterson, *A Statistical History of American Presidential Elections*. New York: Frederick Ungar Publishing, 1963. Updates: Richard Scammon, *America Votes* 19. Washington D.C.: Congressional Quarterly, 1991; *Congressional Quarterly Weekly Report*, Nov. 7, 1992, p. 3552.

Abbreviations:

Admin = Administration supporters
AntiMas = Anti-Masonic
Dem = Democratic
Dem-R = Democratic-Republican
Fed = Federalist

Dem-J = Jacksonian Democrats
Nat R = National Republican
Opp = Opponents of administration
Rep = Republican
Union = Unionist

Contents

Part 3 INSTITUTIONS

Chapter 9 Congress 218

Chapter 10 The Presidency 252

Preface

In 2008 and 2012 young people voted at a higher rate than they have in decades. We write this book in the hope that a greater understanding of and appreciation for American government may encourage those not already engaged in civic and political activities to become more active citizens.

With round-the-clock news and opinions offered by cable television and talk radio, and the thousands of Internet sites offering continual commentary, it is hard to escape from politics. Yet access to information has brought neither enlightenment nor civility to political discussions. Information is not always factual, and opinions often lack fundamental knowledge and context. The continual supply of political opinion, and the ability of all of us to read and hear opinions only of those we agree with, has led to a higher degree of political polarization than we have seen in decades.

We hope students, as they proceed through the book, will practice their critical thinking skills, skills that have wide application throughout their lives. For example, we can describe the substance of the U.S. Constitution and the debates of the Founders as they wrote and ratified it. These are factual. We can also describe the immediate differences that emerged among the Founders about what particular clauses meant and how these differences play out in discussions over political issues today. These are mostly factual, but they do reflect some interpretation as historical debates are summarized and applied to current issues.

In American politics, much of our current polarization is focused on the role and size of government. On some issues, such as health care, Democrats want a more activist government, and on others, such as the regulating of personal behavior, Republicans do. Conflicts over the size and role of government led us to focus on why government is the size and scope that it is. This question is central to understanding government and how it works. After all, government does not create itself; its growth in size and activity reflects the demands placed on it over the decades by citizens. The nature of those demands and why they occur are important to understanding the growth of government and the reactions against it. In a democracy, we assume government is responsive to the citizens, primarily through elections. But some of the constitutional features of our government, the systems of checks and balances, make it, by design, less than responsive. Some argue that the growth of government has not been responsive to the American people, while others argue that over the years Americans have had plenty of opportunities to define the scope and size of government, and they have done so.

Beyond the specifics of current issues, we hope students reading this book will come to understand that much about politics is predictable and rooted in the larger principles of government and political culture. The election of a black president was historic, but predictions of a Democratic victory in 2008 were based on well-known rules of politics—incumbents tend to be voted out when they are unpopular and in times of economic hardship. In 2012, the economy was growing only very slowly, seeming to bode trouble for an incumbent president. Yet the economy's rebound from the Great Recession and Obama's personal popularity combined to predict that he would be reelected. These and other historical regularities of politics are important in interpreting the news of the day in the context of historical trends.

We want to convey to students, whether they are taking this course as an elective or as a requirement, why it is important for every American to understand how our government functions. We hope they find that it is also an interesting and often exciting subject that has relevance to almost every aspect of their lives.

THE ORGANIZATION AND CONTENTS OF THE BOOK

The Introduction sets the stage for a consideration of the size and role of government by looking at the Founders' conceptions of government, how and why government has grown in different historical periods, Americans' general ambivalence about government, and then why antigovernment opinions have taken root during the Obama years.

The organization of the book is straightforward. After the Introduction and material on the American people and core political values, the Constitution, and federalism, the book covers forms of political participation and then institutions. Civil liberties and rights are treated after the chapter on the judiciary. Policy modules on economic, health care, environmental, and foreign policy conclude the book.

But the book is flexible enough—the chapters may stand alone—so that instructors can modify the order of the chapters. Some instructors will prefer to cover institutions before process. Others may prefer to discuss civil liberties and rights when discussing the Constitution.

CHANGES IN THE FOURTEENTH EDITION

Introducing Coauthor MaryAnne Borrelli

For this edition, we welcome a new coauthor to our text: MaryAnne Borrelli, who replaces our longtime coauthor Susan Rigdon. Professor Borrelli brings her wealth of experience as an undergraduate teacher at Connecticut College. She specializes in contemporary U.S. politics and government, women and U.S. politics, environmental policy, bureaucracy, and Congress. She is a fellow with the Goodwin-Niering Center for the Environment and the Joy Shechtman Mankoff Center for Teaching & Learning. Professor Borrelli was a member of an American Political Science Association panel that evaluated more than a hundred introductory American government texts and presented our text with an award for having the best coverage of women.

New Features

This fourteenth edition includes coverage of the 2012 election. It also includes new pedagogical features. Each chapter identifies **Learning Objectives** at the beginning and ends with a **Summary** and **Discussion Questions**. These features highlight the main points of the chapter and help your students identify and understand them. Each chapter also has a box, **CourseReader**, based on a recent article relevant to the content of the chapter. Students can access the article online and after reading it can answer the questions in the box. This feature encourages students to combine their text reading with outside reading for fuller understanding.

Flexible Policy Coverage

For this new edition, we've shortened the policy chapters and focused them on contemporary policy issues. Thus "Economic Policy" has become "Focus On...Spending and Taxing," and "Health Policy" has become "Focus On...Health Care Reform." "Environmental Policy," which was a new chapter in the last edition, is now "Focus On...Environmental Policy," with emphasis on global warming and climate change. "Foreign Policy," now "Focus On...Foreign Policy," retains some breadth but also has been shortened and emphasizes four contemporary foreign policy issues. We hope that you and your students will appreciate the more flexible ways you can use these shorter, policy-focused modules. If, for example, you want to cover deficits or taxes, you can assign the "Focus On...Spending and Taxing" without requiring your students to read a long and more comprehensive chapter. You can slip the Focus module into your semester or quarter schedule without committing too much of your course to the area.

Shorter, Substantive Chapters, Up-to-Date Content

We've also shortened the first fourteen chapters of the book, streamlining them where we could but retaining the interesting examples, anecdotes, and quotations that bring politics to life. This fourteenth edition is 100 pages shorter than the thirteenth edition.

This book has a reputation for clear, straightforward writing. We've continued to hone the writing, while streamlining the chapters, to make the text even more clear and to maintain its reputation as a book that is accessible as well as very substantive.

HALLMARK FEATURES

In addition to including the new pedagogical features just described—Learning Objectives, Summary, and Discussion Questions—each chapter retains some features from the previous editions. The opening section, called "**Talking Points**," is designed to draw students into the chapter. The section features a decision or example of a policy, policy makers, or political debates relevant to the chapter. For example, in Chapter 12 ("The Judiciary"), Talking Points addresses the Supreme Court's decision to uphold the individual mandate of the Affordable Care Act. In Chapter 3 ("Federalism"), Talking Points focuses on state attempts to regulate immigration, and in Chapter 8 ("Elections"), the focus is on negative campaigning.

American Diversity boxes illustrate the impact of the gender, racial, and economic diversity of the American population on political life.

Behind the Scenes boxes examine events, strategies, or other aspects of politics that are illuminating but not widely publicized. These boxes pull back the curtain and shine a spotlight to give students a better understanding of what occurred. For example, a Chapter 8 ("Elections") box describes the spontaneous interchanges between candidates and their supporters on the rope lines following stump speeches and other campaign events. A Chapter 14 ("Civil Rights") box reveals the early efforts to initiate testing, and then halt testing, of women pilots who hoped to become astronauts.

Thinking about Democracy questions ask students to consider how democratic a particular process or institution may be. This feature is intended to alert students to the fact that democracy is not a simple concept and that our Constitution and practices include both democratic and undemocratic features. **Constitution icons**, appear when the text of the Constitution is referred to, making it easy to reference the document in the Appendix and to see how the Constitution deals with the topic at hand. The purpose is to call students' attention to how this founding document shapes our institutions and processes.

Key terms are boldfaced within the text and defined in the Glossary.

We are delighted to have the opportunity to write this fourteenth edition and to improve the text further in ways suggested by our students and readers. We have been extremely pleased by the reaction of instructors and students to our first thirteen editions. We were especially gratified to have won, three times, the American Government Textbook Award from the Women's Caucus for Political Science of the American Political Science Association.

UNDERSTANDING AMERICAN GOVERNMENT: THE HALLMARK TEXTBOOK

It is the leader in DIVERSITY coverage:

- The book emphasizes the significance of our ethnic, religious, and economic diversity in the shaping and implementation of American government, as well as in our historic and future challenges. This important premise is first introduced as the framework for Chapter 1: "The American People" starting on page 1.
- The treatment of women, racial and ethnic minorities, and other marginalized groups is the best on the market. See, for example, the well-respected chapters "Civil Liberties" starting on page 321 and "Civil Rights" starting on page 357.
- *Understanding American Government* is a three-time winner of the American Government Textbook Award for the Best Treatment of Women in Politics, by the Women's Caucus for Political Science. After winning this award three times, the book was put in the caucus's "Hall of Fame."
- Lively American Diversity boxes illustrate the impact of the American population's social diversity on politics. See:
  - *Equality and the Rise of the "Birthers"* p. 26
  - *Founding Mothers* p. 36
  - *Learning Civics State by State* p. 71
  - *Support for a Woman in the White House* p. 78
  - *Media Habits of Men and Women* p. 100
  - *The Origin of Gay and Lesbian Rights Groups* p. 133
  - *Organizing Protest: The Montgomery Bus Boycott* p. 144
  - *The Tea Party as a Third Party?* p. 154
  - *Blacks and Latinos in Office* p. 176
  - *Women in Office* p. 178
  - *Racism in the 2008 Campaign* p. 202
  - *Congress Is Not a Cross Section of America* p. 222
  - *Presidential Candidates: The Pool Deepens, but…* p. 254
  - *Women and People of Color in the Federal Bureaucracy* p. 302
  - *Do Women Judges Matter?* p. 319
  - *Anti-Semitism on the Bench* p. 330
  - *Accommodating and Balancing* p. 354
  - *Black Masters, Red Masters* p. 378
  - *Pain of Recession Is Unevenly Spread* p. 422
  - *Lack of Access to Medical Care Can Affect Life Outcome* p. 446
  - *Environmental Justice* p. 462
  - *Lobbying for the Old Country* p. 485

It has CURRENCY and uses respected SCHOLARSHIP:

- The text, citations, and photo program have been thoroughly updated to include current events through the 2010 election results, cutting-edge research, and the latest scholarship. See Chapter 8: "Elections" starting on page 172 as just one example.

It encourages CRITICAL THINKING and gives an EVALUATIVE, NUANCED VIEW of American government:

- *Thinking about Democracy* questions appear periodically within the narrative and ask readers to consider whether a particular process or institution being discussed is democratic or not. Students become alert to the fact that democracy is not a simple concept and that our Constitution and our practices include both democratic and undemocratic features. See pages 40 and 238 for two examples.

Its ENGAGING writing and features spark students' interest and give them a BEHIND THE SCENES look at American government:

- *Behind the Scenes* boxes give readers a fascinating glimpse into interesting and important aspects of politics not widely publicized. See *An Accidental Classic* on page 63 and *The Rope Line* on page 192 for a few examples.

It uses an ACCLAIMED PHOTOGRAPHY and ILLUSTRATIONS program:

- The art program, which includes carefully chosen photographs, cartoons, and figures, brings the subject matter alive for students. Instructors praise the authors' use of candid, powerful images to reinforce important concepts, relay America's rich diversity, address difficult issues in our country's history and present political landscape, and maintain interest in the topic. Flip through the book, and the photo program will quickly draw you in.

SUPPLEMENTS FOR INSTRUCTORS

For details, please contact your Cengage representative or visit www.cengage.com/sso.

Free Companion Website for *Understanding American Government*, 14e

- ISBN-13: 9781285057859
- This password-protected website for instructors features all of the free student assets plus an Instructor's Manual,

book-specific PowerPoint® presentations, a Resource Integration Guide, and a test bank. Access your resources by logging into your account at www.cengage.com/login.

CourseReader for *Understanding American Government*, 14e

- *Understanding American Government* with Printed Access Card ISBN-13: 9781133955740
- Printed Access Card ISBN-13: 9781111479954
- Instant Access Code ISBN-13: 9781111479978
- In addition to the overviews of important political science theories and quoted excerpts included in the book, we have selected certain readings that highlight the focus of each chapter. Assigning readings can often be a difficult process. Within each chapter, you will come across a reading assignment that is easily accessible within the Cengage Learning CourseReader. We have designed the CourseReader selections to tie in seamlessly with the section material. Keeping in mind the amount of time today's busy students can allocate to extra reading, we handpicked a reading for each chapter that will add the most to their study, reinforce the concepts from the text, and help them apply what they've learned to events around them. You may assign the questions that accompany the readings as graded or completion-based homework or use them to spark in-class discussion.

The readings we've recommended for each chapter can be assigned without any additional set-up, or you can choose to create and customize a reader specifically for your class. CourseReader: American Government allows you to create your reader, your way, in just minutes. This affordable, fully customizable online reader provides access to thousands of permissions-cleared readings, articles, primary sources, and audio and video selections from the regularly updated Gale research library database.

Each selection opens with a descriptive introduction to provide context and concludes with critical thinking and multiple-choice questions to reinforce key points. CourseReader is loaded with convenient tools like highlighting, printing, note taking, and downloadable MP3 audio files for each reading. It can be bundled with your current textbook, sold alone, or integrated into your learning management system. CourseReader 0-30 allows access to up to 30 selections in the reader.

Please contact your Cengage sales representative for details or, for a demo, please visit us at www.cengage .com/coursereader. To access CourseReader materials, go to www.cengage.com/sso, click on "Create a New Faculty Account," and fill out the registration page. Once you are in your new SSO account, search for "CourseReader" from your dashboard and select

"CourseReader: American Government." Then click "CourseReader 0-30: American Government Instant Access Code" and click "Add to my bookshelf." To access the live CourseReader, click on "CourseReader 0-30: American Government" under "Additional resources" on the right side of your dashboard.

Election 2012: An American Government Supplement

- Printed Access Card ISBN-13: 9781285090931
- Instant Access Code ISBN-13: 9781285420080
- Written by John Clark and Brian Schaffner, this booklet addresses the 2012 congressional and presidential races, with real-time analysis and references.

Political Science CourseMate for *Understanding American Government*, 14e

- Printed Access Card ISBN-13: 9781285057835
- Instant Access Code ISBN-13: 9781285057828
- Cengage Learning's Political Science CourseMate brings course concepts to life with interactive learning, study tools, and exam preparation tools that support the printed textbook. Use **Engagement Tracker** to assess student preparation and engagement in the course, and watch student comprehension soar as your class works with the textbook-specific website. An **interactive eBook** allows students to take notes, highlight, search, and interact with embedded media. Other resources include video activities, animated learning modules, simulations, case studies, interactive quizzes, and timelines.

The American Government NewsWatch is a real-time news and information resource, updated daily, that includes interactive maps, videos, podcasts, and hundreds of articles from leading journals, magazines, and newspapers from the United States and the world. Also included is the **KnowNow! American Government Blog**, which highlights three current events stories per week and consists of a succinct analysis of the story, multimedia, and discussion-starter questions. Access your course via www.cengage.com/login.

PowerLecture DVD with ExamView® for *Understanding American Government*, 14e

- ISBN-13: 9781285057798
  An all-in-one multimedia resource for class preparation, presentation, and testing, this DVD includes Microsoft® PowerPoint® slides, a test bank in both Microsoft® Word and ExamView® formats, online polling and JoinIn™ clicker questions, an Instructor's Manual, and a Resource Integration Guide.

The book-specific **PowerPoint® slides** of lecture outlines, as well as photos, figures, and tables from the text, make it easy for you to assemble lectures for your course, while the **media-enhanced slides** help bring your lecture to life with audio and video clips, animated learning modules illustrating key concepts, tables, statistical charts, graphs, and photos from the book as well as outside sources.

The **test bank**, revised by James Goss of Tarrant County College, offered in Microsoft Word® and ExamView® formats, includes 60+ multiple-choice questions with answers and page references along with 10 essay questions for each chapter. ExamView® features a user-friendly testing environment that allows you to publish not only traditional paper- and computer-based tests but also Web-deliverable exams. JoinIn™ offers "clicker" questions covering key concepts, enabling instructors to incorporate student response systems into their classroom lectures.

The **Instructor's Manual,** revised by Sharon Manna of North Lake College, includes learning objectives, chapter outlines, summaries, discussion questions, class activities and project suggestions, tips on integrating media into your class, and suggested readings and Web resources. JoinIn™ offers "clicker" questions covering key concepts, enabling instructors to incorporate student response systems into their classroom lectures. A **Resource Integration Guide** provides a chapter-by-chapter outline of all available resources to supplement and optimize learning. Contact your Cengage representative to receive a copy upon adoption.

The Wadsworth News DVD for American Government 2014

- ISBN-13: 9781285053455
- This collection of two- to five-minute video clips on relevant political issues serves as a great lecture or discussion launcher.

SUPPLEMENTS FOR STUDENTS

Free Companion Website for *Understanding American Government*, 14e

- Access chapter-specific interactive learning tools, including flashcards, quizzes, and more, in your companion website, accessed through www.cengagebrain.com.

CourseMate Political Science CourseMate for *Understanding American Government*, 14e

- Cengage Learning's Political Science CourseMate brings course concepts to life with interactive learning, study tools, and exam preparation tools that support the printed textbook. The more you study, the better the results. Make the most of your study time by accessing everything you need to succeed in one place. Read your textbook, take notes, watch videos, read case studies, take practice quizzes, and more—online with CourseMate. CourseMate also gives you access to the American Government **NewsWatch website,** a real-time news and information resource updated daily, and **KnowNow!**—the go-to blog about current events in American government. In addition, CourseMate for The Enduring Democracy includes "**The Connections App,**" an interactive Web app that helps you better understand the relationship between historical and current events and their connection with basic concepts.

Purchase instant access via CengageBrain or via a printed access card in your bookstore. Visit **www .cengagebrain.com** for more information. CourseMate should be purchased only when assigned by your instructor as part of your course.

ACKNOWLEDGMENTS

We would like to thank the many people who have aided and sustained us during the lengthy course of this project. First, we thank Michael Steinman and John Comer, our original coauthors, and Susan Rigdon, our longtime coauthor. The book still reflects their insights and efforts. Our current and former University of Nebraska and Penn State colleagues have been most tolerant and helpful as we've written and rewritten this book over the years. We thank them all.

We are also grateful to the many reviewers of our manuscript and earlier editions of the book, as listed here. Without their assistance the book would have been less accurate, less complete, and less lively. And thanks, too, to those instructors and students who have used the book and relayed their comments and suggestions to us. The students in our classes have provided invaluable reactions to previous editions.

Our editors at Cengage Publishing also deserve our thanks. We are grateful to Acquisitions Editor Anita Devine for her guidance and vision in preparing this edition. We are also grateful for the continued support of Executive Editor Carolyn Merrill.

Reviewers of the New Edition

Victor Eno, *Florida Agricultural & Mechanical University*
Donna Godwin, *Trinity Valley Community College*
Jack Goodyear, *Dallas Baptist University*
Brian Kreowski, *Cuesta Community College*
Khalil Marrar, *The University of Chicago*
Wendy Martinek, *Binghamton University*
Narges Rabii, *Santiago Canyon College*
Joanna Sabo, *Monroe County Community College*
Arlene Sanders, *Delta State University*
Daniel Sweeney, *University of Scranton*
Robert Whitaker, *Hudson Valley Community College*

Reviewers of Previous Editions

Alan Abramowitz, *State University of New York at Stony Brook;* Larry Adams, *Baruch College–City University of New York;* Danny M. Adkison, *Oklahoma State University;* James Alt, *Harvard University;* Margery Marzahn Ambrosius, *Kansas State University;* Kevin Bailey, *North Harris Community College;* Bethany Barratt, *Roosevelt University;* Kennette M. Benedict, *Northwestern University;* Russell Benjamin, *Northeastern Illinois University;* James Benze, *Washington and Jefferson College;* Melinda K. Blade, *Academy of Our Lady of Peace;* Timothy Bledsoe, *Wayne State University;* Jon Bond, *Texas A&M University;* Paul R. Brace, *New York University;* Joseph V. Brogan, *La Salle University;* James R. Brown Jr., *Central Washington University;* Kent M. Brudney, *Cuesta Community College;* Chalmers Brumbaugh, *Elon College;* Alan D. Buckley, *Santa Monica College;* Richard G. Buckner Jr., *Santa Fe Community College;* Ronald Busch, *Cleveland State University;* Bert C. Buzan, *California State University–Fullerton;* Carl D. Cavalli, *Memphis State University;* Stefanie Chambers, *Trinity College;* Richard A. Champagne, *University of Wisconsin, Madison;* Mark A. Cichock, *University of Texas at Arlington;* Michael D. Cobb, *North California State University;* Michael Connelly, *Southwestern Oklahoma State University;* Gary Copeland, *University of Oklahoma;* George H. Cox Jr., *Georgia Southern College;* Paige Cubbison, *Miami-Dade University;* Landon Curry, *Southwest Texas State University;* Rebecca Deen, *University of Texas at Arlington;* Jack DeSario, *Case Western Reserve University;* Robert E. DiClerico, *West Virginia University;* Ernest A. Dover Jr., *Midwestern State University;* Dennis Driggers, *California State University–Fresno;* Georgia Duerst-Lahti, *Beloit College;* Lois Duke-Whitaker, *Georgia Southern University;* David V. Edwards, *University of Texas at Austin;* Ann H. Elder, *Illinois State University;* Ghassan E. El-Eid, *Butler University;* C. Lawrence Evans, *College of William and Mary;* Dennis Falcon, *Cerritos Community College;* Rhodell J. Fields, *St. Petersburg College;* Robert Glen Findley, *Odessa College;* Murray Fischel, *Kent State University;* Bobbe Fitzhugh, *Eastern Wyoming College;* Jeff Fox, *Catawba College;* Stephen I. Frank, *St. Cloud State University;* Marianne Fraser, *University of Utah;* Jarvis Gamble, *Owens Community College;* Sonia R. Garcia, *St. Mary's University;* David Garrison, *Collin County Community College;* Phillip L. Gianos, *California State University–Fullerton;* Doris A. Graber, *University of Illinois–Chicago;* Michael Graham, *San Francisco State University;* Ruth M. Grubel, *University of Wisconsin–Whitewater;* Stefan D. Haag, *Austin Community College;* Larry M. Hall, *Belmont University;* Edward Hapham, *University of Texas–Dallas;* Peter O. Haslund, *Santa Barbara City College;* Richard P. Heil, *Fort Hays State University;* Peggy Heilig, *University of Illinois at Urbana;* Craig Hendricks, *Long Beach City College;* Marjorie Hershey, *Indiana University;* Kay Hofer, *Southwest Texas State University;* Samuel B. Hoff, *Delaware State College;* Robert D. Holsworth, *Virginia Commonwealth University;*

Jesse C. Horton, *San Antonio College;* Gerald Houseman, *Indiana University;* Timothy Howard, *North Harris College;* Peter G. Howse, *American River College;* David W. Hunt, *Triton College;* Bernard-Thompson Ikegwuoha, *Green River Community College;* Pamela Imperato, *University of North Dakota;* Jerald Johnson, *University of Vermont;* Loch Johnson, *University of Georgia;* Terri Johnson, *University of Wisconsin–Green Bay;* Evan M. Jones, *St. Cloud State University;* Joseph F. Jozwiak Jr., *Texas A&M University–Kingsville;* Matt Kerbel, *Villanova University;* Marshall R. King, *Maryville College;* Orma Lindford, *Kansas State University;* Peter J. Longo, *University of Nebraska–Kearney;* Roger C. Lowery, *University of North Carolina–Wilmington;* H. R. Mahood, *Memphis State University;* Kenneth M. Mash, *East Stroudsburg University;* Alan C. Melchior, *Florida International University;* A. Nick Minton, *University of Massachusetts–Lowell;* Matthew Moen, *University of Maine;* Kenneth W. Moffett, *Southern Illinois University;* Michael K. Moore, *University of Texas at Arlington;* Michael Nelson, *Vanderbilt University;* Bruce Nesmith, *Coe College;* Walter Noelke, *Angelo State University;* Peter Parker, *Truman State University;* Thomas Payette, *Henry Ford Community College;* Theodore B. Pedeliski, *University of North Dakota;* Jerry Perkins, *Texas Tech University;* Toni Phillips, *University of Arkansas;* C. Herman Pritchett, *University of California–Santa Barbara;* Charles Prysby, *University of North Carolina–Greensboro;* Sandra L. Quinn-Musgrove, *Our Lady of the Lake University;* Donald R. Ranish, *Antelope Valley Community College;* Catherine C. Reese, *Arkansas State University;* Linda Richter, *Kansas State University;* Bernard Rowan, *Chicago State University;* Jerry Sandvick, *North Hennepin Community College;* James Richard Sauder, *University of New Mexico;* Eleanor A. Schwab, *South Dakota State University;* K. L. Scott, *University of Central Florida;* Earl Sheridan, *University of North Carolina–Wilmington;* Edward Sidlow, *Northwestern University;* Cynthia Slaughter, *Angelo State University;* Rorie Solberg, *Oregon State University;* John Squibb, *Lincolnland Community College;* Glen Sussman, *Old Dominion University;* M. H. Tajalli-Tehrani, *Southwest Texas State University;* Kristine A. Thompson, *Moorehead State University;* R. Mark Tiller, *Austin Community College;* Gordon J. Tolle, *South Dakota State University;* Susan Tolleson-Rinehart, *Texas Tech University;* Ronnie Tucker, *Shippensburg University;* Bernadyne Weatherford, *Rowan College of New Jersey;* Richard Unruh, *Fresno Pacific College;* Jay Van Bruggen, *Clarion University of Pennsylvania;* David Van Heemst, *Olivet Nazarene University;* Paul Vayer, *Brevard Community College–Cocoa;* Kenny Whitby, *University of South Carolina;* Donald C. Williams, *Western New England College;* James Matthew Wilson, *Southern Methodist University;* John H. Wilson Jr., *Itawamba Community College;* Clifford J. Wirth, *University of New Hampshire;* Ann Wynia, *North Hennepin Community College;* Alex H. Xiao, *Sacramento City College;* and Mary D. Young, *Southwestern Michigan College.*

About the Authors

SUSAN WELCH received her AB and PhD degrees from the University of Illinois at Urbana-Champaign. She is currently Dean of the College of Liberal Arts and Professor of Political Science at the Pennsylvania State University. Her teaching and research areas include legislatures, state and urban politics, and women and minorities in politics. She has edited the *American Politics Quarterly*.

JOHN GRUHL is a Professor of Political Science. He received his AB from DePauw University in Greencastle, Indiana, and his PhD from the University of California at Santa Barbara. Since joining the University of Nebraska faculty in 1976, he has taught and researched in the areas of judicial process, criminal justice, and civil rights and liberties. He has won University of Nebraska campus-wide and system-wide distinguished teaching awards and has become a charter member of the University's Academy of Distinguished Teachers.

SUE THOMAS is Senior Research Scientist at the Pacific Institute for Research and Evaluation (PIRE). Prior to joining PIRE, she served as Associate Professor of Government and Director of Women's Studies at Georgetown University. She received her AB and MEd from UCLA, and her PhD from University of Nebraska, Lincoln. Her research specialty is women and politics, and among her publications are *How Women Legislate* and *Women and Elective Office: Past, Present, and Future* with Oxford University Press.

MARYANNE BORRELLI is Professor of Government at Connecticut College. She received her BA from Wellesley College and her MA and PhD from Harvard University. Her teaching focuses on national institutions and on public policy in the United States, and she has earned awards for teaching excellence from the faculty and from the Student Government Association at Connecticut College. Professor Borrelli's research centers on the workings of gender in the presidency; her publications include *The Politics of the President's Wife* (Texas A&M University Press) and *The President's Cabinet* (Lynne Rienner Publishers).

Introduction: The Role of Government in America

At a town hall meeting in Michigan, one constituent can barely contain his anger toward another.

© Anne Savage

TALKING POINTS

In the scope of all human activity, "government plays a limited role," the historian Garry Wills reminds us. "It cannot be the family, the church, the local club, the private intellectual circle."[1] Few would disagree, but the lines between the responsibilities of government and private institutions are not as sharply drawn in law or practice as some think they are or should be.

Americans are acutely aware of these shifting lines because we have been in continuous debate over the appropriate role for government since 1787. At the convention where our Constitution was written, competing factions argued about the proper scope of government. Our political parties today are direct descendents of these factions and are organized around contrasting views about how big and active government should be.

It is unlikely that most Americans go about daily life thinking about how authority should be distributed across society, but there is no doubt that we do go through periods when some segment of the population becomes convinced that things are out of whack—government is intervening too much or too little in the market or in private life, either taking on functions that should be performed by the community or shirking responsibilities that should be performed by the government.

This is again a time when many Americans are debating the role of government. How big should government be? How active should it be? These perennial questions rose anew during the 2008 presidential campaign and since then have increasingly been a topic of debate, prompted by the expansion of government's reach under President George W. Bush in areas ranging from education to national security; the severe recession of 2008–2009 and the government's actions to combat it; the election of the first black president, who has been open to a more activist role for government; and the efforts of President Obama and Congress to expand health care and reform health insurance for all Americans. Some Americans have been vocal, often furious in their opposition to the federal government, its officials, and its policies. These Americans insist that the federal government should not be as big or as active as its current leaders and their policies call for it to be.

These debates over the role of government have a new focus but are as old as the republic. From the Whiskey Rebellion in 1786–1787 to the Tea (Taxed Enough Already) Party movement today, Americans periodically have rebelled against taxation and curtailment of individual liberties. Even presidents have complained about big government. President Ronald Reagan never tired of talking about his distaste for big government and liked to say he preferred flying over Washington to being on the ground because, from the air, government looked smaller. The historian Garry Wills said it sometimes seems that tradition asks "us to love our country by hating our government."[2]

These developments provide the context in which today's politics occur. This Introduction will provide an overview of these developments before we plunge into the chapters that address our political institutions and processes.

WHY HAVE GOVERNMENT?

To govern, government has to have a measure of control over the people, and it usually has a monopoly on the use of military power. Although any government impinges on personal freedom, people decide to have government because, paradoxically, personal freedom is best protected in some sort of regulated society. The life of people within a society that has no effective government is, in the words of English philosopher Thomas Hobbes, "nasty, brutish, and short."[3]

Today life without an effective government may mean that civil war erupts or neighboring countries invade. Women and children may be at the mercy of marauding bands of soldiers, some of them children themselves, who kill, rape, and plunder at will. Public services outside central cities may be nonexistent—no school system, no health care, no clean water, no good roads or efficient transportation. Children may die of infectious diseases that are easily cured in other societies. People may fend for themselves or their extended family, and they may die in what we consider their middle age. In these societies, individuals are free from the constraints of government but get no protection from government either. For them, life is unpredictable and often painful and short. Contemporary examples include Somalia, where twenty years of civil war and marauding bands leave ordinary people as prey. The world also watched while the Haitian government was unable to provide even the most basic services after the devastating earthquake in 2010.

Very few people argue that we need no government at all. Even those who call for minimalist government, as Libertarians do, argue that we need a military to protect our nation and police forces to enforce our laws.

At the other extreme from powerless or absent governments are dictatorships and totalitarian nations that try to regulate every aspect of life, including what people say and write, where they work, and even what they think. Nazi Germany and Stalinist Russia were modern examples of such governments. Although these two governments were different in their ideology and programs, they were similar in their nearly absolute power. Individuals could be imprisoned or executed for expressing opposition to the state or its leaders or even for being suspected of being a dissident. There were no independent courts or police services, and groups could be singled out for persecution at the rulers' whims.

Democracies fall between these extremes. They have enough power to govern effectively, but they do not control the lives and thoughts of their citizens. In the remainder of the Introduction, we will address the size and scope of the U.S. government.

THE FOUNDERS' CONCEPTION

The Founders expected a limited government with limited input from its citizens.

Early Settlers

Early settlers came to America for multiple reasons, but two groups predominated. Many settlers came for religious reasons. Some had been persecuted by the authorities in their countries, so they sought religious freedom. Others had been tolerated in their communities, but they wanted to live among like-minded people and they hoped to establish religious enclaves where their religion would prevail.[4] Either way, the immigrants who came for religious reasons brought with them suspicion, if not hostility, toward government. They wanted to be left alone so they could practice their religions as they saw fit.

Many other settlers came for economic reasons. Some were impoverished and could afford passage to America only by agreeing to become indentured servants. Others were well off and could pay their own way. But whether poor or rich, these immigrants saw America as a land of opportunity. They saw it as a new continent where they could improve their economic standing, with the poor becoming rich and the rich becoming richer. They too brought with them wariness toward government, in particular, aversion to taxes and restrictions that might limit their economic climb.

Both groups, those who came for religious reasons and those who came for economic reasons, were "runaways from authority."[5] And even though at least 20 percent of the colonists at the time of the Revolutionary War did not want to sever their ties with Britain,[6] those who did set the tone for American society, and they passed down these anti-authority views to their descendents, who in turn would pass down these views to their descendents. Eventually, these views would shape our Constitution and our country for generations to come.[7]

The Constitution

The Articles of Confederation, which governed the country after the Revolutionary War, were our first Constitution. Americans, who as colonists had chafed under rule by the English king and Parliament, wanted to avoid a government that was too strong. But the Articles created a government that was too weak to confront either foreign or domestic challenges. The government was unable to ensure either peace or prosperity. In frustration, the Founders called the Constitutional Convention and wrote a replacement for the Articles, a document we call "the Constitution" today.

The Constitution created a government that is stronger than the one under the Articles. However, the Founders, still wary of a strong government like the English government, wrote the Constitution to limit the power of the federal government. They fragmented governmental power by giving some to the federal government but reserving much for the state governments. They fragmented the power of the federal government further by dividing it into three branches—legislative, executive, and judicial—and then providing checks for each branch over the other branches. (Chapter 2 describes these provisions in more detail.) Founder James Madison wrote that they first had to "enable the government to control the governed, and in the next place to oblige it to control itself."[8]

The Constitution gave authority over foreign affairs and some domestic matters, including regulation of interstate commerce, to the national government. But the Constitution gave authority over many other matters to the states. It gave authority to tax to both levels. The 🏛 **Tenth Amendment,** which reflects the understanding of that time, says that the powers not delegated to the national government are reserved for the states. Although the Constitution's language is quite general and ambiguous, it's clear that the Founders thought they were creating a government that was limited in size and scope and therefore in power over states and individuals.

Yet, the Constitution states the purposes for establishing the United States of America in broad and positive terms, itemizing government's essential functions in its Preamble: to form a more perfect union, establish justice, ensure domestic tranquility, provide for the common defense, promote the general welfare, and secure the blessings of liberty to ourselves and our posterity. Moreover, the authority that the Constitution assigned to the various branches to carry out these functions has allowed the government to grow along with the nation. For example, Article I gives Congress the authority "To make all Laws which shall be necessary and proper for carrying into Execution the foregoing Powers [those enumerated], and all other Powers vested by this Constitution in the Government of the United States...." 🏛 **Art. I, Sec. 8, cl. 18.** This **necessary and proper clause** is also called the "elastic clause" because it can stretch to authorize a wide variety of powers not specifically listed.

When states had to decide whether to ratify the Constitution, the people and the legislators debated how much authority government should have to carry out its specified functions. Just as there was disagreement then, so there are controversies now. The ambiguities in the Constitution, a result of disagreements over the size and scope of government at the time of the Founding, continue to fuel debate.

The Role of the People

In creating the new government under the Constitution, the Founders believed that they should provide a way for the people to express their views and influence their officials. At the same time, the Founders worried that the people—the masses—could not be entrusted to have too direct an influence on national policy. They might be swayed by demagogues or be focused on narrow or local interests rather than the larger good. The Founders talked about "an excess of democracy" and feared "mob rule." Therefore, they wrote the Constitution to allow citizens to vote for members of the House of Representatives, but not for members of the Senate (state legislatures would choose the senators from their states—until the Seventeenth Amendment, mandating popular election, was ratified in 1913) or for the president

(electors in the Electoral College would choose the president—until political changes and state laws made the electors virtual rubber stamps of the voters in their state).

In summary, the Founders expected a limited role for the federal government but also a limited role for the people to influence that government. But they built in flexibility that allowed the Constitution to evolve to meet the changing needs of a growing nation.

GOVERNMENT GROWTH

Throughout history, Americans would confound the Founders' expectations by expanding the power of the government and also by expanding the power of the people to influence the government. Both the role of the government and the role of the people would become more robust than the Founders ever could have imagined.

Reasons for Government Growth

Some people have the impression that the government grows of its own accord. Usually government grows because citizens want it to do more. As crises emerge or society changes, new problems surface and people ask the government to do more to respond to them. To do more, government has to grow, adding departments or agencies or expanding existing ones, thus hiring more workers and budgeting more money to pay the workers or to aid the people directly. In responding to the demand to do something about unemployment, for example, government has to spend money either by providing new tax breaks to persuade businesses to hire more workers; or by building new roads, bridges, and other public works to create more jobs; or by giving unemployed workers more unemployment payments. Whatever the strategy, government has to issue new regulations to govern the expenditure of the money. It probably has to hire some workers to disburse the money and others to make sure that the disbursement is done honestly.

To deal with their near financial collapse in 2008, some large financial firms asked the government to bail them out. Fearing a worldwide depression, the government, then headed by George W. Bush, bailed them out and forced other financial firms to accept government bailouts too. And then, as two of the three major auto manufacturers in the United States, General Motors and Chrysler, teetered on the brink of bankruptcy, and economists and politicians feared the loss of tens of thousands of jobs in the auto industry, including the suppliers to the automakers, the government, then headed by Barack Obama, made massive loans to them too. Although there were some strings attached (General Motors, which was poorly managed, had to accept new management, and Chrysler had to accept a merger with another car manufacturer, Fiat) and the loans were to be repaid, again the government's role in the economy jumped, though temporarily. (Most of the loans were repaid.)

Archive Holdings Inc./Getty Images

As our country grew, our government grew, too. Washington sent soldiers and hired surveyors, road builders, and mail carriers to accommodate the needs of settlers. Here wagon trains head west in 1890.

Once government grows, it creates new clients for its services. These clients then make it difficult for government to cut back. This is true whether the clients are low-income individuals or huge corporations. President Ronald Reagan wanted to eliminate the Department of Education, which had been created under his predecessor, President Jimmy Carter. But Reagan's proposal ran afoul of those who benefited from the existence of federal support for education, including tens of thousands of school districts across the nation, so he wasn't able to eliminate the department.

Periods of Government Growth

Throughout history, the federal government has grown continuously, but it hasn't grown at a constant rate. When the country has experienced a massive crisis or major economic or social changes, the government has grown more because the people have demanded that it do more in response to the crisis or changes. We'll briefly summarize these periods in which the government has grown the most.

Civil War

The first growth spurt occurred during the Civil War. President Abraham Lincoln expanded the size of the government and the power of the presidency as well. Marshaling governmental power, he increased the size of the army to fight the war when Congress was not in session. Taking bold steps, he ordered the blockade of southern ports and denied the states any right to secede from the Union. He even arrested several Maryland state legislators who were going to vote for

Maryland to join the Confederacy, a move that would have left Washington, D.C., surrounded by Confederate states. Lincoln also used his authority as a wartime commander to assume extraordinary powers over domestic policy. And after the war, the government built homes for wounded and indigent Union veterans and paid for their medical care. Though there were earlier government programs to take care of some sailors and soldiers, this might be considered the first widespread social welfare program.[9]

Industrial Revolution

The next spurt occurred in the decades following the Civil War, as the Industrial Revolution transformed our economy in the late nineteenth and early twentieth centuries. Factories sprung up in cities, drawing workers from small towns and rural areas. The factories revolutionized work and society, boosting the economy but creating new problems for workers and consumers. Adults and children often worked in sweatshops—factories where they labored long hours in unsafe conditions for low pay. To cite just one example, in canneries child labor was common, and the new canning machines were dangerous for workers and produced unsafe food for consumers.

In response, Americans demanded reforms. Republican president Theodore Roosevelt used his office as a "bully pulpit" to advocate the improvement of working conditions, consumer protection, and environmental protection. These goals all required more regulation of big business. Roosevelt's concept of government as advocate for the average citizen expanded government and changed its purpose.

Great Depression

The largest spurt occurred during the **Great Depression**, which began when the stock market crashed in 1929 and continued until World War II. With the crash, many banks collapsed and ordinary people lost their savings. Business activity declined, and many workers lost their jobs. Between one-third and one-fourth of the workforce were unemployed. Others toiled for sweatshop wages. In Brooklyn, girls worked for six cents an hour in a pants factory. After paying for carfare, lunch, and child care, one employee took home ten cents a week (about $1.25 today).[10] Without their savings or jobs, many Americans could no longer make payments on their house or farm.

By 1932, one-seventh of the farms in Iowa were auctioned off.[11] On just one day in 1932, one-fourth of the state of Mississippi—12 to 15 percent of property in towns and almost 40,000 farms—was auctioned off in sheriffs' sales, because the banks foreclosed on the property.[12] As the Depression worsened, many people became homeless. Encampments, called "Hoovervilles" (named for the president at the beginning of the Depression, Herbert Hoover), sprung up on vacant lots and under bridges.

Many people also went without adequate food. The desperate walked up and down streets and knocked on doors each night to ask if there was any leftover food from dinner.[13] The really desperate haunted city garbage dumps.[14] Some malnourished men dropped dead in parks and froze to death in abandoned warehouses.[15] Increasing numbers of people

Child labor was common in the 1800s and early 1900s. This boy worked in the coal mines. When Americans no longer tolerated child labor, government passed and enforced laws against the practice. To do so, it expanded the number of its workers, the size of its budget, and the scope of its authority.

were admitted to hospitals for malnutrition, some of whom were so far gone that they couldn't be saved; they literally starved to death.[16]

Unlike today, there was no systematic program of relief—no welfare, no food stamps, no unemployment compensation. Cities and states, which had provided some aid to the poor, were overwhelmed; they did not have the funds or organizations to cope with the increasing needs. Nor did private charities, including churches, which had provided some aid, have enough resources to assume the burden.

Americans turned to the government and the new president, Democrat Franklin Delano Roosevelt (1933–1945), who expanded government power at all levels to mitigate the effects of the Depression, the worst economic crisis the country had experienced. Roosevelt's predecessor, Republican Herbert Hoover, had taken a minimalist approach, and by the time FDR (as Roosevelt was universally known) came to office, the dislocation and suffering of millions of Americans threatened the political stability of the country.

Roosevelt immediately launched an ambitious program, which he called "a new deal for the American people," to stimulate the economy and reduce the suffering. Congress passed Roosevelt's proposals to regulate business and labor and also to establish a national welfare system. Although some people, especially business executives, and corporations resisted the changes, most Americans embraced them.

These **New Deal** programs expanded the size of government more and at a faster rate than anything before or since. In the first six years of Roosevelt's administration, the number of federal employees in Washington, D.C., more than doubled,[17] the number of federal employees in the country almost doubled, and the size of the budget almost doubled as well.[18] Spending by states and localities also expanded greatly. This expansion is considered to be the beginning of "big government" in the United States. These changes were so dramatic that one political scientist said they created a "second American republic."[19] Compared with other Western countries, we got big government late, but in these years we got it fast.

Funds for these new programs came from new taxes levied on personal income, a power Congress acquired only after the 🦅 **Sixteenth Amendment** to the Constitution was ratified in 1913. The power to tax individual income expanded the reach of the federal government by providing fiscal support for many new activities. Some states also funded new programs by adopting new taxes or increasing existing taxes.[20]

Roosevelt's exuberance and experimentation had given people hope. As the country pulled out of the Depression, with help from the economic activity generated by World War II, people gave Roosevelt credit, electing him to an unprecedented four terms and returning Democrats to Congress to support him.

Overall, the New Deal brought a dramatic change in the relationship between the government and its citizens, making the government more prominent because of its greater involvement in daily life, its heavier taxation, and also because of the more visible role for the president. The people saw government's potential to make life better, and their expectations were permanently changed.

World War II and the Cold War

World War II (1941–1945) further stimulated the growth of the national government, especially the military bureaucracy. As Lincoln did during the Civil War, Roosevelt assumed extraordinary powers to meet wartime emergencies, including price controls, the rationing of food and materials for the war effort, and the suspension of some civil liberties (in fact, most civil liberties for most Japanese Americans).

As soon as the war was over, the United States and the Soviet Union, no longer needing to cooperate as allies against Germany, resumed their hostilities in a Cold War. The nuclear arms race ensued, and the government expanded its military in anticipation that the Cold War would become a third world war.[21] President Dwight Eisenhower, a Republican inclined toward small government, supported many new federal programs, ranging from the massive interstate highway system to college programs in science, engineering, and languages. Competition with the Soviet Union drove these initiatives.

AP Images

President Franklin Delano Roosevelt used his unbridled confidence and the public's support for New Deal programs to greatly expand the role of the federal government.

Civil Rights Era

Government expanded again during the 1960s and 1970s as a result of pressure from African Americans for civil rights; women for equal rights; consumers and unions for greater regulation of business; and environmentalists for a healthier environment.

The presidency of Democrat Lyndon Baines Johnson coincided with the peak activism of the modern civil rights movement, whose struggle for political equality was brought into every home by television. As Americans watched protestors being beaten or attacked by police dogs, Johnson, like Eisenhower and John F. Kennedy before him, had to call up, or threaten to nationalize, state militia to force state and local officials to comply with federal law. At the same time, the mass media were making the country aware of the high levels of poverty and hunger in the United States.

Johnson responded to these problems by pushing through Congress civil rights legislation and a massive package of social welfare proposals that he said would promote "a great society." The civil rights legislation prohibited state and local governments and private persons from discriminating against African Americans in public facilities and in hiring, housing, and voting. The **Great Society** programs increased the scope of government and changed the nation-state relationship in important ways. To implement Great Society programs, the federal government began funding work in domains that were formerly state and local preserves, such as law enforcement, fire protection, public education, and urban mass transit. With a tripling of aid to fund new programs, state and local governments became increasingly dependent on federal funding.[22]

Other laws and regulations to reduce discrimination against women and to protect consumers, laborers, and the environment were adopted during the Nixon administration.

To administer, monitor, and enforce these reforms and programs of the 1960s and 1970s, the federal government created and staffed a host of new agencies and even a pair of new departments.

Backlash against Government Growth

None of these major expansions of the size and role of government occurred smoothly or without opposition. All along, some people fought against expansions of federal authority and charged that the government was acting precipitously and in disregard of individual liberties. Just as today, these citizens referred to the Founders' expectations.

During the 1960s and 1970s, however, more people became disenchanted with government. In the 1960s, the civil rights movement, as well as the race riots in many big cities, alienated numerous people. The Vietnam War angered many Americans, both those who wanted leaders to escalate the war to achieve a "victory" and those who thought we shouldn't have been there in the first place and wanted leaders to pull out. Various lifestyle changes led to a generation gap, pitting the young against the old. In the 1970s, the economy slumped, and the Watergate scandal occurred.

The tumult over social issues and the turmoil throughout American society in the 1960s and 1970s produced a conservative backlash. By the mid-1970s, vocal critics began to call for a reduction in the size and scope of government. In 1980, the election of Ronald Reagan began a conservative era that would last into the 2000s. Reagan wanted to shrink government. Essentially, he campaigned on a platform against the federal government, vowing to make it smaller. He insisted, "Government is not the solution to our problems; government is the problem."

Reagan became a voice for Americans who wanted government to stop expanding and to start downsizing. Reagan did persuade Congress to cut spending for domestic programs, such as welfare and enforcement of civil rights and environmental regulations, but he greatly increased military spending and the size of the defense-related bureaucracy. Reagan also persuaded Congress to cut individual income taxes, especially for the wealthy. But when he left office, the government had a larger bureaucracy and a larger budget, and it was running much larger deficits than ever before, due to the combination of increased military spending and reduced tax revenue.

Although the public, with its traditional distrust of big government, cheered when Reagan criticized the government, solid majorities opposed most of the cuts Reagan proposed (except welfare for the poor). Yet, in general, the public, because they agreed with Reagan's rhetoric criticizing the government, gave the president the support he needed to push through Congress the very cuts that many people opposed.

Rather than shrinking government, Reagan shifted the priorities of government, from social and nondefense programs to the military. Indeed, the battle between Republicans and Democrats since the Reagan years has been a war over the priorities of government more than a war over the size of government. Republicans have wanted to deemphasize

President Ronald Reagan capitalized on the public's backlash against governmental growth and societal turmoil in the 1960s and 1970s to cut taxes and social programs in the 1980s.

social and nondefense programs and spend more on the military and national security, while Democrats have wanted to reemphasize social and nondefense programs. Rather than calling for a shift in government priorities, Republicans have called for tax cuts. The lower the taxes, the less money government would have. Although reduced revenues could hamper defense programs as well as nondefense programs, Republican strategists know that Americans will not tolerate a reduction of the military during a time of international tension.[23] Instead, nondefense programs would be cut. Thus their antitax stance has proven to be a more persuasive call to arms than a promise to shift priorities would have been.

George W. Bush, like Reagan, wanted to shrink government, in particular social and nondefense programs, but, also like Reagan, he saw government grow. After 9/11, he claimed vast power for the presidency and for the "war on terror." He presided over two wars—in Afghanistan and Iraq. He also pushed through the largest expansion of federal support for health care since Medicare with a prescription drug subsidy for the elderly and the largest intervention in the public schools with his No Child Left Behind legislation. To administer these programs, the bureaucracy grew. And near the end of his term, he authorized the $700 billion bailout of America's large financial institutions. Bush, too, persuaded Congress to cut taxes, multiple times, and especially for the wealthy. Due to the combination of increased military and domestic spending and decreased tax revenue, Bush also produced huge deficits, and he more

than doubled the national debt accumulated by all previous presidents.

The efforts to cut government by Reagan and Bush show that big government is a permanent presence in the United States. Some programs and some taxes may be reduced or eliminated, but the overall size and scope of government are likely to remain because most Americans want the protection and the programs offered by government. The priorities of government may shift between military and domestic, as national and international events occur or as the dominance among conservatives and liberals switches. It is particularly telling that government has grown most under presidents who decry the size of the federal government (such as Reagan and George W. Bush) and grown least under Democrats who have a more positive view of government (see Figure 1). This is another reason why it is difficult to see dramatic cutbacks in the overall size of government.

Although the public's focus, and this textbook's focus, is on the federal government, government in America also includes the states and their local governments, and they have grown much more since World War II than the federal government.[24] The federal government employs almost 3 million civil servants, fewer than twenty years ago, but the state and local levels employ almost 20 million, nearly a 60 percent growth in twenty years.[25] Some of the government actions that citizens rail against are administered and funded by state and local bureaucracies rather than by the federal government.

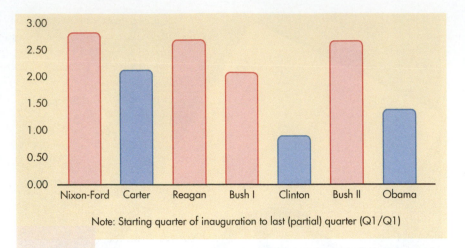

FIGURE 1: ANNUALIZED GROWTH IN REAL PER CAPITA GOVERN-MENT SPENDING Government has grown under all recent presidents. Measured by spending, it has grown the most under Republican presidents.

SOURCE: Derek Thompson, graph—Annualized Growth in Real per Capita Government Spending, from "Obama: Most Fiscally Conservative President in Modern History?" *The Atlantic Monthly*, March 16, 2012. http://www.theatlantic.com/business/archive/2012/03/obama-most-fiscally-conservative-president-in-modern-history/254658/. Copyright © 2012 by The Atlantic.com as published in The Atlantic Online. Distributed by Tribune Media Services. All Rights Reserved. Reproduced by permission.

Compared with Other Countries

Although the United States clearly has a big government, the government is not as big, compared with the governments of modern democracies, as most Americans assume. Ours is in the middle in the number of government workers relative to all workers, and ours is near the bottom in tax levels and public spending.[26] Most other democracies tax more and spend more, and their social programs are more ambitious, often providing paid maternity leave, subsidized day care, comprehensive health care, longer unemployment benefits, more generous pension benefits (than our Social Security); and, in some countries, mandating longer and paid vacations. In some cases, their governments own and operate major industries, such as telecommunications, transportation, and utilities, whereas ours restricts itself to providing services that the private sector finds unprofitable, such as Amtrak. Their bureaucracies regulate more stringently the businesses that remain in private hands.[27] Americans' antipathy toward government, and especially toward taxes, has prevented equally ambitious programs from being adopted in the United States.

THE PEOPLE'S AMBIVALENCE

Americans are ambivalent—of two minds—about government. Thomas Jefferson reflects this ambivalence. Calling his election a revolution, he abolished internal taxes (leaving only taxes on imports and exports, which grew rapidly) and set about making government as small, simple, and informal as possible. He closed down ports and foreign trade but soon found he needed federal policing to enforce his policy.[28] And when the opportunity arose, Jefferson bought the Louisiana

territories from France (a transaction that would become known as the Louisiana Purchase), even though he doubted that a president had the authority to do so. His expansionist vision instantly changed the country's destiny. From a compact coastal nation, the United States became a vast continental empire in which Jefferson's ideal of a small agrarian republic would no longer be possible.

Nonetheless, Jefferson's statement—"That government is best which governs least"—would be cited by Americans for years to come. (Henry David Thoreau's extension of this statement—"That government is best which governs not at all"[29]—would rarely be quoted. Living by himself at Walden Pond, Thoreau rejected society as he rejected government and went too far for most Americans.) In contrast to Jefferson, Abraham Lincoln, who presided over the country during the Civil War, saw a robust role for government and articulated the view of many Americans. "The legitimate object of government," he said, "is to do for a community of people whatever they need to have done, but can not do, at all, or can not so well do, for themselves."[30]

These ambivalent views occur and reoccur in American history and politics. Americans don't like *the idea* of a big, activist government, but they like *the benefits* they get from a big, activist government—the protection and the programs. In 2010, a huge oil rig run by BP in the Gulf of Mexico exploded, killing several workers and gushing 19,000 gallons of oil a day into the ocean, despoiling the coast, coating sea life, and decimating the fishing industry of the Gulf. Suddenly, voices that had been calling for smaller government were stilled, as people across the political spectrum demanded that government *do something* to stop this terrible destruction. Yet many of those calling for government action now had previously opposed

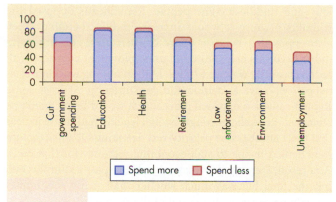

FIGURE 2: PUBLIC SUPPORT FOR GOVERNMENT SPENDING Although the public wants government to spend less in general (*left*), the public wants government to spend more in numerous areas.

SOURCE: The General Social Surveys, conducted by the National Opinion Research Center. These surveys, done every other year, poll national samples of adults. http://www.norc.org/GSS+Website/Data+Analysis/. © Cengage Learning.

government regulation of offshore drilling—the regulation that might have prevented the accident. ("Drill, baby, drill!" was a frequent chant in the Republican campaigns in 2008.)

Public Opinion about Government Spending

Americans' ambivalence can be seen in their opinion about government spending. Normally, government cannot act without spending and cannot grow without spending more, so public opinion about government spending reflects public opinion about government size and activity. Often a majority of Americans say they want government to cut spending. At the same time, large majorities say they want government to increase spending on a variety of domestic matters, as Figure 2 shows, and often on the military too. They want government to help make life better by improving education, health care, retirement security, law enforcement, and environmental protection. These numbers have been quite stable for decades (with some rise and fall in response to government action). In only two areas—foreign aid and welfare programs—have majorities consistently urged less spending.[31]

There are differences between the parties. Republicans tend to be more skeptical of government actions and more opposed to government spending than Democrats. Republicans are especially skeptical of government regulation of the economy and opposed to government assistance, such as health care or unemployment benefits, to needy individuals. However, Republicans like big government in certain areas, including the military, law enforcement, and the regulation of personal behaviors such as abortion and sexuality.

The Libertarian Party, founded in the early 1970s, is the most consistent party in members' attitudes about big government. Libertarians oppose most government activity. In their vision, government would consist largely of a military and police force that would protect the lives and property of the citizens. Almost everything else would be run by private

enterprise. Like most Republicans, they oppose government regulation of the economy. But like most Democrats, they also oppose government intervention in personal decisions like abortion and sexual orientation. Ron Paul, a Libertarian and Republican member of Congress from Texas, ran for the Republican nomination for president in 2008 and 2012.[32]

THE PEOPLE'S OPINIONS IN THE OBAMA YEARS

With an understanding of Americans' historical ambivalence about government, combining suspicion of government's size and scope on one hand but support for government's protection and programs on the other, you can better understand today's contradictory currents. Although government has grown in some ways, with support from the 2008 electorate, there is also a very visible backlash against big government, as shown in the 2010 election. Mitt Romney and the Republicans ran against big government in 2012 but were defeated by a small margin. The electorate of 2012 was much larger than in the 2010 midterm electorate, younger, and less white. Those who voted for Barack Obama were not necessarily saying they liked big government, but many were indicating that they thought government does have a role in helping put people back to work and insuring that every American has access to health care.

The Recession and Government Response

The backdrop to the recent backlash against big government is the severe recession, now called the Great Recession, of 2008–2009 and its slow recovery and lingering unemployment years later. Many Americans were laid off, and many others were unable to pay their mortgages. Countless people were afraid that they, too, would lose their jobs. Middle-class folks were worried that their children would face harder times and never achieve "the American dream." Polls showed widespread despair and loss of confidence.[33] Economic concerns, as well as the 9/11 attacks and two ongoing wars, underscored the events of the decade, which *Time* labeled "The Decade from Hell."[34]

Government Response
Both the Bush and Obama administrations believed that it was necessary to bail out the huge companies—banks, insurers, and automakers—teetering on the brink of collapse. The companies were so big that their failures could cause our entire financial system to collapse. Economists feared that a second Great Depression could ensue. (Now economists, looking back, agree that a second Great Depression was likely without the bailouts.)

The public's sour mood, however, prompted opposition to the bailouts, especially to the Wall Street firms whose risky loans and investments caused the recession. No matter that most economists and most Republican and Democratic leaders considered the bailouts necessary. Many members of the public, conservatives and liberals alike, recoiled. They questioned the cost to taxpayers and the activism of government symbolized by the bailouts. They wondered why Wall Street

"We shouldn't have expected a banker to play by the rules."

bankers were bailed out when the average folks who lost their jobs, and the stockholders who lost their retirement funds, weren't. The public wanted those responsible held accountable. While the economists and political leaders were thinking in pragmatic terms—What will keep this from getting worse?—many people were thinking in moralistic terms—Who deserves help, and who deserves punishment?

Because the economics behind the bailouts was complex, the public did not understand the rationale. So the public saw the bailouts as a gift to Wall Street but no help to Main Street. When people heard economists and politicians say that the huge corporations were "too big to fail," individuals who were struggling felt that they were "too small to notice."[35] They perceived "that one set of rules applies to one group of people—generally wealthy and well connected—and another set of rules applies to the rest. And worse, that the many are subsidizing the few, cleaning up the messes they made."[36] These feelings were rubbed raw when the executives of some failing banks walked away with millions of dollars in bonuses.

Despite initial opposition to the bailouts from many people in both parties and at both ends of the ideological spectrum, sharp differences between Republicans and Democrats, and conservatives and liberals, would emerge. Although many Republicans in Congress voted for the bailout of the financial industry proposed by the Bush administration, most Republicans in Congress voted against Obama's stimulus package, which combined spending for infrastructure, aid to state and local governments, and cuts in payroll taxes. The package was designed to promote economic growth by providing more jobs in the private sector, retaining existing jobs in the public sector, and providing modest tax relief to

low- and middle-income people. Republicans opposed the stimulus because it would increase public spending. They also opposed it because many of their core constituencies didn't need this help; although unemployment cuts across all social classes, it was, and still is, highest among working-class people, who are a Democratic constituency. At least some Republicans also opposed it because it would help Obama be reelected. Republican congressional leaders had made it clear that their number one priority was defeating Obama (though they denied trying to stall economic recovery for that end). As a result, Democratic votes were able to pass a stimulus bill, but the final bill was much smaller than many economists thought necessary to break out of the recession.

The Republicans favored further tax cuts for those at the top of the income scale, under the assumption that those individuals would invest their tax savings in companies that would create jobs. Republicans proposed to compensate for the reduced revenue by cutting programs that provide safety nets for those who are not well off, such as Social Security and various programs that target aid to the poor.

The two parties became so polarized on this issue that government has not used much of its power to end the recession.

Reaction to Government Policies

The election of Democratic majorities to the House of Representatives and Senate in 2006 and larger Democratic majorities and a Democratic president in 2008 brought expectations that the government would become more active in addressing intractable problems that had received scant attention in recent years. The Obama administration proposed an ambitious domestic agenda, calling for health care reform, climate change measures, and education reform as well as stabilizing the economy, all in the president's first term. Obama's chief of staff, referring to the recession, said, "A crisis is a terrible thing to waste." He explained that Americans are more willing to let the government take action during a crisis than at other times.

Yet the administration, and many pundits, misread the election returns, believing that Obama's victory signaled the beginning of a new liberal era. Although there was somewhat more desire for liberal policies than in previous years, the country remained sharply divided, and many Americans remained skeptical, even fearful, of activist government. Some of them had voted for Obama because they considered the Bush administration incompetent rather than because they wanted Obama's policies.

Although Obama's agenda resonated with many voters during the election campaign, once the new president was sworn in and the economic climate showed no signs of improving, the public's priorities focused on creating new jobs rather than on achieving other goals. The president, like President Bush before him, knew that the financial system had to be stabilized or the economy would likely go into a true depression. The president's focus was pragmatic, not ideological. (Helping Wall Street banks is not a liberal priority.) But this focus seemed disconnected from the concerns of average Americans.

AP Images/Ed Andrieski

Tea Partiers protest Obama health care plan.

And the president's efforts to reform health care, while part of his campaign platform, seemed out of sync with the public's concerns during this economic crisis. Coupled with their traditional distrust of big government, Americans' anxiety led to a backlash against Obama's agenda, and his approval ratings fell.

Health care reform especially kindled vocal opposition to activist government. Though Obama's health care plan was based on Republican and conservative plans from the 1980s, 1990s, and 2000s (as will be explained in the Health Care Module), the bill got almost no Republican support. Conservative constituents flooded the town hall meetings held by members of Congress in 2009 when health care reform was under consideration. Some meetings became unruly forums as opponents of reform vented, calling their representatives, the president, and the entire federal government "socialist," "communist," or "fascist" (and sometimes all of these simultaneously) and accusing them of acting like "Hitler" and "Nazis." (As one wag noted, students might be excused for wondering if we fought Germany in World War II because it provided too much health care.) Opponents could barely find language harsh enough to express their outrage. According to a woman who brought three busloads of protestors from Mississippi to Washington, "The consensus is that this is not a left-wing government, but that this is more of a Marxist [government]."[37] This rhetoric was similar to the anti–New Deal rhetoric of the 1930s, but with the pervasiveness of the media today, the charges were multiplied and amplified.

Wild conspiracy theories promoted by Internet blogs, radio talk shows, and television commentators abounded. Rumors warned against "death panels" of government bureaucrats who would deny health care to deformed babies, the disabled, and the elderly. Rumors claimed that the administration would establish reeducation camps for the obese.[38] A woman at a town hall meeting in Virginia said, "I'm really afraid of this president. I mean, they're starting to talk about limits on family size, how many children you can have. In our America."[39]

Tea Party Movement

The town hall meetings grew into the **Tea Party movement**, which represents many conservative voters.[40] Inspired by the Boston Tea Party of 1773 protesting taxation without representation (the colonists had no votes in Britain's Parliament, which levied taxes on them), the Tea Partiers complain that our modern government no longer reflects the Founders' expectations. And they are frightened of the changes taking place in society. They seem especially fearful of "the fast-moving generational, cultural, and racial turnover" reflected in Obama's election and presidency.[41] They are also fearful of the impact of further immigration on the composition of the population. At a town hall meeting in Delaware, a woman wailed, "I want my country baaaaack!"[42] When one Tea Party participant was asked what she hoped the movement would accomplish, she replied, "Well, I want it all to stop. . . . Our way of life is under attack. I truly believe they are trying to destroy this country. It's just hard to say who 'they' is."[43]

The Tea Party movement is a coalition of local groups with no central direction. The Tea Partiers are disproportionately southern, white, male, and older than forty-five. They are very conservative.[44] A majority—nearly three times as many as other Americans—say they are "angry" about the way things are going in Washington.[45] A majority believe that Obama has expanded the role of government too much and is moving the country toward socialism. Most favor a smaller government with fewer programs and benefits. However, they support military spending, and most support Social Security and Medicare, which benefit many of them, though they oppose government programs that benefit other people—especially immigrants, racial minorities, and young people—whom they consider undeserving.[46] They favor reducing the budget deficits, but they also favor cutting taxes, which would increase the deficits.

The Tea Partiers, mostly conservative Republicans, initially were alienated from the party and its leaders but now are squarely within the party. In fact, in many areas of the country, the Republican Party is dominated by supporters of the Tea Party, who by the strength of their numbers and dedication have taken over local party leadership.

To enhance their power, the Tea Partiers have aligned themselves with conservative Christians, who had been motivated by religious issues more than by economic issues. The alliance of Tea Partiers and evangelical Christians has moved the Republican Party in an even more conservative direction. According to one poll, "The most visible shift in the political landscape" in recent years is "the emergence of a single bloc of across-the-board conservatives" who "take extremely conservative positions on nearly all issues."[47]

Occupy Wall Street

Of course, not all Americans, nor even a majority, agree with the Tea Party and the movement's anger toward big government, health care reform, and immigration policy. In 2011, protestors who fashioned themselves as Occupy Wall Street (OWS) emerged with a different set of complaints. They identified different villains and different solutions but reflected shared frustration at "business as usual" and "government as usual."[48]

OWS protestors directed their anger at government's actions benefiting the 1 percent of America's richest individuals at the expense of the other 99 percent. More amorphous and diverse than the Tea Party, Occupy Wall Street began, as its name suggests, with demonstrations on Wall Street, but other protests sprang up around the country. The protests usually involved a camp-in on city parks or other public places. Though the OWS group shared the Tea Party's outrage over the Wall Street bailouts, their solution to the issues was quite different. OWS protesters wanted a stronger government, one that would work to help the poor and middle classes and not just the rich.

A few weeks after OWS burst on the scene, more than 40 percent of the public said they agreed with the goals of OWS, with 30 percent opposing them and the rest uncertain. Young people and liberals were most likely to say they were sympathetic with the goals, while older Americans and conservatives were least sympathetic.[49]

Perhaps the main achievement of OWS was to add concern for the 99 percent to the political debate. Though significant numbers of Americans agreed with the complaints of OWS, the movement never focused on specific policy changes or mobilized its supporters to action beyond the demonstrations. And unlike the Tea Party movement, which was actively promoted by Fox News, OWS never had a cable network supporting its cause and publicizing its rallies. So, a few months after emerging, OWS demonstrations and tent cities were dispersed by local authorities and the movement faded away, leaving behind mostly the renewed awareness that the majority of Americans were not prospering in this economy.

Anger and Polarization

Most Tea Party supporters are not just opposed to government policies; they are angry about them. Plenty of liberals are angry too. This anger, coupled with diverging views on what we should do to fix our country's problems, has led to polarization between the parties and dysfunction within the government.

Our system of government is based on cooperation and compromise. Without the willingness of legislators in one party to join with those in the other party to pass legislation, the business of government grinds to a halt. There are so many places in the legislative process where legislation can be stopped that without some cross-party collaboration, very little gets done. (These checks will be explained in Chapters 2 and 9.)

Though both parties bear some blame for gridlock, in recent years Republicans, reflecting their constituents' anger, have been much less willing to compromise than Democrats. In fact, when running for election or reelection, most Republican members of Congress signed pledges to conservative interest groups—for example, a pledge that they would never raise taxes. Keeping their pledges means that they cannot cooperate

"My doctor says I should take all my bottled-up anger and sell it to a grass-roots movement."

© CHRISTOPHER WEYANT/New Yorker Collection/www.cartoonbank.com

or compromise on many issues. Democrats gave Bush support in his signature issues of educational reform and Medicare drug coverage enhancement. But, except for the bailout of the auto industry, Republicans have been determined not to cooperate with Democrats in issues affecting the economy.

Conservatives' resistance to compromise began with the abortion issue in the 1970s and 1980s. Abortion is especially difficult to compromise—abortion either takes a life, or it doesn't; women either have a right to abortion, or they don't—and conservative Christians believed they represented God's word. Then their reluctance to compromise spread to other religious issues and, eventually, to nonreligious issues, such as global warming, business regulations, and tax rates, which they came to consider religious issues after all.

Sen. Barry Goldwater (R-Ariz.), who was the Republican candidate for president in 1964, sparked the conservative takeover of the Republican Party but years later expressed concern about conservative Christians flocking to the party. "Mark my word, if and when these preachers get control of the party, and they're sure trying to do so, it's going to be a terrible damn problem. Frankly, these people frighten me.... Politics and governing demand compromise. But these Christians believe they are acting in the name of God, so they can't and won't compromise. I know, I've tried to deal with them."[50]

When the Tea Party movement arose, it attracted conservative Christians. The Tea Partiers, who originally focused on economic issues, and the conservative Christians, who originally focused on religious issues, joined forces. Together they pressured Republican leaders and officeholders to adopt conservative positions across the board and to resist Democratic attempts to cooperate and compromise.

In a 2012 book, *It's Worse Than You Think,* two longtime congressional scholars, one a moderate Republican, the other a moderate Democrat, explained that "one of the two major parties, the Republican Party, has become an insurgent outlier, ideologically extreme; contemptuous of the inherited social and economic policy regime; scornful of compromise; unpersuaded by conventional understanding of facts, evidence, and science; and dismissive of the legitimacy of its political opposition."[51] This is a harsh judgment, but the authors point out that today's Republicans have little in common with the party's conservative hero, former President Ronald Reagan, staunchly conservative but deeply pragmatic, and willing to bargain and compromise with his partisan opposites. In contrast, today's take-no-prisoners approach to politics is illustrated by the Republican primary for a Senate seat in Indiana in 2012. Richard Mourdock, the challenger, defeated Richard Lugar, the veteran who was very conservative on domestic issues but a bipartisan leader on foreign policy issues. Mourdock scoffed at bipartisanship, saying that "bipartisanship ought to consist of Democrats coming to the Republican point of view."[52]

Former political scientist E. E. Schattschneider used to say that "democracy is a political system for people who are not too sure that they are right," because democracy requires respect for opponents and willingness to compromise with them.[53] Yet today many Americans are very sure that they are right, and they are disrespectful of their opponents and unwilling to compromise. "Epithets have replaced arguments," and "a sense of common destiny seems lacking."[54] With these attitudes spreading in our population, it's not surprising that dysfunction prevails in our government.

Americans "rail against the nation's capital as if it were a deadly virus implanted on the Potomac by space invaders or the French,"[55] in the words of one columnist, but our representatives are reflecting, at least to some extent, the views of the people. Americans do not agree among themselves. Tea Party supporters believe that most Americans agree with them, but according to polls most Americans don't.[56] And Occupy Wall Street protestors may have thought that they were speaking for 99 percent of the public, but they were speaking for only about 40 percent. Recognizing that your point of view is not shared by everyone is a necessary step toward compromise. (See Figure 3.)

The government must try to reconcile the disparate views held by both ends of the ideological spectrum—the Tea Party supporters and the Occupy Wall Street sympathizers—as well as those in the middle. Congress is the forum where opinions must get translated into policy. The process can be ugly and messy, but ultimately compromises must be made and national problems must be solved.[57] Yet, more than half of the public want their elected officials to "stick to their positions" rather than make compromises.[58] Among those who agree with the Tea Party or who label themselves "conservative Republicans," two-thirds want their representatives to "stick to their positions." And then people complain that government is dysfunctional.

The anger that has driven many Americans to the fringes has led to violent words and images that seem inconsistent with democracy. Rep. Trent Franks (R-Ariz.) called President Obama "an enemy of humanity."[59] At Obama appearances in states with "open-carry laws," men displayed loaded weapons to signal their opposition to "government tyranny."[60] In the 2010 election, a congressional candidate in Nevada proposed "Second Amendment remedies."[61] Another, in Texas, declared that violent overthrow of the government was "on the table" if the election didn't result in new leadership.[62] In 2011, when Rep. Paul Broun (R-Ga.) held a town hall meeting in his district, one constituent asked, "Who's going to shoot Obama?" and the audience broke into laughter. Another constituent responded, "We all want to."[63] In 2012, at a Tea Party rally for a Republican candidate challenging Sen. Claire McCaskill (D-Mo.), one speaker insisted, "We have to kill the Claire Bear, ladies and gentlemen. She walks around like she's some sort of Rainbow Brite Care Bear or something, but really she's an evil monster."[64] It's no longer enough for people to disagree with their opponents over public policies; instead, they consider disagreements as battles between good and evil. All through history, some Americans have given voice to their anger (and many Americans harshly criticized President Bush), but longtime members of Congress say they have never seen nor heard such vitriol as is common today.[65]

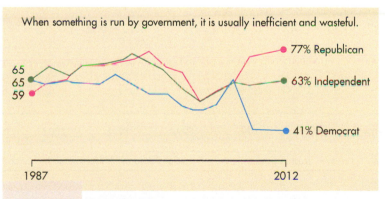

FIGURE 3: CONTRASTING OPINIONS TOWARD GOVERNMENT BY REPUBLICANS AND DEMOCRATS

SOURCE: "Partisan Polarization Surges in Bush, Obama Years: Trends in American Values: 1987–2012," June 4, 2012, Pew Research Center for the People and the Press, 2012. Copyright © 2012 by Pew Research Center. Reproduced by permission.

THE PEOPLE'S TRUST AND CONFIDENCE IN GOVERNMENT

Trust in government and confidence in government rise and fall over time. Trust and confidence vary with the economic conditions of society, the economic status of individuals, the public's confidence in the president specifically, international threats, and other factors.[66] Trust increases when there are external threats, so trust in government soared after 9/11, when the country rallied in support of American victims of the terrorist attack and action against the perpetrators. Trust falls when the public is not pleased with the way the president is handling issues, so trust fell after the government's failure to cope with Hurricane Katrina in 2005 and the recession in 2008 and 2009.[67] Trust decreases when economic times are bad and families suffer.

Thus, during the worst economic crisis since the Great Depression, it is not surprising that overall levels of trust and confidence in government are low (see Figure 4). Eighty-one percent of Americans responding to a 2010 poll said they trusted the government to do the right thing "never" or only "some of the time," the same percentage who said members of Congress did not deserve reelection.[68] But levels of trust in nearly every major institution in American society, including business, labor, media, and education—all except the military—reached historic lows.[69] And when trust in government and trust in business were compared, more Americans trusted government than business.[70]

Among the institutions of government, the public has the most confidence in the Supreme Court, then the president, and last, Congress. Confidence in the president rose in 2009,

Obama's first year, and then fell in 2010 (but not to the level of the last two years of the Bush administration).[71]

The levels of trust and confidence are also diminished because Americans do not like the rough and tumble of politics where interests compete in our governmental institutions and where the process of negotiating, bargaining, and compromising is on full display. In fact, people often make a distinction between their government in theory (or on paper) and their government in action. They cherish the Declaration of Independence and the Constitution and point with pride to the documents and symbols of American democracy. However, they do not like the way their government works or their representatives operate, so they do not trust the government itself.

The historian Garry Wills has written, "Our very liberty depends so heavily on distrust of government that the government itself, we are constantly told, was constructed to instill that distrust."[72] Or, as one public policy scholar has said, "Distrust of government...is hard-wired into the American psyche."[73]

As the 2012 election showed, the public is closely divided on whether government should do more or do less. Those who want it to do less usually target other people's benefits for cutting, not their own, further muddying the water. (Do they really want government to do less, or do they just want government to do less for other people?) These conflicted opinions about government follow in a long tradition. Should government help solve society's problems and improve peoples' lives, or should it remain as small as possible and do as little as possible? You can decide for yourself as you proceed through this course.

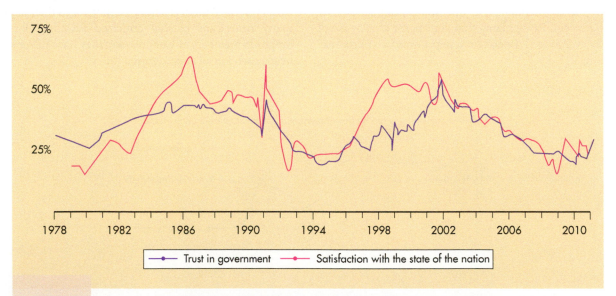

FIGURE 4: TRUST IN GOVERNMENT REFLECTS STATE OF NATION During most times, Americans' trust in government reflects their views about the state of the nation.

SOURCE: "Distrust, Discontent, Anger, and Partisan Rancor: the People and Their Government," Pew Research Center for the People and the Press, a project of the Pew Research Center, April 18, 2010, http://people-press.org/report/?pageid=1698. Copyright © 2010 by Pew Research Center. Reproduced by permission.

The American People

Immigrants celebrate their American citizenship.

AP Images

LEARNING OBJECTIVES

1. Define some important sources of American population diversity, and discuss how they affect politics.

2. List and define the core values endorsed by most people in the United States. Explain why each of these core values sparks controversy, even among supporters.

3. Discuss the concept of political culture, explaining how it is learned. Assess the role played by education, the media, and the government in creating political culture.

4. Analyze conflicts among the core values. Decide whether policies and governmental actions have resolved these disputes.

TALKING POINTS

Most Americans think the United States is the best place in the world to live. Visitors to the nation's capitol marvel at the Washington Monument, the Lincoln Memorial, the Capitol, and the White House. Teachers encourage their students to cherish the Declaration of Independence and the Constitution. Parents nurture patriotism in their children.

At the same time that Americans prize democracy, many condemn the reality of democracy. They refer to debates over issues as "bickering" and call compromises "selling out." They label opponents' views as selfish and narrow, and they tag interest groups and political parties as "special interests." Americans have little tolerance for the slow pace at which government deals with the nation's problems, and in some cases they would rather have no action at all than anything that gives the other side something it wants. In other words, Americans love the concept of democracy and its symbols, but they hate the rough and tumble, the give and take, and the conflict of democracy in action.

Political institutions reflect the public policy disputes within a population, as one would expect in a democracy. Yet, in the United States today, these divisions among the people generate even more bickering, which may or may not lead to compromise. We saw in the previous chapter that most Americans really don't want to compromise; they want their elected representative to hold out for their own position. Sometimes Americans think they would like some non-partisan figure to make decisions, but who would such a figure be?[1]

While these views have not undermined support for the nation, they are reflected in the low esteem that Americans hold their political institutions. Only about 10 percent of Americans approve of the job Congress is doing. Americans feel quite a bit more favorably toward the president and the Supreme Court.[2] Part of the reason is that the justices of the Court do not usually air their differences as publicly as Congress. And the president too can, at least sometimes, stand above partisan differences.

Democracy, when practiced by people who are ethnically, economically, and religiously diverse, and scattered across a vast and varied landscape, is destined to be characterized as much by competition and conflict as by cooperation and community. But Americans do share some political values, at least in the abstract, and this book will describe how those values are expressed in our form of government.

It is ironic that, at the same time that Americans profess to love democracy, they claim to hate politics. For it is through politics that myriad views of the public are considered, debated, and finally reconciled through policy. It is because the people must come together to govern themselves that Aristotle described politics as ennobling. Though popular perceptions today rarely endorse this vision, politics are as central to our nation's life as any of the values that we profess to love.

---

[1] John Hibbing and Elizabeth Theiss Morse, *Stealth Democracy* (Cambridge: Cambridge University Press), 2002.

[2] Jeffrey Jones, "Confidence in U.S. Public Schools at a New Low," *Gallup Politics.* June 20, 2012. http://www.gallup.com/poll/155258/confidence-public-schools-new-low.aspx

Americans are divided about much in the political world, but there is still a deep-seated and widely shared agreement that ideas and ideals matter. In this chapter, we look first at some differences in the backgrounds of Americans and then identify some core values that most Americans share, the American political culture, and the complexities of applying these values to political decisions.

WHO ARE AMERICANS?

The American people are a diverse people and were so long before Europeans arrived.

Racial and Ethnic Diversity

Although sometimes characterized by a single term such as *Indians* or *Native Americans*, the first immigrants of thousands of years ago founded many different civilizations. Their nations were competitive and at times at war, and their differences were substantial enough to doom eighteenth-century efforts to form pan-Indian alliances against European colonization.[1] Today, the U.S. Census Bureau recognizes 564 different tribes, many fewer than there were three hundred years ago, but still suggestive of the wide array of cultures that predated European settlement.

The Europeans who arrived were also a diverse group, emigrating from countries that not only differed linguistically, religiously, and politically but also had often been at war with one another. Migrants carried some of these conflicts with them to America. Africans, too, came from a huge continent that encompassed many languages, cultures, and religions. Even though the European slave trade was concentrated in coastal areas of West Africa, the men and women forcibly removed to the Americas did not share a common tradition, though their experience in the American colonies united them as noncitizens lacking all political and economic rights.

The ethnic and racial composition of the American population broadened in the mid- to late nineteenth century as new waves of settlers came from northern Europe, especially Germany and Ireland; southern and eastern Europe; China; and Japan. Immigration continued at high levels into the twentieth century before peaking in the decade 1905–1914, when more than 10 million immigrants entered the country.

In the late twentieth century, with the removal of the immigration quota system, America's population further diversified as America's door opened to people of every race, religion, and nationality. Preferential treatment was given to those fleeing a communist country, including several million Cubans, Russians, and eastern Europeans during the Cold War, and Vietnamese, Cambodians, and Laotians during and after the Vietnam War. Thousands of Chinese students were granted permanent residency following the 1989 Tiananmen Square massacre in Beijing. (See Figure 1.)

Since 2000, hundreds of thousands have entered the country illegally, most crossing the Mexican border into the southwestern United States. Another group of unauthorized residents entered on temporary visas and overstayed them.

This Italian family arrives at Ellis Island in 1905.

After 2007, this wave of immigration slowed and the numbers of undocumented immigrants fell by a million or more because of the recession and the stepped-up border enforcement.

Protests against Newcomers

Current anti-immigration sentiment and measures are nothing new. Antiforeign, or nativist, sentiments have been common throughout our history. Some native-born Americans have feared economic competition from newcomers or have perceived non-English-speaking people or anyone with different traditions and religious practices as cultural threats. A wave of Germans arriving in Pennsylvania in the 1750s had Benjamin Franklin complaining about the use of bilingual street signs in Philadelphia and warning that if German immigration were not stopped the German language would replace English, and "even our government will become precarious."[2] (Franklin, however, did publish a German-language newspaper.)

Such anti-immigrant sentiments usually are most pronounced when immigration levels are high and economic times are bad, which is why strong nativist sentiments influenced the politics of the mid-1800s, 1920s, and 1990s, and why they are again a force today. Many more people responding to a 2009 poll thought conflict between native-born Americans and immigrants was greater than between black and white Americans.[3]

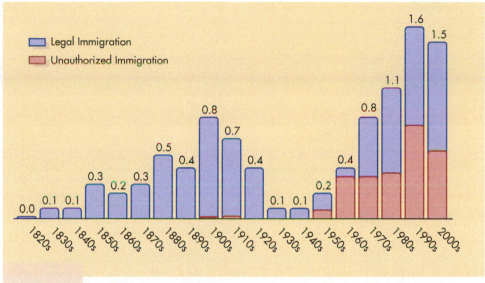

FIGURE 1: IMMIGRATION REACHED AN ALL-TIME HIGH IN THE 1990s
Note: Figures for each decade are annual average number of immigrants in millions. Figures for legal immigration are arrivals only; figures for unauthorized immigration are estimates of net gain (arrivals minus departures).
SOURCE: Jeffrey Passel and D'Vera Cohn, *U.S. Population Projections: 2005–2050* (Washington, D.C.: Pew Research Center, February 11, 2008), 85. http://pewhispanic.org/files/reports/85.pdf. Copyright © 2008 by Pew Research Center. Reproduced by permission.

Religious Diversity

America's religious profile has changed along with its ethnic makeup. Although the vast majority still identify as Christians, they are split among dozens of sects and denominations, and the once dominant Protestants are now barely half of the population. The Catholic Church has lost ground among native-borns but has held its share of the Christian population because of the high level of immigration from Catholic countries such as Mexico. Sixteen percent of Americans claim no religious affiliation, and the percentage is even higher among eighteen- to twenty-nine-year-olds.[4] (See Table 1.)

Increasing religious diversity is partly but not solely a function of immigration. A 2007 survey found that 28 percent of American adults had left the faith they were raised in and that almost half had made some shift in religious affiliation.

To some observers, these figures represent the potential for social fragmentation. Still, as the great French philosopher Voltaire wrote, a nation with one church will have oppression; with two, civil war; with a hundred, freedom.[5] In other words, a proliferation of religious affiliations may both bolster liberty and serve as its measure.[6]

Other Sources of Diversity

America's diversity involves more than differences in national origin, race, and religious affiliation. Where people settle, what they do for a living, how much they earn, when they were born, and how long they have been here are all potential sources for political difference, and over time these factors are probably more important than religion or country of origin.

Economic diversity is very important. In 2009, almost half of Americans believed that conflict between rich and poor was greater than that between blacks and whites.[7] We may think of America as a land of opportunity, but most people who are born poor in the United States stay poor. Opportunities knock harder and more often for those who are born into the upper and middle classes. And although the American society is not as class conscious as many others, its gap between rich and poor is larger than in any other Western industrialized nation. Economic inequality continues to grow: the gap between the lowest and highest income groups in America has grown from 35-fold to 75-fold over the past thirty years.[8] Unlike the post–World War II era, when income growth was shared across all income groups, over the past thirty years the very richest Americans have been the biggest winners, and the poorest 20 percent have actually lost income. More now than a few years ago, a greater number of Americans, of all races and partisan identities, say that there are strong conflicts between rich and poor.[9] The 2011 Occupy Wall Street movement, which focused on the wealth of the 1 percent versus the 99 percent, highlighted this tension. (See Figure 2.)

Regional and residential differences can also be important, especially since they often intertwine with economic interests. The classic and most costly example of regional conflict in our history was the division between South and North over the right of southern states to secede from the Union in order to maintain a regional economic system rooted in slavery. Although in that case economic and political disparities led to the bloodiest conflict in our history, regional diversity usually results in no more than political difference and economic competition. Today, however, with growing income inequality and the residential segregation of gated communities, there is the danger that residential separation will lead the well-off to be politically indifferent to the needs of poor neighborhoods.

		Religious Affiliations of American Adults among the World Religions and within Christianity*		

Table 1

WORLD RELIGIONS	(%)	CHRISTIAN RELIGIONS	(%)
Christian	95.6	Catholic	40.9
Muslim	1.7	Evangelical and Conservative Protestant	34.7
Jewish	1.5	Mainline Protestant	15.7
Buddhist	0.7	Latter-Day Saints	4.4
Hindu	0.4	Historically Black Protestant	3.4
Bahá'i	0.1	Orthodox Christian (Russian and Greek Orthodox)	0.7
		Additional Christian faiths	0.2

*These numbers indicate how many individuals formally associate themselves with the religion or ethical practice. This is a very high standard for participation, which excludes those who only occasionally attend services.

SOURCE: Association of Statisticians of American Religious Bodies, *U.S. Religion Census,* The Association of Religion Data Archives, 2012.

The Political Implications of Diversity

We are interested in these and other sources of diversity in the American population because these differences affect political views and behavior. Of course, each individual is a product of more than his or her race, religion, location, and income level. Yet these characteristics and more have large influences on political attitudes and behavior.

Some racial and ethnic differences contribute to continuing conflict. America's history of slavery, legalized segregation, and discrimination even today provide worse life chances for most African Americans compared to whites, and this situation affects their attitudes toward the role that government should take in equalizing opportunity. As Chapter 12 will explore, Latinos and Indians have faced different kinds of challenges.

Other differences also have political implications. Evangelical Protestants and conservative Catholic groups provide the foundation for the pro-life movement and broader opposition to progressive social policies in areas such as contraception and same-sex marriage. Economic differences affect individuals' likelihood to participate in politics and attitudes toward government activity. Regional differences, and those between urbanites and rural dwellers, play an important role in many policy areas, from gun control to farm aid. Farmers in California and the Midwest, for example, are more likely than city dwellers to be supportive of farm subsidy legislation, and rural residents are more likely to oppose gun control than urbanites.

THE CORE VALUES

Walt Whitman wrote of America, "Here is not merely a nation but a teeming Nation of nations." Despite the diversity of our "nation of nations," most Americans endorse certain basic values. These include liberty, equality, majority rule, rights, and popular sovereignty. If some of these words sound familiar, that may be because our Declaration of Independence asserts "that all Men are created equal, that they are endowed by the Creator with certain unalienable Rights, that among these are Life, Liberty, and the Pursuit of Happiness."

These are broad concepts, and there is considerable debate about what they actually mean for the people and for the government in the United States. Here we briefly examine each of the core values; the next chapter provides a more detailed discussion of how these principles are expressed in and through the Constitution.

Equality

A tenet of Judeo-Christian beliefs, which have influenced so much of U.S. politics, is that all people are equal in the eyes of God. Yet those beliefs do not always lead to a belief in other types of equality, such as political equality.

The words of the Declaration of Independence that "all men are created equal" did not mean that the Founders thought that people were born with equal talents or abilities. In fact, these words championed equality at the same time the Founders lived in a society that justified and relied upon slavery; some of the Founders themselves owned slaves.

The Founders thought all *citizens* are born with equal standing before government and are entitled to equal rights. At this time, as in ancient Greek democracies, full rights of citizenship were conferred only on those thought to have the intellectual and moral judgment to act in the public interest. Such thinking denied political rights to slaves, who were believed incapable of independent judgment. This paradox led an English opponent of slavery and the slave trade to write: "If there be an object truly ridiculous in nature, it is an American patriot, signing resolutions of independency with

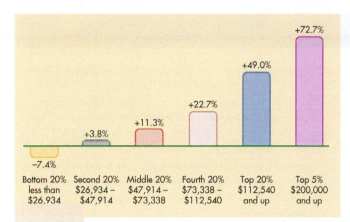

FIGURE 2: CHANGE IN REAL FAMILY INCOME, 1979–2009 After World War II and until the late 1970s, family income grew among all income groups. But since 1979, the income gap among American families has widened. The poorest families have actually lost income while the richest group have seen their incomes soar.

SOURCES: U.S. Census Bureau, Historical Income Tables: "Analysis of U.S. Census Data," in *The State of Working America, 1994–1995* (Armonk, N.Y.: M.E. Sharpe, 1994), 27. Families, Tables F-1 and F-3. http://inequality.org/income-inequality.

one hand, and with the other brandishing a whip over his affrighted slaves."[10]

The Declaration also denied political rights to women, whose knowledge was seen as limited to the private or domestic sphere. When Abigail Adams asked her husband John Adams to "remember the Ladies" in this document, he replied that those drafting the Declaration would not be subjected to "despotism of the petticoat."

It is this reservation of full humanity to a small portion of the population that gives the Declaration of Independence its extraordinary poignancy. Today, we want to read the promise that "all men are created equal" as meaning "all *people* are created equal," but the Founders reserved this status largely to white men of property.

The Constitution continued to protect inequality. **Art. I, Sec. 2 and 9, Art. IV, Sec. 4** It counted slaves as three-fifths of a person and safeguarded the slave trade for almost thirty years. Slaves living in free states, by constitutional dictate, were still slaves. This is why Justice Thurgood Marshall, a renowned civil rights litigator prior to his 1967 Supreme Court appointment, pointed out that the original Constitution was defective and required "several amendments, a civil war, and momentous social transformation to attain the system of constitutional government, and its respect for individual freedoms and human rights, we hold as fundamental today." He concluded, "The true miracle was not the birth of the Constitution, but its life, a life nurtured through two turbulent centuries of our own making, and a life embodying much good fortune that was not."[11]

Important landmarks toward equality in that life of the Constitution included the Thirteenth, Fourteenth, and Fifteenth Amendments, passed after the Civil War, which abolished slavery, provided for due process and equal protection of the laws, and created a constitutional protection against racial discrimination in voting. The Nineteenth Amendment, another landmark, extended voting rights to women. Equality has also been advanced through laws, executive actions, and judicial interpretations during the past century. President Lyndon Johnson signaled the closing of the gap between beliefs in equality before God and equality in the law when, in signing the 1964 Civil Rights Act into law, he declared: "Those who are equal before God shall now also be equal in the polling places, in the classrooms, in the factories."[12] Today, upholding this commitment is a core value for most, though not all, people throughout the United States.

But there is continuing debate about the precise meaning and measure of equality. Does equality mean equality of opportunity or equality of result? **Equality of opportunity** is the idea that every person should have the chance to realize her or his potential economically, intellectually, and socially. **Equality of result** is the idea that all individuals should be guaranteed a certain minimal standard or quality of life. If necessary, the government should help all persons get access to the same services or benefits—for example, adequate health care.

Although Americans indirectly debate these concepts when they talk about public policies—often without realizing that they're doing so—throughout history they have usually favored equality of opportunity over equality of result.[13] There are exceptions. For instance, the Supreme Court has ruled that defense attorneys are so important for fair trials that every defendant has a right to an attorney, even if she or he can't afford one.[14]

But equality of opportunity itself can be difficult to define and controversial to implement. In our capitalist economy, with its huge disparities in income and wealth, what is equality of opportunity? And what should government do to create or maintain it? Should government give a hand to those Americans who are disadvantaged—that is, put them in a position to take advantage of the opportunity that others are able to take advantage of? Or should government stand back and assume that those Americans already have the opportunity (or that private enterprise eventually will provide the opportunity)?[15]

Consider admissions policies used by selective colleges. Many schools take into account a student's race or economic status, giving African American, Latino, American Indian, and poor students a greater chance of admission than they would have from grades and test scores alone. The goal partly is to create a more diverse student body and an enriched educational experience, but the goal also is to compensate for the discrimination or inferior schools that many of these students have experienced—that is, to level the playing field and offer a genuine opportunity to those who have been denied an equal opportunity. Yet these policies also provide a result—admission to this college—that *some* of these students wouldn't obtain otherwise. So, proponents of these policies think they foster equality of opportunity, while opponents think they offer equality of result.

BEHIND THE SCENES

Lady Liberty

In 1882 a group of New Yorkers organized an art exhibit to raise money to pay for the erection of "Liberty Enlightening the World," the monumental sculpture France had given to the United States. One of the organizers asked a prominent New York writer to compose "some verses appropriate to the occasion."[1] Working only from photographs of the statue, which was yet to be shipped from France, Emma Lazarus wrote "The New Colossus," which included these now famous words: "…give me your tired, your poor, your huddled masses yearning to breathe free, the wretched refuse of your teeming shore. Send these, the homeless, tempest tossed to me, I lift my lamp beside the golden door!"

Until Lazarus wrote those lines, no one had associated the Statue of Liberty with immigration. Rather, it stood for the triumph of republican government. The woman with the torch symbolized the Enlightenment philosophy that had so influenced both American and French revolutionaries, reminding the world that the pursuit of enlightenment through reason and science could bring liberty to the world.

Why did Lazarus, whose family had been in America since at least the mid-1700s, and who had shown no prior interest in immigration, want to redefine the statue's meaning? Lazarus was a secular Jew who had been drawn into the cause of resettling Jewish immigrants fleeing persecution in Russia and eastern Europe. Her shock on learning about the conditions driving them from their home countries broadened her interest in all refugees entering the United States, and she believed that the statue in New York's harbor could be used to draw public attention to their plight.

Lazarus's poem *was* read at the fundraiser despite the divergence of her views from those of the statue's benefactors. It was then put aside and virtually forgotten.

But with the rise of fascism in Germany, Italy, and Spain in the 1930s, a new round of refugees began streaming toward America. The country began to celebrate itself as a land of immigrants. Alfred Hitchcock's wartime film, *Saboteur*, ended with the heroine reciting the Lazarus poem while standing in the statue's crown. By the postwar years, Americans were beginning to see the statue as Lazarus had, not as the symbol of liberty through reason, but as "The Mother of Exiles" lighting the way for everyone fleeing oppressive political or economic conditions. Though the United States has not consistently met this promise—Lazarus would have felt betrayed by the decision to refuse most European Jews entry before and during World War II—"Lady Liberty" is still a powerful symbol for many.

[1] This account is based on Esther Schor, *Emma Lazarus* (New York: Schocken Books, 2006), 189–256.

Liberty

Liberty refers to individual freedom. It is also shaped by Judeo-Christian beliefs, in this case the idea that every individual has worth. Therefore, individuals have some ability to control their own lives.

Liberty can be defined as "freedom from" or "freedom to." "Freedom from" means freedom from government interference. "Freedom to" means freedom to maximize one's potential. When liberty is defined as "freedom from," it limits government. When liberty is defined as "freedom to," it encourages individual creativity and self-expression, economically, socially, and intellectually. We can see both aspects of liberty in the First Amendment. This amendment begins with the proclamation "Congress shall make no law…," a "freedom from" assertion. It then lists five "freedoms to": religious worship, speech, press, assembly, and petitioning of the government. "Freedom from" and "freedom to" are intertwined throughout enduring American political traditions. The balance between them, however, varies greatly. And the Constitution encourages this diversity.

The Founding generation's views of liberty were also shaped by the contrasting views of British philosophers Thomas Hobbes and John Locke, who viewed personal liberty and government power from very different perspectives.

Thomas Hobbes, author of *The Leviathan* (1651), argued that people were naturally competitive, glory-seeking, and insecure—a frightening mixture. When people lived in a state of nature, unconstrained by law or government, free to do whatever they wished, they were in "a state of war," with "every man against every man." In one of the most famous passages in English political thought, Hobbes declared that under these circumstances, there would not be a society, a culture, or an economy; there would only be fear and danger of violent death. He concluded with the famous phrase, that in this condition "the life of man [is] solitary, poor, nasty, brutish and short."[16]

To escape these horrors, the people granted extraordinary power to a ruler who would do what was necessary to establish peace. Hobbes named the ruler "Leviathan," describing him as a "Mortal God" who would create a commonwealth that would provide for the people's defense and secure peace.[17] In a Hobbesian government, there was little "freedom from" the government, because the people had to be so closely controlled to avoid strife and war, and little "freedom to," because granting people "freedom to" would lead

Nativist sentiment flared when the waves of immigrants arrived on the shores of America in the 1800s. This illustration depicts Irish and German immigrants, symbolized by whiskey and beer barrels, stealing a ballot box.

to destruction and death. Still, Hobbes saw this absolutist government as achieving good because it ensured safety and security by limiting liberty.

John Locke, in *The Second Treatise of Government* (published about 1688), argued instead that people were rational and social. A civil society—one in which people had property and there were simple markets—was possible even in a state of nature, before there was government to control the people. If Hobbes maintained that people were equal because each could kill the other, Locke insisted that people were equal because God had created them.[18] Where Hobbes saw destruction, Locke saw creativity.

Still, Locke did acknowledge the potential for violence: without a government to enforce shared values, some people would harm others; when this happened, people could not be expected to judge their own cases without bias. To solve these problems—to be more secure and to ensure that power was exercised appropriately—people consented to government by majority rule.[19] In this system, the people would retain their voice and their rights, limiting government and granting comparatively little power to their leaders. For Locke, government was established in order to enhance a people's "freedom to" be creative and distinctive individuals by ensuring their "freedom from" one another's selfishness and bias. Unlike Hobbes's government, Locke's government promised both "freedom to" and "freedom from."

The contrasting views that Hobbes and Locke advanced in the seventeenth century are still heard today. In a time of war or danger, people are more ready to give up their liberty to government; in other times, people are less willing to sacrifice their liberty. Following the September 11, 2001, attacks, Americans felt threatened and fearful. "Homeland security" was suddenly a first priority. When members of

Congress received anthrax-poisoned mailings, the sense of threat became pervasive. In response, Congress passed the USA PATRIOT Act, a law that strengthened counterterrorism efforts but reduced individual liberties. For example, federal agencies could now make more expansive use of electronic surveillance even without warrants or a justification, and in other circumstances they could more readily obtain search warrants; there were also increased penalties for crimes "likely to be committed by terrorists," and the statutes of limitations for these crimes were lengthened or eliminated. Many of the provisions in the USA PATRIOT Act had been repeatedly submitted to Congress before the September 11th attacks occurred, but it was not until 2001 that empowering the government and weakening individual liberties in these ways were acceptable. In defending the act, the government argued that these new laws were within existing legal principles but that changes were needed to protect Americans from terrorists.

The powers of American government also grew during earlier wars—the Civil War, World War I, and World War II—but after the war was over, wartime measures were done away with. The difference between then and now is that, at least during the Bush administration, war was defined as a perpetual state because, after all, terrorists will always exist. The Obama administration has dropped the rhetoric of "war on terror," but Congress renewed most of the PATRIOT Act and Obama has supported many of the measures put in place by the Bush administration. Thus Americans, who like to think of themselves as brave and bold, became timid in the face of immediate international and domestic violence, more aware of the ways in which they could hurt or help one another, and less confident that their limited government would protect them against hostile forces. In this kind of situation,

American Diversity

Equality and the Rise of the "Birthers"

Progress toward racial equality took a big step forward when a majority of voters elected Barack Obama president in 2008. Many Americans were elated that this racial barrier was finally crossed.

Yet this progress is mixed. In 2012, a reporter described an outhouse outside the Montana Republican state convention site in Missoula that had been labeled "Obama Presidential Library" and painted as though it had been shot full of holes.[1] Inside, the reporter continued, "a fake birth certificate for 'Barack Hussein Obama' was stamped with an expletive referring to bovine droppings."

It was clear during the presidential campaign, when some voters admitted that they would never vote for an African American man, that some Americans would never accept an African American president if elected. Some of these individuals, like those who constructed the "outhouse," continue to deny Obama's legitimacy as president. Since the results of the election were not close and there were little grounds to claim he didn't really win, some have decided that he does not meet the qualifications to be president. His mother was a U.S. citizen, which means he automatically became one when he was born. But these "birthers" claim that Obama was born in Kenya, where his father was from, rather than in Hawaii, where he was actually born.[2] If he were not born in the United States, he is not eligible to become the president because Article II, Section 1 of the Constitution states that a president must be a "natural born citizen," that is, born in the United States. For the birthers, then, Obama is not a legitimate president.

The birthers are especially prevalent in the South and among Republicans.[3] Before Obama released his long-form birth certificate (but well after Hawaii officials said state records show he was born there and well after the existence of a 1961 birth announcement in a Honolulu paper was revealed), 45 percent of Republicans nationwide believed he was born in another country, and an additional 22 percent weren't sure.[4] After Obama released his birth certificate, those who believed the "birther" myth decreased by half—but only by half.[5] Some people believe other ridiculous claims circulating on the Internet—for example, that his educational records were fabricated—despite ample evidence to the contrary.

Would these questions have arisen if Obama were white? It is possible. The conservative wing of the Republican Party did all it could to challenge Clinton's legitimacy as president, too. But we also know that there was no "birther" movement that grew up to challenge the legitimacy of John McCain, the Republican presidential candidate who ran against Obama in 2008. McCain was born in Panama. When some people raised the issue that McCain's Panamanian birth disqualified him to serve as president, investigations confirmed that he was born on the military base under U.S. jurisdiction. While the issue was raised intermittently during the campaign by a few people, there was no large-scale "birther" movement that denied the facts, egged on or even led by party leaders.[6] Democrats were generally not supportive of McCain as a possible president, but they respected his legitimacy as a candidate.

This, of course, does not mean that all or even most opponents of Obama are racists or that all or most criticisms of Obama are motivated by racism. Yet it would be naive to discount the role of racism in views of our first African American president.

[1] Dana Milbank, "Nothing Sweet about Heckling Obama in the Rose Garden," *New York Times*, June 19, 2012, http://www.washingtonpost.com/opinions/dana-milbank-nothing-sweet-about-heckling-obama-in-the-rose-garden/2012/06/19/gJQAHgs1oV_story.html?hpid=z2. A message in the structure gave fake phone numbers for Michelle Obama, Hillary Clinton, and Nancy Pelosi "For a Good Time." Milbank reports that the Republican state chairman acknowledged it wasn't in good taste but shrugged it off.

[2] Michael Hirsh and Daniel Gross, "The Wisdom of Crowds; When Populist Rage Leads to Smart Policy," *Newsweek*, February 8, 2010, 27.

[3] A reproduction of his birth certificate is found online at http://latimesblogs.latimes.com/.shared/image.html?/photos/uncategorized/2008/06/13/bobirthcertificate.jp. The Department of Health of the state of Hawaii has a website to deal with inquiries about the birth certificate, including a statement that both the Director of Health and the Registrar of Vital Statistics have personally seen and verified that the State Department of Health has Obama's original birth certificate on record. http://hawaii.gov/health/vital-records/obama.html; http://hawaii.gov/health/about/pr/2008/08-93.pdf.

[4] *New York Times*/CBS News poll, cited in Charles Babington, "'Birther' Claims Force GOP to Take a Stand," *Lincoln Journal Star*, April 23, 2011, A4.

[5] Bill Keller, "Let Me Take Off My Tinfoil Hat for a Moment," *New York Times Magazine*, June 5, 2011, 12.

[6] For a review of this discussion, which took place early in 2008, see http://newsbusters.org/forums/latest-news/q-panamanian-born-john-mccain-natural-born-citizen-united-states-19392.

liberty—both the "freedom to" and the "freedom from"—was seen by many as more threat than opportunity.

But a Hobbesian state existing in perpetuity is not compatible with Americans' views of liberty. The attacks on "big government" are partly about liberty, though few of the attacks in recent years have focused on the decline in liberty brought about by antiterrorism legislation.

Individual Rights

Because of their emphasis on liberty, especially "freedom from," Americans emphasize individual rights. The most important rights are listed in the Bill of Rights to the Constitution. These rights limit the government, establishing a protected sphere for the individual. The government cannot interfere with people's right to speak or practice their religion. The government cannot conduct unreasonable searches and seizures, and it cannot force people to incriminate themselves. The government cannot require excessive bail, or impose excessive fines or cruel and unusual punishments. Individuals are free from such actions.

In the generations since the ratification of the Constitution, rights have continued to be a focus for debate in the United States. "Wedge issues," so called because they push people apart (driving a wedge between groups in the electorate) and polarize the vote, are almost all rights-centered. Gun control, same-sex marriage, reproductive rights, and capital punishment are four examples.

Throughout history, there has also been some demand for "freedom to" individual rights. These rights require government to take action to benefit the individual. Franklin Roosevelt listed many of these rights in his 1944 State of the Union Address when he maintained, "True individual freedom cannot exist without economic security and independence." He argued that, in addition to the political rights in the Bill of Rights, people had economic rights: "The right to a useful and remunerative job... The right to earn enough to provide adequate food and clothing and recreation... The right of every family to a decent home; The right to adequate medical care and the opportunity to achieve and enjoy good health; The right to adequate protection from the economic fears of old age, and sickness, and accident and unemployment; And, finally, the right to a good education."[20]

Notwithstanding Roosevelt's claim that these economic rights rested upon "self-evident" truths, there have been ferocious debates about each of the rights he articulated. For example, "the right to a good education" has become a lightning rod for disagreement. Today, there are ongoing battles over how much support government should offer educational institutions, and how much control government should exercise over curriculum and outcomes.

Both "freedom from" and "freedom to" rights have been valued and challenged. For some, it is critically important to limit government power. In this view, the government poses such an extraordinary threat to individual creativity and self-reliance that it must be limited to performing only the most fundamental of public tasks. This is the judgment endorsed by those in the Tea Party movement. For others, government's power can be channeled to benefit the people. These individuals see an activist government as advancing society, accomplishing good through public initiatives. This is the conclusion reached by progressives. Americans array themselves along a spectrum that includes these views, and everything in between and beyond. Because rights define individuals' relationships with government, as well as with one another and the market, they are core values in the U.S. political system.

Popular Sovereignty

Popular sovereignty means that the people rule. Perhaps President Abraham Lincoln expressed the concept best when he spoke of "government of the people, by the people, and for the people."

Popular sovereignty reflects our form of government, a democracy, meaning "authority of the people." A democracy can be a **pure** or **direct democracy**, such as a New England town meeting. In these local governments, all the residents of a town come together to discuss local issues and then vote on them; the people govern themselves directly.

The national government of the United States, however, is an **indirect democracy** or **republic**. People do not directly make public policy; they select representatives who act in their behalf. It is a democracy because the people elect the decision makers; it is a republic because elected representatives–not the people themselves–are the decision makers in the government. In the U.S. democratic republic, popular sovereignty is a core value, but the people delegate a great deal of power to their representatives.

But government cannot be by the people and of the people unless people participate in politics. Thomas Jefferson said, "Let our countrymen know that the people alone can protect us against the evils" of misgovernment. Americans love the idea that the average person has a say in what government does and serves as a check on its power. Voting is the most basic and easiest way to exert this power, yet participation rates are not high in presidential elections and are quite low for congressional and local elections. Many Americans practice "couch potato politics,"[21] not bothering to learn about candidates and issues and choosing to be disgusted with politics rather than involved with it.[22] But popular sovereignty is a concept that calls on the people to control their government. They can do so only by participating.

Majority Rule

If political authority lies with the people, and if all people are equal, then the majority should rule. Majority rule lies at the heart of democracy, so much so that E. B. White observed that democracy depends upon being able to trust the 51 percent. In other words, democracy requires a deep faith in the wisdom, rationality, and generous self-interest of the people.

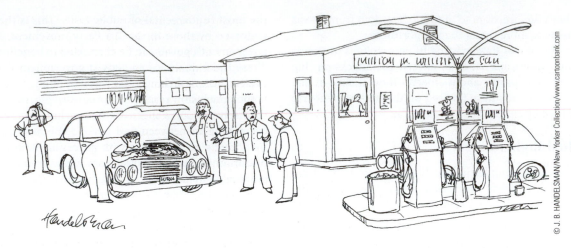

"We can't come to an agreement about how to fix your car, Mr. Simons. Sometimes that's the way things happen in a democracy."

Majority rule is an integral part of U.S. elections. With two parties dominating campaigns and elections, majority rule routinely determines which candidate wins. In legislatures, most votes are decided by majorities, too. Why do minorities go along with majorities? Sometimes they do so because they accept the principle of majority rule and expect that they will be in the majority at other times. The minority also go along because they expect the majority to respect their basic rights. If these expectations are not fulfilled, the minority are less likely to accept majority rule and to tolerate majority decisions. Thus majority rule normally entails minority rights.

Minority Rights

Although we think of the United States government as a system of majority rule, it also is a system of minority rights. The Founders were concerned about the rights of political, religious, regional, and economic minorities (such as land owners). As a result of the expansion of individual rights in the twentieth century, Americans today are also concerned about the rights of racial, ethnic, and sexual minorities.

Fearing that a democratic majority might oppress the minority, the Founders opposed a system of unchecked majority rule and instead constructed a government designed to limit majority rule. Thus, as we will see in Chapter 2, the Founders divided power among different level of government (nation and states) and different branches of government (separation of powers), each with checks on the other (checks and balances). In the legislature, one house—the House of Representatives or the Senate—can check the other. The Senate was also designed to check the majority by giving less populous states the same number of senators as the more populous states. And as we will describe in Chapter 9, some Senate procedures also limit majority rule. Using these constraints on majority rule, then, different minorities at different places and times can check the majority.

The concepts of majority rule and minority rights conflict with each other, and democratic government must strike a delicate balance. Because the majority has more power, it tends to flex its muscles at the expense of the minority. The most egregious example has been the enslavement, segregation, and discrimination directed at African Americans, but other examples occur frequently in our society. The idea that everyone loses when minority rights are trampled is a lesson that does not stay learned.

 Thinking about Democracy

Throughout the text, we will be raising questions about democracy and about how compatible our government and our beliefs are with democracy. To start at the beginning: How do the core values of the United States sustain democracy?

Conflicts between Core Values

As we have seen, in the United States the core values of equality, liberty, individual rights, popular sovereignty, majority rule, and minority rights are abstract and sometimes competing. The USA PATRIOT Act may be viewed as inhibiting or enhancing liberty; and an activist government be viewed as enhancing or undermining individual rights. For this reason, claiming consistency with a core value will not end a political conflict, but it might help by providing a framework for disagreement.

Politics leading to government action is often a process of working out the balance between one core value and another, or the balance between the rights of one group and another. Equality versus liberty, and majority rule versus individual rights, are two perennial examples.

Equality v. Liberty

Equality and liberty can be mutually reinforcing, as when the Thirteenth Amendment abolished slavery. That particular reconciliation of equality and liberty tried to correct a situation that had stretched across two-hundred-plus years of American history and that ultimately ignited a civil war. Since then, the values of liberty and equality for African Americans have required interventions by every branch and level of government.

Equality and liberty may also contradict one another. To the extent that all persons exercise their liberty, taking advantage of their "freedom to" and their "freedom from," there will be inequality. For example, taxation is a limit on liberty, in this case the freedom to spend your own money as you wish, but it is often used to promote equality. Tax money supports police protection in all parts of a city and also supports public education, giving children from middle-class and poor families, who can't afford private schools, a chance to obtain an education. In current political debates about taxation or regulation, Republicans tend to give higher priority to liberty, while Democrats value equality more highly.[23]

Consider the contrasting economic policies debated throughout the 2012 presidential election. Democrat Barack Obama stressed the need for greater government regulation of the economy so that the financial irresponsibilities that led to the stock market downturn and the gutting of the housing market could not be repeated. These policies prioritized equality: information about the market would be more widely disseminated, making it possible for all people to invest more wisely, with greater knowledge of the associated risks and ultimate benefits.

Republican Mitt Romney, the former governor of Massachusetts and once a successful CEO, favored less regulation in order to maximize companies' efficiency and productivity. His proposed policies prioritized liberty: corporate decision makers would be able to act on their own priorities and judgments, making it possible for the market to become more efficient in its consumption of resources and its productivity.

Neither candidate would disavow either core value of equality or liberty: their debate was over which should have priority.

Majority Rule v. Individual Rights

Individual rights often sustain and enrich majority rule. Rights to a free press, to free speech, and to assembly and petition, as well as rights to due process and equal protection of the law, among many others, provide people with the knowledge, the security, and the opportunities to express their views. When women received the right to vote through the Nineteenth Amendment, they were more successful at persuading lawmakers to pass legislation giving women equal employment opportunities, bank credit in their own name, and other rights. Having women become part of a majority promoted individual rights, although even then some restrictions continued. (For example, some employers still would not hire women.)

Yet majority rule and individual rights often oppose one another even more directly. Because majority rule does not necessarily take into account the rights of those not in the majority, the Founders greatly feared majorities that would trample on individual and minority rights. These are the kinds of disputes that have periodically surfaced in gun control policy debates. A majority of Americans favor gun control measures, but gun owners have been able to protect their rights of gun ownership by their political influence in state and national politics. In this case, individual rights have dominated majority rule.

More common is the reverse situation in which majority rule trumps individual rights. Many kinds of regulations can serve as illustrations. Your desire to drive a car while drunk is impeded by majority rule, which trumps your desire in the interests of public safety. You are not free to worship as you want if your religion mandates human sacrifice. You cannot avoid taxes simply because you do not want to pay for the war in Afghanistan or Medicare. In each of these cases, your desire to behave as you want is frustrated by majority rule.

As with the debates about equality and liberty, whenever the conflict is perceived as one of majority rule against individual rights, and those rights are seen as important ones, it is often difficult to find a solution that will be widely supported (see Figure 3).

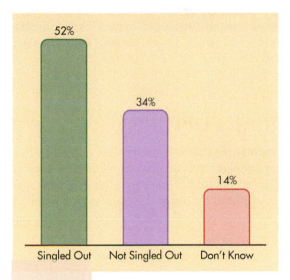

FIGURE 3: A MAJORITY OF AMERICAN MUSLIMS BELIEVE ANTI-TERRORISM POLICIES ARE TARGETED AGAINST THEIR GROUP* Antiterrorism policies enacted after the 2001 attacks generally gave a higher priority to national security than to individual rights. Yet everyone's rights may not be equally affected. Muslim Americans believe their rights were infringed upon.

* Based on a telephone survey conducted from April 14 to July 30, 2011, with 1,033 Muslims in the United States. The margin of error is 5 percentage points. The following question was asked of Muslims in the United States: *Do Government anti-terrorism policies single out Muslims in the United States?*

SOURCE: The Pew Research Foundation, as quoted in Hope Yen, "Poll Shows Muslim-Americans Feel Targeted," *Lincoln Journal Star*, August 30, 2011, A1.

The Founding and Core Values

The Declaration of Independence was an extraordinary statement. Its widely quoted premise has been an inspiration to individuals around the world who seek freedom: "We hold these truths to be self-evident, that all men are created equal, that they are endowed by their Creator with certain unalienable Rights, that among these are Life, Liberty and the pursuit of Happiness." These rights might seem platitudinous now, but they were revolutionary ideas in the eighteenth century. And in the twenty-first century, this document still highlights Americans' core values and aspirations. Yet modern perspectives on the Declaration of Independence vary. For some people, it expresses the core values of equality, liberty, majority rule, and minority rights. It reinforces a belief that the United States is dedicated to human progress. From another perspective, though, the Declaration is seen as favoring a privileged minority, while refusing to recognize most people as citizens.

Martin Luther King, Jr. echoed a nineteenth-century philosopher when he said that "the arc of history is long, but it bends toward justice."[24] In this optimistic view of the world, over time people become freer and more equal, even if there are setbacks along the way. In the United States, though unsteady, inconsistent, and sometimes bloody, the arc of over two centuries of history has bent toward greater fulfillment of the great concepts of the Declaration of Independence.

POLITICAL CULTURE

A **political culture** is a shared body of values and beliefs that shapes perceptions and attitudes toward politics and government and influences political behavior. As this definition suggests, it is very difficult for observers to assess the content or strength of a nation's political culture(s). Political polls can teach us a great deal about a voter's preferences because those preferences are organized around a specific decision. But political culture is more amorphous. As the previous discussion of core values has already shown, political culture often embraces complex and contradictory ideals.

Governments rely on the support of citizens, including their identification with the country and its political values and their actions to sustain the system. Without this support, government will be ineffective or even have to rely on coercion and force to govern. But almost no government requires all its people to adhere to a single political culture. A basic function of government is to establish the rules under which interests can compete. In order for a democratic republic to accommodate conflict and competition, there needs to be popular support for the rules that control competing interests. This keeps the conflict constructive.

The essence of political culture is agreement on the fundamental principles of the country, on the rights and obligations of citizenship, and on the rules for participating in the political process. These shared values reduce the strains produced by our differences and allow us to compete intensely on some issues while cooperating on others.

Creating a National Political Culture

Whether the newly created United States of America came about by "design of Providence," was a "lucky accident," or was the result of the Founders' skill in shaping a workable Constitution, it faced a problem common to all political systems: how to create a national identity among its people.[25] One of the most significant challenges to establishing a national political culture was the dispersion of people among the former colonies. Under the Articles of Confederation, the states were sovereign: people took great pride in their identity as Virginians or New Englanders, for example. It was not until the Civil War, under the influence of Abraham Lincoln's powerful reference at Gettysburg to the "unfinished work" of preserving the Union, that Americans began referring to the United States with the singular *is* rather than the plural *are*.[26]

Throughout U.S. history, political cultures have emerged, flourished, changed, and passed away. Core values have acquired new meanings and new significance and have encountered new challenges and controversies. These changes have been greatly influenced by three factors: the public education system, the media, and government force or coercion.

Public Education

Most of the Founders believed that an educated citizenry was essential to the survival of the new republic, and advocates of public education such as Daniel Webster argued that only educated citizens would be able to understand public issues, elect virtuous leaders, and "sustain the delicate balance between liberty and order in the new political system."[27] Jefferson put it more ominously: "If a nation

"Actually, I prefer the term Arctic-American."

expects to be ignorant and free, in a state of civilization, it expects what never was and never will be." As the public school system emerged, increasing emphasis was placed on the "training of citizens in patriotism, political knowledge and public affairs."[28]

A perennial issue in the debate over what is required to sustain a political culture is whether all citizens should speak a common language. The Founders presumed that English would be the national language, and Noah Webster's 1783 textbook promoting "a new national language to be spelled and pronounced differently from British English" was one of the first attempts to create an American national identity.[29] Webster, a Connecticut schoolteacher, wanted British textbooks banned from the classroom, saying that the wiping out of Old World maxims had to begin in infancy: "Let the first word he lisps be Washington."[30] In 1828 Webster published the *Dictionary of American English*—a dictionary "suited to the needs of the American people"—because, he argued, Americans could never accept the British definitions of senate, congress, assembly, and courts.[31] Another objective was to standardize the multitude of dialects, some mutually unintelligible, that were spoken by Americans of the time.[32] Today the United States has fewer spoken dialects than any other of the world's largest countries, a considerable accomplishment given the diversity of our collective heritage and strong regional cultures. And while schools are still under local control, there is some common content in civic education across the country.

During times of high immigration, many elected officials argued in favor of using the public schools to assimilate the new arrivals. In the late 1800s, a concerted effort was made to establish the American flag as a national symbol.[33] Public schools started flying the flag in 1890, and the Pledge of Allegiance was adopted in 1892.[34] By the mid-twentieth century, most elementary school children were studying current events in their *Weekly Reader* and beginning each day by reciting the Pledge to the flag. Many states required high school students to pass an exam on the U.S. Constitution, and sometimes also their state constitution, to graduate.

In the late 1900s, education was again at the forefront of immigration and assimilation discussions. Those who favored assimilation saw bilingual education and English literacy as opposing priorities. This controversy increased in the 2000s, especially in districts that confronted increasing enrollments as a product of unregulated immigration. When the costs of educating these children contributed to budget shortfalls in a number of states, some began to argue that the children of undocumented persons should not be admitted to the public schools. Although this policy was not adopted, the fact that it was seriously considered suggests that public schools are no longer seen as the leading institutions for assimilating new arrivals to the United States. Now, access to public education is perceived, by some, as reserved to those who have been accepted as permanent residents or as citizens.

The Media

The mass media have always facilitated the dissemination of ideas and information and, consequently, the development of political culture. In the eighteenth century, the question of whether to ratify the Constitution was strongly debated. Some of those writings exercised such influence over people's core values that they continue to be read and studied over two hundred years later. This is certainly true of the *Federalist Papers,* which will be discussed throughout this book.

In the twentieth century, first radio and then television augmented print media, conveying news and public opinion. For several decades, there were comparatively few news outlets, either print or broadcast, which meant that people throughout the nation had similar information and interpretations on which to base their judgments. Yet personal experiences varied widely because of the deep divisions existing among people of different races, ethnicities, genders, religions, regions, and classes, among other identities. These socioeconomic contrasts led to differing interpretations of media reports, ensuring that there continued to be diverse political cultures throughout the United States.

In the late twentieth and early twenty-first centuries, the rise of electronic and social media provided new means of sharing facts, ideas, experiences, and beliefs. These new channels of communication facilitated people's mobilization throughout and across nations. At the same time, the greater number of information sources has meant that each media source typically has fewer consumers. Cable news services and blogs target and are selected by narrower audiences. Each information consumer can seek out the sources closest to her or his own views, which leads some commentators to describe current-day media consumption practices as reading

This Yemeni woman is taking the oath of citizenship in Detroit, having passed a lengthy examination that tested her knowledge and understanding of U.S. political culture.

the "Daily Me." Values and beliefs are still shared, perceptions and attitudes toward politics and government are still developed, and information about political behaviors continues to be disseminated. But whether the narrow and targeted audiences of the electronic age lead to more "group think" and conformity, or greater diversity and creativity, will not be clear for some time.

Government Force

When education and mass communication have failed to persuade people to endorse the mainstream values of the American political system, the society and the government have sometimes turned to force and violence. In the early decades of the twentieth century, for example, the U.S. government obliged all American Indian children to attend government-run boarding schools that required the children to adopt mainstream Anglo-European values, speak English, and dress in uniforms. Children who refused to comply often endured severe corporal punishment. Because parents and grandparents could not teach the children their culture, the effect of these policies was to deny many Indian and native communities a generation of leaders.

Multiple Political Cultures

Throughout much of the twentieth century, different geographic regions of the country were thought to have different political subcultures; although there were similarities in the core values, each region had its own distinctive approach to politics and political participation.[35] The tendency of people in New England and the upper Midwest to believe that politics was a way of improving life, and that they had an obligation to participate politically, was labeled a moralistic political subculture. In the individualistic political subculture, said to be typical of the industrial Midwest, the West, and the East, the objective of politics was to get benefits for oneself and one's group. In the traditionalistic political subculture, associated with the states of the Deep South, politics was seen as a way to maintain the status quo and little value was placed on participation.

Today, these differences are much diminished. Over 40 percent of Americans will move from one state to another.[36] The national economy also leads to a certain sameness throughout the nation. You can hear the same news, eat the same food, shop in the same stores, and buy the same products from Maine to Arizona.

The political effects of this standardization are very evident. In the Deep South, for instance, a much more participatory society has replaced rule by a small white oligarchy. The modern civil rights movement has opened opportunities for participation by the region's large African American population. Religious conservatives have also mobilized.

Still, the most organized attempts to deprive African Americans of voting rights are in the South, through mechanisms such as the removal of voting rights for those convicted

CourseReader ASSIGNMENT

Log into www.cengagebrain.com and open CourseReader to access the full reading "For Many Latinos, Racial Identity Is More Culture than Color," by Mireya Navarro.

What is the definition of "race"? Is it "a set of common physical traits," a description of a person's body? Or is race a social construction, a status that is imposed upon or claimed by individuals? What is the connection between race and ethnicity, which may be defined as "a shared set of cultural traits"? Who should decide a person's race or ethnicity? Should the government be able to do so?

How Latinos perceive themselves, and how they express those perceptions in responding to the census questions, will influence the next ten years of policy making. Whether decision makers have accurate or inaccurate estimations of their numbers, will determine both Latinos' representation in government and their access to government resources. After all, numbers matter in a democracy. But numbers are only part of the whole story. Do Latinos share a common political culture? Will they mobilize on behalf of shared goals? If not, then elected

officeholders may feel they can disregard the people who do claim this identity.

1. Why does the government need information about the identity of the people living in the United States? How should this information be gathered? As you answer this question, think about the potential for this information to be put to appropriate or inappropriate uses, and for information-gatherers to show either respect or disrespect for the people they are profiling.

2. How would you distinguish between "race" and "ethnicity"? How does each affect a person's political culture?

3. The core values of equality, liberty, and rights are focused on the individual. Describing people by their race and ethnicity, however, emphasizes their connection to a group. Given that all these values and identities have been so consistently important in the history of the United States, how do you resolve these fundamental contrasts?

of felonies and attempts to purge the voting rolls. Despite trends toward homogeneity, therefore, distinctive political subcultures endure.

 Thinking about Democracy

> How far should government go in promoting the country's political culture? Should it instill support for the core values? Should it teach a common language? Mandate a common language? Or should it do none of these?

THE ROLE AND RESPONSIVENESS OF GOVERNMENT

As you read this book, you will see questions and issues returning time and again. What is the appropriate role of government? How do our institutions, processes, and policies reflect our core values? To what extent is government responsive to the people? To which people?

Americans' core values support the key role of the people in their governance. To play that role, though, requires participation, and many Americans turn up their noses at politics and politicians. Although much of politics does not reflect the highest ethical standards, its standards are probably similar to those of other institutions in our society, such as business and the media. If government is to be "by the people" and responsive to the people, the people must participate.

Americans often say, "It's all politics." *Of course it is!* It is through politics that decisions are made. If everyone in the United States were in agreement, there would be no need for debate, bargaining, or compromise. But Americans do not agree on most things, so debates about issues and conflicts over elections are necessarily political. They reflect the competition and diverse views inherent in a democratic republic. They are the only way we can ensure governmental responsiveness.

SUMMARY

- Americans are a diverse people who from the beginning have incorporated many different tribes, races, ethnicities, nationalities, and religions. Each wave of immigration has shaped and reshaped the American people and broadened its diversity, even though each new group is resented by some of those already here. Other elements of diversity, such as region and income, are also relevant to the political process and political outcomes.

- Among the core values of U.S. politics are equality, liberty, individual rights, popular sovereignty, majority rule, and minority rights. Each of these is an extremely complicated concept, with several contrasting definitions that are deeply rooted in American history. As a result, there is agreement on the core values, but the meaning and the significance of each value is continually and strongly contested.

- A political culture is a shared body of values and beliefs that shapes perceptions and attitudes toward politics and government, influencing political behavior. Although Americans have a shared political culture that leads us to support our governmental structure and political norms, there are also subcultures based on different values in different regions or groups. Although there is much similarity among these political subcultures, their disagreements are real and vibrant.

- In the United States, government is challenged to respond to the people's needs while balancing the competing priorities of the core values. Doing this requires decision makers to think carefully about the core values, to identify connections between those values and proposed policies, to acknowledge historic biases that have excluded or privileged people in the political system, and always to recognize the government's power to shape people's ideas, interests, and lives.

DISCUSSION QUESTIONS

1. What are the major sources of diversity in the American population? How do these differences affect the U.S. government?

2. What core values have the authors identified in the American democracy? Are there other values that you believe to be similarly important? Describe two current political debates that involve conflicts among the core values.

3. As you think about political culture in the United States, do you think that the nation has one or many political cultures? Do you think that there is a need for less or more diversity in American political culture(s)? Why or why not?

4. Which core value do you consider the most important? Why?

2 The Constitution

Angry protesters attend a Tea Party rally.

AP Images/Steve Helber, File

LEARNING OBJECTIVES

1. Identify the shortcomings of the Articles of Confederation.
2. Identify the goals of the Founders in revising the Articles. Recognize the difficulty the Founders faced in finding a balance between a government strong enough to govern the country but not too strong to threaten the liberty of the people.
3. Understand the need for compromises in drafting the Constitution.
4. Distinguish between direct and indirect democracy, and define a republic.
5. Grasp the general idea of fragmentation of power and the specific concepts of federalism, separation of powers, and checks and balances.
6. Identify the veto points in the American system and understand their implications for political progress.
7. Compare the views of the Federalists and Antifederalists.
8. Recognize how the meaning of the Constitution, especially as it pertains to the size and scope of our government, has evolved in response to major crises, especially the Civil War and the Great Depression.

TALKING POINTS

At Tea Party rallies, signs demand, "Stop Trashing the Constitution" and "Stop Shredding the Constitution." Tea Partiers emphasize the Constitution and revere the Founders. They demand that we "go back" to "following the Constitution." And when did Americans stop following the Constitution? Some Tea Partiers point to the Progressive movement in the late 1800s and early 1900s. That movement led to the Sixteenth Amendment, which allows the federal government to impose income taxes, and the Seventeenth Amendment, which allows people to vote directly for senators (rather than having state legislatures choose senators, as the Constitution originally specified).[1]

After the 2010 congressional elections, when new members of the House of Representatives were sworn in, Tea Party members asked that the Constitution be read aloud, which had never been done in the House before. Tea Party members proposed a flurry of constitutional amendments, intended to undo "the damage" done by previous Congresses, presidents, and federal judges.[2]

Now Americans are talking about the Constitution to a degree they haven't for many years. They debate the meaning of its provisions and the application of its provisions to our government and its policies today.

Some debates revolve around states' rights. At least one Tea Party senator claims that national parks, forests, and wilderness areas are usurpations of the rights of the states in which they're located. The parks are "federal occupations" of state lands.[3] Another claims that federal funding for drug enforcement is unconstitutional because the states have responsibility for drug enforcement (as they do for most crimes).

Other debates revolve around individual freedom. Senator Rand Paul (R-Ky.) asserts that the civil rights laws are unconstitutional because they impinge on individual freedom. Others assert that Social Security; Medicare, which covers some health care expenses for people who receive Social Security; and public housing programs are unconstitutional because they redistribute wealth (taking wealth from some through income taxes and giving it to others through these programs). Likewise, Tea Partiers say that public broadcasting (PBS and NPR) and public art projects are unconstitutional.

Some Tea Party members of Congress insist that environmental regulation is unconstitutional and even entire departments of the government, in particular the Department of Education and the Department of Housing and Urban Affairs, violate the Constitution as well.

Senator Mike Lee (R-Ut.) has spoken favorably of **nullification**, a doctrine that allows states to nullify—ignore—any federal law which they think violates the Constitution. This doctrine was championed by the southern states before the Civil War.[4] Texas governor Rick Perry (R) has even spoken favorably of secession, a doctrine that allows states to secede from the Union. Both Lee and Perry identify with the Tea Party.

Thus the Constitution, written by the Founders over two centuries ago, is the subject of political ferment once again.

Early settlers came to America for different reasons. Some came to escape religious persecution, others to establish their own religious orthodoxy. Some came to avoid debtors' prison, others to get rich. Some came to flee the closed society of the Old World, others to make money for their families or employers in that world. Some came as free persons, others as indentured servants or slaves. Few came to practice self-government. Yet the desire for self-government was evident from the beginning.[5] The settlers who arrived in Jamestown in 1607 established the first representative assembly in America. The Pilgrims, who reached Plymouth in 1620, drew up the Mayflower Compact in which they vowed to "solemnly & mutually in the presence of God, and one of another, covenant and combine our selves together into a civill body politick." They pledged to establish laws for "the generall good of the colonie" and in return promised "all due submission and obedience."[6]

During the next century and a half, the colonies adopted constitutions and elected representative assemblies. Of course, the colonies lived under British rule, so they had to accept the appointment of royal governors and the presence of British troops. But a vast ocean separated the two continents. At such distance, Britain could not wield the control it might at closer reach. It had to grant the colonies a measure of autonomy, which they used to practice the beginnings of self-government.

These early efforts toward self-government led to conflict with the mother government. In 1774, the colonies established the Continental Congress to coordinate their actions. Within months, the conflict reached flash point, and the Congress urged the colonies to form their own governments. In 1776, the Congress adopted the Declaration of Independence. (See box "Founding Mothers.")

After six years of war, the Americans accepted the British surrender. At the time it seemed they had met their biggest test. Yet they would find fomenting a revolution easier than fashioning a government and drafting a declaration of independence easier than crafting a constitution.

This chapter will examine the Founders' efforts to craft a constitution, first the Articles of Confederation and then the Constitution itself. The chapter will also show how later generations modified the Constitution, especially as a result of the Civil War and the Great Depression.

American Diversity

Founding Mothers

Charles Francis Adams, a grandson of President John Adams and Abigail Adams, declared in 1840, "The heroism of the females of the Revolution has gone from memory with the generation that witnessed it, and nothing, absolutely nothing remains upon the ear of the young of the present day."[1] That statement remains true today; in the volumes written about the revolutionary and Constitution-making era, much is said of the "Founding Fathers" but little about the "Founding Mothers." Although no women were delegates to the Constitutional Convention, in various ways—besides birthing and rearing the children and maintaining the homes—women contributed significantly to the founding of the country. Many contributed directly to the political ferment of the time. Their role during the revolutionary and Constitution-making era was greater than it would be again for a century.

Before the Revolutionary War, women were active in encouraging opposition to British rule. Groups of women, some formed as the "Daughters of Liberty," organized resistance to British taxes by leading boycotts of British goods such as cloth and tea; they made their own cloth, hosting spinning bees, and made their own drinks from native herbs and flowers.

A few women were political pamphleteers, helping increase public sentiment for independence. One of those pamphlet writers, Mercy Otis Warren, from Boston, was thought to be the first person to urge the Massachusetts delegates to the Continental Congress to vote for separation from Britain.[2] She also wrote poems advocating independence and plays satirizing British officials and sympathizers among the colonists (although the plays could only be read, not staged, because Puritan Boston forbade theater). Throughout the period before and after the Revolution, Warren shared her political ideas in personal correspondence with leading statesmen of the time, such as John Adams and Thomas Jefferson. Later, she wrote a three-volume history of the American Revolution.

When the Declaration of Independence was drafted, the printer—a publisher in Maryland named Mary Katherine Goddard—printed her own name at the bottom of the Declaration in support of the signers who were in hiding from the British.

Because the Continental Army lacked money to pay, feed, and clothe the troops, women raised funds by canvassing door to door and also made clothes for the soldiers. One group of women in Philadelphia made 2200 shirts.

THE ARTICLES OF CONFEDERATION

Even before the war ended, the Continental Congress passed a constitution, and in 1781 the states ratified it. This first constitution, the **Articles of Confederation**, formed a "league of friendship" among the states that allowed each state to retain its "sovereignty" and "independence." The Articles made the states supreme over the national government.

And the Articles reflected a lack of national identity. Most people did not view themselves as Americans. As Edmund Randolph remarked, "I am not really an American, I am a Virginian."[7] The Articles also reflected the colonial experience under the British government. People feared a central government with a powerful legislature or a powerful executive (like the British king), which could be too strong and too distant to guarantee individual liberty.

Consequently, the American leaders established a weak government that left most authority to the states. The Articles of Confederation included a Congress, but they limited the powers that Congress could exercise, and they provided no executive or judicial branch.

This arrangement proved problematic, and the elites became dissatisfied with their governments. They disparaged the weakness of the national government and feared the democracy of the state governments.

National Government Weakness

After the war, the army disbanded, leaving the country vulnerable to hostile forces surrounding it. Britain maintained outposts with troops in the Northwest Territory (the Midwest today), in violation of the peace treaty, and an army in Canada. Spain, which had occupied Florida and California for a long time and had claimed the Mississippi River valley as a result of a treaty before the war, posed a threat. Barbary pirates from North Africa seized American ships and sailors. (See box "The Black Flag on the High Seas.")

Congress could not raise an army, because it could not draft individuals directly, or finance an army, because it could not tax individuals directly. Instead, it had to ask the states for soldiers and money. The states, however, were not always sympathetic to the problems of the distant government. And although Congress could make treaties with foreign countries, the states made (and broke) treaties independently of Congress. Without the ability to establish a credible army or negotiate a binding treaty, the government could not get the British troops to leave American soil or the Spanish government to permit navigation on the Mississippi River.[8]

During the Revolutionary War, many women followed their husbands into battle. As part of the American army, most filled traditional women's roles as cooks, seamstresses, and nurses, but there are reports of women swabbing cannons with water to cool them and firing cannons when their husbands were wounded. After Margaret Corbin's husband was killed, she manned his artillery piece and was wounded three times. Later she received pay as a disabled soldier, including the ration for rum or whiskey. (Many years later she was reburied at West Point.) Some women disguised themselves as men (this was before a military bureaucracy mandated pre-enlistment physicals) and fought in battle. One wrapped tight bandages around her breasts and served three years, surviving two wounds. Fellow soldiers thought she was a young man slow to grow a beard.[3] Still other women fought to defend their homes using hatchets, farm implements, and pots of boiling lye in addition to muskets.

Women also served as spies. When British soldiers commandeered one house for their quarters, the mother asked if she and her children could remain. One night she overheard the officers plotting a surprise attack on Washington's camp, and she sneaked out of town to warn the camp. A sixteen-year-old girl rode forty miles to warn a militia of another pending attack.[4] Women were so prominent in the war that British general Lord Cornwallis said, "We may destroy all the men in America, and we shall still have all we can do to defeat the women."[5]

Following independence, a few women continued an active political role. Mercy Otis Warren campaigned against the proposed Constitution because she felt it was not democratic enough. Abigail Adams called for new laws that would provide some equality between husbands and wives, unlike English laws, which gave all power to husbands. She also called for formal education for girls.

Yet independence did not bring an improvement in the political rights of women. It would be another century before the rights of women would become a full-fledged part of our national political agenda.

---

[1] Quoted in Linda Grant De Pauw and Conover Hunt, *Remember the Ladies* (New York: Viking, 1976), 9. Also see Woody Holton, *Abigail Adams* (New York: Free Press, 2009).

[2] Alice Felt Tyler, *Freedom's Ferment* (New York: Harper & Row, 1962).

[3] Cokie Roberts, *Founding Mothers* (New York: HarperCollins, 2004), 79–82.

[4] Mrs. Betsey Loring also made a heroic contribution to the cause by keeping a British general so "lustily occupied" in Philadelphia that he failed to move his troops to Valley Forge, where he could have destroyed the Continental Army. Alas, her motive was not patriotism; she sought a position in the British army for her husband. Roberts, *Founding Mothers*, xviii.

[5] Ibid., xix.

In addition to an inability to confront foreign threats, the Articles demonstrated an inability to cope with domestic crises. The country bore a heavy war debt that brought the government close to bankruptcy. Because Congress could not tax individuals directly, it could not shore up the shaky government. At the same time, the states competed with each other for commercial advantage, imposing tariffs on goods from other states. This practice slowed business growth.[9]

In short, the government under the Articles seemed too decentralized to ensure either peace or prosperity. The Articles, one leader concluded, gave Congress the privilege of asking for everything while reserving to each state the prerogative of granting nothing.[10] (A similar situation exists today in the United Nations, which must rely on the goodwill of member countries to furnish troops for its peace-keeping forces and dues for its operating expenses.[11])

Even so, the Articles satisfied many people. Most Americans worked small farms, and although many of them sank into debt during the depression that followed the war, they felt they could get their own state government to help them. They realized they could not influence a distant central government as readily.

But the Articles frustrated the bankers, merchants, manufacturers, and others in the upper classes who envisioned a great commercial empire replacing the agricultural society that predominated then. They wanted national, and even international, trade, not just local trade. To expand national trade, they needed uniform laws, stable money, sound credit, and enforceable debt collection. They needed a strong central government that could protect them against debtors and against state governments sympathetic to debtors. The Articles provided neither the foreign security nor the domestic climate necessary to nourish these requisites of a commercial empire.

State Government Democracy

State constitutions adopted during the American Revolution made the state legislatures more representative than the colonial legislatures had been. Most state legislatures also began to hold elections every year. The result was heightened interest among candidates and turnover among legislators. In the eyes of national leaders, there was much pandering to voters and horse-trading by politicians as various factions vied for control. The process seemed up for grabs. According to the Vermont Council of Censors, laws were "altered—realtered—made better—made worse; and kept in such a fluctuating position that persons in civil commission scarce know what is law."[12] In short, state governments were experiencing more democracy than any other governments in the world at the time. National leaders, stunned by the changes in the few years since the Revolution, considered this development an "excess of democracy."

These leaders, most of whom were wealthy and many of whom were creditors, pointed to the laws passed in some states that relieved debtors of some obligations. The farmers

Impact social, global, historical, economic, political

The Black Flag on the High Seas

Americans faced attacks from pirates as well as threats from foreign powers. As many as a hundred merchant ships sailed from American ports to Mediterranean cities each year, bringing salted fish, flour, sugar, and lumber and returning with figs, lemons, oranges, olive oil, and opium. Barbary pirates from North Africa—Algeria, Morocco, Tripoli (now Libya), and Tunis (Tunisia)—preyed upon ships in the Mediterranean Sea, seizing sailors, holding them for ransom or pressing them into slavery, and extorting money from shippers and governments.[1] Historians estimate that a million Europeans and Americans were kidnapped or enslaved by these pirates in the seventeenth and eighteenth centuries.

Although American ships were protected by the British navy (and by the British government's willingness to pay tribute) during colonial times, they were not shielded after independence. The weakness of the government under the Articles of Confederation left the ships' crews to fend for themselves.

The piracy was driven by financial needs—the Barbary states used the raids to finance their governments—but it also reflected religious conflict. The Barbary states were Muslim, and although their societies would not be called fundamentalist or Islamist today—in fact, they treated their Jewish residents better than most European societies did at the time—their leaders told American officials that the Koran gave them the right to enslave infidels.[2]

The piracy would not cease until the new government under the Constitution created a strong navy and fought the Barbary Wars (1801–1805)—the first deployment of the American military overseas.[3]

[1] Other pirates patrolled the Caribbean or the waters off northern Europe.

[2] Previously, European states had held Muslim slaves.

[3] This led to the line in the Marine Corps anthem "to the shores of Tripoli."

Sources: Christopher Hitchens, "Black Flag," *New York Times Book Review*, August 21, 2005, 7–8; Max Boot, *The Savage Wars of Peace* (New York: Basic Books, 2002), 3–29; Adrian Tinniswood, *Pirates of Barbary* (New York: Riverhead, 2010).

in debt had pressed the legislatures for relief that would slow or shrink the payments owed to their creditors, and some legislatures had granted such relief.

These laws worried the leaders, and **Shays's Rebellion** in western Massachusetts in 1786 and 1787 frightened them. Boston merchants who had loaned Massachusetts money during the war insisted on being repaid in full so they could trade with foreign merchants. The state levied steep taxes that many farmers could not pay during the hard times. The law authorized foreclosure—sale of the farmers' property to recover unpaid taxes—and jail for the debtors, essentially transferring wealth from the farmers to the merchants. The Massachusetts government wasn't as sympathetic to debtors as other state legislatures were. The farmers protested the legislature's refusal to grant any relief from the law. Bands of farmers blocked entrances to courthouses where judges were scheduled to hear cases calling for foreclosure and jail. Led by Daniel Shays, some marched to the Springfield arsenal to seize weapons. Although they were defeated by the militia, their sympathizers were victorious in the next election.

Both the revolt and the legislature's change in policy scared the wealthy. To them it raised the specter of mob rule. Nathaniel Gorham, the president of the Continental Congress and a prominent merchant, wrote Prince Henry of Prussia, announcing "the failure of our free institutions" and asking whether the prince would agree to become king of America (the prince declined).[13]

To a significant extent, then, the debate at the time reflected a conflict between two competing visions of the future American political economy—agricultural or commercial.[14] Most leaders espoused the latter, and the combination of national problems and state problems prompted them to push for a new government.[15]

THE CONSTITUTION

Just months after Shays's Rebellion, Congress approved a convention for "the sole and express purpose of revising the Articles of Confederation."

The Constitutional Convention

The **Constitutional Convention** convened in Philadelphia, then the country's largest city, in 1787. State legislatures sent fifty-five delegates. They met at the Pennsylvania State House—now Independence Hall—in the same room where many of them had signed the Declaration of Independence eleven years earlier. Delegates came from every state except Rhode Island, whose farmers and debtors feared that the convention would weaken states' powers to relieve debtors of their debts.

The delegates were distinguished by their education, experience, and enlightenment. Benjamin Franklin, of Pennsylvania—printer, scientist, and diplomat—was the best-known American in the world. At eighty-one, he was the oldest delegate. George Washington, of Virginia, was the most respected American in the country. As the commander of the revolutionary army, he was a national hero. Washington was

chosen to preside over the convention. The presence of men like Franklin and Washington gave the convention legitimacy.

The delegates quickly determined that the Articles of Confederation were beyond repair. Rather than revise them, as instructed by Congress, the delegates decided to draft a new constitution.[16]

The Predicament

The delegates came to the convention because they thought their government was too weak, yet the Americans had fought the Revolution because they chafed under a government that was too strong. "The nation lived in a nearly constant alternation of fears that it would cease being a nation altogether or become too much of one."[17] People feared both anarchy and tyranny. This predicament was made clear by the diversity of opinions among the leaders. At one extreme was Patrick Henry, of Virginia, who had been a firebrand of the Revolution. He feared that the government would become too strong, perhaps even become a monarchy, in reaction to the problems with the Articles. He said he "smelt a rat" and did not attend the convention. At the other extreme was Alexander Hamilton, of New York, who had been an aide to General Washington during the war and had seen the government's inability to supply and pay its own troops. Ever since, he had called for a stronger national government and had even suggested a monarchy. He did attend the convention but, finding little agreement with his proposals, participated infrequently.

In between was James Madison, of Virginia. The debate revolved around his plan. Throughout the convention, Madison was "up to his ears in politics, advising, persuading, softening the harsh word, playing down this difficulty and exaggerating that, engaging in debate, harsh controversy, polemics, and sly maneuver."[18] In the end, his views more than anyone else's would prevail, and he would become known as the Father of the Constitution.[19] (See box "Small but Savvy.")

Consensus

Despite disagreements, the delegates did see eye to eye on the most fundamental issues. They agreed that the government should be a **republic**—a form of government that derives its power from the people and whose officials are accountable to the people. The term more specifically refers to an indirect democracy in which the people vote for at least some of the officials who represent them.[20]

They also agreed that the national government should be stronger than under the Articles and that it should have three separate branches—legislative, executive, and judicial—to exercise the three functions of government—making, administering, and judging the laws. They thought that both the legislative and executive branches should be strong.

When we refer to constitutional provisions, we'll call attention to them with this icon, and we'll also provide the location in the Constitution (unless the paragraph already indicates the location). The composition and authority of the legislative branch are addressed in Article I, those of the executive branch in Article II, and those of the judicial branch in Article III.

BEHIND THE SCENES

Small but Savvy

James Madison was described as "no bigger than half a piece of soap."[1] Although small and frail, timid and self-conscious as a speaker, he was nonetheless an intelligent and savvy politician.

He operated behind the scenes to organize the Constitutional Convention and to secure George Washington's attendance. Washington was in retirement at his plantation at Mount Vernon and had not planned to attend the convention. Because his presence would lend the convention more legitimacy, Madison notified other delegates that Washington would attend—without asking Washington first. After Madison created the expectation that he would attend, Washington agreed to do so.[2]

Before the convention, Madison, who had studied other countries' governments, concluded that the Articles of Confederation should be replaced rather than reformed. He realized that he would have more influence if he had a plan to offer the delegates, who were disenchanted with the Articles but uncertain what to substitute. Madison secretly drafted a plan for a new constitution, a sharp departure from the Articles. Ultimately, his plan would set the agenda for the convention and lay the foundation for the Constitution.

[1] Quoted in Gary Wasserman, *Politics in Action* (Boston: Houghton Mifflin, 2006), 5.

[2] Fred Barbash, "James Madison: A Man for the '80s," *Washington Post National Weekly Edition,* March 30, 1987, 23.

Conflict

Although there was considerable agreement over the fundamental principles and elemental structure of the new government, the delegates quarreled about the specific provisions concerning representation, slavery, trade, and taxation.

Representation   Sharp conflict was expressed between delegates from large states and those from small states over representation. Large states sought a strong government that they could control; small states feared a strong government that could control them.

When the convention began, the Virginia Plan, drafted by Madison, was introduced. According to this plan, the legislature would be divided into two houses, with representation based on population in each. But delegates from the small states calculated that the three largest states would have a majority of the representatives and could dominate the legislature.

These delegates countered with the New Jersey Plan. According to this plan, the legislature would consist of one house, with representation by states, which would have one vote each. This was exactly the same as the structure of Congress under the Articles, also designed to prevent the largest states from dominating the legislature.

James Wilson, of Pennsylvania, asked for whom they were forming a government—"for men, or for the imaginary beings called states?"[21] But delegates from the small states would not budge. Some threatened to leave the government and align themselves with a European country instead.[22]

The convention deadlocked, and some delegates left for home. George Washington wrote that he almost despaired of the likelihood of reaching any agreement. To ease tensions, Benjamin Franklin suggested that the delegates begin each day with a prayer, but they could not agree on this either; Alexander Hamilton insisted that they did not need "foreign aid."

Faced with the possibility that the convention would disband without a constitution, the delegates, after weeks of frustrating debate, compromised. Delegates from Connecticut and other states proposed a plan in which the legislature, Congress, would have two houses. In one, the **House of Representatives**, representation would be based on population, and members would be elected by voters. In the other, the **Senate**, representation would be by states, and members would be selected by state legislatures. Presumably, the large states would dominate the former, the small states the latter. The delegates narrowly approved this Connecticut Compromise,[23] often called the **Great Compromise** because it not only resolved this critical issue but also paved the way for resolution of other issues.

This decision began a pattern that continues to this day. When officials face implacable differences, they try to compromise, but the process is not easy. It is an apt choice of words to say that officials "hammer out" a compromise; it is not a coincidence that we use *hammer* rather than a softer metaphor.[24]

 Thinking about Democracy

Each state has two senators, regardless of its population. Therefore, small or sparsely populated rural states enjoy disproportionate representation relative to their population. Today the smallest twenty-two states have 44 percent of the senators (44 of 100) but only 12 percent of the population of the United States. Wyoming, the least populous state, has the same number of senators as California, the most populous, which has sixty-eight times more people than Wyoming. Therefore, voters in California have one-sixty-eighth as much representation, or power to elect senators, as voters in Wyoming. Do you think the Senate's representation is democratic? How does the Senate's representation highlight the distinction between democracy defined as the operation of majority rule and democracy defined as the protection of minority rights? What minority is being protected by the Senate's representation? Do you think this minority needs protection?

Slavery   In addition to conflict between large states and small states over representation, conflict emerged between northern states and southern states over slavery, trade, and taxation.

With representation in one house based on population, the delegates had to decide how to apportion the seats. They agreed that Indians would not count as part of the population but differed about slaves. Delegates from the South, where slaves made up one-third of the population, wanted slaves to count fully in order to boost the number of southern representatives. Although slaves had not been counted at all under the Articles or under any state constitution, southerners argued that their use of slaves produced wealth that benefited the entire nation. Delegates from the North, where most states had outlawed slavery or at least the slave trade after the Revolution, did not want slaves to count at all. Gouverneur Morris, of Pennsylvania, said the southerners' position

> comes to this: that the inhabitant of Georgia and South Carolina who goes to the coast of Africa, and in defiance of the most sacred laws of humanity tears away his fellow creatures from their dearest connections and damns them to the most cruel bondages, shall have more votes in a government instituted for the protection of the rights of mankind than the citizen of Pennsylvania or New Jersey who views with a laudable horror so nefarious a practice.[25]

Others pointed out that slaves were not considered persons when it came to rights such as voting. Nevertheless, southerners asserted that they would not support the constitution if slaves were not counted at least partially. In the **Three-fifths Compromise,** the delegates agreed that three-fifths of the slaves would be counted in apportioning the seats.

Art. I, Sec. 2   This compromise expanded the political power of the people who were oppressing the slaves. The votes of southern whites became worth more than those of northerners in electing members to the House of Representatives and also in electing presidents (because the number of presidential electors for each state was based on the number of members in Congress from the state). By 1860, nine of the fifteen presidents, including all five who served two terms, were slave owners.[26] Ultimately, twelve presidents were slave owners.

Southerners pushed through two other provisions addressing slavery. One forbade Congress from banning the importation of slaves before 1808; another required free states to return escaped slaves to their owners in slave states. In these provisions, southerners won most of what they wanted; even the provision permitting Congress to ban the importation of slaves in 1808 would do little to limit slavery because by then planters would have enough slaves to fulfill their needs by natural population increases. In return, northerners, who represented shippers, got authority for Congress to regulate commerce by a simple majority rather than a two-thirds majority. Thus northerners conceded the provisions that reinforced slavery to benefit shippers.[27]

Art. I, Sec. 9
Art. IV, Sec. 2
Art. I, Sec. 8   Yet the framers were embarrassed by the hypocrisy of claiming to have been enslaved by the British while allowing enslavement of African Americans. Their embarrassment is reflected in their language. The three provisions reinforcing slavery never mention "slavery" or "slaves"; one gingerly refers to "free persons" and "other persons."

Slavery was the most divisive issue at the convention. As Madison noted, "The real difference of interests lay, not between the large and small, but between the northern and southern states. The institution of slavery and its consequences formed the line of discrimination."[28] The unwillingness to tackle the slavery issue more directly has been called the "Greatest Compromise" by one political scientist.[29] But an attempt to abolish slavery would have caused the five southern states to refuse to ratify the Constitution.

Trade and Taxation

Art. I, Sec. 9   Slavery also underlay a compromise on trade and taxation. With a manufacturing economy, northerners sought protection for their businesses. In particular, they wanted a tax on manufactured products imported from Britain. Without a tax, British goods would be cheaper than northern products; with a tax, northern products would be more competitive—but prices for northern and southern consumers would be higher. With an agricultural economy, southerners sought free trade for their plantations. They wanted a guarantee that no tax would be levied on agricultural commodities exported to Britain. Such a tax would make their commodities less competitive and, they worried, amount to an indirect tax on slavery—the labor responsible for the crops. The delegates resolved these issues by allowing Congress to tax imported goods but not exported ones.

After seventeen weeks of debate, thirty-nine of the original fifty-five delegates signed the Constitution on September 17, 1787. Some delegates had left when they saw the direction the convention was taking, and three others refused to sign, feeling that the Constitution gave too much authority to the national government. Most of the rest were not entirely happy with the result (even Madison, who was most responsible for the content of the document, was despondent that his plan for a national legislature was compromised by having one house with representation by states), but they thought it was the best they could do.

Features of the Constitution

The American Constitution was unique at the time and remains unusual today. To see why, we'll examine its main features.

A Republic

The Founders distinguished between a democracy and a republic. For them, a *democracy* meant a **direct democracy**, which permits citizens to vote on most issues, and a *republic* meant an **indirect democracy**, which allows citizens to vote for their representatives, who make governmental policies.

Although many small towns in New England used (and some still use) a direct democracy, the Founders opposed a direct democracy for the whole country. Some city-states of ancient Greece and medieval Europe had a direct democracy but could not sustain it. A large country would have less ability to do so because its people could not be brought together in one place to debate and vote. Moreover, the Founders believed that the people could not withstand the passions of the moment, so they would be swayed by a demagogue to take unwise action.

 Thinking about Democracy

What are the implications—for our elections, officials, and laws—of having an indirect democracy rather than a direct democracy?

 Art. I, Sec. 2 & 3
Art. II, Sec. 1 The Founders favored a republic because they believed that the government should be based on the consent of the people and that the people should have some voice in choosing their officials. So the Founders provided that the people would elect representatives to the House. They also provided that the state legislators, themselves elected by the people, would select their state's senators as well as their state's electors for the Electoral College, which chooses the president. In this way, the people would have a voice but one partially filtered through their presumably wiser representatives.

The Founders' views reflect their ambivalence about the people. Rationally, they believed in popular sovereignty, but emotionally, they feared the concept. New England clergyman Jeremy Belknap voiced their ambivalence when he declared, "Let it stand as a principle that government originates from the people; but let the people be taught…that they are not able to govern themselves."[30]

The Founders would have been aghast at the proliferation of such experiments in direct democracy as initiatives, referenda, and recall elections in many states. The **initiative** process allows citizens and interest groups to collect signatures on petitions and place a proposal on the ballot. If enough voters favor the proposal, it becomes law.[31] The **referendum** process allows the legislature to place a proposal on the ballot. **Recall elections** enable voters to remove officials from office before their terms expire.

The Founders considered a democracy radical and a republic only slightly less radical. Because they believed that the country could not maintain a democracy, they worried that it might not maintain a republic either. When the Constitutional Convention ended, Benjamin Franklin reportedly was approached by a woman who asked, "Well, Doctor, what have we got, a republic or a monarchy?" Franklin responded, "A republic, Madam, if you can keep it."

Stronger Government

The Preamble to the Constitution begins, "We the people, in order to form a more *perfect* union.…" The word "perfect" then meant completed, with all necessary parts.[32] In the Constitution, the Founders sought to complete the government, adding the missing parts to the faltering structure created by the Articles.

Instead of just one branch—the legislature under the Articles—the Constitution established three branches. In addition to a legislative branch, it created a new executive branch and a new judicial branch. The executive branch was intended to be strong, to have "energy" to administer the government and undertake diplomacy with foreign governments.[33]

 Art. I, Sec. 8 The legislative branch was intended to be even stronger. Congress was given the responsibility to declare war and unlimited authority to raise an army, even to maintain a standing army in peacetime. It was given extensive authority over economic matters, including the power to print and coin money, impose taxes, regulate commerce, and negotiate and enforce treaties involving trade.

In general, the Constitution established a stronger government to protect the country's territory and its commercial interests. The United States needed a robust military for security—to defend against Britain, France, and Spain, all of whom claimed and possessed territory on the North American continent—and extensive economic authority for prosperity. These goals were related. Tax revenue was necessary to finance the military; the military was necessary to enforce commerce regulations and trade treaties; and the treaties would promote international trade, which would produce tax revenue (that is, imported goods would be taxed).[34] The Founders also desired a larger military to push the Indians, who lived all along the western edge of the United States, even further westward to allow continued expansion and development of the new country.

Art. VI In addition, the Constitution's **supremacy clause** declares that the Constitution is the supreme law of the land and that any laws and treaties made "in pursuance thereof" also are the supreme law of the land whenever they conflict with state laws or actions.

In short, the Constitution granted the federal government the most important powers—over foreign affairs and, in domestic matters, over the economy—and the Constitution proclaimed federal laws supreme over state laws.

Limited Government

When the Founders made our government more powerful than it had been under the Articles of Confederation, they feared that they also had made it more capable of oppression, so they fragmented its power.

The Founders believed that people are selfish, always coveting more property, and that leaders always lust after more power. They assumed that this aspect of human nature is unchangeable. Madison speculated, "If men were angels, no government would be necessary." "Alas," he added, "men are not angels." Therefore, "in framing a government which is to be administered by men over men, the great difficulty lies in this: you must first enable the government to control the governed; and in the next place oblige it to control itself."[35] The Founders decided that the way to oblige the government to control itself was to structure it so as to prevent any one leader, group of leaders, or factions of people from exercising power over more than a small part of it. Thus the Founders fragmented government's power. This is reflected in three concepts they built into the structure of government—federalism, separation of powers, and checks and balances. (The Founders' views are conveyed in the *Federalist Papers*, especially in Nos. 10 and 51, which are included in the Appendix of this text.)

Federalism The first division of power was between the national government and the state governments. This division of power is called **federalism**.[36] The U.S. government under the Articles of Confederation had been **confederal** (as the Confederacy of southern states during the Civil War would be); that is, the state governments wielded most authority. The national government exercised only the powers given it by the state governments. At the other extreme, most foreign governments had been **unitary**; the central government wielded all authority.[37]

The Founders, who had had unhappy experiences with a confederal system (their own government under the Articles) and a unitary system (the British government during colonial times), wanted to avoid both types. They sought a strong, but not too strong, national government and strong state governments as well. So they invented a federal system as a compromise between the confederal and unitary systems.

Federalism was seen as a way to provide sufficient power for the government to function while checking excessive power that could lead to tyranny. The Founders worried about the **"mischiefs of factions"**—groups seeking something for themselves without regard for the rights of others or the well-being of all.[38] According to Madison, factions could be controlled through federalism.[39] A faction might dominate one state but would be less able to dominate many states.

We should note that federalism and democracy do not always go hand in hand. Federalism is not a necessary condition for having a democratic government. Some unitary systems, such as those of England and Sweden, are democratic. Likewise, federalism is not a sufficient condition for having a democratic government. The federalist government of the former Soviet Union was not democratic.

Although the Constitution granted important powers to the national government, it left numerous powers to the state governments, including broad authority to provide for the welfare of their people and concurrent authority to tax. The **Tenth Amendment** underscores the states' role, stipulating that the powers not delegated to the national government are reserved for the states.

Yet the Constitution's language is so general and so succinct that it is very ambiguous. At the time, this language made the document acceptable to advocates of a strong national government and also to supporters of strong state governments, but over time it made the document flexible so that the provisions could be interpreted as later generations desired or critical challenges required. The language could support either nation-centered federalism, which underscores the power of the nation in the arrangement, or state-centered federalism, which emphasizes the power of the states. (These concepts will be explored further in Chapter 3.)

Separation of powers The second division of power was within the national government. The power to make, administer, and judge the laws was split into three branches—legislative, executive, and judicial (see Figure 1). In the legislative branch, the power was split further into two houses. This **separation of powers** contrasts with the parliamentary systems in most developed democracies, in which the

Branch:	Legislative *Congress*		Executive *Presidency*	Judicial *Federal Courts*
	House	Senate	President	Judges
Officials chosen by:	People	People (originally, state legislatures)	Electoral College, whose members are chosen by the people (originally, by state legislatures)	President, with advice and consent of Senate
For term of:	2 years	6 years	4 years	Life
To represent primarily:	Common people	Wealthy people	All people	Constitution
	Large states	Small states		

FIGURE 1: SEPARATION OF POWERS Separation of powers, as envisioned by the Founders, means not only that government functions are to be performed by different branches but also that officials of these branches are to be chosen by different people, for different terms, and to represent different constituencies.
SOURCE: © Cengage Learning.

legislature is supreme. In parliamentary systems, both executive and judicial officials are drawn from the legislature and are responsible to it. There is no separation of powers.

 Art. II, Sec. 2 **Art. III, Sec. 1** To reinforce the separation of powers, officials of the three branches were chosen by different means. Representatives were elected by the people (at that time mostly white men who owned property), senators were selected by the state legislatures, and the president was selected by the Electoral College, whose members were selected by the states. Only federal judges were chosen by officials in the other branches. They were nominated by the president and confirmed by the Senate. Once appointed, however, they were allowed to serve for "good behavior"—essentially for life—so they had much independence. (Since the Constitution was written, the Seventeenth Amendment has provided for election of senators by the people, and the state legislatures have provided for election of members of the Electoral College by the people.)

Officials of the branches were also chosen at different times. Representatives were given a two-year term, senators a six-year term (with one-third of them up for reelection every two years), and the president a four-year term. These staggered terms were designed so that temporary passions in society would not bring about a massive switch of officials or policies.

The Senate was intended to act as a conservative brake on the House, due to senators' selection by state legislatures and

their longer terms. Upon his return, Thomas Jefferson, who was in France during the Constitutional Convention, met with George Washington over breakfast. Jefferson protested the establishment of a legislature with two houses. Washington supposedly asked, "Why did you pour that coffee into your saucer?" "To cool it," Jefferson replied. Similarly, Washington explained, "We pour legislation into the senatorial saucer to cool it."[40]

Separation of powers creates the opportunity for **divided government**. Rather than one political party controlling both elected branches, one party might win the presidency while the other party wins a majority of seats in one or both houses of Congress. Divided government has been common throughout the nation's history. Since the emergence of the Democratic and Republican party system (1856), it has occurred as a result of two of every five elections.[41] Since World War II, it has been the dominant mode of government.[42] In this way, American voters have added another element to Madison's concept of separation of powers.

 ### Thinking about Democracy

> What implications from divided government would you expect? How might divided government affect the ability to pass laws? The need to foster compromise?

Checks and balances To further prevent concentration of power, the Founders built in **checks and balances** (see Figure 2). Madison suggested that "the great security against

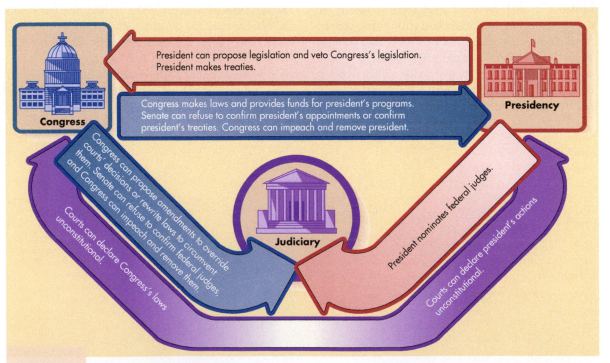

FIGURE 2: CHECK AND BALANCES Most of the major checks and balances among the three branches are explicit in the Constitution, although some are not. For example, the courts' power to declare congressional laws or presidential actions unconstitutional—their power of "judicial review"—is not mentioned.

SOURCE: © Cengage Learning.

a gradual concentration of the several powers in the same department consists in giving those who administer each department the necessary constitutional means and personal motives to resist encroachments by the others.... *Ambition must be made to counteract ambition.*"[43] To that end, each branch was given some authority over the others. If one branch abuses its power, the others can use their checks to thwart it.

Art. I, Sec. 7 Thus, rather than a simple system of separation of powers, ours is a complex, even contradictory, system of both separation of powers and checks and balances. The principle of separation of powers gives each branch its own sphere of authority, but the system of checks and balances allows each branch to intrude into the spheres of the other branches. For example, because there is separation of powers, Congress makes the laws; but because there are checks and balances, the president can veto them and the courts can rule them unconstitutional. In these ways, all three branches are involved in legislating. One political scientist calls ours "a government of separated institutions competing for shared powers."[44]

With federalism, separation of powers, and checks and balances, the Founders expected conflict. They invited the several parts of government to struggle against each other and to limit any one part's ability to dominate the rest. The Founders hoped for "balanced government." The national and state governments would represent different interests, as would the branches within the national government. The House would represent the "common" people and the large states; the Senate, the wealthy people and the small states; the president, all the people; and the Supreme Court, the Constitution. Although each part would struggle for more power, it could not accumulate enough to dominate the others. Eventually, it would have to compromise and accept policies that would reflect the interest of all of the parts and their constituencies.

Veto Points

Because of federalism, separation of powers, and checks and balances, the American governmental system has multiple **veto points**, which are points in the political process where one official or group of officials can block proposals moving through the process. Two veto points are in Congress. For a bill to become law, both houses of Congress must approve it. Either the House of Representatives or the Senate can block it. (As you will see in Chapter 9, Congress is so decentralized, with leaders, committees, and subcommittees all wielding power, that there are multiple veto points in each house. Further, the Senate has adopted rules to thwart its own majorities. But for this discussion in Chapter 2, we'll identify two veto points in Congress—the House of Representatives and the Senate.) A third veto point is the presidency. The president can veto a bill and sometimes derail a bill by threatening to veto it. A fourth veto point lies in the federal courts, especially in a majority—five justices—on the Supreme Court, who can declare laws unconstitutional. When constitutional amendments are proposed,

a fifth veto point lies in the states. As you will see later in the chapter, proposed amendments must be approved by three-fourths of the states to be adopted. Just over one-fourth of the states can block proposed amendments.

In comparison with twenty-three other democracies, the American governmental system has more veto points. Over half have just one veto point; some have two; and only Australia and Switzerland have three. No other country has four or five.[45]

Veto points make it more difficult to pass new laws or constitutional amendments. In practice, veto points make it more difficult for a majority in a country to implement its goals. A minority that controls only one veto point can block any proposal that passes through that point. To prevent gridlock, the majority must control all veto points. Thus the more veto points in a system, the less likely the government will respond to the majority of its citizens.[46]

The Result

The combination of federalism, separation of powers, checks and balances, and multiple veto points (along with the unique method for choosing the president—the Electoral College), makes our government perhaps "the most intricate ever devised"[47] and "the most opaque…, confusing, and difficult to understand."[48]

This fragmentation of power has prevented many abuses of power, although it has not always worked. During the Vietnam War and the Iraq War, for example, one branch—the presidency—exercised vast power while the others acquiesced.[49]

But the system's very advantage has become its primary disadvantage. In their efforts to fragment power so that no branch could accumulate too much, the Founders divided power to the point where the government sometimes cannot marshal enough. In their efforts to build a government that requires a national majority to act, they built one that allows a small minority to block action.

Like a mechanical device that operates only when all of its parts function in harmony, the system moves only when there is consensus or compromise. Consensus is rare in a large, heterogeneous society; compromise is common, but it requires more time as well as the realization by competing interests that they cannot achieve much without it.

At best, the system moves inefficiently and incrementally; at worst, it moves hardly at all. The Constitution has established a government that is slow to respond to change. "By intent," one political scientist noted, "the U.S. government works within a set of limits designed to prevent it from working too well."[50] Therefore, the system tends to preserve the status quo and favor the groups that benefit from the status quo.

Although this arrangement, and its slow pace, may have been suitable for nineteenth-century Americans, it has been frustrating for many contemporary Americans who want the government to tackle the problems we face. Yet other contemporary Americans are more fearful of potential abuse of power by the government than hopeful for the use of power by the government to address these problems. They are satisfied with a government that does not effectively address many problems and apprehensive about a more effective government that would.

Because these Americans are suspicious of government, they may be reluctant to let one party dominate it and use it to advance that party's policies. In surveys, many people—a quarter to a third of those polled—say they think it is good for one party to control the presidency and the other to control Congress.[51] In presidential and congressional elections, more than a quarter of the voters split their ticket between the two parties.[52] As a result, from 1969 through 2000, opposing parties controlled the executive branch and one or both houses of the legislative branch for all but four years. Because of the terrorist attacks of 9/11 and the resulting wars, divided government has been less common after 2000. From 2001 to 2006, the Republicans controlled the presidency and both houses of Congress (except for one year, when a Republican senator defected and gave the Democrats a temporary majority in the Senate). From 2008 to 2010, the Democrats regained the presidency and both houses of Congress and enacted an ambitious agenda. In 2010, however, the voters recoiled and gave the Republicans control of the House of Representatives and reduced the Democrats' majority in the Senate, producing divided government again. In 2012, the voters maintained divided government.

Undemocratic Features

The Founders also left undemocratic features in the Constitution that later generations would have to deal with.[53] They denied some Americans the right to participate in their government and some Americans equal treatment by their government.

The Constitution did not forbid slavery, and it did not allow Congress to halt the slave trade for over two decades. The Three-fifths Compromise actually institutionalized slavery and increased the political power of slaveholders.

The Constitution also did not guarantee the right to vote, allowing states to exclude African Americans, Native Americans, other minorities, and women. For decades, states also excluded white men who didn't own property or those who weren't members of the established church from voting.

The Founders created the Electoral College to prevent the people from choosing the president. Even with the advent of popular election of the electors, the Electoral College still allows the election of a candidate who did not receive the most popular votes (as occurred in 2000). The Founders also allowed the state legislatures, not the people, to choose the senators. By giving each state two seats in the Senate, the Founders gave disproportionate power to the people who happen to live in small states.

The Founders included these features partly because of their need to compromise and partly because of their view that the people could not be trusted. The people were seen as an unruly mob threatening stable, orderly government. As later history would show, however, the Founders exaggerated the dangers of popular majorities. When Americans became more egalitarian in the decades following the adoption of the Constitution, they demanded a greater role for the average person. One political scientist concluded that if the Constitution had been written in 1820 instead of 1787, it would have been a very different, and more democratic, document.[54]

Motives of the Founders

To understand the Constitution better, it is useful to consider the motives of the Founders. Were they selfless patriots, sharing their wisdom and experience? Or were they selfish property owners, protecting their interests? Let's consider the philosophical ideas, political experience, and economic interests that influenced the Founders.

Philosophical Ideas

The Founders were well-educated intellectuals who incorporated philosophical ideas into the Constitution. At a time when the average person did not dream of going to college, a majority of the Founders graduated from college. As learned men, they shared a common library of writers and philosophers.

The Founders reflected the ideals of the Enlightenment, also called the "Age of Reason," an intellectual force throughout Europe in the 1600s and 1700s. In this era, learned men emphasized the use of reason, rather than tradition or religion, to solve problems. So the Founders studied past governments to determine why the governments had failed in the hope that they could apply these lessons to their time. From all accounts, they engaged in a level of debate that was rare in politics, citing philosophers ranging from the ancient Greeks to the modern British and French.

The writings of John Locke, as explained in Chapter 1, underlay many of the ideas of the Founders. The Founders endorsed Locke's views about the relationship between the people and their government as well as his views on natural rights and property rights. Locke maintained that the people come together to form a government through a **social contract**—an implied agreement between the people and their government—that establishes a **limited government**, strong enough to protect their rights but not so strong as to threaten these rights. This government should not act without the consent of the governed.[55]

The views of Charles de Montesquieu, an eighteenth-century French philosopher, also influenced the debate at the convention and the provisions of the Constitution. Although others had suggested separation of powers before, Montesquieu refined the concept and added that of checks and balances. The Founders cited him more than any other thinker.[56] (Presumably, they cited him more than Locke because by this time Locke's views had so permeated American society that the Founders considered them just "common sense."[57])

The principles of mechanics formulated by Isaac Newton, a late seventeenth- and early eighteenth-century English mathematician, also pervaded the provisions of the Constitution. Newton viewed nature as a machine, with different parts having different functions and balancing each other. Newton's principle of action and reaction is manifested in the Founders' system of checks and balances. Both the natural environment and the constitutional structure were viewed as self-regulating systems.[58]

Political Experience

Although the Founders were intellectuals, they were also experienced and practical politicians who had "to operate with great delicacy and skill in a political cosmos full of enemies."[59]

"Religious freedom is my immediate goal, but my long-range plan is to go into real estate."

The Founders brought extensive experience to the convention. Eight had signed the Declaration of Independence, and thirty-nine had served in Congress. Seven had been governors, and many had held other state offices. Some had helped write their state constitutions. The framers drew on this experience. For example, although they cited Montesquieu in discussing separation of powers, they also referred to the experience of colonial and state governments that already had some separation of powers.[60]

As practical politicians, "no matter what their private dreams might be, they had to take home an acceptable package and defend it—and their own political futures—against predictable attack."[61] So, they compromised the difficult issues and ducked the stickiest ones. Ultimately, they pieced together a document that allowed each delegate to return home and announce that his state had won something.

Economic Interests

At the same time, the Founders represented an elite that sought to protect its property from the masses. The delegates to the convention included prosperous planters, manufacturers, shippers, and lawyers. About one-third were slave owners. Most came from families of prominence and married into other families of prominence. Not all were wealthy, but most were at least well-to-do. Only one, a delegate from Georgia, was a yeoman farmer like most men in the country. In short, "this was a convention of the well-bred, the well-fed, the well-read, and the well-wed."[62]

The Founders championed the right to property. The promise of land and even riches had enticed many immigrants to come to America.[63] A desire for freedom from arbitrary taxes and trade restrictions had spurred some colonists to fight in the Revolution.[64] And the inability of the government under the Articles of Confederation to provide a healthy economy had prompted the Founders to convene the Constitutional Convention. They apparently agreed with Madison that "the first object of government" is to protect property.[65] They worried that a democratic government, responding to popular pressures, might appropriate their property or impose high taxes to help less wealthy people. They wanted a government that could resist such populism.

Yet the Founders' emphasis on property was not as elitist as it might seem. Land was plentiful, and with westward expansion, more would be available. Already most men were middle-class farmers who owned some property. Even those who owned no property could foresee the day when they would, so most wanted to protect property.

The Founders diverged from the farmers in their vision to create a national commercial economy in place of the small-scale agricultural economy. Toward this end, the Founders desired to protect other property, such as wealth and credit, in addition to land.[66] So the delegates included provisions to protect commerce, including imports and exports, contracts, and debts, and provisions to regulate currency, bankruptcy, and taxes.[67]

Political scientists and historians have debated which of these three influences on the Founders—philosophical, political, or economic—was most important. Actually, the influences are difficult to separate because they reinforce each other; the framers' ideas, political experience, and economic interests all point to the same sort of constitution.[68]

Ratification of the Constitution

Ratification was uncertain. Many people opposed the Constitution, and a lively campaign against it appeared in newspapers, pamphlets, and mass meetings.[69]

Knowing that opponents would charge the framers with setting up a national government to dominate the state governments, those who supported the Constitution ingeniously adopted the name **Federalists** to emphasize a real division of power between the national and state governments. They dubbed their opponents **Antifederalists** to imply that their opponents did not want a division of power between the governments.

The Antifederalists, more than most Americans, feared strong government. They objected to the Constitution because it didn't express their fear sufficiently.[70] The Antifederalists also distrusted the elites in distant cities. As a result of the Constitution, small farmers expected domination by commercial interests in eastern cities. Provincial rather than cosmopolitan, the Antifederalists were localists at heart. One delegate to the Massachusetts convention debating ratification blasted the Federalists:

> These lawyers, and men of learning and moneyed men, that talk so finely, and gloss over matters so smoothly, to make us poor illiterate people swallow down the pill, expect to get into Congress themselves; they expect to…get all the power and all the money into their own hands, and then they will swallow up all us little folks…just as the whale swallowed up Jonah![71]

The Antifederalists favored amateurism over professionalism in government, so they liked the rotation among government officials under the Articles, which limited officials' terms to one year. This limit promoted close ties between officials and constituents. The Antifederalists worried that under the Constitution Congress—especially the Senate, with just two members per state, but also the House—wouldn't have enough members to represent the variety of towns, villages, and farms in America. And they worried that the terms—again, especially in the Senate, with six years, but also in the House, with two years—wouldn't be short enough. The members wouldn't be responsive to their constituents.[72]

The increase in legislative power was especially troublesome. The Constitution gave Congress unlimited authority to raise an army. Antifederalists felt that a standing army in peacetime was a threat to liberty rather than a guarantor of safety. Moreover, a standing army would be costly and would lead to debt. Repaying debt (with interest) was the largest budget item for European countries at the time. To make matters worse, the Constitution gave Congress authority for "organizing, arming…disciplining…and for governing" the state militias.

Art. I, Sec. 8 Thus the state militias would become subservient to the national government and irrelevant to the state governments.[73]

The Constitution also gave Congress almost unlimited authority to impose taxes. The Antifederalists, who already considered taxes oppressive, worried that under the new government taxes would be even more arbitrary and burdensome and that federal tax collectors would be intrusive, looking into citizens' pantries and cellars for untaxed goods.[74]

The expansion of executive power was also a concern. Although people didn't use the terms *bureaucracy* and *bureaucrats* then, the Antifederalists foresaw "swarms" of new officials appointed to administer new laws of the expanding government.[75]

In short, the Antifederalists anticipated a big, powerful government that wouldn't represent them and wouldn't be responsive to them. They predicted a central government that would resemble a European state—a government that would threaten their liberty.[76] They complained, in particular, about the absence of a bill of rights in the Constitution. The framers had not included one because most states already had one in their constitutions. The framers also thought that fragmenting power would prevent any branch from becoming strong enough to deny individual rights. Yet critics demanded provisions protecting various rights, and the Federalists promised to propose amendments guaranteeing these rights as soon as the government began.

The Antifederalists weren't swayed. They believed that the Constitution betrayed "the American ideal of simple and cheap government."[77]

Parallels between the Antifederalists and today's Tea Party are striking. Most Tea Party adherents live in cities rather than on farms and support government programs like Social Security and Medicare, which benefit them. And,

unlike the Antifederalists, they favor a strong military. In other ways, however, the Tea Partiers' complaints echo the Antifederalists' concerns. The Tea Partiers rail against "the elites." They believe that expertise isn't necessary in government and that average people could make better decisions than professional politicians. They assert that the federal government is too big and too powerful, imposing taxes that are too high and incurring debt that is too large. They want to shrink the size of the government and reduce the number of government workers. They fear that the United States is moving toward the European model and that our officials, manipulated by the elites, have become unresponsive to the people. These trends, they say, threaten our liberty.

Today many Americans—Tea Partiers and others—repeat the arguments of the Antifederalists, even as they think they are supporting the Constitution and revering the Founders who wrote the Constitution. This raises a question: Were the Antifederalists among the Founders of the nation? In a broad sense, they were, as were all Americans at the time. They contributed to the American Revolution and to these political debates as well as to other aspects of society. In a narrow sense, however, the Antifederalists weren't among the Founders. They opposed the Constitution and the people who wrote the Constitution—the people who are usually called "the Founders." Yet the Antifederalists' arguments against the Constitution are often cited, against today's government and its policies, as the views of "the Founders."[78] Today's Tea Partiers, if alive in the 1780s, probably would have rejected much of what the drafters of the Constitution wrote then.

Despite the vehemence of their opposition to the Constitution, the Antifederalists had no alternative plan. They were divided, with some wanting to amend the Articles of Confederation and others wanting to reject both the Articles and the Constitution in favor of some yet undetermined form of government. Their lack of unity on an alternative was instrumental in their inability to win support.[79]

Within six months, nine states ratified the new Constitution, and the new government, with George Washington as president, began in 1788. Within one year, the four remaining states approved the Constitution.

Although this process might seem unremarkable today, it marked the first time that a nation had proposed a new government and then asked the people to approve or reject it. And the process occurred with little violence or coercion. As a constitutional historian observed, "The losers were not jailed, hanged, or politically disabled. They did not boycott, take up arms, or go into exile. They continued, as before, to be full and free citizens, but now living in a new republic."[80]

Changing the Constitution

The framers expected their document to last; Madison wrote, "We have framed a constitution that will probably be still around when there are 196 million people."[81] Yet, because the framers realized it would need some changes, they drafted a Constitution that can be changed either formally by amendment or informally by judicial interpretation or political practice. In doing so, they left a legacy for later governments. "The example of changing a Constitution, by assembling the wise men of the state, instead of assembling armies," Jefferson noted, "will be worth as much to the world as the former examples we had given them."[82]

By Constitutional Amendment

That the Articles of Confederation could be amended only by a unanimous vote of the states posed an almost insurmountable barrier to any change at all. The framers of the Constitution made sure that this experience would not repeat itself. Yet the procedures, though not requiring unanimity, do require widespread agreement. More than nine thousand amendments have been proposed in Congress, but only twenty-seven (including the ten in the Bill of Rights) have been adopted.[83]

Procedures   The procedures for amendment entail action by both the national government and the state governments. Amendments can be proposed either by a two-thirds vote of both houses of Congress or by a national convention called by Congress at the request of two-thirds of the state legislatures. Congress then specifies which way amendments must be ratified—either by three-fourths of the state legislatures or by ratifying conventions in three-fourths of the states. Among these avenues, the usual route has been proposal by Congress and ratification by state legislatures.

Art. V   Amendments   In the first Congress under the Constitution, the Federalists fulfilled their promise to support a bill of rights. Madison drafted twelve amendments, Congress proposed them, and the states ratified ten of them in 1791. This **Bill of Rights** includes freedom of conviction and expression—religion, speech, press, and assembly (First Amendment). It also includes numerous rights for those accused of crimes—protection against unreasonable searches and seizures (Fourth), protection against compulsory self-incrimination (Fifth), guarantee of due process of law (Fifth), the right to counsel and to a jury trial in criminal cases (Sixth), and protection against excessive bail and fines and against cruel and unusual punishment (Eighth). (These will be covered fully in Chapter 13.) It also includes a right to a jury trial in civil cases (Seventh).

Two amendments in the Bill of Rights grew out of the colonial experience with Great Britain—the right to bear arms to form a militia (Second) and the right not to have soldiers quartered in homes during peacetime (Third). The Bill of Rights also includes two general amendments—a statement allowing for additional rights beyond the ones in the first eight amendments (Ninth) and a statement reserving powers to the states that are not given to the national government (Tenth).

Among the other seventeen amendments to the Constitution, the strongest theme is the expansion of citizenship rights:[84]

- Abolition of slavery (Thirteenth, 1865)
- Equal protection, due process of law (Fourteenth, 1868)
- Right of black men to vote (Fifteenth, 1870)
- Direct election of senators (Seventeenth, 1913)
- Right of women to vote (Nineteenth, 1920)
- Right of District of Columbia residents to vote in presidential elections (Twenty-third, 1960)

Authorities empty barrels of beer after the Eighteenth Amendment, which prohibited alcohol, was adopted in 1919. The Twenty-first Amendment repealed the Eighteenth in 1933.

- Abolition of poll tax in federal elections (Twenty-fourth, 1964)
- Right of persons eighteen and older to vote (Twenty-sixth, 1971)

In recent decades, two amendments proposed by Congress were not ratified by the states. One would have provided equal rights for women (discussed in Chapter 14), and the other would have given congressional representation to the District of Columbia as though it were a state.

Although the Constitution expressly provides for change by amendment, its ambiguity about some subjects and silence about others virtually guarantees change by interpretation and practice as well.

By Judicial Interpretation

If there is disagreement about what the Constitution means, who is to interpret it? Although the Constitution does not say, the judicial branch has taken on this role. To decide disputes before them, the courts must determine what the relevant provisions of the Constitution mean. By saying that the provisions mean one thing rather than another, the courts can, in effect, change the Constitution. Woodrow Wilson called the Supreme Court "a constitutional convention in continuous session." The Court has interpreted the Constitution in ways that bring about the same results as new amendments would. (Chapters 12, 13, and 14 provide many examples.)

By Political Practice

Political practice has accounted for some very important changes. These include the rise of political parties and the demise of the Electoral College as an independent body. They also include the development of the cabinet to advise the president and the development of the committee system to operate the two houses of Congress. (Chapters 7, 8, and 9 explain these changes.)

The Founders would be surprised to learn that only seventeen amendments, aside from the Bill of Rights, have been adopted in over two hundred years. In part this is due to their wisdom, but in part it is due to changes in judicial interpretation and political practice, which have combined to create a "living Constitution."

EVOLUTION OF THE CONSTITUTION

The Constitution has evolved since the Founding. This section will introduce the major conceptual changes, which have given us a quite different constitution than the one the Founders drafted.

Early Conflicts

The country faced secessionist threats almost immediately after its creation—by southern states when the Federalists (under John Adams) were in power and then by New England states when the Jeffersonians (under Thomas Jefferson) were in power. These threats were averted, but frequent conflicts between the nation and the states arose.

Supreme Court Rulings

The Supreme Court became the principal arbiter of the Constitution and soon faced questions about federal-state relations. John Marshall, chief justice from 1801 to 1835, was a Federalist, a firm believer in a strong national government, and the decisions of his Court supported this view.

The Marshall Court established the legal bases for the supremacy of national authority over the states. Among the

---

CourseReader ASSIGNMENT

Log into www.cengagebrain.com and open Course-Reader to access the full reading "The Commandments" by Jill Lepore.

Today, the meaning of the Constitution is greatly debated. Tea Party members insist that if people actually read the document they'd force government to follow it. However, the Constitution "doesn't exactly explain itself." Many issues aren't addressed in the Constitution, and some provisions are unclear. Tea Party signs demand, "Find it in the Constitution," but banks, railroads, free markets, and wiretapping, to name a few examples, aren't mentioned in those four pages of parchment. Tea Party activists also accuse political opponents of not understanding the Constitution, but there are multiple ways to interpret its provisions. Tea Party activists want to follow the intentions of the Founders—that is, to interpret the provisions exactly as the Founders intended them—but many other Americans want to interpret the provisions in light of our history and our society as they have developed since the Founding. Is the Constitution flexible so that its provisions can be interpreted as the times require?

1. After reading the article, do you find the views of the author or the Tea Party more persuasive?
2. Benjamin Franklin said that the Founders weren't infallible and the Constitution wasn't perfect. Other Founders thought the same. Does this fact have implications for those who argue that the Constitution should be interpreted exactly as the Founders intended?
3. Important provisions in the Constitution are the result of political compromises rather than deliberate choices. Does this fact have implications for this debate?

Marshall Court's most important rulings was **McCulloch v. Maryland** in 1819.[85] The case grew out of a dispute over the establishment of a national bank. The bank was unpopular because it competed with smaller banks operating under state laws and because some of its branches engaged in reckless and even fraudulent practices. When the government of Maryland levied a tax on the currency issued by the branch in Baltimore, the bank's constitutionality was called into question. The claim was that Congress, by establishing a national bank, infringed on the states' authority.

Marshall's ruling upheld the establishment of the bank and struck down the tax by the state. "[T]he power to tax involves the power to destroy," Marshall wrote, and the states shouldn't have the power to destroy the bank, because the bank was "necessary and proper" to carry out Congress's powers to collect taxes, borrow money, regulate commerce, and raise an army. Marshall maintained that if the goal of the legislation is legitimate, "all means which are appropriate, which are plainly adapted to that end, which are not prohibited, but consistent with the letter and spirit of the Constitution, are constitutional." Marshall interpreted "necessary" quite loosely. The bank was not essential, but it was useful.

 **Art. I, Sec. 8**   Marshall's interpretation of the **necessary and proper clause** recognized the existence of **implied powers**—ones implicit in the explicit powers specifically cited—for the national government. It meant that Congress could legislate in almost any area it wished (including health care), and this meant that the national government could wield more authority than the Constitution appeared to grant. By laying the foundation for a strong national government for our rapidly expanding nation, *McCulloch* would become one of the two most important rulings of the Marshall Court and indeed of the Supreme Court ever. (The other was *Marbury* v. *Madison*, which will be covered in Chapter 12.)

Thinking about Democracy

What might be the implications for democracy of a broad interpretation of the necessary and proper clause and a recognition of implied powers?

Conflicts between the nation and the states continued, and debates over slavery exacerbated them. These conflicts led to southern states' efforts to secede from the Union and to the Civil War.

The Civil War and Reconstruction

The Civil War, from 1861 through 1865, and Reconstruction, from the end of the war through 1876, constituted a "second American Revolution."[86] After the bloodletting and scorched earth, more than six hundred thousand soldiers lay in graves—one of every seven men between the ages of fifteen and thirty—and parts of the South lay in waste. The North's victory preserved the Union, but it did far more than this. It also altered the Constitution—in the minds of the people and in formal amendments to the document.

Although the North's leader, President Abraham Lincoln, a Republican, held views that would be considered racist today (he believed that black people were inherently inferior and that they should emigrate from the United States),[87] he despised slavery because it deprived persons of their unalienable rights to life, liberty, and the pursuit of happiness promised by the Declaration of Independence. But efforts to abolish slavery were constrained by the political climate, and Lincoln was a practical politician. Before the war, he was willing to allow slavery in the southern states as long as the Union was preserved. But one year into the war, he found this goal too limited.[88] Abolitionist sentiment was spreading in the North, giving Lincoln the opportunity to lead efforts to abolish slavery as well as preserve the Union.[89] In the process, he helped reinvent America.

The Emancipation Proclamation

The **Emancipation Proclamation** offered the promise of redefining the Constitution. President Lincoln announced the proclamation in September 1862 and ordered it to take effect in January 1863. The document proclaimed that the slaves "shall be…forever free" in the Confederate states where the Union army was not in control. Its language limited its sweep, for it exempted those parts of the Confederate states where the Union army was in control and also the slave states that remained loyal to the Union (Delaware, Kentucky, Maryland, and Missouri). And despite its language, it could not be enforced in the parts of the Confederate states where the Union army was not in control. Thus, as a legal document, the proclamation was problematic. However, as a symbolic measure, it was successful. The proclamation made clear that the war was no longer just to preserve the Union, but to abolish slavery as well. It captured people's imagination, and when slaves heard about it, many left their plantations and some joined the Union army. The desertion sowed confusion in the South and denied a reliable labor force to the region.

Two decades before the war, Lincoln had suffered from depression and considered suicide. He confided to a friend that he "had done nothing to make any human being remember" that he had lived. Years later, however, he remarked to the friend that the proclamation would justify his existence.[90]

The Gettysburg Address

President Lincoln's **Gettysburg Address** set the tone for new interpretations of the Constitution.[91] The battle at Gettysburg, Pennsylvania, in 1863 was a Union victory and the turning point in the Civil War. Lincoln was invited to deliver "a few appropriate remarks" during the dedication of the battlefield where many had fallen. Lincoln was not the main speaker, and his speech was not long. The main speaker took two hours, recounting the battle and reciting the names of the generals and even some of their soldiers; Lincoln took two minutes

Peter Newark American Pictures/Bridgeman Art Library

Slaves thank President Abraham Lincoln for issuing the Emancipation Proclamation. Although this image may seem demeaning to some people today, it reflected slaves' sentiments at the time. In fact, freed blacks raised funds for a statue with a similar scene in Washington, D.C.

to give a 268-word speech. (He spoke so briefly that the photographer, with his clumsy equipment and its slow exposure, failed to get a single photograph.) Lincoln used the occasion to advance his ideal of equality.

He began: "Four score and seven [eighty-seven] years ago our fathers brought forth on this continent a new nation, conceived in liberty and dedicated to the proposition that all men are created equal." Here Lincoln referred not to the Constitution of 1787 but to the Declaration of Independence of 1776. For Lincoln, the Constitution had abandoned the principle of equality that the Declaration had promised. He sought to resurrect this principle. Lincoln did not mention slavery or the Emancipation Proclamation, which were divisive. A shrewd politician, he wanted people to focus on the Declaration, which was revered.

Lincoln concluded by addressing "the great task remaining before us . . . that we here highly resolve that these dead shall not have died in vain, that this nation, under God, shall have a new birth of freedom, and that government of the people, by the people, for the people shall not perish from the earth." This phrase, which Lincoln made famous, was borrowed from a speaker at an antislavery convention.[92] It depicted a government elected by all the people, to serve all the people.[93] Lincoln's conclusion reinforced his introduction—both emphasized equality.

Although his speech was brief, Lincoln used the word *nation* five times, including the phrase "a new nation." His purpose was not to encourage support for the Union, but to urge people to think of the nation as a whole, its identity now forged in a bloody war of brother against brother, rather than as simply a collection of individual states with separate interests.[94]

Thus the president essentially added the Declaration's promise of equality to the Constitution, and he substituted his vision of a unified nation for the Founders' precarious arrangement of a balance of power between the nation and the states. According to one historian, "He performed one of the most daring acts of open-air sleight-of-hand ever witnessed by the unsuspecting. . . . The crowd departed with a new thing in its ideological luggage, that new constitution Lincoln had substituted for the one they brought with them."[95]

The Gettysburg Address was heard by an audience of perhaps fifteen thousand, but its language was spread through word of mouth and newspapers and eventually by politicians and teachers. It was read, repeated, and sometimes memorized by generations of schoolchildren. Although some critics at the time perceived what Lincoln was attempting—the *Chicago Times* quoted the Constitution to the president and charged him with betraying the document he swore to uphold—most citizens came to accept Lincoln's addition. His speech, which has been called "the best political address" in the country's history, thus became "the secular prayer of the postbellum [post–Civil War] American Republic."[96] (The speech is reprinted in the Appendix.)

The Reconstruction Amendments

If the Gettysburg Address became the preamble of the new constitution, the **Reconstruction Amendments** became its body. These three amendments, adopted from 1865 through 1870, began to implement the promise of equality and the vision of a unified nation rather than a collection of individual states.

The Thirteenth Amendment abolished slavery, essentially constitutionalizing the Emancipation Proclamation.

The Fourteenth Amendment declared that all persons born or naturalized in the United States are citizens, overturning the Supreme Court's ruling before the Civil War that blacks, whether slave or free, could not be citizens.[97] The Fourteenth Amendment also included the equal protection clause, which requires states to treat persons equally, and the due process clause, which requires states to treat persons fairly. The equal protection clause would become the primary legal means to end discrimination, and the due process clause would become the primary legal means to give persons the full benefit of the Bill of Rights.[98] (This amendment and these clauses will be examined further in Chapters 13 and 14.) This amendment, one legal scholar observed, was "a revolutionary change. The states were no longer the autonomous sovereigns that they thought they were when they claimed the right of secession. They were now, in fact, servants of their people. [They] existed to guarantee due process and equal justice for all."[99]

The Fifteenth Amendment extended the right to vote to blacks. Because women could not vote at the time, the amendment essentially provided the right to vote to black men. (This amendment will be addressed further in Chapters 8 and 14.)

As important as the substantive content of these amendments was a procedural provision authorizing Congress to enforce them. ("Congress shall have power to enforce this article by appropriate legislation.") That is, the amendments gave Congress broad power, beyond that granted in the original Constitution, to pass new laws to implement the amendments. Consequently, the federal government would come to oversee and even intervene in the policies of state and local governments to make sure that these governments did not disregard the guarantees of the amendments. These amendments thus marked the start of a trend of federalizing the Constitution by increasing the power of Congress.[100] Five later amendments also would include this provision.

Thinking about Democracy

How do the provisions authorizing Congress to enforce the Thirteenth, Fourteenth, and Fifteenth Amendments have similar implications for democracy as the Supreme Court's interpretation of the necessary and proper clause in the *McCulloch v. Maryland* case?

During Reconstruction, the Union army occupied the South and enforced the amendments and congressional laws implementing them. But southern whites resisted, and eventually northern whites grew weary of the struggle. At the same time, there was a desire for healing between the two regions and lingering feelings for continuity with the past. In 1876, the two national political parties, the Democrats and the Republicans, struck a deal to withdraw the Union army and to allow the southern states to govern themselves again.

The entrenched attitudes of southern whites prompted them to establish segregation and discrimination in place of slavery, thus preventing blacks from enjoying their new rights. As a result, the new constitution stressing equality and powers of the national government to enforce equality, as envisioned by Lincoln, would not really come into being until the 1950s and 1960s, when the civil rights movement, Supreme Court rulings, presidential initiatives, and congressional acts would converge to give effect to the ideal of racial equality. (These developments will be examined fully in Chapter 14.) In the meantime, the new constitution would lie, in our collective consciousness, as an unfulfilled promise, occasionally emerging to foster greater equality.[101]

Thinking about Democracy

Consider the vast implications for democracy of the Civil War, Emancipation Proclamation, Gettysburg Address, and Reconstruction Amendments.

During the industrialization and urbanization that followed the Civil War, the national government continued to extend its reach and expand its power, but more significant changes would occur during the Great Depression.

The Great Depression and the New Deal

In the 1928 campaign, Herbert Hoover, the Republican candidate who would become the next president, predicted, "We shall soon, with the help of God, be in sight of the day when poverty will be banished from this nation."[102] One year later the stock market crashed, and the Great Depression began. As explained in the Introduction to this text, millions of Americans lost their jobs and their savings, and many struggled to find enough food. Unlike today, there were no systematic welfare programs to relieve the suffering.

In the 1932 campaign, Hoover ran for reelection against Democrat Franklin Roosevelt. The choice was stark. Hoover, who favored rugged individualism and expected the economy to right itself, and who was cautious by nature, resisted aggressive action. Roosevelt, who was bold and experimental, urged such action. Hoover proclaimed that the election was not "a contest between two men," but one "between two philosophies of government."[103] He said that Roosevelt's philosophy would "crack the timbers of the Constitution" and "destroy the very foundation of our government."[104] The choice between a relatively passive government and a very active government was clear. The voters chose the latter. Roosevelt won; Hoover carried just six states.

As president, Roosevelt launched his **New Deal** program to stimulate the economy and ameliorate people's suffering. This era also altered the Constitution—not by formal amendments, but through judicial rulings and political practice. In the process, it changed the minds of the people.[105] As a result, we replaced our small, limited government, as envisioned by the Founders, with a big, activist government.

Judicial Rulings

In the late nineteenth and early twentieth centuries, a laissez-faire economic philosophy was popular in this country and was reflected in governmental policies. According to this philosophy, government should not interfere in the economy (*laissez-faire* means "leave it alone" in French). Although government could *aid* businesses, it should not *regulate* them.[106] People who believed this philosophy thought it would create a robust and efficient economy. Indeed, industrialization produced an array of new products for consumers and an increase in personal wealth for owners, but it also led to negative consequences for employees, who were forced to labor in harsh, even dangerous, conditions for long hours and little pay.

For decades, when Congress and state legislatures passed laws regulating child labor, maximum hours of work, and minimum wages for work, the Supreme Court usually followed the traditional philosophy and declared the laws unconstitutional. After Roosevelt took office and Congress passed the laws implementing his recovery program, the Court's majority often declared these laws unconstitutional as well. The impasse reached a climax in 1935 and 1936 when the Court invalidated twelve laws—the core of FDR's program. The Court's resistance made clear that the New Deal reforms were not simply fine-tuning governmental policy toward the economy, but were overhauling the long-standing policy.[107] In response to the Court's resistance, members of Congress introduced thirty-nine constitutional amendments to reverse the Court's rulings.

After Roosevelt was resoundingly reelected in 1936, intense pressure from the president, Congress, and the public prompted two justices who had voted against government regulation of business to switch sides and vote for such regulation in 1937. The switch allowed the government to extend its reach far beyond what was thought permissible just a few years before.

These transformative rulings created a "constitutional revolution."[108] They took the place of formal amendments to the Constitution, which were no longer necessary once the Court acquiesced to the policies of the president and Congress. As a result, government could regulate businesses when the public believed that regulation would be beneficial.

Political Practice

Before the Depression, Washington, D.C., had been "a sleepy southern town," in the eyes of reporters.[109] When Roosevelt took office, he was uncertain exactly what to do, but he was willing to experiment. Roosevelt's personality and ambitious ideas attracted hundreds of thousands of people to the capital, some simply relieved to find a job, but others excited to work for the government. These reformers brought new ideas, even radical ideas for the time, that would receive consideration in the throes of the Depression. As federal efforts to provide relief and regulation spread throughout the country, many other people got jobs in federal offices outside Washington.

Within six years of Roosevelt's taking office, the federal government's workforce and budget nearly doubled, and its power expanded tremendously.[110] The country got a big government and an activist government. The changes were so dramatic that some political scientists believe that they essentially created a new government under a new interpretation of the old constitution.[111]

During the Depression, many people who lost their job lost their ability to put food on the table. Breadlines and soup kitchens were common. Here the unemployed wait for coffee and doughnuts at one of fifty-two relief kitchens in New York City in 1934.

> What implications would these changes during the Depression have, not simply for the size of our government, but for the nature of our democracy?

The changes during the Depression would lay the foundation for the government of the 1960s, which would promote the legal equality advanced during the Civil War. Without a powerful government pushing for change, the entrenched attitudes supporting segregation and discrimination would not have been overcome.

A Combination of Constitutions

As a result of Chief Justice Marshall and the Federalists in the early 1800s, President Lincoln and the Radical Republicans in the 1860s and 1870s, and President Roosevelt and the New Deal Democrats in the 1930s and 1940s, our government is very different from the one the Founders bequeathed us.[112] Later generations of Americans made the eighteenth-century Constitution work in the nineteenth century, and then they made it work in the twentieth century—by remaking that Constitution. Changes in the nineteenth century elevated the national government over the state governments and added the concept of legal equality. Changes in the twentieth century transformed a relatively small, limited government into a very large, activist government.

Even so, these changes didn't alter the fragmentation of power that pervades the Constitution and underscores our system. As a result, we have a more limited government than other advanced industrialized countries have. Contrary to what many Americans believe, our taxes are lower and governmental policies in numerous areas, such as health care, welfare, and transportation, are less ambitious.[113] And our economic inequality is more pronounced.

The original Constitution and the remade Constitution reflect competing visions. Should we emphasize liberty or equality? Should we demand that individuals solve their own problems or ask government to help them? Americans have not reconciled these visions. Sometimes we cling to the Founders' Constitution, or even to the Antifederalists' views

as many Tea Partiers do; other times we embrace the post–Civil War and post-Depression Constitution. In political debates, politicians, commentators, and citizens take positions without articulating, perhaps without even realizing, that these positions hark back to the Founders' Constitution, whereas opponents espouse views that rely on the post–Civil War and post-Depression Constitution. Although, of course, we have only one Constitution on paper, we have at least two constitutions coexisting, sometimes uneasily, in our minds and in government policies.[114] As a consequence of our history, then, we essentially have a combination of constitutions.

IMPACT OF THE CONSTITUTION

Despite the debates—all the sound and the fury—over the meaning of the Constitution, we should acknowledge that the Constitution established a government that has survived for over two centuries. Although the United States is considered a relatively young country, it has the oldest democracy, oldest republic, and oldest federal system in the world.[115]

The Constitution created a mechanism to govern a vast territory and to provide for majority rule while allowing minority rights. This government has enabled more people to live in liberty and in prosperity than the people of any nation before or since.[116]

Despite its status as a political icon, however, the Constitution has been copied by few countries.[117] Although provisions of the Bill of Rights, such as freedom of speech, and of the Fourteenth Amendment, such as the equal protection clause, have been adopted by other countries,[118] the structure of our government has been less popular. Among the twenty-two democratic countries that have remained stable since 1950,[119] only five others have a federal system with significant power at the state level, only three others have a bicameral legislature with significant power in both houses, and only four others have one house with equal representation for the states regardless of their population. No others have a presidential system, and only two others have a judicial system that exercises judicial review of national legislation.[120] Our Constitution and governmental structure are seen more as a reflection of historical factors and political compromises than as a desirable form of government.

SUMMARY

- The Articles of Confederation made the states supreme over the national government, and they created a national government with no executive or judicial branch. The government could not cope with foreign threats or domestic crises.

- The Founders—in particular, the elites at the time—wanted a commercial empire rather than a small-scale agricultural economy. They wanted a stronger government than the Articles of Confederation had created. Yet they feared a stronger government that might threaten their liberty, as they thought the British government had during colonial times.

- At the Constitutional Convention, there were conflicts over representation, slavery, trade, and taxation. Without compromises, the delegates could not have reached agreement on a constitution.

- A direct democracy permits citizens to vote on most issues. An indirect democracy, also called a republic, allows citizens to vote for representatives who make the decisions.

- Because the Founders were creating a stronger government, they sought to fragment, rather than concentrate, its power so it wouldn't become too powerful. This goal is reflected in the concepts of federalism, which divides power between the national government and the state governments; separation of powers, which divides power into three branches within the national government; and checks and balances, which allows each branch to limit the actions of the other branches.

- There are multiple veto points in the American system—in Congress, the House of Representatives and the Senate; the presidency; and, when constitutional amendments are proposed, the states—which make it difficult to pass new laws or adopt constitutional amendments.

- The Federalists favored ratification of the Constitution, while the Antifederalists opposed ratification. The Antifederalists feared that the Constitution would make the national government too strong.

- The Constitution has evolved in meaning through history. In particular, changes from the Civil War era elevated the nation over the states, and changes from the Great Depression period transformed a relatively small, limited government into a large, activist government.

DISCUSSION QUESTIONS

1. What were the shortcomings of the Articles of Confederation? What were the problems they led to?

2. Did the Founders try to create a strong government or a weak government under the Constitution? Argue both sides; then try to synthesize your arguments into an overall understanding of their goals.

3. What do you think would have happened if the delegates to the Constitutional Convention had refused to compromise? Today some politicians resist pleas to compromise because their constituents feel that compromising would dilute their principles. If the Founders could be brought back from the dead, what do you think they would tell us about compromising?

4. What is the difference between a direct and indirect democracy? Which type is the same as a republic? Can you identify examples of direct democracy today?

5. Some political scientists believe that fragmentation of power, as reflected in the concepts of federalism, separation of powers, and checks and balances, is one of the most significant legacies of the Founders. Construct an argument to support this belief.

6. What are the veto points in the American system, and how does the number of veto points compare with the numbers in other countries' systems? What are the implications of these veto pints for political progress today? Imagine that you could eliminate one veto point. Which one would you choose, and why?

7. Assume that the Antifederalists had prevailed over the Federalists. Predict how the United States would be different today.

8. Some Americans want us to follow the Founders' intentions as closely as possible. Can you develop a contrary argument? Incorporate the Civil War and the Great Depression in your argument.

3 Federalism

Mexican immigrants approach the U.S. border, where they will cross into Arizona. They will paint their water cans black to avoid reflections that could alert the border patrol during their trek across the desert.

OMAR TORRES/AFP/Getty Images

LEARNING OBJECTIVES

1. Define, then compare and contrast, unitary, confederal, and federal systems of governance.
2. Explain how the Constitution can be interpreted to justify different allocations of power between the national and state governments in the United States federal system.
3. Define fiscal federalism. Compare and contrast grants and unfunded mandates.
4. Analyze the role of the president, the Congress, and the courts in allocating power among the national, state, and local governments.
5. Describe the strategies used by the states to lobby the national government.

TALKING POINTS

"Who is the sovereign, the state or the federal government?" This question was raised in 2010 by the leader of the Patrick Henry Caucus, formed to assert the "inviolable sovereignty of the State of Utah under the Tenth Amendment to the Constitution."[1] The question of whether state or federal laws are supreme has been asked repeatedly since the earliest days of the Republic. In 2012 it is relevant again in a debate over the enforcement of immigration law.

The Constitution unequivocally puts the regulation and enforcement of immigration and the rules for naturalization in the hands of the federal government. **Art. I, Sec. 8** The federal government pays for border security and provides grants to states for some immigration-related costs, but the states are responsible for most expenses. Federal law requires, for example, that children be educated and that patients be treated in hospital emergency rooms without respect to immigration status. Every day, border state officials deal with the impact of illegal immigration: migrants who die from heat prostration and dehydration; human smugglers (*coyotes*) and drug traffickers; business owners who recruit, employ, and often exploit undocumented workers; and taxpayers who pay for the public services used by undocumented immigrants.

In the mid-2000s, after border enforcement was stepped up in California and New Mexico, human trafficking moved to Arizona. By 2005, crossings along Arizona's 372-mile border with Mexico reached a half-million people per year. Property, livestock, and environmental damages were reported, and correction systems were strained to process an increased number of undocumented persons.[2] Some local law enforcement officers, not empowered to enforce federal laws, looked for any kind of local statute, such as trespassing or loitering laws, to detain people who were in the state illegally.

Some private citizens responded by forming groups, some of which were armed, to conduct patrols along the border. Although the Bush administration and the Mexican government described this as vigilantism, these individuals believed they were continuing a tradition of citizen-based defense. The most well known of these organizations was the Minuteman Project, named after the colonial militias of the American Revolutionary War. Members of this organization spoke of defending the country against an "invasion," claiming their actions were similar to those of World War II civilian defense.[3]

Meanwhile, public officials competed to be the most anti-immigrant. For example, John McCain (R-Ariz.), who previously had a moderate record on immigration, declared that illegal immigrants were responsible for out-of-control fires in the state, a charge with no demonstrable foundation.[4]

Illegal immigration clearly was a problem, even if rhetoric and actions were overheated. By 2007, 9 percent of Arizona's residents were in the country illegally. Arrests were running at over 1400 per day; and, that year, almost 200 died trying to cross the desert, with hundreds more in need of rescue by state and federal law enforcement. The governor responded by asking President Bush to send the National Guard to patrol the border. He eventually did, but in numbers too small to matter. The governor also signed a bill giving local police more enforcement authority, and she billed the U.S. Department of Justice for $217 million to cover the costs of incarcerating illegal immigrants who had committed crimes.[5]

When the recession hit in 2008 and 2009, and state revenues fell as unemployment rose, the situation worsened. After a rancher was killed by men believed to be either *coyotes* or drug smugglers, the legislature passed and the new governor signed a law that made it a state crime to be in residence without federally issued entry papers. In other words, the legislature made it a state crime to be in violation of a federal law.

By the time this law was passed, the number of undocumented residents was on the decline in the nation as a whole, likely because of hard economic times and limited jobs. The Obama administration had also moved to strengthen border security. Still, polls showed that more than two-thirds of Americans supported the Arizona law.[6] State legislators all over the country followed Arizona's lead. In the first part of 2010, they introduced another 1180 bills dealing with immigration and passed more than 200 of them.[7]

The U.S. Department of Justice filed suit against Arizona. In 2012, in a 5-3 decision, the Supreme Court rejected several provisions of the Arizona law. Still, the Court allowed state and local police officers to check the immigration status of individuals detained for a crime; that information could be shared with federal law enforcement authorities, who had the power to deport any individuals who were in the country illegally. Arizona Governor Jan Brewer immediately declared that the Court had upheld "the heart" of the law. Others, however, viewed the ruling as a victory for the federal government, not the states. In his dissenting opinion, Justice Scalia declared: "If securing its territory in this fashion is not within the power of Arizona, we should cease referring to it as a sovereign state." Quite clearly, debates about the balance of power between the national and the state governments would continue, unresolved.

The victory of the Union over secessionist states in the Civil War (1861–1865) established that the Union is indivisible and that the states cannot nullify federal law or the Constitution. However, the war settled little else about the relationship among these governments. Americans continue to disagree about how big and how strong the national government and state governments should be.

Nevertheless, the United States has a strong central government because the country is so large and complex, because expectations of government are so high, and because the nation has such an influential role in world affairs. The central government is much stronger than most of the Founders ever anticipated. But, as the national government has gained extraordinary power, so have the state and local governments. Federal power *and* state power have grown hand in hand, and both are stronger than in the eighteenth century. Yet, even as Americans have supported the continuous growth of the country and the government, many have clung to the belief that there is something more true or representative about small and local government. Some call for more "states' rights."

In this chapter, we look at the politics behind federalism in order to understand how the distribution of power between Washington and the states has changed over time. In describing the everyday workings of federalism, we identify the sources of cooperation and conflict in the allocation of power.

SYSTEMS OF GOVERNANCE

How does a huge diverse country like the United States govern itself? This nation includes people and states with a great many differences. Some states are populated almost entirely by white people, and in others people of color are a significant minority or even a majority, as in Hawaii. Some states have large numbers of poor people, while others have a significant proportion of retirees.[3] Some states have large proportions of fundamentalist Protestants; others have equally large proportions of Catholics. Some states have many first-generation Americans, other states only a few.[4] These and many other differences mean that the lifestyles and political orientations of different state populations are quite diverse.[5]

The institutions for governing such a country must be strong enough to unite the people but flexible enough so that the traditions and beliefs of people in different states and regions have an important role to play. In Chapter 2, we saw how the Constitution is shaped to try to accomplish both of these ends; in this chapter, we focus on how the federal system is an important part of the U.S. constitutional democracy. Because a central government cannot run every local service or deal directly with every local problem, all modern governments must delegate some power. We first lay the foundation for our discussion by examining the allocation of power in unitary, federal, and confederal systems.

Unitary Systems

In a **unitary system**, the national government is supreme. Subnational governments—states, counties, and municipalities, among others—have only as much power as they are granted by the national government. In Britain, for example, the national government can give or take away any power that it previously delegated to the subnational governments; the national government can even abolish subnational governments, as happened in the 1980s when it abolished some city governments.

Some unitary systems are democratic (Britain and Sweden); others are authoritarian (China and Egypt). In the United States, each of the fifty states is unitary with respect to its local governments. Counties, cities, townships, and school districts can be altered or even eliminated by state governments. Yet every state is (and is required to be by the U.S. Constitution) a republic—that is, a representative democracy.

Confederal Systems

In a **confederal system**, the central government has only the powers given to it by the subnational governments. It cannot act directly on citizens, and it can be dissolved by the states that created it.

Perhaps the oldest confederation is the Iroquois League, which has existed for well over five hundred years. Six nations in the United States and Canada—the Cayuga, the Mohawk, the Oneida, the Onondaga, the Seneca, and the Tuscarora—are its constituent members. One of the shortest-lived confederations, in contrast, was Serbia-Montenegro (2003–2006), formed when Yugoslavia dissolved. The confederation was very weak, and Serbia and Montenegro collaborated on only a few foreign policy issues. The confederation was dissolved when each nation passed a resolution of independence.

The first government of the United States, following independence, was a confederation that protected the sovereignty of each of the former colonies, which were now to be individual states. The Articles of Confederation described the national government as "a firm league of friendship" that would allow the states to provide "for their common defence, the security of their liberties, and their mutual and general welfare." The weakness of the national government, including the absence of taxing powers, ultimately prevented it from achieving these goals, and the Founders instituted a very different political system under the Constitution.

When the southern states seceded from the Union, they adopted a confederal system, the Confederacy, that reflected their opposition to a strong national government.

The United Nations is also a confederal system. The UN depends upon agreement among its member states; it cannot act when powerful states refuse to authorize action. In the spring and summer of 2012, for example, two permanent members of the Security Council, China and Russia, blocked Western efforts to stop Syrian President Bashar al-Assad's use of military force against his own people. Despite media coverage that mobilized international public opinion, as well as continuing pressure to condemn the Assad regime or impose sanctions, the United Nations could not intervene. This inability to act is typical of a confederation, which relies heavily on consensus among its members to limit the power of the central government.

Federalism may seem like a dry subject, but Americans did fight a civil war over it, and feelings about the war remain strong. Civil War re-enactors restage a battle in Spring Hill, Tennessee.

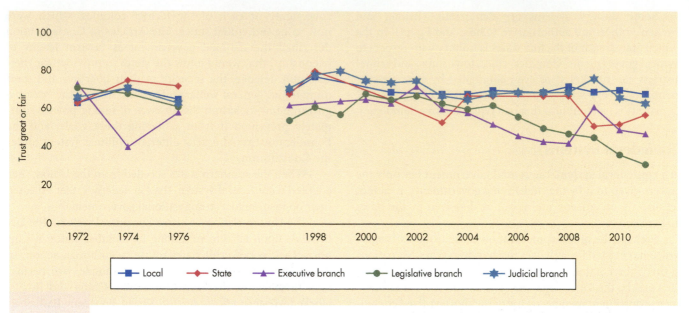

FIGURE 1: PUBLIC TRUST IN LOCAL, STATE, AND NATIONAL GOVERNMENT Respondents nationwide were asked how much "trust and confidence" they had in the executive, legislative, and judicial branches of the national government, in the "government of the state where you live," and in the "local governments in the area where you live." The numbers reflected the combined total for the two responses, "a great deal" and "a fair amount." The governments that are closest to the people (state and local) and the branch of the national government that is most insulated from the public (judicial) have consistently higher scores. The branches of the national government that are elected by the people, the legislative and executive, show the most change.

SOURCE: "Trust in Government," June 5, 2012, www.gallup.com/poll/5392/trust-government.aspx.

Federal Systems

In a **federal system**, the national government is sovereign, but the subnational governments do retain **residual power**. This means that the national government is the most influential, with state and local governments exercising whatever power the national government does not explicitly claim or the Constitution does not explicitly allocate (see Table 1). By the 1960s, as much as half the world's territory was governed through federalism.[8] Some new nations created after World War II chose federalism because they, like the American colonies, were trying to unite diverse states or territories into a single country.

Federal systems are often ethnically, linguistically, religiously, or racially diverse. Agreeing to divide power among levels of government may be the only way to unite people who have a strong motivation to live apart. In 2005, Iraqis wrote a constitution with a federal division of power among the Arab Shia and Sunni Muslims and the non-Arab, but mostly Muslim, Kurds to get the bitterly divided factions to accept the new government. This was a gamble; many federal governments have failed, often because there were not enough shared values to hold the nation together.

Federalism is seen in many very different political systems. It is an element of democratic governments, including Canada, Australia, Germany, and India; and also of several authoritarian governments, including the Congo, the former Soviet Union, and the former Yugoslavia.

In the United States, the Constitution establishes a federal system but gives little information about the details of national-state government relations. This lack of formal constraints, and the continuing differences among the states and regions, all contribute to competition among the various governments. The division of power is constantly changing, and continually questioned. (See Figure 1.) At times, this has led to conflicts that were extremely destructive. The Civil War was fought, in large part, over the power of the states in relation to the national government. Today, this debate continues as the president, Congress, and courts negotiate policy not only with one another but also with state and local governments. Here we should explain a common but confusing term. Although the United States has a federal system, which divides power between the national and state governments, the national government itself is often called the *federal government*.

 Thinking about Democracy

How can federal government strengthen a democracy? Why might federalism fail to build a strong sovereign nation?

FEDERALISM IN THEORY AND PRACTICE

Historically, there have been three interpretations of how the U.S. Constitution defines federalism, each advocating a different allocation of power between the national and state governments. Not surprisingly, then, there have been enduring tensions between the federal government and the states.

Although there is general support for allowing the national government to provide leadership in foreign and defense policy, there is sharp disagreement over which government (national, state, or local) should have the final word in domestic policy. State and local government officials are well aware of how their populations are affected by national problems, and they are pressured to find and implement solutions. But state and local governments often have limited resources; although these governments may see themselves as knowledgeable and skilled policy makers, they are often dependent on the national government for funding.

In this section, we look at the constitutional alternatives for distributing power among the national, state, and local governments. Then we identify the principal points of cooperation and conflict in the everyday workings of federalism. Special attention is paid to the flow of tax revenues between Washington and the states and the conflict over fiscal issues.

Constitutional Federalisms

Nation-centered federalism stresses that the national government is sovereign. It is a philosophy that relies on the **supremacy clause**. **Art. VI** This clause says that treaties, the Constitution, and "laws made in pursuance thereof" are to be the supreme law of the land whenever they come into conflict with state laws or state actions. It also stipulates that when there is a difference of opinion as to whether state actions are in conflict with the Constitution or federal law, the matter is to be decided at the national level.[9] This constitutional interpretation was endorsed two hundred years ago by the Marshall Court in *McCulloch* v. *Maryland* (as explained in Chapter 2) and *Marbury* v. *Madison* (explained in Chapter 12) and was largely settled on the battlefields of the Civil War.

State-centered federalism argues that the states are sovereign. This interpretation of the Constitution highlights the Tenth Amendment, which states, "The powers not delegated to the United States by the Constitution, nor prohibited by it to the States, are reserved to the States respectively, or to the people." As Madison stated in *Federalist Paper* 45, "The powers delegated...to the federal government are few and defined. Those which are to remain in the state governments are numerous and indefinite." In justifying their secession from the Union, members of the southern confederacy held to the extreme version of state-centered federalism: the Constitution had been written by representatives of the states, not the people; because the states had created the Union, they could dissolve it.

BEHIND THE SCENES

An Accidental Classic

Known today as the *Federalist Papers*, the eighty-five essays that James Madison, Alexander Hamilton, and John Jay wrote in support of ratification of the Constitution are widely respected by both theorists and practitioners. They are frequently referenced in popular and scholarly writings, as well as in court decisions. Yet these essays were actually opinion pieces, written to mobilize and win the support of New York's delegates to the ratification convention. The essays were published in newspapers, under the pseudonym of *Publius*.

Though Madison, Hamilton, and Jay all endorsed the Constitution, they frequently disagreed about its provisions and its likely future performance. In fact, John Adams said their essays read like "rival dissertations."[1] These disagreements continued to be expressed when the authors became leaders in the new government: Hamilton was the first treasury secretary and set a strong foundation for fiscal policy; Madison was a U.S. representative, then a secretary of state, and then was elected president; and Jay was the first chief justice of the U.S. Supreme Court.

The debates in the *Federalist Papers* are still heard today, especially those relating to the allocation of power among and within local, state, and national governments in the United States. *Federalist Papers* 10 and 51, which address this issue, among others, are reprinted in the Appendix of this text.

[1] Bernard Bailyn, *The Federalist Papers* (Washington, D.C.: Library of Congress, 1998). p. 8.

Dual federalism maintains that sovereignty is divided among the national and state governments, so that each is essentially equal. This interpretation of the Constitution sees power as divided between the national and state governments so that each is supreme in its own sphere. The different levels of government are essentially equal. The differences between levels derive from their separate jurisdictions, not from an inequality of power.

There has rarely been a national consensus on which interpretation should prevail, though the Civil War was won by those defending the nation-centered view, and that has been the dominant interpretation since. The challenge for people and decision makers in the United States is to balance the fragmentation of governments and people with the need for national unity. Even when there is need for national policy, for issues such as energy, the environment, health care, or defense spending, votes in Congress are still heavily influenced by the members' district and state interests (see Chapter 9).

Federalism Today

Today, the laws of the national government are supreme. In the day-to-day operation of government, however, all levels of government collaborate and sometimes compete. The collaboration is formal and informal, as governments jointly fund and implement a wide range of programs. Political scientists use the term **cooperative federalism** to describe these day-to-day partnerships. Thus, although the term *nation-centered federalism* reflects the dominant interpretation of the Constitution today, the term cooperative federalism accurately reflects the balance of power between the national government and the state governments.

The cooperation may be very formal, as when the national government legislatively delegates responsibility for implementing programs to state and local governments. This occurs in a number of programs. For example, state governments are responsible for enforcing a number of environmental regulations, including those for greenhouse gas emissions, air and water quality, pesticides, pollution prevention and control, transportation, and hazardous waste cleanup. The states also play critical roles in advancing such initiatives as green power, smart growth, clean fuels, water efficiency, and watershed management. Similarly, the Bush-era education law, No Child Left Behind, relies upon state and local governments to administer standardized tests and prepare "accountability plans" assessing each school.

Even programs that are widely viewed as responsibilities of the national government, such as defense and national security, depend upon the states. The National Guard (a militia that is administered by each state) has supplemented regular army troops in Iraq and Afghanistan; the Guard also partners with several national government agencies to provide disaster relief.

Often the cooperation between national and state governments is more informal and depends upon positive relations among agency decision makers. National, state, and local law enforcement willingly, or sometimes reluctantly, share data. Successful collaborations have targeted gang activity related to drug trafficking and distribution, transnational human trafficking, and prostitution. Federal and state governments work together to provide disaster relief when tornados, floods, or hurricanes hit. The Centers for Disease Control and Prevention help state and local governments meet health emergencies and limit the spread of contagious diseases.

More contentious, often less successful, collaborations have centered on immigration and deportation, policing of demonstrators, and intelligence gathering about and surveillance of citizens.[10] When resources are limited, and the law lacks strong public support, collaboration suffers.

Fiscal Federalism

Although the national and state governments cooperate, they also compete with one another. This is especially clear when funding is involved. The relationship is cooperative because the states are dependent upon the national government for

After Hurricane Katrina hit New Orleans in 2005, the National Guard helped to provide disaster relief, handing out emergency meals to residents displaced from their homes.

Vincent Laforet/The New York Times/Redux

money, while the national government is dependent on the states to implement its policy. At the same time, the relationship is competitive because the states want to control the allocation of the money, while the national government wants to set a nationwide policy. For these reasons, **fiscal federalism**—the allocation of government funds among the national, state, and local governments—is routinely controversial. Conflict is most evident in the administration of grants-in-aid and unfunded mandates.

Grants-in-aid are payments made by the national government to states and local governments to fund programs established through national legislation. *Categorical grants* fund specific programs (for example, building a highway); *block grants* fund more general initiatives (for example, improving transportation). Categorical grants have more "strings" than block grants. A categorical highway-building grant requires states to prepare detailed proposals for building specific highways. Block grants give more leeway for states and localities to set priorities within areas (though expenditures have to conform to federal laws involving nondiscrimination, bidding practices, and so on).

In principle, conservatives prefer block grants to categorical grants, seeing the latter as empowering the national government at the expense of states and localities. But in practice, because Congress wants more control over the funding, even Republicans support categorical grants. Today, the vast majority of federal grant programs—80 percent by some estimates—is categorical.[11]

Early grants-in-aid supported the agricultural and industrial development of the United States. Grants helped build the Erie Canal (completed in 1825) and the railroads that first connected the East and West Coasts (1860s). Grants supported the establishment of the land grant universities, connecting instruction in engineering and agriculture to that in the liberal arts (1862), and thus funding the beginnings of America's great public universities. They helped establish and manage state forests (1911), and build a system of highways (1927) and then interstate highways (1956).[12] Thus federal grant funding in the nineteenth century developed the infrastructure that allowed the United States to become a great world power in the twentieth. Some of these investments were even made at the time of America's greatest national crisis, the Civil War (1861–1865).

During the 2008 recession, when unemployment rose and state revenue dropped, federal grants-in-aid accounted for over 25 percent of state spending and supported programs ranging from health care to transportation. Most states sought even more federal aid in an effort to minimize the cuts in their programs and services, including layoffs of teachers, police officers, firefighters, and other public employees. Yet Republican members of Congress resisted efforts to provide this assistance, arguing that reducing the deficit had to take a higher priority. Their resistance illustrates that conflict is especially likely when resources are scarce.

Another kind of conflict occurs when the federal government provides grant funding for some specific purpose but adds standards that some state officials find onerous or

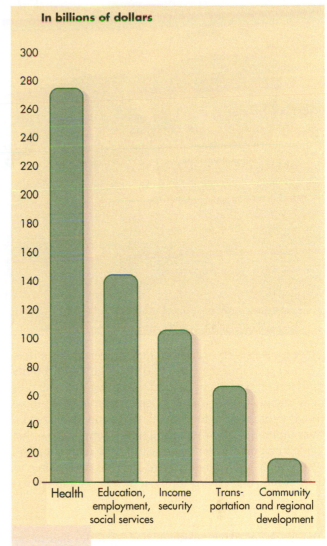

In billions of dollars

FIGURE 2: WHAT DOES THE FEDERAL GOVERN-MENT GIVE THE STATES MONEY TO DO? Ninety-five percent of the estimated $612 billion the federal government sends back to the states is for programs in just five policy areas.

SOURCE: Budget of the United States, Fiscal Year 2011, "Analytical Perspectives" (Washington, D.C.: Government Printing Office, 2011).

disagreeable. If the states do not comply with the standards, the funds are withheld. For example, Congress stipulated that all states must set twenty-one as the legal drinking age or lose highway funds. Although some states did not want to move the drinking age to twenty-one, they needed the highway funds and so complied with federal wishes.

Yet another kind of conflict is a result of **unfunded mandates**. Such mandates are controversial because the national government requires state governments to implement certain policies ("mandates") without compensation for the associated expenses ("unfunded"). For example, federal regulations provided that buildings must have accommodations for disabled people (such as ramps and wide doorways for wheelchairs). In order to receive federal

AP Images

After his state's economy was deeply affected by a massive oil spill into the Gulf, Louisiana governor Bobby Jindal scored political points by meeting with the press almost daily to criticize the federal government's response. But coordination of the federal, state, and local response was different—and more difficult, in some ways—than after a natural disaster because a private company, British Petroleum, caused the damage and was responsible for supervising and paying for most of the cleanup effort.

funds for construction, states and localities had to invest their own funds in such improvements. Antiterrorism laws have also placed new unfunded mandates on states, such as making their drivers' licenses and other identify cards more forgery proof.[13]

In the 1990s—long before the budgetary pressures created by the Great Recession—the financial burden of unfunded mandates led state and local officials to mount a national campaign against them. Congress passed reform legislation in 1995 that required the national government to conduct cost estimates on bills for most matters that would impose costs greater than $50 million on the states. The legislation has had little effect.[14] Facing this burden, and fearing the additional costs imposed by the 2010 health care reform, states pushed back against new mandates.

In 2012, the Supreme Court ruled that the national government could not use a threat to deny funding as a means of forcing state governments to enact certain policies. Specifically, the states could not be required to change the standards for their citizens to participate in Medicaid, a program largely funded by the federal government that provides health care for the disabled and for those with low incomes. Some Republican governors immediately declared that they would not change the current requirements, even if doing

so would bring additional federal dollars for their citizens. Whether the governors will sustain this commitment, and how the Supreme Court ruling will alter national and state budgets more generally, will be critical issues for decision makers in 2013 and beyond.

 Thinking about Democracy

Describe and defend your ideal distribution of power among national, state, and local governments under the U.S. Constitution. As you defend the constitutionality of your ideal, consider the advantages and disadvantages of having governments share power in a federal system. How will your federal system strengthen democracy in the U.S. government?

GOVERNING THROUGH FEDERALISM

Dependent upon the states to implement many of its programs and enforce many of its regulations, the branches of the national government have each had considerable influence over the allocation of power in the federal system. In some instances, the president, the Congress, and the courts have delegated power to the states; in others, they have constrained the states and increased the power of the national government. Meanwhile, the people have also pressured the state governments—and, indirectly, the national government—through ballot initiatives and referenda that push for particular policy outcomes. Surveying these controversies, it becomes very clear why one expert speaks of "competitive federalism": states and the federal government clearly compete for leadership of the nation's domestic policy.[15]

The President

To understand how dramatically a president can influence the workings of federalism, consider the contrasts between Democratic president Lyndon Johnson (1963–1969) and Republican president Richard Nixon (1969–1974). Although one was the immediate predecessor to the other, their differing partisan and political priorities caused them to take very different approaches to federalism.

Shortly after he entered office, following the assassination of President John F. Kennedy, Johnson declared a "war on poverty." His domestic policy agenda, the "Great Society," was focused upon securing the right to vote for African Americans, providing health insurance for seniors and the poor, and strengthening educational opportunities for all. Johnson, a Texan, was steeped in the politics of states' rights and segregation, and he knew that when federal dollars went to some states there would be great resistance in the state-houses to using the money as the law intended. He also knew that rural-influenced state legislatures would be less responsive to the needs of the inner cities. Johnson therefore increased grant-making to local governments, feeling that they, especially the larger cities, where a majority of people live, would be more receptive to his policies than many state legislatures.

Nixon had a less expansive view of government than Johnson; he was determined to gain control of the federal bureaucracy, consolidating programs and increasing the efficiency of the national government. Nixon was, therefore, willing to delegate some programmatic responsibilities to the states. In addition to lessening the decision-making burden of the federal government, the president hoped to create a sense of indebtedness and loyalty among the governors. Where Johnson focused on local governments, Nixon focused on state governments; and where Johnson funded comparatively specific programs (through categorical grants), Nixon funded broader initiatives (through block grants). In the Johnson years, a city could apply for and receive a grant to institute primary education programs; in the Nixon years, a state could apply for and receive a grant to improve public education, which it would then allocate among state and local education programs. In the Johnson years, the power in federalism flowed through local funding; in the Nixon years, the power flowed through state funding.

As these examples illustrate, most federal domestic policies have a role for the states or localities, and that is part of cooperative federalism. How much power should rest there and how much should be retained by the federal government is an ongoing issue. Recent presidents have supported expanded local and state powers, sometimes called devolution. George W. Bush (2001–2009) expanded the powers of the president, as will be discussed in Chapter 10, but he also favored delegating primary responsibility for a range of programs—including Medicaid, Section 8 housing, and the preschool Head Start program—to the states. In addition, Bush reversed executive orders issued by his predecessor that set national standards for arsenic levels in water, pollutants in the air, and health and safety in the workplace. Bush wanted less regulation and expected that many states would use their discretion to reduce regulation in these areas.

Democratic presidents Bill Clinton (1993–2001) and Barack Obama, rather than stressing the limits of the federal government, endorsed the ideal (earlier articulated by Justice Louis Brandeis) of the "states as laboratories"—that is, as places for policy experimentation. Clinton, especially, used the phrase frequently and wrote it into executive orders. Clinton's environmental regulations, as well as his welfare, health care, and education policies, reflected his conviction that the states could help improve the efficiency and effectiveness of policies and programs initially developed by the national government.[16]

Obama's nearly $800 billion stimulus bill, supported by resource-strapped Republican governors, though not by Republican members of Congress, provided significant aid to the states in an effort to limit job loss as the recession

Although marijuana use is prohibited by a federal law upheld by the Supreme Court, it has been legalized for medical use by a number of states, and the Supreme Court has deliberately refrained from overturning those state laws. In at least fourteen states, then, people who use marijuana for medical reasons are protected by state law but may be prosecuted under federal law. Federalism allows states to serve as experimental laboratories for possible changes in federal policy, but those changes are not always smoothly or easily adopted. Here the owner of a dispensary in Boulder, Colorado, prepares marijuana for sale.

worsened. The Obama administration encouraged state governments to take the initiative to regulate in key areas, such as consumer and environmental protection, where Congress and federal agencies have taken little action. It also encouraged state actions opposed by the Bush administration, such as setting higher state standards for clean air.

However, Republican and Democratic presidents have also qualified their support for devolution when it has come into conflict with other policy or ideological priorities. The support that George W. Bush gave to expanding the role of the states in making and implementing welfare policy was countered by his intervention in public education, as the No Child Left Behind Act imposed mandatory national testing on local school systems. Bush also opposed a number of business and environmental regulations that were endorsed by state governments. Mixed messages occurred as well during the Obama administration. Although the Obama administration encouraged states to take initiatives in many policy areas, the 2010 health insurance reform bill was strongly nation-centered, though with many provisions for state experimentation and state differences. Ultimately, thirty-seven states challenged one or more of its provisions as unconstitutional. When the Supreme Court issued its ruling in 2012, it ruled partially in favor of the national government and partially in favor of the state governments: The Court held that the national government could require individuals to have health insurance, but the federal government could not threaten the states with loss of federal dollars if they failed to change their requirements for citizens to gain access to Medicaid. This was a decision that ensured debates would continue about the proper allocation of power among the national and state governments.

Presidents, in brief, favor the balance of power among national and state governments that will advance their own priorities. In this, they are very similar to members of Congress.

The Congress

Members of Congress represent states and districts, and most take this responsibility very seriously. Often, they will devote more time and more resources to advancing the interests of their constituents than to defining and pursuing the national interest. Even when the national interest is discussed, state and local interests continue to be considered. Defense policy, for example, involves careful consideration of the effects of bases and weapon contracts on local economies, and of wars on the National Guard and the lives of all people. Former Speaker Tip O'Neil famously stated that "all politics is local," and in this sense, Congress has a bias in favor of state-centered federalism.

Yet members of Congress have also protected their own interests, asserting the power of the national government over the states and localities. This has been particularly evident in their use of the power to regulate interstate commerce, granted by the Constitution to the legislative branch. **Art. I, Sec. 8, cl. 3** They have, for example, withstood pressures from state governments to tax e-commerce and other Internet activity, a prohibition that cost the states an estimated $23 billion in lost revenues in 2012.[17] Congress has refused to gather this revenue despite growing popular opposition to budget deficits.

As these examples suggest, the power granted or claimed by Congress has historically reflected the political priorities of its members and its voters. Congress supported the tremendous growth of government during Franklin Roosevelt's first three terms, but then many Republicans and southern Democrats wanted to swing the locus of power away from the center and back to the states. Many white southerners were angered when federal laws superseded state and local segregationist policies. Similarly, the growth in social welfare programs during the Johnson era eventually led to the Reagan-Republican smaller-government rebellions of the 1980s, 1990s, and early 2000s, with a reemphasis on states' rights.

One member of Congress summarized all of these actions by saying that fellow members "don't really believe in states' rights; they believe in deciding the issue at whatever level of government they think will do it their way. They want to be Thomas Jefferson on Monday, Wednesday, and Friday and Alexander Hamilton on Tuesday and Thursday and Saturday."[18]

The Courts

Ultimately, it is the Supreme Court that decides which powers the states or the national government exercise. The justices, in keeping with their contrasting jurisprudential philosophies, have variously supported nation-centered, state-centered, or dual federalism. These opinions have also revealed the justices' political priorities, whether conservative or liberal.

Before the Civil War, in the years of small government, the Supreme Court overturned only two congressional and sixty state laws. Beginning in the 1880s, the federal government and (slightly later) state governments took a larger role in regulating business and the economy. From 1874 to 1937, the Court, reflecting its own conservative pro-business bias, found fifty federal and four hundred state laws unconstitutional. These included some of FDR's key New Deal laws.[19] The Court decisions favored limiting government involvement in the economy; to achieve this goal, the justices endorsed state-centered federalism in some cases, dual federalism in others.

When the Court did approve New Deal legislation, beginning in 1937, it also approved more sweeping state regulations of business and labor. With these decisions, the Court enlarged the powers of *both* state and federal government, at a time when the effects of the Great Depression were still profound. Although the Court is expected to stand apart from public opinion, the justices' rulings did seem to respond to the public's demand (and the president's commitment) that government assume greater responsibility for the economic well-being of the nation and of its people.

Similarly, from the 1950s through the 1970s, as the civil rights, women's rights, and environmental movements gained momentum, the courts struck down many state laws that restricted voting rights, criminal defendants' rights, and women's economic and educational opportunities. **Amendments 13–15, 19, 24, and 26** Power shifted to the national government, with the executive branch enforcing court rulings.

Since the 1990s, however, court rulings have trended toward empowering the states at the expense of the national government. In 1992, the Court handed down the first of several key decisions that restricted Congress's ability to impose rules and regulations on state governments; it prevented litigants from bypassing state courts to seek remedies in federal courts. In a 1995 decision, the Court ruled, for the first time since the New Deal, that Congress had exceeded its authority to regulate interstate commerce. In a burst of judicial activism, in the following eight years, the Court "overturned all or parts of thirty-three federal statutes, ten of them on the grounds that Congress had exceeded its authority either to regulate interstate commerce or to enforce the constitutional guarantees of due process and equal protection."[20] Most recently, the Supreme Court ruled on the allocation of power among national and state governments in cases that challenged health insurance legislation and immigration law enforcement. In these cases, the Court upheld the power of the national government and yet reserved important, residual powers to the states.

These and other rulings have encouraged lawsuits by those advocating more limited national government. Efforts to limit Congress's power to extend federal laws to the states have led to court interpretations indicating that while Congress may confer rights on citizens, it cannot tell the states how to protect or enforce them. As a result, it has been difficult to enforce the protections provided by the Americans with Disabilities Act consistently across all the states. Rights, as this example shows, may go unprotected and unenforced. [21]

As was true in the late nineteenth and early twentieth century, the Court's present-day rulings in federalism cases reflect the justices' political priorities as well as their constitutional philosophies. A conservative majority among the nine Supreme Court justices appears to support smaller government at all levels. However, the Court overruled the Florida courts and intervened in the 2000 presidential vote count, awarding the election to George W. Bush. The Court did so, even though the states—not the federal government—have authority over elections, and even though the Constitution specifies procedures to resolve disputed elections. **Art. I, Sec. 4** and **Art. II, Sec. 1** Majorities in various states have also struck down such diverse laws as those that decriminalize "medical marijuana," that regulate guns, and that limit campaign finance donations.

In each instance, the power of state governments has been limited, even as these justices have claimed, in other cases, to be supportive of state-centered federalism. Their conservative policy agenda is focused on reducing the power of both the national and the state governments. While the term *activist judges* has for many years referred to liberal judges, it is now conservative judges who are overturning decades of decisions.

The People

The people also influence the distribution of power throughout the federal system. In addition to electing the president and the members of Congress, voters in many states express their policy judgments through ballot initiatives and referenda.

The ballot initiative and referendum were reforms that emerged in the early years of the nineteenth century, intended to foster democracy by undermining the state and urban political machines. For a **ballot initiative**, sometimes called a citizen initiative, voters sign a petition to have a policy proposal placed on the ballot, which voters will then endorse or reject. In some states, the vote on the initiative is not binding on the legislature, while in other states, the vote is binding, so the initiative becomes law. Over the past fifteen years, voters have approved initiatives that have sanctioned the medical use of marijuana, imposed limits on campaign spending and contributions, expanded casino gambling, and given adopted children the right to know the names of their biological parents.

A **ballot referendum** may originate in a petition signed by the voters (known as a popular referendum) or a measure forwarded by the legislature to the voters for their approval or disapproval (known as a legislative referendum). A popular referendum is an effort to repeal a specific act passed by the state legislature. One popular referendum, for example, overturned state laws instituting affirmative action hiring programs. A legislative referendum may be used to amend the state constitution.

While both citizen initiatives and popular referenda empower the people, the citizen initiative makes law and the popular referendum unmakes it. The National Conference of State Legislatures estimates that there were more than 1300 ballot measures from 1998 to 2010, of which almost two-thirds (857) were legislative referenda, and nearly one-third, or 31 percent (409), citizen initiatives. [22]

Although initiatives and referenda focus on state and local policies, some of them are of interest to political activists and voters in other states, because they could reshape the national

CourseReader   ASSIGNMENT

Log in to www.cengagebrain.com and open Course-Reader to access the full reading "Remaking Federalism to Remake the American Economy" by Bruce Katz.

The Brookings Institution describes itself as a "private organization devoted to analyzing public policy issues at the national level." Widely respected by Democrats and Republicans, though with a somewhat liberal bent, it hosts debates and events and publishes a wide array of papers and books, articulating clear and strong recommendations for government reform. In this Brookings article, Bruce Katz argues that allocating more power to the states—encouraging initiative and innovation in their policy making—could fuel a full recovery from the Great Recession.

Think about the roles that could be assigned to the local, state, and national government: the federal government invests in the states, the states innovate, and "federalist institutions" disseminate state successes throughout the nation. This is an allocation of power that tilts toward state-centered federalism, which claims to be "pragmatic" and which promises "economic prosperity, fiscal solvency and political comity."

1. How did the presidential candidates in 2012 benefit from endorsing these proposals? Did these campaign promises help the president to be a more authoritative chief executive? A more persuasive party leader? A stronger negotiator with Congress? Why or why not?
2. What dangers of state-centered federalism would be avoided by this proposal, given that it reserves a significant role for the national government in financing state-driven innovations?
3. If decision making and policy making in Washington were more bipartisan, and thus more constructive, would nation-centered federalism be more appealing? Why or why not?

Darren Hauck/Getty Images

Stem cell research, such as that conducted at this University of Wisconsin research center, has been another area of conflict in the federal relationship. A number of states passed laws permitting stem cell research after Congress and the Bush administration prohibited federal funding for research that leads to the destruction of human embryos.

political agenda. For example, when California courts upheld same-sex marriages, California voters approved an initiative to make marriage only between a man and a woman. Many organizations and interests outside California, including a number of religions, invested vast amounts in campaigning for and against the initiative because they believed the outcome of the California initiative could influence the outcome of future policy conflicts relating to gay rights.

 Thinking about Democracy

> Having assessed the capacity of the president, the Congress, the courts, and the people to shape the workings of federalism in the United States, which do you think has the greatest potential to threaten democracy?

INTERGOVERNMENTAL RELATIONS

As the federal government continues to devolve responsibilities to the states, and as states have become more dependent on federal aid (see Figure 2), competition among states to get federal dollars has increased. To gain resources and advance their interests, states lobby the national government in several different ways.

Not surprisingly, each congressional delegation advocates on behalf of its constituents, and those states with senior members in the House or Senate usually fare better than others in bringing federal tax dollars to their home districts. Smaller states at times find common interest in voting as a bloc in

the Senate to prevent the largest states from getting a share of aid in proportion to their population or need. An egregious case was the allocation of Homeland Security funding; when the more populous and higher-risk states such as New York attempted to win funding proportionate to their larger populations and greater chance of attack, they were outvoted by smaller states that faced little risk but wanted federal money anyway.[23] It took several years of publicity about irrelevant equipment purchases by small rural states and municipalities to reallocate funding closer to security priorities.

States, and some local governments, also hire lobbyists to represent them in Washington. This may be necessary because the members of a state's congressional delegation may belong to different parties than state leaders. Or members of Congress may disagree with state leaders, as, for example, when Congress waived state sales taxes on e-commerce, which most state leaders strongly favored. Or a state may have an urban majority, whereas its congressional delegation is closer in views to rural and suburban residents. But mainly states hire lobbyists because there is a lot of money at stake.

To make sure that they continue to receive their fair share, or more, of federal funds, a number of individual states and cities have their own Washington lobbyists, some very successful. Many states, for example, use "contingency fee" consultants whose job is to get as much money as possible from Washington to cover state Medicaid outlays. Because the consultants get a share of the money they bring in, they have every incentive to find any way within the law to claim additional payments to the states that employ them.[24]

Finally, there are interest groups that lobby on behalf of the states. Interstate organizations such as the National Conference of State Legislatures (NCSL, est. 1975), the National League of Cities (1924), the American Public Human Services Association (est. 1930), and the National Governors Association (est. 1908) advocate on behalf of favorable legislation for states and localities and also work with federal agencies to ensure that new regulations are implemented in a way that is acceptable to the states. Many of these organizations have multimillion-dollar budgets and employ sizable staffs.

For example, the NCSL looks especially for any new legislation that would undercut state laws, have an impact on state revenue, or tie the hands of state officials in some policy area. Some states are concerned about the free-trade agreements Congress has approved. States that are big exporters do not want to exempt foreign nations from paying import taxes because that could affect the competitiveness of a state's businesses and revenues. Recently, states have been especially concerned about how the new health insurance legislation will affect their budgets over the long term. Many governors ordered their attorneys general to go through the bill and challenge provisions they believed unconstitutional. In 2012, the U.S. Supreme Court agreed to hear one of these cases. The Court ruled in favor of the national government, but with qualifications—the national government could not threaten the states with a loss of funding if they failed to expand access to Medicaid, one of the most important health care programs for the disabled and economically disadvantaged.

As all of these examples demonstrate, the states are in a sometimes competitive, sometimes cooperative relationship with the national government and with one another. Limited resources (including federal funding), contrasting priorities (in public policies such as same-sex marriage, gun regulation, energy, and capital punishment), and contracting economic markets (due to globalization and to the 2008 recession) have resulted in fierce rivalries. These have, in turn, been exacerbated by cultural, political, and regional differences. Environmental stewardship, for instance, has different meanings and consequences for people living in Oregon, Ohio, and Rhode Island. As these states mobilize and lobby, crosscutting pressures emerge at the national, state, and local levels.

Yet scarce resources have also resulted in collaboration. With almost every state having trouble funding even the essentials, some neighboring states have begun to barter for goods and share their services. Wisconsin and Minnesota have negotiated buying in bulk (police bullets, for example), sharing computer systems, and making license plates. Other states are sharing prison and juvenile detention centers.[25] Federalism is as much about mobilizing the governments as it is about leveraging the power and influence of one against the other.

American Diversity

Learning Civics State by State

Local control of K–12 education has led to regional differences in teaching civics and U.S. history. Students in states of the former Confederacy, for example, read a different version of Civil War history than students studying in northern schools. Students in Illinois learn a lot more about Abraham Lincoln than about Jefferson Davis, with the reverse true for Virginia's students. However, until the second half of the twentieth century, children in K–12 were taught, in broad terms, the same story about independence from Britain, the Founders' role, and the expansion of the country. This began to change in the 1960s as a result of scholarly research that shifted the focus from top-down explanations of American history to bottom-up explorations, from studying the Founders and other elites to studying social history, popular culture, and everyday life. This approach assigned much more significance to the role of the people in the making of American history. It also included more coverage of the groups previously excluded or downplayed, such as Native Americans, African Americans, Latinos, women, and gays and lesbians.

In Texas, a single commission, the State Board of Education, almost none of whose members are educators or scholars, rules on content for all textbooks used in the state's public schools. It determines what textbooks they must include and what they must exclude if publishers want to sell their books to the Texas schools. Because Texas is one of the largest markets, choices made by the Texas Board serve as a template for the content of tens of millions of K–12 texts, which are used in as many as forty-six or forty-seven states.[1]

The Board reviews content every five years, at which time interest groups can attend hearings and make a case for those people or events they believe schoolchildren should learn about. The Board tries to be inclusive but insists on a "controlling narrative" of U.S. history rather than a narrative of various groups and forces and struggles. In 2010, the Board's attempt to provide this "through line" included telling publishers that books must make the point that the Founders' intent was to establish a Christian nation. Thomas Jefferson was to be dropped from the list of Founders who influenced the content of the Constitution because of his passionate belief in the separation of church and state. Textbook publishers also were told that books used in Texas schools must define the U.S. government as a "constitutional republic" rather than as a democracy. The U.S. economy was to be called a "free-enterprise system" rather than "capitalist" because the majority of the Board believed capitalism was a word that had negative connotations. They refused to identify hip-hop as a significant cultural movement and eliminated a requirement that sociology students learn about racism in the contemporary United States. They also denied a request from Latino groups to acknowledge a number of Latinos, including those who fought at the Alamo with other Texans.[2]

The Board wants Texas students to learn a common, positive story about the Founding and the development of the United States. It sees a narrative of America as a nation founded on Christianity and western European culture as essential to students' political socialization. Learning political culture is important, and K–12 textbooks are probably not the primary source of this information. But in the battle for the hearts and minds of America's youth, should each state write its own version of American history?

[1] Russell Shorto, "Founding Father?" *New York Times Magazine*, February 14, 2010, 35.

[2] "Conservatives Carry Day for Curriculum in Texas," *Champaign-Urbana News-Gazette*, March 13, 2010, A4.

Thinking about Democracy

Are those who lobby on behalf of state governments acting in the public interest or on behalf of special interests? Are these lobbyists enhancing or undermining democracy in the United States?

POLICY, POWER, AND FEDERALISM

As federalism was designed and is practiced in the United States, the locus of power is never fixed. The sometimes clear, sometimes ambiguous, division of power has meant that struggles between the national, state, and local governments are never-ending. The competition is built into our government as a check on the overconcentration of power at any one level. Whenever the balance of power tips too far toward Washington, there is movement to reinvigorate the states and localities.

Currently a majority appears to be dissatisfied in some way with the national government—it is either doing too much or not doing enough for the average person; it is spending too much or spending for the wrong purposes. This feeling has intensified the movement toward state activism, with states acting because they believe the national government has abdicated its responsibilities or because they believe no one solution will work for all the states. For example, tired of waiting for Washington to act on greenhouse gases, a group of northeastern states has formed the Regional Greenhouse Gas Initiative to control carbon emissions.[26]

But Washington does not want to see state legislatures pre-empting the constitutional authority of the national government, even when the president and Congress are not fulfilling their responsibilities in those areas. And businesses involved in interstate commerce often find it more expensive, time-consuming, and confusing to comply with fifty different versions of a regulation than with a single federal rule.

U.S. history suggests that most people are pragmatic, less concerned about which government makes policy than about ensuring that the policies themselves are working well. In the 1990s, when the public consensus was that Washington was not running welfare programs effectively, much of the responsibility was passed to the states; when state and local governments were judged to be failing at running public schools, Washington stepped in. In 2010, after the federal government passed health insurance reform, three dozen states legislated or sued to regain greater control over state spending on health care programs. And so it has gone for decades.

In the United States, the people are bound together by a shared belief in democracy, equality, and the rule of law. The federal system accommodates regional differences by allowing both state and national governments a role in policy making. In addition, it allows groups and individuals whose demands are rejected at one level of government to pursue

Race relations have often been a source of controversy between the federal government and southern state or local governments that resisted civil rights, claiming "states' rights" instead. Here police unleash dogs on peaceful civil rights demonstrators in Birmingham, Alabama, in 1963.

them at another level. The federal system creates multiple points of access, each with power to satisfy political demands by making policy that was rejected at another level. The challenge is to fragment power and prevent tyranny, while still maintaining a sense of national unity and purpose. One hundred years ago President Woodrow Wilson warned that "it is no longer possible with the modern combinations of industry and transportation to discriminate the interests of the states as they once could be. . . . Interests once local and separate have become unified and national. They must be treated by the national government."

SUMMARY

- The three basic systems of power within a country are unitary (the national government is sovereign), federal (the national government is sovereign and subgovernments exercise real, though residual, power), and confederal (the subgovernments are sovereign). The United States is a federal system, with power divided among the national, state, and local governments.

- The Constitution has been interpreted, throughout the history of the United States, as supporting nation-centered federalism (prioritizing the power of the national government), state-centered federalism (prioritizing the power of the state governments), and dual federalism (where powers are essentially equal). Since the Civil War, a nation-centered federal model has predominated, but within that, states and federal governments collaborate in a system sometimes called cooperative federalism. Although states have certain powers, when the laws of the national and state governments clash, the law of the national government is supreme.

- Fiscal federalism reflects a system in which the national government provides funds for states and localities, but with strings on how those funds can be spent. Poor economic conditions have increased the competition for grants-in-aid among states and local governments, even as they have forced these governments to carefully protect their budgets against unfunded mandates.

- Presidents, Congress, courts, and the people have all shaped the allocation of power among the national, state, and local governments. In part, the allocations have reflected political and partisan ideologies; in part, they have resulted from pragmatic calculations of what would win support from other decision makers and voters, increasing the likelihood that the policies would work as promised.

- To gain the power, policies, and resources that they want and need, state and local governments rely on their members of Congress, on lobbyists, and on interest groups to advance their agendas before the national government.

DISCUSSION QUESTIONS

1. If the U.S. population becomes more geographically segregated along ethnic, religious, or racial lines as it continues to grow, will its survival as a federal republic be threatened?

2. What do you see as the principal weakness of cooperative federalism? Would this be corrected if the United States consistently practiced nation-centered or state-centered federalism? Or would the costs of these approaches outweigh their benefits?

3. Do you think that grants-in-aid or unfunded mandates pose the greater threat to cooperative federalism? Be careful to explain your answer in the context of current economic conditions.

4. Should the president, the Congress, or the courts have more influence over federalism in the United States? What does your answer reveal about your own political views?

5. What problems do well-financed national campaigns to defeat or to pass state ballot initiatives present for Madison's defense of federalism as a way to constrain the "mischiefs of faction"?

6. Given that states and local governments lobby the national government, is federalism in the United States ultimately nation-centered?

4 Public Opinion

A supporter of gay marriage (right) and an opponent face off in Albany, New York.

AP Images/Mike Groll

LEARNING OBJECTIVES

1. Define public opinion, and describe how intensity and stability are key attributes of public opinion.

2. Identify the agents of political socialization.

3. Describe the primary ways public opinion is measured today and how scientific advances have affected the accuracy of polling efforts.

4. Compare how politicians and the mass media use polling results.

5. Distinguish among straw polls, push polls, tracking polls, exit polls, and focus groups; explain how each is used; and identify the benefits and costs attached to each.

6. Explain how informed the general public is about issues and candidates and how levels of knowledge may affect individual participation.

7. Understand the extent to which the red state/blue state concept is accurate or inaccurate.

8. Summarize opinions on social issues of voters who are between eighteen and twenty-nine years of age compared to other age groups, and pinpoint specific differences.

TALKING POINTS

The 2008 presidential election mobilized many young people who had not been interested in politics before but were inspired by one of the candidates, especially by Barack Obama. But the media portrayal of an active and engaged young electorate of 2008 was exaggerated in some ways. Although their turnout increased by 4 or 5 percent from the election of 2004 and two-thirds gave their support to Obama, young adults still had the lowest turnout of any age group.

Moreover, young people remain the least informed and least involved segment of the electorate. For example, in 2010, compared to those over fifty, young people were much less informed on issues ranging from knowledge of the commander of the U.S. forces in Afghanistan (David Petraeus) to estimates of the unemployment rate to the name of the chief justice of the U.S. Supreme Court (John Roberts). On only two questions in the survey were eighteen- to twenty-nine-year-olds more knowledgeable than those over fifty:

that South Africa hosted the 2010 World Cup, and that Twitter is an information-sharing network.[1]

Despite the 2008 surge in interest and participation in the political process, the youth vote since then has been consistent with long-standing trends. Although it is not unusual for off-year elections to attract fewer voters than presidential elections, in the 2009 gubernatorial elections in New Jersey and Virginia fewer than 20 percent of those from eighteen to twenty-nine voted. And in the January 2010 special election in Massachusetts to fill the U.S. Senate seat formerly held by Democrat Ted Kennedy, only 15 percent voted.[2] Worse still, only 9 percent of those eighteen to twenty-nine turned out in the 2010 midterm elections. These results suggest that forecasts of permanent increases in political participation among youth after 2008 were optimistic and that the increase in participation was fueled by other factors, such as dissatisfaction with the direction of the country under George W. Bush and the appeal of the Obama image.

Public opinion is complex and often contradictory. For example, citizens are often angry with political leaders for failing to respond to their needs. At the same time, some complain that leaders follow the latest polls rather than developing well-reasoned political positions. Additionally, many people do not trust government; they think it is too big and spends too much money. Yet they like the services it provides, and, year after year, majorities want to *increase* spending in many areas of government of activity. Few are willing to cut spending to eliminate services or programs that benefit them. This enduring reality of modern American politics was summed up by scholars in 1964 and is equally true today: "Americans are ideological conservatives and operational liberals. Everybody's for less spending and regulation in the abstract. When you try to translate that into specifics—say, lower Medicare benefits or looser standards on pollution—voters run screaming in the other direction."[3]

This chapter explores public opinion to better understand these contradictions. It describes how public opinion is formed and measured, assesses how informed and knowledgeable the public are with respect to public affairs, discusses the role of ideology in American politics, and addresses divisions within the population over some important issues.

NATURE OF PUBLIC OPINION

Public opinion can be defined as the collection of individual opinions about issues, candidates, officeholders, and events of general interest—that is, those that concern a significant number of people. The direction of public opinion can be either positive or negative, that is, for or against something or someone.

 Thinking about Democracy

> In a democracy, should public officials be more responsive to a minority of citizens with very strong feelings about an issue or to the majority with less intense feelings?

Intensity reflects the strength of public opinion. The public may have weak feelings about something or feel strongly about it. Intense opinions often drive behavior. Many people opposed the troop increase in Afghanistan, for example, but only the most intense communicated with their senators or representative or took to the streets to protest this decision. Public opinion is not very intense on most issues. A small minority may feel intensely about an issue or politician, but a majority rarely does.

Opinions also vary in stability. Some opinions change constantly, whereas other opinions never do. Stable opinions are often intense and grounded in a great deal of information—some of it accurate, some inaccurate. Feelings of attachment to political parties tend to be stable, whereas opinions about candidates and public officials, particularly high-profile ones like a president, fluctuate in response to changing events and circumstances. For example, President Obama's initial

approval rating was 68 percent, the highest initial level since President John F. Kennedy. But one year after his election, his approval rate stood at 53 percent, which is near the bottom of post–World War II presidents' first-year ratings.[4] And by January of 2012, it had dropped to 46 percent. The ongoing poor state of the economy, among other issues, accounts for much of this drop (see Figure 1).

FORMATION OF PUBLIC OPINION

People learn and develop opinions about government and politics through the process of **political socialization**. As in other spheres, individuals learn about politics by being exposed to new information supplied or filtered through parents, peers, schools, the media, political leaders, and communities. These **agents of political socialization** introduce each new generation to the rights and responsibilities of citizenship (see Chapter 1) as well as shape opinions and positions toward candidates, officeholders, and political issues. Individuals, particularly adults, also learn about politics and develop opinions through personal experiences.

Political learning begins at an early age and continues throughout life. In young children, learning is influenced by reasoning capacity and expectations.[5] The greater a child's intellect and the demands placed upon her, the more and faster she is likely to learn.

Preschoolers are unable to distinguish political from nonpolitical objects. Some are unable to separate political figures from cartoon characters, and some confuse religion with politics. A significant number of five- and six-year-olds report that the president takes orders from God.[6] By first grade, these confusions are resolved and children begin to see government as separate and unique.[7]

However, children's inability to understand abstract concepts or complex institutions means their conceptions of government are limited. Most identify government with the president.[8] At a very early age, children recognize the president. In one study, 97 percent of a group of fourth graders were able to identify the president by name,[9] a proportion that has stayed constant for several decades.[10] Experiences with parents and other adults give children a basis for understanding their relationship with authority figures with whom they have no contact.[11] Moreover, the feelings children have toward parents are likely to be generalized to presidents.

Older children are introduced to political ideas and political institutions in school and through the media. Their concept of government includes Congress, the act of voting, and ideas such as freedom and democracy. A positive view of government reflected in feelings toward the president gives way to more complex and realistic images. The process can be accelerated by political events and the reaction of others to them. Children were much less positive toward the president and government in the 1970s than in the 1960s. The Watergate scandal in 1973 lowered both adults' and children's evaluations of the president.[12] Even when scandal

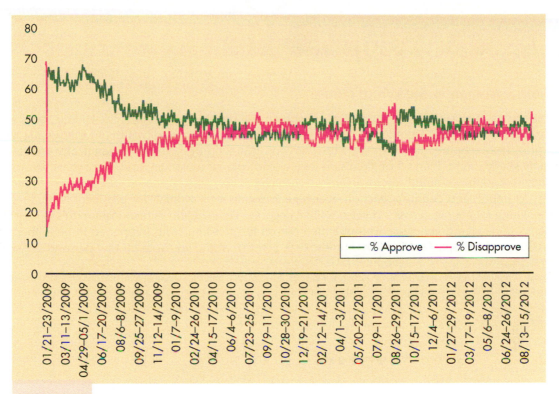

FIGURE 1: PUBLIC OPINION CAN FLUCTUATE: PRESIDENT OBAMA'S APPROVAL RATINGS This graph, based on daily polls of Americans asking if they approve or disapprove of the president, shows week to week fluctuations and trends over time. Like all presidents, Barack Obama started with high ratings, but these sank as the poor economy and other factors eroded his popularity. Daily results are based on telephone interviews of 1,500 adults. Margin of error is 3 percentage points.

SOURCE: From the Gallup polls, reported in Gallup Daily: Obama Job Approval. Copyright © 2012 Gallup, Inc. All rights reserved. The content is used with permission; however Gallup retains all rights of republication.

lowers children's evaluations of government, though, the effect may not last. Negative feelings of children during Watergate diminished as they aged.[13]

In adolescence, political understanding expands still further. Children discuss politics with family and friends. By the middle teens, positions on issues develop.[14] Although they begin to recognize faults in the system, adolescents tend to believe the United States is the best country in the world. Teenagers rate the country low in limiting violence and fostering political morality but high in providing educational opportunities, a good standard of living, and science and technology.[15] For most, the positive feelings toward government learned earlier are reinforced.

In adulthood, opinions about specific personalities and policies develop, and political activity deepens. Although most Americans respect the country and do not want to change the system, many tend to be cynical and distrustful of political leaders. Some of this negative feeling grows out of Americans' dislike of conflict and partisanship in politics.[16] And despite negative feelings about American institutions and politics on the part of some citizens and the violent rhetoric of a minority, the system is stable. Except for the Civil War, criticism and even anger have never boiled over to the point of mass violence directed toward political institutions or leaders.

Critical comments about government and political leaders sharply declined after 9/11, but the drop was short-lived. Though commentators on 9/11 and immediately afterward predicted that nothing would ever be the same, for most Americans life did return to normal quickly, and with it, the usual levels of skepticism toward government.

Agents of Political Socialization

Agents of political socialization—principally the family and schools—embrace the institutions and processes that are the foundations of American democracy, and thus help ensure that each new generation of Americans does too.

Family

Although research suggests that each of us may be born with a biological predilection toward certain traits that manifest themselves in political views (such as conservatism and degree of reaction to threats),[17] children's identification with a political party is strongly shaped by the family.[18]

The family influences opinions in several ways. Parents share their opinions directly with children, and children overhear parents' comments about the political parties and adopt them as their own. Seventy percent of high school seniors, for

American Diversity

Support for a Woman in the White House

Seventy-three percent of American voters believe a woman will become president of the United States within ten years, according to a mid-2011 poll. And 82 percent of likely voters reported that they were willing to vote for a woman president compared to 9 percent who were not. This support increased dramatically over forty years; in 1970, only slightly more than 60 percent said they would vote for a woman, and, forty years before that, less than 40 percent said they would.[1]

One way to understand people's reaction over time to voting for a woman for president is to compare their reactions to voting for people across a diverse set of categories. Figure 2 shows responses to this survey question: "If your party nominated a generally well-qualified person for president who happened to be (either Catholic, black, Jewish, female, Hispanic, Mormon, homosexual, atheist), would you vote for that person?"

[1] "73% Say Woman President Likely in Next 10 Years," *Rasmussen Reports*, June 27, 2011, http://www.rasmussenreports.com/public_content/politics/ general_politics/june_2011/73_say_woman_president_likely_in_next_10_years.

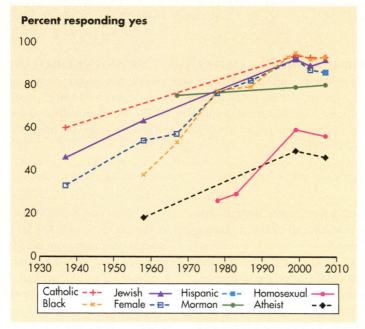

FIGURE 2: DIVERSITY AND PRESIDENTIAL CANDIDATES This Figure shows how people have felt over time about voting for candidates for the presidency who are more diverse than most of those who have held the office. Since 1930, people have become more tolerant, although by 2000, levels of tolerance eroded in all categories except for a Mormon candidate. Governor Mitt Romney's candidacy in 2012 tested that tolerance.

SOURCE: From the Blog of Dr. Philip Brighten Godfrey, Department of Computer Science, University of Illinois at Urbana-Champaign, August 6, 2010. Based on Gallup polls. http://youinfinitesnake.blogspot.com/2008/11/progress.html. Reproduced by permission. See also http://www .gallup.com/poll/3979/americans-today-much-more-accepting-woman-black-catholic.aspx; http://www.gallup.com/poll/26611/some-americans -reluctant-vote-mormon-72 yearold-presidential-candidates.aspx#1

example, were able to correctly identify their political party, but no more than 36 percent could identify their parents' opinion on other issues.[19] Parents may include children in their political activities, such as by taking them when they vote or to hear a candidate speak. Children also transfer feelings toward parents to political objects. When children harbor negative feelings about their parents, they are more likely to be negative toward the president.[20]

The family also shapes the personality of the child. A child who is encouraged to speak up at home is likely to do so in public. Children also inherit their social and economic position from their parents, which influences not only how they view themselves but also how they view the world and how the world views them. For example, a child from a wealthy family begins with advantages and opportunities unshared by a child from a working-class or poor family.

However, even where parental influence is strong, it is not immutable. As young adults leave their parents' circle, agreement declines between their opinions and party allegiances and those of their parents. New influences and experiences come into play.[21] Even among younger children, wider influences matter. Parents do not usually have exclusive control during a child's preschool years, and the number of households with two employed parents or with a single employed parent means that other caretakers and schools play a meaningful role in children's lives. Nevertheless, influence on children regarding political opinions and behaviors is about the same whether one is raised in a two-parent or a single-parent family.[22]

School

A child of our acquaintance who came to the United States at the age of five could not speak English and did not know the name of his new country. After a few months of kindergarten, he knew that George Washington and Abraham Lincoln were good presidents, he was able to recount stories of the Pilgrims, he could draw the flag, and he felt strongly that the United States was the best country in the world. This example illustrates the importance of the school in political socialization and how values and symbols of government are explicitly taught in American schools, as they are in schools in every nation.[23]

Although we do not understand exactly which aspects of formal schooling influence political opinions, education and years of formal schooling make a difference via the skills and experiences they provide. People who have more education tend to be more interested in and knowledgeable about politics.[24] They are also more likely to participate in politics and to be politically tolerant.[25] Yet education does not always prepare citizens for how democracy works in practice, to recognize that disagreement is fundamental to democratic processes, or to build positive feelings toward these processes.

How do the schools influence the political opinions of children? To begin with, schools promote patriotic rituals. Classrooms often begin each day with the Pledge of Allegiance, and schools include patriotic songs and programs in regular activities. In the lower grades, children celebrate national holidays such as Presidents' Day and Martin Luther King's birthday and learn the history and symbols associated with them. In the upper grades, mock elections, conventions, and student government introduce students to the operation of government. School clubs operate with democratic procedures and reinforce the concepts of voting and majority rule. Illinois let the state's elementary school children vote to select the official state animal, fish, and tree, conveying the message that voting is the way issues are decided.

Textbooks also often foster commitment to stability by positively depicting government and the status quo. Those used in elementary grades emphasize compliance with authority and the need to be a "good" citizen. Even textbooks

This boy, at a white supremacist rally, likely was socialized in these views by his parents.

© Robin Nelson//Black Star

in secondary school present idealized versions of governmental processes and overemphasize the ease with which citizens can hold public officials accountable and shape public policy. At the same time, textbooks often fail to stress the importance of fully participating in politics and tolerating the views of others. Nor do many help students understand that conflicts and differences of opinion are inevitable in a large and diverse society and that because the role of politics is to address and resolve these disagreements, compromises and partial solutions are often necessary.

The number of civics courses taken in high school improves students' knowledge of government and politics and fosters the beliefs that government pays attention to people and that elections are important for holding government responsible. Courses during the senior year are particularly important. Because seniors are ready to make the transition to adulthood, government and politics may be more meaningful to them than during their early years.[26]

Reading habits and language skills are also important to democratic citizenship. Compared to those who do not spend time reading, those who do read are more likely to reflect attributes of democratic citizenship—including knowledge of public affairs, interest in politics, and tolerance.[27] Proficiency with language is important, too, as language is the mechanism for communicating and assessing information and evaluating new ideas and arguments.[28] Teachers as role models also contribute to proficiency in significant ways. Perceptions that school administrators and teachers are fair are linked with expressions of trust toward other people.[29]

Thinking about Democracy

Thomas Jefferson wrote: "What signify a few lives lost in a century or two? The tree of liberty must from time to time be refreshed with the blood of patriots and tyrants. It is its natural manure." Is this view more or less supportive of democracy than the alternative of socializing each generation to the existing political authority and routine ways of political participation?

In sum, the major impact of schooling from kindergarten through high school tends to be that it fosters "good" citizens—those who accept political authority and the institutions of our government and who focus their political activities on routine political tasks such as voting in elections. In this way, education contributes to political stability and serves government and the status quo.

Schools may not be as effective, however, at fostering widespread political participation and commitment to a full range of democratic values. Nor do they do a good job of providing students with the skills to critically assess the social, political, and economic structures or policy approaches that are at the root of the nation's problems or strategies for dealing with injustice and effecting political change.[30] If the picture of politics portrayed by socialization in schools is idealized, perhaps it is not surprising that many adults are shocked by the rough and tumble of politics and the sharp disagreements of Americans about the nature of government.

The college experience often broadens students' perspectives and leads to greater understanding of the world around them. They often become more open and tolerant, less rigid and bound by tradition. The latest report of an ongoing survey of college freshman across the nation indicates that students have become more liberal on a range of social issues in the last few years. Seventy-one percent of respondents indicated support for same-sex marriage, which is 6 percent higher than the 2009 figure. Additionally, 61 percent said that abortion should be legal (compared to 58 percent in 2009); and 43 percent indicated that undocumented immigrants should be denied access to education (compared to 47 percent in 2009).[31]

Some commentators argue that college professors indoctrinate students. It is true that college and university faculty have predominantly liberal orientations. One study reports that, from 1996 to 2008, 43 percent of professors identified themselves as liberal and 9 percent identified as conservative. (Liberalism and conservatism are discussed on pages 89–93.)[32] People who are most attracted to the profession tend to be liberal.

But does this mean that college faculty are brainwashing their students? A 2006 study found that 48 percent of those between the ages of eighteen and twenty-five identified with the Democratic Party; 35 percent were Republican, the lowest number since 1987. Fifty-eight percent of those under twenty-six voted Democratic in the 2006 midterm elections. However, in the early 1990s, when college faculty were just as liberal, Republican identification in this age group was 55 percent.[33] Party preferences of students fluctuate in line with those of the public, not their professors.

Other evidence also suggests it is unlikely that professors indoctrinate their students. For example, while faculty strongly opposed air strikes in Afghanistan following 9/11, 79 percent of college students supported the war.[34] In sum, although there is no doubt that college faculty have more liberal political orientations than the general public, it is doubtful that students adopt faculty views wholesale. Moreover, college provides students with the self-confidence and independence that presumably equip them to think for themselves.[35] And, as discussed earlier, faculty members are only one of multiple competing influences on political socialization.

Peers

In many instances, peers reinforce the opinions of the family or school. When there is a conflict between peer and parental socialization, peers sometimes win, but only on issues of special relevance to youth. Peers have the most influence when the peer group is attractive to individuals and when individuals spend time with the group. With growing numbers of single-parent families and employed parents, parental influence may be diminishing while the influence of friends and associates may be growing.

Mass Media

The primary effect of the media on children is to increase their information about politics. The primary effect on adults is to influence what they think about—that is, the issues, events, and personalities they pay attention to.[36] The media also influence opinions about issues and individuals. Research shows that changes in public opinion tend to follow sentiments expressed by television news commentators.[37] The impact of the media is explored in more detail in Chapter 5.

Adult Socialization

Not all political socialization occurs in the pre-adult years. Opinions develop and change throughout life as one experiences new and different things. Marriage, divorce, having children, unemployment, a new job, or a move to a new location can all affect political opinions.[38]

Economic, political, and social events also have the potential to change the way Americans think about politics. Many hard hit by the Great Depression were drawn to politics to seek help. For this reason, most of those voting for the first time in 1932 cast their ballots for FDR and the Democrats

Table 1	Views on Social Issues by Generation*			
	Total	**18–30 Years Old**	**66+ Years Old**	**Difference: Youngest/Oldest**
Favor allowing gays and lesbians to marry legally	46	59	33	+26
Favor legalizing marijuana	45	55	31	+24
What is more important?*				
Protecting gun rights	47	43	49	–6
Controlling gun ownership	49	55	44	+11
U.S. will succeed in achieving its goals in Afghanistan	58	72	43	+29

*"Don't knows" are excluded.

SOURCE: Data from Andrew Kohut, Paul Taylor, Scott Keeter, Carroll Doherty, Michael Dimock, and Kim Parker, *The Generation Gap and the 2012 Election*, Pew Research Center, 2011, http://www.people-press.org/2011/11/03/the-generation-gap-and-the-2012-election-3/ (accessed February 23, 2012).

and continued to vote Democratic throughout their lives. During the Vietnam War, many college students went to the streets in protest, whereas others moved to Canada to avoid the draft. In contrast, the terrorist attacks on the Pentagon and the World Trade Center pushed the public closer to government, although the impact soon dissipated.[39] The ongoing war in Afghanistan, the recently concluded nine-year war in Iraq, and the 2007–2009 recession and its aftermath continue to result in widespread economic dislocation and may shape young Americans in a more lasting way. Elections in 2006, 2008, and 2010 indicated a rise in Democratic Party voting in this age group. (See Table 1.)

Impact of Political Socialization

Each new generation of Americans is socialized to a large extent by the one preceding it, and so in many ways each new generation will look and act much like its predecessor. In this sense, political socialization represents a stabilizing and conserving influence. Typically, it leads to support for and compliance with government and the social order. Although many disagree with particular government policies, few question the basic structure of government.

MEASURING PUBLIC OPINION

Pollsters measure public opinion by asking people to answer questions in surveys or polls. Of course, other techniques are also used to measure opinion, and before scientific polls these techniques were all that were available. Elected officials consider the opinions of people who contact them; journalists gauge public opinion by talking selectively to individuals; and letters are sent to newspaper editors and printed as newspaper and newsmagazine editorials. Blogs, as well as Twitter and Facebook polls, are also indicators of public opinion. Protests and demonstrations reflect public opinion. All of these techniques provide an incomplete picture, however. Those with extreme or deeply held opinions[40] are more likely to engage in these kinds of political actions and may not represent the wider public. The Tea Party movement and Occupy Wall Street protests are illustrations of groups with deeply held, intense opinion about political issues and policy choices that may or may not affect opinions of the broader public.

Well-conducted, scientific polls are the best measure of public opinion, but they are not perfect. Conducting a poll runs the risk of creating public sentiment rather than allowing public opinion to reveal itself. Rather than focus on what the public is concerned about, polls concentrate on what pollsters and their sponsors find most interesting. For this reason, many issues of public importance may never become the subjects of a poll. In spite of this and other problems, polling remains the only accurate way to assess what the nation as a whole thinks about specific political issues and public officials.

Early Polling Efforts

The first attempts to measure popular sentiments on a large scale were **straw polls** (or unscientific polls) developed by newspapers in the nineteenth century.[11] In 1824, the *Harrisburg Pennsylvanian* sent reporters to check on support for the four presidential contenders that year. The paper reported that Andrew Jackson was the popular choice over John Quincy Adams, Henry Clay, and William H. Crawford. Jackson did indeed receive the most popular votes, but John Quincy Adams was elected president after the contest was decided by the House of Representatives. Toward the end of the nineteenth century, the *New York Herald* tried to forecast election outcomes in local, state, and national races. During presidential election years, the paper collected estimates from reporters and political leaders across the country and predicted the Electoral College vote by state.

Straw polls are still employed today. Media outlets of all kinds ask adults about their voting preferences, and major events often trigger media polls. After each presidential debate, national media invite people to cast votes on who won. Straw polls are unscientific because there is no way to ensure that the individuals giving opinions are representative of the larger population. If these polls are unrepresentative, they are unlikely to reflect public opinion accurately.

The famed *Literary Digest* poll is a good example of an unrepresentative poll. The former magazine conducted polls of presidential preferences between 1916 and 1936. As many as 18 million ballots were mailed out to persons drawn from telephone directories and automobile registration lists. Although the *Literary Digest* correctly predicted the winners in 1924, 1928, and 1932, in 1936 its luck ran out: the magazine predicted that Republican Alfred Landon would win, but instead Democrat Franklin D. Roosevelt won by a landslide. This erroneous prediction ended the magazine's polling, and in 1938 the publication went out of business altogether.

Why did the *Literary Digest* miss in 1936? The sample was biased. Working-class and poor people, who were those most likely to vote for Roosevelt, did not own telephones and automobiles in the depths of the Great Depression.[42] Since the sample was drawn from telephone directories and auto registration lists, Roosevelt voters were significantly underrepresented. Today we know that unrepresentative samples lead to erroneous conclusions, but in spite of that knowledge, data from such samples are often accorded equal legitimacy by some media as representative samples. For example, one study reported a very high rate of drinking and unprotected sex engaged in by college women on spring break. Although the report claimed the data were from a random sample, it included only women who volunteered to answer questions.

Moreover, 25 percent of the group never took a spring break trip.[43] Such a "sample" is unrepresentative of college women in the United States.

Emergence of Scientific Polling

Scientific polling began after World War I, inspired by the then new field of marketing research. After the war, demand for consumer goods rose, and American businesses, no longer engaged in the production of war materials, turned to satisfying consumer demand. Businesses used marketing research to identify what consumers wanted and how products should be packaged to attract buyers. The American Tobacco Company, for example, changed from a green to a white package during World War II because it found that a white package was likely to attract women smokers.[44]

Applying mathematical principles of probability to business processes was also important to the development of scientific polling. To determine the frequency of defects in manufactured products, inspectors made estimates on the basis of a few randomly selected items, called a **sample**. It was a simple matter to extend the practice to individuals and draw conclusions regarding a large population based on findings from a smaller, randomly selected sample.

In the early 1930s, George Gallup and several others, using probability-based sampling techniques, began polling opinions on a wide scale. In 1936, Gallup predicted that the *Literary Digest* would be wrong and that Roosevelt would be reelected. Gallup's accurate prediction of the outcome lent credibility to probability-based polls, and in time, Gallup polls became a feature of American politics and probability-based polls the standard for tracking public opinion.

Consequently, government leaders increasingly came to rely on polling and, in 1940, Roosevelt became the first president to use polls on a regular basis, employing a social scientist to measure trends in public opinion about the war in Europe.

Use of Polls

Many major American universities have units that perform survey research, and there are hundreds of commercial marketing research firms, private pollsters, and media polls. For politicians, polls have almost become what the Oracle of Delphi was to the ancient Greeks and Merlin was to King Arthur—a source of divine wisdom. In the 2006 midterm elections and the 2008 presidential elections, polls indicating the intense unpopularity of the Iraq War led the Democrats to promise to end the war in a speedy fashion. In both years, the Democrats' attention to that issue, among others, resonated with voters. They took back control of the House and Senate in 2006 and captured both the executive branch and both houses of Congress in 2008. However, the worsening economic situation between 2008 and 2010 and the Republican charge that it was due to Barack Obama's policy choices led the Republicans to win back the House of Representatives and shatter the sixty-seat supermajority in the Senate in 2010.

President Harry Truman exults in incorrect headlines, based on faulty polls and early returns, the morning after he won reelection.

Polls indicated that citizens blamed the president for concentrating too much on issues other than the economy.

At the time of the 2012 presidential election, although more than 70 percent of voters felt that the economy was poor or not very good, voters tended to blame George W. Bush for the result more than Barack Obama. This is a good illustration of the difference between public opinion and the electoral results of midterm and presidential election cycles.

Use by Politicians

Beginning in the 1960s, presidents have regularly used polls to assess the public's thinking on issues.[45] President Clinton took their use to a new high. He spent more on polling than all previous administrations combined and tested every significant policy idea and the language with which to promote it.[46] Weekly polls shaped his centrist message, leading to his reelection in 1996. He embraced welfare reform, a Republican idea opposed by Democrats in Congress and liberals in his administration, in large part because it was popular.[47] A White House poll in 1997 suggested that Americans preferred using the budget surplus to bolster Social Security rather than administer a Republican-preferred tax cut. In his State of the Union address, therefore, Clinton called on Congress to "save Social Security first." Clinton even used polls to select a vacation spot.[48] Rather than vacation on Martha's Vineyard and play golf, Clinton went hiking in the Rockies because he was told by a consultant that golf was a Republican sport and that the voters he needed to win were campers.

President George W. Bush expressed disdain for the polling done by the Clinton White House. Yet, his administration also made extensive use of polls, but in a different way.[49] Along with its polling, the Bush administration mastered the use of **crafted talk**, which enabled him to cater to the views of the conservative Republican base—while appearing to remain in the middle.[50] Thus, whereas Clinton relied on polls to identify policies with broad public support, Bush relied on them to package policies favored by his conservative base.[51] For example, Bush proposed partial privatization of Social Security. But his pollsters learned that the word *privatization* scared the public by implying that the government would no longer guarantee a lifetime income, as Social Security does. Instead, the president opted to use such terms as *retirement security, personal accounts, choice,* and *opportunity* without changing the substance of his proposal.

President Bush also proposed the elimination of the inheritance tax, which is triggered when wealthy people die and leave their estates to their heirs. Traditionally this tax was called the "estate tax" because it was imposed on people with large estates. But the president and congressional Republicans renamed it the "death tax" to convey the notion that it was imposed on people when they die—that is, on everyone. In fact, it was imposed on only the wealthiest 1 to 2 percent of the population. Yet the phrase *death tax* was a rhetorical success, persuading a majority of middle-class Americans to favor its elimination even though it would never affect them.

Similarly, President Barack Obama has relied on polls and focus group responses to the 2009 stimulus plan to make

his case to Congress and the American people. His staff encouraged legislators to avoid use of the word *recession* and substitute the word *recovery*. *Investment* was used to replace *infrastructure*. During debates about legislation aimed to ameliorate global warming, polling and focus group results convinced the Obama administration to drop phrases like *cap and trade* and substitute phrases like *market-based proposals* and *clean energy jobs*.

Thinking about Democracy

What are the implications for democracy if politicians rely heavily on public opinion to govern the nation?

Misuse of Polls

Sometimes polls are used as a way to manipulate public opinion. These so-called push polls are an egregious example of the misuse of polling. Suppose a pollster for Jones asks whether the person called supports Jane Jones or Mary Smith or is undecided in an upcoming election. If the answer is Smith or undecided, the voter is asked a hypothetical question that leaves a negative impression. "If you were told that Smith mistreats her staff and fudges on her expense reports, would it make a difference to your vote?" The voter is then asked her preference again. The goal is to see whether certain information or disinformation can "push" voters away from a candidate and toward the candidate favored by those doing the poll.[52]

Learning the weaknesses of the opposition has always been a part of politics, but push polls seek to manipulate opinion often by distorting facts, including candidates' records. Before the 2010 Republican caucus in Utah, a push poll by an independent group that supported Republican Mike Lee against incumbent U.S. Senator Bob Bennett aimed to paint Senator Bennett as too liberal on health care and abortion. An automatic call started by asking if the respondent supported or opposed "Obamacare." Then, respondents were asked if they would be more likely to support Lee if they knew that Lee was more strongly opposed to health care reform than Bennett (not mentioning that Bennett voted against health care reform). Next, respondents were asked their position on federal funding for abortions. They were then erroneously told that a health care bill introduced by Bennett would provide such funding, an action opposed by Lee. (Lee won the Republican nomination over Bennett and, eventually, the Senate seat.)

A related tactic, **phony polls**, pump thousands of calls into a district or state under the guise of conducting a poll but with the intent of spreading false information about a candidate. In the 2000 South Carolina primary, Sen. John McCain (R-Ariz.) accused the George W. Bush campaign of spreading false information in the guise of a poll when both were seeking the Republican presidential nomination. Rumors were spread that McCain had become mentally unstable as a result of his imprisonment by the North Vietnamese in the Vietnam

War and had fathered an illegitimate black child (in fact, he and his wife had adopted a Bangladeshi child). This phony poll halted McCain's momentum, which had been surging until this primary. Both push polls and phony polls are violations of polling ethics and corruptions of the political process.

Many private pollsters work for one party or candidate. Although they undoubtedly wish to collect accurate data for their clients, their goal is to present their clients in the most favorable light.[53] They may sometimes manipulate the wording of questions to benefit clients. The results, when publicized, give the impression that the public thinks something that, in fact, it does not.

BEHIND THE SCENES

The Politics of Labels: Public Opinion on Abortion

Policies toward abortion and contraception have been contentious for decades. States and the federal government enacted more than 135 abortion provisions in 2011, most of which restricted access. This was a large increase from previous years, and no slowdown has been seen in 2012.[1]

Though the media portray the abortion debate as between those who are "pro-choice" and those who are "pro-life," in fact, those who are completely pro-choice in every circumstance (around 25 percent) and those who are completely pro-life in every circumstance (about 20 percent) are a minority. Most people are in the middle, supporting abortion under some circumstances but not under others. Even the labels people choose for themselves do not seem to capture the nuances of their views. Polling data show that 50 percent of the population believes abortion should be legal in at least certain circumstances, a higher proportion than the 45 percent who label themselves pro-life. And although more than two-thirds of Republicans identify as pro-life, 50 percent believe that abortion should be legal in some circumstances. Finally, 31 percent of those eighteen to thirty-four years of age support abortion in any circumstances, more than any other age group.[2]

Like other social issues discussed in this chapter, increased support among the youngest voters will affect future trends.

[1] Guttmacher Institute, "Laws Affecting Reproductive Health and Rights: 2011 State Policy Review," http://www.guttmacher.org/statecenter/updates/2011/statetrends42011.html (accessed January 17, 2012).

[2] Data from Lydia Saad, "Americans Still Split along 'Pro-Choice,' 'Pro-Life' Lines," May 23, 2011, http://www.gallup.com/poll/147734/americans-split-along-pro-choice-pro-life-lines.aspx (accessed January 17, 2012).

Use by Media

Along with polling by candidates, polls by news organizations have also increased. **Tracking polls**, in which a small number of people are polled on successive evenings throughout a campaign to assess changes in levels of voter support, began in 1988 and exploded thereafter. Many news outlets feature daily tracking polls that monitor movement of candidates in presidential campaigns.[54] This "horse race" element makes a good story and attracts viewers. Polling on the horse race and related coverage during presidential campaigns have started earlier and earlier. They now start before the primaries and caucuses and are regular features during them.

The ease of conducting polls explains part of the reason for their increasing use. Pollsters can conduct a poll at a moment's notice and have results within hours. The polls are often not very scientific and the questions aren't always asked in a professional way. When people have thought carefully about their views on a clearly defined issue, such as how they will vote in an election taking place in a few days, a well-designed poll can provide an accurate picture of the public's views. However, polls taken well in advance of an election among candidates who are not well known cannot predict the winner because voters do not know the candidates and have not made up their minds. In the 2012 Republican primaries, the races were volatile and many voters did not make up their minds until the day before the election. Thus early polls tend to measure candidate name recognition rather than specific opinions about the candidates.

Even when issues are well defined and opinions are fairly stable, it is increasingly difficult to obtain samples that provide representative pictures of public opinion. Many people refuse to be interviewed,[55] either because they don't want to be bothered or because they fear they'll be asked to buy something or contribute money to a cause. Response rates for telephone surveys have also decreased because of extensive cell phone use and call-screening technologies that allow potential respondents to avoid calls altogether.[56] In fact, an analysis of the 2008 and 2010 elections shows that support for Republican candidates was higher in pre-election poll samples based on data from landline calls than in samples that combine landline and cell phone interviews. Polling young people, who tend to have cell phones and not landlines, is especially challenging, but pollsters increase the number of contacts they make to ensure they have representative samples of the eighteen- to twenty-nine-year-old demographic.[57]

An increasing number of people refuse to answer questions or simply can't be reached. As the proportion of these nonrespondents grows, pollsters are concerned that those who do respond are unrepresentative of the population as a whole.[58] However, currently, those who participate in national polls differ little from those who do not, at least on issues that matter to pollsters.[59]

Other problems make it difficult for pollsters to get accurate readings of public opinion. For example, there is the tendency of some respondents to express an opinion when they don't have one. No one wants to appear uninformed. The problem is getting worse as pollsters probe topics on which the public has no opinion and on which there is little reason to believe it should. For example, pollsters asked citizens whether the U.S. military had enough troops on the ground in Iraq to win the war. Without expert knowledge of military strategy, the general public cannot be expected to provide sensible and useful answers.

Polls taken a few days before an election asking about vote choice, on the other hand, tend to be quite accurate. In 2004, despite the closeness of the election, the average of fourteen major newspaper and network commercial polls had Democrat John Kerry at 47.4 percent and incumbent President Bush at 48.9 percent. The true vote was 48 percent to 51 percent.[60] Similarly, the polls from the 2008 presidential election between John McCain and Barack Obama had high levels of accuracy. According to one study, eight of seventeen national polls predicted the final margin of victory within one percentage point, and most of the others came within three points. Pre-election polls were also highly accurate in predicting the state-by-state vote.[61][62]

Even good polling runs into other kinds of problems, though. In the 1980s, some white voters were reluctant to indicate that they intended to vote against a black candidate and falsely reported their intention. The Obama election has led analysts to conclude that this racial phenomenon of falsely reporting support for a black candidate is no longer a factor. In the 2008 primaries Obama's vote totals were close, sometimes larger and sometimes smaller, than the last pre-election polls. This does not mean that no voters were prejudiced, only that voters who were prejudiced did not try to disguise it by saying they would vote for Obama when they were not intending to.[63]

Election-day **exit polls** are ubiquitous and controversial features of media coverage. The networks identify key precincts around the nation, precincts that are reflective of certain types of voters. Then on election day, as voters leave these precincts, pollsters ask them how they voted. Their responses, coupled with early returns and an analysis of how these precincts voted in past elections, are used to project the winner in the current election. When enough precincts in a state have been analyzed, the networks "call" the state for the winner. Since the 1960s, cable and network television outlets have used exit polls to project the winners before all of the votes have been counted. Usually the exit polls have been accurate, but not always. At 7:50 p.m. on election night in 2000, the networks declared Democratic Al Gore the winner over Republican George W. Bush in Florida. Because the election was very close and Florida had many electoral votes, whoever won this state probably would win the election. About 9:30 p.m., the polling service that conducted the exit polls notified the networks to pull back. Florida was "too close to call." At 2:15 a.m. the next morning, the networks declared George W. Bush the winner in Florida, and thus the next president of the United States. But as more ballots were counted, Bush's lead in Florida eroded. About 3:30 a.m., the networks again pulled back. Florida again was "too close to call." Despite Dan Rather's assertion that if CBS called a state, "you can put it in the bank," the networks botched their calls twice in one night.

What happened? The election in Florida was extremely close and the polling sample was too small to reveal the winner in such a close election. (The networks, which had been bought by corporations such as General Electric, slashed costs so much that the polling service couldn't sample enough precincts.[64]) Those polled were not representative of those who voted.

The wrong calls were not merely an embarrassment to the networks. Because the networks initially called Florida for Gore ten minutes before polling places in the state's western panhandle closed, it is possible that some Republicans on their way to vote might have turned around and gone home. Because the networks later called Florida for Bush, it is likely that many people around the country considered Bush the legitimate winner. Once the election was over and the two sides struggled to make their case regarding who had been elected, the fact that the networks declared Bush the winner made it appear that Gore was trying to take the presidency away from him.

Even accurate and reliable polls can affect politics in a negative way. Poor standing in the polls may discourage otherwise viable candidates from entering a race. In 2000, several potential Republican candidates passed up the presidential race when early polls suggested that George W. Bush was the odds-on favorite to win the Republican nomination. Additionally, polls can have a negative effect on political campaigns. Prior to polling, the purpose of campaigns was to reveal candidates' views on the issues and their solutions to the pressing problems of the day. Instead, polls find out what the voters want, and often candidates adopt positions and develop images to suit the voters. They consider following voters safer than trying to educate the public about complex problems or new solutions. Former senator Daniel Patrick Moynihan (D-N.Y.) decried politicians' addiction to poll results: "We've lost our sense of ideas that we stand by, principles that are important to us."[65]

Poll results also influence fundraising, and without money, a candidate cannot mount an effective campaign. Donors, especially large ones, give money to candidates who have a good chance to win. Candidates and would-be candidates with low poll numbers find it hard to raise the money that could give them visibility and raise their standing in the polls. This was evident in the 2012 Republican primaries and caucuses in the nomination for the presidency. Early in the process, former governor of Minnesota Tim Pawlenty (referred to by the mononym T-Paw) was heavily promoted as a true conservative with effective governing experience who could successfully challenge incumbent president Barack Obama. He received a lot of media attention, but early low polling numbers and a poor showing in the Iowa straw poll made fundraising difficult. He dropped out before the first set of caucuses in Iowa.

In spite of problems and abuses, polls still provide a valuable service to the nation by helping candidates and officeholders understand what citizens think about issues and how important particular issues are to them. If direct democracy, like the New England town meeting, is the ideal, the use of public opinion polls is about as close as the modern state is likely to get. For example, in 2011, for the first time, a majority of Americans (53 percent) indicated support for gay marriage. Prior to that time, significant majorities of Americans believed that lesbians and gays should be permitted to serve openly in the military (as high as 75 percent by 2010). This support helped Barack Obama end the "Don't Ask, Don't Tell" policy in the U.S. military. Polls also help interpret the meaning of elections. When voters cast their ballots for one candidate over another, all anyone knows for sure is that a majority preferred one candidate. Polls can help reveal what elections mean in terms of policy preferences and thus help make the government more responsive to voters. For example, in the 2010 midterm elections, the Republican Party regained control of the House of Representatives and gained Senate seats. But, contrary to what GOP strategists claimed, polls revealed that the election was not a mandate for the GOP. Rather, it was a rejection by the electorate of Democratic policies and priorities. Many Americans believed that, in their attempts to reform health insurance, the Democrats were paying insufficient attention to the economic situation, especially the high unemployment rate.

KNOWLEDGE AND INFORMATION

Asking citizens their opinions on matters of public policy, candidates for public office, and the operation and institutions of government presumes they possess sufficient knowledge and information to form opinions and that expressions of opinion reflect real preferences. But many Americans lack knowledge regarding many issues and aspects of government.

Nearly one-third of Americans do not know the name of the vice president, a proportion that has held constant for the past twenty years.[66] Only one-fourth can name their two senators,[67] and, in 2011, a little more than one-third knew that the Republicans held a majority in the U.S. House of Representatives but not the Senate.[68] However, whereas in most years few people can name the Speaker of the House, almost half could recognize Nancy Pelosi (D-Calif.) when she was Speaker from 2007 to 2010, most likely because of her status as the first woman in that position.[69] In contrast, only 15 percent knew Pelosi's counterpart, Harry Reid (D-Nev.), Majority Leader in the Senate.[70] Generally speaking, more people can identify sports and entertainment personalities than major political figures.[71] Most of the public don't have a factual knowledge about policy either. Only a small percentage can identify a single piece of legislation passed by Congress.[72]

Misperception regarding government policies is widespread. Although polls show that Americans favor reducing the size of the federal government, most have no idea whether government is growing or shrinking.[73] Most Americans feel that the country spends too much on foreign aid, but one-half estimate foreign aid to be about fifteen times greater than it is. Asked what an appropriate spending level would be, the average answer is eight times more than the country spends.[74] In one poll, nearly half of the public had an opinion on a

nonexistent law, the "Public Affairs Act." Fearing to admit that they had never heard of it, people gave an opinion anyway.[75]

Although Americans respect the Constitution and see it as a blueprint for democracy, many do not know what it contains—and what it does not. One-third think it establishes English as the country's official language, and one-sixth think it establishes America as a Christian nation, neither of which is true. One-fourth can't name a single First Amendment right (freedom of religion, freedom of speech, freedom of the press, and freedom to assemble and petition government).[76] Though nearly 90 percent of Americans graduate from high school today and more than half go to college, knowledge about politics has not changed much since the 1940s, when only half of Americans graduated from high school and few went to college.[77]

During the race for the Republican presidential nominee in 2012, many voters were unaware of basic facts about candidates. Though most knew that Newt Gingrich had served as Speaker of the House of Representatives, only 44 percent of voters could identify Ron Paul as the candidate opposed to the U.S. military presence in Afghanistan, despite his success in the New Hampshire primary. Only about half could identify Massachusetts as the state where Mitt Romney had been governor. Tea Party identifiers, however, were able to answer the most items correctly, perhaps because followers of this new movement are heavily engaged in the 2012 election cycle.[78]

Despite this lack of basic knowledge, some argue that the general public knows what it needs to know to make sound political judgments.[79] Most citizens take an active interest in politics and pay attention when they have a personal stake. Eighty percent know that Congress has passed a law requiring employers to provide family leave following the birth of a child or in an emergency. When times are bad, voters tune in to government more. As more and more Americans grew concerned over the direction of the nation, turnout in the 2008 primaries and the general election soared, with many states setting new records and voters reporting greater interest in the campaign than before. In the 2012 election cycle, interest in the campaign is about on par with 2008. This is true for both Democrats and Republicans, even though only the Republican Party has a contested nominating season.

The general public may not know details of government, but most have strong opinions about whether things are going well or not.[80] At the same time, lack of knowledge is an impediment to holding government accountable and responsible to the people. Those who are less politically knowledgeable find it difficult to sort through the claims and counterclaims of politicians. Some support candidates and policies that work against some aspects of their self-interest. By their lack of information, citizens risk being manipulated.[81]

Politicians often contribute to citizen ignorance and misperception. They often avoid discussing issues, especially controversial ones, or worse, mislead by trumpeting suspect or false information. Even after no weapons of mass destruction were found in Iraq, the Bush administration was reluctant to say that they had been wrong to assert there were such weapons.[82] As health care reform became more and more controversial, President Barack Obama mentioned the signature achievement of his years in office less and less, and it got only a passing reference in the 2012 State of the Union address.

It is hard work to stay informed. It takes time and energy. With work and family, many Americans have little time for politics. But failure to stay informed means that politicians can often ignore what the public wants.

Thinking about Democracy

> Can a political system be a democracy when most citizens lack basic knowledge about what their government does?

IDEOLOGY

Americans hold opinions on many different issues. These opinions may be consistent with each other and reflect a broader framework or worldview, what scholars call an **ideology**, or they may be inconsistent and unrelated. One might, for example, express support for government assistance to farmers hit by hard times but oppose it for out-of-work factory workers whose jobs have been outsourced to foreign countries.

© LEE LORENZ/New Yorker Collection/www.cartoonbank.com

Most Americans lack an ideological worldview; that is, they do not have consistent and coherent sets of opinions on political issues. Nor are they consistent in evaluations of candidates for public office or political parties. Yet the major contemporary ideologies, liberalism and conservatism, are useful in thinking about public opinion and understanding the institutions of American politics and political and social conflicts in society. Liberalism is sometimes identified by the label *left* or *left wing* and conservatism by the label *right* or *right wing*. These terms date from the French National Assembly of the early nineteenth century, when liberal parties occupied the left side of the chamber and conservative parties occupied the right.

Modern **liberalism**, used in the American political context, embodies the worldview that government can be a positive and constructive force in society and can assist individuals, businesses, and communities with social and economic problems. Franklin Roosevelt and the Democrats' New Deal policies of the 1930s were enacted to relieve the economic hardships of the Great Depression and limit the harsh consequences of an unrestrained free-market economy. The 2010 health care reform law was enacted to broaden the population with access to medical care. Central to liberalism is the belief that government has a responsibility to make life better for citizens.

While liberalism endorses government action to bring about social equality and ease the hardships of economic distress, it opposes government intrusion into personal matters such as abortion and contraception, or **social issues**. Liberalism is also identified with opposition to government invasions of privacy, such as monitoring phone calls, reading material, and online activity.

Modern **conservatism** generally expresses the worldview that individuals and communities are better off without government assistance and that economic activity should be free from government interference. Conservative calls during the 2012 presidential election to cut government regulation of energy and environmental practices because they believe it will spur job growth are good examples of this perspective. Consistent with this view, conservatives believe that the apparatus and role of government are necessarily small, and where there is a need for government, it is best if it is at the state or local rather than the more distant federal level.

Although conservatives subscribe to the idea of an unfettered free-market economy, this principle has been abandoned in practice throughout the nation's history, as conservatives have promoted commercial and business interests and have favored certain groups, such as farmers, with large subsidies and other benefits. It has been observed that Americans are rhetorically conservative but "operationally" liberal. Americans talk about small government and low taxes, but they remain attached to the services that government provides, especially in economic downturns such as the recent recession.[83]

Both conservatism and liberalism have contradictions. For example, opposed to government interference in the economic domain, many conservatives endorse government intervention when it comes to sexual behavior and its consequences. Many favor severe restrictions on abortion, some favor limiting the availability of contraceptive devices, and most oppose giving lesbians and gays the right to marry or enter into civil unions. Most conservatives want to maintain a large military force, and some conservatives also favor government action in times of war to monitor personal phone calls, restrict political activity, and abolish some rights of defendants. The USA Patriot Act, first enacted under George W. Bush as a response to the 9/11 attacks, is a good example. The act expands the latitude of law enforcement in foreign and domestic intelligence gathering.

However, not all conservatives agree with these policies. Many traditional "small-government" conservatives oppose these invasions of privacy, whether political or sexual, and many oppose what they label big-government conservatism. Individuals who oppose government activity in most domains, including social and economic regulation, are called libertarians. However, the best-known self-described "libertarians," such as Rep. Ron Paul (R-Tex.), who was a candidate for the GOP nomination in the 2012 presidential election cycle, are more libertarian in economic policy than social policy. Paul advocated a reduced federal role in many areas, including lowering taxes and eliminating five cabinet-level departments: Commerce, Education, Energy, Interior, and Housing and Urban Development. He opposed the USA PATRIOT Act because he felt it infringed on the freedom of privacy of the American people. But he favored regulating abortion and other personal activity.

These broad descriptions capture the core ideas of liberalism and conservatism, but individual politicians and most Americans reflect them imperfectly. Though liberalism and conservatism are not political parties, the Democratic Party has a much higher proportion of liberals than does the Republican Party, and the reverse is true for conservatives. The parties, too, are inconsistent.

In reality, most Americans tend to be conservative on some matters and liberal on others. In 2012, 40 percent of Americans considered themselves to be conservative and 21 percent consider themselves to be liberal. Thirty-five percent identified themselves as **moderate**, or middle of the road, neither liberal nor conservative. Since 2010, the proportion of Americans who call themselves conservative has increased, the proportion of liberals has stayed about the same, and the proportion of moderates has declined.[84]

Because moderates are the swing group, not only in voting but also in building support for policies, public officials typically move to the middle or even incorporate ideas from those of different ideologies to garner majority support for their ideas. President George W. Bush, while governing mostly from the right, confounded some conservatives by proposing an expansion of the Medicare program to include a drug benefit for seniors, usually considered a liberal position. President Barack Obama angered some liberals by increasing troop levels in Afghanistan before winding down the war and also by failing to push legislation on climate change or immigration reform.

PUBLIC OPINION IN RED STATES AND BLUE STATES

Liberalism and conservatism also reflect geographical differences. Ideological divisions have strong historical roots stemming from differences between northerners and southerners going back to the time of America's founding. The Civil War (1861–1865) was a stark manifestation of these divisions. Even today, more conservative agrarians in the

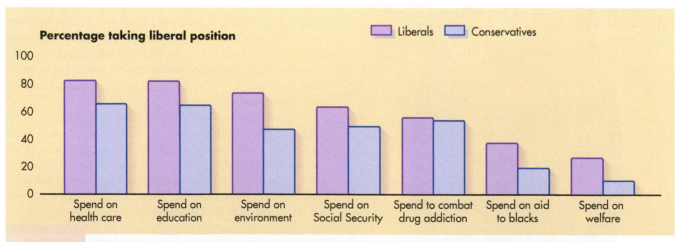

FIGURE 3: LIBERALS AND CONSERVATIVES DIFFER ON SPENDING FOR SAFETY NET AND ENVIRONMENTAL ISSUES The proportions are those who want to increase spending on each area.

SOURCE: General Social Survey, 2002 (Ns = 602 to 1301). Reprinted by permission of NORC, University of Chicago: http://www.norc.org/GSS/GSS +Resources.htm.

CourseReader ASSIGNMENT

Log in to www.cengagebrain.com and open CourseReader to access the full reading "'Haves' and 'Have-nots'" by Andrew Kohut.

The levels of attention that the American public paid to the Occupy Wall Street (OWS) movement may have risen because of the increased income inequality that has resulted from the recent recession and its aftermath. Economic data demonstrate that economic inequality has been rising since the 1970s. Over that time span, there has been a rise in income for the top 1 percent of earners, stagnation among the lowest income earners, and a small rise in growth among middle income earners. Citizens' views about the gap between rich and poor in the nation register this reality: two-thirds of the country believe that there are very strong or strong conflicts between the two groups. Additionally, fully 71 percent of eighteen- to thirty-four-year-olds, the age group associated most with the OWS movement, are more likely than older citizens to feel that strong conflicts are present between the poor and the rich.[1] Think about the movement and the income inequality that impels it as you answer the following questions.

1. Since economic inequality is long-standing, what factors have contributed to the rise of the OWS movement? What role did the Wall Street bailout (technically referred to as the Emergency Economic Stabilization Act of 2008) play in this protest?
2. A fall 2011 survey found that one-third of eighteen- to twenty-nine-year-olds were closely following the Occupy Wall Street movement and about one-fifth supported the movement. How do these figures contrast to the data earlier in the chapter that show high levels of youth support for a number of social issues such as same-sex marriage and abortion rights? Is support or opposition to issues different from support or opposition for direct political action? If so, how?
3. Is support or opposition to the Occupy Wall Street movement likely to affect attention to or participation in the 2012 presidential election cycle by eighteen- to twenty-nine-year-olds? How will youth participation in the 2012 election cycle compare to the relatively high rates of youth participation in the 2008 elections or their relatively low rates of participation in the 2010 midterm elections?

[1]Rich Morin, "Rising Share of Americans See Conflict between Rich and Poor," January 11, 2012, http://www.pewsocialtrends.org/2012/01/11/rising-share-of-americans-see-conflict-between-rich-and-poor/?src=prc-headline.

Midwest have often found themselves in alliance with southern agrarians against the more liberal urbanites in the East and West.

In the parlance of today's media, one conflict is referred to as the **red states** versus the **blue states** (an updated version of the conflict between the "gray" and "blue" in the Civil War). Others have labeled the divide the "retro" states versus the "metro" ones. The red and blue labels stem from the national maps employed by the media, which, on election night, depict states where majorities vote Republican in red and those that vote Democratic in blue. In the 2000 and 2004 elections, the blue states were in New England, the upper Midwest, and the West Coast, and the red ones were in the South, the Border and Plains states, and the Rocky Mountain West. The red states comprise most of the landmass of the United States but are more rural and sparsely populated than the blue states, which include many of the metropolitan centers. As Figures 4 and 5 illustrate, the pattern shifted a bit in 2008 when the Democrats won in more Mid-Atlantic states, some southern states, and more western states. Nevertheless, the basic divisions persist.

For journalists and pundits, red versus blue provides a story line that describes conservative red America as religious, moralistic, patriotic, white, masculine, and less educated, while liberal blue America is depicted as secular, relativistic, internationalist, multicultural, feminine, and college educated. The red state population is stereotyped as church-going and NASCAR watching, while supporting guns, the death penalty, and the Middle East wars. The blue population is stereotyped as supporters of abortion and the environment who read the *New York Times*.[85]

Naturally, many of these stereotypes are exaggerated. But there are real differences among people who live in red states and blue states. Religion is one difference. The red states encompass the **Bible belt**, a broad area of the country where most people identify with a religion and evangelical Protestants are common. This area comprises most of the South and parts of Kansas and Missouri. In contrast, the West Coast and parts of the Southwest are more secular. Forty-four percent of those living in red states identify themselves as born-again Christians; only 26 percent in blue states do. Many fewer people in the blue states identify with any

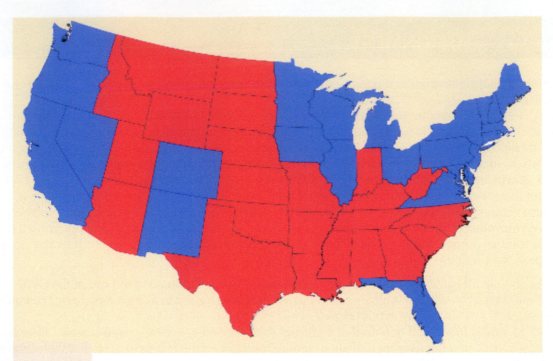

FIGURE 4: ELECTION RESULTS REFLECT GEOGRAPHIC PATTERN The states are colored red if a majority of voters cast their ballots for the Republican candidate, Mitt Romney, in 2012; or blue if a majority voted for the Democratic candidate, Barack Obama. The map, with its large swath of red states, makes it appear that Romney won, but the red states are, on average, less populous than the blue states, so they have fewer electoral votes.

SOURCE: http://www-personal.umich.edu/~mein/election/2008/.

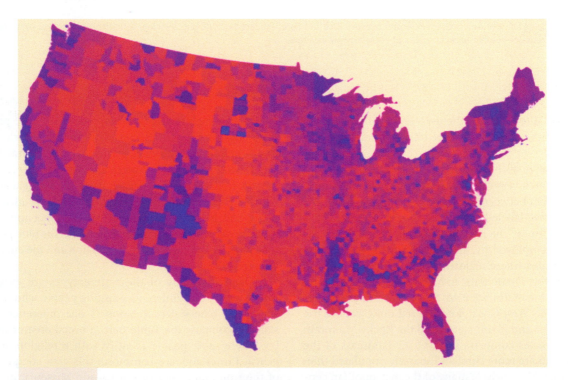

FIGURE 5: MOST STATES ARE PURPLE Despite all the talk about red states and blue states, most states are purple—a combination. This map shades each county according to the way its residents voted in the 2012 presidential election. If they voted heavily Republican, the county is brighter red; if they voted heavily Democratic, the county is deeper blue.

SOURCE: www.-personal.umich.edu/~mejn/election/2008/.

religion. These religious differences are politically significant, because in recent national elections, born-again Christians and regular church attendees have been more likely to vote Republican.

Other differences also reflect more conservative values in the red states. For example, in red states, women are less active in politics, are less likely to hold political office, have lower incomes, and are less likely to be managers and professionals than in the blue states. Red states impose more restrictions on abortion and incorporate more abstinence education in sex education classes (see Figure 6).

Red states are also generally more hostile to labor unions, so they have adopted laws that enable many companies to avoid unionizing their workforce. Wal-Mart, which began in Arkansas and then spread through the nation, strongly discourages its workers from forming or joining unions. In contrast, blue states are more hospitable to labor unions. However, showing that the differences are not always absolute, during the economic recession, Republican governors in "blue" Wisconsin sought to curtail benefits of those in public employee unions.[86]

Sometimes the characteristics of people in red state and blue states are counter to stereotypes of liberals and conservatives. For example, people in the more religious red states rather than the more secular blue states are more likely to divorce and have children out of wedlock, challenging stereotypes of the traditional family.[87] And people in the more conservative red states rather than the more liberal blue states are more likely to be assisted by government payments, such as welfare and Medicaid,[88] and are likely to receive more from the federal government than they send to it in taxes. People in the blue states pay more in federal taxes than their states receive. The explanation for all of these counter-intuitive patterns is that those in the red states tend to have lower incomes than those in blue states, thus contributing to fewer intact families and more government aid.[89]

The biggest differences between red and blue states are those among political activists, people who are the most involved and most interested in politics. Partisans in both parties are increasingly divided, and these divisions affect elections.[90][91] Most elected officials are nominated in primaries, in which only a minority of the most partisan party adherents vote. Thus, Republican candidates target their primary campaigns to conservatives in their party, whereas Democratic candidates target their campaigns to their liberal base. Getting moderate candidates in the general elections who might appeal to the majority of citizens is becoming rarer.

✪ Thinking about Democracy

What are the implications for democracy when citizens or elites are widely divided over the direction that public policy should take?

PUBLIC OPINION TOWARD RACE IN THE AGE OF OBAMA

Public opinion has influenced, as well as responded to, the progress of the struggle for racial equality. For example, polls extending as far back as the 1940s show white America increasingly opposed to segregation between African Americans and whites and to discrimination, at least in principle.[92] Whereas only one-third of whites accepted the idea of black and white children going to the same schools in 1942, in the 1980s more than 90 percent approved. Today nearly everyone approves. The percentage of people believing that whites have a right to keep African Americans out of their neighborhoods is half of what it was In 1963.[93] Thirty-eight percent of whites were against laws forbidding interracial marriage in 1963; 85 percent were opposed in 1996.[94]

Before Barack Obama became a candidate, most Americans said that they would vote for a black candidate

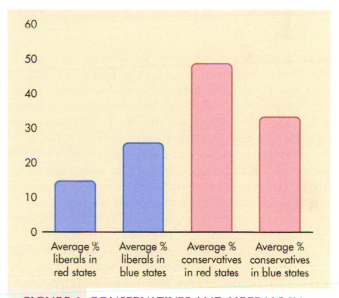

FIGURE 6: CONSERVATIVES AND LIBERALS IN TOP TEN RED AND BLUE STATES The first two bars of the chart show the proportions of liberals in the ten most conservative states and the ten most liberal states in the nation. Each conservative state is a red state and each liberal state is a blue state. The final two bars show the proportions of conservatives in the conservative red states and in the liberal blue states. Although each of the red states has much higher proportions of conservatives than liberals, even the blue states generally have more people who consider themselves ideologically conservative than those who consider themselves to be liberal, except in the most liberal U.S. state—Massachusetts. This comports with the trend among the general population of more conservative than liberal identifiers, as discussed in the "Ideology" section of the chapter.

SOURCE: Data from http://www.gallup.com/poll/125066/state-states.aspx.

© MATTHEW DIFFEE/New Yorker Collection/www.cartoonbank.com

for president. And in 2008, they did. Obama's election indicates that, indeed, many racial barriers have fallen. Still, we don't have a "post-racial nation," as some had hoped.

Public opinion can change because individuals change or because older individuals with one set of opinions are replaced by a new generation with a different set of opinions. Changes in whites' racial opinions through the 1960s occurred for both reasons. Older whites with more stereotyped views of blacks were replaced by a younger generation whose members were more tolerant. At the same time, the civil rights movement prompted many Americans to reconsider their views on race.

Since the 1970s, most changes have occurred because of the replacement of older, more prejudiced whites with younger, less prejudiced ones. More change is likely as today's teens age and replace older Americans. But the Obama election influenced changes in white attitudes in all age groups; older people still have more negative opinions toward African Americans than younger ones, but their positive change was greater during the election campaign than for any but the youngest voters.

In contemporary America, though white Americans accept integration, they have been much slower to accept government initiatives to achieve it. For example, racially segregated schools often are in poor central-city areas and offer inferior education, but busing to achieve racial balance in schools has never had much appeal for whites. Only about one-third support it.

There are at least three reasons why the numbers who believe government should act to help blacks are smaller than the numbers who support integration. First, some whites oppose government help for blacks because they are against government activity more generally. For them, government help violates their sense that individuals have a responsibility to provide for themselves.

A second reason is that, in some cases, unwillingness on the part of whites to endorse government initiatives to end segregation reflects racist sentiments.[95] Although only few white Americans believe that differences in jobs, housing, and income between whites and blacks are the result of biological differences,[96] a plurality assert the racist belief that the cause of these differences is lack of motivation and willpower on the part of blacks.[97]

A third reason for lack of support for government efforts to help blacks is that some do not see the need; they believe that African Americans are just as well off as whites. Anywhere from 40 to 60 percent of whites believe that the average African American is as well as or better off than the average white American in schooling, employment, income, and health care.[98] This is a direct contradiction to the reality that blacks lag behind whites on virtually every social and economic indicator, and the gap has gotten worse during the recent economic downturn. Those who don't see a discrepancy would hardly support efforts to alleviate a problem that in their minds does not exist.

Misperceptions such as these lead many whites to reject any government effort to equalize the social and economic standing of the races. Whites who more accurately recognize the plight of black Americans are more likely to accept the government's role in providing equal education for black and white children and ensuring that blacks are treated equally by courts and police.[99]

Blacks see things differently. A majority view themselves trailing whites in education, income, jobs, and health care, and of course this is the reality.[100] A majority of black men see the economic system stacked against them, but a significant proportion also believe that the problems facing black men result partly from what they have failed to do rather than what white people have done to blacks.[101] Like whites, African Americans have become somewhat less supportive of government initiatives to improve their lots. Support for actions by the federal government to ensure that blacks have fair treatment in jobs and government assistance in school integration has declined since the early 1960s.

The Obama election changed some attitudes of blacks on some measures. One year after the 2008 election, blacks perceived that the state of black America improved more than at any time in the past twenty-five years. Increasing percentages also said that life for blacks in the future will be better than it is now.[102] However, though 75 percent of blacks expected Obama's election to advance cross-racial ties, one year after inauguration, only 51 percent agreed that it had done so. And, two years later, although almost all blacks agreed that civil rights had improved during their lifetime, 60 percent believed that job discrimination persists. The same proportion believed that government should play a major role in improving the social and economic positions of blacks and other minorities. Only 20 percent of whites agreed. Finally, 55 percent of blacks say race relations will always be a problem.[103] Hence, the presidency of Barack Obama reflects how far we have come in race relations, but it also highlights that we still have much to accomplish.

SUMMARY

- Public opinion can be defined as the collection of individual opinions about issues, candidates, officeholders, and events of general interest. The direction of public opinion can be either positive or negative.

- People learn and develop opinions about government and politics through the process of political socialization. Individuals learn about politics by being exposed to new information supplied or filtered through parents, peers, schools, the media, political leaders, and communities. Each new generation of Americans is socialized to a large extent by the one preceding it, and so in many ways each new generation will look and act much like its predecessor. In this sense, political socialization represents a stabilizing and conserving influence. Typically, it leads to support for and compliance with government and the social order.

- Pollsters measure public opinion by asking people to answer questions in surveys or polls. Other techniques are also used to measure opinion. Elected officials consider the opinions of people who talk to them or contact them; journalists gauge public opinion by talking selectively to individuals; citizens contact newspaper editors; newspapers and newsmagazines publish editorials; and citizens blog as well as conduct Twitter and Facebook polls. Finally, protests and demonstrations reflect public opinion.

- The first attempts to measure popular sentiments on a large scale were straw polls developed by newspapers in the nineteenth century. Straw polls are unscientific because there is no way to ensure that the sample of individuals giving opinions is representative of the larger population. If these polls are unrepresentative, they are unlikely to reflect public opinion accurately.

  Scientific polling began after World War I. Applying mathematical principles of probability to business processes was also important to the development of scientific polling. These principles allow pollsters to draw conclusions regarding a large population based on findings from a smaller, randomly selected sample.

- Some members of the public are well informed on matters of public policy, political candidates, and the operation and institutions of government. Others are not. Yet, in interpreting public opinion, we assume that the public is well informed enough to answer knowledgeably.

- Americans hold opinions on many different issues. These opinions may be consistent with each other and reflect a broader framework or worldview, what scholars call an ideology, such as liberalism or conservatism, or they may be inconsistent and unrelated. Not all Americans hold an ideological worldview, however.

  Ideologically, liberalism and conservatism not only find expression in partisan differences but also reflect geographical differences. Voters in "blue" states typically vote for the Democratic candidates; voters in "red" states regularly vote for Republicans. Although appealing as a concept, in reality, this dichotomy stereotypes the differences and similarities across states, and most states are a mix of red and blue characteristics.

- Public opinion has influenced, as well as responded to, the progress of the struggle for racial equality. For example, the Obama election positively changed the attitudes of some whites toward blacks and the attitudes of some blacks about progress in racial equality. Even so, a majority of blacks still say race relations will always be a problem in the United States. Hence, the Obama presidency reflects both the promise of racial equality and the challenges of achieving it.

DISCUSSION QUESTIONS

1. Explain the nature of public opinion, especially with regard to the importance of intensity and stability in understanding its nature.

2. What are the primary agents of political socialization, and in what ways are they influential in people's lives? Can you point to an example in your own life of how one or more of these agents influenced you?

3. How is public opinion measured, and in what ways have scientific advances improved public opinion polling over time?

4. What are the ways in which politicians use polls, and how does this compare to media use of polls? Explain the differences among push polls, tracking polls, exit polls, and focus groups. For what purposes is each of these used?

5. What are the benefits and costs of polling in political life? Can you think of examples of a positive effect and a negative effect from a recent policy debate or an election?

6. To what degree do the concepts of liberalism and conservatism overlap with party affiliation?

7. Is the red state/blue state concept legitimate, and if so, to what extent? What are the major markers of each? How would you categorize your own state?

8. To what extent is the general public informed about political issues and candidates? How does that affect participation? Should it affect participation?

9. To what degree does youth public opinion differ from other age groups in terms of issues or support for candidates? Do your own views fit with these patterns or depart from them?

5 News Media

Senator Patty Murray (D-Wash.) is surrounded by reporters.

Roll Call/Getty Images

LEARNING OBJECTIVES

1. Understand how the media provide a check and balance in our political system.
2. Identify developments in recent decades that have shaken the foundations of traditional journalism.
3. Contrast broadcasting and narrowcasting, and identify reasons why the latter is becoming more prevalent.
4. Recognize the trend toward concentration of the media among chains and conglomerates.
5. Recognize the trend toward fragmentation of the media. Identify the range of media today that offer political news and commentary.

6. Understand the consequences of the trend toward fragmentation of the media.
7. Understand how the 24-hour news cycle affects the relationship between the media and politicians.
8. Compare the symbiotic relationship between the media and politicians with the adversarial relationship between them.
9. Describe the nature of political bias in news coverage by the mainstream media.
10. Distinguish commercial bias from political bias in news coverage.

TALKING POINTS

J. Peter Freire, a young editor of *American Spectator*, a conservative magazine, had given an embarrassing interview on Fox News. Baited by the interviewer, he had called for a boycott of the *New York Times*. So he decided to attend "Pundit School"— actually, the Leadership Institute, a conservative organization that trains hundreds of would-be television pundits each year.[1]

At the school, Freire learned what color suit coat looks best on TV (charcoal), and he learned to use slogans and short phrases (such as "flip-flop"). He learned how to get his message across regardless of what he was asked (by interrupting and saying, "I think the real issue is..."). He gave a practice interview in a mock studio, with coaches critiquing his performance (look down occasionally, which suggests that you're thinking, rather than stare into space, which suggests that you're searching for an answer).

With the proliferation of cable TV channels and 24-hour newscasts, the cable networks need more talking heads to fill their airtime, and the print media and websites want more publicity for their reporters and writers. So the cable networks look for pundits, and the print media and websites supply them. With so much demand, it's no longer necessary for pundits to be established journalists with years of experience. Freire was just twenty-six at the time. Pundit school helped him transition from college dorm debates to prime-time TV.

This example illustrates multiple points about today's media that will become apparent as you read this chapter. The media are no longer dominated by a handful of prominent newspaper reporters and columnists and television newscasters and commentators. News organizations have a lot of space or time to fill, with news or commentary, and they offer a variety of voices, whether expert or not.

A *medium* transmits something. The mass media—which include newspapers, magazines, books, radio, television, movies, records, and the Internet—transmit communications to masses of people. In addition to providing entertainment, they provide information about government and politics. This chapter focuses on the news media—those media that deliver the news about government and politics.

THE MEDIA STATE

The media have become "pervasive…and atmospheric, an element of the air we breathe."[2] Without exaggeration, another observer concluded, "Ancient Sparta was a military state. John Calvin's Geneva was a religious state. Mid-nineteenth-century England was Europe's first industrial state, and the contemporary United States is the world's first media state."[3]

American newspapers originated in colonial times, and political magazines appeared in the 1800s, but there were no "mass media" until the advent of broadcasting. Radio, which became popular in the 1920s, and television, which became popular in the 1950s, reached people who could not or would not read. Television became so central to and influential in American life that one scholar speculated that the second half of the twentieth century will go down in history as "the age of television."[4] The Internet, which became popular in the 1990s, has been drawing users away from other media. The Internet likely will go down in history as even more important than television.

Americans spend more time being exposed to the media than doing anything else. In a year, according to one calculation, the average full-time worker puts in 1824 hours on the job, 2737 hours in bed, and 3256 hours exposed to the media (almost 9 hours a day).[5] Ninety-nine percent of American homes have a radio, and 98 percent have a television. For years, more homes had a television than had a toilet.[6] Almost 20 percent of children younger than two have a television in their bedroom; more than 40 percent of children between four and six do; and almost 70 percent of older children do. A third of children younger than six live in homes where the television is left on all or most of the time.[7] The average child (from eight years old on) or adult watches television 3 hours a day.[8] By the time the average child graduates from high school, he or she has spent more time in front of the tube than in class.[9] By the time the average American dies, he or she has spent one-and-a-half years just watching television commercials.[10] With the development of digital technology, Americans spend even more time being exposed to the media.

Children and young adults, especially, expose themselves to multiple media simultaneously. One study found that eight- to eighteen-year-olds on average pack in 11 hours of media in 7 1/2 hours of time. A third of them pay attention to more than one medium "most of the time," usually music or television while using the computer.[11]

As Internet use has shot up, it has cut into family time more than anything else. Although the average Internet user spends 30 minutes less time watching television than before the Internet, he or she spends 70 minutes less time interacting with family members than before.[12]

Most people use the media for entertainment, but many also use the media for news. More than half of adult Americans say they follow the news "all or most of the time," and another quarter say they follow the news at least "some of the time."[13]

The rest of this section will summarize the traditional roles of the media and our current consumption of news from the media, and it will examine two opposing trends in journalism: the increasing concentration of the media and the increasing fragmentation of the media.

Traditional Roles of the Media

Although the media aren't a branch of government, sometimes they're called the "Fourth Estate" or the "Fourth Branch," because they're powerful enough to check and balance the three branches of government. They provide extremely fast and relatively accurate reports of events. They scrutinize government and officials, evaluating their performance and probing wrongdoing. Thus they serve as a check on government and officials. As a former official noted, "Think how much chicanery dies on the drawing board when someone says, 'We'd better not do that; what if the press finds out?'"[14]

This role emerged as a tradition of serious journalism evolved in the nineteenth and twentieth centuries. Newspapers adopted the concept of objectivity, which emphasizes the publication of facts over opinions and the presentation of both sides in controversies, and the concept of editorial independence. These concepts became, essentially, journalists' religion.[15] Newspapers saw themselves as independent of government and officials. The paper's newsroom even came to see itself as independent of its business side, so the reporters usually paid no attention to what the advertisers may have wanted, and independent of the paper's owners, so the reporters usually paid no attention to what the owners may have preferred (except when the owners insisted on particular editorial positions or candidate endorsements). With objectivity and independence, journalists took on the jobs of educating the public and keeping the government honest. "This vision of a newspaper, one that prevailed at the highest levels of the craft for decades," according to a veteran reporter at the *Philadelphia Inquirer*, "ensured that the paper was not just a propaganda mill, the house organ of some rich man or political party, but a community of street-smart shoe-leather scholars who worked as the eyes, ears, and conscience of their city."[16]

This tradition was extended from major urban newspapers to small local newspapers. Then it was extended to major television and radio networks. At these mainstream media, the journalists saw themselves as representatives of the public

"I'm doing super, but Clark Kent can't find a newspaper that's hiring."

as well as having responsibilities to the public. So, when officials or citizens got upset with news reports and pointedly asked, "Who elected you?" journalists replied that the people—their readers or listeners or viewers—"elected" them by paying attention to their news columns or newscasts. But developments in recent decades have shaken the foundations of traditional journalism, as this chapter will show.

Shifting Dominance among the Media

Newspapers waned when television newscasts became popular in the 1960s. People didn't need their headlines anymore, and many didn't want their in-depth coverage either. Since 1970, the percentage of regular readers has declined, especially the percentage of young adult regular readers.[17] Only 19 percent of Americans between eighteen and thirty-four say they read a daily newspaper. The average age of regular readers is fifty-five.[18] As a result, the number of advertisers has declined. More than three hundred daily newspapers have folded.[19] Ann Arbor, Michigan, a college town, became the first medium-size city without a daily paper,[20] and in 2012 New Orleans became the fist big city without a daily paper. Most surviving newspapers have shrunk, cutting reporters and reducing pages, to save money.[21] Some "daily" papers publish six days a week; Detroit's "daily" papers publish daily but deliver just two or three days a week. So an editor of the *New York Times* says discussing the state of newspaper publishing is like being "a motivational speaker in a hospice."[22]

For several decades, the evening newscasts of the major networks—ABC, CBS, and NBC—replaced newspapers as the dominant medium for political news. The major networks **broadcast**—appealed to the overall audience—to attract the

most viewers. However, cable television—first CNN and later Fox News and MSNBC—and talk radio emerged in the 1980s. They **narrowcast**—appealed to small segments of the audience—and pulled viewers away from the major networks. The Internet, with unlimited sites for news and commentary, appealed to even smaller segments of the public and attracted newspaper readers and television viewers. As cable television, talk radio, and the Internet became available, the audience for the major networks' evening newscasts plummeted. Since the mid-1990s, the percentage of regular viewers dropped from 60 percent to 34 percent.[23] With so many sources of news at their fingertips, people didn't need to tune into the networks at a set time to hear a newscaster read the headlines. They could tune in to cable television or log onto the Internet at any time.

These trends will likely continue. Newspapers will lose more readers while television, especially the broadcast networks, will lose more viewers and the Internet will gain new users (see Figure 1).[24]

The Sources of News Today

Most Americans get news from multiple platforms—local newspaper, national newspaper (for example, the *New York Times, Wall Street Journal,* or *USA Today*), weekly newsmagazine, local radio, national radio, local television, national television, and the Internet. Almost half get news from four or more platforms on a typical day.[25]

Newspapers remain important. Every day 40 percent of Americans read their local paper, and others read a national paper.[26] Further, newspapers provide most content for television news and online news.[27] In fact, the papers' own websites are quite popular. Three-quarters of adults read a newspaper, whether in print or online, each week.[28] Thus most Americans get their news, either directly or indirectly, from newspapers, even as the print versions lose popularity.

Yet newspapers haven't figured out how to get online readers of their websites to pay for news they consume. Although people are willing to pay for texting and pornography online, so far they are reluctant to pay for news online. Most news is generated by professional journalists working for news organizations, especially for newspapers. These organizations cannot continue to generate news for free (or for the limited revenue they get from advertising). In-demand newspapers, such as the *New York Times,* have begun to charge online readers.

Weekly newsmagazines—*Newsweek, Time, U.S. News & World Report*—digest the news of the week and various trends of the times. Every week 8 percent of Americans read one of them.[29] Other weekly and monthly magazines also provide news.

But more people watch television than read newspapers or magazines. Every day 51 percent watch local news, 40 percent watch cable news, 34 percent watch the nightly newscasts of the broadcast networks, and 28 percent watch the nightly newscast of the public television network—PBS.[30]

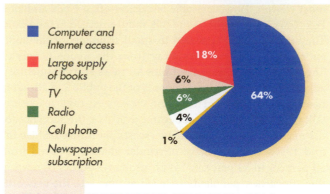

FIGURE 1: IF YOU WERE STRANDED ON A DESERTED ISLAND and could take only one of the following with you, which would you take?

SOURCE: Asked of 1000 households with Internet access. IPSOS Insight U.S. Express Omnibus, August 2004, cited in "Primary Sources," *Atlantic Monthly,* January–February 2005, 54. Copyright © 2005 by The Atlantic.com as published in the Atlantic Online. Distributed by Tribune Media Services. All Rights Reserved. Reproduced by permission.

Radio provides news for people on the go and in their car or at their work. Every day 18 percent listen to the newscasts of the public radio network—NPR—and the same percent listen to local or national talk radio programs.[31]

The Internet is increasingly popular. Every day at least a third of Americans get news from the Internet.[32] And a third of Americans who have cell phones access news from their phone some days.[33]

The Internet fosters two-way communication, more than talk programs on radio and television. Many users not only receive the websites' information but also express their own views in chatrooms or on message boards. They send e-mails with links to stories and videos to their friends and the members of their social networking sites such as Facebook and Myspace. They use this contemporary technology as people traditionally have used word-of-mouth.[34] Thus the Internet has become an important political medium, because in addition to informing it facilitates organizing and mobilizing of citizens with similar interests who form virtual communities. It promotes grassroots engagement.

Today, different media appeal to different groups. Seniors read newspapers and watch TV newscasts, whereas young adults surf the Web (see Table 1). The cable networks attract the least educated, and newsmagazines, political magazines, and the Internet attract the most educated. Conservatives tend to watch Fox News and listen to talk radio, whereas liberals tend to watch MSNBC and listen to NPR.[35] Conservatives and liberals both scan the Web but favor different sites. Even men and women pay attention to different media and to different stories in the media (see box "Media Habits of Men and Women" on page 101).

Concentration of the Media

Journalism is a big business, and it has become a bigger business in recent decades. First, small media organizations owned by local families or local companies were taken over by chains (owning multiple newspapers, radio stations, or television stations) or conglomerates (owning multiple newspapers, radio stations, and television stations). Then large media organizations were taken over by chains or conglomerates. Finally, chains and conglomerates were bought out by larger chains and conglomerates.

A handful of huge companies form the top tier of media conglomerates. Time Warner, the largest, has over eighty thousand employees and $30 billion in annual revenues. It boasts 50 percent of the online business, 20 percent of the cable television business, 18 percent of the movie business, and 16 percent of the record business in the country. It also has 160 magazines, five publishing houses, and "Looney Tunes" cartoons.[36]

The companies' goal is to control the information and entertainment markets of the future. Each conglomerate wants to offer the entire range of media—television stations, radio stations, newspapers, magazines, books, movies, records, and computer services. Each conglomerate seeks to become the sole source of your news and entertainment.[37] The conglomerates are racing to swallow their competitors and influence the government to adopt policies that will lock in their advantage.[38]

As a result of this trend, the news comes from fewer sources than it used to. Although there are tens of thousands of media entities in the United States, the numbers are misleading, because relatively few chains and conglomerates own most media.[39] One analyst observed, "Two dozen profit-driven companies, owned and managed by billionaires operating in barely competitive markets, account for nearly the entirety of the U.S. media culture."[40]

 Thinking about Democracy

Consider the implications of this trend not for consumers, but for citizens in a democracy who rely on the media to inform them about their government and officials.

Just ten companies publish the newspapers that reach 51 percent of the readers.[41] Six companies broadcast to 42 percent of the radio audience, and five companies broadcast to 75 percent of the television audience.[42] Six companies have more than 80 percent of the cable television market. Four companies sell almost 90 percent of all music recordings, and six companies earn more than 90 percent of all film revenues.[43] Moreover, just one wire service—the Associated Press (AP)—supplies the international and national news for most newspapers. Five television networks—ABC, CBS, NBC, CNN, and Fox News—furnish the news for most television stations.

With fewer sources of news, there is a narrower range of views—a smaller marketplace of ideas—than is healthy for

	18–29 Years	30–49 Years	50 and More Years	Gap between Youngest and Oldest
Local TV news	25%	39%	50%	−25%
Sunday network political shows	4	12	21	−17
Nightly network newscasts	24	28	40	−16
Daily newspaper	25	26	38	−13
Public TV newscasts	6	12	14	−8
Morning network shows	18	21	25	−7
Religious radio	5	8	12	−7
Cable network newscasts	35	36	41	−6
National Public Radio (NPR)	13	19	19	−6
Cable network talk shows	12	11	18	−6
Newsmagazines	8	9	13	−5
Talk radio	12	16	17	−5
TV magazine shows	21	19	25	−4
C-SPAN	6	9	9	−3
"Lou Dobbs Tonight"	7	5	8	−1
Late night talk shows	10	8	9	+1
TV comedy shows	12	7	6	+6
Internet	42	26	15	+27

Table 1 News Consumption by Age Percentages who said they regularly learned something about the 2008 presidential campaign from . . .

SOURCE: "Internet's Broader Role in Campaign 2008: Social Networking and Online Videos Take Off," January 11, 2008, Pew Research Center for the People and the Press, a project of the Pew Research Center. Copyright © 2008 by Pew Research Center. Reproduced by permission.

a democracy. Instead, relatively few powerful people provide information and opinion—essentially, define reality—for the rest of the people.

These chains and conglomerates have begun to exercise their power through political activism and censorship. During the Iraq War, Clear Channel Communications, the largest radio chain, organized pro-war rallies in seven cities.[44] Sinclair Broadcast Group, the largest television chain, forbade its ABC affiliates from airing *Nightline* the night it broadcast the names of military personnel killed in Iraq. The company said the show would "undermine" the war effort.[45] Cumulus Media, the second-largest radio chain, halted airplay of Dixie Chicks songs on its country stations after a member of the band criticized President Bush.[46] These instances, though relatively minor in themselves, are ominous signs for the future. It would be naive not to expect more attempts by media chains and conglomerates to flex their muscles through censorship.

In addition, the chains and conglomerates have censored their news divisions when news coverage has threatened corporate interests. ABC killed a story that Walt Disney, its owner, followed employment practices that allowed the hiring of convicted pedophiles at its parks.[47] NBC broadcast a report about defective bolts used in airplanes and bridges built by GE, at the time its owner, and by other companies, but the references to GE were removed. When the president of NBC News complained about the removal and corporate interference in their newscasts, the CEO of GE poked a finger in his chest and shouted, "You work for GE!"[48]

Another problem resulting from concentration of the media is financial pressure to reduce the quality of news coverage. News organizations are expected to match other divisions in their corporations and generate sizable profits each year. Corporate officers feel the heat from Wall Street analysts and major stockholders, who are more concerned with the value of their stock than the quality of their journalism. As a result, costs are cut—some reporters are let go, while others are shifted from time-consuming in-depth or investigative reporting to more superficial stories.[49] ABC News slashed 25 percent of its staff in 2010. A reporter for

Media Habits of Men and Women

Men and women pay attention to different media. Women are more likely to turn on television news, whether a broadcast network or a local station. They are more likely to watch both the morning and nightly newscasts. Men are more likely to switch on a cable network, and they are more likely to check the Internet for news or listen to talk radio for commentary and news.[1] Among men and women who watch the cable networks, men are more likely to watch the most strident programs (such as Sean Hannity's or Bill O'Reilly's on Fox News).[2]

Among more serious sources of news, men are more likely to read newspapers and newsmagazines, though women are equally likely to follow the detailed newscasts of NPR, which is the only "hard-news" source whose audience is about half female.[3]

Men and women also pay attention to different stories in the media. Men tend to favor sports stories and "hard news" examining government and politics. Women tend to prefer entertainment, lifestyle, health, safety, and religion stories. They like "soft news" that has a human interest angle.[4] They also follow crime news more closely.[5]

Men pay more attention to international affairs, while women pay more attention to the weather. Forty percent of men, compared with 27 percent of women, followed articles about the tension between the United States and Iran. During the same time, 40 percent of women, compared with 25 percent of men, followed articles about devastating tornadoes within the United States.[6]

These media habits suggest that men are more interested in politics than women. Indeed, 42 percent of men, compared with 34 percent of women, told pollsters they are "very interested" in government and public affairs. Sixty percent of women, compared with 54 percent of men, said they are only "somewhat interested."[7]

Because men are more interested in politics, they are more likely to discuss politics than women are. According to one survey, 31 percent of men, compared with 20 percent of women, said they discussed national politics nearly every day; and 22 percent of men, compared with 16 percent of women, said they discussed local politics nearly every day.[8]

Social scientists are uncertain why this gender gap exists. Some believe it may be due to the small number of female governmental officials.[9]

[1] Lydia Saad, "Local TV Is No. 1 Source of News for Americans," *The Gallup Poll*, www.galluppoll.com/content/Default.aspx'ci=26053 &VERSION=p.

[2] Louis Menand, "Comment: Chin Music," *New Yorker*, November 2, 2009, 39.

[3] Linda Hirshman, "16 Ways of Looking at a Female Voter," *New York Times Magazine*, February 3, 2008, 41.

[4] Ibid.; "Numbers," *Time*, February 25, 2008, 16.

[5] Hirshman, "16 Ways of Looking at a Female Voter," 41.

[6] "Numbers," *Time*, 16.

[7] Hirshman, "16 Ways of Looking at a Female Voter," 41.

[8] Sidney Verba, Nancy Burns, and Kay Lehman Schlozman, "Knowing and Caring about Politics: Gender and Political Engagement," *Journal of Politics* 59 (November 1997), 1051–1072.

[9] For an examination of some explanations, see ibid. and Kira Sanbonmatsu, "Gender Related Political Knowledge and Descriptive Representation," *Political Behavior* 25 (December 2003), 367–388.

a midsize newspaper in Illinois lamented, "If a story needs a real investment of time and money, we don't do it anymore." He asked, sarcastically, "Who the hell cares about corruption in city government, anyway?"[50]

A decline in local news is a common casualty of the media's concentration. A veteran reporter for the Baltimore Sun noted that the number of staffers on his paper was shrunk from 500 to 300, and "in a city where half the adult black males are unemployed, where the unions have been busted, and crime and poverty have overwhelmed one neighborhood after the next, the daily newspaper no longer maintains a

poverty beat or a labor beat. The city courthouse went uncovered for almost a year...."[51] The executives of the company that runs the paper live in Chicago.

When a train derailed in Minot, North Dakota, and released over 200,000 gallons of ammonia, authorities tried to notify residents to avoid the area and to stay indoors. But when police called the six local commercial radio stations, nobody answered. The stations were all owned and programmed by Clear Channel, based in San Antonio, Texas.[52] By the next day, three hundred people had been hospitalized, and pets and livestock had been killed.[53]

Fragmentation of the Media

Despite the increasing concentration of the media, a contrary trend—a fragmentation of the media—has also developed in recent decades. Whereas concentration has led to a national media, fragmentation has diminished the audience for and the influence of the national media. The major newspapers and broadcast networks have lost their dominance, and other media, some not even considered news organizations, have generated political news that has influenced election campaigns and policy debates.

Segmented Audience

This trend is mostly due to technological changes, particularly the development of cable television and the Internet. Cable television, with an abundance of channels, can narrowcast rather than broadcast as the major networks do. For example, C-SPAN covers Congress on three channels and, unlike the major networks, lingers on members' speeches and committees' hearings.

Cable television can offer 24-hour news, as CNN, Fox News, and MSNBC do. Each network can carve out a niche in this market. After Fox fashioned itself as a conservative network, MSNBC, which had been searching for an identity, became, at least in the evenings, a liberal network. CNN, which pioneered 24-hour news, has tried to build a reputation as the least slanted cable news network (see Figure 2).[54]

Narrowcasting also allows networks to gear programming to minorities and to speakers of languages other than English. National cable networks cater to blacks and Latinos.[55] A cable system in Los Angeles and New York caters to Jews. A cable channel in California broadcasts (24 hours) in Chinese, one in Hawaii broadcasts in Japanese, and one in Connecticut and Massachusetts broadcasts in Portuguese. Stations in New York also provide programs in Greek, Hindi, Korean, and Russian.

Univision is watched by two-thirds of Latinos. In some cities its Spanish-speaking newscasts have higher ratings than local English-speaking newscasts, and on some nights its newscasts have higher ratings than ABC, CBS, Fox, or NBC across the country. The network is the most respected institution (more than the military or Catholic Church) among Latinos, so it has political influence.[56]

The Internet, with unlimited websites, can cater to even smaller segments of the audience than cable television can. Print newspapers post their articles before delivering the papers. Online "magazines" also address political issues. Finally, self-styled "journalists" hawk their news and views in independent web logs—**blogs**.

Blogs are an alternative to mainstream journalism, allowing "citizen journalists" to compete with media giants. Unlike "the sober, neutral drudges of the establishment press, the bloggers are class clowns and crusaders, satirists and scolds."[57] Some bloggers have small operations. Matt Drudge offers political gossip in the Drudge Report, which originated in his one-bedroom apartment.[58] Other bloggers attract thousands or even hundreds of thousands of visitors per day. The most popular political blog—*Daily Kos*—has 600,000 readers each day, which is more than all

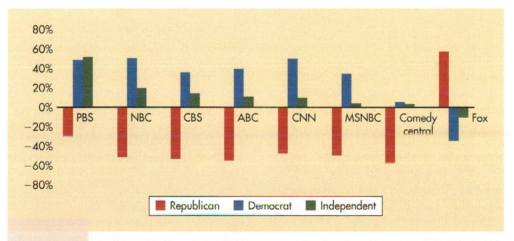

FIGURE 2: MEDIA TRUST AND DISTRUST BY DEMOCRATS AND REPUBLICANS
People were asked which networks they trust and which ones they distrust. The percentage of respondents who said they distrust a network was subtracted from the percentage who said they trust that network. Therefore, a net positive percentage reflects more trust than distrust; a net negative percentage reflects more distrust than trust. Democrats *trust* all networks except Fox, whereas Republicans *distrust* all networks except Fox.

but a handful of newspapers have.[59] Another popular blog—the *Huffington Post*—has more readers than the *Washington Post*.[60] Some bloggers (such as the *Huffington Post*) are "news aggregators," who offer a combination of mainstream news and their opinions.

Mainstream journalists criticize the bloggers as "self-appointed authorities"[61] who offer only opinions, not news, especially not in-depth reporting.[62] A *New York Times* editor said they just "recycle and chew on the news."[63]

Although the variety of blogs enables people to sample a variety of opinions, few do. Readers gravitate to blogs that reflect and then reinforce their political beliefs.[64]

Even YouTube has become a factor in politics, especially in election campaigns, since its inception in 2005. The musician will.i.am made a video, "Yes We Can," that celebrated Barack Obama's candidacy and became the site's most watched political video. Obama's pivotal speech on race, which was presented on a weekday morning to a small audience, was viewed 5 million times during the 2008 campaign. YouTube offered a section of its site, YouChoose, which ran videos from the candidates. And, of course, the site ran "gotcha moments" and snide spoofs that also shaped voters' perceptions of the candidates.[65]

The trend toward fragmentation of the media, which is mostly due to the development of cable television and the Internet, has also been driven by the populist backlash against government officials and established journalists, perceived as "Washington insiders," that has characterized American politics in recent decades. This populism is reflected in the popularity of radio talk shows. Many stations have such programs, and many people, especially conservative men, tune in.[66] Their numbers make talk radio a force in national politics.

Fringe Media

The trend toward fragmentation is also reflected in the attention paid to fringe media by the public. In the 1992 presidential campaign, the *Star*, a supermarket tabloid, published allegations by Gennifer Flowers, a former nightclub singer, that she had a twelve-year affair with Bill Clinton while he was governor of Arkansas. Then Flowers appeared on *A Current Affair*, a syndicated television show, rated Clinton as a lover on a scale from 1 to 10, and sang "Stand by Your Man." Flowers did not need to take her story to the major media; she got the tabloid media to tell it (and pay her—$150,000 from the *Star* and $25,000 from *A Current Affair*),[67] and that got the major media to report it.

In the 2008 presidential campaign, the *National Enquirer* reported an affair between John Edwards, a Democratic presidential candidate, and a campaign staffer, and the tabloid revealed a baby from the affair. The revelations forced Edwards from the race.

Because the public pays attention to fringe media, politicians use these media, especially television shows, to seem "human" and amiable to average voters. Bill Clinton played the saxophone on the *Arsenio Hall Show*, and George W.

Bush kissed the host on the *Oprah Winfrey Show*. Hillary Clinton performed a skit on *Saturday Night Live*, and Barack and Michelle Obama cooked on *Rachel Ray*. Politicians allow themselves to be interviewed on the fake newscasts of Jon Stewart and Stephen Colbert, and they swap jokes with Jay Leno and David Letterman—and pray they won't look silly.

Politicians have to be good sports, because people who pay little attention to political news do pay attention to these shows. Almost a third of adults say they get political information from late-night comedy shows; over a third of those under thirty say they get more information from these shows than from other sources.[68]

The standards of the fringe media are far different than the standards of the mainstream media, because their goal is to entertain rather than to inform. Radio personality Don Imus confessed, "The news isn't sacred to me. It's entertainment ... designed to revel in the agony of others."[69]

Consequences

This trend toward fragmentation of the media has significant implications for political news.

More accessible Many people aren't interested in politics or government, and they don't want to read long articles in newspapers or watch careful presentations of political news on television. They don't want to listen to rational discussions of current events. They want news that's more provocative, even sensational, which they find more entertaining. The fragmentation of the media offers multiple sources that make the news more accessible to these people.

More attention to some issues Blogs enable "issue entrepreneurs" to push an issue onto the public agenda and focus attention on the issue until it "catches fire."[70] In a website from her apartment, Pam Geller opposed plans to build a Muslim community center on a site two blocks from Ground Zero. Calling it the "Ground Zero Mega-Mosque" (although it was neither at Ground Zero nor a mosque), she launched the divisive controversy and drew thousands of protestors to the site in 2010.[71] (For another example, see the CourseReader box in Chapter 6.)

Less factual Although the fragmentation of the media makes the news more accessible to more people, this trend also makes the news less factual. The proliferation of news outlets and the availability of newscasts around the clock create intense competition for news stories. The media have more time or space to fill than information to fill it. So they feel pressure to find new stories or identify new angles of old stories. To fill airtime, television networks offer shows that blend news, opinion, rumor, and speculation, because such shows are cheap to produce and, if the hosts and guests are provocative, entertaining for their viewers. Thus the networks can fill airtime and attract an audience. But the result is a commingling of facts and nonfacts. Then these facts and non-facts are repeated by other media seeking to make sure that they are not left behind. In the rush to broadcast and publish, the media have less time for and put less emphasis on assessing the accuracy of the content they disseminate than they used to.

The Internet also makes the news less factual. Individual bloggers don't have editors or fact checkers—the layers of "review, revision, and correction" that mainstream media have.[72] When hoax e-mails falsely reporting the deaths of various senators were sent to mainstream media and to websites, some bloggers reported the deaths without ever confirming them.[73]

Some blogs push pure hokum—for example, that the World Trade Center was destroyed by the U.S. government rather than by al-Qaeda; that the Pentagon was hit by a cruise missile rather than by a hijacked jet; and that United Flight 93 was shot down by an Air Force fighter rather than forced down by its own passengers.

And some bloggers are partisan operatives who have been trained to engage in "guerrilla Internet activism" while presenting themselves as average people.[74] Their passion for the cause trumps their fealty to the truth. There was a concerted campaign to persuade people that Barack Obama was born in Kenya rather than in Hawaii, and therefore ineligible to be president; that he was educated at an Islamist madrassah (an Islamic school that teaches fundamentalist religious doctrine) as a child in Indonesia; and that he is a secret Muslim rather than a Christian. Despite ample evidence that these accusations are false, the claims continue to ricochet through the blogosphere. Political sophisticates may roll their eyes when they hear such accusations, but many folks believe they are true or at least might be true. An elderly voter in a small town spoke for others when he said he didn't know which biography to believe—the one reported in the mainstream media or the one seen on the Internet and heard at his neighbor's house, at the grocery store, and at his son's auto shop.[75]

Some partisan operatives also originate chain e-mails with bogus claims that reinforce falsehoods in the blogs. The claims range from the trivial—that the Obama administration renamed Christmas trees "holiday trees"—to the serious—that the health care reform law grants free care to illegal immigrants. Chain e-mails spread without a filter. "There's no one between your crazy uncle and his address book."[76]

There's always a current, which one writer calls the "undernews"—stories sometimes true, often false, circulating in the blogs, chain e-mails, or the tabloids—flowing under the news generated by the mainstream media. When this current gets large enough, the mainstream media, or perhaps the politicians who are the subjects of the stories, are pressured to address them.[77] Obama was forced to present his birth certificate. Sarah Palin, campaigning for vice president in 2008, was forced to release her obstetrical records to counter assertions in blogs that her four-month-old baby was actually her teenage daughter's baby—that Palin had faked her pregnancy to cover up her daughter's.[78]

Despite the frequency of falsehoods, bloggers say that blogs are self-correcting because their readers serve as fact checkers. Occasionally, the blogs have corrected inaccuracies in mainstream coverage. When CBS News displayed a letter about the National Guard service of President George W. Bush, bloggers with knowledge of old typewriters identified the letter as a fake.

More angry The fragmentation of the media results not only in news that is less factual but also in newscasts and commentaries that are more angry than they used to be. With the proliferation of media and the trend of narrowcasting, each organization finds its niche and caters to its audience. No longer constrained by the need to appeal to the great middle, each organization can now give vent to the beliefs and fears—and even the delusions—of its audience. Each one can reflect the anger of its audience. Personal attacks and wild claims flourish. Cable news has become "a sandbox" where "people throw things at one another."[79] Talk radio and Internet websites also amplify the angry voices among us. For these media, the "hysteria-to-evidence ratio" is high.[80]

Barack Obama's election and tenure as president generated a virulent backlash from cable television commentators, talk radio hosts, and Internet sites that demonized the president and promoted conspiracy theories.[81] Fox News's Glenn Beck expressed his fear that Obama has "a deep-seated hatred for white people."[82] Rush Limbaugh asserted, "In Obama's America, the white kids now get beat up, with the black kids cheering 'Right on! Right on!'"[83] Limbaugh called Obama's health care plan "Hitlerlike."[84] Numerous commentators claimed, falsely, that the plan included "death panels" of government bureaucrats who would deny health care to the elderly and the disabled. Talk radio hosts Alex Jones and Michael Savage peddled the notion that the Obama administration is creating internment camps—"reeducation camps"—for conservative teens.[85] Then the theory was applied to health care—that the administration is creating "reeducation camps" for the obese. None of these claims was based on facts.

Wild accusations crowd out thoughtful discussions, polarizing society and hamstringing politicians who try to negotiate and compromise with the other side.

Different perceptions of reality Without shared sources of media, people are exposed to different versions of the same events. Without the filter of editors and fact checkers, people are also exposed to false information more often. The result is that different groups of people have different perceptions of reality. Even well-educated, relatively sophisticated people, according to studies, are prone to misperceptions of reality.[86] During the debate over health care reform, people who followed conservative media were told that the law would be "a socialist takeover" of the health care system. People who followed liberal media were told that because it didn't include a public option, the law would be little help to ordinary Americans. Both claims, debunked by political scientists, revealed more about the media than they did about the law. When citizens can't agree about reality, they can't agree about solutions to problems they face.

Concerns of journalists   Professional journalists believe they have a public trust to perform serious journalism. Many have spent years observing and learning about the subjects of their stories. Because of the fragmentation of the media, these journalists see a shrinking role for themselves and their organizations. They see fewer Americans reading newspapers and more flocking to newer media and fringe media, with their shouting and mudslinging, and their playing fast and loose with the facts. These journalists wonder whether the public will continue to want serious journalism and whether media organizations will continue to support such journalism. In particular, they wonder whether in-depth and investigative reporting will continue to survive.

Professional journalists see a role for "citizen journalists" but say such journalists are a supplement, not a substitute, for professional journalists. Although the bloggers insist, "Every citizen can be a reporter," professional journalists doubt that average citizens would spend months covering devastation in places like Haiti or Japan, or any time covering genocide and sex slavery in dangerous parts of the world. Professional journalists

doubt that average citizens would day after day "attend the council meetings, pore over the budgets, decipher the court rulings that help…us understand our cities, nation, and world."[87]

Thinking about Democracy

What are the implications for a democracy when the media are dominated by professional journalists, with their editors and fact checkers? What are the implications when many people pay more attention to citizen journalists and fringe media?

In sum, two opposite trends—concentration of the media and fragmentation of the media—are occurring. How much control will the media conglomerates exercise, and how much news and how many views will emerge through other outlets, especially the Internet? We're witnessing an information revolution, but we don't know what journalism will look like in the future. Comparing the state of the media in our times with Gutenberg's invention of movable type, one observer said, "We're collectively living through 1500, when it's easier to see what's broken than what will replace it."[88]

CourseReader   ASSIGNMENT

Log in to www.cengagebrain.com and open Course-Reader to access the full reading of "Stinger" by Zev Chafets.

James O'Keefe is a conservative activist and an undercover videographer. O'Keefe shoots videos designed to display absurdity or hypocrisy by government officials or liberal organizations. With outlandish costumes and stories for his actors, O'Keefe stages scenarios in which the actors try to get the officials to say embarrassing things while a hidden camera runs. Then he distributes the videos through conservative websites.

O'Keefe misleads his targets and skirts the law, once pretending to be a telephone repairman at the New Orleans office of Senator Mary Landrieu (D-La.). For this, he was convicted of entering federal property under false pretenses. He disdains mainstream journalists, whom he calls "stenographers," and insists that subterfuge is necessary to reveal his targets' true natures.

1. Do you think that O'Keefe's efforts are journalism or just political theater?
2. In what ways does O'Keefe's approach differ from the practices of mainstream journalists? Are there any ways in which they are similar?

3. Put aside your political views, whether conservative or liberal, and think about whether O'Keefe's efforts are beneficial or harmful to society.
4. O'Keefe's video of ACORN, which discredited the community organization, showed a pimp and a prostitute seeking tax advice for a business venture involving underage illegal immigrants. The interview was conducted with O'Keefe dressed like a college student, in slacks and a button-down shirt. Later the interview was edited, with new footage showing O'Keefe dressed like an outlandish pimp. Substituting the new footage for the original footage made the video more outrageous and the responses of ACORN's workers more dubious. The edited version was the one circulated.[1] Does this fact affect your responses to the above questions?

[1]Peter Dreier and Christopher R. Martin, "How ACORN Was Framed: Political Controversy and Media Agenda Setting," *Perspectives on Politics* 8 (September 2010), 781.

Teddy Roosevelt called the presidency a "bully pulpit" from which he could persuade the public and Congress to support his programs. (In his time, "bully" was slang for "jolly good.") Modern presidents, however, have learned that there are real limits to this tactic.

RELATIONSHIP BETWEEN THE MEDIA AND POLITICIANS

"Politicians live—and sometimes die—by the press. The press lives by politicians," according to a former presidential aide. "This relationship is at the center of our national life."[89]

Although this relationship was not always so close—President Herbert Hoover once refused to tell a reporter whether he enjoyed a baseball game he attended[90]—politicians and journalists now realize that they need each other. Politicians need journalists to reach the public and to receive feedback from the public. They scan the major newspapers in the morning and the network newscasts in the evening. President Lyndon Johnson watched three network newscasts on three televisions simultaneously. (President George W. Bush, who boasted that he didn't read the newspapers or watch the newscasts, was an exception to the rule.[91]) In turn, journalists need politicians to cover government. They seek a steady stream of fresh information to fill their news columns and newscasts. This is even more essential in today's **24-hour news cycle**, which provides nonstop news.

When the Berlin Wall was erected in 1961, President John F. Kennedy was on vacation. For six days, reporters didn't expect a reaction from him. When the Cuban missile crisis occurred in 1962, Kennedy informed the nation and then the networks resumed their normal programming. There were no analyses by correspondents or criticisms by opponents.[92] Now, however, reporters expect—and demand—immediate responses from the officials and their opponents and any groups that have an interest in the issue. Journalists report almost continuously. Chuck Todd of NBC

wakes, scans the morning newspapers, and writes the opening page of NBC's blog. Then he appears on the *Today* show on NBC or the *Morning Joe* show on MSNBC. During the day, he conducts eight to sixteen interviews on camera outside the White House. He also writes eight to ten tweets or Facebook postings and three to five blog entries. At night, he hosts an hour newscast on MSNBC.[93] The 24-hour news cycle has an insatiable appetite. With so much background noise, it's difficult for politicians to break through "the cacophony of competing voices"[94] and reach the public.

The close relationship between the media and politicians is both a **symbiotic relationship**, meaning they use each other for their mutual advantage, and an **adversarial relationship**, meaning they fight each other.

Symbiotic Relationship

President Johnson told individual reporters, "You help me, and I'll help make you a big man in your profession." He gave exclusive interviews and, in return, expected favorable coverage. And discreet coverage. On a trip shortly after assuming the presidency upon Kennedy's assassination, Johnson ran into a group of reporters in a hotel bar. After answering their questions, he said, "One more thing, boys. You may see me coming in and out of a few women's bedrooms while I am in the White House, but just remember, that is none of your business."[95]

Reporters get information from politicians in various ways. Some reporters are assigned to monitor a "beat"—that is, to cover the White House, Congress, the Supreme Court, the State Department, the Defense Department, or some other department or agency. Other reporters are assigned to cover specialized subjects, such as economics, energy issues, or environmental problems, which are addressed by multiple departments or agencies.

The government has press secretaries and public information officers who provide reporters with ideas and information for stories. The number of these officials is significant; one year the Department of Defense employed almost fifteen hundred people just to handle press relations.[96]

The government supplies reporters with a variety of news sources, including copies of speeches, summaries of committee meetings, news releases, and news briefings about current events. Officials supply online media with news and features. The White House and members of Congress feed content to blogs, Twitter, and Facebook, and upload video clips to YouTube and still photos to Flickr. Officials also grant interviews, hold press conferences, and stage "media events." The vast majority of reporters rely on these sources rather than engage in more difficult and time-consuming investigative reporting.

Interviews

Interviews show the symbiotic nature of the relationship between reporters and politicians. During the early months of the Reagan presidency, Washington Post writer William Greider had a series of eighteen off-the-record meetings with budget director David Stockman. Greider recounted:

> Stockman and I were participating in a fairly routine transaction of Washington, a form of submerged communication which takes place regularly between selected members of the press and the highest officials of government. Our mutual motivation, despite our different interests, was crassly self-serving. It did not need to be spelled out between us. I would use him and he would use me. . . . I had established a valuable peephole on the inner policy debates of the new administration. And the young budget director had established a valuable connection with an important newspaper. I would get a jump on the unfolding strategies and decisions. He would be able to prod and influence the focus of our coverage, to communicate his views and positions under the cover of our "off the record" arrangement, to make known harsh assessments that a public official would not dare to voice in the more formal setting of a press conference, speech, or "on the record" interview.[97]

Leaks

Interviews can result in **leaks**—disclosures of information that officials want to keep secret. Others in the administration, the bureaucracy, or Congress use leaks for various reasons.

Officials in the administration might leak information about a potential policy—float a trial balloon—and then gauge the reaction to it before committing themselves to it. Officials might leak to prod the president or high-ranking official into taking some action[98] or to prevent the president or high-ranking official from taking some action. When President Obama was deciding whether to send additional troops to Afghanistan, he received a secret report, requesting 40,000 more troops, from his top general in Afghanistan.

Before the president made his decision, Pentagon brass leaked the report to build a public case for the additional troops.

Officials might leak to force public debates on matters that would otherwise be addressed behind closed doors. After Congress investigated the intelligence failures leading up to the terrorist attacks on September 11, 2001, someone leaked the information that the National Security Agency (NSA)—the ultrasecret agency that engages in electronic surveillance around the world—had intercepted al-Qaeda messages on September 10 saying "Tomorrow is zero day" and "The match begins tomorrow" but had not translated the messages from Arabic until September 12.

Officials might leak to shift blame for mistakes. When the Iraqi insurgency cast doubt upon our presumed victory in the Iraq War, officials from the State Department leaked information suggesting that the Pentagon had rushed the country into war. Then officials from the Pentagon leaked information claiming that the CIA had exaggerated the intelligence about Iraq's nuclear weapons program. Then officials from the CIA leaked information indicating that the administration had distorted the intelligence about Iraq's weapons of mass destruction. Each group tried to absolve itself of the blame as the war turned sour.

Officials might leak to hurt an adversary. Diplomat Joseph Wilson was sent to Niger, which exports uranium, to investigate the possibility that Iraq had sought a type of uranium used in nuclear weapons. Wilson found no evidence to support the claim. Yet President Bush included the claim as a fact in his next State of the Union address, and others in the administration repeated it to persuade the public to support a war against Iraq. Breaking his silence, Wilson wrote an article in the New York Times maintaining that the administration had "twisted" the intelligence to "exaggerate" the threat. In retaliation, officials in the administration leaked the identity of Wilson's wife, Valerie Plame, who had worked for the CIA as an undercover spy.[99] Unmasking Plame effectively ended her career as a spy and jeopardized the operations she had established and contacts she had made in foreign countries.[100]

Officials might leak embarrassing information to help an ally or protect themselves. By leaking this information at a particular time or in a particular way, they can minimize the damage it would otherwise cause. After President George H. W. Bush nominated Clarence Thomas to the Supreme Court, an official in the Bush administration leaked the fact that Thomas had experimented with marijuana in college. The official's purpose was to inoculate Thomas from the greater controversy that could have occurred if the press had discovered and revealed this fact closer to the confirmation vote.[101]

Despite the lurking suspicion that leaks are from low-level bureaucrats in the opposite party, most are from high-ranking officials in the president's party. "The ship of state," one experienced reporter noted, "is the only kind of ship that leaks mainly from the top."[102] During the Vietnam War, President Johnson himself ordered an aide to leak the charge that steel companies were "profiteering" from the war. After an executive complained, Johnson assured him that "if I find out some damn fool aide did it, I'll fire the sonuvabitch!"[103]

Rand Paul, now a senator (R–Ky.), awaits an interview at a local television station.

Presidents as far back as George Washington have been enraged by leaks. Reagan said he was "up to my keister" in leaks, and Nixon established a "plumbers" unit to wiretap aides and, once it learned who was responsible, to plug leaks. George W. Bush, embarrassed about leaks revealing that the CIA operated secret prisons in foreign countries and the NSA wiretapped American citizens who made phone calls to foreign countries, launched the most extensive crackdown since Nixon. FBI investigations and CIA polygraph tests targeted government employees considered possible sources for the reports.[104]

Leaks may serve the public by disclosing information that otherwise would not be available, but leaks would serve the public better if reporters explained the leakers' motives so the public could understand the bureaucratic or ideological conflicts behind the stories. Yet reporters are wary of antagonizing the leakers—their sources—for fear of not getting a story next time.

Leaks often enable reporters to break stories before their competitors can report them. Competition for these **scoops** is intense. During the 2004 presidential campaign, CBS displayed a letter about George W. Bush's National Guard service. In its zeal for a scoop, CBS aired the story before verifying the authenticity of the letter.[105] It turned out that the letter had been forged and the network had been snookered, which proved highly embarrassing to CBS and costly to Dan Rather, who lost his anchor position. In 2012, as the Supreme Court announced its ruling on the constitutionality of the Affordable Care Act, CNN and Fox News were in such a hurry to report the ruling that they jumped to the wrong conclusion. They said that the Court's majority invalidated the individual mandate. In fact, the majority upheld the mandate.[106]

Press Conferences

Press conferences also show the symbiotic nature of the relationship between reporters and politicians. Theodore Roosevelt, who was the first president to cultivate close ties to correspondents, started **presidential press conferences** by answering questions from reporters while being shaved.[107] Franklin Roosevelt, who was detested by newspaper publishers, realized that press conferences could help him reach the public. He held frequent informal sessions around his desk and provided a steady stream of news, which newspaper editors felt obligated to publish. This news publicized his policies at the same time that the editors, under orders from the publishers, were writing editorials against them. John Kennedy saw that press conferences could help him reach the public more directly if he allowed the networks to televise the conferences live.[108] Then the editors couldn't filter his remarks.

Presidents and their aides eventually transformed the conferences into carefully orchestrated media shows. Now an administration schedules a conference when it wants to convey a message. Aides identify potential questions, and the president rehearses appropriate answers. (Former press secretaries brag that they predicted at least 90 percent of the questions asked—and often the reporters who asked them.[109]) During the conference, the president calls on the reporters he wants. Although he cannot ignore those from the major news organizations, he can call on others whom he expects will lob soft questions. The George W. Bush administration even gave press credentials to a Republican operative posing as a real reporter so he would ask the questions the president wanted to answer.[110]

Beaming the conference to the nation results in less news than having a casual exchange around the president's desk, which used to reveal his thinking about policies and decisions. Appearing in millions of homes, the president cannot be as open and cannot allow himself to make a gaffe in front of the huge audience.

This transformation of the conference frustrates reporters and prompts them to act as prosecutors. As one press secretary observed, they play a game of "I gotcha."[111] Still, reporters value the conferences. Editors consider the president's remarks news, so the conferences help reporters do their job, and televised conferences also give them a chance to bask in the limelight.

Media Events

"Media events" also show the symbiotic nature of the relationship between reporters and politicians. Staged for television, these events usually pair a photo opportunity with a speech to convey a clear impression of a politician's position on an issue.

The **photo opportunity**, usually called a *photo op*, frames the politician against a backdrop that symbolizes the points the politician is trying to make. Photo ops for economic issues might use factories—bustling to represent success or abandoned to represent failure. Presidential candidates appear at Google headquarters, which represents technological advancement, to identify themselves with the future. The strategy is the same as that for advertisements of merchandise: combine the product (the politician) with the symbols

(the factory or headquarters) in the hope that the potential buyers (the voters) will link the two.[112]

Photo ops can present an accurate or a misleading impression. To persuade people that President Bush's tax cuts, which were designed primarily to benefit wealthy taxpayers, would help working Americans, the Speaker of the House, Dennis Hastert (R-Ill.), asked well-heeled lobbyists who favored the cuts to dress as construction workers and appear in photo ops featuring "a sea of hard hats" and signs proclaiming "Tax Relief for Everyone." The lobbyists were urged to participate: "WE DO NEED BODIES—they must be DRESSED DOWN, appear to be REAL WORKER types, etc."[113]

The speech at a media event is not a classical oration or even a cogent address with a beginning, middle, and end. It is an informal talk that emphasizes a few key words or phrases or sentences—almost slogans, because television editors allot time for only a short **sound bite**. And the amount of time is less and less. In 1968, the average sound bite of a presidential contender on the evening news was 42 seconds; since then, it has dropped to 8 seconds.[114]

Speechwriters plan accordingly. "A lot of writers figure out how they are going to get the part they want onto television," a former presidential aide explained. "They think of a news lead and write around it. And if the television lights don't go on as the speaker is approaching that news lead, he skips a few paragraphs and waits until they are lit to read the key part."[115] This approach doesn't produce coherent speeches, but the people watching on television won't know, and the few watching in person don't matter because they are just props.

 ## Thinking about Democracy

The head of CBS News said, "I'd like just once to have the courage to go on the air and say that such and such a candidate went to six cities today to stage six media events, none of which had anything to do with governing America."[1] Do you agree, or do you think that these media events are beneficial for the voters in a democracy?

[1]David Halberstam, "How Television Failed the American Voter," *Parade*, January 11, 1981, 8

Corbis

After the initial phase of the Iraq War in May 2003, President Bush used the opportunity for a dramatic photo op designed for his reelection campaign. Landing a navy jet on an aircraft carrier off the California coast, he swaggered across the deck, sporting a flight suit and backslapping the sailors. Standing under a banner that proclaimed "Mission Accomplished," he (prematurely) announced the end of major combat in Iraq.

President Reagan's aides were quite skillful at staging media events. Weeks before his appearance, his aides sent advance agents to prepare the "stage"—the exact location, backdrops, lighting, and sound equipment. A trip to Korea was designed to show "the commander-in-chief on the front line against communism." An advance man went to the demilitarized zone separating North and South Korea and negotiated with the Army and Secret Service for the most photogenic setting. He demanded that the president be allowed to use the most exposed bunker, which meant that the army had to erect telephone poles and string thirty thousand yards of camouflage netting to hide Reagan from North

News photo of President Reagan in Korea, staged to reflect "American strength and resolve."

Korean sharpshooters. The advance man also demanded that the army build camera platforms for the media on an exposed hill that offered a dramatic angle to film Reagan surrounded by sandbags. Although the Secret Service wanted sandbags up to Reagan's neck, the advance man insisted that they be no more than four inches above his navel so viewers would get a clear picture of the president wearing his flak jacket and demonstrating "American strength and resolve."[116]

Perhaps more than any other source of news, media events illustrate the reliance of politicians on television and of television on politicians.

Adversarial Relationship

Although the relationship between the media and politicians is symbiotic in some ways, it is adversarial in others. Ever since George Washington's administration, when conflicts developed between Federalists and Jeffersonians, the media have attacked politicians and politicians have attacked the media. During John Adams's administration, Federalists passed the Sedition Act of 1798, which prohibited much criticism of the government. Federalist officials used the act to imprison Jeffersonian editors. Despite this history, once Jefferson himself was elected president, he called for "a union of opinion." Frustrated, he suggested that newspapers be divided into four sections—Truths, Probabilities, Possibilities, and Lies.[117] Later, President Andrew Jackson proposed a law to allow the government to shut down "incendiary" newspapers. Even now, a former press secretary commented, "There are very few politicians who do not cherish privately the notion that there should be some regulation of the news."[118]

Historically the relationship between the media and politicians was more symbiotic than adversarial, but the relationship became increasingly adversarial after the Vietnam War and the Watergate scandal fueled cynicism about government's performance and officials' honesty.[119] Many reporters, according to the editor of the *Des Moines Register*, "began to feel that no journalism is worth doing unless it unseats the mighty."[120] New reporters especially began to feel this way. Sen. Alan Simpson (R-Wyo.) asked the daughter of old friends what she planned to do after graduating from journalism school. "I'm going to be one of the hunters," she replied. When he asked, "What are you going to hunt?" she answered, "People like you!"[121] The relationship has become even more adversarial with the heightened partisanship in American politics and in many media in the 1990s and 2000s.

Politicians, fearing that they will say something that will be used against them, have restricted reporters' access. Reporters, worrying that they will not get the information they need to do their job, have complained that politicians are not accessible. By George W. Bush's presidency, one lamented, "The idea of a truly open press conference, an unscripted political debate, a leisurely and open...conversation between political leaders, or even a one-on-one interview between a member of the press and an undefended politician had become almost quaint in conception."[122]

At the same time, politicians have become more sophisticated in their efforts to **spin** the media—to portray themselves and their programs in the most favorable light and to shade the truth. Politicians' spin prompts reporters to become more cynical. Reporters' cynicism prompts politicians to escalate their efforts to spin the media, which prompts reporters to escalate their comments that politicians are insincere or dishonest. And so the cycle continues.

The increasingly adversarial relationship is also due to other factors mentioned earlier in the chapter. There are so many media, with so much space or time to fill, that they have a voracious appetite for news and a strong incentive to compete against each other for something "new." As a result, they often magnify trivial things. And because the fringe media now play a more prominent role, and because their stories eventually appear in the mainstream media, all media pay more attention to politicians' personal shortcomings with sex, drugs, and alcohol and raise more questions about politicians' "character" than they ever used to.[123] And when there are no concerns about politicians' personal shortcomings, the media pay more attention to their offhand comments or body language—for example, whether President Obama bowed too deeply when he met the Japanese emperor.

President Obama chastises journalists for their frenzied reporting of such trivial matters, calling media coverage "a circus" and comparing cable news in particular to WWF Wrestling—phony fights over nothing of substance.[124] But his charges have had no effect on the coverage.

After repeated salvos of harsh criticism from Fox News, Obama refused to make administration officials available for interviews with Fox reporters. The administration claimed that Fox is an opinion organ rather than a news network. The move, however, was counterproductive. Other organizations, perhaps seeing themselves in Fox's position in the future, pressured the administration to end the freeze-out, and Fox's commentators used the fight to further enflame their viewers.[125]

Despite the combative attitude of some media, relatively few reporters engage in investigative journalism.[126] Before

Franklin D. Roosevelt Library

Because of polio, Franklin Roosevelt spent much of his life in a wheelchair, but journalists didn't photograph him in it. A friend snapped this rare picture. Journalists were reluctant to photograph or write about officials' afflictions or behaviors until the Watergate scandal ushered in a new era of more personal coverage.

Hurricane Katrina, reporters failed to notice that the Federal Emergency Management Administration (FEMA) was headed by political hacks rather than by officials experienced in disaster response. Nor did reporters question why a study found that employees' morale at FEMA was lower than that at any other federal agency.[127] And before the credit bubble burst, which led to the recession of 2008 and 2009, business reporters failed to notice the risky investments of the big banks or the lax regulation by the federal government.[128]

BIAS OF THE MEDIA

Every night, Walter Cronkite, former anchor for *CBS Evening News*, signed off, "And that's the way it is," implying that the network held a huge mirror to the world and returned a perfect reflection to its viewers, without selection or distortion. But the media do not hold a mirror. They hold a searchlight that seeks and illuminates some things instead of others.[129]

From all the events that occur in the world every day, the media can report only a handful as the news of the day. Even the *New York Times*, whose motto is "All the News That's Fit

to Print," cannot include all the news. The media must decide what events are newsworthy. They must decide where to report these—on the front page or at the top of the newscast, or in a less prominent position. Then they must decide how to report them.

When the Wright brothers invited reporters to Kitty Hawk, North Carolina, to observe the first airplane flight in 1903, none considered it newsworthy enough to cover. After the historic flight, only seven American newspapers reported the flight, and only two reported it on their front page.[130]

In making these decisions, it would be natural for journalists' attitudes to affect their coverage. As one reporter acknowledged, he writes "from what he hears and sees and how he filters it through the lens of his own experience. No reporter is a robot."[131]

Political Bias

Early newspapers were established by political parties and echoed the views of their party. Later newspapers were independent, but they too advocated one side or the other. The attitudes of publishers, editors, and reporters seeped—sometimes flooded—into their prose.

But the papers gradually abandoned their editorializing and adopted the **practice of objectivity** to attract and retain as many readers as possible. This means that in news stories (not in editorials or columns) they try to present the facts rather than their opinions. When the facts are in dispute, they try to present the positions of both sides. They are reluctant to evaluate these positions. Even when one side makes a false or misleading statement, they are hesitant to notify their readers. Instead, they rely upon the other side to make a counter statement and hope that their readers can discern which statement is correct.

Although most mainstream media today follow the practice of objectivity, the public still thinks the press is biased. Many people think the press is "out to get" the groups they identify with. Executives believe the press is out to get businesses, and laborers believe it is out to get unions. Conservatives believe the press is biased against conservatives, and liberals believe it is biased against liberals. Republicans believe the press is biased against Republicans, and Democrats believe it is biased against Democrats.[132] For many people, the press is a scapegoat, "a secular devil for our times."[133]

Indeed, the public is more critical today, when mainstream media at least attempt to be objective, than in the past, when the media did not even pretend to be. Back then, citizens could read whichever local paper reflected their own biases. Now, as local newspapers and television stations have given way to national newspapers and networks, and as independently owned newspapers and television stations have given way to large chains and conglomerates, people have fewer choices among the traditional media, so they have less opportunity to follow any media that reflect their views. Many people are dissatisfied with today's relatively balanced coverage in the mainstream media. Their irritation has led to the rise of more slanted media, which some people with strong views prefer. And because the mainstream media don't reflect the partisan views of the slanted media they prefer, people think the mainstream media are biased.

To assess the presence and the direction of **political bias** today, it is necessary to examine the differences in coverage by the advocacy media and the mainstream media and the differences in coverage of elections and issues, including domestic policies and international policies.

Bias in the Advocacy Media

Some media don't try to be neutral. Advocacy media intentionally tilt one way or the other and seek an audience of people who share their views. Advocacy media can be found at both ends of the political spectrum, though far more are conservative than liberal.

Because conservatives perceived a liberal bias in the mainstream media, they established their own media in the 1980s and 1990s. This vocal complex includes newspapers such as the *New York Post*, the *Washington Times*, and the *Wall Street Journal* (especially its editorial pages), various magazines, numerous radio and television talk shows, and Internet websites, plus a network of columnists, commentators, and think tanks. Their business model is to provoke indignation toward political opponents and distrust of mainstream media, so their conservative audience will keep reading and listening.[134]

These conservative journalists see themselves as part of an ideological movement and members of the same team. Some attend regular meetings of conservative activists in which the participants set priorities, plan strategy, and identify talking points for their cause.[135] If a conservative journalist criticizes a conservative politician or the Republican Party, he may be shunned by fellow conservative journalists.[136]

In contrast, the mainstream journalists see themselves as objective reporters rather than as members of any team. They pride themselves on their independence. Those who are liberal criticize liberals and Democrats as well as conservatives and Republicans to demonstrate their impartiality. During the years in which conservatives established their own media, mainstream journalists offered relentless criticism of Bill Clinton and snide portrayals of Al Gore and John Kerry.[137] Today they offer regular criticism of Barack Obama.

The role of conservative journalists in talk radio has been especially powerful. The expansion of talk radio began in the 1980s, when the daytime television audience was mostly female and the daytime radio audience was mostly male, and a gender gap emerged in political preferences, with men becoming more conservative and women remaining more liberal. A backlash against feminism and affirmative action developed among middle-class and lower-middle-class whites, especially the men. During these years, a few large chains, with conservative owners, bought out many stations. To capture conservative male listeners and convey their own political views at the same time, they adopted a talk radio format with conservative hosts.[138]

Today, more than thirteen hundred talk stations fill the airwaves, and about a fifth of American adults consider talk radio

their primary source for news.[139] The vast majority of shows are hosted by conservative commentators,[140] such as Rush Limbaugh, Sean Hannity, Glenn Beck, Bill O'Reilly, G. Gordon Liddy,[141] Oliver North, and numerous others.[142] The Republican National Committee has a Radio Services Department that provides talking points to these hosts every day so that they will reinforce the Republican message.[143] According to one analysis, 91 percent of the talk on the 257 news/talk stations owned by the top five chains was conservative; only 9 percent was liberal.[144]

To titillate his conservative male audience, Rush Limbaugh called a Georgetown law student a "slut" and a "prostitute" and suggested she film her private sex life for the entertainment of others. The woman had testified in Congress on behalf of health insurance that covered contraceptives.

The conservative advocacy media also include Fox News, the first major network to narrowcast rather than broadcast.[145] Owned by a conservative media mogul and operated by a former Republican consultant, Fox appeals to conservatives

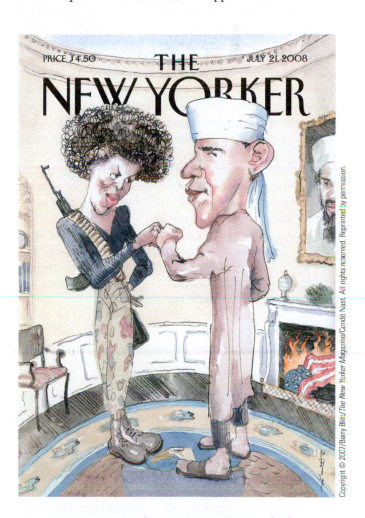

After Internet sites and Fox News questioned Obama's Christianity and his patriotism, a cartoonist depicted Barack and Michelle Obama as radical Muslims bent on destroying America. Through exaggeration, the cartoonist lampooned the false accusations. Some Obama supporters, however, thought the cartoon reinforced the damning perceptions many Americans held.

disenchanted with the mainstream media.[146] The network airs a combination of news and commentary. It blurs the two by alternating its newscasts with commentary programs and also by inserting frequent commentary into its newscasts. The network routinely follows the talking points of the Republican National Committee.[147]

Although Fox claims to be "fair and balanced" and "spin free," this is a marketing strategy to attract conservative viewers. Fox offers them conservative commentary but with the reassurance that this commentary is fact rather than opinion.[148]

During the presidential campaign in 2004, Fox repeatedly called for President Bush's reelection. In 2008, the network questioned Obama's patriotism and compared the candidate to Karl Marx—the communist theorist who called religion the "opiate" of the people.[149] Fox also compared Obama to Nazi leader Adolf Hitler, Soviet dictator Joseph Stalin, and Chinese chairman Mao Zedong, all leaders of authoritarian nations who murdered millions, as well as to Cuban leader Fidel Castro and to the Iraqi insurgents. When Barack and Michelle Obama bumped fists, Fox's E. D. Hill speculated that the gesture could be a "terrorist fist jab." During Obama's presidency, Fox aggressively opposed his policies[150] and actively promoted—not simply reported—the Tea Party protests against the president and his policies.[151] During his presidency and his campaign for reelection, Fox regularly coordinated attacks on Obama, with newscaster after newscaster and commentator after commentator making and reinforcing the same criticisms. The Fox newscast became the journalistic equivalent of a WWF wrestling tag-team match—an orchestrated fight in which the "bad guys" were certain to lose.

A former Fox correspondent said it was common to hear producers remind reporters, "We have to feed the core"—that is, their conservative viewers.[152] A former Fox editor said he was instructed to look for "stories that cater to angry, middle-aged white men who listen to talk radio and yell at their televisions."[153] To satisfy such viewers, a Fox executive admitted promoting ideas that he didn't believe were true (for example, that Obama is socialist).[154]

MSNBC, which had competed with Fox News for conservative viewers, now positions itself, at least in the evenings, as the anti-Fox station to attract liberal viewers. It airs commentary from liberals who chastise both conservatives and President Obama when he compromises or adopts a centrist position.

The conservative media also include Christian radio networks, television organizations, and more than thirteen hundred radio and television stations.[155] These media address political issues as well as spiritual matters.

The advocacy media include many magazines and Internet websites on both the right and the left. Although liberals are well represented in magazines and Internet websites, the only advocacy medium they dominate is documentary films.[156] For example, Michael Moore's films, such as *Fahrenheit 9/11* and *Sicko*, also offer a combination of facts, opinions, and speculation, though from the left rather than from the right.

Bias in the Mainstream Media

Although the advocacy media are far more slanted, allegations of bias are leveled against the mainstream media far more often.

Conservative groups and commentators, especially, claim that these media are biased toward liberal candidates and policies.[157]

Journalists for the mainstream media are not very representative of the public. They are disproportionately college-educated white males from the upper middle class; disproportionately urban and secular, rather than rural and religious; and disproportionately Democrats or independents leaning to the Democrats, rather than Republicans or independents leaning to the Republicans. Likewise, they are disproportionately liberals rather than conservatives.[158]

Focusing on journalists' backgrounds and attitudes assumes that these traits color journalists' coverage. But several factors mitigate the effect of these traits. Most journalists chose their profession not because of a commitment to an ideology—according to veteran columnist David Broder, "There just isn't enough ideology in the average reporter to fill a thimble"[159]—but because of the opportunity to rub elbows with powerful people and be close to exciting events. "Each day brings new stories, new dramas in which journalists participate vicariously."[160] As a result, most journalists "care more about the politics of an issue than about the issue itself,"[161] so they are less likely to express their views about the issue. In addition, mainstream organizations pressure journalists to muffle their views because of a conviction that it is professional to do so and also a desire to avoid the headaches that could arise otherwise—debates among their staffers, complaints from their audience, perhaps even complaints from the White House or Congress.[162] Some organizations fear public perceptions of reporters' bias so much that they restrict reporters' private lives, forbidding any political activity, even outside the office and on their own time.[163] For these reasons, mainstream media don't exhibit nearly as much political bias toward candidates or policies as would be expected from journalists' backgrounds and attitudes.

To measure bias, researchers use a technique called content analysis. They scrutinize newspaper and television stories to determine whether there was an unequal amount of coverage, unequal use of favorable or unfavorable statements, or unequal use of a positive or negative tone. They also consider insinuating verbs ("he conceded" rather than "he said") and pejorative adjectives ("her weak response" rather than "her response"), and for television stories, they evaluate the announcers' nonverbal communication—voice inflection, eye movement, and body language.

Bias in Elections

Researchers have spent the most time examining media coverage of presidential campaigns. Their reports have found relatively little bias: the media typically have given the two major candidates equal attention, have usually avoided any favorable or unfavorable statements in their news stories, and have usually provided diverse views in editorials and columns, with some commentary slanting one way and other commentary slanting the opposite way. The authors of a study examining forty-six newspapers concluded that American newspapers are "fairly neutral."[164] Other studies have reached similar conclusions about various media.[165] An analysis of the data from fifty-nine studies found no significant bias in newspapers, a little (pro-Republican) bias in newsmagazines, and a little (pro-Democratic) bias on television networks.[166]

Media coverage of the 2008 presidential campaign was an exception to the rule. At least on television newscasts, Barack Obama received a boost. In the primary campaign, he garnered 75 percent positive (and 25 percent negative) comments, whereas Hillary Clinton got just 53 percent positive (and 47 percent negative) comments.[167] In the general campaign, Obama had a two-to-one ratio of positive to negative comments, whereas John McCain had the opposite—a two-to-one ratio of negative to positive comments.[168] Partly these differences were due to the fact that Obama was a novelty because of his race, his background, and even his temperament, and the media pay more attention to a novelty.[169] Partly these differences were also due to the fact that Obama ran an effective campaign, whereas McCain ran an inept one, and his choice of Sarah Palin as his running mate was repeatedly questioned on the newscasts. (Obama's running mate, Joe Biden, received light but balanced coverage.) Once in office, however, Obama's coverage was not as positive.

Overall, there is less bias than the public believes or the candidates feel. When candidates complain, they are usually objecting to bad news or are trying to manipulate the media. The strategy is to put reporters on the defensive so that they will go easier on the candidate or harder on the opponent in the future, just as sports coaches "work the refs" over officiating calls.

Yet the way in which the media cover campaigns can have different implications for different candidates. The media report the facts that one candidate is leading while the other is trailing, that one campaign is surging while the other is slipping. "We all respond like Pavlov's dogs to polls," an experienced correspondent explained.[170] This coverage has positive implications for those who are leading or surging—swaying undecided voters, galvanizing campaign workers, and attracting financial contributors—and negative implications for those who are trailing or slipping. It does not benefit one party over the other party in election after election, but it can benefit one party's candidate over the other party's candidate in a particular election.[171] People who support the losers consider such reporting biased. Journalists, however, consider it simply a reflection of reality.

Another habitual practice has different implications for different candidates. The press pays more attention to minor things that are easy to report—and easy to ridicule—than to substantive issues that are difficult to explain.[172] Hence the voluminous coverage about President Clinton's sexual affairs. Although reporters are willing to criticize or even ridicule candidates about minor matters, they are usually reluctant to challenge them on substantive issues. Doing so would require more knowledge about substantive policies or more nerve to draw conclusions about these policies than most reporters have.

Likewise, when covering presidential debates, the press pays more attention to style and tactics than to substantive issues—more attention to how something was said than to what was said.[173] Reporters act more like theater critics than helpful guides to confused voters. These practices don't reflect bias by reporters as much as they reflect superficiality in reporting.

There are two exceptions to the generalization that overt political bias in elections is minimal. First, the media usually give short shrift to third-party candidates.[174] Second, newspapers traditionally print editorials and columns that express opinions. In editorials before elections, papers endorse candidates. Most owners are Republican, and many influence the editorials. Since the first survey in 1932, more papers have endorsed the Republican presidential candidate, except in the elections of 1964, 1992, 2004, and 2008.[175] In columns, writers offer their own opinions. Although most newspapers provide a mix of columnists, the majority are conservative, according to a study of 96 percent of the country's English-language daily newspapers.[176] Sixty percent of the papers print more conservative than liberal columnists, while 20 percent print more liberal than conservative columnists, and 20 percent print an equal number. Evidently the Republican owners want their paper's columns, like their paper's editorials, to reflect their conservative views.

Bias against All Candidates and Officials

Some critics charge that a general bias exists against all candidates and officials—a negative undercurrent in reporting about government, regardless of who or what is covered. President Nixon's first vice president, Spiro Agnew, called journalists "nattering nabobs of negativism." Critics believe that this bias increased after the Vietnam War and the Watergate scandal made reporters more cynical.

There is considerable validity to this charge. Analyses of newspapers, magazines, and television networks show that the overwhelming majority of stories about government and politicians are neutral.[177] However, the rest are more often negative than positive.[178]

Emphasizing the negative conveys the impression that the individuals involved are unworthy of the office they seek or the one they hold. It ultimately conveys the impression that the political process itself is contemptible.[179]

"Larry, you can't blame everything on the media."

Bias toward Issues

The relative lack of bias in the coverage of elections (except for the negative tone against all candidates) doesn't necessarily mean there is the same lack of bias in the coverage of issues. Because elections are highly visible and candidates are very sensitive about the coverage, the media take more care to be neutral for elections than for issues.

Domestic issues   There is some evidence that media coverage of social issues, such as abortion and gay rights, and of some other domestic issues, such as gun control, capital punishment, the environment, and homelessness, tilts toward the liberal positions.[180] At the same time, news coverage exaggerates crimes, drugs, and other urban pathologies that stereotype African Americans and, to a lesser extent, Latinos.[181] In this respect, new reports don't reflect a bias toward the left.

Popular television programs, movies, and records often promote social ideas or trends characterized as liberal, such as diversity, multiculturalism, acceptance of racial minorities, acceptance of casual sex, and disparagement of traditional religion. Conservative Christians, especially, feel that their beliefs are under daily attack by the "liberal media." However, television programs and movies also glorify violence and guns—and since 9/11, torture of suspected terrorists[182]—a bias that does not reflect liberal values. Moreover, television programs and movies rarely have their female characters choose an abortion when they face an unwanted pregnancy.[183] Popular television programs might have as much or even more effect on individuals' views than the news does. But this chapter focuses on the news media, not the entertainment media, which are beyond the scope of this text.

Although debates about bias revolve around liberalism and conservatism, the question actually should be reframed: does the coverage of domestic issues reflect class bias? Analysts insist that for domestic issues the most significant bias is not liberal or conservative but upper middle class over working class.[184] This bias usually favors the liberal positions on social issues and the conservative, or business, positions on economic issues.[185] It closely reflects the suburban origins, college education, and social class of most journalists, who are "unlikely to have any idea what it means to go without health insurance, to be unable to locate affordable housing, to have their children in underfunded and dilapidated schools, to have relatives in prison or on the front lines of the military, [or] to face the threat of severe poverty."[186] Thus, "media bias in our country is not to the left or to the right, but to the top."[187]

Foreign issues   The bias in the coverage of foreign issues is quite different from that of domestic issues. The mainstream media toe the government line, at least until it becomes obvious that the official policy isn't working.[188] The government line is often the conservative position.[189]

This bias was apparent after the 2001 terrorist attacks. The media not only quoted the president and other officials extensively, as would be expected, but also adopted the mindset and language of administration officials. An analysis of the editorials of twenty metropolitan newspapers showed that they echoed the president's rhetoric, magnifying our feelings of fear and portraying a conflict between values decreed by God and the evil perpetrated by the terrorists and their supporters. Like the president, the newspapers emphasized urgent action over debate and national unity over dissent.[190] The television networks also followed the administration, featuring patriotic logos and melodramatic music.

Some media went further. Some newspapers fired columnists who criticized the president, and television networks yanked programs whose hosts (Phil Donohue and Bill Maher) had liberal sensibilities.[191] CNN's head warned the staff, "If you get on the wrong side of public opinion, you are going to get into trouble."[192] The patriotic fervor diminished media coverage and therefore public awareness of important matters, such as Arab opinion, the conflict between the Israelis and the Palestinians, and the disagreements among the countries fighting terrorism.[193]

This bias was also evident in coverage of the Iraq War. In the runup to the war, the sources cited in television news were overwhelmingly pro-war—according to one study, 71 percent were pro-war, whereas only 3 percent were anti-war[194]—and the pundits appearing on television talk shows were heavily pro-war as well. Although there were snippets of doubt and clips of protests on television newscasts, there was no substantive debate.[195] (Ironically, Comedy Central's fake newscasts left a more accurate impression than the major networks' newscasts did.)[196]

CNN, with audiences around the globe, used two news teams to cover the war. One team, beamed to the United States, was overtly pro-war; the other team, beamed to the rest of the world, was more neutral.[197] Even "liberal" newspapers such as the *New York Times* and the *Washington Post* published administration statements without serious scrutiny.[198] In the runup to the war, the *Post* had 140 front-page articles making the administration's case for the war and only a handful questioning the administration's claims.[199]

The media conveyed, without examination, officials' assertions that there was a link between Saddam Hussein and 9/11. They also conveyed, without examination, officials' assertions that Iraq possessed weapons of mass destruction—biological, chemical, and nuclear weapons. For many people, these became primary justifications for the war. (See the box "What You Watch Affects What You Believe.") Yet no evidence of either claim has been found (at least as of fall 2012).

Throughout the war, the American media, compared with European and Middle Eastern media, sanitized the combat. They were slow to report negative news[200] and reluctant to depict the blood and gore—the reality of war—in both words and pictures of both Americans and Iraqis.[201] When the behavior by American soldiers at Baghdad's Abu Ghraib prison was disclosed, the worst abuses weren't covered by many news organizations.[202] The media sanitized the coverage because "the dirty little secret of much war 'news' is that much of the audience wants to entrance itself into emotional surrender, and news officials want to elicit precisely that surrender."[203] The media didn't offer grimmer reports and starker photographs until the insurgency and the lack of real security in Iraq became apparent.

Impact social, global, historical, economic, political

What You Watch Affects What You Believe

A majority of Americans have had serious misperceptions about important questions relating to the Iraq War, according to a study based on a series of polls. Respondents were asked whether world public opinion favored the United States going to war, whether there was clear evidence that Saddam Hussein was working with al-Qaeda, and whether weapons of mass destruction were found during the war. (Responses to the second and third questions are shown in Figure 3.) Respondents were asked what their primary source of news is and how often they watch, listen to, or read this source.

Respondents' misperceptions varied according to the media they followed. Those who watched Fox News had the most misperceptions, whereas those who watched public television or listened to public radio had the fewest.[1] The misperceptions were not due to people's paying little attention to the news. Just the opposite: those who watched Fox News more often had more misperceptions than those who watched it less often. Remarkably, as late as 2006, 50 percent of all Americans still believed that Iraq had weapons of mass destruction right before the war,[2] even though none have been found (as of fall 2012).

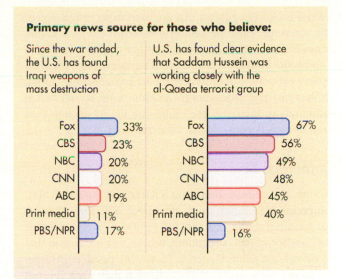

Primary news source for those who believe:

Since the war ended, the U.S. has found Iraqi weapons of mass destruction

Fox 33%
CBS 23%
NBC 20%
CNN 20%
ABC 19%
Print media 11%
PBS/NPR 17%

U.S. has found clear evidence that Saddam Hussein was working closely with the al-Qaeda terrorist group

Fox 67%
CBS 56%
NBC 49%
CNN 48%
ABC 45%
Print media 40%
PBS/NPR 16%

FIGURE 3: MISPERCEPTIONS AND THEIR ORIGINS

SOURCE: Program on International Policy at the University of Maryland and Knowledge Networks. Poll of 3334 adults, conducted January–September 2003, with a margin of error of 1.7 percent (www.knowledgenetworks.com/ganp). Copyright © 2003 by Program on International Policy Attitudes (PIPA). Reproduced by permission.

Not only do these results suggest biased or superficial coverage by some media more than others, but they also have policy implications. Respondents' misperceptions were related to their support for the war: those with the most misperceptions expressed the most support. Without the public's misperceptions, the Bush administration may not have had enough political support to start or continue the war.

[1]Researchers tried to control for the possibility that people presort themselves according to ideology by comparing the same demographic groups for each source and also by comparing similar political groups. For example, they compared people who planned to vote for Bush in 2004 and watched Fox News with people who planned to vote for Bush but followed other media.

[2]Charles J. Hanley, "Half of Americans Still Believe WMD Claims, Polls Show," *Lincoln Journal Star*, August 9, 2006, 1A.

As the aftermath of the invasion revealed serious flaws in U.S. policy, many media became more critical. The *Times* and *Post* acknowledged their one-sided coverage in the runup to the war and in the early stages of the war.[204]

Perceptions of Bias

We've seen that in the mainstream media there is minimal bias in favor of particular candidates or parties in elections, and there is some liberal bias in the coverage of social issues, some conservative bias in the coverage of economic issues, and usually pro-administration bias in the coverage of foreign policy. Overall, however, there is far less political bias than many people believe. In particular, there is far less liberal bias than many conservatives believe.[205] Why do so many people perceive so much bias?

As noted earlier, there is some negative bias against all candidates and officials. People sense this bias against the candidates or officials on their side but don't see it against the candidates or officials on the other side. In addition, people hear aides to the candidates or officials complain about the media without realizing that the aides are simply "working the refs" rather than sincerely lodging a complaint.[206] Also, people hear the steady drumbeat from interest groups and talk shows that the media are biased against their side. Eventually, they come to believe it. They don't realize that the leaders of interest groups and hosts of talk shows are just trying to get them riled up so they will join the group, make a contribution, subscribe to a magazine, or listen to the show.[207] Yet many people assume the existence of a pervasive bias in the mainstream media.[208] Studies show that strong partisans with strong views perceive more bias than average people.[209] When strong partisans evaluate stories that are actually balanced, they perceive a bias against their side.[210] Certain that their side is correct, they consider balanced coverage to be biased coverage because it gives their opponents more credence than their opponents deserve.[211] When strong partisans evaluate stories that are clearly biased toward their side, they see no bias or less bias than average people do.[212] They consider this coverage fair, because in their eyes it reports the "truth."

Even if people's perceptions are inaccurate reflections of media coverage, their perceptions determine which media they pay attention to and which ones they consider less credible and more biased.[213] As a result of conservatives' criticism over the years, some mainstream media have become cowed. CNN has ordered producers to include more conservatives than liberals in their stories.[214] CBS canned its anchor, Dan Rather, to mollify conservative viewers.[215]

Commercial Bias

Although the public dwells on charges of political bias, **commercial bias** is far more pervasive and important in understanding media coverage of politics. As Ted Koppel, former anchor of ABC's *Nightline*, notes, "The accusation that [the] news has a political agenda misses the point. Right now, the main agenda is to give the people what they want. It is not partisanship but profitability that shapes what you see."[216]

Reasons for Commercial Bias

As private businesses (except for public broadcasting), American media are run for a profit. The larger their audience, the more they can charge for their advertising. NBC's news division generates 40 to 50 percent of NBC's overall profit, with its entertainment and sports divisions dividing the rest.[217] Local stations' news programs also provide 40 to 50 percent of the stations' overall profit.[218]

With chains and conglomerates taking over most media, the pressure to make a large profit has escalated. In the 1970s, big-city newspapers expected to make a 7 or 8 percent profit; today, chains and conglomerates expect these papers to make a 20 to 30 percent profit.[219] Corporate executives worry that financial analysts will consider their companies a poor investment and mutual fund managers will refuse to buy or hold their stock if their earnings fall below those available "from investments anywhere else in the financial universe, from a shirt factory in Thailand to the latest Internet start-up."[220]

The pressure to make a profit and the need to attract an audience shape the media's presentation of the news and lead to commercial bias. Sometimes this means that the media deliberately print or broadcast what their advertisers want. CBS bowed to demands by Procter & Gamble that it drop episodes of *Family Law* dealing with gun ownership, capital punishment, interfaith marriage, and abortion.[221] Sometimes the media censor themselves. In 2004, VH1 and MTV pulled clips of, and refused to run ads for, the documentary *Super Size Me*, which shows what happened to a guy who ate every meal at McDonald's for a month. (It wasn't pretty.) They feared losing advertising from fast-food restaurants.[222]

Usually, though, commercial bias means that the media print or broadcast what the public wants, which is to say what

the public finds entertaining. This creates a "conflict between being an honest reporter and being a member of show business," a network correspondent confessed, "and that conflict is with me every day."[223] When Dan Rather was asked why CBS devoted time to the demolition of O. J. Simpson's house two years after his trial, Rather answered, "Fear.…The fear that if we don't do it, somebody else will, and when they do it, they will get a few more readers, a few more listeners, a few more viewers than we do. The result is the 'Hollywoodization of the news.'"[224]

The dilemma is most marked for television. Many people who watch news on television are not interested in politics; a majority, in fact, say that newscasts devote too much time to politics.[225] Some watch newscasts because they were watching another program before the news, others because they were planning to watch another program after the news. Networks feel pressure "to hook them and keep them."[226] Therefore, networks try to make the everyday world of news seem as exciting as the make-believe world depicted in their entertainment programs. One network instructed its staff, "Every news story should, without any sacrifice of probity or responsibility, display the attributes of fiction, of drama. It should have structure and conflict, problem and denouement, rising action and falling action, a beginning, a middle, and an end."[227] As one executive says, television news is **"infotainment"** (see box "Toppling Saddam").[228]

Consequences of Commercial Bias

The media's commercial bias has important consequences.

Sensationalism One consequence is to sensationalize the news. The anthrax infections that occurred after the terrorist attacks in 2001 deserved our full attention, but the media would not let up. Even after the initial flurry of reports, they ran one overwrought piece after another. *Time* magazine featured families who bought gas masks. The *Washington Post* wrote that America is "on the verge" of "public hysteria."[229] In fact, few people panicked. The media had sensationalized the story to prompt people to pay attention to the news.

Human interest Another consequence of commercial bias is to feature human interest over serious news. In 2005, the three main television networks devoted a total of 84 minutes to Michael Jackson's trial for child molesting but only 18 minutes to the massive genocide in Darfur, Sudan.[230] In 2006, *Time* magazine paid a reported $4 million for photos of Brad Pitt and Angelina Jolie's baby but let go two top-notch investigative reporters because the magazine couldn't afford them any longer.[231] In 2007, according to a search of news sources, 985 articles included the words *Britney* and *underwear*.[232]

The media's tendencies to sensationalize the news and to feature human interest over serious news lead to greater emphasis on scandal, sex, and crime. During President Clinton's terms, the media provided saturation coverage of the Whitewater scandal[233] and various other scandals, although a succession of special prosecutors could find nothing more damning than that the president had lied about having sexual relations with White House intern Monica Lewinsky.[234]

BEHIND THE SCENES

Toppling Saddam

Just months into the war, the screen showed a statue of Saddam Hussein, standing larger than life in central Baghdad, but with a rope around its neck. Then the screen showed the statue toppling over and excited Iraqis cheering wildly. It appeared that Bagdad had been liberated from Saddam and that Iraqis were grateful to the United States.

The scene was replayed over and over. Between 11 A.M. and 8 P.M. that day, Fox News showed the film every 4.4 minutes, CNN every 7.5 minutes.[1] Commentators called the event "historic," comparing it to the fall of the Berlin Wall and the collapse of eastern European communism. CNN newscaster Wolf Blitzer said the image "sums up" the war, symbolizing its success and its end.[2]

In fact, the event was only an intermission between the American invasion and the Iraqi insurgency and civil war. The fighting had barely begun.

Contrary to some assertions, the American military did not stage this scene as propaganda for people in the United States.[3] When a battalion of marines reached central Baghdad, they stopped at the square with the statue. Their presence prompted some Iraqis to gather and try, without success, to bring down the statue. The marines decided to help, using a vehicle with a crane. Western journalists, housed in a hotel on the square, filmed the scene for television news. The networks overdramatized the incident and misled the public.

With tight cropping of the scene and close-ups of the Iraqis cheering, the coverage gave the impression of "wall-to-wall enthusiasm throughout Baghdad."[4] The drama made great television. "Pictures are the mother's milk of television," a correspondent explained, "and it was a hell of a picture."[5] So network producers urged continuous coverage, which became the visual equivalent of an echo chamber. With more accuracy, print and radio journalists reported that the square was mostly empty, which could be seen from photographs taken from greater distance than the television cameras were positioned, and that the Iraqis weren't excited—they celebrated only when the television cameras came on. But the editors, who had been watching the TV footage, didn't believe their reporters. At the *San Francisco Chronicle*, an editor changed his reporter's story to say that "a jubilant crowd roared its approval" and onlookers shouted, "We are free! Thank you, President Bush!"[6]

The misleading coverage by the television networks might have reflected political bias, because

© Patrick Robert/Corbis

When Saddam Hussein's statue was toppled, Iraqis erupted for the television cameras. Their shoes symbolize their feelings that Saddam was beneath them—lower than their feet.

most American news organizations accepted the Bush administration's rationales for the war. However, the coverage most clearly reflected commercial bias. The close-up footage, with the statue tumbling and Iraqis cheering, was too compelling for the networks to resist, even when the reporters said the impression was misleading.

[1] Sean Aday, John Cluverius, and Steven Livingston, "As Goes the Statue, So Goes the War," *Journal of Broadcasting and Electronic Media* 49 (September 2005), 322.

[2] Most information in this box is from Peter Maass, "The Toppling," *New Yorker*, January 10, 2011, 42–53. These quotes are from page 50.

[3] A documentary, *Control Room*, shows Arab journalists concluding that the American military staged the scene.

[4] Maass, "The Toppling," 51.

[5] Ibid., 50.

[6] Ibid., 51.

The media frenzy over anthrax prompted some families, like this one in Chicago, to buy gas masks.

The media plunged into the affair with abandon.[235] The *Los Angeles Times* assigned twenty-six reporters to examine Lewinsky's life, interviewing babysitters and kindergarten classmates.[236] The networks interviewed a person who had eaten lunch with her three years earlier. The public was offered breathless reports about phone sex, the president's cigar as a sex toy, and the intern's dress with a semen stain. There was tittering about the "distinguishing characteristics" of the president's genitals—and speculation about how these would be proved or disproved in court.

Although the national media cover crime extensively, the local media cover it even more fully. Local television news is, in Ralph Nader's words, "something that jerks your head up every ten seconds, whether that is shootings, robberies, sports showdowns, or dramatic weather forecasts."[237] The saying "If it bleeds, it leads" expresses, tongue in cheek, many stations' programming philosophy. Thus crime coverage fills one-third of local newscasts.[238] A week before one presidential election, local stations in Columbus, Ohio, devoted more than twice as much time to various crimes than to the election, although the outcome in the state, and in the nation, was in doubt.[239] One station, however, did find time for an undercover investigation of a topless car wash.

A jaded reporter put it bluntly: "It doesn't matter what kind of swill you set in front of the public. As long as it's got enough sex and violence in it, they'll slurp it up."[240] (Even so, American stations don't go as far as the Bulgarian program *The Naked Truth*, which had women disrobe as they read the news.)

Conflict   Another consequence of commercial bias is to highlight conflict. Stories about conflict provide drama. Reporters, one admits, are "fight promoters" rather than consensus builders.[241] So reporters frame issues as struggles between opposite camps. After the murderous rampage at Columbine High School in Littleton, Colorado, the media posed the question, Was the incident caused by the availability of guns in our society *or* by the glorification of violence in the media? In this moronic debate, the media prodded people to choose sides, as though the cause had to be one *or* the other rather than a combination of the two or something else entirely.

The emphasis on conflict prompts the media to focus on the loudest and craziest Americans. A Florida pastor proposed an "International Burn a Koran Day" and then threatened to burn a Koran himself. Even though his congregation numbered only a few dozen, he commanded the media's attention. Such stunts make better television than sane people speaking sane thoughts in sane ways.[242]

Thinking about Democracy

In highlighting conflict and framing issues as though they are debates between two polar opposites, the media polarize the public. What are the implications for a democracy? What are the consequences for the efforts by politicians and parties to find common ground? To forge compromises?

Consequences for television   Commercial bias leads to additional consequences for television especially. One is to emphasize events, or those parts of events, that have visual interest. The networks have people whose job it is to evaluate all film for visual appeal. Producers seek the events that promise the most action, camera operators shoot the parts of the events with the most action, and editors select the portions of the film with the most action.[243] Television thus focuses on disasters and protests far more than their occurrence justifies, and it displays the interesting surface rather than the underlying substance of these events—for example, the protest rather than the cause of the anger.

Another consequence of commercial bias for television is to cover the news very briefly. A half-hour newscast has only 19 minutes without commercials. In that time, the networks broadcast only a third as many words as the *New York Times* prints on its front page alone. Although cable television has ample time, it follows this format, too, endlessly repeating the same stories without adding new information.[244]

Television stories are short—about 1 minute each—because the networks think viewers' attention spans are short. Indeed, a majority of eighteen- to thirty-four-year-olds with remote controls typically watch more than one show at a time.[245] Therefore, the networks don't allow leaders or experts to explain their thoughts about events or policies. Instead, the networks take sound bites to illustrate what was said. Although their correspondents try to explain the events or policies, they have little time to do so. A correspondent was asked what went through his mind when he signed off each night. "Good night, dear viewer," he said. "I only hope you read the *New York Times* in the morning."[246]

Consequences for election coverage   Commercial bias has various consequences for election coverage, whether by the print or broadcast media. The tendency to highlight human interest and conflict leads to **horse race coverage**, with "front-runners," "dark horses," and "also-rans." The coverage features candidates' positions in the race and their strategies and tactics while slighting serious examination of their policies. The race is more interesting and dramatic to most people, so it attracts more readers and viewers.

As a result, reporters often ignore the policy issues in favor of the horse race. After one presidential debate, Ted Koppel, the host of the former late-night newscast *Nightline,* dismissed the candidates' policies, saying, "You know, honestly, it turns my brains to mush. I can't pretend for a minute that I'm really able to follow the argument of the debates…. Parts of it, I haven't a clue what they're talking about."[247] Yet, it wasn't rocket science.

Although the race was a staple of journalism in the nineteenth century,[248] the proportion of election coverage focusing on the race has increased in recent decades.[249] In the 2008 presidential campaign, the major networks devoted 55 percent of their coverage to the race.[250] Because of the economic collapse, the networks devoted more time to policy debates than usual; even so, this was just 31 percent of their coverage.[251]

The quintessential feature of horse race coverage—reporting of candidates' poll standings—has increased greatly. Not only do the media report the results of polls taken by commercial organizations, but they also conduct polls themselves.[252] Nowadays, coverage of polls takes more space than coverage of candidates' speeches, and it usually appears as the lead or next-to-lead story.[253]

Even after elections, horse race coverage continues. When President George W. Bush proposed income tax cuts, *USA Today* printed seventy-eight articles about the cuts, but only six were about the content of the bill. The others were about the politics of the bill.[254]

Thinking about Democracy

What are the consequences of horse race coverage for our elections? Consider the level of voters' interest and participation in the elections and the level of voters' knowledge about the candidates.

Overall, commercial bias in the media results in no coverage or superficial coverage of many important stories. This, more than any political bias, makes it difficult for citizens, particularly those who rely on television, to become well informed. During the year before the September 11 terrorist attacks, al-Qaeda was mentioned only once on the networks' evening newscasts.[255] However, during this time a report predicting a "catastrophic attack" was issued by a government commission, and a statement warning that Osama bin Laden's network was the "most immediate and serious threat" facing the country was made by the CIA director at a Senate hearing. These dire predictions generated little interest among the media. Then, during the runup to the Iraq War and the years before the financial meltdown that led to the Great Recession of 2008 and 2009, the media again missed the real stories. They failed to serve the public interest. The chief foreign correspondent for CBS, who favors more substantive newscasts, remarked, "If I [had] to watch the news that you hear…in the United States, I would just blow my brains out because it would drive me nuts."[256]

SUMMARY

- The media scrutinize government and officials, examining their performance and probing any wrongdoing, and thus serve as a check and balance in our political system. The media can do this because they are independent of government and officials.

- Traditional media have been declining and new media have been increasing in popularity. Newspapers and major networks have lost readers and viewers, while cable networks and Internet sites have gained viewers and readers. In addition, financial pressures have made it difficult for traditional media to thrive and even to survive.

- Broadcasting appeals to a mass audience; narrowcasting appeals to a segment of that audience—a smaller group of like-minded people. Narrowcasting is becoming more prevalent because of technological changes, especially cable television, with more channels, and the Internet, with unlimited sites.

- Huge chains and conglomerates want to become the sole source of Americans' news and entertainment, so they have been buying small media companies and chains and conglomerates.

- At the same time, there's been an opposite trend—fragmentation of the media, with cable television, talk radio, and Internet sites pulling people away from traditional media. Even media such as the tabloids and comedy shows offer political news and commentary.

- The trend toward fragmentation of the media has serious consequences for government and politics today. It makes the news more accessible to more people, and it focuses more attention on some issues ignored by the mainstream media. However, it also makes the news less factual and more angry, and it contributes to different perceptions of reality for Americans, depending on which media people pay attention to.

- The 24-hour news cycle, which has an insatiable appetite, pressures journalists to find new stories or new angles of old stories and thus pressures politicians and officials to keep feeding journalists more information, whether significant or trivial.

- The media and officials have both a symbiotic relationship, meaning that they use each other for mutual benefit, and an adversarial relationship, meaning that they fight each other.

- The mainstream media are relatively even-handed in their coverage of elections. They demonstrate liberal bias in their coverage of some domestic issues, conservative bias in their coverage of economic issues, and a tendency toward pro-administration bias in their coverage of foreign policy. There is no overall liberal bias, though there apparently is some class bias, reflecting a preference for upper-middle-class values and concerns over working-class ones.

- Commercial bias is due not to political views but to the need to attract an audience and generate sizable profits. Commercial bias, unlike political bias, is pervasive. It is reflected in much of what we see and hear through the media.

DISCUSSION QUESTIONS

1. Andrew Card, President George W. Bush's chief of staff, rejected the role that the media have come to play. Card asserted that journalists "don't represent the public any more than other people do" and that news organizations "don't…have a check-and-balance function" (David Remnick, "Comment: Nattering Nabobs," *New Yorker*, July 10 and 17, 2006, 34). What do you think?

2. Why do journalists criticize media coverage of government and politics? List their criticisms—they appear in various parts of the chapter—and then determine which ones have the most merit.

3. Studies show that Americans, especially young people, are less knowledgeable about government, even though they are more educated, than previous generations. Which trends in media coverage may contribute to these findings?

4. This chapter is premised on the assumption that it's important for citizens in a democracy, which entails self-government, to be informed about candidates and issues before voting. Is this assumption, which comes from classical democratic theory, correct in a mass society with different educational levels and individual interests? People aren't required to understand architecture before entering a building or technology before using a computer. Should they be expected to understand, say, the politics of the Middle East before casting a vote? Should they be informed? Why or why not?

6 Interest Groups

Molly Katchpole started an interest group when she launched an online petition to make Bank of America back down from its plan to assess monthly debit card fees.

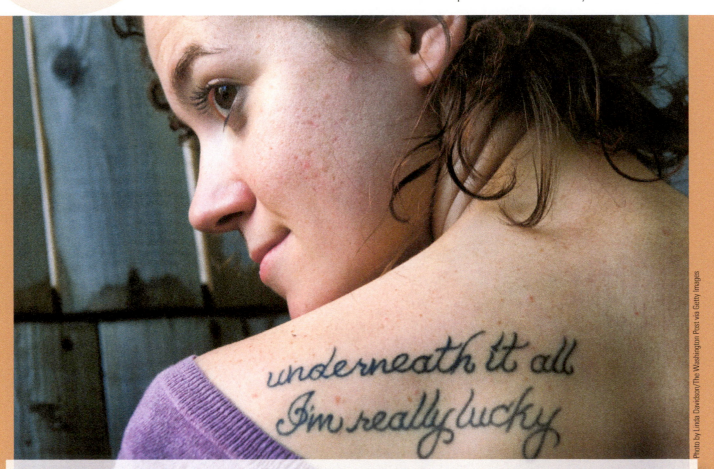

Photo by Linda Davidson/The Washington Post via Getty Images

LEARNING OBJECTIVES

1. Recognize the pervasive presence of interest groups and lobbyists in our political system, and the reasons why groups form and people join.
2. Distinguish between private interest groups and public interest groups. Cite examples.
3. Distinguish between multiple-issue groups and single-issue groups. Cite examples.
4. Describe the types of groups established to donate money to election campaigns, including PACs, Super PACs, and 527s.
5. Understand why in our system it is usually easier for groups to block action that will harm them than to initiate action that will help them.
6. Identify common tactics that interest groups use.
7. Explain why some interest groups are more successful than others.

TALKING POINTS

The average American drinks about 530 cans—50 gallons—of sugared beverages a year. That's almost a can and a half per day and a gallon per week of soft drinks.[1] Scientists think this consumption of sugared drinks, new in human history, is partly responsible for the epidemic of childhood and adult obesity and, in turn, the growing rates of diabetes in children and adults. Adults who drink at least a soda (or, as a midwesterner might say, a "pop") a day are 27 percent more likely than non–soda drinkers to be overweight.[2] Being overweight puts an individual at risk for a variety of serious health issues, including heart disease and stroke as well as diabetes.

For these reasons, many medical professionals, nutrition scientists, and interest groups promoting health and fitness have suggested a modest tax on soft drinks, perhaps a penny an ounce—twelve cents a can. Economists know that taxing a product results in fewer sales of that product. Thus taxing soft drinks would reduce consumption. Some estimates indicate that a tax of a penny an ounce would reduce consumption about 23 percent and reduce health care costs about $17 billion over a decade. At the same time, it would raise about $13 billion in tax revenues each year.[3]

Health activists and some members of Congress thought this idea would be a winner in the discussions about health care reform. Not only would it reduce consumption of something detrimental to our health, but it would also produce new funding for preventive medicine initiatives called for in the reform bills. Thus a product that contributes to our health care costs would help pay for some of these costs.

But of course this idea was anathema to the beverage industry, those who manufacture, can, and deliver soft drinks. The decline in consumption foreseen by health advocates as a very good thing was, naturally, seen by soft drink producers as a very bad thing.

So beverage lobbyists got busy. They launched a $58 million campaign to combat this incipient threat.[4] They enlisted fast-food purveyors, such as McDonald's and Domino's Pizza, who sell a lot of soda. They enlisted businesses that supply fast-food purveyors, such as paper producers, because these restaurants use huge quantities of paper for their cups of soda. Beverage lobbyists also argued that taxes on soda would lead to taxes on other foods. "It's us today; it's you tomorrow." This argument enabled them to enlist other food manufacturers to fight the tax. Even milk producers joined, fearful that chocolate milk might be taxed as well.

To legitimize their cause in the public eye, the beverage industry created a coalition with a public-spirited name, *Americans against Food Taxes*. And the coalition produced a series of television ads, one showing a woman with a grocery bag fretting, "Families around here are counting pennies to get through this economy. So when we hear about another tax it gets our attention.... They say it's only pennies. Well, those pennies add up when you're trying to feed a family."

In the end, the proposal for a beverage tax was dropped, despite the need—almost the desperation—of health care reformers to find ways to finance health care reform. The beverage lobby, with its coalition of other industries, was simply too strong. Members of Congress realized that they would be in trouble with multiple businesses in their district or state if they adopted the tax.

The tanning salon industry, however, isn't as large and powerful as the beverage industry and doesn't have as many allies. When the proposal for a soda tax was dropped, a tax on tanning sessions at tanning salons was suggested instead. Doctors have long criticized tanning salons, saying that the artificial rays in the tanning booths are likely more dangerous than the sun's rays as contributing factors to skin cancer.[5] To the surprise and consternation of the operators of tanning salons, this proposal passed, although it will generate only about $270,000,000 annually, far less than the $13 billion annually that a soda tax would have.

In the United States, everything from fruits to nuts is organized. From apple growers to filbert producers, nearly every interest has an organization to represent it. These organizations touch almost every aspect of our lives. Members of the American College of Obstetrics and Gynecology bring us into the world, and members of the National Funeral Directors Association usher us out.

Organizations that try to achieve their goals with government assistance are **interest groups.** Fruit and nut growers want government subsidies and protection from imported products; doctors want a rational system for reimbursement of health care costs; and funeral directors want limited government regulation and oversight.

The effort of an interest group to influence government decisions is called **lobbying.** Lobbying may involve direct contact between a **lobbyist**—or consultant or lawyer, as they prefer to be called—and a government official, or it may involve indirect action, such as attempts to sway public opinion, which in turn influences government officials.

People organize and lobby to promote their interests and enhance their influence. In our indirect democracy, citizens elect representatives to pass laws and make policies for them. However, elections focus on only a few issues, they occur infrequently, and many citizens don't vote. To supplement the ballot box in our political system, interest groups play an important role. They offer citizens the opportunity to join with others, and they monitor government action and make their views known to public officials. By joining and paying dues or making contributions to a group, citizens essentially hire private representatives—the group's leaders—to act on their behalf much as they elect public officials to do the same. "The modern government," one lobbyist observed, "is huge, pervasive, intrusive into everybody's life. If you just let things take their course and don't get involved in the game, you get trampled on."[6]

However, Americans today complain about interest groups, calling them "special interests" and insisting that Washington caters to them while ignoring the interests of average men and women. Some analysts agree that the constitutional checks don't prevent "special interests" from manipulating government contrary to the interests of the majority or the society as a whole.[7] Indeed, the groups' efforts often prevent government from solving critical problems, even when most citizens want government to address these problems. Ironically, as the groups are making government responsive to their members, they are rendering it unresponsive to the rest of society.

This chapter explores how interest groups work and sheds light on this paradox: although interest groups enhance the influence of average people by providing a way to participate in the political process and by making the government more responsive to them, at the same time they make government less responsive to society as a whole.

FORMATION OF INTEREST GROUPS

The Founders feared the harmful effects of interest groups, which they called "factions." James Madison's answer to the **"mischiefs of faction"** was fragmenting government through federalism, separation of powers, and checks and balances. These elements of the Constitution were intended to prevent a single group or small part of society from dominating or prevailing over the greater good.

Even so, interest groups arose. And as early as the 1830s, the Frenchman Alexis de Tocqueville, who traveled throughout the country, saw the tendency of Americans to form and join groups: "In no country in the world has the principle of association been more successfully used or applied to a greater multitude of objects than in America."[8] Even today, Americans are more likely than citizens of other countries to belong to groups.[9]

Why Interest Groups Form

Groups organize in the United States for a number of reasons. The ⚖ **First Amendment**, which protects the freedom to speak, assemble, and petition government, gives citizens the freedom to form groups, while the proliferation of governments and the extent of diversity in America provide the impetus for many groups to organize. Because our federal structure of government includes the national government, fifty state governments, and thousands of local governments, there are opportunities at each level for groups to develop and influence the government. In addition, our racial, ethnic, and religious diversity, which is greater than in most countries, leads to the proliferation of many groups to represent varying interests and conflicting views.[10]

In addition to these features, which distinguish the United States from other countries, groups form here and elsewhere because of social changes, economic pressures, technological developments, and government actions. When these disturb the status quo, groups form to cope with or benefit from the disturbances. Because historical changes come in waves, the formation of groups occurs in waves too, surging at some times, stable at other times.[11]

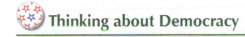

Impact social, global, historical, economic, political

The First Lobbyists

President Ulysses S. Grant had so little to do in his two terms following the Civil War that he often walked from the White House to the Willard Hotel, where he would sit in the lobby and watch the people who passed through. Although the hotel provided him a leather chair and a secluded corner, he was pestered by people with requests and petitions. Grant called them "lobbyists."

SOURCE: Hugh Sidey, "Outsize Slippers for Mr. Lincoln," *Time*, August 25, 1986, 24.

Social changes and economic pressures often lead to these surges. In the decades before the Civil War, debates over slavery led to the formation of abolitionist groups and, in response, to proslavery groups. In the decades after the Civil War, rapid industrialization led to the formation of trade unions and business associations. The greatest surge in group formation occurred between 1900 and 1920, when many groups formed in reaction to the shocks of industrialization, urbanization, and immigration.[12]

Another great surge occurred in the 1960s and 1970s. The success of the civil rights and antiwar movements spurred other groups to form that represented racial minorities, women, consumers, the poor, the elderly, and the environment. Then, in reaction to the success of consumer and environmental groups pushing government to regulate business, the number of business groups surged.[13] In these two decades, the number of groups increased by 60 percent, and the number sending lobbyists to Washington doubled.[14]

Technological changes also accelerate group formation. In the 1960s and 1970s, computer-generated direct mail made it easier to recruit members and raise money. In the 1990s, the spread of personal computers and the growth of the Internet facilitated communication among people with an endless variety of narrow interests. The Internet is particularly useful for those wishing to organize citizen groups on a low budget.[15] It is also useful for groups outside the mainstream who wish to operate anonymously. In the 2000s, the popularity of social media such as Facebook, Twitter, and YouTube made it easy for individuals not just to receive information but also to interact with like-minded others.

Government action also stimulates group formation. When government turns its attention to an issue, interest groups form and flock to Washington.[16] When government passes a law, people who are adversely affected organize to change the law,[17] while other groups spring up to defend it. In 1890, Yosemite National Park was established to preserve a spectacular stretch of the Sierra Nevada Mountains in California. Cattle ranchers, who wanted the land for grazing, proposed that the park be reduced by half. This prompted preservationists to form the **Sierra Club**, an environmental group, to block the ranchers' proposal, which it did. This pattern of action and reaction leads to continuous expansion in the number of interest groups.

Thinking about Democracy

Should the rights of individuals to form or join interest groups be restricted in a democracy? Should the right of interest groups to lobby be restricted?

Why People Join

Although individuals can enhance their political influence by joining an interest group, many groups find it difficult to attract new members. Some people lack a sense of **political efficacy**—the belief that they can make a difference. Instead, they feel that "I'm just one person. What can I do?" Even the people who possess a sense of political efficacy may not join because they're unwilling to bear the costs, such as the dues or their time and effort. They assume that the group will succeed without them, so they let others do the work. But they still expect to share the benefits if the group reaches its goal.[18] For example, if a group prods the government to reduce water pollution in a local river or lake, everyone who uses the river or lake, not just the members of the group, will share the benefits of cleaner water. This is called the **free-rider problem**.[19] Why should individuals join the group if they don't have to?

To overcome this natural human resistance, groups offer a variety of benefits—psychological, social, and economic—to attract members. One benefit is the psychological satisfaction that comes from doing good. So groups emphasize the worthiness of their cause and exaggerate the harm that will occur if their cause doesn't prevail. Groups also offer social interactions among fellow citizens who share similar interests. They host meetings, dinners, and other activities to create feelings of belonging and solidarity among members. The National Rifle Association (NRA), which lobbies against gun control, provides safety and training classes for new shooters and sponsors competitions for the entire family. Groups also offer economic benefits. AARP, formerly the American Association of Retired Persons, provides discounted drugs; health, home, and auto insurance; a motor club; a travel service; investment counseling; and several magazines. These services lure members and generate millions for the organization.

Library of Congress #LC-US262-83799

Preservationists formed the Sierra Club to protect the new Yosemite National Park, which cattle ranchers wanted to reduce by half.

Some people join groups because they are coerced. In a majority of states, lawyers are required to join the bar association, and employees in certain trades are required to join the labor union.

Which People Join

Although America is a nation of joiners, some are more inclined to join than others. Those with more education and income are especially likely to belong. They are more interested in the news and government policies, they can afford membership dues, they have the free time or flexible schedules that allow them to take part, and they have the intellectual ability and social skills that enhance participation. As potential members, they also appear more attractive and so are more apt to be recruited by groups.

Comparing people of similar income and educational levels, men are somewhat more likely to join than women, and whites are somewhat more likely to join than blacks. The elderly and middle-aged participate at higher rates than the young.

People who don't join are less likely to have their interests represented. For example, the poor, including many minorities, are less likely to recognize, or act upon, their interests in public debates over governmental policies. So the unemployed and uninsured, who need representation, are less likely to have effective organizations representing them, while the well-to-do, who have a vested interest in the status quo, do have vigilant organizations representing them.[20] Similarly, the young are less likely to recognize, or act upon, their interests than the elderly, who have strong organizations protecting Social Security and Medicare.

Because people with the least education and the least income are the least likely to join groups, they are less well represented in political struggles. Much of the time, groups don't adequately represent the poor, the working class (except for those in unions), and the politically disinterested. Instead, they disproportionately represent the well-to-do and their businesses. A political scientist's observation from 1960 remains valid today: "The flaw in the pluralist heaven is that the angelic chorus sings with an upper class accent."[21]

Sometimes middle-class lobbies do benefit working-class people, however. For example, the middle-class members of AARP protect the interests of the elderly in all classes. And although those who promoted health care reform—including Big Pharma, the pharmaceutical companies' lobby—weren't always thinking of the interests of the poor, the reform will provide significant benefits to poor people. In general, however, the popular saying "you snooze, you lose" applies to joining and supporting interest groups.

Have People Stopped Joining?

A widely publicized book, *Bowling Alone*, documents the decline in group membership in recent decades.[22] A variety of organizations, from labor unions to churches, PTAs, and bowling leagues, have experienced a decline, for several reasons.

More families today are headed by a single parent or by two parents who work outside the home. Women's lives especially have changed over the past generation, with most women now in the paid workforce while still carrying the largest share of household and child-raising activities. Once the backbone of many local educational, religious, civic, and political groups, women have far less time and energy to devote to these volunteer activities today than women did in the 1950s and 1960s. The entrance of women into the workforce also means that many men do more around the house and with their children than their fathers did. This too decreases the time and energy available for organized groups.

At the same time, technology, such as television, computers, and smartphones, has enabled us to create little islands of our own at our homes; we don't need to join others in person for entertainment. Figuratively speaking, we still bowl, but we bowl alone or we bowl virtually.

However, at the same time that formal membership in interest groups has decreased, membership in issue advocacy groups is increasing.[23] These groups solicit "members" who "join" by donating money—writing an occasional check to support the organization's leaders and activities.[24] These **checkbook members** contribute to the cause but don't interact, face to face, as members of the group.

Jim West/Alamy

The First Amendment protects interest group speech, even repulsive speech such as this message from a church in Topeka, Kansas, whose members believe that God is punishing Americans for tolerating homosexual behavior.

Thinking about Democracy

What implications does the decline in traditional face-to-face groups have for democracy? Consider the roles that interest groups play in representing people, fostering discussions, fashioning compromises, and forging relationships and trust among citizens. Also consider the ways that interest groups conduct their meetings, elect their officers, and decide their positions on issues. How do these procedures reinforce democracy? Do virtual groups fulfill the same functions in a democracy?

Individuals can also be virtual members of groups. They can learn about the activities of a group on the Web, or they can be virtual participants, sharing their views in blogs or social media such as Twitter or Facebook. After the BP oil spill in the Gulf of Mexico, a "Boycott BP" group sprang up on Facebook and had over 800,000 "members" a few months later. But the lifespan of such groups is likely to be short. Moreover, the nature of the Internet doesn't promote workable compromises on difficult issues. Web discussions can be abusive and divisive because anonymity loosens restraints on behavior. If you don't have to interact on a personal basis with others, you don't have the same incentive to be reasonable, let alone compromise.

TYPES OF INTEREST GROUPS

Interest groups come in various sizes and configurations. Some have large memberships, such as the American Federation of Labor–Congress of Industrial Organizations (AFL-CIO), a labor union with 9 million members. Others have small memberships, such as the Mushroom Growers Association with only fourteen members. Some have no members at all. Corporations, which act as interest groups when they lobby government,[25] have managers and stockholders but no members.

Some interest groups are formally organized, with elected or appointed leaders, dues-paying members, regular meetings, and established bylaws. Others are loose-knit, with no leaders and few rules.

Thus, interest groups can be distinguished according to their membership and their organizational structure. They can also be distinguished by their goals, as explained below.

Private Interest Groups

Private interest groups seek economic benefits for their members or clients. Examples include business, labor, and agriculture groups.

Business

Business organizations are the most numerous and, in the aggregate, the most powerful interest groups in Washington. Much of politics is essentially the interaction between business and government.[26] Businesses seek to maximize profit, whereas government, at least sometimes, works to protect workers and consumers from the unfettered effects of profit-seeking businesses through regulation of employees' wages and working conditions, product safety, environmental damage, and monopolistic practices. Thus business groups often oppose government regulation and usually tilt toward the right. (See Figure 1.)

Today, however, there is less confrontation between business and government than in the past. The Republican Party has long favored business, and since the 1990s the Democratic Party, anxious to compete for campaign contributions, has often favored business too.[27] In a capitalist economy, there are powerful incentives and pressures for politicians of all political persuasions to accede to, rather than antagonize, business, which is so important to the nation's economic success.[28] If the economy falters, politicians get blamed. So business usually does well regardless of which party occupies the White House or dominates Congress. Nevertheless, business usually prefers the Republican Party because of that party's more consistent opposition to regulation.

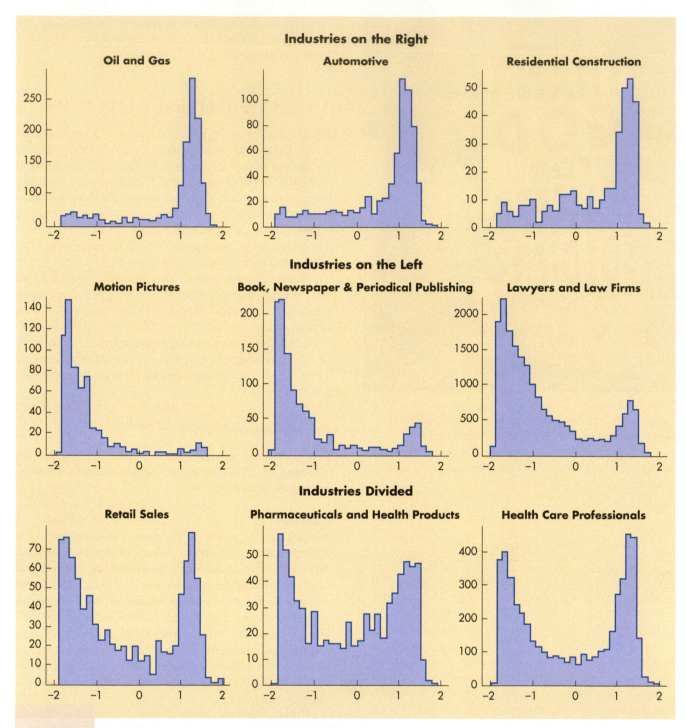

Industries on the Right

Oil and Gas

Automotive

Residential Construction

Industries on the Left

Motion Pictures

Book, Newspaper & Periodical Publishing

Lawyers and Law Firms

Industries Divided

Retail Sales

Pharmaceuticals and Health Products

Health Care Professionals

FIGURE 1: IDEOLOGICALLY ALIGNED INDUSTRIES Although business, in general, tends to sit on the right end of the ideological spectrum, some industries are on the left and other industries are split. (The legal and health care professions aren't usually included in the "business" category but are included in this figure for comparison.)

SOURCE: Graphs were derived from campaign contributions in the 2008 elections. Adam Bonica, "Ideologically Aligned and Ideologically Divided Industries," February 27, 2010. http://ideologicalcartography.com/2010/02/27/which-industries-are-polarized-and-which-are-just-polarizing/. Copyright © 2010 by Adam Bonica. Reproduced by permission.

Business power was evident when President Obama launched his health care reform initiative. At the outset, the administration cut deals with major health care groups—insurance companies, drug companies, and hospital associations. It offered concessions in exchange for support, or at least for promises not to oppose reform. (The administration sought to avoid the united front of opposition that killed President Clinton's health care proposal in the 1990s.) The major health care groups, however, fought specific provisions that applied to them (especially ones that would control costs), and once the legislation passed, they shifted their support to the Republicans in hopes of getting favorable regulations under the law. The pharmaceutical industry alone spent $188 million and employed more than 1000 lobbyists in its lobbying activities and campaign contributions in 2009.

Chamber of Commerce   Each industry has its own business association; at the same time, the **Chamber of Commerce** lobbies for business against regulation by government. Viewing itself as a "shadow-government policymaking body,"[29] it claims to represent all businesses—it boasts 300,000 businesses as members, 96 percent of which have fewer than one hundred employees—but it focuses primarily on the interests of big corporations.[30] It is the most powerful organization opposing progressive reforms, such as health care reform, financial regulation, climate change legislation, and President Obama's budget, which would phase out President Bush's tax cuts for the rich.[31]

The Chamber spends a huge amount of money on its lobbying efforts. In 2009, it spent $120 million. During one stretch in 2010, it spent $800,000 a day to defeat Obama's health care reform. Angry that the legislation passed, the Chamber bankrolled Republican candidates for Congress who vowed to repeal the law.[32] In the 2012 election, the Chamber spent more than $35 million on negative ads to defeat targeted Democratic candidates. Only the Democratic and Republican national committees spent more.[33] But only 5 percent of the Chamber's candidates were successful, leading members and observers to question the Chamber's strategy.

The Chamber finances its efforts with dues from its members and additional contributions from big corporations. A Chamber lobbyist explained how the organization's head, Tom Donohue, taught its lobbyists to solicit contributions: "First, you walk into the room with the CEO and you hit the key issues. Then you sit in closer to them. And you make 'the ask.' You look right into their eyes and say, 'As a result of what the Chamber is doing for your industry, I need a hundred thousand dollars.' Or, 'I need a million dollars.' And then you smile and shut your mouth. Your instinct is to start talking because you're nervous. Don't. Just smile and stare. And wait.... I tell you, there were people in that room who pissed in their pants."[34]

The Chamber's lobbying provides political cover for image-conscious corporations that don't want to risk alienating the public. They contribute money behind the scenes, and the Chamber wields its clout; the individual corporations don't leave any "embarrassing fingerprints" of their own.[35] Donohue admits, "I want to give them all the deniability they need."[36] In 2009, health insurance companies, which had struck a deal with the Obama administration to support health care reform, paid the Chamber $86 million to oppose the legislation.[37]

Although business groups tend to fight the government, sometimes business groups go head-to-head. Movie studios, music companies, and media organizations have pushed for legislation that would crack down on websites offering illegal streaming and downloading of movies and music. The

"What about business—which branch is that?"

legislation would make search engines like Google block copyright violators from appearing in search results. Such regulation raises the specter of other government regulation imposed on other Internet companies. Thus there's a battle between Hollywood and Silicon Valley—two powerful groups with big war chests and well-connected lobbyists.[38]

Labor

Labor unions seek government policies that protect workers' jobs, wages, and benefits and ensure the safety of workplaces. In recent decades they also have been part of a liberal coalition that has fought for civil rights, health care, and environmental protection. Unions channel money to political candidates, chiefly Democrats, though far less than businesses funnel to Republicans. In addition to money, they rely on their membership to distribute campaign literature, man phone banks, and canvass door-to-door to get out the vote.

Winning the right to unionize was a bitter struggle in the late 1800s and early 1900s. Before federal legislation gave workers the right to organize, companies often brought in strikebreakers—men and women willing to cross a picket line of striking workers and to work for the low wages the companies paid. Striking workers were often attacked by police or thugs hired by owners. Many large companies had a more potent arsenal than local police forces. In these confrontations, hundreds or thousands of workers were killed, but brutal incidents shocked the nation and led to the legislation that guaranteed the right to organize.

Union workers made more money than nonunionized workers and were more likely to get paid vacations, health insurance, and pensions.[39] Thus unions boosted workers' standard of living and helped many lower-class families reach the middle class. The union movement, and workers' economic status (relative to others' economic status), peaked in the 1950s and 1960s.

Manufacturing jobs, which had been the backbone of union strength, began to decline in the 1970s and have

IN MEMORY OF

IDA BRAYMAN

17 YEARS OLD

who was shot & killed by an Employer Feb. 5th 1913 during the great struggle of the Garment Workers of Rochester.

Copyrighted 1913 by U. G. W. Local 14 Rochester N. Y.

United States Department of Labor

This postcard commemorates the death of a seventeen-year-old woman murdered while striking for recognition of her union, an eight-hour day, and extra pay for overtime and holidays.

continued to decline since then. Union membership, which had been 35 percent of the workforce in 1955, diminished as manufacturing jobs disappeared. Although the labor movement tried to offset these losses by organizing low-wage service workers, such as those in hotels, nursing homes, and day care centers, union membership today remains low—only 7 percent of the private sector workforce (see Figure 2).[40]

Union membership has also declined because of antiunion attitudes in the South and antiunion practices by businesses throughout the country. Unions were never embraced as enthusiastically in the South as in the North.[41] Historically, white workers and black workers were reluctant to unite, and white employers were determined to prevent them from doing so. Southern-based companies have been especially antiunion, and their practices have been copied by other companies. Arkansas-based Wal-Mart, which is the largest private employer in the United States, sets the standards for other retailers.[42] When meat cutters at a Wal-Mart in Texas

organized, the company shut down the meat counters in the Wal-Marts throughout Texas and five neighboring states.[43]

Unions lack the political power to overcome businesses' antiunion efforts, which have been tolerated by government. The National Labor Relations Board, which is charged with enforcing labor laws, has been underfunded and understaffed and susceptible to business pressure.[44] If a company negotiates with a union in bad faith, the company is simply told to negotiate in good faith. If a company that isn't unionized illegally undermines a campaign by workers to unionize—by firing the workers who are the organizers or by shutting down some facilities—it is usually assessed a minimal penalty. If the workers are fired illegally, they will receive back pay but no additional compensation to deter their company or other companies in the future. The penalties are so small that corporations see them as merely a cost of doing business—a lower cost than tolerating a unionized workforce.[45] Thus business holds most of the power in the relationship, and Congress has made little effort to enforce or strengthen the laws.

Unions have also been hurt by global competition. Fearful of losing their jobs or putting their employers at a disadvantage in a competitive market, workers are reluctant to strike. Without the threat of a strike, there is little reason to heed workers' demands.

The labor movement has gained new members by organizing government workers and teachers. As a result, public employees now are a majority of all union members, and all union members are 12 percent of the total workforce (private and public) in the United States.[46] Public employee unions are loyal constituents of the Democratic Party. Teachers' unions contribute more money to political candidates, mostly to Democratic candidates, than any union representing another industry.[47] (Yet President Obama has championed school reform proposals, including charter schools and merit-based pay, that teachers' unions have opposed.)

Because of the party preference and financial contributions of public employee unions, they have come under attack by Republican officials. In Indiana, Ohio, and Wisconsin, Republican governors and legislators have made efforts to demonize and weaken these unions, especially their ability to raise money through dues.[48] (In Maine, the Republican governor underscored his views by removing the murals of working people from the state's Department of Labor.[49])

Although public employee unions have reinvigorated the labor movement, labor still lags far behind business in its ability to influence government. Its shrunken membership has reduced its political clout.[50] And its heavy concentration in a small number of states—84 percent of private sector union members are located in just twelve states[51]—has limited its political influence to those states. It has not been able to influence the national government.

Labor's decline has led to consequences beyond the unions and their members. When unions were stronger, they pushed for progressive policies for the nation. They were "on the front lines of every major economic battle of the mid-century," from the expansion of Social Security in the 1950s to the creation of Medicare in the 1960s.[52] Their decline,

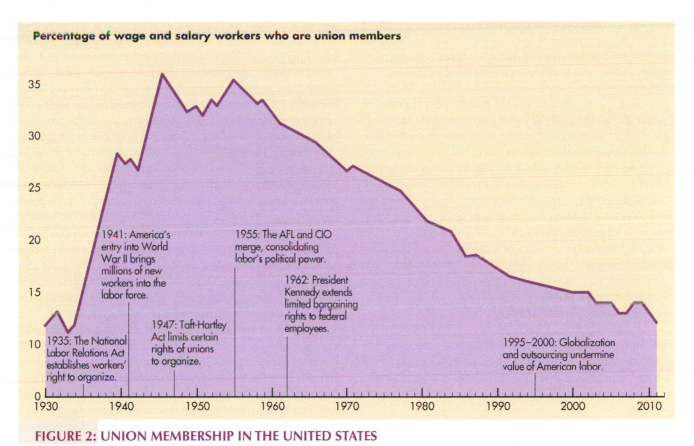

Percentage of wage and salary workers who are union members

1941: America's entry into World War II brings millions of new workers into the labor force.

1935: The National Labor Relations Act establishes workers' right to organize.

1947: Taft-Hartley Act limits certain rights of unions to organize.

1955: The AFL and CIO merge, consolidating labor's political power.

1962: President Kennedy extends limited bargaining rights to federal employees.

1995–2000: Globalization and outsourcing undermine value of American labor.

FIGURE 2: UNION MEMBERSHIP IN THE UNITED STATES

SOURCE: U.S. Census Bureau, *Statistical Abstract of the United States,* online at www.census.gov/prod/www/statistical-abstract-02.html.

according to one study, has led to one-fifth to one-third of the increase in economic inequality in the country since the 1970s.[53] When the recession hit in 2009, labor unions weren't strong enough to get the government to adopt a "jobs bill" that would combat the high levels of unemployment.[54] The unemployed were almost invisible to government policy makers.[55]

Labor's decline may also have led to a decline in voter turnout in elections. Unions engage workers with politics, helping members to identify issues of concern and understand the politics involved, as well as getting members to turn out for elections. With fewer members, unions have fewer get-out-the-vote drives, fewer voter education pamphlets, fewer union advertisements, and fewer union workers talking to relatives, friends, and neighbors about the election.[56]

Agriculture

Agricultural organizations are important in agricultural policy making. Large groups address general farm policy, and hundreds of commodity organizations, representing commodities such as cattle, milk, cotton, wool, and tobacco, promote particular products. Large agribusiness firms such as Cargill and Archer-Daniels-Midland also have influential lobbies in Washington.

Ag groups often compete with each other. The Humane Society and animal rights groups negotiated with major egg companies, who produce 95 percent of the eggs sold in the country, a proposal that would mandate better treatment for chickens—more space and other accommodations.[57] Animal rights groups wanted more humane treatment, and the egg producers wanted one national standard rather than multiple state standards to follow. Despite this rare agreement among groups that often oppose each other, the proposed legislation didn't breeze through Congress. It was fought by beef producers, hog producers, and dairy farmers, who feared that such a law would start a trend that would affect treatment of their animals too.[58]

Because American agriculture is dominated by agribusiness and large corporate farms, agriculture groups are dominated by these interests today. Although lobbyists invoke the small farmer and the family farm in their public appeals—they talk about the need to "save" the family farmer—they ask Congress for subsidies that go primarily to large corporate enterprises. Government spends more than $20 billion subsidizing crop production, or in some situations nonproduction, and most of this money goes to the largest and wealthiest—usually the corporate—farms.[59]

Public Interest Groups

While nearly all groups, even private groups seeking financial gain, think they are pursuing the "public interest," **public interest groups** are those that work for a cause that extends beyond the members of the group. Amnesty International lobbies for the rights of political prisoners around the world even though its members aren't prisoners. The National Taxpayers Union lobbies for reduced taxes; although its members will receive lower taxes if it succeeds, other taxpayers will too.

The term *public interest* doesn't mean that a majority of the public favors the goals of these groups or that their goals are good for all or even most people. Both pro-choice and pro-life groups in the abortion debate are public interest groups, though members of each side don't believe for a minute that members of the other are working in the public interest.

Public interest groups increased dramatically during the 1960s and 1970s.[60] Today there are at least 2500 public interest groups with 40 million members.[61]

Public interest groups can be classified as multiple- or single-issue groups.

Multiple-Issue Groups

Multiple-issue groups address a range of issues.

Racial and ethnic groups   Organizations promoting the interests of racial and ethnic minorities address various issues of concern to racial and ethnic minorities. Chapter 14 discusses these organizations and their role in the civil rights movement.

Women's groups   Groups advocating women's equality range from large, mass-based organizations interested in a number of issues to smaller ones focused on a few. The National Organization for Women (NOW), the largest and most prominent, has 250,000 members and chapters in each state.[62] It lobbies at the national, state, and local levels for a number of issues, including reproductive freedom and economic rights. NOW's success spurred the creation of smaller, conservative groups such as the Independent Women's Forum, which opposes government programs to achieve gender equality.[63] By far the most successful group lobbying for women's election to national office is EMILY's List—*EMILY* stands for Early Money Is Like Yeast (it makes the "dough" rise). The group recruits, trains, and funds pro-choice Democratic women to run for public office. Pro-life and Republican groups promoting women candidates also exist, but none is nearly as successful.[64] Chapter 14 also discusses women's groups and their role in the equal rights movement.

Gay and lesbian groups   Organizations promoting the interests of gays and lesbians fight for equal rights and more recently for same-sex marriage. The Lambda Defense Fund represents gay and lesbian students who have been discriminated against or harassed in school, and it educates teachers, administrators, and legislators about the challenges encountered by these students. (The box "The Origin of Gay and Lesbian Rights Groups" and Chapter 13 discuss these organizations.)

Religious groups   Many religious denominations have organizations representing their interests in Washington. Protestant

groups are found on the left and right as well as in the middle and speak out on a wide range of issues. Catholic groups have long been active in the antiabortion movement and have recently been outspoken on the immigration issue. Jewish groups have long supported liberal causes and stressed Israel's security. Muslim groups lobby for Palestinian rights and favorable policies toward Muslim countries. In the aftermath of 9/11, they have taken up the cause of fair treatment for American Muslims.[65]

Evangelical Protestant denominations—the **Christian right** (sometimes called the "religious right" to encompass conservative Jewish groups as well)—have been the most potent religious force in American politics.[66] Until the 1960s, evangelical Protestants believed that they should not involve themselves in secular government. But in the late 1960s, they came together as a movement to protest an Internal Revenue Service ruling jeopardizing the tax-exempt status of private religious schools that arose to avoid racial desegregation.[67] After this foray into national politics, the Christian right became intensely involved in the hot-button issues of school prayer, abortion, and homosexuality and the related issues of divorce, birth control, and traditional gender roles. The movement supports home schooling and opposes the teaching of evolution in public schools. The movement also opposes restrictions on religious symbols and practices in public schools and buildings. In general, it wants government's laws and policies to be based on Christian principles and to be acknowledged as such. It pushes its agenda through religious schools; religious media, including newspapers, magazines, radio, and television; and thousands of politically mobilized churches.[68]

The Christian right is closely linked to the Republican Party. In the South and Midwest, it is especially influential in state and local organizations of the party. The Christian right called for the resignation or impeachment of President Clinton after his affair with Monica Lewinsky was revealed.[69] The movement also mobilized its followers to vote for George W. Bush in 2000 and again in 2004. Without its support, Bush would not have been elected either time. With his election, the Christian right gained visibility and power in the highest reaches of government. Its leaders, emboldened by having conservative Republicans in control of all three branches of the federal government, flexed their muscles.

Since the 2004 election, the power of the religious right has waned overall[70] but continues to grow within the Republican Party. In 2012, more than 50 percent of the voters in Republican primaries were evangelical Christians.[71]

Some in the movement have become disillusioned because political activity has produced so little. Although their support has helped the Republicans control the presidency or Congress for much of the past quarter-century, their electoral successes haven't led to many policy achievements. The movement hasn't succeeded in eliminating abortion, reinstating school prayers, or reshaping school curricula to teach creationism or intelligent design along with evolution. Although the movement has defeated same-sex marriage in elections, it has been unable to prevent a number of state legislatures and courts from allowing same-sex marriage.

American Diversity

The Origin of Gay and Lesbian Rights Groups

In the 1950s, homosexuals usually kept their sexual orientation private. When their orientation did receive public attention, homosexuals were characterized as deviates and subjected to humiliation. They were often fired (as they still can be in many places).

Consequently, gays and lesbians, especially those who hung out together, were vulnerable to blackmail and police harassment. Following a raid on a gay bar in 1954, a Miami newspaper headlined its story "Perverts Seized in Bar Raid." A decade later, New York's liquor authority declared that a meeting of three or more homosexuals in a bar was reason enough for the bar to lose its license.[1] Through the 1960s, police entrapment of homosexuals was common, with plainclothes officers patronizing gay bars and waiting for propositions.[2]

The modern gay rights movement began when police raided a seedy bar, the Stonewall, in New York's Greenwich Village, in 1969. Run by the Mafia, the bar operated without a liquor license and served as a dope hangout. It was a popular meeting place for a diverse group of gay men, "including drag queens, hippies, street people, and uptown boys slumming."[3] That summer the city's police were cracking down on illegal bars, especially those frequented by gays, Latinos, and blacks. Several gay bars had already been raided without incident before the Stonewall, but each raid heightened the anger and desperation in the gay community.

A small police unit entered the Stonewall at 3 a.m. The employees were arrested for selling liquor without a license, and the customers were lined up and forced to show identification. The transvestites were separated for a "sex check." When a police van arrived to take away the arrested employees and transvestites, the crowd grew hostile and began to throw things—first coins, then cans and bottles, and even an uprooted parking meter. The police took refuge in the club, but the increasingly angry crowd pressed to break in, and the police drew their weapons. Soon lighter fluid and a match were thrown inside the building and a fire was started, although casualties were averted when police reinforcements arrived. The crowd, feeling empowered by its attempt to fight back, moved down the street shouting "gay power" and celebrating newfound strength and solidarity.

After the unrest ended, gays' sense of injustice and pride from the protests were transformed into an organization, the Gay Liberation Front. Its founders were determined to use radical means to fight discrimination against homosexuals. Not long after, politically moderate gays and lesbians broke from the Gay Liberation Front to form the Gay Activist Alliance. Later, other groups evolved that used mainstream politics and legal challenges to support the cause. By the early 1970s, gay pride parades, usually held in late June to commemorate the anniversary of the Stonewall raid, were common in major cities.

Changes in the status of homosexuals soon followed. In 1973, the American Psychiatric Association removed homosexuality from its list of mental disorders. In the 1980s, the AIDS tragedy focused media attention on the gay community and brought public awareness to the discrimination issue. Entertainers and celebrities who acknowledged their homosexuality, including some who suffered from AIDS, raised public consciousness. As more homosexuals "came out of the closet," they received more support from straight people.

---

[1] Robert Amsel, "Back to Our Future? A Walk on the Wild Side of Stonewall," www.gayastrology.com/stonewall.shtml (excerpted from *Advocate*, September 19, 1987).

[2] The source for much of this discussion is Eric Marcus, *Making History: The Struggle for Gay and Lesbian Equal Rights, 1945–1990* (New York: HarperCollins, 1992); see also Jeffrey Schmalz, "Gay Politics Goes Mainstream," *New York Times Magazine*, October 11, 1992, 18ff.

[3] Amsel, "Back to Our Future?"

Meanwhile, it has been unable to slow the shift in public attitudes that increasingly tolerate gay lifestyles and accept the idea of gay rights. Some evangelical Christians feel used by the Republican Party—useful as loyal foot soldiers when it's time to march to the polls, but ignored when the GOP's bigwigs set the party's agenda and priorities.[72]

At the same time, some evangelicals have edged to the left on some issues, expressing interest in protecting the environment, alleviating poverty, tackling AIDS, and promoting human rights rather than focusing mostly on abortion and homosexuality. A third even say that Christian political activism has hurt Christianity.[73]

Environmental groups   Earth Day 1970 marked the beginning of the environmental movement in the United States. Spurred by an oil spill in California, a "teach-in" on college

Olivier Douliery/ABACAUSA.COM/Newscom

Who knew that God had a position on taxes? Although the influence of religious conservatives may have peaked, they increasingly are aligning with economic conservatives to form a more powerful bloc of conservatives within the Republican party.

campuses became a day of environmental awareness for millions of Americans nationwide. A minority movement in the 1970s, the environmental lobby today is large and active, and its values are supported by most Americans.[74]

Some environmental groups, such as the Sierra Club, National Audubon Society, and Natural Resources Defense Council, have permanent offices in Washington staffed with skilled professionals.[75] Other groups, such as Greenpeace, Earth First!, and Sea Shepherds, which seek a green cultural revolution, shun conventional lobbying in favor of confrontation. They are less willing to compromise with businesses and polluters.

Ideology-focused groups   In addition to the categories of public interest groups already addressed, there are a number of prominent and powerful multiple-issue groups with a broader focus than the previous ones. These groups tend to be on the right wing or left wing of the ideological spectrum. They emerged in the 1990s as American politics became more polarized.

On the right wing are Americans for Tax Reform and the Club for Growth, which focus on economic issues and the scope of government programs and regulations. Both groups have small memberships and rely on big donations from wealthy individuals and corporations, including Wall Street financial firms. Americans for Tax Reform, run by Grover

Norquist, favors tax cuts and opposes any increases, regardless of the state of the economy or the size of the deficit. It pressures Republican candidates and officials to pledge never to raise taxes. The Club for Growth, run by Stephen Moore, advocates a flat income tax, in which everyone would pay the same percentage, rather than the current graduated income tax, in which the wealthy pay a higher percentage (at least on paper, if not in practice). The long-term goals of both groups are radical. Moore wants to eliminate all progressivity in the tax code. Norquist wants to reduce taxes, and thus the revenue for government operations, and to shrink government to the point where it would be half as large as it is today—or better yet, "down to the size where you could drown it in the bathtub."[76] Therefore, he says, "Even bad tax cuts are good."[77] The short-term goals of both groups are to force moderates out of the Republican Party and to elect conservatives in their place. These groups are highly influential within the Republican Party, especially in recruiting and funding candidates in the primary elections (when the parties choose their nominees for the general elections against the opposing party).[78]

On the left wing is MoveOn.org, which arose when congressional Republicans launched the impeachment of President Clinton. Husband and wife Wes Boyd and Joan Blakes opposed the impeachment. Instead, they urged Congress to censure the president and then "move on." From their home, they started the website MoveOn.org. Their postings struck a responsive chord among liberal Democrats angered by the impeachment drive and the political circus surrounding it. MoveOn surged during the presidency of George W. Bush, especially after the war in Iraq began. The organization vehemently opposed the war and sharply criticized President Bush and Vice President Cheney for initiating it, but the organization also targeted congressional Democrats for going along. During the presidency of Barack Obama, the organization opposed expansion of the war in Afghanistan and exclusion of the public option from health care reform. Throughout both administrations, the organization has reflected an insurgency against the Democratic Party's establishment, spurning Democratic officials considered too conservative or timid.

MoveOn boasts 5 million members. They don't reside primarily in the liberal citadels on the East and West Coasts. Many live in the suburbs and rural areas of the Midwest. Through MoveOn, they find a connection to liberal causes that they don't find in their communities.[79]

MoveOn sends members e-mails about perceived affronts and outrages in the news, and it solicits donations for commercials to broadcast on television. It also offers interactive opportunities, such as contests for members to create political commercials and to choose which ones to air.

Single-Issue Groups

Single-issue groups focus on just one issue. Because their existence revolves around that issue, they are zealous and reluctant to compromise.

The National Rifle Association (NRA) is an example. Its members are passionate in their opposition to gun control. They live in every congressional district, and they can be mobilized to contact their representatives in Congress. Although a majority of Americans have supported gun control for many years, the NRA has prevented Congress from passing most gun control proposals and has pressed for ever more permissive firearms laws. And it has prevented the Treasury Department's Bureau of Alcohol, Tobacco, and Firearms from strictly enforcing the gun control laws that are on the books.[80]

The NRA campaigned for the election of George W. Bush, with a high-ranking official boasting that a Bush win would guarantee the group's access to the Oval Office.[81] Indeed, the Bush administration was a close ally. Reversing sixty years of government policy, the administration adopted the position that the Second Amendment protects a right for individuals to arm themselves rather than merely ensuring the right of government to arm a militia to maintain domestic security.[82] (The Supreme Court, with Bush's appointees providing the votes to form a majority, agreed with the administration in 2008.[83] Chapter 13 examines the ruling.)

The NRA has been so successful that some politicians, especially in "red" states, where many residents resent gun control measures, have concluded that the risks to their election or reelection are so great and the probability of passing gun control measures is so small that it's prudent to go along with the NRA.

Yet the NRA may be expanding its focus. In recent years, the organization has become increasingly worried about the shrinking wildlife habitat available for hunting and fishing, as continued development near big cities has transformed fields and streams and as government energy policies have opened more federal land for oil and gas drilling. Some members now consider the dwindling habitat a greater threat to hunting and fishing than gun control legislation.[84]

The **pro-life** and **pro-choice groups** in the abortion debate are other examples of single-issue groups. Pro-life groups, such as the National Right to Life Committee, want a constitutional amendment banning all abortions. Because this is unlikely, they have pushed for federal and state laws restricting the availability of abortions, such as laws requiring waiting periods and parental notification or consent for minors. In some states, they have pushed for extra-stringent building codes or staffing requirements for clinics and intrusive and unnecessary medical procedures for women who want abortions. The goal is to make abortions more difficult for the woman, the doctor, and the clinic.[85] Like the Christian right, from which it draws members, the pro-life movement is closely allied with the Republican Party. In 2004, it got the Republican-controlled Congress to forbid the late-term abortions ("intact dilation and extraction") called "partial birth abortions" by the movement and the media.

Pro-choice groups, such as the National Abortion Rights Action League (NARAL) and Planned Parenthood, want to maintain a woman's right to choose. (Often identified with abortion rights, Planned Parenthood also advocates for access to birth control, sex education in schools, and quality reproductive health care for women.) These groups are closely allied with the Democratic Party.

In the early years of the abortion debate, the media referred to the two sides as "the anti-abortionists" and the "pro-abortionists." The "anti-abortionists" realized that it is better to be for something than against something, so they adopted the label "pro-life," which implied that the other side was "anti-life" (or "pro-death"). Then the "pro-abortionists" decided that it is better to be for something recognized as positive than for something considered as controversial as abortions, so they adopted the label "pro-choice." The media accepted the terms used by the two sides, although each side claims that the other side's label is misleading.[86]

Single-issue groups have increased in recent decades, alarming some observers and many politicians. When groups form around highly emotional issues and refuse to compromise, politicians can't deal with them as they deal with other groups, so the issues continue to boil,[87] consuming the time and energy of politicians at the expense of issues that many consider more important. On the other hand, single-issue groups often represent interests that aren't represented by multiple-issue groups.

Some single-issue groups form to influence foreign policy. Often these groups focus on a nation with which members have heritage ties or other emotional attachments. For example, Cuban Americans have formed many organizations

Log in to www.cengagebrain.com and open Course-Reader to access the full reading "Behind an Anti-Shariah Push," by Andrea Elliott.

David Yerushalmi is a Hasidic Jew and little-known lawyer living in Brooklyn. He founded the organization Society of Americans for National Existence, which warns Americans about the threat posed by Islamic law. Called "Shariah," this code guides Muslims' beliefs and actions, telling adherents how to live morally and achieve salvation. Yerushalmi believes that Shariah is more than a code to guide Muslim individuals; he believes that it is a political and legal system that seeks world domination. Although Shariah has seldom been used in American courts, Yerushalmi has sounded the alarm and drafted model legislation that would prevent state courts from using Shariah in their cases. In conjunction with conservative institutes and Christian groups, he has convinced half of the state legislatures to consider his legislation and three states to adopt it.

1. Is the Society of Americans for National Existence more like a grassroots group or an Astroturf group? For definitions of these groups, see page 143.
2. How has Yerushalmi persuaded state legislators to consider his legislation when there's little evidence that American courts are using Shariah?
3. If there's little evidence that American courts are using Shariah, what may be Yerushalmi's motive?
4. Is Yerushalmi's crusade a harmless folly, or may it have real consequences for American Muslims?

to influence U.S. policy toward Cuba, ruled for decades by Communist Fidel Castro and now his brother Raul. These groups have been the driving force behind preferential treatment for Cuban immigrants (special terms of entry and financial help from the government) and the maintenance of an economic embargo against the Castro government.

Another powerful group, AIPAC, the American Israel Public Affairs Committee, promotes close U.S.-Israeli ties. The membership of AIPAC includes Democrats and Republicans, united in their support of Israel, a democratic ally in the Middle East. The group has lobbied for financial support of Israel, which amounted to $3 billion in 2012. AIPAC supports the Israeli government no matter what its politics, leading to charges that AIPAC sometimes undermines U.S. policy and interests. In 2012, as concern grew about the possibility of Iran developing a nuclear weapon, the United States led a coalition that applied strong economic sanctions to Iran, restricting exports to Iran and prohibiting financial transactions between Iranian institutions and U.S. banks. AIPAC supported these strong sanctions. But some in the Obama administration feared that AIPAC was also supporting Israel in its threats to bomb Iranian nuclear installations, a move that the Obama administration, most U.S. allies, and most national security experts thought could lead to a wider Middle Eastern war.

Thinking about Democracy

Do either multiple-issue or single-issue groups pose a threat to democracy? Why or why not?

PACs, Super PACs, and 527s

Political action committees (PACs), which raise and donate money to election campaigns, **Super PACs**, which raise and spend money on political advertising, and 527s, which do the same, are specialized interest groups in modern American politics. Both PACs and Super PACs are authorized by federal law regulating the flow of money to political candidates and the use of money for political advertising.

Most large interest groups and corporations have a PAC. PACs have leaders who articulate the group's views and decide how to spend the group's funds, as well as checkbook members who decide whether the group's views merit their donations.

PACs are funded from dues and "voluntary" contributions from members of labor unions, "voluntary" contributions from employees of businesses, and voluntary contributions from industry groups or public interest groups. Most PACs are small. Only about 400 of the 4000 or so PACs give more than $100,000 in total. These wealthy PACs represent corporate interests, trade interests (groups of professionals or industries, such as the National Pork Producers Council), labor unions, or issue coalitions.

Federal laws limit what PACs can give to individual candidates to $5000 in each election, or $10,000 combined in a primary and a general election. They can also give $15,000 a year to national parties and $5000 a year to another PAC. And, of course, they can give to multiple candidates, parties, and PACs.

By midway through the 2012 primary season, thirteen PACs had given a million or more to candidates. Of those, nine were business and corporate interests, ranging from the

THIS CAMPAIGN MESSAGE PAID FOR BY A SELF-SERVING COALITION OF WEALTHY INDIVIDUALS WITH A VESTED INTEREST IN THE OUTCOME WHO WISH TO REMAIN ANONYMOUS.

WELL, THAT'S CERTAINLY TRANSPARENT.

edStein'10·UFS
EDSTEININK.COM

aerospace firm Lockheed to the beer and sugar industries; two were unions (carpenters and steelworkers); one represented trial lawyers; and one was set up to support Republican candidates.[88]

Super PACs technically have leaders, but most that have emerged thus far are dominated by one or a few major donors. Super PACs are different from PACs in that they can raise unlimited amounts and spend it on advertising for candidates. However, unlike PACs, they are supposed to be "independent" of any candidate or party and thus cannot donate money directly to candidates or parties. That's the theory and the law, but, in fact, most Super PACs have been run by close associates of the candidates. For example, Newt Gingrich's Super PAC, Winning Our Future PAC, which boosted his campaign for the presidency, was run by his former press aide.[89] These close ties make the notion of "independence" only a technicality.

Like PACs, Super PACs must report their donors and targets of spending quarterly to the Federal Election Commission. However, there are so many loopholes in the reporting requirements that the donors of most of the funds raised by the Super PACs are not disclosed. An independent organization, Center for Responsive Government, summarizes these data in user-friendly form on its website, opensecrets.com, but even then, it is often difficult to track what is being received and spent by PACs and Super PACs.

Super PACs rose after the Supreme Court's 2010 decision that limitations on spending for advertising were undue limitations on free speech. In the view of the Court's conservative majority, individuals, corporations, and unions should be free to spend as much as they want to promote their political beliefs as long as they are independent and not connected to candidates and parties.[90] The Court's majority apparently had a naïve view of the relationship between Super PACs and candidates and parties.

The 2012 election was the first with Super PACs playing a role. The Super PACS seemed to play an important role in the primaries, helping Mitt Romney to victory with $40 million of ads. Other PACs provided millions to candidates Newt Gingrich and Rick Santorum, and even Ron Paul had a supportive Super PAC spending $3 million. The biggest donors to the Super PACs were not large corporations or major unions but rather very rich and opinionated individuals. One spent more than $15 million supporting Gingrich, much of it after Gingrich had demonstrated limited appeal to voters. In the general election, tens of millions were spent by Super PACS, the majority supporting Republicans. Yet, in the races where most was spent, the Republicans lost. Thus, the Super PACS did not have the impact that some feared and others hoped for.

Groups called "527s", so-called because of the section of the Internal Revenue Code authorizing them, are set up by party operatives to mobilize voters and advocate for issues. Some 527s are related to political party organizations, and their personnel are often past or future employees of the parties.[91] Other 527s are affiliated with interest groups. Their fundraising and spending are largely unregulated by state or federal laws.

STRATEGIES OF INTEREST GROUPS

Interest groups use several strategies to influence public policy. These include initiating action, blocking action, and influencing appointments.

Initiating Action

Interest groups initiate governmental action that will help them. They lobby Congress to pass new laws, and because the president is involved and influential in this process, they lobby the administration to push these bills.

Groups also lobby the administration to adopt new policies that don't require new laws. When it was uncertain whether the United States would use economic sanctions or military attacks against Iraq in 1991, defense contractors lobbied the first Bush administration for war because they could sell more weapons to the government and see how the weapons performed on the battlefield. The National Wooden Pallet and Container Association, which represents companies that make pallets used to transport supplies, and the Composite Can and Tube Institute, which represents companies that make cardboard containers and the tubes around which toilet paper and paper towels are wrapped, also lobbied the administration for war, because the government would buy more pallets and cardboard containers, toilet paper, and paper towels.

Groups also lobby the administration or bureaucratic agencies to increase or decrease the enforcement of existing laws. As the head of the executive branch, the president is responsible for executing federal laws, but in practice the president has discretion. Some laws are ambiguous, so they can be interpreted multiple ways. Some agencies lack enough trained personnel to enforce all the laws they're responsible for, so they have to choose which ones to emphasize.

Groups also lobby the agencies to adopt new rules. Congress passes general laws, and it delegates considerable authority to the agencies that have expertise in the subject matter to adopt specific rules to implement the laws. When the Federal Aviation Administration (FAA), which regulates air travel, banned firearms from airplanes in the 1960s, the NRA persuaded it to allow knives. This policy was still in effect on 9/11, when the hijackers used box-cutters to subdue the crews. (After 9/11, the FAA changed the policy to ban knives.) The financial regulation law, passed in 2010 in response to the reckless practices of Wall Street banks and the loose regulatory environment that promoted them, is 2000 pages long. The law requires 385 rules,[92] which are being drafted by the Federal Reserve, the Securities and Exchange Commission (SEC), and the Federal Deposit Insurance Corporation (FDIC). The rules can gut or strengthen the law. One part of the law requires the banks to set aside sufficient assets to protect themselves and their depositors against unforeseen losses, but the law doesn't indicate how much. Out of the public's eye, the banks' lobbyists immediately pushed for a small amount. Thus bureaucrats, like members of Congress and officials in the White House, are targets of lobbyists.

Businesses also lobby government agencies to obtain **government contracts**—orders to purchase goods or services. Businesses are anxious to sell everything government wants to buy, whether big or small. Halliburton got lucrative no-bid contracts to supply services to troops in Iraq (so lucrative that the company was charging the government $100 for each 15-pound bag of laundry its workers put in washing machines and $45 for each case of soda).[93] Companies that make playing cards get less lucrative but still profitable contracts for the decks of playing cards that are distributed to people who fly on *Air Force One*—the president's plane. These prized souvenirs are embossed with the presidential seal.

Blocking Action

Interest groups also work to block governmental action that will harm them, doing the reverse of what groups do to initiate action. They lobby Congress not to pass proposed bills and the administration not to push these bills, and they lobby the administration not to adopt new policies under consideration. They lobby the administration or bureaucratic agencies not to increase or decrease the enforcement of federal laws that affect them. They also lobby the agencies not to adopt new rules that affect them. After 9/11, when the FAA finally banned knives from airplanes, airlines lobbied against the change, insisting that their first-class passengers need to cut their steaks with a knife. (Alas, they have to use plastic now.) If these lobbying efforts fail, groups might file lawsuits either to delay the harmful action or to scuttle it altogether by persuading the courts to declare it illegal or unconstitutional.

Of the two strategies, initiating action or blocking action, the latter is more frequent and more successful. In our system of federalism, separation of powers, and checks and balances, power is fragmented and government is decentralized. Initiating action may require a group to clear both federal and state levels. At the federal level alone, initiating action may require a group to clear each part of each branch—at the legislature, to win favorable decisions from multiple committees and both houses of Congress; at the executive, to win favorable decisions from the president and his advisers and from multiple agencies in the bureaucracy; and at the judiciary, to win favorable decisions from several levels of the courts. Groups that want to change a law or policy have to persuade officials at every step in the process. Groups that wish to maintain a law or policy only have to persuade officials at one point, any point, in the process. The American system, which was designed to prevent hasty action by individuals or groups, strongly favors the status quo. According to one study, it takes 3.5 lobbyists working in favor of a proposal to counteract 1 lobbyist working against it.[94]

 ## Thinking about Democracy

> What are the implications for democracy of the bias toward the status quo in our governmental system?

Whether a group is interested in changing or preserving the status quo, the struggle to influence government can be ongoing. Either way, other groups will be adversely affected, so those groups will push back.

Influencing Appointments

To shape government policy and accomplish their goals indirectly, interest groups also try to influence important appointments. The president nominates and the Senate confirms appointees to high positions in the executive branch and judges to the federal courts. Having a friend or ally in a key position can help secure a group's goals.

The financial regulation law passed in 2010 created a new Consumer Financial Protection Bureau, whose mission is to make various financial documents, such as credit-card statements and mortgage paperwork, less confusing and dishonest. Wall Street banks, fearful that potential customers who understand financial documents may refuse to sign them, pressed Senate Republicans to thwart the new agency. When President Obama tried to appoint Elizabeth Warren, a Harvard law professor who had devised this part of the law, to head the agency, Republicans threatened to filibuster her appointment unless Democrats agreed to changes that would weaken the agency. When Obama concluded that Warren would not be confirmed, he nominated Richard Cordray, former Ohio attorney general. But Republicans filibustered his appointment too. Without a director, the agency could not function. Eventually, Obama appointed Cordray on an interim basis (a controversial "recess appointment" for which he did not need Senate confirmation).

Increasingly, interest groups have tried to influence presidential appointments of federal judges, as will be discussed in Chapter 12.

In pursuing these strategies—initiating action, blocking action, or influencing appointments—like-minded groups may join in a **coalition**. For example, amusement parks, lawn and garden centers, Kingsford Charcoal, and 7-Eleven stores joined the Daylight Saving Time Coalition to lobby Congress to extend daylight saving time. All wanted additional evening daylight hours for the users of their services and products: amusement parks so visitors have more time to play; lawn and garden centers so homeowners have more time to work in their yards; Kingsford so picnickers have more time for barbecues; and 7-Eleven so drivers have more time to stop for a snack while it is still daylight.

TACTICS OF INTEREST GROUPS

To implement their strategies, interest groups rely on a variety of tactics. Some try to influence policy makers directly, whereas others try to mold public opinion and influence policy makers indirectly.

Direct Lobbying Techniques

Direct lobbying entails individual contacts between lobbyists and officials. Thirty-two thousand lobbyists are registered in Washington, and many others aren't registered because of various loopholes.[95] Some are salaried employees of the groups they represent; others are contract lobbyists, "hired guns" who represent any individual or group willing to pay for their services. Contract lobbyists include the lawyers affiliated with the capital's prestigious law firms.

Gaining access is the first and essential step in direct lobbying. As busy people, public officials are protected by their receptionists and aides, whose job is to shield them from those who would take their time.

Former members and staffers of Congress, White House aides, and federal bureaucrats are sought as lobbyists. They already have contacts with current officials and knowledge about current policies, and former members of Congress have access to the House and Senate dining rooms and chambers, where no one but members and former members is allowed. Here they can buttonhole current members just before a vote. When they first came to Washington, most members planned to return home after serving, but the longer they experienced the highly charged atmosphere of the most political city in the country, the harder it got to go back. When Bob Dole (R-Kan.) resigned from the Senate to run for president in 1996, he said if he lost he'd have to go back to his hometown of Russell, Kansas. After he lost, however, he became a lobbyist and remained in Washington.

This tendency has led to a **revolving door** tradition, in which high-ranking officials move into high-paying lobbying jobs when they leave public service. Between 1998 and 2006, more than 250 former members of Congress and 275 former aides to the president registered as lobbyists.[96] Between 2000 and 2011, more than 5000 former staffers of Congress became lobbyists.[97] Rep. Billy Tauzin (R-La.), who steered the Bush administration's Medicare drug bill through the House, was rewarded by the pharmaceutical industry with a job as the head of the pharmaceutical lobby—at a salary of more than $11 million a year.[98] He then helped the pharmaceutical companies secure their financial interests in the Obama administration's health care bill.

The door swings the opposite way too. Sometimes lobbyists become staffers of Congress. When the 2010 congressional elections brought new Republican faces to Washington, nearly one hundred hired a lobbyist as their chief of staff or legislative director. Even some Tea Party members, who had vowed to end business as usual, did so.[99]

The revolving door can lead to lax regulations. Officials who hope to move to lobbying positions don't want to antagonize potential employers by advocating strict regulations. And those who move from lobbying positions to Congress are already sympathetic to the industry or the companies they represented. When the BP oil rig exploded in the Gulf of Mexico in 2010, it became apparent that the government's regulations and enforcement were inadequate. BP employed thirty-one lobbyists with government experience, and the American Petroleum Institute, the industry's main association, employed forty-eight more, including former members of Congress who played leading roles in deregulating the industry while in Congress.[100]

Usually both Democrats and Republicans are recruited as lobbyists, so firms have access to both parties. This practice ensures that lobbying firms maintain access when control of government shifts from one party to the other.

When the Republicans controlled Congress in the 1990s, however, they pressured the firms to employ only Republicans as their lobbyists. And then they pressured the lobbyists to make campaign contributions only to Republican officeholders and candidates. The goal was to deprive the Democratic Party of the funds necessary to remain competitive. The plan was dubbed the "K Street strategy" after the K Street corridor,

BEHIND THE SCENES

Access to Legislators? No Problem

The American Legislative Exchange Council (ALEC) is a partnership of state legislators whose main purpose is to promote the conservative agenda in state legislatures. About 99 percent of its budget comes from corporate and trade association partners and the rest from dues paid by state legislators who are members.

To promote pro-business and limited government policies, ALEC drafts laws that its legislative partners introduce in their own states (sometimes without taking off the ALEC name). ALEC's budget then helps fund lobbyists to promote the bills.

Although much of its activity focuses on regulatory and other policies that directly affect business, the organization also advocates for various parts of the right-wing agenda, including laws that promote private schools at the expense of public schools. As a first step, ALEC proposes laws that would provide taxpayer-financed scholarships for disabled children to attend private schools instead of public schools.

The scholarship money would be taken from the public schools' budgets.[106] ALEC also advocates for laws limiting voting (particularly ones requiring photo identification) and the "stand your ground" laws authorizing individuals to use force (including deadly force) if they feel threatened. After an unarmed black teenager was killed by a neighborhood vigilante in Florida, questions were asked about the scope and application of these laws and their implications for safety on the streets, especially for young minorities. Questions were also asked about why many states adopted these laws.

After analysts revealed that ALEC was behind much of this legislation, some corporations withdrew from ALEC because of the public embarrassment of being associated with this non-business-related agenda. Other corporations stayed with ALEC, arguing that it had been very effective in promoting their business agenda. Not surprisingly, another group, Color of Change, an advocacy group for black Americans, began to publicize and criticize the work of ALEC.

home to lobbyists representing the nation's largest business corporations and trade associations.

House Republican leader Tom DeLay (R-Tex.) compiled a list of the four hundred largest contributors to the parties. Their lobbyists were summoned to his office, one by one, and told, "If you want to play in our revolution, you have to live by our rules." Friendly lobbyists were invited to help write legislation affecting their clients. So, chemical industry lobbyists helped decide hazardous waste regulations, oil company lobbyists helped determine energy policies, and defense contractors helped write weapons contracts.[101]

An old adage states, "Power corrupts and absolute power corrupts absolutely."[102] The Republicans' aggressive efforts to maintain control led to corruption, forcing some members of Congress to resign and sending some lobbyists to prison. The spectacle contributed to the Democrats' takeover of Congress in 2006. As a result, the lobbying firms scurried to hire more Democratic lobbyists.[103]

Contacting Officials

Direct lobbying entails paying a visit or making a call to officials. Lobbyists don't need to contact every legislator. Rather, they contact key legislators—party leaders and the members who sit on the committees with jurisdiction over the subject of the lobbyists' concern—and the professional staffers serving those committees.[104]

Successful lobbying is based on friendship. As a former chair of a House committee observed, "The most effective lobbyists here are the ones you don't think of as lobbyists." Referring to one lobbyist, he said, "I don't think of him as a lobbyist. He's almost a constituent, or a friend." Sen. Barbara Boxer (D-Cal.), referring to the same gentleman, described him as "a lovely, wonderful guy. In the whole time I've known him, he's never asked me to vote for anything." She joked that he's almost "a member of the family."[105]

Providing Expertise

When lobbyists contact officials, they might provide expertise that officials lack. Lobbyists make sure that they fully understand their client's business and the industry in which it operates. Consequently, they are an invaluable source of information for members of Congress and aides in the White House, who tend to be generalists rather than experts about policies. Thus officials rely on lobbyists to educate them. Former senator Ted Stevens (R-Alaska) chaired a committee whose jurisdiction included the Internet. His comment that the Internet is "a series of tubes" led to jokes and dismay that the man in charge of congressional action in this area had no idea what he was talking about. His comment underscored the need for information to regulate wisely, and thus the usefulness of lobbyists.

Lobbyists often draft legislation. A legislator may ask a lobbyist known to be an expert in an area to draft a bill, or a lobbyist may draft a bill and ask a legislator thought to be sympathetic to the cause to introduce the bill in Congress.

Giving Money

Lobbyists also give money, in the form of campaign contributions, to candidates for office and incumbents running for reelection. To give money, groups, including businesses and unions, set up PACs, which channel contributions to parties and candidates. Lobbyists give to those with whom they agree and those who are likely to be elected or reelected. The money greases the skids; it ensures access. A longtime financial backer of Ronald Reagan said that having a dialogue with a politician is fine, "but with a little money they hear you better."[107] A Democrat commented, "Who do members of Congress see? They'll certainly see the one who gives the money. It's hard to say no to someone who gives you $5,000."[108]

Although PACs differ in the targets of their donations, they show a distinct preference for Republicans in presidential races and for incumbents—Republicans or Democrats—in congressional races. This preference is especially noticeable when Republicans control Congress. PACs usually want to give to the candidates they believe will win, normally the incumbents, so that they will have access to policy makers. They also give money to members in districts where they have a substantial interest, such as a large number of union members for a union PAC or a large factory for a corporate PAC.[109] They also target contributions to members of key congressional committees. For example, PACs organized by defense contractors give disproportionately to members who serve on the Armed Services Committees, which decide what weapons to purchase.[110]

Women's PACs, including EMILY's List, are unusual in focusing most of their money on nonincumbents. Their goal is to get more women elected, which often means supporting nonincumbents with strong chances of winning. Interest groups often give to candidates they disagree with. Despite its liberal reputation, the entertainment industry donates money to Republican candidates as well as to Democratic candidates. Hollywood studios even donate to conservative Republicans who sit on committees with jurisdiction over issues, such as intellectual property rights, important to the industry.[111] When the Republicans are in the majority, Hollywood moguls, guided by their business interests rather than their ideological views, donate more to the Republicans.

Groups do not always freely decide whether to contribute their money. Once the parties and candidates got used to receiving contributions, and as they faced escalating costs for television advertising, they began to pressure the groups to make contributions, as Republican leader Tom DeLay did when he told lobbyists they had "to pay to play"—that is, to contribute if they wanted to influence congressional bills or obtain government contracts.

Thus leverage is exercised in both directions. The groups give money to the parties and candidates as a way to influence current and future officials, and the parties and candidates demand money from the groups as a way to finance their campaigns. With only some exaggeration, one could say that the groups are practicing a legalized form of bribery and the parties and candidates are practicing a legalized form of extortion.

 Thinking about Democracy

> What are the implications for democracy of this pattern of legalized "bribery" and "extortion"?

Litigating in Court

Although interest groups do not lobby judges the way they do legislators and bureaucrats, some do use litigation to persuade courts to rule for their side in disputes over policies and laws. The groups may file a lawsuit, represent a defendant facing criminal prosecution, or submit a brief—written arguments—in favor of one side in a case.

Although most groups don't use litigation, some use it as their primary tactic, particularly those that lack influence with the legislative and executive branches. Litigation was a successful strategy for civil rights organizations. Throughout the first half of the twentieth century, when Congress and presidents were unsympathetic to the rights of black Americans, the National Association for the Advancement of Colored People (NAACP) fought segregation in the courts. Litigation has been the usual strategy of civil liberties groups, especially the American Civil Liberties Union (ACLU). (These groups' efforts are covered in Chapters 13 and 14.)

Environmental groups use litigation to challenge governmental policies. In local communities, environmental groups file lawsuits against commercial developments that threaten environmental damage. They hope to block the projects or, at least, delay the projects so that the costs will increase and the developers will have an incentive to make modifications.

With the current conservative and activist Supreme Court (see Chapter 12), conservative groups are aggressively using litigation as a strategy. After the passage of the health care reform bill, for example, many lawsuits were filed to prevent its implementation. Conservative groups hoped that conservative justices on the Court would conclude that Congress has no authority to regulate this sphere of the American economy. (The Court's 2012 decision found most of the law constitutional.)

Indirect Lobbying Techniques: Going Public

Traditionally, lobbyists limited themselves to direct lobbying, but increasingly, they have turned to indirect lobbying, known as **going public**.[112] This technique includes mobilizing their supporters and molding public opinion. The goal is to get people to contact officials or to get them to vote in elections. By working through the public, groups lobby indirectly.

Mobilizing Supporters

Groups mobilize their members and supporters—called **grassroots lobbying**—through websites, direct mail, e-mail, texting, and social media. They often exaggerate their opponents' views or strength or the dire consequences that could result if their own supporters don't heed the call. Such communications are "about scaring the hell out of people."[113]

The NRA is especially adept at mobilizing its members. It can generate thousands of letters, e-mails, or calls to members of Congress within days. Calls from irate members led one senator to remark, "I'd rather be a deer in hunting season than run afoul of the NRA crowd."[114]

To be effective, messages from members should appear spontaneous and sincere. Groups often provide sample letters to aid their members, but these aren't as convincing as ones written in a member's own words. Postcards with preprinted messages aren't very convincing either. Some groups use online petitions. Although these aren't as effective as individual communications, a huge number of signatures may have an impact. MoveOn.org, with an e-mail list of over 3 million, can with the click of a mouse send hundreds of thousands of messages hurtling toward Washington.[115]

The Internet facilitates grassroots organizing. For example, in 2009, when health care reform was pending, the Tea Party movement mobilized supporters. Conservative news commentators and talk show hosts had not only criticized the bill but also distorted its provisions, claiming, for example, that the bill would cause elderly people to lose their Medicare and that it would establish "death panels" to decide whether elderly people would receive medical care. Naturally, many people who believed these fictional outrages were irate. When members of Congress hosted "town hall meetings" for their constituents back home, Tea Party groups decided to give their representative or senator an earful. With websites providing the time and location of each meeting and offering transportation, Tea Partiers filled the seats and dominated the meetings.

Astroturf groups—the name comes from the artificial grass on some athletic fields—pretend to be broad-based groups but are run by industry lobbyists.[116] Assuming that average people will be more sympathetic to their cause if the people perceive them to be grassroots groups, they try to mobilize people through efforts similar to grassroots groups and often have misleading names. For example, "Energy Citizens," which was sponsored by a number of industry associations, represented few citizens, but it organized the employees of the industries to attend "citizen rallies" to oppose climate legislation.[117]

Molding Public Opinion

Groups try to mold public opinion through commercials on television and radio and ads in newspapers and magazines. Groups also stage media events, including photo ops, to attract media coverage.

Framing an issue—causing people to view it one way rather than another—can be crucial in winning public support. Those opposing health care reform tried to frame the plan as "socialized medicine," painting the specter of government controlling personal health decisions. Those supporting reform stressed the heavy hand of insurance companies, holding life-and-death power over middle- and low-income individuals who are socked with huge medical bills.

Business groups pushing "tort reform," which would limit the money that courts can award to individuals injured in auto accidents, air disasters, unsuccessful surgeries, and other mishaps, focus on notorious cases in which the victims have received huge awards relative to their injuries, such as the grandmother who spilled McDonald's coffee onto her lap and was awarded $2.9 million for her burns. (But, like many awards, this one was dramatically reduced by the judge, to $840,000, and then further reduced through secret negotiations between the litigants to avoid an appeal.) These groups hope to convince the public that "tort reform" is overdue and necessary to ensure that American businesses will remain competitive or, in malpractice cases, to ensure that American doctors will continue to practice medicine.[118] Lawyer groups that oppose "tort reform" instead focus on the poor victims seriously injured and left penniless by the careless behavior of big corporations or rich doctors.[119] These groups frame the debate as the little guy versus the big bully.

In their zeal to shape public opinion, groups occasionally fabricate information. Although there's a cardinal rule that lobbyists should not mislead officials because they would never be trusted again, there's no comparable rule against misleading the public. ExxonMobil, which opposes government efforts to reduce global warming, has tried to discredit the science of global warming. Although the scientific opinion on the existence of global warming is nearly unanimous (as explained in the Environmental Policy Module), Exxon Mobil, according to one calculation, gave $16 million to forty-three groups between 1998 and 2005 to mislead the public into believing that the science is inconclusive and the scientists are in disagreement.[120] The corporation assumed that it isn't necessary to persuade people that there's no global warming; it is necessary only to convince them that the issue isn't resolved, so difficult steps to counter it don't have to be taken yet.[121]

Engaging in protest   If groups are excluded from the political process or if they simply lack the money necessary to influence the process, they can turn to protest.

The civil rights movement is the best example of a successful protest in twentieth-century America. By demonstrating against legalized segregation, black and some white protestors called attention to the discrepancy between the American values of democracy and equality and the inferior status of blacks in the South. The protestors also called attention to the contrast between their own peaceful behavior and the police and vigilante brutality unleashed against them. In marches, sit-ins, and other demonstrations, the protestors practiced **civil disobedience**—intentionally but peacefully violating laws and getting arrested so they could challenge the laws in court. (See the box "Organizing Protest: The Montgomery Bus Boycott.")

Students sit in at a segregated lunch counter in Jackson, Mississippi, during the civil rights era.

Sometimes protest leads to hostility against, rather than sympathy for, the protesters. Antiwar demonstrations by college students in the 1960s and 1970s angered not only government officials, who targeted the leaders for harassment, but also ordinary citizens, including many who opposed the war. They were more anti-protest than anti-war.

Protest demands skill from the leaders and sacrifices from the followers. Continued participation, essential to real success, robs activists of a normal life. They can face jail, physical harm, or even death, and they need discipline to refrain from violence, even when they are targeted for violence.

Once protest groups find sympathetic officials willing to listen, they often shift to an inside strategy, working with those in power rather than against them. They switch from demonstrations to conventional lobbying techniques.

SUCCESS OF INTEREST GROUPS

Politics is not a game of chance in which luck determines the winners and losers. Some groups are more successful than others because of their resources and goals.

Resources

Money is important for success. Groups with money can establish and operate an organization, hire experienced lobbyists, and make campaign donations. They can also mold public opinion through television commercials and other actions. An economist called the system "survival of the fattest," because those with the biggest wallets have a significant advantage in our system.[122]

Size—number of members—might substitute for money, especially if members can be mobilized. AARP has 35 million members, senior citizens who focus on Social Security and Medicare and who vote in high numbers. (They pay dues, so AARP has a thick bankroll along with its huge membership.) The number of members relative to the number of potential members in a group can also be important. The American Medical Association (AMA) enrolled 70 percent or more of the nation's doctors for years, and it had considerable clout. As its percentage of American doctors declined, its influence declined as well.

The political knowledge and involvement of group members are also very important. Groups with high levels of representation, such as scientists, lawyers, and gun owners, have members who are more involved in politics than those with low levels of representation.[123] Group members follow political news in the media, express their opinions, and vote. That adds to their expertise and clout.

The cohesion and intensity of group members also contribute to group success. Public interest groups, especially single-issue groups such as pro-choice and pro-life groups, have cohesive and intense members who can be mobilized to contact officials, write letters to the editor, persuade their friends, and vote.

American Diversity

Organizing Protest: The Montgomery Bus Boycott

The 1955 Montgomery, Alabama, bus boycott was the first successful civil rights protest, and it brought its twenty-six-year-old leader, Dr. Martin Luther King Jr., to national prominence.

Montgomery, like most southern cities, required blacks to sit in the back of public buses, reserving the seats in the front for whites. In Montgomery, blacks paid their fare in the front of the bus and then had to reboard through the back door. As more whites got on board, blacks had to move further back; they couldn't even sit across the aisle from a white person.

One afternoon, Rosa Parks, a seamstress at a department store and a leader in the local NAACP, got on the bus to go home. The bus was crowded, and when a white man boarded, the driver called on the four blacks in "no-man's land" to move to the back. Three moved, but Parks, tired from a long day and tired of the racial injustice, refused. Under a law that gave him the authority to enforce segregation, the driver arrested her.

Parks was not the first black person in Montgomery to be arrested for not giving up her seat to whites. Two others had before her, but Parks was a better candidate for filing a legal complaint. Not only was she "above moral reproach (securely married, reasonably employed)," but she also possessed "a quiet fortitude as well as political savvy." After consulting her mother and husband, Parks decided to file a lawsuit challenging the constitutionality of the law.

Rosa Parks is fingerprinted in Montgomery, Alabama, after her arrest for refusing to give up her seat on the bus to a white man. Her refusal triggered a boycott of city buses that became the first successful civil disobedience in the civil rights movement and made Parks a hero to black and white Americans alike.

That evening, at Alabama State College, a black college in Montgomery, a group of women professors led by Jo Ann Robinson drafted a letter calling on their brothers and sisters to stay off the buses on Monday. Although fearful for their jobs and concerned that the state would cut funding to the college if it became known that they had used state facilities to produce the letter, they worked through the night, making thirty-five thousand copies of the letter to distribute to the city's black residents.

The following day, black leaders agreed to the boycott, and on Sunday, black ministers encouraged their members to support the boycott. On Monday, 90 percent of black workers walked, shared rides in private cars,

Groups that marshal the greatest resources are the most likely to influence government. They may even overcome the majority view, as reflected in public opinion polls. Supporters of gun control have long had public opinion on their side, but their main group, the National Council to Control Handguns, has less money, fewer members, and less cohesion and intensity among its members than the NRA can boast. As a result, the NRA has triumphed over public opinion for decades.

Goals

As already discussed, groups that promote change, especially sweeping change, usually are less successful than groups that work to preserve the status quo. In our system of federalism, separation of powers, and checks and balances, groups promoting change must persuade numerous officials in multiple institutions; groups opposing change may have to persuade only one key official, or perhaps several important officials, in just a single institution. Thus it is more difficult to produce government action than to prevent such action.

When President Bill Clinton proposed a major health care reform, medical, dental, hospital, and insurance associations and companies voiced their opposition. Different groups opposed different aspects of the proposal, and they came together to fight it. The plan's scope, along with its opponents' power, ensured its defeat.

or took black-owned taxis. The boycott inspired confidence and pride in the black community. Hundreds of blacks jammed the courthouse, as nervous police looked on, to make sure that Rosa Parks was safely released after being convicted.

At a mass rally later that evening, Martin Luther King Jr. cried out, "There comes a time when people get tired of being trampled over by the iron feet of oppression." Noting that the right to protest is the glory of American democracy, King appealed to the strong religious faith of the crowd: "If we are wrong, God Almighty is wrong.... If we are wrong, Jesus of Nazareth was merely a utopian dreamer.... If we are wrong, justice is a lie." These words established King as a charismatic leader of the civil rights movement.

Because of its initial success, the boycott was extended. Each successive day was a trial for the residents and their leaders. Thousands had to find a way to get to work, and leaders struggled to keep a massive carpool going. But each night's rally boosted morale for the next day's boycott. The rallies became prayer services, as the black community prayed for strength to keep on walking, for courage to remain nonviolent, and for divine guidance for their oppressors.

The city bus line was losing money. (Before the boycott, most riders on city buses were black people.) City leaders urged more whites to ride the buses to make up lost revenue, but few did. Black leaders, recognizing that the boycott could not continue forever, agreed to end it if the rules for "no-man's land" were relaxed. In response, city leaders concluded that they were on the verge of breaking the boycott, and they rejected the offer. Police officers began to harass carpoolers and issue bogus tickets for trumped-up violations.

City leaders then issued an ultimatum—settle or face arrest. A white grand jury indicted more than one hundred boycott leaders for the alleged crime of organizing the protest. In the spirit of nonviolence, the leaders, including King, surrendered.

The decision to arrest the leaders proved to be the turning point of the boycott. The white editor of the local paper said it was "the dumbest act that has ever been done in Montgomery." With the mass arrests, the boycott finally received national attention. Reporters from all over the world streamed into Montgomery to cover the story. The boycott became a national event, and its leader, Martin Luther King Jr., became a national figure.

A year later, the U.S. Supreme Court declared Alabama's local and state laws mandating segregation on buses unconstitutional. Only after the city complied with the Court's order did the boycott end.

When Rosa Parks died at the age of ninety-two in 2005, she was lauded as one of the key figures in the civil rights movement. Fifty thousand people filed through the U.S. Capitol Rotunda, where she lay in state, the first woman and second African American to be honored in this way. Thousands attended her funeral, and thousands more lined the streets to witness her casket pulled by a horse-drawn carriage to the cemetery. Parks, however, had a modest view of her own role; as she said, "I did not get on the bus to get arrested; I got on the bus to get home."

SOURCES: Taylor Branch, *Parting the Waters: America in the King Years* (New York: Simon & Schuster, 1988), chs. 4 and 5; Juan Williams, *Eyes on the Prize* (New York: Viking, 1987); quote about Parks is from Rita Dove, "Rosa Parks," *Time Magazine*, June 14, 1999, 168.

President Obama learned from the Clinton experience and made an effort to enlist some of the big interest groups in behalf of his reform plan even if he had to give up some things that he and fellow Democrats wanted. He was able to do this because the cost of health care spiraled between the time Clinton sought reform and Obama did. Many doctors and hospital administrators wanted change, and big pharmaceuticals thought they could position themselves well when health reform passed.

Clinton's welfare reform, which was a major revision of an entrenched policy, was adopted without the controversies that the health reform spawned. It set work requirements for welfare recipients, who are the poorest and least politically active Americans. They don't have strong interest groups, so they weren't able to block the new requirements.

Groups that seek narrow benefits for themselves are usually more successful than those that seek broad policy changes for the entire society. If the proposals are complex, the media are less likely to call attention to them and the public is less likely to be aware of them. Virtually everyone is aware of hot-button issues such as abortion and capital punishment, but relatively few are aware of technical provisions that regulate or tax businesses. Most Americans paid little attention when Wall Street financial firms, such as Citibank and Goldman Sachs, lobbied continuously and successfully to undo some regulations erected during the Great Depression to protect consumers and depositors from future economic crashes. These huge financial firms took advantage of the drumbeat for deregulation during the conservative era of the 1980s, 1990s, and early 2000s, and they persuaded Congress and presidents to repeal existing regulations and allow the firms to engage in new and risky practices. These practices brought the American economy, as well as these big firms, to the brink of collapse in 2008 and 2009.

The tax code is riddled with exemptions for industries and corporations that have slipped through Congress without raising an eyebrow.[124] Some beneficiaries aren't identified by their name. One provision exempts Phillips Petroleum, identified in the law not by its name but as a "corporation incorporated on June 13, 1917, which has its principal place of business in Bartlesville, Oklahoma."[125] A member of Congress from a district with three national bakeries succeeded in inserting a provision into a tax bill that simply deleted "bakery drivers" from the list of occupations treated as employees.[126] The drivers, although hired by the bakeries, would be defined as self-employed rather than as bakery employees. This meant that the bakeries wouldn't have to pay Social Security, Medicare, or unemployment taxes on their drivers. Instead, their drivers would have to pay extra Social Security and Medicare taxes themselves. This rip-off was removed only when a congressional staffer noticed and publicized it.

 Thinking about Democracy

> Does it seem that interest groups enhance or detract from democracy?

Dominance among Interest Groups

Much interest group action in the United States pits those who seek benefits for business and their allies against those who seek benefits for workers and consumers and their allies. With our capitalist economy, business tends to get the upper hand, although workers and consumers have prevailed at times.

In the last century, workers and consumers were the dominant coalition in the 1930s and again in the 1960s and 1970s. In the 1930s, new laws provided a safety net under the elderly (Social Security), the poor (welfare systems), and the unemployed (unemployment insurance), and they protected consumers and investors (banking regulations). In the 1960s and 1970s, new laws provided health care for the elderly (Medicare) and the poor (Medicaid) and promoted civil rights, workplace safety, product safety, and environmental protection.

The role of Ralph Nader reflected the emergence of liberal public interest groups in the 1960s and 1970s. The son of Lebanese immigrants and a crusader for average Americans against the giants of corporate America, Nader spearheaded an array of interest groups, including Public Citizen, which attracted young professionals (dubbed "Nader's Raiders") and fought for safer products and a healthier environment. More than any other person, Nader was responsible for seat belts, air bags, padded dashboards, steering columns that won't impale drivers, and fuel tanks that won't explode upon collision. Because of Nader, drinking water, baby food, and dental X-rays became safer; infant pajamas became less likely to catch fire. To a significant extent, Nader was also responsible for the creation of important government agencies—the Environmental Protection Agency (EPA); the Occupational Safety and Health Administration (OSHA), which tries to ensure safe workplaces; and the Consumer Product Safety Commission (CPSC), which tries to ensure safe products. Nader also pushed for the Freedom of Information Act, which exposes government actions and ensures greater accountability.[127] His work is a testament to how much concerned and active citizens, working through interest groups, can do, even when they are up against powerful opponents.

During the 1970s, business realized that it was losing battle after battle to workers and consumers, and it mobilized, organizing and funding existing and new groups to dominate American politics. Within a decade, the number of corporations with offices in Washington grew from 100 to over 500, the number with registered lobbyists grew from 175 to almost 2500, and the number with PACs grew from under 300 to over 1200.[128] Business donations to political candidates increased just as the cost of political campaigns, which became based on television advertising, increased.[129] Politicians who needed money turned to business.

This growth laid the foundation for business success, which would come in the conservative era that began with the election of Ronald Reagan in 1980. From 1980 through 2008, many regulations on business were swept away, including those on financial firms. Other regulations were laxly enforced, such as environmental and consumer protections. Tax rates on the wealthy were significantly lowered, and IRS enforcement of tax laws abused by the wealthy was intentionally minimized.[130]

During the first years of the Obama presidency, the interests of workers, consumers, and environmentalists gained traction, with the passage of re-regulations on the financial industry and new regulations on the health care industry. But business fought back, helping Republicans gain power in Congress and block proposals by Democrats. In recent years, the contest has often been lopsided. For example, the financial industry has twenty-five of the top sixty-five corporate donors in the United States.[131] It has 2000 registered lobbyists—almost four for every member of Congress. On a bill pitting banks against consumers, the director of the Consumer Federation of America, which represents 280 nonprofit groups, said, "We have three lawyers total working on this.... They can have three people working on a paragraph."[132]

SUMMARY

- Most interests in the United States have an organization to represent them, and most organizations have one or more lobbyists to influence government decisions. In the United States, many groups form because of the First Amendment, the federal structure of our government, and the racial, ethnic, and religious diversity of our society. In addition, groups form because of social changes, economic pressures, technological developments, and government actions. Some people join because they feel they can make a difference; others join because they gain psychological, social, or economic benefits.

- Private interest groups seek economic benefits for their members. Public interest groups work for a cause that extends beyond their members.

- Multiple-issue groups are public interest groups that address a range of issues. Single-issue groups are public interest groups that address one issue.

- PACs, Super PACs, and 527s are interest groups created solely for the purpose of raising funds for political campaigns and causes. They inject massive amounts of money into political campaigns and causes. The amounts that individuals and groups can contribute to PACs and that PACs can give to candidates are limited by federal law. But the amounts that individuals and groups can contribute to Super PACs and that Super PACs can spend on advertising for candidates and causes are unlimited, as long as the spending is "independent" of the candidates and parties. The amounts that individuals and groups can contribute to 527s and that 527s can spend to mobilize voters are largely unregulated.

- In our system of federalism, separation of powers, and checks and balances, power is fragmented and government is decentralized. Initiating action may require a group to clear each level and each part of each branch. Blocking action requires a group to persuade officials at just one point in the system.

- Common tactics of interest groups include direct techniques, such as contacting officials, providing expertise, giving money; and indirect techniques, such as mobilizing supporters and molding public opinion.

- The most successful interest groups have one or more of the following: money, size, cohesion, or intensity. Different groups have dominated at different times, but business groups, which have the most money, tend to prevail over labor unions and consumer groups.

DISCUSSION QUESTIONS

1. Consider the pervasiveness of interest groups and lobbyists in American politics. How do they supplement the role played by elections in American democracy?

2. Which public interest groups do you think are actually in the public interest?

3. What trends in American politics led to the rise and growth of the right-wing and left-wing interest groups? What consequences for American politics do you think these groups have?

4. Super PACs arose because the Supreme Court struck down a congressional law limiting individuals' and groups' spending on election campaigns. What impact may the Court's decision have on (a) the amounts of money in political campaigns and (b) the freedom of speech for individuals and groups who want to spend on election campaigns? Does the impact of either (a) or (b) trouble you?

5. Why is it easier to block political change than to get new laws passed? Illustrate with efforts to pass health care reform.

6. Which interest groups have tried to mobilize your support or mold your opinion? Have any succeeded?

7. Can you think of ways that labor unions or consumer groups might be able to match the power of business groups in the future?

7 Political Parties

Sen. Olympia Snowe, a moderate Republican, got fed up with the extremism and intransigence common in Congress today, so she refused to run for reelection.

AP Images/Charles Dharapak

LEARNING OBJECTIVES

1. Identify the primary characteristics of American political parties.

2. Understand the dynamics of the war within the Republican Party between moderates and conservatives and the role of the Tea Party in this war.

3. Identify multiple reasons why American political parties (a) arose, (b) expanded, and (c) persisted for over two centuries.

4. Grasp the concept of "responsible party government."

5. Understand the process of party realignment in the United States.

6. Cite the factors that prompt people to become Democrats or Republicans.

TALKING POINTS

Olympia Snowe was the most popular politician in Maine. First elected to Congress in 1976, she served in the House of Representatives and then in the Senate, completing her third term in 2012. Snowe and Maine's other senator, Susan Collins, were the most moderate Republicans in the Senate.

Independent and strong-willed, Snowe refused to toe the party line. She occasionally supported Democratic initiatives. Although she has increasingly voted with her party in recent years,[1] she was criticized and isolated within the party. The Tea Party Express had put her on its target list, and a Tea Party candidate had challenged her in the Republican primary in 2012. (In the primary elections, parties choose their nominees for the general election against the opposing party.) Even so, Snowe was considered a shoo-in for reelection. But after almost four decades as a Republican officeholder, she decided to chuck it.

When she announced her retirement before the Republican primary, she denounced the polarization that has increasingly dominated American politics—the "my way or the highway" attitude that has become pervasive in both campaigning and governing.[2] She said that politicians spend too much time battling and not enough time solving problems. Snowe became the last in a string of six centrist senators who decided not to seek reelection in 2012.[3]

Many conservative Republicans cheered Snowe's announcement because it gave them an opportunity to elect a conservative senator from Maine.[4] Snowe's retirement reflects not only the polarization in American politics now, but also the war within the Republican Party. As the party has shifted further and further to the right in recent decades, tension has escalated between the members committed to the party's expansion and other members committed to its ideological purity. The former advocate a **"big tent,"** with diverse people and diverse views. This notion used to be commonplace in both parties but now is disdained by conservative Republicans, who believe that it muddles the coherence of the party's positions and image. Sen. Jim DeMint, a very conservative Republican from South Carolina, said, "I would rather have thirty Republicans in the Senate who really believe in principles of limited government, free markets, free people, than to have sixty that don't have a set of beliefs."[5] With this attitude, conservative Republicans often call moderate Republicans "RINOs"—Republicans in Name Only. So, the number of moderate Republicans has dwindled, and the battle to chart the course of the party into the future continues.

In the 2012 election, the Republican candidate, supported by the Tea Party, lost to an independent, Angus King, who is expected to side with Senate Democrats.

James Madison, the "Father of the Constitution," warned against the "mischief of factions," which today would include interest groups and political parties. George Washington, the "Father of the Country," cautioned against the "baneful" effects of parties and called them the people's worst enemies. Years later, however, a respected political scientist, E. E. Schattschneider, claimed that "political parties created democracy and that democracy was impossible without them."[6]

The public reflects these contradictory views. Americans, especially young adults, are cynical about parties, and many believe the country would be better off without them. People complain that politics is too **partisan**—that candidates and officeholders make decisions based on their party affiliation rather than on the country's needs. People say they're tired of "partisan bickering," as though the parties, like children, argue over nothing consequential. They believe that parties create conflict where none exists. Despite these views, however, most people identify with one of the parties, and many vote solely on the basis of party affiliation.

This chapter examines American political parties to see why they persist—indeed, why they are important—despite the criticism they face.

CHARACTERISTICS OF AMERICAN PARTIES

Political parties consist of three interrelated components: (1) citizens who consider themselves members of the party, (2) officeholders who are elected or appointed in the name of the party, and (3) professionals and activists who run the party organization at the national, state, and local levels (see Figure 1).[7]

The American party system is unusual among Western democracies, as we shall see when examining its distinguishing characteristics.

Two Major Parties

The American party system is a **two-party system**. Only two parties—the **Democratic Party** and the **Republican Party**—have a realistic chance to win the presidency or most seats in Congress. (Occasionally an independent wins a seat; today a socialist—Sen. Bernie Sanders (Vt.)—holds a seat.)

Two-party systems are rare. In western Europe, **multiparty systems** are the rule. Italy has nine national

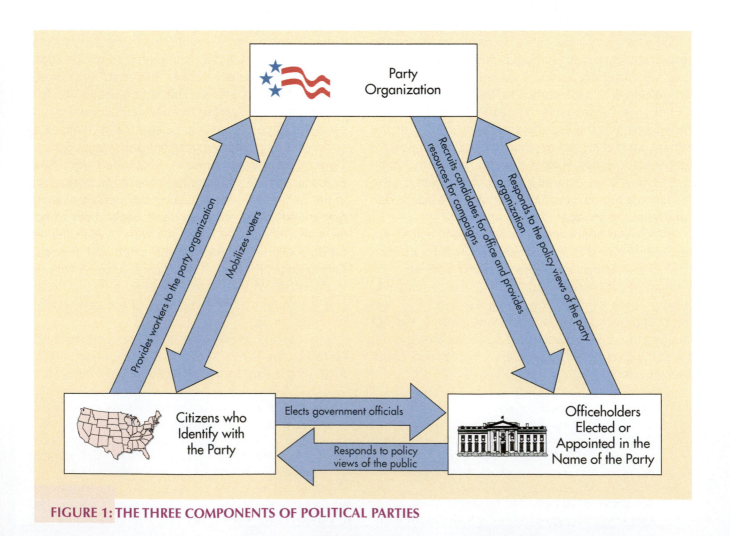

FIGURE 1: THE THREE COMPONENTS OF POLITICAL PARTIES

Party Organization

Provides workers to the party organization

Mobilizes voters

Recruits candidates for office and provides resources for campaigns

Responds to the policy views of the party organization

Citizens who Identify with the Party

Elects government officials

Responds to policy views of the public

Officeholders Elected or Appointed in the Name of the Party

parties and several regional ones; Germany has five national parties. Great Britain, although predominantly a two-party system, has several significant minor parties. Multiparty systems are also found in Canada, which has three parties, and Israel, which has more than twenty.

Why two parties in the United States? The most common explanation is that American elections, with **single-member districts** and a **winner-take-all provision,** favor two parties.[8] These features mean that only one individual—the one who receives the most votes—is elected from a district. Although these features seem natural, even inevitable, to Americans, they contrast with **proportional representation** (PR), which is found in multiparty systems. PR elections employ multi-member districts, where more than one individual is elected. In most, voters cast a ballot for a party slate, and each party receives the number of seats in the district equal to its percentage of votes in the district.[9] (There's no winner-take-all provision.) Consequently, representation in the national legislature is roughly proportional to the popular vote each party receives nationwide.

In single-member-district, winner-take-all elections, only the major parties are likely to win a legislative seat. In PR elections, even a modest showing—15 percent or possibly less—may win a legislative seat, enabling a small party to have a voice and a base to attract more supporters in the next election. This prospect encourages and sustains minor parties.

Minor Parties

Although American elections disadvantage minor parties, also called "third parties," such parties do exist. Most, including the Prohibition Party (since the 1860s), which opposes the sale of alcoholic beverages, and the Communist Party USA (since the 1920s), which proposes the adoption of communism, receive little notice and few votes. But some, such as the Progressive Party in the late 1800s and early 1900s, have had a major impact by proposing a new agenda that the major parties have felt pressured to address or even embrace.

Some minor parties, chiefly in the twentieth century, have been essentially an individual's organization. In 1992, Texas businessman Ross Perot decided to run for president. His willingness to use his personal fortune to fund an expensive campaign made him a viable alternative to the major-party candidates. He received 19 percent of the vote, an extraordinary showing for a minor-party candidate (but his candidacy didn't influence the outcome, as he siphoned votes from both major-party candidates). His campaign pushed the issue of the budget deficit to the top of the national agenda.

Consumer advocate Ralph Nader ran in 2000 and 2004. In 2000, he was the nominee of the Green Party, an offshoot of the antinuclear and environmental movements. He claimed that the major parties were simply pawns of corporate America, and he called for more checks on big business. In 2000, Nader received just 3 percent of the vote nationwide, but his total included 97,000 votes in Florida. Because most Nader voters preferred Al Gore over George W. Bush, many of their votes would have gone to Gore if Nader hadn't been on the ballot. In the tight election, Nader's votes were enough to deny Gore a victory in the state and, consequently, in the Electoral College.[10] (Of course, in such a close election, other factors affected the outcome as well.)

Despite Nader's impact as a spoiler, third parties must overcome substantial barriers to have an impact. Most Americans feel long-standing loyalty to one of the major parties. They also realize that minor-party candidates can't win, so most don't want to "waste their vote" or, worse, help their least-preferred candidate, as Nader's Florida voters helped Bush. For these reasons, minor-party candidates can't raise the money or attract the media coverage they need.[11] Although many Americans—over half in various polls—tell pollsters that they want alternatives to the two major parties, few ever cast a vote for a minor-party candidate.

Historically, minor parties have done well only when the country has faced economic or social challenges that the major parties have failed to address. Then, once the minor parties have made an impact, the major parties have co-opted their ideas, and the minor parties, no longer needed, have faded into oblivion. After Perot focused the country's attention on the budget deficit, the incoming Clinton administration made the deficit its chief economic priority and thus eliminated the reason for supporting Perot.

Moderate Parties

The American party system encourages ideologically moderate political parties. In a two-party system, both parties typically are big tents with diverse members and views. To win, the parties have to attract many voters. Unlike in a multiparty system, where competing parties can gain legislative seats without winning a majority in any district, American parties can't focus their campaigns on just one or a few segments of the electorate. They must appeal to most of the electorate, which clusters in the middle rather than at the extremes (see Figure 2). This means that they usually choose pragmatism over ideology—put forth practical ideas that appeal to many voters over ideological ones that appeal only to their party's staunchest supporters. Therefore, the parties usually pitch their campaigns toward the middle, at least in nationwide contests.[12]

The Democrats are a center-left party. They are a diverse coalition of roughly 40 percent liberals, 40 percent moderates, and 20 percent conservatives.[13] The Republicans historically were a center-right party, though they have increasingly become a far-right party—a departure from the norm for American parties.

For the presidency, the parties usually nominate moderate candidates. When the parties nominate more ideological or extreme candidates—a very liberal Democrat or a very conservative Republican—these candidates usually move to the center or at least obscure their positions during the campaign. In the 2000 election, George W. Bush called himself a "compassionate conservative" to signal moderate voters that he was actually a moderate (but couldn't say so without alienating conservative voters). However, once elected, he pursued very conservative policies that reflected his conservative base.

In 2012, Mitt Romney campaigned as a staunch conservative to appeal to the conservatives who dominate the primary elections in the Republican Party. During the primary elections, a candid adviser told reporters that after Romney won the Republican nomination, he would campaign as a moderate in the general election. "Like an Etch A Sketch," he would shake the slate and start over. In the last month of the campaign, Romney did pivot toward the center, abandoning some positions he had taken earlier in the campaign.

Although the parties aim for the center in national elections, both have members and supportive interest groups—left of center in the Democratic Party and right of center in the Republican Party—tugging them toward their extremes. In recent decades, this tendency has been stronger in the Republican Party.

The Push to the Right

Conservatives began to push the Republican Party to the right in the 1960s, increased their efforts in the 1980s and 1990s, and accelerated their efforts in the 2000s.[14] During these decades, conservatives wrested control of the party's state and local organizations and the party's congressional leadership from moderates. (See Figure 3.)

Conservative interest groups, such as Americans for Tax Reform and the Club for Growth (see Chapter 6), have played a significant role. They have fueled this push to the right by offering political and financial support to Republican candidates while insisting that the candidates sign pledges promising to take conservative positions on various issues. In 2012, for example, Republicans were pressured to sign pledges opposing taxes, reducing deficits, fighting abortions, resisting gay rights, and taking a fourteen-point "marriage vow."[15] If the candidates refuse to sign the pledges, the groups throw their support behind other candidates running for the Republican nomination. If the candidates do sign the pledges, they're locked in. Once elected, they're pressured not to change their mind or compromise with Democratic legislators. If they change their mind or compromise anyway, the groups announce that they broke their pledges and became "untrustworthy" Republicans. Then, in the next election, the groups look for "loyal" Republicans to replace them. This threat has become pervasive within the party. In a message to freshmen Republicans in the House—members who were elected in 2010 and anticipating reelection in 2012—Sarah Palin warned, "Everyone I talk to still believes in contested primaries."[16] So, all but six of the 242 Republicans serving in the House of Representatives in 2012 signed the anti-tax pledge.[17]

The Tea Party movement has also played a significant role in pushing the Republican Party to the right.[18] In primary elections, Tea Party groups and candidates challenged, and defeated, establishment Republicans who had been endorsed by Republican officials. After these elections, Republican officials embraced the Tea Party groups and candidates as a way to tap into the Tea Party anger toward President Obama and the Democratic Party. (See the box "The Tea Party as a Third Party?")

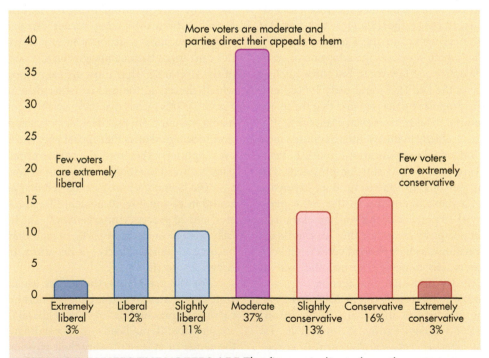

FIGURE 2: WHERE THE VOTERS ARE The figures indicate how the voters characterize themselves. In recent years, more have characterized themselves as conservative than as liberal, but most have characterized themselves as moderate. Thus the parties usually aim their campaigns at the middle.

SOURCE: Data from General Social Survey, 2008.

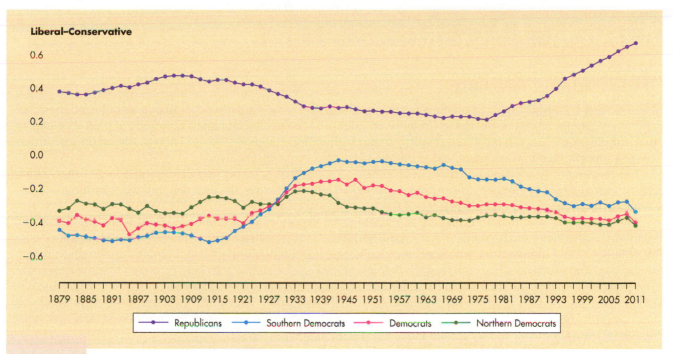

FIGURE 3: IDEOLOGICAL TRENDS OF PARTIES IN CONGRESS The lines indicate the conservative and liberal votes in the House of Representatives for members of both parties. (There are separate lines for southern Democrats and northern Democrats because of their ideological differences. The line for "Democrats" merges the two.) The more conservative the votes, the higher the line; the more liberal the votes, the lower the line. Congressional Republicans' shift further to the right began in the late 1970s, continued through the 1980s, and increased in the 1990s and 2000s.

SOURCE: "An Update on Political Polarization (through 2011)," Voteview Blog, February 9, 2012, voteview.com/images/polar_house_means.jpg. Copyright © 2012 by Keith Poole. Reproduced by permission.

As a result of the pressure from conservative interest groups and the Tea Party, many Republican officeholders fear a primary challenge more than the general election. They try to protect their right flank.

The conservatives' goal has been to mold the Republican Party into a highly disciplined and ideologically uniform party of the right, with a conservative agenda for economic issues, social issues, and foreign policies. By 2010, movement conservatives had succeeded in "silencing, co-opting, repelling, or expelling nearly every competing strain of Republicanism from the party."[19] This development, according to a historian, is unprecedented in American politics.[20]

As a result, the party now is more conservative than it was under Ronald Reagan, an icon of the party. Movement conservatives now don't think Reagan was sufficiently conservative. One Republican representative called Reagan a "moderate former liberal … who would never be elected [in a Republican primary] today, in my opinion."[21]

Fragmented Parties

The American party system also features fragmented political parties, meaning that their power is dispersed among their components. Party voters throughout the country; party officeholders at the national, state, and local levels; and officials in the national, state, and local party organizations are not unified through either a tight structure or a common program. Instead, reflecting the nature of American government itself, which disperses power through federalism, separation of powers, and checks and balances, party elements are relatively independent of one another.

Fragmentation makes it difficult for party leaders to fashion a coherent and consistent program and persuade their officeholders to accept it. Although presidents usually get support from their party members in Congress,[22] some party members go their own way. To get reelected, they need only the votes of their constituents—not the approval of the president or party leaders. When President Clinton proposed an increase in gas taxes to reduce the deficit, Sen. Herbert Kohl (D-Wisc.) told him the increase could be no more than 4.3 cents per gallon. Clinton had to accept Kohl's figure because the bill's outcome was in doubt and the senator's vote was essential. When President George W. Bush proposed immigration reform, conservative Republicans rebelled and refused to pass the bill.

Party Organization

Party organization—the professionals and activists who staff the party apparatus at the national, state, and local levels—reflects the fragmentation of the parties. The organization isn't hierarchical like the military, in which the higher-ups issue commands and the underlings follow them. The national party organization doesn't dictate policies to the state and local levels.

American Diversity

The Tea Party as a Third Party?

The Tea Party movement burst upon the American political scene soon after Barack Obama was elected president and many Democrats were elected to Congress in 2008. The movement launched hundreds of protests claiming that our government is too big and our taxes are too high. ("Tea" stands for "Taxed Enough Already.") Tea Partiers are disproportionately white, male, older, middle class, and very conservative.

The movement is a loose-knit coalition of grassroots clubs that have resisted becoming a large organization with a formal structure. Instead, the clubs have relied on television news, the Internet, and word-of-mouth to disseminate their views and spur attendance at their meetings and rallies.

The movement has criticized both parties, chastising the Republicans for supporting President Bush's increased spending and deficits and, in particular, his bank bailouts. Tea Partiers have derided Republican associations with Wall Street. Some members have complained that Republican leaders are actually liberals rather than true conservatives.[1] The movement has criticized the Democrats more vehemently, attacking President Obama especially. The president reflects the multiracial, multiethnic, and multicultural society that the United States has become rather than the traditional white European culture that Tea Partiers represent. They are suspicious about his background—his nationality, his religion—and his views. When he promised to "transform" America, they recoiled. They claim that he has put the United States on a "socialist" path.

National party organizations   The national party organization, called the **national committee,** is headed by the **national party chair,** who is appointed by the president or, for the opposition party, by its national committee. The chair raises money and speaks out on behalf of the party. The national committees rarely meet, although they do choose the site of the party's national convention and determine the formula for calculating each state's number of delegates.

Both parties also have House and Senate campaign committees, which raise money, recruit candidates, and develop strategy for upcoming campaigns.[23] Rep. Rahm Emanuel (D-Ill.), now mayor of Chicago, headed the Democratic Congressional Campaign Committee in 2006 and was charged with producing a Democratic majority in the House for the first time in twelve years. Emanuel recruited centrist candidates for conservative districts, such

Their criticism of both parties has led to speculation that they might form a third party. Yet most members are longtime Republicans. Their dissatisfaction with Republican officeholders is that they aren't conservative enough or determined enough. Tea Partiers think they are too quick to compromise—too inclined to do "business as usual." When Sen. Lindsey Graham (R-S.C.) was negotiating with Democrats over legislation, he was censored by a South Carolina Tea Party club, despite the fact that he had quite a conservative rating from the American Conservative Union.[2] However, as much as they dislike the Republican leaders and many Republican officeholders, Tea Partiers are well aware that they would split the conservative vote if they formed a third party.

Instead, their goal is to force the Republican Party further right. Before the 2010 congressional elections, they studied the voting records of Republican incumbents and then identified more conservative insurgent candidates to challenge the incumbents in Republican primaries. In seven states, they forced the Republican Party to nominate Tea Party candidates for the Senate over the incumbents or establishment candidates hand-picked by Republican officials.

Even so, Republican officials saw an opportunity to harness the Tea Party's energy and activism for their party, and they courted the movement. Republican representatives formed a Tea Party Caucus in the House. Republican senators funded Tea Party candidates for the Senate. Republican consultants helped the movement stage protests. Wealthy individuals who finance Republican candidates funded Tea Party candidates too. And Fox News, the Republican network that actively promoted the movement, encouraged them to stay within the Republican ranks rather than form a third party.[3]

The efforts by the Republican Party seemed to succeed in the 2010 congressional elections. The Tea Party inspired grassroots conservatives and energized the Republican Party, which had been demoralized by its defeats in the 2008 presidential and congressional elections. As a result, Tea Partiers set the agenda for the election and helped the Republicans regain control of the House of Representatives (though Tea Partiers caused the Republicans to lose three seats in the Senate that they might have won).[4]

Then, the Republican members of the House affiliated with the Tea Party tried to achieve their policy goals. Although they had successes, their extremism was a threat to the Republican leaders of the House, who had a difficult time managing them. In fact, some Republican legislators asked that their weekly meetings be suspended because they became shouting matches and antileader rants. In the end, the Tea Partiers pushed the Republican leadership farther than it wanted to go. Even so, more extreme members wanted to go farther still. They would have shut down the government, if necessary, to force more cuts in its spending.[5]

The movement reflects the war over ideological purity within the GOP (addressed in the Talking Points). The Tea Partiers don't need to form a third party—they plan to dominate the Republican Party. Already Tea Partiers are running for precinct representatives within the GOP, hoping to take over the party one precinct at a time.[6]

[1] Megan Thee-Brenan and Marina Stefan, "'The System Is Broken': More from a Poll of Tea Party Backers," *New York Times*, April 18, 2010, A14.

[2] Robert Draper, "This Year's Maverick," *New York Times Magazine*, July 4, 2010, 25.

[3] For a careful and thorough examination of the Tea Party, see Theda Skocpol and Vanessa Williamson, *The Tea Party and the Remaking of Republican Conservatism* (New York: Oxford University Press, 2012).

[4] Ibid., 158–161.

[5] Paul Kane, "Book: Tea Party Turned into a Monster for Boehner, Other House Leaders," Washington Post, April 22, 2012, http://www.washingtonpost.com/politics/book-gop-freshman-class-turned-into-a-monster-for-boehner-other-house-leaders/2012/04/22/gIQAV15PaT_story.html.

[6] Kathleen Hennessey, "'Tea Party' Activists Filter into GOP at Ground Level," Los Angeles Times, latimes.com/news/la-na-tea-party15-2010feb15,0,1519774.story.

as retired NFL quarterback Heath Shuler of North Carolina. Shuler resisted Emanuel's pleas to run, insisting that he wanted to spend time with his family, but Emanuel persisted, calling him five times a day.[24] Reported Shuler, "He calls one morning: 'Heath, I'm taking my kids to school,' then he just hangs up. At 11:30, he calls and says, 'I'm leaving my office to eat lunch with my kids.' Then, 'Heath, it's 3:30, and I'm walking into school.'"[25] Shuler finally relented—and

won his election—and Emanuel delivered a majority for the Democrats. (But Emanuel discovered that such candidates, once elected, can make governing more difficult. Shuler voted against the Democrats' stimulus, auto bailouts, and health care reform bills.)

State and local party organizations State and local party organizations have committees and chairs to direct party

Log in to www.cengagebrain.com and open Course-Reader to access the full reading "'You're Nuts!' The G.O.P. Elite Tries to Take Its Party Back," by Matt Bai.

The Republican Party has welcomed the Tea Party movement for its energy and its members—foot soldiers marching to the polls on election day for Republican candidates. But the Republican elites have been leery of the extreme positions taken by the Tea Partiers, fearing that these positions will alienate the moderates within the party and among independent voters.

So, while exploiting the movement, the Republican elites have tried to co-opt it and temper it. A Republican strategist explained the approach: "The secret to politics [is] trying to control a segment of people without those people recognizing that you're trying to control them."[1] But the Tea Partiers have resisted entreaties to moderate their positions and have continued efforts to push the Republican Party further right. Thus the Republican Party is attempting to control the Tea Party while the Tea Party is attempting to control the Republican Party.

1. Why do Republican elites consider Tea Partiers "nuts"?
2. How do attitudes toward compromise display differences between the Republican establishment and the Tea Party movement?
3. What consequences do you foresee if the Republican elites control the Tea Party insurgents? If not?

[1] Bai, "'You're Nuts!,'" 46.

activities at these levels. Some communities have strong party organizations made up of volunteers who recruit candidates to run and citizens to work the precincts and staff the telephones. In other communities, the parties are so weak that they have few activities or volunteers.

Now we'll turn to history to see how the parties originated and developed and to see what roles they've played in the American political system.

THE RISE OF AMERICAN PARTIES

The Founders dreaded the prospect of political parties, fearing that rival parties, seeking to win favors for themselves at the expense of the common good, would undermine the new nation and its fledgling government.[26] They hoped, unrealistically, to govern by consensus.

Because of the Founders' misgivings, the Constitution doesn't mention political parties. Nevertheless, the Constitution created a government in which parties would be inevitable. With popular election as the mechanism for selecting political leaders, some agency for organizing and mobilizing the supporters of competing candidates would be necessary.

Birth of Parties

With George Washington's unanimous election to the presidency in 1788, it appeared that the nation could be governed by consensus. But conflicts soon emerged. Alexander Hamilton, Washington's secretary of the treasury, favored a strong national government. He and his supporters in Congress, who called themselves **Federalists,** were opposed by Thomas Jefferson, Washington's secretary of state, who feared a strong central government. This disagreement led Jefferson to challenge John Adams, a Federalist, for the presidency in 1796. Jefferson lost, but his defeat showed him the need for an organization. He recruited political operatives in each state who established newspapers to publicize his views, thus creating the first American political party—the **Jeffersonians.** Backed by his new party, Jefferson won the presidency in 1800. (See the box "Alexander Hamilton, Party Tactician.")

Before Jefferson left office, most members of Congress—more than 90 percent—were either Jeffersonians (later called Jeffersonian Republicans) or Federalists and consistently voted in support of their party's positions.[27]

Development of Mass Parties

Andrew Jackson introduced the idea of a political party with a large following among rank-and-file voters. Running for president in 1828, he reached out to the masses, and his appeals drew five times more voters to the polls than in 1824. Jackson's opponents deplored his approach, calling him a "barbarian" and his campaign "the howl of raving democracy."[28]

Like Jefferson, Jackson saw the strength of American democracy in the common person. He encouraged participation in government and inspired reforms. As a result, property ownership as a qualification for voting was lifted in most states where it still existed,[29] extending the franchise to almost all white men. Members of the Electoral College were elected by the people rather than selected by state legislatures. National party conventions, with representatives from every state and locality, were held to nominate presidential candidates.[30] Looking back on this time and its emphasis on the common person, historians would refer to the era of **Jacksonian democracy.**

With the enhanced participation fostered by these reforms, the idea of a political party with a mass following took root in American politics. The electorate doubled by 1840.[31]

Golden Age of Mass Parties

Parties reached their high point in the late nineteenth and early twentieth centuries, when party leaders controlled nominations for public offices and mobilized voters during election campaigns. Voting rates reached their highest levels ever during this period.

Political Machines

The power of local parties was concentrated in **political machines,** powerful organizations that could deliver the votes. Also known as "urban machines" because they were prevalent in big cities, they flourished during this period, with some lasting until the middle of the twentieth century.

Unlike today's parties, political machines were hierarchical organizations. A city was divided into small neighborhoods called precincts, and the precincts were grouped into larger neighborhoods called wards. Party operatives were designated as "precinct captains" and "ward heelers." Their job was to know their constituents, tend to their needs, and then get their votes for the party's candidates in the next election. The head of the machine was a boss, who often served as the mayor and who directed the organization and ran city government to maintain control for his party. (See the box "A Day in the Life of a Machine Politician.")

The machines relied on the votes of the poor and working class, many of whom had recently immigrated from Europe. Although most accounts of machine politics are negative, dwelling on corruption, the machines provided valuable services for their constituents.

Providing welfare   Political machines served as an informal welfare system for poor people before government established a formal welfare system. Party workers were an early "Welcome Wagon" for new immigrants, meeting them on the dock as they came off the ship and helping them settle into their new community in this strange country. The party provided food, clothing, or housing for people in need.

Longtime Rep. Tip O'Neill (D-Mass.) told the story of Boston mayor James Curley, a leader of the city's Democratic organization in the early twentieth century. As winter approached, Curley called Filene's, a local department store, and told the owner he needed five thousand sweaters. When the owner balked, Curley reminded him that it was time to reassess Filene's property for tax purposes, a none-too-subtle threat that its taxes would go up if the sweaters weren't delivered. So, the sweaters were delivered and then distributed to poor people in the city.[32]

Of course, party leaders were not motivated by altruism but rather by self-interest. They granted favors to get favors (votes) in return. As New York City's boss George Washington Plunkitt said, "If a family is burned out, I don't ask whether they are Republicans or Democrats.... I just get quarters for them, buy clothes for them if their clothes were burned up and fix them up 'til they get things runnin' again. It's philanthropy, but it's politics too—mighty good politics. Who can tell me how many votes one of these fires brings me?"[33]

Providing jobs   Because they controlled government jobs, the machines also served as an informal employment agency. Under their **patronage system,**[34] virtually all government jobs, from the mayor's top aide to street sweepers, went to

political appointees. When one party captured control of city government, city workers who supported the losing party were fired and new workers who supported the winning party were hired in their place. "To the victor belong the spoils," the saying went. So the patronage system came to be known as the **spoils system**. The practice began with the presidency of Andrew Jackson, who wanted common people to get a share of government jobs and so gave jobs to western frontiersmen rather than to eastern businessmen.

In adopting this practice, the machines provided jobs to some middle-class people and to many poor people and new immigrants. By 1900, New York City's machine controlled

BEHIND THE SCENES

Alexander Hamilton, Party Tactician

Alexander Hamilton, who as secretary of the treasury laid the foundation for American capitalism, also was responsible for the first religious attacks on political opponents in election campaigns.[1]

Hamilton was an unlikely advocate of religion. A libertine, he was involved with his sister-in-law and with a woman described as a "grifter" (a swindler).[2] He was not a practicing Christian until the dueling death of his oldest son, just three years before his own dueling death.

Although Hamilton supported separation of church and state, he was a practical politician, and an opportunistic one. Realizing that appealing to the religious sentiments and prejudices of the people was "an important means of influencing opinion,"[3] he urged fellow leaders not to be "overscrupulous" about manipulating the masses.[4]

As the leader of the Federalists, Hamilton opposed the Jeffersonians. In the election of 1800, he launched a smear campaign to portray Thomas Jefferson as a godless and amoral man who, if elected president, would bring depravity to the nation's capital. Hamilton hoped to discourage Christians from supporting Jefferson, who was inspired by philosophy and science more than by religion and who rejected Christian dogma and criticized its clergy.

Hamilton's efforts backfired, as the voters recognized the strategy behind the charges. Nonetheless, his efforts showed savvy politicians how religious issues might be used to manipulate public opinion in the future.

[1] This box is drawn from Brooke Allen, *Moral Minority: Our Skeptical Founding Fathers* (Chicago: Ivan R. Dee, 2006), ch. 6.
[2] Ibid., 123.
[3] Ibid., 130.
[4] Ibid., 131.

In 1828, opponents of Andrew Jackson called him a jackass. Political cartoonists and journalists began to use the donkey to symbolize Jackson and the Democratic Party (*left*). In the 1870s, cartoonist Thomas Nast popularized the donkey as a symbol of the party and originated the elephant as a symbol of the Republican Party. His 1874 cartoon (*right*) showed the Democratic donkey dressed as a lion frightening the other animals of the jungle, including the Republican elephant.

60,000 city jobs. In the 1960s and 1970s, Chicago's mayor, Richard Daley, one of the last of the big-city bosses, controlled 35,000 city jobs and, indirectly through public contracts, 10,000 private ones.[35]

When the parties provided welfare and jobs, the recipients were not only grateful but also indebted to the party. Fearful of losing their jobs, they formed an army of campaign workers, going door-to-door and when necessary taking residents to the polls to cast their votes for the party.

Turnout in elections was sky-high in the era of machine politics. In the 1896 presidential election, party workers got 90 percent of eligible voters (outside the South) to the polls, an astonishing number when many voters lived in isolated rural areas and used horses and buggies for transportation.[36]

Engaging in corruption   Although the machines provided undeniable benefits, they also engaged in undeniable corruption (as the story about the sweaters illustrates). Bribes and kickbacks were common, and payoffs were necessary for businesses to get government contracts. Widespread corruption eventually produced a backlash against the machines, and the middle class, which was less dependent on the machines, pressured legislators to enact reforms that led to their demise.

Thinking about Democracy

Does it seem that the parties in this era made government more democratic or less democratic than the parties of today do?

Functions of Parties

When political parties were at the height of their power, they performed important functions for society. (When we speak of institutions or organizations performing "functions," we mean that institutions or organizations do things that society finds useful. These things become their "functions" for social scientists.) The parties' primary function, then as now, was to get their candidates elected, but to accomplish this goal they had to perform other functions to gain the allegiance of voters.

We've already seen that the parties provided welfare and jobs to many people. They also provided information about politics through party newspapers. Though one-sided, the newspapers helped party supporters learn about politics and government and recognize their stake in upcoming elections.[37] After gaining the allegiance of many people, the parties were in position to mobilize their supporters on election day.

The parties recruited candidates for public office from party workers who had moved up the ladder from low-level jobs to more responsible jobs. (The boss of New York City's machine began by delivering coal to poor people in the winter.) Once the workers had proven themselves, party leaders would consider them for elective office. The party controlled nominations at the local level (city council and mayor), state level (state legislature and governor), and national level (Congress and the president). These nominations weren't open contests in which any aspiring citizen could compete; they were awarded to those who had proven themselves and demonstrated their loyalty. Without the party's blessing, no candidate could secure the nomination or hope to win the election.

Impact social, global, historical, economic, political

A Day in the Life of a Machine Politician

George Washington Plunkitt was a ward leader in the infamous Tammany Hall machine, the Democratic Party organization that governed New York City for seven decades in the late nineteenth and early twentieth centuries. Although Plunkitt was on the city payroll, he did not have a free ride. The demands of his job were exhausting. But providing social services to his constituents created opportunities to build support for his party.

Entries from Plunkitt's diary illustrate the typical tasks he faced each day.

- 2:00 a.m. Aroused from sleep by a bartender who asked me to go to the police station and bail out a saloon keeper who had been arrested for violating the excise law. Furnished bail and returned to bed at three o'clock.
- 6:00 a.m. Awakened by fire engines. Hastened to the scene of the fire . . . found several tenants who had been burned out, took them to a hotel, supplied them with clothes, fed them, and arranged temporary quarters for them.
- 8:30 a.m. Went to the police court to secure the discharge of six "drunks," my constituents, by a timely word to the judge. Paid the fines of two.
- 9:00 a.m. Appeared in the municipal district court to direct one of my district captains to act as counsel for a widow about to be dispossessed. . . . Paid the rent of a poor family and gave them a dollar for food.
- 11:00 a.m. At home again. "Fixed" the troubles of four men waiting for me: one discharged by the Metropolitan Railway for neglect of duty; another wanted a job on the road; the third on the subway; and the fourth was looking for work with a gas company.
- 3:00 p.m. Attended the funeral of an Italian. Hurried back for the funeral of a Hebrew constituent. Went conspicuously to the front both in the Catholic church and the synagogue.
- 7:00 p.m. Went to district headquarters to preside over a meeting of election district captains, submitted lists of all the voters in their districts and told who were in need, who were in trouble, who might be won over [to Tammany] and how.
- 8:00 p.m. Went to a church fair. Took chances on everything, bought ice cream for the young girls and the children, kissed the little ones, flattered their mothers, and took the fathers out for something down at the corner.
- 9:00 p.m. At the clubhouse again. Spent $10 for a church excursion. Bought tickets for a baseball game. Listened to the complaints of a dozen pushcart peddlers who said they were being persecuted by the police. Promised to go to police headquarters in the morning and see about it.
- 10:30 p.m. Attended a Hebrew wedding reception and dance. Had previously sent a handsome wedding present to the bride.
- 12:00 a.m. In bed.

George Washington Plunkitt holds forth in his unofficial office, a bootblack stand at the New York County Court House.

SOURCES: Alistair Cooke, *Alistair Cooke's America* (New York: Knopf, 1973), 290–291; adapted from William L. Riordon, *Plunkitt of Tammany Hall* (New York Dutton, 1963), 91–93.

The parties also ran campaigns for their candidates, mapping strategy, raising funds, and recruiting workers. In the 1896 election, Republican workers brought 750,000 persons from all over the United States to the Ohio home of their candidate, William McKinley, who greeted the visitors from his front porch.[38]

If successful in gaining peoples' allegiance and winning their votes on election day, a party could control the government. Thus the value of political parties in a democracy was to give average people political power. As individuals, ordinary people were powerless; as members of a political party, they could be powerful. Collectively, they could wield power that otherwise only corporations or wealthy individuals could exercise.

In the late nineteenth century and early twentieth century, parties benefited society and in the process strengthened themselves by performing functions that made them indispensable. What, however, would happen if parties could no longer perform these functions? We will return to this question shortly.

THE DECLINE OF AMERICAN PARTIES

Although many Americans think that political parties are too powerful today, they are in fact far less powerful than they were in the late nineteenth and early twentieth centuries.

Progressive Reforms

American political parties began to lose power with the advent of the **Progressive movement,** which morphed into a third party, the Progressive Party, in the early 1900s. Middle-class Americans concerned with the corruption of big-city machines fueled the movement, which sought to wrest control from the machines and from the immigrants and poor people served by the machines. The movement championed numerous reforms that reduced corruption but also weakened the power of political parties and consequently reduced the power of poor and working-class voters.

Election reforms, including voter registration, the secret ballot, and primary elections, brought the golden age of political parties to an end. **Voter registration,** which required voters to register their name and address before an election, made it difficult for parties to stuff ballot boxes with fraudulent votes. The parties could no longer urge their workers to "vote early and vote often." The **secret ballot** prevented party workers stationed at the polls from knowing how any citizens voted—in particular, how their (assumed) supporters voted. Thus parties could no longer reward their supporters for their votes. These reforms reduced the corruption fostered by the machines, but primary elections undermined the parties' control of nominations, which was devastating to the parties' power. **Primary elections,** held several weeks or months before the general election, allowed the party's voters rather than the party's leaders to decide who would be the party's nominees in the general election. The party's leaders could no longer reward the most effective and most loyal workers with nominations. And, after the election, the leaders could no longer demand that the officials remain faithful to the party and its policies. Instead, the officials only had to remain popular with the voters.

Another Progressive reform, the **merit system,** allocated government jobs on the basis of competence rather than affiliation with a party. Once established, merit systems were expanded to cover more and more jobs. Eventually, the merit systems at the local, state, and national levels replaced the patronage systems for all but a small number of jobs—the top aides to the president, governor, and mayor.

Although the Progressive Party never captured the presidency, it became the most influential third party in American history. Its ideas were enacted into law throughout the country.

Welfare Programs

During the Great Depression, which started in 1929, the federal government established welfare programs for the needy and the elderly—basic welfare, now known as Temporary Assistance, and Social Security. In later decades, it added food stamps, Medicaid (health care for poor people), and Medicare (health care for the elderly and others on Social Security). In addition, it provided unemployment compensation to those temporarily out of work. Thus the government substituted systematic welfare programs for the hit-or-miss efforts of the party machines.

Because these benefits come from the government, people don't have to seek them from the parties. Therefore, government welfare programs, along with government merit systems, severed the links between many people and political parties. No longer the source of welfare and jobs, the parties had less hold on the allegiance—and the votes—of lower- and middle-class Americans.

For the most part, the changes during the Progressive era and the Great Depression were desirable. Political corruption was reduced; government jobs went to those individuals competent to perform them, rather than to political hacks; and welfare programs reached everyone in need, not just the supporters of the party in power. But the changes did curtail the parties' power and hence their ability to represent and fight for average people.

Independent Media

The parties also lost their monopoly over political information. In the 1800s independent newspapers replaced party newspapers,[39] and in the 1920s and 1950s radio and television emerged and gained mass audiences. Although many newspapers and radio and television stations expressed political preferences, they were independent of either party. With exposure to multiple news sources, people could, and did, decide for themselves how to vote.

Diminution of Campaign Roles

Today the parties don't even perform their core functions of nominating candidates and running campaigns as they used to.

Party voters in primary elections choose the nominees. The parties still hold their conventions, but the conventions merely ratify the choices of the voters and rally public support for the ticket.

Nor are parties the driving force behind campaigns. Although candidates receive money, advice, and workers from local, state, and national party organizations, most rely on their own campaign teams. Modern media elections require extensive expertise: specialists in polling, fundraising, and

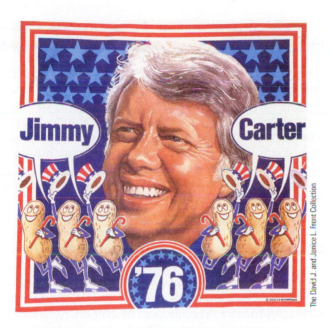

Party officials no longer determine their nominee for president; party voters in primary elections do. In 1976, Democratic officials were reluctant to endorse Jimmy Carter, who was relatively inexperienced, but Democratic voters in the primaries liked his decency. Carter received enough support from them that the party had to nominate him. Although he won the general election (thus vindicating the voters in the primaries), he was unable to govern effectively (thus vindicating party officials). Consequently, in 1980 he lost his reelection bid.

advertising, including experts to design and produce the ads, others to buy television time and newspaper space for the ads, and others to generate direct mail. Now candidates also need specialists to design and maintain web pages and blogs and promote the candidates through social media. They need campaign managers and speechwriters. Some use speech and drama coaches to help them speak, gesture, and move effectively.

This talent is expensive. The 2008 presidential primary candidates spent, collectively, nearly $1 billion. The parties help pay the bills but can't afford the majority of the costs, so the candidates turn to wealthy individuals and interest groups for the rest. Once elected, the officials may feel more beholden to their contributors than to their party.

Thus interest groups play a big role in funding modern campaigns. As the parties have lost power, interest groups have gained it. Picture a teeter-totter with political parties on one end and interest groups on the other. As the power of political parties has gone down, the power of interest groups has gone up.

For these reasons, elected officials are more independent of their party, and less obligated to follow its platform, than they used to be. Therefore, the parties aren't as able to control the government as they used to do.

Erosion of Popular Support?

Because parties don't perform the same functions or don't perform them to the same degree as they used to, people aren't as attached to parties as they once were. *Dealignment* is the term for this lessening of citizens' attachment.[40]

Political scientists pointed to two trends after the 1960s that seemed to reflect dealignment. The percentage of voters who declared themselves independent, rather than a member of either party, increased. And the percentage of voters who split their ticket—voting for both Democrats and Republicans in an election—increased. (However, recent research indicates that most "independents" regularly vote for the candidates of one party, and that numerous voters split their ticket in some years but less in other years. Thus these trends are not as conclusive as they are sometimes portrayed.)

Because of these changes and trends, political scientists in the 1970s and subsequent decades speculated that American parties would continue to decline and perhaps even disappear. But this speculation was premature. Despite some dealignment, there remains considerable support for the parties.

THE RESURGENCE OF AMERICAN PARTIES

The parties have recognized their decline and fought to revitalize themselves. They have adjusted to the changing political landscape by raising substantial amounts of money, bolstering their organizations with professional and specialized staffers, and linking with political consultants. In recent decades they have also benefited from the polarization and heightened partisanship of American society, media, and government.[41] They have been resilient. Although they are weaker today than a century ago, they still play important roles in American politics.

Informing

Parties continue to provide information to supporters by taking positions on issues covered by the media and by advertising in the media and through direct mail. Increasingly, parties provide information via the Internet.

Nominating and Campaigning

Although the parties no longer control the nominations, they do continue to recruit candidates and to provide them with campaign services and financial support. They also host workshops on topics such as raising money and talking to reporters, and they sometimes offer the services of specialized consultants.

Governing

Political parties continue to dominate Congress. The majority party in each house organizes and runs its chamber. It selects the presiding officers, who set the agenda, deciding which issues are debated and voted upon. The majority also designates the chairs of the committees and subcommittees and controls the committees and subcommittees.

Members of Congress usually vote with other members of their party, and members of the president's party usually follow his lead. Partisan voting in Congress has increased dramatically since the 1970s.[42] During the Bush and Obama presidencies, both Republicans and Democrats voted with members of their party, in opposition to members of the other party, about 90 percent of the time.[43] (See Figure 3 in Chapter 9.)

Before the 1980s, congressional Democrats included many southern moderates and conservatives, who sometimes voted with the Republicans, and congressional Republicans included some northern moderates and liberals, who sometimes voted with the Democrats. Thus party voting was less prevalent. Since then, southern conservatives have gravitated to the Republican Party, and northern liberals have moved to the Democratic Party (as we'll explain in the next section). Thus both parties in Congress have become more ideologically consistent.[44]

Party voting in recent decades also reflects the election of conservative Republicans to Congress during the 1990s and 2000s and the election of George W. Bush in 2000 and 2004. Determined to capitalize on their control of Congress and the White House and later on the swell of public support for the president following 9/11, Republican leaders in Congress pushed a very conservative agenda. With the aid of talk radio, Fox News, and conservative interest groups, they pressured the remaining moderate Republicans to go along. In response, Democrats, who traditionally have been less united than Republicans, came together in an attempt to check the very conservative policies of Republicans. These dynamics led to more partisan voting in Congress.

Party-line voting is likely to remain high as long as the parties, reflecting the intense disagreements among the American people, have divergent visions for the country. Party-line voting also is likely to remain high as long as the parties see political gain in such voting. President Obama made overtures toward bipartisanship, but congressional Democrats were less willing, and congressional Republicans were very resistant. Obama believed in bipartisanship but also wanted to show Americans that he could get things done. Republicans wanted to show Americans that he couldn't get things done. Congressional Republicans saw more political advantage in blocking his proposals than in compromising and influencing them. As a result, the Democrats wrote the health care reform bill while the Republicans sat on the sidelines, and most Democrats voted for it while all but one Republican voted against it.

Most Americans deplore partisan wrangling, but clear partisan divisions do help voters recognize the differences between the parties and also help voters hold elected officials accountable for their policies. Thus these divisions increase the likelihood of popular control of government.

Despite the increase in partisan voting, the American party system falls short of what political scientists call **responsible party government**. Under this model, political parties would take clear and opposing positions on major issues, voters would understand these differences and vote on this basis, and officeholders would enact the party's positions into law. Some European democracies, which have much stronger parties, come close to this ideal. Citizens vote for a party, with its positions on the issues, rather than for a candidate. They assume that the party is cohesive enough to enact its positions if it wins the election. Once elected, legislators do vote with their party on major issues. If they defect—a rare occurrence—they risk expulsion from the party and loss of their seat. Even if they abstain, they risk punishment.[45]

In recent congresses, our system has come closer to this model than it typically has in the past. Democrats and Republicans have taken opposing stands on controversial issues, and they have made concerted efforts to enact their party's positions into law. Of course, American citizens vote for individual candidates rather than for a party, and American officials retain more independence than European officials do. Nevertheless, there is mounting pressure on Democratic officials to accept Democratic positions and, especially, on Republican officials to accept Republican positions. Yet it is unlikely that we will adopt the responsible party government model for the long term. In contrast to Europeans, Americans hold individualistic rather than communitarian values. Constituents tolerate, even expect, representatives to deviate from their party at times. They praise representatives who are "independent," and representatives claim to be "independent" of their party and its leaders. To get elected and reelected, of course, representatives need to appease their constituents more than their party.

Further, our separation of powers makes responsible party government unlikely. One party may control the presidency while the other controls one or both houses of Congress. Divided government diffuses and obscures responsibility rather than pinpoints it. With divided responsibility, the voters are unable to determine which party to praise or blame for government policies.

PARTY REALIGNMENTS

Although we have two competitive parties, at any given time the two parties may not be evenly matched. Usually one is dominant, winning the presidency and Congress in election after election. Eventually, some major event, such as a war or a depression, destabilizes voters' party allegiance and triggers a massive movement of voters from one party to the other party, which then becomes the dominant party. The process by which one party loses many supporters to the other party is referred to as a **realignment**.[46]

These upheavals—revolutions without bloodshed—have occurred about every thirty to forty years. Since the party system was established, there have been three major realignments—during the Civil War in the 1860s, the depression in the 1890s,[47] and the Great Depression in the 1930s.[48] There have also been minor realignments limited to certain geographical regions or demographic groups. (See Figure 4.)

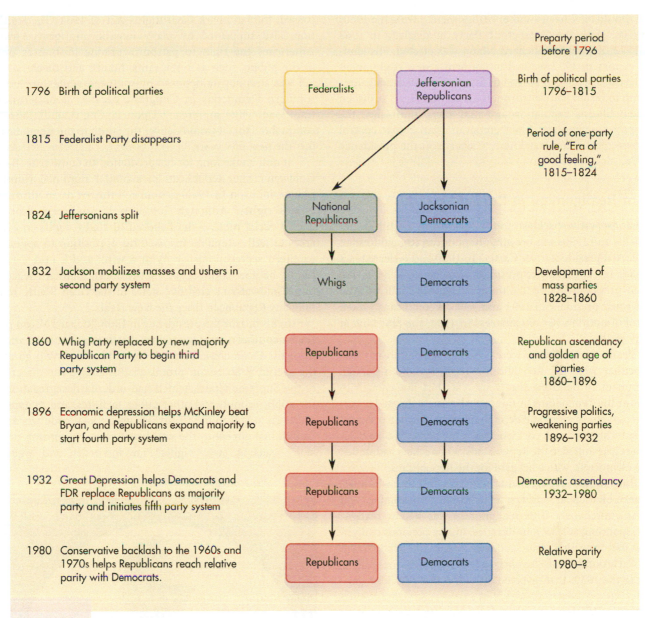

FIGURE 4: EVOLUTION OF THE POLITICAL PARTIES IN THE UNITED STATES

The figure shows a timeline on the left and a corresponding era description on the right, with party boxes in between.

Year	Event	Party line (left)	Party line (right)	Era
				Preparty period before 1796
1796	Birth of political parties	Federalists	Jeffersonian Republicans	Birth of political parties 1796–1815
1815	Federalist Party disappears			Period of one-party rule, "Era of good feeling," 1815–1824
1824	Jeffersonians split	National Republicans	Jacksonian Democrats	
1832	Jackson mobilizes masses and ushers in second party system	Whigs	Democrats	Development of mass parties 1828–1860
1860	Whig Party replaced by new majority Republican Party to begin third party system	Republicans	Democrats	Republican ascendancy and golden age of parties 1860–1896
1896	Economic depression helps McKinley beat Bryan, and Republicans expand majority to start fourth party system	Republicans	Democrats	Progressive politics, weakening parties 1896–1932
1932	Great Depression helps Democrats and FDR replace Republicans as majority party and initiates fifth party system	Republicans	Democrats	Democratic ascendancy 1932–1980
1980	Conservative backlash to the 1960s and 1970s helps Republicans reach relative parity with Democrats.	Republicans	Democrats	Relative parity 1980–?

Major Realignment in the 1930s

The realignment of the 1930s set the stage for the politics of recent decades. The Republicans had dominated since the realignment of the 1890s. When the Great Depression rocked the country, those hit hardest, such as the poor, working men and women, recent immigrants, and black Americans, who had favored Abraham Lincoln's party since the Civil War, turned to the Democrats, electing Franklin D. Roosevelt as president and Democratic majorities to Congress. The 1932 election started a major realignment, from Republicans to Democrats, and marked a new era. Most new voters and some Republicans became Democrats. The Democrats would control the presidency for the next twenty years, electing FDR to an unprecedented four terms, and would control at least one house of Congress until 1954.

Roosevelt's **New Deal coalition,** composed of city dwellers, blue-collar workers, Catholic and Jewish immigrants, blacks, and southerners, was a potent political force, but it was an uneasy alliance—liberal, urban, black and white northerners, and conservative, rural, white southerners committed to racial segregation. After FDR's death in 1945, the coalition began to fray. The party's support for civil rights, which began in 1948 and accelerated in the 1960s, alienated white southerners, and U.S. involvement in the Vietnam War split the party in 1968. The coalition continued to erode. Even though the party would dominate Congress until 1994, it would win the presidency only three more times during the twentieth century.[49]

Remember the historical pattern—a new realignment about every thirty to forty years. If the pattern continued, there should have been another realignment during the 1960s or 1970s. With the Democratic Party in disarray in 1968 and 1972, Republican Richard Nixon was elected. His landslide victory in 1972 seemed to confirm a new realignment toward the Republican Party, but his Watergate scandal, forcing him to resign halfway through his second term, tarnished the Republicans' reputation and may have diminished the anticipated realignment. The Democrats continued to control Congress, and Democrat Jimmy Carter won the presidency in 1976.

Minor Realignment in Recent Decades

But a conservative backlash to the liberalism and turmoil of the 1960s and 1970s was brewing. Republican Ronald Reagan was elected president (over Carter) in 1980 and reelected in a landslide in 1984. His vice president, George H. W. Bush, was elected president in 1988. Although Democrat Bill Clinton was elected president in 1992 and 1996, Republicans gained control of both houses of Congress in 1994, the first time in four decades.

Clearly, the Democrats were no longer the dominant party, but neither were the Republicans. There had been enough realignment to dethrone the Democrats but not enough to enthrone the Republicans. A minor realignment, limited to certain geographic regions and demographic groups, had occurred and had fostered rough parity between the parties. Some blocs of voters had shifted to the Republicans, while others had shifted to the Democrats, with a net gain for the Republicans.

This minor realignment involved southern whites, northern blue-collar workers, white-collar professionals, and regular churchgoers. This realignment was a slow realignment, spanning at least four decades, unlike previous realignments that transpired more suddenly.[50] And this realignment revolved around social cleavages in society, unlike the realignment in the 1930s that revolved around economic cleavages.

Southern Whites

In the 1960s, the combination of the civil rights movement and the federal government's efforts to eliminate racial segregation caused many southern whites to leave their longtime home in the Democratic Party. Their move to the Republican Party was the most significant switch in this minor realignment.

Southern whites' disaffection with the Democratic Party began after World War II, when Democratic president Harry Truman, who took office upon Roosevelt's death, integrated the Armed Forces. In 1948, the president and the Democrats included a civil rights plank in the party's platform. The move prompted Strom Thurmond, Democratic governor of South Carolina, to form a breakaway party, the States' Rights Party, commonly called the Dixiecrats. Thurmond ran for president against Truman and carried four southern states. Although the Dixiecrats returned to the fold, southern discomfort with the party grew in the 1950s when northern Democrats again proposed civil rights legislation.

The exodus gained momentum when Democratic president Lyndon Johnson pushed, and the Democratic Congress

passed, the landmark Civil Rights Act of 1964. The legislation, also supported by many Republicans, gave African Americans the right to patronize private businesses open to the public, such as restaurants, hotels, and theaters. The bill was strenuously opposed by southern whites, including southern Democrats in Congress, because it undermined traditional white supremacy. Upon signing the bill, Johnson commented that it would deliver the South to the Republicans for "the next fifty years."[51]

It didn't take long for his prediction to come true. Barry Goldwater, the Republican presidential nominee running against Johnson in 1964, denounced the act as an affront to **"states' rights."** Although Goldwater himself seemed not to have a racial motive—he believed in states' rights in other areas as well—Republicans used his opposition to appeal to southern segregationists.[52] With a wink and a nod, "states' rights" became code for letting the South maintain segregation. Goldwater carried five states in the Deep South, more than any Republican since the New Deal.

In his bid for the presidency in 1968, Richard Nixon pursued a **southern strategy** to lure disaffected southern whites from the Democratic Party. A top aide said, "We'll go after the racists."[53] So Nixon promised "to change the direction" of the Supreme Court, which had ordered desegregation of the public schools and other public facilities, and to appoint southern judges to the Court. He used racial code words—a "subliminal appeal to the anti-black voter," according to his aide[54]—such as "states' rights," "law and order," and "welfare"

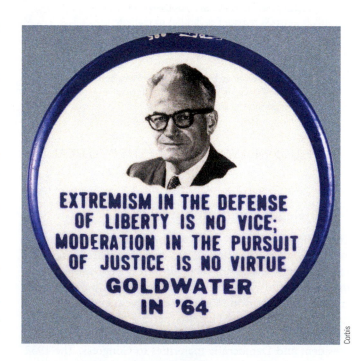

Arizona senator Barry Goldwater captured the Republican nomination for president in 1964. These rousing words in his acceptance speech, quoted on this campaign pin, reflected the new dominance of conservatives over moderates in the party.

to send a clear message that the states should be allowed to handle racial matters; control black demonstrators, rioters, and criminals; and crack down on welfare cheats (who were assumed to be African Americans), all as the states preferred to rather than as federal laws or court decisions told them to. After taping a campaign commercial stressing "law and order in the schools," he said to his aides, "Yep, this hits it right on the nose.... It's all about law and order and the damn Negro-Puerto Rican groups out there."[55]

To accomplish their goal of a realignment, Republican strategists concluded that they would have to polarize the country over racial issues so that whites would remain angry at blacks.[56] After Nixon, Republican politicians continued to fan the flames, from desegregation to busing to affirmative action, and to other issues with racial overtones, such as crime and welfare.

In 1980, Ronald Reagan opened his presidential campaign in Philadelphia, Mississippi, where three civil rights workers had been brutally murdered by local citizens with assistance from law enforcement officers, one of the most notorious crimes of the civil rights era (see Chapter 14). In his campaign, Reagan talked about "states' rights" and "welfare queens," a thinly veiled reference to black women who were assumed to be living the high life on welfare.

In 1988, George H. W. Bush, campaigning against Democratic nominee Michael Dukakis, ran a television commercial featuring a black felon, Willie Horton, who had received a weekend furlough from Dukakis, who as Massachusetts's governor had followed the state's policy. On furlough, Horton raped a white woman. Bush's commercial deliberately linked black criminals and Democratic candidates. The commercial was so powerful that when people were asked after the election what they recalled about the campaign, they mentioned "Bush, Dukakis, and Willie Horton."[57]

Although hardly concealed, the racial strategy of the Republican Party was implemented carefully and cautiously, with code words that stated one thing but meant another. Candidates and party officials rarely praised segregation or used racial epithets, as politicians of both parties had in earlier generations. Whenever confronted about their strategy, Republicans denied that their statements were racist or intended to appeal to racists.[58]

The shift of southern whites to the Republican Party doesn't mean that all or even most are racist. What is clear, however, is that since 1964 the Republicans have used a conservative and sometimes implicitly racist approach to race-related issues to build their dominance in the region, just as the Democrats did for generations before them.[59]

Although racial attitudes were the original factor driving the movement of southern whites, their conservative views on other issues, ranging from foreign policy to gun control to religious matters, also made the Republican Party a congenial home for them.

The southern strategy proved highly successful for the Republican Party. The South went from a solidly Democratic region to a reliably Republican one. Since 1968, the Republicans have carried the South in every presidential

Andy Levin/Photo Researchers, Inc.

The Republican Party has tried to pull blue-collar workers away from their traditional home in the Democratic Party. President Reagan was especially effective in luring these voters.

election except 1976, when the Democrats nominated former Georgia governor Jimmy Carter. Even then, a majority of southern whites voted for the Republican, Gerald Ford. Since 1994, the Republicans have garnered a majority of southern whites' votes for their congressional, state, and local candidates as well. Meanwhile, southern blacks have become the backbone of the southern Democratic Party.[60]

The shift of conservative southern whites to the Republican Party not only makes the South more Republican, but it also makes the Republican Party more conservative and the party system more ideological. The southern Republican members of Congress are more conservative than the southern Democratic members they replaced, and they are more conservative than many northern Republican members. They push their party further to the right. At the same time, their departure from the Democratic Party makes that party more liberal. Thus the transformation of the South has made the parties more ideological, which has made them more polarized and less cooperative than before the shift.

Northern Blue-Collar Workers

Blue-collar workers who were the second- and third-generation sons and daughters of European immigrants, especially from Catholic countries such as Ireland and Italy, were at the heart of the New Deal coalition.[61] But after southern whites left the Democratic Party, some northern blue-collar workers did too.[62]

The economic status of blue-collar workers stagnated in the 1970s and 1980s. Meanwhile, the Democratic Party turned from bread-and-butter issues to the Vietnam War, civil rights, women's equality, and environmental protection—issues that motivated the upper middle class more than the lower middle class. And the Republican Party began to emphasize tax cuts and conservative positions on social issues. As their economic status stagnated, blue-collar workers became more antigovernment and antitax. Eventually, they became more receptive to the Republicans' positions on social issues. Many were drawn to the Republicans' emphasis on "traditional values."[63]

Reagan captured a majority of these voters. In the 2000s, a small majority—no longer a large majority—has supported the Democrats.

White-Collar Professionals

From the Depression through the 1980s, more affluent, better-educated, white-collar workers voted Republican. However, as some blue-collar workers drifted from the Democratic Party, some white-collar professionals, especially teachers, lawyers, doctors, and scientists, gravitated to it. (Most business executives remained in the Republican Party.)

White-collar professionals reject the uncompromising and intolerant approach of the Republican core on social issues. They tend to support abortion rights and have a "live and let live" mindset, rather than a traditional values mindset, toward homosexuality,[64] and they tend to favor civil rights, women's equality, and environmental protection. White-collar professionals also have more liberal attitudes toward foreign policies than blue-collar workers have. (In the 1960s, this split surfaced as student demonstrators with draft deferments—many of whom would eventually become professionals—infuriated the "hard hats" by protesting the Vietnam War.) In recent elections, the Democrats have fared very well in affluent communities populated by white-collar professionals.[65]

Regular Churchgoers

Catholic and Jewish immigrants were also a part of the New Deal coalition. Since the Depression, Catholics and Jews tended to be Democrats because they were largely from the blue-collar immigrant groups helped by the political machines in the big cities. Protestants tended to be Republicans because they were likely to be better off financially and to live in small towns and on farms. As economic issues gave way to social issues, this religious cleavage has declined and a new cleavage has emerged—between those who are very religious and those who are less religious or nonreligious.

Church attendance now is more correlated with party affiliation than either income or education is.[66] Weekly churchgoers congregate in the Republican Party, and less religious or nonreligious people connect with the Democratic Party. Because there are more weekly churchgoers than irregular churchgoers or non-churchgoers, the shift has benefited the Republicans. But the nonreligious group is growing faster. (Among people eighteen to twenty-five years old,

20 percent report no religious affiliation, up from 11 percent in the late 1980s.[67])

Conservative Christians, who deplored the sexual revolution and the secular drift of modern America, were attracted to the conservatism and traditionalism of the Republican Party. As they became politically active, they formed pro-life groups that coalesced into the Christian right. Eventually, the Christian right became one of the strongest forces in the Republican Party. Former senator John Danforth (R-Mo.), himself a minister, observed that his party has been transformed "into the political arm of conservative Christians."[68]

The Net Result

In this minor realignment, the net result has been a gain for the GOP, because the southern whites, northern blue-collar workers, and regular churchgoers who left the Democratic Party far outnumber the white-collar professionals who left the Republican Party. This minor realignment has created a rough parity between the two parties.

A major realignment has not occurred. With the patriotic fervor following the 9/11 attacks, and with the election of Republican majorities in Congress and the reelection of

Republicans have allied themselves with conservative Christians, especially churchgoing Protestant Evangelicals. President Bush spoke their language.

President Bush, the Republican Party had an opportunity to solidify its gains. Karl Rove, the president's chief political adviser, worked to produce a major realignment. But the administration and congressional Republicans overreached, adopting policies to benefit Republican constituencies rather than broaden their appeal to Democrats and independents as well.[69] The administration also pursued an aggressive foreign policy, with the "war on terrorism" used to justify a preemptive attack on Iraq. As the war dragged on and the deficits from tax cuts, war spending, and new entitlements soared, the popularity of the president and the party plummeted.

The Democrats won control of both houses of Congress by small margins in 2006 and larger margins in 2008, and they captured the White House in 2008. New voters, especially young voters, flocked to Democratic candidates. So far, "millennials"—the generation born between 1982 and

BEHIND THE SCENES

The Making of a Partisan Issue

Abortion wasn't always a partisan issue. Before *Roe* v. *Wade*, decided in 1973, almost two-thirds of Americans agreed with the statement "The decision to have an abortion should be made solely by a woman and her physician." More Republicans agreed than Democrats. (Even a majority of Catholics agreed.)[1]

In the 1960s states began to reform their abortion laws. A dozen allowed the procedure for health reasons, birth defects, or when the pregnancy was the result of rape. Four states allowed the procedure for any reason.[2] The move to reform the laws caused the Catholic Church to mobilize in opposition.

Republican strategists saw abortion as a **wedge issue**—one that could split the Democratic coalition. They proposed that the party use the issue to pull Catholics away from their longtime home in the Democratic Party. "Favoritism toward things Catholic is good politics," one concluded; "there is a trade-off, but it leaves us with the larger share of the pie."[3]

In anticipation of his reelection bid in 1972, President Richard Nixon adopted this strategy. He shifted his position on abortion, rescinding a rule (promulgated by his administration) that military hospitals perform therapeutic abortions, and claiming that "abortion on demand" is incompatible with "the sanctity of human life."[4]

In the election campaign, the president and his strategists broadened their focus to lure social conservatives, who had been scattered in both parties, to the Republican fold. At the time, abortion wasn't considered murder (except by the Catholic Church); rather, it was seen as a symbol of the sexual revolution and the permissive behavior of young people and independent women, who could have sex without paying the consequences. It became linked with the feminist movement, working mothers, and day care.[5] To some Americans, abortion represented a loss of respect for tradition and for authority. The use of the abortion issue thus was a political calculation to produce a party realignment of Catholics and social conservatives.

Once Nixon won reelection, he ignored abortion. After Watergate, however, conservative strategists were looking for ways to strengthen the Republican Party. They were "looking for issues that people care about," one admitted, "and social issue[s], at least for the present, fit the bill."[6] They thought the abortion issue, especially, could be used for a longer term than Nixon's reelection campaign. So they formed interest groups and appealed to evangelical Protestants, who previously had considered abortion a Catholic issue.

In 1980, Ronald Reagan, like Richard Nixon before him, changed positions on abortion to reflect this strategy.[7] During the 1980s, the parties' activists took opposing stands on abortion, and the media's coverage linked the parties and their stands, with the Republican Party portrayed as pro-life and the Democratic Party as pro-choice.[8] By the 1990s, the voters recognized the parties' stands. Thus abortion had been transformed from a nonpartisan issue into a highly partisan one, all to spark a party realignment.

[1]Much of this box is drawn from Linda Greenhouse and Reva B. Siegel, "Before (and After) *Roe v. Wade*: New Questions about Backlash," *Yale Law Journal*, June 2011, 2028–2087; statistic on Catholics on page 2031.

[2]Ibid., 2047.

[3]Ibid., 2054.

[4]Ibid., 2053.

[5]Ibid., 2056–2058.

[6]Paul Weyrich, quoted in ibid., 2082.

[7]Ibid., 2067.

[8]Edward G. Carmines, Jessica C. Gerrity, and Michael W. Wagner, "How Abortion Became a Partisan Issue: Media Coverage of the Interest Group-Political Party Connection," *Politics & Policy* 38 (December 2010), 1135–1158.

2003—are registering overwhelmingly as Democrats.[70] This trend suggests the possibility of some realignment toward the Democrats.

Yet American politics is now very volatile. Voters want "to throw the bums out," but they can't decide who "the bums" are. In 2006 and 2008, voters threw the Republicans out, but in 2010 they threw the Democrats out. The 2012 election results show that the country remains sharply split.

In the future, there likely will be further realignments, although they may be minor realignments rather than major realignments and they may be ongoing rather than occurring in a fixed pattern, especially if the dealignment trend continues.[71]

PARTY IDENTIFICATION

Party identification is the psychological link that individuals feel toward a party. Unlike European parties, which have official members who pay dues and sign pledges accepting party principles, American parties have no formal members. You are a Democrat or a Republican if you consider yourself one.[72] (See Figure 5.)

We like to think that we're rational individuals exercising free will when we adopt a party, but that isn't the case for most people. Party identification typically is determined by our parents' party affiliation; our sexual, racial, ethnic, and religious characteristics; and various geographic factors.

The previous section of the chapter has explained the party identification of some groups that have realigned, but we'll recapitulate those groups and address other groups here so you'll have a complete picture of party identification today.

Parents' Party Affiliation

Party identification usually develops through the process of political socialization, explained in Chapter 4. Parents pass down political views, including party identification, to their children. If both parents identify with the same party, their children probably will as well. If the parents identify with different parties, their children receive mixed signals and may identify with either party or be independent. If both parents are uninterested in politics, their children may ignore both parties.

The assumption was that parents' comments and actions influence their children's party affiliation. In recent years, however, new research suggests that parents' genes, passed to their children, may also influence their children's party affiliation. Researchers in biology and politics have argued that there may

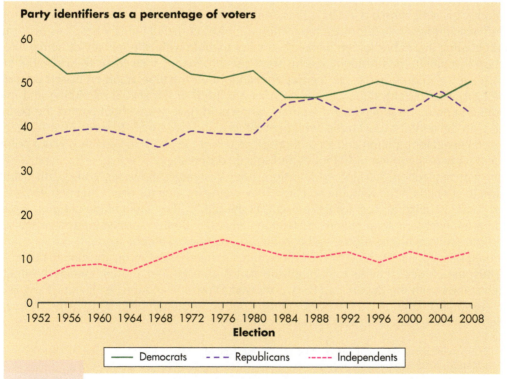

FIGURE 5: PARTY IDENTIFICATIONS OF VOTERS The country is divided between Democrats and Republicans, with relatively few true independents. (For this figure, people who say they are "independent" but say they regularly vote for the candidates of one party—that is, people who are "independent leaners"—are combined with people who say they are members of that party.)

SOURCE: James E. Campbell, "Explaining Politics, Not Polls: Examining Macropartisanship with Recalibrated NES Data," *Public Opinion Quarterly* 74, (October 2010), 612–642. Copyright © 2010 by James E. Campbell. Published by Oxford University Press on behalf of the American Association for Public Opinion Research. All rights reserved. Reproduced by permission.

be a genetic factor in individuals' party identification. There are innate conservative traits (such as caution and aversion to threats) that may link to some party positions (such as views toward the military or various outgroups).[73] Such innate traits may incline people to identify with one party rather than the other.

The party identification of one's parents is the most important determinant of one's own party identification, but other characteristics and factors also come into play.

Sexual, Racial, Ethnic, and Religious Characteristics

The two genders and some racial groups, ethnic groups, and religious groups favor a particular party, so if you belong to one of these groups, it's likely that you'll favor the same party.

For generations, men and women voted similarly. After women got the right to vote, most wives followed their husband's lead. In the 1980s, however, a **gender gap** emerged. During this conservative era, more men moved to the right than women did. Men liked Reagan's anticommunist foreign policies and his pro-business views.[74] Women preferred the Democrats' social policies, which used government to cushion life's hardships and to regulate business's impact on its employees and on the environment. Women also rejected aggressive foreign policies, including military action and military spending. (The gap isn't due to abortion views. Men's and women's views on this issue are similar.)

Today the gender gap persists. It is most marked for working women and unmarried women, who are more likely to be Democrats. Men and stay-at-home moms are more likely to be Republicans.[75]

Most homosexuals are presumed to be Democrats. They are difficult to poll because many feel vulnerable and are reluctant to acknowledge their sexual orientation even in a confidential survey. But the tolerance of alternative lifestyles by the Democratic Party and the opposition to same-sex marriage, civil unions, and antidiscrimination laws by the Republican Party undoubtedly have driven most gays and lesbians into the Democratic camp.

Racial minorities tend to be Democrats. African Americans cast a higher percentage of their votes for Democratic candidates than any other group does. They have never left the New Deal coalition because the Democratic Party has championed civil rights and economic policies favorable to working people.

Latinos are not a monolithic group, so their political preferences vary according to the country they or their parents came from. Cuban Americans in south Florida have been staunch Republicans, although generational differences are beginning to emerge. Mexican, Puerto Rican, and other Latin Americans tend to be Democrats, though to a lesser extent than African Americans are. Even so, in 2008 Latino voters enabled Obama to carry Colorado, Florida, Indiana, and Nevada—states that Republicans usually won.[76] In recent elections, Asian Americans have also supported Democratic candidates.[77]

Although some Latinos and Asians have lived in the United States for generations—Latinos in the Southwest predated the arrival of Anglos in the East—many are immigrants or from families of recent immigrants. As relative newcomers, their party identification isn't as fixed as other Americans' identification is. Both parties are vying for their allegiance, especially for Latinos' allegiance, because their population is the fastest-growing in the United States. As the percentage of (non-Hispanic) white births, relative to all births in the United States, declines—in 2008 it was 52 percent; soon it will be less than 50 percent[78]—Republicans fear that they can't remain competitive if they can't convert significant numbers of Latino voters. The Bush administration made a concerted effort to woo them. The president gave his weekly radio address in Spanish, appointed a Hispanic as White House counsel and then attorney general, and proposed immigration reform that would allow illegal immigrants in the United States for a long time to work toward citizenship rather than be deported. His proposal, however, was rejected by congressional Republicans. The apprehension—sometimes the hostility—toward Spanish-speaking immigrants by its conservative base is a stumbling block for the party's efforts to woo Latino voters.

Most Jews remain Democrats, but Catholics waver between the parties. Among Catholics and Protestants, regular churchgoers are very strong Republicans, and the less religious and nonreligious are almost as strong Democrats.

Socioeconomic Characteristics

Individuals' education, occupation, and income, which indicate their social class, also influence their party identification. Historically, the parties split clearly along class lines, with the upper classes being Republicans and the lower classes being Democrats. The upper class itself still prefers the Republicans, and the lower class itself still prefers the Democrats, but in recent decades the pattern has blurred for the upper middle class and the lower middle class. The emergence of social issues, such as abortion, gay rights, and gun control, has prompted some in the upper middle class, which tends to be liberal on these issues, to become Democrats and some in the lower middle class, which tends to be conservative on these issues, to become Republicans.

In addition, the education and occupation of some in the upper middle class have produced other exceptions to the pattern. Individuals with graduate degrees (beyond undergraduate school) have gravitated to the Democrats. And white-collar workers in the public sector—government and education—have become mostly Democrats. On the other hand, white-collar workers in the private sector—business—remain disproportionately Republicans.

Geographic Factors

Individuals' region of the country and type of community—urban, suburban, exurban, or rural—also influence their party identification.

The Great Plains and the Rocky Mountain West traditionally have been Republican bastions, although the Democrats have made inroads in the latter. The South, in the minor realignment of recent decades, has become another Republican region. The Northeast and the West Coast are mostly Democratic regions. These patterns give rise to red and blue states, discussed in Chapter 4.

Big cities are strong Democratic locales, and small towns and rural areas are strong Republican locales. Suburbs lie in between. Some, which resemble the stereotype with posh homes owned by business executives, are mostly Republican. Others, which lie on the fringe of the city itself, are mostly Democratic. Exurbs, which are the rapidly growing areas just beyond the suburbs, are heavily Republican.

Now consider the last three categories addressed—sexual, racial, ethnic, and religious characteristics; socioeconomic characteristics; and geographic factors. These characteristics and the factors themselves don't make people Democrats or Republicans. Residing on the coast doesn't make one a Democrat any more than residing in the heartland makes one a Republican. The process is more subtle. Each of these characteristics represents a set of experiences or a network of family, friends, and neighbors at home or of colleagues at work that surrounds an individual with other persons who are like-minded. The other persons reinforce the tendency of the individual to identify with one party rather than the other. Black Americans' history of pervasive discrimination and economic hardship prompts most of them to become Democrats. White rural residents' very different set of experiences and network of people prompt most of them to become Republicans.

Changes in Party Identification

Individuals who come into the electorate are influenced by the environment of the time. Most individuals who first voted in the 1930s supported Roosevelt and became Democrats (and most of them still are Democrats). Many individuals who first voted in 1980 supported Reagan and became Republicans (and most of them still are Republicans). Voters who came of age during the Clinton, Bush, and Obama administrations increasingly became Democrats.

Party identification usually remains constant through an individual's life. However, it can change if the country experiences a major economic, political, or social upheaval. The Great Depression was a catalyst for some people, prompting numerous Republicans to become Democrats. The civil rights movement and the Vietnam War were catalysts for other people, prompting numerous Democrats to become Republicans and some Republicans to become Democrats.

Party identification can also change if one's social status changes—for example, if one gets a college degree, especially a graduate degree; pursues a professional career; or moves to a different place. Such changes provide new experiences and more exposure to different people, which can lead to new political views and party identification.

In the next chapter, we'll see that party identification is one factor—a very important factor, but not the only factor—that determines how people vote.

 Thinking about Democracy

In what ways do parties make American government more democratic?

SUMMARY

- The American party system features two major parties—the Democrats and the Republicans—and discourages minor parties. The major parties normally are moderate, with the Democrats leaning left and the Republicans leaning right. In recent decades, however, the Republicans have become increasingly conservative.

- Since the 1960s, the war within the Republican Party has pitted conservatives against moderates, with conservatives wresting control of party organizations and leadership positions from moderates. The Tea Party, which emerged in 2009, has pushed the GOP further right.

- American parties arose during George Washington's presidency because groups took opposing positions on public issues and politicians needed the support of an organization. Parties expanded during the nineteenth century because they performed important functions for

society. They provided welfare, jobs, and information, and they recruited candidates, ran campaigns, and operated government. As a result, parties enabled average people to exercise political power. Even as some functions diminished, parties have persisted because they have played crucial roles in nominating, campaigning, and governing.

- The "responsible party government" model entails parties taking clear and opposing positions on major issues, citizens understanding these differences and voting on this basis, and officeholders enacting party positions into law. Some European democracies come close to this ideal, but American parties traditionally have allowed their members more independence. In recent years, however, American parties, especially the Republican Party, have come closer to this model (though still not as close as European parties).

- When one party loses many supporters to the other party, a realignment of the parties occurs. Historically, a major realignment has occurred about every thirty to forty years, although in recent decades a minor realignment has occurred instead. As a result, the Republicans have achieved rough parity with the Democrats.
- Parents' party affiliation is the most important factor influencing children's party affiliation. Sexual, racial, ethnic, and religious characteristics; socioeconomic characteristics; and geographic factors also are important.

DISCUSSION QUESTIONS

1. Do you think it would be better if the United States had a multiparty system instead of a two-party system? Do you think it would be better if the United States at least had a strong third party? Where do you think a strong third party would lie on the ideological spectrum?

2. Compare the advantages and disadvantages of a party being larger and relatively heterogeneous (a "big tent") or smaller and relatively homogeneous. Which would you prefer to be a member of? Which would you prefer to be a leader of?

3. Why do political scientists consider political parties essential for a democracy? Do we really need them?

4. Make an argument that we (a) would be better off with "responsible party government" but that we (b) could not reach this goal in our system. Then, make a counterargument to each point.

5. What possibilities do you see for future party realignments (major or minor) in the United States?

6. Why are you a Democrat, Republican, or independent? Consider your parents' party affiliation and other characteristics or factors that may have influenced your choice.

8 Elections

President Obama connects with the voters.

AP Images/Toby Talbot

LEARNING OBJECTIVES

1. Understand the early limitations on voting rights in the United States and explain the means by which most Americans got the right to vote. Be able to describe some current limitations to the right to vote.

2. Know the factors promoting and inhibiting voter turnout in contemporary America and understand why many people do not vote.

3. Be able to describe the process by which a person becomes his or her party nominee for president and to analyze the role of the caucuses, primaries, party conventions, and money in this process. Describe how the major candidates in the 2012 Republican primary illustrate successes and failures in primary campaign strategies.

4. Understand general election strategies pertaining to allocation of time and money, use of e-campaigning, and use of the media. Be able to evaluate the importance of negative campaigning.

5. Know the major rules affecting fundraising by candidates, political parties, PACs, and super PACs. Know how these differences affect campaign strategies.

6. Be able to explain the Electoral College, including why we have it, how it affects campaign strategy, and what changes have been proposed. Know who benefits and who loses, compared to a popular vote system, and the extent to which the Electoral College system has had an impact on presidential election outcomes.

TALKING POINTS

The 2008 election was filled with invective tossed at the candidates. Opponents charged that Obama was a secret Muslim (he's really a Christian), foreign born (he was born in Hawaii), or even an anti-Christ. Sarah Palin accused Obama of "palling around with terrorists" because of his community ties with a man who, in the 1960s, was part of the Weather Underground (a violent, communist anti-war group) but who became a distinguished professor of education at the University of Illinois, Chicago.

McCain was a target too. Some charged him with being brainwashed during his years as prisoner of the North Vietnamese. An official Obama ad poked fun of McCain's computer skills, stating he was out of touch, but also implying that he was too old to be president. (McCain's aides say that his war wounds make prolonged typing painful.)

Did the 2008 election reach a new low in mud throwing? Maybe, but American history has been filled with slanderous charges against presidential candidates almost from the beginning. In 1796, a Federalist editorial, supporting John Adams, prophesied that if Thomas Jefferson were elected, "murder, robbery, rape, adultery and incest will be openly taught and practiced."[1]

These two Founding Fathers continued their very low standard in 1800. John Adams accused Jefferson of being an atheistic coward who wanted to "rip Bibles from the homes of God-fearing Americans."[2] Allegedly some people were so frightened by this claim that they buried their Bibles to hide them from Jefferson's imaginary search. Jefferson called the portly Adams "his rotundity" and accused him of tyrannical tendencies.[3]

Twenty-eight years later, when Andrew Jackson ran for president, his mother was called a prostitute, his father a mulatto (someone of mixed races, black and white), his wife a profligate woman, and himself a bigamist.[4] Jackson's wife was so stressed by these charges that she had a heart attack and died before Jackson was inaugurated. Jackson, in turn, called John Quincy Adams, his opponent, a "pimp" and accused him of procuring women for the Russian czar when he served as the American ambassador to Russia.[5]

It appears, then, that campaign nastiness is as American as apple pie. Even our national icons slung mud. A British observer of American elections in 1888 described elections as a "tempest of invective and calumny...imagine all the accusations brought against all the candidates for the 670 seats in the English Parliament concentrated on one man, and read...daily for three months."[6] And now, of course, the campaign is far longer than three months, and cable TV brings us the mud fight 24/7.

Americans have fought and died in wars to preserve the rights of citizens to choose their leaders through democratic elections. Some have even died here at home trying to exercise these rights. Despite this, most Americans take these important rights for granted; about half do not bother to vote even in presidential elections, and fewer still participate in other ways.

Moreover, the process by which we choose our leaders, especially the president, has been sharply criticized in recent years. Critics charge that election campaigns are meaningless and offer little information to the voters, that candidates pander to the most ill-informed and mean-spirited citizens, and that public relations and campaign spending, not positions on issues or strength of character, determine the winners. And in some recent elections, some voters' votes were not counted, largely because of defects in the election process itself.

In this chapter, we analyze why voting is important to a democracy and why, despite its importance, so few do it. Then we examine political campaigns and elections to see how they affect the kinds of leaders and policies we have. We will see that the lack of participation by many reinforces the government's responsiveness to those who do participate, especially those who are well organized.

THE AMERICAN ELECTORATE

During the more than two centuries since the Constitution was written, two important developments have altered the right to vote, termed **suffrage**. First, suffrage gradually was extended to include almost all citizens aged eighteen or over. This expansion occurred largely through federal action: constitutional amendments, congressional acts, and Supreme Court decisions. Second, in recent years serious issues of lack of access to the ballot have arisen. These limitations are largely being imposed by several states under the guise of ensuring that only eligible voters vote.

Early Limits on Voting Rights

Although the Declaration of Independence states that "all men are created equal," at the time of the Constitution and shortly thereafter the central political right of voting was denied to most Americans. States decided who would be granted suffrage. In some, only an estimated 10 percent of the white males could vote, whereas in others 80 percent could.[7] And these were just white males. In the first presidential election, only about 6 percent of all Americans were eligible to vote.[8]

Controversial property qualifications for voting existed in many states. Some argued that only those with an economic stake in society should have a say in political life. But critics of the property requirement repeated a story of Tom Paine's:

> You require that a man shall have $60 worth of property, or he shall not vote. Very well…here is a man who today owns a jackass, and the jackass is worth $60.

> Today the man is a voter and he goes to the polls and deposits his vote. Tomorrow the jackass dies. The next day the man comes to vote without his jackass and he cannot vote at all. Now tell me, which was the voter, the man or the jackass?[9]

Because the Constitution gave states the power to regulate suffrage, the elimination of property requirements was a gradual process. By the 1820s, most were gone, although some lingered to midcentury.

In some states, religious tests also were applied. A voter had to be a member of the "established" church or could not be a member of certain religions (such as Roman Catholicism or Judaism). However, religious tests disappeared even more quickly than property qualifications.

By the time of the Civil War, state action had expanded the rights of white men. However, slaves, Indians, and free southern blacks could not vote, although northern blacks could in a few states.[10] Women's voting rights were confined to local elections in a few states.[11]

Blacks and the Right to Vote

The Civil War began the long, slow, and often violent process of expanding the rights of blacks to full citizenship. Between 1865 and 1870, three amendments were passed to give political rights to former slaves and other blacks. One, the Fifteenth Amendment, prohibited the denial of voting rights on the basis of race and thus gave the right to vote to black men.

For a short time following the ratification of this amendment, a northern military presence in the South and close monitoring of southern politics enabled blacks to vote and hold office in the South, where 90 percent of all blacks lived. During this **Reconstruction** period, two southern blacks were elected to the Senate and fourteen were elected to the House of Representatives between 1869 and 1876. One state, South Carolina, even had a black majority in its legislature. And in Mississippi, historians have discovered that, during Reconstruction, 226 black officials served in a variety of offices, from local to national.[12] In most places, however, blacks did not dominate politics or even receive a proportional share of offices; whites saw blacks' political activities as a threat to their own dominance. White southerners began to prevent blacks from voting through intimidation that ranged from mob violence and lynchings to economic sanctions against blacks who attempted to vote.

Northerners soon tolerated these methods, both violent and nonviolent. The northern public and political leaders lost interest in the fate of blacks or simply grew tired of the struggle, and in 1876, a compromise ended Reconstruction. In the wake of the disputed 1876 presidential election, southern Democrats agreed to support Republican Rutherford B. Hayes for president in return for an end to the northern military presence in the South and a hands-off policy toward activities there. By the end of the nineteenth century, blacks were effectively disfranchised in all of the South. The last southern black member of Congress served to 1901. Another would not be elected until 1972.

Southern constitutions and laws legitimized the loss of black voting rights. **Literacy tests** were often required, supposedly to make sure voters could read and write and thus evaluate political information. Most blacks, who had been denied education, were illiterate. Although many whites also were illiterate, fewer were barred from voting. Local election registrars exercised nearly complete discretion in deciding who had to take the test and how to administer and evaluate it. Educated blacks often were asked for legal interpretations of obscure constitutional provisions, which few could provide.

Some laws had exemptions that whites were allowed to take advantage of. An "understanding clause" exempted those who could not read and write but who could explain sections of the federal or state constitution to the satisfaction of the examiner, and a "good moral character clause" exempted those with such character. Again, local election registrars exercised discretion in deciding who understood the Constitution and who had good character. Finally, the **grandfather clause** exempted those whose grandfathers had the right to vote before 1867—that is, before blacks could legally vote in the South.

The **poll tax** also deprived blacks of voting rights. The tax, though only a couple of dollars, was often a sizable portion of working people's income, as a typical wage in 1870 was $1 to $2 a day.[13] In some states, individuals had to pay not only for the present election but also for every past election in which they were eligible to vote but did not.

In the **white primary**, where party nominees were chosen, blacks were barred from voting. Because the Democrats always won the general elections, the real contests were in the Democratic primaries. The states justified excluding blacks on the grounds that political parties were private rather than government organizations and thus could discriminate just as private clubs or individuals could.

Less formal means were also used to exclude blacks from voting. Registrars often closed their offices when blacks tried to register, or whites threatened blacks with the loss of jobs or housing if they tried to vote. Polling places were sometimes located far from black neighborhoods or were moved at the last minute without notifying potential voters. If these means failed, whites threatened or practiced violence. In one election in Mobile, Alabama, whites wheeled a cannon to a polling place and aimed it at about 1000 blacks lined up to vote.

The treatment of blacks by the southern establishment was summarized on the floor of the Senate by South Carolina senator Benjamin ("Pitchfork Ben") Tillman, who served from 1895 to 1918. As he put it, "We took the government away. We stuffed ballot boxes. We shot them. We are not ashamed of it."[14]

Over time, the Supreme Court and Congress outlawed the "legal" barriers to black voting in the South. The Court invalidated the grandfather clause in 1915 and the white primary in 1944. Through the Twenty-fourth Amendment, Congress abolished the poll tax for federal elections in 1964, and the Court invalidated the tax for state elections in 1966.[15] But threats of physical violence and economic reprisals still kept most southern blacks from voting. Although many blacks in the urban areas of the Rim South (such as Florida, North Carolina, Tennessee, and Texas) could and did vote, those in the rural South and most in the Deep South could not; in 1960, black voter registration ranged from 5 to 40 percent in southern states.[16] (See the box "Blacks and Latinos in Office.")

Blacks line up to vote in Peachtree, Alabama, after enactment of the Voting Rights Act of 1965.

Blacks and Latinos in Office

Before the Voting Rights Act (VRA) in 1965, few African Americans held major public office. Only a handful were members of Congress, and few were state legislators, mayors of major cities, or other important political officers. Following the VRA, southern blacks began to have the political clout to elect members of their own race to office for the first time, and northern blacks began to increase their influence, winning races in districts where blacks were not always majorities. Progress, though slow, has occurred; in 1970, there were only 179 blacks holding state and national legislative seats; by 2001, the number had more than tripled, to 633. Only two African Americans have won a governor's seat in modern times, Virginia's Douglas Wilder and, in 2006, Massachusetts's Deval Patrick. Barack Obama's Senate victory in 2004 made him only the third black person to hold a Senate seat in the modern era.

The first African American mayor of a major U.S. city was not elected until 1968 (Richard Hatcher), but by 2010, more than 600 African Americans were serving as mayors, nearly 50 of them in cities of 50,000 and more, and many in communities where blacks are far less than half the population.[1]

Nationally, the number of black officeholders increased from an estimated 1200 in 1969 to more than 10,500 today.[2] Although this is far from proportional representation, it is a dramatic increase.

Latinos, too, have improved their representation in political office. From a total of little more than 3000 Latino public officials in 1985, their numbers by 2011 had grown to nearly 6000, including more than 280 elected to state and national office.[3] Latino officials are more geographically concentrated than African American officials, reflecting their large populations in the Southwest.

In sum, African Americans and Latinos, like other ethnic groups, are achieving political power through elections. The election of Barack Obama as the president is, of course, the most visible manifestation of that success.

[1] Data from the Joint Center for Political and Economic Studies and the National Conference of Black Mayors, http://ncbm.org/category/about/.

[2] Richard J. Timpone, "Mass Mobilization or Government Intervention? The Growth of Black Registration in the South," *Journal of Politics* 57 (1995), 425–442; Joint Center for Political and Economic Studies, *National Roster of Black Elected Officials Fact Sheet*, http://www.jointcenter.org/sites/default/files/upload/research/files/National%20Roster%20of%20Black%20Elected%20Officials%20Fact%20Sheet.pdf.

[3] NALEO (National Association of Latino Elected Officials) Educational Fund, *2011 Directory of Latino Elected Officials*, http://www.naleo.org/directory.html.

The Voting Rights Act and Redistricting

Despite our shameful history of depriving African Americans the right to vote, today black voting rates approach those of whites. In the Deep South, much of this dramatic change was brought about by the 1965 passage of the **Voting Rights Act (VRA)**, which made it illegal to interfere with anyone's right to vote. This landmark legislation was introduced by President Lyndon Johnson. In an eloquent address urging Congress to pass the legislation, he began by saying, "I speak tonight for the dignity of man and the destiny of democracy," and closed by proclaiming, "We shall overcome." This was the first time any president had echoed the rallying cry of the civil rights movement.

The act abolished the use of literacy tests, and, most important, it sent federal voter registrars into counties where less than 50 percent of the voting-age population (black and white) was registered. The premise of this requirement was that if so few had registered, there must be serious barriers to registration. Registrars were sent to all of Alabama, Mississippi, South Carolina, and Louisiana, substantial parts

of North Carolina, and scattered counties in six other states.[17] Any changes in election procedures had to be approved by the Department of Justice or the U.S. District Court for the District of Columbia. States or counties had to show a clean record of not discriminating for ten years before they could escape this supervision. Those who sought to deter blacks from voting through intimidation now had to face the force of the federal government.

Though black registration had been increasing in the Rim South due to voter registration and education projects, the impact of the VRA in the Deep South was dramatic.[18] Within a year after federal registrars were sent, hundreds of thousands of southern blacks were registered, radically changing the nature of southern politics. In the most extreme case, Mississippi registration of blacks zoomed from 7 to 41 percent. In Alabama, the black electorate doubled in four years. Because of these increases, blacks began to be elected to office and white politicians began to court black voters to get elected.

The VRA was renewed and expanded in 1970, 1975, 1982, and again in 2006, despite some grumbling by white Republican conservatives about the continuing federal scrutiny of voting rights in the South. It now covers more states and other minorities, such as Latinos, Asians, American Indians, and Inuits (called Eskimos in the past), and thus serves as a basic protection for minority voting rights. For example, states must provide bilingual ballots in counties where 5 percent or more of the population does not speak English.

The VRA dramatically changed the face of the electorate in the South and then later in other parts of the nation. Given the success of the VRA and faced with an expanded black electorate, some white officials in areas of large black populations used new means to diminish the political clout of African Americans. Their technique was *gerrymandering*, discussed later in the chapter. Through devices that political scientists call **"cracking, stacking, and packing,"** districts were drawn to minimize black representation, depending on the size and configuration of the black and white populations. *Cracking* divides significant, concentrated black populations into two or more districts so that none will have a black majority; *stacking* combines a large black population with an even greater white population; and *packing* puts a huge black population into one district rather than two, where blacks might otherwise approach a majority in each.

With these practices seeking to limit black voting power, in the 1982 renewal of the VRA, the focus of the legislation turned from protecting the right of suffrage to trying to ensure that voting rights would result in the election of African American and other minority officeholders. Consequently, after the 1990 census, eleven new **majority-minority districts** were created for blacks and six for Hispanics. Partly as a result, blacks and Hispanics dramatically increased their congressional representation. Blacks were elected to Congress for the first time since Reconstruction in Alabama, Florida, North Carolina, South Carolina, and Virginia. Hispanics were elected for the first time

ever in Illinois and New Jersey.[19] However, after this post-1990 redistricting, which used extensive gerrymandering to create the majority-minority districts, some white voters challenged their legality. In a series of cases, the Supreme Court then ruled that racial gerrymandering, the drawing of district lines specifically to concentrate racial minorities to try to ensure the election of minority representatives, is as constitutionally suspect as the drawing of district lines to diffuse minority electoral strength.[20] But despite the consequent redrawing of several majority-minority districts, the African American incumbents were able to win reelection and hold on to the gains made.

Creating majority-minority districts affected the partisan composition of some southern states. Black voters were redistricted from solid Democratic districts to create new majority black districts. This left their old districts with Republican majorities and helped Republicans gain control of numerous districts after the mid-1990s.

Women and the Right to Vote

When property ownership defined the right to vote, women property owners could vote in some places. When property requirements were removed, suffrage came to be seen as a male right only. Women's right to vote was reintroduced in the 1820s in Tennessee school board elections.[21] From that time on, women had the vote in some places, but usually only at the local level or for particular kinds of elections.

The national movement for women's suffrage did not gain momentum until after the Civil War. Before and during that war, many women helped lead the campaign to abolish slavery and establish full political rights for blacks. When black men got the right to vote after the Civil War, some women saw the paradox in their working to enfranchise these men when they

Broadway chorus women train as Home Guards during World War I. Women's contributions to the war effort helped lead to the ratification of the women's suffrage amendment in 1920.

American Diversity

Women in Office

As secretary of state and former senator, Hillary Clinton is probably the most highly visible woman officeholder in the United States, and former Speaker of the House and current minority leader, Nancy Pelosi (D-Calif.), is the most highly visible elected officeholder. But even before women were given the right to vote nationally, they held political office. Women officeholders in colonial America were rare but not unknown. In 1715, for example, the Pennsylvania Assembly appointed a woman as tax collector.[1]

Elizabeth Cady Stanton, probably the first woman candidate for Congress, received 24 votes when she ran in 1866.[2] It was not until 1916 that the first woman member of Congress, Jeannette Rankin (R-Mont.), was actually elected. In 1872, Victoria Claflin Woodhull ran for president on the Equal Rights Party ticket, teamed with abolitionist Frederick Douglass for vice president.

More than 100,000 women now hold elective office, but many of these offices are minor. Inroads by women into major national offices have been slow. Geraldine Ferraro's 1984 vice-presidential candidacy was historic, and in 2008 vice-presidential candidate Sarah Palin galvanized the Republican campaign and millions of conservative Republicans, but they were both part of losing tickets.

As of the 2012 election, women comprise 20 percent of the Senate and 18 percent of the House, record numbers. Most, 80 percent of the Senators and 73 percent of women in the House, are Democrats. Probably the most

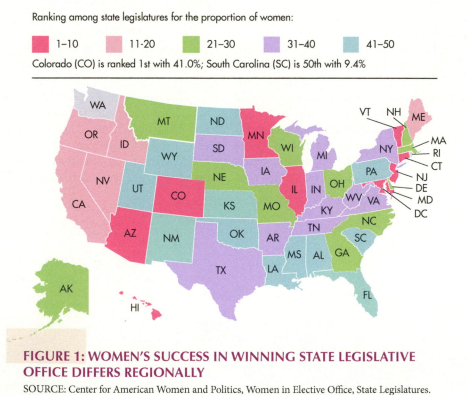

Ranking among state legislatures for the proportion of women:

| 1–10 | 11-20 | 21-30 | 31-40 | 41–50 |

Colorado (CO) is ranked 1st with 41.0%; South Carolina (SC) is 50th with 9.4%

FIGURE 1: WOMEN'S SUCCESS IN WINNING STATE LEGISLATIVE OFFICE DIFFERS REGIONALLY

SOURCE: Center for American Women and Politics, Women in Elective Office, State Legislatures. http://www.cawp.rutgers.edu/. Copyright © 2012 Center for American Women and Politics. Reproduced by permission.

themselves lacked the right to vote. Led by Susan B. Anthony, Elizabeth Cady Stanton, and others, they lobbied Congress and the state legislatures for voting rights for women.

The first suffrage bill was introduced in Congress in 1868 and each year thereafter until 1893. Most members were strong in their condemnation of women as potential voters.

One senator claimed that if women could hold political views different from their husbands, it would make "every home a hell on earth."[22]

When Wyoming applied to join the Union in 1889, it had already granted women the right to vote. Congress initially tried to bar Wyoming from the Union for that reason, but then high-profile new woman Senator was Elizabeth Warren (D-Ma), a national advocate for consumers' rights, who toppled an incumbent. The women newly elected to Congress include the first Asian American woman Senator (Mazie Hirono (D-Hi), the first openly gay Senator (Tammy Baldwin (D-Wi), and the first Hindu in Congress (Tulsi Gabbard (D-Hi).

In achieving state and local offices, women have made real progress. Five women are governors, four of them Republican. When New Hampshire elected a woman governor in 2012, it completed an all-women slate of office-holders: women comprise all of New Hampshire's congressional delegation too. Women hold about 20 percent of the mayorships of medium and large cities.

In 1969, only 4 percent of the state legislators were women; today, nearly 24 percent are. However, the rates of increase have slowed in recent years, with only a 2 percent growth in the past decade.[5] The proportion ranges widely, from 9 percent in South Carolina to 40 percent in Colorado and 30 percent or more in seven more states.[6]

Over time, women have done best in the western states, perhaps due to the ethos of individualism and the strength of female pioneers, or even the exploits of famed cowgirls such as Annie Oakley and Calamity Jane.[7] They have done worst in the southern states, with their history of traditional attitudes. See Figure 1.

Do women officeholders make a difference in policy? Despite a new generation of conservative women officeholders stimulated by the national visibility and success of Sarah Palin, in general women are more liberal than men.[8] Women tend to give issues relating to women, children, and the family higher priority than do male legislators.[9] Across numerous industrialized democracies, legislatures with more women have been more likely to adopt family leave legislation.[10] Women are also less likely to be involved in corrupt activities.

Given women's educational and professional advances, and with strong public support, the trend toward more women in public office will likely continue. In general, women candidates are elected at the same rate as male ones. Even so, sometimes women still face sexism in their quest for office. This was most obvious at the highest levels. As Hillary Clinton's campaign unfolded, so too did evidence of sexism; it was public and needed no code words. John McCain was asked by a supporter how he was going to beat "the bitch," and he did not bother to correct her. The Internet advertises all sorts of campaign-related offensive material slurring candidates, but during the 2008 election a shop on Chicago's Michigan Avenue (a high-end shopping street) prominently displayed a shirt with the motto "Better a Bro than a Ho." The Clinton "Nutcracker" was advertised widely in mainstream outlets that presumably would not have advertised racially offensive items such as an Obama jockey doorstop or minstrel figure.[11] As another example of sexism, a Republican candidate for the gubernatorial position in South Carolina, Nikki Haley, was accused by two men of having inappropriate physical contact. Further investigation revealed that one was working for a primary opponent, and the other was likely gay. Voters ignored the charges and elected her to the governorship.

[1] Joseph J. Kelley, *Pennsylvania: The Colonial Years* (Garden City, N.Y.: Doubleday, 1980), 143.

[2] Elisabeth Griffin, *In Her Own Right* (New York: Oxford University Press, 1983).

[3] Data are from the Center for American Women and Politics, National Information Bank on Women in Public Office, Rutgers University, www.rci .rutgers.edu/cawp/pdf/elective.pdf.

[4] Malcolm Gay, "Mama Bear," *Washington Monthly*, August 5, 2010, www.washingtonmonthly.com/features/2010/1007.tms.html.

[5] Kira Sanbonmatsu, *Democrats, Republicans, and the Politics of Women's Place* (Ann Arbor: University of Michigan Press, 2002),

[6] Data are from the Center for American Women and Politics, Rutgers University, 2012, http://www.cawp.rutgers.edu/fast_facts/levels_of_office/ documents/stleg.pdf.

[7] Rebecca Traister, "Cowgirl Country," *New York Times Magazine*, January 23, 2011, 11.

[8] Susan Welch, "Are Women More Liberal than Men in the U.S. Congress?" *Legislative Studies Quarterly* 10 (1985), 125–134.

[9] Sue Thomas and Susan Welch, "The Impact of Gender on Activities and Priorities of State Legislators," *Western Political Quarterly* 44 (1991), 445–456; Miki Caul Kittilson, "Representing Women: The Adoption of Family Leave in Comparative Perspective," *Journal of Politics* 70 (April 2008), 323–334.

[10] Kittilson, "Representing Women."

[11] See also Jack Hitt, www.harpers.org/archive/2010/06/0082976, Greg Mitchell, "Palin's Porn," http://www.thenation.com/blog/palin-porn.

relented when the Wyoming territorial legislature declared, "We will remain out of the Union one hundred years rather than come in without the women." Still, by 1910, women had complete suffrage rights in only four western states.

Powerful interests opposed suffrage for women. Liquor interests feared that women voters would press for prohibition because many women had been active in the temperance (antiliquor) movement. Other businesses feared that suffrage would lead to reforms to improve working conditions for women and children. Southern whites feared that it would lead to voting by black women and then by black men. Political bosses feared that women would favor political reform. The Catholic Church opposed it as contrary to the proper role of women. According to some people, suffrage was a revolt against nature. Pregnant women might lose their babies, nursing mothers might lose their milk, and women might grow beards or be raped at the polls (then frequently located in saloons or barber shops).[23] Others argued less hysterically that women should be protected from the unsavory practices of politics and should confine themselves to their traditional duties.

About 1910, however, the women's suffrage movement was reenergized, in part by ideas and tactics borrowed from the British women's suffrage movement. A new generation of leaders, including Alice Paul and Carrie Chapman Catt, began to lobby more vigorously, reach out to the working class, and engage in protest marches and picketing, all new features of American politics. Eight more western and prairie states granted suffrage to women between 1911 and 1917, and others had granted the right to vote in presidential elections.[24]

In 1917, the National Women's Party organized around-the-clock picketing of the White House; their arrest and subsequent torture through beatings and forced feedings embarrassed the administration and won the movement some support. These incidents, plus contributions by women to the war effort during World War I, led to the adoption in 1920 of the Nineteenth Amendment guaranteeing women the right to vote. Although only 37 percent of eligible women voted in the 1920 presidential election, as the habit of voting spread, women's voting rates equaled those of men. (See the box "Women in Office.")

Young People and the Right to Vote

Federal constitutional and legislative changes extended the franchise to young adults. Before 1971, almost all states required a voting age of nineteen or more. The service of eighteen-year-olds in the Vietnam War brought protests that if these men were old enough to die for their country, they were old enough to vote. Yielding to these arguments and to the general recognition that young people were better educated than in the past, Congress adopted and the states ratified the Twenty-sixth Amendment giving eighteen-year-olds the right to vote. As we will see, however, young people are a lot less likely to vote than other groups.

Attacks on Voting Rights

Though it may seem that our nation accepts the notion that all citizens should vote, after the 2010 elections a number of states, mostly conservative-dominated states, passed votes to limit suffrage. These restrictions include requiring photo IDs for voters and eliminating same-day registration and early absentee voting. On their face, these laws are designed to reduce voter fraud. However, voter fraud is minimal. Serious studies of voter fraud find an extremely low incidence, perhaps around .0000002 percent. Although the registration rolls do include some outdated or invalid names and addresses, very

few people ever try to vote under these names and addresses. One study concluded, "It is more likely that an individual will be struck by lightning than that he will impersonate another voter at the polls."[25]

While not likely to have an impact on voting fraud, these rules disproportionately affect the elderly, the poor, and racial minorities, who are less likely to be drivers (and have drivers' licenses) and less likely to have checking accounts (and have IDs for them). These groups are more likely to be Democrats. Some legislators make no secret of their desire to reduce the Democratic vote. In Pennsylvania, where an estimated 9 percent of the voters—nearly 1 million people—could losetheir voting rights under voter ID legislation passed in 2012, one Republican state legislator commented, "Voter ID . . . . is gonna allow Governor Romney to win the state of Pennsylvania."[26] When challenged in court, state officials admitted that they knew of no voter fraud in Pennsylvania or elsewhere.[27]

States have a legitimate interest in making sure that voter lists reflect current voters and their addresses, but often this interest is used in less high-minded ways. Thus threats to voting rights also have come from state officials who represent one party and who "update" voter lists in ways that reduce the other party's voters, especially lower-income and minority voters.[28]

Sometimes private companies are hired to purge voter lists and are paid according to how many they purge. Florida election officials purged voting rolls of thousands of people before the 2000 election, including hundreds or thousands—no one knows for sure—of valid black voters. This disproportionately reduced the African American and Democratic vote in this key state in this tight election.[29] In 2012, when Florida was expected to be a toss-up state, officials began doing it again. Originally, they argued that 180,000 people might not be eligible, but on closer inspection they found only 2600 in a voting population of 11 million (.02 percent, if all of them tried to vote). The Justice Department asked Florida to stop the purge because it violated the Voting Rights Act provision to protect voting rolls.[30]

Some states have also tried to limit or ban the use of student IDs as voter identification. Florida even tried to restrict "third-party organizations," including student groups, from registering new voters.[31] Such restrictions, if allowed to stand, could diminish the youth vote, which also tends to favor Democratic candidates.

Felons and the Right to Vote

The restriction of voting rights for felons—those convicted of serious crimes—also seems targeted at the voting power of African Americans. Most states bar felons from voting while in prison or on probation, but many states bar felons from voting after their release. Some states bar them for several years; four states, including Florida and three other southern states with large black populations,[32] bar them forever. These laws in some states stem from post–Civil War policies intended to control blacks. Since 2004, three states have reinstituted voting rights to felons after they serve their time.

Nationally, more than 5 million people are prevented from voting by felony convictions, including one in seven black men (in Alabama, one in three black men).[33] Nationally, 40 percent of those barred from voting are black.[34] Analyses of these laws suggest that they have had a significant effect in putting conservative Republicans in office in states with large black populations.[35]

Loss of voting rights might be seen as part of the punishment for their crimes. However, in theory ex-felons have served their time and paid their debt to society. Moreover, this punishment contradicts the expectation that upon release they should assimilate into society. Many were convicted as young people and have been law-abiding citizens since their release.

VOTER TURNOUT

Paradoxically, as the *right* to vote has expanded, the proportion of eligible citizens *actually voting* has contracted.

Political Activism in the Nineteenth Century

In 1896, an estimated 750,000 people—5 percent of all voters—took train excursions to visit presidential candidate William McKinley at his Ohio home during the campaign.[36] This amazing figure is but one indication of the high level of intense political interest and activity in the late nineteenth century.

In those days, politics was an active, not a spectator, sport. People voted at high rates, as much as 80 percent in the 1840 presidential election,[37] and they were very partisan. They thought independents were corrupt and ready to sell their votes to the highest bidder. In colonial America, voters usually voted by voice, but by the mid-nineteenth century, most states used paper ballots that were distributed by elaborate and well-organized parties. After being coached by party

leaders, voters simply dropped their party's ballot into the box. **Split-ticket voting**—that is, voting for candidates from different parties for different offices—and secrecy in making one's choice were impossible.[38]

Progressive Reforms

The **Progressive reforms** of the late nineteenth and early twentieth centuries brought radical changes to election politics. Progressive reformers, largely professional and upper middle class, sought to eliminate corruption from politics and voting, but they also meant to eliminate the influence of the lower classes, many of them recent immigrants. These two goals went hand in hand because the lower classes were seen as the cause of corruption in politics.

The Progressive movement was responsible for several reforms: primary elections, voter registration laws, secret ballots, nonpartisan ballots (without party labels), and the denial of voting rights for aliens, which removed a major constituency of the urban party machines. The movement also introduced the merit system for public employment to reduce favoritism and payoffs in hiring.

The reforms, adopted by some states at the end of the nineteenth century and by others much later, were largely effective in cleaning up politics. But the reformers also achieved, to a very large extent, their goal of eliminating the lower classes from politics. Taking away most of the reason for the existence of political parties—choosing candidates and printing and distributing ballots—caused the party organization to decline, which, in turn, produced a decline in political interest and activity on the part of the electorate. Without strong parties to mobilize voters, only the most interested and motivated participated. Moreover, the new restrictions on voting meant that voters had to invest more time, energy, and thought in voting; they had to think about the election months in advance and travel to city hall to register. As a consequence, voting declined and politics began to be a spectator activity.

Turnout figures from the nineteenth century are not entirely reliable and not exactly comparable with today's figures. In the days before voter registration, many aliens could vote, and some people voted twice. In some instances, more people voted in a state election than lived there! Nevertheless, it is generally agreed that turnout was very high in the nineteenth century and then diminished substantially, dropping from more than 77 percent in 1840–1896 to 54 percent in 1920–1932, when the Progressive reforms were largely in place. During the New Deal era, when the Democratic Party mobilized new groups of voters, turnout rose again, but it has never achieved the same levels as in the nineteenth century.

Courtesy of the Smithsonian Institution

Election campaigns in the nineteenth century featured more hoopla, which spurred tremendous turnout. This illustration shows the 1840 Whig gimmick—party members rolled a huge ball from town to town—that prompted the phrase "keep the ball rolling."

Recent Turnout

Voting rates were above 60 percent in the 1950s and 1960s, then slowly declined to barely 50 percent in 2000. However, in 2004 that proportion increased significantly, to 58 percent, and remained there in 2008.[39] Looking only at the population

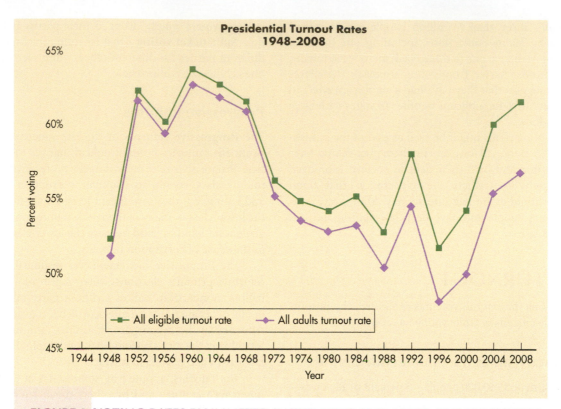

**Presidential Turnout Rates
1948–2008**

Percent voting

■ All eligible turnout rate   ◆ All adults turnout rate

Year

FIGURE 2: VOTING RATES PLUMMETED IN THE 1970S AND 1980S, BUT HAVE RISEN SINCE 2000 This figure illustrates the decline and then the increase in voting rates along with the difference between voting proportions of all eligible citizens and those of all adults. As explained in the text, millions of adults are not eligible because they are felons or non-citizens. Turnout rates appear higher when only those who are eligible to vote are analyzed.

SOURCE: Michael McDonald, "United States Election Project," http://elections.gmu.edu/voter_turnout.htm.

eligible to vote, turnout is slightly higher, over 60 percent, and about the same as in the 1950s. (See Figure 2.)

In 2008, turnout in the primaries was higher than normal, however. In state after state, the turnout far exceeded recent previous turnouts. More than 3 million new voters registered and voted in the primaries,[40] with the increase particularly notable in the Democratic primaries. Senator Barack Obama sparked the enthusiasm of hundreds of thousands of new voters, many of them young or African American, and they registered and voted in huge numbers. Hillary Clinton energized tens of thousands of working-class voters, especially women, to register and vote. The turnouts in many primary states moved into the 30 to 40 percent range—hardly numbers to brag about, but far exceeding the usual dismal primary turnout.[41] Overall primary voting fell in 2012, but comparisons are not meaningful because only one party had competition.[42]

Although nations count their turnouts differently, it is clear that Americans vote at a lower rate than citizens of other Western democracies. Only Switzerland, which has allowed women to vote only since 1971, approximates our low turnout levels. Within the United States, turnout varies greatly among the states. In the 2008 presidential election, for example, 73 percent of Minnesota's citizens voted, but only 45 percent of Hawaii's did.[43] Turnout tends to be lower in the South and higher in the northern Plains, New England, and Mountain states.[44]

Not only do relatively few people vote, but even fewer participate actively in political campaigns. For example, in a recent year, about one-quarter of the population said that they worked for a party or candidate. About an equal proportion claimed that they contributed money to a party or a candidate. Smaller proportions attended political meetings or actually belonged to a political club. However, these rates of campaign participation reflect increases, even while voting rates were declining in the 1970s and 1980s. More people give money to candidates and parties than they used to, probably because, unlike thirty years ago, candidates and parties now use mass mailings and the Internet to solicit funds from supporters.[45] Hundreds of thousands of potential donors can be reached in a very short time.

Who Votes?

There are vast differences in voting habits among different groups of people, especially on the basis of socioeconomic class and age.

Socioeconomic Class

Voting is related to education, income, and occupation—that is, to socioeconomic class. Those who are more educated, have more money, and have higher-status jobs vote more

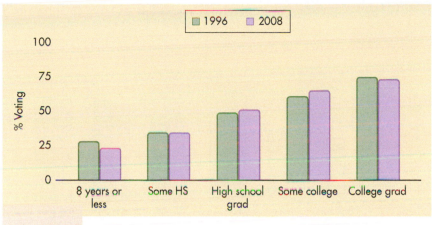

FIGURE 3: CLASS DIFFERENCES IN VOTING ARE STRIKING, AND GROWING

SOURCE: *Statistical Abstract of the United States 2010*, tab. 406. Turnout rates are those in the presidential election. Class is represented by education.

often. If you are a college graduate, the chances are almost 75 percent that you will vote; if you have less than a high school education, the chances are only one-third that.[46] Differences between higher- and lower-income people are also quite large and growing. (See Figure 3.)

Differences between voting rates of the middle and upper classes are much greater in the United States than elsewhere and greater today than in nineteenth-century America.[47] Something unique about the contemporary American political system inhibits voting participation of all citizens, but particularly those whose income and educational levels are below the average. Just as there is a strong class basis to voting, there is also a strong class basis for participation in campaign activities.[48] Those with more education and income are more likely to participate. Those with some college education actually increased their participation over the past twenty years, whereas those with less than a high school education decreased theirs. Thus, the class bias in participation, as in voting alone, has increased.[49]

Age

Voting is also much more common among older people than younger people. Young people are volunteering in their communities in record numbers,[50] so why the low voting rates? Young people's initial tendency to vote or not vote is influenced by their parents' education and political engagement and by their own high school experiences and that of going on to college. This tendency usually stays the same through the life stages of getting married, establishing a stable residence, and becoming active in the community.[51] Thus, low turnouts may reflect many who grew up in homes where there was a low interest in government and the news; they did not learn that politics is important.[52] Then, too, like many of their elders, some young people cannot discern significant differences between the two major political parties, or they believe that candidates do not address issues

of primary concern to young people. Low voter turnout is also a product of mobility: young adults change their residences frequently and do not take time to figure out how and where to register. Finally, many young people are preoccupied with major life changes—leaving home, going to college, beginning their first full-time job, getting married, and starting a family.

The 2008 campaign generated tremendous political interest and enthusiasm among many young voters who had never been engaged in politics before. When asked whether they were paying attention to the campaign, fully 74 percent of those under thirty said "yes," compared with only 42 percent in 2004 and a meager 13 percent in 2000.[53] Still, the turnout of young people was much lower than that of their elders. Turnout in the 2008 election increased for those twenty-one to thirty-four, but all the rhetoric and turnout efforts focused on increasing the participation of college-age students seemed to have no impact at all on overall rates. (See Figure 4.)

Participation in Other Activities

In other kinds of political participation, even taking education into account, men usually participate slightly more than women, whites somewhat more than blacks, older people more than younger people, and southerners more than northerners. But these differences change over time. Young people participated more than their elders, and blacks more than whites, during the late 1960s and early 1970s during the civil rights and anti–Vietnam War movements.[54]

Why Turnout Is Low

In addition to class and age, there are other personal and institutional reasons why more Americans, especially low-income and young Americans, do not vote. Of course, one reason that turnout is lower than in other nations is that millions of American residents are not eligible to vote. However, the rest of this section focuses on reasons why those who *are* eligible

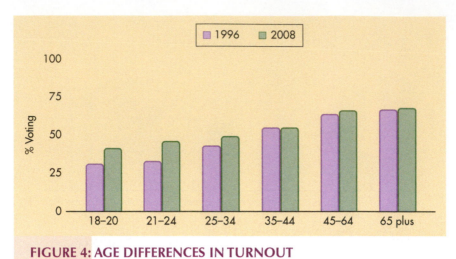

FIGURE 4: AGE DIFFERENCES IN TURNOUT

SOURCE: *Statistical Abstract of the United States 2010,* tab. 406. Turnout rates are those in the presidential election.

do not vote. These reasons include citizens' attitudes, lack of social rootedness, lack of strong labor unions, state barriers to registration and voting, partisan efforts to deter voting, and in the case of legislative elections, noncompetitive districts.

 Thinking about Democracy

> Is our system democratic when the voting rate of those with less income and education is only a fraction of the rate of those higher on the socioeconomic ladder? Would our system be more democratic if we increased the voting rates of those in the lower socioeconomic brackets?

Attitudinal Explanations

Voters' attitudes explain some nonvoting. One reason sometimes given for low rates of voter turnout is that nonvoters are satisfied; failing to vote is a passive form of consent to what government is doing.[55] This argument falls flat. Over the past half century, voter turnout has not fluctuated with public trust in government (Figure 5). Moreover, if staying at home on election day were an indication of satisfaction, one would expect turnout to be lower among the well-off, not among the working class and the poor.

Significant proportions of nonvoters, when asked why they did not vote, say they are disgusted with politics.[56] In explaining low turnout, analysts often point to the hateful advertising, attacks on other candidates, candidates who do not tell the truth about their positions, incessant polling, and lack of thoughtful media coverage.[57]

These analyses might contain some grains of truth, but they don't explain much.[58] People who are most likely to pay attention to the media, watch the ads, hear about the polls, and follow the campaigns are the most likely to vote, not the least likely. Turnout is inversely related to media spending;

the more the candidates spend, the lower the turnout. But negative advertising does not affect turnout much, if at all,[59] and negative advertising and other media attention cannot explain the class bias in nonvoting.

In addition to the *quality* of the campaigns, some people think turnout is lower than it should be because our elections are so frequent, campaigns last so long, and so many offices are contested that the public becomes bored, confused, or cynical.[60] At the presidential level, the sheer quantity of coverage, much of it focused repetitively on "who's winning," may simply bore people. At the local level, voters elect so many officeholders, all the way down to weed and mosquito control commissioners, that many have no idea for whom or what they are voting. This proliferation of elective offices, thought by some to promote democracy and popular control, may promote only voter confusion and alienation. And having elections for different offices at different times contributes to voter confusion and apathy.[61]

By contrast, in Britain the time between calling an election (by the current government) and the actual election is only a month. On April 6, 2010, Prime Minister Gordon Brown asked the Queen to dissolve Parliament, and the election was called for one month later, on May 6, 2010. All campaigning was done during that time. There were no primaries. Moreover, as in most other parliamentary democracies, British citizens vote only for their representative in Parliament and (at one other time) for their local representative. Voters are not faced with choices for a myriad offices they barely recognize.

A more general attitudinal explanation for nonvoting is that it may also be the result of a rational calculation of the costs and benefits of voting. When 35 percent of Americans think voting on *American Idol* is more important than voting for the president, obviously many voters do not think that the stakes in elections are great.[62]

Economist Anthony Downs argued that people vote when they believe the perceived benefits of voting are greater than the costs.[63] If a voter sees a difference between the parties or candidates and favors one party's position over the other,

Obama's candidacy prompted a spike in the turnout of African Americans and young voters.

that voter has a reason to vote and can expect some benefit from doing so. For that reason, people who are highly partisan vote more than those less attached to a party, and people with a strong sense of political efficacy, the belief they can influence government, vote more than others.

Voters who see no difference between the candidates or parties, however, may believe that voting is not worth the effort it takes and that it is more rational to abstain. In fact, as many as one-third of nonvoters gave only the excuses that they were "too busy" or "not interested."[64] Perhaps misled by the continual public opinion polling and the widely publicized results, some may believe that their vote doesn't matter, especially if the race isn't close.

Nevertheless, many people will vote even if they think there is no difference between the candidates because they have a sense of civic duty, a belief that their responsibilities as citizens include voting. In fact, more voters give this as an explanation for voting than any other reason, including the opportunity to influence policy.[65]

Several experiments demonstrate how small things can affect the cost-benefit ratio that determines voting. One researcher demonstrated that going door-to-door to encourage people to vote, presumably enhancing their sense of civic duty, increased voting rates by about 4 percent. But offering a reward for voting (discount coupons for fast foods or rock climbing) increased turnout by 9 percent.[66] Telling people that their neighbors voted or reviewing their own voting history and thanking them for voting also raised turnout.[67] Thus psychological factors are costs and benefits that voters weigh. These experiments attempt to increase the perceived benefits of voting to individuals. Some theorists assume that the costs of voting are minimal, but, in reality, for many people the time, expense of time off from work or transportation costs, and possible embarrassment of trying to register are greater than the perceived benefits of voting. Frequent changes of polling places, for example, can also diminish voting turnout, especially among Democrats.[68] These costs are significant, especially for lower-income people, who may perceive

that neither party is attentive to their interests and who may hear that voters are being challenged at the polls over their right to vote. Finally, the frequency, length, and media orientation of campaigns may lower the perceived benefits of voting for people of all incomes by trivializing the election and emphasizing the negative.

Lack of Social Rootedness

Turnout is lower among those who lack "social rootedness."[69] Middle age, marriage, and residential stability lead to rootedness in one's community. But Americans move around, marry late, and get divorced more than people in other nations, and thus have lower voting rates.

Failure of Parties to Mobilize Voters

Voter turnout in the United States may not increase substantially until one of the political parties works to mobilize the traditional nonvoters through policies that appeal to them. For example, Roosevelt's New Deal mobilized thousands of new voters. If voters believe they have a reason to vote, then their calculation of the benefits of voting increases relative to the costs.

Traditionally, political parties did mobilize voters to turn out. In the 1980s and 1990s, however, the parties spent more time raising funds than mobilizing voters.[70] The failure of parties to mobilize voters is an especially important reason for low turnout among the working class and poor. Because of their low income, a majority of nonvoters are Democrats. If mobilized, they would probably vote for Democrats, but not to the degree many Republicans fear. In many elections, the preferences of nonvoters have simply reflected the preferences of voters.[71]

In recent elections, parties and candidates have worked to mobilize voters, and, consequently, voting has increased. In 2008, both parties used increasingly sophisticated technology to link information about each party supporter with neighborhood information. Each party communicated with its core supporters via e-mail and frequently urged them to register and vote.

Both parties have also developed sophisticated databases that record individuals' residential location, gender, education, race, homeowner status, and many other variables. They gather data not just from public sources such as voter registration rolls and driver's license registrations but also from consumer data from stores ranging from book vendors to auto dealerships. So, for example, we know that Republicans are more likely to drink bourbon and Democrats gin, and Democrats buy Volvos while Republicans buy Fords and Chevys.[72] Parties increasingly use sophisticated polls to develop profiles of voters who are likely to support them. Then they can use census and other neighborhood data to target areas on which to focus their get-out-the-vote drives. Because Republicans have done a better job mobilizing their own supporters, they are more likely to oppose legislation that makes it easier for the general electorate to vote.[73] States with the highest turnout tend to have active and liberal Democratic parties, giving voters a choice and thus a motive to vote.

AP Images/Matt Sayles

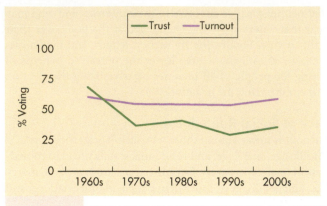

FIGURE 5: TURNOUT IS LITTLE RELATED TO TRUST IN GOVERNMENT

SOURCE: Data on turnout from Michael McDonald, http://elections .gmu.edu/voter_turnout.htm. Data on trust from people-press.org/reports/ images/606-5.gif; trust is the proportion of people saying that they trust the government in Washington all the time or most of the time.

Decline of Strong Labor Unions

Working-class citizens are much less likely to vote than white-collar and professional workers. Yet, among working people, union members are much more likely to vote than are others. Unions inform their members about the stakes of the election and then work to get their members and their families to the polls. Just as parties can increase the perceived benefits of voting by educating voters about the consequences of election choices, unions do the same with their membership. Consequently, as labor union strength has declined, voting turnout has decreased.[74] Although labor strength has declined in other nations as well, most other democracies have much stronger labor unions than the United States and consequently higher rates of turnout among blue-collar workers.

Barriers to Registration and Voting

States can raise or lower the costs of voting by making it easy or hard to register and to vote.

Barriers to registration   Most people who register to vote do vote in the general election for president. But many people never register. In most other democracies, either the state or parties are responsible for registering voters. Voter registrars go door-to-door to register voters, or voters are registered automatically when they pay taxes or receive public services. Usually, these registrar offices are nonpartisan and consider it their duty to register voters. Consequently, almost everyone is registered to vote.

The United States is unique in putting the responsibility for registering on the individual citizen. Moreover, registration is handled at the state level, usually by agencies controlled by one or another party. These conditions are a major impediment to voting, with the result that only about 70 percent of U.S. citizens are registered.[75] Difficult registration procedures have a special impact on low-income Americans, who are 17 percent less likely to vote in states with difficult registration procedures than in other states.[76]

Given that states are laboratories—some things are tried in one state, other approaches in another—we know that some registration procedures encourage people to register and vote and others do not. One estimate is that voter turnout would be 9 percent higher if all states used procedures similar to those used by states that try to facilitate voter registration.[77] Voter registration increases when registration periods last up to election day (most states require registration at least twenty-five days before the election),[78] registration offices are located in neighborhoods rather than just one central county office, registration is by mail, registration offices are open at convenient hours, and voters who vote irregularly are not purged from the registration lists.

Recently Republican majority legislatures have supported, and in some states passed, legislation to eliminate same-day registration. Though designed to reduce Democratic turnout, in fact, it seems to be Republicans who are more likely to register the day of elections.[79]

In other jurisdictions, voter registrars do not provide these options, and some actually try to hinder groups working to increase registration. Some states do not allow volunteers to register voters outside the registration office.[80] Florida tried to impose fines of $250 for every voter registration form filed more than ten days after it was collected, even if a hurricane passed through in the meantime, and a fine of $5000 for every form that was not submitted. The law was declared unconstitutional, and a modified, less draconian, version was implemented.[81] Even so, in the first eight months after the law was implemented, 80,000 fewer people were registered compared to the same period before the 2008 election, and voter registration groups focused their registration drives elsewhere.[82]

To increase registration, a national law—the **motor voter law**—allows people to register at public offices, such as the Department of Motor Vehicles and welfare offices.[83] The law, passed in the early 1990s, led to the greatest expansion of voter registration in American history: 5 million new voters registered. Not all voted, but it is thought to facilitate some of the turnout after 2000.[84]

Barriers to voting   Some states work to facilitate voting turnout of those already registered, while others do not. For example, some states do not provide sample ballots or publicize where voters should go to vote, whereas other states mail sample ballots and information about where to vote to registered voters. Some states have limited polling hours; others open the polls very early and keep them open until 9 p.m. or later so that voters can vote before or after work. About half the states, including most of those west of the Mississippi, allow voters to vote with absentee ballots, even if they are not planning to be absent from their homes on election day. Absentee balloting makes voting something that can be done at the voter's convenience. One observer remarked, "The concept of Election Day is history. Now it's just the final day to vote."[85] Though this is clearly an overstatement, 30 percent of the voters voted before election day in 2008; in Oregon, all of them did.[86] In nine other states, more than 50 percent voted early.[87] To reach these early voters, parties must begin television advertising and flyer mailing much earlier. Providing information, extended polling hours, or using absentee ballots has a positive impact on voting rates, particularly for the young and less educated.[88]

Other states make it harder to vote. The states with the highest barriers to voting tend to be states with the largest minority populations. And we've seen that some states are working to make it even harder to vote.

Noncompetitive Districts

In most states, legislatures draw the boundaries for congressional districts and state legislative districts, so districts are normally drawn to benefit the party in control of the legislature. A district whose boundaries are devised to maximize the political advantage of a party or a racial or ethnic group is known as a **gerrymander** (for more on gerrymanders, see Chapter 9). A gerrymander aims to ensure that one party dominates in a particular district.

One side effect of gerrymanders is that they reduce voter turnout. With the candidate from the dominant party sure to win, the benefits of voting are greatly diminished and so fewer have an incentive to vote. Consequently, accountability to voters is decreased. In 2006 congressional races, voter turnout in districts won by a landslide (defined as 80 percent or more) was only 60 percent that of races where the margin was closer. The best way to ensure district competitiveness is to take redistricting out of the hands of the legislature and put it in the hands of a nonpartisan or bipartisan group, which has been done successfully in Iowa and Washington.[89]

PRESIDENTIAL NOMINATING CAMPAIGNS

In the early days of our nation, it was thought unseemly to "run" for office. John Quincy Adams, our sixth president, refused to campaign for the job. He thought that seeking the voters' approval was "beneath the dignity of the office" and believed that men—and, of course, all candidates at that time were men—who openly wanted the office didn't deserve it.[90]

Today, things are much different. Individuals declare their candidacy and run hard for the office. But not all have an equal chance of winning. Many Americans believe in the Horatio Alger myth: that with hard work anyone can achieve great success. This myth has its parallel in politics, where it is sometimes said that any child can grow up to be president. In fact, only a few run for that office, and even fewer are elected. Most people have little chance of being president: they are unknown to the public; they do not have the financial resources or contacts to raise the money needed for a national campaign; they are the wrong race or gender; they have jobs they could not leave to run a serious campaign; and their friends would probably ridicule them for even thinking of such a thing.[91]

Who Runs for President and Why?

Most candidates for president are senators or governors.[92] In recent decades, governors (George W. Bush, Bill Clinton, Ronald Reagan, and Jimmy Carter) have been more successful than senators (John Kerry, Robert Dole, and George McGovern), but the 2008 election returned a senator to the White House, the first since Richard Nixon. Vice presidents also frequently run, but George H. W. Bush was the only successful candidate during the twentieth century (though Richard Nixon had been vice president in the 1950s, he was a private citizen when he ran successfully in 1968).

Why do candidates run? An obvious reason is to gain the power and prestige of the presidency. But they may have other goals as well, such as to gain support for a particular policy or set of ideas. Ron Paul (R-Tex.) ran in 2008 and again in 2012 to promote his libertarian ideas. (Libertarians combine a conservative disdain for government regulation of the economy with liberal disdain of big-government regulation of personal behavior.) Sometimes candidates run for the presidency to be considered for the vice presidency, probably viewing it as an eventual stepping-stone to the presidency. But only occasionally—as when John Kerry picked John Edwards or Barack Obama chose Joe Biden—do presidential candidates choose one of their defeated opponents to run as a vice-presidential candidate.

How a Candidate Wins the Nomination

The nominating process is crucial in deciding who eventually gets elected. Boss Tweed once said, "I don't care who does the electing, so long as I get to do the nominating."[93] American presidential candidates are nominated through a process that includes the general public, the financial supporters of each party, and other party leaders.

Over time, voters and fundraisers have gained more power at the expense of party leaders. Presidential candidates try to win a majority of delegates at their party's national nominating convention, which takes place in the summer preceding the November election. Delegates to those conventions are elected in state caucuses, conventions, and primaries. Candidates must campaign to win the support of primary voters and those who attend caucuses and conventions.

Dynamics of Primaries

In **primary elections**, candidates of each party run against others of their party to achieve the nomination. Republican voters have to choose among Republicans rather than between a Republican and a Democrat.

Most candidates start with little name recognition. Lots of money and a good strategy are crucial to increasing the candidates' visibility.

In the recent past, candidates have formally announced their candidacies in the year preceding the presidential election year, but many begin laying the groundwork long before. Their aim is to persist and survive the long primary and caucus season that begins in January of election year and continues until only one candidate is left. To maximize their chances of survival, candidates carefully choose the primaries and caucuses where they will devote their resources. They must be successful in enough primaries so that they are seen as national, not regional, candidates, but they cannot possibly devote time and resources to every primary or caucus. Especially important are the early events—the Iowa caucus and the New Hampshire primary—and the larger state primaries. Of course, that strategizing does not always work. In 2012, Michelle Bachman, a Tea Party supporter and member of Congress from Minnesota, decided to spend all her time and money in neighboring Iowa, whose voters, she thought, would be like the voters in her own district. When she finished sixth in the Iowa caucuses, she withdrew from the race. Jon Huntsman, a former governor of Utah and current U.S. ambassador to China, was conservative though in some ways more moderate than the other candidates. He bypassed Iowa in favor of spending his time and money in New Hampshire, thinking that those voters were more independent and more likely to favor his brand of conservatism. He did poorly there and also withdrew from the race.

The Republican primary electorate is a very conservative group of voters, dominated by religious conservatives and Tea Party activists who care a great deal about ideology and policy. To reach this electorate, 2012 candidates had to promote very conservative positions.

The 2012 frontrunner, Mitt Romney, had a more moderate reputation when he served as governor of Massachusetts. The policies he advocated there, including pro-choice opinions on abortion, favoring a ban on assault weapons, and supporting a universal health insurance plan in the state, did not sit well with the Republicans' conservative base. Over the course of two campaigns—2008 and 2012—Romney reversed some of his past moderate or liberal positions and ran as a conservative, hoping voters would look at his current positions instead. A joke by an opponent illustrates the problem he faced in the primaries: "A conservative, a liberal, and a moderate walk into a bar. The bartender says, 'Hi, Mitt.'"[94]

Romney's vulnerability to challenges that he isn't a true conservative prompted eight other candidates to enter the race. In addition to Bachman and Huntsman, Tim Pawlenty, former governor of Minnesota, ran but gained neither financial backing nor support in the polls, so he dropped out long before the first primary. Herman Cain, a wealthy businessman, was the frontrunner in the polls in late 2011, but his candidacy imploded because of charges of sexual impropriety. Rick Perry, governor of Texas, announced his candidacy in August and immediately was considered a frontrunner, but he made many ill-considered comments in the Republican debates, prompting one observer to ask if he had had a stroke.[95] Perry withdrew after poor performances in the early contests.

The beginning of primary season was unusual, because rather than the Iowa winner gaining momentum, the first three contests produced three different winners. Rick Santorum, former senator from Pennsylvania, won the Iowa caucuses, based on his religious conservatism and energetic campaigning that took him all over the state. Mitt Romney won the next contest, in New Hampshire, a neighboring state to his home state of Massachusetts. And Newt Gingrich, former member of Congress from Georgia, won the South Carolina primary.

Santorum and Gingrich vied to be the anti-Romney candidate who would attract Republicans who felt Romney was too moderate. Both had billionaire supporters bankrolling their campaigns. But Santorum's poor campaign organization combined with extreme positions (such as opposing contraception and criticizing Obama's ambition that every student be able to go to college) limited his ability to build a broad coalition of support. His campaign staff was very small and rather amateurish; they did not even get him entered into all the primaries. Santorum finally withdrew in early April. Gingrich's bombastic rhetoric, which initially aroused those Republicans who were most angry toward President Obama, eventually lost its appeal, and Gingrich withdrew in May.

Meanwhile, Ron Paul, former member of Congress from Texas, had an active campaign and many strong supporters, especially young people, but his libertarian philosophy did not resonate with most Republicans. He probably did not expect to win any states, and he didn't, but he did pick up delegates along the way.

Money in Primary Campaigns

Money helps win elections. It's not the only factor, of course. Many candidates have tried and failed to "buy" elections with their own money. But money certainly aids in getting the candidate's message out.

Other things being equal, spending does influence voting in primaries. Some candidates are never considered serious contenders because they do not have sufficient money to mount a large campaign. Money is most important in multicandidate races, as is often typical early in the primary season when candidates are seeking to distinguish themselves from other little-known contenders.[96] Money is less important in two-candidate primary contests, often the situation late in the primary season when voters are aware of both candidates or one has emerged as the frontrunner.

Primary candidates who appear to be doing well generally attract money.[97] "Doing well" includes getting favorable media coverage that suggests the candidate is gaining popularity and momentum. Actual success in early primaries also stimulates giving. George W. Bush started strong in the 2000 primaries because he had raised millions more than all his opponents combined. Barack Obama's fundraising success gave him a large advantage in the 2008 primary campaign. Money, in turn, allows further purchases of media ads so candidates can become known for the next primaries.

However, in 2012, some new dynamics emerged. In *Citizens United*, the Supreme Court nullified campaign finance laws governing donations and spending not directly related to candidates. So, although wealthy donors cannot give as much as they want directly to campaigns, they can spend as much as they want on ads supporting one candidate and trashing the others. For candidates in 2012 to be competitive, they had to find a wealthy patron to bankroll "independent" political advertising. That became of equal or greater importance than raising funds from a large group of less wealthy supporters. Several of the Republican candidates, including Romney, Santorum, and Gingrich, had such wealthy supporters who spent millions out of their own pockets to advertise.

The ability to fund much of a television campaign with only one or two large donors affects the dynamics of the primary race. In multicandidate races in years past, most of the weaker candidates would drop out by the end of January because if they were unable to ignite popular support, their funding would dry up. In 2012, with no limits on the funds that supporters can spend as long as they don't give to candidates directly, candidates could continue if their patrons remained committed. Even when he lost primary after primary, Gingrich's campaign continued for some time because it was bankrolled by the multibillionaire owner of the Las Vegas Sands casino.

Where is the money spent? The media often expose inappropriate personal expenditures, such as 2008 Democratic candidate John Edwards' $400 haircuts or vice-presidential candidate Sarah Palin's $150,000 clothes shopping spree paid for by the Republican National Committee. But most spending is more mundane, even if the sums are staggering. During the 2008 primaries, the candidates spent about $1 billion. The best-funded candidates, Barack Obama and Hillary Clinton, spent more than $1 million a day. The beneficiaries of campaign spending are not just the staff who run the campaigns, but also a variety of private firms, consultants, media contacts, telemarketers, pollsters, event planners, and even credit card companies.

Media and consulting constitute more than one-third of all spending (see Figure 6). A number of private firms benefit from this fact, most particularly, in recent elections, the firms that plan and execute media buys for the candidates. Salaries and benefits (such as insurance and tax contributions) have been the next largest spending category. Although campaigns are largely staffed by volunteers, the top managers and campaign strategists who set the overall directions for the campaign, as well as local operatives who organize the volunteers, are on the payroll.

During the 2008 campaign, direct mail and telemarketing firms together received nearly $150 million of business from the candidates. Travel is another big item; in addition to flying the candidate and the staff around the country, the campaigns must also provide for the press. When money is flush, the press may be able to ride on comfortable large planes. When money is tight, they may be riding a bus and staying in cheap motels.

Candidates also use event planners to stage rallies and election night celebrations and to make bumper stickers and banners. The residual spending is for things like running local offices, renting space and furniture, obtaining phone service, and paying credit card fees. The Clinton campaign was widely criticized because early on it assumed that the primaries would be over after "Super Tuesday" in early February 2008. Therefore, campaign staff stayed at expensive hotels and their election day parties were catered expensively. Even the Dunkin' Donuts bill during one month was $1200.[98] As the primaries moved along, the campaign stretched their dollars much further.

Primary Message

Candidates try to find the position, slogan, or idea that will appeal to the most voters. In 1984, Ronald Reagan presented himself as the candidate embodying traditional America. As one of his staff aides wrote in a campaign memo, "Paint RR as the personification of all that is right with, or heroized by, America."[99] Barack Obama was the candidate for "change," rallying his supporters around the slogan "it's our time" to change the country. In 2008, it took Hillary Clinton several months to find a theme that resonated. Then she combined the "ready on day 1" theme with a strong populist message of fighting for the underdogs, a message that especially resonated with many women and blue-collar workers.

In 2012, both candidates struggled to develop a theme that resonated. Romney argued that his business success prepared him for the presidency and that the sluggish economy disqualified Obama, but Romney did not articulate a larger theme. As sitting president, Obama could no longer argue that he was the candidate of change and hope, though he tried to replicate these notions with the theme "Forward!" Yet his major messages were slow to develop.

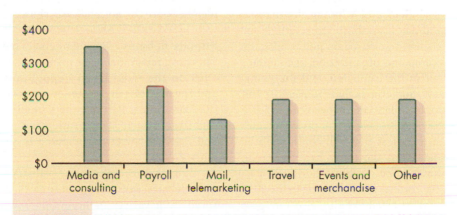

FIGURE 6: WHAT PRIMARY CANDIDATES SPENT MONEY ON IN 2012
SOURCE: © Cengage Learning.

Log in to www.cengagebrain.com and open Course-Reader to access the full reading, "The Citizen's United Catastrophe" by E. J. Dionne. A columnist for the *Washington Post,* E. J. Dionne critiques the Supreme Court's decision in *Citizen's United,* calling it "one of the most naïve decisions ever rendered by the court." Dionne describes how the Court's decision overturned decades of public policy and case law allowing regulation of campaign spending.

1. Why does Dionne believe the decision was naïve? He offers an alternative explanation that it was a deliberate attempt to remake our political system in a more conservative direction. But are there other, less negative interpretations to put on the Court's decision?
2. Freedom of speech is a value we hold dear. How do campaign finance laws limit or regulate free speech? In your view, is that a tradeoff worth making? Why or why not?
3. Dionne quotes another commentator who said that "little attention is being paid to the fact that our system of electing a president is under siege." How is it under siege?
4. Do you believe that unlimited campaign spending undermines democracy or strengthens it? Why or why not?

Primary Media Coverage

Media coverage of primaries is multifaceted, including free media—news reports and editorials, including coverage of debates, and candidate appearances on local and national shows—and paid ads.

Candidates need considerable free media coverage. They must convince reporters and the public that they are serious candidates with a real chance of winning. Journalists, with prodding from candidates, establish expectations for how well each candidate should do based on poll results, the quality of a candidate's campaign organization, the amount of money and time spent in the campaign, and the political complexion of the state. Sometimes these journalists and campaign pros are jokingly called "the expectorate."[100] If a candidate performs below expectations, the press assumes that the candidate has a weakness that will continue to be exploited and may be fatal. On the other hand, a strong showing when expectations are low can give a boost to a candidate's campaign. Rick Santorum's great showing in the 2012 Iowa caucuses when he was expected to be an "also-ran" gave him credibility in primary races throughout the first two months of the campaign.

Candidates must avoid making a big mistake or, worse yet, being caught covering up a mistake or untruth, especially about one's personal life. Senator Gary Hart's 1988 candidacy collapsed when the media discovered that his marriage did not prevent him from having affairs with other women. He compounded the damage by lying, thereby raising questions about his character and honesty. In contrast, during the primary campaign, Clinton admitted that his marriage was not perfect. (The Monica Lewinsky scandal occurred after he was in the White House and was already a popular president.)

In 2012, paid political ads for the Republican primaries were overwhelmingly negative, as candidates and their supporters sought to distinguish themselves by painting their opponents as less conservative than they were. Super PAC ads were much more negative than ads sponsored by candidates themselves; 72 percent of the ads sponsored by Super PACs (political action committees that raise money for political advertising; see Chapter 6) were negative. The Romney Super PAC spent the most money and had the greatest proportion of negative ads targeting his opponents.[101] In the Florida primary, 90 percent of ads run by Romney or his supporters were negative, and most focused on Gingrich. As a result, voters became much more negative about Gingrich during the Florida campaign. Only 0.1 percent (one-tenth of 1 percent) of Romney ads were positive.[102]

Super PAC ads can be so negative because they are usually anonymous, with the sponsors identified with vacuous names like "Winning Our Future" (supporting Gingrich), "Restore Our Future" (supporting Romney), and "Red, White, and Blue Fund" (supporting Santorum). Although these groups identify themselves, they don't identify their donors.[103] Thus big corporations and wealthy individuals can donate to these groups and attempt to influence the election without the public becoming aware of their efforts. Big corporations, especially, welcome the anonymity because they don't want to alienate any customers. But the public has no idea which businesses and persons are trying to manipulate their vote.

Some Republican insiders despaired during the primary season because candidates threw so much mud at each other. But, as usual after a hard-fought primary, the party did come together once the nominee was chosen.

Primary debates Primary debates have become the norm. The first debate between primary candidates occurred in 1948 on the radio when Republicans Thomas E. Dewey and Harold Stassen debated for an hour on the topic "Shall the Communist Party in the United States Be Outlawed?" Eight years later, Democratic candidates Adlai Stevenson and Estes Kefauver participated in the first televised primary debate.

In more recent years, the primary season has seen multiple debates with many candidates that have been sponsored by a variety of nonprofit, media, and commercial groups. In the eighteen months before the general election in 2008, Democrats debated twenty-five times, and in

2012, Republicans debated twenty-four times. [104] The early debates featured as many as eight or nine candidates, and the later ones became two-person debates for Democrats in 2008 and three- or four-person debates for Republicans in 2012.[105]

The early debates with multiple candidates are difficult, as all candidates struggle to make their views heard. When some candidates drop out, the focus becomes clearer, with the remaining candidates tearing down the frontrunner and the frontrunner trying to avoid damaging mistakes. Positions become more visible as the field melts from eight or nine to two or three. These smaller numbers allow candidates to articulate their positions and focus their criticisms more sharply.

Though audiences for primary debates are relatively small, the debates are important for voters who are interested in the presidential election at this early stage. The debates, one observer noted, are "choppy and awkward" and sometimes have "howling studio audiences," but they are "of inestimable value" by allowing voters to "see and hear the candidates in a sustained manner."[106]

The common wisdom about presidential primaries is that the key ingredient is "momentum." That is, a candidate needs to win early, or at least do better than expected, to gain momentum, and then keep winning to maintain momentum. The "expectorate" needs to pronounce him a winner. In 1976, Jimmy Carter, then an unknown governor from Georgia, won the Iowa caucuses; this performance attracted tremendous media attention, which, in turn, led to further primary wins

and eventually the nomination. John Kerry, by winning Iowa and then New Hampshire in the 2004 Democratic primaries, gained so much momentum that he knocked the other candidates out of the race very quickly, in what was originally billed as a tightly contested race. In 2008, however, on both the Republican and Democratic sides, the momentum seemed to shift back and forth.

Incumbent presidents seeking renomination do not have the same problems as their challengers. Incumbents usually have token or no opposition in the primaries. No incumbent who sought renomination was denied it in the twentieth century.

In addition to these general strategies, candidates must deal specifically with the particular demands of caucuses, conventions, and primaries.

Presidential Caucuses and Conventions

Some states employ caucuses and conventions to select delegates to attend presidential nominating conventions. A caucus is a neighborhood meeting of party members who discuss the candidates and then vote for their preference. These results are then added across the state. A convention, on the other hand, is usually a statewide event. Delegates to the convention are elected at the local level by party voters.

Iowa, as the first state to hold its caucuses, normally gets the most attention, but the Iowa caucuses, except for their timing and newsworthiness, are similar to those in other

BEHIND THE SCENES

The Rope Line

Though presidential campaigns are conducted primarily through the media, candidates do make personal appearances in towns and cities across the United States. And usually, after a speech or event, the candidate will stay for a few minutes—or longer—to shake hands and speak briefly with some of those who came to see him or her. This ritual takes place at the "rope line," now usually a metal barrier separating the candidate and the surging crowd.

At the rope line, a member of the public might shake a candidate's hand, give her a memento (a coin, rabbit's foot, book, photograph, or any number of other odd items), ask to have a photo taken with the candidate (usually with a cell phone camera), get an autograph, give the candidate advice about a policy or even about getting enough sleep, or tell the candidate of a personal problem—all in a few seconds. Sometimes these brief encounters are reflected in later speeches, where the candidate will mention a person, sometimes by name, who told of a harrowing personal story that could be alleviated or avoided with better government policies or procedures.

The rope line offers a relatively spontaneous moment in what are usually very tightly controlled appearances. "I got to smell him, and it was awesome," said one Obama fan, caught between him and another woman trying to hug him. "I can't believe she picked me out of a crowd," said a Clinton supporter, after she gave him a bottle of water and signed a photograph for him. (The reporter noted that the man had fainted in front of her, so he was easy to pick out.)

Observers reported that Obama is not much of a hugger or handshaker and does "about 20 voter touches per 30 seconds." He rarely signs autographs on the spot. By contrast, Hillary Clinton was "a rope lining dynamo," charging into the crowd, spending time with supporters, signing autographs on everything from T-shirts to Krispy Kreme boxes, and, like her husband, seeming to enjoy the experience. Mitt Romney can be "chatty" on the rope line, so his staff, fearing that he might say something that could be used against him, tried to limit reporters' access to his rope line comments.

Of course, the Secret Service does not like rope lines either because it is hard to control people pressing in on the candidate. One man on a Hillary Clinton rope line reported that he was asked to take off his respirator mask but was "allowed to keep his goggles and blue rubber gloves on." (He wanted to talk about the chemical industry.)

SOURCE: Mark Leibovich, "Where to Catch the Sights, Sound and Smell of a Campaign," *New York Times*, May 24, 2008, www.nytimes.com/2008/05/24/us/politics/24rope.html. See also Michael Barbaro and Ashley Parker, "Romney Camp Tries to Limit Reporters' Access, and Rope Line Ruckus Erupts," *New York Times*, May 16, 2012, http://www.nytimes.com/2012/05/17/us/politics/romney-camp-tries-to-limit-reporters-access-and-rope-line-ruckus-erupts.html.

Mitt Romney works a "rope line."

states. Thousands of representatives of the media cover these caucuses, which have gained importance beyond what one would normally expect for a small state. Although only a handful of delegates to the national convention are at stake, a win with the nation's political pros watching can establish a candidate as a serious contender and attract further media attention and the financial donations necessary to continue the campaign.

Presidential Primaries

Delegates to presidential nominating conventions are also selected in direct primaries, sometimes called **presidential preference primaries**. In these elections, governed by state laws and national party rules, voters indicate a preference for a presidential candidate, or they vote for the delegates committed to a candidate, or both. (In states where voters merely indicate their preference, the delegates are actually selected in conventions or caucuses and the primaries are called "beauty contests" because they are meaningless in terms of winning delegates, though they can be important in showing popular support.) Like other primaries, presidential primaries can be open (to all voters) or closed (to nonparty members).

Through the 1960s, presidential preference primaries usually played an insignificant role in presidential nominations because only a handful of states employed primaries to select delegates. Thus Vice President Hubert Humphrey gained the Democratic Party's nomination in 1968 without winning a single primary. A majority of the delegates to the Democratic convention were selected through party caucuses and state conventions, where party leaders supportive of Humphrey had considerable influence. Humphrey's nomination severely divided the Democratic Party. Many constituencies within the party, particularly those opposed to the Vietnam War, charged that the nomination was controlled by party elites out of touch with rank-and-file Democrats.

Delegate Selection Reform

In response, the Democratic Party changed delegate selection procedures to make delegates more representative of Democratic voters. One change established quotas for blacks, women, and young people to reflect the groups' percentages in each state's population. These reforms significantly increased minority and female convention representation and, quite unexpectedly, made the primary the preferred method of nomination. Criteria of openness and representativeness could be more easily satisfied through primary selection. In recent years, more than 70 percent of the Democratic delegates have been chosen in primaries. Although the Democrats have replaced quotas for minorities with guidelines urging minority involvement in party affairs, the quota for women remains: half the delegates must be women.

The Republican Party has not felt as much pressure to reform its delegate selection procedures, but Republicans have tried to eliminate discrimination and increase participation in the selection process.

Reforming the Nomination Process

Each election year political observers discuss changing the presidential nomination process. They correctly complain that primaries weaken political parties by removing the decision from party officials and that primaries have very low, unrepresentative turnouts. But while caucuses empower the party elite, they are a barrier to broad participation and even more unrepresentative than primaries.

The Caucuses

The caucus system came under attack in 2008, especially by Clinton supporters. Although Clinton's campaign did not pay close enough attention to the rules that gave caucuses significant power, it is also true that, as they alleged, caucuses favor individuals who have a good deal of flexible time, such as independent professionals. They do not empower working-class people because participation in a caucus requires several hours. Thus, those who have child care responsibilities, are out of town, are ill or disabled, or have inflexible work schedules are disfranchised.

Moreover, the small number of participants means that caucuses can be very unrepresentative of the overall primary electorate. In 2008, in the four states that had both primaries and caucuses, Obama won the caucuses by margins 5 to 34 percent greater than the popular vote and thus piled up huge delegate margins. (In three of the four states, the primaries were only "beauty contests"; the vote didn't count in the delegate selection.) On the Republican side, McCain did very poorly in the caucuses because of his organizational problems yet was able to win most of the big primaries, which, because of the Republicans' method of delegate allocation, he converted into large numbers of delegates.

The Primaries

The primary electorate, often in the 25 to 35 percent turnout range, is much larger than the number of caucus participants but significantly smaller than the number of voters in the general election. Primary voters include the citizens who are most interested in politics and tend to hold more extreme views than other people. Thus Democratic primaries have a disproportionate number of liberals, and Republican primaries have a disproportionate number of conservatives. These primary voters pull the Democratic candidates further to the left and the Republican candidates further to the right than the candidates might choose to position themselves or than the electorate as a whole might want the candidates to position themselves.

Moreover, until 2008, the system gave disproportionate influence to two small states, Iowa and New Hampshire, that come first in the process. Voters in most other states did not get to see most candidates; they had already been weeded out by the time the April, May, and June primaries occurred. There are some advantages to having the small states go

Republicans keep looking for the next Ronald Reagan who can unify the party and win over independent voters.

first,[107] particularly the fact that campaigns in small states can be personal and relatively inexpensive compared to the costs of the big media markets in large states. But in 2008, the system changed. Legislators in the larger states moved to get their states into the early action. The Iowa caucus and then the New Hampshire primary remained first, but a month later twenty-two states, including many large states, held primaries. This new lineup put a much bigger premium on having money and gaining support early, since only media buys allowed candidates to be visible in so many large states simultaneously.

Rearranging the schedule does not address the central problem: that primaries remove power from political parties. Many people are glad that we no longer have the "smoke-filled rooms" where party bosses chose the nominees. Nevertheless, the primary system has weakened political parties, and the small primary electorate is unrepresentative of the general public, though it is more representative than the caucuses. It is possible that primary voters are even less representative of the public than the party bosses who met in smoke-filled rooms. Certainly they know less about the nominees than the party bosses did. But the days when party leaders could anoint the nominees are probably gone forever.

Another issue with primaries is how the votes are counted. In 2008 the Republicans operated with a winner-take-all system; that is, the candidate winning the most votes won all the delegates in the state. This is analogous to the Electoral College system for determining the general election winner. The Democrats, on the other hand, split each state's delegates according to the proportion of votes they received in the primary or caucus. Thus, a 51 percent victory for John McCain gave him all the state's delegates; a similar victory for Barack Obama gave him only 51 percent. Several commentators have pointed out that had the Democrats operated under the Republican rules, Hillary Clinton would have been the Democratic nominee.

 ## Thinking about Democracy

Can we know whether caucuses or primaries are more representative of the party? Of the general electorate? Are caucuses or primaries more democratic?

The National Conventions

Once selected, delegates attend their party's national nominating convention in the summer before the November election. Changes in party rules have reduced the convention's role from an arena where powerful party leaders came together and determined the party's nominee to a body that ratifies a choice based on the outcome of the primaries and caucuses. In other words, the conventions now routinely nominate whichever candidate wins the most primaries.

In the "old" days, often many ballots were necessary before a winner emerged. In 1924, it took the Democrats 103 ballots to nominate John W. Davis. Now nominees are selected on the first ballot. Sometimes commentators predict a close nomination race, which would force the decision to be made at the convention, but this hasn't happened since the primaries have been used extensively. Instead, the national party conventions served other purposes: to endorse the nominee and his choice for vice president, to construct a party platform, to whip up enthusiasm for the ticket among party loyalists, to showcase rising talent and popular party elders, and to present the party favorably to the national viewing audience. Thus even without choosing the nominee, the national conventions give meaning to the notion of a national party.

After the reforms of 1972, convention delegates have become a more diverse group, especially on the Democratic side. In 2004, 50 percent of the Democratic and 43 percent of the Republican delegates were women; 18 percent of the Democratic and 6 percent of the Republican delegates were black. (Only 2 percent of Republican voters are black, compared with 28 percent of Democratic voters.) Similarly, Democratic delegates are much more likely to be Latino and very slightly more likely to be Asian than are Republican delegates.[108] Compared to the population, delegates to national party conventions are well educated and financially well-off. Delegates also tend to be more ideologically extreme than each party's rank and file. Democratic delegates are more liberal and Republican delegates more conservative than their party's supporters and the public in general. (See Figure 7.)

The Activities of the Convention

National party conventions are full of color and portray at least a semblance of excitement. They are a montage of balloons, placards, and demonstrations. Candidates and their lieutenants scurry around in search of uncommitted delegates, while behind-the-scenes negotiators try to work out differences among factions of the party. Journalists are everywhere, covering the trivial and occasionally the momentous. The keynote address reviews the party's glorious past, speaks to a promising future, and levels attacks, usually relatively gentle, at the opposition. Each candidate is placed in nomination by a party notable who reviews the candidate's background and experience. The roll call of the states ratifies the party's choice, and on the last night delegates cheer the acceptance speeches of the presidential and vice-presidential nominees. Those who contested the nomination often join the nominees on the platform at the end in a display of party unity.

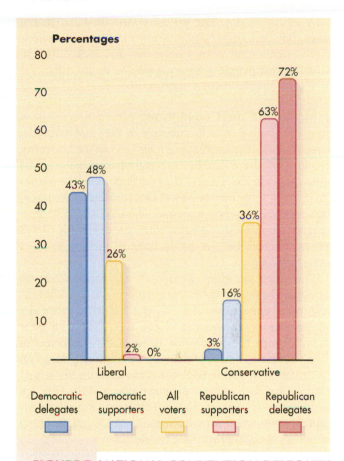

FIGURE 7: NATIONAL CONVENTION DELEGATES ARE MORE IDEOLOGICALLY EXTREME THAN RANK-AND-FILE MEMBERS The numbers represent the percentages of those who identify themselves as liberal or conservative. For example, of Democratic delegates, 43 percent consider themselves liberal and 3 percent conservative. (Others are middle of the road.)

SOURCE: Data from 2008 delegate and public surveys reported in the *New York Times*, September 1, 2008, graphics8.nytimes.com/packages/pdf/politics/20080901-poll.pdf?scp=5&sq=delegate%20survey&st=cse.

During the convention, each party endorses a platform, a statement of what it plans to do dressed up in flowery language about how it is the only possible choice for patriotic Americans. Although platforms are filled with platitudes, they do have some substance. Most of the platforms contain pledges of proposed future actions, and most of those pledges are fulfilled.[109] Platforms do provide observant voters with information about what the party will do if elected.

Finally, the conventions close with the acceptance speeches of the presidential and vice-presidential nominees, which are the highlights for most viewers, though watched predominantly by the partisans of the party. The conventions have a noticeable impact on mobilizing those partisans and contributing to a more positive image of the party's candidate among independents as well as the party's supporters.[110] And, as one observer commented,

"Conventions are now like bar mitzvahs. They are rites of passage. But rites of passage are very important in society. The guy is changing from a politician and a candidate to one of the two people who are going to be president for sure; it gives them a certain majesty."[111]

The Media and the Convention

With the beginning of radio coverage in 1924 and television coverage in 1940, the conventions have become media events. In recent years, there have been several times as many media representatives as delegates at the conventions.[112] The parties try to put on a show they hope will attract voters to their candidates, controlling who speaks and when. Polls usually show the party's candidate doing better during and after the party's convention, called the "convention bounce," though the effect does not last long.

When there are deep divisions in the party, it may be impossible to prevent them from surfacing at the convention during prime time. This has not happened since the 1968 Democratic convention, which was filled with conflict, both inside the convention between the supporters of Hubert Humphrey and opponents of the Johnson policies on the Vietnam War, and outside the convention on the streets of Chicago between antiwar demonstrators and the Chicago police. Television covered both events, associating the division in the convention with the turmoil outside and dimming Humphrey's chances of winning the election.

Because subsequent conventions have been predictable, with few controversial issues, the major networks are no longer showing them "gavel to gavel," leaving that coverage to public television or specialty cable networks such as CNN and C-SPAN. The major networks showed only a few prime-time events of each 2012 national convention: the keynote speech and an occasional speech by a party luminary, including President Bill Clinton at the Democratic convention and Ann Romney at the Republican one. The vice-presidential and presidential nominees' acceptance speeches are also given extensive coverage. In 2008, coverage of the Democratic convention focused on whether Hiliary Clinton supporters would rally around Obama, and the media gave extensive coverage to speeches by Hillary Clinton and Bill Clinton. At the Republican convention, the focus was on whether Romney could generate enthusiasm from among the party's conservatives and on his choice of Paul Ryan as the vice presidential candidate. This limited coverage is the logical outcome of the successful attempt of party leaders to control the conventions. Still, even if there's no controversy, the media's talking heads will work hard to create conflict and excitement.

Selecting a Vice-Presidential Nominee

In modern times, the vice-presidential candidate is selected by the party's presidential nominee and then merely ratified at the convention, although in 1956, Democratic presidential nominee Adlai Stevenson broke with tradition and left the decision to the convention. In earlier years, party bosses chose the running mate. When Rutherford B. Hayes (1877–1881) first got word that William Wheeler was to be his running mate, Hayes responded, "I'm ashamed to say: Who is Wheeler?"[113]

Presidential candidates usually select a vice-presidential nominee who can balance the ticket. What exactly does "balance" mean? A careful analysis of vice-presidential choices of both parties since 1940 revealed that presidential candidates tend to balance the ticket in terms of age—choosing a running mate from a different age cohort, as John McCain did with Sarah Palin.[114] Those with little Washington experience usually balance the ticket by choosing a Washington insider as a running mate (as, in 2008, relative outsider Obama did by choosing Joe Biden and as, in 2012, outsider Mitt Romney did by choosing Paul Ryan). Sometimes candidates will balance the ticket in terms of region (for example, John F. Kennedy from Massachusetts chose Texan Lyndon Johnson in 1960) or ideology. In 2012, voters were uncertain about Romney's true ideological beliefs; he chose very conservative Paul Ryan to try to assure the Republican core of his own commitment to conservatism.[115]

In the 1950s, at the dawn of the television age, Democratic Party leaders instruct their delegates how to behave on camera.

Gender traditionally was not part of a ticket-balancing effort, but since Walter Mondale's historic choice of Geraldine Ferraro in 1984, women are sometimes among those given consideration. Much discussion of both parties' tickets in 2008 swirled around the issue of whether a woman would be asked to join the ticket. Though Barack Obama passed over Hillary Clinton as his choice in favor of Sen. Joe Biden (Del.), John McCain did choose Sarah Palin. Though his primary aim may have been to woo disaffected Clinton supporters (an attempt that failed), the major impact was to rally the religious right to his ticket. Palin, a conservative Republican, energized the Republican base and gave the ticket new excitement but also raised questions about McCain's judgment in putting someone so inexperienced on the ticket, questions that grew more frequent as Palin interacted with the press.

Pundits often opine that choosing a vice-presidential candidate from a large state will help win that state in the November election.[116] In fact, this is not true; the added advantage of a vice-presidential candidate in his or her home state is less than 1 percent, and the bigger the state, the less the advantage.[117] About one-third of the vice-presidential candidates since 1960, including Paul Ryan, did not even carry their home state.[118] In recent elections, no presidential candidates have chosen running mates from large states, and Dick Cheney, Sarah Palin, and Joe Biden came from the nation's smallest states, with three Electoral College votes each.

Do vice-presidential choices affect the election outcome? In most cases, no, although Kennedy's selection of Johnson probably enabled him to carry the state of Texas in the tight 1960 race. Without Texas, Kennedy would have lost. In recent years, presidential candidates have been more attentive to the possible contributions a vice president would make after being elected. Other than that, as one commentator quipped, "picking a running mate is…like picking a pet. How much time are you planning to spend with the little fellow? How much exercise will he be getting on an average day? On the one extreme, you have the William Wheeler model [Rutherford B. Hayes's vice president]. There's the living room, go find a corner and sleep in it. On the other end, there's the Cheney version in which the pet takes over the checkbook, diversifies the family investment portfolio and starts strafing the neighbor's cat."[119]

Independent and Third-Party Nominees

Independent and third-party candidates are part of every presidential campaign. Most of the candidates are invisible to all except the most avid political devotee. It's not easy for independents to get on the ballot; state laws control access to the ballot, and state lawmakers are Republicans or Democrats. But in recent elections, strong independents have emerged with some frequency, including Ross Perot in 1992 and 1996 and Ralph Nader in 2000. The Nader candidacy probably cost Al Gore the election by taking some liberal votes away from him in closely fought states.

Paul Ryan, vice-presidential candidate, campaigns with Mitt Romney.

THE GENERAL ELECTION CAMPAIGN

We take it for granted that the election campaign is what determines who wins, and it does have a modest effect.[120] But consider this: only twice since 1952 has the candidate who was ahead in the polls in July, before the national conventions, lost the election. Those years were 1988, when Dukakis led, and 2000, when Al Gore led (and since Gore won the popular vote, perhaps his case is only a partial exception to the rule).[121] This suggests that although campaigns can make a difference, a lot of other factors determine who is elected.

Campaign Organization

Staffing the campaign organization is crucial, not only hiring talented people but also getting those with considerable national campaign experience and a variety of perspectives. The candidate's own personal organization is only one part of the overall campaign organization. The national party organization and state parties also have some responsibilities, including the very important functions of registering potential party voters and getting them to the polls, as well as trying to make sure that the presidential candidate's local appearances will help the party's congressional and state candidates. Individuals and groups who raise and spend money to influence the election also must be considered.

Obama's campaign organization in 2008 and 2012 was far superior to that the Republicans mounted. In 2012 this might be partly attributed to the fact that Romney did not secure the nomination until late March and had spent most of his funds doing so. The leadership of the Obama campaign was highly disciplined, resisting the temptation to respond to distracting events that occur during the campaign. Their "ground game," the deployment of campaign workers in communities and neighborhoods was highly strategic, and they had two to three times as many local offices and workers as the Romney campaign in 2012. One illustration of the Obama field organization's efficiency is that their poll watchers were trained and equipped with the material they needed on the weekend before the election, while many Romney poll watchers did not receive instructions until Monday night before the Tuesday election, and then many were not provided with their certified badges allowing them to be poll watchers. The Obama poll watchers in key precincts texted the Chicago headquarters with turnout numbers at prescribed intervals, whereas the Romney campaign's computer tallying system broke down on election day.

Campaign Money

Waging a campaign is expensive. Fundraising for national elections is done by the party committees, candidates themselves, and private groups that support candidates. Although candidates for president can receive some public money, most funding is private, so candidates for office must continually look for funding sources. Potential presidential candidates appear on television and fly around the country to woo potential donors and fundraisers and to attend fundraising functions. Without money, even the best candidates with the best ideas will go nowhere. In the 2008 presidential and congressional campaigns, spending to influence the elections totaled over $5 billion. That's a lot of money, but Americans spend about $300 million on their phones each year and in 2008 spent more than $340 million on entertainment.[122]

There are some laws regulating campaign finance, but beginning in 1976[123] and continuing through the *Citizens United* ruling in 2010,[124] the Supreme Court gutted serious efforts to regulate spending. In its weakening of campaign finance laws, the Court joined forces with Republicans in Congress, most of whom adamantly oppose regulating campaign money (Senator John McCain of Arizona is a notable exception).

There are some rules worth noting, however. Money raised for the candidates' own campaigns is regulated. Donors' names are made public, individuals and political action committees (PACs) are limited in the amount they can give, and corporations and unions are prohibited from giving directly to candidates. The Court has accepted these limits.

There is a system of public funding in place for presidential elections, and candidates who accept public funding are limited in the amount of money they can spend. But no significant candidate has accepted public funding for primaries in the last several elections, and in 2008 Obama rejected public funding for the general election too. Obama rightly knew that he could raise more than that limit. John McCain did accept public funding, probably because he suspected he could not raise more than the limit. In 2012, both candidates rejected public funding and thus any limit on their overall spending.

We described the organization and spending rules for PACs, Super PACs, and 527 organizations in Chapter 6. PAC fundraising, spending, and gifts to candidates and political parties are regulated by federal legislation, and such donations and gifts are a matter of public record. Super PACs may receive money without revealing sources and spend an unlimited amount as long as they are technically separate from the candidate's or the party's organization. In *Citizens United,* the Court overturned sixty years of precedent that barred corporations and unions from giving to political candidates. In particular, it overturned a 2002 law passed by Congress that forbade corporate and union contributions to groups supporting candidates.[125]

The 2012 election is the first operating under the new rules, and candidates and observers quickly learned how to use the system to their advantage.

Raising Money

If the presidential candidate is running for reelection, the chief fundraiser is likely to be him. This certainly creates awkwardness and can diminish the president's stature. To raise soft money for the Democratic National Committee and thus for his campaign, President Bill Clinton invited big donors to the White House to have coffee with him and, in some cases, to stay overnight. These and other revelations about fundraising practices prompted cries of outrage from Republicans. Said candidate George W. Bush, "Will we use the White House…as a fundraising mechanism—in other words, you give money and you get to sleep in the Lincoln Bedroom? The answer is no."[126] But once in office, the Bush administration just as blatantly exploited the office for partisan fundraising, as the president invited big donors to dine with diplomats at an embassy and meet with cabinet officials.[127] Indeed, Bush and his organization were by far the biggest fundraisers ever among political candidates. They used their close connections to industry to raise staggering amounts from corporate executives eager to have high-level access to the president and his team.

Whether the candidate is already in office, or not, a significant part of his or her time must be spent raising money. This deters some potential candidates from even running. And once a candidate, asking for money is a job that few candidates enjoy. Former astronaut and unsuccessful presidential candidate John Glenn once remarked, "I'd rather wrestle a gorilla than ask anyone for another 50 cents."[128]

 ## Thinking about Democracy

> Is it more democratic to let individuals and corporations spend as much as they want to influence elections, or is it more democratic to limit spending? Why?

Campaign Strategies

In developing a strategy, candidates primarily seek to do two things: mobilize those who are already loyal to them and their party and persuade independent voters that they are the best candidate. At the national level, given entrenched party loyalties, little effort is spent trying to convert the opposition. Democrats have to work harder at mobilizing their voters than do Republicans because Democratic voters, especially the poor and the young, often do not vote.

Most partisans vote for their party's candidate, so the job is to mobilize them. Both parties must try to persuade independent voters, who are swing voters and can determine the outcome, even though true independents are only about 7 percent of the electorate. (See box "Are Independents Really Independent" on page 213) Most of those who say they are "independent" lean strongly to one party or another and vote accordingly.[129]

The crucial strategic question is where to allocate resources of time and money: where to campaign, where to buy media time and how much to buy, and where to spend money helping local organizations. Skill in raising money is, of course, also one of the keys to a successful political campaign.

Allocating Resources among States

Candidates know that they have to win a majority of the Electoral College vote (see "The Electoral College" section later in this chapter). The most populous states, with the largest number of electoral votes, are vital. However, compared to thirty years ago, more states are now "safe" (see the box "America the Sorted"). So candidates focus their resources

on a decreasing number of so-called **battleground states**, or **swing states**, where the results are in doubt. That includes not just the large states of Ohio, Pennsylvania, and Florida, but also medium-sized states such as Wisconsin and Iowa and even smaller states such as New Mexico, with its five electoral votes, and New Hampshire, with its four.

Thus in both the 2008 and 2012 presidential campaigns, there was little advertising or activity in several of the largest states—California, New York, and Texas—because the first two were considered sure Obama states and the last a sure Republican state. Meanwhile, the swing states received massive attention. For example, in 2008, Obama and McCain totaled twenty-seven visits to Pennsylvania and twenty-nine to Ohio, while California and New York received less than half that. Smaller swing states, including Missouri, Colorado, Virginia, and Florida, had presidential candidate visits more frequently than New York and California, even though they had many fewer electoral votes.[130] And Texas, safely in the Republican column, received only two visits. In 2004 the same dynamics were at work, where in 2012, Ohio was a particular focus, with both candidates visiting frequently as they competed for what they thought would be the key state in the electoral map.[131]

In focusing on swing states, candidates are attempting to expand their existing bases of support. Most of the Rocky Mountain states have been solidly Republican in their presidential loyalties. Republicans must build on this base and their strength in the South by carrying some of the large eastern or midwestern industrial states.

Democrats have a strategic problem stemming from the fact that Republicans locked up most of the Rocky Mountain and southern states in the 1970s and 1990s. Between the end of Reconstruction (in 1877) and 1948, the South was solidly Democratic. Since 1976, the Democrats have consistently lost the South, as we discussed in Chapter 6. President Clinton, himself a southerner, proved that Democrats could win without most of the South. (This strategy was also used successfully by the Republicans between the 1870s and the 1920s, when they were able to capture the White House regularly without ever winning a southern state.)

The Republicans' strategic problem is that the party has become heavily reliant on the thirteen states of the old Confederacy. Those states have provided more than half of the Republicans' electoral votes in every election since 1992 (as well as almost half of the Republicans' congressional representation).[132] As the South becomes more multicultural and diverse, especially with the growth of the Latino population, Republicans' grip on parts of the South is threatened.

In 2008 and 2012, Obama campaigned heavily in areas of population growth, particularly where the Latino and Asian population was increasing.[133] His strategy paid off when, in 2008, he won North Carolina and Virginia in the South and broke the Republicans' hold in the Mountain states by winning Nevada and Colorado, solidly Republican in the Bush years, as well as New Mexico.[134] In 2012, Obama held all these states except North Carolina, which he lost by a narrow margin.

BEHIND THE SCENES

America the Sorted

Americans today are much more likely than previous generations to live among others of similar economic statuses and cultural beliefs. For example, whereas in 1970 people with college degrees were fairly evenly spread across cities, today college graduates are leaving some areas and congregating in others. Those areas are booming, while other areas are declining.

Because cultural differences influence political choices, this **Big Sort** has had dramatic political consequences. As the author of the book by that name illustrates, before 1980, only about a third of voters lived in counties where one or the other presidential candidate won by a landslide (at least 20 points). In 2004, nearly half of the voters did.

That sorting, in turn, has consequences for democracy. Communities of like-minded individuals can become homogeneous and even extreme in their political attitudes because there is little diversity of opinions generated by individuals of widely different circumstances. Central cities are overwhelmingly Democratic, while many suburbs and small towns are overwhelmingly Republican.

This sorting extends to lifestyle differences too. Commercial marketers divide Americans into small segments and target consumer goods to each segment, a practice called microtargeting. And political and brand microtargeting are converging.

For example, in 2008, Obama carried 81 percent of the counties that had a Whole Foods chain store (a high-end grocery store) and just 36 percent of the counties with Cracker Barrel chain restaurants (a restaurant appealing to an "old country" constituency with southern roots).[1] Al Gore and Bill Clinton also were more successful in Whole Foods than in Cracker Barrel counties, though the difference was smaller than Obama's.

Americans, then, increasingly live in areas with people like themselves, in terms of foods they eat as well as political preferences. There is little need to compromise on those preferences. Those who want Whole Foods, or Cracker Barrel, can live in a place that has one. Perhaps it is not surprising that the people they elect to represent them in Congress are not that interested in compromise either. As diversity of income and life styles within a community declines, so too does the need to find a middle ground. Elections reflect that polarization.

[1] David Wasserman, "Will the 2012 Election be a Contest of Whole Foods vs. Cracker Barrel Shoppers?" *Washington Post*, December 9, 2011, http://www.washingtonpost.com/opinions/will-the-2012-election-be-a-contest-of-whole-foods-vs-cracker-barrel-shoppers/2011/09/28/gIQAMuXDiO_story.html.

SOURCE: Bill Bishop, *The Big Sort* (Boston: Houghton Mifflin, 2008); Sheryl Gay Stolbert, "You Want Compromise? Sure You Do," *New York Times*, August 14, 2011, 5.

Creating Images

Largely through the media, candidates try to create a favorable image and portray the opponent in an unfavorable way. In 2012, Barack Obama was successful in painting Mitt Romney as a heartless businessman who made tens of millions by taking over companies and then firing their employees. Romney was not able to overcome that image, which was amplified by his opposition to bailing out the auto industry and letting auto companies go bankrupt. These statements hurt him significantly in the midwestern states where he needed to win an electoral college majority. In 2008 and 2012, McCain, then Romney, tried to portray Obama as different, radical, and out of touch with ordinary people. These charges resonated with the Republican base, many of them still believing that Obama was not born in the United States, but the charges did not take hold in the larger electorate. In 2004, Bush successfully defined himself as a resolute war leader and Kerry as a "flip-flopper" with no principled positions.

Issues can also be the basis for an appeal to voters. Democrats traditionally have used "pocketbook" issues, arguing that economic times are better with Democratic presidents. They did the same in the 2008 election. Given the problematic

state of the economy, high gas prices, and the slumping housing market, the Democrats fought the 2008 campaign on economic issues. McCain tried to gain advantage on foreign policy and war issues, arguing that Obama was an untried leader and that Obama would rather win an election than the war. As a war hero himself and an experienced senator, McCain had some advantage on these issues. Republican surrogates even cast doubt on Obama's patriotism, while far-right ideologues tried to make an issue out of Obama's middle name, Hussein. But, even with two ongoing wars, economic issues touched people the most, and Obama and the Democrats were seen by the electorate as better on those issues.

Issue appeals are usually general, and often candidates do not offer a clear-cut choice even on the most important controversies of the time. In 2008, it was hard to see any differences between McCain and Obama on the war in Afghanistan, but, on Iraq, Obama pushed for a timetable for withdrawal, while McCain argued for staying until the United States achieved "victory." In 2012, Romney had difficulty distinguishing his foreign policy positions from those of Obama, and he focused on domestic policy differences, including his opposition to the Affordable Care Act (which he called "Obamacare") and his view that he could do a better job with the economy.

Ideally, the major campaign themes and strategies have been put into place by the end of the summer, but these themes and strategies are revised and updated on a daily, sometimes hourly, basis as the campaign progresses. Decisions are made not only by the candidate and the campaign manager but also by a staff of key advisers that includes media experts and pollsters. Campaigns use sophisticated polling techniques to produce daily reports on shifts in public opinion across the nation and in particular regions. Campaign trips are modified or scratched as the candidate's organization sees new opportunities. And media events can be planned to complement the paid advertising the candidate runs.

Campaign Communication

Candidates use multiple ways of communicating with their supporters and with the millions of swing voters who might vote either way. Campaign advertising, appearances on television, candidate debates, mass mailings, and many forms of electronic communication are all part of campaign communication. They inform, they help set the campaign agenda, and they help persuade voters.[135]

Media Advertising

Paid advertisements allow candidates to focus on points most favorable to their cause or to portray their opponents in the most negative light. Most of the cost of campaigns is in advertising, and in that category in 2008, Obama outspent McCain by $83 million.[136] Obama's campaign had so much money that it even ran ads on evangelical radio stations "just to hold down the McCain margin."[137]

Most advertising is done through television, increasingly on cable channels, although radio and the Internet also reach significant audiences.[138] Television ads were first used in the 1952 campaign. One, linking the Democratic Truman administration to the unpopular Korean War, showed two soldiers in combat talking about the futility of war. Then one of the soldiers is hit and dies. The other one exposes himself to the enemy and is also killed. The announcer's voice says, "Vote Republican."[139] Today's ads are shorter and less melodramatic but still appeal to emotions. The 1984 Reagan commercials hearkened back to an idyllic past before the turmoil of the 1960s and 1970s and proclaimed American greatness again. Their cheerful tag line was "It's morning in America."[140] (Many historic ads are available for viewing online at http://www.livingroomcandidate.org/.)

Targeting advertisements Designing campaign ads is both an art and a science. Most political ads are quite short, thirty or sixty seconds in length. Campaigns are sophisticated in placing ads, targeting them to demographic groups they hope will be sympathetic to their candidates. This technique, called **"narrowcasting,"** is possible today because of the many cable TV and local radio stations in existence. BET attracts blacks, Univision appeals to Hispanics, ESPN to men, Lifetime to women, Fox to conservatives, and MSNBC to liberals. Although these are generalizations, if your target audience

is moderates and liberals, for example, you won't advertise on Fox. Radio stations also have particular demographics. Conservative talk radio shows, pop stations, and NPR have different demographics, as well as a local audience.

Narrowcasting relies on the fact that Democrats and Republicans prefer different programs even on the same network. Excluding sports and news programming, PBS's *Masterpiece Theater* is first among liberal Democrats' top twenty-five shows, while PBS's *This Old House* is second among conservative Republicans' shows.[141] Republicans prefer *Jay Leno*; Democrats favor *David Letterman*, *The Daily Show*, and the *Colbert Report*. Republicans like *Swamp Loggers* and *NCIS*, while Democrats enjoy comedies like *30 Rock* and *The Office*.

These kinds of preferences influence the advertising that parties and candidates do.

Republicans tend to advertise more than Democrats on crime and sports shows, whereas Democrats advertise more than Republicans on television talk shows and situational comedies. The Republicans try to activate middle-aged male voters, and Democrats try to reach more women voters.[142] In the 2010 congressional elections, for example, programs featuring mostly Republican ads included pro and college football, NASCAR racing, and major league baseball. All of these have more than two-thirds Republican ads. Programs featuring mostly Democratic ads included *Two and a Half Men*, *Everybody Loves Raymond*, *Smallville*, *Dr. Oz Show*, and *Rachel Ray*.[143]

Both campaigns focus on the battleground states and waste little of their advertising budget on states already thought to be sure for one candidate.[144] But within the battleground states, Republicans generally focus more on rural and outer suburban areas than do Democrats.

Negative or positive campaigning Campaigns also have to decide what combination to run of positive ads that introduce the candidates, their ideas, and their programs; negative ads that attack their opponents; and response ads that respond to opponents' charges.

We described at the beginning of the chapter how negative advertising is nothing new in American politics. Even the Founders engaged in it. In the more immediate past, negative ads have been prominent.[145] In 2008, negative ads were the staple of the McCain campaign, while the Obama campaign had a greater balance of positive and negative. The Obama campaign could do this, not only because it was the frontrunner throughout the campaign, but also because it outspent McCain on advertising by a substantial margin, so it could do both positive and negative advertising. With a more limited budget, the McCain campaign used negative ads, which were more effective.[146] Many of the most negative ads are run not by the candidates and their campaigns but by independent groups supporting them.

Because negative ads do provide some helpful information about issues, they supplement media news coverage, which focuses heavily on personalities, conflicts, and the "horse race" aspect of campaigns.[147] Many, though not all, negative ads contain a grain of truth. Obama *was* more supportive of government spending than McCain, and McCain *was* more hawkish on the Iraq War than Obama.

American Diversity

Racism in the 2008 Campaign

With the election of Barack Obama, the racial barrier to the presidency fell. Some other barriers had fallen in earlier decades. In 1960, only 71 percent of all voters said they would vote for a Catholic for president, and some doubted whether a Catholic could ever be elected.[1] But in 1960, John F. Kennedy was elected, and that barrier was broken. Twenty years later Ronald Reagan became the first divorced person to be elected. Race, however, is a much more distinctive barrier than religion or divorce.

In some ways, the 2008 election seemed light-years away from earlier eras, when the idea of a woman of any color or an African American man running for president would have seemed ludicrous. Both Hillary Clinton and Barack Obama had millions of campaign supporters who included men, women, blacks, and whites (and, of course, Americans of other ethnicities too), and both their campaigns broke fundraising records. In these ways, their campaigns were much different than Jesse Jackson's 1984 campaign, which appealed mostly, though certainly not entirely, to black Americans, or earlier bids for the presidency by Shirley Chisholm in 1972, who never had a chance to become a mainstream candidate.

In 2008, few, if any, mainstream commentators made blatantly racist comments. Yet race was injected into the campaign in several ways. A significant minority of voters stated in pre-election and exit polls that race was a factor in their vote. While some of these were African American voters positively inclined toward Obama, others were white voters stating they would not vote for a black person. But surveys cannot tell us exactly how many such voters there are because people aren't always honest with surveyors or don't really understand their own motivations.

One researcher, however, devised a strategy to measure the impact of race in the election. He obtained data of the frequency of Google searches for the word *nigger* by people in nearly two hundred media markets in the four years before Obama was a candidate (so the searches weren't related to feelings toward Obama.) Those searches, about as frequent as searches for *economists, Lakers,* and the *Daily Show,* usually turn up stereotype-based jokes using coarse language.[2] People living in West Virginia, upstate New York, rural Illinois, eastern Ohio, southern Mississippi, western Pennsylvania, and southern Oklahoma were most likely to undertake such searches. Then the researcher compared the votes received by Democratic candidate Kerry in 2004 and Obama in 2008. He found that the areas with the greatest decline in the Democratic vote from 2004 to 2008 were the areas where searches for the N-word were the most numerous. Thus the decline in the Democratic vote in these areas reflected prejudice.[3] Overall the negative effect of prejudice measured in this way cost Obama 3 to 5 percent of the vote, not enough to affect the 2008 election, but enough to affect a closer race.

Obama rarely brought race into the election, but McCain frequently articulated the idea that Obama was different, that he was "the other," even when race was not explicitly mentioned. Republican rallies, taking a cue from conservative commentators, often called attention to Obama's middle name, Hussein, to imply that he was foreign and Muslim. (He is Christian.) On the Internet, questioning of his American ancestry continued (as it did into his presidency). The goal was to convey the feeling that Obama was not "one of us."[4]

The election results showed that enough Americans cast aside their doubts about a relatively inexperienced African American candidate to elect him by a large margin. In fact, the campaign itself seemed to bring about a modest change in whites' attitudes about blacks.[5] Though Obama did not win a majority of white votes, he won a higher proportion than any Democrat since Jimmy Carter. Even some voters who admitted prejudice against an African American candidate voted for him because they thought he would better protect their economic interests or they doubted whether the McCain-Palin team was up to the job.

[1] Barry Sussman, "A Black or Woman Does Better Today than a Catholic in '60," *Washington Post National Weekly Edition,* November 21, 1983, 42.

[2] Seth Stephens-Davidowitz, "The Effects of Racial Animus on a Black Presidential Candidate: Using Google Search Data to Find What Surveys Miss," November 2011, http://www.people.fas.harvard.edu/~sstephen/papers/RacialAnimusAndVotingSethStephensDavidowitz.

[3] Obama ran a more effective campaign than Kerry did and took less liberal positions than Kerry did, so these factors wouldn't account for the decline in the Democratic vote in these areas.

[4] Shankar Vedantam, "Why Those Rumors Stick," *Washington Post National Weekly Edition,* October 20–26, 2008, 37.

[5] Lee Sigelman and Susan Welch, "The 'Obama Effect' and White Racial Attitudes," *Annals of the American Academy of Political and Social Science* 634 (March 2011), 207–220, http://ann.sagepub.com/content/634/1/207.refs.

SOURCE: www.cbsnews.com/htdocs/pdf/ 020306woman.pdf; Gallup poll data from www.atheists.org/flash.line/atheism9.htm.

However, some negative ads are simply false. Political observers are still talking about the anti-Kerry negative ads in 2004. The so-called Swift Boat Veterans for Truth attacked Kerry's war record, which had been a strong point of his campaign appeal. (Kerry, as a young naval lieutenant, commanded a "swift boat" in the Vietnam War and won medals for heroism as well as for his wounds.) The Swift Boat Veterans did not serve with Kerry, and several were angry with him for opposing the war after returning from Vietnam. The Kerry campaign was slow to respond to these ads because the Kerry staffers knew that the substance of the ads was false.[148] But the Swift Boat ads were so effective that reporters coined a new verb—"to swift-boat"—meaning to produce a commercial that is dishonest but plausible to viewers.

Negative ads, whether true or false, tend to reinforce viewers' previous beliefs. So, if you believed that Kerry wouldn't be a strong leader or that Democrats wouldn't stand up to foreign threats, you would be more likely to believe the Swift Boat ads that implicitly drew those damning conclusions.

Campaign advisers think that negative ads are very effective, even though most people say they do not like them.[149] One adviser said, "People won't pay any attention [to positive ads]. Better to knock your opponent's head off."[150] Some negative ads focus on policies, such as opposition to the Democrats' health care reform or the Republicans' plans to lower taxes for the wealthy. But, increasingly, negative ads go beyond critiques of policies. In the 2012 election season, a billionaire proposed to spend $10 million on an advertising campaign that would resurrect a racial issue from the 2008 election. The goal was to promote opposition to Obama among whites. In a memo, the advertising agency noted that "voters aren't ready to hate this president," as if encouraging hatred was a desirable objective of political ads.[151] (The plan was scratched after it was publicized.)

Political scientists disagree about how much effect negative ads have on changing votes or reducing turnout. Some suggest that negative ads depress turnout of those whose candidate is the subject of the attacks.[152] However, in today's campaign settings, candidates trade negative attacks, so everyone's candidate is a target. Whether negative ads reduce turnout or not, they do tarnish the election in voters' minds. A strategist for George W. Bush's reelection campaign in 2004 admitted, years later, that negative campaigning is like "poisoning the water table."[153]

Some checks do exist on negative campaigns.[154] One check is the press, which could point out errors of fact. In recent campaigns, the press has tried to do this. Since 2004, fact checkers have been more active, and many papers ran critiques of the truthfulness of ads and statements made by candidates while campaigning. In the process, however, the press often simply gave more attention to the negative messages.[155] Another potential check is the voters, who might become outraged. But although the voters complain, negative ads may still influence swing voters, and any lies are often discounted by the candidates' supporters.

E-Campaigning

Increasing numbers of people are using the Internet as a source of news. In fact, during the 2008 election, nearly half of Americans said they looked online for news about the campaign or got e-mails about it. Seventeen percent claimed to look for campaign news online on a daily basis.

Not surprisingly, then, candidates are increasingly relying on electronic communication to keep supporters informed about the campaign and the issues, to raise money, and to solicit volunteer activity. Their tools include websites, e-mail, blogs, YouTube, text messaging, and social networking sites like MySpace, Facebook, and Friendster.

Use of e-mail and texting is a particular form of narrowcasting, sometimes called **microtargeting**, that targets specific groups of people. Electronic communications are critical to microtargeting, allowing communication with hundreds of thousands of people, making them feel like insiders and encouraging their continued support, allegiance, and activity. These e-mail messages and texts supplement the use of direct postal mailings, which are more expensive and less responsive to breaking events. An e-mail can be prepared and sent in a few hours and can be linked to a website or streamed video.

In 2008, Barack Obama led, by far, in using the Internet to attract supporters and keep them engaged. "Our e-mail list had reached 13 million people. We essentially created our own television network, only better, because we communicated directly with no filter to what would amount to about 20 percent of the total number of votes we would need to win," claimed his campaign director.[156] The Obama campaign sent

"Remember, it's not enough to say what's great about mac'n'cheese. We've got to go negative on tuna noodle casserole."

more than 1 billion e-mails and included 1 million people in its texting program.[157]

Whether as a cause or effect of this aggressive program, Democrats favoring Obama were the most likely group to be online. Though McCain's supporters were about as likely as those of Obama to use the Internet, they were much less likely to use it to get political news or to promote their views (such as by signing an online petition or forwarding a link to someone else).

Obama's Internet activity also fit well with the overall demographics of Internet users. Younger people, the core of Obama's support, are more likely to use the Internet as a news source: half of those under fifty look online for news, compared to only 15 percent of those over sixty-five. Similarly, less educated and lower-income people are less likely, by a considerable margin, to go online. However,

there are few racial differences in using the Internet for political news.[158]

As another example of Obama's Internet presence, his Facebook site showed more than 1.2 million supporters, and his website linked to many general social networking sites and those targeted to African Americans, Asian Americans, religious believers, baby boomers, gays and lesbians, Latinos, business professionals, and Democrats. Estimates are that individuals, collectively, spent "more than 14 million hours watching over 1800 Obama-related videos on YouTube that garnered more than 50 million views."[159]

The Republican candidates, with the exception of Ron Paul, were not as effective in using the networking capacities of the Internet. For example, even in summer 2008, the McCain website offered places for supporters to sign up and keep in contact but did not offer links to networking sites.

BEHIND THE SCENES

Blogs and the Big Sort

Political blogs are an increasingly common way to keep track of politics. About one-third of individuals claim to read blogs, and of those about half read political blogs. One survey identified 476 political blogs, though that probably only scratches the surface.

Most blogs are read by only a few people, perhaps friends and acquaintances of the blogger. On the other hand, blogs such as the Huffington Post and Daily Kos (both on the left) and the Drudge report (on the right) are read by millions. Some nonpartisan blogs are widely read too, such as RealClearPolitics, which posts articles and information from many political perspectives.

As we would expect, blog readers are more likely to be educated and highly interested in politics (not just marginally interested).[1] They are likely to be strong Democrats and individuals who consider themselves liberal or very liberal rather than moderate or conservative, though very conservative individuals also read blogs more than those with more moderate positions. Thus, though fewer Republicans than Democrats are bloggers, those that do blog are disproportionately very conservative. Consistent with the "Big Sort" models of the American electorate, blog readers tend to read the blogs that are consistent with their political views. More than 94 percent of blog readers read only blogs from one side of the spectrum, and only 6 percent read blogs from both sides. With few exceptions, only liberals read the Daily Kos and only conservatives the Drudge report, for example.

Blog reader polarization is even more extreme than television news audiences. Even though Fox viewers are mostly conservative, they have some moderate and liberal viewers. And the network newscasts, MSNBC, and CNN have many moderate viewers and a few conservatives. Readers of right-wing blogs are considerably to the right of Fox News viewers, and readers of left-wing blogs are to the left of mainstream network viewers.

Blogs are another way that individuals can interact with people like themselves. That's true for self-help groups and also true of politics. Rather than widening individuals' perspectives, they largely provide a way to reinforce them. For example, in a one-month scan, information scientists found that those who searched the Web for "Obama" and who went to the liberal blogs were interested in his accomplishments and his recent press conference; those who went to middle-of-the-road blogs were interested in his poll numbers; and those who went to conservative blogs were interested in the cost of his recent foreign trip and views on "Obamacare." Those who looked up "violence" on liberal sites were interested in right-wing violence, whereas those who went to conservative blogs were interested in left-wing violence.[2]

[1] Information for this box is drawn from Henry Farrell, Eric Lawrence, and John Sides, "Self Segregation or Deliberation? Blog Readership, Participation, and Polarization in American Politics," *Perspectives on Politics 8* (March 2010), 141, http://home.gwu.edu/~jsides/blogs.pdf.

[2] Erik Borra and Ingmar Weber, "Political Insights: Exploring Partisanship in Web Search Queries," *First Monday* 7 (July 2012), http://firstmonday.org/htbin/cgiwrap/bin/ojs/index.php/fm/article/view/4070/3272.

Thus, it is not surprising that the McCain Facebook address had less than 200,000 supporters.

YouTube is increasingly used as a campaign tool. Of course, it can be a negative, because a candidate's dumb statements or actions, if captured on camera, live on forever in cyberspace and are easily retrievable. In 2012, Romney's campaign was dealt a blow when a talk he gave to a group of wealthy donors was secretly recorded and played on YouTube millions of times. The talk labeled 47 percent of Americans as takers and victims, showing disdain for millions of Americans. The video slowed the momentum of the campaign and distracted it from the messages that he was trying to convey.

Blogs also have become a campaign tool. Candidates and their supporters can air their views and attack opponents through blogs; a few prominent ones are read by millions.[160] Although talk radio is dominated by conservative Republicans, the most popular political blogs are those on the liberal side.

Of course, the Internet spreads lies as well as truth. Those receiving e-mail in the last part of the 2008 campaign were more likely than others to believe Obama was a Muslim, for example, and that he "palled around with terrorists."[161] And the Internet has other limitations too. Obama intended to use his powerful Internet presence to generate support after he was elected, but this plan has fallen short. It is easier to mobilize people for a short time around the rhetoric of change than it is to rally them for a prolonged period around the nitty gritty business of compromise and governing.

Television Appearances and Media Events

As we described, mass media buys are the biggest part of a campaign's expenses. It is true that "for the large majority of voters, the campaign has little reality apart from the media version."[162] Media exposure includes paid advertisements focused on selected states and areas. Given the increasing sophistication of the campaigns, most television and radio ads never appear in states that are solid for one candidate or another. Although voters in battleground states might be delighted not to have to listen to an onslaught of campaign ads, voters in other states may feel less connected to the campaign.

But some media exposure is free. One way to garner media attention is to appear as a guest on various television shows. Before the 1990s, presidential candidates appeared only on "serious" shows, such as the Sunday morning talk shows, where candidates would be interviewed by one or more members of the press. Now it is common for candidates to appear in more informal, sometimes humorous, settings, such as late-night talk shows, daytime shows targeted to women, or comedy shows. The candidates hope to use these settings to show voters that they are approachable and down-to-earth. They also give candidates a chance to poke fun at their own foibles and thus possibly defuse opponents' attacks. Candidates' appearances on such shows often become major stories themselves, prolonging the impact of the appearance. (And, then, in 2008 there were Tina Fey's impersonations of Sarah Palin on *Saturday Night Live* that poked fun at her lack of preparation for major interviews,

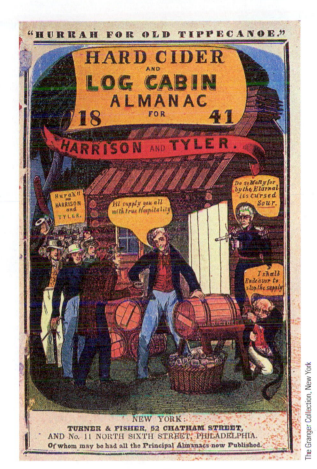

The Granger Collection, New York

Long before television cameras, candidates shaped their image. In 1840, William Henry Harrison campaigned as the log cabin and hard cider candidate—a common man—even though his father was a wealthy planter, a Virginia governor, and a signer of the Declaration of Independence. To underscore his purported origins, Harrison gave Indian war whoops at rallies.

and *those* shows also became news stories even though Palin was not actually there.)

The candidates also vie for media attention at the local level. In fact, candidates spend most of their time going from media market to media market, hoping to get both national and local coverage.[163] Vice-presidential candidates often appear in the smaller media markets, while the presidential contenders hit the major metro areas. They stage media events with photo opportunities in front of enthusiastic crowds and patriotic or other positive symbols.

Televised Debates

A third form of free media exposure is the televised debate. In 1960, Kennedy challenged Nixon to debate during their presidential campaigns. Nixon did not want to debate because as vice president he was already known and ahead in the polls. He remembered his first election to the House of Representatives when he challenged the incumbent to debate and, on the basis

National Archives and Records Administration

Families all across the country gathered in front of their TVs to watch the first tele-vised presidential debates in 1960, featuring Senator John F. Kennedy and Vice President Richard Nixon.

of his performance, won the election. Afterward he said the incumbent was a "damn fool" to debate. Nevertheless, Nixon did agree to debate, and when the two contenders squared off, presidential debates were televised to millions of homes across the country for the first time.

Nixon dutifully answered reporters' questions and rebutted Kennedy's assertions. But Kennedy, to compensate for his youth and inexperience, projected an image of vigor. He also sought to contrast his attractive appearance and personality with Nixon's. So he quickly answered reporters' specific questions and then directly addressed viewers about his general goals. Kennedy's strategy worked. He appealed to people and convinced them that his youth and inexperience would not pose problems. While Kennedy remained calm, Nixon became nervous, smiling at inappropriate moments, with his eyes darting back and forth and beads of sweat rolling down his face, which had a five-o'clock shadow that projected a somewhat sinister look.

According to public opinion polls, people who saw the debates thought that Kennedy performed better in three of the four. (The only debate in which they thought Nixon performed better was the one in which the candidates were not in the same studio side-by-side. They were in separate cities, and with this arrangement Nixon was less nervous.) Yet people who heard the debates on radio did not think Kennedy performed as well. They were not influenced by the visual contrast between the candidates or the Kennedy strategy of looking directly into the camera. Clearly, television made the difference.

No more presidential debates were held for sixteen years. The candidates who were ahead did not want to risk their lead. But in 1976, President Ford decided to debate Carter, and in 1980, President Carter decided to debate Reagan. Both incumbents were in trouble, and they thought they needed to debate to win. Although President Reagan was far ahead in 1984, he decided to debate Mondale because he did not want to seem afraid. By agreeing to debate, he solidified the precedent begun anew in 1976.

In 2000, the media's low expectations for Bush's performance, coupled with his congenial, personal style, helped him hold his own or even win the debates in the view of many, even though the debates revealed his limited grasp of issues and misstatements of facts. Gore's mannerisms seemed stiff and overbearing. And the press, which is far more inclined to evaluate the debates as theater performances than as policy discussions, addressed Gore's body language more than Bush's grasp of issues and misstatements of facts.

Because candidates have different strengths, each campaign wants a debate format that builds on its candidate's strengths. The "debate about debates" has become as predictable a part of campaigns as the debates themselves. Representatives of candidates debate the number of debates, the formats, the topics to be covered, the size of the audience, even the size and shape of the podia. The 2004 debates were governed by a thirty-two-page set of rules agreed to by the candidates' representatives.

In 2004, those negotiating for Bush argued that the first debate should be about foreign policy, ostensibly Bush's strength. He thought he could easily show Kerry to have an uncertain grasp and a vacillating policy. Instead, Kerry looked assured and confident and attacked Bush's foreign policy mistakes throughout the debate. When cameras focused on Bush listening to Kerry, he looked surly and angry at being attacked. And when Bush responded, he wasn't able to offer a coherent defense of his policies. Consequently, although Kerry had been trailing in the polls before the debate, his performance in this debate narrowed the gap. The president prepared more for the second and third debates and looked more confident and pleasant.[164]

In 2008, the first and second debate came in the middle of a free fall in the economy, with the Dow stock market index losing more than 2500 points between the first and last debate and one of Wall Street's largest investment firms, Lehman Brothers, collapsing. McCain was quoted as saying the economic fundamentals were strong, a view held by almost no one else and that played into the hands of the Obama campaign, which had been arguing that McCain was out of touch.

This economic context favored Obama, who pounded home the point that the economic disaster was a result of failed Bush policies that McCain would continue.[165] Moreover, Obama, who had not done well in the primary debates against Clinton, prepared thoroughly for the debates. McCain hated to prepare.[166] "Not today" was a frequent response to the suggestion that he practice. As a result, whereas Obama came over as assured and knowledgeable, McCain came over as grumpy and dismissive of Obama. Said one commentator afterwards, "Do people want to put up with four years of that? Of [him] sitting there, angrily, grumpily, like a codger?"[167]

In 2012, the first debate was a disaster for Obama and gave the Romney campaign new hope. Like Bush in 2004, Obama did not prepare well for the first debate, despite advisors' warnings that presidents usually do not do well in those first debates. He even took time out from debate preparations to visit nearby Hoover Dam.[168] In the debate, Obama looked tired, bored, and distracted and made very few compelling points. Romney, in contrast, prepared well and looked vigorous and confident in making his arguments. Democrats were aghast, and Republicans triumphant. Obama spent considerable time in the next few days reassuring supporters and donors that he would do better next time. A week later, Biden dominated the vice presidential debate, stopping the Romney poll gains, and then in the following two weeks, Obama did well in the second and third debate.

The Electoral College

In the United States, we do not have a direct election of the president. All planning for the campaign has to take into account the peculiar American institution of the **Electoral College**, described by one wit as "the exploding cigar of American politics."[169] Most of the time it works fine as "little more than a question on the citizenship test and a subject for political thriller novels." Then, every so often, "it blows up in our faces, throwing whole elections in doubt and making a mockery of the popular will."[170]

The last time it blew up in our faces was in 2000, when although Al Gore had over 500,000 more votes than George W. Bush, he lost the election. The Electoral College is another feature of the American constitutional system that limits democracy.[171]

The Way the System Works

What counts is the popular vote in each state, because that vote determines which candidate will receive the state's electoral votes. Each state has as many electors as its total representation in Congress (House plus Senate). The smallest states (and the District of Columbia) have three, whereas the largest state—California—has fifty-five. Voters choose electors of the Electoral College when they vote for president. Technically, they vote for the electors pledged to the candidate and whose names are on file with the state government. The outcome is not official until these electors gather in each state capital in December after the presidential election to cast their votes for president and vice president.

With the exception of Maine and Nebraska, which divide some of their Electoral College votes according to who wins in each congressional district, all of each state's electoral votes go to the candidate winning the most votes in that state. If one candidate wins a majority (270) of the electors voting across the United States, then the election is decided. If the electoral vote is tied, or if no candidate wins a majority, then the election is decided in the House of Representatives, where each state has 1 vote and a majority is necessary to win. This has not happened since 1824, when John Quincy Adams was chosen. But it nearly happened in 1976 with the shift of a few thousand votes in Delaware and Ohio. If voting in the Electoral College for the vice president does not yield a majority, the Senate chooses the vice president, with each senator having one vote. If it should get to that stage, the largest and smallest states would have equal weight, a very undemocratic procedure.

Strategic Implications

The campaign strategies that candidates use are shaped in part by the Electoral College system. In general, candidates have incentives to spend more time in the large states where the majority of the electoral votes are. A 1-vote margin in Pennsylvania, for example, yields 21 votes for the winning candidate compared to only 3 votes in North Dakota. Thus it is more important to get that extra vote in Pennsylvania. Given the need to focus on a small number of swing states, more time is consequently spent in the larger ones than the smaller ones.

However, as we described earlier, only some large states get attention. So, in 2012, we expected political activists from California not to spend much time there, but rather head for Colorado or New Mexico or Oregon, where there was competition. The Electoral College system, then, favors "states" over "people." As one observer pointed out, gun owners or women, for example, live all over the country, but only those in swing states get wooed.[172]

Smaller states tend to favor the Electoral College system because their Electoral College votes give them a larger influence on the Electoral College than their population proportion would. But unless they are swing states, they are ignored as well. The safe Republican states in the South and the Great Plains are largely ignored by the candidates.

Rationale and Outcomes of the Electoral College

The Founders neither wanted nor envisioned a popular election of the president; selection of the president was placed in the hands of state elites, the electors. The Founders also agreed to enshrine the influence of small states (at that time, disproportionately southern, slaveholding states) in the fundamental framework of the Constitution, and the Electoral College was one way to do that.[173]

The Founders assumed that the Electoral College would have considerable power, with each elector exercising independent judgment and choosing from among a large number of candidates. They did not foresee the development of political parties or of a political climate in which the popular vote was considered the source of legitimacy for a candidate. In practice, as state parties developed, the electors became part of the party process, pledged to party candidates. Therefore, electors usually rubber-stamp the choice of voters in each state rather than exercise their own judgment.

A discrepancy between the Electoral College and the popular vote outcome occurred three times in the nineteenth

century (1824, 1876, and 1888). However, after more than a century of presidential elections whose outcome was known once the popular vote was tallied, and since the principle of "one person, one vote" has become enshrined in law and political culture, the American public has become used to thinking of elections as an expression of the will of the people.

When the 2000 election yielded an Electoral College winner who had not won the popular vote, there were immediate calls for the elimination or reform of the Electoral College system. However, these calls went nowhere, and the Electoral College remains (see Figure 8).

Possible Reforms

The Electoral College was designed both to temper the influence of voters by establishing an intermediate body of electors who actually choose the president and to make sure that the South had a disproportionate influence on the choice of the president.[174] It is a distinctly undemocratic mechanism that institutionalizes in the presidential election process part of the excess weight given to smaller states in the U.S. Senate (because the number of electors for each state is based on the number of senators and representatives in each state).

Over the years, several proposed reforms have been considered. One reform would be to abolish the Electoral College

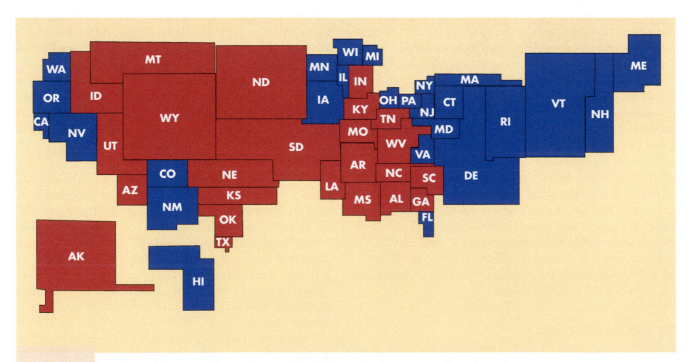

FIGURE 8: THE ELECTORAL COLLEGE VOTE Each state is drawn to reflect the relative power of its average voter. Because the electoral vote for a state is based on the number of its representatives in the House plus its two senators, and because small states are overrepresented in the Senate, the voters in small states have more power than the voters in large states. For example, California has nearly 12 percent of the U.S. population but only 10 percent of the Electoral College votes, whereas Wyoming has 0.17 percent of the population but 0.5 percent of the Electoral College votes. So the average vote in Wyoming is worth more than the average one in California. The states are colored according to the winner in the 2012 election, with blue for Obama and red for Romney.
SOURCE: © Cengage Learning.

altogether and leave the choice of president to the popular vote because direct election is a more understandable system. This change would require a constitutional amendment (which requires a two-thirds approval by members of Congress and three-quarters of the states), which is very difficult because the small states that think they benefit from the current system and the swing states that do benefit from the existing system will block it.

Another target of reform is the constitutional requirement that if the electoral vote is tied, the presidential choice is to be thrown to the House of Representatives. There is no expectation that each state's House delegation would vote for the presidential candidate that its state's voters chose; rather, states would reflect the majority party in their House delegation. Moreover, each state would have an equal vote: Alaska would carry the same clout as California. This would be a very undemocratic feature and would probably cause a crisis if actually used to elect a candidate with a minority of the popular vote.

Another undemocratic feature of the Electoral College is that not all states require their electors to cast their votes for the candidates who won the state vote. The **faithless elector** is one who casts his or her vote for a personal choice, even someone who was not on the ballot. Even though the intent of the Founders was to allow electors to cast their votes any way they desired, modern reformers have proposed that, in our more democratic era, electors should be bound by the wishes of the voters in their states. It is true that no faithless elector has ever made a difference in the outcome of an election, but in the 2000 election, as few as three faithless electors could have made a difference.

A current reform proposal is the National Popular Vote, a movement gaining some ground. The idea, supported by a group of electoral reform advocates, is that each state would pass a law entering into an agreement to award all its electoral votes to the candidate who receives the most popular votes nationally. The proposal, then, could take effect when states whose total electoral votes equal 270, the Electoral College majority, have entered the agreement. Nine states have now endorsed the measure, states that provide about half of the 270 electoral college votes.

 Thinking about Democracy

Why do Americans tolerate the undemocratic features of the Electoral College?

The 2000 Election: A Perfect Storm

The election of 2000 demonstrates the antidemocratic nature of the Electoral College. It was won by George W. Bush, who got fewer popular votes than his rival, Al Gore. In another antidemocratic twist, the election was decided by the U.S. Supreme Court, when, by a 5–4 vote, it stopped the recount of votes ordered by the Florida Supreme Court. The division

in the Electoral College was very close, and the outcome rested on the winner in Florida, where election mismanagement, partisan politics, and unavoidable human error came together to create chaos in a closely divided race.

Election day exit polls of Florida voters showed Gore winning by a small margin. But after first declaring Gore the winner, the television networks declared Bush the winner, and then in the early morning hours decided it was too close to call. The election hung in the balance. Bush had a tiny lead of several hundred ballots.

Confusion reigned in the days afterward. The press and election observers reported several problems, some of them serious. Thousands of Gore votes were lost because of the strange "butterfly ballot" configuration in Palm Beach County, a heavily Democratic liberal county. The odd format, designed by the supervisor of elections in the county, made it difficult for some voters to determine which punch hole corresponded to which presidential candidate. More than 3000 voters punched the hole registering a vote for Patrick Buchanan, listed to the right of Gore's name on the ballot. This is particularly ironic because the areas of Palm Beach County casting the most votes for Buchanan were those inhabited by mostly Jewish voters, the least likely group to support Buchanan, who is considered anti-Semitic. As one elderly Jewish woman exclaimed after mistakenly voting for Buchanan, "I would rather have had a colonoscopy than vote for that son-of-a-bitch Buchanan."[175]

Nearly 3000 voted for Gore and the socialist candidate whose punch hole was underneath Gore, apparently thinking they voted for Joseph Lieberman, Gore's vice-presidential running mate, whose name was under Gore's. (Bush lost about 1600 votes from those who voted for him and Buchanan.) Although some spoiled ballots are normal in every election, this erratic pattern in one county was the result of a badly designed ballot. But there was nothing the Gore campaign could do. The ballot was designed by a Democratic supervisor of elections who made the candidates' names larger so elderly voters could read them better and without an intention to deceive any voters.

There was also a problem with overseas ballots. Americans overseas have the right to vote. They must ask for a ballot before the election and mail it by the day of the election, but the ballot need not be received by local officials until ten days after the election, to allow for mail delays. There are strict rules about how these ballots are to be certified to avoid vote fraud, but hundreds of these ballots came in lacking postmarks (or having U.S. postmarks) or lacking a witness and from voters who were not registered. Many military personnel whose home state was Florida must have decided to vote after the election when the outcome appeared uncertain, and some may have been persuaded to do so by partisan groups. Under law, these ballots shouldn't have been counted, but the Bush campaign, assuming the ballots were mostly Republican, claimed that it would be unpatriotic not to count them. The Gore campaign was put in the unenviable position of choosing either to accept the illegal Republican ballots or to appear to deny our overseas military personnel their right to vote.

After the election, Gore pursued a conservative strategy to deal with these problems that likely cost him the election. He did not call for a complete recount, and he did not challenge the likely fraudulent overseas ballots. Nothing could be done about the butterfly ballot problem save a revote.[176] Finally, when the Florida Supreme Court mandated a recount in every county, so much time had elapsed that the U.S. Supreme Court threw up its hands and gave the election to Bush.

Gore's biggest mistake was to refrain from challenging the overseas votes, even the hundreds that were patently illegal under Florida laws. As a consequence of the illegal military ballots alone, Gore lost Florida by 537 votes when his election day margin—that is, the margin given him by people who voted on election day rather than by mail ballot—was a 202-vote victory.[177]

The Bush postelection campaign was more skillful and more aggressive. Republican representatives urged election officials in Democratic-majority counties to follow the law in handling overseas ballots, so that illegal ballots would not be counted; in Republican counties, they urged election officials to disregard the law, so that illegal ballots would be counted.[178] (There is nothing illegal or even immoral about Republican supporters doing this; that is, they had the legal right to challenge ballots. But the election officials should not have given in and should have upheld the law, and the Democratic representatives should have argued that the laws be followed.) At one point the Bush campaign even organized a demonstration to intimidate election officials in Miami-Dade County to stop conducting the recount they were in the middle of. Demonstrators barged into the building, yelling and pounding on doors. Photos from that event showed that many of the "demonstrators" were staffers in conservative congressional Republican offices who had been sent to Florida to do this, though at the time the election officials recounting the ballot did not know that. The demonstration succeeded in getting the officials to halt the recount.

Thinking about Democracy

How democratic is it to attempt to intimidate election officials? Is that just a normal part of political activity, or does it go beyond what we would expect in a democracy?

In addition, the Bush campaign had strong political allies in Florida who held the levers of power. Bush's brother, the governor, and the secretary of state, who oversees the election system, were cochairs of Bush's Florida campaign. At every opportunity the secretary of state ruled in favor of the Bush campaign and forced the Gore campaign to go to court to obtain recounts and redress. Time also worked in favor of the Bush campaign, because it held a narrow lead throughout the post–election day period and because it knew that the deadline for certifying Florida's electors would put pressure on the courts to stop the recount. Thus the Bush campaign used delaying tactics to slow and stop the recounts.

The outcome of this election will long be argued. It is likely that a bare majority of Florida voters, in fact, favored Gore.[179] Systematic analyses have proven that the Buchanan vote was inflated by at least 2500 votes intended for Gore in Palm Beach County.[180] As one commentator noted, "No election analyst will say with a straight face that the butterfly design didn't cost Al Gore the presidency."[181]

Of course, the overseas ballots contributed, too, by an unknown amount. That is, we know how many ballots were illegal, but we don't know for sure their distribution between Bush and Gore. Nearly two-thirds of the 2400 overseas ballots counted after November 7 were for Bush. Presumably the illegal overseas ballots also broke for Bush. Two independent scholars argue that the probability is about 99 percent that Gore would have won if the invalid overseas ballots had been handled properly and a statewide recount had been allowed under any reasonable standard.[182]

The confusion surrounding the 2000 election outcome highlights an important aspect of our electoral process: state law and local policies determine the mechanics of presidential elections. The election brought into stark relief the problems that shoddy election procedures can create. Former president and Nobel Peace Prize winner Jimmy Carter, who, through his Carter Center, now works for peace and social justice around the world, is often invited to monitor elections in Asia and Africa and to attest to their fairness. He remarked, "I was really taken aback and embarrassed by what happened in Florida. If we were invited to go into a foreign country to monitor the election, and they had similar standards and procedures, we would refuse to participate at all."[183]

VOTING BEHAVIOR

Voting behavior is shaped by party identification, candidate evaluations, and positions on the issues.

Party Identification

Party identification is crucial in predicting how a person votes. Because we discussed this extensively in Chapter 7, we will not revisit it here. Keep in mind that overwhelming proportions of individuals with party identifications vote for candidates of their party. In the 2012 election, around 92 percent of members of each party did so.

Candidate Evaluations

Candidates' personalities and styles have had more impact since television has become voters' major source of information about elections. Bush's popularity in 2000 is an example of the influence of a candidate and his personality.

BEHIND THE SCENES

Are Independents Really Independent?

"The independent voter" is a popular topic in the press. Since most party loyalists vote for their party's candidate, the movement of the independents can, supposedly, swing the election. But how many independents are there?

Newspaper accounts often peg the number of independent voters as around 30 percent or even more. This is pretty much a fiction. Political scientists who study elections report that most independents actually support one party most of the time. Perhaps they like to think of themselves as independent or perhaps they say they're independent because they don't want to reveal their preferences to pollsters. If pressed, they will then say they are closer to one party or the other. In fact, only about 7 to 10 percent of the "independents" are really independent. Most vote like those who claim to be party supporters.

An examination of the vote of independents in the 2008 election illustrates what political scientists have found:[1]

Percentage Vote for Obama	
Strong Democrats	92
Weak Democrats	83
Independents "leaning Democratic"	88
Independent independents	50
Independents "leaning Republican"	17
Weak Republicans	10
Strong Republicans	2

In sum, there are few truly independent "independents." The rest tend to vote like party loyalists.

[1] Data for the 2008 election from Paul Abramson, John Aldrich, and David Rohde, *Change and Continuity in the 2008 Election* (Washington, D.C.: CQ Press, 2009), xx; "Three Myths about Political Independents," http://www.themonkeycage.org/2009/12/three_myths_about_political_in.html.

SOURCE: Mark Blumenthal, "How Independent Are the Independents?" *NationalJournal.com*, February 22, 2010, http://www.nationaljournal.com/njonline/mp_20100219_9614.php; John Sides, "Three Myths about Political Independents," *The Monkey Cage*, http://themonkeycage.org/blog/2009/12/17/three_myths_about_political_in/.

The perceived competence and integrity of candidates are other facets of candidate evaluation. Voters are less likely to support candidates who do not seem capable of handling the job, regardless of their issue positions. Jimmy Carter suffered in 1980 because of negative evaluations of his competence and leadership among voters.

Clinton's popularity puzzled some observers. Many voters did not like his evasions and his adulterous behavior, but they voted for him anyway. During the impeachment debates, many journalists expressed amazement that Clinton's popularity remained high. The public, more than journalists, seemed to be able to separate his public and private roles. They continued to support him because they felt he was doing a good job as president, not because they admired him personally.

In 2008, McCain often seemed out of touch with the average person, while Obama had a kind of star quality that drew people to him. However, neither candidate in 2012 had a personality that engaged voters much. Obama lost his star quality as the economy rebounded too slowly for most people, and he revealed a cool and detached persona. Romney struggled to connect with average people and sometimes tried too hard to do so.

Issues

Issues are a third factor influencing the vote. Although Americans are probably more likely to vote on issues now than they were in the 1950s, issues influence only some of the voters some of the time. In 2000 and 2004, though voters elected George Bush, they saw themselves as much closer to the Democratic candidates than to Bush.[184]

To cast an **issue vote**, voters obviously must have a position on an issue. In recent elections, more than 80 percent of the public had a position on issues such as government spending, military spending, and women's rights.[185] An issue vote also requires the candidates to differ with respect to their issue positions and for the voters to recognize this difference. A substantial minority of voters are able to detect some differences among the issue positions of presidential candidates.[186] Lastly, voters must cast their vote for the candidate who reflects their position on the issue or at least is the one closest to that position.

In every election since 1972, more than 70 percent of voters who met these conditions cast issue votes.[187] The highest proportion of issue voting was on those issues that typically divided Republicans and Democrats, such as government spending, military spending, and government aid to the unemployed and minorities. In 2008, issue voting on health care was also high, with most voters identifying different Obama and McCain positions. More than 70 percent who agreed with Obama on health insurance voted for him, compared to less than 30 percent whose position on universal health insurance was closer to that of McCain.[188] However, because many in the electorate were unable to define both their own and the candidates' positions on each issue, the proportion of the total electorate that can be said to cast an "issue vote" is usually less than 40 percent, and for some issues it is much less.[189]

Because abortion is a salient issue for many, it attracts issue-related votes. In 2008, for example, about 70 percent of the voters cast issue-related votes on abortion, similar to previous years. Of those voters (who had a position and also knew the candidates' position), 16 percent of those who opposed abortion under any conditions voted for Obama, a supporter of abortion rights, compared with 79 percent of those who believed that abortion should be a matter of personal choice.[190]

Issue voting may be mostly an evaluation of the current incumbents. If voters like the way incumbents or their party has handled the job in general or in certain areas—the economy or foreign policy, for example—they will vote accordingly, even without much knowledge about the specifics of the issues.

Voting on the basis of past performance is called **retrospective voting**. There is good evidence that many people do this, especially according to economic conditions.[191] Voters support incumbents if national income is growing in the months preceding the election. Since World War II, the incumbent party has won a presidential election only once when the growth rate was less than 3 percent (Eisenhower in 1956) and lost only twice when it was more than 3 percent (Ford in 1976 and Gore in 2000).[192] For example, in 2008, 89 percent of voters who strongly approved of Bush's handling of the economy voted for McCain, and only 11 percent voted for Obama. However, only 30 percent of the public approved of Bush's handling of the economy by 2008, and those who disapproved gave Obama 67 percent of their votes.[193]

Parties, Candidates, and Issues

All three factors—parties, candidates, and issues—clearly matter. Party loyalties are especially important because they help shape our views about issues and candidates. However, if issues and candidates did not matter, the Democrats would have won every presidential election between 1932 and 2000 because the plurality of voters were Democrats. Republican victories suggest that they often have had more attractive candidates (as in 1952, 1956, 1980, and 1984) or issue positions (in 1972 and, in some respects, in 1980). However, the Democrats' partisan advantage shrank throughout the 1980s. Although there are still more registered Democrats than Republicans, the margin is slight and the number of independents, though not high, is high enough to tilt the outcome.

Party loyalty, candidate evaluations, and issues are important factors in congressional elections just as in presidential ones. Chapter 9 discusses voting in congressional elections.

Voting Patterns in the 2012 Election

The 2012 election followed the traditional script. Obama won the votes of 92 percent of those identifying themselves as Democrats and lost 93 percent of those identifying themselves as Republicans. Independents broke 50-50.[194] Obama's winning coalition included majorities of several groups that

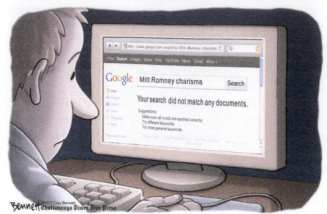

Although voters were dissatisfied with Obama's handling of the economy, they weren't excited by Romney's personality.

have been loyal to the Democratic party for decades: urbanites, Jews, Catholics, and blacks. The coalition expanded to include Latinos and Asian Americans, growing portions of the electorate who gave the Democrats more than 70 percent of their vote.

Women have also been an important part of the Democratic coalition in recent elections. About 55 percent of women voted for Obama, while men gave Romney about a 52 percent majority. Thus, the gender gap was significant, about 7 percent. It was heightened by well publicized statements of prominent Republican senatorial candidates whose extreme statements about rape and abortion disgusted and offended many. In trying to justify their views that abortion should be banned even in the cases of rape, the Missouri Senate candidate used the phrase "legitimate rape" to argue that women can't get pregnant from rape, and the Indiana candidate commented that when a woman is impregnated during a rape "it's something God intended."[195] These comments spotlighted the restrictive views of the Republican platform on the issue of abortion, views that were widely discussed during the Republican primary when at least one of the candidates also argued against contraception and Romney argued to remove funding from Planned Parenthood. The latter organization provides abortions at some locations, but at all locations provides to low and moderate income women contraceptive services and connections to providers of low-cost services for mammograms and other vital women's health tools.

Whites have not given a majority of votes to the Democratic candidate since Johnson in 1964. In this election, whites gave a solid majority to Romney, about 60 percent, slightly higher than in 2008. Obama received only 39 percent, about the same proportion as Clinton received in 1992 and generally on par with all recent Democratic candidates except Jimmy Carter, from Georgia, who received 47 percent in 1976. Still, the legacy of racism was evident in that, compared to the white Democrat John Kerry, Obama's vote total dipped the most in Alabama and Mississippi, the heart of the Confederacy and states that historically have been the most resistant to breaking down the barriers of segregation and inequality. Indeed, a study of racist tweets on days before and after the election (using the "N" word or "monkey" to describe the president in a tweet about the election) found the ratio of these tweets was highest in Mississippi and Alabama.[195a]

Latinos flocked to the polls in 2012 and gave a resounding majority to the Democrats. Support for Obama among Latinos rose as high as 89% in New York, and nationally 70 percent voted for Obama. Asian Americans are a smaller portion of the electorate, but also were strongly Democratic. These were presumably policy based votes. An anti-immigration position is the cornerstone of the Tea Party movement, and that stance became the party's official position. In the primaries, Romney swerved to the far right, trying to demonstrate his conservative credentials. Thus, he encouraged immigrants without papers to "self deport," and argued against the plan that Obama put in place to defer any moves to deport young people in college or the military even if they were not legal immigrants. Republicans also opposed the Dream Act, an initially bipartisan bill which was the model for Obama's executive action. The Dream Act would go further to allow immigrants to qualify for permanent residency and eventually citizenship if they have served honorably in the armed forces or received a college degree.

As they did in 2008, young people voted Democratic in astounding proportions, around 60 percent and a small majority of those from 30 to 44. Romney won a significant majority of those over 65 and a small majority of the 45-64 age group.

These age-related voting patterns suggest difficulty for Republicans in the years ahead if these patterns hold, because individuals usually retain their initial voting allegiances. For example, a majority of those who came of voting age during the New Deal remained Democrats throughout their lives, and a majority who first voted during the Reagan years held on to their Republican loyalties.[196] Republicans must also confront another demographic trend. Their support among whites is much stronger than among blacks, Latinos, and Asians, and yet the white portion of the electorate is shrinking, from about 86 percent in 1992 to an estimated 72 percent in 2012.[197] Also this proportion is projected to continue to decline by 1.5 to 2 percent each election cycle. States like Texas, and even Arizona, may come into play for the Democrats on the basis of these demographic changes.

As in past elections, Democrats won large majorities of the votes of the unmarried and of gays, lesbians, and bisexuals. With his support of gay marriage, and elimination of the "don't ask, don't tell" policy about sexual orientation in the military, Obama won the vote of more than three-quarters of those self-reporting as gay or lesbian. Republicans won large majorities of those currently married, white Protestants, and those who are born-again or evangelical Christians. Though the Catholic vote went overwhelmingly to Obama, white Catholics gave a small majority to Romney. Romney also won the majority of voters in small cities, whereas Obama won large majorities in big and mid-sized cities, and the two parties split the suburban vote evenly.

The geography of the election results is portrayed in Figure 8. Republicans continue to do well in the Great Plains, the Mountain West, and the South, though they again lost Colorado, Nevada, and New Mexico in the West and Virginia in the South. Indiana and North Carolina, which had given majorities to the Democrats in 2008, returned to the Republican fold in 2012. Democrats swept the Northeast and mid-Atlantic, the industrial Midwest, except for Indiana, and the west coast.

Issue voting was also evident. Generally, economic issues are highly salient to voters, especially in hard times. In this election, 90 percent who thought the economy was good or excellent voted for Obama. Romney took 60 percent of those who thought it was not so good or poor. It is surprising that the latter number is not larger, except that many voters were attuned to Obama's repeated reminder that the economy was in a free-fall when he took office and he had been successful in stabilizing it. Indeed, the economy shrank in 2008, the last year of Bush's administration and in the first nine months of 2009, Obama's first nine months in office. Helped by the stimulus, it began slow but steady growth in October, 2009 and continued throughout the rest of the term. The Dow Jones average (one measure of the stock market) was only 7900 in January 2009, after a long fall, but grew during the next four years to around 13,000, not matching its pre-recession high, but exhibiting significant growth. So, while Romney had a strong case when he claimed that most Americans were not better off in 2012 than in 2009, Obama's case was also strong that he avoided financial catastrophe and set the economy on a better course.

The Republican vote was strongest in the oldest, whitest, and slowest-growing part of the population. The increasing diversity of Americans now poses a challenge, even in Republican strongholds of the South and Plains. The party must find a way to win Hispanic and Asian American votes. The day after the election, Republican leaders were vocal about that challenge, and looking for ways to modify their immigration positions while still retaining their base. This is not to say that the Republicans are doomed to become a minority party. With new issues, changing voter concerns, and party adaptation, they will most likely revitalize.

THE PERMANENT CAMPAIGN

The **permanent campaign** is a term coined by political scientists to describe the current state of American electoral politics.[198] During each election cycle, the time between the completion of one election and the beginning of the next gets shorter and shorter. No longer does the election campaign start in the election year; now it is nearly a four-year process, as candidates hire consultants and fundraisers, assemble field operations, and commission polls.

Several factors are responsible for this change, some political and some technological. The political process has changed a great deal during the past thirty years. Primaries have become the chief means by which candidates get nominated, and parties have shrunk in importance in the nominating process. The necessity to win primaries in different regions of the nation means that potential candidates must start early to become known to key political figures, and ultimately to the voting public, in these states. In the "old days," candidates had to woo only party leaders, a process that, though not easy, was much less public and much less expensive than campaigning for primary victories.

Technology has also contributed to the permanent campaign. Certainly, in comparison to the turn of the twentieth century, transportation and communications technologies have revolutionized campaigns. Then travel was by rail, ship, or horse, and candidates could not dart about the country spending the morning in New York City and the afternoon in Seattle. Telephone communication was primitive, and there were no radios or televisions. The idea of potential candidates spending four years publicly campaigning for office under these conditions would have been ludicrous.

But even in comparison with only thirty years ago, the media and information technologies have revolutionized campaigning and thus have contributed to the permanent campaign. Modern computer and telephone technology enables the media and private organizations to take the pulse of the public through opinion polls almost continually. As polls have become more common, they have become a source of fascination to the media (and as pollsters have discovered that the media's appetite for polls is nearly insatiable, polls have proliferated). Whereas in the 1950s polls were rarely done and poll results were rarely discussed in media coverage of elections, by the 1980s hundreds of stories about each election campaign focused on poll results. Indeed, much of the media coverage of the campaign focuses on exactly that. In 2012, there was daily polling from the beginning of the primaries. During the general election, there were often twenty to thirty national polls daily, easily accessible at websites such as RealClearPolitics, fivethirtyeight.com, and many other sites. Candidates, donors, and campaign operatives pay considerable attention to these polls, so candidates must begin campaigning early to earn name recognition from the public. A new breed of poll analysts sprang up (fivethirtyeight.com; http://election.princeton.edu/, http://votamatic.org/) aggregating and analyzing these polls on a daily basis. (Figure 9 is drawn from fivethirtyeight.com). All the "aggregators" predicted the Obama win with great accuracy (in fact, most called all the states correctly as well as most Senate races). Republican pundits challenged these findings beforehand as being biased toward the Democrats and one even set up his own site "unskewedpolls.com" which used a different model to give Republicans more weight. Presumably, Romney and his campaign believed the Republican pundits and poll-deniers and were shocked that he lost (unlike Obama, he had not written an alternative concession speech for election night).

And, more generally, the fact that campaigns have become media events means that candidates must begin early to establish themselves as worthy of media attention. Until candidates have organizations, fundraisers, and pollsters, the media do not take them seriously. Nor would it be very rational to do otherwise, because a modern campaign cannot succeed without these things. The same is true of the blogosphere. Political bloggers begin to track candidates, their activities, and their poll results from the beginning of their campaign. To develop momentum, to be discussed, a candidate must be doing or saying something.

All of these factors—the decline of the party organizations and the increased importance of primaries, the growth of polling, the ubiquity of Internet news and commentary, and the overwhelming role the media now play in campaigns—have contributed to the perpetual motion that modern elections have become. These trends seem irreversible. Only eliminating the primary system would seem to make much difference, and that change is nearly impossible.

Elections, Mandates, and the Role of Government

Do elections contribute to the growth of government and to what government does? Unequivacally yes! Government grows primarily because the electorate wants it to do more. Candidates promise to do things, usually to provide more and better services or to stimulate the economy. It is a brave and rare candidate who promises to cut a popular program (candidates often talk about cutting the deficit or slashing waste—but that's easy talk). Even in 2012, when the public was concerned about the deficit, they were far more concerned about jobs and what government could do to help create them.

Even though elections are the mechanism by which the public decides what it wants from government, in fact, it is hard to interpret what voters want. In the popular press, we hear a lot about "mandates." A president with a **mandate** is one who is clearly directed by the voters to take some particular course of action—such as reduce taxes or begin arms control talks. Barack Obama won by a comfortable majority in 2012. Did he have a mandate? If so, what for? The largest proportion of the public was concerned about the economy and jobs issues.[199] Large majorities of those who felt the economy was in bad shape voted for Romney, but Obama too campaigned on the basis of increasing jobs.[200] He also campaigned on raising taxes on those with incomes over $250,000. Two days after the election, he said he was ready to sign legislation holding taxes constant on those making less than $250,000 but not those making more. Clearly, he believes he has a mandate on this issue; but Republicans in the House might not see it that way since the public also gave Republicans the majority of seats in that body.

In 2008, Obama campaigned partly on a pledge to reform health care and provide health insurance for everyone. Once elected, he worked successfully to do this and Congress passed the Affordable Care Act (popularly known as Obamacare) with little Republican support. After the 2010 election, House Republicans tried to get rid of this legislation and Mitt Romney campaigned with a pledge to end Obamacare, though that would be hard for a president to do. Still he could have delayed implementation and impeded enforcement. Clearly, Obama's election was a signal that the

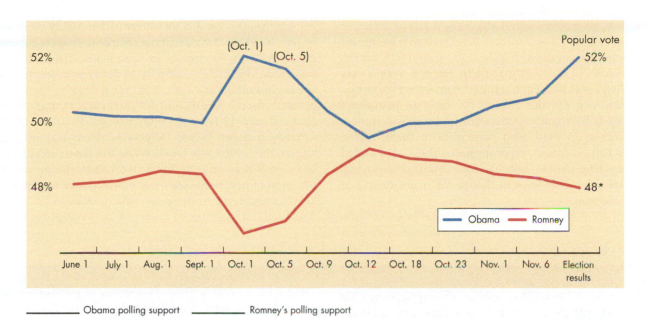

Obama polling support _____   Romney's polling support

*Final popular vote counts are not available as of this writing. It appears that Obama will win between 52 and 53 percent of the two party vote and Romney between 47 and 48.

FIGURE 9: PUBLIC OPINION CHANGED LITTLE DURING CAMPAIGN Despite the events of the campaign, Obama and Romney's poll numbers were very constant through the election with two exceptions. Obama received a positive bump in his numbers after the Democratic convention held September 4 to 6 with a small increase in his numbers peaking around October 1 and then declining after the first debate, October 3. With excellent first debate performance, Romney received a positive bump until around October 12, the day after the vice presidential debate. Then Obama's numbers crept up slowly through the rest of the campaign. The polls never registered "momentum" for Romney after about October 12. But note that these changes were tiny, even when the polls seemed to move.
SOURCE OF POLLING DATA: Nate Silver Fivethirtyeight.com, Nate Silver's Political Calculus; Now cast; popular vote. The polling data are a combination of all national polls taken that day, weighted by past poll accuracy.

majority of people do not want to eliminate Obamacare, though the legislation remains controversial.

Because voters' issue positions influence their party loyalties and their candidate evaluations, it is primarily political parties that translate the mix of various issues into government action. Over time, a rough agreement usually develops between public attitudes and policies.[201] Same-sex marriage is a contemporary example. Opposition to same-sex marriage varies widely by state. Constitutional amendments denying the right to same-sex marriage have passed mostly in states where support for same-sex marriage is weakest, and almost all states where support is highest now legally recognize same-sex couples.[202] A vote for the candidate of one's own party is usually a reflection of agreement on at least some important issues. Once in office, the party in government helps sort out the issues for which there is a broad public mandate from those for which there is not.

In close elections, few would argue that there is a mandate. In 2000, voters favored the Democratic policy positions and did so in a time of peace and prosperity. A plurality gave their votes to Gore. Yet Bush became president and acted as though his narrow Electoral College victory was a mandate in support of his foreign policies and conservative domestic policies.

On the other hand, elections that appear to be clear mandates can become "mandates for disaster." More than one observer has pointed out that every twentieth-century president who won the election by 60 percent or more of the popular vote soon encountered serious political trouble. After his landslide in 1920, Warren Harding had his Teapot Dome scandal involving government corruption. Emboldened by his 1936 triumph, Franklin D. Roosevelt tried to pack the Supreme Court and was rebuffed on that issue. Lyndon Johnson won by a landslide in 1964 and was soon mired in Vietnam. Richard Nixon smashed George McGovern in 1972 but then had to resign because of Watergate. Ronald Reagan's resounding victory in 1984 (a shade less than 60 percent) was followed by the blunders of the Iran-contra affair. Of these presidents, only Roosevelt was able to recover fully from his political misfortune. Reagan regained his personal popularity but seemed to have little influence on policy after Iran-contra. One recent observer has argued that these disasters come because "the euphoria induced by overwhelming support at the polls evidently loosens the president's grip on reality."[203]

Elections can point out new directions for government and allow citizens to make it responsive to their needs, but the fact that many individuals do not vote means that the new directions may not reflect either the needs or wishes of the public. Those of lower income vote less and government is less responsive to them.[204] If election turnout falls too far, the legitimacy of elections may be threatened. People may come to believe that election results do not reflect the wishes of the majority. For this reason, the increase in turnout since 2004 is heartening. If elections promote government responsiveness to those who participate in them, higher turnouts help increase responsiveness. Those dissatisfied Americans who want to "take back our country" are saying, presumably, that they want to change the majority vote in the next election.

On the other hand, if we believe in democracy, we should be concerned about the declining competitiveness of congressional elections. Essentially, in most states, state legislative majorities have had the capacity to determine election outcomes, including their own seats, for a decade. The impact of this is that the bare majority of votes cast in Congressional elections in 2012 favored Democrats, yet Republicans won a handy majority (when Democrats dominated the state houses, the reverse was true). While the power to redistrict has always been in state legislative hands, the power and precision of new technology makes this power even greater. This is a significant challenge to responsiveness.

SUMMARY

- When our country was founded, suffrage was limited almost entirely to white males—in many cases, white male property owners and sometimes only if they were of the right religion. Within fifty years after the Founding, most property and religious qualifications were dropped. Through the Fifteenth Amendment, black people were granted the right to vote after the Civil War, but in the South quasi-legal laws, violence, and economic sanctions severely limited that right. Women gained the right to vote through a constitutional amendment in 1920. Since then, African Americans have been fully enfranchised and the right to vote has been extended to almost all, including eighteen-year-olds. However, conservative majorities in several state legislatures have legislated to curtail voting rights through requirements of ID cards and in other ways. In several (mostly southern) states, felons are also barred from voting for life.

- Several factors deter people from voting, including feeling that their vote does not count and apathy, multiplicity of elections and possibly negative campaigning, lack of rootedness in a community, failures of political parties to mobilize voters, decline in labor unions, and barriers erected by states to minimize voting.

- The process of nominating a party's candidate is a complex one, involving candidate self-identification, caucuses, primaries, and then the party convention held in late summer. Fundraising is a key part of a successful campaign, but sound strategy, effective use of the media, and a compelling message are also important. The erasure of restrictions on donating to and spending on Super PACs changed some of the dynamics of the 2012 race, as donors scrambled to find wealthy backers who could finance significant parts of their campaigns. Early departures of some Republican primary candidates illustrate the effects of failures to define campaign strategies or to have a clear message.

- Once the nomination is won, candidates must focus their time and resources strategically. Because of the structure of the Electoral College, of prime importance is allocation of resources among states, focusing on those states that are likely to have close but winnable elections. The use of media, free media, paid advertising, and debate strategies is key to getting a candidate's message out. In recent years, negative campaigning has grown, but political scientists do not agree on whether negative campaigning has a special influence on voting choice or turnout.

- Donations to, and spending by, candidates and campaign organizations are regulated by federal election law. However, overall donations and spending are unlimited because regulations targeting what are known as Super PACs have been thrown out. People, corporations, or unions can give as much as they want to Super PACs, which can spend as much as they want. Most Super PAC money comes from billionaire donors rather than corporations or unions. Super PACs are supposed to be independent of campaigns, but in fact, they are usually run by friends or operatives of the candidates. In 2012, Super PAC support extended the campaigns of some candidates who were not winning many votes, and advantages in Super PAC funding helped Romney stamp out his opponents.

- The Electoral College is a system designed by the Founders to remove people from direct control of the presidency. Each state receives the same number of electoral votes as it has senators and representatives, thereby overrepresenting smaller states. As it currently works, each state allocates its electoral votes in accord with the popular vote in its state. This system means that candidates focus on winning states, and thus devote most of their personal time and campaign advertising to a relatively few states that are likely to be close races.

Many large states receive little attention because they are likely to be strongly for one party or the other. The Electoral College is another undemocratic feature of the American system. It tends to benefit smaller, more rural states at the expense of states with large urban populations.

- Political party identification is the single most important predictor of voting for president. Around 90 percent of Republicans vote for the Republican candidate, and the same proportion of Democrats vote for their candidate. Issues and candidates' personalities do matter at the margin. Economic issues can be very important when the economy is doing poorly. In 2008, issues favored Obama because of the downturn in the economy late in 2008 and the public's loss of trust in Bush's ability to handle the job. Though unemployment remained high in 2012, the slow economic growth and slow decline in unemployment, combined with a superior campaign organization, were enough to allow Barack Obama to be reelected.

- The decline of the party organizations and the increased importance of primaries, the growth of polling, the ubiquity of Internet news and commentary, and the overwhelming role the media now play in campaigns have created a permanent campaign. Primaries create the need for candidates to assemble an organization four years before the next election and then begin visiting people and party leaders around the country. The 24-hour news cycle, the need to raise funds for a national campaign, and continual polling all mean that we have a nearly permanent campaign.

- A mandate election is one in which voters clearly send a signal about what they want. Very few elections are mandates, even landslide elections. Some of the landslide elections of the twentieth century led presidents to exceed what voters expected and led to poor endings of the presidencies. Those have been called mandates for disaster.

DISCUSSION QUESTIONS

1. Describe the voting population when the Constitution was ratified, and outline how suffrage has been extended in different eras. What new threats to voting rights have emerged, and how might these be a response to the changing American electorate?

2. List and explain five reasons why millions of people do not vote. In what ways do states encourage and prohibit voting?

3. What are the major stages in primary elections? How do caucuses, primaries, and conventions differ? What role does money play in primary elections? How does the Electoral College influence how candidates decide to allocate their time among states? Describe the contributions of free media, paid advertising, and debates to the campaigns.

4. If you were the Republican nominee for president, how would you allocate your time and resources among New York, Texas, Pennsylvania, Nebraska, and Florida? Would you buy ads that featured positive messages or negative ones? Why?

5. Describe the major elements of federal campaign finance regulations. What advantages do Super PACs have in getting their messages out?

6. What is the Electoral College? Why do we have it, and how does it work? Who benefits and who loses from the Electoral College compared to a system of electing the president by popular vote?

7. Discuss the role of party identification in presidential voting. Include a discussion of the voting behavior of independent voters. What other factors shape voters' decisions? Illustrate by analyzing the 2012 general elections.

8. What is a permanent campaign, and why do we have it?

9. Do most elections provide a mandate to presidential victors? Illustrate your answer by giving examples of those that do and do not. Were presidents able to carry out the mandates when they had them?

9 Congress

Public opinion about Congress today is very negative.

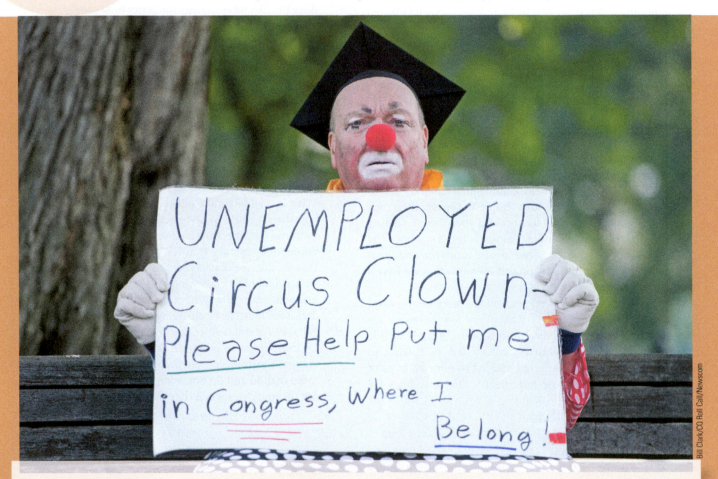

UNEMPLOYED Circus Clown- Please Help Put me in Congress, where I Belong!

Bill Clark/CQ Roll Call/Newscom

LEARNING OBJECTIVES

1. Define the terms "acting for" and "standing for" representation, provide an example of each, and explain how representative Congress is according to each of these concepts.

2. Explain the process of reapportionment of the House of Representatives, how often it is performed, and its consequences.

3. Describe the advantages of incumbency for members of Congress who run for reelection.

4. Identify, contrast, and compare the leadership positions in the modern House and the Senate.

5. Committees are the place where the details of legislation are often hammered out. Distinguish the types of committees and identify the role played by each.

6. Explain how a bill becomes a law, and distinguish policy bills from budget bills.

7. Identify the informal norms of Congress, and explain what role they play in facilitating congressional work. Discuss which norms have atrophied and which still exist.

8. Summarize public opinion toward Congress, and explain the difference between views of the institution and views of one's own member of Congress.

TALKING POINTS

Many members of Congress, expert observers, and the public consider the modern Congress and its rules to be inadequate to the complex national and global challenges that face us today. As a result, public evaluation of Congress is at a low ebb, sometimes with only about 9 to 10 percent of Americans approving of the work it has been doing.

Thus, it's hard to read or hear about Congress without someone mentioning the need to reform it. One possible reform has received scant public debate: increasing the size of the U.S. House of Representatives. With 435 members of the House and 100 members of the Senate, conventional wisdom says that it is impossible for an institution with that many people to deal expeditiously with the complex world in which we find ourselves. But, looked at another way, the path to public approval and effectively addressing our national problems may lie not in reducing the size of Congress, as has been widely advocated over the years, but in increasing its size dramatically, at least in the House of Representatives, the branch intended by our Founders to be closest to the people.

The argument for an increase in size is that there are no longer strong ties between representatives and the represented. Since the first Congress, the House has grown from 59 members to today's 435. And because the size of the House has been fixed since 1929, as the population increases, the number of people in each congressional district rises as well. Compared to the earliest Congress, where each member represented only about 33,000 people, today an average district has over 700,000 people. With so many people and so many varied interests competing for the support of representatives, some observers believe that special interests have it easier than ever before to gain influence and dominate policy choices because the House, in particular, is much more distant from the people than ever before. And the center of opinion is not what is being represented in Congress; rather, it is the interests of those at one extreme or the other of issues, those who lobby and donate the most money, that gain the most attention.

Some say that the solution is to use the representation ratio planned by the Founders of one member for every 50,000 people. That would make today's House an institution of just above 6000 members. Or, doubling that, one member for every 100,000 people would create a more manageable 3000 members.

Of course, such a large institution would create challenges. Moreover, when representatives are only representing 50,000 or so people, it is possible that individual representatives would be even more extreme than now because districts would be less diverse. But large assemblies are not unheard of around the world, and with a larger House, we would have a wider range of people to represent us and a closer relationship between members and the people. This radical notion of expanding representation may be one worth debating.[1]

In creating our system of government, the Founders intended Congress to be the dominant branch. The description of Congress and its powers in Article I of the Constitution 🏛 comprises almost half the document. James Madison could not have stated it more clearly than he did in *Federalist Paper* 51: "In republican government, the legislative authority necessarily predominates." He believed this because Congress alone had "access to the pockets of the people." In this new system of government, the lower chamber, the House of Representatives, was conceived as the one closer to the people, with smaller constituencies, frequent elections (every two years), and the power to originate revenue (tax) legislation. But the framers were also concerned about balancing deliberation with popular, and possibly erratic, political enthusiasm. Therefore, the upper chamber, the Senate, was smaller, faced less frequent elections (every six years), and was granted the power to ratify treaties and approve executive appointments. Originally, senators were not even elected by the people but rather by state legislatures. In 1918, however, the Seventeenth Amendment mandated that popular elections replace the original procedure.

In this chapter, we explore how representative Congress is, how the legislative branch does its work, and how the public understands and evaluates the institution.

CONGRESS AS A REPRESENTATIVE BODY

Is Congress a representative body? That depends on what we mean by *representation*. During the Revolutionary War, John Adams said that the legislature "should be an exact portrait, in miniature, of the people at large, as it should think, feel, reason, and act like them."[2] Benjamin Franklin said simply that Congress should be a mirror of the people. But neither clarified whether it is was more important for Congress to reflect a demographic cross section of the public or to reflect constituents' issue preferences. They also did not elaborate on whether members of Congress should sometimes or always vote as the people wish or use their own judgment to make decisions in the national interest, even if not supported by a majority of their constituents.

Types of Representation

We consider two features of representation. Do representatives reflect population demographics? And do they make policy choices that are consistent with the scope and depth of public sentiment?

"Standing For" Representation

A Congress that reflects the demographic mix of the country can be referred to as having "standing for" representation. This kind of representation is rooted not in what legislators *do* but in their personal characteristics—what they *are*, or *are like*.[3] Congress does not represent the demographic diversity of America, though in the last several decades it has been more representative than it was when almost all legislators were white, male, and Protestant. Today, females, Latino, African American, Asian, American Indian, and lesbian and gay legislators are more common, as are citizens from different economic classes, professions, ages, and religions. But Congress is still quite unrepresentative in terms of demographic characteristics. For example, few members are working class or poor, and only a minority is female (see the box "Congress Is Not a Cross Section of America"). And the people living in America's large urban and suburban areas are woefully underrepresented in the Senate.

"Acting for" Representation

If Congress still has a way to go to *look* like the American public, a related question is whether its members have the same beliefs as their constituents and act in a way reflecting their constituents' beliefs.

One important type of "acting for" representation is when members provide economic and other benefits to their district, such as a new federal government building, contracts, or services. In making these provisions, members must consider what will benefit their districts and the subgroups within each district, such as party voters, socioeconomic groups, and personal supporters.[4] In general, if districts are filled with farmers, the members must represent farmers; if the district economy depends on defense contractors, members must advocate for projects to keep or bring jobs to their district.

Another type of "acting for" representation is when members cast votes on policy issues. On the whole, members' issue positions are usually not far from those of their party or the majority of the constituency who votes. In any case, members are more likely to reflect the issue position of constituents when the issue is important to the public and when opinions are strongly held. On many issues, though, constituents are less informed, divided, or undecided, in which case members can vote their personal issue preferences, or with their party, or with those constituents or donors who most vigorously make their positions known. Social media technology has made it much easier for constituents to actively communicate with their legislators. E-mails, tweets, texts, and Facebook messages flow in to Congress along with phone calls and letters. And of course, lobbyists make their positions known continuously, and most of the time without public attention.

"Acting for" representation can also concern segments of the population that are underrepresented in Congress. Women, African Americans, Hispanics, Asian Americans, and American Indians, among others, are seen as having *national* constituencies with distinct issue priorities in addition to their geographic constituencies. For example, Rep. Gwen Moore (D-Wisc.) spoke for women across America when she took the House floor to defend the anti–domestic violence legislation in 2012, saying that such violence "is epidemic and it is only with the passage of the Violence against Women Act in 1994 that we have been able to put a dent in violence against women, and women have had a place to go."[5]

Research also suggests that congressional members from underrepresented groups serve their constituents differently than their counterparts. For example, women in Congress are more likely than men to introduce and vote for women's issues such as those involving sexual harassment, sex equity in education, and family leave. Thus, there is a relationship between "standing for" and "acting for" representation, and, as Congress begins to look more like a cross section of the population, legislation may become more representative of the wishes of the broadest segment of the electorate.

MEMBERS AND CONSTITUENCIES

In this section we describe who can run for Congress, the terms of service, and the compensation and perks of the jobs. We also explain what is meant by "constituency," the areas and people that members of Congress represent.

Members

Alexis de Tocqueville, a nineteenth-century French political theorist who traveled throughout the United States to understand its politics and culture, came away unimpressed with the status of members of Congress and commented that they were "almost all obscure individuals, village lawyers, men in trades, or even persons belonging to the lower class." Tocqueville's view was shared by another European visitor, Charles Dickens, who, in 1842, was shocked to find Congress full of tobacco spitters who committed "cowardly attacks upon opponents" and seemed to be guilty of "aiding and abetting every bad inclination in the popular mind."[6]

Observers of Congress are still prone to negativism about the institution. But many of the opportunities and constraints of congressional service have changed since the nineteenth century.

Who Can Serve?

The Constitution places few formal restrictions on membership in Congress. One must be twenty-five years old to serve in the House and thirty in the Senate, and one must have been a citizen for at least seven years to be elected to the House and nine years to be elected to the Senate. Members must reside in the states from which they were elected, but House members need not reside in their own districts. As a practical matter, however, it is highly unlikely that voters will elect a person to represent their district who is not from the district. **Art. I, Sec. 2**

Local identity is not as significant a factor in Senate races as it is in House races; national figures such as Robert Kennedy and Hillary Rodham Clinton, who established in-state residency within weeks or months of the election, both ran successful campaigns in New York. However, it is a rare occurrence.

Length of Service

Members of the House serve two-year terms and senators serve six-year terms, with one-third of the membership standing for election every two years. Although the Articles of Confederation set a limit on the number of terms a representative could serve, the Constitution placed no caps on service. Perhaps the Founders thought that no one would want to serve more than a few terms. In the late eighteenth and early nineteenth centuries, leaving one's home to serve in Congress was considered a great sacrifice. Washington was a muddy swamp, with debris-filled streets and farm animals running loose, and in the pre-railroad, pre-airline age, transportation was so poor that almost no one got home during a session. In fact, during Congress's first forty years, 41 percent of House members, on average, dropped out every two years, and in the early 1900s, the median length of service for a representative was still only five years.[7]

But, as Washington became a power center and a much more livable and accessible city, members became receptive to longer periods of service. Today, the average representative has served ten years. Serving thirty or forty years is no longer unusual, and a few serve even longer. Sen. Daniel

In its early years, Washington, D.C., was described as "a miserable little swamp." When this photo was taken in 1892, it still retained the look and feel of a small rural town.

American Diversity

Congress Is Not a Cross Section of America

Congress is not now, and never has been, a cross section of the American population. Despite the progress made since the earliest Congresses, the citizens who serve are still disproportionately white and male. Women, who make up 51 percent of the nation's population, are a particularly underrepresented demographic group, at just 17 percent of the 112th Congress (see Table 1). As a result of the 2012 election cycle, the percentage of women will rise to 18 percent in the 113th Congress.

Table 1   Demographics of the 112th Congress (2011–2012)

DEMOGRAPHIC GROUP	CONGRESS (NUMBERS PER CATEGORY OUT OF 535)	PERCENT
Women	93	17%
Men	445	83
African American	43	8
Hispanic	27	5
Asian Pacific	9	2
American Indian	1	0.1
White	458	86
Married	455	85
Divorced	37	7
Protestant	312	58
Catholic	160	30
Jewish	36	7
Mormon	15	3
Buddhist	3	1
Muslim	2	0.4
Former governors	10	2
Lawyers	207	39
Farmers or ranchers	6	1
College graduates	507	95
Veterans	113	21
Millionaires	196	37
Average age	57	

SOURCES: R. Eric Petersen, "Representatives and Senators: Trends in Member Characteristics since 1945," Congressional Research Service, 7-5700, Report R42365, February 17, 2012; "Congressional Demographics," http://congress.org/congressorg/directory/demographics.tt?catid=all (accessed April 20, 2012); "Congress Profile: The Backgrounds and Groups among Members of Congress," http://www.thecapitol.net/FAQ/Congress_Profile .html#5_16 (accessed April 20, 2012).

Hispanics, Asians, African Americans, and American Indians are also below parity with their numbers in the population, although thirty-seven of the forty-one congressional districts whose populations are one-third or more African American have elected an African American to represent them.[1]

Congress is also unrepresentative of the range of religious views among the general public. Seventeen percent of the population claims "other" or no religious affiliation, but just 1 percent of congressional members claim no affiliation, and only approximately 2 percent adhere to religions other than Christianity and Judaism.[2] However, two Buddhists, Mazie Hirono (D-Hawaii) and Hank Johnson (D-Ga.), and the first Muslim (Keith Ellison (D-Minn.) were elected to the House in 2006. A second Muslim member was elected in 2008 (André Carson (D-Ind.). As result of the 2012 election cycle, the first Hindu was elected to Congress, Tulsi Gabbard (D-Hi).

Members are much better off financially than the average householder; 172 of 535 members of the 111th Congress were millionaires, and a number were multimillionaires.[3] The median net worth of a member of Congress in 2011 was $913,000, more than 35 times that of an average American.[4] Thus, few members of Congress face the financial struggles of working-class and middle-class Americans.

Representatives Linda Sanchez (*left*) and Loretta Sanchez, both Democrats from southern California, are the first sisters in Congress. Linda was also the first unmarried pregnant member of Congress.

Members also tend to rank well above average in education; nearly all have college degrees, and more than four hundred have graduate or professional degrees. Although blue-collar workers constitute nearly one-quarter of the working population, only seventeen members of Congress claim blue-collar backgrounds. In the 112th Congress, one member of the House even graduated from college while in office. Rep. Kristi Noem (R-S.D.), who had to drop out of college when her father died, went back to school while she was in the state legislature and was awarded a degree in political science from South Dakota State University in 2012.

The most common occupational background of members has been the law. But this pattern is changing, especially in the House. Although almost 60 percent of senators name law as their primary occupation, there are now more House members with backgrounds in public service and business than in law.

Increasingly, Congress is drawing its members from professional politicians; in 2009, over half of all House members and 40 percent of senators had served in their state legislatures. Others have been mayors, judges, governors, cabinet officials, ambassadors, law enforcement officials, and congressional or White House staffers. Another dent in the citizen-legislator ideal has been the presence of "dynasty" families (the Adamses, Harrisons, Kennedys, and Bushes).

Members of the Senate are even less a cross section of the American population than the House, but the Senate was designed to represent the interests of the states, not the people. Representation in the Senate is based on a one-state, two-vote standard, not one person, one vote. As such, it is far from a democratic institution in terms of representing major population groups. It vastly overrepresents the interests of low-population states, and the people in them, particularly rural, ranching, and agricultural interests, and significantly underrepresents the interests of those who live in metropolitan areas, both urbanites and suburbanites, and those who are minorities.

[1] Unless otherwise indicated, data on members of the 110th Congress are taken from Mildred Amer, "Membership of the 111th Congress: A Profile," Congressional Research Service, Report R40086, December 31, 2008, 1–6.

[2] Estimates of how many Americans have no religious affiliation are from a Pew Research Center survey published June 24, 2008, pewresearch.org. Congressional affiliations are from Amer, "Membership of the 111th Congress," 5.

[3] These are estimates drawn from members' financial disclosure statements; a complete list is posted at opensecrets.org. Members must file statements in May of every year but need only report income and assets within a broad dollar range; so, for example, the net worth of one of the wealthiest members of the House can only be estimated at somewhere between $112 and $377 million.

[4] "The Growing Wealth Gap between Congress and Constituents: By the Numbers," *The Week*, December 27, 2011, http://theweek.com/article/index/222880/the-growing-wealth-gap-between-congress-and-constituents-by-the-numbers.

Inouye (D-Hawaii) has served since 1963, and Rep. John Dingell (D-Mich.) has served since 1955. Lengthy service has an important impact on politics because senior members of Congress amass power inside the institution and can affect public policy in important ways.

Term Limits

During a period of heightened public anger with government in the 1990s, a nationwide movement arose to limit the number of terms that state and national legislators could serve, and most Americans favored such limitations.[8] Some supporters of term limits believed that not having to worry about getting reelected would free legislators to consider the "public interest." Others saw term limits as a way to weaken the power of government by having frequent turnover of members.

Although Congress narrowly defeated term-limit legislation, several states enacted laws to limit state legislative and congressional terms of office. However, in 1995, the U.S. Supreme Court held that term limits for members of Congress were unconstitutional, ruling that permitting individual states to have diverse qualifications for Congress would "result in a patchwork of state qualifications, undermining the uniformity and national character that the framers envisioned and sought to ensure."[9] The holding also affirmed that the Constitution can be amended only through the processes of adoption and ratification it specifies, not by state or congressional laws or ballot initiatives.

By the late 1990s, public enthusiasm for term limits in the state legislatures had also waned; courts eventually overturned them in four states and, in two others, the state legislatures repealed them.[10] By 2010, only fifteen states still had legislative term limits, although the governors of almost all states, like the U.S. president, are term-limited.[11]

Constituencies

The district a member of Congress represents is called a **constituency**. The term is used to refer to both the area within the electoral boundaries and its residents. There are two senators from each state, so each senator's constituency is the entire state and all its residents. Most states have multiple House districts, although seven states (Alaska, Delaware, Montana, North Dakota, South Dakota, Vermont, and Wyoming) have populations so small that they are each allotted a single seat in the House of Representatives. Except for those states, in accordance with the one-person, one-vote rule, every House district must have roughly the same number of residents, so the number of districts in each state depends on its population.

Reapportionment

Initially, the House of Representatives had 59 members, but as more states joined the Union, the size of the House increased. Since 1911, it has had 435 voting members. Every ten years, in a process called **reapportionment**, the 435 House seats are allocated among the states based on the latest U.S. census.

Art. I, Sec. 2

Within a now constant 435-seat House, states with the fast-growing populations gain seats, whereas those with slow-growing or declining populations lose seats. Since World War II, population movement in the United States has been toward the South, West, and Southwest and away from the Midwest and Northeast. For example, after the 2010 census, Illinois, Massachusetts, Michigan, New Jersey, New York, and Pennsylvania lost seats, and Arizona, Florida, Georgia, South Carolina, Texas, Utah, and Washington gained them. Thus political power has shifted away from traditional centers of geographical power and political culture to newer ones.

Redistricting

States that gain or lose seats and states with internal population shifts (rural to urban or urban to suburban) must redraw their district boundaries every ten years in a process called **redistricting**. This is always a hot political issue because the precise boundaries of a district determine the election prospects of candidates and parties. In most states, the state legislature controls the redistricting process, so districts are normally drawn to benefit the party in control or to protect incumbents, making races less competitive than they might be otherwise. A district whose boundaries are devised to maximize the political advantage of a party or a racial or ethnic group is known as a **gerrymander** (as explained in Chapter 8). This boundary manipulation can result in bizarrely shaped districts because district lines are drawn to secure partisan advantage, not to maximize contiguity or voter interests (for example, a community may be divided into many different districts even if its size suggests it could make one contiguous district). With modern geographical information systems, voting patterns down to the block level are available, and legislators can draw district lines to maximize the number of districts the majority party controls.

After the 2010 census and that year's midterm elections, Republicans won control of legislatures in 25 states and had control of one chamber in an additional 8 states. Democrats had control of only 16 state legislatures. Thus, in the subsequent redistricting process, Republicans made as many seats safe for their candidates as possible. That means that they had the redistricting advantage in the 2012 electoral cycle, and ever more districts are no longer competitive.

Over time, redistricting has become such a political battleground that there is growing support in a number of states to take responsibility away from the legislatures and put it in the hands of bipartisan commissions, which are thought to have fewer partisan incentives. This is what happened in California when voters approved a law mandating that a commission draw the boundaries for all congressional and state legislative districts. The desired outcome is that voters in more districts will have a choice between candidates, each of whom will have a decent chance of winning, rather than having the district outcome largely predetermined.

Tenure

As members of Congress have become more career-focused and as congressional seats have generally become safer, congressional tenures have become longer.[12] In the modern era, a seat in Congress has become a career for many; the average tenure of a representative is about ten years, and the average tenure of a senator is about thirteen years. In contrast, in the post–World War II years, the average tenure for representatives was about seven years and the average tenure for senators was about eight years.[13]

Thinking about Democracy

If gerrymandering is used to make the majority of House seats safe for one party or another, what is the potential for increasing voter apathy and decreasing voter turnout, and how does that affect democracy?

ELECTING MEMBERS OF CONGRESS

Elections determine who represents the rest of us. Because reelection is an important objective for most members of Congress and *the* most important objective for many, they work at being reelected throughout their terms.[14]

The Nomination Process

Typically, members of Congress are nominated in party primaries, as described in Chapters 7 and 8. Sometimes state party conventions nominate the candidates with a primary held only to ratify or reject the party leaders' nomination. Incumbents are usually renominated.

In some cases, though, reelecting one's own member of Congress is far from assured. In 2010 and again in 2012, the Tea Party movement has had success in ousting or threatening conservative Republican incumbents who were considered not conservative enough. In 2010, incumbent senator Robert Bennett (R-Utah), who, apart from supporting the Wall Street bailout, voted in a reliably conservative manner, was defeated at the state party convention by a Tea Party candidate who eventually won the general election. In 2012, Sen. Richard

Lugar (R-Ind.), who sometimes voted with Democrats on foreign policy issues and was considered one of the Senate's leading experts in that area, was defeated in his state's primary by a conservative who claimed that no compromise is acceptable unless it means that the Democrats come to agree with him. Also in 2012, after massive organization, fundraising, and campaigning to avoid the same fate, six-term senator Orrin Hatch (R-Utah) survived the state party convention vote despite a strong Tea Party challenger.

Campaigns

In the nineteenth century, political parties organized congressional campaigns, and the candidates had relatively little to do. Today, congressional campaigns are candidate-centered. That is, candidates typically hire staff, raise money, and organize their own campaigns rather than rely on the party organizations to do so. To be successful, members of Congress must attend constantly to these challenges. Here, the advantages of incumbency are vital. In large part because of them, vast majorities of incumbents who seek reelection win, even in so-called "anti-incumbent" years.

In most election years, reelection of members of Congress is almost certain unless the member has been accused of corruption or is involved in a scandal (see Figure 1). Indeed, one Republican member remarked, "Let's face it, you have to be a bozo to lose this job."[15] Sometimes that happens. In 2010, Rep. Alan Grayson (D-Fla.) stood for reelection against Tea Party candidate Daniel Webster. Grayson ran a TV ad with the title "Taliban Dan Webster." The ad's famous line was "Daniel Webster wants to impose his radical fundamentalism on us." The widespread attention to the veracity and reasonableness of the ad did nothing to help his reelection bid, and, in the end, Grayson lost.

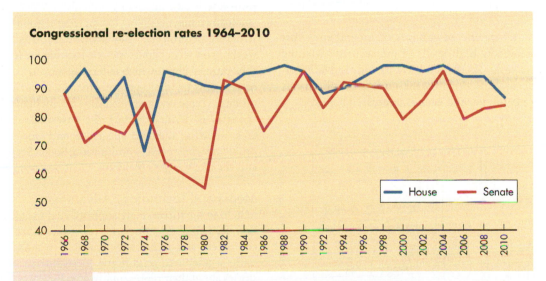

FIGURE 1: CONGRESSIONAL REELECTION RATES, 1964–2010 House members have generally had higher reelection rates than senators. Low rates for either have tended to occur during recessions, such as in 1980 or 2010, or during political scandals, such as Watergate in 1974. In the House of Representatives, reapportionment has also affected reelection rates.

SOURCE: Data from www.opensecrets.org Center for Responsive Politics.

There are also election years in which national issues, such as a poor economy, a war, an unpopular president, or a combination of these factors makes incumbent reelection less certain. Voter displeasure with the domestic and foreign policies of President George W. Bush, such as his response to Hurricane Katrina and the prosecution of the war in Iraq, resulted in more Republicans than usual being defeated (though the overall reelection rate for incumbents was still high). Because of the defeat of several Republican incumbents, including Sen. Rick Santorum from Pennsylvania, who campaigned for the Republican presidential nomination in 2012, Democrats took control of the House of Representatives and the Senate, and several high-profile Republican incumbents lost their races.

Similarly, in the 2010 midterm elections, voter anger at President Obama's economic record, especially high unemployment rates, resulted in many incumbents being defeated, this time Democratic ones, so the Republicans won back the majority in the House of Representatives and gained seats in the Senate.

The Advantages of Incumbency

To avert losses, incumbents work hard to serve their home districts, raise money for reelection campaigns, vote with district policy preferences to the greatest degree possible on high-profile votes, and raise their public profiles to boost their name recognition in their districts and states. When incumbents are successful at these tasks, and when the national mood is consistent with electoral safety, serious rivals are less likely to run, thereby increasing the chances of success.[16]

Incumbent reelection rates over time make the advantages of incumbency clear. Even in the anti-incumbent election of 2010, of those who sought reelection, about 83 percent of senators and 87 percent of members of the House were reelected.

What are the specific advantages of incumbency that lead to these relatively high levels of job security? Mailing privileges, casework, media and technology advantages, fundraising success, and pork-barrel funding are all aspects of this overall advantage, and each is addressed below.

"There's nothing wrong with you, Steve—it's just you're the incumbent."

© ROBERT MANKOFF/New Yorker Collection/www.cartoonbank.com

Mailing Privileges

An important advantage of incumbency is the opportunity to communicate with constituents and to do favors for them. For example, members send constituents calendars, newsletters, U.S. flags that have flown over the Capitol, and publications of the federal government. Members also correspond with constituents about issues, and the volume of correspondence has increased many-fold as electronic communication has become omnipresent. For example, mail volume to Senate offices increased 548 percent since 2002 (most of it e-mail), and volume to House offices increased 158 percent. Members and their staffs spend a great deal of time responding to these communications, and members take this work very seriously because it raises their profiles and provides a positive view of their work on behalf of their districts.

In order to communicate with constituents, members of Congress have taxpayer support for office and mailing costs. For correspondence sent through the mail, the franking privilege allows members to send items without paying for postage out of pocket or using campaign funds. The frank is a facsimile of the member's signature, and it works like metered mail, with the frank appearing where the stamp would be. The use of the frank has declined by about two-thirds over the past twenty years, partly because of tighter regulation of its use and partly because various forms of electronic communication have displaced regular mail. Altogether, for the 112th Congress (2011–2012), taxpayers are slated to provide more than a half billion dollars for office and franking expenses.[17, 18]

Casework

The work of doing personal favors for constituents who write or call for help is called **constituency service** or **casework**. Congressional staff function as red-tape cutters for everyone from elderly citizens having difficulties with Social Security to small-town mayors trying to win federal grants for local infrastructure or projects. They provide information to students working on term papers, people looking for federal jobs, citizens puzzled about which federal agency to ask for assistance, or residents trying to get information about a relative in the military. Typically, responsibility for mediating with federal agencies is divided among the casework staffers by issue area, allowing them to specialize and resolve constituents' problems—passports, immigration, Social Security payments, and the like—more efficiently.

Media and Technology Advantages

Matching the increasingly sophisticated means that members have for communicating with constituents are the production equipment and technology available to make television and radio segments to send home. Constituents may see or hear stories about their representatives on local television and radio news programs produced in congressional studios by the representatives' staff and paid for out of campaign or party funds. Often, stations run these productions as news features without telling their viewers that the stories have not been independently reported. Congressional staffers also write press releases

Impact *social, global, historical, economic, political*

Pay and Perks of Office

The first members of Congress made $6 a day, which paid for boardinghouse accommodations near the Capitol, firewood, candles, meals, and a mileage allowance for travel from their home states.[1] (In current dollars that $6 per day is around $58,000 a year.) Today, members receive a salary about three times that large, $174,000, along with health care and retirement benefits, and money for office, staff, mailing, and travel.[2] Leaders are paid more. Congress has indexed members' pay to inflation so that members do not have to vote directly on increases unless they want to refuse them. Although these incomes don't put members of Congress in the top 1 percent of wage earners in the United States, they do put them in the top 5 percent.

Benefits That Help Reelection Chances

Office and Clerical Support

Representatives are authorized to hire staff members out of their member's representational allowance (MRA), which amounts to about $1.5 million per year. Salaries take up almost two-thirds of the MRA; the remainder is for mailing, travel, and office expenses in both the Capitol and in their districts. Senators' annual allowances vary with the population of their states and range from $3 million to almost $5 million. Additionally, members who serve as committee chairs or in leadership positions are allowed additional staff and more money for expenses.[3]

Other Perks

Members of Congress enjoy many other perquisites, including subsidized travel abroad, subsidized meals in the Senate and House dining rooms, free parking in Washington and at airports, free car washes, a gymnasium, and a child care center.

A Final Benefit

Taxpayers fund life insurance policies and a death benefit equal to a year's salary for each member of Congress. And if a legislator desires, the sergeant-at-arms will arrange for an undertaker to plan the member's final journey.

[1] Per diem and travel allowances for the first members were verified in 2002 when Senate custodial staff found an eighteenth-century ledger with payment accounts.

[2] Patrick J. Purcell, "Retirement Benefits for Members of Congress," Congressional Research Service, Report RL30631, February 9, 2007, 1–13.

[3] Ida A. Brudnick, "Congressional Salaries and Allowances," Congressional Research Service, Report RL30064, October 28, 2009, 1–3.

---

about the accomplishments of their bosses and send them to local newspapers, which often print them as written.

Every member of Congress has an official website. Though these focus on congressional business and cannot be used to solicit funds or do campaigning, they provide voluminous information about the member. Typical websites allow constituents to ask for help or order American flags that have flown over the Capitol, and they have a section for press releases, information about the member's policy positions, and headlines about what the member has done for her district or state lately.

Fundraising

In order to ward off quality challengers and to run reelection campaigns, incumbents must raise substantial sums of money. Thus, members of Congress are aggressive in soliciting for donations. They fear defeat in the next election and think that raising a lot of money can protect them.

A senator in a typical state, for example, must raise more than $20,000 each week during all six years of her or his term to fund an average winning reelection campaign, which totals more than $6 million. A senator from a populous, high-cost state or in a hotly contested election needs to raise much more.[19] In 2008, the high-profile Democratic challenger Al Franken defeated incumbent Norm Coleman in a tightly contested Minnesota race in which the two together spent $35 million. Many incumbents raise millions even when they face little-known opponents.

In the House, an average winning race costs just over $1 million. That means the average House member has to raise about $10,000 a week over the course of a two-year term.

Until the 1960s, most fundraising by members of Congress was done in their home districts because members did not want their constituents to think they were influenced by Washington lobbyists. In contrast, today members of Congress are heavily supported by political action

Courtesy of Congresswoman Lucille Roybal-Allard

The "Constituent Services" section of Congresswoman Lucille Roybal-Allard's (CA) website illustrates how members of Congress serve their states or districts.

committees (PACs), and the majority of PAC funds are raised in Washington.[20] Members of Congress continually hold fundraisers, and well-known lobbyists get hundreds of invitations to congressional fundraisers every year.[21]

Raising money for congressional campaigns is becoming nationalized in other ways too. Individual donors from across the country pour money into districts that are considered competitive or otherwise important. Interest groups and political parties may raise the call to their donors to send contributions to key targeted districts. In 2010, in the high-profile California Senate race between the incumbent Democrat Barbara Boxer and the Republican challenger, the former CEO of Hewlett Packard, Carly Fiorina, money flooded in from all over the nation—more than $30 million by midsummer 2010. This nationalization of fundraising strengthens parties and gives members of Congress reasons to weigh national interests, as seen by those parties, alongside their local interests.

Incumbency is key in fundraising. Many PACs make generous donations to make sure they have the ears of members of Congress. In addition, committee assignments help a member gain large donations. Membership on a powerful committee that considers legislation important to big-money interests or that appropriates money greatly increases the chances of attracting large campaign donations. Another benefit of incumbency for fundraising is that national party campaign organizations, such as the National Republican Campaign Committee in the House or the Democratic Senatorial Campaign Committee, contribute substantial funds to the races of many incumbents, especially those who are most vulnerable. Said one Democratic congressional campaign chair, "I'm not looking for liberals or conservatives.... I'm looking for winners."[22]

Pork-Barrel Funding

Incumbents can gain the attention of or win over constituents by obtaining funds for special projects, new programs, buildings, or other public works that bring jobs, benefits, and business to their districts or states. Such benefits are widely known as **pork-barrel projects**. Virtually every annual budget contains money for military spending such as weapons or military construction projects. Universities also feature frequently in annual budgets, with large amounts allocated for campus projects. "Acting for" representation is a feature of pork-barrel funding. For instance, black members of Congress are three to five times more likely than their white counterparts to secure funding for historically black colleges and universities and to secure projects in predominately black counties.[23]

Because members consider pork-barrel projects crucial to their reelection chances, there is little support in Congress for eliminating projects most know to be unwise or wasteful. David Stockman, director of the Office of Management and Budget during the Reagan administration, observed, "There's no such thing as a fiscal conservative when it comes to his district."[24] Liberals and conservatives, Democrats and Republicans, protect these kinds of projects.

HOW CONGRESS IS ORGANIZED

An institution with 535 voting members that must make thousands of policy decisions every year is not likely to work quickly or efficiently.[25] Like all organizations, legislatures need structure to be able to accomplish their purposes. The House and the Senate have a leadership system and a

BEHIND THE SCENES

The Politics of the Post Office

The United States Postal Service (USPS) is an independent agency of the federal government explicitly authorized by the Constitution. The USPS began in 1775 during the Second Continental Congress, with Benjamin Franklin as postmaster general.

Today, the USPS is legally obligated to serve all Americans at a uniform price and quality, but, with small exceptions, it has not been funded directly by taxpayers since the 1980s. Since the early part of the 2000s, declining mail volume due to electronic communication and competition from rival firms such as FedEx and UPS has meant sharp drops in revenue and a corresponding and growing budget deficit.

In response, in late 2011, the USPS announced it would close more than 3500 post offices, eliminate almost 30,000 jobs, and end overnight delivery of first-class mail. Shortly thereafter, in response to a public outcry and congressional reaction, the postal service announced a delay in closures until mid-2012 to give Congress a chance to explore the best path to reform and deficit reduction.

The politics of postal closure is directly tied to the chances of reelection for members of Congress and has therefore received a great deal of attention. First, the USPS is the second-largest civilian employer in the nation. Additionally, many rural areas are much more dependent on their post offices than are urban areas because alternative delivery systems are less convenient and more expensive. Finally, particular demographic groups are affected to a greater degree than others. So, members of Congress have made saving their local postal facilities and services a high priority in order to protect their constituencies.

One constituency that has been especially active on this issue is seniors. For Rep. Chris Van Hollen (D-Md.), whose district includes Leisure World, a large seniors-only community with a post office, fighting to keep the post office has been imperative. Those in senior communities may not be as physically active and able as younger people, and the closeness of their essential services is important. Seniors are also the most reliable voting demographic, and the Leisure World residents of Van Hollen's district have let him know that this is a "real-world" problem for them. "We need to look at the post offices and how they are being used," Van Hollen said. "Communities are in a good position to know how used their post offices are, and anyone who knows Leisure World in my district, knows that you have a senior population that does use postal services; they are still writing a lot of letters, so they rely on that post office."

In the end, the postmaster general announced that rural post offices would not be closed; instead, hours were cut to a minimum. After two years, if cuts in hours and some other costs savings were not enough to close the deficit, a commission and independent control board would be authorized to do more drastic cost-cutting.

SOURCES: United States Postal Service website, "Postal History," http://about.usps.com/who-we-are/postal-history/welcome.htm; Humberto Sanchez, "For Some, All Politics Is Postal," *Roll Call*, April 19, 2012, http://www.rollcall.com/issues/57_124/For-Some-All-Politics-Is-Postal-213928-1.html.

---

committee structure with each organized along party lines. Alongside this partisan organization exist dozens of other groups—caucuses, coalitions, work and study groups, and task forces—whose membership cuts across party lines or reflects the division of interests within parties.

The Evolution of Congressional Organization

The Constitution calls for the members of the House of Representatives to select a **Speaker of the House** to act as its presiding officer and for the vice president of the United States to serve as president (or presiding officer) of the Senate. **Art. I, Sec. 2 & 3** But the Constitution does not say anything about the powers of these officials, nor does it require any further internal organization.

The first House, meeting in New York in 1789, had cumbersome procedures. For its first several sessions, Congress's legislative work was accomplished by appointing ad hoc committees. By the Third Congress, there were about 350 committees, and the system had become unwieldy. Soon permanent committees were created, each with continuing responsibilities in one area, such as taxes or trade.[26]

As parties developed, the selection of the Speaker became a partisan matter, and the Speaker became both a party leader and a legislative manager. The seventh Speaker, Henry Clay (Whig-Ky.), who served ten of the years between 1811 and 1825, transformed the Speakership from a ceremonial office to one of real leadership, maintaining party discipline by controlling perks like committee appointments and chair positions. Under Clay's leadership, the House was the dominant branch, but its influence declined when it, like the rest of government, could not cope with the divisiveness of the slavery issue. At the time it was said that "the only people in Congress who are not carrying a revolver are those carrying two revolvers."[27] By 1856, it took 133 ballots to elect a Speaker. Physical fights broke out on the House floor; duels were held outside.[28]

Library of Congress

Vitriolic exchanges are not a new phenomenon in Congress. Here is a fight in the House in 1798. After Rep. Matthew Lyon (Vt.) spit on Rep. Roger Griswold (Conn.) and the House refused to expel Lyon, Griswold attacked Lyon with a cane. Lyon defended himself with fire tongs as other members looked on—with some amusement, it seems.

The Senate, a smaller body than the House, was less tangled in procedures, less rule-bound, and more effective in its operation. Its influence rose as visitors packed the Senate gallery to hear the great debates over slavery waged by Daniel Webster (Mass.), John C. Calhoun (S.C.), and Clay (who had moved from the House). During this era, senators were elected by state legislatures, not directly by the people. **Art. I, Sec. 3** But the Senate, too, became ineffective as the nation moved toward civil war. Senators also carried arms to protect themselves as debates over slavery turned to violence.

After the Civil War, with the presidency weakened by the 1868 impeachment of Andrew Johnson for efforts to undermine congressional policy, strong party leadership reemerged in the House, and a period of congressionally centered government began. Speaker Thomas Reed (R-Maine), who served as Speaker from 1889 to 1891, was nicknamed "The Czar" by his colleagues because he exerted dominance over legislative rules, committee assignments, and party discipline generally.

At the same time, both the House and the Senate became more professional. The emergence of "national" problems and a proactive Congress made a congressional career more prestigious. And an accompanying desire for permanent careers in the House produced an interest in more broadly dispersed power and the related ability to garner support for reelection efforts. Members wanted a chance at choice committee seats and did not want to be controlled by the Speaker.

By 1910, members' interest in loosening the grip of congressional leaders and participating in a system of more dispersed power through committee chairs produced a successful revolt in the House against Speaker Reed's successor, Joseph

Cannon (R-Ill.). The result was a substantial loss of Speaker-centered power.

The Senate of this time was also undergoing a major reform. As part of the Progressive movement, pressure built for the direct popular election of senators. The election of senators by state legislatures had made many senators beholden to special interests, especially the big monopolistic corporations (called trusts) and railroads. Even in a day when millionaires were less common than today, the Senate was referred to as the "Millionaires' Club" because that is whose interests senators were thought to represent.

The Senate first refused to consider a constitutional amendment providing for its direct election. Finally, under the threat of a call for a constitutional convention, which many members of Congress feared might lead to other changes in the Constitution, a direct-election amendment was passed in the House and Senate in 1912 and ratified by the states a year later. **Seventeenth Amendment** These early twentieth-century reforms dispersed power in both the House and the Senate and weakened leadership.

Modern Leadership Positions

The Speaker of the House is the only leadership position specified in the Constitution. Other leadership positions arose along with political parties.

House Leadership Positions

The leaders of each party are selected by their members meeting as a group to conduct party business. **Party caucuses, sometimes called party conferences,** refer both to party meetings and to the party members collectively. For example, the House Republican caucus (or conference) consists of all Republicans serving in the House, and the Senate Democratic one consists of all Democratic members of the Senate. When independents or third-party members are elected to the House, they can ask to caucus with one of the major parties. Independent senator Bernie Sanders (Vt.) caucuses with the Democratic Party.

The full House must elect the Speaker, but as this vote occurs along party lines, the real selection is made in the majority party's caucus. Once elected, the Speaker becomes second in line to succeed the president, after the vice president. The Speaker's institutional task is to act as presiding officer and to see that legislation moves through the House.

The Speaker also has duties to maximize partisan advantage in committee and staff appointments and to secure the passage of measures put forward by the party or the president, if the majority party also controls the White House. For this reason, the person selected usually has been someone who has served in the House a long time and is a skilled parliamentarian who can negotiate compromises and put together legislative majorities.

Trying to win partisan support is often difficult, but the Speaker has some rewards and punishments to dispense for loyalty and disloyalty. Speakers have a say in who gets to sit on which committees, they control some material benefits, such as the assignment of extra office space, and they have the power to name the chair of the powerful Rules Committee as well as their party's members on that committee. Speakers also have influence over which committees will be given jurisdiction over complex bills, such as financial reform, which bills will come to the House floor for a vote and under what rules they will be considered, and how their party's congressional campaign funds are allocated. Finally, the Speaker decides who will be recognized to speak on the floor of the House and whether motions are relevant.

Despite these formal powers, the job is challenging. As one veteran legislator has described the Speaker's role, "It's all about your caucus. Never, ever, use your power to twist the results.... The Speaker must be empowered at all times to make the call. But you must be sure that your decisions don't cost you and your membership the majority."[29]

When Nancy Pelosi (D-Calif.) was Speaker from 2007 to 2011, she took on the high-profile role as party spokesperson in the two years before the Democrats won the White House. Inside the House, however, she crafted an effective legislative strategy by negotiating a path between the liberal and conservative wings of her caucus and by being willing to bend to the issue needs of more conservative caucus members. As one of the conservative Democrats said, "She's a very practical, tough strategist who knows what people can and what they can't do."[30] Or, as a House ally said, "she's recognized from Day One that you have to find the center of gravity in your caucus."[31] By being attentive to the district needs of all caucus members, Pelosi built loyalty and increased the chances of achieving consensus on party votes. She used this power to shepherd through the House almost every major piece of legislation backed by the Obama administration, including health care reform. As a result, in her fourth year as Speaker, Pelosi was

being ranked among the great floor leaders, some saying she had become the most powerful Speaker in the modern era.[32] Even after the huge House losses in 2010, Pelosi was elected House minority leader, an indication of how effective her legislative leadership was regarded within her own caucus.

John Boehner (R-Ohio), Pelosi's successor as Speaker, has had a more laissez-faire approach to his role. His hands-off style avoids providing sticks along with carrots and can encourage dissension and defiance within the caucus, especially its most conservative elements in the Tea Party. Conservatives defied Boehner during negotiations over the first debt limit increase and a payroll tax cut, among other legislative business. In the end, Boehner successfully guided that debt ceiling increase and other efforts. Still, observers from both sides of the aisle note that his inability to provide a united front in negotiations with Democrats in the House and Senate and the lengthy negotiations to get results have made Boehner a weak Speaker compared to his historical predecessors.

Additional party leadership positions in the House have evolved through practice and include a majority leader, a minority leader, and majority and minority whips. The **majority leader** is second in command to the Speaker and is in charge of the party's legislative agenda, since the Speaker is technically an officer of the House, not of her or his party. The majority leader, working with the Speaker, also schedules votes on bills. The **minority leader** is the top-ranking member of the opposition party. **Whips** originated in the British House of Commons, where they were named after the "whipper in," the rider who keeps the hounds together in a fox hunt. In Congress, party whips maintain contact with party members, determine which way they are leaning on votes, and seek their support. Assisting the majority and minority whips are a number of deputy and assistant whips who keep tabs on their assigned state delegations.

Party organization in the House also includes committees that assign party members to standing committees (described later in this chapter), work out the party's stance on major policy issues, plan legislative and campaign strategies, and allocate funds to party members running for reelection.

Senate Leadership

The Senate has no leader comparable to the Speaker of the House. The vice president of the United States is the president and may preside any time he chooses. In reality, the vice president attends infrequently and has relatively little power. However, when sitting as Senate president, he is allowed to cast tie-breaking votes in those rare instances when the Senate is evenly split. **Art. I, Sec. 3** Vice President Joe Biden performed in this role in 2010 when the Senate voted on the controversial health insurance reform bill.

The Senate has an elected president pro tempore who, by tradition, is the senior member of the majority party. It is an honorific post with few duties except to preside over the Senate in the absence of the vice president. In practice, during the conduct of day-to-day business, presiding duties are divided among junior senators. This division releases the senior member from routine work while giving the Senate's newest members a chance to learn the rules and procedures of the chamber.

The position of Senate majority leader was not created until 1911 and has none of the Speakership's potential for control of chamber organization and proceedings. Still, the majority leader is a spokesperson for his (no woman has ever held the position) party's legislative agenda and works to line up members' votes on key issues. This is difficult as, procedurally, the Senate is a free-for-all compared to the House, with "every man and woman for him- or herself."[33] At least two former majority leaders, Howard Baker (R-Tenn.) and Trent Lott (R-Miss.), described the job as "herding cats."

Another reason the job is difficult is that the majority leader has little power to stop a filibuster—a procedural maneuver that allows a minority to block a bill from coming to the floor by monopolizing the session with nonstop speeches or, in recent years, by threatening to do so. This means that a majority leader needs to do much more than keep his own party in line to keep legislation moving through the Senate. He can influence the general atmosphere of deliberation by working with the minority party in a way that is either conciliatory or partisan. But whichever approach is chosen, the majority leader must take into account the low tolerance senators have for being forced to act. As former senator Arlen Specter said, "Senators don't get here to be pushed around."[34] And in recent years, with the hyper-partisanship in the Senate as well as the House, the majority leader has had little influence over members of the other party.

The instances of powerful majority leaders are few, the most notable being Lyndon Johnson (D-Tex.). Johnson assumed office at a time when the Democrats had a slim hold on the Senate, giving him an opportunity to exercise his extraordinary powers of personal persuasion to keep party members in line on key votes. Johnson's reputation was made through a combination of his forceful personality and his mastery of the legislative process (he had been a staff aide to the House Speaker and then served in the House before election to the Senate). He made it his business to know everything about his colleagues—"what they drank, where their wives wanted to go on junkets, whether they had a mistress" or were "happy with their parking space [and] what the interests and needs of their constituents were." Acquiring this information and being "ruthless" in using it made him, by one estimation, the "greatest vote counter ever in Congress."[35]

The Senate minority leader's job is similar to that of the majority leader in that its effectiveness depends on a limited package of incentives and procedural ploys to enforce party discipline. Historically, the Senate's majority and minority leaders have worked closely together to conduct Senate business. But if either or both are seen as overly partisan, or more interested in personal political ambition than in running the Senate, it can weaken the collegial relationship and slow the legislative process. A sign of the deterioration of cross-party cooperation in the Senate in recent years is that majority and minority leaders have gone out on the campaign trail to defeat their counterparts in their reelection bids, something unheard of under old rules of collegiality.[36]

In representing the party, Senate leaders also may undercut their political viability at home if their constituents are more conservative or liberal than the leadership of the national parties. Harry Reid (D-Nev.), who became Senate majority leader in 2007, has had to walk that fine line.

As Senate majority leader, Lyndon Johnson (D-Tex.), shown (*left*) with Sen. Theodore Green (D-R.I.), "used physical persuasion in addition to intellectual and moral appeals. He was hard on other peoples' coat lapels." If the man he was trying to persuade was shorter, Johnson would "move up close and lean over." If the man was taller (and few were), Johnson would "come at him from below, somewhat like a badger." Quotes are from Eugene McCarthy, *Up 'til Now* (New York: Harcourt, 1987).

A Democrat from a Republican state, Reid is more conservative (an opponent of abortion rights, for example) than the mainstream of his party. As the spokesman for the more liberal Senate Democratic caucus, he risked his own reelection in 2010. With approval ratings in the low thirties, Senator Reid avoided losing his seat, thanks to a Tea Party opponent who ran to the right of most Nevada Republicans.

As in the House, both parties also elect assistant floor leaders and whips to help maintain party discipline. These are important, if not essential, positions for working one's way into the top leadership posts.

Committees

Because of its size (435 members of the House and 100 members of the Senate), much of the legislative work of Congress is done in committees. This division of labor enables Congress to consider a vast number of bills each year. If every member had to review every measure in detail, it would be impossible to deal with the workload of approximately 10,000 bills biennially. Instead, most bills are killed in committee, leaving many fewer for each member to evaluate before a floor vote. Committees also help members develop specializations. Members who remain on the same committee for some time gain expertise. As detailed below, there are several different types of committees, including standing committees, select committees, joint committees, and conference committees, in addition to the subcommittees that further divide the work among standing committees.

Standing Committees

In the 112th Congress (2011–2012), there were twenty **standing committees** in the House and sixteen in the Senate. Each deals with a different subject matter, such as finance or education or agriculture. Each has a number of subcommittees, totaling more than one hundred in the House and about seventy-five in the Senate.[37] The number of committees and subcommittees fluctuates, declining during years of reform and cost-cutting and increasing during years of government growth. In the wake of the terrorist attacks on New York and Washington during the George W. Bush administration, as government grew with the new cabinet-level Department of Homeland Security, so did the number of congressional committees.

The number of seats on any committee also can change from one session to another as party caucuses try to satisfy as many of their members' preferences as possible. Party ratios—the number of Republicans relative to Democrats on each committee—are determined by the majority party in the House and negotiated by the leadership of both parties in the Senate. The ratios are generally set in rough proportion to party membership in the particular chamber, but the majority party gives itself a disproportionate number of seats on key committees, such as Appropriations, to ensure control.

Committee membership Committees are essential not only to the legislative process but also for building a power base within Congress, attracting campaign donors, gaining the influence and name recognition needed for reelection,

AP Images/Pablo Martinez Monsivais

Senate majority leader Harry Reid (D-Nev.), heading left, and Senate minority leader Mitch McConnell (R-Ky.), heading right, usually go in opposite directions. Reid has tried to pass legislation proposed by President Obama and Democratic colleagues, while McConnell has tried to block virtually all of these proposals.

and even running for a higher office. The party tries to accommodate members' requests for assignments that will be most beneficial to their constituencies, but there is some self-selection by seniority.

Historically, junior members did not ask for the most prestigious posts, but this tradition has eroded as freshmen have become bolder in their requests. And if there are freshmen members whose reelection races are likely to be tough or who the party leadership believes have the potential to be future leaders, those members will likely be given helpful committee assignments. Barack Obama was given a position on the influential Foreign Relations Committee in his freshman year, just as Hillary Rodham Clinton had been given a seat on the important Armed Services Committee in 2001 to burnish her credentials for a possible future role as commander in chief.

The committees dealing with appropriations, taxes, and finance are always sought after because having a say in the allocation of money and how the tax burden falls on individuals and businesses gives members power, enhances their ability to help their home districts, and provides leverage to raise campaign funds. For the last-mentioned reason, these are sometime called "juice committees" because of the advantage they give members in squeezing interested parties. Most members also want committee assignments that let them tell constituents they are working on problems of the district. Members from rural districts, for example, seek seats on committees that deal with agricultural and trade issues.

The practice of filling each committee with representatives whose districts have an especially strong economic interest in its work helps bring long experience and expertise to complex issues. But it also encourages committees to be parochial in their outlook and can lead to wasteful legislation and bloated appropriations. If committee members' constituents benefit from programs under their jurisdiction, the members have no incentive to eliminate them or pare them back. Thus, although committees allow the large legislative agenda of Congress to proceed, they also lead to the substantial weaknesses of seemingly locking in programs and funding streams that may not be serving the public well and furthering the unseemly influence of private interests on public policy making.[38]

Media coverage is another criterion that is important in members' choice of committee assignments. The work of some committees is more likely to be covered by television. In 2008, committees scrambled to hold attention-getting hearings on the investigation of subprime mortgage lenders, and in 2010, hearings on the causes and consequences of British Petroleum's massive oil spill into the Gulf of Mexico was the attention-grabbing issue. When a journalist once asked then Senator Joe Biden (D-Del.) why he was so newsworthy, Biden replied, "It's the committees, of course." Biden served on the committees with the greatest media exposure, such as Judiciary and Foreign Relations, which made him a credible potential candidate for the presidency in every Democratic primary season for twenty-five years and, finally, a vice-presidential candidate who could convincingly balance Barack Obama's lack of foreign policy experience.

A consequence of specialization and committee government is that committees are often filled with members who have financial interests in the businesses for which they make policies. Most members who sit on the banking committees own bank stock, many on agriculture committees own agribusiness stock, and those on the armed services committees hold stock in defense industries.[39] Federal farm subsidies illustrate these conflicts well. For example, Ron Paul (R-Tex.), who owns shares in gold-mining companies worth about $1.5 million, served as ranking minority member of the subcommittee that oversees monetary policy, mints, and gold, and he advocated for a U.S. return to the gold standard.[40] Along with other congressional beneficiaries of farm subsidies, rancher Jon Tester (D-Mont.) and his wife receive about $200,000 annually from these programs.[41]

Committee chairs The chair is usually the most influential member of a committee. Chairs have the authority to call meetings, set agendas, and control committee staff and funds. In addition, chairs usually have strong substantive knowledge of the matters that come before their committees, and this, too, is a source of influence. Chairs are generally selected on the basis of seniority by special committees set up by both parties in the House and the Senate, but the seniority preference is not iron-clad, and, in the past few decades, chairs have usually been party loyalists.

Subcommittees Each standing committee is divided into subcommittees with jurisdiction over part of the committee's area of responsibility. For example, the Senate Environmental and Public Works Committee has seven subcommittees, including Green Jobs and the New Economy, Clean Air and Nuclear Safety, and Superfund, Toxics, and Environmental Health. The subcommittees in the House and Senate operate semi-autonomously from their parent committees and do the bulk of the substantive work on legislation.

Select, Special, Joint, and Conference Committees
Select or *special committees* are typically organized on a temporary basis to investigate a specific problem or to hold hearings and issue a report on special problems that arise, such as the impeachment of a federal official or an investigation into a policy failure, such as the government response to Hurricane Katrina. Select and special committees are usually disbanded when their work is completed; however, some select committees are permanent, such as the Senate committee on Indian Affairs.

Four *joint committees* include members from both houses, with the chair alternating between a House and Senate member. An example includes the Joint Committee on Taxation, whose duties include investigating methods for the simplification of taxes. Its job may not have been done very effectively, as in 2010 alone, there were 579 changes to the federal tax code consisting of 3.8 million words.[42]

Conference committees, appointed whenever the Senate and the House pass different versions of the same bill, also have joint membership. Members from the committees that managed the bill in their respective chambers work out a single version for the full membership to vote on. Conference committees are dissolved after the compromise version is completed.

Task Forces
The traffic jams and turf wars around some committee work have led members of Congress with strong interests in particular policy areas to look for ways to bypass the committee structure. Task forces and ad hoc committees have existed in the House for decades to study major issues and draft legislation, sometimes to speed action on a bill when a committee is dragging its feet or producing an outcome not in accord with leadership priorities.[43] For example, former Speaker Pelosi bypassed the standing committee and named a bipartisan House task force to write an ethics reform bill in 2007. The Senate makes less use of task forces, but there are a number of cross-chamber study groups, most devoted to health issues like AIDS or smoking.

Staff and Support Agencies
The legislative branch is staffed by more than 30,000 employees, about 17,000 of whom work directly for the House and Senate as personal or committee staffers.[44] Without its own information base, Congress cannot serve its proper role as a check on the executive branch.

Photo by Sarah L. Voisin / The Washington Post via Getty Images

Staffers sit behind their representative or senator at committee hearings. Staffers are so valuable to busy members of Congress that Sen. Jay Rockefeller (D-W.V.) admitted, during consideration of the health insurance reform bill, that "The staff is the whole ballgame."

SOURCE: Quote from Manuel Roig-Franzia, "The Washington Whisperers: Quietly but Forcefully, Hill Aides Have Their Lawmaker's Ear," *Washington Post*, October 1, 2009, http://www.washingtonpost.com/wp-dyn/content/article/2009/09/30/AR2009093005042.html.

Apart from personal or committee staff, support agencies for the legislature carry out various research functions. For example, the Government Accountability Office (GAO) checks on the efficiency and effectiveness of executive agencies, the Congressional Budget Office provides the expertise and support for Congress's budgeting job, and the Congressional Research Service provides comprehensive policy analyses for members. The cost of funding the legislative branch as a whole in 2011 was more than $5 billion.[45]

WHAT CONGRESS DOES

The centrality of Congress's task is reflected in the major, explicit constitutional powers the Founders gave it: to lay and collect taxes, coin money, declare war and raise and support a military, and regulate commerce with foreign governments and among the states. **Art. I, Sec. 7 & 8** Most of the named powers that the Constitution invests in the national government—including "All legislative Powers herein granted"—were given to Congress. **Art. I, Sec. 1** These and other powers specifically mentioned in the Constitution are called the *enumerated powers* of Congress.

Congress also has *implied powers*; that is, it is permitted to make all the laws "necessary and proper" to carry out its enumerated powers. Although the Founders did not necessarily

foresee it, this tremendous grant of power covers almost every area of human activity.

Lawmaking

In each recent congressional session, more than ten thousand bills and resolutions are introduced, although most don't go far in the legislative process. Of those enacted, many are noncontroversial, including "sense of the chamber" measures, such as resolutions congratulating the winners of the Super Bowl. However, even these nonpolitical resolutions are sometimes grist for the partisan mill. A former Republican Senate majority leader refused to allow a vote on a congratulatory resolution offered by New Jersey's two Democratic senators on behalf of their constituent, Bruce Springsteen, who was celebrating the thirtieth anniversary of his "Born to Run" album.

How does Congress decide which of the bills introduced each year it will pass? The Constitution says virtually nothing about the legislative process itself, and the way bills work their way through the House and Senate evolved with the development of party caucuses and the committee system. The procedures can be very arcane, but the general steps in the process are bill introduction and referral, subcommittee hearings and markup, full committee hearing and markup, calendar and rule assignment by leadership, floor debate, vote, resolution of differences in House and Senate versions through

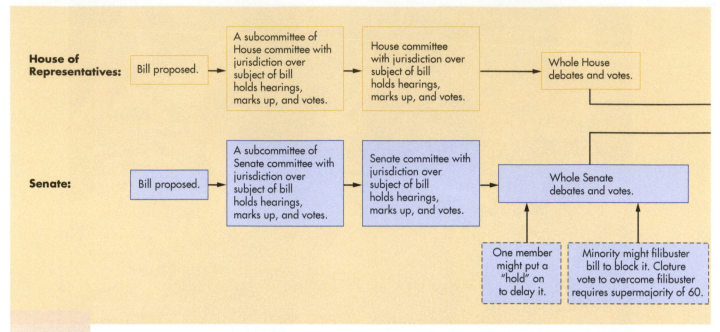

FIGURE 2: HOW A BILL BECOMES A LAW Of the approximately 10,000 bills introduced in Congress each year, only about 125 to 400 become law. This diagram highlights the key steps in the process. At every step, bills are subjected to political pressures that can't be conveyed in a diagram. Bills can be killed at any step. Most are killed in the subcommittee of the committee. If they pass the committee, they usually pass the whole chamber. Although the process looks similar for the two chambers, House leaders have more power to influence the process than do Senate leaders. And the use of holds and filibusters allows the minority in the Senate to delay and block bills. A filibuster requires a supermajority of 60 votes to get the bill to the floor for an up-or-down vote.

conference committee, president's signature or veto, and vote to override veto when applicable (see Figure 2).

These formal steps are important, but they do not reveal the bargaining and trade-offs at every step in the process. Often, turning a bill into a law is like running an obstacle course. Opponents have an advantage because it is easier to defeat a bill than to pass one. Will Rogers's observation in the 1930s still reflects the modern difficulty of passing legislation: "Congress is so strange. A man gets up to speak and says nothing. Nobody listens—and then everyone disagrees."[46] Because of the need to win a majority at each stage, the result is always a compromise. In defending the compromises that then Speaker Nancy Pelosi made to get the health care reforms through the House, one observer explained, "The real world has limits, and one of them is that there will never be a major bill to emerge from the House of Representatives that doesn't have something regrettable in it."[47]

Bill Introduction and Referral

Bills may be introduced in either the House or the Senate, except for tax measures, which, according to the Constitution, must be initiated in the House, 🏛 **Art. I, Sec. 7** and appropriations bills, which, by tradition, are introduced in the House. This practice reflects the Founders' belief that the chamber directly elected by the people should control the purse strings.

Although the White House initiates some of the legislation Congress enacts, only members can introduce bills for consideration. The president, like interest groups or constituents who suggest legislation, must find congressional sponsors for each bill in his legislative agenda. After a bill's introduction, it is referred to a standing committee by the Speaker of the House or the presiding officer in the Senate. The content of the bill largely determines where it will go, although the Speaker has some discretion, particularly over complex bills that cover more than one subject area. Many such bills are referred to more than one committee simultaneously.

Committee Action

Once the bill reaches a committee, it is assigned to an appropriate, subject-specific subcommittee. One of the functions of subcommittees is to screen bills with little chance of passage. If a subcommittee decides to take up a proposed piece of legislation, it may call hearings. Unless otherwise specified, hearings are open to the public. Witnesses are heard, amendments are considered, and substantive and procedural votes are taken. Although hearings are open to the public, it is lobbyists who fill most of the hearing rooms. For critical meetings, lobbyists will hire messengers to stand in line for them, sometimes all night, and then pack the hearing room. If the bill is approved, either as is or with revisions after the hearing, it is sent to the full committee along with a report explaining the subcommittee's action and reasoning. The standing committee may hold additional hearings and markup sessions before voting to move the bill to the chamber floor, tabling it for further, future consideration, or killing it.

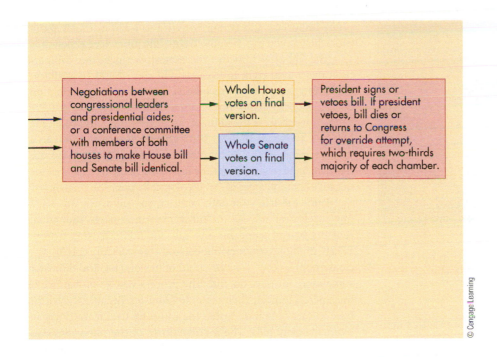

© Cengage Learning

Scheduling and Rules

Once a House committee approves a bill, it is placed on one of five "calendars," depending on the subject matter of the bill. The Senate has just two calendars: one for private bills (applies to an individual, group, or corporate entity) and public bills and another for treaties and nominations. In the House, the powerful Rules Committee sets the terms of the debate over the bill by issuing a rule on it. The rule either limits or does not limit debate and determines whether amendments will be permitted. A rule forbidding amendments means that members have to vote yes or no on the bill; there is no chance to change it. If the committee refuses to issue a rule, the bill dies.

Because the Senate is a smaller body, it can operate with fewer rules and formal procedures. A lot of work is accomplished through the use of unanimous consent agreements negotiated between the majority and minority leaders that allow the Senate to dispense with existing standard rules and define terms for debating and amending a specific bill. As the Senate's workload has increased and its sense of collegiality has decreased, it has become more difficult to get opponents to accept a unanimous consent agreement. A single senator can use parliamentary tactics to freeze the agenda. A senator once held up an antibusing bill for eight months with 604 amendments.

Debate

Debate on a bill in both chambers is controlled by bill managers from the committee that sent the bill to the full chamber. "Debates" are not a series of fiery speeches of point and counterpoint. They are often recitations delivered to a handful of members, some of whom may be reading, conversing, or walking around the floor. In the House, after the time allotted for debate is over (typically five minutes per speaker), the bill is reported for final action. And if a bill is brought to the floor under a rule allowing no amendments, even a day's debate can lead to no more than an up-or-down vote on the bill as presented.

In the Senate, the lack of fixed rules on debate and the majority leader's inability unilaterally to set them have made unrestricted debate a principal method of defeating or delaying consideration of a bill. The major mechanism for doing this is to threaten a **filibuster**, a continuous speech made by one or more members to prevent a piece of legislation from being brought to the floor for a vote. The word *filibuster* comes from a Dutch term for pirates who held ships for ransom.

When the first Congress met, the rulebooks of the House and Senate allowed for debate to be cut off by a simple majority. But in 1805 Vice President Aaron Burr, acting as Senate president, encouraged the streamlining of the Senate rulebook, and during this process the rule allowing for a simple majority to end debate was eliminated by accident.[48] Still, the use of the filibuster as a legislative tactic did not begin in earnest until 1837, when it was used periodically to block election reform, nominations, and civil rights legislation.[49] Up into the early twentieth century, Senate leaders tried many times to reinstate the original simple majority rule. Failing, they developed rules such as unanimous consent to avoid the possibility of filibusters.

In 1917, under pressure from President Wilson, citing wartime needs, the Senate adopted the **cloture** rule, which allowed debate to be cut off by two-thirds of those present and voting. In 1975, the rules were changed again to allow three-fifths of the membership (sixty senators) to end debate. When the Senate invokes cloture, debate must end within thirty hours and the measure must be brought to a vote.

The public became aware of the use of the filibuster to block legislation during the 1960s civil rights movement, when it took a cloture vote to end fifty-four days of debate and get the 1964 Civil Rights Act to the floor for a vote.

The filibuster was not widely used again until the 1990s, when Republicans used it frequently during President Clinton's administration. Then Democrats used the same tactic for

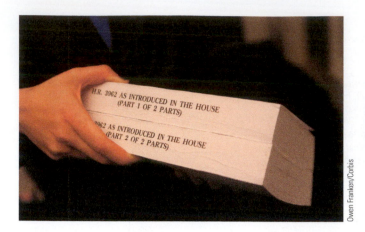

Owen Franken/Corbis

Proposed bills often are long and complex, in part because of references to provisions of past legislation that they are required to include.

most of George W. Bush's presidency, and the practice continued with even greater frequency during Obama's first term in office. For instance, had there been no opportunity for filibustering, a climate and energy bill to reduce global warming and the DREAM Act (Development, Relief and Education for Alien Minors, which would provide conditional permanent residency to illegal immigrants who have arrived in the United States as minors and who meet several other conditions) would likely be the law of the land. And more than two hundred judicial nominees would be seated in open judicial slots.

In practice, actual filibusters rarely occur because the threat of one is now sufficient to stop action on a bill or other piece of Senate business. In effect, this has meant that a **supermajority** of 60 votes is often necessary to pass a bill in the Senate. In the past two Congresses, more than 30 percent of the roll-call votes in the Senate have required 60 votes for success, a historic high.[50] Said one senator, "If you're not comfortable with delay, frustration, and impatience, get out of the Senate. It's the nature of the institution, but I think we've taken it to an art form."[51]

 ### Thinking about Democracy

Minority rights are a foundational element in our form of democracy, but how far does this principle extend to the legislative process? Should a minority be able to block bills that are supported by a majority of elected officials? Are there any benefits to this approach?

Impediments to Deliberation

The filibuster is of importance beyond voting on bills or nominations; the threat of one can also be used by the minority to stop routine procedural motions and bring Senate business to a halt. Senate minority leader Mitch McConnell (R-Ky.) has boasted of his success in leveraging Senate rules to stop the majority from acting. He said he learned fairly early "that it is

pretty important and certainly useful to learn as much about procedure as you can, because frequently procedure is policy."[52]

The filibuster impedes the majority's (including a bipartisan majority's) right to legislate and contributes to gridlock, but it also can prevent precipitous action or total domination by the majority party. Some argue that by dragging out the deliberative process the filibuster rule contributes to producing bills that are better thought through and more acceptable to a broader range of the membership and the public. Others are more inclined to see the routine use of the filibuster as one of the negative consequences of "an ideologically polarized Senate."[53]

Until the late twentieth century, the filibuster was used only rarely and only for the most important issues. Individual senators had to stand up and talk for hours to stop action. When multiple senators filibustered, they set up cots in the cloak room so each senator could filibuster, rest, and filibuster some more for days on end. The process was an ordeal. Now, they merely indicate their *intent* to filibuster. Because they don't have to carry out a filibuster, the minority uses it routinely to block majority bills. The increased use of the filibuster is an impediment to Senate action, and thus congressional action, and is an anti-majoritarian aspect of American government.

Senate rules also encourage gridlock in another way by allowing a single member to place a hold on any nomination (or bill) anonymously, for any reason, thus preventing an up-or-down vote. A senator who places a hold must identify herself or himself six days after a vote has been called for. However, if, prior to the sixth day, the senator withdraws the hold and gets a colleague to place it anew, the originator can remain anonymous. And, by passing a hold from one senator to another within the six-day limit, all can remain anonymous. By mid-2010, secret holds had stalled confirmation of presidential nominations for an average of 106 days.[54]

The hold originated as a courtesy in the days when senators had to travel by horse; holding a vote allowed members time to reach the capital and read a bill or consider a nominee before voting.[55] Today the hold is used occasionally to stall a nomination for political or policy reasons, but most holds have little to do with policy, qualifications, or personalities, and certainly not with travel delays from slow horses. They are more often used by senators as a bargaining chip to get something they want. Senator Richard Shelby (R-Ala.) placed a blanket hold on seventy nominees because he wanted assurances that the work on a new tanker for the Pentagon would be done in his state and also that a planned new FBI facility would be located in Huntsville.[56] This quid pro quo leveraging of a vote is why the hold has been described as the "bare-knuckled politics of obstruction."[57]

The Senate was created to make sure that Congress did not rush to pass ill-considered legislation; as one senator noted, it was not created to be efficient, but rather inefficient.[58] George Washington is alleged to have made this point when he compared the Senate with a saucer: you pour your hot coffee (the more populist measures passed by the House) into a saucer to cool it. But carried to extremes, this deliberate gridlock of the Senate legislative process has created bad feelings in the House, where, with its simple majority rule, legislation continued to move either by Democrats in the first two years

President Obama meets with Sen. Susan Collins (R-Maine), one of the few remaining moderate Republicans in the Senate. Early in his administration, the president tried to negotiate the content of proposed legislation with moderate Republicans to win their votes.

of the Obama administration or by Republicans in the next two years. More importantly, it has helped to create public disdain for the institution of Congress. The public assumes that Congress operates according to majority rule, so it does not understand why Congress cannot act. As one longtime Senator remarked, "senators are so proud of being the saucer" that "the Senate no longer has the ability to answer the problems of this nation in real time."[59] And, some political scientists have said that today's Senate, rather than being a cooling saucer for legislation, has become "a deep freezer."[60]

The Vote

When a bill ever makes it to an up-or-down floor vote in the House and Senate, the vote may be taken in several different ways—by voice, a standing count, or recording of individual votes—depending on the level of support and the importance of the legislation. When a measure passes, it is sent to the other chamber for action.

At the time members cast their votes on the floor of the House or Senate, they are usually voting on the general aim of the bill without knowing its exact provisions. Rarely do members read bills in full. This sometimes becomes grounds for partisan rhetoric. For example, Republicans complained that the 2010 health care reform bill was long and complicated and was being rushed through without the chance for members to read it. At more than 2000 pages, it was indeed long, but not out of line with the size of bills or speed of passage of other laws passed by Republican Congresses, such as the educational reform measure called the No Child Left Behind Act, the anti-terror PATRIOT Act, passed shortly after 9/11, and the prescription drug benefit for seniors, which ran from 800 to more than 1000 pages. Neither was the health care reform bill rushed through

compared to other bills, particularly the PATRIOT Act, which was signed a month and a half after the attacks of 9/11.

Conference Committee

The House and Senate must agree on an identical version of a bill before it can become law, and since this rarely happens, the two versions must be reconciled. Sometimes the chamber that passed the bill last will simply send it to the other chamber for minor modifications. But if the differences between the two versions are not minor, a **conference committee** is set up to try to resolve them. The presiding officers of each chamber, in consultation with the chairs of the standing committees that considered the bill, choose the members of the committee. Both parties are represented, but there is neither a set number of conferees nor a rule requiring an equal number of seats for each chamber.

Conference committees have tremendous latitude in how they resolve the differences between the House and Senate versions of a bill. Officially, nothing can be added to the bill that is not germane to it, and no part of a bill can be amended that had not been amended prior to passage. But sometimes a bill is substantially rewritten, and occasionally a bill is killed. Or, as President Reagan once said, "an apple and an orange could go into a conference committee and come out a pear."[61] The power of conference committees to alter bills after their passage is why they are sometimes called the "Third House" of Congress.[62]

Once a conference committee reaches an agreement, the bill goes back to each chamber, where its approval requires a majority vote. It cannot be amended at that point, so it is presented to the membership on a take-it-or-leave-it basis. In practice, both House and Senate accept most conference reports because members of both parties in each chamber have participated in working out the compromise version.

© Bettmann/CORBIS

Senator Strom Thurmond, at the time a Democrat from South Carolina, is congratulated by his wife for setting a record for the longest filibuster. He talked for twenty-four hours and eighteen minutes to prevent a civil rights bill from being voted on in 1957. In preparing for the ordeal, he took a steam bath to eliminate excess fluids and brought throat lozenges. After criticizing the bill, he talked about whatever came to mind, including his grandmother's biscuit recipe. His effort was in vain, as the bill was adopted.

Knowing how to win a seat on a conference committee is an essential skill for any legislator who wants to wield influence. However, in periods when one party controls the White House and both houses of Congress (most of George W. Bush's terms and the first two years of Obama's presidency, for example), few bills go to conference committee. The White House and congressional leaders pre-empt the conference process by working out final wording of bills among themselves. Minority parties often feel so blocked out of the negotiations that they refuse to sign on to conference committee reports. In the last years of the Bush presidency, only 2 percent of public bills were passed through conference committees.[63]

Presidential Action and Congressional Response

The president may sign a bill, in which case it becomes law. Or the president may veto it, in which case it returns to Congress with the president's objections. The president also may do nothing, and the bill will then become law after ten days unless Congress adjourns during that period. 🏛 **Art. I, Sec. 7**

Most presidents have not used the veto lightly, but when they do veto a bill, Congress rarely overrides them. A two-thirds vote in each house is required to override a presidential veto. Congress voted to override only nine of former President Reagan's seventy-eight vetoes, only one of President George H. W. Bush's forty-six, only two of Clinton's thirty-four, and two of George W. Bush's ten. President Obama used the veto twice in his first three years in office and they stood.

After the bill becomes a law, it is assigned a number (which always begins with the session of Congress that passed it), published, and entered in the United States Code.

Oversight

As part of the checks-and-balances principle, it is Congress's responsibility to make sure that the bureaucracy is administering federal programs as Congress intended. This monitoring function, called **oversight**, has become more important as complex legislation has resulted in increased congressional delegation of authority to the executive branch. Laws such as those enacted to prevent future terrorist threats to the United States or the health insurance reform law are good examples of this practice.

Congressional oversight is primarily exercised through control over the federal budget. Congress can cut or add to agencies' budgets depending on the political focus of the day and the party or parties in power in the House, the Senate, and the executive branch. Members with authority over an agency's budget can also use that power to get benefits for their constituents, and by going along with the members' wishes, agencies may stand a better chance of having their budget requests approved.

Committee hearings on policy issues are another method of oversight. They give members an opportunity to query presidential nominees to executive positions such as cabinet secretaries or Supreme Court nominees and to question executive branch staff on the operation of their agencies.

Congress can also exercise its oversight function through informal means.[64] One way of doing this is to request reports on topics of interest to members or committees. In a given year, the executive branch might prepare 5000 reports for Congress.[65] Moreover, senior members of an agency consult regularly with the chair and staff of the committee or subcommittee relevant to the agency's mission.

As important as it is, oversight, formal or informal, is not the first priority of most members of Congress. There is little electoral or other incentive to do it most of the time because it does not contribute to a higher public profile, a constituency benefit, or a new law for which a member can claim credit. On the other hand, when a crisis arises or public confidence in the economy or government institutions is threatened, the opportunities for members to claim credit for a strong and effective response make them much more willing to engage in oversight. When that happens, heavily media-saturated hearings are held and members are profiled.

A good example of such after-the-fact oversight is a congressional investigation into a lavish, four-day Las Vegas conference of the General Services Administration (GSA). The GSA provisions products, services, and offices for federal government departments and agencies. In 2012, it came to light that one GSA conference in 2010 cost the federal taxpayers a whopping $822,000. Soon, four separate committees in the House and Senate investigated and judged the event to be extravagant, wasteful, and excessive. Some of the spending was declared impermissible, such as outlays for a clown show, mementos for those who attended the conference, tuxedo rentals, and the purchase of commemorative coins intended

"After months of partisan bickering, Congress has finally agreed to put a Slinky on an escalator and see if it goes forever."

to reward all conference participants for their work.[66] Had Congress been monitoring the GSA more routinely, such expenditures may never have occurred.

Although one-time investigations, such as the efforts to order the GSA to conduct its business efficiently and within the scope of its mandate, are useful, waiting to do oversight until there is a crisis can have very negative, widespread, and ongoing consequences. For instance, serious hearings about the practices of financial institutions did not materialize until after the subprime mortgage crisis threatened economies in the United States and around the world.

Responding to crises also can make oversight more of a partisan weapon than an attempt to right a wrong. So, when the Republicans took back control of the House in 2010, they began to hold hearings intended to challenge the Obama administration's responses to the economic downturn. The purpose of these hearings was to position the parties for electoral advantage more than to improve policy making.

Partisan oversight is common when the party that controls the White House is different from the party that controls at least one house in Congress. But when the party in Congress is the same as the party that controls the executive (unified government), oversight is rarely seriously considered. Recent Republican majorities have been particularly lax in investigating fellow party members. During most of the Bush administration, compliant Republicans did not want to investigate anything that made the administration look bad. In the wake of 9/11, the Bush administration encouraged Congress to neglect oversight of defense policy and intelligence operations by arguing that the president needed a free hand to wage the war on terrorism.

Budget Making

An increasingly large and critical part of the job of Congress is to pass a budget. Real priorities are reflected not in rhetoric but in the budget. The Constitution gave Congress the power to appropriate money and to account for its expenditure, **Art. I, Sec. 9** but in the 1920s, Congress delegated its authority to prepare the annual budget to the president. In years when the president's party does not control Congress, the congressional majority also produces its own budget, with priorities distinctly different from the president's.

Characteristics of Budgeting

Historically, congressional budgeting has had three basic characteristics. First, the process is usually incremental; that is, budgets for the next year are usually slightly more than budgets for the current year. Normally, Congress does not radically reallocate money from one year to the next. Second, Congress tends to spend more in election years and in times of unemployment. Third, the process, while similar to the one for passage of any other bill, is more complex and contains multiple layers and many different participants, as described below. There are also exceptions to these general rules, such as times of war or domestic crisis. The first budget submitted after 9/11, for example, requested a huge increase in defense spending.

The House and Senate Budget Committees

Since 1974, the House and Senate have subcommittee-free budget committees whose membership includes representatives from the leadership of both parties. The job of the budget committee is to craft and recommend an annual budget resolution that dictates the overall amount of money for that year's budget as well as how much should go into the almost two dozen basic functional budget categories, such as defense. This resolution is intended to be the first step in the process and to guide the rest of the work on the budget. Congress is aided in budget review by the Congressional Budget Office (CBO), which provides expertise on matters related to both the budget and the economy. Because the CBO is responsible to both parties in Congress, it provides less politically biased

Michael Reynolds/Landov

The CEOs of financial firms prepare to testify before a congressional committee investigating the financial collapse of 2008, which was driven by the risky practices of the huge firms. Congressional committees hold hearings as part of their oversight of federal agencies.

analyses than the administration or the leadership of either party would.

Authorizations and Appropriations

To understand the next steps in the process, it is important to consider the distinction between budget authorizations and budget appropriations. **Authorizations** are acts that enable agencies and departments to operate, either by creating them or by authorizing their continuance. They also establish the guidelines under which the agencies operate. Although authorization bills might specify funding levels, they do not provide the funding. **Appropriations** are acts that give federal agencies the authority to spend the money allocated to them. Both authorization and appropriation bills must pass each house, and differences must be resolved in conference.

Typically, authorizations precede appropriations, although this is not always the case. Budgetary procedures are not defined in the Constitution but are determined by House and Senate rules, which can be, and often have been, changed. The standing committees that oversee the work of the agency or program being funded usually work out the authorizations. The House Natural Resources Committee and the Senate Energy and National Resources Committee, for example, review the authorization of the Park Service in the Department of the Interior, and the agricultural committees write authorizations for the Department of Agriculture. Close ties often exist between the agency being reviewed and the authorizing committee, which can cause proposed funding levels to be set without consideration of the overall demand on federal revenues. This puts pressure on latter stages of the budget process.

Each chamber also has an Appropriations Committee with subcommittees corresponding to functional areas into which budget allocations are divided, such as Homeland Security or Labor, Health and Human Services, Education, and Related Agencies. The Appropriations Committee assigns a spending limit for each area, and the relevant subcommittee then decides how to apportion it among the agencies in its jurisdiction. The bills that the full Appropriations Committees send to the floor for a vote may reflect increases or decreases to previous year's funding levels, or they can recommend the elimination of an agency altogether. The power of Appropriations Committees is vast, and those who chair their subcommittees are nicknamed "The College of Cardinals" to indicate that power.

Problems with the Budget Process

Most participants and knowledgeable observers are critical of congressional budget making. One reason is that, especially in recent years, members simply cannot agree on spending for any fiscal year. Failure to pass a budget resolution, which sets the overall spending totals for the appropriations process, has become common. It is also common for a new fiscal year to begin before Congress has passed all the necessary appropriations bills. To avoid government shutdown, members of Congress routinely pass stopgap measures called continuing resolutions (CRs) that keep allocations steady until the process can be concluded after the new fiscal year has already begun.

Another problem is that even when Congress enacts budget resolutions, it does not always honor them. Congress has frequently outspent the dollar limit that it set.[67] This happens with emergencies such as natural disasters like Hurricane

Rep. Joe Walsh (R-Ill.) was elected in the Tea Party surge of 2010. Although he won by less than 300 votes, he saw his victory as a mandate. "I came here ready to go to war. The people didn't send me here to compromise." Reflecting the extremism common in the House today, he vowed to "shut down government" because the deficits are "so serious that this country needs to crash." In 2012, Walsh lost his re-election bid.

SOURCES: Quotes from Alex Altman, "A Tale of Two Freshmen," *Time*, March 14, 2011, 38–39.

Katrina, but Congress often simply allows important parts of the budget to be allocated separately in what are called "supplemental" bills. Spending on Iraq and Afghanistan has been done with supplemental bills even though the spending, unlike for Katrina, was not unforeseen. This sleight-of-hand was useful because it offered the convenient illusion that the cost of the wars in Iraq and Afghanistan was zero and thus reduced pressures to increase taxes to pay for them, even though paying for these wars has increased the U.S. budget deficit significantly.

The budgeting process also suffers from the dynamics of committee government. By developing expertise in a few areas, House members are often more responsive to narrow interests and constituencies and less responsive to national priorities when deciding how to spend money. Over time, members of congressional subcommittees develop close relationships both with lobbyists for interest groups whose goals are affected by committee decisions and with the staff in executive branch agencies that the subcommittee oversees. The lobbyists also are likely to be among the legislators' campaign contributors. These relationships can result in favorable treatment of special interest groups or reluctance of committee members to decrease funding levels for an agency.

Another concern about congressional budgeting is the lack of transparency. Although the annual budget is published and available to everyone online, the sheer size and complexity of the budget and budget tricks such as paying for wars off budget make it hard for all but the most seasoned pros to understand.

In recent years, the attention paid to lack of transparency has focused on earmarks, which are specific amounts of money set aside in budget bills at the request of a member. Earmarks include funds for a building, road, museum, park, research center, or another targeted benefit. These mean a great deal to the economy of localities and offer representatives and senators a chance to claim credit for their acquisition.

Earmarks have been prevalent since about 1970, and in recent years their existence has been a political issue. Senator John McCain attributed much of the deficit problem to earmarks during his 2008 campaign for the presidency, even though earmarks are only approximately 2 percent of the budget. Earmarks have been a convenient target for those who are concerned about the deficit, though they have not focused on war spending, which has an impact many times greater than earmarks.[68] One pundit said that trying to balance the budget by eliminating earmarks was like trying to solve global warming by banning bathroom night lights.[69] (For more on global warming, consult Focus on ... Environmental Policy.)

Because of the public outcry against earmarks, Congress has officially dispensed with them. Yet, in practice earmarks persist because of the reelection benefits of targeted appropriations. To get around their self-imposed ban, members of Congress press agencies to allocate existing available funds to specific local projects or attempt to get their pet projects directly into the president's budget. In the 112th Congress, the House Armed Services Committee voted to add an antimissile battery on the East Coast, even though the Pentagon said it is both expensive and not needed.

A final issue that critics raise is that, in the end, most members of Congress have no real role in the budget process. Party leaders negotiate with the White House to arrive at final dollar amounts on functional budget areas and budgetary totals, and the rest of Congress is often left with a take-it-or-leave-it budget package. They feel excluded from these crucial decisions and question whether citizens are represented if most members of Congress are shut out of these deliberations.

In general, the breakdown in the budget process reflects the heightened partisanship and increased extremism of Congress combined with the checks and balances from the days of our Founders that slow or halt action. As a consequence, commentators sometimes compare our budget processes to those of banana republics, where budgets are mostly fictional, produced behind the scenes, and not reflective of real spending and revenue.

MEMBERS ON THE JOB

To be successful in all their roles, representatives and senators must not only serve their constituents and get reelected but must also know how to work with their colleagues and how to maneuver within the intricate system of parliamentary rules, customs, and traditions that govern the House and Senate.

Congressional Norms

First among the many lessons every new member must learn are the customary ways of interacting with colleagues both on and off the floor of Congress.[70] These **informal norms** help keep the institution running smoothly by attempting to

When President Obama gave his State of the Union speech to Congress in 2009, he asserted that his health care proposal did not cover illegal aliens. Rep. Joe Wilson (R-S.C.) interrupted and yelled, "You lie!" (Obama's proposal in fact did not cover illegal aliens.) The outburst reflected the incivility that is sometimes evident in Congress.

minimize friction and allowing competition to occur within an atmosphere of civility. Although these norms are often not followed today, they are not entirely extinguished and thus are guides to how members learn and maintain their jobs.

In 1801, Thomas Jefferson wrote the foundational rules for in-chamber conduct in an effort to contain the inevitable conflict between Federalists and Antifederalists, abolitionists and slave owners. His notes laid the groundwork for Congress's system of informal norms.

Throughout much of the twentieth century, the most important norm was institutional loyalty, the expectation that members would respect other members and Congress itself, especially their own chamber. Personal criticism of one's colleagues was to be avoided, and mutual respect was fostered by such conventions as referring to colleagues by title, such as "the distinguished senator from New York," rather than by name. Clearly those norms have broken down, as members criticize their institution and each other. Language is often informal and not always polite. In 2012, former Rep. Allen West (R-Fla.) publicly claimed that more than seventy-five House Democrats are members of the Communist Party. His assertion was based on membership in the Congressional Progressive Caucus. This unfounded allegation illuminates how cross-party ill feeling is created and extended. And while this accusation won Representative West media publicity and undoubtedly contributed to his and his followers' sense that he is an important member of Congress, such name-calling contributes to the poor public perception of Congress as an institution.

In recent years, hostility among members of Congress seems as sharp as among those delegates to the First Congress. And the consequences of weakening informal norms are

serious. Lower legislative productivity results from incivility and hostility among members.[71]

Scholars differ on the origins of this decline in civility. Some say it dates back decades to the time Democrats had a lock on both chambers, leaving Republicans permanently aggrieved. Some say it began with Watergate—that Nixon's enemies list and Congress's impeachment hearings poisoned the atmosphere. Others tie it to the hearings on the nominations of Robert Bork and Clarence Thomas to the Supreme Court, which were notorious for their overheated exchanges and character bashing. Still others trace the decline to Newt Gingrich's strategy as a minority tactician in the 1980s prior to his ascension to the Speakership. At that time, he attacked not only the Democratic leaders but also Congress as an institution, calling it "sick." This was a severe departure from the institutional loyalty norm, but he and his Republican colleagues found it useful as a strategy to turn the public against the Democrats, who controlled Congress at that time. And, once the Republicans captured control of the House and Gingrich became their leader, he continued to encourage an aggressive, combative style on the floor of the House.

We can test these different explanations by looking at the numbers of highly partisan votes in each session of Congress. Figure 3 shows the proportion of all votes in which majorities of one party oppose the majority of the other, which is one way to define a partisan vote. The proportion of votes cast along party lines stayed about the same from the 1950s through the 1970s, thus giving little support to the idea that it was a strong Democratic majority or Watergate that caused the upturn in partisan voting. Then the proportion of these votes began to increase and did so through 2011. The exception was a dip right

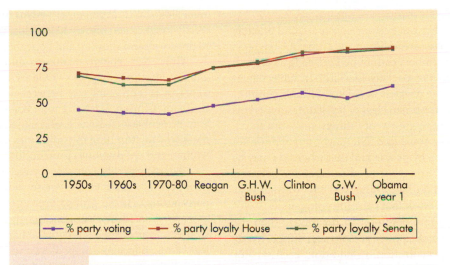

FIGURE 3: DURING PAST DECADES, MORE CONGRESSIONAL VOTES ARE PARTISAN Note: "% party voting" are the percentage of votes where a majority of one party opposes a majority of the other; "% party loyalty" are the proportions of each party who support their party when party voting occurs.

SOURCE: *CQ Weekly*, January 11, 2010, 125. CQ weekly by Congressional Quarterly, Inc. Copyright © 2010. Reproduced with permission of CQ-ROLL CALL, INC. via Copyright © Clearance Center.

after 9/11, but during the last four years of the Bush administration, the proportion returned to the Clinton-era levels.

Another way to think of partisanship in congressional voting is what proportion of each party goes along with its majority on party votes. That increase is also vivid. From the 1950s through the 1970s, between 63 and 70 percent of party members voted with their party. This proportion rose in the Reagan years, but the increase was dramatic in the Clinton and George W. Bush years. In recent years, on party majority votes, nearly 90 percent of all members in both the House and Senate have voted with their party. Thus, party unity voting has increased between 20 and 30 percentage points in the House and Senate after the peak years of Democratic dominance in the 1950s through 1970s.[72]

The voting data give support to the Bork, Thomas, and especially the Gingrich explanations of heightened partisanship. Partisanship increased somewhat in 1987, and in 1992 and 1993 at the time of the Bork hearing. But it increased dramatically in 1995, after Gingrich became majority leader. Along with the increase in party voting came continuing investigations of the Clinton administration by the Republican-controlled Congress. They spent more time in hearings on his holiday card list one year than a later Republican-controlled Congress did in investigating the failures of the government response to Hurricane Katrina. It was in this climate of extreme partisanship that Republicans launched the impeachment hearings against President Clinton, leaving many Democrats wanting revenge for what they felt was an outrageous diversion of time and energy from crucial business.

The strengthening of party leadership and unity voting has continued during the first Obama term, and centrist collaboration across party lines that continued, albeit somewhat diminished, into the early 1990s has not returned. There were

some bipartisan moments in the George W. Bush administration, when many Democrats supported his "No Child Left Behind" education reform and the introduction of prescription drug benefits to Medicare, but there have been few bipartisan efforts during the Obama administration. Republicans uniformly opposed Obama's legislative initiatives, even when those initiatives were based on ideas and legislation the Republicans had supported in the previous decade. This hyper-partisanship has created the appearance, and usually the reality, of gridlock. As one veteran congressional scholar has described Congress in recent years, it is "a situation in which producing the party program trumps any institutional concerns. There is no one tending to the institutional maintenance of Congress."[73]

In fact, in a provocative book entitled *It's Worse Than You Think*, two veteran congressional scholars, one liberal and one conservative, have labeled the current situation deeply dysfunctional, with Congress unable to rise to the nation's challenges. In addition to an extreme Republican majority, they point out that the existence of two highly partisan parties is not compatible with the system of checks and balances that allows minorities to stop action but that also envisioned a desire to compromise in the middle.

The only reassuring aspect of the intense degree of partisanship is that it is neither new nor destined to last. Congress passes through cycles of greater and lesser civility. Although members may be name-calling now and having the occasional shoving match, they are not beating up or shooting at one another as members were in the years leading up to the Civil War. And Jefferson's ears were hardly virgin; a frequent target of gossip and character attacks, he could dish it out with the best and used paid agents to spread slander about his Federalist opponents.

Specialization

By specializing, a member can become an expert, and possibly influential, in a few policy areas. Given the scope of Congress's legislative authority, members cannot be knowledgeable in all areas, so House members especially specialize in subject areas important to their home districts or related to their committees. The leader of one freshman class of legislators advised his new colleagues, "If you've got twenty things you want to do, see where everything is. You'll find that maybe ten of those are already being worked on by people and that while you may be supportive in that role, you don't need to carry the ball.... If you try to take the lead on everything, you'll be wasting your time and recreating the work that's already going on."[74]

Specialization is more common in the House than the Senate. The Senate's smaller membership can support only a smaller degree of specialization. In addition, each senator represents an entire state with interests in a much broader range of issues than those of a single House district. For those senators considering a run for the presidency, there is also a need to be well versed on a variety of issues.

Reciprocity

Tied to specialization is the norm of reciprocity. Reciprocity, or "logrolling," is summarized in the statement "You support my bill, and I'll support yours." The term *logrolling* dates to the 1780s, when an Ohio Federalist said that he did not really understand the terminology but he thought it meant "bargaining with each other for the little loaves and fishes of the State."[75]

Reciprocity helps each member get the votes needed to pass legislation favored in his or her district. The traditional way in which reciprocity worked was described by the late Sam Ervin, Democratic senator from tobacco-growing North Carolina: "I got to know Milt Young [then a senator from North Dakota] very well. And I told Milt, 'Milt, I would just like you to tell me how to vote about wheat and sugar beets and things like that, if you just help me out on tobacco.'"[76]

Reciprocity is another informal norm that is weakening. Open meetings, media scrutiny, stronger party leadership, and more partisan position taking have made it more difficult for members to "go along" on bills unpopular in their constituency or with the party leadership. However, it is still important for winning acceptance of earmark requests (don't oppose the new museum for my district and I won't oppose the road work in your district) and other legislation important to members' districts. Former senator Henry Jackson (D-Wash.) explained how he put together enough votes to pass a complex bill this way: "Maggie said he talked to Russell, and Tom promised this if I would back him on Ed's amendment, and Mike owes me one for last year's help on Pete's bill."[77]

Making Alliances

Any member who wants to get legislation passed, move into the party leadership, or run for higher office needs to develop a network of allies. Members of the more egalitarian House may be able to move faster on this than their colleagues in the Senate, but all newcomers have to be sensitive to the prerogatives of the senior members and committee chairs. Former senator

Alan Simpson (R-Wyo.) described his first two or three years as "really tough...you just try to look like you're smart. I just tried to dress well and show up and hope they'd think I was smart."[78]

Crossing ideological lines to find sponsors or votes for a bill sometimes happens. One of the most unusual alliances of recent years was between former senators Hillary Rodham Clinton (D-N.Y.) and the Christian conservative Sam Brownback (R-Kans.), who joined forces to promote new measures to stop human trafficking, especially the selling of women and children into prostitution.

An increasingly common venue for cooperation among members, especially in the House, is informal party or cross-party groups. **These groups are** organized by members who share partisan, ideological, issue, geographic, or identity interests so they can pool their strengths to highlight an issue and pass legislation. Informal groups have memberships ranging from a handful to more than a hundred members, and almost every member belongs to at least one. The House and Senate have 250 such organizations. Some have a narrow focus, such as those promoting bikes, ball bearings, boating, or wireless technology. Some are rooted in personal experience, such as the caucuses of Vietnam veterans and cancer survivors.[79] Others are to promote awareness of public health issues, such as the Congressional Caucus on Fetal Alcohol Spectrum Disorders. In the full fury of partisan battles and perceptions of congressional gridlock, some members even started the Fix Congress Now Caucus.

Among the most significant of the caucuses are those designed to leverage the collective power of women and minorities. These caucuses develop policy in key issue areas and serve national constituencies. The Caucus for Women's Issues, working across party, ideological, racial, and ethnic lines, has managed to recruit almost all women members and many male colleagues as well. With a Republican and a Democrat serving as cochairs, the caucus is regarded as one of the most bipartisan in Congress. Its legislative agenda includes supportive measures for women-owned businesses, pay equity, and women in the military.

Hispanics, East Asians, Native Americans, Asian Indians, and African Americans also have special interest caucuses. The Black Caucus was organized in 1970 by thirteen House members determined to raise the visibility of issues about which they cared. Since then, almost all members have been Democrats, as there have been few black Republican members of Congress. In the 112th Congress, there were two African American Republicans, Allen West of Florida and Tim Scott of South Carolina, but only Representative West joined the caucus. In 2012, the caucus focused on opposition to the proposed Republican budget. Said its chair, Emanuel Cleaver II (D-Mo.), "Our nation's communities of color have been hit hardest by the effects of the recession and the Republican Budget does little to address the priorities of these communities."[80]

Personal Friendships

In some cases, informal groups are the source of a House member's closest political allies. But with the exception of its Centrist Coalition, these groups are not as important in the much smaller Senate. There, personal friendships might count for more than committee or caucus membership. "Acquire a friend" by helping someone when he needs it, "and

Rep. Earl Blumenauer (D-Ore.) cochairs the House Bicycle Caucus, which promotes the bicycle as a green alternative to the car.

you'll never regret it," is the advice of former senator and 2012 candidate, Bob Kerrey (D-Nebr.) to those new to the Senate.[81]

Strong relationships of trust sometimes develop across party lines. John Kerry (D-Mass.) and John McCain (R-Ariz.), two decorated Vietnam War veterans, became friends while working together on veterans' issues. Sometimes the chair of a committee develops both a close working relationship and personal friendship with the ranking minority member, as happened, for example, between former senators Richard Lugar (R-Ind.) and Joe Biden (D-Del.) of Foreign Relations, before Biden became vice president. In both houses, much of the work gets hammered out in personal conversations and exchanges away from official venues.

Political Action Committees

The most influential members of Congress have their own PACs for raising campaign funds to disperse to colleagues. When Hillary Rodham Clinton was a junior senator, she was able to use her celebrity and connections to raise millions of dollars for her PAC, Friends of Hillary. She used the funds to support the reelection campaigns of colleagues, building a network of supporters. She could then cash in these favors when looking for a committee chair or a leadership position and, later, during her

run for the presidency. Nancy Pelosi was able to beat out rivals for the minority leader position in 2001 largely because of her ability to raise campaign donations for colleagues. By the time she announced that she wanted the position, dozens of fellow House members were in her political debt. Speaker of the House John Boehner (R-Ohio) won his position based, in part, on his superior fundraising skills. Boehner's leadership PAC, called Freedom Project, raised $3.1 million for the 2010 electoral cycle. Partly as a result, Republicans gained control of the House.

Using the Media

Forty years ago, the workday routine in both House and Senate for resolving most issues involved bargaining with other members, lobbyists, and White House aides. Working privately, one on one in small groups, or in committees, members and staff discussed and debated issues, exchanged information, and planned strategies. Even though many issues are still resolved through these private channels, much has changed in the way Congress operates since that time.

The way Congress operates reflects its own rules for opening up its processes, such as opening committee hearings to the public and lobbyists, and the modern world of social media and 24-hour cable news networks. In that world, for members to further their goals, it is often important to reach beyond colleagues and appeal directly to the larger public.[82] **Going public** means taking an issue debate to the public through both the "old" media, as Congress does when it televises floor debates and important hearings, and new media. The most media-oriented members of Congress are experts in providing short and interesting comments for the nightly network news, writing articles for major newspapers, appearing on talk shows and as commentators on news programs, using their websites and Facebook pages to publicize their priorities and opinions, posting speeches on YouTube, maintaining their own blogs, and sending a steady stream of tweets. House minority leader John Boehner (R-Ohio) reported more than 100,000 Facebook friends in 2010, and John McCain (R-Ariz.) led the Senate and placed second only to Oprah Winfrey in number of Twitter followers.[83]

Of course, television remains important in publicizing activities of members. Cable Satellite Public Affairs Network, or C-SPAN, which was created and funded by cable companies as a public service, televises the proceedings of the House and Senate and follows candidates on the campaign trail. C-SPAN reaches 100 million households and has about 40 million regular viewers. Although viewership is small compared with that of commercial networks, the C-SPAN audience has a higher educational level and is better informed and more interested in both local and national government than the general public. Viewers are equally divided among liberals and conservatives, and nine out of ten viewers voted in the 2008 election.[84]

The congressional leadership goes public, too. Leaders of both parties regularly call producers of television talk shows to suggest guests. They meet with the press and use social media. Before important congressional votes on key issues, the leadership plans letters to the editors of important newspapers and floor speeches designed for maximum television coverage.

However, openness can hinder the work of the institution. Before committee deliberations were open to the public and to lobbyists, members could put together compromises on bills that satisfied no one completely but had a chance of winning support. Now, it is difficult to make compromises in the glare of the public eye and with the knowledge that your partisan supporters will be critical of these compromises. This has been especially true of Republicans, with Tea Party adherents ready to sweep out members of Congress who sometimes vote with Democrats. It is also true of members of both parties who worry about losing support of powerful interest groups that fund their campaigns.

Balancing the Work

Multiple committee assignments, in combination with party caucus work, fundraising, and visits to the district, mean that members have impossible schedules. At times, committees cannot obtain quorums because members are tied up with other obligations. It is the norm for members to attend meetings with legislative staff in tow to take notes and to consult with during hearings. If they cannot attend or have to leave for floor business or another meeting, a staffer takes notes and briefs the member later.

But, to the extent that legislators do not directly participate in the work of legislating, the reputation of Congress can be affected negatively. Whenever it comes out, as it did in the case with the health insurance reform law, that many members have not read the bills on which they are voting, public trust in the institution can erode. Former Senate majority leader Tom Daschle (D-S.D.) discussed how common this is:

> Sometimes you are dialing for dollars, you get the call, you've got to go over to vote, you've got fifteen minutes. You don't have a clue what's on the floor, your staff is whispering in your ears, you're running onto the floor, then you check with your leader—you double check—but, just to make triple sure, there is a little sheet of paper on the clerk's table: The leader recommends any aye vote, or a no vote. So, you've got all these checks just to make sure you don't screw up, but even then you screw up sometimes. But, if you're ever pressed, "Why did you vote that way?"—you just walk out thinking, Oh, my God, I hope nobody asks, because I don't have a clue.[85]

Use of Staff

Compared to members of early Congresses, members today employ many staff members. Staffers do most of the background work on the complex foreign and domestic issues that cross the members' desks every day. The Senate Appropriations Committee alone has 150 staff members, each of whom specializes in a specific aspect of the budget. In the Senate, where staff are often better versed on an issue than the member, cultivating colleagues' chief aides may be essential to winning support for legislation. "You can get the senator on your side, and that works nine times out of ten, but if you don't have the staffer on your side too, it is very, very difficult."[86]

Formal Standards of Conduct

In addition to the informal norms of Congress, members are expected to conform to the ethical standards of conduct they have set for themselves. The Constitution gives each chamber

---

CourseReader ASSIGNMENT

Log in to www.cengagebrain.com and open Course-Reader to access the full reading "For New Congress, Data Shows Why Polarization Abounds" by John Harwood.

Congress has changed over time across many types of demographic indicators, such as age, proportion of members with business background, sex, and race. According to commentators, one consequence of these changes is increased polarization. The following three questions will help you think further about the implications of increased diversity in Congress.

1. At the beginning of the chapter, the concepts of "acting for" and "standing for" representation were raised. Based on this article, what links do you see between these two types of representation?
2. With increased diversity, Congress begins the process of "looking like America." What are the benefits of this process? Are there any negatives?
3. In what concrete ways can increased diversity be linked to polarization in Congress? Is this outcome worth the cost?

---

the power to establish rules, pass judgment on conduct, and, by a two-thirds vote, expel a member. **Art. I, Sec. 5** Each chamber has a select committee to hear ethics complaints; it is the only committee where membership is equally split between the parties rather than in proportion to the number of seats they hold. Unethical behavior includes such action as using one's position for personal enrichment, using it for financial gain of a family member or campaign contributor, misusing campaign funds, violating codes of conduct toward other members, or being found guilty of criminal conduct.

Corruption was one of the issues voters cited as extremely important in how they voted in the 2006 elections, and the Democrats promised to make ethical reform an issue if they won control of either or both houses. In 2007, therefore, legislation authorized a new Office of Congressional Ethics and strengthened ethics standards. The main goal of the reform was to reduce the influence of lobbyists by restricting their ability to make gifts to members and do favors for them.[87]

Despite these actions, reforms have not changed the ways members and lobbyists interact. Private financing of congressional campaigns gives lobbyists an easy route to provide money to members. Money previously spent by lobbyists on members' meals and gifts now goes to the members' campaign committees.

Relationships between members and their family who are lobbyists or campaign employees are another murky area. Many members of the House and Senate, including the Senate majority leader Reid, have close relatives who lobby Congress. And some members employ family with campaign funds or use their positions in other ways to financially benefit relatives. As evidence of how little has changed, nineteen House members and three senators were believed to be under investigation during 2009–2010.[88]

Congress also benefits by the lower standards it applies to itself. Unlike the case for the rest of us, until recently, it has not been against the law for members of Congress to engage in insider investment trading or to make financial investments based on privileged knowledge of particular companies' records and plans. Members are not prohibited from owning shares in companies that are regulated by their committees. After these facts were revealed on a 2012 television news show, both Republican and Democratic members rushed to introduce legislation to prohibit members from doing market trading based on nonpublic information obtained during congressional work. The STOCK act was quickly passed. In this case, openness served the public interest, as the media spotlight motivated members to give priority to restoring public trust over their own financial interests.

CONGRESS AND THE PUBLIC

One of the perplexing things about Congress for the public is the messiness, length, and malleability of the legislative process. Not only is the process of crafting laws long and complex, but it also provides opportunities for legislators and interest groups to secure concessions from legislative sponsors of bills and, therefore, water down their intent. When, as has been especially true in recent years, partisan bickering escalates, with Democrats picking a proposal apart simply because a Republican introduced it or vice versa, and both parties introducing bills with "poison pills" (provisions that are guaranteed to make the other party look bad), some observers wonder if the legislative process is consistent with good and effective governance. A good recent example is the Republican attempt

to add a provision to strip funding from the public health and prevention fund of the 2010 health care reform law to a bill that will prevent student loan interest rates from doubling.

Media attention is valuable because we prize open government in a democracy. Yet media coverage sensationalizes insignificant details to improve ratings. As one observer commented, "A member's every twitch is blared to the world, thanks to C-SPAN, open meetings laws, financial-disclosure reports, and every misstep is logged in a database for the use of some future office seeker."[89] Add to that YouTube, Facebook, Twitter, other social network sites, and blogs that report what members had for lunch and if they were wearing a flag pin on their clothing, and it is no wonder that the public often does not think much of Congress or its members.

Media, especially cable news and talk radio, also seem to scorn nonpartisan or bipartisan efforts at problem solving and instead prize bold and even outrageous statements and actions. As news becomes purely entertainment, much more coverage is given to name-calling than to policy proposals.

Coverage of Congress rarely discusses the fact that the design of the legislature and the checks and balances in the system were intended to slow the process to make room for careful reflection of the nation's problems. "Bickering" can reflect true divisions in the country. The public *is* divided on most issues. These divisions require deliberation and compromise, which takes time. Members of the public who want Congress to act quickly no doubt want it to act in ways consistent with their own views, views that other Americans might find abhorrent.

Indeed, of the three branches of government, the public has been least supportive of Congress, probably because partisan wrangling is at its most obvious in this branch. But the public's attitudes about Congress are also conflicted (see Figure 4). In recent decades people's approval of their

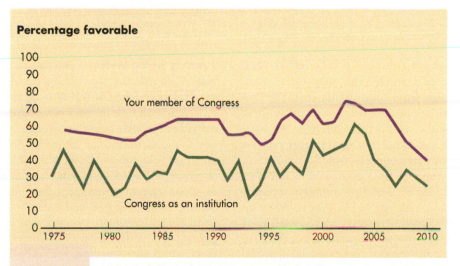

FIGURE 4: PUBLIC OPINION TOWARD CONGRESS People were asked whether they approve of the way Congress is handling its job and whether they approve of the way the representative from their congressional district is handling his or her job. People consistently voice more approval of their member than of Congress itself. In 2012, levels of support ranged from 9-15 percent through September.

SOURCE: Combined responses from similar surveys by the Gallup Organization and the Harris Survey. Roger H. Davidson, Walter J. Oleszek, and Frances E. Lee, *Congress and Its Members,* 11th ed. (Washington, D.C.: CQ Press, 2008), 490.

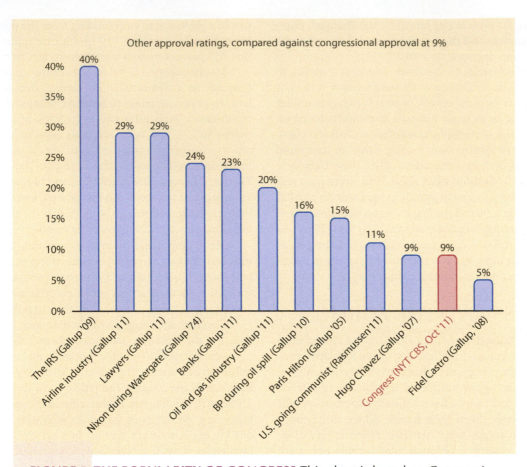

Other approval ratings, compared against congressional approval at 9%

- The IRS (Gallup '09) — 40%
- Airline industry (Gallup '11) — 29%
- Lawyers (Gallup '11) — 29%
- Nixon during Watergate (Gallup '74) — 24%
- Banks (Gallup '11) — 23%
- Oil and gas industry (Gallup '11) — 20%
- BP during oil spill (Gallup '10) — 16%
- Paris Hilton (Gallup '05) — 15%
- U.S. going communist (Rasmussen '11) — 11%
- Hugo Chavez (Gallup '07) — 9%
- Congress (NYT CBS, Oct '11) — 9%
- Fidel Castro (Gallup, '08) — 5%

FIGURE 5: THE POPULARITY OF CONGRESS This chart is based on Congress' approval ratings of October 2011 as measured by *The New York Times* and compares it to approval ratings of other institutions and individuals at different points in time as noted. The other ratings were measured by Gallup polls. The Gallup ratings of Congress are quite consistent with the *New York Times* poll as shown in Figure 4.
SOURCE: Ezra Klein, "14 Reasons Why This is the Worst Congress Ever," *The Washington Post*, July 13, 2012, http://www.washingtonpost.com/blogs/ezra-klein/wp/2012/07/13/13-reasons-why-this-is-the-worst-congress-ever/.

own representative was 20 or more points higher than approval for Congress as a whole. This may be, in part, because members benefit from local media coverage that is overwhelmingly positive, in part because many of these stories are prepared by the members themselves. But local press stories on Congress as a whole are also far more positive than those written by the national press corps.[90]

Even with public support for Congress at a low ebb, however, incumbents' odds of reelection are high, typically above 80 percent. Occasionally the public gets so down on Congress that it affects constituents' attitudes toward their own representatives. It was true, for example, before the 2010 midterms, when some polls showed congressional approval ratings below 20 percent; nevertheless, 86 percent of incumbents were reelected. Almost all of the fifty-four House and three Senate incumbents who lost their seats were Democrats, reflecting public displeasure with the Democratic majority.

During 2012, public support for Congress was at a low ebb. Early in the year, most voters said that most lawmakers didn't deserve to be reelected. In the pre-election period through September, the approval rating of Congress ranged from

9 percent to just under 15 percent, the lowest levels in many years.[91] Yet, reflecting the ongoing paradox, 53 percent of registered voters said their own House member deserves reelection.

Despite all this, the idea of Congress as a constitutionally mandated "people's house" is esteemed by the public. It is the way Congress works that the public dislikes. This is a fault of both the institution and its members. Our system of separation of powers and checks and balances was designed for compromise and centrist government, but our current parties have become more polarized and extreme. They behave like the parties in parliamentary systems, which are cohesive and disciplined. But parliamentary systems produce unified government, which allows majorities to act even in the face of sharp and deep disagreements. Our system often features divided government. The use of anti-majoritarian rules (such as the Senate's filibuster and holds), combined with the growth of hyper-partisanship and the breakdown of the congressional norms that had facilitated the policy process, has led to gridlock.[92] Our current system of campaign finance, which permits lobbyists to fund candidates' campaigns, is another factor that prevents congressional action and leads to public dissatisfaction.

SUMMARY

- The extent to which Congress is representative depends on what we mean by the term. This chapter highlights two types of representation, "acting for" and "standing for" representation, and explains the connection between the two.
- Every ten years, in a process called **reapportionment,** the 435 House seats are allocated among the states based on the latest U.S. census. In this process, states that have lost population can lose seats while states that have gained population can gain seats in the House.
- Incumbents who run for reelection have many advantages over their challengers. These include mailing privileges, performance of casework, media and technology opportunities, fundraising, and pork-barrel funding.
- The Constitution calls for the members of the House to select a **Speaker of the House** and for the vice president to serve as president of the Senate. But it does not specify any further internal organization. Additional positions in both chambers, such as majority and minority leaders in the Senate, and all other positions have evolved over time with parties.
- The legislative work of Congress is done in committees. Many types of committees are discussed in this chapter, including standing committees, subcommittees, select and special committees, joint committees, and conference committees, along with their specific roles in the process.
- The standard path through which a bill becomes a law includes bill introduction and referral, subcommittee hearings and markup, full committee hearing and markup, calendar and rule assignment by leadership, floor debate, vote, resolution of differences in House and Senate versions, president's signature or veto, and vote to override veto when applicable. Filibusters and holds can deter the process from moving forward, and both of these have become more frequent in this era of hyper-partisanship.
- Informal norms of Congress help structure the processes through which members of Congress do their work. Among these are civility toward fellow members, respect for the institution of Congress, reciprocity, and specialization. Reciprocity helps members get their agenda done, and specialization allows a member to become an expert. There has been a breakdown in respect for other members and for the institution itself, which in the past facilitated congressional effectiveness.
- Of the three branches of government, the public has been least supportive of Congress. But the public's attitudes about Congress are also conflicted. Citizens' approval of their own representative is usually much higher than approval for Congress as a whole. Additionally, the public dislikes the way Congress works, including the contemporary gridlock and the current system of campaign funding, both of which create a negative impression and perhaps reflect the reality of congressional accountability. Still, the idea of Congress as a constitutionally mandated "people's house" is esteemed by the public.

DISCUSSION QUESTIONS

1. What are the definitions of "acting for" and "standing for" representation, and how are these two concepts linked?
2. What is reapportionment, how often is it performed, and what are its consequences?
3. What advantages do incumbent members of Congress have in relationship to reelection bids?
4. What are the main leadership positions in the modern Congress, and how do they differ in the House and the Senate?
5. What are the main types of committees in Congress, and what roles do they play?
6. How does a bill generally become a law, and what is different for budget bills compared to policy bills? Define and illustrate the use of filibusters and holds.
7. What are congressional norms, and how do they facilitate congressional work? How has the breakdown of norms become an impediment to congressional functioning?
8. How does the public generally view Congress, and how does this view differ from citizens' evaluations of their own members of Congress? What are some reasons for the discrepancy?

10 The Presidency

President Obama is not a typical glad-handing, back-slapping politician. More cerebral and detached, his personality has enabled him to form effective policies but has hindered him in relating to average people.

AP Images/Susan Walsh, File

LEARNING OBJECTIVES

1. Name the requirements for becoming president, both formal and informal.
2. List the ways in which a president may be removed from office. Understand why it is so difficult to impeach a president.
3. Define the powers of the president.
4. Evaluate the power of the president within the constitutional context of checks and balances and separation of powers.
5. Describe the principal offices of a presidential administration, explaining their functions and evaluating their contributions.
6. Assess why the White House Office has become so important and influential,

using the first lady and the vice president as examples.
7. Assess the balance of legislative and executive powers. Build hypotheses about congressional versus presidential leadership.
8. Analyze the standards by which the public and the media have judged modern presidents to be effective or ineffective leaders.
9. Summarize legislative-executive relations from the presidency of Franklin D. Roosevelt to the present.
10. Conclude whether—and when—the president is an authoritative decision maker, an influential negotiator, or a persuasive speaker.

TALKING POINTS

In 1967, Lyndon Johnson faced every president's dilemma, the hard truth that governing is all about making choices. Johnson was a legendary legislator who had become one of the most ambitious—some say overreaching—presidents of the twentieth century. He was the principal backer of, and legislative strategist for, much of our social safety net, including Medicare and Medicaid and greater income support for the poor, programs collectively known as the Great Society. Johnson also worked with Congress to enact the major civil rights legislation of the modern era, all while backing the expansion of American military power and the war in Vietnam.

Most presidents accede to the limitations of public support and of presidential power. They make hard choices, set priorities, and shorten their political agendas. Johnson refused to do so. "I was determined," he said, "to be a leader of war *and* a leader of peace. I refused to let my critics push me into choosing one or the other."[1] Yet he knew that the war in Vietnam could cost him everything he had accomplished domestically. As he expressed it, the war could tear away "all my programs . . . all my dreams. . . ."[2]

As Johnson feared, his failures as a commander in chief are widely viewed as overshadowing his domestic successes. Historians acknowledge that Johnson

"did more for racial justice than any president since Abraham Lincoln. He built more social protections than anyone since Franklin Roosevelt. He was probably the greatest legislative politician in American history." But these same scholars maintain that Johnson is "largely responsible for one of the greatest disasters in American history"—the Vietnam War, which he inherited and sharply escalated.[3]

Voters demand much from presidents. They expect presidents to be leaders. As the head of state and head of government, presidents are supposed to keep their campaign promises, protect the interests of the nation, provide for their supporters and win over their opponents, and correct market failures domestically and globally. Many presidents, at least early in their terms, think they can do all these things. But most successful presidents have been skilled decision makers who respected the limits of public support and the constraints of the constitutional system of checks and balances, realizing they could not do everything.

How does—how will—this gap between expectations and performance affect the political fortunes of presidents in our time? How will it affect the lives of ordinary people in this country? These are the questions you need to answer as you study the president and the presidency.

At its inception in a fledgling country that had few international ties and virtually no standing army, the presidency was not a very powerful office. The first presidents were drawn from among the Founders, and a few of them, especially Washington and Jefferson, served with some reluctance. Jefferson called the office a "splendid misery," and one of his successors, John Quincy Adams (1825–1829), said, "No man who ever held the office would congratulate another on attaining it." Throughout the nineteenth century, except during the Civil War, the real power at the national level resided in Congress, so much so that Woodrow Wilson, who was a political scientist before becoming president, characterized our national government as a "congressional government."[4]

During the twentieth century, however, presidents assumed a more powerful and influential role in the national government. They began to take greater initiative and exercise more authority in decision making and policy making, and their influence was perceived by elites in Washington and by people throughout the nation. The social and economic programs of the New Deal, the Fair Deal, the New Frontier, and the Great Society; the military, defense, and homeland security actions taken throughout World War II, the Cold War, the Vietnam War, the Gulf War, the War on Terror, and countless other confrontations; the contests between the legislative and the executive branches, whether those branches were led by the same or different parties—these were only some of the instances in which the president's responsibilities and powers were made obvious to the Washington community and to the country as a whole.

As power has been revealed, however, it has also come to be more closely scrutinized. Issue networks and interest groups, the media, other officeholders and decision makers, and other nations all watch presidents and their administrations closely, assessing the consequences of their actions for their own interests and priorities, as well as for the balance of power among the branches of the national government; among local, state, and national governments; and, in a globalizing world, among nations. There have been no continuous increases or decreases in the chief executive's power throughout the modern presidency. Instead, all presidents have had to forge alliances, mediate conflicts, and negotiate decisions with other actors throughout the nation and the

American Diversity

Presidential Candidates: The Pool Deepens, but . . .

The informal requirements for the presidential office are very well established. Every president has been male. All (but one) have been white. All (but one) have been married. All (but one) have self-identified as Protestant. In more recent elections, presidential candidates have also had to prove their athleticism, their virility, and their toughness—to present themselves as heroically masculine. In the United States, these traits are deemed requisite to success as a president because the office itself is strongly associated with what have been historically masculine leadership practices of command.[7]

When presidential candidates have not conformed to these standards, they have paid a heavy price. In 1972, Rep. Shirley Chisholm (D-N.Y.), the first black woman to seek a major party nomination for president, encountered both racism and sexism throughout her campaign. One reinforced the other, though she thought she encountered more discrimination as a woman than as an African American. The 2008 Democratic primaries forced consideration of whether the public would require the president to be white and to be male. Poll respondents thought Hillary Clinton had more experience and was more prepared to be commander in chief than Barack Obama, but she was ultimately unable to convince enough voters that she could be both feminine and tough. Referring to the 18 million votes she received in primary elections, Clinton remarked in her concession speech to her supporters, "Although we weren't able to shatter that highest, hardest glass ceiling this time, thanks to you, it's got about 18 million cracks in it."[8]

When Obama won the presidency, many throughout the nation congratulated themselves on entering a post-racial era. Yet President Obama was repeatedly targeted. He endured racial slurs and caricatures; nativist criticisms; and religious stereotyping.

Republican candidates have also encountered discrimination. In 2008 and 2012, Mitt Romney dealt with religious bigotry. A bishop in the Church of Jesus Christ of Latter-Day Saints (familiarly referred to as the Mormons), a church whose claim to be Christian is questioned by a number of evangelicals, Mitt Romney found that his faith and religion were major campaign issues. Though Romney did not win the 2012 election, he won support throughout the nation, suggesting that this particular religious barrier to the Oval Office had been removed.

world. Their successes and failures, from one presidency to the next, reveal the strengths and weaknesses of their office.

This chapter explores those strengths and weaknesses. We begin by defining the central features of the Office of the President. Then, we examine the powers formally granted to the president in the Constitution, and the powers that are only implied in the Constitution but which have been claimed and exercised by the presidents. This leads us to examine the organization of the presidency, looking at the role of staff and of presidential appointees. Finally, we discuss the ebb and flow of presidential power.

THE OFFICE OF THE PRESIDENT

The Constitution specifies only three conditions to be eligible for the presidency: the person must be a "natural-born citizen," at least thirty-five years old, who has resided in the United States for at least fourteen years before taking office. **Art. II, Sec. 1**

Historically, presidents have typically been white males with roots in small towns; Protestants of English, German, or Scandinavian ancestry; residents of populous states; and "good family men." In recent decades, this profile has broadened considerably as society has become more inclusive, the electorate more diverse, and social norms more tolerant of divorce. Still, sexual, racial, and religious barriers remain. (See the box "Presidential Candidates: The Pool Deepens, but ….")

Most modern presidents have been well-to-do and college educated, but the public expects presidents to understand their everyday experiences. So even though nine of the ten presidential nominees from the major parties since 1988 have had a degree from Harvard or Yale, they have deliberately presented themselves as similar to average Americans,[5] as self-made individuals with empathy for the average citizen. They claim that their self-reliance and toughness will make them effective national leaders.[6] As Republican Mitt Romney proclaimed in the 2012 elections, "I will not apologize for my success."

Yale-educated George W. Bush, the heir to significant wealth, presented himself as a down-to-earth Texan, complete with cowboy boots. Barack Obama was not born into an elite family, but his degrees were from Columbia and Harvard Law School. He presented himself as a community organizer committed to grassroots change. Like other presidential candidates, then, Obama presented himself as both exceptional and as accessible, a balance that was particularly significant for an African American man seeking the nation's highest elective office.

Experience

History suggests there is no clear correlation between experience in government and being effective as a president. Abraham Lincoln had little experience compared to his predecessor James Buchanan or his successor Andrew Johnson, but he was an incomparably greater president. Washington insiders such as Harry Truman and George H. W. Bush only

rarely saw their policy agendas enacted and implemented. As former White House chief of staff and cabinet veteran James A. Baker concluded, "There's no such thing as presidential experience outside of the office itself."[9] The fact that most presidents are more successful in their first than in their second term suggests that experience does not go hand in hand with achievement.

Pay and Perks

The Constitution authorizes Congress to award the president "a Compensation," which can be neither increased nor decreased during a president's term of office. This was $25,000 a year for our first seventeen presidents; then it jumped in increments to $200,000, where it stayed for many years. It did not reach $400,000 until 2001. In real dollars, President Obama makes less than George Washington, despite the vast increase in responsibilities and scope of the job.

In addition, there are **substantial** fringe benefits. Most are obvious—the White House, the rural Camp David retreat, the best health care, and *Air Force One*. After leaving office, the president is entitled to a taxable lifetime pension equal to the annual pay of a cabinet secretary ($199,700 in 2012). Former presidents are also given money for travel; an office and staff; Secret Service protection, though this is limited to ten years for presidents George W. Bush onward; health care; and a state funeral with full military honors.

Tenure and Succession

Presidents serve four-year terms. The **Twenty-second Amendment** limits a president to two terms (or ten years if they complete the term of an incumbent who dies or resigns). Four presidents died in office from illness (Harrison, Taylor, Harding, and Franklin Roosevelt), and four were assassinated (Garfield, McKinley, Lincoln, and Kennedy). In each instance, when a president has left office, the vice president has completed the term of office.

The **Succession Act** and the **Twenty-fifth Amendment** ensure that there is a smooth transition of power if a president is unable to serve. The Succession Act, passed in 1947, establishes the order of succession among legislative leaders and cabinet secretaries if the president and vice president are both unable to hold office. The immediate successor is the Speaker of the House, then the president pro tempore of the Senate, and then the cabinet secretaries in the order in which their departments were established. Any foreign-born individual is, as noted above, ineligible. Although she was fourth in the presidential line of succession, Clinton's secretary of state, Madeline Albright, could not have served as president because she was born in Czechoslovakia.

The Twenty-fifth Amendment, ratified in 1967, has two crucial provisions. One provides for the presidential selection and congressional approval (by majorities in both houses) of a vice president in the event that the elected vice president leaves office. This procedure has been used twice, during and after the Nixon presidency. When Nixon's vice president,

Spiro Agnew, pleaded no contest to bribery and tax evasion charges, Nixon selected and won legislative approval for Gerald R. Ford (then the House minority leader) to be the new vice president. When Nixon resigned and Vice President Ford became president, Ford selected and won legislative approval for Nelson Rockefeller (the wealthy philanthropist and former governor of New York) to be vice president.

The second crucial provision of the amendment provides a procedure to determine whether a president is mentally or physically incapable of exercising power. If so, the vice president serves as the "acting president" until the president notifies Congress in writing of recovery. If the vice president and cabinet dispute this claim, they also must notify Congress in writing. Then, Congress must decide whether the president can reclaim the office. Though these provisions have made for dramatic Hollywood scripts—including the confrontations in *Air Force One,* the plot themes in *24,* and the elaborate cover-up in *Dave*—no modern vice president or cabinet has had to make this judgment.[10] Still, when Reagan and George W. Bush underwent surgery, they sent letters to their respective vice presidents, authorizing them to act as president while they were unconscious.

Impeachment

Presidents can be removed from office by impeachment and conviction. The House has the power of **impeachment**, which is the authority to bring formal charges against a president (similar to an indictment in criminal proceedings) for "Treason, Bribery, or other high Crimes and Misdemeanors." **Art. II, Sec. 4** In an impeachment inquiry, the House votes the articles of impeachment—the charges—and the Senate conducts the trial, with the chief justice of the Supreme Court presiding. Conviction requires a two-thirds vote of members present in

the Senate and results in removal from the presidency. As a limit on the power of the parties, the Founders made it very difficult for Congress to remove a president.

Only three presidents have been targets of full impeachment proceedings.[11] Andrew Johnson, who came to office after Lincoln's assassination, was a southerner who was unpopular in his own party; he was impeached following a dispute over Reconstruction policies in the post–Civil War South. By a single-vote margin, the Senate failed to convict. A century later, the House Judiciary Committee voted to impeach Richard Nixon on obstruction of justice and other charges stemming from the Watergate break-in and cover-up. Nixon resigned to avoid impeachment. He was subsequently granted a full (and pre-emptive) pardon by his successor, President Gerald Ford. In 1998, the House voted two articles of impeachment against President Clinton—one for perjury and one for obstruction of justice—both stemming from statements he made about his sexual relationship with a White House intern. The Senate found the president not guilty of perjury with a vote of 55–45 and not guilty of obstruction of justice with a 50–50 vote.

Thinking about Democracy

When should the House of Representatives impeach a president? When should the Senate convict a president? (Be careful to give your definition of "high Crimes and Misdemeanors.") Should it be easier for Congress to remove a president from office? Why or why not? How do these procedures safeguard democracy?

As revelations of the Watergate scandal emerged, President Richard Nixon was defiant, but ultimately he resigned.

PRESIDENTIAL POWERS

A president's powers are rooted in the Constitution. Enumerated powers, such as the veto, are described in relative detail in the Constitution. Implied powers are extrapolated from powers that are more specifically assigned. For example, because presidents are granted executive power, they have been allowed to issue executive orders. Especially compared to Congress, the president's powers are more often implied than enumerated. **Art. II, Sec. 2 & 3** As will be seen, the constitutional system of checks and balances often constrains presidents in exercising power, but the Constitution does allow a president to take some **unilateral actions**.

Head of State

A **head of state** is the official representative of a country and its people. He or she symbolizes the identity and the unity of the nation. In contrast, a **head of government** is the leader of a political party with a partisan agenda. In most Western democracies, the state and government are separate entities headed by different people. The state is the society, the history, the traditions, and the people of the nation. The head of state, then, is typically expected to be above partisan politics. The government, in contrast, consists of elected and appointed officials advancing partisan interests. In Great Britain, the head of state is the queen, a hereditary office, while the head of government is the prime minister, an elected office. In the United States, however, the president is both head of state and head of government.

As the head of state, the president performs ceremonial and symbolic functions such as throwing out the first baseball of the season, receiving foreign dignitaries, and lighting the nation's holiday tree. In these (and other) instances, the president expresses and reinforces national priorities, from sports to foreign policy to religion.

One of the most important—and familiar—acts performed by the president as head of state is the annual delivery of the State of the Union address. The Constitution requires the president to make this report, but it does not stipulate a particular format. **Art. II, Sec. 3** For over a hundred years, presidents submitted their statement in writing, not wanting to mimic the monarchical speeches that open parliamentary sessions. When Woodrow Wilson delivered his report in person, one senator labeled the action a "cheap and tawdry imitation of English royalty."[12]

Today, the public expects these addresses to be delivered publicly; they are given before a joint session of Congress and are nationally televised. Intensely negotiated with members of the administration and with legislators, the addresses set out a policy agenda for the coming year. The State of the Union Address mixes reassurance and aspiration, real priorities and hoped-for initiatives.

Even when presidents are mired in political controversy—Nixon during the Watergate investigation or Clinton delivering the 1998 State of the Union address just weeks after the revelation of personal misconduct—congressional

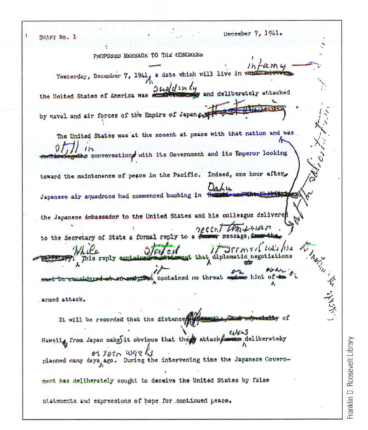

President Franklin Roosevelt edited his speech to Congress about the Japanese attack on Pearl Harbor. The word *infamy*, which made memorable the phrase "a date which will live in infamy," was one of his corrections.

leaders remind the membership to show respect for the presidential office. A break with this tradition occurred in 2010, when a U.S. representative, a white male Republican from the South, shouted, "You lie!" in the middle of President Obama's address. His words led to a national debate about racism and partisanship in legislative-executive relations.

Presidents have also acted as heads of state when providing leadership after tragedy. Some of the most famous presidential statements have come from speeches delivered on these occasions. There was Franklin Roosevelt's description of the Pearl Harbor attacks as "a day that will live in infamy" and Ronald Reagan's eulogizing of the *Challenger* crew as having "'slipped the surly bonds of earth' to 'touch the face of God.'"[13] In 2001, George W. Bush, leading the memorial service at Washington's National Cathedral for the victims of the September 11 attack, announced, "This conflict was begun on the timing and terms of others; it will end in a way and at an hour of our choosing."

The president gains a tremendous advantage by fusing and blurring the roles of head of state and head of government. Addressing the public from the Oval Office, the president implicitly claims to represent the entire nation, not a single political party. Members of Congress, the press, or the public may attack the president freely as a partisan head of government. However, they usually show more—some say too much—deference when the president is acting as a head of state.

BEHIND THE SCENES

If They Can't Get Back from the Moon . . .

When a tragedy strikes, the president is expected to be the "mourner in chief." In the days before American astronauts were sent to the moon in 1969, government officials feared that a malfunction might leave the astronauts stranded on the moon, unable to return to earth. According to documents that surfaced at the National Archives years later, the Nixon administration had prepared for this contingency. A speechwriter penned the following speech for President Nixon in the event the astronauts were still alive but had no hope of returning:

> Fate has ordained that the men who went to the moon to explore in peace will stay on the moon to rest in peace.
>
> These brave men . . . know that there is no hope for their recovery. But they also know that there is hope for mankind in their sacrifice.
>
> These . . . men are laying down their lives in mankind's most noble goal: the search for truth and understanding.
>
> In ancient days, men looked at stars and saw their heroes in the constellations. In modern times, we do much the same, but our heroes are epic men of flesh and blood.
>
> Others will follow, and surely find their way home. Man's search will not be denied. But these men were the first, and they will remain the foremost in our hearts.

Before giving the speech, the president would contact the "widows-to-be." After giving the speech, he would instruct NASA to cut off all further communications with the astronauts to cut short the public agony over their deaths. Then a clergyman would follow the protocol used for a burial at sea and conclude with "The Lord's Prayer."

The president didn't have to implement these plans, as the astronauts, after twenty-one hours on the moon, returned home safely.

SOURCE: "Nixon Had Words Ready for Moon Disaster," *Lincoln Journal Star*, July 10, 1999.

Chief Executive

The president is typically referred to as the **chief executive**, meaning that the president is at the top of all the hierarchies in the executive branch. Yet the Constitution provides few details about the president's executive powers. It stipulates only that the "executive power shall be vested in a president," and charges the president to "take care that the laws be faithfully executed." Art. II **Sec. 1 & 3** This is in keeping with assertions in the *Federalist Papers* that the president's responsibilities, with respect to lawmaking, would be "mere execution" and "executive details."[14]

The executive powers of the president have been formally and informally reinforced through the years. For example, the Constitution stipulates that the president will nominate and the Senate will confirm officers in the executive branch. As the branch expanded, however, Congress exempted some offices from Senate confirmation. Today, the president unilaterally appoints the members of the White House staff; the Senate has nothing to say about these personnel decisions. The executive powers granted to the president have expanded far beyond the powers enumerated in the Constitution.

Executive Orders

Executive orders, as the term suggests, are unilateral commands issued by the president; they have the full force of law, as long as they do not violate the Constitution or a valid statute. The power to issue executive orders is derived from the constitutional provision assigning "executive power" to the president. It is unclear how many orders have been issued, because their publication was not standardized until 1935. By the beginning of 2012, however, presidents had issued an estimated 13,596 executive orders.

Presidents argue that executive orders allow the chief executive to act when Congress is unable or unwilling to act, either because it lacks the requisite information and expertise, or because it is constrained by partisan disagreements. As President Obama declared, "We can't wait for Congress to do its job. So where they won't act, I will."[15] But executive orders allow a president to implement significant, and sometimes contentious, policies without the benefits of legislative deliberation and partisan negotiation.

Among the most notable executive orders issued during the modern presidency are those inhibiting or advancing civil rights. Roosevelt issued an executive order that led to the internment of people of Japanese ancestry—over two-thirds of whom were American citizens—in camps during World War II. Truman advanced civil rights with an executive order that racially integrated the military. Kennedy ended racial discrimination in federally funded public housing. Lyndon Johnson required affirmative-action hiring by firms with federal contracts. More recently, in 1998, through an executive order, President Clinton prohibited discrimination based on sexual orientation in federal government employment.

For those who think that command is an efficient approach to decision making, executive orders may seem very appealing. Yet executive orders do have their limitations.

National Archives

A three-year-old Japanese girl awaits relocation during World War II. Yukiko Llewellyn later became an assistant dean of students at the University of Illinois.

When presidents have used executive orders to implement controversial policies, their successors have sometimes reversed or rescinded those orders. George W. Bush issued environmental regulations through executive orders, several of which were rescinded by Barack Obama. Executive orders can also be challenged in federal court. George W. Bush ordered signs posted in union shops informing workers that they were not required to allow union dues to be withheld from their paychecks. A federal court ruled that this was a misuse of an executive order. Thus the changes effected by executive orders may be immediate, but they will not necessarily be lasting.

 Thinking about Democracy

The first sentence of the Constitution assigns "all legislative Powers" to Congress. Do executive orders undermine that assignment of powers? Why or why not? Is the United States still a democracy if the president can make law unilaterally?

Appointment and Removal Powers

Appointment power refers to the president's power to appoint or to nominate senior executive officials and judges. Appointments are unilateral actions by the president that name an individual to a post. The greatest concentration of presidential appointees is in the White House Office. Nominations occur when presidents name an individual for an office but the Senate must confirm the nomination before the appointment is made. All federal judges are nominated by the president and confirmed by the Senate. In the executive branch, presidential nomination and Senate confirmation are reserved for the highest offices. All those who lead executive branch departments and independent agencies, as well as most of the senior executives leading units in the Executive Office of the President, are subject to Senate confirmation.

The Founders feared that, without the check of a Senate confirmation, a president would become an autocrat with complete power over the executive branch. Requiring Senate confirmation has given U.S. senators real power. Senators in the president's party expect to strongly influence judicial nominations to district and circuit courts—a practice referred to as **senatorial courtesy**. Similarly, confirmation requirements for executive offices have given senators an opportunity to pressure presidents and nominees to make policy promises that advance the priorities of the senators and the interests of their constituents.[16] When made by department secretaries, these promises have imposed significant constraints on the president.

The Constitution grants Congress the power to impeach and remove all "civil Officers of the United States." **Art. I, Sec. 3 & 4; Art. II, Sec. 4** But presidents have, more generally, claimed the power to remove nominees from office, whether by requesting resignations or by simply firing the individuals. This power is not in the Constitution; it has been resisted by the legislative branch and limited by the courts. Still, the battle over removal powers was fought and largely won by Grover Cleveland, who insisted on naming his own people to decision-making posts when he entered office in 1885. His persistence, which overcame strong Senate objections, helped revitalize a presidency weakened by impeachment proceedings during Andrew Johnson's administration. Fifty years later, the Supreme Court ruled that presidents do have the power to remove appointees from purely administrative jobs but not from those with quasi-legislative and judicial responsibilities. This ruling actually protects many appointees, since distinguishing quasi-legislative and judicial positions from those with no policy-making authority is not easy.[17]

Presidents cannot remove officials appointed to policy-making positions with fixed terms, such as those on regulatory boards and the Federal Reserve Board. A president cannot remove federal judges from office, either. These individuals serve for life, making their selection and nomination among the most lasting of a president's decisions.

Political pressure often influences executive branch resignations and firings, as it does nominations. There can be considerable pressure to remove department executives who alienate the legislative branch or influential constituencies. Yet the president may rely on these individuals, valuing their loyalty and trusting them to implement critical policies. George W. Bush, for example, often resisted pressures to request the resignations of department executives. Among those he protected was Attorney General Alberto Gonzalez, who was strongly criticized for playing a pivotal role in the expansion of presidential powers. When Bush did concede to critics and exercise his removal power, he did so because the pressure was overwhelming. Defense Secretary Donald Rumsfeld, whose positions on torture and other war-related policies were widely criticized, was fired only after the Republican Party lost its majority in the House of Representatives in the 2006 elections. Loyalty, policy expertise, and politics, as well as constitutional considerations, are all part of a president's calculations in nominating individuals to office and removing them from office.

Executive Privilege

Executive privilege allows presidents to refuse requests to publicly disclose the contents of internal documents and conversations with their aides and advisers. This power is intended to ensure that presidents receive full and frank advice from their staff.

Presidents since George Washington have asserted executive privilege, usually in response to congressional requests for information. Though the courts have endorsed executive privilege and upheld many presidential claims, they have also ruled that it is limited and not absolute. Rather than issuing general guidelines for the exercise of this power, however, the courts have issued narrow rulings tailored to each case and question. There is no definitive ruling on what information or documents a president can choose to withhold from the public or Congress.

U.S. v. *Nixon* is perhaps the most well-known Supreme Court ruling on executive privilege. President Nixon had refused requests to provide recordings of Oval Office conversations, which investigators believed would document his knowledge of the attempted burglary of the Democratic Party's national headquarters at the Watergate Hotel in 1972. The Court ordered the president to turn over the tapes, ruling that executive privilege could not be invoked to withhold evidence relating to a criminal investigation. When Nixon ultimately complied, the Congress gained evidence that the president had participated in covering up the complicity of the White House in the break-in. Just seventeen days after the ruling that stripped him of the protection of executive privilege, after the House Judiciary Committee had passed articles of impeachment, Nixon resigned.

George W. Bush claimed executive privilege a number of times, arguably as part of a larger strategy to expand presidential powers. Perhaps the most notable instance of this strategy was seen when Vice President Cheney, chairing an energy policy task force, rejected requests for documents related to the task force deliberations. Maintaining that the task force was addressing issues related to national security, Cheney argued that releasing the information would compromise the decision-making authority of the president, even though the president had not necessarily attended any of the meetings. In essence, the vice president was claiming executive privilege on behalf of the president, with the effect of greatly increasing the power of the president.[18]

Reorganizing Agencies

As part of their efforts to control the huge executive branch and implement their own policy agendas, presidents propose reorganization plans. Dwight D. Eisenhower brought together a number of agencies to create the Department of Health, Education, and Welfare. Twenty-five years later, Jimmy Carter reorganized this department, creating a Department of Education and a Department of Health and Human Services. In both instances, the president's intent was to signal the higher priority that he would assign to domestic social programs. Presidents also promise that reorganization will eliminate waste and redundancy. These were the reasons why the 9/11 Commission recommended, and George W. Bush supported, the creation of the Department of Homeland Security.

Because reorganization can drastically alter programs that benefit legislators' constituents, members of Congress insist upon reviewing and approving all major reorganization plans. Legislators have great incentives to protect "their" programs and the associated relationships and budgets. And because legislators have often served in government for many years, building strong relationships that extend deep into executive branch agencies and bureaus, they often have the expertise and the information to challenge and modify (or even defeat) presidential reorganization plans. A number of Republican presidential candidates and presidents have promised to abolish the Department of Energy, but it endures. As this book goes to press, President Obama and several Republican presidential candidates are proposing to reorganize the Department of Commerce. Time will show whether this department is significantly changed. During the 2012 primaries, President Obama and several Republican candidates proposed to reorganize the Department of Commerce. Time will show whether this department is significantly changed. Voters can see reorganization as less important than the pursuit of policy initiatives, failing to realize that the two may be connected. Reorganizing the Commerce Department may or may not contribute to economic expansion and job creation.

Legislative Powers

Presidents have significant lawmaking power and influence, both formally and informally. Formally, the Constitution assigns legislative powers to the president as checks on the Congress; an example is the veto, which can only be overridden if two-thirds of the members in each chamber vote to do so. Informally, presidents have claimed powers that were later confirmed by the courts, as in regard to signing statements, which are discussed in a later chapter. In still other instances, Congress has abdicated or ceded responsibility to the president, especially when presidents were skillful negotiators who knew how to secure success for their policies. Though Congress has the power of the purse, for instance, the president submits the original budget proposal. (More will be said about this in "Focus On… Spending and Taxing.")

The president also enjoys a number of organizational advantages. First, the president is one person, whereas Congress includes 535 members in two houses, each with many committees and subcommittees. Legislative leaders struggle to develop and articulate policy goals acceptable to their party and to keep party members committed to these goals. Even in a time of partisan polarization, narrow majorities also force some negotiation across party lines. While the members of Congress talk and negotiate, the president can decide and act.

Second, and related to this first advantage, the president can attract the attention of the media. Focusing on the single president, rather than the many and diverse members of Congress, often yields a more understandable and more dramatic news story.

Third, the president has more information, which is collected and analyzed by the executive branch bureaucracy. Executive privilege empowers a president to keep many of the most important pieces of information confidential, even secret.

In studying lawmaking, therefore, we study the workings of both separation of powers and checks and balances: the president and Congress each have their distinctive responsibilities, but they are engaged in a competitive relationship.

Negotiating with Congress

When asked how a president should deal with Congress, Lyndon Johnson replied, "continuously, incessantly, and without interruption."[19] Not every president has Johnson's stamina or zest for the job, but effectiveness does depend on the president's knowledge of Congress and skill as a negotiator. Presidents discuss, cajole, negotiate, bargain, and compromise to get as much as they can.

Partisan polarization has made legislative-executive negotiations progressively more difficult and bipartisan compromise more of a rarity. Throughout the summer of 2011, Democratic and Republican differences, expressed by the president and by legislative leaders, pushed the country to the point of defaulting on its loan obligations. Without significant budget concessions from the president, Republicans refused to increase the government's debt ceiling, thus risking the nation's defaulting on its loan obligations and perhaps sending the world economy into a crisis.

Nominations have also become more contentious. High-level executive and judicial nominations are no longer unanimously approved, but instead receive close scrutiny by the media, the public, and the Senate. Hard bargaining takes place throughout the selection, nomination, and confirmation process. President Clinton's nomination of Alexis Herman as labor secretary, for example, was repeatedly delayed in the Senate, sometimes by members of the president's own party, as legislators tried to force the president to accept their labor policy priorities.

In both the George W. Bush and the Obama administrations, a number of nominations were never brought to a Senate floor vote. Some nominees became so frustrated that they withdrew their names. Sometimes the stalling had little to do with the qualifications of the candidate, but rather with one or more senators' grievances or priorities. In 2010, for example, Sen. Richard Shelby (R-Ala.) held up more than seventy of President Obama's nominations in an effort to secure defense contracts for his home state, which would provide employment for his constituents.[20] These and other confrontations made

bargaining time-consuming for the president, led to uncertain outcomes, and left key positions filled by interim officials or no one at all. In fact, from 1977 to 2005, on average, top positions in the executive departments and agencies were empty or filled by "acting" officials 15 to 25 percent of the time.[21] Gridlock carries heavy costs for the chief executive, the presidential administration, the executive branch, Congress, and the nation.

Veto Power

If Congress passes legislation strongly opposed by the president, then the president can exercise the **veto power**. Latin for "I forbid," the veto is arguably the most significant legislative power granted to the president in the Constitution. It is not listed among the president's formal powers in Article II, but rather is included in Article I as a check on Congress's power to legislate.   **Art. I, Sec. 7**

The veto is actually one of three options for a president who is responding to a bill passed by Congress. A president can sign the bill into law.

Or, a president can refuse to sign the bill. If Congress adjourns within ten working days after sending the bill to the White House, the bill is dead. This is called a **pocket veto**. Because Congress has adjourned, there is no possibility of an override. If, however, Congress does not adjourn within the ten working days, then the bill becomes law without the president's signature. This allows a president to sidestep responsibility for the legislation.

Or, a president can exercise the veto, returning the bill to Congress with a veto message explaining why the president considers the proposed legislation unacceptable. If two-thirds of both houses vote to override the president's veto, then the bill will become law despite the president's opposition. Mobilizing these supermajorities, however, is very hard. As a result, the threat of a veto can carry real influence if members want to see the bill become a law.

Historically, presidents have used the veto for different reasons, and more or less frequently. George Washington cast the first veto, but only once in each of his two terms. In both instances, he believed the bills contained provisions that were unconstitutional. He was acting as one who had to execute the law, not as one trying to write law. Congress rewrote those provisions rather than trying to override.[22]

Only seven presidents never vetoed a bill (both Adamses, Jefferson, Harrison, Taylor, Fillmore, and Garfield).[23] Clinton, who confronted Republican majorities in Congress throughout the last six years of his presidency, issued thirty-seven vetoes, only two of which were overridden. George W. Bush, however, did not use the veto until his sixth year in office; his White House staff was exceptionally skilled in legislative negotiations and benefited from having the president's party hold slim but well-disciplined majorities in Congress. After Democrats gained the majority in the House in 2006, Bush issued eleven vetoes, four of which were overridden. Presidents who use the veto too often may appear isolated or uncooperative or may seem to be exercising negative leadership. But the fact that presidents are rarely overridden is a reminder of their power to check the legislature.

Signing Statements

When presidents sign a bill into law, they may also set out their interpretation of the new law, indicating which provisions they find problematic either constitutionally or politically. Known as **signing statements**, these written comments are deposited with new laws and recorded in the *Federal Register*.

Signing statements allow a president to undermine specific provisions in a bill without the possibility of a congressional override, which might have occurred if the president had vetoed the bill. And the Supreme Court has ruled that the president has the power, as the chief executive responsible for implementing law, to issue these statements. Recent presidents have made increasing use of signing statements as a means of winning policy battles with the legislative branch without the publicity of a veto. President Reagan issued 71 signing statements and President Clinton, 105. [24] Yet it was President George W. Bush who made the greatest use of signing statements.

In his two terms in office, Bush attached signing statements that challenged 1200 sections of bills. [25] The legislation included foreign and military policy, as well as "affirmative action, immigration, whistleblower protections, and safeguards against political interference in federally funded research." [26] In many instances, these signing statements significantly expanded the power of the presidency. For example, Bush issued signing statements that exempted him from providing information to congressional oversight committees, a controversial expansion of executive privilege. As another example, when Bush signed a bill forbidding the use of torture, he wrote a signing statement indicating that the legislation would not be enforced to the extent that it compromised the president's powers and responsibilities as commander in chief. The Bush signing statements often provided constitutional interpretations of the laws, mandated how the laws would or would not be implemented, and vetoed specific provisions. Through these statements, therefore, President Bush claimed and exercised judicial, executive, and legislative powers.

Signing statements became an issue in the 2008 presidential election when candidate Barack Obama promised to issue them only to "protect a president's constitutional prerogatives," not to "undermine the legislative intent." As of November 2012, Obama had issued twenty signing statements, which he described as addressing "constitutional concerns… as a means of discharging my constitutional responsibilities." [27] Judicial scholars describe this rationale as being among the most controversial reasons for issuing a signing statement, especially when it leads a president to refuse to enforce the law, yet comparatively few signing statements are challenged, either in the courts or during congressional oversight hearings. [28]

Foreign Policy Powers

Some of a president's most formidable powers are centered on foreign policy. These give the president so much influence over foreign affairs that they have sometimes endangered the constitutional balance of power among the branches. For example, in 1998, President Clinton committed American

BEHIND THE SCENES

Trading Favors

In 1962, President John Kennedy received a call from Senate minority leader Everett Dirksen (R-Ill.) requesting a favor. An aide to former president Dwight Eisenhower was under investigation for income tax evasion and expected to be formally charged the next day. Eisenhower's wife, Mamie, was a close friend of the aide's wife, who worried that the aide might commit suicide if indicted. Eisenhower did not know Kennedy, so he asked his fellow Republican, Dirksen, to approach the president and ask "as a personal favor to me, to put the . . . indictment in the deep freeze. . . . Advise him he'll have a blank check in my bank if he will grant me this favor."

Kennedy had no knowledge of the matter but said he would do what Eisenhower asked. He called his brother Robert, the attorney general, and told him not to sign the indictment. His brother objected on the grounds that granting a special favor to a tax evader would be politically disastrous. But the president told him to do it or submit his resignation.

Weeks later, the nuclear test ban treaty with the Soviet Union was pending in the Senate, where ratification required a two-thirds vote. This was especially difficult to obtain at the height of the Cold War. Americans didn't trust the Soviets, and conservatives claimed that a treaty banning the testing of nuclear weapons would give the Soviets the upper hand. A head count showed the treaty falling short of a two-thirds majority. Kennedy rang Dirksen and called in his chits. He asked the senator to change his vote and to get Ike to endorse the treaty too, saying the treaty was important to him, the country, and all mankind. If both men lent their support, Kennedy would consider his favor repaid. With public support from the minority leader and the popular former president, enough Republicans joined the Democrats to ratify the treaty.

SOURCE: The account of this deal appeared in Bobby Baker (with Larry L. King), *Wheeling and Dealing: Confessions of a Capitol Hill Operator* (New York: W. W. Norton, 1978), 97–99.

ground forces to war in Yugoslavia without legislative authorization. The House subsequently prohibited the use of appropriated funds for deploying ground forces unless Congress first authorized their deployment. The House further rejected a motion to declare a state of war between the United States and Yugoslavia, but it also rejected a motion requiring the removal of forces from Yugoslavia. Meanwhile, the Senate tabled several similar motions. In this instance, the president acted without statutory or constitutional support, and also without strong checks from the legislative branch, endangering the constitutional order.[29] And, as is often the case, Congress was not unified in its strategies to oppose this executive action.

In addition, many of the powers previously discussed apply to both domestic and foreign policy making. Executive orders, for example, allow a president to act unilaterally at home and internationally. Reagan, George H. W. Bush, and George W. Bush each issued executive orders banning abortion counseling in federally financed clinics at home, as well as financial aid to United Nations–sponsored family planning programs abroad. Clinton and Obama reversed these orders. Presidents also nominate individuals to serve in the executive branch domestically and internationally, in civilian and military posts. Presidential nominees with foreign policy-making powers include ambassadors and the Joint Chiefs of Staff; the latter are the president's highest-ranking military advisers.

Diplomatic Powers

The Constitution authorizes the president to negotiate treaties with foreign countries, appoint ambassadors, and receive foreign ambassadors. **Art. II, Sec. 2** It may seem that the president is the nation's "chief executive," yet none of these powers are unchecked.

Treaties   Though authorized to negotiate **treaties**, a president is also constrained by the constitutional requirement that they must be ratified by a two-thirds vote in the Senate. Just as it is difficult to organize a supermajority to override a presidential veto, it is difficult to mobilize a supermajority to ratify a treaty. The requirement of a two-thirds vote for treaty ratification means that the Senate has leverage to bargain with the president. After Jimmy Carter negotiated a treaty to give the Panama Canal to Panama and put the Canal Zone under its authority, the Senate demanded, as a condition of ratification, partial renegotiation of treaty terms. The Senate wanted to ensure that U.S. ships would receive priority passage during wartime and that the United States would retain the right to intervene militarily against any threats to the canal. During the Clinton administration, the Senate narrowly rejected a treaty banning underground nuclear testing. Under international law, however, even treaties not ratified by the U.S. Senate may be binding on the United States.[30]

However, the president evidently can terminate treaties without any involvement by the Senate. The Supreme Court allowed Carter to terminate the 1903 treaty with Panama to make way for the new one.[31] A more striking example of unilateral termination came in 2001 when George W. Bush withdrew the United States from the ABM (anti–ballistic missile) treaty not long after taking office.[32]

Executive agreements   **Executive agreements** are international agreements other than treaties that are binding on the United States under international law. Executive agreements, therefore, have the same status as treaties, internationally.

They may be authorized by treaties (the NATO Treaty has authorized hundreds of agreements), by Congress through statutes (Congress has authorized the president to reach agreements with the United Nations and many other international organizations), or by the president acting unilaterally. Executive agreements are far more numerous than treaties. For example, in his first term in office, George W. Bush reached agreement on 504 executive agreements and just 39 treaties. And yet executive agreements are not mentioned in the Constitution.

Because the Constitution assigns responsibility for foreign trade to Congress, Congress ratifies, by majorities in both houses, these executive agreements. Yet even when congressional authorization is not required, presidents have found it advantageous to secure approval, for two reasons. First, by tradition, an executive agreement requires only a majority in both houses; this is much easier to get than the two-thirds majority in the Senate, which the Constitution requires for treaty ratification. Second, having the House approve an executive agreement can make it easier for a president, later, to secure the legislation and the appropriations needed to actually enforce the agreement.

Executive agreements unilaterally negotiated and declared by the president are the smallest percentage of executive agreements and the most controversial. Although the president's power to reach executive agreements is not enumerated in the Constitution, the State Department argues that it is implied by other powers, namely, the executive, commander in chief, and recognition powers. The Constitution also charges the president with responsibility for law enforcement. The danger is that the president's unilateral power to negotiate executive agreements could essentially erase the constitutional check of treaty ratification. Although the Supreme Court has limited unilateral executive agreements, it has not abolished them. It has, for example, struck down unilateral trade agreements, as this is a congressional policy responsibility. It has also struck down unilateral agreements that abridged constitutional rights.

Nominating and receiving ambassadors   An ambassador represents one country to another; on a daily basis, the ambassador is the highest-ranking diplomatic official and has corresponding influence. Though ambassadors to many nations are State Department careerists, some ambassadorial posts—those in Europe and the larger Asian nations, for instance—are presidential nominees, confirmed by the Senate. As is true of other nominations, this requirement provides senators with an opportunity to elicit policy commitments from individuals who might otherwise be perceived as the president's representatives.

When ambassadors from other nations arrive in the United States, they are each required to present their credentials to the president. This highly symbolic action has profound significance: when the president "receives" the ambassador, the United States officially recognizes the nation that the ambassador is representing. This is referred to as the president's **recognition power**. When a government has come to power by revolution, coup, or fraudulent elections, the United States may refuse to recognize that nation and so will refuse to receive its ambassadors. The United States did not recognize the governments of the Soviet Union and of mainland China for many years after their leaders gained power.

War Powers

War powers are divided between Congress and the president. The Constitution charges Congress with declaring war and the president with waging war. This allocation of responsibilities and powers reflected the Founders' fears that presidents would be too eager to go to war.[33] In James Madison's words, "the executive is the branch of power most interested in war and most prone to it. [The Constitution] has, accordingly, with studied care, vested the question of war in the legislature."[34]

This arrangement seems to place a very strong check on the executive because Congress has numerous incentives not to declare war. The legislative branch is the branch closest to the people, and frequent elections ensure its accountability. As the branch with the "power of the purse," it decides how wars will be paid for and by whom; and as the lawmaking branch, it determines who serves in the military and thus who dies in a war. In dividing war powers between the legislative and the executive, therefore, the Founders seemed to give the advantage to Congress.

As weaponry has become more sophisticated, however, power has shifted in favor of the president. During the time of the modern presidency, the only congressional declaration of war was for World War II. All other wars were fought without a congressional declaration of war (as was true of the Korean War and the Vietnam War), or with the lesser congressional authorization to exercise force (as was true for the Persian Gulf War and the wars in Iraq and Afghanistan). In many instances, the president committed troops without the knowledge of Congress (as when Reagan sent aircraft to bomb Libya in 1986) or dramatically expanded the scope of conflicts (as when Nixon covertly sent troops from Vietnam into Laos and Cambodia). Once the troops have been committed, lawmakers have been reluctant to limit their resources or insist that the hostilities cease, not wanting to appear lacking in patriotism or resolve.

War powers are among the most contested arenas of legislative-executive power, a situation that is likely to continue into the future. Here, we seek to understand why and how this is true.

Commander in chief The Constitution designates the president **"Commander in Chief** of the Army and Navy... and of the Militia of the Several States, when called into the Actual service of the United States." **Art. II, Sec. 2** In writing this, the Founders were designating the president "first general" and "first admiral," as Hamilton wrote in *Federalist Paper* 69, making it clear that civilian authority has primacy over military authority. This also means that presidents may

National Archives

As commander in chief, the president appoints military officers. During the Civil War, President Lincoln couldn't understand why the Union Army hadn't pressed its advantage over the Confederate Army. When he visited the Antietam battlefield, he discovered that his top general, George McClellan (facing Lincoln), was both pro-Union and proslavery. Hoping for a stalemate in the war, McClellan tried to block Confederate advances but refused to rout Confederate troops. Lincoln replaced him.

determine military strategy. President Johnson reviewed and approved bombing runs throughout the Vietnam War. President George H. W. Bush made the decision not to pursue the defeated Iraqi forces into Baghdad, ending the war with a negotiated truce rather than unconditional surrender.

At times, presidents have demonstrated their control over the military by relieving their senior officers of command, insisting that the president's orders be respected and followed. Douglas MacArthur, a five-star general, ignored President Truman's express orders to the contrary and sought to expand the Korean War to include China. Truman relieved MacArthur of his command, ending his military career. When Eric Shinseki, then a four-star general and chair of the Joint Chiefs of Staff, testified before Congress in 2002 that the president's estimates regarding troop commitments for the Iraq war were too low, President Bush forced his retirement. In 2010, President Obama relieved four-star General Stanley McChrystal from his command of the U.S. forces in Afghanistan after repeated instances of insubordination, which culminated in a *Rolling Stone* interview that belittled the policies and persons of the president, the defense secretary, and State Department personnel.

Presidents have also exercised their power as commander in chief domestically, maintaining that the wars threatened the nation's survival. Acting under his expansive definition of commander in chief, Franklin Roosevelt put approximately 100,000 Americans of Japanese descent into camps during World War II. He also had the government seize and operate many industries important to the war effort, pre-empting any possibility of strikes. And Roosevelt created special agencies to control the consumption and price of gasoline, meat, shoes, and other goods.

Wars that do not threaten our national survival tend not to generate high levels of support for executive actions. Truman had his secretary of commerce seize many of the nation's steel mills during the Korean War to keep them operating, pre-empting a possible labor strike, but in 1952 the Supreme Court ruled that Truman had not exhausted other, legal remedies to the problem. His actions as a commander in chief were not constitutional.[35] Decades later, however, George W. Bush would take an even more expansive approach to the powers of the commander in chief at home and abroad. The consequences of these actions for the president and for the nation are discussed below and in "Focus On ... Foreign Policy."

The War Powers Act   In an effort to reinstate a balance of war powers between the president and Congress, Congress passed the War Powers Act in 1973, overriding Nixon's veto. The War Powers Act requires a president to notify Congress within forty-eight hours of committing troops to hostilities. Troops must then be removed from harm's way within sixty days, though the president may request Congress to issue a thirty-day extension, unless the Congress declares war or authorizes the use of force. Nixon and every one of his successors in the Oval Office have considered the War Powers Act an unconstitutional limitation on the president's authority as commander in chief. Each of these presidents has resisted congressional involvement in the use of troops, though some presidents—most notably, George W. Bush—have negotiated congressional authorizations that expanded their power to wage war.

For example, when President George H. W. Bush sent troops to invade Panama in 1989, he did not even refer to the War Powers Resolution in the two-page letter he sent to Congress justifying the invasion, sixty hours *after* the invasion began. He also ordered 250,000 troops to the Persian Gulf between August and November 1990 on his own authority, and he delayed announcing his decision to double this number until after the November elections. This kept the decision that changed the mission from defense (Operation Desert Shield) to offense (Operation Desert Storm) from coming to Congress until after Bush had mobilized U.S. and world opinion, and gained United Nations support. By the time Congress authorized using force in January 1991, the question of whether it should be used was, practically speaking, already decided. As another example, in 2002 President George W. Bush negotiated a congressional authorization to use force in Iraq that, as one of its provisions, authorized the president to "to use the armed forces of the United States as he determines to be necessary and appropriate."[36] With this statement, Congress arguably removed all checks on the executive as commander in chief.

Ultimately, the War Powers Act is ineffective because Congress hesitates to oppose the president after troops are deployed into combat. There is almost always a "rally 'round the flag" effect on these occasions. Any vote that can be framed as a lack of support for the troops becomes an electoral and political problem for the Congress member. Still, the presidential advantage can be short-lived, as Presidents George H. W. Bush, George W. Bush, and Barack Obama learned.

The War on Terror   No president made more expansive claims for the commander in chief role than did George W. Bush. The national emergency precipitated by the attacks of September 11, 2001, led the Bush administration to claim more latitude for unilateral action. In planning a response immediately after the attacks, for example, Vice President Cheney articulated the "One Percent Doctrine," arguing that if there was even a 1 percent chance that a person or a situation was a threat, the government had to act.[37]

Following Cheney's lead, Bush claimed that, as commander in chief, he had unilateral powers that allowed him, on his own authority, to identify any persons as enemy combatants; to hold them for any length of time without bringing charges or allowing access to lawyers or courts; to have them interrogated under rules set independently of international laws and treaties signed by the United States; and to bring them to trial in tribunals established outside the military or civilian justice systems.

Bush relied upon his powers as commander in chief and as chief executive to expand the actions taken by law enforcement and intelligence agencies within the executive branch. Without legislative or judicial oversight, these executive agencies, acting on the president's instructions, were to collect intelligence by opening postal and electronic mail, seizing library and bank records, and wiretapping telephones.[38] Although some of these actions were subsequently critiqued in the media and in academic publications, and several court cases resulted, many were endorsed by Congress through passage of the USA PATRIOT Act—Uniting and Strengthening America by Providing Appropriate Tools Required to Intercept and Obstruct Terrorism. This acronym, and the strong bipartisan majorities that passed the act in 2001 (98–1 in the Senate, 357–66 in the House), indicate that Congress cannot be depended upon to limit the president in times of crisis.

In the past, when presidents have used war or other national crises to justify the expansion of their powers, checks and balances have been reasserted when the crises eased. But the powers that Bush claimed for his office present a greater threat to maintaining a balance of power among the three branches, and to personal liberties, because the "war on terror," as Bush defined it, would last into the indefinite future. As a presidential candidate, Barack Obama promised to curtail the executive powers Bush had claimed as a wartime commander in chief, but it is not yet clear just how much of that authority he has renounced as president.

Pardon Power

The **pardon power** Art. II, Sec. 2 allows a president to "exercise leniency toward persons who have committed federal crimes." This can be done by commuting a person's sentence or by issuing a pardon. If a president commutes a sentence, it is reduced or eliminated entirely, but the conviction and the associated "civil disabilities" remain. A criminal conviction can restrict a person's right to vote, to hold state or local office, or to sit on a jury; it can affect the individual's eligibility for various licenses, including gun ownership, and employment opportunities. If a president issues a pardon, however, these civil disabilities are removed. "A pardon is an expression of the President's forgiveness and ordinarily is granted in recognition of the applicant's acceptance of responsibility for the crime and established good conduct for a significant period of time after conviction or after completion of sentence." Blanket pardons have been issued to Confederate Army veterans and Vietnam draft evaders, but most pardons have been granted to individuals. This is consistent with Chief Justice Marshall's definition of a pardon as "a private, though official act of grace."[39] Each year hundreds of people petition the president for pardons, the overwhelming majority of which are denied.

During the modern presidency, the number of pardons granted has varied greatly, though there has generally been a trend toward issuing fewer in each term. President Truman, for example, issued 1913 pardons and President Eisenhower issued 1110; President Johnson granted 960 pardons and President Nixon granted 892. But then President Reagan granted just 393 pardons, and President George W. Bush lowered the number further, to 189. As of November 2012, President Obama had issued only 22 pardons, more than Bush though less than Clinton in the same period. President Clinton was widely criticized when he issued most of his pardons—218 of his 396—in the final days of his presidency.

Individual pardons have sometimes been controversial, especially when linked to partisan politics. President Ford pardoned then-former President Nixon, in advance of impeachment or trial, for all actions relating to the Watergate break-in. Ford described this as one of his most important decisions as president, and many believe it contributed to his loss in the 1976 election. President George H. W. Bush pardoned the six Reagan officials charged with or convicted of crimes related to the Iran-Contra scandal. Like Ford, Bush had been a vice president in the administration whose officials he pardoned; also like Ford, Bush found his decision and his ethics questioned. Clinton's pardon of a fugitive commodities trader whose ex-wife was a large donor to the Democratic Party and to the Clinton presidential library raised concerns about inappropriate ties between pardons and financial support. Though George W. Bush expanded presidential powers in many ways, he was very cautious in his use of the pardon power. He did, however, commute the sentence of Cheney aide and administration loyalist Lewis "Scooter" Libby. Bush commuted the two-and-a-half-year prison sentence Libby received for perjury and obstructing justice during the investigation into the leak of an undercover CIA agent's identity. Libby still had to pay a $250,000 fine and serve two years' probation. "I respect the jury's verdict," said the president, "but I have concluded that the prison sentence given to Mr. Libby is excessive."[40]

Party Leader

The president's role as party leader is not defined in the Constitution. Parties did not exist then, so the power as it has developed is not mentioned or referred to in that document.

Presidents try to speak more as a head of state than as a partisan in an attempt to appeal to everyone. But presidents also must rely on their party in Congress, among interest groups, and in the public to gain support for presidential initiatives. Two measures of a president's success as a party leader are, first, the president's approval ratings among party members in the general public; and, second, the midterm election outcomes.

Approval ratings can be measured in many ways, but among the most revealing of the public's priorities and of its perceptions of the president are the approval ratings among the members of the president's party and among those in the opposing party. Since the mid-2000s, the increasing polarization in Washington has been reflected in how differently members of the two parties evaluate the president. By 2007, after the unity of the 9/11 attacks had faded, the difference between Democrats' and Republicans' approval of President Bush was 58 points, an all-time high. But that was exceeded during the Obama years. In 2011, for example, 80 percent of Democrats, but only 12 percent of Republicans, approved of Obama. This 68-point gap is the highest ever.[41]

Midterm election returns may also be indicative of the public's assessment of the president's performance. Since 1934, the president's party has lost an average of 28 House seats and 3 to 4 Senate seats in off-year elections. Among the modern presidents, there have been wide swings in the wins and losses of the president's party at midterm, though typically the president's party loses at least some seats in the midterm election. In their first terms Reagan (in 1982) saw his party lose 26 House seats, Clinton 54 seats, and Obama (in 2010) 63 seats. In an exception to the general rule, after 9/11 and the rallying of support behind President George W. Bush, the Republicans gained 6 seats in 2002 but then lost 31 seats in the midyear election during Bush's second term.[42]

In addition to specific historical and political events, these electoral outcomes are also affected by congressional politics. In the House of Representatives, districts are drawn to protect incumbents. And both representatives and senators have significant advantages as incumbents, including name recognition, war chests and fundraising networks, well-organized campaigns and constituent outreach offices, and innumerable other resources. Congress members, then, may capitalize on presidential popularity or may have the resources to cushion themselves against presidential unpopularity.

The political advantages that a president can gain from being the leader of the party are unpredictable. The power of public opinion, the dynamics of party polarization, the advantages enjoyed by congressional incumbents, and many other events will impact the effectiveness of the president as a partisan leader. Fate also plays a role. In 2012, just days before the election, President Obama's responsiveness to the states devastated by "Superstorm Sandy" earned national praise. When New Jersey Governor Chris Christie, a fierce partisan, endorsed and hugged the president, many felt that Obama's status as a bipartisan leader had been reinvigorated.

ORGANIZING THE PRESIDENCY

As the chief executive, the president leads a vast bureaucracy. There are cabinet departments, independent agencies, government corporations, and many other entities. The vast majority of the over 2 million workers in the executive bureaucracy are careerists, whose employment with the federal government is largely unaffected by the president. Yet the upper echelon of the executive branch—the executives who lead the departments, independent agencies, and various other units—are typically presidential nominees. These individuals, who mediate between the president and the careerists in order to advance the president's agenda, are commonly referred to as the presidential administration.

In selecting the individuals who will have the power and the responsibility to make decisions in their administration, presidents must consider and prioritize at least four different kinds of expertise. These include the following:

- knowledge about substantive policy, so that the decision maker can assess different options for using government resources and taking action;
- knowledge of the Washington, D.C., community, so that the decision maker knows who to talk to and how to get things done in the capital city;

- knowledge from the presidential campaign, so that the decision maker understands the electoral reasons for making and keeping promises; and
- knowledge of the president, so that the decision maker understands the president's values, ideology, and commitments.[43]

As this list makes clear, a president's nominees and appointees are valuable political resources. They are expected to transform campaign promises into functioning programs, to facilitate the president's exercise of his powers within the confines of a system of checks and balances, and to find ways to prevent or correct bad presidential decisions. Having individuals with multiple areas of expertise is critical to a president's success.

Chapter 11 studies the work of the executive branch bureaucracy. Here, we survey the major units that comprise a presidential administration.

The Cabinet

The **cabinet** is composed of the top executives of the executive branch departments. A unit within the executive branch is identified as a "department" when its policy and programmatic responsibilities are recognized as being nationally significant. The top executive in a department is referred to as the secretary, except in the Department of Justice, which is headed by the attorney general; all of these individuals are nominated by the president and must be confirmed by the Senate.

In addition to the department secretaries, the president, and the vice president, the cabinet often includes individuals that the president has designated as having **cabinet rank**. Though not leading departments, these individuals are viewed as having responsibilities that are of similar importance. For example, the director of the Office of Management and Budget (OMB), an agency in the Executive Office of the President, is usually given cabinet rank. One of the OMB's functions is to compile the budget for the executive branch, a task that is of critical importance to the government and to the nation.

Individual cabinet secretaries are often influential decision makers. They lead large organizations with broad policy jurisdictions and many employees, which also require large budgets. The secretary of defense leads a department that includes four branches of the armed services; the secretary of health and human services administers a budget that will exceed $1 trillion in 2014. (By way of comparison, the Department of Defense budget is expected to be $572 billion in 2014, down from $678 in 2011.)[44] The secretaries are also representatives of the president, and they spend a great deal of time meeting with presidential constituents and Congress members. In many instances, the secretaries' work bridges national and international politics. Though the secretary of state is an obvious example, the effects of globalization have made the secretaries of the treasury, commerce, and labor (among others) increasingly attentive to international markets. Yet cabinet secretaries typically have less access to the president than do many members of the Executive Office of the President, especially those who serve in the White House Office.

The Executive Office of the President (EOP)

The **Executive Office of the President** is not a single office but a group of offices, councils, and boards devoted to specific functional or issue areas such as national security, trade, the budget, drug abuse, the economy, and the environment. Though many EOP staffers are careerists, the top executives in each unit, like the top executives in the departments, are nominated or appointed by the president. Whether the post is filled through presidential nomination and Senate confirmation, or through presidential appointment, is decided when the unit is recreated or reorganized. It is a matter for intense executive-legislative negotiation. Because the executives in the EOP work closely with the president, the chief executive wants as much discretion as possible in naming these decision makers. For the same reason, the Senate wants the opportunity to examine and oversee these individuals. Today, nominees that require Senate confirmation lead most of the EOP units, except the White House Office.

Today, the average person presumes that the president requires and has specialized personnel to lead the nation. Yet the Executive Office of the President only dates back to the Franklin Roosevelt administration. Then, overwhelmed by the administrative responsibilities that came with the New Deal programs, FDR called upon a team of public administration experts to bring structure to the presidency; it would no longer be an *ad hoc* arrangement of the president and a few aides. Subsequent changes and developments in the EOP have reflected a wide range of priorities, many but not all presidential. The Office of Management and Budget emerged from a Nixon reorganization, undertaken to secure greater control over the executive branch. The Council of Economic Advisors, however, was part of a congressional initiative to force the president to more systematically consult economic policy experts. Because the EOP provides expertise that enhances the power of the president, congressional oversight tends to be close and careful.

The White House Office

The **White House Office** "extends the president's reach" by gathering and analyzing information, and it "magnifies the president's voice" by repeating the president's **message**. Of the units within the Executive Office of the President, the White House Office may be the most well known. Among the most familiar are the **chief of staff** (with responsibility for advising the president and managing the White House Office) and the press secretary (who conducts the daily briefings for the White House press corps). Less familiar are the communications and congressional liaison staff, though the work of these individuals is on public display in every

The Cabinet

Vice President
Secretary of State
Secretary of the Treasury
Secretary of Defense
Attorney General
Secretary of the Interior
Secretary of Agriculture
Secretary of Commerce
Secretary of Labor
Secretary of Health and Human Services
Secretary of Housing and Urban Development
Secretary of Transportation
Secretary of Energy
Secretary of Education
Secretary of Veterans Affairs
Secretary of Homeland Security

Cabinet Rank

The White House Chief of Staff
Administrator of the Environmental Protection Agency
Director of the Office of Management and Budget
United States Trade Representative
United States Ambassador to the United Nations
Chair of the Council of Economic Advisors
Secretary of the Small Business Administration

The Executive Office of the President

Council of Economic Advisors
Council on Environmental Quality
Executive Residence
National Security Staff
Office of Administration
Office of Management and Budget
Office of National Drug Control Policy
Office of Science and Technology Policy
Office of the United States Trade Representative
Office of the Vice President
White House Office

SOURCES: The Cabinet, http://www.whitehouse.gov/administration /cabinet (accessed February 23, 2012); Executive Office of the President, http://www.whitehouse.gov/administration/eop (accessed February 23, 2012).

presidential event and congressional contact. And then there are the individuals who make the presidency "work," such as those in the office of the White House counsel who craft the legal statements of the president, including veto messages and signing statements; in the personnel office, who recruit and vet prospective nominees and appointees for posts throughout the administration; and in the office of management and administration, who organize the details of White House life from dining privileges in the White House mess to allocating office space. All of these responsibilities come with real challenges. As one Reagan staff member in the management and administration office remarked, "Well, it can be intense and things can also be very emotional. You start with office space. People will take a closet to say they're in the West Wing rather than take a wonderful office in the Old Executive Office Building."[45]

As the responsibilities of the president have grown and changed, so also has the White House Office.[46] Since the Nixon administration, however, presidents have generally adopted a similar set of specialized offices. For example, a chief of staff has emerged in each of these presidential administrations. Several presidents—including Ford, Carter, and Clinton—initially resisted having a chief of staff, fearing that they would become distanced from staff decision making. Yet each of these chief executives ultimately relied on a chief of staff to bring order to the White House Office and to conserve the president's time. Perhaps even more importantly, chiefs of staff have often had the responsibility of saying "No" to the president. As one chief of staff explained, "You've got to have a person who can *tell you what they think* . . . and it's rare when you're President. Most people come up to me as Chief of Staff and say I'm going in and tell him it's the dumbest thing I've ever seen and he's simply got to change it. They get in there, slobber all over him, kiss his ring, tell him how wonderful he is, leave and walk out and say, gee, I really told him. I'd say that's the most groveling, sycophantic behavior I've ever seen in my life. And they say, no, I told him.... People just simply do not walk in, point their finger at the President and say, look: that's wrong."[47]

The Office of the First Lady   This unit within the White House Office provides the president's wife with the specialized staff necessary to fulfill the duties that are assigned to her by tradition and by each chief executive. Since the Carter administration, the first lady's office has included a chief of staff, a press secretary and communications director, a correspondence director, policy experts, and travel and advance teams. The first lady's office routinely works closely with other units in the White House Office; the president's chief of staff, especially, maintains close contact with the first lady. The demands placed upon the first lady by the president, and by the wider administration, have become so heavy and so consistent that she requires a specialized staff and good relations with other offices in the administration.

Among the more consistent responsibilities assigned to the first lady have been those associated with hosting social and cultural events at the White House. Working with the social secretary, first ladies have organized state dinners (integral to the president's diplomatic outreach as chief of state), concerts (showcasing artistic genius, with a number of events publicly broadcast), and holiday events

Lyndon B. Johnson Library

President Johnson worked continuously. When he awoke, he read newspapers, ate breakfast, and met with his staff—all before getting out of bed.

(ranging from holiday parties to the Easter egg roll). These are highly ritualized events, but there is still the expectation that each first lady will seize them as opportunities to deliver important political messages. In the modern presidency, Lou Henry Hoover and Lady Bird Johnson invited a wider array of women's organizations to the White House, signaling the accessibility of the presidency to women who were mobilized. Mamie Eisenhower desegregated the Easter egg roll; she invited Lucille Ball and Desi Arnaz to sit next to her even though Senator Joseph McCarthy had questioned them as communist sympathizers. These actions were taken as evidence of the first lady's commitment to civil rights and due process. Years later, Michelle Obama linked social and cultural priorities to presidential initiatives, arguing for inclusivity in the arts while her husband argued for universal health care insurance. In these and virtually every other administration, first ladies and their staff have put traditional events to untraditional uses.

First ladies have also been decision makers, contributing to partisan, policy, and presidential politics. Their partisan contributions have included extensive campaigning on behalf of their husband and congressional candidates in the president's party. The first lady has been an especially active campaigner when she has been a less polarizing figure than her husband. While many Republican candidates did not want President Bush to campaign for them in 2006, Laura Bush was a welcome guest. As policy makers, first ladies have advocated on behalf of social justice (Roosevelt), medical research funding (Truman), White House restoration (Kennedy), environmental and urban development programs (Johnson), voluntarism (Nixon), the equal rights amendment (Ford), mental health care reform (Carter), opposition to drugs (Reagan), literacy (B. Bush and L. Bush), human rights (Clinton), and childhood health and healthy eating (Obama). As veterans of winner-take-all elections and checks-and-balances government, first ladies have been formidable participants and advisers in presidential politics. Bess Truman, Nancy Reagan, and Hillary Clinton are just three of the first ladies who influenced presidential staffing decisions.

For the first ladies, balancing tradition and advocacy is never easy. Gender roles do not change easily, and approval ratings for nontraditional first ladies often fluctuate, heading downward. First ladies Eleanor Roosevelt, Nancy Reagan, and Hillary Clinton all endured intense scrutiny and criticism. Concerns about the influence of a wife over the president endure, and there is little that the president can do to reassure the public about the condition of his marriage. It is important to note, however, that Congress has formally authorized the first lady's post and, also formally, has appropriated funds for her staff. Equally important, the courts have ruled that the first lady is a *de facto* public official, who may conduct policy meetings behind closed doors with other public officials without having to later disclose the content of those dialogues to interest groups or other interested parties. Recognizing the first ladies as presidential advisers, Congress and the courts have provided these women with the resources and powers they need to fulfill this role.[48]

The Office of the Vice President

The EOP also includes the Office of the **Vice President**. The vice president has his own budget for office and staff (housed adjacent to the White House), an official airplane (*Air Force Two*), and his own white mansion (the former home of the chief of naval operations).[49]

The vice president has few formal duties—to preside over the Senate, which he rarely does (junior senators are assigned this routinely thankless task to help them learn rules and procedures); to cast tie-breaking votes, which he rarely needs to do; and to succeed to the presidency, if necessary. Benjamin Franklin suggested that the vice president should be addressed as "His Superfluous Excellency" because he had so little to do. "Standby equipment" is how Nelson Rockefeller described the job. Franklin Roosevelt's first vice president, John Nance Garner, was less elegant, observing that his job was not worth a "pitcher of warm piss."

Historically, presidents gave their vice presidents little information and few opportunities to prepare for succession. They were usually chosen to balance the ticket geographically or ideologically, not because they were men with whom presidents wanted to work. When Harry Truman became vice president, he had no knowledge of the ongoing research into atomic

Michelle Obama has used her position as First Lady to promote exercise and healthy eating.

President Obama assigned important responsibilities to Vice President Biden, including the winding down of the Iraq War.

power and no preparation for the extraordinary decisions he would confront after four months in office, in determining whether to use the atomic bomb in the war against Japan.

Yet vice presidents have succeeded to office unexpectedly nine times, following eight presidential deaths and one resignation. In the modern presidency, three vice presidents unexpectedly became president, and serious presidential illnesses or near-assassinations could have resulted in two other vice presidents becoming chief executive. These circumstances have led to more attention and power being given to this office in more recent administrations.

Throughout the modern presidency, chief executives have decided how much work and authority to give their vice presidents based upon their personal relationship, the president's own need for assistance, the president's generosity in sharing power, and the vice president's own ambitions. (Vice presidents planning their own presidential campaigns may be working to build an independent political base, qualifying their loyalty to the president.) As a former governor without Washington experience, President Carter included his vice president, Walter Mondale, in important White House staff meetings.[50] Presidents Reagan, Clinton, and George W. Bush were also Washington outsiders, and they continued this practice of drawing upon the expertise of their vice presidents.[51] It was George W. Bush, however, who granted his vice president, Dick Cheney, the most authority.

Dick Cheney was well known to Bush from his service in George H. W. Bush's administration as defense secretary. Cheney's career included six terms in the House of Representatives and senior positions in the White House Office and the cabinet; he had far more administrative and political experience than the new president. Cheney came to office with the goal of "merging" the vice president's office with the president's to create a "single Executive Office" in which the vice president would serve as the president's "executive and implementer."[52] He was also deeply involved in the president's legislative strategy, went to Capitol Hill at least once a week to meet with the Republican caucus, and kept an office in the House of Representatives (the only vice president to do so). He headed the most important policy-making groups in the White House and was the author of its energy policy. He created his own national security staff, placed his own people in key defense and state department offices, and worked closely on military policy with Bush's defense secretary, Cheney's old friend Donald Rumsfeld. By virtually everyone's judgment, Cheney was the most powerful vice president in U.S. history. Few people who reach the White House are as willing as Bush was to gamble their professional reputations on their second-in-command.

The Obama-Biden relationship reinforces the conclusion that Bush-Cheney did not set a lasting precedent. Elected to the presidency during his first term in the Senate, President Obama is a Washington outsider compared to

LARRY DOWNING/Reuters/Landov

Vice President Dick Cheney was the driving force behind many Bush administration policies.

Vice President Biden. With six terms in the Senate, including service as chair of the Senate Foreign Relations Committee, Biden has substantive policy expertise, extensive knowledge of the Washington community and of congressional procedures, and long-standing collegial relationships among Democrats and Republicans. Bringing these resources into the administration, Biden meets regularly with the president, sits in on any meeting of his choosing, and has been an important adviser on foreign and security policies and on relations between the White House and Congress. But he has none of Cheney's skill in behind-the-scenes bureaucratic maneuvering, and Obama has not charged him with these responsibilities. Biden also has not asked for independent spheres of operation or policy initiatives as Cheney did. Rather, Biden is said to aspire to Cheney's role as most influential adviser, or "the last voice in the room."[53]

Thinking about Democracy

As president, how would you assert control over your cabinet? Your White House Office? To what extent would you centralize your decision making in the White House staff? When would you include your department secretaries in your policy-making deliberations? How would your decisions and actions reflect your commitment to a democratic form of government?

Presidents as Managers

Just as the structure of the White House Office has slowly—in fits and starts—become somewhat standardized across administrations, so also have presidential managerial styles become somewhat similar.

Prior to the Nixon administration, the modern presidents' management styles were typically a reflection of their political and personal style. In most presidential administrations, most staff members were generalists, who expected to perform a wide range of tasks at the request of the president. Presidents Franklin Roosevelt and John Kennedy fostered a sense of competition among staff members, sometimes assigning the same task to multiple individuals in order to see who would serve them best. President Lyndon Johnson took this approach even further and pushed his staff to achieve ambitious goals, to the point that some described him as bullying and abusive.[54] In marked contrast to the flexibility and fluidity of these staffing arrangements, President Dwight Eisenhower favored a comparatively formal and hierarchical structure for his White House Office. Work assignments and office responsibilities were clearly and consistently defined, and information was communicated through well-established relationships. Though many factors influence a chief executive's management of the White House, it is significant that Roosevelt, Kennedy, and Johnson gained most of their experience in elective political offices, while Eisenhower was a career military officer.

From the Nixon administration onward, presidents' management styles have shown some important similarities, especially as their term has progressed and they have been exposed to the full pressures of policy making and decision making on a national and global scale.

Like Eisenhower, President Nixon valued formal lines of authority. Particularly influential was the chief of staff, H. R. Haldeman, who was effectively the president's second-in-command, controlling access to the president and taking responsibility for virtually every aspect of White House life. In Haldeman's words, "Every president needs a son of a bitch, and I'm Nixon's. I'm his buffer and his bastard. I get done what he wants done and I take the heat instead of him."[55] The high value placed on loyalty, combined with an expansionist view of presidential powers, led to descriptions of this administration as "an **imperial presidency**" and to its White House staff as "the palace guard."

Responding to these criticisms, and to the scandal of the Watergate break-in, Presidents Ford and Carter stressed that their White House Offices would be more transparent and that they would be more directly engaged in decision making. Both of these presidents initially refused to name chiefs of staff; both eventually relented. President Ford later concluded that "anybody who doesn't have [a chief of staff] and tries to run the responsibilities of the White House…is putting too big a burden on the President himself. You need a filter, a person that you have total confidence in…. I just can't imagine a President not having an effective Chief of Staff."[56] When President Clinton resisted naming a chief of staff, he became so bogged down in details that his wife referred to him as the "mechanic-in-chief."[57]

There was no one to check the president's preference for discussions without fixed agendas, his disregard for schedules and appointments.[58] Clinton ultimately appointed individuals who tightened the lines of authority and communication and who were willing to say "No" to the president.

George W. Bush employed a near-opposite approach to management. With experience as an enforcer of political loyalties on his father's campaign, and as the only president to have earned a master's in business administration, Bush set out to run his White House along corporate lines. He tried to delegate work along crisp lines of authority, kept to a tight schedule, and demanded complete team loyalty with no public dissent from administration policy.[59]

As Bush's term progressed, however, he found that these managerial practices had serious limitations and drawbacks. The tight hierarchy sometimes isolated the president, preventing him from receiving important information and inhibiting constructive disagreement. "The first time I told him he was wrong," a young aide said, "he started yelling at me. Then I showed him where he was wrong, and he said, 'All right, I understand. Good job.' He patted me on the shoulder. I went and had dry heaves in the bathroom."[60] Friction and dissent among senior officials was publicly expressed, raising questions about the administration's policy commitments. Secretary of State Colin Powell and Secretary of Defense Donald Rumsfeld strongly disagreed over the use of intelligence and the conduct of the war in Iraq. And Bush's willingness to delegate power, especially to his vice president, led to his sometimes appearing a secondary figure in his own administration. There are few more damning descriptions of a president than that given by Bush's own treasury secretary, Paul O'Neill, who wrote that, in cabinet and private meetings, the chief executive seemed disengaged and uninformed.[61]

Barack Obama centralized policy decisions in his White House, appointing a number of "czars" to coordinate policies across departments and agencies. Energy and climate change policy, economic policy, health care insurance reform, urban affairs, auto industry restructuring, financial bailouts, terrorism, drug control, and American Indian affairs were among the policies that White House aides coordinated. The president devoted a great deal of his own time and resources to health care, economic recovery, and the war in Afghanistan.[62] Following Democratic losses in the 2010 midterm elections, and throughout 2012, as it became increasingly clear that the Republican House majority would not allow the president to advance major policy initiatives, the president relied more on unilateral powers such as executive orders. Centralizing decision making in the White House Office and policy making in the person of the president established Obama as an energetic and controversial chief executive.

Public expectations for President Obama were sky-high and unrealistic.

PRESIDENTIAL LEADERSHIP

Pharaohs, consuls, kings, queens, emperors, tsars, prime ministers, and councils had served as executives in other governments before 1789. But no national government had a president, an elected executive with authority equal to and independent of a national legislature, until George Washington was elected president of the United States.

As explained at the beginning of this chapter, Congress held most of the national power for most of the nineteenth and some of the twentieth century, prompting Woodrow Wilson to call this government a "congressional government."[63] From the administration of Franklin Roosevelt onward, however, presidents asserted and often expanded the powers of their office. Nixon pursued this goal so strongly that, as we described earlier, his was called an imperial presidency. Even so, all the modern presidents have become frustrated with the limits on their power. At times, they consider themselves stuck with an imperiled or impossible presidency.[64]

Consider our most recent presidents. Bill Clinton saw much of his policy agenda sidetracked by successive congressional investigations. Most of his second term was consumed by impeachment proceedings. George W. Bush enacted much of his policy agenda, including major tax cuts, education and regulatory change, and the prosecution of two wars. Yet Bush's failure to end the wars, coupled with a prolonged economic recession and high unemployment, led to deep public discontent with his leadership. Barack Obama achieved notable legislative successes before starting his reelection campaign, including health insurance reform, an extension of child health insurance, the Lily Ledbetter Fair Pay Act, an economic stimulus package, foreclosure assistance, credit-card regulation, financial services regulation, tobacco regulation, food safety regulation reform, and an expansion of hate crimes legislation. Yet continuing troop commitments abroad, enduring unemployment, and a rising national debt lowered his approval ratings throughout the first term, though Obama sustained his 2008 voter coalition sufficiently that he won re-election in 2012.

Imperial, imperiled, or impossible? What is the current state of the presidency in the United States today?

The Personal President?

The Founders envisioned a president chosen by the Electoral College and removed from the public, and the earliest presidents had little direct public contact. George Washington and Thomas Jefferson averaged only three speeches a year to the public; John Adams averaged one.[65] Abraham Lincoln thought it prudent to make few speeches. He told people gathered at Gettysburg the night before his famous address, "I have no speech to make. In my position it is somewhat important that I should not say foolish things. It very often happens that the only way to help it is to say nothing at all."[66]

This is not an option for presidents today, who win office, in significant part, on the basis of promises made to the voters. "Everybody now expects the man inside the White House

When President Franklin Roosevelt died, most Americans, reflecting the personal presidency, felt a personal loss. Chief Petty Officer Graham Jackson plays "Nearer My God to Thee" as the president's body is carried to the train that returned him to Washington for burial.

to do something about everything."[67] More bluntly, people expect presidents to cause change. Throughout the modern presidency—and earlier—most presidents have entered the Oval Office with a legislative agenda. As the president's legislative role has grown, and as mass communications have become increasingly attentive to political decision makers and decision making, the president has been identified as the voice of the people and the most visible figure in government.[68] In the words of one presidential scholar, "The great powers of the American people have been invested" in this one office, "making it the most powerful office in the world . . . precisely because it is truly the people's power."[69]

Franklin Roosevelt is credited with (some say, blamed for) doing most to develop and institutionalize this personal relationship with the public, greatly expanding the powers of the presidency in the process. His radio addresses, some of which were framed as "**fireside chats**," were among the first to systematically and deliberately use the media to speak directly and regularly to people. These addresses made the president the focal point and public face of the government. Roosevelt's tone was warm and conversational, as evidenced by his reference to the people as "my friends." Listening to the radio became a family event; one listener said that, on a summer day, with windows open, one could walk down the street and never miss a word of the president's address because every family was listening. Roosevelt also made use of public opinion polls to gauge the public's views. Thus he created a communications loop—to the people and from the people—that helped him sell his policies.

This "personal presidency" has both advantages and disadvantages for the president and for the country. On the one hand, it helps presidents marshal public support for important goals, overcoming the inertia of a system with fragmented power. On the other hand, it encourages tendencies to see presidents as all-powerful. It causes people to give the president too much credit when things go right, too much blame when they fail, even when the president has little to do with either outcome, as when the economy sags or surges.

Wanting to win their office, and then wanting to sustain their approval ratings, candidates and presidents make unrealistic promises and typically work hard to keep those commitments. Barack Obama promised health care to every American, reform of the educational system, victory in Afghanistan, and the restoration of America's image abroad. As president, Obama sought to follow through on these promises, making health care insurance reform a first priority. As his term progressed, Obama found, as had his predecessors, that it is necessary to set some promises aside, to counter congressional opposition to others, and to devote considerable resources to others. The prison at Guantanamo was still open, more than three years into Obama's presidency, despite promises that it would be closed within the first year; pro-consumer regulatory reform encountered strong Republican opposition in Congress; and health care insurance reform, though it ultimately passed, dominated the presidential agenda for months, to the exclusion of other much-needed initiatives. Whether they fail or succeed in keeping their promises, presidents often pay a heavy price for the statements they make as candidates. (See Figure 1.)

The public also may pay a heavy price for promises that they pressure the presidential candidates to make and uphold. When presidents are unsuccessful in negotiating with Congress—perhaps because they lack the support of their own party, perhaps because the opposing party is skilled in political obstruction—presidents often decide to exercise power more unilaterally. Though Barack Obama consistently spoke of his desire for bipartisan policy making, the resistance of congressional Republicans to his agenda led him to make use of signing statements, though many fewer than Bush, to achieve some of his legislative priorities. Unilateral presidential powers such as this have the potential to disrupt the balance among the three branches. When presidents justify the use of such powers on the grounds that a majority of the voters have endorsed their policy agenda, the challenges and contradictions of leading a democratic republic multiply.

The President and the Media

Presidents' media relations involve managing the flow of information and the interpretation of that information. To achieve these goals, presidents rely upon a press secretary and a press office within the White House Office to explain their actions. Also within the White House Office is the communications office, which creates events at which the president can demonstrate leadership through words (such as speeches, interviews, town hall meetings) and visuals ("photo ops"). It is tempting to think that the press secretary focuses on "what is," while the communications director is devoted to "what could be," but that would be a mistake. After Bush's second press secretary resigned, he wrote a book describing how the White House staff manipulated intelligence information to convince the public that an invasion of Iraq was necessary.[70] Both press secretaries and communications directors are

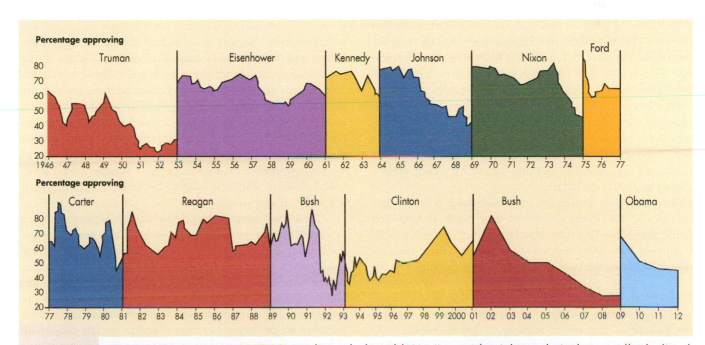

FIGURE 1: PRESIDENTIAL POPULARITY Since the end of World War II, presidential popularity has usually declined over time. Only two presidents—Reagan and Clinton—left office with ratings at a level comparable to that when they entered.

SOURCE: Gallup polls, reported in *Public Opinion* and updated at www.presidency.ucsb.edu/data/popularity.php. The question asked is "Do you approve or disapprove of the way [name of president] is handling his job as president?"

dedicated to securing coverage that endorses the president and the president's agenda.

Though their functions are different, the press and communications offices are both dedicated to delivering a focused message for every day and every week. The goal is for everyone in the administration to "stay on message"—to repeat the message and to avoid distracting issues. In this way, it is hoped, the president's priorities and policies will be coherently and persuasively presented. Inevitably, however, other issues will arise, and the administration's message will fracture. Presidents are rarely able to control the media's coverage of their administration.

The Reagan White House was, however, particularly effective in managing presidential communications. Having acted in theater, movies, and television, Reagan had mastered the art of speaking and performing in front of live audiences and on camera.[71] Tall, handsome, and poised, he knew exactly how to use an inflection, a gesture, or a tilt of his head to keep all eyes and ears focused on him. His speeches and even his casual comments were highly effective. Reagan's aides capitalized on these talents. As one explained, "The media, while they won't admit it, are not in the news business; they're in entertainment. We tried to create the most entertaining, visually attractive scene to fill that box [the TV screen], so that the networks would have to use it."[72] This strategy meant that the aides controlled the president: aides, not the president, determined "the line of the day" and instructed the president in what to say. They also instructed him not to answer reporters' questions about other matters. The administration, not the media, would determine what was covered in the news and what would be a priority for the president.[73]

The George W. Bush administration was also very disciplined about staying on message, especially during the first four years. On most days, newscast viewers and talk radio listeners heard administration officials delivering the same message. Running such an operation is a high-pressure job, and press secretaries and communications directors usually do not last long. When Bush's first press secretary resigned after two years, he said he wanted to do "something more relaxing, like dismantling live nuclear weapons."[74]

Crafting the message is only one aspect of the president's media relations. The message also has to be picked up and relayed by the media in terms that support the president. To achieve this goal, presidents have embraced technological advances in mass communication—from radio to television to social media—and have traveled throughout the nation. Presidents have used technology to convey their message more directly to the public, trying to limit the filters of the media. Travel is undertaken for similar reasons: once outside Washington, presidents can circumvent the White House press corps, stating their message through local and regional media outlets. This is the strategy of **going public**. [75] As always, the goal is to secure favorable coverage for themselves and their administration.

For presidents, of course, the real test of a communications strategy is whether it wins public support for their

President Kennedy cultivated a persona of youthful vigor and cool elegance.

policy agenda. Yet careful study of public opinion polls before and after speeches suggests that any changes in the presidents' approval ratings are small and of limited duration. This is true even for State of the Union Addresses, which are major political events that receive extensive coverage. When presidents have conducted lengthy and focused campaigns on behalf of their policy priorities, they have rarely altered the prevailing judgment of the public. For example, George W. Bush worked hard to win popular support to privatize Social Security, with little success, because the public favored the program as it was.

These circumstances have led observers of the presidency to conclude that presidential speechmaking persuades the public only under certain conditions. First, presidents have more success in reinforcing than in changing public opinion. When there is already widespread agreement in the public, or among elites, the words of the president are accepted more readily. Second, presidents are more persuasive when their speeches are perceived as ethically and politically consistent. When the public finds a president sincere, the president's words are more readily accepted. Finally, presidents can more readily persuade the public to accept the importance of an issue than to take a particular stance on that issue.

Jimmy Carter's campaign to prioritize human rights in U.S. foreign relations transformed these apparent constraints into guidelines for success. The members of his administration consistently spoke on behalf of human rights; this policy meshed closely with the president's persona and political agenda; and it was congruent with the nation's self-perception as a democratic advocate. Human rights were also a policy priority that built upon the initiatives of prior administrations; it was continued, sometimes debated, by Carter's successors. As this example suggests, however, the persuasiveness of a presidential communications campaign may not be evident for decades—a problem for chief executives trying to change policy and win reelection in a matter of months or years.[76]

Presidential Communications

The observation that "politics is theater" is intended as ridicule, but the best political presentations are like the best theater: they reveal truths about the human condition. And the actors who convey these insights, educating the audience, gain respect and influence. The evolution of these practices, and the changing relationships among the president and the media, can be seen in modern presidents' televised presentations.

Though television became popular in the 1950s, not all politicians immediately recognized its potential. Dwight Eisenhower shunned televised speeches because, he said, "I can think of nothing more boring, for the American public, than to have to sit in their living rooms for a whole half hour looking at my face on their television screens."[77]

Television became a powerful political tool in the 1960s. President John Kennedy initiated live television coverage of his presidential press conferences. By answering reporters' questions with intelligence and wit, he reached out to the viewers. When asked how he felt about the Republican National Committee adopting "a resolution saying you were pretty much of a failure," Kennedy grinned and replied, "I assume it passed unanimously." More generally, he made extensive use of visuals throughout his presidency. Photographs and films showed the president sailing and playing touch football, hosting elegant White House gatherings, presiding over meetings with his senior staff, and representing the United States at international summits. Almost twenty years younger than his predecessor at the time of his inauguration, Kennedy presented himself as a dynamic, authoritative head of state and head of government, even though he endured chronic back pain and suffered from Addison's disease.

Years later, Ronald Reagan, George H. W. Bush, and George W. Bush crafted public personae that connected their lives and leadership to enduring American values. These presidents cast themselves as symbols and embodiments of the nation, drawing upon western mythologies of the cowboy as self-reliant, strong, and tough. Reagan and George W. Bush regularly provided photo ops at their ranches, where they wore cowboy boots, rode horses, and cut brush. The presidents' faith in these self-presentations gave them authenticity. Yet, like Kennedy, their lives were much more complicated

The public didn't always agree with President Reagan's views or policies, but he remained popular partly because of his image as a rugged individualist.

than they were admitting. Reagan grew up in the Midwest, became an influential union leader in Hollywood, and converted from the Democratic to the Republican Party. Bush was the son of a president and the beneficiary of generations of wealth whose companies weathered serious financial reversals. Their characterizations were simplifications and, as such, were challenged.

George W. Bush, with his communications staff, presented himself as a forceful and successful wartime president. In 2003, Bush flew on a fighter jet—many observers thought he was the pilot—to an aircraft carrier. Climbing down from the cockpit in a fighter suit, and striding to a podium flanked by the carrier crew and by an enormous banner that declared "MISSION ACCOMPLISHED," Bush staged one of the most dramatic photo ops of the modern presidency. It was an outstanding example of a gesture designed to shape public perceptions and gain public support.[78] The advantage of such bold efforts is that the visual image lingers. But for Bush that was also the disadvantage. He had announced the end of the war in Iraq far too soon. The photo-op came back to haunt him as war dragged on for years in Afghanistan and Iraq, as the Middle East remained destabilized, and as threat levels in the United States remained high.

As Bush found, if a president fails to manage his image, the press or his opponents will do so, in ways that the president is likely to find objectionable. This was a lesson that Bush should have learned from President Clinton. Clinton, too, crafted a public persona that linked his life and his leadership with enduring American values. Clinton was the "man from Hope," a self-made individual whose success testified to his own abilities and to the fluidity of American society. Clinton was the "comeback kid," the underdog who never stopped fighting and who believed in the rightness of his cause. And Clinton was a talented communicator, with a gift for changing and shifting public perceptions. Clinton so strongly framed the 1995–1996 government shutdowns as Republican failures that these events contributed to his 1996 reelection win. Yet even Clinton's persuasiveness had its limits. Though he won reelection despite threats of impeachment, media coverage was far from positive. The president appeared to be a self-indulgent adulterer, whose personal choices severely compromised the effectiveness of his presidency.

President Obama established his persona in memoirs written in 2007 and 2008, just before and in the midst of his presidential campaign. His presented himself as a cosmopolitan, multiracial man with roots in the rural Midwest, who had lived in Hawaii and Indonesia. The traditions and values that Obama claimed to embody included those of immigration (his father was a Kenyan), socioeconomic mobility, personal talent and communal outreach (educated at elite schools, he had been a community organizer and a state legislator), and inclusivity and optimism ("Yes, we can!" was more mantra than slogan). As president, Obama was rarely an eloquent or inspiring speaker, though his speeches began to regain their energy and intensity as the reelection campaign gained momentum. As president, Obama was rarely an eloquent speaker, and he was slow to regain his inspirational style in his re-election campaign. After a dismal first presidential debate, which undermined his lead against challenger Mitt Romney, Obama finally returned to a style that was succinct, intense, and responsive to his audience.

 ## Thinking about Democracy

As a voter, do you think that a president should use the media to disseminate information or to gain support? From the voter's perspective, are these different tasks? Why or why not? How would a journalist respond to your judgments? What would a president say?

Legislative-Executive Relations

When a president enters office during a time of economic prosperity and unified government, the opportunities for legislative success are great. But even when government is divided and economic conditions are not bright—as was the case throughout Franklin Roosevelt's presidency and the early years of the Reagan and Clinton presidencies—a skilled

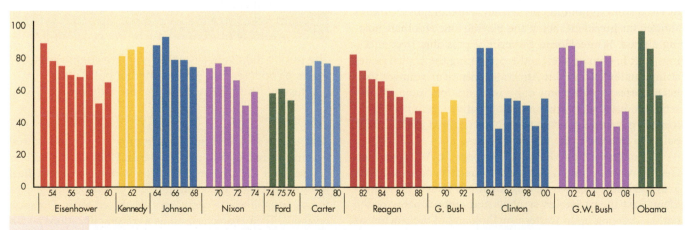

FIGURE 2: PRESIDENTIAL SUCCESS ON CONGRESSIONAL VOTES A president's legislative success rate measures the number of presidential "wins" on roll call votes, on which the president has clearly stated a position. Though some presidents have been more successful in their second year than in their first, their winning percentage typically declines with time.

SOURCE: *CQ Weekly*, January 11, 2010, 113. CQ weekly by Congressional Quarterly, Inc. Copyright © 2010 Reproduced with permission of CQ-ROLL CALL, INC. via Copyright Clearance Center.

chief executive can still capitalize on the electoral mandate for change, the media's desire for a story, the opposing party's internal divisions, and the members' concern to secure their reelection by providing for their constituents' needs.

Among the most important factors affecting legislative-executive relations are the partisan majorities in the two houses and the electoral pressures felt by the members. When the president's party has strong majorities in both the House and the Senate, the president's first priority is keeping party members together in support of his agenda. The legislative agenda needs to include both presidential and congressional priorities, but negotiations about those priorities can be conducted within the party. Members of the minority party are reduced to obstructionist tactics. For the first six years of his presidency, George W. Bush enjoyed just this political situation. Though there were some tough negotiations within the Republican Party, majorities of the House and the Senate were generally strongly supportive of the president. The September 11, 2001, attacks also generated a willingness to defer to the president, a common practice in wartime (sometimes called the "rally 'round the flag" effect). In the second year of his presidency, Bush won 87.8 percent of the roll call votes on which his administration had taken a clear position. His success rate remained above 70 percent so long as his party was in the majority. (See Figure 2.)

When, however, the president confronts a Congress with one or both houses controlled by the other party, the situation changes. Depending on the strength of the party controlling Congress and whether or not it controls both houses rather than just one, compromise may lead to major changes in the legislation, forcing a president to qualify even highly publicized commitments. After the Democratic Party suffered significant losses in the 2010 midterm elections, President Obama agreed to extend the Bush-era tax cuts for two years—breaking his own campaign promise to end these cuts for the wealthy—in return for Republican support in extending unemployment benefits and a cut in the Social Security payroll tax. If the minority party is internally fragmented, however, and the president is able to capitalize on those divisions, then the compromises may be more limited. Rather than having to find common ground with an entire party, the president appeases influential individuals. This tactic has been used less frequently in recent administrations, as partisan polarization has caused members of the opposing party to be less interested in—and less willing to—abandon their party. During the fight to secure passage of its health care reform legislation, for example, the Obama White House struck a number of deals with Senate Democrats, not Republicans, to secure support for passage of the legislation.

Sometimes, when a president has to deal with a Congress controlled by the opposite party, gridlock ensues as neither side has enough clout to put together winning coalitions of votes and neither side is willing to compromise. This situation emerged frequently during George W. Bush's second term and Obama's tenure. This frequently came at a very high

CourseReader ASSIGNMENT

Log in to www.cengagebrain.com and open Course-Reader to access the full reading "America Isn't a Corporation," by Paul Krugman.

Paul Krugman is a Nobel Prize–winning economist who is famed for his work in international trade and economic geography. He has also won wide respect for his writing as a New York columnist and for his skill in advancing strong and clear arguments for the everyday relevance of economic analysis. In the column "American Isn't a Corporation," however, Krugman is more modest in his claims for economics. Stating that business expertise and political expertise are distinct, that "running a business and managing an economy" are quite different undertakings, Krugman cautions against presuming that success as a corporate leader will lead to success as a president. Why not? Do you find this argument convincing?

1. Krugman focuses on the claims of Mitt Romney, but many presidential candidates have highlighted their private sector accomplishments. Jimmy Carter's success in running his family's peanut business, Ronald Reagan's negotiating skill as a union executive, George H. W. Bush's performance as an oil executive, and George W. Bush's promise to be a "CEO president" are just a few examples. Why is private sector experience and success so appealing to American voters when they assess a presidential candidate?

2. What powers can a president actually exercise in order to affect the economy? What connections exist between the executive branch and the economy? Between the national government and the nation's economy? What experience, prior to entering the Oval Office, can prepare a president to exercise these powers and improve these connections?

3. What policies do you think the government should institute to improve the performance of the national economy? Do you think that the president should initiate these policies? Why? If not the president, which branch or which government leader should exercise this leadership?

price, as when lengthy budget and debt ceiling negotiations cost the nation its Standard & Poor's AAA credit rating in the summer of 2010.

Presidents tend to be less successful later in their administrations. For members of Congress of the president's party, their constituents' priorities become more important as the midterm elections draw closer, and those are not always congruent with the president's priorities. In addition, members of the opposition party may believe that standing against the president's priorities is a winner in their own districts. So, for example, in 2010 Republicans voted against Obama's proposals in Congress and then ran against him and his priorities in the midterm elections that year. As the presidents' influence with the voters lessens and as politics become more polarized, legislative-executive relations become gridlocked.

THE FLUCTUATING POWERS OF THE PRESIDENCY

Despite its advantages, presidential power should not be exaggerated. Most presidents since World War II have seemed at times almost powerless to shape events affecting the national interest. The immensely popular war hero Dwight Eisenhower (1953–1961) was unable to buck Cold War sentiment and prevent the buildup of the military-industrial complex. John Kennedy (1961–1963), who enjoyed an extraordinary success rate in a conservative Congress, was stymied in getting civil rights legislation accepted. The domestic goals of Lyndon Johnson (1963–1969), along with his chances for reelection, were derailed by a war that took Richard Nixon (1969–1974) years to end. And Nixon, for whom the "imperial presidency" phrase was coined, was forced from office on obstruction of justice charges for covering up criminal activity in the Watergate scandal.

Reaction against the arrogant use of presidential powers led to the modest presidencies of Gerald Ford (1974–1977) and Jimmy Carter (1977–1981). Each presented himself as more humble than Nixon and less interested in power for its own sake. Ford, who became president when Nixon resigned, was a kind of accidental president and could not get reelected. Nor could Carter; he had ambitious programs, especially in energy and conservation, but his ascetic, if not dour, demeanor and demands for American sacrifice put him at a disadvantage against the sunny disposition of his election opponent and successor, Ronald Reagan. But Reagan, one of our most popular recent presidents, was so frustrated when Congress thwarted his foreign policy initiatives that he condoned illegal activities, producing the Iran-Contra scandal

Opposition to President Obama's policies and to the president himself has been fierce. In Mason City, Iowa, a Tea Party group, reflecting the over-the-top anger and irrationality common today, erected this billboard comparing Obama to the Nazi Adolf Hitler and the communist Vladimir Lenin.

and tarnishing his personal reputation. Reagan, George H. W. Bush, and Bill Clinton all had ambitious agendas, although Reagan's and Bush's were directed more toward foreign than domestic policy.

Under Clinton, the presidency seemed to be imploding as the personal presidency reached a new level. A former employee of Arkansas state government sued him, and the Supreme Court ruled that he had no immunity while in office because the conduct occurred before he took office.[79] The judges, in a colossal misjudgment, doubted that the case would take much time or attention. In fact, it not only took time but also diverted attention away from the president's domestic agenda. Then came impeachment.

The continuous investigations of Bill Clinton by Congress, special prosecutors, and conservative groups resulted in media saturation of the most private and intimate details of a president's life ever revealed. "It is entirely possible," one reporter observed, "that the Clinton era will be remembered by historians primarily as the moment when the distance between the President and the public evaporated forever."[80]

Some historians speculated that Clinton's impeachment would leave a legacy similar to Andrew Johnson's, which weakened the presidency for the next half-century.[81] But when George W. Bush came to office in 2001, he brought a retinue of Washington professionals and set out to restore the presidency to its former pre-eminence. Then, despite the successes of his first term, Bush also fell prey to the ills that beset second-term presidents. He watched his popularity plummet to historic lows as his wars dragged on at an increasing cost and as the economy fell into recession.

Wars and crisis situations are always temptations for presidents who believe this office needs to be even stronger. This tendency has been strengthened by the evolution of the personal presidency, increasing the likelihood that the public will look first to the president to act in a crisis. The ability of the president to command the stage in these situations may tempt Congress to abdicate its constitutional obligations, especially in a unified government. But the Bush administration's interpretation, according to one Republican legal adviser, "staked out powers that [were] a universe beyond any other administration."[82] In the political climate created by the September 11, 2001, attack, the Republican leadership in Congress was reluctant to exercise oversight of executive branch actions. It was just as reluctant five years later. Frustrated critics in Congress charged that Bush acted as if the system of checks and balances did not exist.

There is no doubt that the public, after the spectacle of the Clinton impeachment, wanted to see dignity returned to the White House and Congress get back to the real business of governing. But there is no reason to believe that the public was looking for more power to gravitate to the presidency, or for Congress and the courts to abandon their responsibility to act as checks on executive power. In other words, the move to expand presidential powers was not necessarily government responding to the people, but rather government officials trying to institutionalize their personal vision of the presidency.

Eventually the Bush-Cheney reach for imperial powers led to the same kind of rebuff experienced by other presidents with long arms. Cheney's approval ratings fell to single digits, Bush's to the high twenties, and in 2007 *Time* magazine did not even list the president among the world's most influential people.[83] With a divided government in his last two years, Bush's congressional success rate fell to 38 percent and he began to exercise his previously unused veto power. In his last year in office, *The Daily Show* began referring to him as "Still" President Bush.

This "diminished presidency" was matched by a weak Congress, with approval ratings even lower than the president's.[84] The powerful executive-driven government that Bush and Cheney tried to put in place led instead to a stalemated government in which no branch was carrying out its role. These developments seemed to indicate that those presidents who overreach in trying to make a lasting imprint on the office can do serious harm to their own legacies. Meanwhile, the office itself will be reshaped by its next occupant.

Barack Obama rode into office on a wave of public adulation, with high expectations that he would reduce partisanship and bring a new way of governing to Washington. But despite his remarkable first-year success with Congress and the passage of several major pieces of legislation, partisanship was worse than ever. George W. Bush had successfully used the "rally 'round the flag" effect to dampen Democratic opposition in his first term, but congressional Republicans showed little deference to Obama's huge electoral victory. Most Democrats had supported Bush's No Child Left Behind school reform and his foreign policy. Some even helped pass tax cuts for the highest earners, his other major legislative innovation. Obama, on the other hand, was unable to win more than a few Republican votes for any of his top legislative priorities. Obama's early successes with Congress would have been impossible if he had not had, in his first two years, the largest congressional majorities of any Democrat since Lyndon Johnson. Even so, during his first eighteen months in office, Obama saw his approval ratings drop by twenty points, but those for Congress stood as much as thirty points lower.

It is too soon to conclude that we now have a diminished presidency. One of the most interesting aspects of this unusual office is its resilience and elasticity. The Constitution does not give the presidency the dominant role in government; the office does change from one administration to another, or even within a single administration. How the individuals we elect to the Oval Office will use the powers of the presidency—formal and informal, to act as head of the government and head of state—will reflect the ideologies and talents of the president, the historical forces at work in and on the office, and the needs of the time. Understanding how and when each of these influences is felt, and to what extent, is the challenge confronted by scholars and voters who see the constructive potential of the leadership that presidents could and will provide.

SUMMARY

- The Constitution sets few requirements for presidential candidates; the electorate, however, has identified as "presidential" individuals with a very specific profile. Throughout the twentieth and twenty-first centuries, chief executives have consistently been white heterosexual males, married with children, educated at elite institutions, and possessed of graduate degrees. Highly ambitious, these individuals have typically been governors (chief executives in state politics), U.S. senators, or vice presidents.

- Presidential removal and succession are governed by the Constitution and by supplementary laws. The Constitution sets out the procedures for impeachment; the Twenty-fifth Amendment provides guidelines for replacing a vice president in the event of resignation or impeachment; and the Succession Act defines the order in which federal officers will serve as president in the event the vice president is unable to do so.

- The constitutional powers granted to the president allow this decision maker to influence the executive branch (as chief executive and commander in chief), the legislative branch (through lobbying, through the veto, and through signing statements), and the judicial branch (by exercising the pardoning power).

- Presidential powers are checked by law and by tradition. Presidents conduct extended negotiations with Congress on behalf of their proposals, for example, especially when the opposing party controls one or both houses.

- A president's administration is critically important to the chief executive's success in making decisions and implementing policy because presidential appointees and nominees transform a president's words into programs.

- Senior members of the White House Office typically have a close relationship with the president; their access adds to their influence. At the same time, because they are so closely associated with the president, the work performed by these individuals is closely scrutinized and criticized by the public, the media, and other decision makers.

- Presidents find it very difficult to stay "on message" and almost impossible to control their media coverage. The challenges have increased with the 24/7 news cycle, which has helped created an insatiable demand for information.

- Though modern presidents have repeatedly presented themselves as decisive, most have found themselves constrained by the Congress, by their own and the opposing party, and by the electorate.

- Presidents rely on speechmaking and communication events to build support throughout the public, issue networks, and the Washington community. Though some observers question the power of a president's words, others point to presidential statements that have mobilized the society and changed long-standing political agendas.

- Legislative-executive relations have varied greatly throughout the modern presidency. Among the factors influencing a president's legislative success are the majority or minority status of his party, and the extent to which members feel they can reach bipartisan agreements.

DISCUSSION QUESTIONS

1. How do the requirements for being president, both formal and informal, define the constitutional Office of the President?

2. Do you think that it should be easier to impeach a president? Why or why not? How would your answer alter the balance of power among the three branches of the national government?

3. As president, which presidential powers would you rely upon? Which would you want to expand? Why? Would your priorities change if your party controlled (or did not control) the legislative branch? Why or why not?

4. Do you think it is more important to empower or to check a president? Defend your answer with constitutional and party-based arguments.

5. Compare and contrast appointments and nominations. Imagine you could change cabinet secretaries into presidential appointees. Would this be a good reform? Why or why not?

6. If you were vice president, what responsibilities would you want the president to give to you? How much power would you want to exercise? How would your functions be similar to or different from those of the first lady?

7. Do we still have the same Office of the President that the Founders designed, given all that has happened throughout the modern presidency?

8. When do you think that "going public" will most help a president?

9. Which modern president's relationships with Congress do you think have been most constructive? What does your answer reveal about your expectations of legislative leadership?

10. What is your definition of an effective president? How does your definition compare and contrast with prevailing popular expectations?

11

The Bureaucracy

An FDA inspector examines beef for contaminants at a meat-packing plant in Fort Morgan, Colorado.

© Kevin Moloney/Aurora Photos/Corbis

LEARNING OBJECTIVES

1. Define, then compare and contrast, private and public bureaucracies. Analyze the goals of responsiveness, accountability, and equity.

2. Explain the major functions of bureaucracies.

3. List the reasons why policy implementation is complicated. Assess how well the federal bureaucracy is fulfilling this responsibility, with illustrative examples.

4. Name the major causes of growth in the federal bureaucracy. Examine the significance of each for bureaucratic performance.

5. Describe the principal types of federal bureaucracies, delineating the extent to which each is independent of the president.

6. State why and how the law limits the political activities of federal bureaucrats. Discuss why and how presidents have nonetheless sought to politicize these agencies.

7. List the principal ways that oversight is conducted by the president, the Congress, and the courts; and by interest groups, corporations, and the public. Hypothesize which will be most effective in controlling the federal bureaucracy.

8. Defend and critique the role of the bureaucracy in the U.S. democratic republic.

TALKING POINTS

After Sen. Dennis Kucinich (D-Ohio) bit into an olive pit in a sandwich and broke a tooth, which then required extensive dental work, he sued operators of the congressional cafeteria. Kucinich settled his case out of court for an undisclosed sum, despite the fact that in any bottle of olives 1.3 percent may contain pits or pit fragments.[1] Who says so? The presence of olive pits and many other food contaminants is regulated by the federal Food and Drug Administration (FDA).[2]

The FDA is charged with regulating impurities in food and drugs as well as certifying the safety and effectiveness of drugs. Some of its work is well publicized, including its regulations on labeling of foods (including vitamin and calorie content and ingredients), its drug testing, and its announcement of outbreaks of food poisoning and recall of food found to be contaminated or to contain life-threatening allergens not found on the label (such as milk products or nuts, to which some people are severely allergic). Other work gets less attention, such as its standards for contaminants in food products.

All food, whether grown at home in an organic garden or grown in an industrial farm and processed, canned, or frozen, contains some contaminants: insect parts; mold and mildew; excreta from rodents, insects, and other living beings; parasites; insect eggs; and all sorts of other icky things. It also contains other nonfood items, such as sticks and stones…or olive pits. But how much of these objectionable items is too much? How much is unhealthy or simply too disgusting to look at? What is the balance between allowing a certain amount of such contaminants in food, on the one hand, and the cost of removing it on the other?

It falls to the FDA to determine that. And its list of acceptable contaminants is found in a booklet, *The Food Defect Action Levels: Levels of Natural or Unavoidable Defects in Foods That Present No Health Hazards for Humans* (http://www.fda.gov/food/guidancecomplianceregulatoryinformation/guidancedocuments/sanitation/ucm056174.htm#CHPT3). In it you can learn about the acceptable contaminant levels of dozens of common foods: for example, 3 percent of canned peaches can be wormy or moldy, peanut butter can contain 30 insect fragments and a rodent hair per 100 grams, 5 percent of potato chips can contain rot, and pizza sauce can contain 30 fly eggs or 2 maggots per 100 grams. At these levels, the contaminants are not a danger to health, but, as the booklet notes, they can have "aesthetic significance." At higher levels, the FDA considers the food adulterated and subject to punitive action.

Individuals probably ingest, according to one estimate, 1 or 2 pounds a year of flies, maggots, and mites, and such a diet does no harm.[3] It is the regulators' job to make sure that not too many of them are in one meal!

When George Wallace ran for president in 1968, he campaigned against "pointy-headed bureaucrats" in Washington making decisions that regulated good people's lives. Bureaucrats, according to Wallace, were out of touch with everyday citizens and their concerns. Wallace was not the first to bash the bureaucracy, but he increased the appeal of such bashing as an electoral strategy. That appeal has continued to grow, especially as voters have become more polarized and policy making has become more contentious.

In truth, the bureaucracy is involved in our lives because we expect government to serve diverse purposes and interests. For example, we expect the canned and processed food we buy in the store to be safe and the medicines prescribed by our doctor to be helpful. We take for granted that our grandparents will get their Social Security checks on time, and that if we are granted a student loan, it will appear on our student accounts. We expect safe water to flow from the tap and certified doctors to practice in our local hospital. We expect law enforcement to protect us from domestic criminals and our military to protect us from enemies abroad. To do all that, and more, government bureaucrats check manufacturers' claims about their products, inspect mines, send out Social Security checks, authorize Medicare payments, administer student loan programs, run hospitals and utilities, check for soil and water contamination, fight drug trafficking, develop high-tech weapons systems, and regulate air traffic, to mention only a few responsibilities.

But while bureaucrats perform many tasks, their actual power is limited. The bureaucracy's official role is to implement and enforce policies made by elected officials, that is, by Congress and the president. Congress establishes bureaucratic agencies and can close them or trim their budgets. The bureaucracy's actions and decisions are also subject to review by the courts. And there is additional, constant scrutiny by interest groups, by the media, and by the public. A bureaucratic agency may exceed its authority or fail, but it is likely that these flaws will be exposed and dissected.

In this chapter, we study how and why the federal bureaucracy works. We draw contrasts between private and public bureaucracies. Then we describe the functions of the federal bureaucracy and the different kinds of structures that exist to perform those functions. Finally, we examine the rules governing the work of the bureaucrats and the political and popular oversight that evaluates their performance. Throughout, we consider whether the federal bureaucracy enhances or undermines democratic-republican government in the United States.

THE NATURE OF BUREAUCRACIES

Many people associate the word *bureaucracy* with the federal government. They visualize rows of cubicles with nameless clerical workers inefficiently shuffling papers. Trying to cash in on this stereotype, a Virginia company sold a "Bureaucrat" doll as "a product of no redeeming social value. Place the Bureaucrat on a stack of papers on your desk, and he will

just sit on them."[4] The problem with this joke is that these parodied traits are no more common among government bureaucrats than among workers in the bureaucracy of a private company.

What Is a Bureaucracy?

All organizations, private and public, structure work in order to achieve goals, but bureaucratic organizations have certain distinctive characteristics. First, **bureaucracies** rely upon a **division of labor**, allocating work among personnel so that each worker or each set of workers performs specific tasks. In this way, bureaucracies focus and coordinate their workers. Second, bureaucracies are **hierarchical**, stipulating which workers have the power to issue commands, about what, to whom. Then bureaucrats can be held accountable for their actions and decisions, even when there are layers of supervisors. Finally, bureaucracies rely heavily on **formal rules**: written job descriptions and guidelines for good performance, for promotion, and for grievances are essential to bureaucracies.

As this brief and abstract definition suggests, bureaucracies are expected to be impersonal, even mechanical. They are to be efficient and productive, accomplishing agreed-upon goals by adhering to established routines.

The military is a well-known government bureaucracy illustrating these characteristics. The work assigned to the military—to defend the nation, to keep the peace, to win wars, to conduct rescue missions—is sometimes dangerous and uncertain. To make this work more manageable, it has been divided across five armed services: the Air Force, Army, Coast Guard, Marines, and Navy. Within each service, the work has been further divided among numerous occupations and professions. Soldiers, sailors, and aviators spend years learning, refining, and mastering specific tasks, performing them in specific ways. Personnel are held accountable through strict hierarchies, especially when deadly force is used. Promotion is dependent upon leadership, the exercise of power in formally defined ranks, and mastery of a particular set of job-related skills. There are handbooks and regulations for every office and rank, and it is expected that these guidelines will be followed. "Bureaucracy," as an organizational tool, makes it possible for the military to accomplish difficult goals.

Yet no bureaucracy, private or public, lives up to all its goals. Assessing the performance of a government, or public, bureaucracy is not easy. On the one hand, many of these organizations function well. They provide customers with services and goods that are of good quality, while providing their own workers with good wages and productive occupations. A number of government bureaucracies—including the military, the National Park Service, the U.S. Forest Service, the Federal Bureau of Investigation, the Secret Service, the Foreign Service, and many others—engender such loyalty that people commit themselves to an entire career in that one agency.

On the other hand, even well-functioning bureaucracies may have severe limitations. Government bureaucracies sometimes fail to meet the needs of the public, or to take advantage of new technologies, or to capitalize on the talents of their workforce. Throughout the wars in Iraq and Afghanistan, misconduct by U.S. military personnel has sometimes caused or resulted in civilian deaths or deaths of military personnel. In other bureaucracies, applications that are not processed, information that is not provided, and checks that are not issued are bureaucratic failures that deny people access to public services. A bureaucracy may not value its workers' creativity, undermining its own productivity. For example, teachers who are obliged to "teach to the test," drilling students in facts rather than fostering critical thinking skills, resent the lost opportunities to encourage students to think more analytically and imaginatively. Presidential appointees at the Federal Emergency Management Agency (FEMA) ignored the warnings of agency careerists and focused on terrorism following the 9/11 attacks. The result was disaster management programs that were so compromised, the agency could do little to alleviate the suffering caused by Hurricane Katrina. On or off the battlefield, government bureaucracies have the power to change (even threaten) lives.

Private bureaucracies may also be inefficient or corrupt. Enron's looting of shareholders and taxpayers, and customer service departments that provide frustratingly slow and often inaccurate services, are other examples of ineffectiveness or misguided goals in private bureaucracies.

Bureaucracy, in brief, is a way of organizing workers to perform tasks and achieve goals. It coordinates workers through a division of labor, through hierarchy, and with formal rules. Like every other form of organization, bureaucracies have the potential to achieve and to fail. Understanding the different incentives that are confronted by bureaucracies in government and in the private sector helps to reveal when success is the more likely outcome.

Bureaucracies operate in the private (business) and public (government) sectors. Though all bureaucracies share organizational similarities, the precise environment in which they operate affects every aspect of their performance. For this reason, those who are successful in private bureaucracies will not necessarily be successful in public bureaucracies. This has

The Federal Emergency Management Agency (FEMA) was ill prepared to evacuate, rescue, or aid New Orleans residents when Hurricane Katrina hit in 2005. Some residents were stranded on their rooftop, waiting for days to be rescued, and water and food supplies were limited.

been especially true for several treasury secretaries; although they had been influential leaders of private corporations, they failed to establish themselves as strong leaders of government departments. Here, we will explore how private and public bureaucracies are similar, how they are different, and why it all matters for a bureaucracy's executives and workers—and for us, the bureaucracy's clients.

Private Bureaucracies

Private bureaucracies measure success or failure by their profits. These organizations prioritize efficiency and use market standards to value their workers, their performance, and their products. They seek to maximize revenue or minimize costs. There has often been an expectation that as companies prospered, so also would their workers, the idea that a rising tide lifts all boats. But this link is not always valid; in recent years, corporate profits have been very high but so have been unemployment and poverty.

The public does not generally think private organizations are wasteful as long as they make a profit. Marketing a hundred different kinds of breakfast cereal in packaging twice the size of the contents may not be an efficient use of resources or energy efficient, but if they sell, most consumers say, "Why not?"

Private bureaucracies are usually spared negative press unless they become embroiled in scandals or are perceived as corrupt or criminal. The housing market failure, which caused so many to lose their savings and their homes, was such a case. Although the banks and investment firms were granting risky mortgages and then selling the "toxic assets" to escape responsibility for their actions, the public, government officials, and the press only became critical when these banks and investment firms lost hundreds of billions of dollars. Until that point, their behavior did not come under much scrutiny. More routinely, the governance of private bureaucracies is in the hands of shareholders, not taxpayers. Private bureaucracies are not accountable to the public, even when government provides financial aid to private bureaucracies, as it did during the financial crisis in 2008 and 2009, in this case to help stave off a worldwide economic crisis.

Public Bureaucracies

Public bureaucracies are not evaluated according to whether they make a profit. They are supposed to serve the "public interest," so their success or failure is measured more subjectively by elected officials and by the public, who assess how well bureaucracies serve the public.

Evaluating whether bureaucracies serve the public interest is highly subjective and dependent on any person's view of what the public interest is. We evaluate bureaucracies on the basis of *effectiveness* in serving that interest. The effectiveness of a public bureaucracy might be thought of as some combination of *responsiveness, accountability,* and *equity*. Public bureaucracies are expected to be responsive to their clients and to elected officeholders, to be accountable for public programs and funds, and to administer government services

equitably.[5] Educational equity, for example, requires bureaucrats to be fair, ensuring that individual circumstances (such as gender, wealth, or ethnicity) are not obstacles to achieving educational potential, and inclusive, ensuring that everyone has a chance.[6]

The measure of effectiveness is subjective, so people can come to different conclusions about whether a bureaucracy is performing well or failing. For example, if you do not value public education or if you do not have children in the public schools, you may believe that schools are ineffective because they cost more than you want to pay, which perhaps is nothing. Your neighbor may value public education very highly and see the same outcome and same cost as resulting in a highly effective school. If you think small towns need to be preserved, you may believe that local post offices are a good investment. If you do not value small town life, you may regard the network of very small post offices as wasteful of public spending. These debates will be vigorous for three good reasons: people have different ideas about the objectives of public policy, public bureaucracies have power over people's lives, and bureaucracies spend public money. Because of their power and influence, and because they are supposed to be accountable and responsive to the public, government bureaucracies are more regularly and closely scrutinized by the media and by the general public than private bureaucracies.

Contrasting Public and Private Bureaucracies

Openness

Public bureaucracies must be more open than private ones, and their greater visibility helps make them more responsive. Successful leaders in the public bureaucracy are public figures and skilled communicators. For example, cabinet secretaries are regularly expected to testify at congressional hearings and to conduct press conferences. These high-ranking individuals are also selected for their campaign skills, as they are expected to sell the president's policy priorities in both congressional and presidential elections. Senior executives in private bureaucracies, in contrast, rarely appear in the news, and then they may do so largely as part of a public relations campaign to control the negative effects of scandal, corruption, or poor performance. For example, a company may have to recall a product or confront outrage over a failure, such as the oil spill of a BP well in the Gulf of Mexico.[7] For the leaders of public bureaucracies, public presentations are routine; for the leaders of private bureaucracies, public presentations are often crisis-driven.

The actions of bureaucrats in public bureaucracies are also on record. *The Federal Register*, for instance, publishes all government rules and regulations.

Different Protections for Workers

Other differences between public and private bureaucracies relate to the protections that each gives its workers. Although anti-discrimination statutes, worker safety regulations, and other laws protect workers in the private sector, their supervisors still have a great deal of discretion in hiring and firing.

In the federal bureaucracy, there are many more limitations on executives and many more protections for the workers to ensure that qualifications, rather than whether a person is a member of the party winning an election, determine whether the person is hired by the government. We will discuss this aspect of public bureaucracies more later in the chapter.

Different Goals

Perhaps the most marked contrast between private and public bureaucracies, and the greatest challenge to the successful performance of a public bureaucracy, lies in the simple fact that public bureaucracies are often established to do what private bureaucracies have failed or are unwilling to do. The private sector fills needs that generate a profit. This is not a criticism of the private sector; it is an acknowledgment that most private bureaucracies exist to make a profit. (Charitable or religious bureaucracies, which provide much-needed services and goods on a not-for-profit basis, have their own distinctive goals and performance standards.) Generally, though, when needs cannot be met while still generating a profit (such as through postal service in small towns, rail transportation between smaller cities, or housing for people who cannot pay prevailing prices), private sector bureaucracies will have little incentive to meet public demand. Then the public demands that these services be provided, and public bureaucracies are created and funded. Effectiveness, not efficiency, becomes the first priority—and the debates about responsiveness, accountability, and equity begin.

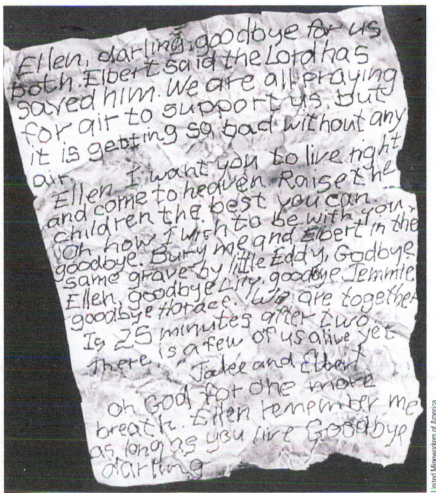

United Mineworkers of America

Jacob Vowell wrote this letter shortly before suffocating after a mine collapse in Fraterville, Tennessee, in 1902. Such disasters prompted government regulation of mining, which has since saved many lives. Still, some companies continue to resist the regulations. In West Virginia, Massey Energy Company thought safety regulations caused unnecessary delays, so the company disregarded some regulations. Investigators found that the 2010 explosion at its Big Branch Mine, which killed twenty-nine, could have been prevented if the company had complied with safety standards.

How does democracy shape bureaucracy in the United States? Does it influence private and public bureaucracies differently? Should it do so?

WHAT BUREAUCRATS DO

The executive branch bureaucracy provides continuity in governing. In many agencies, bureaucrats have decades-long careers that allow them to acquire expertise about their programs and their clients. They know a lot more about their programs than the presidential appointees who come to head the department for a relatively short time. This long-term expertise protects agencies from radical shifts in direction but may make them less responsive.

Policy Implementation

The principal responsibility of the public bureaucracy is to implement the law. Implementation requires administering and enforcing the laws that have been passed by Congress and signed by the president, promulgated by the bureaucracy, or issued through court rulings. When the president and Congress decide to go to war, for instance, they empower the Department of Defense (DOD) to acquire weapons, recruit and train soldiers, and devise a winning strategy. Through implementation, the government bureaucracy makes policy, transforming words into action.

Implementation encompasses thousands of different kinds of activities. Street-level bureaucrats interact directly with their clients, as doctors in veterans' hospitals, as rangers in the national parks, as statisticians gathering census data. Other federal bureaucrats are more distanced from the public. They may conduct research or review citizens' claims to government services. For example, members of the Women's Bureau in the Department of Labor compile a statistical record of women's employment in the United States. In the Social Security Administration, legal professionals review citizens' claims to health insurance. However different the tasks, all of these bureaucrats are fulfilling legal directives issued by Congress, the president, or the courts. The medical care provided by doctors in veterans' hospitals must be congruent with the veterans' health care benefits authorized by Congress. Census questions and categories are of intense interest to Congress members, because these statistics may determine whether a district or a state is eligible for federal programs. And the list continues: bureaucrats translate legal generalities into specific programs.

Industrialization, population growth, urbanization, and profound changes in science, transportation, and communications have put increasingly complex problems on the government's agenda. The large number and technical nature of these problems—think about writing environmental protection rules, for example—as well as polarization and policy differences among the legislators, often lead Congress to draft and pass laws that are more general, setting out broader goals rather than detailed or specific policy responses. Power is then delegated to the bureaucracy, whose workers have the expertise to develop more specific rules and guidelines. Because Congress has explicitly empowered the bureaucracy to take action, these rules have the same power and authority as the laws that are passed by Congress. The great benefit of this partnership between Congress and the executive bureaucracy is that it allows each to do what it does best: members of Congress are generalists, skilled in deliberation and negotiation, while members of the executive bureaucracy are specialists, focused on problem solving and implementation. Well-designed, clear, specific, effective policies require all of these talents, as well as the support of the public.

Despite its advantages, this policy-making and policy-implementing arrangement has strong critics. These analysts argue that the members of Congress are simply avoiding hard work, failing to conduct much-needed negotiations. Although these are difficult, they are a legislator's responsibilities. When the members of Congress delegate decision-making power to the bureaucrats, these critics conclude, they are abdicating their responsibilities and failing to meet their voters' expectations. In a democratic republic, policy should be made and developed by the people's representatives, not by unelected bureaucrats.

As is often true of U.S. politics, both the supporters and the critics are stating important truths. The 2010 legislation to re-regulate the financial industry provides a good illustration of the positives and negatives associated with the delegation of power from Congress to the executive bureaucracy. The need for this legislation had been made very clear, the unrestrained activities of Wall Street firms having sent the housing market and then the entire economy into a tailspin beginning in 2008. The legislative battles were fierce—lobbyists were paid a reported $1 billion to argue the industry's case to influential congressional committee members[8]—and the law passed by Congress was very broad. Because the public was so outraged by the role of Wall Street in precipitating the Great Recession, the law favored tighter regulation. Or rather, the law suggested support for regulation—it delegated the power and the responsibility to draft and implement the actual regulations to the bureaucracy.

Lobbyists now shifted their attention from the legislative to the executive branch, advocating on behalf of weaker regulations and enforcement. Because there is less media and public scrutiny of unelected bureaucrats than of elected members of Congress, the lobbyists may be more successful in achieving their goals. If so, then the critics will be right: delegating power to the bureaucracy is undemocratic and fails to protect the people. But if the bureaucrats do uphold the congressional mandate to re-regulate, then those who support delegating power to the bureaucracy will be vindicated: delegating power to the bureaucracy results in a creative partnership of elected generalists (the members of Congress) and policy specialists (executive branch bureaucrats) who make good policy. But this will be a long process;

the debates continued for two years in Obama's first term, were a campaign issue in 2012, and show little sign of resolution following the elections.

Regulation

A special kind of policy making, called regulation, produces rules, standards, or guidelines conferring benefits and imposing restrictions on business conduct and economic activity. Regulations have the force of law and are made by agencies whose directors and board members are appointed by the president. An estimated quarter-million federal workers are paid to write and enforce regulations, and their work has become one of the most contested areas of the bureaucracy's role in government.

Regulations derive from laws passed by Congress that direct agencies to accomplish the goals established in the legislation. Developing rules to carry out the financial reform act, described above, is an example of regulating. Another contested area of regulation is environmental regulation, which stems from legislation requiring regulatory agencies to, among other things, set standards for clean air, safe disposal of toxic wastes, and safe workplaces.

Data Collection and Analysis

Much of what we know about ourselves as a people comes from the government's collection and analysis of data. Government reports range from basic facts on births, deaths, and population to specialized information about the incidence of abortions, the export of zinc, how much celery we eat, how we spend our money, and how the government allocates revenues. This information is more available today that at any time in the past, as federal agencies have established websites profiling their policies and programs, the data and the reports gathered in the course of their work, and "contact us" links for feedback. Among the most frequently accessed websites

are those of the National Park Service, the Forest Service, and the Bureau of Land Management, which allow people to plan travel to the public lands; those of the Departments of Defense, Health and Human Services, and Veterans Affairs, which provide people with information about essential employment, social, and medical services; and the Internal Revenue Service, which provides links so that people can file their tax returns electronically.

The bureaucracy conducts research as well. A prime example is the Department of Agriculture, which for nearly 150 years has researched how to grow bigger and better crops and to transport and market food products more effectively. At the National Institutes of Health and the Centers for Disease Control and Prevention, government researchers do a great deal of medical research. Every cabinet department has careerists—geologists, chemists, physicists, engineers, social scientists—carrying out research relevant to its policies. For the bureaucracy, it is critically important to perform research, conduct analysis, and inform the public if programs are to successfully meet their constituents' needs.

 Thinking about Democracy

> In practice, bureaucracies make policy. What features of our constitutional system make this consistent with democracy? Under what circumstances can it be undemocratic?

THE SIZE OF THE FEDERAL BUREAUCRACY

Article II of the Constitution mentions "executive Departments" and "Heads of Departments" in listing presidential powers. Art. II, Sec. 2 Thus, the Constitution did anticipate the

The Transportation Security Laboratory in Atlantic City, New Jersey, tests bomb-detection equipment by making bombs with various explosives (*left*) and planting them in abandoned luggage purchased by the government. This luggage is then used to test and upgrade security equipment.

BEHIND THE SCENES

Project MEDEA: The CIA and Climate Change

The government's Project MEDEA has nothing to do with Euripides' classic play about a woman so full of revenge she murders her children. It is just another government acronym, in this case for Measurements of Earth Data for Environmental Analysis, a scientific group established in 1992 to advise the government on environmental surveillance. The group's main purpose is to see if any of the data collected by intelligence agencies, as a byproduct of their search for other kinds of information, could help scientists reach a better understanding of the "hidden complexities of environmental change." The scientists look for images of clouds, glaciers, deserts, and tropical forests picked up by spy satellites and other classified sensors that would help them determine, for example, why and how fast glaciers are melting.

MEDEA is run by the CIA, which arranges for scientists to have access to highly classified data collected by the National Reconnaissance Office (NRO) that would otherwise be unavailable to climate researchers. All participating scientists, most from academia, have security clearances and work under the guidance of the National Academy of Sciences, which advises the government.

One climate scientist said the data sharing was vital to scientists' research because academic researchers "have no way to send out 500 people" to the Arctic to collect data that are the equal of what the government's reconnaissance satellites and other highly sophisticated imaging and detection equipment can gather. Their analysis can in turn have significant economic implications for any industries, such as shipping and fisheries, that utilize the Arctic waters, or for oil companies looking for new places to drill. The scientists' predictions on ice floes and what they may mean for the navigation in the Arctic Sea and the possible opening of new sea lanes also have military implications, matters of great interest to the CIA.

Despite the promising applications of the data collected, Project MEDEA was shut down in 2001 after George W. Bush took office. Bush did not like the idea of America's top spies sharing information with some of America's top scientists, even less with those studying climate change. But in 2009, after a plea from former vice president Al Gore to the Senate Intelligence Committee, the project was reinstated. It has received tacit backing from the Obama administration and especially from then-CIA director Leon Panetta, who believes "it is crucial to examine the potential national security implications of phenomena such as desertification, rising sea levels, and population shifts."

Despite official backing, little is said publicly about the collaboration. For security reasons, images captured by satellites that have been declassified are made less sharp to avoid revealing satellite capabilities to enemies. (Some of these images can be seen at the National Academy of Science's website.) But the sharing of classified data with environmental scientists is still politically controversial. One senator said the agency should be using its sophisticated equipment to fight terrorists, "not spying on sea lions."

SOURCE: William J. Broad, "C.I.A. Is Sharing Data with Climate Scientists," *New York Times,* January 5, 2010, A1. The final quote was by Sen. John Barrasso (R-Wyo.).

---

creation of an executive bureaucracy. It provided for raising an army and a navy, for levying taxes and allocating revenues, for creating a diplomatic corps and a judiciary, and for other tasks that need to be conducted by a bureaucratic organization.

George Washington's first cabinet included only three departments and the offices of attorney general and postmaster general, and it employed just a few hundred people. More people worked at Mount Vernon, Washington's plantation, than in the executive branch in the 1790s.[9] The Department of State had just nine employees. By 1800, the bureaucracy, though still small, had grown to have 3000 civil servants. Throughout the nineteenth century, civil war and the subsequent peace, economic downturns and recoveries, and industrialization and urbanization fueled growth in the federal bureaucracy. In this section, we analyze that growth and its consequences.

Why the Bureaucracy Has Grown

Because the bureaucracy implements the law and administers policies, it has grown as the government has been assigned more responsibilities by its citizens. Over time, presidents and members of Congress responded to public wishes by creating federal agencies to assist and promote the emerging economic interests of business, agriculture, and labor and to provide health and economic protections for workers, consumers, retirees, and other groups.[10] As these agencies meet the needs of their constituents, they also gain the political influence needed to protect their programs and increase their budget allocations. While presidential candidates have often promised to cut the size of the bureaucracy, presidents have found it difficult to do so without incurring significant political costs.

More specifically, much of the growth in the federal bureaucracy can be attributed to three factors. First, extraordinary social and economic change has prompted the establishment of new agencies. During the Progressive Era of the earlier twentieth century, reformers lobbied for government agencies that would protect workers, women, and children, all of whom were seen as vulnerable to the dislocations caused by industrialization and urbanization. Among the agencies established in this period were the Bureau of Reclamation (1902), which built dams and water conservation projects throughout the West, the Food and Drug Administration (FDA, 1906), the Federal Reserve Board (1913), and the Federal Trade Commission (FTC, 1914).

By the 1930s, the hardships caused by the Great Depression led to the establishment of a number of social service agencies to protect individuals against the harm done by an unregulated market. Federal agencies were also established to hire the unemployed to build roads, bridges, post offices, and other public buildings in an effort to stimulate the economy. They included the National Youth Administration (NLRB, 1935), the Civilian Conservation Corps (CCC, 1933), and the Public Works Administration (1933). These agencies did not persist. Other agencies, founded to regulate business and impose controls on the market, still exist today: the Federal Deposit Insurance Commission (FDIC, 1933), the National Labor Relations Board (1935), the Federal Housing Administration (FHA, 1934), and the Securities and Exchange Commission (SEC, 1934).

Few new organizations were created in response to the "Great Recession," but the Bush and Obama administrations and Congress added regulatory responsibilities to the federal bureaucracy, especially to monitor the financial industry.

Second, wars and prolonged foreign policy crises have increased the personnel, budgets, and responsibilities of the federal bureaucracy. The buildup to and conduct of a war obviously increase the size of the armed forces and the DOD. And there are many other responsibilities and expenses associated with wars and conflicts. World War II dramatically increased the size of the bureaucracy and the city of Washington, D.C. Following each war and conflict, new obligations emerge. Humanitarian, military, and economic forms of aid need to be negotiated and administered. We see this today, as the United States negotiates what will be its continuing relationships with Iraq, Afghanistan, and countries throughout the Middle East. Obligations at home are even greater, as disabled veterans need medical care, families whose lives have been changed forever by the war must be tended to (because family members were killed or disabled), and opportunities for education and training need to be provided to surviving veterans In fact, veterans' pension, medical care, education, and employment needs have increased the size of the federal bureaucracy since at least

Early in the twentieth century, many young children worked twelve-hour days in unhealthy conditions, such as in this vegetable cannery. Eventually, public demands to stop this practice led to government regulations on child labor and to the creation of bureaucratic agencies to enforce the regulations.

BEHIND THE SCENES

Privatizing National Security

Privatization, or outsourcing government programs to private industry, is one route to downsizing the federal bureaucracy. It is also perceived as a means of making government more efficient and less costly. But does privatization achieve these goals? And does it meet the standards of responsiveness, accountability, and equity that are expected of programs administered in the public interest?

The most publicized practice of privatization has been in the military. In the first Gulf war, about 10 percent of the personnel worked as private contractors. The same was true of the Clinton-ordered military involvement in Bosnia in the 1990s. But at points during the wars in Iraq and Afghanistan there were more private contractors than military personnel.[1] According to the Department of Defense, in 2011 (the most recent year for which the data are available) contractors still accounted for 32 percent of the DOD's workforce in Iraq and 53 percent in Afghanistan (see Figure 1).

A less noticed area of privatization has been intelligence gathering and analysis. The attacks of 9/11 led many to believe that the United States was not prepared for a war against terrorists and that intelligence work had to be expedited. To that end the Bush administration made it easier for intelligence agencies to outsource work to private contractors. A two-year *Washington Post* investigation found that by 2010, "1,271 government organizations

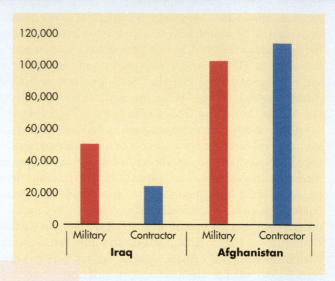

FIGURE 1: A SUBSTANTIAL PORTION OF AMERICA'S CURRENT WARS HAVE BEEN PRIVATIZED Contractors have been extraordinarily important—and sometimes extraordinarily controversial—in Iraq and Afghanistan. In Afghanistan, contractors were a higher percentage of American forces in 2011 because they were in the midst of hostilities. Lower numbers in Iraq reflected the withdrawal of DOD personnel from that country; just two years previously, there had been 111,000 military personnel and 100,000 contractors in Iraq.

SOURCES: *CQ Weekly Report,* April 12, 2010, 889; "Contractor Support of US Operations in the USCENTCOM Area of Responsibility, Iraq, and Afghanistan," 1st Quarter FY 2012, www.scribd.com/doc/80807835/Contractor-Support-OF-USCENTCOM-AOR-1st-Quarter-FY-2012; Department of Defense Manpower Data Center, "Active Duty Military Personnel Strengths by Regional Area and by Country (309A)," December 31, 2011.

---

the Civil War. Especially during the past seventy years, the United States has been at war much of the time, a continuing involvement that has dramatically increased both the wartime bureaucracy and the number of veterans who must be assisted. In 2012, the Department of Veterans Affairs was responsible for services to an estimated 21.8 million veterans. Other war- and foreign policy–related bureaucratic developments are no less significant, revealing the ways that domestic and defense spending may blur together. For example, the interstate highway system was deemed essential to national defense during the Cold War, as decision makers realized the extent to which mobility in the nation was compromised by poor roads. Roads are expensive and complicated to build and maintain, a circumstance that led to increased federal support and funding, and eventually to the establishment of a cabinet department of transportation.

Third, the federal bureaucracy has expanded in response to constituent pressures. Through electoral politics, issue campaigns, and sometimes the sheer force of public opinion, the public has encouraged members of Congress and

presidents to expand the roles, responsibilities, and power of the federal bureaucracy.

For example, consider the origins of three very different innovations in the federal bureaucracy. The idea for the Peace Corps can be traced to a campaign speech that John Kennedy delivered at the University of Michigan. Delivered at 2 a.m. and only a few moments in length, it was nonetheless remembered for its inspirational call. Kennedy insisted that students see a "greater purpose" to their education than providing graduates with "an economic advantage in the life struggle." "How many of you who are going to be doctors are willing to spend your days in Ghana? Technicians or engineers, how many of you are willing to work in the Foreign Service and spend your lives traveling around the world? On … your willingness to contribute part of your life to this country, I think will depend the answer whether a free society can compete. I think it can! … [T]he effort must be far greater than we have ever made in the past." Once in office, Kennedy found himself virtually forced to take action and proposed an agency and a program that would give bureaucratic expression to this ideal. In 2012, and 1,931 private companies work on programs related to counterterrorism, homeland security and intelligence in some 10,000 locations across the United States." Of the 854,000 people who then had top-secret security clearances, 265,000 were working on contract.[2]

Today, private businesses perform almost 30 percent of intelligence work, and the agencies are heavily dependent on private contractors to maintain essential operations. All sixteen agencies in the intelligence community rely on corporations to set up their computer networks and their communications systems with other agencies, and on private contractors to serve as translators and linguists. The ultra-secret National Reconnaissance Office (NRO) "cannot produce, launch or maintain its large satellite surveillance systems...without the four major contractors it works with."[3] The former undersecretary of defense for intelligence (later, the director of the Office of National Intelligence) said that God was the only "entity in the entire universe" that had a view of all the ultra-secret projects known as Special Access Programs. "The complexity of the system defies description," said a former Iraq troop commander who was assigned to track DOD's top-secret programs. "I'm not aware of any agency with authority, responsibility or a process in place to coordinate all these interagency and commercial activities."[4] In other words, there is no reason to think that privatization has increased either responsiveness or accountability in intelligence work.

We might also question whether privatization has enhanced equity or efficiency. The sheer volume of contracts has made oversight nearly impossible. The DOD alone has eighteen commands and agencies handling information operations. When former Defense Secretary Robert Gates set a goal of cutting contractors back to their pre-9/11 level, he said he had to make a "terrible confession": he was unable to "get a number on how many contractors" worked for his own office.[5] The work has grown so fast that it has been called a "jobs program," and the proliferation of agencies so great that no one is sure who is in charge or if anyone is capable of coordinating the work.

[1] On the privatization of defense and foreign policy work, see Allison Stanger, *One Nation under Contract: The Outsourcing of American Power and the Future of Foreign Policy* (New Haven: Yale University Press, 2009).

[2] Dana Priest and William M. Arkin, "A Modern World, Growing beyond Control," *Washington Post*, July 19, 2010, A1. The text, graphics, and supplemental material from the *Post's* investigation are at TopSecretAmerica.com.

[3] Michael D. Shear, "National Security, Inc.," *Washington Post*, July 20, 2010, A9.

[4] Lt. Gen. John R. Vines, quoted in Priest and Arkin, "A Modern World, Growing beyond Control."

[5] Ibid, A8.

---

the Peace Corps had over 9000 volunteers serving in 75 countries and an alumni network estimated at more than 181,250.

The National Park Service (NPS) prospered because its early directors cultivated the support of presidents and Congress members, established partnerships with industries that fostered tourism, and transformed casual park visitors into dedicated supporters. These policy entrepreneurs and their successors created an agency that now administers 84 million acres in national parks identified as the nation's "Crown Jewels," world historic sites, biosphere reserves, and national historic sites, among others.

After 9/11, a frightened public wanted greater safety. Congress passed legislation, including the USA PATRIOT Act, to increase the responsibilities of the federal government to ensure public safety, to reorganize agencies and create a new Department of Homeland Security, and to wage the war on terror. All of this increased both the size of the bureaucracy and its intrusion into private lives. This legislation passed with bipartisan support and the leadership of a conservative Republican president, and few of either party questioned the need for a more activist government,

though some then, and more now, question the balance struck between personal liberties and national security.

One scholar has explained the bureaucracy's growth as evidence of Americans' discovery that "government can protect and assist as well as punish and repress."[11] Great social and economic change has consistently resulted in great political change; and mediating among social, economic, and political pressures has been a task delegated largely to the bureaucracy. The federal bureaucracy has been charged with providing social services, stimulating economic growth, and guarding against market failure. And the federal bureaucracy waged the wars declared or authorized by Congress, advanced the diplomatic initiatives that prefaced and followed hostilities, and cared for those who fought for the nation. The federal bureaucracy has been expected to keep the campaign promises of elected officials, to respond to the lobbying of policy entrepreneurs, and to allay public fears. As this list suggests, the federal bureaucracy has grown because the needs, wants, and hopes of the nation have grown and because war has become more common in the past century.

Controlling Growth

When new bureaucracies are created, the intent is to hold them to their original size, but most grow over time because once they are in place, additional responsibilities are assigned to them. Consolidation or elimination is rare. And sometimes they get so big they subdivide.

Almost every president since Lyndon Johnson (1963–1969) has tried to streamline or downsize the bureaucracy. Presidents often think they can encourage efficiency and then cut personnel. But this usually doesn't work. For all of Ronald Reagan's (1981–1989) talk against big government, it grew by over 200,000 employees during his administration. The size of government grew under George W. Bush too, largely because of hiring in the homeland security area. Within two years of its founding, the new Department of Homeland Security had twenty-one levels of administration.[12] Under President Obama, the size of the federal bureaucracy grew by 6 percent, though during his first term, state and local government shrank because of financial pressures on the states during the recession.

On the other hand, Bill Clinton (1993–2001) had a "reinventing government" initiative, a brainchild of Vice President Al Gore. During the Clinton administration, the size of the government really did fall (due in part to outsourcing and privatization) by 20 percent.

For the past fifty years, presidents have warned against the dangers of big government and have tried to downsize and streamline it. Yet, because of the pressures of national needs, war and its aftermath, and constituent pressures, the government continues to grow even under conservative presidents, or perhaps more correctly, especially under conservative presidents.

 Thinking about Democracy

Given the forces that have increased the size of the federal bureaucracy, is the growth of bureaucracy a reflection of democracy or not? To what extent is the bureaucracy a reflection of our priorities as a democracy?

TYPES OF FEDERAL AGENCIES

The Constitution says little about the organization of the executive branch other than indicating a need for the president to have a cabinet. As government's role expanded, it became clear that a single type of organization would not be appropriate for every task assigned to the bureaucracy. While every unit within the federal bureaucracy is expected to respond to elected officeholders, is held accountable for its programs and expenditures, and is required to value equity, not every agency is expected to fulfill these obligations in the same way. By learning which federal bureaucracies are more closely tied to the political parties, to issue networks, to the legislative branch, or to the presidency, we learn more about the calculations that lead to the agencies' programmatic and policy priorities.

Departments

Departments are the largest bureaucracies within the executive branch. There are fifteen executive departments, each of which is responsible for an issue area of national significance. The State Department is primarily responsible for diplomatic outreach to other nations, for example, while the DOD is home to four of the military services. (The fifth, the Coast Guard, is currently located in the Department of Homeland Security.) Even the names of the departments are indicative of the breadth of their jurisdictions, as, for example, Transportation, Health and Human Services, Education, Housing and Urban Development, and Energy.

Identifying an agency as a department raises its status within the executive branch. The senior executive in a department is a member of the president's cabinet, with opportunities to lobby the chief executive and other elite decision makers in the presidential administration. When presidents elevate an agency to department status, therefore, they are sending a message about their priorities to interested publics. The newest departments are the departments of Homeland Security (2002), Veterans Affairs (1989), Energy (DOE, 1977), and Education (1979), reflecting priorities that arose during these decades (see Figure 2).

The Department of Homeland Security was established in response to the September 11, 2001, attacks. The legislation mandated bringing together diverse agencies in an effort to provide a more coherent and forceful response to threats to the nation, whether from terrorism or natural disasters. The Department of Energy, like Homeland Security, brought together a diverse set of agencies, each with a specific energy-focused interest, such as oil, coal, and natural gas, nuclear power, and energy sources such as wind and sun. To give greater status to the national interest in education and in providing services to Veterans, the Departments of Veterans Affairs and Education were raised from agency to departmental status after lobbying by powerful veterans' and teachers' groups.

Although all cabinet departments have a certain prestige in the bureaucracy, and though frequent reference is made to members of the president's cabinet in the media and by Congress, cabinet secretaries vary widely in their influence over politics and policy. Typically the secretary of state, the attorney general, and the secretaries of treasury and defense are high-visibility cabinet members who are frequently called on for advice. Perhaps not coincidentally, these are heads of the four original cabinet departments organized by George Washington.

Independent Agencies

The "independent" in **independent agencies** has two possible meanings. First, and most broadly, these units are not located within a cabinet department. This is a deliberate decision by the agencies' founders, who hope that keeping them independent will also protect them against the influence wielded by a department's constituents. Even so, an independent agency may be susceptible to whatever political forces are currently dominant. This outcome has been seen in several agencies, including the Environmental Protection Agency (EPA, 1970).

The EPA was charged with comprehensively regulating environmental pollutants, to safeguard human health and environmental quality. It could have been placed in the Department of the Interior or the Department of Commerce. But there was a fear that if it was in the Department of the Interior, which administers many of the nation's natural resources, the agency would come to favor more environmental protection. Alternatively, if the EPA had been placed in the Department of Commerce, the agency might have acceded to business preferences for less regulation and less environmental protection. In seeking to protect the agency from these influences, however, the president and the Congress have left the EPA vulnerable to both. In the forty-plus years of EPA's existence, the EPA senior executives named by Democratic presidents have sought to enforce pollution controls more stringently, while those named by Republican presidents have supported less stringent standards.

Although independent agencies lack the status of departments, their leaders exercise considerable influence. They are nominated by the president and confirmed by the Senate, and their selection receives close scrutiny by the media and interested publics. All of these decision makers want some influence over these agencies, and they seize every opportunity to gain that influence. Examples of independent agencies include the Central Intelligence Agency (CIA, 1947), the National Aeronautics and Space Administration (NASA, 1958), the National Archives and Records Administration (NARA, 1934), and the Peace Corps (1961).

The second definition of "independent" is much narrower. **Independent regulatory agencies** are a specific subset of independent agencies. The president appoints members to a commission or board of five to ten individuals who lead this type of agency. Commissioners' terms of office are usually longer than a president's four-year term, and the commissioners serve staggered terms so that the leadership turnover is gradual. In several independent agencies, the law specifies that equal numbers of Democrats and Republicans be named as board or commission members. These requirements limit the president's options in selecting the leadership and setting the agenda for these agencies.

Regulation is the primary function of board- or commission-led independent agencies. Among the most familiar of these agencies are the Federal Communications Commission (FCC, 1934), which regulates radio, television,

Though bureaucracies rely on conformity, predictability, and routine in administering their programs, they also foster creativity, innovation, and change. In addition to a wide range of research projects, there are also U.S. government agencies dedicated to advancing the creative arts. Artists in the Federal Art Project (1935–1943), which was established to put unemployed artists to work while improving public buildings and recording American history, painted more than 2500 murals in public buildings, produced more than 108,000 paintings and 18,000 sculptures, provided photographic documentation of the New Deal projects, and designed recruitment and publicity posters for government agencies, including the military. In the words of its director, the project "brought the artist closer to the interests of a public which needs him, and which is now learning to understand him."[14]

BEHIND THE SCENES

Turf Wars in the Federal Bureaucracy

Sometimes the agencies of the executive branch are more committed to preserving and protecting their own resources than preserving and protecting the people of the United States.

A prime example is the Federal Aviation Administration's (FAA) passenger safety practices before 9/11. When the 9/11 Commission investigated the breaches in security that allowed the terrorists to succeed, it learned that the FAA had a "no fly" list of twelve names that included none of the 9/11 hijackers.[1] The FAA had not consulted the FBI, which had been seeking two of the hijackers. FAA officials did not even know that the State Department had a list of 61,000 known or suspected terrorists whose travel was to be restricted. Instead, the FAA had devoted considerable effort to resisting passenger safety rules proposed by the

National Transportation Safety Board (NTSB). The FAA was determined to protect its constituents in the airline industry from additional costs, which was contrary to the NTSB's mission of safeguarding passengers.[2]

The federal bureaucracy may seem to be an impenetrable monolith devoted to frustrating individuals, but it is actually hundreds of agencies, each focused on its own mission and constituencies. Positions and projects are jealously guarded from budget cutters and from other agencies with similar programs. In other words, there are **turf wars** within the federal bureaucracy. The costs of these wars can be extraordinarily high.

[1] Thomas H. Kean and John Farmer Jr., "How 12/25 Was like 9/11," *New York Times*, January 6, 2010, A23. The authors were the cochair and chief counsel of the 9/11 Commission.

[2] Al Baker, "Collision Bares Longtime Rift over Air Safety," *New York Times*, August 14, 2009.

---

wire, satellite, and cable communications. The Securities and Exchange Commission (SEC, 1934), which regulates stock market transactions, has often been in the news in recent years as the financial industry has imploded and lax regulations have appeared to be part of the reason. Because independent regulatory agencies enforce the law, it is especially important that they be impartial. Yet these agencies have sometimes been "captured" by the industries they police. For example, investigators found that the Federal Aviation Administration (FAA), from 2006 to 2008, allowed airlines to operate planes that were not in compliance with safety codes. When violations were publicized, hundreds of planes had to be grounded and Southwest was fined $10.2 million.[13]

Independent agencies were established as "independent" from the departments in the hopes of limiting the influence of partisanship and politics. Whether this leads to greater effectiveness or greater corruption depends on the oversight conducted by other branches of the government, the media, the public, and the bureaucrats themselves. The FAA's failure to enforce the law, described above, was brought to light by FAA bureaucrats who were determined to see their agency fulfill its responsibility to protect the public.

Over time, presidential appointments can bolster either those who act on behalf of the industry they are supposed to regulate or those who are independent of the industry and committed to its regulation. Which possibility is realized depends on the president's policy priorities and, as will be seen, the president's willingness to conduct oversight of these agencies.

Government Corporations

Legally distinct from the government, **government corporations** are expected to be the most politically independent

of the different kinds of organizations that constitute the federal bureaucracy. The most familiar government corporations are the Corporation for National and Community Service (AmeriCorps, 1993); the Corporation for Public Broadcasting (1967); the Federal Deposit Insurance Corporation, which ensures your bank deposits (FDIC, 1933); the National Railroad Passenger Corporation (Amtrak, 1971); and the Tennessee Valley Authority (TVA, 1935). All of these government corporations are owned by the government. Other government corporations, such as the mortgage giant Freddie Mac, are owned by private stockholders.

Government corporations charge for their services or products, but their primary objective is to provide a needed service, not to make a profit. When a government corporation does become profitable, it may be sold to private stockholders. For example, the Consolidated Rail Corporation (CONRAIL) consolidated the holdings of six bankrupt freight railroads in a single government corporation. When the corporation became profitable, it was sold to private stockholders for nearly $2 billion.

 ### Thinking about Democracy

As citizens in a democracy, we want the law to be administered fairly and consistently. The different types of federal bureaucracies are designed to act on these democratic priorities. Which type of bureaucracy—department, independent agency, independent regulatory agency, or government corporation—do you think is most likely to achieve these goals? What is at stake in its success or failure?

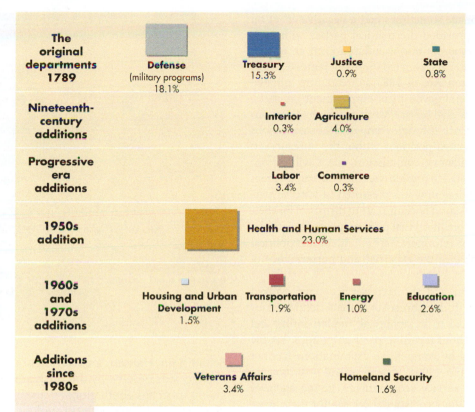

FIGURE 2: THE DEVELOPMENT AND RELATIVE SIZE OF CABINET DEPARTMENTS Percentages are each department's estimated share of the budget authority for Fiscal 2012. The figures add to less than 100 percent because they do not include budget allocations to the many other executive branch agencies and to the legislative and judicial branches. The relatively large square for HHS includes mandatory spending on Social Security and Medicare, while the Treasury square includes interest on the debt, which will continue to grow. The Defense square is for military programs only. SOURCE: United States Budget for Fiscal Year 2011 (Washington, D.C.: Government Printing Office, 2010).

PARTISAN POLITICS AND THE BUREAUCRACY

Because it is responsible for implementing programs, the bureaucracy is lobbied constantly. However, bureaucrats are legally required to prioritize professional standards and expertise and to discount political loyalties and partisan politics. They are not to implement policy in a partisan manner; they are governed by laws that give priority to professional competence over political loyalty. After all, most Americans want the bureaucracy to be fair and apolitical. They want the quality of their government services and goods to be unaffected by partisan beliefs.

The Merit System

For decades, public bureaucracies were staffed under the **patronage system**, which allowed elected officials to fill administrative jobs on the basis of political loyalty. By providing their supporters with jobs, elected officials strengthened their political base. Many people accepted this as a way for government agencies to provide employment to citizens. Patronage hiring was usually referred to as the **spoils system** because it operated in rough accordance with the principle "to the victor belong the spoils."

The most obvious problem with staffing the bureaucracy with political supporters is that jobs may go to people who are not competent to perform their duties. This became a major problem as government work became more technical and specialized. Furthermore, patronage could and frequently did lead to corruption, with deal making between candidates and voters, or between candidates and those who controlled blocs of voters. In small towns, for example, the postmaster was routinely the leader of the president's party organization at the local level. She or he (it was usually a he back then) was responsible for ensuring a high turnout of loyal voters in each election; a victory for the party meant continued employment for the local party leader.

Although patronage sometimes had a negative effect on the government, it provided the political parties with such extensive political resources that it endured until an unsuccessful federal job seeker assassinated President James Garfield in 1881. The Pendleton Act of 1883 subsequently initiated major reforms in federal government employment practices. This law created a new civil service; workers who had demonstrated their competence through competitive examinations would now fill designated positions within the bureaucracy. An independent regulatory commission, the Civil Service Commission, was created to preside over the new employment system. Bureaucrats were now less pressured to vote for particular candidates and faced fewer threats of dismissal for their political ideologies. Convinced that partisan politics were necessarily corrupting, the reformers were confident that political neutrality would enhance the expertise and performance of the bureaucracy.

The merit system and the civil service have evolved through the decades. Today, careerists in the federal bureaucracy are still expected to be apolitical, implementing and enforcing the law without regard to partisan politics. Yet the number of jobs filled by competitive examinations has not increased since the mid-1900s. Instead, many positions are exempted from civil service requirements, giving agencies some flexibility in setting professional criteria for their hires. Meanwhile, presidential nominees and appointees, while a small percentage of the whole, have increased in number over the past thirty years, as presidents have sought to gain greater control over the executive bureaucracy.

Neutral Competence

The merit system established neutral competence as the professional standard for civil service employees. It requires that individuals filling merit positions be chosen for their expertise in doing the job and that they carry out their work in a nonpartisan or neutral way. This standard assumes that there is no Republican or Democratic way to build a sewer, collect customs duties, or fight a war. It also implies that bureaucrats should not profit personally from the decisions they make. Yet it is very difficult for the U.S. government, which is intensely partisan, to uphold this standard.

Science is an area where neutral competence often conflicts with political agendas. The thousands of government scientists, mathematicians, engineers, investigators, and data analysts who provide the information that informs policy making and implementation were hired specifically for their professional knowledge. It is up to elected officials whether they choose to act on the information these experts provide.

All administrations vet scientific reports, and on many issues there is no clear consensus in the findings. There are many examples, such as whether there is enough evidence to approve or ban a new medical procedure. Even when there is consensus among experts, presidents are not obligated to act on it and may even cherry-pick reports for the evidence that supports their own policy preferences. Government researchers whose findings are not followed may not be happy with the

Scientist Jim Hansen, a government expert on climate change, was ordered by the Bush administration to stop giving speeches about global warming because his conclusions, based on scientific evidence, contradicted the administration's policies.

policy results, but if they are not pressured to change their data or their conclusions, their expertise has not been challenged.

The threat comes when a president's appointees suppress data or actually edit the content of research reports to fit policy. These actions are most egregious when there is a consensus among experts.

Falsifying or suppressing scientific research in the interest of political goals can work in the short run. In the long run, however, it undermines the public's faith in government and in science, and it can delay government action on issues crucial to public welfare and national security. As the chair of the House Committee on Science remarked on his retirement, "This is a town where everyone says they are for science-based decision making—until the science leads to a politically inconvenient conclusion."[15]

Political Activism

Banning patronage from federal hiring did not end participation in partisan politics by federal employees. In 1939, following the massive expansion of the federal bureaucracy throughout the Roosevelt administration, Congress passed the Hatch Act. This law expressly prohibited federal employees in the executive branch (except the president, vice president, and presidential appointees and nominees) from active participation in partisan campaigns, even at the state and local levels. Included in the ban are party-sponsored voter registration drives, candidate endorsements, and campaign volunteering. Political activities were restricted to voting, attending rallies, and having private conversations.[16] These regulations also applied to employees of state and local government who were primarily supported by federal funds.

The Hatch Act was controversial from the beginning. Supporters argued that it insulated federal bureaucrats from partisan influences. Critics said it denied civil servants their First Amendment rights of freedom of speech and association, though the Supreme Court repeatedly ruled otherwise. In 1993, Congress changed the law to allow most federal employees to hold office within a political party, to participate in political campaigns, and to raise funds for political action committees when they are not on duty. However, employees of law enforcement and national security agencies are still governed by the earlier, more stringent standards.

 ### Thinking about Democracy

In limiting the political speech and activities of federal bureaucrats, are we sacrificing their constitutional rights? Is it necessary to do this? Why? Is this sacrifice congruent with our core values as a democracy?

Politicizing the Bureaucracy

No president has spoken against the basic principle of merit hiring, but some have challenged it in practice.

For decades, the White House has linked the announcement of federal grants to the president's campaign for reelection. In the George W. Bush administration, these practices were refined and systematized. Grants and policy decisions were used to build electoral support for the president and for White House–endorsed congressional candidates in battleground states. Numerous and extensive briefings were conducted to explain how department and agency resources could be "deployed" to achieve these goals. However, federal agency decisions on the use of public money and other assets cannot be made on the basis of political needs or election campaigns. Having conducted an extensive investigation, the Office of Special Counsel concluded that at least one of the briefings violated the Hatch Act.[17] In response to the report, the Obama administration closed the White House Office of Political Affairs.[18]

Bush appointees also systematically violated merit-based hiring standards. A 2005 directive from the White House to its executive branch liaisons recommended that Internet searches be conducted on applicants for federal jobs to look for evidence of their political views and activities and their attitudes toward the president. As successive investigations revealed, aides researched the partisan affiliations and personal lives of applicants for nonpolitical posts as well as political ones. Candidates were assessed for their stances on "god, guns + gays." Applicants with actual or rumored Democratic or liberal connections were not hired.[19] The Department of Justice's inspector general

found that the department had broken the law and violated departmental practices in using political criteria for the hiring of federal prosecutors, immigration judges, and other nonpolitical offices. At least one of the individuals involved in the hires admitted to a congressional committee that she had "crossed the line."[20]

Whistleblowers

A **whistleblower** is a person who reports a bureaucracy's performance failures—to superiors within the specific agency, to other government authorities, or to the media—in an effort to force significant change and improvement. Whistleblowers are typically very loyal employees who are determined to see their agency fulfill its legal, professional, and political responsibilities. The failures they publicize are often long-standing problems, with severe consequences for the public, that are dismissed or discounted by others in the agency. One of the most famous whistleblowers was Pentagon employee Daniel Ellsberg, who leaked the Pentagon Papers, revealing the conduct of the Vietnam War, to the *New York Times*. Henry Kissinger claimed that Ellsberg was the most dangerous man in the world. Ellsberg's acts, however, helped the public understand that the Johnson and Nixon administrations were fighting the war for very different reasons than they had publicly stated. More than forty years later, when army intelligence analyst Bradley Manning leaked diplomatic cables, video, military logs, and diaries—perhaps the largest cache of confidential documents ever released into the public domain—the debate about whistleblowers and national security was renewed. Manning was charged with at least twenty-two offenses, including the capital offense of providing aid to the enemy.

Although they are protected by at least twenty federal statutes, whistleblowers have often suffered retaliation for their disclosures. In recent years, airport baggage screeners, border patrol agents, and the chief of the United States Park Police have been disciplined or fired for reporting problems in their agencies. Worse, investigators found that the director of the Office of Special Counsel had, from 2005 to 2008, abused his office, which provides legal protection to whistleblowers. The director had not only failed to provide this protection but had also retaliated against whistleblowers in his own office and destroyed evidence on his office computer.[21]

It is the rare person who will set aside collegial relations and professional ambitions to challenge established agency practices. Most people, whether working in the private or the public sector, find it difficult to expose the failings of their superiors and their peers. Being a whistleblower also has high costs, personally and professionally. About half of all whistleblowers are fired. With neither income nor professional standing, half of these individuals lose their home and half again lose their families.[22] Under these circumstances, it is remarkable that so many people continue to step forward and demand that their agencies meet their obligation to serve the public.

American Diversity

Women and People of Color in the Federal Bureaucracy

In recruiting people to work in a bureaucracy, attention is supposedly focused on their occupational and professional credentials. Yet there is a long history of discrimination in hiring in the United States. Historically, people of color and women have encountered great difficulty in gaining employment and promotions. When government bureaucracies discriminate in this way, there are added concerns. Those who seek employment and are denied posts because of their identity are being denied access to public employment resources. In addition, if bureaucrats share a common and limited identity, clients with other identities and experiences may find that their needs and interests go unrecognized. And, again, public resources are reserved to a few members of the society and denied to many others.

Following critical studies of the bureaucracy's hiring procedures and standards, and several initiatives to broaden recruitment, there has been some progress in diversifying the profile of federal bureaucrats. In 2010, the most recent year for which data are available, people of color constituted 31 percent of the American population and were 33.8 percent of the civilian federal workforce, a 5.0 percent increase over the previous year (see Figure 3).

African Americans were a significantly larger portion of the federal workforce (18 percent) than of the general civilian workforce (10 percent). American Indians, Asian Americans, and Pacific Islanders were a slightly larger portion of the federal than of the overall citizen workforce, but Hispanics are underrepresented in the federal workforce (8 percent compared to 13 percent of the civilian workforce). This may be partly because significant numbers of Hispanics are not yet citizens and thus are not eligible for the federal workforce.

Women were 44 percent of the federal workforce, slightly less than their representation in the private labor force (46 percent) and considerably below parity with their 51 percent share of the population. Women of color are 18 percent of the federal workforce, slightly more than their 14 percent of the civilian workforce.

Some progress has also been made in diversifying the top management positions. Collectively, people of color held about 18 percent of all senior positions. Women filled 31 percent of these offices, more than twice the share that they held in 1990. Federal court rulings and out-of-court settlements in discrimination cases, as well as changing generations in leadership positions, account for some of this upward mobility.

Even so, 56 percent of all federal bureaucrats, with 69 percent of those at the senior pay levels, are men; and 66 percent, with 82 percent at the senior pay levels, are white. Given that bureaucracies reward conformity and that formal rules change only incrementally, the distinctive interests of previously marginalized peoples will only gradually be incorporated in the policies of the federal bureaucracy.

SOURCE: All percentages cited are from U.S. Office of Personnel Management, Federal Equal Opportunity Recruitment Program report to Congress for fiscal year 2010. Diversity statistics in hiring by agency can also be found at www.data.gov.

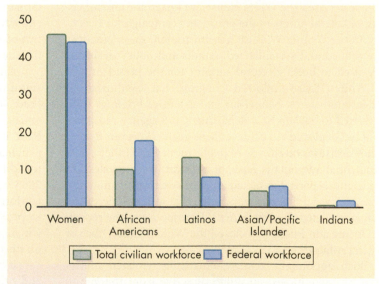

FIGURE 3: HOW REPRESENTATIVE IS THE FEDERAL WORKFORCE? African Americans are overrepresented and Latinos underrepresented in the federal workforce compared to the overall civilian workforce.

SOURCE: All percentages cited are from U.S. Office of Personnel Management, Federal Equal Opportunity Recruitment Program report to Congress for fiscal year 2010. Diversity statistics for hiring by agency can also be found at www.data.gov.

OVERSIGHT OF THE BUREAUCRACY

The principal overseers of the bureaucracy are, of course, the president, who heads it and appoints its top policy makers; the Senate, which holds confirmation powers; Congress as a whole, which has authority to create, monitor, and fund agencies; and the federal courts, which often have to interpret the meaning of regulations or rule on their constitutionality. Congress has also given the public a significant, if vastly underused, role through legislation that mandates openness in government through public hearings, access to agency documents, and whistleblower protection. This scrutiny sometimes improves and at other times undermines the bureaucracy's performance.

In essence, oversight is a struggle for power over government programs and resources. As a result, it may challenge or it may reinforce a bureaucracy's commitment to responsiveness, accountability, and equity.

President

As the chief executive, a president wants to control and to lead the executive branch. Oversight helps a president achieve these goals, because it provides the chief executive with an opportunity to review the work of the federal bureaucracy on a continuing basis. This will require both staff resources and time, however, and not all presidents have been willing to make these investments. Richard Nixon and George W. Bush, however, did so. They saw continuous oversight as critical to their success as presidents and devoted considerable effort to ongoing evaluative reviews, assessing how agencies were administering programs and acting on their priorities. Presidential oversight is conducted in at least three ways: through appointment power, budgeting, and administrative reform.

Appointment Power

Presidential oversight is made easier when the senior executive in the department or agency is a presidential nominee, such as a cabinet secretary, because it is accepted that those individuals will be loyal to the president and the presidential agenda. Although partisan polarization has increased conflict throughout the Senate confirmation process, senators still usually confirm nominees who share the president's views. Thus, in the Reagan and the two Bush administrations, environmental posts were held by individuals who supported more commercial development and less regulation. In the Clinton and Obama administrations, however, environmental posts were held by individuals who favored regulation to promote clean water and air and to protect natural resources. Policy priorities are also important in the independent regulatory agencies. Republican presidents tend to nominate people who favor business, while Democratic presidents appoint those who lean toward the interests of consumers and organized labor. Reagan chose heads for regulatory agencies such

as OSHA, the Consumer Product Safety Commission, and the EPA who agreed with his goal of reducing government regulation. In contrast, Obama named individuals who advocated on behalf of workers, consumers, and environmental protection. In each instance, the presidential appointees set important agendas for their agencies.

Budget Process

Presidential oversight is also conducted through the budget process. The president has had the power to draft the annual budget since 1921, and that power was strengthened in 1937 when Congress approved an executive branch reorganization that moved the Bureau of the Budget into the Executive Office of the President to help the president manage the bureaucracy. Later the Bureau of the Budget became the Office of Management and Budget (OMB). All departments and agencies submit their budgets to OMB, whose director is nominated by the president and confirmed by the Senate. OMB then compiles the proposed budget for the government, reviewing the requests of the various bureaucracies in light of the president's priorities. To the extent that the president's priorities are strong and clear and are incorporated into the proposed budget by the OMB, the budget gives the president an opportunity to set the policy agenda for the executive bureaucracy.

The president submits the budget to Congress, which takes it as the starting point for congressional deliberations. As the president's term continues and the bureaucratic agencies submit successive budgets, presidents can see whether and how the bureaucracy is acting upon their priorities and policies.

Administrative Reform

Presidents sometimes try to curb the bureaucracy by proposing sweeping organizational changes. President Reagan wanted to abolish the Departments of Education and Energy, but Congress would not support him. President Bush pushed through the massive reorganization of intelligence and emergency bureaucracies into the Department of Homeland Security (DHS). After DHS's disastrous response to Hurricane Katrina, Congress reorganized the chain of command and gave the Federal Emergency Management Agency (FEMA) more responsibility for responding to natural disasters.

Despite these powers, there are limits to the president's oversight capabilities. Given the size and complexity of the federal bureaucracy, the president cannot possibly influence every important decision. He must focus on a relatively few high priorities. Moreover, the Civil Service system deliberately insulates the bureaucracy from presidential control. Although presidents have more authority to appoint top-level and emergency appointments, 90 percent of the bureaucracy consists of civil servants. These are the individuals who actually implement the regulations and programs that are promised in presidential campaigns and sought by presidential appointees. Because they know that presidents come and go while civil servants remain, they may or may not work hard to implement the priorities of the current administration. Civil servants are hard to remove, even when they are poor performers.

Some presidents are surprised by the need to conduct oversight; they expect the bureaucracy to simply follow their requests and orders. But agencies are responsive to others as well, including Congress, interest groups, and sometimes the public. Although chief executives have the edge in setting the political agenda for the executive branch, they still must focus attention on those parts of the bureaucracy that are most important to their policy agenda.

Congress

Although the president has the leadership role in the bureaucracy through appointment powers, Congress has great scope for oversight and control. Much of the bureaucracy's power is authority delegated by Congress, and much of its work is implementing laws passed by Congress. Congress has the power to create, reorganize, or eliminate agencies and also has the ultimate instrument of control, the power of the purse. Thus Congress and the president compete for control over the executive branch, and checks and balances ensure that their competition will be fierce. For example, although the president nominates individuals to lead the executive branch departments and agencies, those nominees must be confirmed by the Senate. The president proposes a budget, but Congress decides which parts to accept and which to reject or change.

Members of Congress also have a strong electoral motivation to conduct oversight: they want to provide services to their constituents. Thus members routinely try to influence agencies to take some action on behalf of constituents, districts, or states. As a result, agencies and departments are often responsive to the preferences of the congressional committees that authorize their programs and appropriate their funds. At times, agencies may even adjust their priorities to match the ideological preferences of their oversight committees. For example, decisions by members of independent regulatory commissions are sensitive to the views of members of their congressional oversight committees. When the membership of the committees becomes more liberal or more conservative, so do the decisions of the regulators.[23]

Congressional oversight is most consistently exercised in three ways. First, it is exercised through the budgetary process. The Constitution grants the power of the purse to the House of Representatives, though the budget is submitted by the president and must also be approved by the Senate. The need to review and approve government expenditures on an annual basis gives members of Congress an opportunity to ask questions and lobby on behalf of particular programs. Members see this as an opportunity to advance the interests of their constituents, to argue for implementation of their priorities, and to advocate on behalf of their ideologies. Conservative Republicans affiliated with the Tea Party movement have pushed hard for heavy cuts in the federal budget. Yet both Democrats and Republicans have worked hard to secure and safeguard government programs (and government dollars) for their districts.[24]

Second, Congress receives mandatory reports from a number of agencies that provide members with the information needed to query the bureaucracies about their performance. In 2009, the DOD provided more than seven hundred reports to Congress.[25] And while members were willing to acknowledge that this number was excessive, they still pushed the department to disclose more about its decision-making processes and conclusions.

Third, Congress conducts investigations. Though Congress cannot send officials to jail for wrongdoing, the public exposure that comes through investigatory hearings carries high costs for the individuals who are accused of wrongdoing. These are occasions of great drama and importance; they receive considerable coverage in the media and influence the public's perception of the government. The Watergate hearings (1973–1974), the Iran-contra investigation (1987), joint hearings on the space shuttle *Challenger* disaster (2003), and hearings on the taxpayer-funded bonuses for financial executives (2009) have been just a few of these high-profile oversight events.

Partisanship, politics, and policy are all powerful motivators for oversight by Congress, as they are for the president. For the legislative branch, however, there is the added incentive of gaining some control over the "president's branch," issuing an unmistakable challenge to the president as the head of the government.

Courts

Federal courts act as another check on the bureaucracy. Courts cannot intercede in an agency's decision making unless some aggrieved person or corporation has filed a suit against an agency. Still, in almost any controversial agency action, someone will file a suit. In deciding on suits against the bureaucracy, the courts provide the federal bureaucracy with clear and strong feedback about its performance, the essence of oversight. The courts cannot reach beyond the case that is filed; they cannot address additional and broader issues. Even given these constraints, however, courts can profoundly influence the decisions and actions of the bureaucracy.

Courts try to interpret lawmakers' intentions when judging agency actions. However, understanding what the Congress and the president had in mind can be difficult. Lawmakers may be divided among themselves and may omit critical aspects of their reasoning, perhaps leaving a bill deliberately ambiguous in order to gain a majority for its passage. In the current Supreme Court, the conservative majority has increasingly used its authority to interpret the intent of congressional acts in ways that expand the Court's own powers. (Chapter 12 will discuss the Court's discretion and power.)

Regulators and other agency policy makers appear to be quite sensitive to federal court decisions. For example, when the courts overturn the National Labor Relations Board's decisions in a pro-labor direction, the board's decisions become more pro-labor. Similarly, decisions drift the other way when courts overturn agency decisions in a pro-business direction.[26]

The Public: Interest Groups and Individuals

Interest groups and individuals interact with agencies in the federal bureaucracy so frequently that they may seem to be immersed in oversight. But providing feedback that systematically evaluates and changes agency performance is a complicated task, far different from routine interactions with program administrators. Oversight requires interest groups and activists to gather and analyze information about the agency's performance, recruit allies and build a network of committed supporters, and develop strategies to lobby on behalf of change. Interest groups may work with congressional committees to put pressure on the agency, or they may rally public opinion to pressure members of Congress or the president to take action. Individuals may also employ these tactics, using social media to mobilize people in greater numbers. When citizens weigh in by the thousands, as happens with some rules posted for comment at agency websites, they can cause real change.

This oversight is facilitated by laws that require federal agencies to provide the public with opportunities to comment on proposed rules and regulations (the Administrative Procedures Act), to gain access to internal documents (the Freedom of Information Act), and to attend the meetings at which issues are debated and decided (the Sunshine Act).

The Administrative Procedure Act

The **Administrative Procedure Act (APA)**, passed in 1946, requires public participation in the bureaucratic rule-making process. All federal agencies must disclose their rule-making procedures and publish all regulations at least thirty days in advance of their effective date to allow time for public comment. Today, citizens can often post comments on proposed rules at an agency's website. It is also common for public hearings to be held on controversial rules or those with wide impact. Environmental rules frequently provoke citizen reactions, with comments sometimes numbering in the tens of thousands. Often, interest groups and issue networks will mobilize their members to provide these responses, lobbying agencies to implement one set of reforms rather than another.

The Freedom of Information Act

Congress increased public access to the bureaucracy by passing the **Freedom of Information Act** (FOIA) in 1966. This law allows any person (corporate or individual) to apply to an agency, through a formal procedure, for access to unclassified documents in its archives. The act was updated in 1996 to provide access to electronic records.[27] A "deliberative process" exemption allows the withholding of records describing behind-the-scenes decision making and is most frequently used by government agencies. Once obtained, the documents can be published and shared with the wider public, exposing government corruption or failure.

Federal agencies receive hundreds of thousands of FOIA requests annually, and each agency is required to make public the number of requests it receives. In addition to those filed

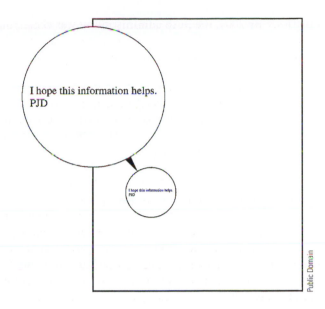

The Freedom of Information Act requires the release of documents, but sometimes the government will censor information within them. This comment was all that remained of an e-mail that the Bush administration censored before releasing.

by the media, many FOIA requests are filed by businesses and interest groups. These organizations want access to information that will help them to develop better strategies for influencing agency decision making.

Efforts to make government agencies more open often run up against the agency's desire to limit the distribution of critical or embarrassing information. It is the rare public or private bureaucracy that wants to reveal its failures. The FBI is one agency that has developed a reputation for finding ways not to comply with requests, and the proportion of successful FOIA requests to the FBI is much lower than it is to other agencies.

As chief executives, presidents have variously increased and limited access to government documents. President Clinton, for example, issued an executive order authorizing the declassification of most documents twenty-five years old or older. An FOIA request was to be met unless there was "foreseeable harm" in the document's release.[28] Clinton put a ten-year limit on the classified status of new documents unless a review had determined that they must remain secret.[29] During Clinton's presidency, four times as much material was declassified as had been in the previous fifteen years.[30]

George W. Bush, also by executive order, tightened access to documents. He wanted to strengthen executive control of the bureaucracy and weaken the oversight powers of Congress and the public. Bush directed agencies to deny FOIA requests if there was any "sound legal basis." He also reversed the Clinton policy that prohibited department and agency heads from stamping documents "secret" on their own authority. During Bush's first term the number of classified documents doubled and declassification dwindled to about 10 percent of what it had been at the end of the nineties.[31] By 2004, the Bush administration was classifying a historic high of 125 documents per minute, in large part by creating vague new security classifications, at an estimated cost of $7.2 billion.[32]

The Obama administration has also limited FOIA access in some important ways. The national security and deliberative process exemptions were cited as reasons for not releasing photos taken at the Abu Ghraib prison in Iraq and for not making available complete logs of White House visitors. The administration has also had to defend itself against numerous FOIA lawsuits filed by newspapers or press agencies about key decisions such as the bank bailouts.[33] It has not always been successful in doing so. In 2009, for example, a FOIA lawsuit forced the FBI to release its "Domestic Investigations and Operations Guide," giving the public a better understanding of how far the law allows the agency to go in spying on American citizens with little or no judicial oversight.[34]

The Sunshine Act

The **Sunshine Act** (1976) requires that meetings be conducted openly, with advance notice provided to the public, unless there is a formal vote taken in favor of a closed door meeting. In this way, those who are opposed to public access find their opposition made part of the public record, which means that the denial of public access can subsequently be challenged. Even if the meeting is closed, a transcript must be kept and provided to the public. However, testimony relating to trade secrets or other confidential information, criminal accusations or actions that may interfere with a person's right to a fair trial, and other such pieces of information can be redacted from this account. The goal of the Sunshine Act is to abolish unwarranted secrecy so that political deliberations and decisions are all conducted openly. The expectation is that, if members of Congress know that their statements will be made available to the public, these decision makers will be demonstrably fair and ethical as they write the law. Decisions that follow from meetings conducted in closed, unannounced sessions may be challenged in the media and in court.

 Thinking about Democracy

Which type of oversight—presidential, congressional, judicial, or public—most promotes democracy? What does this answer reveal about your expectations for democratic governance?

CourseReader ASSIGNMENT

Log in to www.cengagebrain.com and open Course-Reader to access the full reading "More Bureaucrats, Please" by John Gravois.

Even some critics of the federal government acknowledge the challenges confronting its workforce and argue that more government workers are needed if programs are to be well managed and regulations well enforced. Otherwise, economic failures, defense purchasing overruns, and environmental disasters will multiply, to the point that government begins to break down.

In essence, some experts recommend that resources be invested in the government; private bureaucracies often conduct and act upon such self-studies similar to this assessment. However, a public bureaucracy is assessed by standards that are very different from those applied to private bureaucracies. And with just a few years in office, presidents are less concerned with being good administrators than with being strong innovators. Similarly, electoral pressures lead members of Congress to undervalue management and favor more dramatic partisan priorities. Think about the political feasibility of the reforms that place an emphasis on investing in government. How could you make them happen, if you were a president, a cabinet member, a senator, a representative?

1. Some argue that government bureaucrats work hard to fulfill the responsibilities that Congress and the president have assigned to their agencies. Why does the general public judge these individuals so harshly?

2. To what extent are government bureaucrats asked to do the impossible (for example, regulating new technologies whose capacities are still uncertain), and to what extent are government bureaucrats asked to do the necessary (for example, safeguarding the health and well-being of the nation)? Given that the public bureaucracy is often assigned tasks that private bureaucracies could not make profitable, what is the real difference between the "impossible" and the "necessary"? How does your assessment relate to your argument for or against providing government agencies with more staff and more expertise?

BUREAUCRACY IN A DEMOCRATIC REPUBLIC

Without a bureaucracy, none of the laws passed or programs established by Congress could be implemented. But has the bureaucracy become an impenetrable forest or an uncontrollable fourth branch of government, as some portray it? The turf wars, miscommunication, and fragmented authority that surfaced after 9/11 and that continue today certainly indicate that at least part of the federal bureaucracy is an impenetrable forest.

It is not surprising that most of the agencies that failed so badly at that time (for example, the CIA and the FBI) were among the least open to citizens or the media and even to congressional oversight. More than ten years after 9/11, the problems of interagency information sharing have still not been resolved and may have been worsened by the rapid growth and privatization of work that most agree is rightfully a job for government. However, how large government's role in intelligence gathering can become without infringing on another of its essential functions—protecting individual liberty—is a highly controversial issue.

There is a vaguely defined but frequently articulated public suspicion that any bureaucracy is destined to be intransigent and inefficient. We have tried to show that some of that attitude stems from lack of consensus on what the work of government should be. If you do not like the work that Congress and the president have assigned to the bureaucracy, there is not much chance you will view the bureaucracy as functioning within its constitutional role.

But the bureaucracy is not an errant fourth branch of government. Most of the bureaucracy is subject to presidential and congressional control, if these elected officials exercise their powers. Indeed, the Bush administration's attempt to increase presidential control of the executive branch reawakened Congress to the importance of its oversight responsibilities. The public can also directly influence how bureaucrats do their work, and can lobby Congress and the president to effect change.

Despite people's negative feelings about the bureaucracy, the mail is delivered, Social Security checks are written, and passports are issued. The bureaucracy usually does what it is supposed to do. Some public agencies, such as Social Security and Medicare, operate far more efficiently than their private counterparts. When government fails, the human cost can be enormous. But today there is a more serious concern for and greater awareness of the costs of poorly functioning government agencies. The head of one government watchdog group summarized the feeling this way: "Before September 11 there was a bit of a blasé attitude of 'OK, the government screwed up again.' Now people see the consequences on their lives and see the necessity of government functioning well."[35]

SUMMARY

- All bureaucracies are characterized by the division of labor, by hierarchy, and by a reliance on formal rules. However, there are many differences between bureaucracies in the private (business) and the public (governmental) sectors. Because private bureaucracies are profit driven, they prioritize efficiency. Because public bureaucracies serve the public interest, they prioritize responsiveness, accountability, and equity.

- The primary responsibility of the federal bureaucracy is to implement the laws passed by Congress, signed by the president, and interpreted by the courts. This also requires the bureaucracy to gather and analyze information. Implementation is contentious because, in allocating resources and exercising power, government agencies directly affect the lives of individuals and the profits of private companies.

- Growth in the federal bureaucracy can generally be attributed to the following three factors: widespread social and economic change throughout the nation; wars and prolonged foreign policy crises; and constituent pressure, exerted through elections, issue campaigns, and public opinion. Attempts to slow the growth of bureaucracy, or to shrink its size, have usually been failures, especially in recent years under Republican presidents.

- Departments, independent agencies (including independent regulatory agencies), and government corporations are three different types of federal agencies. These types of agencies systematically vary in their relationships with political parties, issue networks, the legislative branch, and the presidency.

- To ensure that federal bureaucrats uphold professional standards of neutral competency, they are prohibited from engaging in many political activities. However, presidents, seeking to gain control over the federal bureaucracy, have used political standards in recruiting careerists for key departments.

- The performance of the bureaucracy is subject to review by the president, the Congress, and the courts; and by interest groups and the general public. Each of these political institutions and actors has distinctive resources that can be used to gain information from the bureaucracy, to critically assess its work, and to effect significant change in bureaucratic routines.

- Although the federal bureaucracy may be perceived as inefficient or ineffective, there is considerable evidence that it accomplishes the goals assigned by elective officeholders. Moreover, it does so while being responsive, accountable, and equitable in its relationships with constituents.

DISCUSSION QUESTIONS

1. Private bureaucracies prioritize efficiency, while public bureaucracies prioritize accountability, responsiveness, and equity. When do you think that accountability, responsiveness, and equity should be important for private bureaucracies? When do you think that efficiency should be important for public bureaucracies? What do your answers suggest about your expectations of how well business and government will meet human needs?

2. Given the social, economic, and geographic diversity of the United States, how much power should Congress, the president, and the courts delegate to the bureaucracy so that it can effectively implement the law?

3. Of the various factors that have fueled the growth of the federal bureaucracy throughout history, which do you consider the most important? Which do you think is most valid? Be careful to consider how your historical judgments and your ideological preferences are influencing one another as you answer these questions.

4. In analyzing the different types of federal agencies, scholars focus on the extent to which an agency is insulated from the political process. Why is this an important factor? What are ways in which an agency can be politically insulated? Which of these practices is likely to be successful?

5. Bureaucrats are supposed to demonstrate a neutral, professional competence. They are also supposed to value equity and to be responsive and accountable to elected officeholders and to the public. Does the Hatch Act balance these somewhat competing priorities? Is it necessary for presidents to "politicize" the bureaucracy in order to secure responsiveness, accountability, and equity?

6. As you study the various ways in which different political institutions and actors exercise oversight of the federal bureaucracy, which do you think will be most effective in evaluating and reforming these agencies? Having decided upon your response to this question, are you answering from the perspective of an overseer or a bureaucrat? How does changing your perspective from one to the other change your assessment? How does changing your perspective affect your definition of "effective" and your attitude toward reform?

7. Is the bureaucracy political? Is this a good or a bad situation? What does this mean for democratic-republican governance in the United States? Be careful to explain and defend your definition of "political" as you answer these questions.

12

The Judiciary

A disappointed minister is comforted by a fellow opponent of the Affordable Care Act after the Supreme Court upheld the law's individual mandate.

Photo by Lucian Perkins/The Washington Post via Getty Images

LEARNING OBJECTIVES

1. Understand the process of appointing federal judges and the role of politics in this process.
2. Understand, specifically, why the process has become more politicized in recent decades.
3. Grasp the concept of judicial independence and its importance for a strong judicial branch.
4. Understand why judges must interpret statutes and constitutional provisions.
5. Understand why judges usually follow precedents.
6. Distinguish between judicial restraint and judicial activism.
7. Understand why judges may make law when they decide cases.
8. Understand why Chief Justice John Marshall is considered a towering figure in the development of American law.
9. Understand the power of judicial review for our courts and the role of judicial review in our system.

TALKING POINTS

As soon as Congress passed the Affordable Care Act—President Obama's health care reform proposal—opponents filed lawsuits claiming that the act is unconstitutional. They objected especially to the individual mandate, which requires Americans to have health insurance. Those who don't get health insurance through work must buy it. (Those who can't afford it will receive subsidies to buy it.) The mandate is considered necessary to reach the goal of universal coverage and also to facilitate the regulations on insurance companies included in the act. Opponents hoped that the courts would invalidate the mandate and render the law unworkable.

Legal scholars scoffed at the suits[1] because Congress has considerable authority over economic matters, especially over commerce and taxes, which relate to the act. Ever since the Great Depression, the Supreme Court has interpreted congressional authority over these areas very broadly. (The Constitution's provisions, the Court's doctrine, and the law's provisions are complex, and we don't have space to elaborate here.) On the other hand, conservatives felt that the law is an interference with individual freedom, because it requires people to buy a product—health insurance. In particular, they claimed that the mandate isn't a legitimate exercise of congressional authority over commerce or taxes.

Normally congressional acts are presumed constitutional and ruled constitutional. This practice reflects judges' respect for Congress and its members, who are elected by the public. Yet judges do have discretion. For this act, they had discretion to interpret the constitutional provisions involving commerce and taxes to allow or disallow the mandate.

When the Supreme Court heard the case in 2012,[2] it had five conservative justices and four liberal justices. Despite the views of legal scholars that the act is clearly constitutional, some observers predicted that the justices would vote along ideological and partisan lines—that the five conservative Republicans would vote to strike down the mandate and the four liberal Democrats would vote to uphold it.

When the Court announced its decision, the four liberal Democrats did vote to accept it, and four conservative Republicans did vote to reject it. This left Chief Justice John Roberts, a conservative Republican who was appointed by President George W. Bush. In his tenure on the bench before this case, Roberts had voted consistent with his conservative ideology. In this case, however, Roberts decided to uphold the mandate, providing the fifth vote and creating a bare majority for it.

According to a leak from a justice or a clerk on the Court (evidently one who was angry with Roberts and sought to embarrass him), the chief justice initially planned to rule the mandate unconstitutional, joining the other conservatives and providing the fifth vote for a majority against the mandate. Roberts even wrote the opinion for this majority. Before the Court announced its decision, however, he changed his mind and voted to hold the mandate constitutional after all.

It's not clear why Roberts switched sides. He may have been concerned about the Court's prestige or his own legacy as the chief justice. If the Court had struck down the mandate, legal scholars would have criticized the justices' departure from the Court's doctrine (as they saw it). And although public opinion toward the law was split, many Americans would have accused the conservative majority of substituting their policy preferences for the congressional law enacted by our elected representatives. Public opinion toward the Court was already at a low ebb.[3] Roberts may have feared a reaction like the firestorm that followed the Court's ruling to settle the presidential election of 2000 between George W. Bush and Al Gore. In the opinion of one legal scholar, the chief justice may "[love] the Supreme Court more than he loves political conservatism."[4]

Or he may have decided to act as he promised at his confirmation hearings. He said, "Judges are like umpires. Umpires don't make the rules; they apply them.... [I]t is a limited role.... I will remember that it's my job to call balls and strikes and not to pitch or bat."[5]

But conservative politicians and commentators were furious with Roberts. Representative Mike Pence (R-Ind.) compared the ruling to the 9/11 attacks. Radio host Glenn Beck called Roberts a coward and sold t-shirts labeling him a coward.[6]

The public expresses more support for the Supreme Court than for the president or Congress.[7] It dislikes the disagreements and debates and the negotiations and compromises among governmental officials, and it deplores the efforts of interest groups to influence governmental policies. These messy features of democratic government, which are visible in the executive and legislative branches, aren't visible in the judicial branch.

Consequently, many people assume that courts *are* nonpolitical and that judges *are* objective. These people say we *have* "a government of laws, not of men." Other people, who criticize their decisions, assume that courts *could be* nonpolitical and that judges *could be* objective. These people say we *could have* "a government of laws, not of men." But both views are myths. At any time in our history, "it is individuals who make, enforce, and interpret the law."[8] When judges interpret the law, they are political actors and courts are political institutions. As we'll see, judges are simply people who interpret the law.

Thus public support for the Supreme Court and the lower courts rests partly on false assumptions about the absence of politics in this branch. In fact, there is a lot of politics in the courts, as will be seen in each of the topics covered in this chapter.

COURTS

Due to federalism, the United States has a complete system of national courts side by side with complete systems of state courts, for a total of fifty-one separate systems.[9]

Structure of the Courts

The Constitution mentions only one court—a Supreme Court—although it allows Congress to set up additional lower courts, 🏛 Art. III, Sec. 1 which it did in 1789 and again in 1891, completing the basic structure of the federal judiciary.

The **federal district courts** are trial courts. There are ninety-four, based on population, but with at least one in each state. They have multiple judges, although a single judge or a jury decides each case.

The **federal courts of appeals** are intermediate appellate courts. They hear cases that have been decided by the district courts and then appealed by the losers. There are twelve, based on regions of the country known as "circuits."[10] They have numerous judges, from six to twenty-eight, although a panel of three judges decides each case.[11]

The Supreme Court is the ultimate appellate court. It hears cases that have been decided by the courts of appeals, district courts, or state supreme courts. (Although it can hear some cases—those involving a state or a diplomat—that have not been heard by the lower courts first, in practice it hears nearly all of its cases on appeal.) The group of nine justices decides its cases.

Only the district courts conduct trials; the courts of appeals and the Supreme Court do not have juries or witnesses to testify and present evidence—just lawyers for the opposing litigants. Rather than determine guilt or innocence, these courts evaluate arguments about legal questions arising in the cases.

The state judiciaries have a structure similar to the federal judiciary. In most states, though, there are two tiers of trial courts. Normally, the lower tier is for criminal cases involving minor crimes, and the upper tier is for criminal cases involving major crimes and for civil cases. In about three-fourths of the states, there are intermediate appellate courts, and in all of the states there is a supreme court (although in a few it is called another name).

Jurisdiction of the Courts

Jurisdiction is the authority to hear and decide cases. The federal courts can exercise jurisdiction over cases in which the subject involves the U.S. Constitution, statutes, or treaties; maritime law; or cases in which the litigants include the U.S. government, more than one state government, one state government and a citizen of another state, citizens of more than one state,[12] or a foreign government or citizen. **Art. 🏛 I, Sec. 2** The state courts exercise jurisdiction over the remaining cases. These include most criminal cases because the states have authority over most criminal matters and pass most criminal laws. Consequently, the state courts hear far more cases than the federal courts.

Despite this dividing line, some cases begin in the state courts and end in the federal courts. These cases involve state law and federal law, frequently a state statute and a federal constitutional right—for example, a criminal law and a legal question about the search and seizure (Fourth Amendment) or interrogation (Fifth Amendment) conducted by the police. For these cases, there are two paths from the state judiciary to the federal judiciary. One is for the litigant who lost at the state supreme court to appeal to the U.S. Supreme Court.

The other path, available only in a criminal case, is for the defendant who has exhausted all possible appeals in the state courts to appeal to the local federal district court through a writ of **habeas corpus** ("Bring the body!" in Latin). This order demands that the state produce the defendant and justify his or her incarceration. If the district court decides that the state courts violated the defendant's constitutional rights, it will reverse the conviction. After the district court's decision, the losing side can try to appeal to the courts of appeals and the Supreme Court (see Figure 1).

 Thinking about Democracy

Consider the implications of *habeas corpus* for our democracy. It gives criminal defendants several opportunities (by the district court, the court of appeals, and the Supreme Court) to get the constitutional rights they are supposed to get. Thus *habeas corpus* helps protect minority rights, which is one aspect of democratic government. (Although we often think of racial minorities when we speak of minority rights, criminal defendants also are a minority who have various rights.) Toward this end, *habeas corpus* enables the federal courts to oversee the state courts, forcing state judges to provide these rights.

JUDGES

The judges, of course, are the key component of the federal judiciary. This section will examine how they are chosen, who they are, and whether they are qualified.

Selection of Judges

Benjamin Franklin proposed that judges be selected by lawyers because lawyers would pick "the ablest of the profession in order to get rid of him, and share his practice among themselves."[13] The Founders rejected this unique idea, instead deciding that the president and the Senate should share the appointment power. The Constitution stipulates that the president shall nominate judges and the Senate shall provide "advice and consent"—that is, recommend judges and then confirm or reject them.[14] **Art. II, Sec. 2** There are no other requirements in the Constitution, although there is an unwritten requirement that judges be trained as lawyers.

 Thinking about Democracy

Does the appointment of federal judges contradict the essence of democracy by denying our citizens the opportunity to choose their judges through elections?

Mechanics of Selection

For the lower courts, lawyers who want to become judges get politically active in their party and make financial contributions to the party and its candidates. When vacancies arise, they lobby political officials, bar association leaders, or interest group leaders in the hope that these elites will recommend them to the administration.

They especially focus on their senators, who play a role through the practice of **senatorial courtesy**. This tradition allows senators in the president's party to recommend, or veto, candidates for judgeships in their state. Senatorial courtesy applies not only to district courts, which lie within individual states, but also to courts of appeals, which span several states. For courts of appeals, senators informally divide the seats among the states within the circuit. (This practice doesn't apply to the Supreme Court because it has too few seats to divide among the states.)

Senatorial courtesy can limit the president's choices. During President Kennedy's term, the practice was ironclad. In deference to southern senators, the president, who advocated civil rights, was forced to appoint southern judges who favored segregation. One of them characterized the Supreme Court's desegregation ruling as "one of the truly regrettable decisions of all time," and another even called black litigants "niggers" and "chimpanzees" from the bench.[15] However, senatorial courtesy is not as ironclad now as it was then. Since the 1970s, most administrations have sought certain candidates for their ideology or diversity, so they have pressured senators to cooperate. Consequently, there is more give-and-take between the senators and the president than there used to be.

For the Supreme Court, lawyers who want to become justices also try to become prominent in the legal profession by writing articles or giving speeches designed to attract officials' attention. When vacancies arise, political officials, bar association leaders, and interest group leaders urge consideration of certain candidates. The administration also conducts a search for acceptable candidates. Sometimes even sitting justices make a recommendation. Chief Justice Warren Burger discouraged President Nixon from choosing a woman, claiming that not one was qualified. Instead, he recommended Harry Blackmun, a childhood pal and the best man at his wedding. Justice William Rehnquist recommended Sandra Day O'Connor, a law school classmate whom he had dated occasionally.

Once the president has chosen a candidate, he submits the nomination to the Senate, where it goes to the Judiciary Committee for hearings. Senators question the nominee about his or her judicial philosophy, and interest groups voice their concerns. If a majority of the committee consents, the

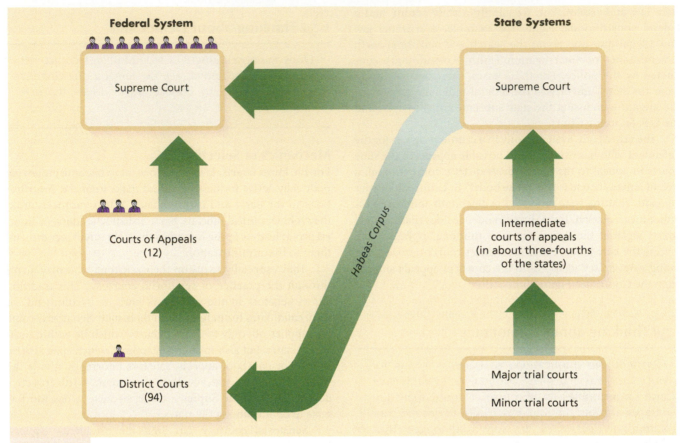

FIGURE 1: FEDERAL AND STATE COURT SYSTEMS The arrows indicate the primary avenues of appeal, and the heads indicate the usual number of judges who hear cases in the federal courts.

SOURCE: © Cengage Learning

nomination goes to the whole Senate. If a majority of the Senate consents, the nomination is confirmed.

The Judiciary Committee is the battleground for controversial nominations. The committee is controlled by the party that has a majority in the Senate, so it reflects the views of that party. If the committee confirms the nominee, usually the whole Senate will confirm the nominee. If the committee rejects the nominee, usually the president will have to submit another one.

The mechanics of selection for all federal courts are similar, but the process of selection for the Supreme Court is more politicized at every stage because the Court is more powerful and visible, so its seats are fought over more intensely.

Criteria of Presidents

Although presidents want judges who have merit, they choose judges who meet various political criteria as well. Presidents normally nominate members of their party. In fact, they normally nominate active members who have served in public office or contributed to the party and its candidates. In the twentieth century, presidents selected members of their party from 82 percent of the time (William Howard Taft) to 99 percent of the time (Woodrow Wilson).[16] This practice has become so established that senators of the opposite party usually vote to confirm nominees of the president's party.

Some presidents want judges who hold certain ideological views. President Theodore Roosevelt sought judges who opposed business monopolies and supported labor unions, and President Franklin Roosevelt sought judges who favored his New Deal policies. President Nixon sought conservatives who would reverse the direction of the Supreme Court and prompt southern whites to join the Republican Party.[17]

The Reagan administration was the first to establish systematic procedures for choosing lower court judges as well as Supreme Court justices according to ideology. The George H. W. Bush administration did the same. These two administrations sought conservatives who would roll back the rulings of previous courts. They had candidates fill out lengthy questionnaires and then submit to daylong interviews probing their positions. They expected candidates, for example, to oppose the right to abortion, the Supreme Court's ruling establishing the right, and the Supreme Court's reasoning in the case.[18]

In the George W. Bush administration, an unusual feature was the role of Vice President Dick Cheney, who took the lead within the administration. Cheney sought conservative judges, especially those who had a broad interpretation of presidential power and a narrow interpretation of congressional authority, so that they would uphold the administration's sweeping claims of presidential power in the war on terror. After rigorous screening and interviewing of the candidates, Cheney

American Diversity

Do Women Judges Matter?

Although presidents have begun to appoint women to the bench in significant numbers, women are still vastly underrepresented on the bench. Only 30 percent of federal judges are women.[1] Some people believe that there should be more women judges because women are entitled to their "fair share" of all governmental offices, including judgeships. Others believe that there should be more so women will feel that the courts represent them too. Still others believe that there should be more because women hold different views than men and therefore would make different decisions.

A study of Justice Sandra Day O'Connor, the first woman on the Supreme Court, shows that although she generally voted as a conservative, she usually voted as a liberal in sex discrimination cases. Moreover, her presence on the Court apparently sensitized her male colleagues to gender issues. Most of them voted against sex discrimination more frequently after she joined the Court.[2] A study of federal courts of appeals judges found the same pattern among female judges and male colleagues.[3]

Some studies found similar results for women justices on state supreme courts. Even women justices from opposite political parties supported a broad array of women's rights in cases ranging from sex discrimination to child support and property settlement.[4] But studies that compare voting patterns on issues less directly related to gender have less clear findings. Women judges appear more liberal than men in cases involving employment discrimination and racial discrimination. Perhaps the treatment they have experienced as women has made them more sympathetic to the discrimination others have faced. They're also more liberal than men in cases involving asylum for immigrants.[5] On the other hand, women judges don't appear more liberal or conservative than men in cases involving obscenity, criminal rights, or other areas of the law.[6]

Studies that compare the sentencing of criminal defendants in state courts find scant differences between men and women judges.[7] However, women judges do tend to sentence convicted defendants somewhat more harshly.[8] Women judges in Harris County, Texas, which includes Houston, have applied the death penalty with "greater ferocity" than their male predecessors. This *county,* a majority of whose judges are female, has given the death penalty to more defendants than all other *states* but one.[9]

But the studies comparing men and women judges find more similarities than differences. This should not be surprising, because the two sexes were subject to the same training in law school and the same socialization in the legal profession, and they became judges in the same way as others in their jurisdiction.

Perhaps the greatest difference women judges have made is to protect the credibility of women lawyers and witnesses. In court, some men judges and lawyers have made disparaging remarks about women lawyers, suggesting that they should not be in the profession—for example, calling them "lawyerettes." Many male judges and lawyers have made paternalistic or personal remarks to female lawyers and witnesses, referring to them by their first name or by such terms as "young lady," "sweetie," or "honey." Sometimes, in the midst of the proceedings, men have commented about their perfume, clothing, or appearance. "How does an attorney," one asked, "establish her authority when the judge has just described her to the entire courtroom as 'a pretty little thing'?"[10] Even if the men considered their remarks harmless compliments rather than intentional tactics, their effect was to undermine the credibility of women lawyers and witnesses in the eyes of jurors. Women judges have squelched such remarks.

[1] "Women in the Federal Judiciary: Still a Long Way to Go," National Women's Law Center, April 27, 2012, nwlc.org/resource/women-federal-judiciary-still-long-way-go-1.

[2] Karen O'Connor and Jeffrey A. Segal, "Justice Sandra Day O'Connor and the Supreme Court's Reaction to Its First Female Member," in *Women, Politics, and the Constitution,* ed. Naomi B. Lynn (New York: Haworth Press, 1990), 95–104.

[3] Christina L. Boyd and Lee Epstein, "All Else Being Equal, Choose a Woman," *Washington Post National Weekly Edition,* May 11–17, 2009, 26.

[4] David W. Allen and Diane E. Wall, "Role Orientations and Women State Supreme Court Justices," *Judicature* 77 (1993), 156–165.

[5] Julia Preston, "Big Disparities in Judging of Asylum Cases," *New York Times,* May 31, 2007.

[6] Sue Davis, Susan Haire, and Donald R. Songer, "Voting Behavior and Gender on the U.S. Courts of Appeals," *Judicature* 77 (1993), 129–133; Thomas G. Walker and Deborah J. Barrow, "The Diversification of the Federal Bench," *Journal of Politics* 47 (1985), 596–617; Boyd and Epstein, "All Else Being Equal."

[7] John Gruhl, Cassia Spohn, and Susan Welch, "Women as Policymakers: The Case of Trial Judges," *American Journal of Political Science* 25 (1981), 308–322.

[8] Darrell Steffensmeier and Chris Hebert, "Women and Men Policymakers: Does the Judge's Gender Affect the Sentencing of Criminal Defendants?" *Social Forces* 77 (1999), 1163–1196.

[9] Jeffrey Toobin, "Women in Black," *New Yorker,* October 30, 2000, 48.

[10] William Eich, "Gender Bias in the Courtroom: Some Participants Are More Equal than Others," *Judicature* 69 (1986), 339–343.

Qualifications of Judges

Given the use of political criteria in selecting judges, are judges well qualified?

Political scientists who study the judiciary consider federal judges generally well qualified. This is especially true of Supreme Court justices. Presidents realize that they will be held responsible for their appointees. Moreover, presidents have so few vacancies to fill that they can confine themselves to persons of their party and political views and even to persons of a particular region, religion, race, and sex and still locate good candidates. This is less true of lower court judges. Presidents and senators (through senatorial courtesy) jointly appoint them, so both can avoid taking responsibility for them. These judges are also less visible, so a lack of merit is not as noticeable.

Presidents do appoint some losers. President Truman put a longtime supporter on a court of appeals who was "drunk half the time" and "no damn good." When asked why he appointed the man, Truman candidly replied, "I . . . felt I owed him a favor; that's why, and I thought as a judge he couldn't do too much harm, and he didn't."[58]

Sometimes presidents appoint qualified persons who later become incompetent. After serving for many years, they incur the illnesses and infirmities of old age, and perhaps one-tenth become unable to perform their job well.[59] Yet they hang on because they are allowed to serve for "good behavior," and they prevent other lawyers from filling their seats on the bench.

This problem has prompted proposals for a constitutional amendment setting a term limit of eighteen years[60] or a mandatory retirement age of seventy. Either of these changes would have a substantial impact because over one-third of all Supreme Court justices have served longer than twenty years and past seventy-five years old. But constitutional amendments are difficult to pass, and mandatory retirement ages are out of favor now. Furthermore, some of the best judges have done some of their finest work late in their career. Recently, however, some observers of appointment battles have argued that having fixed terms might lessen the stakes, and therefore the fights, over the appointments. This may be wishful thinking.

Independence of Judges

Given the use of political criteria in selecting judges, can judges be independent on the bench? Can they decide cases as they think the law requires? That is, do they have **judicial independence**? Or do they feel pressure to decide cases as presidents or senators want them to?

Because judges are not dependent on presidents for renomination or senators for reconfirmation, they can be independent to a great extent. When President Nixon claimed executive privilege to keep the Watergate tapes secret, three of his appointees joined the other justices in ruling against him.[61] When President Clinton asserted presidential immunity from Paula Jones's lawsuit charging sexual

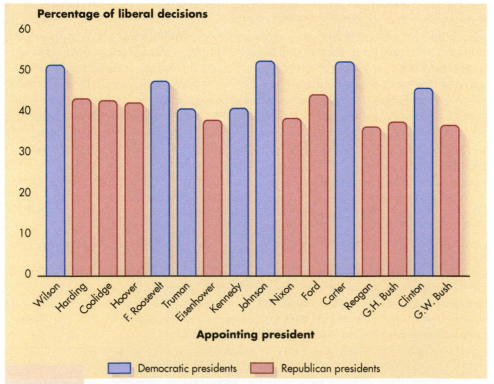

FIGURE 2: DEMOCRATIC APPOINTEES ARE MORE LIBERAL Appointees of Democratic and Republican presidents tend to decide cases somewhat differently.

SOURCE: Robert A. Carp, Ronald Stidham, and Kenneth L. Manning, *Judicial Process in America*, 6th ed. (Washington, D.C.: CQ Press, 2004), fig. 7-1. Copyright © 2004. Reproduced with permission of CQ PRESS via Copyright Clearance Center.

harassment, both of his appointees joined the Republican justices in deciding against him.[62]

After surveying the Warren and Burger Court decisions involving desegregation, obscenity, abortion, and criminal defendants' rights, one scholar observed, "Few American politicians even today would care to run on a platform of desegregation, pornography, abortion, and the 'coddling' of criminals"[63] (as the Courts' decisions were characterized by critics).

Presidents have scoffed at the notion that their appointees become their pawns. A study concluded that one-fourth of the justices deviated from their president's expectations.[64] Theodore Roosevelt placed Oliver Wendell Holmes on the Court, believing that Holmes shared his views on trusts. But Holmes voted against Roosevelt's position in an antitrust case, prompting Roosevelt to declare, "I could carve out of a banana a judge with more backbone than that!"[65] Holmes had ample backbone; he just didn't agree with Roosevelt's position in this case. Likewise, President Eisenhower placed Earl Warren on the Court, assuming that Warren was a moderate. But Warren turned out to be a liberal. Later Eisenhower said his appointment of Warren was "the biggest damn fool thing I ever did"[66] (although many legal scholars rank Warren as a great justice). President Truman concluded that "packing the Supreme Court simply can't be done.... I've tried it and it won't work.... Whenever you put a man on the Supreme Court he ceases to be your friend."[67]

Truman exaggerated, although some presidents have had trouble "packing" the courts. They have not been able to foresee the issues their appointees would face or the ways their appointees would change on the bench. (During Harry Blackmun's confirmation hearings, no senators asked about his views on abortion law, yet within six months *Roe* v. *Wade* would reach the Supreme Court, and Blackmun would author the controversial opinion.[68]) Nevertheless, presidents who have made a serious effort to find candidates with similar views usually have been able to.[69]

ACCESS TO THE COURTS

In our litigation-prone society, many individuals and groups want courts to resolve their disputes. Whether these individuals and groups get their "day in court" depends on their case, their wealth, and the court involved.

Courts hear two kinds of cases. **Criminal cases** are those in which governments prosecute persons for violating laws. **Civil cases** are those in which persons sue others for denying their rights and causing them harm. Criminal defendants, of course, must appear in court. Potential civil litigants, however, often cannot get access to court.

Wealth Discrimination in Access

Although the courts are supposed to be open to all, most individuals don't have enough money to hire an attorney and pay the costs necessary to pursue a case. Only corporations, wealthy individuals, or seriously injured victims suing corporations or wealthy individuals do. (Seriously injured victims with a strong case can obtain an attorney by agreeing to pay the attorney a sizable portion of what they win.) In addition, a small number of poor people supported by legal aid programs can pursue a case.

The primary expense is paying an attorney. New lawyers in law firms charge more than $100 an hour; established partners may charge several times that.[70] Other expenses include various fees for filing the case, summoning the jurors, and paying the witnesses, as well as lost income from missed work due to numerous meetings with the attorney and hearings in court.

Even if individuals have enough money to initiate a suit, the disparity continues in court. Those with more money can develop a full case, whereas others must proceed with a skeletal case that is far less likely to persuade judges or jurors. Our legal system, according to one judge, "is divided into two separate and unequal systems of justice: one for the rich, in which the courts take limitless time to examine, ponder, consider, and deliberate over hundreds of thousands of bits of evidence and days of testimony, and hear elaborate, endless appeals and write countless learned opinions," and one for the non-rich, in which the courts provide "turnstile justice."[71] (During the week that one judge spent conducting the preliminary hearing to determine whether there was sufficient evidence to require O. J. Simpson to stand trial for murdering his ex-wife and her friend, other judges in Los Angeles disposed of 474 preliminary hearings for less wealthy defendants.) Consequently, many individuals are discouraged from pursuing a case in the first place.

Interest Group Help in Access

Interest groups, with greater resources than most individuals, help some individuals gain access to the courts by sponsoring and financing their cases. Of course, the groups don't act out of altruism; they choose the cases that will advance their goals. An attorney for the **American Civil Liberties Union (ACLU)**, which takes criminal cases to prod judges to protect constitutional rights, admitted that the defendants the ACLU represents "sometimes are pretty scurvy little creatures, but what they are doesn't matter a whole hell of a lot. It's the principle that we're going to be able to use these people for that's important."[72]

Some liberal groups—especially civil liberties organizations such as the ACLU, civil rights organizations such as the National Association for the Advancement of Colored People (NAACP), environmental groups such as the Sierra Club, and consumer and safety groups such as Ralph Nader's organizations—use litigation as a primary tactic. Other groups use it as an occasional tactic. In the 1980s and 1990s, some conservative groups began to use litigation as aggressively as these liberal groups. The Rutherford Institute arose to help persons who claimed that their religious rights were infringed upon, representing children who were forbidden from reading the Bible on the school bus or praying in the school cafeteria. Today, the Alliance Defense Fund, which

STEVE PETTEWAY/UPI /Landov

The first female justices—former justice Sandra Day O'Connor (left) and current justices Sonya Sotomayor, Ruth Bader Ginsburg, and Elena Kagan. O'Connor was appointed by President Reagan, Ginsburg by President Clinton, and Sotomayor and Kagan by President Obama.

sponsors eighty to one hundred cases at a time, prods the courts to reflect conservative Christian values in disputes involving education, homosexuality, and embryonic stem cell research.[73]

Interest groups have become ubiquitous in the judicial process. About half of all Supreme Court cases involve a liberal or conservative interest group,[74] and many lower court cases do as well. Even so, interest groups can help only a handful of the individuals who lack the resources to finance their cases.

Proceeding through the Courts

Cases normally start in a district court. Individuals who lose have a right to have their case decided by one higher court to determine whether there was a miscarriage of justice. They normally appeal to a court of appeals. Individuals who lose at this level have no further right to have their case decided by another court, but they can appeal to the Supreme Court. However, the Court can exercise almost unlimited discretion in choosing cases to review. No matter how important or urgent an issue seems, the Court doesn't have to hear it.

When the husband of Terri Schiavo, who was brain dead but physically alive in a persistent vegetative state, sought to have her feeding tube removed, her parents, aided by pro-life groups, sued to take custody from her husband, then to maintain the feeding tube, and, once taken out, to

reinsert it. They appealed to the Supreme Court six times. Although congressional leaders, thundering about federal judges, made her situation a political cause, the Supreme Court refused to hear the case each time it was appealed. Sen. Tom Coburn (R-Okla.) responded, "I don't want to impeach judges; I want to impale them."[75] Still, the Court refused to hear the case.

Litigants who appeal to the Supreme Court normally file a petition for a **writ of *certiorari*** ("made more certain" in Latin). The Court grants the writ—agrees to hear the case— if four of the nine justices vote to do so. The rationale for this "rule of four" is that a substantial number, though not necessarily a majority, of the justices should deem the case important enough to review. Generally, the Court agrees to review a case when the justices think an issue hasn't been resolved satisfactorily or consistently by the lower courts.

From eight to ten thousand petitions each year, the Court selects eighty or fewer to hear, thus exercising considerable discretion.[76] The oft-spoken threat "We're going to appeal all the way to the Supreme Court" is usually just bluster. Likewise, the notion that the Court is "the court of last resort" is misleading. Most cases never get beyond the district courts or courts of appeals.

That the Supreme Court grants so few writs means that the Court has tremendous power to determine which policies to review. It also means that the lower courts have considerable power because they serve as the court of last resort for most cases.

DECIDING CASES

In deciding cases, judges need to interpret statutes and the Constitution and determine whether to follow precedents. In the process, they exercise discretion and make law.

Interpreting Statutes

In deciding cases, judges start with **statutes**—laws passed by legislatures. Because these statutes are often ambiguous, judges need to interpret them in order to apply them.

Congress passed the **Americans with Disabilities Act** to protect people from discrimination in employment and public accommodations (businesses open to the public, such as stores, restaurants, hotels, and health care facilities). The act applies to people who have a "physical impairment" that "substantially limits" any of their "major life activities." The statute does not define these terms. Thus the courts have to do so, and in the process they determine the scope of the act.

When a dentist refused to fill a cavity for a woman with HIV, she sued, claiming discrimination under this act. The Supreme Court agreed by a 5–4 vote.[77] The majority concluded that HIV was a "physical impairment," although the disease was in its early stages and didn't prevent the woman from performing any activity yet. The majority also concluded that HIV would limit the "major life activity" of reproduction, because the disease could infect her fetus if she got pregnant. The dissenters interpreted "major life activities" to mean repetitive activities that are essential for daily existence rather than important activities that rarely occur in a person's life. Therefore, they denied that reproduction is a "major life activity." (None of this relates to dentistry, but the justices were defining the scope of the statute for future cases involving HIV as well as for this case.)

When a woman developed carpal tunnel syndrome on the assembly line at a manufacturing plant, she sued, claiming that the company didn't make the reasonable accommodation—give her a different job that didn't require repetitive manual labor—that was required under the act. She said her condition limited her "major life activities" of performing manual tasks at work and at home, including lifting, sweeping, and gardening; playing with her children; and driving long distances. The Court ruled that these aren't "major life activities,"[78] because they aren't of central importance to daily life, as seeing, hearing, and walking are.

Thus the Court had discretion. It interpreted the act broadly when it covered persons with HIV but narrowly when it refused to cover workers with less serious ailments.

Interpreting the Constitution

After interpreting statutes, judges determine whether the statutes are constitutional. Or if the cases involve actions of government officials rather than statutes, judges determine whether the actions are constitutional. For either, they need to interpret the Constitution.

Compared to constitutions of other countries, our Constitution is short and general and therefore ambiguous. It speaks in broad principles rather than in narrow details. The Fifth Amendment states that persons shall not be "deprived of life, liberty, or property without due process of law." The Fourteenth Amendment states that persons shall not be denied "the equal protection of the laws." What is "due process of law"? "Equal protection of the laws"? Generally, the former means that people should be treated fairly and the latter means that they should be treated equally. But how fairly? How equally? These are broad principles that need to be interpreted in specific cases.

Sometimes the Constitution uses relative terms. The Fourth Amendment provides that persons shall be "secure... against unreasonable searches and seizures." What are "unreasonable" searches and seizures? In 2012, the Supreme Court had to decide whether the FBI could attach a GPS device to the underside of a car driven by a suspected drug dealer. The device monitored his movements and led the agents to a house occupied by another drug dealer. Was use of the device reasonable or unreasonable? The Constitution doesn't tell us. (The majority decided that it was unreasonable.[79])

Other times the Constitution uses absolute terms that appear more clear-cut but aren't. The First Amendment provides that there shall be "no law ... abridging the freedom of speech." Does "no law" mean literally no law? Then what about a law that punishes someone for falsely shouting "Fire!" in a crowded theater and causing a stampede that injures some patrons? Whether relative or absolute, the language needs to be interpreted in specific cases.

Occasionally, politicians, following the lead of Richard Nixon, assert that judges ought to be "strict constructionists," that they ought to interpret the Constitution "strictly." This is nonsense. Judges can't interpret ambiguous language strictly. When politicians or commentators use this phrase, they're trying to persuade voters that judges from the other party are deciding cases incorrectly, as though they are departing from some clear and fixed standard. (For another method of interpreting the Constitution, see the CourseReader box.)

When judges interpret the Constitution, they exercise discretion. As former Chief Justice Charles Evans Hughes candidly acknowledged, "We are under a constitution, but the Constitution is what the Supreme Court says it is."[80]

Restraint and Activism

All judges exercise discretion, but not all engage in policy making to the same extent. Some, classified as restrained, are less willing to declare laws or actions of government officials unconstitutional, whereas others, classified as activist, are more willing to do so.

Restrained judges believe that the judiciary is the least democratic branch because federal judges are appointed for life rather than elected and reelected. Consequently, they should defer to the other branches, whose officials are elected.

Log in to www.cengagebrain.com and open Course-Reader to access the full reading "If Scalia Had His Way" by Jeffrey Rosen.

Some judges and legal commentators, acknowledging the need to interpret the Constitution, say that all judges should interpret the general provisions in the document according to the Founders' intentions at the time the Constitution was written. This approach is called **originalism**. Justice Antonin Scalia of the Supreme Court advocates this approach.

Originalism became popular among conservatives who opposed the liberal decisions of the Supreme Court in the 1960s and 1970s. They maintain that it would keep judges from using their own values when deciding cases. Instead, it would force judges to interpret constitutional provisions as the Founders intended.

Those who advocate originalism use it when constitutional provisions are ambiguous, but some also use the term when the language is clear. The Fourteenth Amendment, adopted after the Civil War to protect newly freed slaves, says that states can't deny "any person" equal protection of the laws. (That is, states can't discriminate—they must treat people equally.) Because the goal was to prohibit racial discrimination, not sexual discrimination, Justice Scalia insists that the amendment should apply only to men, not to women (or to homosexuals), despite its language.

Thus the implications of originalism could be extreme if a majority of the Court subscribed to this approach. But many originalists pick and choose, taking this approach in some areas of the law but not in others. Justice Scalia, for example, brushes aside charges that originalism would be extreme. He says that he wouldn't approve flogging as punishment, despite its use at the time of the Founding, because he isn't "a nut." Yet originalists who follow the Founders' intentions in some areas of the law but not in others appear to be using their own values in individual cases—exactly what they criticize other judges of doing—rather than following a consistent approach.

1. Do you see any difficulties in determining the Founders' intentions?
2. Are you more comfortable with judges interpreting the Constitution as the Founders intended or as people today understand the provisions?
3. In what ways would legal doctrine differ if a majority of the Court adhered to originalism?
4. Originalists claim that this approach prevents judges from using their own values. Do you think the advocates adopt this approach because it reflects their own values—that is, because it leads to their preferred results?
5. Do you see any parallels between originalism and the Tea Party's views? (Chapters 2 and 7 have discussions of the Tea Party's views.)

That is, they should accept the laws or actions of the other branches rather than substitute their own views. They should be wary of "government by judiciary." They should recognize, Justice Harlan Stone said, that "courts are not the only agency of government that must be presumed to have the capacity to govern. For the removal of unwise laws from the statute books, appeal lies not to the courts, but to the ballot and the processes of democratic government."[81]

Restrained judges also maintain that the power to declare laws unconstitutional is more effective if it is used sparingly. Justice Louis Brandeis concluded that "the most important thing we do is not doing."[82] That is, the most important thing judges do is declare laws constitutional and thereby build up political capital for the occasional times that they declare laws unconstitutional.

Ultimately, restrained judges contend that showing appropriate deference and following proper procedures are more important than reaching desired results. When a friend taking leave of Justice Oliver Wendell Holmes one morning said, "Well, Mr. Justice, I hope you do justice today," Holmes replied, "My job is not to do justice but to follow the law."[83] Justice Harry Blackmun reflected this view in a capital punishment case:

I yield to no one in the depth of my distaste, antipathy, and, indeed, abhorrence for the death penalty, with all its aspects of physical distress and fear and of moral judgment exercised by finite minds. That distaste is buttressed by a belief that capital punishment serves no useful purpose that can be demonstrated. For me, it violates childhood's training and life's experiences, and is not compatible with the philosophical convictions I have been able to develop. It is antagonistic to any sense of "reverence for life." Were I a legislator, I would vote against the death penalty.

But as a judge, he voted for it in 1972.[84]

Activist judges are less concerned with showing appropriate deference and following proper procedures. Some are more concerned with the results; others are more outraged at injustice. Chief Justice Earl Warren said that the courts' responsibility was "to see if justice truly has been done."

BEHIND THE SCENES

Do Personal Preferences Matter?

The Supreme Court ruled that Michigan and New York can't prohibit out-of-state wineries from shipping wine to customers in their states while allowing in-state wineries to ship wine to residents in their states.[1] That is, the states can't discriminate against out-of-state wineries, which these states did to boost the business of their in-state wineries. The ruling means that wine connoisseurs can order fine wine from wineries throughout the United States.

The question was whether the commerce clause (Art. I, Sec. 8), which prohibits states from interfering with interstate commerce, or the Twenty-first Amendment, which repealed Prohibition and which allows states to regulate liquor, should prevail. A plausible argument could be made either way.

The majority emphasized the commerce clause, which opened the states to shipments from out-of-state wineries, rather than the Twenty-first Amendment. One insider observed that the five justices in the majority (Breyer, Ginsburg, Kennedy, Scalia, and Souter) happened to be the wine aficionados on the Court. Justice Breyer called the majority "the rosy-cheeked caucus."[2]

[1] *Granholm* v. *Heald*, 161 L.Ed.2d 796 (2005).

[2] Jeffrey Toobin, *The Nine: Inside the Secret World of the Supreme Court* (New York: Doubleday, 2007), 306.

He asked lawyers who emphasized technical procedures during oral arguments, "Yes, yes, yes, but is it right? Is it good?"[85]

Activist judges don't believe that the judiciary is the least democratic branch. Warren, who had served as governor of California, saw that the legislators, though elected, were often the captives of special interests. As a result of these attitudes, activist judges have a flexible view of separation of powers. District court judge Frank Johnson, who issued sweeping orders for Alabama's prisons and mental hospitals, replied to critics, "I didn't ask for any of these cases. In an ideal society, all of these . . . decisions should be made by those to whom we have entrusted these responsibilities. But when governmental institutions fail to make these . . . decisions in a manner which comports with the Constitution, the federal courts have a duty to remedy the violation."[86]

Activist judges don't believe that the power to declare laws unconstitutional is more effective if it is used sparingly. Rather, they claim that the power is enhanced if it is used frequently—essentially, they urge their colleagues to "use it or lose it"—because the public gets accustomed to it.

Thus judicial restraint and judicial activism are belief systems and role concepts that people think judges should follow when they decide cases. Some judges tend to be restrained, whereas others tend to be activist; most fall somewhere in between.

Both conservatives and liberals have practiced both restraint and activism depending on the political climate at the time. In the late nineteenth and early twentieth centuries, the Court was conservative and activist, striking down regulations on business. After its switch in the 1930s, the Court was liberal and restrained, upholding regulations on business. Then in the 1950s and 1960s, the Court was liberal and activist, striking down restrictions on individual rights. Today the Court often is conservative and activist.

Although restraint and activism are useful concepts, we shouldn't make too much of them. It's usually more important to know whether a judge is conservative or liberal than whether the judge purports to be restrained or activist. Political science research shows that justices' votes reflect their ideology: conservative justices vote for the conservative position, and liberal justices vote for the liberal position in most cases. When justices claim to be restrained, their decision, allowing a particular law or policy to continue, produces the conservative or liberal outcome they prefer.[87] Thus some political scientists conclude that "judicial restraint" is little more than "a cloak for the justices' policy preferences."[88] It enables them to proclaim their "restraint" while actually voting on the basis of their ideology—without ever admitting this to the public.

Following Precedents

In interpreting statutes and the Constitution, judges are expected to follow precedents established by their court or higher courts in previous cases. This is the rule of ***stare decisis*** ("stand by what has been decided" in Latin).

Stare decisis provides stability in the law. If different judges decided similar cases in different ways, the law would be unpredictable, even chaotic. "*Stare decisis,*" Justice Brandeis said, "is usually the wise policy; because in most matters it is more important that the applicable rule of law be settled than that it be settled right."[89] *Stare decisis* also promotes equality in the law. If different judges decided similar cases in different ways, the courts would appear discriminatory toward some litigants.

In 1962, the Supreme Court held unconstitutional a New York law requiring public school students to recite a nondenominational prayer every day. This ruling became a precedent.[90] The following year, the Court held unconstitutional a Baltimore school policy requiring students to recite Bible verses.[91] The Court followed the precedent it had set the year before. In 1980, the Court held unconstitutional a Tennessee law forcing public schools to post the Ten Commandments in all classrooms.[92] Although this law differed from the previous ones in that it did not require recitation, the majority concluded that it reflected the same goal—to use the public schools to promote the Christian religion—so it violated the same principle—separation of church and state. In 1992, the Court ruled that clergy cannot offer prayers at graduation ceremonies for public schools.[93] Although this situation, too,

Justice Clarence Thomas shares a laugh with his clerks in his chambers.

differed from the previous ones in that it did not occur every day at school, the majority reasoned that it, too, reflected the same goal and violated the same principle. Finally, in 2000, the Court ruled that schools cannot use, or allow clergy or students to use, the public address system to offer prayers before high school football games.[94] For almost four decades, the Court followed the precedent it originally set when it initially addressed this issue.

Stare decisis is considered so important that judges sometimes follow precedents that they don't agree with. In *Roe* v. *Wade* in 1973, the Supreme Court established a right to abortion.[95] After five straight Republican appointments to the Court since the ruling, it appeared that a majority on the Court might be willing to reverse the ruling. Pennsylvania passed a law denying a right to abortion—essentially inviting the justices to reverse the ruling. In 1992, the law reached the Court. A bare majority overturned the state law and upheld the Court's precedent.[96] Three justices in the majority said they disagreed with the precedent but felt obligated to follow it. One of these, Justice Souter, wrote,

> For two decades of economic and social developments, people have organized intimate relationships and made choices … in reliance on the availability of abortion in the event that contraception should fail. The ability of women to participate equally in the economic and social life of the nation has been facilitated by their ability to control their reproductive lives.… [O]nly the most convincing justification … could suffice to demonstrate that a later decision overruling the first was anything but a surrender to political pressure.… So to overrule under fire in the absence of the most compelling reason to re-examine a watershed decision would subvert the Court's legitimacy beyond any serious question.

Thus the right to abortion remained only because three justices who disagreed with it decided to follow the precedent rather than their preference. (Of course, not all justices feel equally obligated to follow precedents.)

Making Law

Many judges deny that they make law. They say that it is already there, that they merely "find" it or, with their education and experience, "interpret" it. They imply that they use a mechanical process. Justice Owen Roberts wrote for the majority that struck down a New Deal act in 1936:

> It is sometimes said that the Court assumes a power to overrule… the people's representatives. This is a misconception. The Constitution is the supreme law of the land.… All legislation must conform to the principles it lays down. When an act of Congress is appropriately challenged in the courts as not conforming to the constitutional mandate, the judicial branch of government has only one duty—to lay … the Constitution … beside the statute … and to decide whether the latter squares with the former.[97]

In other words, the Constitution itself dictates the decision.

However, by now it should be apparent that judges do not use a mechanical process. They *do* exercise discretion, and they *do* make law: when they interpret statutes, when they interpret the Constitution, and when they determine which precedents to follow or disregard.[98] In doing so, they reflect their own political preferences. As Justice Benjamin Cardozo said, "We may try to see things as objectively as we please. Nonetheless, we can never see them with any eyes except our own."[99] They do not shed their attitudes, even their prejudices, when they don their robes.

But to say that judges make law is not to say that they make law as legislators do. Judges make law less directly, in the process of resolving disputes brought to them. They usually make law by telling governments what they cannot do, rather than what they must do and how they must do it. And judges make law less freely. They start not with clean slates, but with established principles embodied in statutes, the Constitution, and precedents. They are expected to follow these principles. If they deviate from them, they are expected to explain their reasons, and they are subjected to scrutiny by the legal profession.

 ### Thinking about Democracy

> Once we realize that judges make law as they decide cases, do we have to alter our conception of democratic government?

Deciding Cases at the Supreme Court

The Supreme Court's term runs from October through June. Early in the term, the justices decide which cases to hear, and by the end of the term, they decide how to resolve those cases.

After the Court agrees to hear a case, litigants submit written arguments. These "briefs" identify the issues and marshal the evidence—statutes, constitutional provisions, and precedents—for their side. (The word *briefs* is a misnomer, as some run to more than one hundred pages.)

Often interest groups and governments, whether federal, state, or local, submit briefs to support one side. These **friend of the court briefs** present additional evidence or perspectives not included in the litigants' briefs. Major cases can prompt many briefs. The health care case had a record 136 briefs.[100]

Several weeks after receiving the briefs, the Court holds oral arguments. Normally the Court schedules an hour per case (a half hour per side). Due to the magnitude and complexity of the health care law, however, the Court scheduled six hours stretched out over three days for this case.

For oral arguments, the justices gather in the robing room, put on their black robes, and file into the courtroom, taking their places at the half-hexagon bench. The chief justice sits in the center, with the associate justices extending out in order of seniority. The crier gavels the courtroom to attention and announces:

> The Honorable, the Chief Justice and Associate Justices of the Supreme Court of the United States! Oyez, oyez, oyez! [Give ear, give ear, give ear!] All persons having business before the Honorable, the Supreme Court of the United States are admonished to draw near and give attention, for the Court is now sitting. God save the United States and this Honorable Court.

The chief justice calls the case. The lawyers present their arguments, although the justices interrupt with questions whenever they want. When Solicitor General Donald Verrilli defended the Affordable Care Act, he was interrupted

180 times—once every 22 seconds, on average.[101] The justices ask about the facts of the case: "What happened when the defendant …?" They ask about relevant precedents that appear to support or rebut the lawyers' arguments: "Can you distinguish this case from …?" They ask about hypothetical scenarios: "What if the police officer …?" These questions help the justices determine what is at stake, how a ruling would relate to existing doctrine, and how a ruling might govern future situations. They are experienced at pinning lawyers down. Chief Justice Rehnquist, who was affable toward his colleagues, was tough on the lawyers appearing before him. When asked whether the lawyers were nervous, he replied, "I assume they're all nervous—they should be."[102] Occasionally, one faints on the spot.

In the process of questioning the lawyers, the justices are also trying to persuade each other. Their questions, while directed at the lawyers, are designed to reveal the weakness of the position they oppose and to convey this weakness to their colleagues.[103] Often, according to Chief Justice Roberts, the justices "are debating among themselves and just using the lawyers as a backboard."[104]

On the current Court, Justice Antonin Scalia is an aggressive interrogator; Justice Thomas, on the other hand, rarely asks any question. In her first term, Justice Sotomayor was the "most exuberant rookie interrogator" since Scalia's first term. "Like a transfer student who picks a fight on the first day of school, Sotomayor seemed to be showing that she was not to be taken—as she variously had been, in the months leading up to her debut—for a pushover, a token, or a slouch. She would not be cowed by the pomp of the setting—the velvet draperies, the spittoons—nor would she be inhibited by the Court's finicky codes of seniority and decorum."[105]

When the allotted time expires, a red light flashes on the lectern, and the chief justice halts any lawyer who continues. Rehnquist, who valued efficiency and punctuality, cut lawyers off in mid-sentence when their time was up.

The oral arguments identify and clarify the major points of the case for any justices who did not read the briefs, and they assess the potential impact of the possible rulings. The oral arguments also serve as a symbol: they give the litigants a chance to be heard in open court, which encourages the litigants to feel that the eventual ruling is legitimate. However, the oral arguments rarely sway the justices, except occasionally when a lawyer for one side is especially effective or ineffective.

As a lawyer before becoming chief justice, John Roberts argued thirty-nine cases at the Court. He was considered especially effective.[106]

After the lawyers have presented the case, the Court holds Friday conferences to make tentative decisions and assign the opinions. The decision affirms or reverses the lower court's decision. The opinion explains why. It expresses principles of law and establishes precedents for the future, thus telling lower courts how to resolve similar cases.

A portrait of Chief Justice John Marshall presides over the conference. To ensure secrecy, no one is present but the justices. They begin with handshakes. (During his tenure,

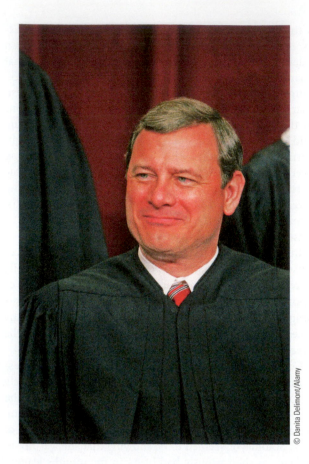

© Danita Delimont/Alamy

Supreme Court Chief Justice John Roberts

Chief Justice Marshall suggested that they begin with a drink whenever it was rainy. But even when it was sunny, Marshall sometimes announced, "Our jurisdiction extends over so large a territory that the doctrine of chances makes it certain that it must be raining somewhere."[107] Perhaps this accounts for his extraordinary success in persuading his colleagues to adopt his views.) Then the justices get down to business. The chief justice initiates the discussion of the case. He indicates what the issues are and how they ought to be decided, and he casts a vote. The associate justices follow in order of seniority. Although the conference traditionally featured give-and-take among the justices, discussion became perfunctory under Rehnquist, and the conference became a series of quick votes.[108]

The Court reaches a tentative decision based on these votes. If the chief justice is in the majority, he assigns the writing of the opinion to himself or another justice. If he is not in the majority, the most senior associate justice in the majority assigns it. This custom reveals the chief justice's power. Although his vote counts the same as each associate justice's vote, his authority to assign the opinion can determine what the opinion says. He knows that certain colleagues will use strong language and lay down broad principles, whereas others will use guarded language and hew closely to specific facts in the case.

Before Marshall became chief justice, each justice wrote his own opinion. But Marshall realized that one opinion from the Court would carry more weight. He often convinced the other justices to forsake their opinions for his. As a result, he wrote almost half of the more than eleven hundred opinions the Court handed down during his thirty-four years. Recent chief justices have assigned most opinions—82 to 86 percent—but have written just slightly more than their share—12 to 14 percent.[109]

After the conference, the Court produces the opinion. This is the most time-consuming stage in the process. After Justice Brandeis died, researchers found in his files the thirty-seventh draft of an opinion he had written but still had not been satisfied with.

Because the justices are free to change their vote anytime until the decision is announced, the justice assigned the opinion tries to write it to command support of the justices in the original majority and possibly even some in the original minority. The writer circulates the draft among the others, who suggest revisions. The writer circulates more drafts. These go back and forth as the justices attempt to persuade or nudge their colleagues toward their position.

Unlike legislators, however, the justices don't engage in horse-trading—if you join me on this, I'll join you on that. According to one justice, there's "[n]one of that, zero. The coalitions float. Each … case is a new day."[110]

Sometimes the outcome changes between the tentative vote in the conference and the final vote in the decision. According to Justice Blackmun's notes, eleven times during his last three years on the Rehnquist Court, one or more justices switched sides to fashion a new majority from the original minority. In the case involving graduation prayers, Justice Anthony Kennedy was writing the **majority opinion** to allow such prayers, but he was unable to persuade himself. He abandoned the majority and joined the minority, thus making it the eventual majority.[111]

These inner workings underscore the politicking among the justices. Justice William Brennan, a liberal activist on the Warren and Burger Courts, was a gregarious and charming Irish American who was well liked by his colleagues. After drafting an opinion, he sent his clerks to other justices' clerks to learn whether their justices had any objections. Then he tried to redraft it to satisfy them. If they still had qualms, he went to their offices and tried to persuade them. If necessary, he compromised. He didn't want "to be 100 percent principled and lose by one vote," a law professor observed.[112] Brennan was so "attuned to the concerns and passions of his colleagues"[113] and so adept at persuasion that some scholars consider him "the best coalition builder ever to sit on the Supreme Court."[114] In fact, some say the Warren and Burger Courts should have been called the Brennan Court.

Justice Scalia, a conservative activist on the Rehnquist and Roberts Courts, is a brilliant and gregarious Italian American who, when appointed by President Reagan, was expected to dominate his colleagues and become the leader of the Court. Yet he has not fulfilled this expectation. He has been brash and imprudent, appearing to take more pleasure in insulting his colleagues than in persuading them.[115]

In a case in which Justice O'Connor, who also was conservative but more cautious, did not want to go as far in limiting abortion rights as he did, Scalia wrote that her arguments "cannot be taken seriously."[116] In another case in which Chief Justice Rehnquist, who usually voted with Scalia, voted opposite him, Scalia wrote that his arguments were "implausible" and suggested that any lawyer who advised his client as Rehnquist urged should be "disbarred."[117] As a result, Scalia has not been as effective in luring moderates as Brennan was or in forging a consensus among conservatives as Brennan was among liberals.

Leadership, by someone, is necessary with nine strong-willed individuals, each of whom has risen to the top of the legal profession and each of whom is essentially operating a one-person law firm. (See the box "Anti-Semitism on the Bench.") Sometimes the chief justice becomes the informal leader. Marshall set the standard; Warren and Rehnquist were also effective leaders. Burger, however, possessed neither the interpersonal skills nor the intellectual firepower to earn the respect of his colleagues. It is not yet clear whether Roberts will be an effective leader.

If the opinion does not command the support of some justices in the original majority, they write a **concurring opinion**, which indicates that they agree with the decision but not the reasons for it. Meanwhile, the justices in the minority write a **dissenting opinion**, which indicates that they do not agree even with the decision. Both concurring and dissenting opinions weaken the force of the majority opinion. They question its validity, and they suggest that at a different time with different justices, there might be a different ruling. Chief Justice Hughes used to say that a dissenting opinion is "an appeal to the brooding spirit of the law, to the intelligence of a future day."[118]

Unlike the high courts of many other countries, which don't report any dissents, the Supreme Court of the United States routinely does, and the American people usually accept the existence of such disagreements.[119] In recent terms, about 60 percent of the Court's cases have had dissents.[120] But too many dissents indicate a fractious Court. One-third of the Rehnquist Court's cases were decided by a 5–4 vote in 2001, possibly the highest proportion ever.[121]

Finally, the print shop in the Court's basement prints the opinions, thus preventing the leaks that might occur if the opinions were printed elsewhere, and the Court announces its decisions and distributes the opinions in public session.

EXERCISING POWER

The Founders expected the judiciary to be the weakest branch of government. In the *Federalist Papers*, Alexander Hamilton wrote that Congress would have power to pass the laws and appropriate the money; the president would have power to execute the laws; but the courts would have "merely judgment"—that is, only power to resolve disputes in cases brought to them. In doing so, they would exercise "neither force nor will." They would not have any means to enforce

decisions, and they would not use their own values to decide cases. They would simply apply the Constitution and laws as written. Consequently, the judiciary would be the "least dangerous" branch.[122]

This prediction was accurate for the early years of the Republic. The federal courts seemed inconsequential. The Supreme Court was held in such low esteem that some distinguished men refused to accept appointment to it; others accepted appointment but refused to attend sessions. The first chief justice thought the Court was "inauspicious,"[123] without enough "weight and dignity" to play an important role.[124] So he resigned to be governor of New York. The second chief justice resigned to be envoy to France.

When the nation's capital was moved to Washington, D.C., in 1801, new homes were built for Congress and the president but not for the Supreme Court. Planners considered the Court too insignificant for more than a small room in the Capitol. But the Court couldn't even keep this room. For decades, it would be shunted from one location to another, from the marshal's office to the clerk's office, from the clerk's home to the Capitol's cellar—a dark and damp chamber in which visitors joked that Lady Justice wouldn't need to wear a blindfold because she couldn't see anyway—and from one committee room to another.[125] It wouldn't get its own building until 1935.

However, the status of the Court began to change after the appointment of the fourth chief justice, John Marshall. Under his leadership, the Court began to develop "weight and dignity" and to play an important role in government. The use of judicial review by the courts and the exercise of political checks against the courts show the extent of their power.

Use of Judicial Review

We'll examine two eras—the Founding era and the modern era—to see how the Court has used judicial review.

The Founding Era

In the Founding era, the **Marshall Court** established judicial review and national supremacy.

Establishing judicial review   The authority to declare laws or actions of government officials unconstitutional is called **judicial review**. The Constitution doesn't mention judicial review. Although the idea was proposed at the Constitutional Convention, it was strongly opposed by some delegates who feared that it would strengthen the federal courts too much and, ultimately, weaken the state governments. The delegates who favored judicial review didn't press for its inclusion because they worried that doing so might jeopardize the Constitution's ratification.[126]

Nevertheless, the Supreme Court claimed the authority of judicial review in the case of **Marbury v. Madison** in 1803.[127] The dispute originated in 1800, when the Federalist president, John Adams, was defeated in his bid for reelection by Thomas Jefferson and many Federalist members of Congress

American Diversity

Anti-Semitism on the Bench

President Woodrow Wilson admired James McReynolds's zeal as a trust-busting attorney, so he chose McReynolds as his attorney general. But after brief service in this post, McReynolds's "violent temper and abusive nature" made Wilson anxious to get rid of him, so Wilson appointed him to the Supreme Court in 1914,[1] where McReynolds exercised his violent temper and abusive nature for twenty-seven years. He was called "the rudest man in Washington."[2]

The product of a severe upbringing along the Kentucky-Tennessee border, McReynolds was especially prejudiced toward Jews. When Louis Brandeis, the first Jew on the Supreme Court, was appointed, McReynolds refused to speak to him for three years. And for the annual photograph of the justices one year, McReynolds refused to sit next to Brandeis, where he was assigned according to seniority, and the chief justice was forced to cancel the photo shoot. McReynolds also refused to join the other justices at a ceremonial event in Philadelphia because, he wrote the chief justice, "I am not always to be found when there is a Hebrew abroad." For the same reason, the chief justice had to divide the justices into two groups when he invited them to dinner. Years later, when Benjamin Cardozo, the second Jew, was sworn in, McReynolds conspicuously read a newspaper while muttering, "another one." When Felix Frankfurter, the third Jew, was appointed, McReynolds exclaimed, "My God, another Jew on the Court!" and refused to attend Frankfurter's robing ceremony.[3]

McReynolds didn't want any Jews to visit his Washington apartment, and he didn't even want his aides to fraternize with the aides of the Jewish justices.[4] He was so cantankerous and intemperate that Justice William Douglas named a card game after him, called "Son of a Bitch."[5]

It wasn't only McReynolds's sour personality that dismayed Washingtonians, but also his evident shift from a progressive attorney for the government to a reactionary member of the Court. McReynolds became one of the "Four Horsemen" who, when they were able to obtain the vote of another justice, struck down government regulations on businesses and stymied President Franklin Roosevelt's New Deal program for years.[6]

Yet, after McReynolds retired from the Court, European newspapers reported that this lifelong bachelor was financially supporting thirty-three English children left homeless by the German blitz during World War II. And when he died, he willed most of his estate to charities for needy children.

Nonetheless, based on his jurisprudence and his personality, McReynolds has gone down in history as perhaps the worst justice ever to sit on the Supreme Court.[7]

[1] Henry J. Abraham, *Justices and Presidents: A Political History of Appointments to the Supreme Court,* 2nd ed. (New York: Oxford University Press, 1985), 175.

[2] Dennis J. Hutchinson and David J. Garrow, eds., *The Forgotten Memoir of John Knox: A Year in the Life of a Supreme Court Clerk in FDR's Washington* (Chicago: University of Chicago Press, 2002), xix.

[3] Abraham, *Justices and Presidents,* 176.

[4] Hutchinson and Garrow, *Forgotten Memoir,* 36–37.

[5] Ibid., 177.

[6] The other three "Horsemen" were Justices Butler, Sutherland, and Van Devanter.

[7] Abraham, *Justices and Presidents,* 178, 377–379.

were defeated by Jeffersonians. With both the presidency and Congress lost, the Federalists tried to maintain control of the judiciary. The lame-duck president and lame-duck Congress added more judgeships, most of which were unnecessary. (Forty-two were for justices of the peace for the District of Columbia, which was a sparsely populated swamp.) They hoped to fill these positions with loyal Federalists before the new president and new Congress took over.

In addition, Adams named his secretary of state, John Marshall, to be chief justice. At the time, Marshall was still secretary of state and responsible for delivering the commissions to the new appointees. But he ran out of time, failing to deliver five commissions for District of Columbia justices of the peace. He assumed that his successor would deliver them. But Jefferson, angry at the Federalists' efforts to pack the judiciary, told his secretary of state, James Madison, not to deliver the commissions.[128] Without the signed commissions, the appointees could not prove that they had in fact been appointed.[129]

William Marbury and the three other appointees petitioned the Supreme Court for a writ of *mandamus* ("we command" in Latin), an order that forces government officials to do

© The Granger Collection, New York

Chief Justice John Marshall (*right*) swears in President Andrew Jackson in 1829. Although Marshall's party, the Federalists, had dissolved, Marshall remained as chief justice, serving for thirty-four years.

something they have a duty to do. In this case, it would force Madison to deliver the commissions.

The Jeffersonians were furious when the Court agreed to hear the case, so they threatened to impeach Federalist justices and they abolished the next term of the Supreme Court. Thus the case was held over until the following year, when it was finally decided.

As chief justice, Marshall was in a position to rule on his administration's efforts to appoint these judges. Today this would be considered a conflict of interest, and he would be expected to disqualify himself. But at the time, people were not as troubled by such conflicts.

Marshall could issue the writ, but Jefferson would tell Madison to disobey it, and the Court would be powerless to enforce it. Or Marshall could decline to issue the writ, and the Court would appear powerless to issue it. Either way, the Court would reflect weakness rather than project strength.

Marshall shrewdly found a way out of the dilemma. He interpreted a provision of a congressional statute in a questionable way and then a provision of the Constitution in a questionable way as well.[130] As a result, he could claim that the statute violated the Constitution. Therefore, the statute was unconstitutional, and the Court couldn't order the administration to give the commissions. Thus Marshall exercised judicial review. He wrote, in a statement that would be repeated by courts for years to come, "It is emphatically the province and duty of the judicial department to say what the law is."

Marshall sacrificed the commissions—he couldn't have gotten them anyway—and established the power of judicial review instead. In doing so, with one hand he gave the Jeffersonians what they wanted—permission not to deliver the commissions—while with the other he gave the Federalists something much greater—judicial review. And all along he claimed he did what the Constitution required him to do.

Jefferson saw through this. He said the Constitution, in Marshall's hands, was "a thing of putty,"[131] adding that Marshall's arguments were "twistifications." But the decision didn't require Jefferson to do anything, so he couldn't do anything but protest. Most of Jefferson's followers were satisfied with the result. They weren't upset that the Court had invalidated a Federalist law, even though it had established judicial review to do so.

Of course, they were shortsighted because this decision laid the cornerstone for a strong judiciary. A case that began as a "trivial squabble over a few petty political plums"[132] became perhaps the most important case the Court has ever decided.

Establishing national supremacy   After *Marbury*, the Marshall Court declared numerous state laws unconstitutional.[133] These decisions solidified the authority of judicial review and symbolized the supremacy of the national government over the state governments.

The Court also advanced the supremacy of the national government by broadly construing congressional power. In **McCulloch v. Maryland**, discussed in Chapter 2, the Court interpreted the **necessary and proper clause** to allow Congress to legislate in many matters not mentioned in the Constitution and not anticipated by the Founders.[134]

In the Founding era, the Court laid the foundation for judicial review and national supremacy. Of course, it would take the Civil War to resolve the conflict between the nation and the states and to enable the Court to build upon this foundation.

Now let's leap forward to the modern era, where we'll see how the Court has used judicial review and national supremacy to grant civil liberties and civil rights.

The Modern Era

The modern era for the Supreme Court began when President Dwight Eisenhower, fulfilling a campaign pledge to a presidential rival, Earl Warren, appointed him chief justice. In the 1950s and 1960s, the **Warren Court** decided many cases involving civil liberties and civil rights that pitted individuals against the government. Often they pitted minority individuals—whether a racial minority, a political minority, or a religious minority—against the majority of the public, whose views were reflected in government policy.

Historically, the courts had paid little attention to civil liberties and civil rights, allowing the government to ignore these constitutional rights. But the Warren Court reversed this lax attitude. It completely replaced traditional legal doctrine involving racial segregation, legislative reapportionment, criminal defendants' rights, libel, obscenity, and religion. It also modified traditional legal doctrine involving political speech. In the process, it held many laws, especially state laws, unconstitutional. The Warren Court was more activist in civil liberties and civil rights cases than any Supreme Court had ever been (see Figure 3).

The Warren Court sympathized with powerless groups and unpopular individuals when they challenged government policies. Thus the most elite institution in our government used its power to benefit many nonelites in our society. In its sympathies, the Warren Court differed sharply from previous Courts, which typically favored the haves over the have-nots and the efforts to preserve the status quo over the struggles to change it.[135]

The Warren Court's decisions brought about a conservative backlash.[136] President Richard Nixon vowed to change the Court's direction, and after Earl Warren retired Nixon appointed Warren Burger to be chief justice. Then Nixon and his former vice president, President Gerald Ford, appointed four more justices as vacancies occurred, seeking to slow, halt, or even reverse the Court's liberal doctrine. They expected the **Burger Court** to bring about a "constitutional counterrevolution."

But the Burger Court in the 1970s and 1980s did not. Although it eroded some liberal doctrine,[137] it left most intact. And it initiated new liberal doctrine in two areas where the Warren Court had been silent—sexual discrimination and abortion. Although it was not as committed to civil liberties and civil rights as the Warren Court, the Burger Court was more committed to them than any earlier Court.

President Ronald Reagan and his former vice president, George H. W. Bush, also sought to reverse the Court's liberal doctrine. When Burger retired, Reagan elevated William Rehnquist, the most conservative associate justice, to be chief justice. Then Reagan and Bush appointed five more conservatives as vacancies occurred. By this time, Republican presidents had named ten justices in a row.

President Bill Clinton's election led to the first Democratic justices since 1967. Although these two moderate liberals (Breyer and Ginsburg) slowed any further swing to the right, the conservative justices controlled the **Rehnquist Court** in the 1980s, 1990s, and early 2000s. But conflicts among the conservatives splintered their bloc. Some were bold, eager to sweep away liberal precedents and substitute conservative principles. Others were cautious, willing to uphold liberal precedents they would not have agreed to set in the first place and inclined to decide cases on narrow bases rather than on broad principles. In some terms, the former group dominated, but in other terms the latter group dominated.[138] Overall, the Rehnquist Court, though markedly more conservative than the Burger Court,[139] did not bring about a "constitutional counterrevolution" either.

The Rehnquist Court also practiced judicial activism, though from the right rather than from the left. For example, it struck down laws implementing gun registration, affirmative action, legislative districts that help racial minorities elect their candidates, and governmental policies that help religious minorities practice their religion. It also invalidated

Chief Justice Earl Warren

FIGURE 3: LAWS REGULATING ECONOMIC ACTIVITY AND RESTRICTING CIVIL LIBERTIES AND RIGHTS DECLARED UNCONSTITUTIONAL BY THE SUPREME COURT SINCE 1900 The Supreme Court was nearly as activist in striking down laws in the 1910s, 1920s, and 1930s as it was in the 1950s, 1960s, and 1970s. But in the former years, it was activist in economic cases (usually those involving government regulation of business), whereas in the latter years, it was activist in civil liberties and civil rights cases.

SOURCE: Lawrence Baum, The Supreme Court, 9th ed. (Washington, D.C.: CQ Press, 2007), 176. Copyright 2007. Reproduced with permission of CQ PRESS via Copyright Clearance Center.

a series of congressional laws regulating the states. In one eight-year stretch, the Rehnquist Court invalidated thirty-three federal laws, the highest annual average—over four per term—ever.[140]

In **Bush v. Gore**, which arose from the disputed presidential election of 2000, the conservative majority deliberately intervened—essentially, picked the president—even though the Constitution gives Congress, not the courts, primary authority to choose the president in electoral deadlocks.[141] The Court's ruling was clear judicial activism.[142]

President George W. Bush, like recent Republican presidents, tried to fashion a more conservative Court. When William Rehnquist died in 2005, Bush appointed John Roberts to be chief justice. He then appointed another conservative, Samuel Alito. The **Roberts Court** is emerging as an even more conservative court than the Rehnquist Court. It, too, has practiced judicial activism, overturning precedents while striking down campaign finance laws and gun control laws and limiting affirmative-action policies. The five justices who form the conservative majority on the Roberts Court all were either appointed by President Reagan or worked as lawyers in the Reagan administration.[143]

After the Warren Court, there was a steady trend toward more conservative justices. Justice John Paul Stevens, who was appointed by President Ford in 1975, observed that every justice, except one, appointed between 1971 and 2009 was more conservative than the justice he or she replaced. Stevens was a moderate Republican, but as the Court shifted to the right, he wound up on the left—the most liberal justice on the Rehnquist Court and the early Roberts Court.[144] President Obama

appointed two liberals, one replacing Stevens, which maintained the division of five conservatives and four liberals on the Court.

Nonetheless, the Roberts Court is the most conservative Court in the past seventy-five years.[145] It includes four of the five most conservative justices since 1937. (The fifth was Rehnquist.)[146] Its decisions are decidedly, though not uniformly, conservative. They are especially pro-business,[147] such as the Citizens United ruling that allows unlimited corporate spending in elections.[148] The Court thus reinforces the power of business, which was examined in Chapter 6.

In the modern era, the Supreme Court has used judicial review to be a policy maker. The Warren Court was a liberal policy maker, the Burger Court was a moderate policy maker, and the Rehnquist and Roberts Courts have been conservative policy makers. All four Courts have been activist rather than restrained. (For the time periods of these Courts, see Table 1.)

The Role of Judicial Review

Judicial review is the most powerful tool courts use to wield power. When the courts declare a law or action unconstitutional, they not only void that law or action but also might put the issue on the public agenda, and they might speed up or slow down the pace of change in the government's policy.

When the Supreme Court declared Texas's abortion law unconstitutional in Roe v. Wade in 1973, the Court put the abortion issue on the public agenda. Abortion hadn't been a raging controversy before the Court's ruling.

The Court also used judicial review as a catalyst to speed up change in the desegregation cases in the 1950s. At the time, President Eisenhower wasn't inclined to act, and Congress wasn't able to act because both houses were dominated by senior southerners who, as committee chairs, blocked civil rights legislation. The Court broke the logjam.

In the first third of the twentieth century, the Court used judicial review as a brake to slow down change in business cases. After the Industrial Revolution swept the United States, powerful corporations abused their employees, their customers, and their competitors. Although Congress and state legislatures passed laws to regulate these abuses, the Court, dominated by justices who had been lawyers for corporations, often struck down the laws. The Court delayed some policies for several decades.

Judicial review, an American contribution to government, was for years unique to this country. It is now used in numerous other countries, but not as extensively or as effectively as in the United States.

Table 1	Modern Supreme Courts
Warren Court	1953–1969
Burger Court	1969–1986
Rehnquist Court	1986–2005
Roberts Court	2005–present

SOURCE: © Cengage Learning.

The Supreme Court alone has struck down over 160 provisions of federal laws and over 1300 provisions of state and local laws.[149] The number of laws struck down, however, isn't a true measure of the importance of judicial review. Instead, the ever-present threat of review has prevented the legislatures from enacting many laws they feared would be struck down.

By using judicial review to play a strong role in government, the Court has contradicted the Founders' expectation that the judiciary would always be the weakest branch. Usually it has been the weakest branch, but occasionally it has been stronger. Arguably, these times include some years during the early nineteenth century, when the Court established national supremacy; the late nineteenth century and early twentieth centuries, when the Court thwarted efforts to regulate business; and the 1950s and 1960s, when the Court extended civil liberties and civil rights.

Nevertheless, the extent to which the Court has played a strong role in government shouldn't be exaggerated. At any given time, the Court has focused on one broad area of the law—in the modern era, civil liberties and civil rights—and has paid little attention to other areas. Moreover, this area has always involved domestic policy. Traditionally, the Court has been reluctant to intervene in foreign policy.[150]

Use of Political Checks against the Courts

The courts have exercised judicial review cautiously because they're subject to various political checks by the other branches.

Checks by the Executive

Presidents can impose the most effective check. If they dislike courts' rulings, they can appoint new judges when vacancies occur. Many appointees remain on the bench two decades after their president has left the White House.[151] President Nixon resigned in disgrace in 1974, but his appointee William Rehnquist stayed on the Court until he died in 2005.

Presidents and state and local executives, such as governors and mayors and even school officials and police officers, can refuse to enforce courts' rulings. School officials have disobeyed decisions requiring desegregation and invalidating class prayers. Police officers have ignored decisions invalidating some kinds of searches and interrogations. Yet executives who refuse to enforce courts' rulings risk losing public support, unless the public also opposes the rulings. Even President Nixon complied when the Court ordered him to turn over the incriminating Watergate tapes.

Checks by the Legislature

Congress and state legislatures can overturn courts' rulings by adopting constitutional amendments. They have done so four times (with the Eleventh, Fourteenth, Sixteenth, and Twenty-sixth Amendments).[152]

They can also overturn courts' rulings by passing new statutes. If courts make decisions when there are no relevant statutes, legislatures can pass new statutes that effectively overturn the decisions. The Court ruled that the Air Force didn't have to allow an ordained rabbi to wear his yarmulke with his uniform, because neither the religious guarantees of the First Amendment nor any congressional statute obligated the military to allow its personnel to wear religious apparel while in uniform.[153] The next year, Congress passed such a statute.

If courts base decisions on their interpretations of existing statutes, legislatures can amend the statutes, or pass new statutes, with clear language that effectively overturns the decisions. The Civil Rights Act of 1964 prohibits employment discrimination on the basis of gender as well as race. The act requires employees to file a complaint within 180 days after the discrimination occurs. Lilly Ledbetter discovered that she had been paid less than her male counterparts at a Goodyear Tire and Rubber Co. plant in Alabama. Apparently she had been paid less for nineteen years, although she didn't realize it until receiving an anonymous note from a co-worker. The legal question was, When did her 180-day clock start? The statute was ambiguous. The government interpreted the statute so the clock would start after each incident of discrimination—that is, the clock would restart after each paycheck reflecting the discrimination. Goodyear, however, interpreted the statute so the clock would start only once—after her first paycheck reflecting the discrimination. She wasn't aware of the discrimination then. Thus Goodyear, while acknowledging the discrimination, concluded that she couldn't sue because she didn't file her complaint within the first 180 days. The Roberts Court interpreted the statute as Goodyear, and other corporations, wanted. The effect was to nullify the statute for most employees, and protect the corporations from most lawsuits, because most employees wouldn't be aware of any discrimination at first. In 2009, however, Congress passed a new statute—the Lilly Ledbetter Fair Pay Act—to clarify the ambiguous provision. The new statute specifies that the 180-day clock restarts after each incident of discrimination.

Legislatures can refuse to implement courts' rulings, especially when money is necessary to implement them. The legislators simply don't appropriate the money.

Although these checks are the most common, Congress has invoked others, though only rarely. It can alter the structure of the lower federal courts, it can limit the appellate jurisdiction of the Supreme Court, and it can impeach and remove judges.

Checks by the Public

Checks by the executive and legislature are more likely if the public is upset with the courts. However, the public knows little about the courts and judges; more adults can identify the character names of the Three Stooges than a single justice on the Supreme Court.[154] They also know little about the cases, but they do remember controversial decisions, and they do recognize broad trends.[155] If they dislike these decisions or trends, their opinions pressure the executive or legislature to respond to the courts.

Thus the courts tend to reflect the views of the public. Studies comparing 185 Supreme Court rulings from the mid-1930s through the mid-1990s with public opinion polls on the same issues found that the rulings mirrored the polls in approximately 60 percent of the cases.[156] The justices reflected the views of the public about as often as elected officials did. Thus the justices either responded to the public or, having been appointed by political officials chosen by the public, simply reflected the views of the public as political officials did.

In short, the courts are part of the political process and are sensitive to others in the process, especially to the president and Congress, but ultimately to the public, which makes its wishes known to, and through, these branches. Although the courts enjoy relative independence, they aren't immune to political pressure. They have therefore "learned to be a political institution and to behave accordingly" and have "seldom lagged far behind or forged far ahead" of public opinion.[157]

As a result of occasional checks or threatened checks, the courts have developed a strong sense of self-restraint to ensure self-preservation. This caution, more than the checks themselves, limits their use of judicial review.

 Thinking about Democracy

Is judicial review compatible or incompatible with democratic government? In what ways is it compatible? Incompatible? Does the existence of political checks against the courts make judicial review more compatible with democratic government than it would be without them?

SUMMARY

- The president nominates and the Senate confirms federal judges. Politics is pervasive in this process because political parties and interest groups want judges who represent their "side." There is no requirement or tradition that judges be chosen by merit.
- Judicial appointments have become more politicized since the 1960s because Americans have been divided and government often has been divided, with one party occupying the presidency and the other dominating Congress. The parties have fought over the judiciary to tip the balance. And because of the Supreme Court's activism at that time, the parties realize the impact that a favorable or unfavorable Court can have on their agenda. Interest groups that support one side also jump into the fray.
- Judicial independence means that judges can decide cases as they think the law requires rather than feel pressure to decide cases as presidents or senators want them to. Judicial independence strengthens the courts. It enables them to check and balance the other branches.
- Judges must interpret statutes and constitutional provisions because many are ambiguous.
- Judges usually follow precedents because doing so promotes stability, predictability, and equality in the law.
- Judicial restraint reflects reluctance by judges to insert themselves in policymaking; judicial activism reflects willingness to do so. More specifically, restraint reflects reluctance to use judicial review—to declare the laws or actions of government officials unconstitutional; activism reflects willingness to do so.
- Because judges have discretion when they interpret statutes and constitutional provisions and when they decide whether to follow precedents, they may essentially make law when they decide cases.
- Chief Justice John Marshall laid the foundation for a strong judiciary and a strong national government by articulating judicial review in *Marbury* v. *Madison* and broadly interpreting the necessary and proper clause in *McCulloch* v. *Maryland*.
- Judicial review enables the courts to check and balance the other branches. Without judicial review, the courts would be weaker and the other branches would be stronger than they are. Through American history, however, the courts have been cautious in exercising judicial review and challenging the other branches.

DISCUSSION QUESTIONS

1. Do you think we should take the politics out of the process of appointing federal judges? Is it possible to do so?
2. Do you foresee any developments that might reduce the politicization of the process in the future?
3. Some developing countries lack judicial independence. What problems can you predict with this arrangement, even if you don't understand the government or politics of these countries?
4. At his confirmation hearings, Chief Justice Roberts said that judges are like umpires—they don't make rules; they just apply them. Perhaps Roberts was simply signaling his willingness to defer to Congress, or perhaps he was actually intending his statement to be taken more literally. If the latter, explain why his statement was misleading. Then explain why a nominee would make this analogy even if he realized it was misleading.

5. Think of a Supreme Court decision that you disagree with. Then construct a persuasive argument for why judges should follow the precedent anyway.

6. When the next vacancy on the Supreme Court occurs, will you care more whether the nominee is restrained or activist or whether the nominee is conservative or liberal?

7. Explain to someone who hasn't taken this course why the saying "a government of laws, not of men" is misleading.

8. Throughout his tenure on the Court, Chief Justice Marshall expected to be impeached. How might American government be different if he had been more cautious in deciding cases or his opponents had been bolder in pursuing impeachment?

9. It may sound cynical to say that judges are political actors and courts are political institutions, but can you construct an argument that makes this sound positive? (Perhaps you can build upon Aristotle's view that politics is noble because it helps people to know themselves and communities to govern themselves.)

13

Civil Liberties

Gun activists in Virginia promote the open carrying of weapons.

AP Images/HALEY/SIPA, Sipa via AP Images

LEARNING OBJECTIVES

1. Become familiar with the individual rights in the Bill of Rights.
2. Explain the importance of freedom of expression for American government and society.
3. Distinguish between speech that is allowed and speech that isn't allowed under the First Amendment.
4. Identify the two religion clauses in the Bill of Rights, and understand how they work in tandem to provide freedom of religion.
5. Describe the concept of "separation of church and state."
6. Understand how the rights for criminal defendants in the Bill of Rights make the criminal process fairer for these defendants.
7. Learn where the constitutional right to privacy comes from and what it applies to.

TALKING POINTS

The **Second Amendment** states, "A well regulated militia being necessary to the security of a free state, the right of the people to keep and bear arms shall not be infringed." When the amendment was adopted, there was no standing army to protect people from foreign invasions, Indian uprisings, or mob riots. The amendment was intended to protect people from these threats. The language implies that the right belongs to a local or state militia.[1] At the Founding, the militias were the ragtag bands of civilians in each community; today they would be the National Guard of each state. However, the National Rifle Association (NRA), in statements to its members and to the public routinely deletes the first half of the amendment and only quotes the second half to emphasize its view that the amendment provides an *individual* right rather than a *collective* right for each community or state. The NRA adopted this position after a conservative faction took over the organization in the 1970s.

For years, the courts rejected the NRA's view.[2] Conservative chief justice Warren Burger criticized the NRA for misleading the American public in its efforts to thwart gun control legislation. Burger said that the amendment "has been the subject of one of the greatest pieces of fraud—I repeat the word 'fraud'—on the American public by special interest groups that I have ever seen in my lifetime."[3] The courts' interpretation meant that the Second Amendment was a useless anachronism. It merely allowed the National Guard to have weapons, which was never doubted. But the NRA's advocacy and the public's predisposition to believe it undermined the courts' interpretation.[4] Conservative politicians and even judicial nominees were expected to offer an enthusiastic endorsement of the NRA's view, which reflected the conservative agenda against regulation and government.

In 2008, a case challenging the District of Columbia's thirty-one-year-old ban on handguns gave the Roberts Court an opportunity to address the issue. In *District of Columbia* v. *Heller*,[5] the divided Court ruled 5–4 that the Second Amendment does provide an individual right after all. The five most conservative justices banded together to challenge settled precedents and overturn the law.

The case shows that the justices need to interpret constitutional provisions, and the ruling shows that their interpretation may reflect their ideology. The ruling also demonstrates that conservative justices can be activists, as they were here in disregarding the precedents and invalidating the law. Ultimately, of course, the ruling shows how the law—even the Constitution—can change as the membership of the Court changes.

However, the ruling doesn't mean that most gun control laws will be struck down. The amendment refers to a "well regulated militia," meaning that the new right is not an absolute right. It can be limited because guns are dangerous. Certain weapons, such as assault rifles, and any weapons for felons and mentally ill people may still be banned. Carrying weapons into schools and other government buildings may still be forbidden. Various restrictions on the sale of arms may still be enacted. Other limits on the right may also be imposed.[6]

Americans value their "rights." Eighteenth-century Americans believed that people had **"natural rights"** by virtue of being human. Given by God, not by government, the rights could not be taken away by government. Contemporary Americans do not normally use this term, but they do think about their rights much as their forebears did.

Yet Americans have a split personality when assessing their rights. Most people tell pollsters they believe in constitutional rights, but many don't accept these rights in concrete situations. During the Cold War, for example, most people said they believed in free speech, but many also said that communists, socialists, or atheists shouldn't be allowed to speak in public or teach in schools.

Surveys show that Americans remain divided over their support for civil liberties. Many would ban expression that might upset others.[7] In one survey, one-third said they wouldn't allow a rally that might offend community members. Two-thirds said they wouldn't allow people to say things in public that might offend racial groups, and over one-half said they wouldn't allow people to say things in public that might offend religious groups. One-fifth said they wouldn't allow newspapers to publish without government approval of the articles.[8]

Conflicts over civil liberties and rights have dominated the courts since the 1950s. This chapter, covering civil liberties, and the next, covering civil rights, explain how the courts have interpreted these rights and tried to resolve these conflicts. The chapters show how judges have acted as referees between the litigants, brokers among competing groups, and policy makers in the process of deciding these cases.

THE CONSTITUTION AND THE BILL OF RIGHTS

The term **civil liberties** refers to individual rights in the Constitution. Some rights are identified in the body of the Constitution, and more rights are listed in the Bill of Rights.

Individual Rights in the Constitution

The Constitution bans religious qualifications for federal office. **Art. VI** (England had required its citizens who sought public office to profess their allegiance to the Church of England, which kept Catholics and religious dissenters on the sidelines.) The Constitution also guarantees jury trials in federal criminal cases. **Art. III, Sec. 2** It bans bills of attainder, which are legislative acts rather than judicial trials pronouncing specific persons guilty of crimes, and *ex post facto* ("after the fact") laws, which are legislative acts making some behavior illegal that wasn't illegal when it was done. **Art. I, Sec. 9 & 10** The Constitution also prohibits suspension of the writ of *habeas corpus,* except during rebellion or invasion of the country. **Art. I, Sec. 9**

The Bill of Rights

The civil liberties people usually think of are listed in the Bill of Rights.

Origin and Meaning

The Constitution originally didn't include a bill of rights; the Founders didn't think traditional liberties needed specific protections because federalism, separation of powers, and checks and balances would prevent the national government from becoming too powerful. But to win support for ratification, the Founders promised to adopt constitutional amendments to provide such rights. James Madison proposed twelve, Congress passed them, and in 1791 the states ratified ten of them, which came to be known as the **Bill of Rights**.[9]

The first eight grant specific rights. (See the box "Civil Liberties in the Bill of Rights.") The Ninth Amendment says that the listing of these rights does not mean they are the only ones the people have, and the Tenth says that any powers not granted to the federal government are reserved for the state governments.

The Bill of Rights provides rights against the government. According to Justice Hugo Black, it is a list of "Thou shalt nots" directed at the government.[10] In practice, it provides rights for political, religious, or racial minorities against the majority, because government policy toward civil liberties tends to reflect the views of the majority.

As explained in Chapter 2, the Founders set up a government to protect property rights for the well-to-do minority against a jealous majority. The Constitution's fragmentation of power and some specific provisions were designed to prevent the masses from curtailing the rights of the elites. However, as Americans became more egalitarian and as the masses gained more opportunity to participate in politics in the nineteenth and twentieth centuries, the relative importance of property rights declined while the relative importance of political rights increased. Thus the Bill of Rights became the means to protect the fundamental rights of political, religious, and racial minorities and of criminal defendants—people who are out of the mainstream and often unpopular and powerless—when they come in conflict with the majority.

Thinking about Democracy

Does the emphasis upon minority rights in the Bill of Rights contradict democracy or enhance democracy? What implications does this emphasis have for a conception of democracy that is based on majority rule?

Responsibility for interpreting the Bill of Rights lies with the federal courts. Because federal judges are appointed for life, they are more independent of majority pressure than elected officials are.

Application

For many years, the Supreme Court applied the Bill of Rights only to the federal government, not to the state governments (or to the local governments, which are under the authority of the state governments). That is, the Bill of Rights restricted the actions only of the federal government.[11]

Impact *social, global, historical, economic, political*

Civil Liberties in the Bill of Rights

- First Amendment grants

  freedom of religion

  freedom of speech, assembly, and
  association

  freedom of the press

- Second Amendment grants

  right to keep and bear arms

- Third Amendment forbids

  quartering soldiers in houses during
  peacetime

- Fourth Amendment forbids

  unreasonable searches and seizures

- Fifth Amendment grants

  right to a grand jury in criminal cases

  right to due process

- Fifth Amendment forbids

  double jeopardy (more than one trial for the
  same offense)

  compulsory self-incrimination

  taking private property without just compensation

- Sixth Amendment grants

  right to speedy trial

  right to public trial

  right to jury trial in criminal cases

  right to counsel in criminal cases

  right to cross-examine adverse witnesses

  right to present favorable witnesses

- Seventh Amendment grants

  right to jury trial in civil cases

- Eighth Amendment forbids

  excessive bail and fines

  cruel and unusual punishment

In ruling this way, the Court followed the intentions of the Founders, who assumed that the states, with their capitals closer to their people, would be less likely to violate the liberties of their people.[12] The Founders didn't realize that the states would in fact be more likely to violate the liberties of their people. Because the state governments represent smaller, more homogeneous populations, they tend to reflect majority sentiment more closely than the federal government, so they often ignored—and sometimes obliterated—the rights of political, religious, or racial minorities or of criminal defendants.

However, in the twentieth century there was a growing sense that individual rights are important and that the state governments as well as the federal government should protect them. Starting in 1925[13] and continuing through 1972,[14] the Supreme Court gradually applied most provisions of the Bill of Rights to the states.[15] In addition, the Court established some rights not in the Bill of Rights, and it applied these to the states, too—presumption of innocence in criminal cases, right to travel within the country, and right to privacy. Thus most provisions in the Bill of Rights, and even some not in it, now restrict the actions of both the federal and the state governments.

By forcing the states to grant national constitutional rights, the Supreme Court strengthened national governmental authority. This development was one factor that contributed to the evolution from the state-centered federalism favored by some Founders to the nation-centered federalism evident today. (Recall the discussion of these concepts in Chapter 3.)

To see how the Court has interpreted these provisions, we'll look at four major areas—freedom of expression, freedom of religion, rights of criminal defendants, and right to privacy. We'll put the major rulings of the Supreme Court in italics because the Court's doctrine is complex.

FREEDOM OF EXPRESSION

The **First Amendment** guarantees freedom of expression, which includes freedom of speech, assembly, and association, and freedom of the press.[16] The amendment also guarantees freedom of religion, which will be addressed in the next section. (Take note, in case you're asked. Americans can name more members of *The Simpsons* and more judges on *American Idol* than they can rights in the First Amendment.)[17]

The amendment states that "Congress shall make no law" abridging these liberties. The language is absolute, but no justices interpret it literally.[18] They cite the example of a person who falsely shouts "Fire!" in a crowded theater, which causes a stampede that injures someone. Surely, they say, the amendment doesn't protect this expression. So the Court needs to draw a line between expression the amendment protects and that which it doesn't.

Freedom of Speech

Freedom of speech, Justice Black asserted, is "the heart of our government."[19] There are important theoretical justifications for freedom of speech. By creating an open atmosphere, it promotes individual autonomy and self-fulfillment. By encouraging a wide variety of opinions, it furthers the advancement of knowledge and the discovery of truth. The English philosopher John Stuart Mill, who championed freedom of speech, observed that individuals decide what is correct by comparing different views. Unpopular opinions might be true or partly true. Even if completely false, they might prompt a reevaluation of accepted opinions. By permitting citizens to form opinions and express them to others, freedom of speech helps them participate in government. It especially helps them check inefficient or corrupt government. Finally, by channeling conflict toward persuasion, freedom of speech promotes a stable society. Governments that deny freedom of speech become inflexible. Eventually, their inflexibility fosters rebellion among their people.[20]

Thinking about Democracy

Why would philosopher John Dewey say that "democracy begins in conversation"?[21]

Because of our tradition and constitutional guarantee, almost all speech is allowed. However, there are some restrictions on the content of speech—what is said—and other restrictions on the manner of speech—how it is said. We'll first examine the restrictions on the content of speech, focusing on seditious speech, offensive speech, hate speech, and sexual speech. We'll then examine the restrictions on the manner of speech.

Seditious Speech

Seditious speech is speech that encourages opposition to or rebellion against the government.[22] The public becomes most hostile to seditious speech, and the government becomes most likely to prosecute people for such speech, during or shortly after war, when society is most sensitive about patriotism and loyalty. Criminal prosecution for seditious speech undermines our freedom of speech, which is supposed to protect individuals and groups who criticize the government and its officials.

World War I and the Russian Revolution, which brought the communists to power in the Soviet Union in 1917, led to numerous prosecutions for seditious speech. After World War II, the uneasy alliance between the United States and the Soviet Union gave way to the Cold War between the two countries in the 1950s and led to more prosecutions. Politicians, especially Sen. Joseph McCarthy (R-Wisc.), exploited the tensions, claiming that many government officials were communists. He said he had a list of 205 "known communists" in the State Department alone. He had little evidence—and provided no list.[23] Other Republicans also accused the Democratic Truman administration of covering for communists in government and goaded it into prosecuting communists outside government so it would not appear "soft on communism."

In 1940, Congress had passed an act that prohibited advocating overthrow of the government by force and organizing or joining individuals who advocated overthrow.[24]

During the Cold War, the government used the act against the communists. The Court upheld the act and affirmed the convictions of eleven upper-echelon leaders of the American Communist Party.[25] Although these leaders organized the party and the party advocated overthrowing the government by force, the leaders had not attempted to overthrow the government. (If they had, they clearly would have been guilty of crimes.) Even so, the Court concluded that *they were "a clear and present danger."* In reality, there was nothing clear or present about the danger; the defendants' efforts—essentially, the defendants' speech—had little effect. The Court, reflecting our society at the time, was scared and intolerant of dissent. After the Court's decision, the government prosecuted and convicted almost one hundred lower-level communists as well.

The public's fear was so consuming that the government's actions extended beyond criminal prosecutions to other measures, and beyond active communists to former communists—some Americans had dabbled with communism during the Great Depression in the 1930s—and even to

During the Cold War, Americans feared communism so much that some built bomb shelters in their yards, believing that taking refuge would protect their family in a nuclear attack.

individuals who had never been communists but who were lumped together as "commie dupes" or "comsymps" (communist sympathizers).

In the midst of this fear, the federal government and some state governments required government employees to take "loyalty oaths" and then fired those who refused, even on principle, and those who (purportedly) lied. Some state governments banned communists, former communists, and alleged subversives from public jobs such as teaching or private jobs such as practicing law or serving as union officers. Federal and state legislative committees held hearings to expose and humiliate them. These actions cost an estimated ten thousand Americans their jobs.

Eventually, the Cold War thawed somewhat, and the Senate condemned McCarthy after he tried to bully the army. His method was likened to witch hunts, and the tactic of making political accusations or name-calling based on little or no evidence came to be known as **McCarthyism**. (However, McCarthyism began before and continued after McCarthy's tenure in the 1950s, as other politicians and the Senate's Internal Security Committee and the House's Un-American Activities Committee used similar tactics.)[26]

Although McCarthy and others were bullies who hurt many innocent or harmless people, there actually were communist spies in the federal government, from the atomic labs at Los Alamos, New Mexico, to the State Department and the White House, according to records revealed after the collapse of the Soviet Union. Apparently most spies were discovered before the 1950s, but some were never uncovered.[27]

In the meantime, two new members, including Chief Justice Earl Warren, joined the Supreme Court. In a series of cases in the mid- to late 1950s and early 1960s, the Warren Court made it more difficult to convict the communists.[28] (See the box "The President Summons the Chief Justice.")

Ultimately, the Warren Court created a new doctrine for seditious speech.[29] The justices drew a distinction between advocacy and incitement. *People can advocate, enthusiastically, even heatedly, as long as they don't incite illegal action—that is, urge immediate action to violate any laws.* This doctrine protects most criticism of the government, whether at a rally or through the media, and it remains in effect today.

Thus after many years and many cases, the Court concluded that the First Amendment protects seditious speech as much as other speech. Justice William Douglas noted that "the threats were often loud but always puny."[30] Even the attorney general who prosecuted the major communist cases later admitted that the cases were "squeezed oranges. I didn't think there was much to them."[31] Nevertheless, the Court had permitted public fear to overwhelm the First Amendment for a long time.

The Vietnam War didn't prompt the same concerns as the Cold War, and Congress didn't pass any comparable laws. Nonetheless, the federal government took some actions against individuals and groups. Antiwar groups were harassed by federal grand juries, and their leaders were spied on by the U.S. Army. Some outspoken opponents were prosecuted for conspiring against the draft.[32] However, opposition to this war was so widespread that the government's actions didn't silence the protesters' speech.

Although the collapse of the Soviet Union and the demise of the Cold War made communism less threatening, the seditious speech doctrine remains important. After the Oklahoma City bombing in 1995, government surveillance of right-wing militia groups increased, but prosecution of the members, under terrorism laws, was limited because most of the evidence was fiery rhetoric, which is protected speech (unless it urges immediate action to violate any laws).

After the terrorist attacks in 2001, pressure to conform mounted. Conservative organizations and commentators sought to stifle inquiry and dissent and promote support for the administration's policies. One organization, in an attempt to prod colleges and universities to restrain faculty, identified forty professors who had "un-American" agendas.[33] Another group pressured the University of New Mexico to discipline a tenured professor who cracked, "Anyone who can blow up the Pentagon gets my vote." After the professor was reprimanded by the university, the group filed a lawsuit demanding that he be terminated.[34] During the Iraq War, critics were branded as "unpatriotic" and "disloyal" by commentators who stoked their listeners' anger.[35] But pressure to conform came from political organizations and commentators; little came from the government because First Amendment doctrine had been so fully developed by this time. (Other threats to civil liberties did come from the government, especially threats to privacy from the surveillance that followed 9/11.)

The state and federal governments have also limited offensive speech, hate speech, and sexual speech, which we'll turn to now.

BEHIND THE SCENES

The President Summons the Chief Justice

When the Supreme Court made it more difficult to convict American communists in the 1950s and 1960s, the justices incurred the wrath of the public, Congress, and President Dwight Eisenhower, who summoned Chief Justice Warren to the White House. In a private conversation, the president criticized the rulings. Warren asked Eisenhower what he thought the Court should have done with the communists. Eisenhower replied, "I would kill the SOBs."[1] Warren ignored the remark.

[1] Earl Warren, *The Memoirs of Earl Warren* (Garden City, N.Y.: Doubleday, 1977), 6.

Offensive Speech

Arrests for swearing, especially at police officers or in the presence of police officers, were numerous for many years. In the District of Columbia, for example, about ten thousand people per year were arrested for swearing (and charged with "disorderly conduct").[36] As swearing in general became more common in the 1960s and 1970s, and as swearing at police became a clear manifestation of the poor relations between inner-city residents and the officers who patrolled their neighborhoods, the justices decided that *swearing in many situations is protected speech* (though not on radio or television, as we'll see). They expected police, who are trained to face emotionally charged situations, to tolerate swearing.[37]

During the Vietnam War, a man on his way to observe a trial walked through the corridors of the Los Angeles County courthouse wearing a jacket with the words "Fuck the Draft" emblazoned on the back. A cop arrested him, and a judge convicted him. The Supreme Court reversed the young man's

The First Amendment prevents governments—not businesses—from restricting your speech. When Lorrie Heasley boarded a Southwest Airlines plane, she wore a T-shirt featuring President Bush, Vice President Cheney, Secretary of State Rice, and the title of the movie *Meet the Fockers*—except an expletive was substituted. The flight crew removed her from the plane. Although the government could not restrict this expression, the airline could.

conviction, as seventy-two-year-old Justice John Harlan remarked that "one man's vulgarity is another's lyric."[38] Harlan recognized that "much linguistic expression serves a dual communicative function: it conveys not only ideas capable of relatively precise, detached explication, but otherwise inexpressible emotions as well. In fact, words are often chosen as much for their emotive as their cognitive force.... [The former] may often be the more important element of the overall message." Thus the First Amendment protects emotional speech just as it does rational speech.

Hate Speech

Hate speech is derogatory speech—racial, ethnic, sexual, or religious slurs—usually aimed at a group rather than at an individual. When aimed at an individual, the speech impugns a characteristic the individual shares with the group. Hate speech demeans people for characteristics that are innate, such as race, ethnicity, or sexuality, rather than chosen (except for religious faith). Such speech can cause emotional or psychological harm.

Even so, it can be difficult to distinguish hate speech from other speech. What one person considers hate speech another may consider a simple observation or a valid criticism. And because of the First Amendment, *hate speech normally can't be prohibited by governments.*[39]

In 1978, lower federal courts required the Chicago suburb of Skokie to permit the American Nazi Party to demonstrate.[40] The Nazis intentionally chose Skokie as the site for their demonstration because many Jews lived there—forty thousand of the seventy thousand residents. Hundreds were survivors of German concentration camps during World War II, and thousands were relatives of people who were murdered by the Nazis. The city, in anticipation of the demonstration, passed ordinances that prohibited wearing "military-style" uniforms and distributing material that "promotes and incites hatred against persons by reason of their race, national origin, or religion." These ordinances were an attempt to bar the demonstration, and the courts threw them out. One court quoted Justice Oliver Wendell Holmes's statement that "if there is any principle of the Constitution that more imperatively calls for attachment than any other it is the principle of free thought—not free thought for those who agree with us but freedom for the thought we hate."[41]

Thinking about Democracy

Does the outcome of this case suggest another theoretical justification for freedom of speech? Does freedom of speech make people more tolerant, because they can't silence those they disagree with? Tolerance is essential in a multiracial, multiethnic, multicultural nation like the United States. If we can tolerate the Nazis' venomous speech, we should be able to tolerate the less hateful speech of other groups.

Cross-burning by the Ku Klux Klan presents a more difficult question. In the Klan's heyday, a cross-burning was a clear threat to the black families it was directed toward, and even today it might be used this way. But in other circumstances, a cross-burning *might* be intended only as a rallying symbol to the Klan's members. The Supreme Court ruled that persons who burn a cross to intimidate or to threaten—for example, to frighten their black neighbors—can be prosecuted, but those who burn a cross at a KKK rally in a private field hidden from other people and passing cars cannot be prosecuted.[42]

Despite the First Amendment, many colleges and universities adopted hate speech codes in the 1980s and 1990s because they worried that such speech created a hostile and intimidating environment for the victims.[43] A student who was jeered nightly by taunts of "Faggot!" said, "When you are told you are not worth anything, it is difficult to function."[44] Some students were disciplined under the codes. But colleges and universities, more than other institutions in our society, have traditionally fostered free expression and debate. And the codes, which were inherently difficult to write, were often too broad or too vague. Some were struck down by lower courts, and others were abandoned by the schools. Some were rewritten to focus on harassment and threats, which can be prohibited, and to apply to computers using university networks. George Mason University forbade students from using computers "to harass, threaten, or abuse others." Virginia Tech disciplined a student for posting a message on the home page of a gay men's group calling for gays to be castrated and to "die a slow death."[45]

Some conservative Christians, funded by evangelical ministries and interest groups, have launched an attack on tolerance policies toward gays and lesbians. They demand that schools and workplaces revoke their policies, including speech codes and, in lower grades, dress codes prohibiting antigay T-shirts. A Georgia Tech student who was reprimanded for sending a letter that berated students who came out as gay filed suit, claiming that her faith compelled her to speak out against homosexuality.[46]

These disputes highlight the fine line between harassment and free speech. So far, the Supreme Court hasn't addressed college and university speech codes or school tolerance policies.

In contrast to the United States, most Western countries, including Canada, England, France, and Germany, and other countries such as India and South Africa, ban hate speech and make it a crime to provoke racial or religious hatred. French actress Brigitte Bardot, an animal rights activist, was fined $23,000 by the French government for criticizing a Muslim ceremony that entails a sheep slaughter.

In 2010, Ireland banned "blasphemy," which was defined as speaking critically of anything sacred to any religion.[47] Islamic countries have campaigned for an international treaty banning blasphemy in an attempt to protect religious symbols, personalities, and dogmas from criticism or ridicule. The proposed treaty, of course, would limit freedom of speech, and the United States has announced that it will not join any such treaty.

Sexual Speech

In some contexts, sexual speech—here we're referring to language or situations that fall short of obscenity—has been prohibited. (Obscenity, whether in print or film or on radio or television, is never allowed. But its legal definition and judicial doctrine are complex and beyond the scope of this text.)

Governments can forbid nude dancing,[48] even though it may be expression. Through zoning, *governments can restrict pornographic theaters or sex shops* from most (though not all) parts of their cities.[49]

The Federal Communications Commission (FCC) can forbid radio and television stations from broadcasting some sexual language and situations. A California radio station broadcast a monologue by comedian George Carlin. Titled "Filthy Words," it lampooned society's sensitivity to seven words that "you couldn't say on the public airwaves…the ones you definitely wouldn't say, ever." The seven words, according to the FCC report, included "a four-letter word for excrement" repeated seventy times in twelve minutes. A majority of the Court ruled that although the monologue was part of a serious program on contemporary attitudes toward language, it was not protected under the First Amendment because people, including children, who were tuning in the radio could be subjected to the language in their homes.[50] The Court also ruled that the FCC can ban even "fleeting profanities"—single spontaneous expletives voiced in a nonsexual context.[51] Now the FCC forbids indecent material on radio and noncable television between 6 a.m. and 10 p.m. and fines any media that violate the ban. (Large fines were levied on the *Howard Stern Show,* before it moved to satellite radio, and on a New York City radio station that broadcast a tape of a couple having sex in Saint Patrick's Cathedral.)[52] Yet the Court struck down a Utah law restricting indecent material on cable television. By subscribing to and paying for cable television, its customers are accepting exposure to its programming.[53]

In each of these areas we have covered—seditious speech, offensive speech, hate speech, and sexual speech—courts allow more freedom for individuals today because the Supreme Court broadened its interpretation of the First Amendment during the second half of the twentieth century.

We'll now examine the restrictions on the manner of speech, focusing on demonstrations and symbolic speech.

Demonstrations

Protesters want people to see or hear their demonstrations, so they seek locations where people congregate and provide an audience. Although some people won't like their message or their use of public places to disseminate the message, protesters have a right to demonstrate.

Individuals are allowed to use public places, such as streets, sidewalks, parks, theaters,[54] and the grounds around public buildings,[55] *to express their views on public issues.* These places constitute the **public forum** and serve as "the poor person's printing press."

Private property is not part of the public forum, so *individuals have no right to demonstrate on private property.*[56] They need the owner's permission. Shopping malls usually forbid demonstrations. During the runup to the Iraq War, a sixty-year-old man wore a T-shirt with the slogan "Give Peace a Chance" at a mall in Albany, New York. Security guards ordered him to take off the shirt or leave the mall. When he refused, he was arrested.[57] Although wearing a shirt is not what we normally consider as staging a demonstration, the shirt did express his views, and the mall could forbid such expression.

Even in the public forum, individuals can't demonstrate whenever or however they want. The streets, sidewalks, parks, and theaters in the public forum are used for purposes other than demonstrations—especially for transportation and recreation—so individuals can't disrupt these activities. They can't, Justice Arthur Goldberg remarked, hold "a street meeting in the middle of Times Square at the rush hour."[58]

To ensure that potential demonstrations don't disrupt the normal activities of the places in the public forum, governments can require groups to obtain a permit, which can specify the place, time, and manner of the demonstration. Officials can establish restrictions to avoid disruptions. However, officials cannot use these restrictions to censor speech. They cannot allow one group to demonstrate but forbid another, no matter how much they dislike the group or its message. They cannot forbid the group even if they say they fear violence (unless the group actually threatens violence).

In recent years, questions have arisen about demonstrations at abortion clinics and at funerals. In their zeal, protesters have interfered with staffers and patients of abortion clinics and attendees at funerals. Abortion protesters can demonstrate on public streets and public sidewalks near abortion clinics, and they can approach staffers and patients who come and go, but *protesters cannot block access* (and to ensure this, judges can order them not to come within a certain distance—for example, fifteen feet—of driveways and doorways).[59] Moreover, they cannot demonstrate at the doctor's house even if they stand on a public sidewalk. After protesters repeatedly picketed at a doctor's residence in a Milwaukee suburb, the town passed an ordinance forbidding such picketing. The Court upheld the ordinance, ruling that protesters can march through residential neighborhoods but *cannot focus on particular houses,* because such picketing interferes with the privacy of the home for the doctor and the family.[60]

Members of a church in Topeka, Kansas, that opposes homosexuality began picketing at funerals of American soldiers killed in Afghanistan or Iraq. The church claims that God is punishing America—that is, killing soldiers—for tolerating homosexuality. (The church members picket regardless of the sexual orientation of the slain soldier.) In response, most states have passed laws restricting picketing at funerals, usually banning picketing within five hundred feet of funerals or funeral processions. The Supreme Court has not ruled on this issue,[61] but most lower courts have upheld these restrictions.

Symbolic Speech

Some demonstrations feature **symbolic speech**, which is the use of symbols rather than words to convey ideas. Sometimes symbolic speech has been prohibited when actual speech, with the same message, would have been permitted.

© Hiroji Kubota/Magnum Photos

When young men illegally burned their draft cards to protest the Vietnam War, the Supreme Court refused to protect their action as symbolic speech.

During the Vietnam War, some young men burned their draft cards to protest the war and the draft. Their action was powerful expression—symbolic speech was a novelty in the 1960s—and Congress tried to stifle it by passing a law prohibiting the destruction of draft cards. The justices upheld the law and expressed their discomfort with the concept of symbolic speech.[62]

But the Court came to accept symbolic speech in the late 1960s and early 1970s.[63] To protest the war, a Massachusetts man wore a flag patch on the seat of his pants and was arrested and sentenced to six months in jail. A Washington student taped a peace symbol on a flag and then hung the flag upside down outside his apartment. The Court reversed both convictions.[64]

When a member of the Revolutionary Communist Youth Brigade burned an American flag outside the Republican convention in 1984, the justices faced the issue of *flag desecration*—the ultimate symbolic speech. A bare majority of the Rehnquist Court *permitted* this symbolic speech.[65] Justice William Brennan wrote that the First Amendment can't be limited just because this expression offends most people. "We do not consecrate the flag by punishing its desecration, for in doing so we dilute the freedom that this cherished emblem represents." The ruling invalidated the laws of forty-eight states and the federal government.

In a dissent, Chief Justice William Rehnquist emotionally criticized the decision. He said the First Amendment shouldn't apply because the flag is a unique national symbol. In page after page, he recounted the history of "The Star-Spangled Banner" and the music of John Philip Sousa's "Stars and Stripes Forever," he quoted the poems by Ralph Waldo Emerson and John Greenleaf Whittier that refer to the flag, and he discussed the role of the Pledge of Allegiance. He relied on these historical manifestations of the flag's symbolism because the legal doctrine had become so robust by this time that it favored the symbolic speech.

Civil liberties advocates praised the decision, but veterans' groups were outraged and many Americans were upset. As a result, Congress passed a federal statute prohibiting flag desecration. (The previous case involved a state statute.) Yet the justices, dividing the same way, declared the new statute unconstitutional for the same reasons they reversed the prior conviction.[66]

European countries are less willing to accept symbolic speech. As they struggle with high numbers of Muslim immigrants and the reluctance of these immigrants to assimilate, some prohibit Muslim symbols. France banned the hijab (headscarf), worn by some young Muslim women, in public schools and the burqa (full veil), worn by some older Muslim women, in public places. In another backlash against Muslim immigrants, Swiss voters adopted a constitutional provision banning minarets—the towers on some mosques.[67]

In this chapter so far, we've focused on adult speech. Now we'll turn to student speech. Students below the college level are considered children rather than adults, so they aren't afforded full First Amendment rights.

Student Speech

During the Vietnam War, junior and senior high school students in Des Moines, Iowa, wore black armbands to protest the war. When they were suspended, their families sued school officials. The Warren Court ruled that the schools must allow the students freedom of speech as long as the students

Student speech that celebrates or condones drug use can be prohibited by school administrators.

don't disrupt the schools.[68] Public schools, Justice Abe Fortas said, "may not be enclaves of totalitarianism."

However, this case, which involved political speech, has proven to be the exception to the rule. According to the Burger, Rehnquist, and Roberts Courts, *administrators in public or private schools can restrict student speech for educational purposes.* They can restrict speech or clothing that is lewd or vulgar[69] or that promotes sex, drugs, or violence.

When the Olympic Torch Relay passed through Juneau, Alaska, for the 2002 Winter Games, high school students were released early to watch.[70] As the relay approached and television cameras filmed the scene, some students unfurled a banner that said, "BONG HiTS 4 JESUS." The principal was not amused and suspended the student who initiated the prank. (When the student quoted Thomas Jefferson on free speech, the principal doubled his suspension.) Although the student said the phrase was "meaningless and funny, in order to get on television," the Roberts Court, by a 5–4 vote, upheld the suspension because the phrase might have been understood to celebrate or condone drug use.[71]

Administrators restrict hate speech as well. Conflicts over hate speech arise in public schools because many administrators and teachers believe they should encourage tolerance. Disputes over antigay speech have been especially controversial, but the Supreme Court hasn't ruled on this issue.

Administrators can also censor student publications, even serious articles that don't promote sex, drugs, or violence or contain hate speech. The Rehnquist Court allowed censorship of student newspaper articles about the impact of pregnancy and of parents' divorce on teenagers.[72]

After the ruling, a Colorado principal blocked an editorial criticizing his study hall policy while allowing another editorial praising it. A Texas principal banned an article about the class valedictorian who succeeded despite the death of her mother, the desertion of her father, and her own pregnancy. North Carolina administrators shut down a high school newspaper and fired its adviser because of three articles, including a satirical story about the "death" of the writer after eating a cheeseburger from the school cafeteria.

Some principals have tried to restrict their students from using the Internet to criticize school officials or policies. But like the underground newspapers of the 1960s and 1970s, web pages created off campus (rather than in class) can't be censored and their creators can't be disciplined by administrators, unless the pages urge illegal action or make terrorist threats. A Georgia student was arrested for suggesting that the principal be shot, his daughter kidnapped, his car keyed, and its locks clogged with Superglue.

Freedom of Association

Although the First Amendment does not mention *association,* the Supreme Court has interpreted the right to speak, assemble, and petition the government for a redress of grievances, all of which the amendment does list, to encompass a **freedom of association** for individuals to join with others to do these things.

The right is strongest when the organization forms for "expressive association"—that is, when it speaks, assembles, and petitions the government for a redress of grievances. The right is also strong when the organization forms for "intimate association"—that is, when it is relatively personal, selective, and small, such as a social club or a country club.

This freedom implicitly entails a right not to associate as well. Therefore, *organizations formed for expressive or intimate association can exclude others.* The Supreme Court allowed organizers of Boston's Saint Patrick's Day parade to exclude a group of gays, lesbians, and bisexuals.[73] Because the organizers were private individuals—the parade wasn't sponsored by the city—and because a parade is an expressive activity, the organizers didn't have to allow any views contrary to their views. The Supreme Court also allowed the Boy Scouts of America to expel an assistant scoutmaster who was openly gay.[74] The Court concluded that the Boy Scouts is an expressive organization, which espouses values, including opposition to homosexuality.

The right is weakest when the organization forms for "commercial association"—that is, when it is designed to enhance the business interests of its members and is relatively large, unselective, and impersonal. *Organizations formed for commercial association, such as civic clubs, can't exclude others* (in states or cities that adopt nondiscrimination laws; elsewhere, they can). Their right to associate can be overridden by the individual's right to be free from discrimination.[75] Therefore, the Jaycees (the Junior Chamber of Commerce), which was a business organization of young men, and the Rotary Club, which was a civic organization of men, can't discriminate against women in states that have laws forbidding sex discrimination.[76]

Freedom of the Press

Freedom of the press entails freedom from prior restraint and from restrictions on gathering news.

Prior Restraint

The core of **freedom of the press** is freedom from prior restraint—censorship. If the press violates laws prohibiting, for example, libelous or obscene material, it can be punished after publishing such materials. But freedom from prior restraint means the press can disseminate the information it considers appropriate and the public can see this information.

Yet freedom from prior restraint isn't absolute. During the Vietnam War, the secretary of defense in the Johnson administration, Robert McNamara, ordered a thorough study of our engagement. The study, known as the **Pentagon Papers**, laid bare the reasons the country was embroiled, reasons not as honorable as ones the officials had fed the public, and it questioned the effectiveness of military policy. The study was so revealing that McNamara confided to a friend, "They could hang people for what's in there."[77] He classified the papers "top secret" so few persons could see them. One of the authors, Daniel Ellsberg, who was a planner in the war, originally supported the war but later turned against it.

Haunted by his involvement, he photocopied the papers and passed them to the *New York Times* and *Washington Post* in the hope that their publication would sway public opinion and force the government to halt the war. (He also passed them to the television networks—ABC, CBS, and NBC—but they were afraid to use them.)[78]

The newspapers began to publish excerpts of the papers. Although the information implicated the Kennedy and Johnson administrations, the Nixon administration, which was still fighting the war, sought injunctions to restrain the newspapers from publishing more excerpts. In the *Pentagon Papers Case*, the Supreme Court refused to grant the injunctions.[79] Most justices said they would grant the injunctions if publishing the papers clearly jeopardized national security. But the information in the papers was historical; its disclosure didn't hinder the current war effort.[80] Thus *the rule—no prior restraint—remained, but some exceptions could be made.* (See box "The Road to Watergate.")

One exception occurred in 1979 when *The Progressive*, a monthly political magazine, planned to publish technical material about the design of hydrogen bombs. The article, "The H-Bomb Secret: How We Got It, Why We're Telling It," argued against secret classification of this material. Although the article wasn't a "do-it-yourself guide," it might have helped a medium-size nation develop a bomb sooner than the nation could otherwise. At the government's request, a federal judge granted an injunction prohibiting the magazine from publishing the article.[81]

The press in the United States is freer than the press in Great Britain, where freedom from prior restraint began. Britain, which has no constitutional provision comparable to the First Amendment, tolerates more restrictions on the press.

For example, the government banned radio and television interviews with all members of the outlawed Irish Republican Army and its political party, including its sole representative in Parliament.[82] The French government banned the sale of a song critical of the West during the Persian Gulf War, and it blocked the broadcasting of anti-Semitic programming by an Arab channel in 2005. The German government, which has prohibited the display of the Nazi swastika since World War II, banned the sale of music by skinhead groups after neo-Nazi violence in recent years. The Austrian government imprisoned a British historian for publicizing his book denying the Holocaust.

Restrictions on Gathering News

Although prior restraint is an obvious limitation on freedom of the press, restrictions on gathering news are less obvious but no less serious. They also keep the news from the public.

The Burger Court *denied reporters the right to keep the names of their sources confidential.* In investigative reporting, reporters frequently rely on sources who demand anonymity in exchange for information. The sources might have sensitive positions in government or relations with criminals that would place them in jeopardy if their names were publicized. A Louisville reporter was allowed to watch persons make hashish from marijuana if he kept their names confidential. But after publication of his story, a grand jury demanded their names. When the reporter refused to reveal them, he was cited for contempt of court, and his conviction was upheld by the Supreme Court.[83] The majority said reporters' need for confidentiality isn't as great as courts' need for information about crimes. So reporters face a difficult choice: either do not guarantee anonymity to a potential source, which means they might not obtain information for an important story; or do guarantee anonymity, which means, if the courts demand their source, they might be cited for contempt and jailed for months. Grand juries have demanded reporters' sources increasingly in recent years.[84]

Invasion of Privacy

Freedom of the press can result in an invasion of privacy when the press publishes personal information. In these conflicts, the Supreme Court has favored freedom of the press.

The Court has *permitted the press to publish factual information.* For example, although Georgia law prohibited the press from releasing the names of crime victims, an Atlanta television station announced the name of a high school girl who was raped by six classmates and left unconscious on the lawn to die. Her father sued the station, but the Court said the press can publish factual information from the public record so that citizens can scrutinize the workings of the judicial system.[85] (A need to scrutinize the workings of the judicial system wasn't apparent in this case, but the justices established a precedent that would apply to other cases in the future.)

When a man in a crowd watching President Gerald Ford noticed a woman, close by, pull out a gun, he grabbed the gun and prevented an assassination. Reporters wrote stories about this hero, including the fact that he was a homosexual.

The press chief of the *Washington Post* hails the Court's decision allowing publication of the Pentagon Papers.

BEHIND THE SCENES

The Road to Watergate

When the *New York Times* and *Washington Post* began to publish excerpts of the Pentagon Papers, President Richard Nixon was furious. He hated the press, especially the eastern press, and he feared the liberal groups who were criticizing—undermining, he believed—his Vietnam policies and his entire administration as well. He barred *New York Times* reporters from the White House and *Air Force One,* and he ordered his staff members to have no dealings with "any of those Jews." He ordered his attorney general to prosecute "those bastards."[1] But Nixon still wasn't satisfied. He summoned his chief of staff and his national security adviser and demanded:

> I have a project I want somebody to take....This takes eighteen hours a day. It takes devotion and loyalty and diligence such as you've never seen....I really need a son of a bitch...who will work his butt off and do it dishonorably....And I'll direct him myself. I know how to play this game and we're going to start playing it....I want somebody just as tough as I am for a change. ...We're up against an enemy, a conspiracy. They're using any means. We're going to use any means.[2]

This tirade set in motion the developments that would culminate in the Watergate scandal. The president and his underlings initiated a series of actions challenging the rule of law. Among these actions was a directive to party operatives to break in and steal Daniel Ellsberg's records from his psychiatrist's office and then leak the records to the press in an effort to tarnish his reputation.

[1] Quoted in Garry Wills, *Bomb Power: The Modern Presidency and the National Security State* (New York: Penguin, 2010), 171.

[2] Erwin N. Griswold, "No Harm Was Done," *New York Times,* June 30, 1991, E15.

This coverage caused him considerable embarrassment and practical problems as well, so he sued. The courts sided with the press again. The man's good deed made him newsworthy, whether he wanted to be or not.[86] Persons who become newsworthy are granted little privacy. Justice Brennan said this is a necessary evil "in a society which places a primary value on freedom of speech and of press."[87]

However, the Court has prohibited the press from sending reporters and photographers with law enforcement officers when they conduct a search or make an arrest at someone's home.[88] The Court decided that the police department's desire for good publicity and the local media's desire for interesting stories don't justify the invasion of a resident's privacy.

When press freedom and individual privacy conflict, European countries are far more sensitive to the invasion of individual privacy. They consider privacy a fundamental human right. Perhaps because of their bitter experience with the Nazis' Gestapo and East Germany's Stasi (secret police), they recoil from the public exposure of individuals' private lives. In 2010, an Italian court convicted three Google executives for not blocking a video posted on YouTube that showed an autistic boy being bullied by his schoolmates. The video was up for two months before a complaint led to its removal. The court ruled that Google should have a process in place for blocking such videos.[89] These rulings have serious implications not only for Internet companies but also for the flow of information across borders.

Thinking about Democracy

> Recall the assertion earlier in the chapter that freedom of speech is "the heart of our government." Some commentators claim that freedom of the press is just as important, or more important, for a democracy in modern times. Why would they claim this?

Libel

Libel consists of printed or broadcast statements that are false and that tarnish someone's reputation. Victims are entitled to sue for money to compensate them for the harm done.

Historically, the justices considered libelous material irrelevant to the exposition of ideas and search for truth envisioned by the framers of the First Amendment. The minimal benefit such material might have had was outweighed by the greater need to protect persons' reputations. For many years, the Court allowed the states to adopt libel laws as the states saw fit.

However, the Warren Court recognized that state libel laws could be used to stifle legitimate political criticism; they could be used to thwart freedom of the press. The justices forced radical changes in these laws in the landmark case *New York Times* v. *Sullivan* in 1964.[90]

The *Times* ran an ad by black clergymen criticizing Montgomery, Alabama, officials for their response to racial protests. The ad contained trivial inaccuracies. Although it didn't name any officials, the commissioner of police claimed that it implicitly referred to him, and he sued. A local jury ordered the *Times* to pay him a half-million dollars. Meanwhile, another local jury ordered the *Times* to pay another commissioner another half-million dollars for the same ad. It was apparent that traditional libel laws could be used to wreak vengeance on a critical press, in this case, on a detested northern newspaper for its coverage of controversial civil rights protests.

The Court, ruling against the commissioner, made it more difficult for public officials to win libel suits. It held that *officials must show not only that the statements made about them* were false, but also that the statements were made with "reckless disregard for the truth." This standard gives the press some leeway to make mistakes—to print inaccurate statements—as long as the press is not careless to the point of recklessness.

This protection for the press is necessary, according to Justice Brennan, because the "central meaning of the First Amendment" is that citizens should have the right to criticize officials. This statement prompted one legal scholar to herald the decision as "an occasion for dancing in the streets."[91]

In later cases, the Court *extended this ruling to public figures*—other persons who have public prominence or who thrust themselves into public controversies. These include candidates for public office[92] and activists for various causes.[93] The Court reasoned that it should be more difficult for public figures, as for public officials, to win libel suits because they also influence public policy and also are newsworthy enough to get media attention to rebut false accusations against them.[94]

In sum, the Warren Court's doctrine shifted the emphasis from protection of personal reputation to protection of press freedom. This shift in emphasis has helped the press report the news—and helped the public learn about the government—during a time when media coverage of controversial events has angered many people. Since the 1960s, individuals and groups have sued the press not primarily to gain compensation for damage to their reputation, but to punish the press for its coverage. For example, a lawyer for a conservative organization that sued CBS for its depiction of the army general who commanded the U.S. military in Vietnam admitted that the organization sought the "dismantling" of the network through libel suits.[95]

FREEDOM OF RELIGION

Some people came to America for religious liberty, but once they arrived, many didn't want to grant this liberty to others. Some communities became as intolerant as those in the Old World from which the people had fled.[96] But the colonists came with so many religious views that the diversity gradually led to grudging tolerance. By the time the Constitution and the Bill of Rights were adopted, support for religious liberty was fairly widespread.

Both the diversity and the tolerance are reflected in the two documents. Unlike the Declaration of Independence, the Constitution is a secular document. It doesn't mention "God," "Creator," "Providence," or "divine."[97] It doesn't claim to be a compact between the people and God (or, like some monarchies, between the rulers and God); rather, it's a compact among the people, as the Preamble underscores—"We the people. . . ."

The Bill of Rights grants freedom of religion in the First Amendment, which states, "Congress shall make no law respecting an establishment of religion, or prohibiting the free exercise thereof." These two clauses—the establishment clause and the free exercise clause—were intended to work in tandem to provide freedom for people's religions and, by implication, freedom from others' religions.

The Founders recoiled from Europeans' experience of continuous conflict and long wars fought over religious schisms. Consequently, Thomas Jefferson explained, the clauses were designed to build "a wall of separation between church and state."[98] Each would stay on its own side of the wall and not interfere or even interact with the other. **Separation of church and state** was a novel idea; according to one historian, although the phrase isn't in the Constitution, it's the "most revolutionary" aspect of the Constitution.[99]

When the District of Columbia was designed, a triangular configuration popular at the time was adopted. In one corner was the Capitol building for Congress, and in another was the White House for the president. In the third corner in many other nations, a large church representing the state religion reflected the spiritual power. Because of separation of church and state, however, the Founders didn't want a church in that corner. (They could have put the Supreme Court there, but the Court wasn't considered important then and wouldn't get its own building until 1935.) Instead, they located the Patent Office in that corner to represent the spirit of innovation. They anticipated many inventions.[100] (Now the building houses the National Portrait Gallery and the Museum of American Art.)

Today some deeply religious people scorn the idea of separation of church and state, thinking it devalues the importance of religion. But the Founders saw it as a means to preserve the peace that had eluded European states. In addition, they saw it as a way to protect religion itself. Without interference by government officials, whether to hinder or to help, churches would be free to determine their dogma and establish their practices as they saw fit. They would be free to flourish. Indeed, religion is stronger in the United States than in western Europe, where the churches endorsed and supported by the government sit mostly empty and most people are not believers. Some scholars think that religion is stronger in the United States *because of* separation of church and state.[101]

Despite the Founders' intention to separate church and state, as society became more complex and government became more pervasive, church and state came to interact, sometimes to interfere, with each other. Inevitably, the wall began to crumble, and the courts had to devise new doctrine to keep church and state as separate as possible while still accommodating the needs of each, as we'll see.

The disputes that lead to court cases usually pit a religious minority against the government, which tends to reflect the views of the Christian majority. Thus freedom of religion, like freedom of expression, revolves around the conflict between majority rule and minority rights.

Free Exercise of Religion

The **free exercise clause** allows individuals to practice their religion without government coercion. From time to time, however, government has restricted the free exercise of religion, either directly or indirectly.

Amish children head for the cornfields to avoid school officials in Iowa.

Direct Restrictions

Government has occasionally restricted free exercise of religion directly. Early in the country's history, some states prohibited Catholics, Quakers, or Jews from voting or holding office, and as late as 1961, Maryland prohibited nonbelievers from holding office.[102] In the 1920s, Oregon prohibited students from attending parochial schools.[103] More recently, prisons in Illinois and Texas prohibited Black Muslims and Buddhists from receiving religious publications and using prison chapels.[104] The Supreme Court *invalidated each of these restrictions.*

A suburb of Miami tried to ban the Santeria religion in 1987. Santeria blends ancient African rites and Roman Catholic rituals, but its distinguishing feature is animal sacrifice. Adherents believe that animal sacrifice is necessary to win the favor of the gods, and they practice it at initiations of new members and at births, marriages, and deaths. They kill chickens, ducks, doves, pigeons, sheep, goats, and turtles. When adherents, who had practiced their religion underground since refugees from Cuba brought it to Florida in the 1950s and 1960s, announced plans to construct a church building, cultural center, museum, and school, the city passed ordinances against ritualistic animal sacrifice, essentially forbidding adherents from practicing their religion. The Court struck down the ordinances.[105] "Although the practice of animal sacrifice may seem abhorrent to some," Justice Anthony Kennedy wrote, "religious beliefs need not be acceptable, logical, consistent, or comprehensible to others in order to merit First Amendment protection."

Indirect Restrictions

Government has also restricted free exercise of religion indirectly. As society has become more complex, some laws have interfered with religion, even when not designed to do so. The laws have usually interfered with minority religions, which don't have many members serving as state legislators and looking out for their interests.

At first the Court distinguished between belief and action: individuals could believe what they wanted, but they could not act accordingly if such action was against the law. In 1878, male Mormons who believed their religion required polygamy could not marry more than one woman.[106] The Court rhetorically asked, "Suppose one believed that human sacrifices were a necessary part of religious worship?" Of course, belief without action gave little protection and scant satisfaction to the individuals involved.

In the 1960s, the Warren Court recognized this problem and broadened the protection by *granting exemptions to laws.* A Seventh-Day Adventist who worked in a textile mill in South Carolina quit when the mill shifted from a five-day to a six-day workweek that included Saturday—her Sabbath. Unable to find another job, she applied for unemployment benefits, but the state refused to provide them. To receive them, she had to be "available" for work, but the state said

Photo by Thomas DeFeo, Copyright 1965, The Des Moines Register and Tribune Company. Reprinted with permission.

she wasn't available because she wouldn't accept any jobs that required Saturday work. The Court ordered the state to grant an exemption to its law.[107] The Burger Court articulated a general standard: employers need to make a reasonable effort to accommodate employees' requests to fit work schedules around their Sabbath.[108]

Congress, too, granted some exemptions. It excused the Amish from participating in the Social Security program because the Amish support their own elderly. And in every draft law, it excused conscientious objectors from participating in war.

The Court, however, was reluctant to exempt individuals from paying taxes. It didn't excuse either the Amish[109] or the Quakers, who as pacifists tried to withhold the portion of their income taxes that funded the military.[110] The Court worried that many other persons would try to avoid paying taxes, too.

The Rehnquist Court, which was less sensitive to minority rights, *refused to grant such exemptions.*[111] The Native American Church uses peyote, a hallucinogen derived from a cactus, in worship ceremonies. Church members believe that the plant embodies their deity and that ingesting the plant is an act of communion. Although peyote is a controlled substance, Congress has authorized its use on Indian reservations, and many states have authorized its use off the reservations by church members. But when two members in Oregon, a state that didn't allow its use off the reservations, were fired from their jobs and denied unemployment benefits for using the drug, the Court refused to grant an exemption.[112] A five-justice majority rejected the doctrine and precedents of the Warren and Burger Courts. Justice Antonin Scalia, a Catholic, admitted that denying such exemptions will put minority religions at a disadvantage but insisted that this is an "unavoidable consequence of democratic government." (See box "Accommodating and Balancing.")

 ## Thinking about Democracy

Compare the implications for democracy of (a) the Warren and Burger Courts' doctrine granting exemptions to religious minorities with (b) the Rehnquist Court's doctrine denying exemptions to these groups. Is one more democratic? Or do they emphasize different facets of democracy? What would be the consequences if the Rehnquist Court's doctrine were extended to other provisions of the Bill of Rights?

As a result of the decision, some adherents of minority religions weren't allowed to practice the tenets of their religions. Families of deceased Jews and Laotians, whose religions reject autopsies, were overruled. Muslim prisoners, whose religion forbids them to eat pork, were denied other meat as a substitute. Sikh construction workers, whose religion requires them to wear turbans, had been exempted from the law mandating hard hats at construction sites; after the decision, their exemption was rescinded.[113]

National Archives and Records Administration

The country's religious diversity has led to demands for some exotic exemptions. Inspired by the Bible's statement that Jesus's followers "shall take up serpents" and "if they drink any deadly thing, it shall not hurt them," members of the Holiness Church of God in Jesus's Name handle snakes and drink strychnine. Some become enraptured and entranced to the point of hysteria, and occasionally some die. The Tennessee Supreme Court forbade such practices, saying that the state has "the right to guard against the unnecessary creation of widows and orphans." However, these practices continue in some places.

Even mainstream churches worried about the ruling's implications, and a coalition of religious groups lobbied Congress to overturn it. Congress passed an act reversing the ruling and substituting the previous doctrine from the Warren and Burger Courts. But the Rehnquist Court invalidated the act because it challenged the justices' authority and altered their interpretation of the First Amendment without going through the process required to amend the Constitution.[114]

Establishment of Religion

Two competing traditions reflecting the role of government toward religion have led to intense conflict over the **establishment clause.** Many settlers were Christians who wanted the governments to reinforce their religion, yet the framers of the Constitution were products of the Enlightenment, which emphasized the importance of reason and deemphasized the role of religion. Many Founders, including the most important ones, were Deists rather than Christians, believing in a Supreme Being but rejecting much religious dogma.[115]

American Diversity

Accommodating and Balancing

The annual Sun Dance is the Northern Arapaho Indians' most important religious ceremony. Winslow Friday, who lives on the Wind River Reservation in Wyoming, shot an eagle to obtain its tail fan for the ceremony. He was arrested for violating the Bald and Golden Eagle Protection Act, which prohibits killing these once endangered species. In defense, he cited the free exercise clause of the First Amendment.

The federal district court ruled for Friday, but the federal appellate court ruled for the government. The Supreme Court declined to hear the case.

In a diverse country, it's difficult to accommodate the needs and desires of all religious groups. And it's difficult to balance the needs and desires of any religious group with the commands of the secular laws. In the eagle, "You have a precious commodity," a federal official remarked. "It's precious to Native Americans, but it's also precious to the American people. How do you balance that?"

Members of Congress recognized the conflict when they passed the law, and they sought a balance. They created an exception for Native Americans who use the eagles in religious ceremonies. The law established the National Eagle Repository in Commerce City, Colorado, to collect dead eagles—usually struck by cars or electrocuted by utilities—and provide them to Indians. But many carcasses are poor specimens, and the repository, which collects about two thousand carcasses a year, has a waiting list of six thousand requests. Alternatively, the law established a permit process for Indians to kill eagles. But the process is obscure and unknown to most Indians, apparently by design. "We're not in the business of trying to generate interest in the taking of wildlife," another official said. So, some Indians, like Friday, shoot an eagle and risk an arrest.

After the Supreme Court declined to hear this case, federal prosecutors also sought a balance. They agreed to transfer the case from federal court, where the sentence could be harsher (a maximum fine of $100,000 and prison term of one year), to the reservation's tribal court, which sentenced Friday to a fine of $2,500 and a suspension of his hunting privilege on the reservation for one year.

SOURCES: DeeDee Correll, "Bald Eagle Case Raises Issue of Religious Liberty," *Los Angeles Times*, September 21, 2009, latimes.com/news/nationworld/nation/la-na-eagle-feather21-2009sep21,0,7225203.story; "Eagle-Killing Case Ends in Tribal-Court Guilty Plea," *Billings Gazette*, December 22, 2009, billingsgazette.com/news/state-and-regional/Wyoming/article-35cd45f2-6e5c-11df-001cc4c002e0.html. Quotes are from Correll article.

The two considered most responsible for the religious guarantees in the First Amendment, Thomas Jefferson and James Madison, especially feared the divisiveness of religion. They wanted separation of church and state, advocating not only freedom *of* religion for believers but freedom *from* religion for others.[116]

Even some religious groups wanted separation of church and state. The Baptists had been harassed and persecuted by the Anglicans (Episcopalians) and Congregationalists—for example, from 1760 to 1778, fifty-six Baptist preachers had been jailed in Anglican Virginia[117]—and they feared that these larger groups would use the power of the state to promote their views and practices.[118]

The Supreme Court initially reflected the first of these traditions. In 1892, Justice David Brewer proclaimed that "this is a Christian nation."[119] But as the country became more pluralistic, the Court moved toward the second of these traditions. Since the 1960s, the Court has *generally interpreted the establishment clause to forbid government not only from designating an official church,* like the Church of England, which receives tax money and special privileges, *but also from aiding one religion over another or even from aiding religion over nonreligion.*

School Prayers

Courts have used the establishment clause to resolve disputes about public school prayers. In 1962 and 1963, the Warren Court initiated its prayer rulings. At the start of each day, New York had students recite a nondenominational prayer, and Pennsylvania and Baltimore had students recite the Lord's Prayer or Bible verses. The Court, with only one justice dissenting, ruled that *these practices violated the establishment clause.*[120] Although the prayers officially were voluntary—students could leave the room—the Court doubted that the prayers really were voluntary. The justices noted that nonconforming students would face tremendous pressure from teachers and peers. The Court therefore concluded that the prayers fostered religion. According to Justice Black, "Government in this country should stay out of the business of writing and sanctioning official prayers and leave that purely religious function to the people themselves and to those the people...look to for religious guidance." Although schools could teach religion as a subject, they could not promote religion. For similar reasons, the Court ruled that Kentucky *could not require public schools to post the Ten Commandments* in classrooms.[121]

Many people sharply criticized the rulings. A representative from Alabama lamented, "They put the Negroes in the schools, and now they've driven God out."[122] Yet students, of course, can still pray on their own at any time.

Empirical studies in the years after the rulings found that prayers and Bible readings decreased but by no means disappeared, especially in the South.[123] A Tennessee school official asserted, "I am of the opinion that 99 percent of the people in the United States feel as I do about the Supreme Court's decision—that it was an outrage.... The remaining 1 percent do not belong in this free world."[124]

News reports in recent years indicate that some schools, especially in the rural South, still use prayers or Bible readings in violation of the Court's rulings. These practices are reinforced by social pressure. A woman whose family had moved to Pontotoc, Mississippi, discovered that Christian prayers were being broadcast on the intercom and the Bible was being taught in a class. When she objected, rumors circulated that she was an outside agitator paid by the ACLU to force the town to change. One of her children had a teacher who told the class that the child didn't believe in God, while another of her children kept "getting jumped" in the bathroom. Then the woman lost her job in a convenience store after customers threatened to boycott the store.[125] News reports also indicate that officials in Kentucky and Ohio allowed volunteers to put the Ten Commandments inside or outside public schools in violation of the Court's ruling.[126]

Although many people wanted a constitutional amendment to allow official prayers in public schools, Congress never passed one. Some people supported the rulings. Other people, who disagreed with the rulings but supported the authority of the Court, didn't want to challenge its authority and set a precedent for other groups on other matters. Some religious leaders doubted that the religious groups would ever agree on specific prayers. America's religious diversity means that any prayer would offend some students or parents. Prayers that suit Christians might offend Jews; those that suit Jews might offend adherents of other faiths. Recent immigrants from Asia and the Middle East, practicing Buddhism, Shintoism, Taoism, and Islam, have made the country even more pluralistic. Now, according to one researcher, America's religious diversity is greater than that of any country in recorded history.[127] Asking the students in this country to say a prayer would be like "asking the members of the United Nations to stand and sing the national anthem of one country."[128]

However, many small communities don't reflect this nationwide diversity, and their residents often assume that everyone, or at least "normal" people, share their views toward religion.

In lieu of an amendment, about half of the states have passed laws providing for a "moment of silence" to begin each school day. A majority of justices indicated that they *would approve a moment of silence if students were not urged to pray.*[129]

The Rehnquist Court reaffirmed and extended the prayer rulings of the Warren Court. It held that *clergy can't offer prayers at graduation ceremonies* for public elementary, middle, and high schools.[130] The prayers in question were brief and nonsectarian, but the majority concluded, "What to most believers may seem nothing more than a reasonable request that the nonbeliever respect their religious practices, in a school context may appear to the nonbeliever or dissenter to be an attempt to employ the machinery of the state to enforce a religious orthodoxy." Although attendance at the ceremony was voluntary, like participation in school prayers, the majority didn't consider it truly voluntary. Justice Kennedy wrote, "Everyone knows that in our society and in our culture high school graduation is one of life's most significant occasions.... Graduation is a time for family and those closest to the student to celebrate success and express mutual wishes of gratitude and respect."

Although the Court's language here was emphatic, its stance on student-led prayers has been ambiguous. In 1992, the Court refused to review a federal court of appeals ruling that allowed student-led prayers at graduation ceremonies.[131] A Texas school board permitted the senior class to decide whether to have a prayer and, if so, which student to give it. The appellate court held that this policy wasn't precluded by the Supreme Court's ruling because the decision wasn't made by officials and the prayer wasn't offered by a clergy member, so official coercion wasn't present. But in 1996, the Court also refused to review a federal court of appeals ruling from a different circuit that prohibited student-led prayers.[132] The Court's reluctance to resolve this controversy means that the ruling of each court of appeals remains but applies only to the schools in its circuit.

The first appellate court's holding encouraged opponents of the Supreme Court's rulings to use the same approach to circumvent these daily prayer rulings as well. Several southern states passed laws allowing student-led prayers to start each school day. Some school officials, who selected the students, let them give the prayers over the intercom. Federal courts in Alabama and Mississippi invalidated these laws because school officials were involved and because all students were required or at least pressured to listen to the prayers.

The Rehnquist Court also invalidated the use of schools' public address systems by clergy or students to give prayers at high school football games.[133] Although student attendance is voluntary (except for the players, cheerleaders, and band members), the games are official school events.

The public desire for official school prayers is fueled by nostalgia for the less troubling times before the 1960s. As one writer perceived, the desire "doesn't have much to do with prayer anyway, but with a time, a place, an ethos that praying and pledging allegiance at the beginning of school each day represent."[134] For some people, buffeted by the upheavals and dislocations of our times, the reinstitutionalization of school prayers would symbolize that our society still stands for appropriate values.

The public desire for official school prayers is also fueled by occasional reports of school officials who mistakenly believe that court rulings require them to forbid all forms of religious expression. Some confused administrators have prohibited a few students from wearing religious jewelry, reading the Bible while riding the bus, and praying before eating their lunch.[135]

Students from diverse backgrounds mix at a Dearborn, Michigan high school.

Now we'll turn to several cases that illustrate an attempt by the justices to strike a balance in this area. The Burger Court held that the University of Missouri at Kansas City had to make its meeting rooms available to students' religious organizations on an equal basis with other organizations, even if the religious organizations use the rooms for prayer or worship.[136] Otherwise, the university would be discriminating against religion.

After this decision, Congress passed a law that *requires public high schools as well as colleges and universities to allow meetings of students' religious, philosophical, or political groups outside class hours.* The Court accepted this law.[137] Justice Sandra Day O'Connor said that high school students "are likely to understand that a school does not endorse or support student speech that it merely permits on a nondiscriminatory basis." Students have established Bible clubs in many high schools. As an unintended consequence of this act, students have also established gay-straight clubs—organizations of gay and straight students who support the rights of gays, lesbians, and bisexuals—in many high schools.[138]

The Rehnquist Court held that the University of Virginia had to provide funding, from students' fees, to students' religious organizations on an equal basis with other campus organizations, even if a religious organization sought money to print a religious newspaper.[139] Following this precedent, a federal court of appeals ruled that the University of South Alabama had to provide funding to a gay organization.

The Roberts Court, however, ruled that a public university doesn't have to recognize or fund students' religious organizations that don't allow all students to join. Therefore, a university can deny recognition or funding to a Christian group that bars gay students, even though the group's beliefs oppose the students' homosexuality.[140]

In these cases, the Court has emphasized equality. Public schools can't discriminate against students' religious organizations, and students' religious organizations can't discriminate against any students.

Religious Symbols

Despite its prayer rulings, the Court has been *reluctant to invalidate traditional religious symbols.* It has not questioned the motto "In God We Trust," on our coins since 1865 and paper money since 1955, or the phrase "one nation under God," in the Pledge of Allegiance since 1954.[141]

In 2002, a federal court of appeals held the phrase "under God" in the Pledge unconstitutional when recited in the public schools. The court said it promotes religion as much as if it professed that we are a nation "under Jesus" or "under Vishnu" or "under Zeus" or "under no god." It promotes Christianity and leaves out not only atheists and agnostics but also believers of other deities, such as Buddhists and many Native Americans. Although the ruling was a logical extension of the prayer rulings, it was a lightning rod for the public's anger, and the Supreme Court sidestepped the issue (deciding that the student's father, an atheist, lacked authority to bring suit on the student's behalf because the student's mother, a born-again Christian, had custody of the child after their divorce).[142]

The Burger Court upheld the display of a nativity scene on government property, at least when it's part of a broader display for the holiday season.[143] Pawtucket, Rhode Island, had a crèche, Christmas tree, Santa Claus, sleigh with reindeer, and talking wishing well. The Court said that Christmas had become a secular as well as a religious holiday and that the secular decorations diluted any religious impact the nativity scene would have. A crèche by itself, however, would be impermissible.[144]

The Rehnquist Court addressed Ten Commandments displays and ruled much like the Burger Court did for Christmas nativity scenes. A Ten Commandments monument on the Texas capitol grounds could remain because it was just one of sixteen other monuments and twenty-one historical markers, which were secular, and because it had been there for forty years.[145] But copies of the Ten Commandments in two Kentucky courthouses could not remain because they were not part of historical displays[146] and they were posted recently for religious purposes.[147]

Evolution

Courts have also used the establishment clause to resolve disputes about teaching evolution in schools. In 1968, the Supreme Court invalidated Arkansas' forty-year-old law forbidding schools from teaching evolution.[148] Arkansas and Louisiana

then passed laws requiring schools that teach evolution to also teach "creationism"—the biblical version of creation.[149] In 1987, the Court *invalidated these laws because their purpose was to advance the fundamentalist Christian view.*[150]

Evolution remains controversial. In recent years, many states have considered antievolution proposals. In 2005, a suburban Atlanta school district pasted disclaimers onto ninth-grade biology textbooks stating, "Evolution is a theory, not a fact" and should be "critically considered." A federal court ordered the disclaimers removed because their denigration of evolution reflected a religious view.

Critics of evolution also promoted "intelligent design"—the notion that some life is so complex that it must have been designed by an intelligent creator rather than have evolved through natural selection and random chance, as the theory of evolution posits.[151] In 2005, the Dover, Pennsylvania, school district required teachers to discuss intelligent design. A federal court invalidated the policy because intelligent design isn't a science. Its proponents invoke a supernatural designer—that is, God[152]—whereas science deals with natural phenomena. Although intelligent design proponents make scientific critiques of evolution, intelligent design itself isn't based on empirical evidence and doesn't offer testable hypotheses.

Despite the Court's rulings and the scientific consensus supporting evolution, the majority of high school biology teachers don't teach evolution. A recent study concluded that only 28 percent make a real effort to do so. Over half try to

A megachurch with twelve thousand members in Memphis, Tennessee, unveiled its "Statue of Liberation through Christ" in 2006. In contrast to the Statue of Liberty, this monument holds a cross rather than a torch and, with the other arm, the Ten Commandments. She also has a tear running down her cheek because of modern secularism, legal abortions, and the absence of school prayers. According to the pastor, the purpose of the monument is to let people know that "God is in the foundation of our nation." Hence the merger of church and state.

avoid the controversy in various ways, and 18 percent actually advocate creationism or intelligent design instead.[153]

Other Policies

Conservative Christians have pushed Republican officials to adopt policies and programs reflecting their beliefs. Despite the establishment clause, the Bush administration limited scientific research with stem cells, withheld federal money from family planning organizations and programs in the United States and abroad, gave federal money to abstinence education programs, and gave federal money to hundreds of church-run marriage, child care, and drug treatment programs. As a result, for example, the government gave federal money to Louisiana, which funneled it to Protestant groups to teach abstinence through Bible lessons and to Catholic groups to hold prayer sessions at abortion clinics.[154] So far, the courts haven't ruled that these policies and programs violate the establishment clause.

The modern interpretation of the religion clauses, which began in the 1960s, has reduced the legal dominance of Christianity, especially of Protestantism, and enhanced the legal standing of minority religions and nonreligion. This change mirrors broader changes in American society, which also began in the 1960s. The first Catholic, John F. Kennedy, was elected president, signaling greater tolerance of Catholics; American Jews faced fewer barriers to acceptance; new immigrants from Asia and the Middle East made American society more pluralistic; and increasing numbers of Americans became nonreligious.[155] The courts, as explained in Chapter 12, reflect societal trends. With these changes in society and doctrine has come a backlash from religious conservatives, especially evangelicals, who have gotten more involved in politics (as explained in Chapters 6 and 7).

In this maelstrom, the wider public is ambivalent (or confused?). While surveys show that two-thirds of the public believes that the First Amendment requires separation of church and state, half of the public also believes that the Constitution "establishes a Christian nation."[156]

Despite ever-present tensions and very frequent conflicts, the effort to separate church and state has enabled the United States to manage, even nourish, its religious pluralism. The effort has kept many religious fights out of the political arena. Today, however, this practical arrangement is opposed by those religious conservatives who most fear the changes in modern society. They consider their religion a shield protecting their family against these changes, and they want the authority of the government to reinforce their religion. In one of her last opinions, Justice O'Connor, a moderate conservative, addressed these religious conservatives: "At a time when we see around the world the violent consequences of the assumption of religious authority by the government, Americans may count themselves fortunate.... [Those] who would renegotiate the boundaries between church and state must therefore answer a difficult question: Why would we trade a system that has served us so well for one that has served others so poorly?"[157]

RIGHTS OF CRIMINAL DEFENDANTS

The Fourth, Fifth, Sixth, and Eighth Amendments provide numerous **due process** rights for criminal defendants. When the government prosecutes defendants, it must give them the process—that is, the procedures—they are due; it must be fair and "respect certain decencies of civilized conduct,"[158] even toward uncivilized people.

One defense attorney said that many of his clients "had been monsters—nothing less—who had done monstrous things. Although occasionally not guilty of the crime charged, nearly all my clients have been guilty of something."[159] Then why do we give them rights? We give criminal defendants rights because we give all individuals rights in court. As Justice Douglas observed, "respecting the dignity even of the least worthy...citizen raises the stature of all of us."[160]

But why do we give all individuals rights in court? We do so because we have established the **presumption of innocence**. This presumption is "not...a naive belief that most or even many defendants are innocent, or a cavalier attitude toward crime." It reflects a mistrust of the state, as it recognizes the possibility of an overzealous prosecutor or an unfair judge. It requires the state to prove the defendant's guilt, essentially saying, "We won't take your word for it."[161] Of course, when the crime rate is high or a particular crime

Impact social, global, historical, economic, political

When a Court Reverses a Conviction...

...the defendant does not necessarily go free. An appellate court only evaluates the legality of the procedures used by officials; it does not determine guilt or innocence. Therefore, when it reverses a conviction, it only indicates that officials used some illegal procedure in convicting the defendant—for example, evidence from an improper search and seizure. Then the prosecutor can retry the defendant, without this evidence, if the prosecutor thinks there is enough other evidence. Often prosecutors do retry the defendants, and frequently judges or juries reconvict them.

is heinous, many people fear the state less than the criminals. Then they want to give officials more authority and defendants fewer rights. But doing so sets a precedent for doing so again and again in the future, and could diminish the rights of all people eventually. (See box "When a Court Reverses a Conviction…")

Search and Seizure

England fostered the notion that a family's home is its castle, but Parliament made exceptions for the American colonies. It authorized writs of assistance, which allowed customs officials to conduct general searches for goods imported by the colonists without paying taxes to the crown. The English tradition of home privacy combined with the colonists' resentment of these writs led to adoption of the Fourth Amendment, which forbids **unreasonable searches and seizures**.

In these cases, the Supreme Court has tried to walk a fine line between acknowledging officials' need for evidence and individuals' desire for privacy. This judicial doctrine is so complex that we will note just its basic principles here.

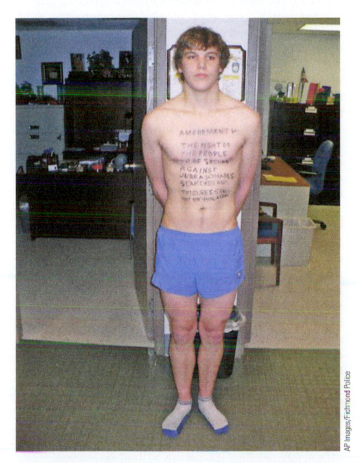

Aaron Tobey stripped to his shorts at the Richmond, Virginia airport, with the Fourth Amendment written across his chest, to protest airport searches. He was arrested for disorderly conduct, but the charge was dropped.

One type of seizure is the arrest of a person. *Police must have evidence to believe that a person committed a crime.*

Another type of seizure is the confiscation of illegal contraband. *The general requirement is that police must get a search warrant from a judge by showing evidence that a particular thing is in a particular place.*

However, *the Court has made numerous exceptions to this requirement* that complicate the law. These exceptions account for most searches. If persons consent to a search, police can conduct a search without a warrant. If police see contraband in plain view, they can seize it; they don't have to close their eyes to it. If police have evidence to arrest someone, they can search the person and the area within the person's control. If police have reason to suspect that someone is committing a crime but lack evidence to arrest the person, they can "stop and frisk" the person—conduct a pat-down search. If police have reason to believe that a person's life is in jeopardy, they can search for weapons. In some situations, if police want to search a motor vehicle, they can do so because vehicles are mobile and could be gone by the time police get a warrant.

These exceptions make search and seizure law quite flexible, enabling police to exercise much discretion. In the "war on drugs," police aggressively use these exceptions to target and search racial minorities (as Chapter 14 will explain).

Exclusionary Rule

To enforce search and seizure law, the Supreme Court has established the **exclusionary rule**, *which bars from the courts any evidence obtained in violation of the Fourth Amendment.* The purpose is to deter illegal conduct by police officers.

Although the Court created this rule for federal courts in 1914,[162] it didn't impose the rule on state courts until 1961 in *Mapp* v. *Ohio*.[163] Until this time, police in many states had ignored search and seizure law. *Mapp* was one of the Warren Court's most controversial rulings. Many people didn't think that evidence of guilt should be barred from court, even if search and seizure law had been violated by police.

The decision still hasn't been widely accepted, and the Burger and Roberts Courts created exceptions to it.[164] Nonetheless, the rule remains for most situations.

Electronic Surveillance of Suspected Criminals

The Fourth Amendment traditionally applied to searches involving a physical trespass and seizures producing a tangible object. Electronic surveillance, however, does not require a physical trespass or entail a tangible object.

This posed a problem for the Supreme Court when it heard its first wiretapping case in 1928. Federal prohibition agents tapped a bootlegger's telephone by installing equipment on wires in the basement of the bootlegger's apartment building. The Court's majority rigidly adhered to its traditional doctrine, saying that this was not a search and seizure, so the agents did not need a warrant.[165]

In a classic example of keeping the Constitution up-to-date with the times, the Warren Court overruled this precedent in 1967.[166] Because electronic eavesdropping might threaten privacy as much as traditional searching, *officials must get judicial authorization,* similar to a warrant, *to engage in such eavesdropping.*

Because GPS devices also threaten privacy, the Roberts Court ruled that officials must get judicial authorization before attaching a GPS device to a vehicle. The government argued that all persons driving on public streets have waived their privacy, so they can be tracked everywhere they go. (The defendant in this case was tracked everywhere he drove for a month.) At the time of the decision, the FBI was operating about 3000 GPS devices. The justices, however, decided that modern technology doesn't permit law enforcement to become Big Brother.[167]

The decision raises questions about tracking persons through their cellphones, many of which have a GPS device built in (designed for emergencies like child abductions or suicide calls).[168] With little or no judicial oversight, law enforcement has been using phone tracking for surreptitious surveillance. The practice has become so common that cellphone companies have set "surveillance fees" for police departments.[169] The Court has not decided this issue.

Electronic Surveillance of Possible Terrorists

The law is quite different for surveillance of possible terrorists than for ordinary criminals. Soon after 9/11, the Bush administration encouraged the National Security Agency (NSA) to conduct an electronic "fishing expedition" to locate terrorists or people connected to terrorists in the United States and around the world. The NSA began to intercept international calls and e-mails *between people in the United States and people in foreign countries* (whether Americans or foreigners). It gained access through American telecommunications companies, which had created a robust network of fiber-optic cables that carry most worldwide communications that travel on wires. Then it used computer searches to look for telltale words and phrases that might be spoken or written by terrorists. Although the administration claimed that it was obtaining calls and e-mails "from very bad people to very bad people,"[170] the program was not restricted to suspected terrorists. It was far broader.[171]

The NSA also began to analyze calls *between people within the United States* to uncover terrorists through social network analysis. By correlating callers' and receivers' numbers and the date, time, and duration of the calls,[172] computers can map patterns of interactions among people. If the government knows that one person is a member of al-Qaeda, this analysis might identify other members too.

The administration didn't seek judicial authorization for either of these programs. The interception of calls and e-mails between people in the United States and people in foreign countries was definitely a violation of the law.[173] (The analysis of calls between people within the United States may also have been a violation of the law.) After the programs were revealed by the press, the administration pressured Congress to amend the law to allow the programs to continue.[174] Now the law legalizes eavesdropping that had previously been illegal.

It's not known how extensive either the international surveillance or the domestic surveillance has been or is now,

although both have examined the calls of many ordinary Americans.[175] The programs are sweeping dragnets, rather than targeted searches, with little or no oversight.[176] They show how a combination of technological advances and terrorist attacks can challenge our liberties.

Self-Incrimination

The Fifth Amendment stipulates that persons shall not be compelled to be witnesses against themselves—that is, to incriminate themselves. Because defendants are presumed innocent, the government must prove their guilt.

This right means that *defendants on trial don't have to take the witness stand and answer the prosecutor's questions,* and neither the prosecutor nor the judge can call attention to their decision to exercise this right. Neither can suggest or imply that the defendants must have something to hide and must therefore be guilty. (But if the defendants do take the stand, they thereby waive their right, so the prosecutor can cross-examine them and they must answer.)

This right also means that *prosecutors can't introduce into evidence statements or confessions from defendants that weren't voluntary.* The meaning of *voluntary* has evolved over time.

For years, police used physical brutality—"the third degree"—to get confessions. After 1936, when the Supreme Court ruled that confessions obtained in this manner were invalid,[177] police used psychological techniques. They held suspects incommunicado, preventing them from contacting relatives or lawyers and delaying them from going to court, to pressure them to confess.[178] They interrogated suspects for long periods of time without food or rest, in one case with alternating teams of interrogators for thirty-six hours straight,[179] to wear them down and break their will. The Court ruled that confessions obtained by these techniques were also invalid.

The Warren Court still worried that many confessions weren't truly voluntary, so it issued a landmark decision in 1966. Arizona police arrested a poor, mentally disturbed man, Ernesto Miranda, for kidnapping and raping a woman. After the woman identified him in a lineup, police interrogated him, prompting him to confess. He hadn't been told that he could remain silent or be represented by an attorney. In *Miranda* v. *Arizona,* the Court concluded that his confession wasn't truly voluntary.[180] Chief Justice Warren, as a former district attorney, knew the advantage that police officers have in an interrogation and thought the suspects needed more protection. The Court ruled that *officials must advise suspects of their rights before their interrogation.* These came to be known as the **Miranda rights**:

> You have the right to remain silent.
> If you talk, anything you say can be used against you.
> You have the right to be represented by an attorney.
> If you can't afford an attorney, one will be appointed for you.

The Burger, Rehnquist, and Roberts Courts haven't required police and prosecutors to follow *Miranda* as strictly as the Warren Court did, but, contrary to expectations, they didn't abandon it. In 2000, the Rehnquist Court reaffirmed *Miranda* by a 7–2 vote.[181]

Even with the warnings, most suspects talk anyway. Some don't understand the warnings. Others think the police, who may rattle off the warnings very fast or in a monotone, give them as a formality but won't follow them. Also, suspects being interrogated face a coercive atmosphere and law enforcement tactics designed to exploit their weaknesses. Detectives are trained to persuade suspects to talk despite the warnings. One said, "Before you ever get in there, the first thing an investigator usually thinks about is…how can I breeze through this *Miranda* thing so I don't set the guy off and tell him not to talk to me, song and dance it, sugarcoat it, whatever?"[182] So detectives frequently lie and trick suspects.

Counsel

The Sixth Amendment provides the **right to counsel** in criminal cases. Initially, this meant that defendants could hire an attorney to help them prepare a defense, and later it meant that defendants could also have the attorney represent them at the trial. But it was no help to most defendants because they were too poor to hire an attorney for either. Consequently, in 1938 the Supreme Court required federal trial courts to furnish an attorney to all indigent defendants.[183] But most criminal cases are state cases, and the Court was reluctant to require state trial courts also to furnish an attorney.[184]

However, the Warren Court was willing to do so in 1963. It heard the case of Clarence Earl Gideon, who was charged with breaking into a pool hall and stealing beer, wine, and change from a vending machine. At trial, Gideon asked the judge for a lawyer. The judge wouldn't appoint one, leaving Gideon to defend himself. The prosecution didn't have a strong case, but Gideon wasn't able to point out its weaknesses. He was convicted and sentenced to five years. On appeal, the Warren Court unanimously declared that Gideon was entitled to be represented by counsel.[185] Justice Black explained that "lawyers in criminal courts are necessities, not luxuries." The Court finally established a broad rule: state courts must provide an attorney to indigent defendants in felony cases.

When he was tried again, Gideon was given a lawyer, who proved the Court's point. The lawyer did an effective job defending him, which Gideon hadn't been able to do himself. This time Gideon wasn't convicted.

The Burger and Rehnquist Courts expanded the rule: state courts must provide an attorney to indigent defendants in misdemeanor cases, too, except those that result in no incarceration (or probation),[186] because misdemeanor cases

National Archives and Records Administration

Clarence Earl Gideon, convinced that he was denied a fair trial because he was not given an attorney, read law books in prison so he could petition the Supreme Court for a writ of *certiorari*. He wrote his petition by hand. Although he had spent much of his life in prison, he was optimistic. "I believe that each era finds an improvement in law [and] each year brings something new for the benefit of mankind. Maybe this will be one of those small steps forward."

as well as felony cases are too complex for the defendants to defend themselves. Thus *all courts must offer an attorney to indigent defendants in all cases except the most minor ones, such as traffic violations.* The Supreme Court also decided that, in addition to an attorney for the trial, *the courts must provide an attorney for one appeal.*[187]

Receiving counsel doesn't necessarily mean receiving effective counsel, however. Some assigned attorneys are inexperienced, some are incompetent, and most are overworked and have little time to prepare the best possible defense.

Some jurisdictions make little effort to provide effective counsel, even in murder cases where capital punishment looms. In Illinois, at least thirty-three convicts on death row had been represented at trial by attorneys who were later disbarred or suspended.[188] In Louisiana, a defendant was represented by an attorney who was living with the prosecutor in the case. In Florida, a defendant was represented by a part-time attorney who was a deputy sheriff. In Georgia, a black defendant was represented by a white attorney who had been the Imperial Wizard of the local Ku Klux Klan for fifty years.[189] Also in Georgia, an attorney was so unversed in criminal law that when he was asked to name criminal rulings he was familiar with, he could think of only one (*Miranda*).[190] In three murder cases in one recent year in Texas, defense attorneys slept through the trials. When one of these defendants appealed his conviction on the ground that he didn't receive his constitutional right to counsel, the appellate court announced that "the Constitution doesn't say the lawyer has to be awake."[191] (Stung by criticism, the appellate court sat *en banc*—that is, the entire court, rather than a three-judge panel, reheard the case—and overruled itself.) At least these attorneys were present. In Alabama, a defendant was represented by an attorney who failed to appear when his case was argued before the state supreme court. The defendant lost and was executed.[192]

In recent years, the issue of legal counsel for the defendants subject to capital punishment has received more scrutiny because new investigations and technologies, involving DNA analysis, have demonstrated that dozens of inmates on death row didn't commit the murder they were convicted of and sentenced for (and hundreds of inmates didn't commit the lesser crimes they were convicted of and sentenced for).[193] Nonetheless, there is little effort to provide effective counsel for criminal defendants because few groups, other than lawyers' associations, urge adequate representation. Criminal defendants have no political power in our system, and the public has limited sympathy for their rights.[194]

Jury Trial

The Sixth Amendment also provides the **right to a jury trial** in "serious" criminal cases. The Supreme Court has defined "serious" cases as those that could result in more than six months' incarceration.[195]

The right was adopted to prevent oppression by a "corrupt or overzealous prosecutor" or a "biased...or eccentric judge."[196] It has also served to limit governmental use of unpopular laws or enforcement practices. Regardless of the evidence against a defendant, a jury can refuse to convict if it feels that the government overstepped its bounds.

The jury is supposed to be impartial, so persons who have made up their minds before trial should be dismissed. It is also supposed to be "a fair cross section" of the community, so no group should be systematically excluded.[197] But the jury need not be a perfect cross section and in fact need not have a single member of any particular group.[198] Most courts use voter registration lists to obtain the names of potential jurors. These lists aren't closely representative because poor people don't register at the same rate as others, but the courts have decided that the lists are sufficiently representative. And the "motor voter law," which requires drivers' license and welfare offices to offer voter registration forms, has prompted more people to register to vote and thus to make themselves available to serve on juries.

Cruel and Unusual Punishment

The Eighth Amendment forbids **cruel and unusual punishment** but doesn't define such punishment. The Supreme Court had interpreted the phrase to mean torture or punishment grossly disproportionate to the offense. Thus the Roberts Court invalidated life terms for juvenile defendants who did not commit murder.[199]

The death penalty was used at the time the Eighth Amendment was adopted, so for many years it was assumed to be constitutional.[200] But in 1972 the Burger Court narrowly ruled that *the death penalty, as it was then being administered, was cruel and unusual punishment.*[201] The laws and procedures allowed too much discretion by those who administered the punishment and resulted in too much arbitrariness and discrimination for those who received it. The death penalty was imposed so seldom, according to Justice Potter Stewart, that it was "cruel and unusual in the same way that being struck by lightning is cruel and unusual." Yet when it was imposed, it was imposed on black defendants more often than on white defendants.

The decision invalidated the laws of forty states and commuted the death sentences of 629 inmates. But because the Court didn't hold capital punishment cruel and unusual in principle, about three-fourths of the states adopted revised laws that permitted less discretion in an attempt to achieve less arbitrariness and discrimination.

These changes satisfied a majority of the Burger Court, which ruled that *capital punishment isn't cruel and unusual for murder if administered fairly.*[202] But it can't be imposed automatically for everyone convicted of murder, because the judge or jury must consider any mitigating factors that would justify a lesser punishment.[203] Also, it can't be imposed for rape, as some states legislated, because it's disproportionate to that offense.[204]

The revised laws have reduced but not eliminated discrimination. Where past studies showed discrimination against black defendants, recent studies show discrimination against black or white defendants who murder white victims.

People who affect the decision to impose the death penalty—prosecutors, defense attorneys, judges, and jurors—appear to value white lives more. Despite evidence from Georgia that those who killed whites were more than four times as likely to be given the death penalty as those who killed blacks, the Rehnquist Court, by a 5–4 vote, upheld capital punishment in the state.[205]

The revised laws have not addressed an equally serious problem—inadequate representation given to poor defendants who face the death penalty—which we discussed in conjunction with the right to counsel.

For years, most people dismissed any suggestions that innocent defendants might be put to death. They assumed that, at least in these cases, the criminal justice system used careful procedures and made no mistakes. However, since capital punishment was reinstated and stricter procedures were mandated in the 1970s, at least 134 inmates awaiting execution have been released because new evidence, including DNA tests, revealed their innocence.[206] This number represents one exoneration for every seven to eight executions—a disturbing frequency for the ultimate punishment.[207] And apparently at least one inmate who was innocent was executed (in Texas in 2004).[208] Some defendants were the victims of sloppy or biased police or overzealous prosecutors; some were the victims of mistaken witnesses; others were the victims of emotional or prejudiced jurors. Many were the victims of inadequate representation.

Because of the patterns of racial discrimination and inadequate representation, the American Bar Association and some state governors have called for a moratorium on the use of capital punishment.[209] Although a majority of the public still supports capital punishment, that support is declining as more inmates are being found innocent through new investigations and DNA analysis.[210] Consequently, more jurors are becoming reluctant to impose the death penalty, instead opting for life in prison.[211]

Even the Rehnquist Court, long a staunch supporter of the death penalty, reflected the changing mood. In 2002, it ruled that states cannot execute the mentally retarded.[212] Previously, it had allowed execution of the retarded, including a man who had the mental capacity of a seven-year-old and still believed in Santa Claus.[213] Now, the six-justice majority observed, there is a new "national consensus" against such executions. In 2005, it ruled that states cannot execute juveniles who were younger than eighteen when they killed.[214] Previously, it had allowed execution of juveniles as young as sixteen. Now, Justice Kennedy noted, there are "evolving standards of decency" in society.

In recent years, some states have abolished the death penalty, but most still retain it for adults, even though nearly all other developed countries (except Japan) have abolished it.[215]

Rights in Theory and in Practice

Overall, the Supreme Court has interpreted the Bill of Rights to provide an impressive list of rights for criminal defendants (although the Burger, Rehnquist, and Roberts Courts have narrowed the rights established by the Warren Court in some ways). Yet not all rights are available for all defendants in all places. Some police, prosecutors, and judges don't comply with Supreme Court rulings.

When the rights are available, most defendants don't take advantage of them. About 90 percent of criminal defendants plead guilty, and many of them do so through a **plea bargain**. This is an agreement among the prosecutor, the defense attorney, and the defendant, with the explicit or implicit approval of the judge, to reduce the charge or the sentence in exchange for a guilty plea. A plea bargain is a compromise. For officials, it saves the time, trouble, and uncertainty of a trial. For defendants, it eliminates the fear of a harsher sentence. However, it also reduces due process rights. A guilty plea waives the defendants' right to a jury trial, at which the defendants can present their own witnesses and cross-examine the government's witnesses and at which they can't be forced to incriminate themselves. A guilty plea also reduces the defendants' right to counsel because it reduces their lawyers' need to prepare a defense. Most attorneys pressure their clients to forgo a trial so that the attorneys don't have to spend the time to investigate and try the case. Despite these drawbacks for due process rights, the Supreme Court allows plea bargaining, and the trial courts encourage the practice, because it enables judges and attorneys to dispose of their cases quickly.[216]

RIGHT TO PRIVACY

Neither the Constitution nor the Bill of Rights mentions privacy. Nevertheless, the right to privacy, Justice Douglas noted, is "older than the Bill of Rights,"[217] and the framers undoubtedly assumed that the people would have a right to privacy. In fact, the framers did include several amendments that reflect their concern for privacy: the First Amendment protects privacy of association (groups can keep their membership lists confidential); the Third, privacy of homes from quartering soldiers; the Fourth, privacy of persons and places where they live from searches and seizures; and the Fifth, privacy of knowledge and thoughts from compulsory self-incrimination. The Supreme Court would use these provisions to establish an explicit **right to privacy**.

So far, the Court's right-to-privacy doctrine reflects a right to autonomy—what Justice Louis Brandeis called "the right to be left alone"—more than a right to keep things confidential. As noted earlier in the chapter, the Court has been reluctant to punish the press for invading people's privacy by publishing personal information.[218]

Birth Control

The Warren Court explicitly *established a right to privacy* in *Griswold* v. *Connecticut* in 1965. The case began when Planned Parenthood and a professor at Yale Medical School opened a birth control clinic in New Haven. This action violated a nineteenth-century Connecticut law that prohibited distributing or using contraceptives or even disseminating information about them. After the state shut down the clinic, its founders challenged the law and the justices invalidated it.[219] To enforce the law, the state would have to police people's bedrooms. The very idea of policing married couples' bedrooms, the Court said, was absurd. Then the Court struck down Massachusetts and New York laws that prohibited distributing contraceptives to unmarried persons.[220] "If the right of privacy means anything," Justice Brennan said, "it is the right of the individual, married or single, to be free from unwarranted governmental intrusion into matters so fundamentally affecting a person as the decision whether to bear or beget a child."[221]

Abortion

When twenty-two-year-old Norma McCorvey became pregnant in 1969, she was distraught. She had one young daughter, she had relinquished custody of two previous children, and she was divorced. She sought an abortion, but Texas prohibited abortions unless the mother's life was in danger. "No legitimate doctor in Dallas would touch me," she discovered. "I found one doctor who offered to abort me for $500. Only he didn't have a license, and I was scared to turn my body over to him. So there I was—pregnant, unmarried, unemployed, alone, and stuck."[222] Unaware of states that permitted abortions, McCorvey put her baby up for adoption. But the state law rankled her. When she met two women attorneys who recently graduated from law school and also disliked the law, they offered to take her case to challenge the law. She adopted the name Jane Roe to conceal her identity. (Years later she switched sides, proclaiming herself pro-life.)

In *Roe* v. *Wade* in 1973, the Burger Court *extended the right to privacy from birth control to abortion.*[223] Justice Harry Blackmun surveyed the writings of doctors, theologians, and philosophers over the years and found that these thinkers didn't agree when life begins. Therefore, the majority on the Court concluded that judges shouldn't proclaim when life begins—whether at conception, which would make a fetus a person and abortion murder, or at birth. Without this factor in the equation, a woman's privacy, or control, of her body became paramount.

The Court ruled that *women have a* **right to abortion** *during the first six months of pregnancy.* States can prohibit an abortion during the last three months because the fetus becomes viable—it can live outside the womb—at this point. (However, states must allow an abortion during this time for a woman whose life is endangered by continuing her pregnancy.) Thus the right is broad but not absolute. The justices, as revealed in memos discovered years later, acknowledged that their division of the nine-month term was "legislative," but they saw this as a way to balance the rights of the mother in the early stages of pregnancy with the rights of the fetus in the later stage.[224]

Almost 90 percent of abortions are performed during the first trimester. Barely 1 percent are performed after twenty-one weeks, which is several weeks before the end of the second trimester.[225]

The *Roe* case has had an enormous impact on American politics. The Court's ruling invalidated the abortion laws of forty-nine states[226] and increased the number of abortions performed in the country (see Figure 1). It put abortion on

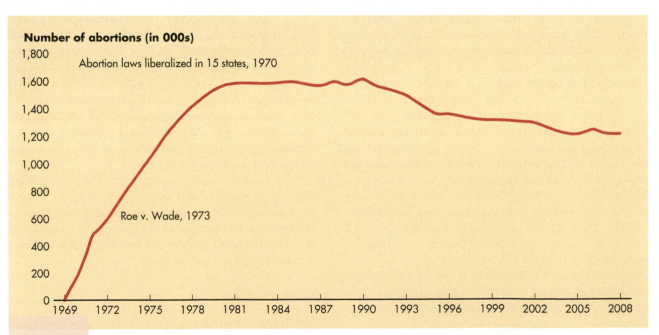

FIGURE 1: ABORTION RATE SINCE *ROE* The abortion rate climbed after *Roe* and peaked in the 1980s. Since then it has declined steadily (at least until the recession that began in 2008).

the public agenda, galvanizing conservative groups, who saw the decision as a symbol of loosening social restraints at a time of rampaging social problems. Disparate groups, such as Roman Catholics and evangelical Protestants (and some Orthodox Jews), rural residents and urban ethnics, who rarely saw eye to eye, coalesced around this issue and exercised leverage within the Republican Party.

In hindsight, some observers believe that the justices may have been imprudent or at least premature (even though majorities in both parties at the time supported leaving the decision to the woman and her doctor).[227] Before the ruling, some states began liberalizing their laws, but there wasn't time for others to follow or for citizens to ponder the issue. There was little public debate, let alone the extended debate necessary to develop a broad consensus. The Court's ruling short-circuited the normal political process and prompted opponents to mobilize and supporters to counter-mobilize. Both sides scorned the compromises that typify political solutions to most issues.[228]

The right-to-life movement pressured presidents and senators to appoint justices and lower court judges who opposed the ruling. The movement also lobbied members of Congress and state legislatures to overturn or circumvent the ruling. Although Congress refused to pass constitutional amendments banning abortions or allowing states to regulate them, Congress and state legislatures did pass statutes limiting abortions in various ways.

The Burger Court invalidated most of these statutes,[229] but it upheld a major limitation. The Medicaid program, financed jointly by the federal and state governments, began to pay for abortions for poor women. As a result, the program came to pay for a third of the abortions in the country each year.[230] But Congress eliminated federal funding (except when pregnancy threatens the life of the mother or is the result of rape or incest), and thirty-three state legislatures eliminated state funding. In these states, poor women need to pay the entire cost. The Court upheld these laws, ruling that *governments have no obligation to finance abortions,* even if this means that some women cannot take advantage of their right to have them.[231] For some women, these laws delay abortions while the women search for the money. For other women, these laws deny abortions because the women can't obtain the money.[232]

Many people, including pro-choice advocates, support these bans because they dislike welfare spending. Yet according to an analysis of the states that do provide abortion funding for poor women, the states save money. For every $1 they spend on abortions, they save $4 in welfare and medical expenses in what would have been the first two years of the child's life.[233] They save much more over a longer period. Ironically, public distaste for welfare spending actually leads to more welfare spending here.

Presidents Reagan and George H. W. Bush sought justices who opposed *Roe,* and after they filled their fifth vacancy on the Court, pro-life advocates expected the Court to overturn it. Yet the Rehnquist Court didn't overturn it.[234] In 1992, a bare majority reaffirmed the right to abortion.[235] At the same time, the majority *allowed more restrictions on the right—as long as the restrictions don't place an "undue burden" on the women seeking abortions.* In other words, states must permit abortions but can discourage them.[236]

Therefore, the majority upheld Pennsylvania's 24-hour waiting period between the time a woman indicates her desire to have an abortion and the time a doctor can perform one. Although a 24-hour waiting period is not a burden for many women, it can be for poor women who live in rural areas and must travel to cities for abortions. One Mississippi woman hitchhiked to the city and planned to sleep on outdoor furniture in the Kmart parking lot until the clinic offered to pay for her motel room.[237]

A waiting period can also affect teenagers. Some pro-life groups note the license numbers of cars driven to clinics by teenagers. After looking up the name and address of the family, they inform the parents in the hope that the parents will persuade or pressure their daughter to change her mind during the waiting period.

The majority did strike down Pennsylvania's requirement that a married woman notify her husband before having an abortion.[238] This was considered an undue burden because a woman who fears physical abuse from her husband would be deterred from seeking an abortion. Justice O'Connor wrote that a state "may not give to a man the kind of dominion over his wife that parents exercise over their children."

However, the Court upheld thirteen states' requirement that unmarried minors notify their parents and twenty-one states' requirement that unmarried minors obtain their parents' consent before having an abortion.[239] For either requirement, if a daughter doesn't want to tell her parents, she can seek permission from a judge. She must convince the judge that an abortion would be in her best interest or that she is mature enough to make the decision herself. If she's not mature enough, she's expected to become a mother.

Pro-life groups advocated these laws with the expectation that they would result in fewer abortions. They believed that many teenagers would go to their parents rather than face the forbidding atmosphere of a court hearing before an unknown judge and that their parents would persuade or pressure them not to have the abortion. Some evidence indicates that the laws have had this effect.[240]

When teenagers do go to court, they routinely get waivers in some states but not in others.

Many states adopted other restrictions designed to discourage abortions. Some require clinics to distribute a pamphlet about fetal development and a list of adoption agencies. Some require clinics to conduct an ultrasound of the fetus, on the assumption that the patient will change her mind after seeing the image.[241] In the first trimester, the fetus is so small that this ultrasound is not "the jelly on the belly" scan performed later in pregnancy, but a vaginal ultrasound—inserting a wand inside the body. The original laws required clinics to offer to show the image to the patient, but more recent laws require clinics to place the screen to face the patient and require doctors to explain, in detail, physical features of the fetus.[242]

The pro-choice movement uses this symbol, referring to the history of coat-hanger abortions in the back alleys before *Roe.* Sarah Weddington, an attorney who challenged Texas's law in *Roe,* often wears this pin while traveling. Once a young flight attendant asked, "What do you have against coat hangers?"

Mississippi requires doctors to tell the patient that abortions increase the risks of breast cancer and infertility, although the scientific research shows no clear link.[243] South Dakota requires doctors to tell the patient that abortions "terminate the life of a whole, separate, unique living human being" and that the patient already has an "existing relationship" with her fetus. When the requirement was challenged, the U.S. Court of Appeals for the Eighth Circuit upheld the language. The conservative majority asserted that life begins at conception, despite *Roe's* conclusion, and that the state can force doctors to say so, despite the First Amendment's guarantee of freedom of speech. (Six of the seven justices in the majority were appointed by President George W. Bush.)[244]

After the Rehnquist Court reaffirmed the right to abortion, pro-life groups tried to prohibit one abortion procedure known as "intact dilation and extraction" in medicine but referred to as "partial-birth abortion" in politics—a rhetorical success of antiabortion supporters. In this procedure, a doctor delivers the fetus except for the head, punctures the skull and drains the contents, and then removes the fetus from the woman.[245] Because the procedure seems gruesome, pro-life groups used it to sway undecided people in the abortion debate. The groups prompted some states to pass laws banning the procedure. A bare majority of the Rehnquist Court struck down the laws.[246] But Justice Sandra Day O'Connor, who supported abortion rights, retired, and Justice Samuel Alito, who opposes abortion rights, was appointed by President Bush to replace her. When Congress passed a similar law for the whole country, a bare majority of the Roberts Court upheld the law.[247] Writing for the majority, Justice Kennedy said the law protects women from themselves. "While we find no reliable data to measure the phenomenon," he concluded that some women "regret their choice to abort," so the law prevents other women from making that choice.

For the time being, a five-justice majority, including Kennedy, supports the basic right to abortion.

Nonetheless, in 2010 Nebraska banned abortions after twenty weeks based on the questionable conclusion that the fetus at that point feels pain from the procedure.[248] Other states followed. (As of fall 2012, the Supreme Court had not ruled on this direct challenge to the trimester foundation of the *Roe* ruling.)

The pro-life movement is divided over its current tactics. Some factions prefer an incremental strategy, passing numerous restrictions that might go unnoticed by most people, rather than a frontal attack that might prompt a backlash by the majority. When South Dakota, which had no doctors who performed abortions—Minnesota doctors flew in to the state's sole facility—banned all abortions in 2005, abortion supporters petitioned to put the issue on the ballot in 2006. Voters repealed the law.

In some states, pro-life groups have quietly pressed the legislatures to enact extra-stringent building codes for abortion clinics. These codes specify such things as the heights of ceilings, widths of hallways and doorways, dimensions of counseling rooms and recovery rooms, rates of air circulation, and types and angles of jets in drinking fountains. (Although all states have construction codes for their buildings, these new laws apply only to abortion clinics.) Some codes require equipment or levels of staffing, such as a registered nurse rather than a licensed practical nurse, beyond the norms for these clinics. Although the stated goal is health and safety, the real purpose is to drive up the clinics' expenses so they have to increase their patients' fees to the point where many women can no longer afford to have an abortion.[249] When South Carolina's law, which mandates twenty-seven pages of requirements just for abortion clinics, was challenged, a lower court upheld the law and the Supreme Court refused to hear the case, thus allowing the law to stand.

Despite dissatisfaction by activists on both sides of this controversy—pro-life groups are disappointed that the conservative Supreme Court has upheld the right to abortion, whereas pro-choice groups are critical that it has upheld some restrictions on abortion—it is worth noting that the non-elected, non-majoritarian Supreme Court has come closer to forging a policy reflective of public opinion than most politicians have. Polls show that the public is conflicted. The majority (52 percent) believes that abortion is morally wrong, but the majority (56 percent) also believes that abortion should be legal in all or most cases. (Even a majority of Catholics agree.) Moreover, the majority (58 percent) says that health care professionals in their communities should provide legal abortions.[250] Thus many people support the right to abortion but are uncomfortable with it and willing to allow restrictions on it. The Court's doctrine articulates this position.[251]

But the Court's rulings aren't necessarily the final word in this controversy, as they haven't been the final word in some other controversies. Frustrated by the Court's refusal to overturn *Roe,* activists in the pro-life movement (not most of the pro-life supporters) adopted more militant tactics. First they targeted abortion clinics. Organizations such as Operation Rescue engaged in civil disobedience, blockading clinics and harassing workers and patients as they came and went. Some activists sprayed chemicals inside clinics, ruining carpets and fabrics and leaving a stench that made the clinics unusable. Such incidents occurred fifty times in one year alone.[252]

Then activists targeted doctors, nurses, and other workers at the clinics. Operation Rescue ran a training camp in Florida that instructed members how to use public records to locate personal information about clinic employees, how to tail them to their homes, and how to organize demonstrations at their homes. Activists put up "Wanted" posters, with a doctor's picture, name, address, and phone number, and then encouraged people to harass the doctor, the doctor's spouse, and even their children. (One thirteen-year-old was confronted in a restaurant and told that he was going to burn in hell.)[253] Letters containing powder and threatening death by anthrax were sent to over one hundred doctors and clinics.[254] Some extremists even advocated killing the doctors. One minister wrote a book—*A Time to Kill*—and marketed a bumper sticker reading "execute abortionists-murderers."[255]

In this climate, four doctors, two clinic employees, and one clinic volunteer were killed, and seven other doctors, employees, and volunteers were wounded.[256] Numerous clinics were firebombed.

The tactics have had their intended effect on doctors.[257] Because they have made the practice of providing abortions seem dangerous and undesirable, fewer medical schools offer abortion classes and fewer hospitals provide abortion training, so fewer doctors study abortion procedures.[258] As a result, the number of abortion providers has dropped significantly.[259]

One pro-life leader proclaimed, "We've found the weak link is the doctor."[260] Another observed, "When you get the doctors out, you can have all the laws on the books you want and it doesn't mean a thing."[261]

As a result of these actions, abortions remain available in most metropolitan centers but not in most rural areas. Eighty-seven percent of U.S. counties, containing 32 percent of the American women aged fifteen to forty-four, have no doctor who performs abortions. Some states have only one, and others have only two cities where women can obtain abortions in clinics.[262] However, some obstetrician-gynecologists and family physicians perform abortions on the side.[263]

Nevertheless, an abortion is still a common surgical procedure for American women. At some point in their life, a third of American women have an abortion.[264] Moreover, the French abortion pill—RU-486, whose brand name is Mifeprex—offers a nonsurgical procedure (if used by the seventh week of pregnancy), allowing women to take one pill in the doctor's office and another at home. This procedure is increasingly being used.[265]

Birth Control, Revisited

The pro-life movement, stimulated by the conservatism of the Bush administration, trained its sights on contraception in addition to abortion.[266] Initially the pro-life movement was dominated by Catholics, whose church opposes contraceptives, but the leaders muted their views to avoid scaring off potential supporters. (Over 90 percent of all Americans, and 90 percent of Catholics, support contraceptives.)[267] Eventually, the pro-life movement was joined by conservative Protestants who didn't oppose birth control. In recent years, however, more movement leaders, Protestants as well as Catholics, have voiced opposition to contraception. The president of the American Life League declared, "We oppose all forms

of contraception."[268] Now religious interest groups, such as the Christian Coalition and Focus on the Family, address birth control; increasing numbers of evangelical theologians oppose it and evangelical churches discuss it; and a cluster of representatives and senators spearheads congressional efforts against some forms of birth control. At least one evangelical organization proposes allowing birth control only for married couples.[269]

Current opposition to contraception makes it difficult for the two sides in the abortion controversy to find common ground. In the past, some on each side had called for greater availability of contraceptives so there would be less need for abortions. But now this common ground is giving way as more who oppose abortion also oppose contraception.

This opposition suggests that, for some leaders in the pro-life movement, the issue is sex as much as abortion. One leader said, "We see a direct connection between the practice of contraception and the practice of abortion." They both reflect "an anti-child mindset."[270] Both serve "the selfish demands of the individual."[271] The president of the Southern Baptist Theological Seminary stated, "The effective separation of sex from procreation may be one of the most important defining marks of our age—and one of the most ominous."[272] Their goal is to reverse the sexual revolution of the 1960s, when "the pill" became commonplace, and to confine sex to marriage.

A new dimension of the contraception issue arose with passage of the health care reform law. Under rules issued by the Obama administration, insurance plans will have to cover contraception along with other preventive care for women, and the plans will have to cover all methods, including the emergency or morning after pill ("Plan B"), which the Catholic Church believes induces abortions rather than prevents pregnancies. (Some scientists and doctors disagree.) The rules exempt churches but not schools and hospitals operated by churches. The Catholic Church objects—Catholic bishops even compared President Obama to Adolf Hitler and Joseph Stalin[273]—but the administration and women's groups maintain that the women employees, many of whom aren't Catholic, shouldn't be given less insurance than other women.[274] A majority of the public (and Catholics) favors the policy.[275]

Homosexuality

Homosexuals have faced pervasive discrimination. In recent years, federal, state, and local governments have begun to combat this discrimination, especially in the areas of sex, marriage, employment, and military service.

Although the debates over these issues feature the words *discrimination* and *equality*, the courts consider homosexual rights to be a matter of civil liberties—encompassed within the right to privacy, like abortion rights—so the text will cover this topic in this chapter rather than in the civil rights chapter.

Running through the debates over these issues is a broader debate: Are homosexuals seeking equal rights or "special rights"? Homosexuals claim the former; opponents claim the latter. Homosexuals think it is self-evident that they want equal rights with heterosexuals. How, they ask, can protection from discrimination be considered special treatment rather than equal treatment? Indeed, they want to end their special status as pariahs in law and society. Opponents, especially conservative Christians, insist that homosexuality is a lifestyle choice rather than an immutable characteristic like race or gender. (This conclusion is debatable and is rejected by most homosexuals, who claim to have been born as they are.) Therefore, opponents say, homosexuals could renounce their homosexuality and alter their behavior. Then they would face no discrimination. Instead, they want governmental protection for a chosen lifestyle. Fundamentally, opponents find homosexuality abhorrent and contrary to biblical teachings, and they fear that equal rights will lead to full acceptance in society.[276]

Opponents also use the term *special rights* for political reasons. The phrase separates homosexuals' demands from previous demands by racial minorities and women for equal rights. To listeners, the phrase makes homosexuals' demands seem less defensible. To those who are leery about gay rights, the phrase provides an excuse for opposing such rights.

Sex

For years, states prohibited adultery, fornication, and sodomy. Reflecting Christian doctrine, the statutes targeted various forms of nonmarital sex and nonprocreative sex (including masturbation and withdrawal prior to ejaculation).[277] After the "sexual revolution" of the 1960s, many states repealed these statutes. However, most states retained their sodomy statutes, which prohibited oral or anal sex (performed by heterosexuals or homosexuals) because of legislators' disgust at homosexual practices and their opposition to the emerging gay rights movement.[278] Although these statutes were primarily symbolic, they were occasionally enforced against homosexuals.

When an Atlanta police officer, serving a warrant, entered a bedroom of an apartment, he found two men engaged in sodomy, and he cited the men for violating state law. When the case reached the Supreme Court in 1986, five justices refused to extend the right to privacy to protect homosexual practices.[279] Justice Lewis Powell, a moderate conservative and a swing vote, seemed baffled by the case. He told his clerk, "I don't believe I've ever met a homosexual."[280] Yet his clerk was a homosexual. Powell ultimately cast the deciding vote to uphold the Georgia law.

Although Powell was uncertain, Chief Justice Burger was adamant in supporting the state law. Quoting an English jurist, Burger called sodomy a "crime against nature"—a crime so vile that it was "not fit to be named."

In 2003, however, the Court reversed itself. In *Lawrence v. Texas,* the Court overturned a Texas statute and *invalidated the sodomy laws* of the thirteen states that still had them.[281] By this time, the justices had openly gay clerks and heard prominent gay attorneys argue cases before them. In a broad opinion, Justice Kennedy wrote, "Liberty presumes an autonomy of self that includes freedom of thought, belief, expression,

"If you don't hurry up, you're never going to be the first openly gay anything."

and certain intimate conduct." Therefore, homosexuals are entitled to "dignity" and "respect for their private lives."

A sizable shift in public opinion had occurred in the seventeen years between the two rulings.[282] As more homosexuals came out, they gained greater acceptance from straights. Most Americans say they know someone who is gay or lesbian, and a majority say they are sympathetic to the gay and lesbian communities. Numerous states repealed their sodomy statutes after the 1986 ruling (even though that ruling allowed the states to keep the statutes). Thus in the *Lawrence* case, according to one law professor, "the Court legitimized and endorsed a cultural consensus."[283]

Marriage

Although the majority in *Lawrence* said the ruling would not apply to same-sex marriages, the dissenters feared that establishing a right to privacy for homosexual practices would lead to a right to marry for homosexual couples. Congress adopted the Defense of Marriage Act, which allows states to disregard same-sex marriages performed in other states. (About forty states have passed laws to do so.) The act also forbids federal recognition of same-sex marriages and thus denies federal benefits, such as Social Security, to same-sex couples.[284]

Although marriage was a fantasy for most homosexuals, their lack of legal rights was both a cause for concern and a source of anger. In the 1980s and 1990s, the AIDS epidemic swept gay communities across the United States. "Lovers, friends, and AIDS 'buddies' were spooning food, emptying bedpans, holding wracked bodies through the night. They were assuming the burdens of marriage at its hardest."[285] Yet gay partners had no legal rights. They encountered problems involving health insurance, hospital visitation, disability benefits, funeral planning, and estate settling. Gays were often unable to participate fully in these life-and-death matters because of legal impediments that didn't exist for married couples. In the same decades, lesbians gave birth with

Chris Melzer/dpa/picture-alliance/Newscom

Stephanie Figarelle (left) and Lela McArthur marry on the viewing platform of the Empire State Building. They came from Alaska, which doesn't allow same-sex marriage.

donated sperm, and gays got children through adoption and surrogate mothers, yet homosexual couples realized that they didn't have legal protections for their families. These developments increased the calls for legal rights commensurate with the rights of heterosexual couples.[286]

In 1999, the Vermont Supreme Court ruled that the state must either legalize same-sex marriages or equalize the rights and benefits received by same-sex couples and traditional married couples. The legislature decided to equalize the rights and benefits. To implement this policy, the legislature established "civil unions," with procedures for couples to become official partners (similar to marriage) and procedures for them to dissolve their relationship (similar to divorce).

Although these civil unions provide most of what regular marriages provide, the unions don't apply when couples move from Vermont to other states. And they don't apply to federal benefits. By one count, 1138 federal laws apply to married couples that don't apply to unmarried couples. Some impose responsibilities; most provide rights and benefits, such as tax breaks.[287] Also, of course, the unions don't provide the symbolism that regular marriages do. Instead, they imply that homosexuals are "subcitizens... regarded as defective by the law."[288]

So the pressure for same-sex marriages continued. In 2004, the Massachusetts Supreme Judicial Court, hearing a suit brought by seven couples, ruled that same-sex marriages are allowed under the state's constitution. Otherwise, same-sex couples would be relegated to "a different status.... The history of our nation has demonstrated that separate is seldom, if ever, equal."[289]

In quick succession, officials in San Francisco; Portland, Oregon; and smaller cities in New York, New Jersey, and New Mexico were inspired to issue marriage licenses to same-sex couples. State courts halted the licenses, but not until thousands of beaming couples had married and posed for news photos. Although the marriages were pronounced invalid, the head of the Lambda Legal Defense and Education Fund observed, "You can't put the toothpaste back in the tube."[290]

There was an immediate backlash. Polls showed that a majority of the public opposed same-sex marriages. President Bush proposed a constitutional amendment. One congressional sponsor claimed, "There is a master plan out there from those who want to destroy the institution of marriage." Another senator, comparing the threat of gay marriage to that of terrorism, called the amendment "the ultimate homeland security." And an evangelist predicted that "the family as it has been known for five millennia will crumble, presaging the fall of Western civilization itself."[291] Yet there was more fire from the pulpits than there was in the pews. Evangelical leaders expressed puzzlement and frustration that there was no loud outcry from their faithful.[292] The fact was that many people who oppose gay marriage don't feel threatened by it. Consequently, the amendment failed to pass.

Nevertheless, voters in about thirty states adopted such amendments to their state constitution, most by a wide margin. Opponents to same-sex unions found that the most effective tactic was to claim that same-sex marriages would lead to teaching homosexuality in school. A California commercial portrayed a field trip to a lesbian wedding.[293]

Despite many people's objections, gay rights leaders predicted that once homosexuals began to marry and straights saw that "the sky didn't fall," people would stop opposing their marriages.[294] They also noted that time is in their favor. Young people are the most supportive, and old people are the most opposed. Seventy percent of Americans between eighteen and thirty-four support same-sex marriage; 53 percent of those between thirty-five and fifty-four do; and just 39 percent of those over fifty-five do.[295]

Other states followed Massachusetts, with Connecticut, New Hampshire, Vermont, New York, and Iowa (and the District of Columbia) also allowing same-sex marriage. In these states, the supreme court or the legislature and governor changed the law.

The California Supreme Court ruled that the state's domestic-partnership law wasn't sufficient and that same-sex marriages must be allowed in that state too. Yet this ruling was negated by voters.[296] After the ballot measure, the California court decided that the eighteen thousand couples who were married in the five months in which same-sex marriage was legal would remain married.

In 2012, voters in Maine, Maryland, and Washington State voted for same-sex marriage. These victories were the first after 32 losses in state elections.

In addition to the states that allow same-sex marriage, more states allow civil unions or equivalent rights.[297]

Even states that don't allow same-sex marriage or civil unions find that a body of law indirectly supporting same-sex relationships is emerging, as couples who move from states that do allow these relationships are forcing courts to resolve legal issues such as divorce, custody, and inheritance. Judges must resolve cases before them, even if their state has no law on the books.

Through executive orders, President Obama has extended some benefits to the partners of federal workers, including access to medical treatment, long-term disability insurance (though not to full health care coverage), fitness centers, credit unions, and relocation assistance. His administration has also refused to defend in court the sections of the Defense of Marriage Act that deny federal benefits to same-sex couples married in the states that allow such marriages.

Employment

About half of the states and some cities have passed laws barring discrimination against homosexuals in employment and also in housing, credit, insurance, and public accommodations. (And thirteen states have passed laws barring discrimination against transgendered persons—those who are born as one gender but live as the opposite gender.)[298]

In response, Colorado adopted a constitutional amendment that prohibited laws barring discrimination against homosexuals. But the Supreme Court rejected the claim that such laws amounted to "special rights." The majority struck down the amendment because it singled out homosexuals and denied them opportunity to seek protection from discrimination.[299] This ruling put the brakes on a drive to adopt similar provisions in other states.

Log in to www.cengagebrain.com and open Course-Reader to access the full reading "A Risky Proposal" by Margaret Talbot.

After the California Supreme Court ruled that same-sex marriages are allowed in the state, voters passed Proposition 8, which overturned the ruling, in 2008. Two prominent lawyers, Theodore Olson, a conservative, and David Boies, a liberal, joined to invalidate the proposition. Olson had represented George W. Bush in his effort to be chosen president in 2000, while Boies had represented Al Gore in that contest, but they see eye-to-eye on marriage equality. They expect their lawsuit (originally called *Perry* v. *Schwarzenegger* but now called *Perry* v. *Brown*) to reach the U.S. Supreme Court and hope the case will do for homosexual marriage what *Loving* v. *Virginia* did for interracial marriage in 1967. Since the article was written, the federal district court and appellate court ruled the proposition unconstitutional. These rulings only apply to California.

1. How does the strategy used by Olson and Boies differ from the strategy favored by gay rights organizations?
2. Why is this lawsuit considered high stakes for the plaintiffs?
3. Whether you favor or oppose same-sex marriage, do you welcome or dread this lawsuit?

Yet homosexuals remain vulnerable at workplaces in states and cities without laws barring discrimination. Because Congress rejected a bill barring discrimination in employment at the same time it passed the Defense of Marriage Act, in many states employees can be fired for being homosexual.

Even so, homosexuals have gained equal benefits at more workplaces. Some state and city governments, universities, nonprofit organizations, and many large corporations offer health care packages to same-sex couples as a way to attract and retain good workers.

Military Service

Since World War II, the military rejected recruits and discharged troops who were homosexuals, fearing that they would disrupt the morale and unit cohesion essential for fighting forces. When Bill Clinton, campaigning for president, pledged to end the ban, he ignited a firestorm that burned throughout his presidency. His proposal rallied evangelical groups, who launched an attack against the proposal and the president himself. They persuaded military officers to pressure Congress and their followers to flood Congress with petitions and phone calls against the proposal.

Although opponents claimed that military performance was their concern, the experiences of other countries belied this claim. European countries, Canada, Japan, and Israel, which has a battle-tested military, all tolerated homosexuals in their services.[300] Rather than military performance, the opponents' motives were mostly cultural and religious. They wanted the military to remain "a bastion of traditional male values," and they wanted the military and the nation to retain their "Christian character."[301]

The opposition prompted Congress to block the proposal and forced Clinton to accept a compromise, called "don't ask, don't tell." Under this policy, the military (including the Reserves and National Guard) was not allowed to ask members about their sexual orientation but was allowed to discharge members for statements admitting homosexuality or conduct reflecting homosexuality (or bisexuality). The restrictions applied off base as well as on.

The policy didn't work well. Some commanders were confused, and others were unwilling to follow the policy. They continued to ask and discharge. The policy led to speculation among troops as to which ones might be homosexuals. One soldier joined his colleagues on a trip to a brothel to avoid such speculation. (He sat with a prostitute in a room.)[302] As a result, more homosexuals were discharged after the policy went into effect than before.[303] Over thirteen thousand service members were forced out, including almost sixty Arabic specialists who were in demand in Afghanistan and Iraq.[304] As a candidate, Barack Obama opposed the policy, but as president he moved cautiously. Aware of Clinton's experience, he was leery about alienating the public and rallying

conservative Christians while trying to push through his major initiatives. In his second year, he initiated the process to repeal the policy, ordering the military to assess the policy, with an expectation that the brass, despite their reservations about gay soldiers "in the foxholes," would conclude that the policy was not necessary for military readiness. Then congressional Democrats, over Republican opposition, passed a law permitting the president and defense secretary to repeal the policy when the study was completed. In 2011, they did so, and homosexuals were allowed to serve openly. Although one representative warned that the change will lead to "hermaphrodites" in the ranks,[305] the reaction in Congress and by the public was mostly positive. Three-fourths of the public supports allowing homosexuals to serve openly.[306]

Animus toward gays and lesbians is far less than it used to be. Unlike public opinion toward abortion, which has remained relatively stable since *Roe,* public opinion toward homosexuality has changed dramatically. Until 1973, the American Psychiatric Association believed that homosexuality is a mental illness. In 1992, a gay leader said, "What we were begging Bill Clinton about—literally—[was] whether he was going to say the word *gay* in his convention speech. Even say it. We had to threaten a walk-out to get it in."[307] But now more than four hundred openly gay and lesbian officials hold elected office in the United States.[308] A majority of Americans, including men, who traditionally were the most averse, consider "gay and lesbian relations" morally acceptable.[309] And another barometer of public opinion, *Archie Comics,* added its first openly gay character to the cast of teenagers in Archie's "Riverdale"—the quintessentially American town.

In Ashland, Oregon, Steve Mason suffered from terminal lung cancer and waited until he could no longer eat or sleep. Then he took the lethal drugs (on the table) prescribed by his doctor. He said, "I've lived my life with dignity. I want to go out the same way."

Right to Die

The Court has broadened the right to privacy to provide a limited right to die. When Nancy Cruzan's car skidded off an icy road and flipped into a ditch in 1983, doctors were able to save her life but not her brain, and she never regained consciousness. She lived in a vegetative state, similar to a coma, and was fed through a tube. Twenty-five at the time of the accident, she was expected to live another thirty years. When her parents asked the doctors to remove the tube, the hospital objected, and the state of Missouri, despite paying $130,000 a year to maintain her, also objected. This issue became entangled in other issues. Pro-life groups contended that denying life support was analogous to abortion; disability groups, claiming that her condition was merely a disability, argued that withholding food and water from her would lead to withholding treatment from others with disabilities.[310]

When Cruzan's parents filed suit, the Rehnquist Court established a limited **right to die**.[311] The justices ruled that *individuals can refuse medical treatment, including food and water, even if this means they will die.* But individuals must make their decision while competent and alert. They can act in advance, preparing a "living will" or designating another person as a proxy to make the decision if they're unable to.

Cruzan's parents presented evidence to a Missouri court that their daughter would prefer death to being kept alive by machines. Three of Cruzan's coworkers testified that they recalled conversations in which she said she'd never want to live "like a vegetable." As a result, the Missouri court granted her parents' request to remove the feeding tube. She died twelve days later.

Although the legal doctrine is clear, various practical problems and emotional issues limit its use. Many people don't make their desires known in advance. Approximately ten thousand people in irreversible comas now didn't indicate their decision beforehand.[312] Some people who do indicate their decision beforehand waver when they face death. Some doctors, who are in the habit of prolonging life even when

their patients have no chance of enjoying life, resist their patients' decision.[313]

Although the Rehnquist Court established a right to die, it *refused* patients' pleas *to expand the limited right into a broader right to obtain assistance in committing suicide.*[314] The Court drew a distinction between stopping treatment and assisting suicide; individuals have a right to demand the former but not the latter. As is typical with an issue new to the courts, the justices seemed tentative. Chief Justice Rehnquist emphasized, "Our holding permits this debate to continue, as it should in a democratic society."

Oregon decided to allow assisted suicide, but its law provides some safeguards. The patient must submit written requests in the presence of two witnesses, get two doctors to concur that he or she has less than six months to live, and wait fifteen days. The George W. Bush administration challenged Oregon's law, claiming that individual states can't allow assisted suicide. But the Supreme Court rebuffed the Bush administration and *allowed the state law to stand.*[315] So far, a modest number of terminally ill patients—about thirty a year—have taken advantage of the law.[316] (Washington and Montana also allow assisted suicide now.)

A majority of the public favors a right to assisted suicide,[317] but conservative religious groups oppose it, insisting that people, even when facing extreme pain and no hope of recovery, shouldn't take their own life. In addition, ethicists worry that patients will be pressured to give up their life because of the costs, to their family or health care provider, of continuing to live. They fear that a right will become a duty.

Meanwhile, the practice, even where officially illegal, is widely condoned, much as abortion was before *Roe.* Almost a fifth of the doctors who treat cancer patients in Michigan admitted in a survey that they have assisted suicide, and over half of two thousand doctors who treat AIDS patients in San Francisco also admitted that they have done so.[318]

Moreover, many doctors treat terminal patients with a strong sedative to relieve pain. The sedative, which can make it impossible to drink or eat, can hasten death. The treatment is called "palliative sedation," "terminal sedation," or, more provocatively, "slow euthanasia."[319]

SUMMARY

- The Bill of Rights is a list of "Thou shalt nots" directed at the government. It provides freedom of expression and religion, multiple rights for criminal defendants, and some rights invoked less often.
- Freedom of expression, which includes freedom of speech, assembly, and association and freedom of the press, is essential for American government and society. Freedom of speech promotes individual autonomy and

self-fulfillment and the advancement of knowledge and discovery of truth. It helps citizens participate in their government and check inefficient government.

- Almost all speech, including criticism of government, is allowed under the First Amendment. There are some restrictions on the content of speech: people can't incite illegal action, they can't harass or threaten others, and in some situations they can't use sexual speech. There are also some restrictions on the manner of speech: people have no right to demonstrate on others' property, and they have no right to disrupt the normal activities of the public places where they can demonstrate.

- The free exercise clause allows individuals to practice their religion without government coercion, and the establishment clause prohibits government from aiding one religion over another or aiding religion over nonreligion. Thus individuals are free to follow their religion, and government is forbidden from helping or hindering.
- Although the phrase "separation of church and state" isn't in the Constitution, the concept is reflected in the religion clauses and in the Founders' intent that church and state should not interfere, or even interact, with each other.
- The rights in the Fourth, Fifth, Sixth, and Eighth Amendments provide minimal procedures that government officials—police, prosecutors, judges, and jurors—are expected to follow toward criminal defendants. Without these procedures, the process would be less fair.
- Although the Constitution doesn't include an explicit right to privacy, several amendments reflect a concern for privacy, and historical evidence indicates that the Founders had an expectation of privacy. So far, the right to privacy entails a right to obtain contraceptives and abortions and to refuse medical treatment. So far, the right to privacy entails a right to obtain contraceptives and abortions, to practice homosexual sex, and to refuse medical treatment.

DISCUSSION QUESTIONS

1. Civil liberties in the United States reflect Americans' desire for "freedom from" governmental interference. People in some countries, however, conceptualize *freedom* as "freedom to" improve their lives with governmental assistance. Can you think of examples of the latter? Can you explain why Americans conceptualize *freedom* as "freedom from" rather than "freedom to"?
2. Construct an argument that freedom of speech is the most important civil liberty we have.
3. The Supreme Court hasn't decided whether picketing at or near funerals is allowed under the First Amendment. Argue that it should be allowed. Then argue that it shouldn't.
4. The Supreme Court has tried to be neutral between religions and between religion and nonreligion. Do you think it has succeeded? If not, what do you think it has favored?
5. Why do some Americans oppose the concept of separation of church and state? What would they prefer instead? In your opinion, what consequences would result?
6. Which right in the Bill of Rights do you think is most important for criminal defendants? Why?
7. Should the right to privacy be extended from a right to autonomy to a right to keep information confidential? Consider the implications for modern technology and also for freedom of the press.

14

Civil Rights

Mug shots of "Freedom Riders," who attempted to desegregate buses in Alabama and Mississippi, after they were arrested in Jackson in 1961. The Freedom Riders and other civil rights protestors paved the way for average African Americans to become the first nurse, plumber, postal clerk, or bank teller of their race in their city or state. John Lewis (top row, second from left) became a member of Congress (D—Ga.).

Mississippi Department of Archives and History

LEARNING OBJECTIVES

1. Learn the historical practices, beginning with slavery, that fostered discrimination against African Americans.
2. Learn how the civil rights movement fought discrimination against African Americans.
3. Understand the rulings and the impact of *Plessy* v. *Ferguson* and *Brown* v. *Board of Education*.
4. Understand why residential segregation has led to school segregation and why efforts to desegregate the schools have not succeeded.
5. Understand the ways in which African Americans still face discrimination, despite the progress they have made.

6. Understand why the black underclass is an exception to African American progress.
7. Learn who Latinos are and where they came from.
8. Learn what discrimination Latinos face.
9. Grasp how traditional gender roles led to sex discrimination.
10. Learn how the women's movement overcame discrimination.
11. Learn what affirmative action is and what it applies to.

TALKING POINTS

Dorothy Allen was the first black probation officer in Saginaw, Michigan. Nancy Hodge-Snyder was the first black registered nurse in Kalamazoo. Marjorie Grevious was the first African American woman licensed as a funeral director and embalmer in Kentucky. Eugene Smith was the first African American licensed as a plumber and master electrician in Spartanburg, South Carolina.

A search of the website Legacy.com, which includes obituaries from over 750 newspapers in the United States, found more than 300 people who died in 2011 who were the first African Americans to hold their job or position in their city or state.[1]

Walter Lee was the first black postal clerk in Winter Park, Florida. Camillus Wilson was the first African American meter reader for the Baltimore Gas and Electric Company. Bernice Ellis Riley was the first black teller at the First Federal Bank in Rocky Mount, North Carolina. Leon Gates was the first African American business agent for Heavy Construction Laborers' Union Local 663 in Kansas City, Missouri.

"How mundane the positions were, how modest the dreams had been," wrote Isabel Wilkerson, the first African American woman who won the Pulitzer Prize in journalism. But they reflect individual decisions and risks, accompanied by considerable "anxiety and second-guessing," by the African Americans who sought the job or license and by the white persons who hired or certified them.

Eddie Kroger was the first black bus driver in South Carolina. Marshall Arnell was the first black teacher at Dover High School in Dover, Delaware. Bayleas Bingham was the first black female school bus driver in Newport News, Virginia.

Most of these pioneers got their jobs between World War II and the 1980s, when the United States was opening up to the people who had been denied these opportunities for so long. Their obituaries show how far the country has come.

Donald Dickerson was the first African American firefighter in Statesboro, Georgia. Wilbert Coleman was the first African American narcotics detective in Hackensack, New Jersey.

For Barack Obama to become the first African American president, Dorothy Allen, Walter Lee, Eddie Kroger, Donald Dickerson, and all the rest had to pave the way.

The term *civil rights* means equal rights for persons regardless of their race, sex, or ethnic background. The **Declaration of Independence** proclaimed that "all men are created equal." The author, Thomas Jefferson, knew that all men were not created equal in many respects, but he meant that they should be considered equal in their rights and equal before the law. This notion represented a break from Great Britain, where rigid classes with unequal rights existed and nobles enjoyed more rights than commoners.

The Declaration's promise didn't include nonwhites or women, however. So although colonial Americans advocated equality, they envisioned it only for white men. Although other groups eventually gained more equality, the Declaration's promise remains unfulfilled.

RACE DISCRIMINATION

African Americans, Latinos, and American Indians all have endured and continue to experience discrimination. This chapter recounts the struggle for equal rights by these groups.

Discrimination against African Americans

Discrimination against African Americans occurred during the long and sordid history of slavery, neoslavery, segregation, and violence.

Slavery

The first Africans came to America in 1565 as slaves. They were brought to Florida by the Spanish, who settled St. Augustine.[2] Fifty-four years later, other Africans were brought to Virginia by the British as indentured servants, like many whites. In exchange for their passage across the ocean, indentured servants were bound to an employer, usually for four to seven years, and then freed.[3] Later in the seventeenth century, however, the British colonies passed laws making the Africans and their children slaves for life.

Once slavery was established, the slave trade flourished. In the South, slavery provided the foundation for an agricultural economy with huge and prosperous plantations. In the North, too, slavery was common. Plantations in Connecticut, Massachusetts, and Rhode Island used slaves to grow products sent to the West Indies in exchange for molasses used to make rum. Tradesmen and households in the cities also used slaves. In the mid-1700s, New York City had more slaves than any city in the colonies except Charleston (and in the early 1800s, it would have more slaves than any city in the country, including Charleston). About 40 percent of its households owned slaves—although, unlike southern plantations, the households had an average of only two slaves.[4] The northern cities, with their merchants and bankers, served as the hub of the international trade in the commodities produced by slave labor—cotton, sugar, and tobacco.

At the outbreak of the Revolutionary War in 1776, one-fifth of the American population was enslaved. The British, in an attempt to disrupt American society, promised freedom for the slaves. (The promise was a tactical maneuver rather than an ethical stand, as British generals themselves had slaves.) Perhaps as many as eighty thousand escaped and fought alongside the Redcoats.[5] After the war, some fled to Canada with the Loyalists, some sailed to Caribbean islands, where they would be enslaved again, and others shipped to Sierra Leone. Most remained in America.

During and after the war, abolitionist sentiment grew in the North. By the Constitutional Convention, there were sharp differences between northern and southern attitudes toward slavery. In most parts of the North, slavery was condemned and slaves were freed,[6] whereas in the South slavery was accepted and ingrained.

As a result of the compromises between northern and southern states, the Constitution protected slavery. It allowed the importation of slaves until 1808, when Congress could bar further importation, and it required the return of escaped slaves to their owners.

In 1808, Congress did bar the importation of slaves but not the practice of slavery, which continued to flourish because there were so many slaves that their natural reproduction provided an ample number for the southern plantations. Yet Thomas Jefferson, a Virginia slave owner, foresaw its demise, "whether brought on by the generous energy of our own minds" or by a "bloody process."[7]

 Thinking about Democracy

Ancient Greece developed democracy but also held prisoners of war as slaves. We can ask the same question of the antebellum (pre–Civil War) United States as we ask of ancient Greece: Is slavery compatible with democracy?

Meanwhile, abolitionists called for an end to slavery. In response, southerners began to question the Declaration of Independence and to repudiate its notion of natural rights, attributing this idea to Jefferson's "radicalism."[8] And they began to claim that slavery was ordained by God and sanctioned by Scripture.[9] Eventually, they came to believe that slavery was necessary for the slaves' own good, because the slaves weren't smart enough or virtuous enough to live independently.[10]

The Supreme Court tried to quell the antislavery sentiment in the **Dred Scott case** in 1857.[11] Dred Scott, a slave who lived in Missouri, was taken by his owner to the free state of Illinois and the free territory of Wisconsin and, after five years, was returned to Missouri. The owner died and passed title to his wife, who moved and left Scott in the care of people who opposed slavery. They arranged for Scott to sue his owner for his freedom, arguing that Scott's time in a free state and a free territory made him a free man even though he was returned to a slave state. Because his owner opposed slavery, she could have simply freed Scott, but they all sought a major court decision to keep slavery out of the territories.

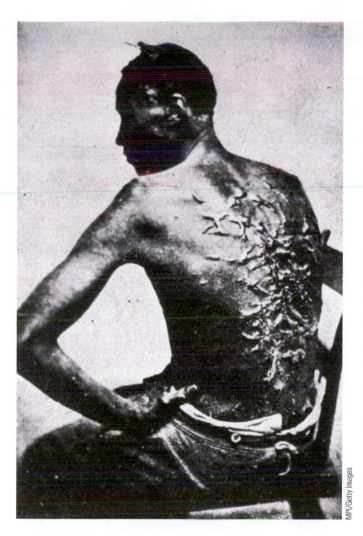

his own slaves, whom he had inherited from his parents, and he remained with the Union when the war broke out.)[12]

Although Scott received his freedom from his owner, most slaves weren't so lucky (see the box "Black Masters, Red Masters"). When the Civil War began, only one of every nine black people in America was free; the rest were slaves. By this time, slaves collectively were the largest financial asset in the United States—worth more than America's banks, factories, or railroads—and cotton was the most valuable export.[13] Slaves were so integral to the southern economy that the paper money of some Confederate states pictured slaves harvesting cotton.

As soon as the Civil War erupted, southern slaves began to flee their masters—first in a trickle, eventually in a flood—and seek refuge in Union forts and behind Union lines. At least tens of thousands, probably hundreds of thousands, did so before the Emancipation Proclamation.[14] More did so after President Lincoln announced the Emancipation Proclamation (as Chapter 2 explained).

The North's victory in the Civil War led to abolition of slavery. But as the following sections show, blacks would find short-lived solace.

Reconstruction

After the war, Congress passed and the states ratified three constitutional amendments. The Thirteenth Amendment prohibited slavery. (In 1995, Mississippi became the last state to ratify the amendment, but of course the state's ratification was merely a symbolic act by then.) The Fourteenth Amendment granted citizenship to blacks, thus overruling the *Dred Scott* decision, and also granted "equal protection of the laws" and "due process of law." The **equal protection clause** would eventually become the primary guarantee that governments would treat people equally. The Fifteenth Amendment gave black men the right to vote.

These amendments not only granted specific rights for African Americans but also transformed the relationship between the federal and state governments. Each amendment included the stipulation that "Congress shall have power to enforce" the provisions of the amendment. (In the wake of the war, Congress didn't trust the southern states to enforce the constitutional provisions.) This stipulation granted the federal government new power—whatever power was necessary to guarantee these rights—in marked contrast to the Founders' original intention to limit federal power. The Civil War and these amendments together thus constituted a constitutional revolution (as explained in Chapter 2).[15]

Congress also passed a series of Civil Rights Acts that allowed blacks to buy, own, and sell property; to make contracts; to sue; and to serve as witnesses and jurors in court. The acts also allowed blacks to use public transportation, such as railroads and steamboats, and to patronize hotels and theaters.[16]

During Reconstruction, the Union army, which occupied the South, enforced the new amendments and acts. Military commanders established procedures to register voters and hold elections. The commanders also started schools for the

This photo, which shows a slave named Gordon who was whipped by his master in Mississippi, was taken after the slave escaped (by rubbing himself with onions to confuse the bloodhounds) and reached the Union army. The photo was printed in a magazine and circulated as a postcard by abolitionists—an early example of photographs used as propaganda.

In this infamous case, Chief Justice Roger Taney, from Tennessee, stated that blacks, whether slave or free, were not citizens and were, in fact, "so far inferior that they had no rights which the white man was bound to respect." Taney could have stopped here—if Scott wasn't a citizen, he couldn't sue in federal court at the time—but Taney went on to declare that Congress had no power to control slavery in the territories. This meant that slavery could extend into the territories that Congress had declared free. It also raised the possibility that slavery might extend into the states that had prohibited it.

By this time, slavery had become the hottest controversy in American politics, and this decision fanned the flames. It provoked vehement opposition in the North and produced bitter polarization in the country, leading to the Civil War. Today it is cited among the worst decisions ever made by the Supreme Court. (Yet three decades earlier, Taney had freed

American Diversity

Black Masters, Red Masters

Although most slave owners were white, some were black and some were red. In the South, as many as 3700 were black.[1] William Ellison of South Carolina was one. Born a slave, he bought his freedom and then his family's by building and repairing cotton gins. Over time, he earned enough money to buy slaves himself and operate a plantation. With sixty-three slaves, Ellison ranked in the top 3 percent of all slaveholders, black or white. Ellison was unusual, but he was not unique. In Charleston, South Carolina, alone, more than one hundred African Americans owned slaves in 1860. Most black owners, however, had fewer than four slaves.[2]

Some black slaveholders showed little sign that they shared the concerns of black slaves. Indeed, Ellison freed none of his slaves.

As a member of the slave-owning class, Ellison was allowed to sue a white man who didn't pay his bills (and even to win the case), and Ellison's family was granted a pew on the main floor of the Episcopal church. Yet in most respects the black owners weren't seen as equals by whites. They were expected to maintain the norms of black-white relations, especially to act deferentially toward whites.

As the Civil War approached, whites increasingly viewed free blacks, even slaveholders, as a threat to the established order, and state legislatures passed harsh legislation to regulate free blacks. For example, they had to have a white "guardian" to vouch for their moral character, and they had to carry special papers to prove their free status. Without these papers, they could be sold back into slavery.

The southeastern Indian tribes also adopted the practice of slavery. By 1820, they were buying and selling slaves in the markets and stealing slaves from other tribes. As a result, runaway slaves could no longer find refuge in Indian villages. By the time of the Civil War, the Cherokees, who were considered the "most civilized" of the southeastern Indians, owned four thousand black slaves and joined the Confederacy against the Union.

Several factors led to Indians' adoption of this practice. Outnumbered by both blacks and Indians, southern whites fostered hostility between the two groups to prevent them from joining forces. For example, white owners told their slaves hair-raising stories about Indian cruelty, and at times they armed their slaves to kill local Indians. Yet they also paid the Indians to capture escaped slaves. In addition, white missionaries who brought Christianity to the Indians were slaveholders themselves, and federal agents who implemented government policies toward the tribes encouraged the tribes to emulate white farmers and thus become assimilated and "civilized." Of course, the most visible agriculture was the plantation system with slave labor.

Dominated by whites, Indians saw slavery as an opportunity to rank higher than at least one group—black slaves—in the racial hierarchy. Indeed, although Indian masters initially weren't as brutal as white masters, they eventually treated their slaves as badly as whites did.[3]

---

[1] Loren Schweninger, *Black Property Owners in the South, 1790–1915* (Urbana: University of Illinois Press, 1990), cited in David Brion Davis, *Inhuman Bondage: The Rise and Fall of Slavery in the New World* (New York: Oxford University Press, 2006), 373, n. 17.

[2] For an acclaimed novel exploring the moral intricacies for black slave owners, read Edward P. Jones, *The Known World* (New York: Amistad, 2003).

[3] The Seminoles apparently were an exception. They required slaves to pay a nominal tribute but otherwise allowed them to run their own lives.

Sources: Michael Johnson and James L. Roark, *Black Masters* (New York: Norton, 1984); William McLoughlin, *The Cherokee Ghost Dance: Essays on the Southeastern Indians, 1789–1861* (Macon, Ga.: Mercer University Press, 1984), 261–283.

---

children of former slaves. But the army didn't have enough troops in the region to maintain Reconstruction policies. And in state after state, the South resisted.[17]

Eventually, the North capitulated. The 1876 presidential election between Republican Rutherford Hayes and Democrat Samuel Tilden was disputed in some states. To resolve the dispute, Republicans, most of whom were northerners, and Democrats, many of whom were southerners, agreed to a compromise: Hayes would be named president, and the remaining Union troops would be removed from the

South. Without Union troops, there was no way to enforce Reconstruction policies.

The collapse of Reconstruction limited the impact of the Civil War. In effect, the South was allowed to nullify one result of the war—granting legal and political rights to blacks—in exchange for accepting two other results—preserving the Union and abolishing slavery.

In hindsight, it isn't surprising that Reconstruction didn't accomplish more. It was difficult, if not impossible, to integrate 4 million former slaves into a society that was bitter in its defeat and weak economically. Northerners who expected progress to come smoothly were naive. When it didn't come quickly, they grew weary. At the same time, there was a desire for healing between the regions and lingering feelings for continuity with the past.

Public attitudes during Reconstruction thus began a recurring cycle that continues to this day: periodically the public gets upset about the treatment of African Americans and is determined to improve their conditions. But the public is naive and impatient, and when the efforts don't produce the results it expects as soon as it expects, the public becomes disillusioned with the efforts and dissatisfied with their costs. Then the public forces the government to put the race problem on the back burner until some future generation picks it up again.[18]

Neoslavery

Despite the outcome of the Civil War and the passage of the Thirteenth Amendment, many southern blacks were subjected to **neoslavery**, which entailed new forms of slavery or near slavery.

One type of neoslavery was **sharecropping**. After the war, Congress had rejected proposals to break up the plantations and give former slaves "forty acres and a mule" or to provide aid to establish schools. Without land or education,

the former slaves had to work for their former masters as hired hands, or sharecroppers. They were dependent on the landowners, who had designed a system to bind the workers to the plantations. A landowner contracted with former slaves to work on his fields and live at his plantation. The sharecroppers were allowed to sell half of their crop to the landowner and keep the proceeds, but they were paid so little, regardless of how hard they worked, that they had to borrow to survive the winter. The next year, they had to work for the same landowner to pay off their debts. The cycle continued, year after year. And lacking education, most sharecroppers didn't keep any records, so they didn't know how much they were owed, and many were cheated.

Another type of neoslavery was even harsher. Landowners or factory owners who needed more workers conspired with local officials to charge black men with minor crimes, such as vagrancy, gambling, "selling cotton after sunset," or changing employers without permission.[19] The men would be tried, convicted, and fined more than they could afford, so they would be jailed. Then they would be leased to local plantations, mines, mills, lumber camps, turpentine camps, brick companies, or steel factories to work off their fines. The arrest rates seemed to fluctuate according to the labor needs of the local businesses. (Some factories owned by northern corporations also benefited from this scheme.)[20]

Black men and boys were arrested and used like slave laborers for local landowners and factory owners. This boy is being punished in a forced labor camp in Georgia in the 1930s.

The prisoners were guarded—some were shackled to their bed at night—and many were worked to their death. One, convicted of "gaming" in 1903, was leased to a mine. His fine could be worked off in 10 days, but his "fees" to the sheriff, court clerk, and the witnesses at his trial required 104 more days. He didn't survive long enough to be released.

This industrial servitude was pervasive in rural Alabama and common in other southern states. It continued until the mid-1940s.

Segregation

In both the South and the North, blacks became segregated from whites.

Segregation in the South   As already mentioned, the reconciliation between Republicans and Democrats—northerners and southerners—was effected at the expense of blacks. Removing the troops enabled the South to govern itself again, and the former slave states used this opportunity to establish segregation.

Before the Civil War, there was no segregation in rural areas, where slaves' shacks sat near plantation mansions, or in urban areas, where few blocks were solidly black. Segregation would have been inconvenient, with blacks and whites working in proximity, and it would have been unnecessary—slavery itself kept blacks at the bottom of society. But after slavery was abolished, southerners established segregation as a new way to keep blacks "in their place."

By the turn of the century, the southern states had established a pervasive pattern of **Jim Crow laws** that segregated city blocks or whole neighborhoods.[21] Some small towns excluded blacks altogether, either by passing explicit laws or by adopting **sundown laws**, which required blacks to be off the streets by 10 p.m. Other Jim Crow laws segregated schools, which blacks had been allowed to attend during Reconstruction, and even textbooks: black schools' texts had to be stored separately from white schools' books. Many laws also segregated public accommodations, such as hotels, restaurants, bars, theaters, and streetcars. Others segregated sporting events, circuses, and parks. They separated black and white checkers players in Birmingham and districts for black and white prostitutes in New Orleans.

The laws were pervasive, segregating entrances, exits, ticket windows, waiting rooms, restrooms, and drinking fountains. They segregated the races in prisons, hospitals, and homes for the blind. They even segregated the races in death—in morgues, funeral homes, and cemeteries.

Although blacks were denied access to better locations or facilities, the greatest damage from segregation was that they were degraded. The system of Jim Crow laws was "an officially organized degradation ceremony, repeated day after day." Segregation told blacks that they were inferior and did not belong in the communities in which they lived.[22]

At the same time, segregation told poor whites that they were superior at least to the blacks. Thus segregation drove a wedge between poor whites and poor blacks (the former slaves) so they would be less likely to form an alliance, based on economic interests, that could challenge the power of the white elite.[23]

In addition to the laws, blacks were forced to defer to whites in informal settings as well—for instance, to move off the sidewalk when a white pedestrian approached. Failure to defer could bring punishment for being "uppity." Blacks were "humiliated by a thousand daily reminders of their subordination."[24]

Meanwhile, northern leaders, who had championed the cause of the slaves before and during the Civil War, abandoned African Americans a decade after the war. Congress declined to pass new laws, presidents refused to enforce existing laws, and the Supreme Court gutted the constitutional amendments and Civil Rights Acts.[25]

Then the Court upheld segregation itself. When Louisiana passed "an Act to promote the comfort of passengers," which mandated separate accommodations in trains, New Orleans black leaders sponsored a test case challenging the act's constitutionality. Homer Adolph Plessy, who was seven-eighths white—an "octoroon" in the parlance of the time—nonetheless was considered black, and he sat in the white car. When the conductor ordered him to move to the black car, Plessy refused, maintaining that the act was unconstitutional under the Fourteenth Amendment. In **Plessy v. Ferguson** in 1896, the Court disagreed, claiming that the act was not a denial of equal protection because it provided equal accommodations.[26] The Court established the **separate-but-equal doctrine**, which allowed separate facilities if they were "equal." Of course, government required separate facilities only because people thought the races were not equal, but the Court brazenly commented that the act did not stamp "the colored race with a badge of inferiority" unless "the colored race chooses to put that construction on it." Only Justice John Harlan, a former Kentucky slaveholder, dissented: "Our Constitution is color-blind, and neither knows nor tolerates classes among citizens."

Three years later, the Court accepted segregation in schools.[27] A Georgia school board turned a black high school into a black elementary school without establishing a new high school for blacks or allowing them to attend the existing high schools for whites. Nevertheless, the Court said this action was not a denial of equal protection. Its ruling set a pattern in which "separate but equal" meant separation but not equality.

Segregation in the North   Although Jim Crow laws were not as pervasive in the North as in the South, they were quite common.[28] In fact, sundown laws were more prevalent in the North, especially in the Midwest. In the 1930s, Hawthorne, California, posted a sign at its city limits: "Nigger, Don't Let The Sun Set On YOU In Hawthorne."[29] Jim Crow laws in the northern states prompted one writer to proclaim, "The North has surrendered!"[30]

Yet job opportunities were better in the North. While southern blacks were sharecropping—as late as 1930, 80 percent of those who farmed were working somebody else's land[31]—northern factories were offering jobs. Between 1915 and 1940, more than a million southern blacks headed north in the **Great Migration**.[32] Although they got decent jobs, they were forced to live in black ghettos because they couldn't afford better housing and they weren't allowed to live in some areas.

Denial of the Right to Vote

With the adoption of the Fifteenth Amendment, many African Americans voted and elected fellow African Americans to office during Reconstruction, but southern states began to disfranchise them in the 1890s (as explained in Chapter 8).

Violence

To solidify their control, whites engaged in violence against blacks. In the 1880s and 1890s, whites lynched about one hundred blacks a year, and vigilante "justice" continued in the 1900s (see Table 1). For example, a mob in Livermore, Kentucky, dragged a black man accused of murdering a white man into a theater. The ringleaders charged admission and hanged the man. Then they allowed the audience to shoot at the swinging body—those in the balcony could fire once; those in the better seats could empty their revolvers.[33]

Table 1   Why Whites Lynched Blacks in 1907

Whites gave the following reasons for lynching blacks, who may or may not have committed the acts cited.

REASON	NUMBER OF LYNCHINGS
Murder	5
Attempted murder	5
Manslaughter	10
Rape	9
Attempted rape	11
Burglary	3
Harboring a fugitive	1
Theft of 75 cents	1
Having a debt of $3	2
Winning a fight with a white man	1
Insulting a white man	1
Talking to white girls on the telephone	1
Being the wife or son of a rapist	2
Being the father of a boy who "jostled" white women	1
Expressing sympathy for the victim of mob violence	3

SOURCE: Adapted from Ray Stannard Baker, *Following the Color Line* (New York: Harper & Row, 1964), 176–177.

Lynchings often began with a false report of a white woman being sexually assaulted by a black man. An irate mob would gather and, after locating the man, sometimes already in jail, would subject him to an excruciating ordeal of beating and torture. Usually, they castrated him before they killed him. Frequently, they hacked off his fingers and ears as well.[34]

Lynchings were not the result of a few troublemakers; rather, they were a social institution in the South. The ritualized spectacles were a desperate attempt to cling to the antebellum order upset by the Civil War. At the same time, lynchings were related to the increase in white women who worked outside the home at the turn of the century. As these women experienced greater independence, insecure men feared that they would become too independent, perhaps even leave them for black men. Hence the ritual of castration.[35] Through lynchings, then, white men could remain in charge—at home and in the community—while appearing to defend women's honor.

Lynchings were considered entertaining as well as essential to maintain the racial order. They would be photographed and, later, postcards would be sold (though after 1907, postal regulations banned them from the mail). Many of the photographs show gleeful crowds around the body of the person lynched.

Whites engaged in other forms of violence as well. In 1919, twenty-five race riots erupted in six months. White mobs took over cities in the North and South, burning black neighborhoods and terrorizing black residents for days on end.[36] In 1921, ten thousand whites burned down thirty-five blocks of Tulsa's black neighborhood. The incident that precipitated the riot was typical—a report of an assault by a black man on a white woman. The report was false, fabricated by the woman (and later retracted), but residents were inflamed by a racist newspaper and encouraged by the city's officials. Almost three hundred people were shot, burned alive, or tied to cars and dragged to death. Survivors reported corpses stacked like firewood on street corners and piled high in dump trucks.[37]

The white-supremacist **Ku Klux Klan**, which began during Reconstruction and started up again in 1915, played a major role in inflaming prejudice and terrorizing blacks. It was strong enough to dominate many southern towns and even the state governments of Oklahoma and Texas. It also made inroads into some northern states, such as Indiana, Ohio, and Pennsylvania.[38]

In addition, bands of white farmers known as "Whitecaps" nailed notes, with a drawing of a coffin and a warning to leave or die, on the doors of black farmers. Their goal was to drive black farmers off the land. Then the local governments put the land up for auction or simply gave it to the white families who owned the adjacent land.[39] The impact of this intimidation continued for many generations and, in fact, continues to this day. The black families lost wealth for themselves and their descendants, and the white families gained wealth that is appreciating in value for their descendants today, many of whom may be unaware of how "their" land changed hands.

Lynching occurred not only in the South but also in northern cities such as Marion, Indiana, in 1930. The girls on the left hold pieces of the victims' clothing, torn off as "souvenirs."

Despite all this violence and injustice, federal officials contended that racial violence was a state problem. Presidents refused to speak out, and Congress refused to pass legislation making lynching a federal offense—yet state officials did nothing. For at least the first third of the twentieth century, white supremacy reigned, not just in the southern states but also in the border states and in many northern states. It also pervaded the nation's capital, where President Woodrow Wilson instituted segregation in the federal government.[40]

Overcoming Discrimination against African Americans

African Americans fought white supremacy primarily in three arenas: the courts, the streets, and Congress. In general, they fought in the courts first and Congress last, although as they gained momentum they increasingly fought in all three arenas at once.

The Movement in the Courts
The first goal was to convince the Supreme Court to overturn the separate-but-equal doctrine of *Plessy* v. *Ferguson*.

The NAACP   In response to racial violence, a group of blacks and whites founded the National Association for the Advancement of Colored People, or **NAACP**, in 1909. In its first two decades, it was led by W. E. B. Du Bois, a black sociologist. In time, it became the major organization fighting for blacks' civil rights.

Frustrated by presidential and congressional inaction, the NAACP decided to appeal to the courts, which are less subject to political pressure from the majority. The association assembled a cadre of lawyers, mainly from Howard University Law School, a historically black school in Washington, D.C., to bring lawsuits attacking segregation and the denial of the right to vote. In 1915, they persuaded the Supreme Court to strike down the grandfather clause (which exempted persons whose ancestors could vote from the literacy test);[41] two years later, they convinced the Court to invalidate residential segregation laws.[42] But the Court continued to allow most devices to disfranchise blacks and most efforts to segregate.

In 1938, the NAACP chose a thirty-year-old attorney, Thurgood Marshall, to head its litigation arm.[43] Marshall—whose mother had to pawn her engagement and wedding rings so he could go to an out-of-state law school because his in-state school, the University of Maryland, didn't admit blacks—would become a tireless and courageous advocate for equal rights. (In 1946, after defending four blacks charged with attempted murder during a riot in rural Tennessee, he would narrowly escape a lynch mob himself.)[44]

Desegregation of schools   In the mid-twentieth century, seventeen states and the District of Columbia segregated their schools (and four other states allowed cities to segregate their schools). The states gave white students better facilities and white teachers larger salaries. Overall, they spent from two to ten times more on white schools than on black ones.[45] These states provided few graduate schools for blacks. As late as 1950, they had fifteen engineering schools, fourteen

Tulsa's black neighborhood smolders after whites burned it down in 1921.

medical schools, and five dental schools for whites and none for blacks; they had sixteen law schools for whites and five for blacks.

The NAACP's tactics were first to show that "separate but equal" actually resulted in unequal schools and then, attacking the concept head-on, to argue that "separate but equal" led to unequal status in general.

The NAACP challenged segregation in graduate schools. It got the Supreme Court to require these states to provide more grad schools for black students or to admit black students to the white schools.[46] Then it got the Court to require the schools for black students to be equal to the schools for white students.[47] In these decisions, the Court did not invalidate the separate-but-equal doctrine but made segregation almost impossible to implement in graduate schools.

The NAACP then turned its attention to the lower levels of the school system. Marshall filed suits in two southern states, one border state, one northern state, and the District of Columbia. The suit in the northern state was brought against Topeka, Kansas, where Linda Brown could not attend the school just four blocks from her home because it was a white school. Instead, she had to go to a school twenty-one blocks away.[48]

When these cases reached the Supreme Court, the justices were split. Although Chief Justice Fred Vinson might have had a majority to uphold the separate-but-equal doctrine, the Court put off a decision and rescheduled oral arguments for its next term. Between the Court's terms, Vinson suffered a heart attack, and President Dwight Eisenhower appointed Earl Warren to take his place. When the Court

reheard the case, the president pressured his appointee to rule in favor of segregation. Eisenhower invited Warren and the attorney for the states to the White House for dinner. When the conversation turned to the segregationists, Eisenhower said, "These are not bad people. All they are concerned about is to see that their sweet little girls are not required to sit in schools alongside some big overgrown Negroes."[49] However, Warren would not only vote against segregation but would also use his considerable determination and charm to persuade the other justices to vote against it too. Later, Justice Felix Frankfurter said that Vinson's heart attack was "the first indication I have ever had that there is a God."[50]

In the landmark case of **Brown v. Board of Education** in 1954, the Warren Court ruled unanimously that school segregation violated the Fourteenth Amendment's equal protection clause.[51] In the opinion, Warren asserted that the separate-but-equal doctrine produced unequal schools and also was inherently unequal because it made black children feel inferior.

In overruling the *Plessy* doctrine, the Court showed how revolutionary the equal protection clause was. The Court required the segregated states to change their way of life to a degree unprecedented in American history. (See box "The Social Code.") After overturning laws requiring segregation in schools, the Court overruled laws mandating segregation in other places, such as public parks, golf courses, swimming pools, auditoriums, courtrooms, and jails.[52]

In *Brown*, the Court had ordered the schools to desegregate "with all deliberate speed."[53] This standard was a compromise between justices who thought schools should do

BEHIND THE SCENES

The Social Code

At the time the Supreme Court was deciding *Brown* v. *Board of Education,* a strict social code governed interactions between blacks and whites in the South. The code, which differed from place to place, was barely visible yet clearly understood by residents and very effective in keeping blacks "in their place"—and discouraging sympathetic whites from challenging the norms.

The experience of one white woman who had moved from the North to Alabama in the 1950s illustrates how the code worked. While shopping, the woman accidentally bumped into a black woman, causing her to drop her packages. The white woman picked up the packages and handed them to her. After this courtesy, the store clerks, while making no comments, refused to wait on the white woman. In another store on another day, the white woman and her daughter were shopping when a black child offered her daughter a piece of candy. After her daughter accepted the candy, these clerks also refused to wait on the woman.

SOURCE: Tinsley E. Yarbrough, *Race and Redistricting: The Shaw-Cromartie Cases* (Lawrence: University Press of Kansas, 2003), 30.

so immediately and those who thought communities would need to do so gradually.[54] The ambiguity of the phrase, however, delayed the implementation of the ruling.

The South engaged in massive resistance. The Court needed help from the other branches, but southerners controlled Congress and President Eisenhower criticized the decision. With his power and popularity, he could have speeded implementation by speaking out in support of the ruling, yet he offered no help for three years. When nine black students tried to attend a white high school under a desegregation plan in Little Rock, Arkansas, the governor's and state legislature's inflammatory rhetoric against desegregation encouraged local citizens to stage a riot. Finally, Eisenhower acted, sending federal troops and federalizing the state's National Guard to quell the violence.

President Kennedy also used federal marshals and paratroopers to stop the violence after the governor of Mississippi blocked the door to keep James Meredith from registering at the University of Mississippi. Kennedy again sent troops when the governor of Alabama, George Wallace, proclaiming "segregation now, segregation tomorrow, segregation forever," blocked the door to keep blacks from enrolling at the University of Alabama.

After trying outright defiance, some states attempted to circumvent the ruling by shutting down their public schools and providing tuition grants, textbooks, and recreation facilities for students to use at new private schools, which at the time could segregate. The states also tried less blatant schemes, such as "freedom of choice" plans that allowed students to choose the school they wanted to attend. Of course, virtually no whites chose a black school, and due to social pressure very few blacks chose a white school. The idea was to achieve desegregation on paper, or token desegregation in practice, in order to avoid actual desegregation. But the Court rebuffed these schemes and even forbade private schools from discriminating.[55]

To black southerners, the Court's persistence raised hopes. Chief Justice Warren, according to Thurgood Marshall, "allowed the poor Negro sharecropper to say, 'Kick me around Mr. Sheriff, kick me around Mr. County Judge, kick me around Supreme Court of my state, but there's one person I can rely on.'"[56]

To white southerners, however, the Court's rulings reflected a federal government, a distant authority, that exercised too much control over their traditional practices. The rulings engendered intense bitterness. Justice Hugo Black, who was from Alabama, was shunned by former friends from the state, and his son was driven from his legal practice in the state. Years later, the justice wasn't even sent an invitation to his fiftieth reunion at his alma mater, the University of Alabama.[57]

The segregationists tried to resist, then to evade, and finally to delay. In this they succeeded. In 1964, a decade after *Brown,* 98 percent of all black children in the South still attended all-black schools.[58]

By this time, however, the mood in Congress had changed. Congress passed the Civil Rights Act of 1964, which, among other things, cut off federal aid to school districts that continued to segregate. The following year, it passed the first major program providing federal aid to education. This was the carrot at the end of the stick; school districts complied to get the money.

 Thinking about Democracy

Does the role of the Supreme Court in the civil rights era reflect or contradict the concept of democracy? That is, was it democratic for the nonelected justices to mandate equality to the elected officials of the southern states and cities? (Consider the tension between popular sovereignty and political equality and that between majority rule and minority rights.)

Finally, by 1970, only 14 percent of all black children in the South still attended all-black schools. Of course, many others went to mostly black schools. Even so, the change was dramatic.

Busing   *Brown* and related rulings addressed **de jure segregation**—segregation enforced by law—which can be attacked by striking down the law. *Brown* didn't address **de facto segregation**—segregation based on residential patterns.

The first day for desegregated schools in Fort Myer, Virginia, brings apprehension and curiosity.

This segregation was typical of northern cities and large southern cities, where most blacks lived in black neighborhoods and most whites lived in white neighborhoods. Students attended their neighborhood schools, which were mostly black or mostly white. This segregation was more intractable because, for the most part, it didn't stem from particular laws, so it couldn't be eliminated by striking down any laws.

To address de facto segregation, civil rights groups proposed busing some black children to schools in white neighborhoods and some white children to schools in black neighborhoods. They hoped to improve black children's education, their self-confidence, and eventually, their college and career opportunities. They also hoped to improve black and white children's ability to get along together.

The Burger Court, which succeeded the Warren Court, authorized busing within school districts—ordinarily cities. These included southern cities where there was a history of de jure segregation and northern cities where there was a pattern of de facto segregation and evidence that school officials had located schools or assigned students in ways that perpetuated this segregation.[59] However, busing for desegregation was never extensive. In one typical year, only 4 percent of students were bused for desegregation. Far more students were bused, at public expense, to segregated public and private schools.[60]

Even so, court orders for mandatory busing ran into a wall of opposition from white parents. Their reaction stemmed from a mixture of prejudice against black people, bias against poor persons, fear of the crime in inner-city schools, worry about the quality of inner-city schools, and desire for the convenience of neighborhood schools.[61]

Because of the opposition of white parents, busing—and publicity about it—prompted an increase in "white flight" as white families moved from public schools to private schools and from the cities to the suburbs to avoid the busing in the cities.[62] This trend overlapped other trends that altered the racial and economic composition of our big cities, especially a reduction in the white birthrate and an increase in the nonwhite immigration rate. As a result, there were fewer white students to balance enrollments and fewer middle-class students to provide stability in the cities' schools.

Therefore, even extensive busing couldn't desegregate the school systems of most big cities, where blacks and other minorities together were more numerous than whites. Consequently, civil rights groups proposed busing some white children from the suburbs to the cities and some black children from the cities to the suburbs. This approach would provide enough of both races to achieve balance in both places.

The Burger Court rejected this proposal by a 5–4 vote in 1974.[63] It ruled that busing isn't appropriate between school districts unless there is evidence of intentional segregation in both the city and its suburbs. Otherwise, such extensive busing would require too long a ride for students and too much coordination by administrators. Although there was intentional segregation by many cities and their suburbs,[64] the evidence was not as clear-cut as the de jure segregation by the southern states, so it was difficult to satisfy the requirements laid down by the Court. The ruling made busing between the cities and their suburbs very rare.

Thurgood Marshall, by then a Supreme Court justice, dissented and predicted that the ruling would allow "our great metropolitan areas to be divided up each into two cities—one white, the other black." Indeed, the ruling was the beginning of the end of the push to desegregate public schools in urban areas.

In 1991, the Rehnquist Court, which succeeded the Burger Court, ruled that school districts have no obligation to reduce de facto segregation. The Court also diminished their obligation to reduce the vestiges of de jure segregation.[65] This ruling relieved the pressure on school districts, and most stopped busing.[66] The result was increasing resegregation.

Some districts tried other ways to balance enrollments. The county that includes Louisville, Kentucky, voluntarily adopted a "managed choice" program in which parents indicated their preference for their children's schools, but the school district kept the black enrollment in each school between 15 and 50 percent through extensive busing. Yet the plan was popular with most parents, including white parents, who got their first or second choice of schools.[67] Louisville became one of the most desegregated cities in the nation. In 2007, however, the Roberts Court, which succeeded the Rehnquist Court, invalidated the Louisville program and a limited program in Seattle.[68] The five-justice majority ruled that school districts can't use race as a basis for assigning students. The ruling jeopardized the programs in a thousand school districts across the country.[69]

The Court's decisions in the 1990s and 2000s reflect none of "the moral urgency of *Brown*."[70] Instead, they reflect hostility toward government efforts, even school districts' voluntary efforts, to achieve desegregation. For most justices, desegregation is relatively unimportant, certainly less important than allowing white parents unfettered choice where they send their children. In this way, the Court's majority mirrors the views of the Republican presidents who appointed them.

Some districts have tried to integrate the races by integrating social classes. Because black students disproportionately come from the lower classes, assigning a percentage of poor students to middle-class schools would also integrate the races to some degree. This may require students to attend schools far from home and ride buses for long distances. But Raleigh, North Carolina, which used this approach, saw a dramatic improvement in poor students' performance (along with gains in other students' performance).[71] Such plans, based on class, aren't likely to be overruled by the courts because they aren't based, at least directly, on race. Yet these plans, too, have been opposed by white parents. In Raleigh, which was the model for other cities, a new school board halted its plan in 2010.

The Movement in the Streets

After the NAACP's early successes in the courts, other blacks, and some whites, took the fight to the streets. Their bold efforts gave birth to the modern civil rights movement.

The movement came to public attention in Montgomery, Alabama, in 1955, when Rosa Parks refused to move to the back of the bus. Her courage, and her arrest, roused others to boycott city buses. For their leader they chose a young Baptist minister, Dr. Martin Luther King Jr. The boycott catapulted

the movement and King to national attention (as explained in Chapter 6).

As the first charismatic leader of the movement, King formed the Southern Christian Leadership Conference (SCLC) of black clergy and adopted the tactics of Mahatma Gandhi, who had led the movement to free India from Britain. The tactics included direct action, such as demonstrations and marches, and civil disobedience—intentional and public disobedience of unjust laws. The tactics were based on nonviolence, even when confronted with violence. This strategy was designed to draw support from whites by contrasting the morality of the movement's position with the immorality of the opponents' discrimination and violence toward blacks.

For a long time, southern whites deluded themselves into thinking that "outside agitators"—northerners or communists—were responsible for the turmoil in their communities.[72] But the movement grew from the grassroots and eventually shattered this delusion.

The movement spread among black students. In 1960, four students of North Carolina A&T College sat at the lunch counter in Woolworth's, a chain of dime stores, and asked for a cup of coffee. The waitress refused to serve them, but they remained until they were arrested. On successive days, more students sat at the lunch counter, as whites jeered and waved the Confederate flag.[73] Within a year, sit-ins occurred in more than one hundred cities.

When blacks asserted their rights, whites often reacted with violence. In 1963, King led demonstrators in Birmingham, Alabama, seeking desegregation of public facilities. Police unleashed dogs to attack the marchers. In 1964,

Dorothy Counts, the first black student to attend one white high school in Charlotte, North Carolina, is escorted by her father in 1957.

Firefighters turn their hoses on demonstrators in Birmingham, Alabama, in 1963.

King led demonstrators in Selma, Alabama, for voting rights. State troopers clubbed some marchers, and vigilantes beat and shot others.

In the summer of 1964, black and white college students mounted a voter registration drive in Mississippi. By the end of the summer, 1000 had been arrested, 80 beaten, 35 shot, and 6 killed.[74] When a black cotton farmer, trying to register to vote, was shot in the head in broad daylight by a white state legislator, the act wasn't even treated as a crime.[75]

Perpetrators of the violence usually were not apprehended or prosecuted. When they were, they usually were not convicted. Law enforcement was frequently in the hands of bigots, and juries were normally all white.[76]

During these years, whites told pollsters they disliked the civil rights movement's speed and tactics: "They're pushing too fast and too hard." At the same time, most said they favored integration more than ever. And they seemed repelled by the violence. The brutality against black demonstrators generated more support for black Americans and their cause.

The media, especially national organizations based in northern cities such as the *New York Times*, the Associated Press, and the major television networks, played a role simply by covering the conflict. The leaders of the civil rights movement staged events that captured attention, and violent racists played into their hands. As northern reporters and photographers relayed the events and violence to the nation, the movement gained public sympathy in the North. Yet the national press became as vilified as the federal government in the South. (This anger would fuel southerners' distrust of the media for many years.)[77]

Although the movement's tactics worked well against southern de jure segregation, they didn't work as well against northern de facto segregation or against job discrimination in either region. By the mid-1960s, progress had stalled and dissatisfaction had grown. Young blacks from the inner city, who

hadn't been involved in the movement, questioned two of its principles: inter-racialism and nonviolence. As James Farmer, head of the Congress of Racial Equality (CORE), explained, they asked, "What is this we-shall-overcome, black-and-white-together stuff? I don't know of any white folks except the guy who runs that store on 125th Street in Harlem and garnishes wages and repossesses things you buy. I'd like to go upside his head. [Or] the rent collector, who bangs on the door demanding rent that we ain't got. I'd like to go upside his head."[78] These blacks criticized King and his tactics.

In place of the integration advocated by King, some leaders began to call for "black power." This phrase, which implied black pride and self-reliance, meant different things to different people. To some it meant political power through the ballot box, and to others it meant economic power through business ownership. To a few it meant violence in retaliation for violence by whites. The movement splintered further.

The Movement in Congress

As the civil rights movement expanded, it pressured presidents and members of Congress to act. President John Kennedy, who was most concerned about the Cold War, considered civil rights a distraction. President Lyndon Johnson, who was a champion of "the poor and the downtrodden and the oppressed"—a biographer calls him our second most compassionate president, after Abraham Lincoln[79]—supported civil rights but felt hamstrung by southerners in Congress who, through the seniority system, chaired key committees and dominated both houses. As a result, the presidents considered the civil rights leaders unreasonable, because their movement alienated the southerners on whom the presidents had to rely for other legislation.

However, once the movement demonstrated real strength, it convinced officials to act. After 200,000 blacks and whites marched in Washington in 1963, President Kennedy

Yoichi R. Okamoto/Courtesy LBJ Library

President Lyndon Johnson and Martin Luther King Jr., compatriots with a tense relationship.

introduced civil rights legislation. After Kennedy's assassination, his successor, President Johnson, with consummate legislative skill, forged a coalition of northern Democrats and northern Republicans to overcome southern Democrats and pass the Civil Rights Act of 1964. Then Johnson pushed through the Voting Rights Act of 1965 and the Civil Rights Act of 1968. These acts prohibited discrimination in public accommodations, employment, voting, and housing. Passed within a span of four years, they would become the most significant civil rights acts in American history.

Today it is hard to imagine how controversial these laws were at the time. In 1964, the Republican nominee for president, Sen. Barry Goldwater of Arizona, opposed the Civil Rights Act. He had been assured by two advisers—Phoenix attorney William Rehnquist and Yale professor Robert Bork—that it was unconstitutional.[80] The conservative Republican Ronald Reagan, preparing to run for California governor, also strongly opposed the act.[81] The opponents called the bill "a usurpation of states' rights" and claimed that it would create "a federal dictatorship." They also claimed that it would "destroy the free enterprise system."[82] (Years later, as president, Reagan would appoint Rehnquist as the chief justice and nominate Bork as an associate justice on the Supreme Court. Bork wasn't confirmed, in part because of his views toward civil rights laws and rulings.)

Although President Johnson believed he was doing the right thing, he realized the political ramifications. In pushing for civil rights, he said he was handing the South to the

Republican Party "for the next fifty years."[83] And that's exactly what happened. In less than a decade, the South went from the nation's most Democratic region to one of the most Republican.[84]

After the 1966 congressional elections, when it was evident that the party was losing southern voters, Democratic governors in southern and border states demanded a meeting with Johnson. They criticized administration efforts to desegregate the schools and even suggested that the president was a traitor to his heritage. The next day Johnson was still fuming. To an aide he vented, "'Niggah! Niggah! Niggah!' That's all they said to me all day. Hell, there's one thing they'd better know. If I don't achieve anything else while I'm president, I intend to wipe that word out of the English language and make it impossible for people to come here and shout 'Niggah! Niggah! Niggah!' to me and the American people."[85]

Desegregation of public accommodations   The **Civil Rights Act of 1964** prohibits discrimination on the basis of race, color, religion, or national origin in public accommodations.[86] The act doesn't cover private clubs, such as country clubs, social clubs, or fraternities and sororities, on the principle that the government shouldn't tell people who they may or may not associate with in private. (The Court has made private schools an exception to this principle to help enforce *Brown*, so they can't discriminate.)

Desegregation of employment   The Civil Rights Act of 1964 also prohibits employment discrimination on the basis of race, color, religion, national origin, or sex and (as amended) age, physical disability, or Vietnam-era veteran status. The act covers employers with fifteen or more employees and unions.[87]

In addition to practicing blatant discrimination, some employers practiced more subtle discrimination by requiring applicants to meet standards unnecessary for the jobs, a practice that hindered blacks more than whites. A high school diploma for a manual job was a common example. The Supreme Court held that the standards must relate to the jobs.[88]

Desegregation of housing   Although the Supreme Court had struck down laws that prescribed segregation in residential areas, whites maintained segregation by making **restrictive covenants**—agreements among neighbors not to sell their houses to blacks. In 1948, the Court ruled that lower courts could not enforce these covenants because doing so would involve the government in discrimination.[89]

Real estate agents also played a role in segregation by practicing **steering**—showing blacks houses in black neighborhoods and whites houses in white neighborhoods. Unscrupulous real estate agents practiced **blockbusting**. After a black family bought a house in a white neighborhood, the agents would warn the white neighbors that more black families would move in. Because of prejudice and fear that their house values would decline, the whites would panic and sell to the agents at low prices. Then the agents would resell to black families at higher prices. In this way, neighborhoods that might have been desegregated were instead resegregated—from all white to all black.

Bank and savings and loan officers also played a role. Some refused to lend money to blacks who wanted to buy houses in white neighborhoods, and some, engaging in **redlining**, refused to lend money to people who wanted to buy houses in racially changing neighborhoods. The lenders worried that if the buyers couldn't keep up with the payments, the lenders would be left with houses whose value had declined.

The government also played an important role. The Veterans Administration and the Federal Housing Authority, which guaranteed loans to some buyers, were reluctant to authorize loans to blacks who tried to buy houses in white neighborhoods (but they did provide loans to whites who fled from the cities to buy houses in all-white suburbs). In addition, the federal government, which funded low-income housing, allowed local governments to locate such housing in ghettos. In these ways, the governments fostered and extended residential segregation.[90]

The **Civil Rights Act of 1968** bans discrimination in the sale or rental of housing on the basis of race, color, religion, or national origin and (as amended) on the basis of sex, having children, or having a disability. The act covers 80 percent of the housing in the United States and prohibits steering, blockbusting, and redlining.

Restoration of the right to vote   The Voting Rights Act of 1965, which implemented the Fifteenth Amendment, includes measures that enable blacks to vote (as explained in Chapter 8).

 ## Thinking about Democracy

> Consider the actions of the people who participated in the civil rights movement and the efforts by Congress during these years. In what ways do they reflect democracy?

Continuing Discrimination against African Americans

Although African Americans have overcome much discrimination, they still face lingering prejudice. Overt laws and blatant practices have been struck down, but subtle manifestations of old attitudes persist—and in ways far more numerous and with effects far more serious than this one chapter can convey.[91] Moreover, African Americans must cope with the legacy of generations of slavery, segregation, discrimination, and for many, the effects of poverty.

They must also cope with the attitudes of whites. Although few people say they want to return to the days of legal segregation, about half reject the dream of an integrated society.[92]

Discrimination in Education

Most black students attend segregated schools, and most schools for black students are unequal to the schools for white students.

Segregated schools   Some black children, especially those who have affluent parents who pay for private schools or live in well-off neighborhoods with good public schools, go to integrated schools. However, most black children who live in big cities or areas where private schools predominate go to segregated schools.

Although de jure segregation of schools has been eliminated, de facto segregation remains. In fact, this segregation is getting worse. After progress in the 1960s, 1970s, and 1980s, the trend toward desegregation reversed itself in the 1990s. "For the first time since the *Brown* v. *Board* decision," one study concluded, "we are going backwards"[93] (see Figure 1). Smaller percentages of black students and Latino students attend schools that have a majority of white students than at any time since 1968.[94] Almost 40 percent of black students and fully 40 percent of Latino students attend schools that are 90 to 100 percent minority.[95]

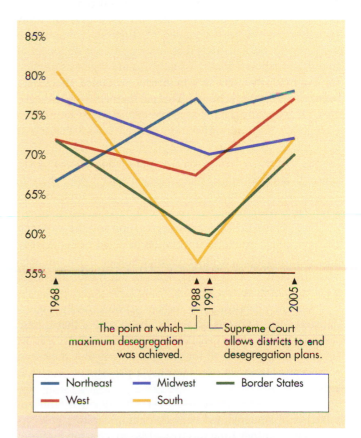

FIGURE 1: RESEGREGATION OF SCHOOLS Percentage of students attending predominantly minority schools (schools in which 50 to 100 percent of students are nonwhite).

SOURCE: Gary Orfield and Chungmei Lee, "Historic Reversals, Accelerating Resegregation, and the Need for New Integration Strategies," The Civil Rights Project, UCLA, August, 2007, 28. This report is based on data through 2005, which are the most current data available.

The segregation is worse in the North, where it has been de facto, than in the South, where it had been de jure.[96] The segregation is worse in big cities, but it is spreading to their suburbs, especially to the inner-ring suburbs where numerous minorities live now.[97]

This **resegregation** is due to white flight to private schools and to the suburbs, leaving fewer white children, and also due to higher nonwhite birthrates and immigration rates, bringing more nonwhite children to the public schools. These changes affect the decisions of white parents who look for schools with low numbers of racial minorities.[98] Although many say they move for "better schools," few ever visit the schools or check the schools' test scores before moving. They use racial composition as a proxy for school quality. The more racial minorities, the poorer the quality, they assume.[99]

This resegregation is also due to a shift in government policies and court decisions resulting from conservative dominance of American politics from 1980 through 2008. Conservative presidents, beginning with Ronald Reagan and continuing through George W. Bush, and conservative justices on the Supreme Court, especially on the Rehnquist and Roberts Courts, based their social policy decisions on the assumptions that "race should be ignored, inequalities should be blamed on individuals and schools, and existing civil rights remedies should be dismantled."[100] Their decisions sent a message to school districts that desegregation is no longer an important national goal.[101] Usually this message was implicit; for example, the Reagan administration ended the federal program that aided school districts in their efforts to desegregate. Occasionally the message was explicit; for example, the George W. Bush administration advised school districts to cut back on their efforts to desegregate.[102] In short, the three branches of the federal government have done "nothing significant" to foster school desegregation since 1981 (when the Reagan administration ended the federal program that aided school districts).[103]

The persistence of de facto segregation and the waning of society's commitment to integration have led national, state, and local officials to adopt a resigned attitude: "We still agree with the goal of school desegregation, but it's too hard, and we're tired of it, and we give up."[104]

Reforms proposed for urban schools rarely include desegregation. Officials speak of a ghetto school that is more "efficient" or one that gets more "input" from ghetto parents or offers more "choices" for ghetto children. But they seem to accept segregated education as "a permanent American reality."[105]

A writer who visited many central-city classrooms and talked with students, teachers, and administrators observed that Martin Luther King was treated as "an icon, but his vision of a nation in which black and white kids went to school together seemed to be effaced almost entirely. Dutiful references to 'The Dream' were often seen in school brochures and on wall posters in February, when 'Black History' was celebrated in the public schools, but the content of the dream was treated as a closed box that could not be opened without ruining the celebration."[106]

Indeed, many cities have a school named after King—a segregated school in a segregated neighborhood—"like a terrible joke on history," a fourteen-year-old, wise beyond her years, remarked.[107] In fact, if you want to find a school that's really segregated, look for schools named after champions of integration—Jackie Robinson, Rosa Parks, and Thurgood Marshall.[108]

The resegregation has consequences for the education of minority students. Those who attended desegregated schools were more likely to graduate from high school and to attend and graduate from college than those who attended segregated schools. Those who spent five years in desegregated schools now earn 25 percent more than those who did not. In their thirties and forties, they are also healthier—the equivalent of seven years younger—than their contemporaries who did not attend desegregated schools. Why? Desegregated schools spent more per pupil than segregated ones, so they offered smaller classes and better equipment. Their teachers had higher expectations, and their schools included students from better-off families who also fostered higher expectations. At the same time, the performance of white students in desegregated schools did not decline.[109]

Unequal schools   In areas where the schools are segregated, their quality varies enormously—from "the golden to the godawful," in the words of a Missouri judge.[110] And of course, blacks and Latinos are more likely to be in the "godawful" ones. By virtually every measure of school quality—school funding, class size, teacher credentials, teacher salaries, breadth of curriculum, number of computers, opportunities for gifted students—these black and Latino children attend worse schools.[111]

Public schools are financed largely by property taxes paid by homeowners and businesses. Wealthy districts in cities, where property costs more to buy and is assessed more in taxes, collect more in taxes than poor ones. In modern America, this means that suburban school districts have more to spend per pupil than central-city school districts.[112]

In about three-fourths of the states, school districts with the highest percentages of black and Latino children receive less funding than the districts with the fewest.[113] Nationwide, the difference amounts to $25,000 less per *classroom* per year for school districts with the most black and Latino children. In Illinois, the difference totals $47,000 less per classroom, and in New York, it totals $50,000 less.[114] And these official figures don't count the extra money that affluent parents, on their own or through PTAs, contribute to hire additional teachers to reduce class sizes or to provide art and music instruction, or to buy books for the library or equipment for the gym and playground.

Spending-per-pupil figures also don't take into account the fact that the needs of poor children, after years of neglect and with scores of problems in their homes and neighborhoods, are greater than the needs of other children. Schools for poor children would require *more* funding to provide their students an *equal* education.[115]

So, many inner-city schools are bleak institutions, filthy and in disrepair. A thirty-year veteran of seven District of

Columbia schools said all should be condemned. Of her current school, she said, "I have to cover books, computers, and student work stations with plastic to catch the falling plaster and water from the leaking roof. In the school cafeteria, 55-gallon garbage cans are strategically placed to catch the water from gaping holes in the ceiling."[116] Teachers in some Los Angeles schools said the children count the rats.[117]

Most inner-city schools are overcrowded. They lack up-to-date texts and paper and pencils. They lack books for literature classes, chemicals for chemistry classes, and computers for computer classes. (Teachers *talk* about using computers.)[118]

Most inner-city schools also can't attract enough good teachers. A New York City principal said he is forced to take the "tenth-best" teachers. "I thank God they're still breathing."[119] In Illinois, which measures the quality of its teachers, just 11 percent of the teachers in majority-white schools are in the lowest quartile of the teachers in the state, but 88 percent of the teachers in almost-all-minority schools are in the lowest quartile.[120] Yet the quality of its teachers might be the most important factor in the success of a school.[121]

Despite the pattern of unequal funding, cash alone wouldn't solve the problems of inner-city schools. Cultural and economic factors in these communities also limit the education provided. Minority children enter kindergarten behind their peers.[122] And minority students say their school is a more rowdy, disrespectful, and dangerous place, with more drugs, weapons, and fights, than white students report in their school.[123] Nevertheless, cash would help, not only for the reasons cited so far, but also to fund intensive programs for lagging students, such as family counseling, language development, and longer school days and school years.[124]

Some states have equalized funding for public schools, but the attempts to do so in other states have encountered fierce opposition. As an alternative to equalized funding, some states have considered supplementary funding for inner-city schools, but people's priorities run in other directions. In 1999, the Pennsylvania legislature approved $160 million of public financing for new stadiums for the Eagles and Phillies and another $160 million of public financing for new stadiums for the Steelers and Pirates, while the schools in Philadelphia and Pittsburgh languished.[125]

Charter schools are not a panacea for these problems. Numerous cities are experimenting with charter schools, which are operated by private companies or nonprofit organizations and are allowed to disregard some rules established by school districts and teachers' unions. With more leeway, they're expected to produce better results. Yet their results are mixed. Some charter schools are a real improvement over the public schools in their neighborhood; others, however, show a noticeable decline in test scores. Regardless, charter schools tend to reinforce existing segregation.[126]

Because of the persistence of segregated schools and unequal schools, one study concluded, "Millions of nonwhite students are locked into 'dropout factory' high schools, where huge percentages do not graduate, have little future in the American economy, and almost none are well prepared for college."[127]

Discrimination in Employment

Although the Civil Rights Act of 1964 and affirmative action (discussed later in the chapter) have prompted more employers to hire and promote African Americans, discrimination in employment remains.

Many blacks who are hired encounter negative stereotypes that question their competence on the job. These workers are passed over when they could be promoted.[128] Other blacks who are hired face racial slurs in comments, notes, and

Because Chicago public schools don't have an adequate budget, they have to rely on contributions from businesses for school supplies.

graffiti from coworkers. They endure an unfriendly or hostile environment.[129] Although most upper-level executives realize that it is economically advantageous to have a diverse workforce, some middle-level white managers and lower-level white workers interact poorly with black employees.

Discrimination in Housing

The Civil Rights Act of 1968, which prohibits discrimination in housing, has fostered some desegregation of housing, but extensive segregation persists.

One reason is economic. Many blacks don't have enough money to buy homes in white neighborhoods. Another reason is discrimination. Social pressure discourages blacks from moving into white neighborhoods. Continuing discrimination by homeowners, real estate agents, lenders, and insurers also stymies them. Many blacks who escape the ghetto end up in black neighborhoods in the suburbs.[130]

The federal government makes virtually no effort to enforce the act.[131] Victims of discrimination make the only attempts to enforce it when they file lawsuits. Yet residential segregation is slowly declining, especially in growing suburban areas in the West and South, more than in stagnant "rust belt" cities in the East and Midwest.[132]

Segregation doesn't persist because black people "want to live among their own kind," as some whites insist. Surveys show that only about 15 percent want to live in segregated neighborhoods, and most of them cite their fear of white hostility as the reason. Eighty-five percent would prefer mixed neighborhoods. Many say the optimal level would be half black and half white. But whites tend to move out when the concentration of blacks reaches 8 to 10 percent.[133] These contrasting attitudes make residential integration an elusive goal. And because residential segregation is at the heart of school segregation, they make school integration an elusive goal as well.

Another form of housing discrimination emerged in the crisis over subprime mortgages in recent years. Major banks targeted minority neighborhoods for predatory loans—housing loans with inferior terms, such as high up-front fees, high interest rates, and lax underwriting practices. Many aspiring minority homeowners were financially unsophisticated, without prior experience owning a home and without financial advisers or lawyers. The banks marketed these loans to black ministers as a way to gain the trust of their parishioners.[134] The terms made it more likely that minority homeowners, with a tenuous foothold in the middle class, would be unable to make their payments and unable to keep their home. When the crisis hit, these homeowners were among the first to lose their home.[135]

Discrimination in Law Enforcement

African Americans encounter discrimination from law enforcement, due to racial profiling and the "war on drugs."

Racial profiling   The practice of **racial profiling**, which is based on the assumption that minorities, especially males, are more likely to commit crimes, especially those involving drugs, targets minorities for stops and searches. Without evidence, officers stop minority drivers and search them and their vehicles.[136] Sometimes officers stop minority pedestrians

African American communities often have tense relationships with local police departments. After Hurricane Katrina, Leonard Thomas's family were living in their flooded home when a SWAT team burst in, believing that they were squatting in another family's house.

as well. Although police departments deny profiling, statistics show clear evidence of the practice.

Nationwide, black, Latino, and white drivers are equally likely to be stopped, though black and Latino drivers are twice as likely to be searched. Black and Latino drivers are also more likely to be given a ticket, rather than a warning.[137] In some places, profiling is more pronounced. Interstate 95, especially through Maryland, has a notorious reputation. In Los Angeles, blacks are two times as likely to be stopped and four times as likely to be searched as other drivers. Yet they are less likely to be found with illegal substances.[138] Therefore, the higher rates of stops and searches aren't because police have more evidence, or better hunches, of illegal substances in the cars of black drivers.

African Americans speak of the moving violation "DWB"—*driving while black*. A school administrator was stopped twenty times in one decade.[139] Former Rep. J. C. Watts (R-Okla.) was pulled over six times in one day in his home state.[140]

Police can engage in profiling because they have extraordinary discretion to stop, search, and interrogate whoever they want. Although the Fourth and Fifth Amendments provide protections against stops, searches, and interrogations (as explained in Chapter 13), the Supreme Court has created numerous exceptions to maximize police authority and flexibility. Police discretion allows officers' conscious or unconscious racial prejudice to come into play. And even when some officers exceed their discretion and violate the law or court rulings, they may lie in their report and in the courtroom. This is so common in some places that it has a name: "testilying."[141]

Police exercise their discretion freely. In one recent year, New York City police stopped more than a half million people—1400 per day—most of whom were black.[142]

So, cautious parents teach their children how to avoid sending the wrong signals to the police. Some schools offer survival workshops for police encounters. Minority officers instruct the students what to do when they get stopped: don't reach for an ID unless the officer asks for one; don't mumble or talk loudly; don't antagonize by asking for a badge number or threatening to file a complaint.[143]

But the encounters humiliate those who are stopped and spark animosity toward the police in these communities (as the movie *Crash* so clearly depicts). The first time young black males are stopped, searched, and interrogated tells them that "this is what it means to be black."[144] The stop defines their relationship not only to the police, but to the government and our society as well. It alienates them from all of these.

Profiling might be justified if it led to the apprehension of dangerous criminals, but apparently it does not. When police stop motorists, they find no greater evidence of crimes by blacks and Latinos than by whites.[145]

Some states and many counties and cities have taken steps to reduce profiling, such as recording data on every stop to see whether the police, or individual officers, are prone to profile. Yet the cops on the beat have discretion and are reluctant to change their habits.

"War on drugs"   The "war on drugs" was launched by the Reagan administration and joined by Congress and the Supreme Court in the 1980s. Congress passed numerous laws to support the war, and the Court decided drug cases to deny defendants' rights and bolster police's authority. The pattern of decisions was so pronounced that some scholars claimed that the Court had created a "drug exception" to the Bill of Rights. For instance, the Court ruled that police can use minor traffic violations—failing to use the turn signal to change lanes or failing to use the turn signal at the appropriate distance before an intersection—as a pretext to conduct drug searches, even when they have no evidence of drug activity.[146] One justice had to remind his colleagues that there was "no drug exception" in the Constitution.[147]

The war appears to be race neutral. However, this war has been waged primarily against racial minorities. Huge numbers of blacks and Latinos have been swept into the criminal justice system by police who conduct drug operations mostly in poor and minority neighborhoods.

Although young black men do commit a larger percentage of violent crimes, and violent crimes are concentrated in the ghettoes,[148] they do not commit a larger percentage of drug crimes, contrary to the stereotypes fostered by the media. All races, according to multiple surveys, appear to use and sell drugs at similar rates. (If there's any difference, white youths may actually use cocaine and sell drugs at greater rates than racial minorities.)[149] Therefore, more users and sellers are white (because more Americans are white), yet three-fourths of the people imprisoned for drug crimes are black or Latino.[150]

Since the war on drugs began, 31 million people have been arrested for drug offenses—most for possession, not for sale; and most for marijuana, not for hard drugs.[151] In New York City, 50,000 people—one every ten minutes—were arrested for possession of small amounts of marijuana in 2011. Eighty-seven percent were black or Latino.[152]

The war on drugs and the "tough on crime" movement, pushed by conservatives also in the 1980s, have led to a system of mass incarceration. At the same time that the federal government was initiating the war on drugs, the federal and state governments were sharply increasing the length of sentences (for drug crimes and other crimes) and also reducing or eliminating the discretion of judges for sentences. This combination led to much longer sentences, especially for drug crimes. From the 1980s to the 2000s, the federal and state prison populations skyrocketed. Two-thirds of the federal increase and over half of the state increase were due to drug cases.

"We are told by drug warriors that the enemy in this war is a thing—drugs—not a group of people, but the facts prove otherwise," one analyst concluded.[153] In fifteen states, black drug offenders are sent to prison at rates 20 to 57 times greater than white male offenders. In seven states, they constitute 80 to 90 percent of all drug offenders sent to prison.[154]

Consequently, 41 percent of federal and state prisoners are black, although only 13 percent of the U.S. population is black. In Illinois, there are nearly 20,000 more black men in the state's prisons than in the state's universities. In the Chicago area, 55 percent of the black men have a felony record.[155]

Nationwide, more blacks are under control of the corrections system—in prison or jail or on probation or parole—than were enslaved in 1850. Because so many black men are incarcerated, a black child is less likely to be raised by both parents than a child in slavery was. "The absence of black fathers from families across America," one scholar remarked, "is not simply a function of laziness, immaturity, or too much time watching Sports Center."[156]

After release from prison, most offenders have a felony label,[157] which makes it hard to integrate into mainstream society. They are ineligible for food stamps and barred from public housing and from private apartments by many landlords. They are rejected for jobs by many employers.[158] They are denied federal grants or loans for higher education (for a number of years). They also are denied the right to vote in many states—some for a number of years, others forever.

Because people assume that the "war on drugs" is race neutral, and because they believe that blacks use and sell drugs at greater rates, they aren't troubled by the fact that black men, especially, are the casualties in this war. One scholar, however, has called the war and its system of mass incarceration "the New Jim Crow," because its impact is to isolate, and thus segregate, so many blacks from mainstream American society.[159]

Summary

Overall, discrimination against African Americans continues. Whites speak of "past discrimination"—sometimes referring to slavery, sometimes to official segregation, and sometimes to the pattern of pervasive discrimination. These are history because of the civil rights movement, Supreme Court decisions, and congressional acts. However, "past discrimination" is not all past.[160] The effects linger, and the discrimination itself persists. As a black journalist observes, "Modern bigotry usually isn't some nitwit screaming the N-word. It is jobs you don't get and loans you don't get and health care you don't get and justice you don't get, for reasons you get all too clearly, even though no one ever quite speaks them."[161]

When blacks point out the discrimination, some whites insist that little discrimination remains. These whites apparently assume that they know more than blacks do about what it is like to live as a black person. This perceptual gap between blacks and whites about the existence of discrimination is a real barrier to improved race relations. Whites who believe nothing is wrong don't favor actions to fix what they consider a nonexistent problem.

A solid majority of Tea Party supporters (61 percent) and almost half of Republicans (47 percent) in 2010 agreed with the statement that government "has paid too much attention to the problems of blacks and other minorities." In fact, for many whites, the real problem is "reverse discrimination." Majorities of Tea Party supporters (61 percent) and Republicans (56 percent) think that "today, discrimination against whites is as big a problem as discrimination against blacks and other minorities."[162]

Improving Conditions for African Americans?

Despite some continuing discrimination, African Americans have taken long strides toward achieving equal rights. These strides have led to much better living conditions for many and to a healthier racial climate in society. For those in poverty, however, serious problems remain.

Progress

As a result of the civil rights movement, Supreme Court decisions, and congressional laws, the United States has undergone a racial transformation in just one generation. As a black law professor observed, racism has become "unlawful, immoral, and, perhaps more important, declasse" (out of style).[163] Antiracism has replaced racism as the dominant ideology toward race relations in our major institutions, such as the schools, the military, the media, big corporations, and labor unions. And the civil rights movement has become "as much a part of American nationalist lore as the Boston Tea Party or Paul Revere's midnight ride."[164]

Consequently, blacks' lives have improved in most ways that can be measured.[165] Blacks have a lower poverty rate and a longer life expectancy than before. They have completed more years of education, with larger numbers attending college and graduate school. They have also attained higher occupational levels—for example, tripling their proportion of the country's professionals[166]—and higher income levels. Many—well over half—have reached the middle class.[167] At least before the Great Recession, almost half owned their homes,[168] and a third moved to the suburbs.[169]

During the years that blacks' lives have improved, whites' racial attitudes have also improved. Numerous polls show that whites' views have changed significantly (even assuming that some whites gave socially acceptable answers rather than their real feelings).

Since the 1960s, whites and blacks both report more social contact with members of the other race and more approval of interracial dating and marriage (see Figure 2), which is especially significant because these practices were the ultimate taboos. Interracial couples represented the clearest breach and their potential offspring the greatest threat to continued segregation.[170]

When the Supreme Court struck down Virginia's law barring interracial marriage in 1967, sixteen states had such laws.[171] Almost three-fourths of Americans disapproved of interracial marriages. People fretted about the problems the children of such marriages would face, because they were "neither black nor white." Interracial couples encountered stares and ostracism. According to a psychiatrist, most had "deep-seated psychological sicknesses." According to *Time* magazine, a white husband in an interracial marriage would face career setbacks. When the daughter of Secretary of State Dean Rusk married a black man, Rusk offered to resign to save President Johnson embarrassment. (Johnson did not accept his resignation.)[172]

Interracial marriage has evolved "from being illegal, to being taboo, to being merely unusual." And each year, it

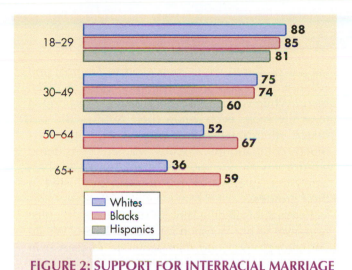

FIGURE 2: SUPPORT FOR INTERRACIAL MARRIAGE
Percentages of those who would be fine with a family member's marriage to someone of any other race or ethnicity. Whites include only non-Latino whites. Blacks include only non-Latino blacks. Latinos are of any race. There were insufficient numbers of Latinos ages 50–64 and 65+ for analysis.

SOURCE: "Almost All Millennials Accept Interracial Dating and Marriage," Pew Research Center, February 1, 2010. http://pewresearch.org/pubs/1480/millennials-accept-iinterracial-dating-marriage-friends-different-race-generations. Copyright © 2010 by Pew Research Center. Reproduced by permission.

becomes less unusual.[173] In 2010, 15 percent of all marriages in the United States were interracial.[174] Asians and Latinos have the highest rates,[175] but blacks have a higher rate (17 percent) than before. (Whites have the lowest rate—9 percent—but a higher rate than before.)[176] Many cohabitations are interracial as well.

Some whites, of course, remain blatant racists. For socioeconomic reasons, these whites are more likely to come into contact with blacks—living near them and working with them—than are tolerant whites, who are more educated and more prosperous. Even so, overt racist behavior occurs less frequently and is condemned more quickly than before. In some circles today, a blatant racist is considered not only a "fossil," but a "moral pervert" as well.[177] Yet covert racist attitudes persist in the minds of many whites, resulting in more subtle distrust and disapproval, rather than outright antipathy, toward blacks and toward policies that involve, or are perceived to involve, race, such as affirmative action and welfare spending.[178]

The election of Barack Obama shows how far we've come. In fact, his campaign appears to have decreased negative stereotypes about blacks held by many whites, especially older whites, who tend to be the most prejudiced.[179] But the reaction to Obama's campaign and presidency also shows how far we've got to go. During his campaign, numerous voters confided to reporters that they wouldn't vote for a black candidate. During his presidency, many Americans have internalized the frantic attempts, not just by the loco fringe, to portray Obama as "the Other"—a foreigner, Muslim, fascist, socialist, communist—not a real American or a legitimate

president. Even commentators and politicians, who are quoted often enough to be more careful, have let slip revealing remarks. Commentator Patrick Buchanan referred to the president as "your boy." Representative Lynn Westmoreland (R-Ga.) called him "uppity." Representative Doug Lamborn (R-Colo.) compared him to "a tar baby."[180] These views and comments are fueled, at least in part, by Obama's race. "Some people just can't believe a black man is president and will never accept it."[181]

Of course, this does not mean that all or most of his opponents are motivated by racism, but it would be naive to believe, as some pundits speculated after the election, that we're now living in a "post-racial society."[182] Most talk about a "post-racial society" comes from whites who want to congratulate themselves or those who want to pressure government to abandon efforts to promote equality.

Although we're not living in a post-racial society, we're living in a more equal society than previous generations ever experienced. Journalist Ellis Cose interviewed middle-class blacks for a 1993 book that he titled *The Rage of a Privileged Class*.[183] He found that even successful blacks faced numerous racial slights and insults and, as a result, seethed with anger and expressed pessimism that American society would ever treat them well. Cose interviewed more middle-class blacks for a 2011 book that he titled *The End of Anger*.[184] The anger and pessimism had given way to real optimism, especially among the successful blacks of the next generation. His interviewees, while maintaining that they've had to work harder than whites to get ahead and had to overcome institutional impediments along the way, are very hopeful for the future.

Problems

Although the push for civil rights has opened many doors, some blacks aren't in a position to pass through. About a quarter of the black population live in poverty—two and one-half times the rate among the white population—and about a tenth, the poorest of the poor, exist in a state of economic and social "disintegration."[185] This "underclass" is trapped in a cycle of self-perpetuating problems from which it is extremely difficult to escape.

The problems of the lower class and the underclass have been exacerbated by economic changes that intensified in the 1970s and have continued since then. These changes hit the poor the hardest. Good-paying manufacturing jobs in the cities—the traditional path out of poverty for immigrant groups—disappeared. In two decades, Chicago lost over 300,000 jobs, New York over 500,000.[186] Many jobs were eliminated by automation, while many others were moved to foreign countries or to the suburbs. Although service jobs increased, most were outside the cities and required more education or paid lower wages than the manufacturing jobs had.

As black men lost their jobs, they lost their ability to support a family. And many went to jail for minor drug offenses. This led to a decrease in the number of "marriageable" black men and an increase in the number of households headed by black women.[187] The percentage of such households rose from 20 percent of all black families in 1960 to 45 percent in

BEHIND THE SCENES

What Online Dating Tells about Racial Prejudice

The online dating site OkCupid analyzed its users' responses. The users post a profile, identifying their characteristics, interests, and preferences. Other users (the "senders") who see their profile may contact them (the "receivers"). Then the receivers decide whether to respond to the senders. The site examined the frequency with which the receivers responded to the senders.

For analysis, OkCupid pulled a random sample of a half million users, including whites, blacks, Latinos, American Indians, Asians, (Asian) Indians, Middle Easterners, and Pacific Islanders. It controlled for looks (through a picture-rating feature on the site) and, among men, for height.

Its primary finding was that black women and black men are not considered desirable dates or mates. Black women were the least sought racial-gender combination. They got the cold shoulder even from black men.

White women, Hispanic women (Latinas), and Asian women all preferred white men. (That is, Latinas preferred white men even to Latinos, and Asian women preferred white men even to Asian men.) White women disproportionately responded to white men, even when their profiles did not match—that is, when their profiles did not predict much compatibility. White women considered white race more important than the other characteristics, interests, or preferences they listed in their profiles.

Perhaps this finding is not a surprise, given users' responses to one question for their profiles: "Would you strongly prefer to date someone of your own skin color/racial background?" The majority (54 percent) of white women said yes. A large minority (40 percent) of white men also said yes. But just small percentages (in the teens and twenties) of almost all other racial-gender combinations said yes.

The operators believe that this site has younger, better-educated, and more progressive users than other online dating sites.

SOURCE: Christian Rudder, "How Your Race Affects the Messages You Get," *OkTrends* (blog), October 5, 2009, blog.okcupid.com/index.php/your-race-affects-whether-people-write-you-back/.

2000.[188] And 60 percent of black children live in such households. These families are among the poorest in the country.

Meanwhile, the gains from civil rights enabled the black middle class to flee the inner cities for the suburbs. Their migration left the ghettos with fewer healthy businesses and strong schools to provide stability and fewer role models to portray mainstream behavior.[189] By the mid-1990s, one Chicago ghetto with 66,000 people had just one supermarket and one bank but forty-eight state-licensed lottery agents and ninety-nine state-licensed liquor stores and bars.[190]

Today many ghetto residents have "almost no contact with mainstream American society or the normal job market."[191] Too few jobs are available, and very few jobs pay a living wage. Serious crimes are ever present. As a result, many residents have developed understandable but dysfunctional social norms, rejecting the work ethic, deferred gratification, and any investment in their future, all of which may seem pointless in their environment.[192]

It is commonly recognized that the plight of young black men is worse than that of any other group in society. More black men receive their GED (high school equivalence degree) in prison than graduate from college.[193] About half as many black men as black women attend college. A black man in Harlem has less chance of living past forty than a man in Bangladesh.[194]

After widespread riots in the 1960s, the Kerner Commission, appointed by President Johnson to examine the cause of the riots, concluded, "What white Americans have never fully understood—but what the Negro can never forget—is that white society is deeply implicated in the ghetto. White institutions created it, white institutions maintain it, and white society condones it." After the riots, however, governments did little to improve the conditions that precipitated the riots.

After the riots in Los Angeles in 1992 following the trial of police officers who beat up Rodney King, there was more talk about improving the conditions in the ghetto. But a columnist who had heard such talk before commented, "My guess is that when all is said and done, a great deal more will be said than done. The truth is we don't know any quick fixes for our urban ills and we lack the patience and resources for slow fixes."[195]

And we lack the will to make the effort. A national focus on our big cities and their impoverished residents dissipated in the furious backlash against government and taxes that arose in the late 1970s and has continued for over three decades since then.[196] This backlash has starved governments of the revenue and sapped them of the desire necessary to act.

During these decades, the cities have lost political power as they have lost population due to white flight and black migration. Since 1992, more voters have lived in the suburbs than in the cities. (More than 40 percent of blacks live in the suburbs too.) Suburban voters don't urge action on urban problems, and sometimes they resist action if it means an increase in their taxes or a decrease in their services.

For the black lower class, and especially for the black underclass, it is apparent that civil rights aren't enough. As one black leader said, "What good is a seat in the front of the bus if you don't have the money for the fare?"[197]

But most blacks don't fall in the lower class or underclass, and most don't dwell in the inner cities. It would be a serious mistake to hold the stereotypical view that the majority reside in the inner cities and that most of them live in dysfunctional families filled with crackheads and prone to violence. Although black men lag behind, black women have vastly improved lives—academically, professionally, and financially—over the span of one generation.[198]

Discrimination against Latinos

Latinos (often called Hispanics) are people in the United States who have a Spanish-speaking background. Although sometimes they are considered a separate race, in fact they can be of any race. Some are brown skinned, others black skinned, and still others white skinned. Many are an amalgam of European, African, and American Indian ancestry that makes it impossible to classify them by race. Thus Latinos should be regarded as an ethnic group rather than a distinct race. (But Latinos are so diverse that some scholars are reluctant to consider them even an ethnic group, preferring to consider them simply a statistical category for the convenience of government reports, academic research, and media coverage.)

About 60 percent of America's Latinos trace their ancestry to Mexico.[199] They are heavily concentrated in the Southwest but are increasingly spreading throughout the United States, including the Midwest and the South. About 10 percent are from Puerto Rico, which is a commonwealth—a self-governing territory—of the United States. As members of the commonwealth, they are U.S. citizens. Most live in New York, Boston, Chicago, and other cities in the North. Another 4 percent are from Cuba. Following the establishment of a communist government in Cuba in 1959, many fled to the United States and settled in south Florida. A significant number are also from the Caribbean islands and Central American countries, where emigrants left turmoil and oppression. A smaller number are from South American countries or from Spain.

Despite the diversity of their origins, Latinos are heavily concentrated in six states. More than half live in California and Texas, where they make up one-third of the population. Already they outnumber non-Latino whites (now often called Anglos when compared with Latinos) in Los Angeles and Houston.[200] Many of the rest live in Florida, New Jersey, New York, and Illinois, but there are growing pockets all around the United States.

Representing more than 16 percent of the population, Latinos have overtaken blacks as the largest minority in the United States. (This number includes legal and illegal residents.) Fueled by high immigration rates and birthrates, this group is the fastest-growing minority (slightly faster growing than Asians) in the United States.

Latinos never endured slavery in this country[201] but have faced discrimination. Although some Latinos are Caucasian, many Puerto Ricans and Cubans have African ancestry, and many Mexicans have Indian ancestry, so they have darker skin than Anglos.[202] Like blacks, Latinos, especially Mexicans and Puerto Ricans,[203] have faced discrimination in education, employment, housing, and voting.[204]

Cuban Americans are more likely than other Latinos to be middle class.

Discrimination Due to Immigration

Latinos also endure discrimination because of immigration. The flood of illegal immigrants pouring in from Latin America, especially from Mexico, has produced a wave of anti-immigration sentiment throughout the United States, even in the states and cities with few immigrants.[205] This sentiment affects not only illegal immigrants but also the Latinos who are legal residents and U.S. citizens, including those who are native-born Americans, because the average person or law enforcement officer often can't tell, simply by watching or listening, which Latinos are legal and which ones are illegal.

Because illegal immigrants can't get driver's licenses and most don't get driver's insurance, police officers expect to identify illegal immigrants by demanding these documents. As a result, border patrol agents and local police officers often stop Latinos for questioning. Agents stopped the mayor of Pomona, California, a hundred miles from the Mexican border, and ordered him to produce papers proving that he's a legal resident. Local police officers also assume that many Latinos are involved in drug trafficking, so they practice profiling, as they do toward blacks.[206] Even when the officers are well intentioned, their conduct—stopping and questioning and demanding documents—seems like harassment to law-abiding residents and citizens.

This profiling was a problem even before 2010, when frustrated states began to withdraw the welcome mat. Arizona adopted a policy of "attrition through enforcement." The state passed a law (further explained in Chapter 3) with harsh provisions in the hope that illegal immigrants would leave or be deported. Five states passed similar laws, and hundreds of cities passed narrower laws.[207]

One provision of Arizona's law requires police to verify the legal status of every person they stop if they have a "reasonable suspicion" that the person is an illegal immigrant.[208] The law prohibits profiling,[209] but the prohibition is unenforceable. The standard of "reasonable suspicion" is vague, and the officers have discretion.

The debate over Arizona's law unleashed strong emotions and nativist comments. At times the debate became irrational. Even Sen. John McCain (R-Ariz.), who previously cosponsored a bill that would reform immigration law and provide a path to citizenship for illegal immigrants, backtracked as he heard his constituents' views during his reelection bid. Defending Arizona's law, he said, "It's the…drivers of cars with illegals in it that are intentionally causing accidents on the freeway."[210]

Fearing a wave of similar laws in other states, the federal government sued Arizona, claiming that the law is unconstitutional because the federal government is responsible for immigration. The Supreme Court agreed that the federal government is responsible for immigration, and it struck down several provisions of the law. However, it upheld the controversial provision that police determine the legal status of the people they stop if they suspect the people are in the United States illegally.[211]

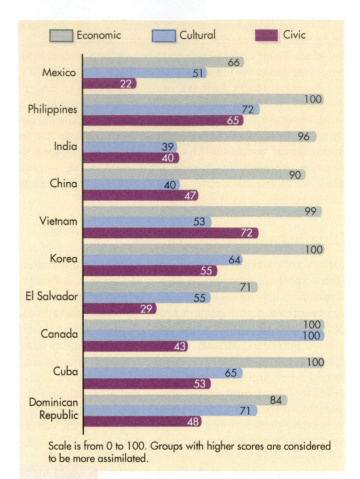

Scale is from 0 to 100. Groups with higher scores are considered to be more assimilated.

FIGURE 3: ASSIMILATION OF IMMIGRANTS, BY COUNTRY OF ORIGIN Researchers created indices reflecting the economic, cultural, and civic assimilation of immigrants, and they assessed immigrants from the ten countries that provide the most immigrants to the United States (listed in order). The figure shows the extent of each nationality's assimilation, based on data from 2006. Economic assimilation reflects the similarity of foreign and native-born populations in their labor force, educational attainment, and home ownership patterns; cultural assimilation reflects the similarity of their English-speaking ability, marriage, and childbearing patterns; civic assimilation reflects the similarity of their citizenship rates, voting rates, and military service.

SOURCE: Manhattan Institute.

But more pervasive than the occasional stops by law enforcement officers is the hostility from ordinary Americans who are opposed to the influx of immigrants. In their looks and comments, some Americans send a message that immigrants, especially Latinos, aren't welcome here.

This message has stalled the proposed DREAM Act,[212] which has been filibustered by conservatives in Congress. The act would provide legal residency for illegal immigrants who were brought to the country as children and who graduated from a U.S. high school and completed two years of a

U.S. college or served two years in the U.S. military. With legal residency, they could eventually attain U.S. citizenship. Opponents say the act amounts to "amnesty" and rewards illegal behavior, even though the potential beneficiaries were brought to the country by their parents or other relatives.

In lieu of the DREAM Act, President Obama issued an executive order in 2012 that halts deportation for at least two years of young illegal immigrants who were brought to the United States as children. The order applies to those who were brought here before the age of 16, have lived here continuously for at least five years, and who have not reached the age of 31 (as of June 15, 2012). They need to be in school or to have graduated from a U.S. high school or served in the U.S. military, and they need to have no record of serious crimes. The order also allows these immigrants to obtain work permits, which will enable them to work legally. The order doesn't provide a path to citizenship, and it's a stopgap measure rather than a permanent fix. It can be rescinded by a future president.

To dampen anti-immigrant sentiment and to pave the way for the DREAM Act and other immigration reforms, the Obama administration has enforced federal immigration laws aggressively, deporting record numbers of illegal immigrants—nearly 400,000 in 2011.[213] The administration wants to show the public that the federal government can secure the country's borders, but the deportations have split Latino families, which often include both legal and illegal immigrants.

Actually, the controversy over illegal immigrants may be less about illegal immigration than about immigration in general—polls show that people who say they oppose illegal immigration tend to oppose legal immigration as well. The controversy may even be less about immigration in general than about assimilation into the American culture and adoption of the English language.[214] Among some Anglos, there is widespread unease about the Latino culture and real anxiety about whether, and how fast, these recent arrivals will discard their culture in favor of Anglo culture. There are fears that immigrants will change white Americans more than white Americans will change them. In Arizona, supporters of the state's immigration law also sought to remove Mexican-studies classes from the public schools.[215]

These fears are aggravated by the fact that 40 percent of Latinos are first-generation immigrants, meaning that they themselves came from other countries.[216] In general, these immigrants haven't assimilated or learned English, just as the first generation of previous immigrant groups didn't assimilate or learn English.[217] With so many new immigrants in recent decades, Anglo Americans often encounter first-generation immigrants, and they draw conclusions about all Latinos from these immigrants.

Yet clear patterns of cultural assimilation and language acquisition are emerging. Immigrants' children, especially, do assimilate and learn English.[218] Illegal aliens live in the shadows, fearing deportation. They can't assimilate. Among legal residents, many immigrants came to the United States to work for a few years and then to return to their home country. They don't want to assimilate. But the rest do remain

and do assimilate. In fact, immigrants in the past quarter-century have been assimilating at a faster rate than previous immigrants. They are assimilating economically, by holding jobs and earning money and by buying homes; culturally, by learning English and intermarrying with U.S. citizens; and politically, by becoming citizens, voting, and serving in the military. (See Figures 3 and 4.) A study concluded that "the nation's capacity to assimilate new immigrants is strong."[219]

Immigrants in the past quarter-century have also been learning English. Cuban Americans are learning English as fast as or faster than any group in history.[220] Mexican Americans are learning English slower than other groups, but they are learning it as they reside longer in the United States. Although many who come for work and plan to return to Mexico don't speak English, most who remain in the United States learn to speak some English, and almost all of their children learn to speak fluent English.[221] Most of these second-generation Americans are bilingual, speaking Spanish at home with their parents and relatives and English outside of home. But many of *their* children—the third-generation Americans—are monolingual, speaking only English. The drive to learn English is so strong that just a third of Latinos born in the United States are bilingual. Most can't speak Spanish.[222] (See Figure 5.)

It is true that some immigrant communities, especially Cubans in south Florida and Mexicans in some parts of the Southwest, are so large that residents can survive without learning English. But most feel pressure to learn English to function in society and for their children to succeed in school. Indeed, 89 percent of Latinos believe that those who immigrate must learn English to succeed in the United States.[223] Children do learn English in schools, though it is harder for

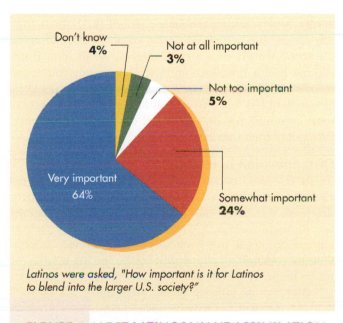

Latinos were asked, "How important is it for Latinos to blend into the larger U.S. society?"

FIGURE 4: MOST LATINOS VALUE ASSIMILATION

SOURCE: *Time*, August 22, 2005, 56. Poll conducted by phone, with interviews in English and Spanish. *N* = 503.

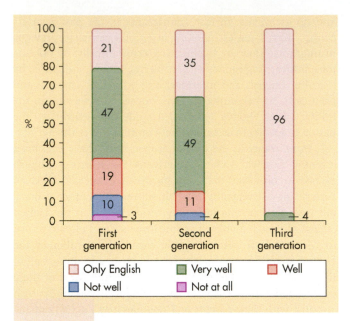

FIGURE 5: IMMIGRANTS' CHILDREN LEARN ENGLISH This figure shows the extent to which immigrants' children in California know English. By the third generation, all know English very well, and most know English only.

SOURCE: Laura Hill, "English Proficiency of Immigrants," March, 2011. PPIC, 2011. Copyright © 2011 by Public Policy Institute of California. Reproduced by permission.

adults to find English classes that fit with their work schedules, especially given the long hours and multiple jobs that many immigrants have.[224]

While illegal immigration doesn't lead to all of the harms that its opponents charge, it certainly causes some problems. The communities and states near the Mexican border bear a disproportionate share of the burden from this immigration. Their education costs rise as children fill the schools; their health costs increase when immigrants without health insurance go to the emergency room; and their law enforcement costs expand too. Because the federal government has failed to reform immigration, residents of these communities and states feel overwhelmed by problems not of their making.

Discrimination in Education

As late as the mid-twentieth century, Latino children were not allowed to attend any schools in some places. In other places, they were segregated into "Mexican" schools that were inferior to Anglo schools.[225] When the Supreme Court declared segregation illegal, many school districts achieved "integration" by combining Latinos with blacks, leaving non-Latino whites in their own schools.[226]

Although de jure segregation has been struck down,[227] de facto segregation exists in cities where Latinos are concentrated. Many Latinos attend schools with more than 90 percent minorities, and most attend schools with more than 50 percent minorities.[228]

Predominantly Latino schools, like predominantly black schools, aren't as well funded as other schools because they're located in poor communities that don't get as much revenue from property taxes. In San Antonio, wealthy families, who were concentrated in one section of the city, got their section incorporated as a separate school district, although it was surrounded by the rest of the city. As a separate district, its property taxes financed its schools only. When Mexican American parents sued, the Burger Court ruled that the Fourteenth Amendment's equal protection clause doesn't require states to equalize funding among school districts, even where artificial districts have been carved out of a city.[229] Despite the Court's ruling, this case highlighted the problem of unequal funding, prompting some states to equalize funding, though most states did not change the status quo.

Latinos' primary problem in education, however, is the language barrier. Many, because they are unable to speak English, fail in school and drop out of school at higher rates than other students, even African Americans. One-third of Latinos drop out before graduating from high school.[230]

Bilingual education was created in the 1970s to help such students. Bilingual classes used the students' native language to teach the students English and their other subjects. The goal was to transition them from their native language to English rather than to immerse them in a foreign language—English—that they didn't understand.[231] Around the country, more than 150 languages were offered; Spanish was the most common.[232]

However, bilingual programs faced numerous problems. They were expensive because they required more teachers and smaller classes, and they were impractical because schools couldn't find enough teachers in various languages. Schools in California, where half of all students in bilingual programs lived, fell 21,000 teachers short in one year.[233] Thus the schools couldn't offer bilingual education to most students who were eligible for it.[234]

Bilingual programs were controversial as well. Although Latino groups advocated for these programs as a way to preserve Latino culture, many Latino parents worried that these programs would delay their children's mastery of English.[235] Many Anglos also opposed these programs for the same reason that Latino groups favored them. For all of these reasons, California citizens voted to abolish bilingual programs in 1998. Some states have followed California's lead, while other states have maintained bilingual programs.

Discrimination against Farmworkers

Latino farmworkers have encountered particular problems. Agribusinesses have long avoided regulations imposed on other businesses, and for decades the minimum wage law didn't apply to farm workers. Even today, the laws providing overtime pay and the right to organize don't apply. In many states, laws establishing workers' compensation and unemployment benefits programs don't apply either. Farmworkers' lack of governmental protection, coupled with their economic desperation, makes them vulnerable to unscrupulous employers. The Department of Justice has investigated more than one hundred cases of involuntary servitude—slavery—and has prosecuted a half dozen from south Florida in the 2000s.[236]

Combating Discrimination against Latinos

In the 1960s, Latino advocacy groups tried to imitate African American groups by using protests and other forms of direct action. The Chicano movement attempted to forge a powerful bloc from the diverse population of Latinos. Cesar Chavez successfully led a coalition of labor, civil rights, and religious groups to obtain better working conditions for migrant farmworkers in California, but few other visible national leaders or organizations emerged.

Latinos remain more diverse and less cohesive than blacks. Most don't even consider themselves part of a common group.[237] They identify strongly with their national origin and have little contact with Latinos of other national origins. And they lack a shared, defining experience in their background, such as slavery for blacks, to unite them.

Where Latinos are highly concentrated, they are increasingly powerful at the local and state levels of government. Yet Latino politicians haven't shaped a common agenda, perhaps because Latino people don't share a common agenda.[238]

They are potentially powerful at the national level as well. When Congress considered harsh measures toward illegal immigrants in 2006, many Latinos were concerned because often their families include both legal and illegal residents—children who were born here living with parents who are illegal, or nuclear families who are legal residents living with grandparents or aunts and uncles who are illegal. They were also angered by politicians' comments that immigrants are taking jobs from citizens and not contributing anything to society. As a result, hundreds of thousands rallied against the

Latinos are gradually improving their status as more go to college and graduate school and become professionals, such as this doctor.

© Paul Kuroda/SuperStock

Undocumented college students, who were brought to the United States when young, are chafing at their life "in the shadows" and yearning for a life in the open. Risking deportation, they are attending rallies, even engaging in sit-ins, for the DREAM Act while wearing shirts or displaying signs proclaiming their "undocumented" status.

1. Why do these students trumpet their illegal status?
2. Do you see parallels between these students' tactics and the civil rights movement's tactics?
3. Why are most of these demonstrators women rather than men?
4. Do you think these students are brave or reckless?

measures. In their passion, some observers saw the stirrings of political activism, especially among young Latinos.

Yet many Latinos aren't citizens, and many of those who are citizens don't register and vote. Although the Latino population is slightly larger than the African American population, far fewer Latinos are registered to vote. Nonetheless, with their huge numbers, Latinos are a coveted bloc of voters, especially in the swing states in presidential elections.

Meanwhile, Latino individuals are moving up society's ladder. More attend college and become managers and professionals. At least those who speak educated English appear to be following the pattern of earlier generations of immigrants from southern and eastern Europe—arriving poor, facing discrimination, but eventually working their way up. Along the way, they are also assimilating through high rates of marriage to non-Latinos.

Discrimination against American Indians

More than 2 million American Indians live in the United States. Most live in the West, and half live on reservations. Although some Native Americans are Eskimos and Aleuts from Alaska, most are Indians, representing more than 560 tribes with different histories, customs, and languages. Proud of their tribal heritage, they prefer to be known by their tribal name, such as *Cheyenne* or *Sioux*, than by the collective terms *Indians* or *Native Americans*.[239] (Of the collective terms, they prefer to be called *Indians*, so our text will follow their preference.) American Indians have endured treatment quite different from what African Americans or Latinos have experienced.

EMILY MICHOT/MCT/Newscom

Undocumented immigrants—students at Miami-Dade College—learn about President Obama's policy to defer deportation of young illegal immigrants who were brought to the United States as children.

Government Policy toward American Indians

Government policy toward Indians has ranged from forced separation at one extreme to forced assimilation at the other.

Separation   The Constitution treats Indian tribes as separate entities. The commerce clause grants Congress authority to "regulate commerce with foreign nations, and among the several states, and with the Indian tribes." In early cases, Chief Justice John Marshall described the tribes as "dependent domestic nations."[240] They were within U.S. borders but outside its political process.

Reflecting this interpretation of the Constitution and this characterization of the tribes, early government policy promoted separation between Indians and non-Indians. Treaties established boundaries between Indians and non-Indians to minimize conflict, and white hunters or settlers who ventured across the boundaries could be punished by the Indians.

People believed that the North American continent was so vast that most of its interior would remain wilderness and would be populated by Indians who would have ample room to live and hunt. But as the country grew, it became increasingly difficult to contain the settlers within the boundaries. Mounting pressure to push the Indians farther west led to the Indian Removal Act of 1830, which mandated removal of tribes east of the Mississippi River and relocation on reservations west of the river. At the time, people considered the Great Plains (now such states as Kansas, Nebraska, and the

Dakotas) as a great desert, unfit for habitation by whites but suitable for Indians.

Assimilation   As more settlers moved west, the vision of a separate Indian country far beyond white civilization faded. In the 1880s, the government switched its policy to assimilation.[241] Prompted by Christian churches, government officials sought to "civilize" the Indians—to integrate them into American society, whether they wanted to be integrated or not. In place of their traditional means of subsistence, rendered useless once the tribes were removed from their historical homelands, the government subdivided reservation land into small tracts and allotted these tracts to tribe members in the hope that they would turn to farming as white and black settlers had. Bureau of Indian Affairs (BIA) agents, who supervised the reservations, tried to root out Indian ways and replace them with white dress and hairstyles, the English language, and the Christian religion. To instill these new practices, government boarding schools separated Indian children from their families.

As long as their tribes were considered separate nations, American Indians were not considered citizens.[242] In 1890, after government policy had switched to assimilation, Congress permitted Indians who remained on reservations to become citizens. In a formal ceremony marking his new citizenship, the Indian shot his last arrow and then took hold of the handles of a plow to demonstrate his assimilation.[243]

After World War I, Congress granted citizenship to those who served in the military during the war, and finally, in 1924, Congress extended it to all who were born in the United States.

Citizenship enabled Indians to vote and hold office, although some states effectively barred them from the polls for decades. Arizona denied them the right to vote until 1948, Utah until 1956.[244]

Tribal restoration   By the 1930s, the government recognized the consequences of coerced assimilation. Most Indians, though able to speak English, were poorly educated. And with their traditional means of earning a living gone, most were poverty-stricken. The policy had led to the destruction of native culture without much assimilation into white society. Consequently, in 1934 Congress implemented a new policy of tribal restoration that recognized Indians as distinct persons and tribes as autonomous entities that were encouraged to govern themselves once again. Traditional cultural and religious practices were accepted, and Indian children, no longer forced to attend boarding schools, were taught some Indian languages.

Reflecting the policy of tribal restoration and the efforts of other minorities in the 1960s and 1970s, Indian interest groups became active. Indian law firms filed lawsuits, seeking to protect not only tribal independence and traditional ways but also land, mineral, and water resources.

The diversity and the dispersion of the tribes, divided by culture and by geography and often located in the remotest and poorest parts of the country, make it difficult for them to present a united front. Nevertheless, they have been able to wrest some autonomy from the government. In particular, they have gained more authority over the educational and social programs administered by the BIA for the tribes.[245]

In recent years, Indians have fought for the return of some tribal land and for an accounting of the money owed them for the use of their individual land held in trust by the government. In the early nineteenth century, the government took tribal land and put it in trust for the Indians. But then the government divided the land, classified large tracts as "surplus" land, and offered the tracts to white settlers. In return, it paid individual Indians a pittance. In this way, the Indians lost two-thirds of their territory. The government held the remaining land in trust for the Indians, leasing it to ranchers, loggers, and miners. Although the government collected the rents and royalties for the Indians, the BIA didn't bother to keep accurate records or even to preserve its records. A class-action lawsuit sought a reckoning of the accounts and a payment to the Indians who were owed money.[246] The case was resolved in 2012, and the Indians received a portion of the money they had lost.

After a Supreme Court ruling and a congressional law in the 1980s underscored tribal sovereignty on tribal land, tribes could establish gambling casinos on reservations, even if their state didn't allow any casinos.[247] Almost three hundred tribes have done so, although less than a dozen have found a bonanza—mostly small tribes in populous states where their casinos attract numerous customers.[248] And many of the casinos are bankrolled by unknown investors who keep most of the profits. A Malaysian businessman owns one, a South African developer another. From these casinos, little money trickles down to tribal members.[249]

Nevertheless, with their casino businesses, some tribes have begun to buy into the political process, as other groups have done. Threatened by gambling interests in Las Vegas and Atlantic City, which fear that tribal casinos will lure away their customers, the tribes have formed a lobby, the National Indian Gaming Association, and made political contributions. These contributions reportedly total more than the contributions by individual corporations such as AT&T, Boeing, or General Motors.[250]

 Thinking about Democracy

Do you think that any one of the government's policies toward Indians—separation, assimilation, or tribal restoration—is more democratic than the others?

Now more Indians share the views of one activist who says, "You have a federal government, state governments, and tribal governments—three sovereigns in one country. This is the civil rights movement of Native Americans."[251] Indeed, enjoying renewed pride, tribes have established programs to preserve their language and culture.[252]

Nevertheless, Indians remain at the bottom of America's racial and ethnic ladder. They are the least educated and most unemployed group, and also the poorest and sickest group, of any people in the country, with the highest alcoholism rates and lowest life expectancy.

SEX DISCRIMINATION

Most sex discrimination has been directed at women, although some has been directed at men.

Discrimination against Women

The traditional view of gender roles fostered discrimination against women, but the vigorous efforts by the women's movement and by Congress and the Supreme Court have led to greater equality for women.

The Traditional View

People used to believe that natural differences between the sexes required men and women to occupy separate spheres of life. Men would dominate the public domain of work and government, and women would dominate the private domain of the home. Both domains were important, and men were considered superior in one and women were considered superior in the other.

"I love the way you make those yams. You'll have to give me the recipe before your culture is obliterated from the face of the earth."

Thomas Jefferson, the most egalitarian of the male Founders, reflected this view when he said, "Were our state a pure democracy there would still be excluded from our deliberations women, who, to prevent deprivation of morals and ambiguity of issues, should not mix promiscuously in gatherings of men."[253] That is, women are more moral than men, so they would be corrupted by politics, and they are more irrational, so they would confuse the issues. For both reasons, they should not participate in politics.

So, women were denied the right to vote, and married women were denied other rights—to manage property they acquired before marriage, to manage income they received from jobs, to enter into contracts, and to sue. Some states eventually granted these rights, but when disputes arose within families, male judges hesitated to tell other men how to treat their wives.

Even women's citizenship was tied to their husbands' citizenship. If a foreign woman married an American man, she automatically became a United States citizen. But if an American woman married a foreign man, she automatically lost her United States citizenship. (Women's citizenship wouldn't become independent of their husbands' citizenship until 1922.)

Women were barred from schools and jobs. Before the Civil War, they weren't admitted to public high schools. Because they were being prepared for motherhood, education was considered unnecessary, even dangerous. According to the *Encyclopaedia Britannica* in 1800, women had smaller brains than men.[254] Education would fatigue them and possibly ruin their reproductive organs. For the same reasons, women weren't encouraged to hold jobs. Those who did were shunted into jobs that were seen as extensions of the domestic domain, such as producing textiles, clothes, and shoes in sex-segregated factories.[255]

This traditional conception of gender roles created problems for women who didn't fit the standard mold. After the Civil War, Myra Bradwell ran a private school, founded a weekly newspaper, and worked for various civic organizations. She was active in the women's suffrage movement and instrumental in persuading the Illinois legislature to expand women's legal rights. After learning the law, however, she was denied a license to practice it solely because she was a woman. The Supreme Court upheld the Illinois policy in 1873.[256] Justice Joseph Bradley declared:

> Law, as well as nature itself, has always recognized a wide difference in the respective spheres and destinies of man and woman. Man is, or should be, the woman's protector and defender. The natural and proper timidity and delicacy which belongs to the female sex evidently unfits it for many of the occupations of civil life.... The constitution of the family organization... indicates the domestic sphere as that which properly belongs to the domain and functions of womanhood. The harmony...of interests and views which belong, or should belong, to the family institution is repugnant to the idea of a woman adopting a distinct and independent career from that of her husband.... The paramount destiny and mission of woman are to fulfill the noble and benign offices of wife and mother. This is the law of the Creator. And the rules of civil society must be adapted to the general constitution of things, and cannot be based upon exceptional cases.

This view applied to various issues. In the 1860s and 1870s, the doctors who practiced scientific medicine formed the American Medical Association (AMA) to drive out other people who offered medical services. These people included not only hucksters and quacks but also women who served as midwives or abortionists. Although abortions had been widely available, the AMA, drawing on popular fears about the women's suffrage movement, convinced state legislatures that abortions were "a threat to social order and to male authority." The woman who seeks an abortion, the AMA explained, is "unmindful of the course marked out for her by Providence, she overlooks the duties imposed on her by the marriage contract. She yields to the pleasure—but shrinks from the pains and responsibilities of maternity.... Let not the husband of such a wife flatter himself that he possesses her affection."[257]

Traditional notions in some states allowed a husband to "correct" his wife. The Mississippi Supreme Court acknowledged a husband's right to beat his wife.[258] Using the "rule of thumb," the court held that a husband could not beat his wife with a weapon thicker than his thumb.

The Women's Movement

Early feminists were determined to remedy these inequities. Many had gained political and organizational experience in the abolitionist movement. Because that movement was associated with religious groups, it wasn't considered "unladylike" for women to join. Yet women weren't allowed to participate fully. When Abigail Kelley was nominated as an official of the American Anti-Slavery Society, almost three hundred men

Dilos Lonewolf became Tom Torlino during his transformation at a boarding school in Carlisle, Pennsylvania. Indians were shorn of their hair and clothes and trained to adopt white ways.

left the meeting to form another antislavery society in which women couldn't vote or hold office. Later, when Kelley rose to speak at a meeting of the Connecticut Anti-Slavery Society, the chair insisted,

> No woman will speak or vote where I am moderator. It is enough for women to rule at home. It is woman's business to take care of the children in the nursery; she has no business to come into this meeting and by speaking and voting lord it over men. Where women's enticing eloquence is heard, men are incapable of right and efficient action. She beguiles and blinds men by her smiles and her bland winning voice.... I will not submit to PETTICOAT GOVERNMENT.[259]

Shunned by the men, in 1848 the women convened a meeting to discuss the "social, civil, and religious rights of women." This Women's Rights Convention adopted a declaration of rights based on the Declaration of Independence, proclaiming, "We hold these truths to be self-evident: that all men and women are created equal." The convention also passed a resolution calling for women's suffrage.

After the Civil War, the women who had worked in the abolitionist movement expected that women as well as blacks would get legal rights and voting rights. When the Fourteenth and Fifteenth Amendments did not include women, they felt betrayed. They disassociated themselves from the black movement and formed their own organizations to campaign for women's suffrage. This movement, led by Susan B. Anthony and Elizabeth Cady Stanton, succeeded in 1920, when the Nineteenth Amendment gave women the right to vote.[260]

Then dissension developed within the movement. Many groups, feeling that the Nineteenth Amendment was just the first step in the struggle for equal rights, proposed the Equal Rights Amendment to remedy remaining inequities. Other groups felt that the battle had been won. They opposed the Equal Rights Amendment, arguing that it would overturn labor laws recently enacted to protect women. Because of this dissension and the conservatism in the country at the time, the movement became dormant.[261]

The movement reemerged in the 1960s when the civil rights movement led many women to recognize their own inferior status. Female writers sensitized other women. The most famous statement was Betty Friedan's book *The Feminine Mystique,* which grew out of a questionnaire she circulated at her fifteenth college reunion. The book addressed the malaise that afflicted college-educated women who were socialized into the feminine role but found it unsatisfying.[262] Friedan observed that women reared the children, shopped for groceries, cooked the meals, and cleaned the house, while secretly wondering, "Is this all?" Friedan's manifesto became the best-selling nonfiction paperback in 1964. Its popularity spurred Friedan and other upper-middle-class, professional women to form the **National Organization for Women (NOW)** in 1966. They resolved "to bring women into full participation in the mainstream of American society *now.*"

Other upper-middle-class women, who were veterans of the civil rights and antiwar movements, had developed a taste for political action and formed other organizations. Whereas NOW fought primarily for women's political and economic rights, the other organizations fought broadly for women's liberation in all spheres of life. These organizations sought to transform American society, upending traditional practices at home and at work. Together these organizations pushed the issue of women's rights back onto the public agenda.

Nevertheless, they weren't taken seriously for years. In 1970, *Time* magazine reported, "No one knows how many shirts lay wrinkling in laundry baskets last week as thousands of women across the country turned out for the first big demonstration of the women's liberation movement. They took over [New York City's Fifth Avenue], providing not only protest but some of the best sidewalk ogling in years."[263]

Although the movement tried to broaden its base beyond upper-middle-class and college-educated women, it was unable to do so. As a result, it fostered an image of privileged women who looked on other women with disdain. Some activists considered *housewife* a derisive term, and traditional women viewed the movement as antimotherhood and antifamily and, when it became more radical in the 1970s, prolesbian. This image gave "women's liberation" a bad name, even though most women agreed with most goals of the movement.[264] This image persists. More Americans believe that extraterrestrials have visited the earth than think that the word *feminist* is a compliment.[265] (It is unclear, however, whether this says more about Americans' attitudes toward gender equality or their penchant for paranoid conspiracy theories.)

The Movement in Congress and the Courts

Congress initially didn't take the women's movement seriously either. When the House debated a bill forbidding racial discrimination in employment, eighty-one-year-old Rep. Howard Smith (D-Va.) proposed an amendment to add sex discrimination to the bill. A staunch foe of equal rights for blacks, Smith thought his proposal so ludicrous and so radical that it would help defeat the entire bill. Indeed, during their debate on the amendment, members of Congress laughed so hard that they could barely hear each other speak.[266] But the joke was on these members, because the amendment, and then the bill—the Civil Rights Act of 1964—passed. (For another reflection of officials' attitudes toward gender roles at this time, see the box "The Mercury 13.")

Equal Rights Amendment Congress also passed the **Equal Rights Amendment (ERA)**. The amendment simply declared, "Equality of rights under the law shall not be denied or abridged by the United States or by any state on account of sex." Introduced in 1923 and every year thereafter, the amendment was finally passed in 1972.

It looked like the amendment would zip through the states. Both parties endorsed it, and a majority of the public supported it. But the amendment stalled. Observers speculated that it could make women subject to the draft for the military (if there was another draft). Opponents charged, falsely, that it would result in unisex restrooms and homosexual rights.

The main problem, however, was the amendment's symbolism. For many women, the ERA represented an attack on the traditional values of motherhood, the family, and the home. Early feminists had emphasized equal employment so much that they gave some women the impression that they opposed these values. Traditional women sensed implicit criticism for being housewives.[267] To underscore the symbolism,

the women in anti-ERA groups baked bread for state legislators scheduled to vote on ratification.

Consequently, numerous women, even some who favored equality, opposed the amendment. Although many young women supported it, fewer middle-age and elderly women did; and although many working women supported it, fewer housewives did. Women's organizations hadn't created an effective grassroots campaign to sway traditional women. Their disaffection allowed male legislators to vote according to their male attitudes. They didn't need to worry about a backlash from their female constituents.[268]

In 1980, the Republican Party became the first party not to endorse the ERA since 1940, and President Reagan became the first president not to support the amendment since Truman. When the deadline for ratification set by Congress expired in 1982, the ERA fell three states short of the three-fourths necessary. As with the Nineteenth Amendment, it was opposed primarily by the southern states.

Supreme Court rulings Historically courts upheld laws that limited women's participation in the public domain and occasionally even laws that diminished their standing in the private domain. As late as 1970, the Ohio Supreme Court ruled that a wife is a husband's servant with "no legally recognized feelings or rights."[269]

The Burger Court finally reversed this pattern. In 1971, for the first time, the Court struck down a law that discriminated against women,[270] heralding a long series of rulings that invalidated a variety of such laws. The Court used the congressional statutes and broadened the Fourteenth Amendment's equal protection clause to apply to women as well as to racial minorities.

The change was especially apparent in a pair of cases involving the selection of jurors. For the pool of potential jurors, some states drew the names of men, but not women, from voter registration or other lists. These states allowed women to serve only if they voluntarily signed up at the courthouse. Consequently, few women served. In 1961, the Court let Florida use these procedures because the "woman is still regarded as the center of home and family life."[271] In 1975, however, the Court forbade Louisiana from using similar procedures,[272] thus overturning a precedent only fourteen years old.

The Court's rulings rejected the traditional stereotypes that men are the breadwinners and women the child rearers in society. For example, the Court invalidated Utah's law that required divorced fathers to support their daughters until eighteen but their sons until twenty-one.[273] The state assumed that the daughters would get married and be supported by their husbands, whereas the sons would need to get educated for their careers. But the Court noted, "No longer is the female destined solely for the home."

Laws on discrimination in employment The Civil Rights Act of 1964 forbids discrimination on the basis of both sex and race in hiring, promoting, and firing. It prohibits discrimination on the basis of sex, except where sex is a "bona fide occupational qualification" for the job. Sex is considered a legitimate qualification for very few jobs, such as restroom attendants, lingerie salesclerks, models, and actors. It is not considered a legitimate qualification for jobs men traditionally held, such as those that entail heavy physical labor, unpleasant working conditions, late-night hours, overtime, or travel. Employers can no longer reserve these jobs for male applicants.

However, discrimination in hiring, promoting, and firing persists, even forty years after the act. A major study examined the records in lawsuits alleging sex discrimination in one recent year. A surprising and staggering number, they required employers to pay $263 million to the female plaintiffs in that year alone.[274] Testimony by midlevel managers revealed that higher executives instructed them, "We do not employ women," or, "The day I hire a woman will be a cold day in hell." In dozens of cases, the managers were told to throw women's applications into the trash.[275]

The same result occurs when male managers decide according to their "gut instinct" that a man is more qualified. Their "gut instinct" may be biased without them realizing it.

The discrimination occurs up and down the ladder. Huge lawsuits have been brought against both Merrill Lynch and Wal-Mart in recent years. But the discrimination appears most prevalent for traditional male, blue-collar jobs. Some men don't want to work with women; they don't want to break up the "good-ol'-boys' clubhouse."[276] Mysteriously, a woman's application disappears; or the letter telling her when to come for the interview gets lost in the mail; or her examination is invalidated for some reason.[277]

Some companies that fill their positions through hiring agencies instruct the agencies to send them only men for traditional male jobs and only women for traditional female jobs.[278]

Discrimination in firing, especially for pregnancy, continues as well, despite the **Pregnancy Discrimination Act** of 1978, which forbids firing or demoting women when they become pregnant or after they return from maternity leave.[279] Some women have been fired as soon as they mentioned being pregnant, others as soon as their body showed it. Many have seen their performance evaluations drop as their bellies swelled, even though their actual performance did not decline.[280] Others have been demoted after giving birth. "When I returned from maternity leave," a lawyer recounted, "I was given the work of a paralegal and I wanted to say, 'Look, I had a baby, not a lobotomy.'"[281]

The cases examined in these studies probably represent the tip of the iceberg. To sue an employer for sex discrimination is to embark on an expensive and exhausting legal battle that will take several years of one's life. It requires a strong-willed woman who has experienced discriminatory behavior egregious enough for her to persuade a lawyer to take the case and then a company to settle or a judge or jury to find for her. Although there are some frivolous lawsuits in our legal system, there is more discriminatory behavior in our workplaces than is ever brought to court.

The **Equal Pay Act** of 1963 requires that women and men receive equal pay for equal work, with exceptions for merit, productivity, and seniority. As a result of the act, the gap between women's and men's earnings has slowly shrunk. In the 1960s, working women earned just 59 cents for every dollar men earned.[282] Today, working women earn 77 cents for every dollar men earn—an improvement but far short of real equality.[283]

However, a contrary trend is emerging for young women and young men. Women from twenty-two to thirty who are unmarried and childless are making 8 percent more than their male counterparts, because young women are more likely than young men to be college educated.[284] (This doesn't mean that young women are making more than young men who are college educated, and it doesn't mean that young women are making more than young men who have the same job. Young women who are college educated have better-paying jobs than young men who aren't.) It's not clear whether this trend will continue after these women get married and have children.

There are several reasons for the overall gap between women's and men's earnings. One is old-fashioned sex discrimination. Despite the Equal Pay Act, some male employers with ingrained attitudes are reluctant to pay women equally. The act allows exceptions for merit and productivity, which usually are determined subjectively. The employer may insist, whether sincerely or not, that the man is more meritorious or productive. Legions of women believe that they need to perform better to be paid equally.[285]

Although the Roberts Court made it more difficult for women to bring lawsuits for pay discrimination, Congress overrode the Court when it passed the Lilly Ledbetter Fair Pay Act (as explained in Chapter 12).

Another reason for the gap is that women and men have different jobs, whether due to discrimination or to choice. Despite the Civil Rights Act of 1964 and the societal changes—the blurring of lines between genders— many women have traditional women's jobs and most men have traditional men's jobs. And traditional women's jobs pay less.

Although the Equal Pay Act mandates equal pay for equal work, it does not require equal pay for comparable work—usually called **comparable worth**. According to a study in Washington State, maintenance carpenters and secretaries performed comparable jobs in terms of the education, the skill, or other qualifications required, but the carpenters, mostly men, made about $600 a month more than the secretaries, mostly women. In general, "men's jobs" paid about 20 percent more than comparable "women's jobs." Yet courts rejected demands by public employees that government employers boost the pay for "women's jobs." Private companies have also resisted requests to boost the pay for such jobs.

Although the push for comparable worth has stalled, in recent years grassroots campaigns organized by labor unions and church groups have called for laws mandating a **living wage**.[286] These laws would require employers to pay more than the federal minimum wage, to pay whatever is necessary so a full-time worker doesn't fall below the poverty line.

Some proposals would apply only to government employees and to the employees of those companies that do business with the government. Other proposals would apply to all employees within a city or state. Still other proposals would apply just to the employees of "big-box stores," such as Wal-Mart and Home Depot, because these companies drive down the wages for workers throughout society. Most proposals would exempt small businesses with fewer than twenty-five workers.

So far, some cities (Baltimore, San Francisco, and Santa Fe) and one state (Nevada) have adopted such laws.[287] If many cities and states did, living wage laws would have a significant impact on women and minorities, because women and minorities hold a disproportionate number of the lowest-paying jobs. In addition, living wage laws would have a ripple effect, prompting employers to raise the wages of the workers just above the lowest level.

Another reason for the gap between women's and men's earnings is that women have children. Some interrupt their career until their children start school. Others continue to work but shift from the fast track to the so-called "mommy track," working fewer hours due to child care and household responsibilities.[288] Still others fall victim to stereotypes—that mothers aren't serious about their careers, that mothers aren't dependable because they won't show up when their children get sick, or that mothers will quit sooner or later anyway.[289] Through such stereotypes, managers move mothers to the "mommy track" in their own minds, whether the mothers want that track or not.

For whichever reasons, the difference in pay makes a difference in life. Early in her career, it means that a woman might not be able to pay off her credit card debts or college loans as quickly. She might not be able to have as nice a car or an apartment as her male counterpart. Later in her career, she might not be able to have as nice a house or as exotic vacations. Then, if her husband divorces her or dies before her, she might not be able to have as comfortable a retirement. The accumulated shortfall in her retirement savings means that she might struggle in her old age.[290]

Despite the barriers to equal pay, almost 40 percent of women in two-income households have become the primary breadwinner.[291]

BEHIND THE SCENES

The Mercury 13

The Soviet Union shocked a complacent America in 1957 when it launched the first satellite into space. In the midst of the Cold War, Americans feared that this achievement would signal the superiority of the communist system over our capitalist system to other nations around the world. A year later, the National Aeronautics and Space Administration (NASA) was established to spearhead the U.S. program, and a year after that the first astronauts—the Mercury 7—were selected. In 1960, John F. Kennedy was elected president. Vowing to catch up with the Russians, he challenged NASA to put "a man on the moon" within the decade.

The promise of space exploration lured not only men who had been test pilots in the military, but also some women fliers. Although women weren't allowed to serve as pilots in the military and therefore weren't hired as pilots by passenger airlines, they were employed as pilots by charter airlines and flight schools. Some hauled cargo or ferried planes to South America, while others competed in the women's air-racing circuit.

Yet in the 1950s and early 1960s, the feminine ideal still prevailed—people "expected women pilots to look like fashion models when they stepped out of a cockpit, even if they had been up all night with their arms covered in grease"—so the pilots wore a dress

AP Images

Aspiring astronaut Jerrie Cobb was an experienced pilot.

Mothers with young children confront more obstacles than unequal pay. Male employers do little to accommodate the demands of child rearing. Most companies don't provide paid maternity leave, on-site day care, or flexible schedules. The United States lags far behind most other countries, including all wealthy countries, in creating family-friendly policies. Of 173 countries, all but the United States, Papua New Guinea, and three African countries guarantee paid maternity leaves. Sixty-five countries even provide paid paternity leaves. (In the United States, only California provides partly paid family leaves.)[292]

Congress passed and President Clinton signed a bill requiring employers to grant unpaid maternity and paternity leaves. Companies must allow unpaid leaves for up to three months for workers with newborn or recently adopted children or with seriously ill family members. The act applies to companies that have fifty employees and to workers who work twenty-five hours a week for a year.[293] This covers about half of American workers.

But relatively few workers take advantage of these leaves. Most workers can't afford to take unpaid leaves. Moreover, many managers don't support such measures, and some coworkers resent the additional burdens, so employees are reluctant to ask for leaves. When companies are laying off workers to cut costs, "If you look like you are not career oriented, you can lose your job."[294]

Because of the influx of women workers, the workforce has changed enormously since 1970 (then two-thirds of married couples had a stay-at-home spouse—normally a wife; today just 40 percent do[295]). But the workplace is "stuck in a time warp, modeled for *[Leave It to Beaver's]* Ward and June Cleaver when the reality feels more like … 'Survivor.'"[296] Workers in the United States put in longer hours than those in other industrialized countries, and these hours, for both sexes, have increased since the 1970s.[297]

The result is that mothers and fathers with young children often face unreasonable demands on their time. Neither spouse has the time to do what the housewife once did. (It's not really a joke when someone quips, "They both need a housewife.") In many families, the woman tries to do these tasks at night and on weekends.

Married women and men, with or without children, work almost exactly the same number of hours per week. Although

---

under their flight suit and put on high heels and touched up their lipstick before emerging from the plane.

Two doctors who tested the men who applied to be astronauts wondered if any women might also qualify. The doctors knew that NASA was encountering problems developing rockets with sufficient payload, and they realized that women astronauts, weighing less and consuming less oxygen and food, might alleviate these problems. But they didn't know whether women would be physically or psychologically capable. The assumption at the time, of course, was that women wouldn't be. Plus, officials said, when women menstruate, their brain changes, and they can't think clearly enough. NASA, reflecting the conventional wisdom, was leery of expanding its program to encompass women astronauts.

The doctors, however, weren't convinced. Without official approval, they began recruiting women pilots who were interested in space flight. Eventually, they winnowed their list from over a hundred to thirteen. All had logged many hours in the air, and one held world records for long-distance and high-altitude flights. In 1960 and 1961, the women were put through the same rigorous tests as the men had been subjected to.[1] The doctors found that the women performed as well as the men in all respects—physical capability, endurance, and resilience.

As word of potential women astronauts spread, the air force and the navy recoiled from the prospect of "girl astronauts"—or "astronettes," as they were dubbed by reporters. If women could become astronauts, they might also become test pilots and ultimately destroy the masculine culture in the air force and navy.

After two years of unofficial testing, Vice President Lyndon Johnson, who was the president's liaison with NASA and an enthusiast of space travel, met with two of the aspiring women astronauts. If women were allowed, he said, blacks, Mexicans, Chinese, and other minorities would also want a chance. Despite his sympathy for civil rights, after the meeting Johnson sent a message to his aides: "Lets [sic] Stop This Now!" Whether from NASA, the military, or the White House, officials weren't ready to foster this change in American culture.[2]

Barring women from the program became a Cold War blunder, as the Soviet Union put the first woman into space in 1963. The United States would not put a woman into space until Sally Ride two decades later.

---

[1] Ultimately, the doctors completed the first two batteries of tests; they weren't allowed to complete the final battery required of men.

[2] President Kennedy showed no interest in expanding the program either. There was some sentiment in Congress to do so, but that reflected a minority view.

SOURCE: Martha Ackmann, *The Mercury 13: The Untold Story of Thirteen American Women and the Dream of Space Flight* (New York: Random House, 2003). Quotations from pages 4 and 148.

women put in more time doing child care and household chores, men log in more hours on the job.[298] The combination of paid and unpaid work leaves both spouses feeling stretched thin and stressed out. Two-thirds of parents say they don't have enough time with their children, and nearly two-thirds of married workers say they don't have enough time with their spouse.[299]

So even though women have gained greater acceptance in the workplace, they—and their spouses—have not overcome the expectations that developed long before they were ever allowed in the workplace. And these expectations are exacerbated by Americans' glorification of work and, with new communications technology, a perverse celebration of a "24/7 workweek." "We glorify an all-work, all-the-time lifestyle," notes one commentator, "and then weep crocodile tears for kids whose parents are never home."[300]

Laws against sexual harassment   In addition to their difficulties in getting hired, promoted, and paid equally, some women also face sexual harassment. The Supreme Court has ruled that sexual harassment is a form of job discrimination prohibited by the Civil Rights Act of 1964,[301] and Congress has passed a law allowing victims to sue employers and collect money for distress, illness, or loss of their job due to such behavior. Although sexual harassment can be directed toward either sex,[302] it is usually directed toward women.

Courts recognize two types of **sexual harassment**. The most obvious is quid pro quo, in which a supervisor makes unwanted sexual advances and either promises good consequences (for example, a promotion or pay raise) if the employee goes along or threatens bad consequences (for example, an undesirable reassignment) if the employee refuses. The less obvious type is creating a hostile environment that interferes with the employee's ability to perform the job. To prove that a hostile environment existed, the employee must demonstrate that the offensive conduct was severe or persistent.

As Arkansas' governor, Bill Clinton allegedly asked Paula Jones, a state employee, for oral sex. Her lawsuit was dismissed because his sexual advance was deemed neither severe enough nor, as a single incident, persistent enough to constitute a hostile environment. If it happened, the judge said, it was "boorish and offensive" but not technically harassment.

Despite some men's fears, occasional innocuous comments, jokes, or requests for dates would not be classified as harassment. Justice Antonin Scalia emphasized that the law did not create "a general civility code."[303]

Women in traditional female jobs, such as secretaries, are more likely to be subjected to quid pro quo harassment from supervisors, whereas women in traditional male jobs, especially blue-collar jobs, are more likely to be subjected to hostile-environment harassment from coworkers. Examples abound of male laborers posting sexual pictures or writing sexual messages in women's lockers or restrooms or leaving plastic penises in their toolboxes; taunting the women with sexual questions and comments or addressing them as "Bitch," "Slut," or "Whore"; and grabbing their breasts, buttocks, or genitals. Worse for new workers, however, is having supervisors or coworkers who refuse to train or help them, or who sabotage their work or equipment, making them appear slow and shoddy.

The dynamics of sexual harassment don't revolve around sex as much as they reflect abuse of power. (In fact, the law doesn't forbid sex between workers, even if one supervises another.) A supervisor or coworker who practices harassment makes a woman feel vulnerable and thus exercises psychological dominance over her. He wants her to leave the workplace or, at least, to suffer inferior status if she remains there.

Laws on discrimination in education   The Education Amendments of 1972 (to the Civil Rights Act of 1964) forbid discrimination on the basis of sex in schools and colleges that receive federal aid. The amendments were prompted by discrimination against women by undergraduate and graduate colleges, especially in admissions and financial aid.

The language of the amendments, often referred to as **Title IX**, is very broad, and the Department of Education, which administers the law, has established extensive rules that cover more aspects of education than Congress expected.[304] The department has used Title IX to prod institutions into employing and promoting more female teachers and administrators, opening vocational training classes to girls and home economics classes to boys, and offering equal athletic programs to girls and women. If institutions don't comply, the government can cut off their federal aid. (See Table 2.)

Title IX has affected athletic programs especially. Before, schools provided far fewer sports for females than for males, and they spent far fewer dollars—for scholarships, coaches, and facilities—on women's sports. Now the department interprets Title IX to require a school either to have approximately the same percentage of female athletes as female undergraduates, or to expand the opportunities for female athletes, or to accommodate the interests and abilities of female students. (The latter, which is the least stringent of

Table 2	Women's Gains in Higher Education:	
Percentage of Degrees Earned by Women		
	1971–1972	**2008–2009**
Bachelor's	43%	57%
Master's	41	60
Doctoral	16	52
Law	8	46
Medicine	9	49

Women's gains in education have been dramatic since the modern women's movement arose.

SOURCE: National Center for Education Statistics, reported in Nancy Gibbs, "What Women Want Now," *Time*, October 26, 2009, 27.

the three standards, would occur if female students at a school were satisfied that there were sufficient opportunities for them, given their interests and abilities, even if their opportunities were unequal to men's.)

Very few colleges meet the first requirement. To comply, most are trying to meet the second requirement by expanding the number of women's sports. But they worry that they will have to fulfill the first requirement eventually and will have to cap the squad size of their football team, which has the most players and costs the most money, to do so. This would lessen the imbalance in the numbers of male and female athletes, and it would free more money for women's teams.

Title IX has had a major impact. Colleges have increased their women's teams—more than three times as many as in the early 1970s—and their female athletes—more than ten times as many as before.[305] Women now make up 42 percent of all college athletes and receive 42 percent of the scholarship money, though their teams have lower coaches' salaries and operating expenses than men's teams, as well as a smaller proportion of women coaches than they used to.[306]

Colleges with successful football or basketball programs have increased their women's teams the most because these sports generate revenue that funds women's sports. Colleges with no football program have also increased their women's teams. Colleges with football programs that don't generate a profit (as most don't) lag behind. They pour money into football but lack revenue from television or bowl contracts to fund women's sports.[307]

To reduce the gender imbalance, many colleges have eliminated low-profile men's teams, especially wrestling, gymnastics, tennis, and track. Marquette University eliminated men's wrestling even though the team was financed mostly by private donations.[308]

Men resisted the expansion of women's athletics. The Boston Marathon was traditionally for men only. When the first woman tried to participate in 1967, a marathon official assaulted her.

Some colleges have resisted the enforcement of Title IX, partly because athletic departments are struggling to balance their budgets and partly because the act threatens deeply ingrained cultural values reflected in men's athletics. Administrators and boosters fear that women's sports will take money from men's sports and thereby weaken the primacy of men's athletics.

Title IX has also had a major impact on high schools, which have increased their girls' teams. Before Title IX, 1 of every 27 girls played on a high school team; now 1 of every 2.5 girls does.[309]

But supporters have a broader goal in mind as well. "If girls are socialized the way boys are to take part in sports," the editor of a women's sports magazine says, and "if boys and girls grow up with the idea that girls are strong and capable, it will change the way girls and women are viewed—by themselves and by society."[310]

Overall, Congress and the courts have moved steadily toward legal equality for the sexes. Women have accomplished through congressional and judicial action much of what they would have accomplished with the ERA. It is an indication of the success of the movement that young women today take their equality for granted and focus on their personal lives rather than on the need for further progress.

Discrimination against Men

The traditional conception of gender roles has also created problems for men who don't fit the standard mold.

When the Burger Court rejected stereotypes that led to discrimination against women, it also rejected some that led to discrimination against men. For example, it invalidated Mississippi's law barring men from a state university's nursing school.[311] It also invalidated Alabama's law allowing only women to seek alimony upon divorce.[312] Thus the Court rejected stereotypes that only women become nurses and only women are dependent on their spouses.

On the other hand, the Burger Court upheld some laws that were designed to protect women but discriminate against men. It affirmed laws prohibiting statutory rape— intercourse with a minor, with consent—by males but not by females.[313] It also affirmed a law mandating draft registration for males but not for females.[314] The rationalization was that registration eventually could lead to the draft and the draft eventually could lead to combat, and it insisted that most women aren't capable of combat. Thus the Court accepted the stereotypes that only men initiate sex with underage partners and only men can fight in a war.

In the absence of a draft, the most significant discrimination against men may occur in divorce cases, where the norm is to grant custody of children to mothers and require payment of support by fathers. Although courts give fathers visitation rights, they permit mothers to move miles away, making visitation difficult and sporadic. And although governments have taken steps to enforce support payments, they have done little to enforce visitation rights. This practice reflects the stereotype that fathers are capable of funding

Although most single parents are women, an increasing number are men, such as this father of an eleven-year-old in Dallas.

their children but not of raising them. The Supreme Court has ignored this problem.

Other discrimination against men may occur in cases of unintended pregnancy. Women may choose abortion, adoption, or raising the child. Men have no choice. The Supreme Court invalidated laws requiring a husband's consent before his wife's abortion, because the woman carries the fetus so she is most affected by the decision.[315] The Court's ruling affects unmarried couples as well. And if the woman decides to raise the child, the man must pay child support (probably for eighteen years).

AFFIRMATIVE ACTION

Assume that a black runner and a white runner compete at a track meet. But the officials force the black runner to carry heavy weights, and he falls behind. Eventually, the officials realize that this is unfair, and they take the weights off. Of course, the black runner is still behind. Would this be fair? Assume instead that the officials not only take the weights off but also allow him to catch up. Would this be fairer?

This scenario, sketched by President Johnson, captures the dilemma of civil rights policy today. Although most discrimination has been repudiated by the courts and legislatures, the effects of past discrimination persist. Now the question is whether civil rights policy should ignore race and sex or take race and sex into account to compensate for the effects of

past discrimination. That is, should the policy require nondiscrimination only or **affirmative action** as well?

Affirmative action applies to employers when hiring and promoting minorities and women, colleges and universities when admitting minorities and women, and governments when reserving a portion of their contracts for businesses owned by minorities and women. We will examine affirmative action in employment and in education. We do not have sufficient space to discuss the pros and cons of affirmative action, but we will explain the policy, the law, and the primary consequences of affirmative action.

In Employment

The Civil Rights Act of 1964, which bars discrimination in employment, does not mention affirmative action, but it does authorize the bureaucracy to make rules to end discrimination. In 1969, the Department of Labor called for affirmative action by companies doing business with the federal government. Later, the Equal Employment Opportunity Commission called for affirmative action by governments themselves, and the Office of Education called for affirmative action by colleges as well. Presidents from Nixon through Carter supported it with executive orders, and the Supreme Court sanctioned it in a series of cases.[316]

Affirmative action requires positive steps to ensure that qualified minorities and women receive a fair share of the jobs at each level. What the positive steps and the fair share should be are the subjects of considerable controversy.

If the percentage of minorities or women who work in a government agency or in a private company that has government contracts is less than the percentage in the local labor force, the agency or company must agree to recruit more minorities or women or, in serious cases, draw up an affirmative-action plan that includes goals to hire or promote more minorities or women. If the agency or company does not reach the goals, it must show that it made an effort to do so. If the company does not satisfy the government, it can be denied future contracts (though in reality companies rarely are penalized).

Although affirmative-action plans speak of "goals," critics charge that they mandate quotas and that quotas amount to "reverse discrimination" and result in lower standards.[317] The terms do blur; if employers are pressured to meet goals, they might interpret *goals* to mean *quotas*. But only after a finding of deliberate and systematic discrimination does affirmative action entail actual quotas.[318]

The plans must allow white men, as well as minorities and women, to be hired and promoted, and the plans must be temporary (usually until the percentage of minority or female employees reaches the percentage of minority or female workers in the community).

Affirmative action applies to hiring and promoting but not to laying off workers. Because of a belief that affirmative action shouldn't impose much burden on innocent individuals, the Court has struck down the use of affirmative action—any protection for minorities and women—when employers pare their workforce for economic reasons. Instead, the Court

© Mike Thompson, Detroit Free Press. Reprinted by permission Copley News Service.

has accepted the traditional practice, based on seniority, that the last hired can be the first fired, even if the last hired were minorities and women.[319]

In addition to these long-standing limits on affirmative action, the Rehnquist Court made it more difficult for the government to mandate affirmative action for government agencies or private companies.[320] The government must show clear evidence of particular past discrimination by a government agency or a private company (or by the entire industry in which the company is a part), rather than simply point to pervasive historical discrimination in society as the justification for affirmative action by the agency or company.

Affirmative action has helped minorities and women. White men dominate public and private institutions, and as the personnel director of a *Fortune* 500 company observed, "People tend to hire people like themselves."[321] Thus affirmative action has prodded employers to hire more minorities and women.[322] It has also prodded managers to promote more minorities and women who had been stuck in low-level positions.[323] In fact, the most significant consequence of affirmative action may have been to pressure employers to hire and promote workers who should have been hired or promoted all along—that is, to pressure employers to stop discriminating against minorities and women.

Although affirmative action is controversial among the public, it is routinely used and even championed, under the name of "diversity," by big businesses, which see it as a way to locate untapped talent in overlooked groups and to gain new insights for selling their products to minority and female

consumers.[324] Corporations' use of "diversity" also provides a competitive advantage in the global economy.[325]

Whether affirmative action is mandated by the government or practiced by big businesses, it has helped some blacks move up a rung—from the lower middle class to the middle class or from the middle class to the upper middle class.[326] But affirmative action has not pulled many blacks out of the underclass. In families mired in poverty, these individuals often lack the education and skills necessary to compete for available jobs.[327] And, of course, affirmative action has not created new jobs or better jobs, so it has not helped minorities or women as much as a flourishing economy would.

In short, affirmative action should not be given more credit, or saddled with more blame, than it deserves. It has boosted some minorities and women but has not helped many others. It has displaced some white men but has not affected most others.

Yet 13 percent of white men think they have lost a job or promotion because of their race, and 10 percent think they have because of their sex.[328] Many others claim they have "heard about" another white man who did. However, affirmative action is not as pervasive as most people assume.[329] Many people view affirmative action as they do handicapped parking. When looking for a parking space in a crowded lot, many drivers see an empty handicapped space and think, "If it weren't for that, I could park here." Of course, if the space weren't reserved for handicapped drivers, only one other driver could park there.[330] So it is with affirmative action. Many white men think they would get a particular job if it weren't for affirmative action, but only one would. Meanwhile, the rest feel victimized by the policy. In fact, white men are victimized far more by global competition, business downsizing, and cutbacks in government services.

In College Admissions

Colleges and universities began to use affirmative action in the 1970s. Some schools used limited programs that gave a boost to minority applicants, while other schools used extensive programs that reserved seats—essentially, set quotas—for minority applicants. The medical school of the University of California at Davis reserved sixteen seats in its class of one hundred students for minorities. The Burger Court upheld the use of race as a factor in admissions, emphasizing the value of diversity, but struck down the use of quotas (unless the school has a history of intentional discrimination).

The Rehnquist Court narrowed the use of affirmative action. In a pair of cases from the University of Michigan, one directed at undergraduate admissions and one directed at law school admissions, five justices upheld affirmative action, though only as part of a "holistic review" that gives "individualized consideration" to each application. Rather than use formulas that add points for minority status, schools must use a more labor-intensive review.[331] The decision to uphold affirmative action came as a surprise, because the Rehnquist Court had limited affirmative action in employment cases. The majority's decision—or at least its fifth vote—evidently was influenced by friend-of-the-court briefs from *Fortune* 500 companies insisting that affirmative action is necessary to compete in the global marketplace, and from generals and admirals insisting that affirmative action is necessary to produce a diverse officer corps to lead a twenty-first-century military.[332]

The future of affirmative action is in doubt, however, because Justice O'Connor, the swing justice on affirmative action, retired and was replaced by the more conservative Justice Alito. Now four, possibly five, justices on the Roberts Court are opposed to any use of race to ameliorate past discrimination.[333] As this book went to print, the Supreme Court agreed to decide a case challenging the use of affirmative action by the University of Texas. Meanwhile, some states (including Michigan) have outlawed the use of race or "preferential treatment" in education.

Just as some white men believe that affirmative action has cost them a job or promotion, some white students believe that it has cost them, or will cost them, a seat in the college or university of their choice. But 60 percent of colleges admit nearly all students who apply; only 20 percent are selective enough to use affirmative action.[334]

Students who apply to elite schools that do use affirmative action are more likely to be rejected because these schools give preferential treatment to their "legacies"—the sons and daughters of their alumni—than because these schools practice affirmative action. (Giving preferential treatment to their legacies encourages their alums to donate to the school.) Typically, a fifth of Harvard's students receive preferential treatment because their parents attended the school. Harvard's "legacies" are more than twice as likely to be admitted as blacks or Latinos. A similar advantage exists at other selective schools, including public schools such as the Universities of California and Virginia.[335]

Affirmative action may be more widespread in graduate and professional schools.[336] For some beneficiaries of affirmative action in law schools, recent social science research has found a mismatch between these students' abilities and the schools' demands. These students attended law schools that were too difficult for them, making it harder for them to graduate, pass the bar exam, and join the legal profession.[337] These findings are controversial, but, if confirmed, they suggest that some schools may need to adjust the scope of their affirmative-action programs.

For both sides in the controversy, affirmative action, whether in employment or education, has become a symbol. For civil rights leaders, it represents fairness and a step toward equality and progress. For critics, it represents unfairness and an attack on individuality and merit. It's important to debate these values, but it's also important to recognize that affirmative action is neither the key public policy for racial and sexual equality, as some supporters portray it, nor a big stumbling block for individual achievement, as some detractors characterize it. Indeed, affirmative action reaches so few individuals that in the eyes of some observers the policy is a "distraction,"[338] or even an attempt to achieve "racial justice on the cheap," without adopting the more extensive programs that would be necessary to address the much greater problem of the underclass.[339]

 ## Thinking about Democracy

How do the existence and operation of affirmative action highlight the contradictions among the core values of democracy (discussed in Chapter 1)?

SUMMARY

- African Americans have endured slavery, neoslavery, segregation, and violence as well as pervasive discrimination in other ways. These practices were more pronounced and entrenched in the South but, except for neoslavery, occurred in the North too.

- The civil rights movement attacked segregation and discrimination in the courts, in the streets, and in Congress. The result was a landmark ruling by the Supreme Court—*Brown* v. *Board of Education*—and the most important civil rights acts in history by Congress—the Civil Rights Act of 1964, the Voting Rights Act of 1965, and the Civil Rights Act of 1968.

- *Plessy* v. *Ferguson* established the separate-but-equal doctrine, which led to separation but not equality. *Brown* v. *Board of Education* overturned *Plessy* and invalidated the separate-but-equal doctrine. *Brown* led to some desegregation of schools.

- In northern cities and large southern cities, residential segregation is the usual pattern, so school segregation is one common result. Although busing was used to desegregate schools for a while in the 1970s, more conservative Courts following the Warren Court rejected extensive efforts to reduce de facto segregation.

- African Americans still face discrimination in education, due to segregated and unequal schools; in employment; in housing; and in law enforcement, due to racial profiling and the "war on drugs."

- Despite tremendous progress for African Americans, the underclass—the poorest of the poor—is trapped in a cycle of self-perpetuating problems in the ghetto. Economic changes eliminated manufacturing jobs, and the black middle class fled the inner cities for the suburbs, leaving fewer healthy businesses and strong schools and fewer role models.

- Latinos are people in the United States who have a Spanish-speaking background. They are an ethnic group rather than a separate race. A majority came from Mexico, but others came from Puerto Rico, Cuba, the Caribbean, or Central America.
- Latinos have faced discrimination due to immigration. The flood of illegal immigrants has prompted an anti-immigrant and anti-Latino backlash from Anglos who fear that Latinos won't assimilate into the American culture and learn the English language. Latinos have also faced discrimination in education, primarily due to language barriers.
- Traditional gender roles, which relegated women to the private domain of the home, kept women from the public domain of work and government. These roles also denied women legal rights.
- The women's movement won the right to vote in 1920. The modern women's movement reemerged in the 1960s to pressure the Supreme Court to strike down laws that discriminated against women and Congress to pass new laws that prohibited sex discrimination in employment and education.
- Affirmative action is a policy that takes race and sex into account to compensate for past discrimination. It applies primarily to employers when hiring and promoting workers and to colleges and universities when admitting students.

DISCUSSION QUESTIONS

1. Why do you think it took so long for African Americans to move from slavery to legal equality?
2. How did the civil rights movement's protests help achieve its goals?
3. Why was "separate-but-equal" not equal?
4. Do you think it's important to have an integrated society? What gains, and what costs, might come from new efforts to integrate society? Do you think the gains or the costs would be greater?
5. Do you think that more attempts to equalize funding among public schools in an urban area or in a state should be made? Why or why not? Do you think that the "war on drugs" should continue as is or should be revamped, reduced, or eliminated? Explain.
6. Why are the problems of the underclass largely ignored by society?
7. Why do Latinos have trouble advancing their agenda, despite their increasing population?
8. Do you favor or oppose the DREAM Act? Why?
9. Why do you think society evolved from traditional gender roles to fluid gender roles?
10. What problems should the women's movement focus on now?
11. What consequences of affirmative action may be beneficial? Detrimental?

Focus On... *Spending and Taxing*

The Great Recession of 2008-09 and the slow recovery since then have left high unemployment rates.

LEARNING OBJECTIVES

1. Describe the tensions between democracy and capitalism. Explain why even healthy economies have unemployment and inflation.
2. Discuss the impact of the U.S. government on the nation's economy. Identify when the federal budget will strongly influence the economy.
3. Analyze the reasons why the U.S. tax code is complex. Assess whether it should be, and can be, reformed.
4. Compare and contrast the principal economic theories of the Democratic and Republican Parties. Evaluate the links between campaign promises and policies.

Why doesn't the U.S. government have a balanced budget? Why do we have to pay taxes? And if we have to have them, why don't the rich pay more in taxes? Why do Democrats and Republicans have such different ideas about the economy?

These are just a few of the questions that are asked every day, often by people who are both confused and angered by the government's economic policies. That is probably why they phrase the questions as negatives: it seems a matter of common sense that the government should balance its budget, impose fair taxes, and administer bipartisan policy. After all, families have to balance their budgets, retailers have to charge fair prices, and daily life is about compromise. Shouldn't we hold the government to these same standards of financial responsibility?

In this "Focus On … Spending and Taxing," we begin to find answers to these questions by studying the spending and the taxing of the U.S. government. Who is taxed and at what rates reflects the country's political goals and values. The size of the government's annual budget and how it is allocated reveals the nation's priorities. This is why decisions about the proper size and role of government in a democracy and a largely free-market economy often begin with discussions about taxing and spending. Taxes and budgets measure the power of the government, politically and economically.

GOVERNMENT AND THE ECONOMY

Americans take great pride in describing their economy as a free-enterprise system, celebrating individual ambition, private property, and capitalism. In actuality, however, the United States has historically had a **mixed economy**, in which there is both private and government ownership. Building a strong economy was a priority for the Founding generation, and their successes created enduring expectations that public and private would mix together in the market. As Henry Adams remarked, "A people which had in 1787 been indifferent or hostile to roads, banks, funded debt, and nationality, had become in 1815 habituated to ideas and machinery of the sort on a grand scale."[1]

Consider, for example, the Louisiana Purchase. In a deal struck by President Jefferson in 1803, the geographic size of the country was nearly doubled. Then the Congress proceeded to pass laws and provide grants that encouraged the settlement and development of these lands, establishing a postal system, building canals, and sponsoring farmers and industrialists.[2] Similarly, the West was settled by both private initiative and strong government support in the form of land grants to settlers and railroads. And in any subsequent era of American history, government and the private sector worked together to make infrastructure investments.

Today, the U.S. government owns power-generating dams, some railroads, and 29 percent of all the land in the country, to name just a few of its resources. It also participates in the economy in many other ways. For example, it is an insurer of last resort for individual and corporate assets. It has loaned money to corporations to save them from bankruptcy. It has "bailed out" large banks, most notably in 2008 when it assumed almost a trillion dollars in bad debt. In the 1980s, it bailed out the entire Texas savings and loan industry at a cost of about $75 billion to taxpayers all over the country. This bailout, which occurred because of risky failed loans, was equal to about one-quarter of the entire Texas economy at that time.[3] The government also regulates many industries, setting policies for everything from workplace health and safety to interest rates. Public and private ownership are still inextricably interwoven throughout the U.S. economy.

Though the Constitution does not specify a particular kind of economic system, it defines the basic parameters for the relationship between the government and the economy by giving the federal government a wide range of economic powers, including the power to tax and to spend, to regulate commerce, to borrow money, and to coin money and set its value. **Art. I, Sec. 8** The Constitution also protects the private ownership of goods by individuals and corporations. **Art. VI, Amendments IV, VII, IX** Exactly how these government powers and individual rights are mixed has been negotiated with every policy decision since the Founding.

Government spending and taxation are essential to this mixture of the public and private in the economy. Decisions about how much money the government spends on which of its programs have always affected the nation's wealth and income. For example, major reforms in welfare policy throughout the 1990s resulted in many people losing access to these programs. As they lost this government aid, their income dropped even further and they had less to spend. Community and philanthropic organizations tried to compensate, but their resources could not match those that had previously come from the government. This is just one example of a policy decision that changed both individual incomes and the economy.

Tax policy is no less influential. "Who" pays "how much" on "what" to the government affects the spending decisions of individuals, organizations, and the government. Should all persons pay the same percentage of their income to the government? Or should those with higher incomes pay a higher percentage in taxes because they have more disposable income? Or should those with lower incomes pay more because they may use more public services? Each of these possibilities has been extensively debated in the United States.

Today, those with higher incomes are required to pay a higher percentage to the federal government. However, the government also allows tax deductions (sometimes referred to as tax loopholes) that are more likely to be claimed by those with a higher income. Those with more income, for example, are more likely to have a home with a mortgage, to make larger charitable donations, and to have significant business expenses. They also get more income from investments, which are taxed less. For these reasons, billionaire CEO Warren Buffett has famously and repeatedly proclaimed that he pays a smaller percentage of his income in taxes than does his secretary. A tax where the rich pay a greater percentage is called a **progressive tax**. If the poor pay proportionately more, it is called a **regressive tax**.

The framers knew that the power to tax and to spend would determine the power of the national government. They included these powers in the Constitution to help ensure that the national government would be strong enough to unite states that had previously been connected only through a loose confederation. **Art. I, Sec. 7, 8, & 10 Art. IV, Sec. 1.** Yet the framers also limited direct taxation on individuals by the central government by requiring that individual taxes must be in proportion to each state's population. **Art. I, Sec. 9** The national government could only begin to tax its citizens' income directly in 1913, after passage of the Sixteenth Amendment. Today, as then, taxing and spending are essential powers of the U.S. government. To understand why, we need to consider the basic issues associated with capitalism and democracy in the United States.

Capitalism and Democracy

An economy in which the country's capital or productive capacity, businesses, factories, and farms are owned by individuals and corporations is called a **capitalist economy**. In practice, there are no pure capitalist systems and there never have been. Virtually all economies are a mix of private and government ownership. These mixed economies are distinguished from one another by the degree of government ownership and intervention in the economy through taxing, spending, and regulation of both business and consumption. Government action through taxing and spending policies can make the rich richer and the poor poorer, or they can make the poor better off at the expense of the rich. Most Western democracies have fairly elaborate social welfare systems that redistribute some wealth from the rich to the poor in order to provide them with a minimal standard of living. We do less of this in the United States than do most other industrial nations.

Capitalism and American Values

Capitalist systems are not inevitably democratic, nor, obviously, are democratic systems purely capitalistic. Many presume that capitalism will foster democracy because liberty, individualism, and private property are of such importance to a capitalist economic system. Yet the tensions between equality and liberty that are seen in politics are also seen in the economy. As individuals exercise their liberty, pursue their personal preferences, and use their property, they will succeed or fail to increase their income. Capitalism does not value equality of result. Capitalism doesn't necessarily promote equality of opportunity, either. As income disparities increase, those with income and wealth will be able to afford a more extensive and better education and will gain more access to economic and political decision makers. As a result, those with higher incomes and greater wealth can expect to have more opportunities to develop their talents and profit from their investments. Liberty and equality are the foundations of democracy, but liberty and *in*equality are intrinsic to capitalism.

Capitalism and Market Regulation

It is partly because of this tension that increasing democracy in the United States, as measured by the expansion of the vote, was gradually accompanied by increasing regulation of the market. In nineteenth-century America, government focused on encouraging economic expansion and development by supporting railway and canal construction, giving away farmland through the Homestead Act, and developing transcontinental communication through a postal service and the telegraph. The government moved toward an even more proactive role in the twentieth century because of abuses by big business: child labor was widely used, workers were paid a pittance, filthy and unsafe working conditions (sweatshops were the norm) led to thousands of workers' deaths, food and drugs were routinely unsafe, and a few large producers controlled prices and wages for some products. As public anger focused on these economic injustices, the government, through the New Deal (1932–1940) programs, increased regulation of such things as wages, working conditions, and the content of food and drugs. Meanwhile, as more and more diverse peoples were voting, elected officials began paying more attention to the needs of average people. Today, there is general agreement that the government should be involved in the market, but how much and what kind of involvement are still contested. The Great Recession stimulated many heated discussions about the government bailouts for Wall Street and for car manufacturers, about stimulating the economy through public works such as highways and educational research programs, and about extending unemployment insurance coverage. These are all disagreements about what a government should do to stimulate or slow the growth of a "free-market" economy, to alter the distribution of wealth or provide a measure of equality.

Keynesian Economics

Most, but not all, economists subscribe to the notion propounded by John Maynard Keynes in 1935 when he argued that the government can stimulate the economy by increasing spending in a time of high unemployment and cutting spending in times of low unemployment. By pumping more money into the economy in times of high unemployment, government increases the demand for goods and services in the private sector, which leads to less unemployment. Therefore, the government can safely run a budget deficit in order to increase its spending because higher employment will eventually lead to an increase in tax revenues, which in turn will ultimately lead to payment of the debt that was created by the deficit spending. This scenario became known as **Keynesian economics**.

President Roosevelt's New Deal package tested this theory and engineered growth during the Great Depression. Local public buildings, roads and highways, bridges, and other public works throughout the nation were built as part of New Deal stimulus programs. But, fearful of government debt, the president and Congress put the brakes on in 1938, and the economy shrank again. It was the entry of the United States into World War II and the economic stimulus of manufacturing armaments and other military necessities that brought a final end to the Great Depression.

President Obama and the Democratic Congress tried to stimulate the economy with an economic stimulus package, passed in 2009, that funded some infrastructure, gave households tax breaks, and provided state and local governments with funding. While it did produce an upturn in growth, at the time some Keynesian economists said it was much too small relative to the size of the economy to have a longer-term effect. (Misjudgments by economists about the depth of the recession, and fears by the administration that there would not be congressional support, limited the president's stimulus package.) And indeed, though there was a short-term boost in employment, when the stimulus ended state and local governments laid off thousands of workers, demand for goods and services decreased, and the economy sagged again.

Other economists argue that spending that increases the national debt makes the economy worse. That was the thinking in 1938 when Roosevelt and Congress cut government spending after the earlier New Deal stimulus; now it's clear that this thinking was incorrect during the Depression—it caused the economy to tank again. But this desire to limit debt led some European governments, in 2010–2012, to pare back spending even though they were still in recession. This is also the thinking of most congressional Republicans who have opposed President Obama's plans to stimulate employment through continuing aid to state and local governments and new investments in infrastructure.

Recurring Economic Problems

Economic cycles of boom and bust have been a constant in human history. Good times with rising living standards are followed by bad times when economic activity slows, investment income declines, people go hungry, unemployment is

Sally Ryan/The New York Times/Redux

As unemployment increased during the Great Recession and more Americans fell behind on mortgage and rent payments, poor women in rental housing were most likely to be evicted.

rife, tax revenues decline, and living standards decline. Until modern times, governments did little to regulate these cycles, although some tried to ease the consequences of the bad times by distributing grain to people who were starving or by providing temporary shelters for the homeless. In the United States, it was not until the 1930s that government tried to prevent these cycles from occurring.

The idea that government intervention could ease the boom-and-bust cycle of the economy was revolutionary. Classical economists had argued that the market would adjust itself without government action. But as governments became larger and more powerful, people expected government to at least try to alleviate economic problems. Since the Great Depression, government has almost always been linked in the public mind to poor performance by the economy, whether or not government policies have contributed much to the failures. This assumption gives elected officials an incentive to solve economic problems or to blame the opposing party for those failures.

Unemployment

Unemployment is a familiar economic problem that modern government is expected to address. Its effects are sometimes obvious (people cannot pay their debts and fall into poverty), sometimes less so (unemployed workers are less healthy and suffer higher mortality rates—even years after they re-enter the labor market—than workers with uninterrupted employment). As unemployed workers lose their job skills, the likelihood that they will be able to find work declines and a high unemployment rate becomes the norm, to the detriment of

the economy.[4] But unemployment cannot always be eliminated, whether times are good or bad.

Even in a "full-employment" economy, 3 to 5 percent of the labor force will be out of work—people who quit their jobs to look for something better, those just entering the workforce, those unable to work, and those who do not want to work for one reason or another. But most Western countries experience periods when many people are unemployed because the economy does not create enough jobs.

Depressions   A **depression** is a period of decline in the gross national product (GNP), the total dollar value of all goods and services produced over a specific time period, and is usually characterized by prolonged high unemployment. If the GDP declines by more than 10 percent, then the country is in a depression. Using this standard, the last depression in the United States was the **Great Depression** from 1929 to 1933 (GDP declined by almost 33 percent); then, after a recovery period, a less severe depression occurred in 1937 and 1938 (in which GDP declined by over 18 percent). (The Great Depression is further examined in the Introduction and Chapter 2.)

Recessions   A less severe and briefer decline in GDP is referred to as a **recession**. There are many definitions of a recession; most analysts think that the nation is in a recession when the GDP has declined for two or more consecutive quarters (six months or longer). Falling GDP is linked to high unemployment: when more people are unemployed, fewer goods and services are produced. According to another

"I'm not huffing and puffing. I'm foreclosing."

foreclosed on their loans. Child poverty rates increased dramatically: 13 states had child poverty rates of 20 percent or higher before the Great Recession; the number had doubled to 26 states by the end of 2011.[6]

When European nations, including such major economies as that of Spain, encountered economic problems in 2012, fears of another downturn took deep root in the United States and began to affect the presidential campaigns. As one influential decision maker described the U.S. economy relative to those in Europe, "We're the healthiest horse in the glue factory."[7]

Inflation

Another intermittent economic problem is **inflation**, which occurs when prices for goods and services rise and purchasing power falls. Inflation erodes the value of savings because the dollar will be worth less in the future than it is in the present. For this reason, inflation gives people an incentive to spend money (taking advantage of their comparatively greater purchasing power right now) and to hoard goods (guarding against the drops in the purchasing power of the dollar).

Inflation has contributed to social unrest and political revolutions throughout history. Part of the reason for German enthusiasm for Hitler in 1933 was the inflation of the early 1920s. In 1923, German inflation was so high that a wheelbarrow of money barely sufficed to buy a bag of groceries. Contributing to the hyperinflation were the World War I reparations that the victors imposed upon Germany and banking purchases made in the international money markets. The government finally ended the inflation by issuing new currency, one unit of which was equal to one trillion of the old. This made the lifetime savings of many people worthless and contributed to the unrest that eventually toppled the democratic government and installed the Nazi government.

As inflation grows, bankers increase interest rates in an effort to compensate for the declining value of the dollar. This is also intended to slow the pace of inflation by reducing the incentive to borrow and spend. However, these increased interest rates make it difficult for businesses and industries to expand, and if interest rates rise too high, the economy can slow down too much and lapse into a recession.

The ultimate goal in any economy is to have low unemployment, low inflation, and increasing productivity, with a steady growth in total economic output. Achieving all of these simultaneously is rare, however. Often, low inflation is accompanied by higher unemployment because production sags. Higher inflation is often associated with lower unemployment, as production increases. But from the 1980s onward, increased productivity did not result in similar increases in wages for the 32 percent of the labor force that are production and non-supervisory workers.[8] The negative effects were masked in the 1990s, when the United States boasted the lowest unemployment rate (3.9 percent) in a quarter-century, and a low, stable inflation rate (about 2 percent). For many, but not all, this economic growth boosted wages and standards of living and created a prosperous economy. But this was the calm before the storm of the Great Recession.

informal standard, a recession turns into a depression when unemployment is 10 percent or higher. This number is the reason why the Obama administration has always taken such care not to "round off" unemployment statistics. When unemployment in 2008 was at 9.8 percent, rounding off (to 10 percent) would have indicated that the country was in a depression. Yet some states endured depression-level unemployment, including Michigan (over 18 percent in October 2009) and Nevada (13 percent in October 2009). In Nevada, Rhode Island, and California, unemployment was typically above 10 percent from 2008 through 2012.

Economists have sometimes referred to the period of 2008 to 2012 in the United States as the **Great Recession** because of its severity and long duration. Economic growth was sluggish, though mostly positive, job creation was slow, and high unemployment was prolonged. While many banks and corporations were thriving again by 2010, the economy was unable to replace the millions of jobs lost after the housing boom crashed and banks collapsed, let alone keep pace with the normal growth in job demand. Layoffs of government workers, teachers, police, and other civil servants by state and local governments offset gains in private sector jobs. Disagreement among the experts over whether the economy remained in recession or was in a "jobless recovery" illustrated the problem of interpreting the meaning of leading economic indicators.

Regardless, the Great Recession wiped out nearly two decades of increases in wealth for middle-class families. It slashed the value of their stocks and their homes, pulling Americans back to where they were in 1992.[5] (The increases in the value of stocks and homes in the intervening years were only on paper—not real unless the stocks or houses were sold before the recession—but most Americans believed the gains were real, so the losses were a jolt.) The Great Recession also saw many Americans losing their houses; when people could no longer meet their mortgage payments, the banks

Still, inflation remained low during the Great Recession. This occurred despite near-record government spending and borrowing for the bailouts of Wall Street banks and the auto manufacturers and for the stimulus. Government borrowing can certainly trigger inflation if the private sector is chasing money as well and banks are willing to lend. But when times are uncertain, individuals and businesses are less willing to borrow money for consumption and expansion, and sometimes the banks will not extend them the credit to do so. Under these conditions, even low interest rates do not stimulate economic growth because individuals and businesses are unwilling to risk starting new projects and companies, which involves borrowing and incurring added debt.

Deflation

Most economists believe that moderate inflation is preferable to deflation. **Deflation** occurs when prices fall so low that there is a disincentive to buy because consumers keep waiting for prices to fall lower.[9] The result is a sluggish economy, falling wages, and no job creation.

Japan experienced severe deflation beginning in the early 1990s and extending into the early years of the new century.

Pain of Recession Is Unevenly Spread

The effects of hard economic times hit different groups of people very differently. For example, discrimination in hiring and compensation leaves African Americans and Latinos more vulnerable even in good times, and the impact is exaggerated in times of high unemployment. The typical gap between white and black unemployment, for example, is about 5 percent. At the height of the recession, in 2010, the unemployment rate for whites was nearly 9 percent, but it was 16 percent for African Americans. Not only did unemployment increase significantly for both groups, but the gap between them increased too. Latino unemployment is less than that of blacks and more than that of whites; the white-Latino gap also increased during the recession. This can be explained in part because African American and Latino workers have been concentrated in some of the sectors with the greatest job losses, such as manufacturing, the auto industry, and construction. (See Figure 1.)

Paradoxically, women, another group subjected to wage discrimination and occupational segregation, have fared better than men during the recession, because their employment has been concentrated in health care and education, areas where there has been job growth. Only a little more than 30 percent of the workforce in 1964, women are now close to a majority. Typically unemployment rates for men and women are similar, but male

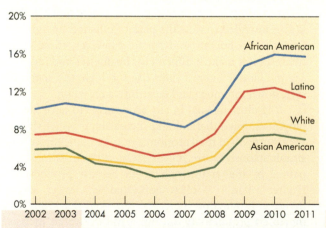

FIGURE 1: THE IMPACT OF THE 2008 RECESSION ON UNEMPLOYMENT BY RACE AND ETHNICITY
African Americans and Latinos were hardest hit by the recession.
SOURCE: Economic Policy Institute, www.economytrack.org/unemployment.php.

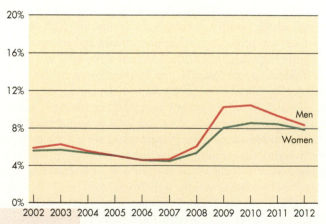

FIGURE 2: RECESSION HAS HIT MALE WORKERS HARDER THAN FEMALE WORKERS
SOURCE: Economic Policy Institute, www.economytrack.org/unemployment.php.

During this time period, which some refer to as Japan's "lost decade," its economy came to a near standstill.

Some fear that the United States will experience deflation in the coming years. Government spending and borrowing are now at record levels, yet there is virtually no inflation and prices are stagnant or falling. With an uncertain economic outlook, consumers are afraid to spend and employers afraid to hire. As productivity and profits fall, factories and companies are likely to close, unemployment rises, and debt and loan defaults increase. If this continues or accelerates, the nation could fall into depression.[10]

The Misery Index

The sum of the unemployment rate and the inflation percentage is the **misery index**. This is not an official index put out by government economic agencies, but rather a measure constructed around election time by those wanting to evaluate economic progress or lack of it during a president's term. The misery index is so named because it gets higher as the number of people looking for work and the prices people have to pay for basic goods and services rise. Then it is likely that more people are unhappy. It has been as high as 21 when both

unemployment rose more than that of women in 2010 and 2011. By 2012, the numbers began to converge again. As with men, African American women and Latinas experience considerably higher unemployment rates than white women. (See Figure 2.)

Education has a huge impact on unemployment. College graduates saw their unemployment levels rise only minimally, while unemployment among those with high school degrees or some college rose significantly and unemployment among those without even a high school degree skyrocketed. Whites (and Asian Americans) have the advantage of having more years of education, on average, than blacks and Latinos; but even whites (and Asian Americans) without high school diplomas are more successful in finding jobs than workers in other categories. (See Figure 3.)

Sources: All statistics are provided by the Bureau of Labor Statistics. For further information about women, see Andrea Orr, "Women Now Hold Close to Half of All Jobs," Economic Policy Institute, May 6, 2010, www.epi.org/economic_snapshots/women_now_hold_close_to_half_of_all_jobs/; Bureau of Labor Statistics, "Women in the Labor Force: A Data Book" (2009 edition), www.bls.gov/cps/wlf-intro-2009.htm. Statistics focusing on Asian American women were not available.

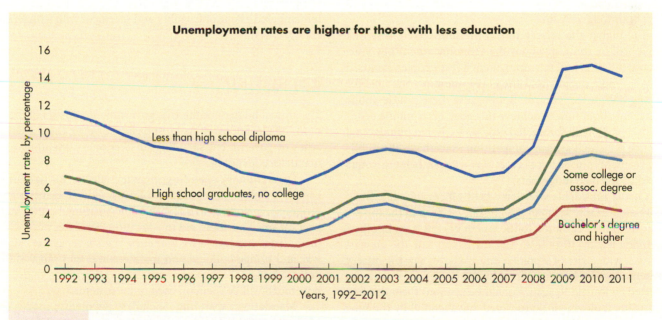

FIGURE 3: UNEMPLOYMENT AND EDUCATION Unemployment rates are higher for workers with less education. These workers also suffer more in economic downturns, which was especially true in the recession that began in 2008.

SOURCE: U.S. Bureau of Labor Statistics, Labor Force Statistics from the Current Population Survey, http://data.bls.gov/pdq/SurveyOutputServlet.

Hyperinflation in post-World War I Germany caused the money to become virtually worthless; baskets of money were necessary to purchase even a few groceries. The hyperinflation was caused by the German government's printing ever more money to pay penalties it was assessed by the victors of World War I. The government finally ended the inflation by issuing new currency, one unit of which was equal to one trillion of the old. This made the lifetime savings of many people worthless and contributed to the unrest that eventually toppled the democratic government and installed the Nazi government.

unemployment and inflation were very high and as low as 3 when both were very low.

The higher the misery index, the more likely it is that people will be thinking about the economy when they vote. Because inflation and unemployment affect people's standard of living, most people hold the government accountable for keeping both under control. But because there is little public agreement about how to achieve this goal, even among economists, it is difficult for elected officials to design popular and effective policies. Partisan competition exacerbates the public disagreement, polarizing perceptions without helping voters to make informed judgments.

Of the presidents who have held office since the Great Depression, Harry Truman saw the largest drop in the misery index from the beginning to the end of his full term in office; the index fell by 10 points. Richard Nixon saw the greatest increase, with a rise of 9 points. Jimmy Carter saw the misery index increase by 7 points during his term in office, and he was defeated by Ronald Reagan. Ronald Reagan saw the index first rise, as unemployment skyrocketed, but then fall by the time of his reelection. When Obama became president, the misery index was 7.7. It rose to more than 12 as the impact of the recession hit, then fell to less than 10 midway through 2012.

The misery index does affect popular perceptions and memories of the presidents, for better or for worse. Reagan's presidency is widely remembered as a time of prosperity (despite an early recession), while Carter's presidency is remembered as one of frugality and sacrifice (with a lingering energy crisis).

SPENDING

The annual budget for the U.S. government consists of thousands of allocations. At its most basic, however, there are two types of government spending: discretionary spending and mandatory spending.

Discretionary spending includes salaries for operating expenses and employee salaries of most federal agencies and programs, including, as a few examples, national parks, support for small business, aid to education, regulatory agencies, the judicial and legislative branches, the space agency, highway and bridge building and maintenance, and most of the defense budget. Each year, Congress has discretion to decide how much will be spent on each of these items.

Mandatory spending includes payments made for Medicare and Medicaid, various government subsidies such as farm price supports, interest on the national debt, and unemployment insurance. Money for each of these items is required by law; if Congress wants to change the allocation, then it must change the relevant law. For example, Congress cannot refuse to fund welfare programs, nor can it drastically cut their funding. But Congress can amend the laws that created these programs to reduce eligibility, or it can repeal the laws and remove any need for appropriations. This is what was done to federal welfare programs in 1995 and 1996. The laws that made welfare spending mandatory were rewritten, with eligibility standards changed and many responsibilities devolved to the states. A few mandatory expenditures cannot be changed in this way. Paying the interest on the national debt is unequivocally mandatory; the only way to reduce this spending is to pay the debt.

For fiscal year 2011, actual spending was $3.603 trillion. Of this, 55.9 percent was for mandatory spending, and 5.6 percent was allocated for paying the interest on the national debt. Only 38.5 percent was for discretionary spending. (See Figure 4.)

Whether discretionary or mandatory, government spending affects the economy in three ways: first, by its size relative to the overall economy; second, by what it is used for; and finally, by whether, or by how much, it exceeds revenues.

How Much?

How great an impact government has depends on how much it spends in relation to the size of its economy. Under normal circumstances, spending by the U.S. government is a sufficiently small part of all economic activity that it limits the influence of the government in the market. When government does try to slow inflation through reduced spending or to stimulate the economy through increased spending, it is very difficult to determine how much additional spending will be necessary and in which areas it should be concentrated, though estimates can be made. Moreover, our economy is linked to the global market and thus is affected by conditions over which the U.S. government has little control, such as energy prices or the economic policies of other nations.

From 1970 through 2008, federal spending as a proportion of the GDP ranged from 18.2 percent in the last year of the Clinton administration and the first year of the George W. Bush administration, to 23.5 percent in 1983 during the Reagan administration. State and local governments spent another 10 percent of the GDP. Beginning in 2009, the financial industry bailout and counter-recessionary measures (such as the economic stimulus bill) increased government spending and its percentage of the GDP. That proportion peaked in 2009 at 25 percent before falling to 24.1 percent in 2011, which exceeds the forty-year maximum by about half a percent.[11]

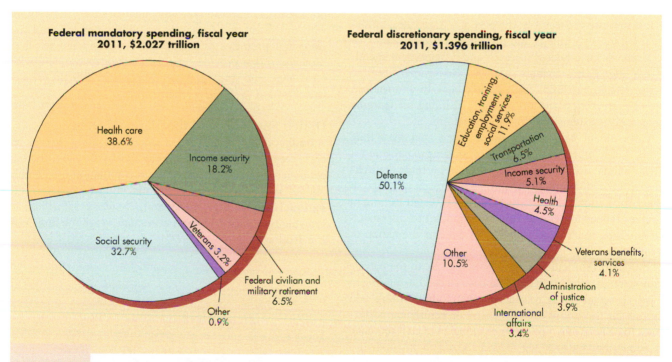

FIGURE 4: BUDGETED FEDERAL SPENDING, 2011: $3.8 TRILLION Mandatory spending accounted for 55.9 percent of the federal budget in FY 2011, discretionary spending for 38.5 percent, and interest on the national debt for the remaining 5.6 percent. The largest percentage of mandatory spending, after Social Security programs, went to health care; Medicare ($560 billion) and Medicaid ($275 billion) consume most of this spending. Income security programs include unemployment compensation ($119 billion), earned income and child tax credits ($78 billion), and the Supplemental Nutrition Assistance Program ($77 billion). The largest percentage of discretionary spending was defense-related, which included expenditures ranging from personnel to maintenance to research and development.

SOURCE: Jonathan Schwabish and Courtney Griffith, "The U.S. Federal Budget, Discretionary Spending," "The U.S. Federal Budget, Mandatory Spending," Congressional Budget Office, April 2012.

On What?

As Keynes argued, much government spending can stimulate economic growth. It creates jobs directly, as when government hires more workers, and indirectly when it buys goods and services from the private sector, which then hires more workers.

Sometimes government spending has less of an impact, as when government aid is spent abroad to finance wars or to provide military or civilian aid (though if the development aid is used to buy U.S. goods and services it has some impact; military aid often yields purchases of arms from U.S. manufacturers). Military spending can boost the civilian economy. The massive spending on World War II finally ended the Great Depression. It was an overwhelmingly large stimulus package, and much of it was spent at home, manufacturing weapons, planes, and ships. At the midway point in the war, the government had spent six times the amount allocated for all of the New Deal programs. As in all previous wars, taxes were raised to pay for the war, though the national debt still increased.

Money used to pay for our recent wars in Iraq and Afghanistan was borrowed money because President Bush and Congress refused to increase taxes to pay for them. As a consequence, deficits increased significantly, and so did the interest on the national debt. While some of the spending stimulated the American economy, an unknown proportion was lost to waste and fraud on the part of U.S. private contractors, the Iraqi government, and the Afghan government.

Some defense-related research and development spending has significant civilian benefits. Government-funded defense-related research, for example, led to innovations in food preservation and preparation, clothing for extreme climates, GPS systems, and Internet development.

Government can also spend in areas that over time become a drag on economic growth. Spending to pay interest on the national debt, for example, does not promote the well-being of the nation, unless the money borrowed was used to protect the nation's vital interests or was invested in human resources (education and health, for example) or infrastructure (building roads and bridges) that benefits the nation in the long run.

Much government spending goes directly to the private sector through purchase of goods and services. Outsourcing to the private sector can be routine, as when food, clothing, and weapons for the troops are purchased or equipment is purchased for offices, labs, and other workplaces of civil servants. But sometimes outsourcing replaces government activities with those of the private sector. For example, in Iraq, much of the security for U.S. officials was provided not through our military forces but by private security firms. As we saw in Chapter 11, while outsourcing is often justified as a cost savings, it tends to increase cost and reduce accountability.

Relation to Revenue

Government spending and government revenues (collected through fees, fines, and taxes, among other sources) have a complex relationship. Projecting the revenues that will come into the government is no less complicated than projecting the need for government spending. In both instances, budget writers have to project future rates of inflation, unemployment, and productivity. If there is an economic slowdown, factories will idle, workers will be laid off, tax revenues will fall, and more spending will be required for unemployment insurance, welfare, and health care, among many other programs. If there is economic growth, taxes will generate greater revenue and spending needs will drop. External events, such as wars or natural disasters, will have even more drastic effects on spending and taxes, and are even more difficult to anticipate. Yet small errors in predictions make an astoundingly large difference. Underestimating unemployment by 1 percent can lead to a multibillion-dollar budgeting problem, as revenue drops and expenditures rise.

Campaigns and elections further complicate spending and revenue projections. During campaigns, incumbents have an incentive to accept optimistic projections that will win public support for themselves and their policies. Challengers, conversely, have reason to present the most negative projections, attacking the incumbent and drawing sharp contrasts with their own policy proposals. Not surprisingly, election outcomes often influence consumer behavior and corporate decision making. During their first year in office, presidents are eager to take advantage of their "honeymoon" with the voters and Congress by fulfilling as many of their campaign promises as possible. New presidents select the projections that provide support for their recommendations for change, and since all projections are so difficult to calculate, it is hard to challenge their choices.

Deficit Spending and the National Debt

A **budget deficit** occurs when federal spending exceeds federal revenues in a single year. For fiscal year 2011, the budget deficit was $1.3 trillion.[12] The accumulation of all annual budget deficits (minus the occasional budget surpluses) is the **national debt**. In 2011, the federal debt was $13.9 trillion and growing by almost $4 billion every day.[13] (See the box "What Is a Trillion Dollars Anyway?")

"Did he say the budget was going to be a zillion billion krillion dollars or a krillion billion zillion dollars?"

Impact social, global, historical, economic, political

What Is a Trillion Dollars Anyway?

When economists and politicians talk about the deficit and the debt, they throw around numbers in the billions and trillions. These numbers are hard to comprehend. Just writing out a trillion dollars is astounding: $1,000,000,000,000. But what does it mean? It is a million million dollars.

Here are other ways to put it in perspective:

A million seconds ago was only 11½ days ago. A trillion seconds ago was 31,700 years ago, about the time modern human beings evolved.

If someone handed you a $100 bill every second, you would be a millionaire eight times over in one day. But, to be a trillionaire, you would have to be handed a $100 bill every second for 317 years.

If you laid $1 bills end to end, 1 million of them would only go about 100 miles. One billion would get you around the earth four times. One trillion would allow you to go to the sun and several million miles beyond.

If you packed $1 bills into railroad boxcars, you could get $63.5 million in each boxcar. To get $1 trillion loaded in, you would have almost 16,000 boxcars and the train would be 167 miles long.

Sources: Boyce Rensberger, "$1,000,000,000,000—We're Talking Real Money," *Washington Post National Weekly Edition*, January 19, 1987, 32.

When the government faces a deficit, it sells investments (for example, government bonds) to individuals and corporations in the United States and foreign countries and to governments of foreign countries (especially China).[14] The government uses the proceeds to offset its deficit. The individuals, corporations, and governments who hold these investments will eventually cash them in. That is, they will be paid back, with interest.

It is important to remember that deficits occur because Congress spends more than the government takes in through tax revenues. As a result, deficit spending results from both spending and taxing decisions. It is a product of the amount of spending, the level of tax rates, and the growth of the economy. If tax rates remain constant, tax revenues will be higher in prosperous times because individual and corporate incomes will be larger, and lower in hard times because incomes will be smaller.

In fiscal year 2011, about one dollar in every ten received by the government in revenues was spent on interest on the debt, and deficits of at least $600 billion a year were forecast through fiscal year 2020.[15] If we don't raise tax rates or reduce annual spending, we will see a $3 trillion deficit by 2030, $9 trillion by 2050.[16] Obviously, as deficits increase, less and less will be left in the budget to meet national security needs or urgent needs in education, health care, research, and the infrastructure improvements, all of which contribute to economic growth and competitiveness in the global economy.

A balanced budget is generally regarded as sound policy in ordinary times, though it is a rare year when we achieve it. The last balanced budget came in the Clinton administration. But a budget in deficit can be helpful in a recession or depression to fuel economic growth, and may also be necessary in wartime. The Revolutionary War, the Civil War, and the Second World War all left the country with huge debts, but we repaid them when more normal times returned.

The United States entered into a new period of deficit spending in the 1980s with Reagan's adoption of supply-side economics and massive military spending. As deficits continued to soar in the administration of George H. W. Bush, the Republican president and the Democratic-controlled Congress set caps on spending and adopted the **pay-as-you-go** system, or simply **paygo**. If the president or Congress wanted to pass a tax cut or increase spending on a program, they had to pair this change with spending cuts elsewhere or new revenues.

In 1993, against the wishes of many Democrats, Clinton supported renewal of the spending caps and the pay-as-you-go principle. A few years later, he committed to achieving a balanced budget by 2002. Clinton was fortunate: continued economic growth and low unemployment produced greater-than-anticipated federal revenues, while spending caps and paygo rules limited spending. With these advantages, the budget balanced three years ahead of schedule.[17]

Once there appeared to be budget surpluses, however, Congress began modifying the constraints on spending. The spending caps were raised annually, beginning in 1999, and the paygo law expired in 2002.[18] It was reinstituted as a procedural rule—giving Congress much more discretion than the original law—after the 2006 elections.

At the same time, George W. Bush increased discretionary spending by an amazing 36 percent during his first term, the largest increase since FDR's presidency.[19] Much of this increase was caused by spending on the War on Terror. At the same time, the Bush tax cuts reduced federal revenues; the tax cuts alone increased the national debt by $1.8 trillion. (Slow economic growth also reduced revenues, by an additional $1.4 trillion.[20]) Ultimately, the cost of all of Bush's policies from 2001 to 2009, including the wars in Iraq and Afghanistan ($853 billion), the financial bailout ($224 billion), and other discretionary defense spending ($616 billion), was $5.1 trillion. In contrast, the cost of policies enacted during Obama's first term will amount to $983 billion by 2017.[21] Though members of the Republican Party stress the need to cut spending, Republican

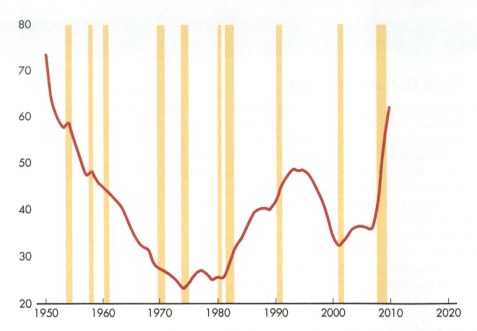

FIGURE 5: U.S. DEBT RELATIVE TO GDP The ratio of debt to GDP shows that the United States faced a large debt from World War II but paid it back during the booming decades of the 1950s and 1960s. The debt rose under President Reagan in the 1980s, receded under President Clinton in the 1990s, and rose again during the Great Recession in the late 2000s. The shaded areas indicate U.S. recessions.

SOURCE: Paul Krugman, "Sixties Madness," *New York Times* Opinion Pages, July 10, 2012, http://krugman.blogs.nytimes.com/. Data from Economic Research, Federal Reserve Bank of St. Louis, http://research.stlouisfed.org/fred2/graph/#.

policies have played a greater role than Democratic policies in increasing the size of the national debt.

As the economy picked up steam in the middle of the decade, so did revenues, but government spending still outran these increases. And unlike FDR's social spending—which "hired about 60 percent of the unemployed in public works and conservation projects," which included building or renovating "2,500 hospitals, 45,000 schools, 13,000 parks and playgrounds, 7,800 bridges, 700,000 miles of roads, and a thousand airfields"[22]—Bush's spending created few jobs and did not improve the nation's infrastructure. The financial bailouts implemented during the Bush administration and the economic stimulus programs of the Obama administration produced deficit levels not seen since World War II. (See Figure 5.)

There is no prospect that deficits will disappear in the coming decade. Spending will far outrun revenues. Consider the costs that are associated with defense, war, nation building in Iraq and Afghanistan, Social Security, Medicare, Medicaid, unemployment insurance, and job creation. At the same time, there have been sizable cuts in estate taxes and in personal and corporate income taxes. There are no nonpartisan projections that near-term economic growth alone will produce the additional revenue needed to balance the budget. All evidence indicates that reducing the annual deficit will require either drastic cuts in spending or significant increases in taxes.

Deficits, Debt, and Economic Health

Those who focus on having a balanced budget often use the analogy of a family budget: no family can keep on overspending

its resources indefinitely. In fact, of course, families frequently go into debt. Very few families can pay cash for a house, so they take out mortgages, a substantial long-term debt. If they did not, very few houses would get built or sold. Many families also take out loans to help their children through college. In both cases, families are investing in their future, just as government debt is often run up to invest in a country's future.

But a country is not a family, and the family budget analysis is not particularly helpful in thinking about the national debt or annual deficits. Unlike family debt, a country's debt consists heavily of money it owes itself. It borrows from those who buy its bonds and from parts of the government with surpluses. A family cannot raise taxes or issue bonds to produce more revenue.

Economists and elected officials disagree about how urgent it is to pay down the debt. Those who give high priority to debt reduction point to the amount of money tied up in annual interest payments on the national debt. They also point out that we are increasingly indebted to foreign individuals, corporations, and governments, not all of whom are allies. This makes us more vulnerable to economic and political forces outside our borders. And the outflow of dollars to cover these interest payments contributes to our trade deficit, weakens the dollar, and makes us even more vulnerable to the uncertainties of international markets. This is a strong argument for lowering our annual budget deficits.

Others point out that the United States has had a national debt during most years of its existence, with no particular harm done. Still others point out that government spending should be high during hard times, despite deficits, but then should pivot toward a balanced budget when the economy revives and extra spending is not needed. As far as public opinion goes, there actually is more support for increasing spending than for decreasing it, despite the attacks on "big government" (see Table 1).

Although there is disagreement about the urgency of paying off the public debt, there is general agreement that large deficits are unsustainable over the long term. Deficits can only be reduced and debt paid back by a combination of tax increases and spending decreases. However, there is sharp partisan disagreement on this issue. During the past several years, increasing taxes has become anathema to Republicans, with many members of Congress even signing a pledge not to raise any taxes. Some now identify Republicans as "the Party of the Rich," because its tax reforms offer so little to the working and lower classes.[23] This has happened at a time when taxes, especially taxes on the wealthy, are at a modern low point, much lower than they were in conservative President Reagan's era or the Clinton era with its good economic times

and brief balanced budget. The Republican support for tax cuts has also signaled that the party is no longer upholding deficit reduction as a major policy objective. As Vice President Cheney remarked, "Reagan proved that deficits don't matter" to the voters.[24] However, with no possibility of negotiations to raise more revenue, and Democrats having agreed to many spending cuts, bipartisan agreements on dealing with deficits are stalemated. Various public officials, Republican and Democrat alike, offer plans to reduce the deficit, but few are willing to tackle the revenue side of the equation, and no plan that fails to tackle that is feasible.

TAXING

Taxes, said Oliver Wendell Holmes, are the price of civilization. They provide all the governmental benefits that we enjoy, from roads to insured bank accounts, from public

Table 1 There Is More Public Support for Increasing Than for Decreasing Government Spending

Policy	Increase Spending	Decrease Spending
Education	62%	11%
Veterans' benefits, services	51	6
Health care	41	24
Medicare	40	12
Combating crime	39	18
Energy	36	23
Scientific research	36	23
Environmental protection	36	26
U.S. anti-terrorism defenses	33	21
Agriculture	32	23
Military defense	31	30
Unemployment assistance	27	28
Global poverty assistance	21	45

A 2011 Gallup survey found that 64 percent of respondents felt that "big government" would be "the biggest threat to the country." In the same year, however, the Pew Research Center found that there was more support for increasing than for decreasing government spending for many programs. This seemingly contradictory finding has been echoed in news reports about citizens who feel that "too many Americans lean on taxpayers rather than living within their means," even as their children participate in school breakfast and lunch programs, their senior parents rely on government health programs, and they claim various tax deductions. The expanded dependence on government benefits by the middle class has generated a wide range of emotions, ranging from guilt and frustration, to relief and appreciation. In 2012, the federal government had 2,238 assistance programs and government benefits accounted for 17.6 percent of all personal income. And the most expensive programs benefited the middle class. In a *Time* cover story, a reporter listed all the benefits his middle-class family derived from government programs. He then cautioned against cutting these same programs because the members of his family were "the kind of moochers who vote."[25] References to "moochers" surfaced throughout the 2012 presidential campaigns, especially when vice presidential candidate Paul Ryan's stump speeches advocated extensive budget cuts.

SOURCES: Table: Pew Research Center, February 2–7, 2011. Caption: Binyamin Appelbaum and Robert Gebeloff, "Even Critics of Safety Net Increasingly Depend on It," *New York Times*, February 11, 2012. Ezra Klein, "Liberalism's Problem in One Graph," [Gallup data] December 12, 2011, www.washingtonpost.com/blogs/ezra-klein/post/liberalisms-problem-in-one-graph/2011/08/25/gIQAVuVTqO-blog.nthl?wpisrc=nl_politics. Pew Research Center, February 2–7, 2011. Bureau of Economic Analysis data, as quoted in Jeremy White et al., "The Geography of Government Benefits," *New York Times*, February 11, 2012.

schools to national parks, and from local police protection to the national defense. As this list suggests, tax policy is used to achieve a number of social goals and to regulate the economy; see Figure 6). The desire to encourage some activities and discourage others through tax policy means that our tax laws are extraordinarily complex. Franklin Roosevelt once said that our tax code "might as well have been written in a foreign language," and it is much more complex now, with more than 650 different IRS forms and thousands of pages of directions. Even the careerists in the IRS find the rules difficult to decipher; a 2003 study found that the agency either did not answer or did not answer correctly 43 percent of citizens' walk-in questions.[26]

It is important to study taxes in both their political and their economic context. Taxes in the United States claim a relatively small portion of the GDP, just over 30 percent (counting state and local taxes as well as federal taxes). Among Western industrialized nations, only Australia has tax revenues that are a smaller share of GDP. In Norway and Denmark, total government receipts amounted to almost 60 percent; in Germany and the Netherlands, almost 50 percent; in Canada and Portugal, almost 40 percent.[27]

Achieving Social Goals

The social goals upheld through the tax code are closely connected to the constituents that it rewards. The tax code implicitly or explicitly favors some activities over others. Tax exemptions or deductions favor some activities by reducing the income that can be taxed (an exemption) or allowing expenses to be subtracted from the person's income (a deduction). As a person's taxable income decreases, his or

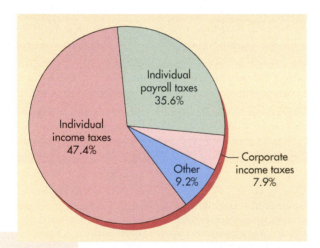

FIGURE 6: PAYROLL TAXES Note: "Payroll taxes" are the taxes for Social Security and Medicare deducted from paychecks. In addition to these revenues, the government borrows money—more than the revenue from individual income taxes—by selling investments to individuals, corporations, and foreign countries.

SOURCE: Derived from baseline budget projections in Congressional Budget Office, "Updated Budget Projections, Fiscal Years 2012–2022," March 2012.

her taxes also decrease because the U.S. tax code allows those with lower incomes to pay a lower percentage of their income in taxes.

Perhaps the most well-known exemption is the one granted for dependent children. Families can reduce their taxable income by a certain amount for each dependent child. Well-known deductions include the interest on home loans, the cost of child care, and the value of charitable donations. A few years ago, deductions were allowed for expenses incurred in weatherproofing homes to obtain more energy efficiency. The intent of these exemptions and deductions is to encourage families and children, home ownership, philanthropy, and energy efficiency, all goals strongly endorsed in American society.

Activities not considered socially desirable can be discouraged through extra taxes. For example, states levy a tax on alcohol and tobacco, with an eye toward limiting consumption as well as raising revenue. The federal government taxes tobacco and, in the health care law, tanning salons to decrease their use and raise revenue. (The federal government also taxes gasoline, primarily to raise revenue. Economists and environmentalists have proposed that the government sharply increase gas taxes to discourage the purchase of "gas guzzling" vehicles.)

The American tax system was designed to be mildly progressive, that is, to impose higher tax rates on wealthier people, but in fact because of numerous deductions and exemptions, the tax system does little to reduce inequality. On paper, wealthier people pay a higher percentage of their income, but in practice most wealthy people pay a lower percentage of their income in federal taxes than middle-class Americans do. Of all the modern nations, only Chile, South Korea, and Switzerland have tax systems that are less progressive—that reduce income inequality less—than the United States.[28]

Rewarding Constituents

Exemptions and deductions reward specific constituencies and networks. Charities, including educational institutions, benefit because people's donations can be deducted from their taxable income, so some people, especially big donors, are more inclined to donate. Builders, developers, and bankers, as well as home owners, gain because the home ownership deduction creates economic incentives to build and buy homes. Deductions for energy-saving home improvements also benefit these groups, with the added social value of conserving energy resources and preserving the environment. Exemption by exemption, deduction by deduction, these provisions in the tax code reduce the amount of money that is paid to the federal government and complicate tax policy. In 2011, taxpayers claimed approximately $1.7 trillion in deductions.[29]

Cumulatively, all these exemptions and deductions create an extraordinarily complicated tax code. It is also a tax code that favors wealthier Americans, who are more able to take advantage of the greatest number of exemptions and deductions.

"Well, we've licked taxes—that just leaves death."

Managing the Economy

Tax policy generates so much controversy because it affects people's daily lives, the economic fortunes of diverse industries, the debt burden of the government, and the productivity of the economy. In other words, the nation's tax policy and its economic prosperity are inextricably connected.

The tax code helps manage the economy in several ways. As people respond to its incentives, their spending and saving behaviors are altered. Because the U.S. tax code provides a deduction for home mortgages, for example, a larger proportion of the population own homes and the home-building market and the building trades are larger than they might otherwise be.

Even more generally, the amount of money that individuals pay in taxes affects their purchasing power. Increased taxes lessen individual spending power and can slow the economy. In contrast, tax cuts, which decrease taxes, leave more money in the hands of the consumer, stimulating spending and thus the economy.

However, an individual reduction in taxes does not stimulate the economy as much as an equal dollar of government spending. This is because not all individuals will spend all their tax refund or reduction. The higher the income scale, the more likely the individual is to save money or invest it in stocks or bonds. This form of behavior may be healthy for the economy too, but it does not provide an immediate economic stimulus. A significant part of the Obama stimulus package was in the form of tax cuts, which dampened its impact.

Reforming the Tax Code

Public officials frequently say they are in favor of a simpler tax code. But every time the tax code is revised, it becomes more complex. That is because the tax reform goals of members of Congress and the president are quite different and sometimes contradictory. It is also because every provision in the tax code benefits some groups, and no group wants to step forward and give up its special tax break.

Liberals who support reform want to create a more progressive tax code, with higher-income people paying more. Reform-minded conservatives want to make the tax code less progressive so that the middle and lower classes pay a greater proportion of government programming costs—they favor increasing the tax burden of the middle and lower classes. Most people want to close some tax loopholes—that is, exemptions and deductions—but disagree about which ones. Some want to close tax loopholes for corporations; others want to open more. Some want to further reduce the taxes on capital gains (profits from investments); others want to increase these taxes. Some would like to see tax reform produce more revenue so that government could do more; others want just the reverse, so that government would have to do less. In other words, though there is general agreement that the tax code needs simplification, there is no agreement at all on the objectives.

As a former Republican senator who helped pass Reagan's 1986 tax reforms remarked, "Every person who's going to lose a deduction regards their deduction as having come with the Bill of Rights, or even Moses."[30] A significant reform will require support of a broad coalition of people, most of whom are benefiting from the existing system.[31]

It is because of this contentiousness that elected politicians rarely propose any significant reforms in the tax code: tax policy is considered a "career killer."[32] Reagan and Clinton made only marginal changes, altering the tax rates without significantly altering exemptions or deductions. The George W. Bush tax cuts were much larger but did nothing to make the code simpler. And they were phased in over several years, with an end date on which they were supposed to lapse. That due date, well after the election. December 2012.

The effectiveness and success of lobbyists for interest groups and corporations are especially evident when Congress approves extenders, which are annual tax breaks for special categories of taxpayers, typically businesses. In 2012, there were over 129 extenders being considered in the Senate, which would cost the government up to $35 billion in revenues.[33]

Frustration with the existing code and the continual attempts to use it to favor one group or another has prompted some people to propose eliminating all exemptions and deductions. That is, they have proposed a policy of **tax neutrality**, which does not favor one kind of economic activity over another. As we have seen, our current tax code is definitely not neutral. For example, it favors home ownership over renting, and raising children over having none. It favors oil exploration and extraction over solar energy and wind power, and income from investments over income from salaries and wages. Supporters of greater tax neutrality say that it is inefficient to have a tax system that determines "where investment flows or who spends how much on what."[34] This is another idea that is more accepted in theory than in practice, because most people want to retain the advantages they have in the current code.

"I would not be opposed to a cat tax."

GREGORY

PARTISAN DEBATES

The public perception of Republicans as the party of business and fiscal restraint, and of Democrats as the party of labor and social spending, has not disappeared, but actual spending and taxing during Republican and Democratic administrations paint a more complex picture.

Most people agree that taxes are needed and some services must be provided. The issue is really *how much* taxation and *how much* spending. (See Figure 7). The deep compromise that is necessary to develop responsible, transparent, accountable tax and budgetary policy is always hard to achieve, and it can be nearly impossible in a time of strong partisanship and polarized politics. Little progress was made throughout 2011 and 2012 on economic policy because the political parties were more interested in framing the electoral choices to their own advantage than in developing workable economic policies. A bipartisan working group in Congress was charged with coming up with some compromises to reduce the debt but could not reach any agreements.

In this section, we compare and contrast Democratic and Republican stances on government spending and tax policy, seeing how these ideas are expressed during elections and acted upon while governing. This survey allows us to consider the extent to which partisan differences contribute to a creative or a destructive tension among policy makers.

Ideological Contrasts

Democrats and Republicans disagree about the extent to which government should use taxing and spending to redistribute wealth among income groups. Democrats are more likely to believe that government action can be a force to improve people's lives. Thus they are more supportive of government economic programs that provide assistance to the poor, sick, and elderly. They are also more likely to favor regulations that protect individuals from health hazards or from being duped by unscrupulous businesses. They are more likely to agree with Keynesian economics. As President Franklin Roosevelt stated in 1936, "The true conservative seeks to protect the system of private property and free enterprise by correcting such injustices and inequalities as arise from it.... I am that kind of conservative because I am that kind of liberal."[35] Democrats emphasize the core value of equality, as both equality of opportunity and equality of result.

Republicans are much less likely to think that the power of government is good, except when its power is expressed through military force or is used to control what many Republicans see as undesirable personal behavior, such as gay marriage or abortion. With those exceptions, they favor a less active government, with fewer market interventions and social programs. They are less favorable to government regulation, believing that the market can regulate most companies and that the cost of government regulation outweighs its benefits. As Ronald Reagan declared in responding to the recession that hit in the early years of his presidency, "In the present crisis, government is not the solution to our problem; government is the problem."[36] Republicans emphasize the core value of liberty, as both "freedom from" government intrusion and "freedom to" make economic decisions.

Keynesian economic theory, the idea that government can play a big role in managing the economy by spending more during high unemployment and less in times of nearly full employment, was partially tested during the Great Recession. One of the first legislative initiatives of the Obama administration was a stimulus package of $787 billion, which provided tax cuts, extended unemployment benefits, and expedited funds for public works. A year later, unemployment was down and economic growth was up. The Congressional Budget Office estimated that between 1.4 and 3.3 million jobs were created by the stimulus and that it caused the economy to grow by an additional 1.7 to 4.4 percent, relative to its likely growth without the stimulus.[37] But the spending and tax relief provided by the stimulus lasted only two years, and the economy stalled when these provisions ended. The period after the stimulus was almost an anti-stimulus, with state governments, no longer receiving federal aid from the stimulus, laying off thousands of workers.[38]

Supply-Side Economics and the Republicans

In 1981, the administration of Ronald Reagan came to the White House with a new policy and theory, **supply-side economics**, to simultaneously reduce inflation, lower taxes, and balance the budget. (This is also known as "trickle down" economics or as "Reaganomics.") The basic premise of this theory is that as government lowers taxes, more money is freed for private investment. The assumption is that people will save or invest some of the money they would have paid in taxes, thus making more money available to lend to businesses for expansion and modernization. But people will also spend some of this money, thus causing businesses to increase production and hire more workers. With higher employment and rising wages, more people will pay more taxes. The lost

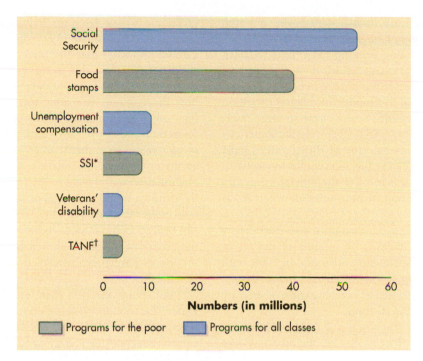

FIGURE 7: A LARGE PROPORTION OF AMERICANS RECEIVE INCOME SUPPORT More than 100 million Americans receive direct federal aid. This figure does not include indirect subsidies or tax subsidies. (The numbers in this figure add up to more than 100 million because many people benefit from more than one federal program.)

*Supplemental Security Income, the program that provides additional aid for the elderly poor and for the disabled who qualify for Social Security.

†Temporary Assistance for Needy Families, the program that replaced Aid to Families with Dependent Children. This program is what most people think of when they think of "welfare."

SOURCE: Budget of the United States Government, Fiscal Year 2008, www.ssa.gov; www.usda.gov; www.va.gov; www.cms.hhs.gov/url./fsn; www.hhs.gov.

tax revenue caused by the tax cuts will be recovered as the economy improves. These ideas appeal to conservatives and Republicans because they provide an economic rationale for a smaller budget and a smaller government, and also because the short-term gains go mostly to the wealthiest Americans (and as it has turned out, so do the long-term gains).

Keynesians and supply-siders have fundamentally different views about government regulation of the economy. Keynesians believe that government intervention can be effective both in steering the economy and in controlling boom-and-bust economic cycles. Keynesian economics has justified across-the-board tax cuts to stimulate consumer spending and fund programs for people with lower incomes. Here is the Democratic emphasis on equality of opportunity and even of results.

Supply-siders believe that taxing and spending for these purposes are inappropriate and inefficient uses of government powers. They believe it is better to leave as many decisions on spending and investing, and as much money as possible, with the market. Economic growth will come through increased production. This is the Republican emphasis on liberty, "freedom from," and "freedom to."

Though supply-side economics was popularized during the Reagan era, there was never any evidence that the theory worked as it was supposed to. The projected growth did not occur to the degree that it offset the revenue loss from the tax cuts. Increased spending for the military and the loss of

billions of dollars in tax revenues during the twelve years of the Reagan and George H. W. Bush I administrations left the country with $2.5 trillion of new debt.

Even so, George W. Bush followed a similar policy of using huge tax cuts for the wealthy to stimulate economic growth. Savings rates among the wealthy did not increase, however. Although the economy did grow at a faster rate for a few years, revenues as a percentage of GDP were lower in 2004 than at any time since World War II. Because Bush increased both military *and* social spending, more than $5 trillion of new debt was added during George W. Bush's eight years in office.

Tax breaks have contributed significantly to the deficit and have driven the level of income inequality to an extent not seen since the 1920s. There is less talk of supply-side economics now, though the claim that tax breaks will provide enough stimulus to the economy to overcome the revenue loss is still a popular one among conservatives and Republicans.

Economic Issues and Elections

Democrats and Republicans emphasize their opposing views of the economy in election campaigns and their votes in Congress. But both parties seek to gain electoral advantage from economic policies and so sometimes come together on legislation.[39]

During election years, tax reductions and spending increases are more likely than tax increases or budget cuts. Predictions of multiyear budget deficits did not stop President George W. Bush or Congress from proposing additional tax cuts and extending existing tax breaks in 2002, even with one war in progress and another on the horizon. In 2004, Bush pushed a prescription drug benefit to seniors, and many Democrats voted to support this biggest extension of Medicare since its inception. Seniors vote in large numbers and are represented by AARP (formerly the American Association of Retired Persons), one of the country's most powerful interest groups. Before the 2006 midterm elections, Republicans sponsored a bill to raise the federal minimum wage, a measure they had opposed for a decade when it was sponsored by Democrats.

Congressional spending on earmarks and pork-barrel projects almost always increases by billions of dollars in election years, and both parties support them. In 2008, both Congress and the White House supported a tax rebate, despite a record deficit. Congress passed a tax rebate and a health care bill in 2009, a year before the election.

There is little evidence that voters cast their ballots on the basis of one or a few legislative acts, though the economy does play a role in their decisions. In Bill Clinton's campaign against George H. W. Bush in 1992, Clinton's staff kept reminding Clinton and aides that "it's the economy, stupid," to emphasize how important this factor was. When they consider the economy in their decision, people tend to look backward at how the economy has done in the recent past rather than forward to how it might do in the future. And they tend to focus on whether their own family is better off now than two or four years ago, rather than on larger economic trends such as unemployment or inflation. (Obviously, unemployment and inflation are relevant to their personal situations if a family member, friend, or neighbor is unemployed or the household budget is stressed from rapidly rising prices.) Incumbents can easily become scapegoats for economic declines or heroes for economic spurts, deserved or not. Voters assume that presidents have more control over the economy than they actually do.

But in any election there are likely to be other salient issues. The economy did not do well in George W. Bush's first term, with few new jobs created, the budget surplus from Clinton's second term eliminated, and new massive deficits

Library of Congress

Photo by Bill Ganzel, from *Dust Bowl Descent*, University of Nebraska Press

The American economy after World War II lifted millions of families into middle-class status. At left are thirty-two-year-old Florence Thompson and her three daughters in 1936 after drought and the Depression drove them from Oklahoma to look for a better future in California. The family was living in migrant labor camps and surviving on vegetables dug up from fields and birds killed by the children. Publication of the photo prompted the government to send 20,000 pounds of food to the camp. At right is the same family forty-three years later in Modesto, California, where Mrs. Thompson's children were eventually able to buy her a home. But before her death in 1983, they had to solicit contributions to pay for her medical care.

emerging, yet Bush was reelected and Republicans gained seats in Congress because people put their concern about terrorism and the war in Iraq ahead of their anxiety about poor economic and fiscal performance.

In 2012, however, voters clearly prioritized the economy. As President Obama began his second term, respondents to a Gallup poll identified three of the top five "most important problem[s] facing this country today" as the recession, unemployment, the federal budget deficit.[40]

Governing

The realities of economic conditions during recent presidential administrations do not always support public stereotypes of partisan differences. For example, deficit spending was much greater under most of the recent Republican presidents; with few exceptions, Democrats were in the Oval Office when there were budget surpluses. (See Figure 5.) This fact challenges the Republicans' reputation as the party of fiscal restraint and balanced budgets. Reagan and George H.W. Bush doubled the national debt, and George W. Bush doubled it again. While the Republican supply-siders accepted these deficits as short-term necessities, the deficits turned out to be long-term problems. Conservatives have grown increasingly upset about this change in the Republican Party's historical stance in favor of fiscal restraint and balanced budgets. There is also evidence that Democratic administrations were more supportive of business than were the Republican administrations, at least as measured by the stock market. It rose 46 percent under recent Democratic administrations and 32 percent under recent Republican administrations.[41] To the extent that the economy tends to expand more during Democratic administrations, it is not surprising that the stock market reflects this expansion. This finding runs counter to the view held by many businesspeople that Republicans are better for business because Democrats are more likely to push regulation.

One way in which Democratic and Republican administrations have pursued economic policies that conform to popular views of the parties is the degree to which they foster or reduce economic inequality. The income gap between higher and lower income groups increased under Presidents Eisenhower, Nixon, Ford, Reagan, and both Bushes, while under the five Democrats who served during the same period, with the exception of Jimmy Carter, the income gap decreased.[42] (See Figure 8.) This fact is not surprising given that the wealthiest Americans tend to be Republicans and the working class and lower class are more likely to be Democrats. The parties adopt economic policies that reflect the views of their constituents.

During the current recession the traditional policy orientations have held: although both Republicans and Democrats supported the Bush administration's bailout of the financial industry, only a handful of Republicans voted for the Obama administration's economic stimulus bill or extensions for unemployment compensation. And no Republican supported health care reform. Generally, Republicans complained about

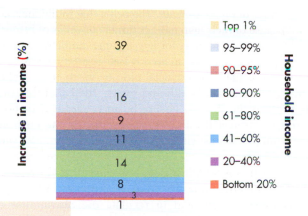

FIGURE 8: UPPER-INCOME EARNERS HAVE GAINED THE MOST DURING THE PAST THIRTY YEARS (PERCENT GAINED 1979–2007) The figure shows that during this twenty-eight-year period, the top 10 percent of income earners gained nearly 65 percent of the increased income. The bottom 40 percent gained only about 3 percent.

SOURCE: Economic Policy Institute analysis of Congressional Budget Office Average Federal Tax Rates and Income, 2010. Data comparing 1979 and 2007. www.epi.org/page/-/img/090810-snapshot.jpg.

spending and inflation (which was low, ranging between 1.5 and 3.0 percent during Obama's first term) and demanded drastic cuts in social spending. Democrats worried less about the deficit and more about high unemployment and the increasing need for social services and income support.

During the first years of the Obama administration, spending increased as a proportion of GDP. Beginning in 2011, spending began to fall because the stimulus and bailouts were one-time events, unlike tax cuts and other spending, which may persist over many years.

POLITICS, THE ECONOMY, AND THE BUDGET

The health of any economy depends on many factors, only some of which government can influence and none of which it can completely control. Private spending accounts for the majority of our economy, so the economic policies of the private sector and the consumption and saving habits of Americans play an enormous role in the state of the economy.

The country remains divided over how, if at all, government should respond to growing income disparity and how much it should try to regulate the economy. This debate was highlighted in the Occupy Movement, which presented itself as acting on behalf of the 99 percent versus the 1 percent, and which indicted the current economic system as accelerating income inequalities. Although the United States has a mixed economy, it also has a very individualistic, capitalistic ethic. The idea that government should be small and that the private sector should provide most social welfare services influences a wide range of public policies. The belief that individuals are poor because of their own failings limits our sense of responsibility to provide support for low-income families. The idea that private business is inherently self-regulating makes it difficult to regulate the financial industry or to enact higher standards for worker health and safety. The belief that private profit is the singular goal of business means that those fighting to protect the individual investor or the environment from abuse must either defeat or find compromise with powerful lobbies.

The Clinton administration argued that a responsible government is one that uses fiscal policy both to foster economic growth and to regulate the distribution of income generated by that growth. George W. Bush and the Republican-controlled Congress argued that the country's economic difficulties stemmed precisely from this interventionist, Keynesian approach. In their view, the role of government most consistent with our economic system is one that leaves an unfettered market to "grow" the economy and distribute its wealth. This is the essence of the long-standing debate in U.S. politics over the proper relationship of government to the economy. Disagreements are suspended only in extreme crises when the public believes the stability of the entire economic system is at stake, such as during the Great Depression or the collapse of the financial services industry in 2008—and for some, not even then.

SUMMARY

- A democracy values equality, but capitalism generates inequality along with liberty. Competing values of equality and liberty make it difficult for the government to manage the problems of unemployment, inflation, and deflation.
- The impact of the government budget on the economy is largely determined by the amount of government spending relative to the overall economy and to a lesser extent by the programs and functions that the budget pays for.
- U.S. tax policy is complex and often lacks transparency because it is expected to achieve so many goals, some of which are contradictory. The tax code seeks to achieve widely endorsed social goals, to reward constituents of the president and members of Congress, and to manage the economy. The number and inconsistency of these goals make it difficult to reform the code, and most presidents have made only small changes.
- Democrats and Republicans endorse contrasting economic theories and policies, though their differences are sometimes exaggerated. Democrats tend to be Keynesians, using government spending to stimulate the economy. Republicans favor less government intervention, trusting that consumer spending and investments will result in a healthy economy.

DISCUSSION QUESTIONS

1. As president, would you prefer your first term in office to occur during a time of low inflation or low unemployment? Why? Would current leaders of the Republican and Democratic Parties agree with you? What are the consequences of low inflation for a president's reelection chances?
2. Under what circumstances, if any, would you support a budget deficit? Justify your choice. How would the current leaders of the national Republican and Democratic Parties view your ideas? What do these answers reveal about the connections between your economic and political values?
3. Name three tax policy reforms that you support. What goals do you think these reforms would achieve? Do you think that these reforms are politically feasible?
4. If you were a member of Congress and the nation was in a recession, would you favor a stimulus package? Or would you choose a more supply-side approach? Justify your choice with examples of successes or failures of these policies. Would your choices differ if you were representing a district with a large number of poor people rather than a district with high proportions of wealthy people?

Focus On...

Health Care Reform

Stephen Boitano/Barcroft Media/Landov

LEARNING OBJECTIVES

1. Explain the origins of the U.S. government's involvement in health care and describe its current involvement.

2. List the successes and failures of the U.S. health care system.

3. Identify responses to the U.S. health care system that compensate for or correct its failures.

4. Assess the largest health insurance programs currently administered by the U.S. government.

5. Describe the Affordable Care Act of 2010. Contrast it with a single-payer system. Explain why this law is so controversial.

6. Discuss the electoral, presidential, legislative, and judicial politics of health care reform in 2009–2012.

The United States spends a greater amount of its national wealth on health care than any other industrialized nation. It has world-class medical facilities and medical scientists equal to none. But in some ways, the United States is more like a "Third World," or developing, country in terms of the quality of health care received by its citizens. Infant and maternal mortality are high. Life expectancy is lower than for citizens of forty-nine other countries.[1] Moreover, citizens of almost every other developed country are happier with their health care system than are Americans. The United States is the only Western industrialized nation that does not provide universal health care. Thousands of American families face bankruptcy each year when a health catastrophe strikes. As one observer noted, "In no other industrial country do we see communities organizing bake sales to help defray the cost of an uninsured neighbor's cancer treatments."[2]

So the health care system has mixed success. Attempts to change the system are controversial because Americans disagree about what is wrong. Some Americans want government to do more; others cry "socialism" and even "communism" at proposals to provide health coverage to all. Yet, even before health care reform legislation passed in 2010, government—including both the federal and state governments—was already paying about half of all costs for health care and prescription drugs.

Currently, one of every six dollars in the American economy goes to health care. Health spending uses 17 percent of our national income and increases each year. The amount that the United States spent on health care in 2010, $2.6 trillion, was equal to the entire GDP of the fifth largest economy in the world, France.[3]

Why aren't Americans healthier, given the medical spending and the medical advances made in this country? Why has it taken until 2010 to adopt nearly universal health care? In this "Focus On…Health Care Reform," we will answer these questions by looking at the health care programs and reforms instituted to ensure care for Americans, exploring why government has become so deeply involved in this issue and why its involvement is so controversial.

THE GOVERNMENT AND HEALTH CARE

The government has had a role in health care since the Founders' generation. Health care is so fundamental to the nation's well-being—to its physical security, economic stability, and social justice—that the government had to become involved in its provision.

The U.S. government began to provide personal health care in 1798, when President John Adams signed an "Act for the relief of sick and disabled Seamen." It was paid for by a tax collected from shipmasters, which was used to build hospitals and provide medical care for merchant and naval seamen. These marine hospitals were gradually established throughout the country and were locally administered but funded under federal law. The same law established the U.S. Public Health Corps, or **Public Health Service (PHS)**, as it came to be known. The PHS was responsible for preventing returning sailors from spreading diseases they may have contracted in foreign ports. The primary motivation for the corps' creation was the public's security, which was reflected in the corps' mission—"health defense"—and in its quasi-military organization.[4]

In subsequent decades, the PHS has assumed a number of other health defense responsibilities. In 1878, the National Quarantine Act gave the service the power to prevent the spread of contagious diseases by quarantining the homes of the infected.[5] This controversial policy required significant intrusion into homes and family life by local officials. Congress later extended the PHS's responsibilities to examining newly arrived immigrants for contagious disease; controlling the spread of life-threatening communicable diseases such as smallpox, cholera, yellow fever, measles, and whooping cough; and inspecting water and sewer systems in an effort to halt the spread of disease.

Today, after numerous reorganizations, the PHS exists as the Public Health Service Commissioned Corps, a 6,000-strong uniformed organization headed by the surgeon general. Physicians, nurses, dentists, and engineers working for the service wear military uniforms, as does the nation's surgeon general, a presidential appointee. They assist with recovery from manmade and natural disasters, and they continue to combat and control contagious diseases and epidemics. PHS personnel also provide medical care to individuals, working for the Indian Health Service and the Bureau of Prisons, among other federal agencies.

But the PHS is just the tip of the iceberg in government's involvement in health care. Over time, the activity of the government in this area has grown, and, as the nation sought to respond to needs over time, the people and their representatives created a complex bureaucracy with extensive responsibilities and a sometimes confusing array of powers, all of which exist side-by-side with an even more complex array of private entities involved in health care.

WHY GOVERNMENT IS INVOLVED IN HEALTH CARE

Government involvement in health care has developed over time in a piecemeal fashion, with government programs emerging to meet specific needs at specific times. Underlying specific needs are general rationales for government action: protecting the physical security of the country and its people, ensuring economic security, and promoting human rights and social justice. Yet not all of these rationales are accepted by everyone.

Physical Security

Government involvement in health care came first for those who served their country in the navy or merchant marine. And today, the government maintains a huge network of hospitals and health care providers for veterans from all military services. There is little disagreement that national security includes taking care of the health care needs of those who are serving, or who have served, in the armed forces.

Most people also readily accept government's responsibility for protecting their safety when presented with a health threat from lethal substances released into the atmosphere (as after a nuclear power plant accident), mass outbreaks of contagious diseases, or illness from food contamination. Examples of agencies that protect public health in these ways include the National Institutes of Health (NIH, which traces its origins to 1798), whose work develops drugs, vaccines, and treatments that led to drops in death rates and advances in treatment of many dreaded diseases, and the Centers for Disease Control and Prevention (CDC, which traces its origins to 1942), which seeks to prevent and control infectious and chronic disease, injuries, workplace hazards, disabilities, and environmental health threats.

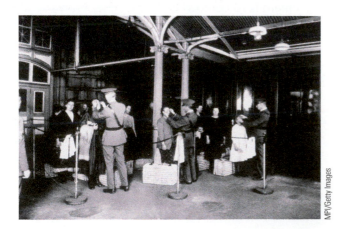

MPI/Getty Images

From its earliest days, the government has been involved in protecting and promoting public health. Here inspectors from the Public Health Service screen immigrants entering the country in the early 1900s, looking for evidence of contagious disease.

Economic Stability

Every economy relies on a healthy labor force, and every government needs a healthy economy. Thus both private business and government have a stake in the general health of the population. Because government has become a major health insurance provider over the past fifty years, it also has an interest, at minimum, in keeping medical costs from rising faster than GDP. If the cost of medical care spirals out of control, there is no way for businesses to remain competitive with those in other countries, and no way for government to keep public spending under control.

While the government pays for approximately half of all spending on health care, private individuals and corporations pay for the other half, largely through insurance premiums. Private insurance is provided to many workers through their employers, who subsidize part of the costs. Therefore, a middle-income family with employer-based insurance will spend 8 percent of its income on health care, but a comparable family with private insurance (through the open market rather than through an employer) will spend a significant percentage, even one-fifth or more, of their income to obtain coverage. However, as health care costs have escalated in recent decades, thousands of firms have dropped health care coverage for their workers.

Despite the high levels of spending by government, businesses, and private insurers, there is a great deal of evidence that the care provided by our health system is inferior to that of many other nations. Millions of people without health insurance do not have access to preventative care, or care that treats diseases in early stages. Millions do not seek treatment until after their diseases have progressed to stages where treatment is costly or impossible. As health premiums and out-of-pocket costs have risen faster than incomes, health insurance and medical bills stress household budgets and limit the ability of families to save. As more employers discontinue this benefit for their workers, the income drain for families continues. Those with low incomes either rely on need-based government assistance or receive no health care at all.

Lost productivity and the cost of health insurance are a burden on corporations as well as families. After corporate income taxes, employee benefits are the largest structural cost to business. By one estimate, if we had had a government-funded national health insurance plan similar to those in Canada and Europe, U.S. automakers, who have been losing ground to foreign competitors for two decades, could have saved at least $1,300 per vehicle.[6] High health costs encourage employers to relocate abroad where the cost of labor is low, as in developing countries, or where the government picks up the costs of health care, as in Canada, Europe, and Japan.

Human Rights and Social Justice

The degree to which health care is a government responsibility because of commitments to human rights and social justice is more controversial than the physical and economic security rationales. Although it has signed two international conventions that explicitly identify access to health care as a fundamental human right, the United States is one of the few industrialized nations that does not treat access to health care as a right. The Universal Declaration of Human Rights (1948) states, "Everyone has the right to a standard of living adequate for the health and well-being of himself and of his family, including...access to medical care and necessary social services...." Eleanor Roosevelt, a vigorous spokesperson for social justice and whose late husband, as president, had identified the right to health care as one of the "economic truths [that] have become accepted as self-evident," chaired the Declaration's drafting committee. Almost twenty years later, the United States reiterated its commitment to health care as a fundamental right in signing the U.N. International Covenant on Economic, Social, and Cultural Rights (1966), which also recognizes the right of everyone to the medical service and medical attention that will keep them in good health.

At the foundation of human rights is a concern for social justice. In our society, we are concerned that infants and children who lack needed medical care may be ill throughout their entire lives. They may be unable to succeed in school, may never realize their full potential or make their full contribution to the community, and may never achieve full independence, all because by accident of birth they had illnesses that went untreated.

Medical care in the United States, however, is largely rationed by the patient's ability to pay. If you can afford it or if you have the right insurance, you can have the most expensive treatment, even if it will prolong your life only a short while or improve your condition only a little bit, or not at all. If you do not have the money or insurance coverage, you may die at an early age even though you have a treatable condition. It is telling that the poorest Americans have a lifespan that is three to five years less than those who are most well off.[7] (See the box "Lack of Access to Medical Care Can Affect Life Outcome" on page 446.)

Over 17 percent of Americans, more than 50 million, were uninsured in 2011. That is, more than 50 million had no coverage at all, through private insurance or government programs that provide health care. (Thus this number does not include those who receive Medicare or Medicaid.) Fifty million is about equal to the entire population of the twenty-five smallest states.[8] About one-sixth of these people could afford insurance at market prices,[9] but the rest do not have the means to buy it and still pay for life's other necessities.

Members of different racial and ethnic groups have differential access to health care. Racial differences in health outcomes are decreasing but still significant.[10] People of color are disproportionately among the uninsured. In a recent year, 16 percent of non-Latino whites were uninsured, but more than 20 percent of members of other groups lacked insurance, including more than one-third of American Indians and Latinos. Infant morality rates for babies born to African Americans, Puerto Rican Americans, and American Indians are higher than those for babies born to white mothers.

Some Americans oppose expanding government's reach in health care. Some have reasons relating to their belief that government's range of activities should be small or that they fear government indebtedness. Others resent government underwriting the health care costs of low-income people. A few very conservative commentators write about "the moocher class." The moocher class, said one, "is made up of people who are 'perfectly content to live at the expense of others."[11] In this view, providing a means for the uninsured to get insurance is a way to give shiftless people benefits paid for by everyone else.

In fact, though there are undoubtedly some "moochers" out there, most of the 50 million uninsured are employed but are working low-wage jobs in companies that do not provide health insurance; or working part-time (up to thirty-nine hours a week), so employers who cover full-time workers do not cover them; or just starting in the workforce and have not landed jobs with health coverage; or are self-employed, earning enough to make ends meet but not enough to buy insurance. (Six million of the uninsured are undocumented immigrants who are not eligible for government-funded health insurance.) Very few of the uninsured are able-bodied people who are shirking work. Ironically, those attacking the "moocher class" often are recipients of government aid themselves, particularly Social Security and Medicare.[12]

GOVERNMENT'S ROLE IN PROVIDING HEALTH INSURANCE

America has a complicated health care system mixing private and public entities. The vast majority of doctors and other health providers are part of clinical practices that are privately owned, though a minority work for the government in Veterans Affairs, the Bureau of Indian Affairs, or other agencies. Many hospitals are operated by corporations or churches. Insurance companies and pharmaceutical companies are corporations, owned by their stockholders. But, as we have already seen, government also has a major role in health care. It supplements private medical care. Until 2011, its primary contributions were in providing medical insurance for the elderly through Medicare, for the poor through Medicaid, and for some children through the State Child Health Insurance Program (S-CHIP). It also provides direct care to military personnel, through the Department of Defense, and to more than 22 million veterans through the Department of Veterans Affairs and its nationwide network of hospitals and clinics. With the Affordable Care Act, government's role has expanded, as we will see later, though the private-public mix remains.

Medicare

Older people are a lot healthier than they were fifty years ago. There are numerous reasons, including scientific breakthroughs in prevention and treatment of some diseases. But the government's underwriting of health care costs through **Medicare** is responsible for much of the improvement. Medicare is a public health insurance program for Social Security recipients that funds basic medical expenses for seniors and the disabled (see Figure 1). Medicare recipients still choose their own doctors and medical facilities, but the doctors and medical facilities send their bills to Medicare rather than to private insurance companies. This is unlike a "socialized medicine" system (or even our own veterans system), in which government hires the doctors and runs the hospitals.

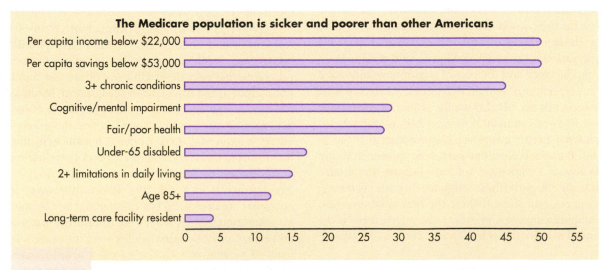

FIGURE 1: RECIPIENTS OF MEDICARE ARE SICKER AND POORER THAN OTHER AMERICANS
The numbers are the proportion of Medicare recipients having each condition. For example, 50 percent of Medicare recipients have a per capita income of less than $22,000. This profile demonstrates the income limitations and health problems of recipients. The average Medicare household has a family income of $30,966 and spends approximately 15 percent of that income on health care, while the average non-Medicare household has a family income of $50,143 and spends less than 5 percent on health care.

SOURCE: Kaiser Family Foundation, "Fact Sheet: Medicare Policy," November 2011. This information was reprinted with permission from the Henry J. Kaiser Family Foundation. The Kaiser Family Foundation, a leader in health policy analysis, health journalism and communication, is dedicated to filling the need for trusted, independent information on the major health issues facing our nation and its people. The Foundation is a non-profit private operating foundation, based in Menlo Park, California.

Medicare was adopted in 1965 as part of President Lyndon Johnson's "Great Society" and was augmented in 2004, with prescription drug benefits, as an election-year initiative of President George W. Bush. Today almost 50 million Americans receive Medicare benefits. Compared with the period before 1965, more seniors are able to see doctors now. Their hospital stays are more numerous, but also shorter. There also have been declines in death rates from diseases that particularly affect seniors, such as heart attacks and strokes, and a decrease in the number of days that seniors experience restricted activity.[13] The financial burden on families has been reduced too, as adult children are not forced to either push their parents into Medicaid or sacrifice their own financial well-being when an elderly parent has a catastrophic illness.[14]

Medicare is financed by payroll taxes—a percent of each paycheck for every employee throughout his or her lifetime—just as Social Security is, plus premiums paid by recipients for some coverage. Medicare has four "parts," covering hospitalization, doctor visits, preventive care, and prescription drugs. Recipients receive hospitalization coverage and may buy supplementary (optional) coverage for the remaining parts. Over 90 percent of recipients buy the optional insurance.

Medicare is a major item in the federal budget. In 2011, it covered 49 million people at an estimated cost of almost $563 billion. Medicare spending accounted for approximately 15 percent of all U.S. government spending and more than 20 percent of the nation's total spending on health care.

Despite its substantial accomplishments, Medicare has not been a complete success. It is expensive, and many of those who need it have trouble paying their portion of the costs. Yet the maximum fees the government has set for services are lower than some doctors have been willing to accept, and as a consequence, some refuse to treat Medicare patients. Patients have been criticized for driving up costs by making unnecessary doctor or hospital visits and by having unrealistic expectations about what medical care can do to resolve their health problems. There has also been fraud in the program—an estimated $47 billion in 2009 alone—most of it attributed to unnecessary treatments or overbilling by doctors.

However, the government's spending on overhead and administrative costs for Medicare is far lower than insurance companies' spending on these costs for private insurance. For this reason, the government's program is considered the more efficient. This is why some policy experts favor the eventual adoption of "Medicare for all" as a way to control health care costs.

Although Medicare was controversial when proposed by President Johnson—critics claimed that it was "socialism," and some, like Ronald Reagan, claimed that it marked the end of American freedom—it is widely accepted now, even by those who dislike government spending. Most Tea Party members who talk about "moochers" aren't referring to Medicare recipients, perhaps because many in the Tea Party are benefitting from this program.

Nonetheless, Medicare spending is increasing, especially with the rising number of older Americans and rising health costs. Even though Medicare spending is increasing at a lower rate than private health insurance spending (3.5 percent a year compared to 5.4 percent), it is unclear how the program will be paid for in the future. Thus there are calls for reform. U.S. Representative and 2012 vice presidential candidate Paul Ryan, for example, has pushed very strongly for a comprehensive reform of Medicare—some describe him as abolishing the program—which would institute a voucher system for medical care.

Medicaid

Also established in 1965 as part of President Johnson's "Great Society," **Medicaid** is a federal-state program that provides medical coverage for low-income and severely disabled people: those whose income falls below thresholds set by the states, within federal guidelines. The great majority are children, pregnant women, the aged, and the disabled. Before the 2008 recession swelled its rolls, 49 million Americans received health coverage through Medicaid. The program paid for one-third of all births, two-thirds of nursing home stays, and nearly half of public expenditures for AIDS patients.[15]

Although most of the Medicaid costs are paid by the federal government, the state governments also contribute significantly.[16] In the years before the recession, Medicaid funding required, on average, 17 percent of state general funds. Even when the economy was growing rapidly, rapid growth in demand for the program was crowding out spending for other programs.[17] Recognizing these pressures, the federal government in these years granted the states more authority to set Medicaid eligibility standards.

During the 2008–2009 recession, as unemployment increased and more people fell into poverty, Medicaid enrollments rose dramatically. By 2012, about 60 million Americans received Medicaid,[18] half of them children and another 25 percent elderly and disabled. The highest enrollments were in California, where 30 percent of its population relied on Medicaid. (The national average was 20 percent.)[19] In an effort to ensure access to health care for the poor and unemployed, Congress denied the states the power to reduce eligibility. It did, however, allow states to reduce the services and raise the costs for recipients.[20]

Acknowledging the problems confronting the states and their citizens, Congress increased federal funding for Medicaid through the 2009 stimulus bill.[21] But by 2011, the president's budget proposed cuts in Medicaid (and in the State Children's Health Insurance Program). As one analyst concluded, this means "stripped-down health care coverage for the poor and bigger burdens for the states."[22]

State Children's Health Insurance Program (S-CHIP)

Congress passed the **State Children's Health Insurance Program (S-CHIP)** in 1997 to provide greater health insurance coverage for children. Working through existing state programs, S-CHIP set a goal of insuring all children whose parents did not qualify for Medicaid but who could not afford private insurance. Almost 8 million children have received coverage under this program, but there are many more who are eligible.

The federal government funds about 70 percent of S-CHIP costs, but states have considerable leeway to determine eligibility. As medical costs have soared and the recession has cut revenues, different states have established different standards for access; some have made it more difficult for children to qualify, while others have broadened coverage to provide for all children. Even after these changes, more children are insured by the government-funded Medicaid and S-CHIP programs than by private insurance programs.

Although President George W. Bush vetoed Democratic efforts to expand this program, President Obama signed a bill to do so. The Affordable Care Act extends these appropriations until 2015, when the program will expand and funding will increase. Then, the federal government will pay approximately 90 percent of the program's costs unless a state refuses to participate in the Medicaid expansion. Under those circumstances, federal government funding will continue at the earlier levels.

PROBLEMS WITH THE EXISTING SYSTEM

The push to reform health care insurance in the early months of the Obama administration had its origins in widespread perceptions of the health care system as deeply flawed, even as failing. These problems included high costs, limited coverage, inadequate quality, and excessive waste and inefficiency.

High Costs

Costs have been escalating, outpacing inflation, for years. At this rate, and without reform, health care spending would consume an unsustainable 40 percent of the GDP by 2080. Reining in the costs of health care, both that financed by government and that financed by individuals with insurance, is necessary even for middle-class Americans to afford health insurance in the future.

New drugs and new technologies make it possible to do more for more people. Everyone wants the state-of-the-art

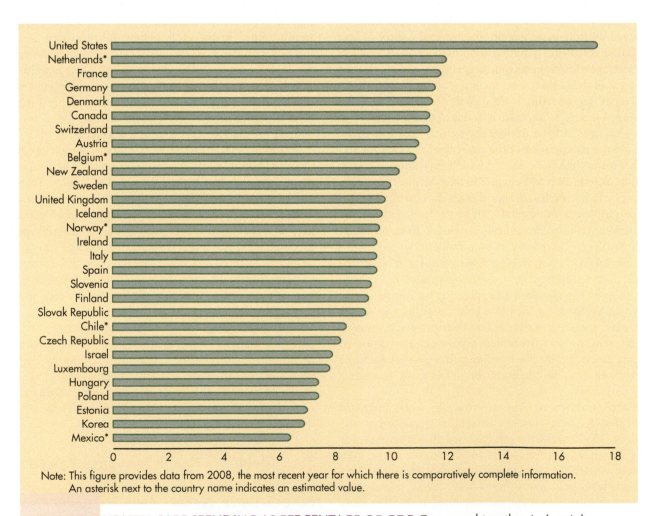

Note: This figure provides data from 2008, the most recent year for which there is comparatively complete information. An asterisk next to the country name indicates an estimated value.

FIGURE 2: HEALTH CARE SPENDING AS PERCENTAGE OF GDP Compared to other industrial or developed nations, the United States consistently spends a much higher percentage of its gross domestic product on health care.

SOURCE: Organisation for Economic Co-operation and Development, "Total Expenditure on Health, % GDP" (Paris: OECD, 2011).

treatments, which are often more expensive as well as more effective. In some systems, such as Canada's, the government negotiates prices with drug companies for drugs used in the system. However, as a result of intense lobbying by pharmaceutical companies, American law prohibits the government from conducting these negotiations.

Unnecessary tests and other procedures are commonly performed, whether because doctors are cautious and thorough, are fearful of malpractice lawsuits, or simply want to show patients and relatives that everything possible is being done. In the United States, most doctors are paid for each procedure they perform. Rates of procedures vary wildly among regions and hospitals, suggesting that local norms or community pressures affect their use. For example, people in Alabama have twice as many gall bladder surgeries (standardized for population) as in Hawaii, and people in North Dakota have more than twice as many hip replacements as in West Virginia.[23] Great differences occur within states too.[24] Although the differences may reflect better care offered in some states or communities, the differences also reflect unnecessary tests and procedures performed in other states or communities.

A large proportion of health care resources is spent on people in the last year of their lives. Thirty percent of all Medicare costs are incurred for the last year of care, much of it for the last month of treatment. This strains the health care system. (See Figure 2)

Limited Coverage

The United States has a patchwork of public and private programs that leave large holes in coverage. Military personnel and veterans and the elderly have systems that provide insurance for all. The young do not. Some workers obtain insurance at discounted rates through their employer. Other workers do not. Some persons can afford to purchase their own insurance. Other persons cannot.

Even some who can afford to purchase their own insurance cannot obtain it. Insurance companies are private corporations run for a profit. They don't want any policyholders who will cost them more than the policyholders will pay them in premiums. Therefore, before the 2010 reforms, insurance companies often denied coverage to individuals who had pre-existing conditions and even terminated coverage of individuals who incurred a serious illness or injury that would cost a lot to treat.

Most of us know or have read about individuals who could not afford coverage, or who were denied coverage, and whose seemingly secure middle- or working-class existence was destroyed by unforeseen medical bills.

In most other industrialized countries, health care is guaranteed and paid for through taxes. Differences in individuals' costs between these countries and the United States are shocking. In Belgium, a cancer patient pays only $36 for a three-day treatment (and the cost to the government is only $2,000).[25] In Sweden, a patient never has to spend more than $118 a year for doctors' visits or $236 a year for total medical bills. Vacationing in France, one author's spouse had a nasty fall and spent an afternoon in the emergency room receiving treatment. The charges came to $7.

Inadequate Quality

If cheaper care meant worse care, these examples from other nations wouldn't be so revealing. We aspire to high-quality care. But in these other nations, care is much better as measured by the outcomes of life expectancy, infant mortality, and other indicators of good health. This does not mean that our best health care doesn't match theirs. Our best health care is among the world's best, and in some specific areas we

"Uh-oh, your coverage doesn't seem to include illness."

American Diversity

Lack of Access to Medical Care Can Affect Life Outcome

Lack of access to medical care in lower-income groups can have an impact on quality of life, upward mobility, and lifespan. African Americans and Latinos (excluding Cuban Americans) are disproportionately represented in low-income groups, and consequently a higher percentage of these groups have been unable to buy private health insurance. The difference in access is reflected in the shorter lifespans for poorer Americans, especially African Americans, and the higher infant mortality rate for Puerto Ricans, American Indians, and African Americans (see Figure 3). Latinos overall, however, now have a longer lifespan than whites.

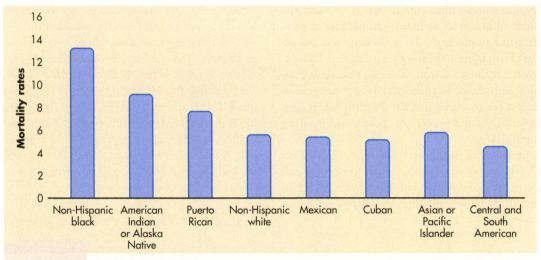

FIGURE 3a: INFANT MORTALITY RATES, BY RACE AND HISPANIC ORIGIN OF THE MOTHER (2007)

SOURCE: Marian F. MacDorman and T. J. Mathews, "Understanding Racial and Ethnic Disparities in U.S. Infant Mortality Rates," *NCHS Data Brief*, No. 74 (September 2011).

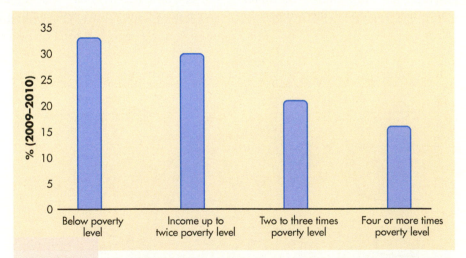

FIGURE 3b: POOR AMERICANS ARE MORE LIKELY TO HAVE CHRONIC ILLNESSES THAN MORE AFFLUENT AMERICANS The figures are the proportions in each category of middle-age adults (ages forty-five to sixty-four) with two or more chronic health conditions. A chronic illness is one that persists and should be treated, like asthma, diabetes, cancer, respiratory diseases, heart conditions, and kidney diseases.

SOURCE: Centers for Disease Control and Prevention, *Health, United States, 2011* (Atlanta, Ga.: CDC), 40.

perform well compared to other nations, such as breast cancer survival rates. But lack of access to good health care on the part of millions means that overall we don't stack up well. For example, the poorest one-third of the population in England are healthier than the richest one-third of Americans, even though Britain's per capita health expenditures are 40 percent of those in the United States.[26] A recent study ranking quality and access ranked the United States seventh out of seven countries examined, despite spending about twice as much per capita.[27]

In the United States, we spend more than other nations on end-of-life care and less on preventive care that can detect and treat disease at early stages. Health insurance has not emphasized preventive care, and medical costs have discouraged many people from seeking such care. In the United States, people visit the doctor less and early detection of disease is lower. For example, many Americans have untreated diabetes. If no preventive measures are taken, the disease progresses and eventually leads to serious problems, such as the need to amputate feet or legs and the possibility of strokes and blindness. The cost to treat such problems is many times higher than prevention would have been, but prevention depends on getting routine treatment. Britain is five times more productive at managing diabetes than the United States but spends half as much per person. France, despite higher smoking rates and more lung diseases than in the United States, spends one-eighth the amount spent by the U.S. on treatments per person with one-third the deaths from lung disease.[28]

In the U.S. preventive care is sacrificed to end-of-life care; a very large proportion of health care spending goes to hospital stays in the last month or so of life. None of us want the life of a friend or family member to be terminated prematurely, and none of us want friends or family members (or ourselves) to suffer at the end, but balancing these wishes in an ethical fashion is a challenge that most families, hospitals, and doctors do not address.

Excessive Waste and Inefficiency

Why do we spend more and get less than many other nations? One reason is that waste and inefficiency account for at least one-third, and perhaps as much as one-half, of U.S. health care costs.[29] The cost of administration alone accounts for about one-quarter of all costs, largely because there are so many different providers and insurers, each with its own rules and systems for managing paperwork and billing. U.S. hospitals spend about 25 percent of their budgets on billing and administration, about twice as much as what Canadian hospitals spend in their simpler, single-payer system. And American doctors spend a lot more time on paperwork, too. [30]

Short-Term Solutions

Obviously, Americans have found ways to live with this system. Many people, unaware that other developed countries provide better outcomes than the United States, assume that American health care is superior, so they tolerate its shortcomings. Other people, who lack health insurance, have received some care through private charity, medical tourism, or state experiments.

Private Charity

Charitable organizations often organize to provide free clinics, dental care, eyeglasses, and other health aids. Private charities also contribute food to those in need. And individuals, churches, and community groups may band together to help particular people hard hit by medical bills, as alluded to by the reference to bake sales to pay for cancer treatment. Obviously, these options, however generous, are spotty in coverage and unavailable to most people. Neighborhoods with the most poor and the most uninsured are less likely to have access to the private resources that will help neighbors.

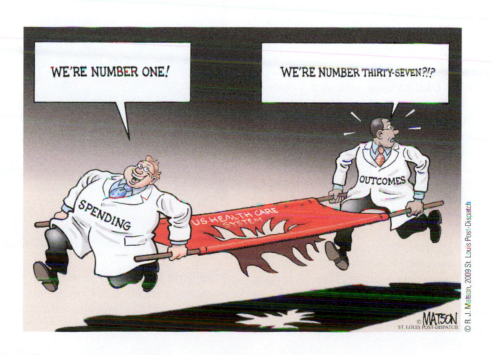

Medical Tourism

To avoid high costs of medical care and drugs, many Americans purchase drugs abroad. Purchase of prescription drugs in Canada has become so common that American drug manufacturers have lobbied on behalf of stronger enforcement of the laws prohibiting the importation of drugs.

Others travel to Canada, Mexico, and further abroad for medical services. Medical tourism is not a new phenomenon, as ancient Greeks and Romans and travelers throughout the centuries traveled to other destinations to worship at shrines of healing gods and to bathe in waters thought to be healthful. Today's tourism, however, has spawned travel agencies specializing in making air travel, hotel, and hospital arrangements for such visits.

Estimates of how many Americans have become medical tourists range from 75,000 to 750,000 per year. The savings can be impressive. A heart operation that would have cost $130,000 in the United States in 2009 cost $18,500 in Singapore and $10,000 in India. Internet sites now allow patients to comparison-shop for the best deals. At www .allmedicaltourism.com, for example, a shopper can select the treatment or procedure, and then compare the cost of that service in each country where it is offered.

Some businesses take advantage of this approach to health-care. One supermarket chain with employees in five states agreed to send employees needing hip and knee replacements to Singapore. The costs were so much lower that the employer could pay all travel costs for the patient and a companion, make the patient's copayments, and still come out well ahead compared to paying the cost of treatment in the United States.[31]

International medicine has significant risks, including different standards and unsavory practices, such as a black market in transplant organs. And it requires more research than most patients can do, and more experience or comfort with foreign travel than many patients have. Consequently, medical tourism is most often used by those who have considerable resources, either of their own or through their employer. It does little to solve problems of those with limited or no insurance.

State Experiments

State governments have tried to cope with rising costs of medical care and holes in coverage. Some states expanded the Children's Health Insurance Program (S-CHIP) to all children. Other states created exchanges for the uninsured, bringing individuals together, as employers bring employees together, so they could enjoy the lower insurance costs offered to groups. More ambitious states, such as Massachusetts and Hawaii, adopted more comprehensive programs.

The Massachusetts plan is of greatest interest because it was a forerunner of the plan eventually passed by Congress. The reform passed in 2006 with bipartisan support, including the support of Mitt Romney, then Massachusetts's Republican governor and later a presidential candidate. There were three key elements to the reform. First, insurance companies could not deny coverage to people with pre-existing conditions and could not charge people more because they were ill. Second,

everyone was required to buy health insurance, and those who failed to obtain health insurance were fined. This averaged the risk for insurance companies. Third, low-income families had their health insurance subsidized.[32]

As judged by coverage and public acceptance, the plan has been a success. Four years after its adoption, over 95 percent of the state's residents were covered, and 79 percent of the public thought the reforms should be continued. Almost as many of the state's physicians—75 percent—favored retaining the policy.[33]

There are two apparent drawbacks to the Massachusetts reform. One is its complexity, due to the mix of private and public insurers. The other drawback is cost, as the reform has not yet reduced the amount the commonwealth is spending for health care. In fairness, however, the goal of the 2006 law was cost containment, not cost reduction. Costs were expected to increase as thousands entered the health care system, but covering everyone, which initially drove up costs, should, over time, contain spending. Health care is the largest industry in Massachusetts, which only makes it more important to fine-tune health care insurance reform.[34]

HEALTH CARE REFORM, 2009–2012

President Obama was not the first president to tackle health care coverage. It has been a staple on the American political agenda since at least the presidency of Harry Truman (1945–1953), who proposed universal coverage. President Dwight Eisenhower (1953–1961) signed legislation to provide generous health care benefits for federal employees. Medicare

After Scott Janis had a stroke in 2009, the insurance company cancelled his insurance, claiming an omission in his original application. His girlfriend offers encouragement.

and Medicaid were adopted with the leadership of President Lyndon Johnson (1963–1969). His successor, President Richard Nixon (1969–1974) supported, without success, legislation to provide universal coverage for all Americans. In the wake of a lingering recession, President Ronald Reagan (1981–1989) signed a law that allowed employees to continue their health insurance coverage for several months after they leave employment. During the Clinton administration (1993–2001), coverage for children through the State Children's Health Insurance Program (S-CHIP) was adopted even though President Bill Clinton's more ambitious plan for universal coverage was defeated. President George W. Bush's administration (2001–2009) won increased prescription drug coverage for seniors. Of the modern presidents, only Presidents Gerald Ford and George H. W. Bush failed to lobby on behalf of, or actually expand, the government's provision of health care.

The Context of Reform

The rising costs of health care both for individuals and federal and state government, coupled with the millions who have no access to affordable health care, intensified the debate over health care reform in 2009. President Obama and his strongest Democratic opponent, Hillary Clinton, both called for universal health insurance when they ran for president in 2008, so it was no surprise that Obama made it a priority when he took office.

Several other factors combined to lay the groundwork for government action. The rising costs of insurance had caused many businesses to drop health care as a benefit, leaving more workers on their own to find insurance or pay bills without it. The recession and increased unemployment left millions more Americans without health insurance. The medical care industry, which in Harry Truman's time had been solidly opposed to universal health care, was no longer unanimously

against it. In 2004, almost eight thousand U.S. doctors (about 1 percent of all practicing physicians) published a letter in the *Journal of the American Medical Association* arguing that private sector solutions had failed; they called for the creation of a government-financed health insurance system covering every American and argued that this change would save billions.[35] The pharmaceutical industry had reaped benefits with the expanded Medicare drug benefit; now, the industry believed it could work with Congress to fashion a bill it could support. Nurses and some other allied health workers advocated reform, too.

Public opinion had become much more supportive of government-funded health insurance. In 2007, fully 64 percent of Americans said they believed government should guarantee health insurance.[36] And of course, Obama's victory put into office an avowed supporter of universal coverage, though at the same time contributing to partisan polarization on the issue.

Despite this more favorable climate, reformers faced many challenges, given the nation's private-public health care patchwork and the powerful stakeholders invested in the existing system. Some reformers wanted a single-payer system, which meant that government would pay all or most costs, like Medicare. Extending Medicare to those of all ages would have been a relatively simple solution. With Medicare, people choose their own doctor and other medical providers and government covers the cost. Private insurers are part of the Medicare picture, but only in a supplementary role.

But a single-payer solution was strongly opposed by many in the health care industry. Insurance companies benefit from being able to decide to whom to provide coverage and operating with minimal regulation. They opposed reforms that would subject them to further regulation. They feared that government control would lead to efforts to contain medical costs, which would squeeze their profits. The insurance industry alone (including life insurance companies) spent

Mike Keefe, The Denver Post and inToon.com

Damon Winter/The New York Times/Redux

"You are trampling on our Constitution," Craig Anthony Miller shouts at the late Senator Arlen Specter (at the time, a Republican) in Lebanon, Pennsylvania. Members of Congress got an earful from irate constituents when the health care bill was moving through Congress.

nearly $90 million from 2007 through 2010 in campaign contributions, most to Republicans but also to Democrats.[37] The American Medical Association, despite the support of many members, also opposed a single-payer system. Some hospitals also opposed reform. The health care industry has been one of the largest lobbies in Washington, and spent $1 million a day at the height of the health care debate in an effort to influence legislation.[38]

And many people wanted no reform at all. Americans who had health insurance, despite its escalating costs, were willing to maintain the status quo. Many were leery of change, and more so after opponents sketched scary scenarios they claimed would follow the reform. Conservatives especially were opposed to the reform because they were against any expansion of government's role in health care. They wanted to improve the workings of the private market. For example, John McCain, the 2008 Republican candidate, called for increased tax credits for individuals to buy insurance, the end of tax deductions for businesses to provide insurance to employees, more competition among insurers that might result in lower prices for consumers, and state involvement in creating risk pools and stimulating that competition. His vision was that people would be able to bargain more effectively to drive down prices. This was still the essence of the Republican position on health care reform in the 2012 presidential campaign. Ultimately, individuals would be expected to manage their finances well enough that they could afford health insurance.

Market-based solutions, such as McCain's plan, do not address three key issues with the current system. One is that private insurance is a moneymaking business, and thus it is not in the insurance companies' interest to enroll people who are sick and need insurance or to lower prices and reduce their

profits. This is not a criticism, but a recognition of how profit-making entities work. Second, market-based solutions do not accommodate people who simply can't afford insurance. And third, their solution to reducing the cost of the medical care system rests on trying to increase competition. There is, however, little evidence that the health care market responds to normal market forces because people are ill-equipped to make choices among different treatments and providers.

The challenge of reform was to design a system that would win support from those who wanted a single-payer system, the government; those who wanted a system that made private insurers the key in providing insurance, regulated by the government; and those who thought reform was best achieved through only private market mechanisms. In the end, though there were many concessions made to the private market group, only the first two groups, and only Democrats, supported the Affordable Care Act.

The Affordable Care Act

The Affordable Care Act (ACA) was arguably the greatest legislative achievement of Obama's early presidency. The debate was highly polarized among not just members of Congress but also within the public and interest groups.

The Politics of the Act

The debate over health reform was contentious and confusing. President Obama, aware that President Clinton had presented a detailed bill for health care reform to Congress only to see Congress reject it, did not offer any bill to Congress. Instead, he proposed features and parameters—for example, universal coverage—and stressed that he wanted a bill with support from both parties, and from the insurance and pharmaceutical companies. He left the details and the drafting to Congress in hopes that members would become invested in a bill they wrote.

To win the support of insurance and pharmaceutical companies, and to try to win the support of some Republicans, the president dropped the idea of a single-payer system—essentially, "Medicare for all"—that would shut out private insurers. Instead, the president indicated that he would support a plan that had been offered by Republicans in previous decades, a plan whereby everyone who could afford it would have to buy insurance or pay a penalty (a fine or a tax). This mandate was the centerpiece of the plan. The idea was originally developed by the Heritage Foundation, a conservative Washington think tank, in the 1980s. Recognizing the shortcomings of our health care system, the think tank sought a conservative solution. By forcing individuals to buy insurance, the mandate forced them to accept responsibility for their care.[39] The idea was championed by Republican members of Congress in the 1990s as an alternative to the reform proposed by President Bill Clinton. And the idea had been adopted by then-Governor Mitt Romney, who had played a major role in reforming health care in Massachusetts in 2006.

Insurance companies also supported the idea of a mandate because it would force more people to buy insurance even if they were healthy. Without a mandate, the insurance companies would pay for the sickest people while many healthy people, especially young adults, would opt out. With a mandate, however, the insurance companies could afford to cover the sickest people.

The expansion of coverage to many people without coverage before prompted the drug companies to support the bill. Millions of people would now be able to afford medication, thus opening a huge new market for prescription drugs. As negotiations progressed, insurance companies and drug companies angled to get the most benefits, and the fewest regulations, they could but in the end supported the proposal.

The Republicans did not put forward a comprehensive bill, so they were fighting something but not offering an alternative, though they did identify a series of reforms to provide more tax incentives, slightly expand federal health care insurance programs, and allow insurance companies to sell policies across state lines (a proposal that was incorporated, in limited form, in the final bill). Republicans also hoped to control costs by shifting more of it to the individual patient, forcing patients to choose more wisely among treatments, doctors, and hospitals.

Republicans also proposed medical malpractice reform so that injured patients could not sue doctors and hospitals for as much money as they can now. Although Democrats rely on trial lawyers for campaign contributions, and trial lawyers oppose malpractice reform, Obama had tentatively agreed to this proposal but ultimately abandoned it when Republicans refused to support the bill. Politicians don't give their opponents something for nothing; they expect an exchange.

Many Democrats were displeased with Obama's positions on the bill. Liberal Democrats criticized him for conceding the single-payer system before the debate and the "public option" during the debate. (The public option would have allowed the federal government to offer health insurance in competition with insurance companies as a way to force the companies to lower their costs. The public option was anathema to insurance companies, whose support was considered necessary for the bill's passage.) Conservative Democrats were also opposed to provisions of the bill, including the individual mandate. In the end, Republicans all voted against the bill, so Obama's concessions alienated his supporters without gaining any votes across the aisle. Still, most liberal Democrats ultimately supported the bill.

During the nearly yearlong consideration of the bill, opponents and supporters of health care legislation organized and lobbyists covered Capitol Hill. Opponents stirred up fears about what new legislation might do to existing health insurance arrangements, to the level of benefits, to doctor-patient relations, to the budget deficit, and to the size of the federal bureaucracy. In addition, they raised the specter of rationed care and bureaucrats making life-and-death decisions in "death panels." (This notion grew out of a provision in the initial bill that insurance would pay for counseling for dying patients and their families to help them make the decision about end-of-life care. Because of the misleading claims, this provision was removed from the final bill.) Led by extreme conservatives, later to organize as the Tea Party, opponents loudly and sometimes rudely expressed their opposition in town hall meetings and other constituency gatherings hosted by members of Congress. Some members encouraged such opposition, repeating the misinformation (in addition to "death panels," claims that the government would choose your doctor or force you to have abortions), while other members, intimidated by the opposition, refused to correct the misinformation.

The ugly atmosphere carried over to a joint session of Congress. Representative Joe Wilson (R-S.C.) cried "You lie!" when the president declared that the reforms would not provide undocumented persons with health care. (The bill explicitly prohibited undocumented persons from obtaining insurance coverage, though the traditional practice of hospital emergency rooms to treat all persons who came through the doors with serious injuries or illnesses presumably would continue.) Although the House formally rebuked Wilson for this breach of protocol, his campaign fundraising surged.

Other lobbying was more traditional as interested parties sought to shape the bill to their liking. The American Medical Association endorsed the bill only after removal of a tax on cosmetic surgery and of an antifraud fee to be assessed on physicians with Medicare patients. Pro-life advocates and Catholic bishops lobbied for assurance that the bill would not allow federal money to pay for abortions. In the end, the Catholic bishops opposed the bill while a national group of nuns, who work among the poor and sick, supported it. Lobbyists for drug makers (as we saw in Chapter 6), the NRA, and small businesses also demanded and got changes.

In the House, Speaker Nancy Pelosi (D-Calif.) needed only a simple majority for passage, and the Democrats commanded a large majority. Still, she confronted a daunting task. She had to organize the Democratic caucus behind a version of the bill that many opposed—most because it didn't go far enough, some because it went too far—and hold them in line through passage. Pelosi's accomplishment was also significant in light of the public polarization and vociferous opposition by many Americans. Democratic members felt vulnerable with the 2010 elections approaching. The final vote was 219–212, with about three dozen Democrats and all Republicans in opposition.

In the Senate, Majority Leader Harry Reid (D-Nev.) held the support of all Democrats (and two independents who usually voted with the Democrats) to get 60 votes to block a threatened filibuster. (As Chapter 9 explained, frequent use of the filibuster in the Senate now means that 60 votes, rather than 51, are necessary to pass most bills in that chamber.) The 60 votes reflected member-by-member negotiations, which were continuous, public, and infuriating to many. In return for their votes, many senators demanded and received special provisions for their home states, such as additional funds for hospital construction and for Medicare and Medicaid programs; and additional medical care for their constituents. This bargaining was intended to benefit constituents and win the senators electoral support, but the bill came to be associated with self-interested backroom deals, rather than being seen as a hard-won solution to a national problem. The most notorious was $100 million to help pay Nebraska's Medicare costs. Obtained by Sen. Ben Nelson (D-Nebr.), whose support was uncertain, it was dubbed the "Cornhusker Kickback." (After negative publicity, the provision was removed from the bill.) The 60 votes included Al Franken (Minn.), who won a cliff-hanging race after a months-long recount; a Democratic appointee to replace Edward Kennedy (Mass.), who died during the process; and ninety-three-year-old Robert Byrd (W.Va.), who was wheeled from a hospital during a blizzard for a vote. (Republican senator Tom Coburn [Okla.] encouraged people to pray that "somebody can't make the vote."[40] Senator Byrd did die three months after the bill was passed.) The final Senate vote was along party lines, 60–39. Because the Republican filibuster required a Democratic supermajority, the bill barely squeaked by, without a single vote to spare.

What the New Law Provides

Key elements of the ACA include the individual mandate, a provision that Americans must take responsibility to obtain health insurance. They may get it from their employer, or they must buy it if they can afford to, or pay a penalty or tax (when they file their income tax return). Those who cannot afford to buy it are eligible for a subsidy from the government. Eligibility for Medicaid is broadened so that more low-income people can receive it. Initially the federal government will pay most of the additional costs, but after a few years the states must pick up 10 percent of the costs. For those whose income is above the new eligibility level for Medicaid but who cannot afford insurance on the private market, financial aid will be provided and the states will set up insurance pools to negotiate and bargain with private insurance companies (an idea supported by Republicans in other contexts). If some states refuse to set up the pools, the federal government will do it for citizens of those states.

The law requires insurance companies to cover young adults up to age twenty-six on their parents' insurance if the family wants to. The law also prohibits insurance companies from denying coverage to people because they have a pre-existing medical condition or dropping coverage of people who incur a serious illness or injury. The law encourages businesses to provide health insurance for their employees, offering additional tax breaks if they do and penalties if they don't. (It exempts small businesses from the penalties.) The law closes the "donut hole" gap in prescription coverage left by the original Medicare prescription drug legislation. (That term refers to the fact that the government paid for 75 percent of drug coverage for Medicare recipients up to $2800; then recipients had to cover the next $1700 themselves, before Medicare again kicked in.) To help finance the program, the law eliminates the generous subsidies for some optional packages available under Medicare, and it levies a tax increase on high-income individuals.[41]

The bill is also designed to reduce the rate of cost increases in health care, though not necessarily to lower them. It relies on continuing diffusion of best practices to reduce costs and improve patient care. As one pro-market advocate argued,

"In America, no one has incentives to make quality and cost-effective outcomes the goal. There are so many stakeholders and they each want to protect themselves."[42] Opponents of the bill challenged these government estimates of cost savings and predicted rising costs. How can we afford to cover 20 to 30 million more people?

This is a key debate, though it has received less attention than the one over individual mandates. The U.S. health system, as we have shown, is less effective and efficient, while being more expensive, than many peers. These comparisons are why the ACA focuses efforts by doctors and hospitals to diffuse best practices for patient care and cost-effectiveness and mandates insurance plans to offer preventive care.

These provisions are being phased in over time. By 2012, tens of millions of dollars had been awarded to states to design and establish the health insurance exchanges that would pool the uninsured and facilitate comparison shopping. Several popular ACA provisions had gone into effect, including those that allowed young adults to remain on their family's insurance plan until age twenty-six and those that removed financial limits on Medicare prescription drug coverage. In addition, insurance companies were prohibited from dropping people who became ill, from setting lifetime or annual limits on coverage, and from denying coverage to people with pre-existing health conditions. The individual mandate was to become effective in 2014.

This summary of the main provisions of the bill illustrates, yet again, the mix of private and public that characterizes the American health care system. After the act is fully implemented, government will underwrite more of the cost of medical care and will regulate the insurance system more tightly, but the system will continue to rely on private insurance companies, patient-chosen doctors and hospitals, and private employers providing health insurance to their employees.

Reactions to the Bill

Few people believed that the law was optimum. The process was messy, and the law seemed jerry-rigged. But after sixty-five years of failed attempts, beginning with President Harry Truman in 1945, the Democrats were pleased—relieved—to get comprehensive health care reform passed. Although many wished the law went further, they recognized its accomplishment: by providing health care to most Americans, the nation was fulfilling its promise to its citizens.[43] The Republicans saw the law quite differently, perceiving it as a radical change that promised to increase the nation's debt and take over activities previously left to private enterprise. Ironically, the Affordable Care Act was built on Republican ideas, yet all Republicans voted against it.

The law was a contentious issue in the 2010 congressional elections. Deriding the law as "Obamacare," Tea Party members and other Republicans ratcheted up the rhetoric, claiming that Democrats "evoked people's fear of dying to make way for a federal takeover of the U.S. health-care system and to turn the management of our health, our very lives, into public utilities, essentially creatures of Congress and the Health and Human Services Department."[44] Motivated by intense dislike of the bill, the Republicans mobilized their voters and won big in the 2010 elections. They regained their majority in the House and gained seats in the Senate. Due to Tea Party candidates and pressure, the Republicans who held office after the election were even more conservative than those who had held office in the previous Congress. It was a "rightward lunge" greater than any previous shift from one Congress to another.[45] Republicans also captured many governorships and majorities in state legislatures. They were positioned and determined to be formidable obstructionists at least, reluctant negotiators at best.

House Republicans, from 2010 through 2012, passed bill after bill repealing the act but, of course, had no support from the Democratic majority in the Senate. By July 2012, House Republicans had held thirty-three separate debates and votes to voice their opposition to the law. Even so, they did not offer an alternative vision of how to address health care issues, possibly because the ACA contains so many of their ideas.

Opponents also fought the law in the courts. Approximately thirty lawsuits to overturn the ACA, one initiated by the attorney generals in Republican-dominated states, were filed in federal district courts. The Court accepted several cases, heard arguments, and reached its decision in 2012.

The law was challenged on several dimensions. The most important was the charge that the individual mandate was unconstitutional. The Court, by a 5–4 decision (the majority included the conservative chief justice and the four more liberal members of the Court), held that the individual mandate was constitutional. The Court justified it under Article I, Section 8, which gives Congress substantial power to tax and spend. The Court considered the penalty for violating the mandate to be a tax. **Art. I, Sec. 8**

However, a second key part of the ruling struck a blow at the Medicaid part of the ACA. To broaden eligibility for Medicaid, the ACA used a carrot and a stick. The carrot was a promise that the federal government would pay all costs for the additional enrollees for ten years; then the states would pick up 10 percent of the medical costs and 50 percent of the administrative costs. The stick was a threat that the states could lose all their federal Medicaid funding (existing as well as new funding) if they refused to broaden eligibility. A narrow majority (for this issue, the chief justice switched sides) ruled that this penalty was too draconian because it would force—not just encourage—states to comply. Thus the penalty violated the federal spending power (Article I, Section 8), despite its similarity to dozens of other programs with federal strings. As a result of the ruling, the ACA can still provide financial incentives for the states to broaden eligibility, but the law can no longer require the states to do so.

The Court's decision clarified the statute's constitutionality so that implementation plans could move along. Yet several Republican governors indicated that they will not expand their Medicaid program, which will leave some low-income people without the newly constructed safety net. These governors and

Representative Nancy Pelosi (D-Calif.), who as Speaker of the House had shepherded health reform through that chamber, celebrates with staffers upon hearing that the Supreme Court upheld the individual mandate.

their legislators are ideologically opposed to the ACA and to the Medicaid expansion, and they are fearful of the eventual costs. Some are also reluctant to give benefits to poor Americans. Some states with conservative leadership also are resisting setting up insurance pools. Here, however, the federal government will step in to organize pools for states without them.

With President Obama winning reelection, his administration will have the opportunity to solidify the ACA. The law will be fully in place and Americans will be well aware of its provisions by the time he leaves office. If Americans like the provisions, it will be difficult for any future Congress and president to repeal the law.

GOVERNMENT'S EXPANDING ROLE IN HEALTH CARE

Government's role in health care has expanded as its commitment to equality of opportunity and social justice has increased. In the United States, we like to think that everyone can have a chance to achieve to the best of his or her ability and that parents can have a reasonable hope that their children's lives will be better than their own.

Moreover, democracies function better when there are no permanent classes of haves and have-nots. Both goals are difficult, if not impossible, to reach unless everyone has adequate health care.

The commitment to ensuring broader access to health care led to the great expansion of government's role: it stepped into a health insurance void left by the private sector. For decades, private insurers excluded from coverage people with existing health problems or those at risk for contracting expensive-to-treat illnesses. These policies became especially problematic for the poor, the disabled, and the aged. But even with vast government programs, millions of Americans had no access to health care. And even for Americans who had insurance, the cost of providing that coverage continued to grow until it threatened the viability of the programs and the country's fiscal health. That led Congress in 2010 to pass a law to force change in the health insurance industry. It has also forced government to begin adjusting its own health spending and concentrate more heavily on disease prevention and better patient care at lower prices. These changes remain unpopular with those fearing increased government debt and increased government power.

SUMMARY

- The U.S. government first became involved in providing health care in 1798, with medical care for sick and disabled sailors that was paid for by a tax on shipmasters. The same law established what is today known as the Public Health Service (PHS). Today, there are specialized health-oriented government agencies working to enhance health care and accessibility to health care.
- The U.S. health care system is widely respected for its advances in research and technology, but it is equally notable for its failures in cost and coverage. Its cost has been increasing at an unsustainable rate while nearly 20 percent of Americans have not had any form of health insurance. Because of this problem, the health system does not contribute optimally to the physical and economic security of the nation. It also falls short of the nation's human rights and social justice objectives, denying health care to those who cannot afford its high costs. Failing to uphold the international covenants that the United States has signed, current health policies and practices actually contribute to shortening the lifespan of those who are economically disadvantaged.
- Individuals, corporations, and states have tried to compensate for the failures of the health care system. Reform has most consistently focused on the economics of health care. Religious organizations, neighbors, and

community groups often step in to provide charity, including medical care, to those whose medical bills are driving them to bankruptcy. Individuals and corporations have resorted to medical tourism, leaving the country to find cheaper medical care and prescription drugs. States have sometimes expanded, sometimes contracted, their health insurance programs as part of their effort to balance coverage with costs. But none of these efforts addresses the overarching national health care issues.
- Medicare, Medicaid, and the State Children's Health Insurance Program (S-CHIP) are three of the government's largest health insurance programs. These programs have provided coverage for the elderly (Medicare) and for many, though not all, of the poor and disabled (Medicaid and S-CHIP). With the Department of Veterans Affairs also providing help for veterans, the government is by far the largest health care spender in the country.
- To expand health care coverage to all Americans, the Affordable Care Act (ACA) was designed to provide all Americans with health coverage through a combination of private insurance, Medicare and Medicaid, and state-run insurance pools. The system reflects the hybrid public-private nature of health insurance in America.

- Though the Supreme Court ruled the ACA constitutional, it faces implementation challenges from state leaders who are threatening not to expand their states' roles in Medicaid or the insurance pools. Following President Obama's re-election, deadlines were extended to facilitate state compliance even as the federal government signaled that it would continue to push for full compliance with ACA provisions.

DISCUSSION QUESTIONS

1. How does the history of the Public Health Service help us understand government's role in today's health care system?

2. What were the major positives and negatives about the functioning of the health care system before passage of the Affordable Care Act? How was the ACA designed to improve the health care system? How does it illustrate the public-private partnership that has been characteristic of the American health care system for decades?

3. How does the ACA contribute to the objectives of protecting human rights and social justice, economic stability, and physical security in the health care system? Does the ACA set the United States back on any of these objectives?

4. For Medicare, Medicaid, and S-CHIP, describe who is covered and how the systems are funded. As a member of Congress confronting the need for budget cuts, how would you prioritize spending among Medicare, Medicaid, and S-CHIP? Consider both electoral and party politics in defending your answer.

5. Why did Congress pass a nearly universal health care law in 2010 after years of rejecting the approach? What individuals and groups played important roles? What does your judgment reveal about your view of politics, the law, and health care?

6. Now that the ACA has been passed and ruled constitutional, how do separation of powers and checks and balances help retain it?

Focus On...

Environmental Policy

This oil refinery symbolizes, perhaps unintentionally, the link between our consumption of oil and our way of life. This link makes it hard for Americans to acknowledge and address environmental problems stemming from the use of fossil fuels.

David McNew/Getty Images

LEARNING OBJECTIVES

1. Identify major federal action on key environmental issues over the last forty years, such the creation of the Environmental Protection Agency (EPA) and legislation that addresses air pollution, clean water, and endangered species; explain its significance.

2. Summarize the challenges to development of effective government regulations to protect the environment. Focus especially on the factors that propel and inhibit federal action, the interests involved in the ongoing controversy about policy direction, the role of experts, and the costs of action and inaction.

3. Explain the many forces that contribute to, or detract from, the effective implementation of environmental regulation, including changing science, public pressures, interest group activity, and differences of opinions and strategies among elected officials.

4. Define global warming, its major causes, and its major effects.

5. Describe the scientific evidence in support of global warming, the extent to which consensus exists among scientists, and the views of climate skeptics.

6. Explain the public's view of the causes of global warming and the trends in public opinion over time.

7. Identify major U.S. efforts to reduce greenhouse gas emissions, and assess the adequacy of these efforts.

How active should the federal government be in pursuing energy and environmental goals, including reducing the greenhouse gas emissions that create global warming? Who should pay the costs of making our environment safer: the government, private companies, or citizens? Or, if everyone should contribute, on whom should the primary burden fall?

In this "Focus On…Environmental Policy," we explore the governmental role in a broad range of environmental protection issues, including climate change, the forces that lead us toward addressing these issues, and those that reinforce the status quo.

Everyone breathes the air, drinks the water, and experiences the effects of climate change, and many Americans—one in four—live or work in proximity to a hazardous waste site.[1] About 127 million Americans live in counties that violate at least one air quality standard.[2] As a result, a majority of the public has long been in favor of spending for environmental protection. In fact, over the last forty years, government action to safeguard public health through protection of the environment has had broader public and more bipartisan legislative support than almost any area of regulation. Its importance has been proclaimed by leaders from President Richard Nixon—who called a clean environment the "birthright" of every American—to former vice president Al Gore, who helped bring the concept of global warming (a rise in the earth's temperatures due to an increase in greenhouse gas emissions that trap heat in the atmosphere resulting from human activity such as the burning of fossil fuels) to public consciousness. But public support and changes in individual behavior are two different things, especially when behavioral changes require increased costs.

In the modern era, the United States has confronted environmental challenges and reduced pollution levels in the air, water, and ground. It has reduced the dangers from acid rain and hazardous waste sites and implemented national testing programs that require screening and testing of newly manufactured chemicals. It has also saved the American bald eagle and other plant and animal species threatened with extinction, as well as committed the nation to regional and international treaties to reduce the global **ozone hole** caused by damage to the protective layer of the stratosphere from certain chemicals in propellants and spray cans.

Still, there are significant challenges ahead. The American Lung Association's 2010 report on air quality noted that six in ten Americans—or about 175 million people—live in cities with air quality that is frequently at dangerous levels. The worst is Los Angeles, California, which has the highest levels of ozone pollution in the nation. And more than half the nation's citizens live with poor air quality, polluted rivers and other bodies of water, and exposure to thousands of chemicals about which the risks are little understood. For instance, a 2009 survey found traces of 212 environmental chemicals in the population, including arsenic, pesticides, flame retardants, and perchlorate, which is an ingredient in rocket fuel.[3]

Today, however, the federal government is providing diminishing revenue for adequately addressing these issues and the problem may be getting worse. Despite more people, cars, and activity affecting the environment, budgets for environmental protection were no greater in 2008 than they were in 1980.[4] Additionally, climate change as a result of the greenhouse gas effect is causing widespread damage to our environment. And experts have confirmed that, in 2010, energy-related carbon emissions reached a record level.[5]

How our government has responded to these challenges and how it should respond are ongoing, critical debates.

EVOLUTION OF GOVERNMENT'S ROLE IN ENVIRONMENTAL POLICY

The crucial question in the debate over government's role can be stated simply, but it cannot be answered simply. How can we define standards that protect society's interest in having a clean, healthy, and sustainable environment and at the same time not unreasonably handicap economic growth and individual action? Historical and current debates over environmental policy revolve around this issue.

The Constitution contains no hint of concern about preserving and protecting the environment. Indeed, the Founders' and our own orientation to the environment are rooted in the Western, Judeo-Christian tradition that the physical world exists to serve human needs.[6] This sentiment was reinforced during the eighteenth-century period known as the Enlightenment, which led people (including the Founders) to believe that, through science and learning, we could conquer almost any obstacle to human progress.[7] Awareness of the negative consequences of science and technology for the environment was far into the future.

In the nineteenth century, concern grew about the effect that the Industrial Revolution, coupled with rapid population growth, might have on the environment. Late in that century, a conservationist movement to preserve some of the natural environment from farmers, ranchers, and loggers resulted in the creation of the national forests and a national park system.[8]

Awareness of pollution came along with concern about saving some forests and other areas of scenic beauty. The first federal government effort to combat water pollution was an 1899 law requiring that individuals dumping waste into navigable waters obtain a permit from the U.S. Army Corps of Engineers. In 1924, Congress banned oceangoing ships from dumping oil in coastal waters. Neither of these acts was enforced very well, but the legislation did indicate a growing concern with pollution.

The modern environmental movement probably stemmed from a book that was published in 1962: Rachel Carson's *Silent Spring*. In it, Carson argued that pesticides used in agriculture find their way into the air and water and harm crops, animals, and people. Moreover, she demonstrated that scientists and engineers neither knew the extent of these harmful effects nor seemed particularly concerned. After the book's publication, the chemical industry immediately attacked Carson, accusing her of hysteria and misstatement of facts, and calling her un-American. But the industry's attacks created widespread publicity for her views and raised the environmental consciousness of millions of Americans. Indeed, President Kennedy cited Carson's work as his reason for ordering a review of government regulation of pesticides.[9] The decade and a half following the publicity over Carson's book was characterized by a burst of regulatory activity by the government. By this time, public concern about the environment also peaked. Huge oil spills, such as one off Santa Barbara, California, rivers catching fire, such the Cuyahoga River in Cleveland, Ohio, and the growing impact of automobile use on air quality lent substance to these concerns.

By 1970, public opinion polls showed that the most frequently cited national problem was protecting the environment.[10] In response, in April 1970, Earth Day was inaugurated, and hundreds of thousands of citizens across the nation demonstrated to show their concern. That event and the activism that followed, including the targeting and defeat of twelve members of Congress dubbed "The Dirty Dozen," led directly to major new environmental legislation. Every year since, April 22 has been set aside to celebrate the planet's resources and to heighten environmental awareness. And since 1972, June 5 has been commemorated as World Environment Day.

Since the birth of the modern environmental movement, more than forty major federal environmental laws have been enacted. Progress in cleaning up our water, air, and land has, on one hand, been impressive. Increased development of renewable sources of energy has put us closer to the time when heavy reliance on fossil fuels will no longer be routine. Yet, as frequent headlines about climate change and its dangers to the planet attest, our greatest challenges—those of sustainability—may lie ahead of us.

GraphEGO/Shutterstock

The first recycling logo, introduced on the first Earth Day in 1970, was designed by Gary Dean Anderson, a twenty-three-year-old student at the University of Southern California, in response to a competition by the Container Corporation of America. The company used recycled paper in its production process and wanted to spur more widespread recycling.

MAJOR FEDERAL ACTION

In the modern political era, the federal government has enacted major legislation to clean up air, ground, and water pollution. It has also passed legislation to protect endangered species and to contain and ameliorate damage done by the use of toxic substances such as asbestos, radon, and lead-based paint. These efforts have resulted in a better environmental situation than would be the case otherwise.

The Role of Citizens in Protecting the Environment

In 1970, Congress gave citizens a formal way to influence environmental policy. New legislation required that government agencies prepare **environmental impact statements** for internal projects or projects they fund.[11] These analyses must detail the effects, including any negative consequences, that a proposed project or activity would have on the environment. No new buildings, dams, sewers, pipelines, or highways may be built, or any research or other government projects initiated, until these statements are filed and reviewed.

Not only did the law give federal agencies the power to comment on each other's environmental impact statements, but it also gave citizens access. Early environmental legislation was the first to incorporate the 1960s ethic of public involvement. These provisions became an important device for organizations interested in protecting the environment. Within a few years, more than four hundred legal suits were filed to force the government to comply with the act's provisions; by 1980, thousands had been filed.[12]

EPA

Another landmark event marking the growing federal involvement in environmental protection was the 1970 creation of the **Environmental Protection Agency (EPA)** by President Nixon.[13] Recognizing that responsibilities for pollution control were spread throughout the executive branch, Nixon brought them together in this one regulatory agency with a single head who reported to the president. During the EPA's first years, several foundational pieces of environmental protection legislation were passed by Congress and were followed by additional enactments in subsequent decades.

Clean Air

The Clean Air Act of 1970 mandated that the EPA set limits on air pollutants (the result of producing energy using fossil fuels) by giving it authority to reduce emissions from chemical plants, utilities, steel mills, and other sites across the nation.[14] From 1970 to 1990, the Clean Air Act relied on risk-based assessments of air quality and issued few standards. After that time, technology-based standards were developed for major sources of air pollution that focused on the maximum degree of reduction in emissions.

State and local governments do much of the work of implementing the Clean Air Act. They monitor air quality, inspect facilities, and enforce the act's regulations, and the EPA has the authority to sanction states that do not meet the national standards.

Clean Water

The Clean Water Act of 1972 is intended to protect surface water quality by mandating reductions in pollutant discharges

SARAH LEEN/National Geographic Stock

Environmental concerns have spurred some Americans to take action themselves. Jacques Chiron of Corvallis, Oregon, powers his green (Astroturf) car with vegetable oil from a potato chip factory.

into waterways and wastewater treatment facilities and by setting standards for management of polluted runoff. Early regulatory efforts concentrated on sewage plants and industrial sites. More recent efforts focus on runoff from construction sites, streets, and farms. There has also been a shift over time from dealing with individual sources of pollution to what is called a coordinated "watershed approach" in which both the public and private sectors are responsible for protecting healthy waters in specific geographic areas and restoring impaired ones.

Toxic Substances

In 1976, congressional legislation broadened the powers of the EPA and directed it to regulate the chemicals used in manufacturing and commerce, including **polychlorinated biphenyls (PCBs)**, asbestos, radon, and lead-based paint. Thus, the manufacture or importation of chemicals that are not on what is called the allowable Toxic Substances Control Act Inventory is prohibited. If the EPA concludes that a certain chemical would pose an unreasonable risk to human health or the environment, its staff may take a range of actions, including limiting its use, requiring warning labels at point of sale, or banning its use entirely, although the agency is directed to use the least burdensome option possible.

Although, over time, there has been regulation of some chemicals, several constraints on action, including the high burden of proof required by an unreasonable risk to human health and the grandfather clause for chemicals that existed prior to 1976 (approximately 62,000 of the over 80,000 in inventory), have resulted in required testing for only a few hundred chemicals, and the agency has only partially restricted five chemicals. Thus, the vast majority of chemicals used today are unregulated. One result is that the amount of toxic chemicals released into the environment in 2010 increased 16 percent over the year before, driven largely by metal mining and the chemical industry.[15]

Superfund

A federal law, popularly known as **"Superfund,"** was enacted in 1980 in the wake of a public health tragedy referred to as **"Love Canal"** in which many residents of a community in upstate New York were relocated because of groundwater contamination from a chemicals and plastics plant that once inhabited the neighborhood. The statute created a tax on the chemical and petroleum industries and provided federal authority to respond to releases of hazardous substances, including radioactive waste, that may endanger public health or the environment. The tax went into a trust fund for cleaning up hazardous waste sites. The law also established legal liability of those responsible for waste at Superfund sites when they could be identified. Subsequently, however, the Superfund tax expired, and the fund ran out of money. The Obama administration has been pushing to reinstate the

Superfund tax, which hasn't been collected since 1995, but, to date, has not been successful.

Endangered Species

The Endangered Species Act of 1973 mandates conservation of threatened and endangered plants and animals as well as their habitats. The government manages a list of endangered species that includes fish, birds, insects, reptiles, crustaceans, mammals, grasses, trees, and flowers and must be consulted when actions are taken that might jeopardize any of the species on the endangered list or any of their habitats.

The government reports that, in the United States alone, over 600 animal and 700 plant species are on the threatened or endangered lists. Since the law was enacted, some animal species have become extinct, but others have repopulated to sustainable levels and been removed from the list, including the American bald eagle, the gray wolf, the gray whale, the grizzly bear, and the California southern sea otter. But the forces that created the problems originally can sometimes lead to recurring dangers for these animals. For instance, scientists are studying the gray whale population to determine if this animal should be put back on the endangered list. Other forces, such as global warming, may jeopardize the existence of additional animals. By 2050, scientists predict that polar bears will live mostly in zoos, because global warming is melting the Arctic ice that is their habitat.

EFFECTIVENESS OF ENVIRONMENTAL LEGISLATION

Passing laws is one thing, enforcing them another. Congress and the president can mandate certain environmental goals, but governmental agencies, such as the EPA, must then write rules for reaching those goals and monitor implementation of them by states. That process, while producing some good effects, has also been fraught with slowness, controversy, changes in strategies, and high costs. Part of the reason is that multiple entities are responsible for oversight. At the federal level, twelve different cabinet departments, agencies such as the EPA and the Nuclear Regulatory Commission, and approximately twenty Senate and twenty-eight House committees play roles in this process.

Regulating Air Pollution

Under the Clean Air Act, the EPA was ordered to establish air quality standards for major air pollutants, a task that required writing hundreds of rules. States were also mandated to draw up plans to bring local air quality into compliance with federal standards. In keeping with the commitment to public involvement in the regulatory process, the Clean Air Act also permitted citizens to sue to enforce its provisions.[16] Of course, the industries and public utilities subject to the new rules also had the right to challenge them.

Early efforts focused on a "standards" approach to writing rules, but these proved to be ineffective. Penalties for failure to achieve the pollution standards were often not assessed, and when they were, the fines were usually far less than the cost of compliance. Although the EPA can have a noncomplying company closed, the agency has been reluctant to enforce standards against large companies with political clout or small profit margins, especially industries crucial to the nation's economic health. To take action against a large industry requires significant political will all the way to the White House. That kind of commitment is rare.

Presidential administrations have developed more effective means to enforce environmental air standards. The Carter administration allowed compliance in some industries to be based on the **bubble concept**, which allows companies to meet an overall standard for emission of pollutants. Imagine that a bubble has been placed over a factory with ten smokestacks. Under original rules, each smokestack would have to meet EPA standards. Under the bubble concept, one or more smokestacks might exceed the limits on emissions as long as the total emissions within the bubble met the standard. Rather than bringing all ten smokestacks into compliance, the company might find it easier or cheaper to install equipment on only five smokestacks—if doing so would reduce total emissions to the required level. The bubble concept provided greater flexibility in determining how a standard could be met and reduced the cost, resulting in greater levels of compliance.

Eventually, an even more flexible system evolved that allowed for a multifactory bubble. A limit or cap is placed on the amount of a pollutant that can be emitted in a geographic area, and factories within that area are allowed to buy, sell, or trade rights to pollute as long as collective emissions do not exceed the cap. Utility companies can then decide whether it is cheaper to buy and install scrubbers to reduce plant emissions or to buy permits that allow them to pollute. This policy, called **cap-and-trade**, gives industries some flexibility in meeting pollution standards, but if they do pollute, they have to pay in advance.

The evolution of regulation of air quality is a good illustration of how industry and public responses to the implementation of rules can influence reassessment and revision. The goals of the original Clean Air Act were not weakened but strengthened by subsequent modifications because the rules were revised to make them less cumbersome and more cost-effective. And new procedures have been applied to multiple situations. For example, the cap-and-trade approach has been adopted by international environmental agencies to achieve worldwide reductions in the emission of greenhouse gases, such as carbon dioxide (CO_2) and others linked to global warming, with nations, rather than businesses, buying and trading permits to pollute.

Nonetheless, legislation before Congress in 2010 to institute a cap-and-trade system for greenhouse gas emissions in the United States was declared a nonstarter. Because the Republican Party opposes environmental regulation, even proposals it once supported, President Obama avoided making this an issue before the November 2010 midterm elections. The topic was not even raised by either presidential candidate in the 2012 presidential elections, and references to it were excised from President Obama's 2012 Earth Day proclamation.

Regulating Water Quality

Before 1972, at least eighteen thousand communities regularly dumped untreated raw sewage into rivers and lakes. Food, textile, paper, chemical, metal, and other industries discharged approximately 25 trillion gallons of wastewater each year. These activities occurred despite federal attempts to improve water quality. For example, a 1948 law authorized the federal government to give funds to local governments to build sewage treatment plants. Thousands of communities used the grants for this purpose. In 1965, Congress mandated that states establish clean water standards to get these sewage treatment grants. But the law was not effective. States did not want to establish stringent quality standards because they were concerned that industries would leave, and they did not want to lose revenue to neighboring states.

In 1972, with the opportunity afforded by the Clean Water Act, the federal government tried again, aiming to achieve "fishable and swimmable" waters by 1983 and zero discharges into water by 1985. Industries were to be given permits to discharge wastes and to make sure that discharged pollutants were the lowest amounts possible. And the EPA set uniform national standards for discharge control for each type of industry so that states did not have incentives to set lax standards to keep industries in their borders.

It took years to implement water quality standards effectively, for many of the same reasons that initially confounded air quality enforcement. Finally, in 1991, Congress passed new, more stringent safety standards for tap water, requiring more frequent testing for lead levels in municipal water supplies, only to see them threatened by a subsequent round of **deregulation**.

The difficulty achieving the goals of clean water was not all due to resistance to regulation and its costs. When the first rules were written, they covered only industries and municipal sewage plants, which account for only part of the water pollution problem. But "nonpoint sources" (discharges that do not come from a specific pipe) account for as much as half of all water pollution. Examples include farmlands, which produce fertilizer runoff, and sewers connecting drains and grates in city streets, which collect gas, oil, fertilizers, pesticides, animal excrement, and other substances. These toxins end up in the nearest waterways. Current rules are written to achieve clean water goals that stress pollution from these nonpoint sources.

For all the difficulties implementing the law, the Clean Water Act has improved the safety of many of our water sources since it was enacted. Much of today's drinking water is much safer than it was, and 60 percent of all rivers and lakes are now safe for swimming and fishing. But, in part because of still inadequate enforcement, even today, approximately 20 percent of Americans have some form of unsafe drinking water.[17]

Regulating Nuclear Waste

Most hazardous waste—toxic chemicals such as those in Love Canal—are generated by private industry. But some hazardous waste is created by the government, especially in the development of nuclear weapons and nuclear power. At issue is the fact that nuclear waste, which is highly toxic and radioactive for tens of thousands of years, cannot be recycled. And science has not provided a safe way to dispose of these wastes.

At the start of the U.S. nuclear program during World War II, policy makers and scientists believed that spent fuel from nuclear weapons programs, power plants, uranium mining, hospitals, and research centers could be reprocessed. This turned out not to be the case, and what has occurred instead is an ever-increasing amount of radioactive waste temporarily stored in civilian and military facilities, many of which have safety and leakage issues. Federal plans to construct permanent nuclear waste facilities, focused on Yucca Mountain, Nevada, have never been implemented, mostly because state

American Diversity

Environmental Justice

Issues of environmental justice are an ongoing concern in debates over pollution and global warming policies. As defined by the EPA, environmental justice means involving people and treating them fairly in "the development, implementation, and enforcement of environmental laws, regulations and policies." The goal is to provide the same protection from environmental and health hazards for low-income people and minority racial groups as for those with higher incomes and those in white neighborhoods.[1]

An example of how environmental justice or injustice is manifested in water pollution comes from Dickson, Tennessee, where government officials were long aware that local water wells had become contaminated with trichloroethylene (TCE) via decades of dumping in a local landfill. White residents of the community were warned about the danger and included in the municipal water system, but the African American residents were not—at least until Sheila Holt-Orsted lost her dad and several neighbors to cancer and was shortly thereafter diagnosed herself. After a nine-year legal battle, Holt-Orsted won a settlement in 2011 that provided the entire community with access to safe water, something that should have been afforded them from the start.[2]

Environmental justice issues have also been prevalent with respect to the effects of radioactive contamination. Mining for uranium, a naturally radioactive element, began in the Navajo Nation near the end of World War I. Navajo workers were paid very low wages and given no information about the hazardous effects of the job. In time, the consequences became clear: the miners had a much higher incidence of cancer than the general population. By the 1950s, miners demanded compensation from mine companies. But it was not until 1990 that a federal law was enacted that required redress to the cancer victims. Still, getting the money proved to be very difficult. The government imposed certification guidelines that were hard for the Navajo people to fulfill. Because tribal culture did not value keeping family and medical records, few miners had proof and few received compensation. Those who did received less than they were entitled to receive.

[1]U.S. Environmental Protection Agency, "Environmental Justice," http://www.epa.gov/compliance/ej/ (accessed May 15, 2012).
[2]Natural Resources Defense Council (NRDC), *Nature's Voice*, March–April 2012, 2.

residents are concerned about the possible harmful effects of housing radioactive material. The Obama administration called the Yucca Mountain plan unworkable, shut down the project, and set up a blue-ribbon commission to figure out an alternative plan. To date, the United States is still entirely without permanent repositories for these materials.

These nuclear dangers have already exacted enormous health costs. During the Cold War, six hundred thousand people in thirty-seven states worked in the nuclear weapons industry and were routinely exposed to radioactive substances. Thousands of other people have suffered health problems as a result of living near weapons industries or serving as subjects in weapons research. For example, no one warned the citizens of Yucca Flats, Nevada, about radioactivity, even though the government exploded more than one thousand bombs in their state to test nuclear weaponry. According to a study by the U.S. Centers for Disease Control, eleven thousand people died because of exposure to radioactive fallout from aboveground weapons testing. The testing also contributed to a minimum of twenty-two thousand cancers.[18]

Similarly, the nuclear weapons plant in Hanford, Washington knowingly released massive amounts of radioactive materials, including iodine, into the air for test purposes. Researchers from the U.S. Centers for Disease Control believe that twenty thousand children in eastern Washington may have been exposed to unhealthy levels of this iodine by drinking milk from cows grazing in contaminated pastures.[19] And the dangers continue; a new analysis indicates that the amount of plutonium at the Hanford Nuclear Reservation is almost three times greater than acknowledged in previous reports. More than two decades after the incident, none of the 53 million gallons of toxic waste has been cleaned up.

Problems emanating from nuclear power plants are equally disturbing. In 2011, 104 nuclear power plants operated in the United States, and no new ones have been ordered in several decades. The halt in building new plants stems from the worst nuclear power plant accident in the United States, which occurred in 1979 at Three Mile Island (TMI) near Harrisburg, Pennsylvania. As a result of equipment malfunctions, design problems, and human error, a partial meltdown of a reactor core occurred, releasing small amounts of radioactivity. The dosage of radiation to which the area's residents were exposed was estimated to be a year's worth of natural background radiation. Subsequent studies of the air, water, vegetation, food, and soil found minimal contamination, but, fortunately, to date few adverse health effects to the population are detectable.

Even though the damage from the Three Mile Island accident was less severe than the worst nuclear power plant disaster in history, the 1986 **Chernobyl** accident in the former Soviet Union, and the second most severe disaster, the 2011 release of radioactive materials at the Fukushima nuclear power plant in Japan, the TMI accident eroded public trust in nuclear power. It also triggered important changes to the nuclear power industry, such as improved operator training, increased radiation protection, enhanced emergency response planning, and increased oversight by the Nuclear Regulatory Commission. Today, the reactor that malfunctioned is permanently shut down.

In the face of ongoing concerns about public health, few new plants have been completed since TMI. However, in 2005 Congress passed a law offering incentives for construction of new plants. In 2012, the Nuclear Regulatory Commission approved plans for two new nuclear reactors in Georgia, the first approval of a new project since 1978. These may come online as early as 2016 and 2017, and they will be developed with $8.3 billion in loan guarantees from the Obama administration.

Containing the danger from nuclear waste—whether from weapons programs, power plants, or other sources—and nuclear accidents is a most difficult and consequential problem, particularly when the government must regulate itself rather than industry.

FORCES SHAPING REGULATION

Once standards are worked out and rules are written, implementing begins. This step is challenging because fundamental disagreements exist about calculating the benefits and costs of regulation. What monetary value should be put on intangibles such as human health, comfort, appreciation of clean air, or loss of individual liberties?[20] Is it even possible or desirable to put a price on these?

The best estimates for the costs and benefits of air pollution regulation show that, although pollution control equipment costs millions of dollars to industry and requires additional employees to deal with federal regulations, reducing pollution also offsets other industry costs. Equipment life is longer because corrosion is reduced, employee productivity rises because fewer days are lost due to illness, and medical costs for employers are reduced.[21] Cleaning up the air also increases agricultural output. However, company executives faced with complying with federal regulations see mostly the costs and not the benefits, which may be long term and not specific to them.

Environmental cleanup also results in considerable job creation. Sixty thousand public and private companies are engaged in environmental activities, employing almost 1.5 million people and generating annual revenues in the billions.[22] Reducing greenhouse gases by moving to renewable sources of energy will also create jobs in a new **green economy**, jobs such as constructing and installing solar panels and producing electric vehicles.

But even with these benefits, environmental regulations can be unpopular. The speed of scientific change, public pressures, interest group advocacy, and lack of consensus among policy makers all contribute to implementation challenges.

Changing Science and Disagreements about Science

Sound regulatory policy has to be based on good science, and the scientific process does not always yield definitive or static answers. Because disagreement among scientists exists about the best regulatory course, the right path is not always clear. Additionally, rapid changes in high technology and the massive changes brought by globalization have made it difficult for scientists and policy makers to keep pace with change. Sometimes scientific findings of one era are over-ridden by later research, and policies based on the earlier findings become invalid. And sometimes proceeding with cutting-edge solutions is very risky. Human interventions in the environment may have unintended consequences. On top of all this uncertainty is cost and the disagreements about the right level of safety versus the economic costs of producing it. A former EPA director once said that the EPA's mission is like trying to give someone an appendectomy while the person is running the hundred-yard dash.[23]

One example of the risks of human intervention focuses on proposals to address the harmful effects of global warming. Many scientists believe that, at this point, curbing greenhouse gas emissions will not be effective enough to reverse severe damage to the earth. Therefore, some advocate new technologies such as reducing incoming sunlight to earth by injecting sulphurous fluids into the stratosphere, injecting salt particles into clouds to create more reflection and less sunshine,

capturing carbon dioxide in the atmosphere and trapping it, or seeding oceans with iron to accelerate the growth of algae, which can then sink to sea beds, taking carbon with them. Yet all these potential technological "fixes," often referred to as geoengineering, come with attendant dangers. No one knows how deliberate tinkering with the environment may destabilize it and create unforeseen and potentially very dangerous consequences.[24]

Even in cases where scientific solutions are relatively clear and cost-effective, sometimes policy makers deliberately ignore or misuse scientific findings in pursuit of their own ideological goals. One prominent example from the George W. Bush administration was the deletion of conclusions from an EPA report on global warming. The scientists' findings reflected a consensus that global warming exists, that human behavior contributes to it, and that it is a serious problem that requires immediate and extensive action (see Figure 1). The president ignored this conclusion because it was contrary to his beliefs, claimed that no scientific consensus existed, and

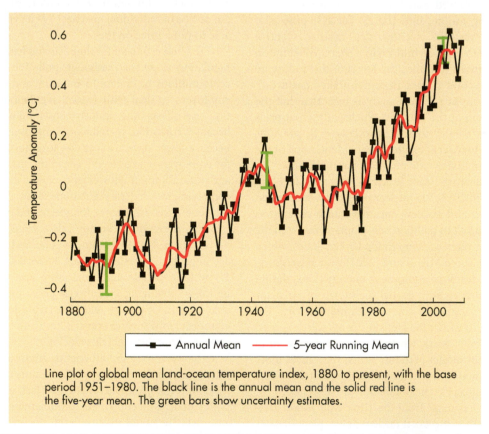

Line plot of global mean land-ocean temperature index, 1880 to present, with the base period 1951–1980. The black line is the annual mean and the solid red line is the five-year mean. The green bars show uncertainty estimates.

FIGURE 1: THE EARTH HAS GOTTEN WARMER DURING THE PAST CENTURY This figure shows the global warming of the earth between 1880 and 2000. The peaks and valleys also show the climate variability—with some years warmer or cooler than others—that occurs from year to year. The effects of the increase in average global temperature during this time are expected to be strong and significant. Additionally, the National Oceanic and Atmospheric Administration's (NOAA) 2009 *State of the Climate* report, which uses ten warming measures, confirms that this past decade has been the warmest ever recorded. Sea levels and air temperatures over land and oceans rose, while spring snow in the Northern Hemisphere and Arctic sea ice declined.

SOURCE: National Oceanic and Atmospheric Administration's (NOAA) National Climatic Data Center, *State of the Climate in 2009*. As appearing in the July 2010 issue (Vol. 91) of the *Bulletin of the American Meteorological Society* (BAMS).

stated that more research was needed before any commitment to remedial action was made.

Public Pressures

Trying to formulate policy based on sound science is also complicated by conflicting pressures from the public. With widespread information available about how exposure to toxic substances in our water, land, and air may be linked to cancer and other illnesses, Americans have become increasingly concerned about avoiding such risks. And information about energy-related accidents, such as the underground coal mine explosion in Montcoal, West Virginia, and the **Deepwater Horizon** oil rig explosion and oil spill, both of which occurred in 2010 and resulted in death and destruction of the environment and property, has heightened awareness of the risks associated with our energy choices. Thus, the public has increased pressure on the government to protect us from both toxic substances and poorly regulated energy extraction and delivery processes, but it has not necessarily committed to the costs inherent in doing so.

And although environmental concerns have widespread support among the public, that support is not necessarily consistent or even very deep, and it fluctuates over time. For instance, among the data reported in an annual environmental poll is a question about how much people are worried about a range of environmental issues. As Figure 2 shows, in every category reported, Americans worried less about the environment in 2012 than they did twelve years earlier, and no category rose to the 50 percent level. These declines may indicate that people believe some problems have gotten

better, as indeed they have. But several, like global warming, have gotten worse.

Another explanation for lesser levels of worry may be that, in times of economic stress, environmental issues decrease as a priority.[25] As one citizen commented, "How do you expect me to believe in global warming if I don't even know how I'm going to put my five-year-old kid through college?"[26]

A third explanation is that the leaders of the Republican Party do not accept the scientific consensus about global warming. Some take an anti-science position, and others are against regulation in general; moreover, many Republican Party supporters (the oil and gas industry in particular) would be subject to greater compliance costs if actions to reverse the trend were taken.

These attitudinal fluctuations make it unsurprising that the public's willingness to change behavior to reverse the dangers of global warming is not entirely compatible with the goals it supports. We want clean air and water and a sustainable planet, but we do not want to give up gas-powered vehicles for individual use, disposable products, high levels of home, office, and business energy use, airline travel, and other pollution-causing aspects of our lifestyles. In the United States, we use far more energy per person than do the people of any other nation except Canada. Part of this heavy consumption is due to our level of economic development and to consumer wealth, and part is due to wastefulness. Sustainability is best illustrated in the oft-repeated phrase "reduce, reuse, renew, recycle." But, as a nation, we are far more likely to acquire more than to make the effort to reduce our use or create multiple uses for what we already have.

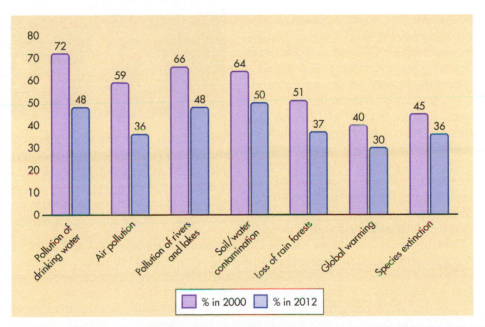

FIGURE 2: AMERICANS WORRY ABOUT THE ENVIRONMENT THOUGH LESS THAN IN 2000 The figures reflect the percent who say they worry "a great deal."

SOURCE: Jones, Jeffrey M. "Worry about U.S. Water, Air Pollution at Historical Lows; Americans' Concerns about Environmental Threats Remain Lower than in the Past." Gallup, Inc. April 13, 2012. http://www.gallup.com/poll/153875/Worry-Water-Air-Pollution-Historical-Lows.aspx. Accessed May 24, 2012. Copyright © 2012 Gallup, Inc. All rights reserved. The content is used with permission; however, Gallup retains all rights of republication.

From a broader perspective, a very small percentage of citizens are willing to take any action that will result in increased costs to themselves. Surveys have asked people what they might be willing to pay per year to ensure that renewable energy is produced. In 2009, one-third would not be willing to pay *anything* to achieve that goal; another third would only be willing to pay between $1 and $49 a year. To many people struggling to make ends meet in the recession, $49 is a significant amount. But, to many Americans, this sum is less than buying a single coffee drink each week. And only 5 percent of the public would be willing to spend between $250 and $500 or more a year.[27] Perhaps in relationship to these inclinations, a survey of people in 17 nations found that Americans are the most confident that their individual actions can help the environment. Yet, the U.S. trails other nations in sustainable behaviors, and our citizens are the least likely to feel guilty about that fact.[28] Thus, the environment is not a very high priority, especially when the economy is poor and some political leaders and the press are telling citizens that they don't need to worry about these issues.

Sometimes emergencies or crises cause us to reduce our harm to the environment. For example, high oil prices in the 1970s curbed energy use for a time, but we quickly returned to our high-consumption ways. Similarly, although there were many calls for reduction in our dependence on Middle Eastern oil after 9/11, our reliance on it is greater than it was before the attack. After the BP Deepwater Horizon oil rig explosion and oil spill in the Gulf of Mexico, public opinion polls showed that, although the public wants better regulation, it supports offshore oil drilling in the United States.[29] And environmental groups report that, unlike with other large environmental disasters, they gained little traction after the Deepwater Horizon accident when they attempted to advocate for legislation that would reduce our dependence on oil, imported or otherwise.

Impact social, global, historical, economic, political

The Environmental Costs of Oil and Gas Extraction

The environmental costs of oil and gas extraction are significant. In the best-known recent example, the 2010 BP Deepwater Horizon oil rig explosion in the Gulf of Mexico resulted in the deaths of eleven oil rig workers and a massive oil spill. It was deemed the single worst environmental event in U.S. history and illuminates the dangers inherent in lax environmental regulation. After the disaster, which spewed oil for eighty-seven days before it was fully contained, the public discovered that the federal government had long been doing an inadequate job of regulating and monitoring oil drilling.

Oil drilling, especially in deep water, is a dangerous activity. Without stringent rules, consistent enforcement activity, and careful implementation of business policies, the probability of serious accidents is real. In the case of the Gulf oil spill, none of these requirements was met. Not only had several presidential administrations given too much leeway to and performed too little oversight of the oil industry, but BP itself has a long history of overlooking safety concerns, as have other companies. Indeed, federal records indicate frequent oil spills,

JIM LO SCALZO/EPA/Landov

Fracking has made water in some parts of Pennsylvania non-potable. One way that has happened is that methane has leaked into residential water wells as a result of the fracking process. In this photo, Sherry Vargson lights the water coming from her sink on fire to demonstrate the effects of the presence of methane.

consisting of 517,847 barrels of petroleum into the Gulf of Mexico, between 1964 and 2009.[1] In 2012, the U.S. government filed a legal suit against BP charging that the company engaged in a culture of corporate recklessness.[2]

A second type of fossil fuel extraction, fracking, is supported by many as a way to bridge the gap between the end of reliance on oil and coal and the beginning of large-scale reliance on solar, wind, and other non-fossil energy sources. Fracking, which has grown considerably in the past decade, is a shorthand for hydraulic fracturing, a method that allows producers to extract gas or oil from hard-to-reach places by drilling into rock formations using water, sand, and chemicals.

The fracking process results in significant environmental damage and requires a massive use of natural resources. For instance, almost six hundred chemicals, many of which are carcinogenic, are used in fracking

Interest Groups

Interest groups on all sides of regulatory issues sometimes exaggerate in making their claims, thus making it difficult to sort out the likely implications of regulation or lack of it. In recent years, antiregulatory forces have successfully played on public fears. Businesses and industries sometimes try to scare the public with visions of huge individual and industry costs associated with action and ignore the benefits. For example, industry groups claim that family budgets will be decimated in any switch from primary reliance on burning fossil fuels (oil, gas, coal), even though critics of these estimates claim that the cost of capping greenhouse gases will come to less than 1 percent of household budgets over the next twenty years.[30] And critics of plans to address climate change rarely consider the long-term costs of ignoring it.

For their part, environmental groups sometimes make unachievable demands for safety standards for all pollutants. Their critics say this has caused a great deal of money to be spent on less critical goals while more threatening hazards are ignored. Environmental interest groups counter by speaking of the consequences to people's lives if the full range of public health harms are not addressed; they prefer to err on the side of safety. They are also sometimes unwilling to admit their successes because of the intense competition among environmental groups for membership and financial support.[31] Their critics argue that this competition has led them to make "apocalyptic prophecies to raise more money and further their political objectives." One fundraising letter from the National Audubon Society, for example, claimed that it could "project with some accuracy the eventual end of the natural world as we know it."[32]

fluid, and between 1 and 7 million gallons of water are necessary to frack a natural gas well just once. As a result of the process, dangerous pollutants are released into the air and water, and accidental leaks of fracking fluid can create even more damage. Indeed, in several communities in which fracking has been prevalent, air pollution levels are among the highest in the nation, drinking water has been poisoned with toxic chemicals, and residents have experienced health problems, including eye irritation, headaches, sore throats, and difficulty breathing. In Dimock, Pennsylvania, the tap water is so contaminated that it is flammable. Even so, fracking has been subject to little regulation and even has been granted exemptions from some laws such as the Clean Drinking Water Act. The lack of governmental action is consequential enough that the pioneer of the fracking method, an oil and gas drilling executive, has called for stepped up regulation to protect the environment.[3]

Today, environmental groups and their allies in Congress are working toward requiring better reporting of chemicals used in fracking and applying existing environmental regulations to the process. However, legislation has gone nowhere so far. For its part, the Obama administration has launched a study of the effects of fracking (while being careful to say that the action won't necessarily lead to more regulation) and has made small efforts to regulate the practice. One such effort is a requirement that chemicals used have to be disclosed—although not until after a fracking project has been completed.

In the absence of serious federal action, several states are requiring disclosure of chemicals involved in the process. In 2012, Vermont became the first state in the nation to ban fracking entirely.[4]

These risky oil and gas extraction methods illustrate the challenges of policy making in this area. In the case of the Deepwater Horizon, shortly after the spill, President Obama ordered a six-month moratorium on permits to drill new (although not existing) wells in order for the experts to review and revise safety mandates. Yet the pressure was on to end the ban as quickly as possible, and, less than a month before the 2010 midterm elections, it was lifted. More recently, Shell Global was granted a permit by the Obama administration to drill in the Gulf, even though its technology to address blowouts is similar to the technology in place before the Deepwater Horizon tragedy. The company plans to drill exploratory wells in environmentally delicate areas such as the Chukchi and Beaufort Seas (referred to as the Polar Bear Seas since a polar bear research station is situated there) near Alaska.

[1] Steven Mufson, "Federal Records Show Steady Stream of Oil Spills in Gulf since 1964," *Washington Post,* July 24, 2010, http://www.washingtonpost .com/wp-dyn/content/article/2010/07/23/AR2010072305603.html.

[2] Voice of America, "US Accuses BP of 'Gross Negligence' in Deadly 2010 Oil Spill," September 5th, 2012, http://blogs.voanews.com/breaking -news/2012/09/05/us-accuses-bp-of-gross-negligence-in-deadly-2010-oil-spill/ (accessed September 17, 2012).

[3] Christopher Helman, "Billionaire Father of Fracking Says Government Must Step Up Regulation," *Forbes,* July 19, 2012, http://www.forbes.com/sites/ christopherhelman/2012/07/19/billionaire-father-of-fracking-says-government-must-step-up-regulation/?utm_source=forbespicks%3Dpartner%3Dfo rbespicks%3Dforbespicks&google_editors_picks=true (accessed September 18, 2012).

[4] Andrew Chow, "Vermont Bans Fracking, Citing Injury Concerns," Reuters, May 23, 2012, http://www.reuters.com/article/2012/05/23/ tagblogsfindlawcom2012-injured-idUS3652343241201205 23 (accessed May 28, 2012).

Caroline Cannon, an advocate for the Inupiat people of Point Hope, Alaska, has fought to prohibit offshore oil and gas drilling that would harm her community and the environment. She became a co-plaintiff in a federal lawsuit that successfully challenged planned drilling in the Arctic Circle. In 2012, she won the Goldman Environmental Prize, considered the "Green Nobel Prize."

Lack of Consensus among Elected Officials

We do not have a public consensus on how much we should regulate, in what ways, and at what cost for any given amount of benefit. Defending environmental protection in principle has remained good politics, but *implementing* governmental rules is not always seen as popular.

In the 1970s, environmental enthusiasm was high, and substantial bipartisan support in Congress resulted in rapid adoption of environmental protection laws. During this period, laws to clean up air, water, and ground pollution were enacted and national wilderness areas more than doubled. Less positive results were achieved on energy issues after the oil embargo of 1973. Although the threat of reduced ability to obtain oil and gas from foreign sources made energy independence popular, and although support for increasing domestic oil and gas exploration grew, little progress was made. And President Jimmy Carter's preferences for development of alternatives to fossil fuels met with limited success.

The environmental protection enthusiasm of the 1970s quickly gave way to a backlash in the 1980s during the presidency of Ronald Reagan. His administration limited government regulation and shifted more of the responsibility for environmental protection to the states and the private sector. This change resulted in reduced budgets for the EPA and the Department of Energy and the appointment of administration officials who were ideologically opposed to the policies of the Carter era. Reagan even removed solar panels from the roof of the White House that were installed during the Carter administration. Still, because public support for environmental protection was fairly high, during this period Congress was able to enact legislation to promote clean water and protect drinking water.

The administration of George H. W. Bush began with an intention to frame a more positive environmental agenda than the one under Ronald Reagan. During this time, clean air legislation was strengthened. Still, because there was division within the administration about the costs and direction of environmental regulation, little else was done.

When President Bill Clinton and Vice President Al Gore took office in 1992, hopes were high for environmental improvement. Although Clinton's leadership on the issue was episodic, he reversed many of the Reagan-Bush actions that favored industry over environmental regulation. Still, compared to the 1970s, the national appetite for strong regulation was limited; instead, the trend appeared to be toward finding an elusive balance between economic development and improvements to our environment.

Like the Reagan administration, George W. Bush focused on deregulation. He advanced voluntary efforts by the timber, agriculture, mining, and oil industries rather than federal mandates. He also supported transferring responsibility for environmental protection from the federal government to the states as an effort to save federal funds and perhaps to weaken regulation entirely. This approach prevented the establishment of a single federal standard and left the states with new responsibilities but without funds to carry out the job.[33]

The Obama administration has reversed the Bush approach and committed to a series of environmental efforts, including increasing conservation efforts, reducing the use of fossil fuels, promoting biofuels, ordering motor vehicle fuel standards to be doubled by 2025, and issuing more stringent standards for sulfur dioxide emissions, mercury emissions from power plants, and carbon dioxide emissions from new power plants. The administration has also issued stricter pollution controls for wetlands and streams and provided greater protection to oceans.

However, in response, some Republicans in Congress have pushed to eliminate the Environmental Protection Agency's (EPA) authority to limit greenhouse gases, to abolish the EPA entirely, and to weaken environmental protection more generally. To date, those legislative efforts have stalled. Nonetheless, the Obama administration has bowed to the political pressure and has dropped several regulatory initiatives and abandoned efforts to set a national energy policy.

Thus, in recent years, environmental policy has been a roller coaster driven by the party in power. Democratic presidents have pushed for greater environmental protection, while Republican presidents have tried to limit environmental regulations.

Regulatory Choices

From the beginning of the modern environmental movement, there has been contentiousness about the way implementation is handled. Regulations prescribing rules for individuals and industries to comply are sometimes unpopular.[34] Ensuring compliance requires monitoring by a government agency, and that contributes to the growth of government. Effective enforcement is also a significant challenge. One example is the explosion in the coal mine in Montcoal, West Virginia, that killed twenty-five miners in 2010. It was the worst U.S.

mining disaster in more than twenty-five years. The mine, owned by Massey Energy, was cited for hundreds of safety violations in the year before the explosion, and federal inspectors had fined Massey Energy almost $400,000. Despite the more than 1300 citations on the mine since 2005, serious problems involving ventilation plans and equipment failures were not fixed.

Thus, regulations are not always effective. But without any regulations, the cost of producing certain chemicals, for example, is borne by the workers who suffer diseases, ailments, or death. It is also borne by individuals who become ill from toxic chemicals released into the air or who die from energy-related mishaps, communities that cannot attract clean business and industry, and property owners who cannot sell their properties at reasonable prices because of poor environmental conditions. These problems are called **negative externalities**.

Most people agree that some regulation is needed; the issues are how much regulation is needed and how we can make it most effective. Reformers stress the need to make greater use of economic incentives to encourage desired behavior and to reduce the cost of enforcing regulations. Instead of trying to control behavior after the fact, many argue that individuals and businesses should be made to "face up to the full costs and consequences" of harmful actions at the time they make their decisions.[35] So polluters could be required to incorporate at least some of the costs of the negative externalities into production costs. One solution is high-cost pollution permits for companies that decide to pollute or taxes on manufacturing or purchasing environmentally harmful products, waste disposal processes, and energy use. Environmental groups also support heavy "green" taxes on polluters and their products. Such taxes would help pay for mounting cleanup costs

and would provide a market incentive to avoid actions that endangered the public.

On the other hand, there are those who want no government intervention into the market, even to bring about outcomes they view as desirable. Regulation opponents place individual and private property rights above the obligation to protect **the commons** (that is, mineral resources, waterways, the air, parklands, etc.) for the public good. They posit that the marketplace is the only arena for resolving the question of what is rational and appropriate economic behavior. This view fits well with a small-government philosophy.

Seeking a middle ground, still other supporters of deregulation believe it is possible for the government to set standards for health and safety and environmental protection but to have a limited role in writing the rules. The underlying assumption is that the federal government cannot protect against every public danger, and trying to do so leads to an excessive number of rules that try to anticipate every eventuality.[36]

CURRENT CHALLENGES: GLOBAL CLIMATE CHANGE

One of the key issues of environmental policy is global climate change, also often referred to as global warming and, by the Obama administration, as "global climate disruption."

Scientific Evidence of Global Warming

Scientists have found that global warming results from the release of greenhouse gases—mostly carbon dioxide (CO_2) and methane—into the atmosphere. Scientists have traced

"Long term I'm worried about global warming— short term, about freezing my ass off."

atmospheric CO_2 levels through millennia by drilling through ice cores that formed hundreds of thousands of years ago. These studies show a sharp rise in greenhouse gas emissions beginning with the Industrial Revolution. Although nonhuman activities produce greenhouse gases, human activity, especially since the Industrial Revolution and the widespread burning of fossil fuels, now accounts for over 85 percent of greenhouse gas emissions.[37] The most common causes of these emissions are burning gas in cars, burning coal, oil, and gas in industrial processes, and using fertilizer in agricultural production. All these human uses have long been prevalent in the developed world and are increasing dramatically as the developing world tries to catch up with heavily industrialized countries. The result is rising temperatures across the globe. In the United States, July 2012 featured the hottest temperature ever recorded, eclipsing even the Dust Bowl of the 1930s which caused farmers to flee from Oklahoma, Texas and the Great Plains.[38]

Higher temperatures cause a host of negative consequences, such as more extreme weather patterns (stronger and more long-lasting hurricanes and tropical storms), more prolonged and intense droughts, changes in ocean currents, rising sea levels, reductions in sea ice, and melting of glaciers and ice caps. The impact of these changes on people all over the world is already being seen and is projected to become more significant. Loss of low-lying coastal areas from flooding, on the one hand, and increased desertification inland, on the other, is already resulting in climate refugees. The tiny island nation of Tuvalu, which is famous as one site of the reality TV show *Survivor*, has already lost one-fifth of its population to a climate exodus as the sea has been rising, frequently flooding dwellings and salinating soil. Since 1997, Tuvalu has been campaigning to bring the world's attention to the current consequences of global warming.

Global climate change may seem remote and hypothetical to most people outside Tuvalu, but the predicted effects may be devastating. When more areas become deserts, agricultural patterns will become disrupted, challenging our ability to ensure food security and increasing starvation in some parts of the globe. The production of corn, which is a dietary staple for hundreds of millions of people worldwide, is expected to be reduced by 20 to 25 percent in the African and Latin American countries that produce the bulk of it.

Public health and well-being will also be endangered due to loss of rainforests, reductions in biodiversity, transformation of natural animal habitats that result in species extinction, and increases in tropical diseases. For example, the mosquitoes that carry malaria are usually found in low-lying areas, but now they are found at higher and higher elevations than ever before, such as on Mount Kenya, which has experienced them since 2006.

Rising ocean levels and melting polar icecaps are already changing the ecology of the ocean. Because of depleted oxygen levels, there are now huge dead areas where there are no fish or other sea life, and these areas are expanding. This too could threaten the food source of millions of people.

The effects of rising temperatures will not be consistent across the planet, but no area or region will remain unaffected. Some areas might become more fertile and hospitable to

agriculture as others become hotter and more arid. Nonetheless, the potential impact is dire: the loss of resources, relocation of populations, and increased threats to public health are predicted to be catalysts for increased military conflict. Moreover, the costs associated with these changes are projected to be very high. In the United States alone, they are projected to be $14 billion over a decade and targeted toward addressing the problems of pollution, heat waves, hurricanes, insect-borne infectious disease, river flooding, and wildfires. Health care costs will increase for the treatment for insect-borne infectious diseases, asthma, and allergies, among other health challenges.[39]

As the population expands, development continues, standards of living rise, and the demand for energy use rises, worldwide carbon dioxide levels are predicted to be four times greater than the entire amount to date, which would double the total amount in the atmosphere. In fact, global carbon dioxide emissions from fossil fuels rose by the largest amount on record in 2010,[40] and continued to rise in 2011.[41] These dynamics have caused some scientific experts to argue that earth is near a tipping point where it will be impossible to sustain a climate as it is, with a consequent impact for human habitation, and, by the end of our century, the earth will be a very different place than it is today.

Although global warming has only come to widespread public attention in the last few years, climate scientists have been concerned about the effects of greenhouse gases on the sustainability of the planet for nearly two centuries. The scientists who first warned of the possibility of global warming did so in 1824, and the first scientific mention of the greenhouse effect was in 1896 by a Swedish Nobel laureate.[42] In the United States, early concerns came from military planners, who had long paid attention to its effects on the prosecution of war and other military actions.

By the 1970s, climate scientists were arguing for a unified federal climate studies program to investigate the growing suspicion that rising CO_2 levels could raise the earth's temperature and imperil civilization. By 1988, in response to increased concern, the United Nations established the **Intergovernmental Panel on Climate Change (IPCC)**, charging over 2500 scientists from more than 130 countries with determining how much the climate changed over time and why. After nearly twenty years of study, the IPCC's 2007 report concluded that **greenhouse gases** have risen to levels that are likely unprecedented; that the evidence for **global warming** is "unequivocal"; and that the human production of energy is largely responsible. Major scientific organizations agreed with this conclusion, and the IPCC, along with former vice president Al Gore, whose documentary, *An Inconvenient Truth*, drew attention to their work, won the 2007 Nobel Peace Prize for its efforts. Today, many scientists refer to our era as the anthropocene, the first geological period in which human activity is the primary driver of environmental change.

Climate Skeptics

There are many who reject the consensus findings of the scientific community. Known as **climate skeptics** or **deniers**, they have organized an energetic campaign to assert that the science of global warming is unsettled. They argue that temperature variation over time is normal and that human activity has little to do with that natural cycle. Because they see no problem, skeptics oppose governmental action to ameliorate the damage from global warming. Most are political conservatives to whom regulation is distasteful in any area. Others are religious conservatives who believe that only God controls changes in the earth's climate. Senator James Inhofe (R-Okla.), one of the Senate's strongest opponents of governmental action to reduce CO_2 emissions, expresses both views. He has written a book entitled *The Greatest Hoax: How Global Warming Conspiracy Threatens Your Future.*

Skeptics charge that legislation and other efforts, such as ratification of international climate change treaties to reduce production of greenhouse gases, are at best unnecessary and at worst will be drags on the American economy and will lead to restrictions on individual freedom and liberty. Says the author of *Climate of Corruption*, climate change "has little to do with the state of the environment and much to do with shackling capitalism and transforming the American way of life in the interests of global wealth distribution."[43]

Given the views of their supporters, U.S. political parties have also diverged in their views of global warming. Democrats tend to support the scientific findings and action to address the issue, while Republicans tend to repudiate the findings and oppose such action. This is especially true in Congress. In the 2010 election cycle, in which Republicans took control of the House of Representatives and lost the supermajority in the Senate (see Chapter 9 on Congress), the result was widespread efforts by some Republican members of Congress to limit or abolish federal efforts to address the issue. Indeed, a report from the Democrats on the U.S. House of Representatives Committee on Energy and Commerce claimed that the House in the 112th Congress was arguably the "most anti-environment House in the history of Congress." There were 191 votes taken that, if enacted, would have weakened environmental protections.[44]

As a consequence of the efforts of skeptics, an overwhelming scientific consensus on global warming has often been portrayed in the American media as a matter on which reasonable people may disagree, much more of an opinion-based matter than a scientific one. (In other nations, the scientific consensus is accepted by most parts of the political spectrum.) In the United States, media discussions frequently feature one person who supports the scientific foundation of global warming and one person who challenges that scientific evidence (much like some publications pitted World War II historians against Holocaust deniers in the 1990s). Giving precisely equal weight to each side presents a distorted view of the evidence for global warming (among scientists, the representation would likely be 97 to 1)[45] and of the widespread national and international support for addressing the problem. Indeed, a Fox News executive ordered reporters to counter discussion of climate change with skepticism about the scientific data and conclusions.[46]

Skeptics are supported by the mainstream energy industry, which has a vested interest to resist regulations intended to address global warming, and conservative research organizations, such as the Heartland Institute, which is funded, in part, by energy corporations such as ExxonMobil (see Chapter 6 for additional discussion of ExxonMobil's direct attempts to mislead the public about climate science). And one study found that nine of the ten scientists who have written the most papers skeptical of global warming have links to the corporation.[47] Not only does the fossil fuel industry oppose further regulation, but its members also want to preserve their tax breaks. Although one often hears the declaration that "we can't choose winners and losers" by giving tax breaks to green energy sources, we do that now, and the fossil fuel industry is one of the big winners.

Photo: REUTERS/Landov

The Heartland Institute, which advocates against government regulations and is funded by big corporations, put up this billboard in Chicago in 2012 to compare those who accept global warming to "murderers, tyrants, and madmen." The Institute had planned to put up more billboards featuring Osama bin Laden and mass murderer Charles Manson. But, after a vociferous outcry, it pulled down the original billboard within twenty-four hours and canceled plans for the others. Soon after, Al Gore's Climate Reality Project erected billboards in Chicago that asked, "Who to believe on climate—Heartland?...or EVERY National Scientific Academy in the world?"

Public Perceptions of Global Warming

It is difficult for laypeople to judge the science behind the consensus that global warming is occurring. But public opinion polls have long shown majority agreement with scientific conclusions that climate change is occurring and support for government action to reverse it. Differences in levels of support are apparent, however, among subsets of the population. For example, Republicans are much less likely than Democrats or Independents to believe that global warming is occurring or that its origin is human activity.[48]

Generational variations have also been documented. The Millennial generation, born between 1982 and 2000, is the most likely to believe that there is scientific evidence for global warming, that developing alternate energy sources should be a high priority, and that stricter environmental laws are worth the cost.[49] Nevertheless, a recent study found that civic orientation (interest in social problems, political participation, trust in government, and willingness to take political action, particularly action to help save energy and the environment), had declined from Generation X (born between the mid-1960s and the early 1980s) to the Millennial generation.[50]

As climate skeptics garner media attention from reporters trying to be fair and unwittingly (in many cases) undermining the scientific view, the likely effect is an increase in public skepticism about global warming, a decrease in trust in science, and a decrease in support for public policy to combat global warming. Said one Republican political consultant, as long as "voters believe there is no consensus about global warming within the scientific community," governmental action will be curtailed.[51]

And in fact, the tactics appear to have worked. People who believe there is a lot of disagreement among scientists are less sure that global warming is true than those who correctly note that there is little disagreement among scientists.[52] Additionally, the number of people who distrust scientists' work on the topic has increased.[53] Finally, public support for the scientific consensus about global warming has eroded over time. As Figure 3 illustrates, over the last ten years, there has been a modest decrease in the proportion of people who believe that global warming results from human activity rather than natural causes.

National Policies on Climate Change

In 1973, the Persian Gulf states withheld their oil from the market, creating an energy crisis in the United States and around the world. With long lines at the gas pumps and angry consumers, interest in alternative energy sources grew. President Jimmy Carter created a cabinet-level Department of Energy, and later in the decade Congress passed a law that established a national climate program to better understand and respond to natural and human-induced climate change.

By 1980, a prominent geophysicist declared that "the CO_2 problem is the single most important and the single most complex environmental issue facing the world."[54] Since then, American policy has been erratic, though mostly conservative. Reagan administration officials were early skeptics of climate science and directed little attention to this issue beyond signing a law passed by Congress that required a plan to stabilize the level of greenhouse gases. His Republican successor, George H. W. Bush, was more receptive to scientific understanding of the effects of greenhouse gas emissions, but his administration did relatively little besides adopting modest efforts to promote energy efficiency. It also failed to support the first report of the Intergovernmental Panel on Climate Change, which documented evidence of global warming and which was adopted at the first Earth Summit in 1992. Although many in the environmental advocacy community expected substantial attention to global warming from the Clinton administration, little was accomplished beyond endorsement of a U.S. Climate Action Plan.

At the start of the twenty-first century, the George W. Bush administration embraced climate change skeptics, arguing

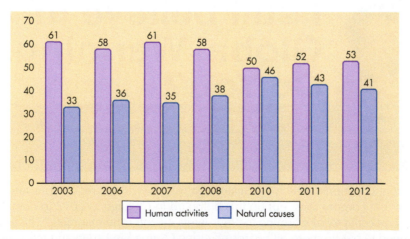

FIGURE 3: CHANGING OPINIONS ABOUT GLOBAL WARMING The bars reflect the changing proportion of people who attribute global warming to human activities versus those who believe it is due to natural causes.

SOURCE: Saad, Lydia. In U.S., Global Warming Views Steady Despite Warm Winter. Gallup Politics. March 30, 2012. http://www.gallup.com/poll/153608/Global-Warming-Views-Steady-Despite-Warm-Winter.aspx. Accessed May 22, 2012. Copyright © 2012 Gallup, Inc. All rights reserved. The content is used with permission; however, Gallup retains all rights of republication.

that there was no good evidence that human activity contributed to global warming, although it was not always the case that Republicans opposed environmental action. In fact, the first EPA administrator under George W. Bush has said, "Republicans have been part of the environmental movement since the get-go, and it just drives me nuts that we now seem to be walking away from it as if it were something bad or we don't believe in the science of the environment."[55] On the campaign trail and in the early days of his administration, Barack Obama called climate change one of the defining challenges of our time. Recognizing that the United States is the largest emitter *per person* of any nation (although China, which only has about a fourth of our per person emissions, is the largest total emitter due to its population size), his administration has taken several steps toward increased sustainability. These include funding for green job training, provision of loan guarantees to green energy firms (although one to a solar panel manufacturer, Solyndra, garnered much media and legislative attention when the firm went bankrupt), higher fuel efficiency standards, and support for development and implementation of a smart grid (a sophisticated electricity transmission and distribution network that relies on information technology to improve efficiency, reliability, and security).

Despite these policy efforts intended to reduce emissions of greenhouse gases, the president has also disappointed environmentalists by withdrawing a proposed regulation to reduce ground-level ozone (the main ingredient in smog), providing loan guarantees for new nuclear power plants, supporting increased oil and gas drilling in the United States, delaying clean air regulations of wood-fired power plants, cutting fossil fuel research, and supporting **"clean coal"** and **biofuels** made from corn ethanol, both politically popular policies for constituencies such as farmers and coal-mining regions, but rejected by climate scientists and environmentalists as contributors to the problem rather than as steps toward any reasonable solution. Indeed, former vice president Al Gore has criticized the president for failing to engage in bold action, repudiate dishonest attacks on science, and educate Americans about the extent and consequences of the climate crisis.[56]

The result is that, after more than forty years of episodic and partial attention to environmental issues, the United States still has no comprehensive energy policy or climate policy.

"The Focus On...Foreign Policy" section of the text discusses efforts by other nations to address the issue of global warming.

THE RE-GENERATION?

The consequences of environmental pollution and global warming will affect the youngest generations most heavily. Yet young people have a mixed reaction to this issue. Those under age thirty-five, especially those college-aged, are more likely than older generations to believe that there is a scientific consensus on global warming and that global warming is caused by humans. Nevertheless, by some measures, the younger generations, including college-age people, are more disengaged than their elders. Eighteen- to twenty-two-year-olds

express concern less than their elders that global warming will affect them personally and are less likely to report that they are very worried about it. And they are more confident that specific steps are possible to ameliorate the problem.[57]

At the same time, among those college-age people who are concerned with environmental issues, there is a great deal of activism. For example, Pick Up America, which was founded by a group of college graduates, began a local, regional, and nationwide initiative to reduce plastic waste in communities and waterways. The team members started to pick up trash in Assateague Island, Maryland, in 2010 and plan to continue their cleanup efforts across the country until they reach San Francisco, California, in November 2012. The goal of the founders is to reverse the "throw-away mentality" and encourage people to reduce consumption and the trash that accompanies it. Indeed, Americans throw away about 29 percent more than Europeans or Japanese.[58]

Perhaps students have had the most impact on campuses. The Energy Action Coalition joined the efforts of student and youth energy leaders across the United States and Canada. Their first event, the Campus Climate Challenge, was run on over 700 college and university campuses and resulted in more than 550 of those campuses making institutional commitments of carbon neutrality, and many are moving toward that end. The Coalition has also organized other events to raise awareness of climate change. Most recently, it worked in opposition to the proposed Keystone XL tar sands pipeline, which would carry almost a million barrels of oil from Alberta, Canada, to refineries on the Texas Gulf coast. (Tar sands oil is considered to be the dirtiest type of oil production because extracting it produces lakes of toxic waste, creates air pollution, and generates three times more global warming gases than production of regular oil.)

The journalist Thomas Friedman hopes that college-age people will join with their parents and grandparents to become the **"Re-Generation,"** one that will ensure that sustainability is central to all our activities. Friedman likens this call to action to the imperatives within previous American struggles such as World War II and civil rights. However, he warns that this will take a lot more than changing a few of our consumer-centered actions; rather, it will take "learning how Congress works, how campaign finance gets done, how utilities get rate increases, and how major firms lobby the government...if the Re-Generation wants to play in this game, it has to get out of Facebook and into somebody's face."[59]

Indeed, the politics of the environment well illustrates the American political system. Because of checks and balances, greatly augmented in the last decade, it is far easier to do nothing than to take action. Those who want significant policy changes have a steep hill to climb. Those who do not want change have been effective in simply raising questions about the need to change. None of us can predict the future, even though, year by year, the predictions of climate scientists are being shown to be accurate. But, as long as the American electorate is so evenly divided between the parties, and one party opposes action to address the problem, it is unlikely there will be much change unless, and until, even more catastrophic events occur.

REUTERS/China Photo/Landov

Americans use more than 50 million bottles of water each year—and recycle less than a quarter. When Americans do recycle, companies ship the bottles to China and thus add to greenhouse gases.

SUMMARY

- Since the birth of the modern environmental movement, more than forty major federal environmental laws have been enacted. Progress in cleaning up our water, air, and land has, on one hand, been impressive. Increased development of renewable sources of energy has put us closer to shedding reliance on fossil fuel. Yet our greatest challenges may lie ahead, especially the challenge of global warming.

- Congress and the president can mandate environmental goals, but governmental agencies, such as the EPA, must then write rules for reaching those goals and monitor their implementation. That process, while producing some good effects, has also been fraught with slowness, controversy, changes in strategies, and high costs.

- Implementing environmental regulation is challenging. The chief forces that contribute to the challenges include the speed of scientific change, public pressures, interest group advocacy, and lack of consensus among policy makers.

- Global warming results from the release of greenhouse gases, such as carbon dioxide, into the atmosphere. Human activity and the widespread burning of fossil fuels are the primary causes. Higher temperatures from global warming are already yielding negative consequences such as more extreme weather patterns, more prolonged and intense droughts, changes in ocean currents, rising sea levels, reductions in sea ice, and melting of glaciers and ice caps. The impact of these changes on people all over the world will be significant.

- Despite nearly unanimous scientific consensus about global warming and the resultant public health harms, climate skeptics argue that temperature variation over time is normal and that human activity has little to do with that natural cycle. Skeptics make ample use of media outlets to advance a false picture of "unsettled" science and are supported by the fossil fuel industry, which currently receives favored treatment in public policies such as taxation.

- Public opinion polls have long shown majority agreement that climate change is occurring and support for government action to reverse it, although a downward trend is apparent. Additionally, there are sharp differences in public opinion among population subsets: Republicans are much less likely to believe that global warming is occurring and that its origin is human activity. Age cohort matters also: the younger generation is the most likely to believe that there is scientific evidence for global warming.

- National policy efforts on environmental issues including global warming have occurred in fits and starts. The 1970s saw strong governmental action on pollution and conservation; the 1980s and 1990s saw moderate governmental action, and the 2000s saw retrenchment. Most recently, the Obama administration has taken a number of positive steps to address energy use and global warming, although it has failed to advance a comprehensive national energy policy or to pursue strong efforts to reduce greenhouse gas emissions.

DISCUSSION QUESTIONS

1. Give a brief description of major federal legislation that has emerged since 1970 to address environmental issues such as clean air, clean water, and endangered species. How successful have these efforts been, and what remains to be accomplished?

2. What are the major challenges to developing effective government regulation of the environment? Describe the effects of slow regulatory development, policy disagreements among the public, experts and politicians, strategic obstacles, and high costs.

3. How have the speed of scientific change, public pressures, interest group activity, and differences of opinions and strategies among elected officials contributed to difficulties in implementing regulatory policy?

4. What is the definition of global warming, and what are its major causes and its major effects?

5. How settled is the science of global warming? On what basis do climate skeptics assert that global warming is not the result of human activity, but is a natural occurrence over which people have no influence? How have climate skeptics influenced the policy debate?

6. Does public opinion support the science of global warming? What are the trends in public opinion, and which subgroups are most likely to accept the scientific consensus?

7. What efforts has the U.S. government made to reduce greenhouse gas emissions, and how adequate are these efforts?

Focus On... *Foreign Policy*

Since 9/11, the United States has emphasized military force in its foreign policy, launching wars in Afghanistan and Iraq and hunting suspected terrorists with unmanned drones. Here soldiers are airlifted to Afghanistan.

Damon Winter/The New York Times/Redux

LEARNING OBJECTIVES

1. Know America's foreign policy goals and be able to give an example of how the United States seeks to achieve each.

2. Understand the role of the president and his inner circle, specialists, Congress, interest groups, and public opinion in making U.S. foreign policy. Be able to describe the conditions under which each might have an important influence.

3. Define isolationism, containment, and détente; identify the period in which each was a dominant foreign policy objective of the United States; and be able to give an example of each.

4. Describe how the Cold War ended, including the role of Mikhail Gorbachev and Ronald Reagan.

5. Be able to compare and contrast the foreign policy objectives and means of achieving them of Bill Clinton and George W. Bush. Define and contrast multilateralism and unilateralism and illustrate with some of Barack Obama's policies.

6. Identify and describe four contemporary foreign policy challenges.

The foreign policy of the United States has a substantial impact on the world, yet we are not all-powerful. We are one of many nations; decisions about war and peace and about trade and diplomacy are made by people in all nations. In this sense, Americans' expectations about what we can achieve have often been unrealistically high. But we still have the world's largest economy and most powerful military. Thus our power, and how we use it, have a tremendous impact on people throughout the world.

In recent years, we have shifted from a world divided between East and West to one increasingly linked by the forces of globalization. Much of the world left behind the great power struggles of the Cold War and immersed itself in trade rivalries and economic competition. Yet, although the United States is unrivaled in its military power, it has been embroiled in costly and not always successful wars against smaller states and nonstate armies for much of the past fifty years. We continue to evaluate what *strength* and *effectiveness* mean in foreign policy.

In this "Focus On...Foreign Policy," we examine past and present foreign policy goals and how we pursue them, discover how foreign policy decisions are made, and review changes in U.S. foreign policies over time. Then we discuss foreign policy challenges in an era of globalization.

FOREIGN POLICY GOALS

The goals any nation has and the means it uses to pursue them are influenced by its traditions, core values, ideology, and the advantages and limitations imposed by its geographical location, size, and wealth relative to other nations. Foreign policies are the strategies adopted and the actions taken by a government to achieve its goals in its relationships with other nations. These actions range from informal negotiations to waging war, from writing position papers to promoting our products abroad. They may require economic, political, cultural, or military resources.

The art of foreign policy making includes choosing means suitable to the objective sought. Because of our size and great wealth, huge diplomatic corps, military forces, and intelligence establishment, we have the fullest possible range of foreign policy instruments at our disposal.

Physical Security

Our primary foreign policy goal, like that of every other nation, is to protect our physical security. Until the era of long-range bombers and ballistic missiles, achieving this goal meant preventing land invasions, and in this we were successful. Our success was due largely to our separation from the other major powers by two oceans and being bounded on the north and south by two friendly countries. In the nuclear era, when we could be attacked by air by long-range bombers and intercontinental ballistic missiles launched by land or sea, we had to develop an air as well as a ground defense.

In an era when terror has become a major tactic of our enemies, physical security must be defended against both external and internal attacks. Since September 11, 2001, greater emphasis has been placed on how to prevent terrorist attacks by conventional, biological, chemical, or nuclear weapons, both from within and without, and how to stop the proliferation of weapons of mass destruction (WMDs).

Physical Security of Neighbors and Allies

A second goal is to help protect the physical security of our neighbors and major democratic allies. Since World War II, we have committed ourselves, through the North Atlantic Treaty Organization (NATO), to join in the defense of Canada and western Europe. These are our principal military allies, with whom we share a cultural heritage and commitment to democratic government. Some eastern and southern European nations and Turkey are now also part of NATO.

The original purpose of NATO, protecting the physical security of western Europe by deterring Soviet aggression, seems far less relevant now with the end of the Soviet Union. With its dominant purpose gone, there are questions about the alliance on both sides of the Atlantic. In Europe, there is popular opposition to several U.S. policies, including having hundreds of tactical nuclear weapons deployed in five NATO countries. In the United States, policy makers complain that the U.S. taxpayer is paying more per person to defend Europe than are taxpayers in Europe.[1]

The United States has treaty and bilateral security relationships with many other countries, including Japan, South Korea, and the nations of Latin America, but none as close as the original working relationship in NATO. Since the post–World War II occupations, the United States has maintained tens of thousands of troops in South Korea and Japan. At the end of the Cold War, it appeared that we would significantly reduce the numbers of those troops, but the nuclear aspirations of North Korea and the emergence of China as a military as well as a preeminent economic power in the Pacific have led us to continue these costly deployments.

Whatever the difficulty in maintaining the old alliances, there is an explicit and pronounced commitment to keeping and strengthening them in current security policy. The nature of security threats demands multilateral cooperation, and the United States is simply no longer in an economic and military position to go it alone.

Economic Security

A third goal of foreign policy is to protect our economic security. Although the United States is blessed with many natural resources, we must purchase such essential resources as oil, manganese, titanium, and tin elsewhere. Safeguarding access to these resources may include stabilizing the governments of producing nations or protecting oil pipelines and the sea lanes in which goods are shipped.

Even in our dealings with our closest allies, economic self-interest is almost always a factor in foreign policy. We are economic competitors as well as political and military allies. Thus trade missions and participation in the international organizations that govern trade relations are crucial to achieving our foreign policy goals, even though most of the public pays scant attention to them.

Today the electronic flow of capital into and out of the country is also essential to our economic viability, so ensuring the privacy of information transfers, including financial transactions, and securing computer systems against hackers are as important to national security as protecting sea lanes.

Global economics are now linked. Foreign creditors underwrite a large share of our huge national debt, and we in turn help stabilize other nations' finances. In 2008, when the financial industry in the United States started to collapse under the weight of bad mortgages and other debt, one motivation behind the government's bailout plan was to keep the crisis from spreading abroad, a task that proved impossible precisely because the world's economies are so closely linked.

The interconnectedness of world economies can work in our favor, however. Foreign investors holding trillions of dollars or other assets in the United States have no interest in seeing their holdings decline in value, nor do they want to see a decline in the buying power of American consumers, because that would mean they wouldn't be able to export as

Evelyn Hockstein/The New York Times/Redux

In an exercise of soft power, the United States has joined international efforts to improve the health and educational opportunities for children in poor countries. These displaced children are on their way to school in West Darfur, Sudan.

many goods to the United States. Even when the U.S. financial system melted in 2008, the worldwide economic uncertainty was so great that investors worldwide decided that investments in the United States were still the safest. China and other countries put their money in "safe" U.S. Treasury notes and bonds.

Our economic well-being is also dependent on selling our goods abroad, which in turn depends on how cheaply we can manufacture products or grow crops desired in other parts of the world and how willing our trading partners are to buy them. At the end of World War II, half of all world trade passed through our ports. Today, the United States is still the largest single exporter of goods and services, but because of economic growth around the world, our share of world trade has fallen to 11 percent, and we have lost much of the power we once had to regulate the flow of trade.[2] This is especially significant because trade accounts for about 30 percent of our gross domestic product (GDP) and one-third of our economic growth.[3]

Extending Our Sphere of Influence

A fourth, overlapping, foreign policy goal is to extend our sphere of influence. Historically, this has meant keeping foreign powers out of the Caribbean and Latin America.

In the 1780s, Thomas Jefferson said he hoped Spain would hold on to its territory in South America until "our population can be sufficiently advanced to gain it from them piece by piece."[4] There is still a tendency to see Latin America as "our turf" (a view certainly not shared by those countries, however). After World War II, we extended our sphere of interest and sought to influence security arrangements on all continents. We still have more military bases and more troops outside our borders than any other country.

More generally, we try to spread our influence by promoting democracy, capitalism, and Western cultural values. Former president Bill Clinton asked: "Do we lead by the example of our power or by the power of our example?" "Leading by the power of our example" is an important way to promote our values. It is a succinct way of describing the use of **soft power**, getting your way through shared ideas or values instead of through military power or coercion (hard power).

Like Clinton, Obama has stressed economic progress and the need to reassert America's soft power, deemphasizing the military instruments of foreign policy in favor of leading by moral example. He advocated admitting the excesses and violations of our own legal principles in actions against al-Qaeda and in the Iraq War, saying he wanted to restore America's image and leadership position in the world. However, his decision to widen the war in Afghanistan and to retain a number of the Bush administration's practices in the war against terrorism undermined his message to some of those around the world he was trying to reach.

Concrete ways of sharing values include a system of public libraries around the world, maintained by the U.S. Department of State, to disseminate information on our government, economy, and popular culture. The Department also funds thousands of cultural and academic exchanges between American and foreign artists and scholars each year.

We use our vast military and medical resources in disaster relief in conjunction with private relief efforts organized by prominent Americans. Former Presidents Clinton and George H. W. Bush organized a fundraising drive to help the victims of the 2004 tsunami in the Indian Ocean, which complemented the relief effort led by U.S. armed forces. In Indonesia, the world's largest Muslim country and one very important to us in fighting Islamist terrorism, the number of Indonesians who looked on the United States favorably increased substantially after direct contact with soldiers and other aid workers. And in 2010, when Pakistanis living in isolated areas were victims of some of the worst flooding in the country's history and without government assistance, U.S. troops brought in food and medical equipment, in part to counter aid being provided by the Taliban and al-Qaeda.

The past three administrations, all of which not coincidentally have had women secretaries of state, have made a special effort to spread Western ideas of gender equality. This has meant encouraging universal education for women, opposing the practice of genital mutilation of adolescent girls (including granting them asylum in the United States), supporting microfinancing projects for women entrepreneurs, and focusing aid efforts on mother-child health. All these efforts serve both humanitarian and political ends and are also examples of the effective use of soft power.

The United States promotes democracy by supporting groups in other nations who are opposing their dictators. We helped fund the Orange Revolution that brought down Ukraine's authoritarian government after it tampered with election results in 2004, and we supported other popular movements in former Soviet nations. In 2011, when Libyan insurgents rose against dictator Muammar Gaddafi, France, the United States, and Britain provided air support for the insurgents by bombing Libyan troops and their sanctuaries. As insurgents continued to protest in Iran in 2012, the United States and other nations imposed severe economic sanctions on the government of Iran.

The Internet is another way of extending our influence by supporting insurgents fighting against dictators. The United States has offered direct or indirect support to pro-democracy activists around the world who try to coordinate their movements via the Internet. The State Department has been providing information technologies, such as instant-messaging and anti-filtering software, that facilitate communications among dissidents and make it easier to coordinate opposition movements. The Obama administration State Department also promotes American policies through the use of YouTube, Tweeting, and Facebook pages.[5] Like other strategies, this one can be a two-edged sword: though the Internet communication focuses attention on dictatorial regimes, it opens an avenue for those regimes to identify insurgents when computer security is faulty. It also can create backlashes against American attempts to meddle in other nation's policies.

Of course, American presidents do not have to be directly responsive to worldwide opinion and hostile attitudes toward the United States. But negative public opinion can have serious consequences if it encourages people to pressure their governments to refuse to help the United States achieve its objectives. And when the United States tries to extend its sphere of influence through violence, whether by encouraging coups in other countries such as Iran in 1953, or by invasion as in Grenada, Panama, and Iraq, it can decrease our influence in these countries or elsewhere in the world. When Bush had to ask NATO to send more troops to Afghanistan and ask allies to share the burden for reconstructing Iraq, he found himself working against public sentiment in those countries. It is a consequence of living in an intensely interdependent world that the leaders of activist governments must court world, as well as domestic, opinion (see Table 1).

MAKING FOREIGN POLICY IN A DEMOCRACY

Alexis de Tocqueville was one of the first to remark that it is difficult to have a coherent foreign policy in a democracy. His sentiments have been echoed thousands of times since. Why, when there has been basic agreement on the broad goals of our foreign policy, has the United States had such difficulty articulating a coherent and consistent set of objectives?

Historically, inconsistencies in our foreign policy were rarely caused by differences among policy makers over fundamental goals but rather over the specific actions to achieve the goals. But between the end of the Soviet threat and the 9/11 attacks, disagreements emerged over even the fundamentals. There was confusion about what constituted the primary threats to national security and exactly who and what we should be protecting ourselves from. After 9/11, Americans united behind the goal of destroying al-Qaeda's terrorist network, just as they had earlier agreed on containing Soviet influence during the Cold War. But once again disagreement emerged on how much intervention in the internal affairs of another country is justifiable, what form that intervention should take, and to what extent fundamental principles of government should be compromised in the name of national security.

Here we look at some of the groups and individuals who influence the foreign policy-making process and how division and conflict among them can affect the content and execution of U.S. policy.

The President and His Inner Circle

As head of state and commander in chief of the armed forces, the president is in control of the nation's diplomatic and

Table 1	Around the World, Confidence in Obama Has Fallen but Still Greatly Exceeds Confidence in Bush		
	2008 (Bush)	**2009 (First Year of Obama Term)**	**2012**
Western Allies and Japan			
Germany	14	93	87
Britain	16	86	80
France	13	91	86
Japan	25	85	74
Spain	8	72	61
Middle East and Turkey			
Egypt	11	42	29
Turkey	2	33	24
Pakistan	7	13	7
Other Large Powers			
Russia	22	37	36
China	30	62	38

The numbers are percentages of those with a lot or some confidence in Obama.

military establishments. In addition, as the nexus of the vast diplomatic and military communications and intelligence networks, he has the most complete and privileged access to information of anyone in the policy-making network. In times of crisis, without immediately available alternative sources of reliable information, members of Congress and the public have historically almost always relied on the president's sources.

Given the central role of the president in foreign policy making and the fact that most presidents enter office with very little foreign policy expertise, it is important to know who advises them. No firm rules dictate whom the president must consult on foreign policy, but usually he gives at least a perfunctory hearing to people who head departments and agencies involved with making or implementing policy. The government officials best positioned to advise the president on foreign policy include the secretaries of defense and state, the national security adviser, and the head of the National Intelligence Agency (NIA). The president also frequently consults others, including the Joint Chiefs of Staff, influential members of Congress, and, on trade issues and foreign debt especially, the secretary of the treasury.

These individuals represent a wide range of experience and bring different perspectives to the analysis of foreign policy issues. The secretary of state is usually concerned with the nation's diplomatic relations and the use of diplomatic channels to implement the president's policies. The secretary of defense (a civilian) is primarily concerned with military and security issues and the use of the military to pursue foreign

policy goals. The national security adviser heads the National Security Council, a team of security specialists working within the Executive Office of the President. They are essentially political advisers whose job is to vet all security-related information coming into the White House and make recommendations to the president.

Members of the Joint Chiefs of Staff are military professionals who give advice to the president on both the readiness of their service arms and the appropriateness of their use in specific situations. Members of Congress may be consulted because they are political allies of the president, because they are in leadership positions crucial for mobilizing support on an issue, or because they have developed expertise in military or foreign policy issues through their committee assignments.

The president may also consult family or friends and advisers outside government, not because of their policy expertise, but because he trusts their good judgment and wants the perspective of people close to him who have no organizational interests or policy agenda to advance.

Who the president draws into his inner circle of advisers depends in large part on his experience and decision-making style. President Kennedy, the son of an ambassador, who had studied abroad and fought in World War II, had considerable knowledge of international affairs but almost no policy-making experience. After a confidence-shaking first encounter with Soviet premier Nikita Khrushchev in which Kennedy felt he had been bested, he assembled a committee of cabinet heads and close advisers to help him construct a response to Khrushchev's actions during the Cuban missile crisis. But during the Persian Gulf crisis, the first President Bush, a former fighter pilot, ambassador, and CIA director, reportedly made the decision to send troops to Saudi Arabia relying almost exclusively on his own judgment and that of a few close advisers.

If a president comes to office with a foreign policy agenda and expects to make his political reputation and leave his mark on history in this policy area, as Richard Nixon and Bush Sr. did, he will surround himself with like-minded people and replace those who disagree with him or ignore their advice. Those with less foreign policy experience, such as ex-governors Carter, Reagan, Clinton, and George W. Bush, can compensate for their lack of foreign policy experience when they become president by surrounding themselves with experts. Nevertheless, Carter and Reagan chose foreign policy advisers with limited experience and had difficulty maintaining unity among them. In contrast, Clinton appointed an experienced team of advisers, including a number from the Carter administration.

George W. Bush chose his entire first tier of foreign policy advisers, and part of the second tier, from those who had served in his father's and other earlier Republican administrations. Although, or perhaps because, they were probably the most experienced group of foreign policy advisers assembled by any president since the end of World War II, many came with predetermined worldviews and their own policy agendas. Donald Rumsfeld wanted to transform the military and brought with him neoconservatives associated with his longtime colleague Dick Cheney. This subset of advisers also favored overthrowing Saddam Hussein and worked behind the scenes to initiate a war to do so.[6] Their influence dwarfed advice received from the State Department and the president's own National Security Council.

Barack Obama came to office with little experience beyond spending significant time abroad and a brief time on the Senate Foreign Relations Committee. To bolster support from Republicans, he retained Bush's secretary of defense, and to obtain experience, he recruited many Clinton administration veterans, including his political rival Hillary Clinton as secretary of state.

Specialists

Much further removed from the president are the career specialists in the federal bureaucracy who are not political appointees: the staff of intelligence agencies, area specialists in the State and Defense Departments, and almost all members of the Foreign Service. Although they must implement the president's policy as directed, when giving advice their job is to exercise neutral competence, not to serve a political

President Obama and his team monitor the operation that killed Osama bin Laden. The White House received a live feed from an unmanned drone. At the left is Vice President Joe Biden, and at the far right are Secretary of State Hillary Clinton and Secretary of Defense Robert Gates. The president said it was "the longest forty minutes" of his life, except when his daughter got spinal meningitis.

agenda. However, their briefings may simply be ignored if they do not support policy choices preferred by their superiors. Agency separation, competition, and even antagonism led to many of the failures and misuses of intelligence prior to and after the September 11 attacks.

Foreign Service Officers

The principal office for carrying out the president's foreign policy, the State Department, has almost nine thousand Foreign Service officers who are experts on every policy area and region of the globe. Ambassadors, the president's personally appointed emissaries to other countries, are often career professionals, but in some of the largest and most important embassies and in some of the smaller but very desirable posts, the ambassador may be a political appointee chosen from among the president's friends or campaign contributors.

Political officers in Washington and in our embassies and consulates abroad write daily summaries of important political and economic events occurring in the countries to which they are assigned. This information is used to provide daily briefings for higher-level officials, but almost none of it ever reaches the president's desk, and only a small portion of it can be read even by the secretary of state.

We should not assume that these experts present neutral information that is somehow mechanically cranked out as public policy. Even if the experts do their best to provide the most accurate information and most comprehensive policy alternatives possible, top policy makers see the information through their own perceptual and ideological lenses. Specialists can be ignored or downgraded when their recommendations do not support the preferred policies of a particular administration. Our Vietnam policies failed in part because many of our best Asia experts had been purged from the State Department during the McCarthy era in the 1950s. George W. Bush's administration ignored both intelligence reports and advice from experts in the State Department in its rush to war in Iraq, leading to another exodus of specialists, including the head of the al-Qaeda desk at the CIA.[7]

The impact of high turnover in specialist positions is magnified by the fact that almost all of the policy-making positions within the foreign policy establishment are held by political appointees who usually stay only a few years. The lack of expertise at crucial times, or an unwillingness to rely on career professionals, can put us at a disadvantage relative to our adversaries and allies.

Intelligence Agents

One of the important components in formulating foreign and military policy is economic, military, and diplomatic information gathered by operatives of the government's intelligence agencies. The best known of these is the CIA, but in all, we have fifteen intelligence agencies, some part of cabinet offices, others part of the military, and others in separate agencies. Some are so secret that their employees cannot be photographed and most of their funding—some fraction of the $80 billion spent annually on intelligence—is part of the **"black budget,"** unknown to the public and even to many in Congress.

Though novels written about intelligence work focus on undercover agents, and our agencies have many of those, in fact most of the work done by intelligence agencies, including CIA agents, involves routine fact collecting, research, and report writing rather than covert operations. Fully 60 percent of the data used to prepare the president's daily intelligence briefing comes from electronic and satellite surveillance, another type of intelligence gathering.[8]

In 2005, all intelligence operations were put under the supervision of a sixteenth agency, the National Intelligence Agency (NIA), whose head, rather than the CIA director, now briefs the president daily. Though the consolidation was undertaken to correct the rivalry and turf wars between agencies that contributed to inefficiencies in data sharing and analysis so criticized after 9/11, in fact, it may have increased turf wars.[9] (See Chapter 11.)

Congress

The leading members of congressional committees on foreign affairs and armed services and of the oversight committees for intelligence agencies play a larger role in foreign policy than the average member plays. But Congress as a whole has specific constitutional authority to act as a check on the president's policies through its power to declare and fund wars and the requirement for Senate ratification of treaties and most trade agreements. The Senate also has confirmation power over ambassadorial appointments and nominations to high-level positions in the State and Defense Departments and intelligence agencies. Because Congress appropriates all money for carrying out foreign policy, the president is limited in the scope of the actions he can take without congressional approval or at least acquiescence.

Rivalry between the White House and Congress in foreign policy making varies with the issue in question. Nowhere is conflict greater than over the use of the military to achieve foreign policy goals. Politicians and scholars have been arguing for more than two hundred years about how Congress's constitutional authority to "declare war" limits the president's authority as commander in chief. The Founders, believing it too dangerous to give war powers to the president alone, were also unwilling to accept wording that would have given Congress the power to "make war." **Art. I, Sec. 8** Instead, they gave Congress the power to "declare war," leaving the president, according to James Madison's notes on the debate, "the power to repel sudden attacks."[10] This left Congress and the president to struggle over what constitutes an attack on the United States and when a military intervention becomes a war.

There have been more than two hundred occasions when the president has sent troops into combat situations without congressional approval. In fact, Congress has exercised its power to declare war only five times, and on only one of those occasions, the War of 1812, did it conduct a debate before issuing the declaration. Yet the two undeclared wars in Korea and Vietnam alone produced almost 100,000 American deaths, more than the combined losses of our declared wars, except World War II and the Civil War.[11]

The War Powers Resolution, which was intended to curb what Congress believes is presidential usurpation of its authority, has been opposed by every president since Lyndon Johnson, with the exception of Barack Obama, who argued it did not apply to our military actions in Libya because it was not a full-blown war. No prior approval was sought for sending troops to Lebanon, Grenada, or Panama, and both Presidents Bush sought it for their actions in Iraq only under pressure. During the Clinton administration, Democrats tried to strengthen the resolution and Republicans to repeal it; neither effort was successful. As one supporter of the act commented, "Every president finds Congress inconvenient, but we're a democracy, not a monarchy."[12] In 2008, a committee of former State and Defense Department officials concluded that the resolution was something worse than useless and recommended its overhaul. (This issue is discussed in greater detail in Chapter 10.)

In his dealings with Congress over use of the military, George W. Bush paid little attention to the War Powers Resolution, concentrating instead on establishing a new interpretation of the president's powers as commander in chief. **Art. II, Sec. 2** Justice Department attorneys claimed virtually unchecked powers for the commander in chief in committing and directing the armed forces in combat.[13]

Whatever their differences with Congress, presidents in the postwar era have usually proclaimed their desire to have a "bipartisan" foreign policy, that is, to get support from both parties to present a united front to the world. Presidents will often try to frame policies in a national security context as a way to pressure Congress into accepting their position, but Congress's role is not simply to rubber-stamp executive branch policies. Presidents especially need bipartisan support when treaties are to be ratified because it is rare for one party to have the necessary two-thirds majority in the Senate or for members of each party to be united in their ranks.

Presidents like to say that, in facing the rest of the world, Americans are all on the same side. But this view is too simplistic. Americans come from all over the world and, once here, look out on the rest of the world from very different vantage points. And there are significant differences between the two major parties, not to mention the factions within them. Democrats tend to favor lower levels of military spending and higher levels of foreign aid than Republicans do, and to support interest group demands for worker and environmental protection restrictions on trade agreements, the funding of international agencies, and working with other nations to achieve goals. Republicans are more likely to support unrestricted trade and military intervention to protect U.S. economic interests and to oppose support for family planning programs in poor countries, working through the United Nations, and placing U.S. troops under foreign command as part of multilateral forces. Despite these partisan differences, Republican candidate Mitt Romney earned condemnation from many of his Republican counterparts when his first reaction to the 2012 murder of America's ambassador to Libya by Libyan terrorists was to condemn Obama.

Once troops are fighting, it is very difficult for the opposition party to oppose the president's policy. There are notable exceptions, such as bipartisan criticism of Johnson's and Nixon's Vietnam policies, but this dissent came late in the course of the fighting, when public opinion was turning against the war and administration policies did not seem to be working. Even then, Congress approved virtually all

"What's amazing to me is that this late in the game we still have to settle our differences with rocks."

expenditures requested to wage the war. And even as criticism of George W. Bush's handling of the Iraq War mounted, very few members of Congress of either party voted against supplemental funding to pay the costs. Members know that their votes will be portrayed by their opponents as refusal to support U.S. troops rather than opposition to the war policy. War, in the short term, is popular.

Interest Groups and Lobbyists

A multiplicity of interest groups are concerned with foreign policy issues: international businesses; public interest groups, such as those that lobby on environmental and human rights issues; veterans' organizations; farmers who grow crops for export; labor unions; and ethnic groups interested in their ancestral lands, such as African, Jewish, Muslim, Arab, Irish, Cuban, Mexican, and Polish Americans.

Foreign governments also lobby, and some former members of Congress and high-level political appointees become their lobbyists, raising questions of conflict of interest.[14] For example, Henry Kissinger, former secretary of state, advises some of the world's largest corporations about the international economy while providing advice to the U.S. government through his service on various influential advisory boards.

In general, it is harder for interest groups to affect foreign policy than to influence domestic policy. Part of the reason is that the president and the executive branch have greater weight than Congress in day-to-day foreign policy decision making. But interest group activity has always been effective in some policy areas, especially those related to containing communism and managing trade and foreign investment. For example, electronics industries lobby against national security restrictions that keep them from exporting computer equipment and software that have military applications. Farm and business organizations lobby on behalf of import quotas and tariffs to protect their domestically produced goods and against trade restrictions and embargoes that prevent them from selling their products abroad.

During the past quarter-century, four factors have opened up the foreign policy decision-making process to greater influence by interest groups. The first is the growing importance of campaign spending and the rise of political action committees (PACs). Both the president and members of Congress

American Diversity

Lobbying for the Old Country

Americans have a long history of trying to win favorable U.S. policy for their countries of birth or ancestry. Some have even undertaken private action in support of home countries: Irish Americans have sold guns to the Irish Republican Army and Jewish Americans to Jews in Palestine trying to establish an independent state (in the territory that became Israel). Cuban Americans have trained a military force on U.S. soil to overthrow the Castro government in Cuba (even though it is illegal to do so under U.S. law).

Cuban Americans, who have particular clout because they are located in Florida with its large number of electoral votes, were responsible for an economic embargo against the Cuban government. For fifty years the embargo has been singularly ineffective in achieving its goal of unseating the Castro government. With declining support for it among younger Cuban Americans, U.S. farm and business lobbies, tired of losing export and investment opportunities on the island to Canada and Europe, finally succeeded in getting Congress to lift the sanctions on food exports and to lighten travel restrictions. George W. Bush did not oppose this change, though he toughened sanctions on travel and family remittances to Cuba before the 2004 election, hoping to solidify support among Cuban Americans. The Obama administration lifted the restrictions Bush had placed on family visits and remittances and is trying to increase telecommunication links with the island.

CARLOS BARRIA/Corbis

Cuban Americans carry a sculpture of the head of Cuban leader Fidel Castro to a garbage truck for a mock burial. Cuban Americans in south Florida have driven U.S. policy toward Cuba, restricting trade and travel by other Americans.

depend on large campaign contributions from interest groups and are thus more vulnerable to their demands. For example, the National Rifle Association (NRA) supports arms dealers and exporters and has worked to prevent government from stopping the sale of guns and other armaments by American dealers to middlemen for or operatives in Mexican drug cartels. It was successful even though guns are being used in the war between cartels that has made border security more difficult and dangerous.

Women's and religious interest groups have also become important lobbies, affecting policies on foreign aid, family planning, abortion, immigration, and women's rights. Women's groups found an advocate in Madeleine Albright, the first woman to serve as secretary of state. Albright identified women's rights and ending the trafficking of women and children as among the Clinton administration's priority issues. Condoleezza Rice, the second woman to head the State Department, continued the strong emphasis on ending the trafficking in women and children but gave priority to education over family planning. Hillary Clinton, too, has given priority to women's issues, especially education and mother-child health, and meets with women's interest groups everywhere she travels.

Third, the globalization of economic activity has intensified interest groups' efforts to influence trade policy because of their concern about its impact on wages, job opportunities, child labor, worker safety, and the environment. This has led to new and very vocal alliances among trade unions and environmental and human rights groups who oppose some aspects of current trade policy.

Fourth, the extraordinary expansion of the media has given foreign policy issues far greater exposure than ever before. No one with a cause has to wait for the mainstream press to cover it. In addition to round-the-clock cable television news, blogs allow individuals to participate in discussions of issues large and small. The 24/7 media coverage of virtually everything has helped create what some call a celebrity culture, and celebrities have used their heightened exposure to mobilize public opinion on behalf of causes they support.[15]

Think Tanks

Experts outside government who are associated with various think tanks are also sometimes influential in foreign policy making. Primarily located in Washington, close to decision makers and the national media, these institutions—such as the Institute for Policy Studies on the left of the political spectrum, the Libertarian Cato Foundation and the conservative Heritage Foundation on the right, and the Brookings Institution, the American Enterprise Institute, and the Council on Foreign Relations in the middle—conduct and publish research on policy issues and seek to influence American foreign policy.

Public Opinion

Overall, the views of the public on foreign policy are not that different from those of elected policy makers. When they do vary, public opinion has little direct effect except on high-profile issues that could make a difference at the polls. One reason is that much of our foreign policy is made incrementally over a long period of time and out of public view. Public opinion also has little short-term impact on decisions made in "crisis" situations or in secrecy for national security reasons.

Another factor limiting the public's ability to influence foreign policy decisions is that only a minority of Americans know much about even the most publicly discussed issues, and many have no opinion about them. The public has always been more interested in domestic issues that impinge directly on daily life, such as the availability of jobs, gas prices, and the cost of consumer goods. Although there is growing awareness about the impact of foreign policy, especially trade issues, on daily life, it is difficult for the public to be well informed on the technical problems involved in trade and tariff negotiations.

People who rely on television as their main news source, as a majority of Americans do, see only a few minutes of foreign coverage each day. After 9/11, when viewers began expressing more interest in foreign policy and information about other countries, especially those with Muslim populations, television news increased coverage of international affairs. But in polls taken one month after the attacks, Americans were saying again that their primary concerns were jobs and the economy, and coverage was reduced.

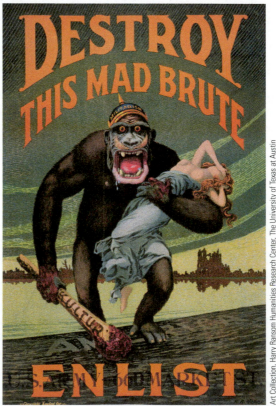

In World War I, government rhetoric and propaganda shaped public opinion by portraying German opponents as bloodthirsty gorillas. This army enlistment poster was printed in 1917.

In general, the public is more likely to concede its ignorance on a wider range of issues in foreign policy than in domestic policy and to accept the judgments of decision makers. Therefore, on most issues, it is easier for the president to influence public opinion on foreign affairs through use of the media than it is for public opinion to change the president's foreign policy. President Bush's consistent linking of al-Qaeda and Iraq was hugely successful in convincing the public that Iraq had had a role in the 9/11 attacks, which it did not. Three years later, long after the president and secretary of defense conceded publicly that there was no evidence for such a link, 40 percent of Americans continued to believe that Saddam Hussein had been "personally involved" in the attacks.[16]

That belief appeared to be an important factor in Bush's reelection in 2004, a campaign in which national security was the main issue. Only after public opinion turned against the war in Iraq did the public show signs of separating it from the 9/11 attacks, but even then it was possible for the Republican vice-presidential candidate Sarah Palin to equate the Iraq War with an attack on the perpetrators of the 9/11 attacks.

Sometimes public opinion does resist attempts to change it. When the Bush administration discounted our ties to our traditional western European allies when they refused to support the invasion of Iraq, 66 percent of the public disagreed. They believed that our partnership with western Europe on security and diplomatic matters should remain as close as it has always been.[17] Deeply held opinions like these are more resistant to administration pressure.

Trade policy illustrates the limits on the ability of public opinion to change the president's position on a foreign policy issue. Interest group opposition to the North American Free Trade Agreement (NAFTA), which eliminated trade barriers between Mexico, Canada, and the United States, was so strong that it led most Democrats, who were then the majority in Congress, to openly oppose their own party's president on this issue. Despite this opposition, Clinton never wavered in his support for NAFTA because increasing trade was the cornerstone of both his domestic and his foreign policies.

Ultimately, without some public support, foreign policy objectives that require substantial commitments of time and resources will prove unsuccessful. So to curry public support, governments try to withhold negative information, such as casualty rates, civilian deaths, and lack of progress. During the Bush administration, the Department of Defense prohibited photographing soldiers' coffins as they were returned to the United States for burial. The department said it was to protect family privacy, but it was also a way to divert public attention from the rising body count. In addition, official casualty counts did not include casualties of troops wounded or killed in noncombat activities. And no tally at all was kept of Iraqi civilian casualties. A few years into the war, the Defense Department was forced to change its policy because interest groups and international agencies posted casualty figures on websites for all the world to see.[18] Similarly, the public learned about prisoner abuse in the Abu Ghraib prison camp—which the International Red Cross and government officials had known about months earlier—because digital photos taken by troops at the site were e-mailed to friends and relatives and were circulating on the Internet. In 2010 the Obama administration tried unsuccessfully to stop the website Wikileaks from making public thousands of classified documents whose contents challenged the military's claims of progress in the war in Afghanistan.

The expansion of media coverage has somewhat strengthened the impact of public opinion on foreign policy decisions. Because of the revolution in information technology, it is becoming harder for the president, or the president and Congress together, to appeal for public support based on a claim of privileged information. The press, interest groups, and the general public now have many more sources of information on foreign policy issues than they had even a decade ago. More Americans are in e-mail contact with people in other countries and have access to the websites of foreign newspapers, governments, and think tanks, as well as to declassified documents in electronic archives. Private firms here and abroad will even sell satellite reconnaissance photography to order, and Internet sites such as Google Earth regularly show high-altitude shots of secret locales, such as North Korea's suspected nuclear test sites.[19]

CHANGING APPROACHES TO U.S. FOREIGN POLICY

Isolationism

Historically, noninvolvement with other nations outside the Americas, or **isolationism**, was a principal goal of our foreign policy. In the nineteenth and early twentieth centuries, Americans generally stayed aloof from European conflicts and turned inward, busy with domestic expansion and development.

One important exception was our continuing military and political involvement in Latin America, which was justified by the **Monroe Doctrine** of 1823. In articulating this doctrine, President James Monroe warned European powers that were not already in Latin America to stay out. This was a brazen move because we were a fledgling country challenging the major powers of the time.

As European powers withdrew from the region in the late nineteenth and early twentieth centuries, the United States began to play an increasingly active and at times interventionist role. With little regard for national sovereignty, we sent troops to protect U.S. citizens or business interests and to replace existing governments with those more sympathetic to our wishes. Paradoxically, the Monroe Doctrine derived primarily from isolationist, not interventionist, sentiment. By keeping foreign powers on their side of the ocean and out of our hemisphere, we believed we would be less likely to be drawn into conflicts abroad.

During this time, Americans did not think it appropriate to intervene in the problems of Europe or to keep a large standing army at home. Americans were focused on economic growth and feared a strong central government. Isolationism was also a realistic position in the sense that the United States was not yet a world power. Americans also thought that the United States was unique and that the more entangling alliances it entered into with foreign countries, the more likely it would "be corrupted and its unique nature…subverted."[20] This isolationist sentiment lapsed briefly in 1917–1919, when America entered World War I on the side of the British and French against Germany, but rapidly revived at its close. Despite the wishes of President Woodrow Wilson, the U.S. Senate refused to join the League of Nations, the ill-fated precursor to the United Nations. Although we have no public opinion polls from these early years, 70 percent of Americans polled in 1937 thought, in hindsight, that it had been a mistake to enter World War I.

Yet the United States was never truly isolationist in its actions. We frequently intervened diplomatically and militarily in the Caribbean and Central America and consistently sought to expand U.S. commercial and cultural influence throughout the world. Theodore Roosevelt, at the turn of the twentieth century, intervened freely in Latin America. Polls from the post–World War I era show that Americans overwhelmingly favored joining an international peacekeeping body like the League of Nations.[21]

Americans have almost always been willing to participate in world affairs to defend their national interests. But before World War II we were slow to recognize just what was at stake. In 1939, we refused to join Britain in its war to stop Nazi Germany's attempted conquest of Europe. It was not until the December 1941 Japanese attack on Pearl Harbor, Hawaii, that the public was willing to support entry into World War II. When Germany and Italy then declared war on the United States, we fought in Europe alongside Britain, the Soviet Union, and remnant armies from the occupied nations of Europe.

Containment

Containment policies began after World War II, when the Soviet Union, which suffered devastating losses in the war, sought a ring of friendly countries to serve as a buffer and installed communist governments in neighboring countries. Fearing that the Soviet Union was seeking to expand its territory and its influence, the United States tried to "contain" the Soviet Union so it could not expand further. Containment policies included economic and military aid to developing countries, cultural exchanges, covert activity, alliance building, nuclear deterrence, and, as in Korea and Vietnam, limited wars fought with conventional weaponry. During the Korean War (1950–1953), President Truman steadfastly refused to allow U.S. troops, fighting as part of a UN coalition, to expand the war's objectives to oust the communist government in North Korea and unify the country. He also refused to authorize the use of tactical nuclear weapons, knowing it could end the limited nature of the war and draw in the Soviets. The division of Korea into the communist North and the Western-allied South stands today as it did at the end of the Korean War.

During the Cold War, communism generated real fear among Americans, as this poster for a 1962 Hollywood documentary shows. Soviet Premier Nikita Khrushchev had proclaimed, "We'll bury you!"

Containment philosophy also was at work in the **Marshall Plan**, which provided economic relief to the nations of western Europe in 1947 (aid was offered to some eastern European governments, but they refused it), and in military alliances with friendly nations in Europe and Asia to stop the spread of Soviet influence or even to roll it back. As we have previously described, the most important of these was the **North Atlantic Treaty Organization, NATO**. Building these military alliances to compete with the Soviet Union and its eastern European allies was a response to the **Cold War** era that we had now entered. We were not in a military battle (or hot war) with the Russians, but the deep hostility between the two nations threatened to turn any conflict into a major armed confrontation.

Nuclear Deterrence

The nuclear era began in 1945, when the United States dropped atomic bombs on the Japanese cities of Hiroshima and Nagasaki. Although the debate on the necessity and ethics of dropping these bombs still continues, Japan did surrender after the bombing of Nagasaki, ending the war in the Pacific and making an invasion of the island by the Allies unnecessary.

At the close of the war, the United States was the only nuclear power. The Soviet Union exploded its first bomb in 1949, but it did not have an operational warhead until the mid-1950s. But our nuclear weapons were of little use in the pursuit of most foreign policy objectives because the threat of inflicting mass destruction to achieve a nonvital objective was not credible to opponents.

With Soviet advances in their own nuclear technology, everyone agreed that neither side could attack the other without the certain knowledge that both the attacker and the attacked would suffer enormous damage. No sane leader would risk so much damage by striking first. This capability is called **mutual assured destruction**, referred to by the fitting acronym **MAD.** MAD was not a strategy for defeating the Soviet Union but for containing it within its existing sphere of influence.

Successive administrations found that "rolling back" communism in the nuclear age was not possible without the kind of risk and commitment of resources most Americans were unwilling to assume. Although the Kennedy administration did risk nuclear war over Soviet placement of nuclear weapons in Cuba, ninety miles from our shores, we avoided such risks by taking no action when the Soviet Union invaded Hungary in 1956, Czechoslovakia in 1968, and Afghanistan in 1979. And the Soviet Union stayed out of the fighting when we sent military forces to oppose a Russian-backed nationalist movement in Vietnam, just as it had stood down when we tried to overthrow Castro in the 1961 Bay of Pigs invasion and when we forced the removal of Russian missiles from Cuba in 1962.

In the 1960s, the seemingly monolithic communist bloc of nations began to splinter. Yet, the U.S. became engaged in an effort to defeat communists in Vietnam, a small country in Southeast Asia.

Vietnam

If one were ranking the landmark events of the twentieth century, surely World War II would be at the top. We live in a completely different world than would have existed had Hitler not been defeated. Fighting alongside Britain and the Soviet Union, the United States achieved its greatest military victory and forged the alliance with western Europe that led to our most important treaty relationship. Yet the Vietnam War has had a far greater impact on U.S. military policy since its end in 1975. We will try to explain why.

Early period When we became involved in Vietnam, it was still part of the French colonial territory of Indochina. After the defeat of the Japanese occupying forces in World War II, the Indochinese Communist Party, led by Ho Chi Minh, engaged the returning French forces in a war for independence. Ho asked the United States for help in this anticolonial struggle, but was rebuffed. As the war in Indochina dragged on, the Cold War settled in, and containment became the organizing concept in American foreign policy, we began to support the French, eventually underwriting 80 percent of their war costs. But after considerable deliberation, the Eisenhower administration refused to provide troops or air support to try to produce a French military victory, because Eisenhower believed this could bog us down in a long war requiring many troops, certainly a prescient view.

"He's been so much more attentive since he found out I have the bomb."

At a conference in Geneva in 1954, a temporary boundary was established separating the territory of Ho's government in the North from that of the French- and U.S.-backed government in the South until elections could be held to choose leaders for all of Vietnam. But the South Vietnamese government, with influential friends in the U.S. religious community and Congress, refused to participate in the elections scheduled for 1956. The United States backed the South Vietnamese government because it feared that Ho's communist government would win the election. The temporary partition between the North and South continued, and after the assassination of Diem in 1963, it soon became clear that the South Vietnamese government would collapse without more U.S. intervention.

Armed intervention   In 1964, President Lyndon B. Johnson won congressional approval for massive intervention in Vietnam. Falsely telling Congress and the public that two U.S. destroyers had been attacked by North Vietnamese torpedo boats while on routine patrol in international waters near the Vietnam's Gulf of Tonkin, he asked Congress to endorse the Gulf of Tonkin Resolution authorizing him "to take all necessary measures to repel any armed attack against the forces of the U.S. and to prevent further aggression." Johnson later said the resolution was like "grandma's nightshirt. It covers everything."[22] He and his successor President Nixon used the Tonkin Resolution to justify each act of escalation in the war.

In early 1965, Johnson sent in U.S. troops in the belief that the war would be over "in a matter of months." But three years later, after a half-million U.S. troops had been committed to combat, the Vietcong—North Vietnam's southern allies—were able to launch a major offensive that demonstrated that all our military efforts had not made one square foot of Vietnam truly secure. When the Joint Chiefs of Staff requested more than 200,000 additional troops, a stunned President Johnson decided to undertake a review of Vietnam policy. Even the Joint Chiefs were not sure how many years and troops it might take to win. As public opposition to the war grew, Johnson called for peace talks and announced that he would not run for reelection in 1968. The talks began in May 1968 and dragged on through the administration of Johnson's successor, Richard Nixon.

President Nixon wanted to leave Vietnam without appearing to have lost the war. To accomplish this, he tried "Vietnamizing" the war by forcing the South Vietnamese government to give more responsibility to its own army. He authorized the massive bombing of Hanoi and began withdrawing U.S. troops. He also expanded the war into neighboring Cambodia, supposedly to destroy a huge underground headquarters of the North Vietnamese army near the Vietnamese border. In addition to igniting the largest public protests of the war, the invasion finally led to significant congressional opposition. The Gulf of Tonkin Resolution was repealed, and a resolution was passed prohibiting the president from using budgeted funds to wage a ground war in Cambodia. Nixon withdrew the troops from Cambodia but continued bombing in Cambodia until 1973, when Congress

Jack Kightlinger/Lyndon Baynes Johnson Library

President Johnson listens in anguish to a tape sent by his son-in-law (Charles Robb, then an officer in Vietnam and later a U.S. senator from Virginia), talking about the men lost in battle in Vietnam.

forbade the use of funds for this purpose. This was the only time Congress actually blocked presidential policies in the war. The victory of the Vietcong and North Vietnamese finally occurred in 1975 as the South Vietnamese army disintegrated in the face of a communist attack.

Lessons from Vietnam   Much of our thinking about the use of the military today is still informed by the lessons of policy failures in Vietnam.[23] Opponents of our interventions in Iraq and Afghanistan argue that we did not really learn those lessons well. Even though at its peak in 1968–1969 our military force in Vietnam exceeded half a million, had sophisticated equipment and training, and had complete air superiority, we were eventually defeated.

We failed for several reasons. We did not have clear goals and were not even sure who we were fighting (China, North Vietnam, the Soviet Union, rebels in the South?). In justifying the war, policy makers shifted focus from one to another.

We did not understand the political aspects of the war. We ignored the vast indigenous opposition to the South Vietnamese government from communists, other nationalists, and Buddhists, and we underestimated the incompetence of the South Vietnamese army (our allies) and the strength and determination of the North Vietnamese.[24] President Johnson himself, at the very time he was making large troop commitments, was saying, "I don't see any way of winning."[25]

This photo of a naked South Vietnamese girl screaming after a napalm attack by "friendly" forces became one of the most famous photographs of the war and a major incitement to antiwar protest. The girl, Kim Phue, survived, despite enduring pain and long-term treatment for her wounds.

We did not understand the nature of guerrilla warfare. For much of the war, we did not fight against a standing army dressed in the uniform of an enemy force. We fought people who dressed like civilians and blended in with civilians. We killed tens of thousands of civilians, turning them against us.

We were impatient with the war and were unwilling to devote unending resources to winning it. No leader dared tell the public that we must commit massive numbers of troops for many years. And since our goals were unclear, few wanted to risk use of nuclear weapons that could have destroyed the North. Although this stance was rational, it did not seem to lead to the obvious question of whether our objectives were worth the effort we were making.

Finally, we did not have public support. Although public opinion was supportive during the first years of the war, support eroded as it became clear that we were bogged down in an interminable and indecisive conflict. Support for withdrawal grew to overwhelming proportions as the war dragged on.[26]

The United States persisted in Vietnam for nearly eleven years because most policy makers believed in standing firm against what they saw as communist aggression and because no president wanted to be responsible for losing a war. But for much of the post-Vietnam generation, the experience shattered U.S. illusions that it could serve as the world's police force.

Differences over the lessons of Vietnam persist among policy makers today. Colin Powell, former chairman of the Joint Chiefs of Staff and George W. Bush's first secretary of state, did two tours of duty in Vietnam. This experience led him to believe that we should never commit U.S. forces to combat abroad without clear goals and an exit plan. He was initially opposed both to committing troops to the Persian Gulf War in 1991 and to unilateral military action against Iraq in 2003. On the other hand, John McCain, a Vietnam veteran who opposed the American pullout in 1975, argued

during his 2008 presidential campaign that he knew how to use lessons from our failures in Vietnam to bring the Iraq War to a successful conclusion. President Obama withdrew most American forces from Iraq in 2011, but it is too early to describe our involvement as successful or not.

And the debate over how comparable the Vietnam, Afghani, and Iraq experiences are continues when we again find ourselves in wars against guerrillas, supporting corrupt and ineffective leaders, causing heavy civilian casualties, and with uncertain popular support. We cut our losses in Iraq by withdrawing most of our troops, but we continue to fight in Afghanistan.

Détente

Richard Nixon came to office after public opinion had begun to turn against the war, and he immediately began looking for ways to shape international relations in the post–Vietnam War era. As a man whose career was built on making political hay out of his staunch anticommunism, President Nixon was well placed to make diplomatic overtures to the Soviet Union without fear of being attacked by any but the most die-hard Cold Warriors. Thus Nixon and his national security adviser and later secretary of state, Henry Kissinger, developed a policy called **détente**, which was designed to deescalate Cold War rhetoric and to promote the notion that relations with the Soviet Union could be conducted in ways other than confrontation.

The détente doctrine recognized that although the Soviet Union would remain our adversary, it, too, had legitimate interests in the world. Détente also recognized the growing military strength of the Soviet Union and the fact that it was in our interests to pursue bilateral agreements, such as on arms control, that would try to limit this strength.

During this era of new diplomacy with the Soviet Union, President Nixon also opened normal relations with China. Even though it was home to one-fifth of the world's population, China had been shut out of the mainstream diplomatic community, largely due to U.S. pressure, since the communist victory in 1949. After lengthy negotiations, the first cultural exchange, a visit by the U.S. table tennis—ping-pong—team, was arranged in 1971. Full diplomatic recognition by the United States did not come, however, until the Carter administration several years later.

The resumption of diplomatic relations between China and the United States was one of the most remarkable achievements of Nixon and Kissinger's attempts to break the Cold War stalemate. The Nixon-Kissinger visits to China were all the more remarkable because they occurred while U.S. troops were still fighting in Vietnam. It had been the specter of a Sino-Soviet communist bloc and a near paranoid fear of "yellow hordes" (in the racist parlance of the time) advancing throughout Asia that led us to fight in Korea and Vietnam. Within a few short years, China's image was recast from dreaded enemy to friendly ally, and Cold War fears of world communist domination were greatly diminished.

Jimmy Carter and his advisers also saw the world as far more complex than Cold War rhetoric suggested.[27] They thought that the United States should work with other nations to address substantial threats to world order such as global poverty, inequitable distribution of wealth, abuse of human rights, and regional competitiveness.

In 1979, Carter signed a new agreement with the Soviet Union placing limits on offensive missiles. But the Soviets' stunning invasion of Afghanistan that same year ended the chance of gaining Senate approval for the treaty. Public and

A major achievement of the Nixon-Kissinger policy of détente was to establish normal relationships with the communist government of the People's Republic of China. Here Nixon attends a state banquet in Beijing with then-Premier Zhou Enlai.

National Archives and Records Administration

elite opinion shifted, and Cold War views, never completely abandoned, became much more respectable again.

Cold War Revival and End

The Reagan administration took office in 1981 determined to challenge the Soviet Union in every way possible. During his first term, Ronald Reagan renounced the Nixon-Kissinger principle of détente and labeled the Soviet Union an "evil empire." He painted a simple picture of an aggressive, reckless, and brutal Soviet Union and a peace-loving and virtuous United States. Despite the rhetoric, however, the administration did not risk direct confrontation.

Reagan's approach differed from containment because it was more ideologically than strategically driven; he sought not just to contain the Soviets but to roll back their power and to topple communist rule if possible. One method Reagan endorsed was stepping up the arms race and, by forcing them to keep pace, driving the Soviets into economic ruin. American military spending on building up the U.S. military increased to record peacetime levels, dramatically increasing our national debt.

Though the election of Reagan put a Cold Warrior in the White House, the public was not willing to buy Cold War arguments wholeheartedly. By Reagan's second term, a dramatic drop in public support for increased military spending and growing public pressure for progress on arms control helped push the administration toward a less belligerent stance. Violent rhetoric was toned down, and conciliatory gestures multiplied.[28]

The moderation in Reagan's rhetoric was also a response to changes in the Soviet Union. In 1985, Mikhail Gorbachev, the new general secretary of the Communist Party of the Soviet Union, called for "new thinking" and began to shake up Soviet society as it had not been shaken since the Russian Revolution in 1917.[29] Faced with a stagnating economy and an antireform Soviet leadership, Gorbachev encouraged competition in the economy, criticism of corruption and inefficiencies by government agencies, and free elections of some government legislative bodies.

Gorbachev also challenged the status quo in the international community by opening to the outside world. He encouraged foreign investment and requested foreign aid to help rebuild the Soviet economy. He pulled Soviet troops out of Afghanistan and reduced aid to Soviet-backed governments in Nicaragua and Cuba. Gorbachev also took the initiative in resuming arms control negotiations with President Reagan. In 1987, the two men reached an agreement on intermediate-range nuclear forces. To ensure compliance, the United States sent inspectors or monitors to the Soviet Union and the Soviets sent them to western Europe and the United States to observe production facilities and the dismantling and removal of the missiles.

During the first two years of George H. W. Bush's administration, the Soviet empire in eastern Europe disintegrated rapidly, stunning policy makers (and experts) all over the world. The Soviet-dominated governments were dismantled, communist parties changed their names, opposition parties formed, and free multiparty elections were held. In late 1989, demonstrators tore down the most visible symbol of the Cold War, the Berlin Wall (built by the Soviets in 1961 to divide Soviet-occupied East Berlin from NATO-occupied West Berlin). A year later, Germany was reunified and the Soviet Union passed from existence as the non-Russian states of the Soviet Union declared their independence. This was clearly a new world order.

Americans were relieved at the disintegration of the Soviet Union, but uncertain about the new foreign policy challenges. Without the Soviet threat to justify expenditures, the United States began to shrink its military. With the Cold War over, Americans seemed weary of trying to understand and change the world. They were more impressed by the failures of foreign aid, military intervention, and diplomacy than by foreign policy successes, more weighed down by problems at home than by those in other countries.

Despite this sentiment, George H. W. Bush led the United States into another military engagement, this time intervening in the Persian Gulf to protect Kuwait from invasion by Iraq. Reflecting public sentiment, at least in part, Bush chose a multination approach with cost sharing and participation of an international force under UN auspices.

Clinton: Economic Interests and Multilateralism

Bill Clinton's foreign policy themes were shaped more by the skepticism of the Vietnam era than by memories of the Allied victory in World War II. In his campaign, he reminded voters that we had not defeated the Soviet Union in battle but that it had collapsed from within due to "economic, political, and spiritual failure." He believed that the best foreign policy is to have a strong economy.[30] Thus Clinton emphasized economic instruments of foreign policy, using our economic strength to achieve political goals, such as promotion of democracy and human rights.

Clinton's foreign policy was so rooted in the pursuit of national economic interests that almost all issues were discussed in terms of their value to U.S. trade relations. (Clinton's second-term national security adviser was an international trade lawyer.) This led some observers to label his foreign policy "merchant diplomacy."[31] Deemphasizing the military in favor of economic diplomacy suited the public mood, which, although not one of withdrawal from world affairs, was leery of new political entanglements.

Clinton also emphasized multilateralism, that is, working with other nations to achieve our goals. When he ordered troops to Haiti in 1994 to oust a military dictatorship and restore the elected president, it was only after gaining UN backing. Clinton believed that every country should assume part of the burden for maintaining international peace and security. This approach can be cumbersome. The stake that each country has in any international dispute varies, making military or even diplomatic cooperation sometimes impossible to achieve. For example, the failure of the United States

(or any other country) to act unilaterally to stop ethnic cleansing in the breakaway republics of Yugoslavia cost tens of thousands of lives. However, when we did get involved, it was as part of a NATO force, with shared costs and troop commitments, and one could argue that it was with greater legitimacy and a more effective force than the United States could have provided by acting on its own. However, conservatives generally oppose multilateralism, arguing that it erodes U.S. sovereignty and freedom of action.

Although Clinton's multilateralism slowed U.S. response to crises, this approach rationed the use of U.S. military force and spending, maintaining the bulk of strength for response to vital national security threats. Avoiding costly military entanglements also helped end the huge budget deficits run up by the military spending and tax cuts of the Reagan era. Multilateralism slows response time, but it can prevent precipitous entry into situations we do not fully understand.

The most glaring failure of multilateralism during Clinton's administration was the decision to follow the UN's lead in not intervening to stop the genocide in Rwanda, a conflict that cost an estimated 800,000 lives. Both Clinton and the intervention-shy UN leadership later admitted that this was a drastic failure of preventive diplomacy and international peacekeeping.

Bush: Pre-emptive War and Regime Change

George W. Bush's foreign policy views were radically different. He did not believe in multilateralism, preferring unilateralism, with the United States acting on its own whenever possible.

Under Bush, the United States did not withdraw from international organizations, but Bush suggested that he would only *consult* with other countries, not deal with them as equals. He announced his opposition to a number of treaty arrangements, including the Kyoto agreements on global warming, which Clinton had signed. In withdrawing the United States from the treaty, Bush said he thought it placed unreasonable burdens on American businesses and too few on those in poorer countries. He refused to renew the ABM treaty because it would keep him from pursuing the development of the space-based antimissile defense system Reagan had begun, and he refused to agree to U.S. participation in an international court to try war crimes and human rights abuses because he thought it would make American peacekeeping troops subject to false accusations.

The terrorist attacks by al-Qaeda on September 11, 2001, changed policy dramatically. With world public opinion in sympathy with the United States as a victim of unprovoked attack, Bush enlisted several of our traditional allies, such as Britain, Australia, and several NATO allies, to strike against the Taliban-controlled government of Afghanistan, the country that had sponsored al-Qaeda. (The Taliban was a radical Muslim group that controlled Afghanistan.) Within a month of the attack, U.S., British, and other armed forces entered Afghanistan and overthrew the Taliban leadership, which fled to Pakistan, and the United States and its allies quickly established a presence in many parts of the country.

Bruno Stevens/Cosmos/Aurora

The U.S. invasion of Iraq unleashed a near civil war between two rival Muslim sects, which also led to more attacks on American troops.

But Bush had declared a war on terror, so initial successes in Afghanistan were not enough. At the time and since, analysts have pointed out the strategic and practical errors of this approach. Terrorism has always existed and will always exist. A war on terror, thus, is a perpetual war, and perpetual war is not kind to democratic ways of doing things. Moreover, declaring a war on terror took the focus off the specific enemy that attacked us, al-Qaeda, and its sponsors. Bush further diffused a strategic focus by labeling three nations—Iraq, Iran, and North Korea—an "axis of evil" and agents of state-sponsored terrorism. Though these governments were led by individuals who were called evil, none of these nations was the sponsor of the al-Qaeda attacks on the United States. (U.S. allies Pakistan and Saudi Arabia had much more to do with al-Qaeda than the so-called "axis of evil" countries did.)

The conviction that an international ring of state-sponsored terrorists was lying in wait to launch other attacks led to a major redefinition of U.S. defense policy. The Bush national security team endorsed the strategy of pre-emption, or striking first in a preventive or **pre-emptive war**.[32] In a much-quoted speech delivered at West Point after 9/11, Bush said, "We must take the battle to the enemy, disrupt its plans, and confront the worst threats before they emerge." Reinforcing this point, Vice President Cheney added, "this struggle will not end with a treaty or accommodation of terrorists [but] with complete and utter destruction" of terrorist networks.[33]

Pre-emption had never been a policy of the United States, though it has always been an option.[34] It is unlikely that any

president would fail to strike first in a situation where it was certain it would prevent a lethal attack on the United States. But Bush's position that pre-emption was a guiding principle in defense policy was unprecedented in U.S. history. It suggested the possibility of launching wars of choice rather than confining ourselves to wars of necessity. Evidence can often be cited to claim a threat from another country, even if the perceived threat is bogus or questionable or unlikely to lead to any attack by that country.

In 1954, at the height of the Cold War, some Cold Warriors were advising President Eisenhower to take action against the Chinese government, then under the control of communist leader Mao Tse-tung. Eisenhower, a West Point graduate and supreme commander of the Allied Forces in Europe during World War II, told a reporter, "I don't believe there is such a thing [as preventive war] and, frankly, I wouldn't even listen to anyone seriously that came in and talked about such a thing."[35] Despite continued pressure, Eisenhower refused to launch a pre-emptive war against China. He told the reporter that "the easy course for a president...is to adopt a truculent, publicly bold, almost insulting attitude," but that approach he was convinced would lead to war. He knew from experience where a wartime mentality led: everyone gets behind the troops and unifies against the enemy, and a fervor builds to the point of "exhilaration." That attitude, Eisenhower said, bred "impulsiveness and hubris. The hard way is to have the courage to be patient."

Bush put his preventive policy into effect by calling for a pre-emptive strike against Iraq, a country that was governed by what most observers agreed was a murderous tyrant. It was not, however, a country that had attacked the United States, nor was there any evidence that it was intending to. But Bush's Iraq policy was based not on known capabilities or actual plans but on *assumed intent*. In opposing this policy, many members of Congress argued that sending thousands of combat troops to invade a sovereign nation encroached on Congress's constitutional prerogative to declare war. Many foreign policy analysts argued that pre-emptive war was a terrible precedent to set in the international community. Attacking a country to prevent the possibility that it *might* one day attack us sets a frightening precedent for international rules of engagement, legitimizing pre-emptive military or nuclear strikes by other countries against their enemies.

Thus, after less than two years in office, Bush's approach to foreign policy had been drastically revised from a passive unilateralism to an interventionist unilateralism and reluctant multinationalism. Bush did put together a "coalition of the willing" to participate in the invasion of Iraq, but of the more than thirty countries signing on, only Great Britain contributed any significant contingent of combat troops. Troops and civilian personnel from other countries served mainly in support and humanitarian roles and sometimes numbered only a handful. Except for Great Britain and Australia, we paid most of our coalition partners to participate. (This is in contrast to the first Gulf War, when our coalition partners paid most of the war's cost.)

Bush's pre-emptive unilateralism, with its token multilateralism, pushed U.S. military strength to its limits. We did not have the economic and military resources to stabilize and reconstruct Iraq and carry on the war in Afghanistan. Though Bush did not believe that nation building was a role for the U.S. military, in fact, by overthrowing the governments in both Afghanistan and Iraq, nation building fell to us.

The drain on our resources, and increasing public skepticism, led to diplomacy, even in negotiating with "the axis of evil." The government reached agreement with North Korea to dismantle its nuclear weapons facilities in return for various kinds of assistance—the same Clinton approach Bush had rejected on entering office. An opponent of the Iraq War, Obama announced that we would withdraw our troops in 2011, which we did. A supporter of the war in Afghanistan, he increased troop strength there but said we would leave in 2014.

Bush's strategy of pre-emptive war and regime change unleashed a wave of anti-Americanism throughout Europe and parts of Asia as well as the Middle East. After 9/11, world opinion was almost entirely sympathetic to the United States, but the U.S. decision to launch a pre-emptive war to overthrow the government of a sovereign country triggered fear and hostility in many parts of the world. Public opinion was against the war, even among our closest allies, including Britain, Canada, Germany, and Australia. Though not the intention of the U.S. government, our wars in Iraq and Afghanistan were interpreted as wars against Islam, both in the Arab world and by some at home. International criticism increased after revelations of U.S. actions not in conformity with U.S. law, democratic norms, or international law, including sending prisoners to countries whose laws do not prohibit torture, secret CIA prisons for holding suspected terrorists, and the use of torture in American-run prisons in Iraq and Afghanistan. Animosity deepened when Bush claimed he did not have to abide by all terms of the Geneva Convention on prisoners of war.

Obama's Pragmatic Strategies

President Obama came to office on a wave of good will from around the globe. People believed he would be a force for change. As a black man, Obama appeared to those of color around the world as a potential ally and a symbol of an America where a black person could be elected president. As Table 1 shows, the confidence of the world's population in presidential leadership soared.

But of course, good will is not a foreign policy, and some of the initial good will has dissipated in light of subsequent events. It is still very high relative to the last years of the Bush term.

Obama developed a mixed strategy of unilateralism and multilateralism. The United States has gone-it-alone on issues immediately crucial to its national security, such as locating Osama bin Laden and killing him in a firefight with Navy Seals. It has also gone-it-alone in launching unmanned vehicles (drones) to attack and kill various al-Qaeda leaders (and in the process also killing quite a few Pakistani and Afghan civilians). The United States has engaged in multilateral strategies, such as continuing NATO involvement in Afghanistan, joining with a small number of western Allies in helping Libyan rebels topple Muammar Gaddafi, and taking the lead, but in conjunction with the United Nations Security Council, in imposing a trade embargo on Iran in an attempt to deter it from developing nuclear weapons capability.

Obama's pragmatism was also indicated by his action to withdraw U.S. fighting forces from Iraq but then to add combat forces to fight the war in Afghanistan in 2010. Then his growing realization that the Afghan government was not taking steps to reduce its corruption or improve the quality, honesty, and efficiency of its local infrastructures led to a decision to withdraw by 2014 and a reduction of troops throughout 2012 and continuing. The failures of the Afghan government to govern local areas meant that there would be no long-term success in the central government's ability to hold the allegiance of civilians in areas threatened by the Taliban. Thus U.S. military successes were only temporary, creating what one American general called "a bleeding ulcer."[36] Though this withdrawal, like that in Iraq, was opposed by some Republicans (though not all), there appears to be little appetite by anyone for reentering the fray in Iraq and only a few argue openly that we should make an open-ended military commitment to Afghanistan.

NEW AND OLD CHALLENGES IN THE GLOBAL ERA

The United States faces significant foreign policy challenges in the global era, and not all Americans agree on the right ways to tackle them.

Confronting Nonstate Actors

When we think of "war," we usually think of massed armies, as in World War II. But among the major forces in contemporary international relations are "nonstate actors." These are groups of individuals, not part of a recognized government, who are using armed force to try to topple their own government or intervene in other nations to pursue their objectives. Sometimes they are guerilla soldiers or militia, rebels, warlords, or even criminal gangs that control communities, such as the powerful drug cartels in Mexico. If they are our opponents, we sometimes call them terrorists. All of our wars since the 1950s have involved nonstate actors as our enemies.

The Vietcong, one faction of our enemies in the Vietnam War, were an example of a nonstate actor that fought successfully against the U.S. presence in their country to bring about a communist government in the south of Vietnam. Al-Qaeda, the terrorist group that attacked the United States on 9/11, are another example. Though supported by the government of Afghanistan (then run by the Taliban), an Islamic extremist group, and backed by governments in Pakistan and Saudi Arabia, they were not the official army of any of these states. Al-Qaeda's attacks were successful to a degree because, not only did they murder nearly 3000 people, mostly civilians, but they also challenged the United States's view of itself as safe from enemy attack. And they prompted the United States to react in ways that harmed our international image and our own values.

The security threats of these groups are very different from the Cold War threats of Soviet nuclear attacks and massive armies. We were able to protect against nuclear attacks by our mutually assured destruction policies already described. But the rise of nonstate actors poses new vulnerabilities.[37] Unlike states, even secretive ones like North Korea, which are visible to everyone, nonstate actors are more difficult to track. The 9/11 attack was made by only nineteen individuals, part of an organization that used the openness of our society to its own ends in training for and carrying out attacks. Terrorist groups may come and go and change organization and shape. The CIA had intelligence about al-Qaeda before it attacked us, even intelligence about the attack, but because this group was only one of many, we did not give this priority or coordinate information.

Powerful countries often support rebel groups that they think support their own national goals. For example, the United States provided arms to the mujahedeen, the Islamist group resisting the Soviet occupation of Afghanistan in the 1970s and 1980s. Later, this group became the Taliban, controlled Afghanistan, and turned its hostility on the United States. In 2011, the United States and some of its Western allies supported the Libyan rebels fighting Muammar Gaddafi with air power and arms. The rebels succeeded in overthrowing Gaddafi, though whether this will be a success for Western democracies in the long term remains to be seen.

Combatting nonstate actors requires a transformation of traditional military strategies and weaponry, with more emphasis on mobility and quick response than on heavy weapons. Moreover, it requires powerful nations to rely on their soft power, including their strong economies and the power of their ideas, rather than the hard power of their armies and navies. Yet despite widespread agreement that the most immediate security threats may come from nonstate actors, we still spend far more on conventional warfare abroad.

Of course, some experts believe that we have not seen the last of traditional ground warfare and are reluctant to prepare for new kinds of warfare. But there are also political pressures that make change difficult, especially the tight grip that arms manufacturers, military leaders, and their congressional allies have on the defense budget.

The United States as a Military State

We noted earlier in the book that when America has been in a major war, government has grown to support it. And because we have spent so many of the last decades at war, military conflict has changed the nature of American government. Not only has government grown, but a powerful coalition of industries supporting military activities, their congressional allies, and military leaders has emerged. This so-called iron triangle is the military-industrial-political complex President Dwight Eisenhower spoke of as he left office in 1961. Recognizing the potential for profit-hungry defense industries and pork-hungry congressional allies to drive military spending, determine the kind of weaponry purchased, and encourage the use of military force to achieve objectives, Eisenhower warned: "The conjunction of an immense military establishment and a large arms industry is new in the American experience," and "we must not fail to comprehend its grave implications.... The potential for the disastrous rise of misplaced power exists and will persist. We must never let the weight of this combination endanger our liberties or democratic processes."[38]

Eisenhower's prediction came true decades ago, and the alliance of industry, military, and political professionals created a set of powerful vested interests driving up spending and budget deficits and, once the United States becomes involved in a military action, providing support for military solutions. Being continually at war also leads to a diminution of liberties, as we have seen in the decade after 9/11, when Congress accepted historic invasions into the private communications of our own citizens and public opinion became inured to the use of torture on our enemies.[39]

Getting control of defense spending is one of the greatest challenges we face in formulating effective national security policy, both to better target preparedness to the most urgent threats and to reduce deficit spending, something that cannot be achieved without containing the Pentagon budget as well

President Dwight Eisenhower, who served as an army general in World War II, was leery about overreliance on military force. He cautioned against preventive war and warned about the increasing influence of the "military-industrial complex."

as domestic spending. (Over 90 percent of defense spending is discretionary.) Defense spending has grown by 7 percent a year (adjusted for inflation) for the past decade, in part because of the wars in Iraq and Afghanistan.[40]

Presidents, past and present, dramatically underrepresent the cost of military actions, sometimes as a strategy to diminish opposition to those actions. Members of Congress and interest groups who are normally concerned about deficit spending usually do not challenge those estimates either, perhaps because they are afraid of seeming unpatriotic, or because they are political supporters of defense spending.

The Civil War cost more than thirteen times original estimates and the Vietnam War eleven to fifteen times more than was first thought. The Bush administration's initial predictions that the war in Iraq would cost $60 to $80 billion were grossly underestimated.[41] They assumed that the war would be over in months, that there would be no civil war and therefore no occupation, and that Iraq's oil industry would soon be operating at normal levels and its revenues would pay for reconstruction. All of these assumptions were dramatically wrong and were seen to be so by many at the time. One well-known economist estimated, before the war started, that the overall cost could be $1.9 trillion.[42] Even that is an underestimate of what the real cost has been.

By 2010 the *direct* costs of the Iraq War were at least three-quarters of a trillion dollars, or about ten times the original estimate.[43] These direct costs do not include health care and disability pay for veterans, lost productivity, impact on oil prices, and interest payments on money borrowed to pay for the wars. The real cost of the war may run as high as

$3 trillion, and one recent estimate has total costs exceeding $4 trillion.[44]

Some of these indirect costs are indisputable, such as interest payments on the debt. So is the long-term cost of medical care for veterans, although we will know the exact figure only years from now. By 2010, 600,000 of the 2.1 million troops who had served in both wars had received medical treatment; the most recent estimate of these costs is that they may top $900 billion. If they continue to grow, total war costs could reach $6 trillion.[45]

Not only were the costs of the war grossly underestimated, but there was no revenue-raising plan put in place to pay for it other than to borrow money. So far all of the money to pay for the war has been borrowed, much of it from foreign lenders. With the exceptions of the Mexican-American War and the first Gulf War, taxes have always been raised during wartime to pay the costs, but during the Iraq War, Americans received a tax cut.[46]

As politicians debate deficits in the Obama administration, there is little sustained attention to the impact that the wars of the last decade have had on these deficits and how military spending might contribute to the problem. The military-industrial-political complex is largely deaf to these concerns.

In addition to its impact on the budget, war erodes civil liberties. For example, as we saw in Chapter 13, after 9/11, the Bush administration encouraged the National Security Agency (NSA) to intercept international calls and e-mails between people in the United States and those abroad. It gained access to American telecommunication companies and then used computer searches to look for words that might be written or spoken by terrorists. The program was not restricted to suspected terrorists; it was much broader.[47] The NSA also examined calls between people within the United States. None of this had judicial authorization and was probably in violation of the law. Congress, once it found out, didn't stop these moves, but legalized them.[48]

Relations with China

In 2010, China became the world's second-largest economy, and it remains the United States principal competitor for export markets. China has built its economy by exporting the goods it makes rather than by encouraging domestic consumption of its own or imported products (the opposite of the U.S. approach; China has done this by keeping the value of its currency artificially low, a subject we leave for your economics course). Exports to the United States account for 6 percent of China's entire economic output, or thirteen times as large a share of the Chinese economy as exports to China represent for the U.S. economy. In 2009 the United States was buying $4.46 worth of Chinese goods for every $1 worth of American goods sold to China.[49]

However, China is investing enormous diplomatic energy in increasing markets for its goods in other parts of the world and is becoming increasingly less dependent on the United States as a buyer of its products.[50] The less interdependent our economies become, the more our massive debt gives China leverage over our foreign policy.

In fact, we exist in what some economists call a new balance of terror with countries like China, which holds more dollars than any other government, an amount equal to 10 percent of its GDP. China cannot stop underwriting our debt by loaning us huge sums of money because the failure of our economy would reverberate through China's own economy in a kind of mutual economic destruction.[51]

Though the U.S. economy, along with its military might, is far superior to that of China, our continuing failure to get our deficit under control means that we will be even more indebted to creditor nations, and the primary one is China. Thus they will have an increasing influence on America's behavior in the world. We cannot dismiss Chinese viewpoints because of their economic leverage on us. This has implications for our relations with many other nations, particularly Asian nations who are Chinese neighbors.

It is also a limitation on our ability to pressure China to reform its internal policies, such as its human rights policies. Though China presents a largely peaceable face to the world, it does not allow internal dissent and will arrest and imprison dissenters. Though, over time, the right of Chinese citizens to protest local injustices has grown somewhat, there is no analog to the rights of free speech typical of democratic societies. Americans, and the rest of the world, were alerted to that fact when a Chinese dissident, Chen Guangcheng, escaped to the U.S. Embassy in the days before Secretary of State Clinton arrived in China on a diplomatic mission in 2012. He wished to flee to the United States after having been confined to his home, isolated from friends and family, and physically

mistreated. Chen Guangcheng decided to leave the embassy, but he later made statements suggesting that the United States had not supported him, thereby undermining the American mission. After a few days, a compromise solution was worked out allowing him to come to the United States on a student visa, thus saving face for all involved.

It is in our interest to develop working ties with China. One of the centerpieces of the Obama administration's foreign policy has been to try to engage the Chinese in a partnership to help solve problems in other parts of the world. One of those efforts is to reduce the likelihood that North Korea, a communist state, will develop nuclear weapon capabilities. China is one of North Korea's few allies, and its leverage could be critical. Enlisting the partnership of China in issues of global climate change is another objective of American foreign policy.

The Middle East

The Middle East poses continuing foreign policy challenges to the United States. It is the home of a large proportion of the world's oil supply, so it has a strategic value. Because of that strategic interest, for several decades we have supported the authoritarian governments of some of these states, such as Saudi Arabia, Egypt, and sometimes Iraq.

The Context

The only democracy in the Middle East is our ally Israel (which has no oil). Israel was created by Jews who fled from or, in more cases, were survivors of, the Holocaust (Hitler and Nazi's attempts to murder the entire European Jewish population during World War II). During the years leading up to World War II, and during the war, the world stood by while about 6 million of Europe's Jewish population were murdered by the Germans and their allies in occupied territories of Europe. Tens of thousands had fled to the British-occupied area of Palestine before the war; and during and after the war tens of thousands of survivors emigrated to Palestine. These refugees fought against the British who controlled the area, and in 1948, when the British withdrew, the United States and the United Nations recognized the new government of Israel.

Many of the issues involving the Middle East stem from the fact that while Israelis consider Palestine their ancient homeland, going back to biblical times, so do the Arabs. Since 1948, Middle Eastern politics has focused on military conflict and attempts at negotiations to try to resolve this fundamental divide.

In 1948, after the Israeli declaration of independence, Arab states tried to throw the Jewish population out of Israel, but they were defeated. In 1967, as several Arab countries mobilized their troops to invade Israel, Israel launched a preemptive air and land strike. Within a few days, it captured the Gaza Strip and the Sinai Peninsula from Egypt, the West Bank (including East Jerusalem) from Jordan, and the Golan Heights from Syria. These areas became known as the "occupied territories."

Some see China, with its rapidly growing economy and surging nationalism, as a possible rival, especially in trade. But we remain one of China's best customers, and it remains one of our chief creditors.

In 1973, after an invasion of Israel by Egypt and Syria, both sides began to consider negotiations more seriously. Early Arab successes in the war meant that Israel could no longer simply assume that it could easily defeat its Arab neighbors. But the failure to recapture any territory lost in the 1967 war encouraged Egyptian leader Anwar Sadat to begin to think of a settlement with Israel. In 1979, at Camp David, the U.S. president's retreat, President Jimmy Carter helped broker a historic agreement between Egypt and Israel. Egypt agreed to normal diplomatic relations with Israel, recognizing Israel's right to exist, and Israel returned the Sinai Peninsula to Egypt. Fifteen years later, Jordan also signed a peace treaty with Israel.

Key Issues in the Region

But peace has not come to the region. The United States and other nations try periodically to broker peace agreements, but tensions remain high. The list of grievances on both sides is lengthy and complicated, but three important and intertwined issues are (1) Israel's right to exist; (2) the right of Palestinians displaced by Israel to return to their ancestral homes; and (3) the question of a "two-state" solution with a Palestine state existing side by side with Israel.

The Arab states that have not reached any agreement with Israel deny that Israel has a right to exist. The most extreme case is Syria, whose leader, a radical anti-Semite, denies the Holocaust and makes no secret of his desire to eliminate the Jewish population of Israel. Israeli leaders, understandably, insist that a statement that Israel has a right to exist is a precondition to any peace agreement.

The right of return has been contentious since 1948. After the 1948 war, somewhere over 700,000 Arabs fled Israel (in some cases they were forced to leave by threats and violence, and debates continue about how many left voluntarily). Many were relocated on the Gaza Strip, a narrow strip bordering Egypt, Israel, and the Mediterranean Sea, which was created as a refugee camp. Over time, however, Gaza has developed into a set of communities with a population of nearly 2 million, most born in Gaza. Other Palestinian Arabs fled to other Arab nations of the Middle East, such as Jordan or Egypt. At the same time, between 1948 and 1973, perhaps 1 million Jews fled their homes in Arab nations (in many cases they were persecuted, had their citizenship and assets stripped, and forced to leave) to settle in Israel. The once vibrant Jewish communities of the Arab Middle East are gone.

While Jews who emigrated to Israel from Arab lands are not claiming they should have a right to return to their ancestral homes, those Palestinians who fled Israel or who were forced to leave through threats of violence believe they should have the right to return and reclaim their land and property. Israel resists this right of return, pointing out that others now own the land, including the Jewish immigrants from the Arab world, and that most of those who left are dead so that the returnees would never have lived in these ancestral homes. This "right of return" issue continues to be an impediment to any settlement between Israel and its neighbors.

A third issue is the legal status of the occupied West Bank. The Palestinians created their own state in the occupied West Bank, including Gaza, but it is not a fully sovereign state because Israel still controls it militarily and imposes many restrictions on travel within the area and between the area and Israel. In the decades since the 1967 war, Israel has settled parts of the West Bank, planting settlements of Jewish Israelis in a largely Arab population. Also during this time, the Arabs have periodically rebelled against the Israelis occupying this area (these uprisings have been labeled "intifadas"). The situation of the West Bank, including part of Jerusalem that is primarily occupied by Arabs, is perhaps the most contentious issue. The Israeli government is now dominated by those who believe that Israel has a right to these territories as the home of the ancient Israelites. Arabs want the settlements disbanded before they will agree to any peace arrangements, and not all Palestinian leaders recognize Israel's right to exist. The situation of East Jerusalem is especially controversial because it includes religious shrines sacred to people of both Jewish and Muslim faiths (as well as many Christian shrines). Israel considers Jerusalem its capital, but the United States and the rest of the world do not recognize it as the capital, preferring to wait until there can be a settlement between Israel and Palestine to determine the fate of Jerusalem.

Hundreds of books have been written about Israeli-Arab relations. This brief description hardly does justice to the situation except to illustrate that the issues are complex and the different groups in the region have different understandings of the realities. The situation is especially inflammatory because each religious group intensely believes that the other group has no territorial rights on land it controls, or used to control. The situation is also very unstable. Nearly 20% of the Israeli population is Arab, including Arab Christians but mostly Muslims. This group is growing faster than the Jewish population. Arab Israelis are citizens of Israel with political rights, though they do not serve in the military. But as the group grows, this will certainly change the nature of Israeli politics, and attempts to stifle the voice of the Arabs will threaten the democratic nature of Israel.

The ongoing Arab-Israeli controversy that periodically results in bloodshed is a hot political issue all over the Middle East. The United States has supported dictatorial regimes that have either recognized Israel (such as Egypt) or that seem willing to live with the status quo (such as Saudi Arabia and Iraq).

Arab Spring

In 2011, in what many observers called "the Arab spring," the Middle East status quo was overturned. Several longtime dictators were overthrown, largely through peaceful protests and civil disobedience, by the citizens of Egypt, Tunisia, and Yemen. The rebels used military force in Libya, with aid from the United States and other Western countries. In Syria, the nonviolent initial protests were met with military force on the part of the Syrian government, leading to what is now a civil war with an uncertain outcome. The genesis of the rebellions seems to have been a hunger for more democracy and a better life for the average person. Young Arabs saw the rest of the world, including Israel, on TV and realized that in their countries the opportunities for education were small; income distributions were highly unequal, with rulers and their friends

Libyan rebels, with help from Britain, France, and the United States, overthrew the ruler Muammar Gaddafi. The Libyan uprising was part of the Arab Spring in 2011.

and family bilking the state, piling up money, and living high while most of the population was mired in poverty; and hopes for better jobs and a better world were dim. In these nations, there were few avenues for peaceful change: no free elections were ever held, no opposition parties were allowed, and certainly no free press existed.

So citizens rebelled and in many cases were successful. But the outcomes of these protests have not yet been greater democracy, and some Arabs hold extreme anti-Israel attitudes, wanting to exterminate Israel. Within these new democracies, moderate groups are battling with more extreme groups for control. Still, the motivations sparking the protest hold within them the seeds for a better future, and the United States and other Western democracies are trying to support these transitions, even while those transitions have created further instability and uncertainty in the region. Instability in the area was demonstrated yet again when violent protests were launched against the U.S. in 2012 in several nations, ostensibly protesting a crude video lampooning the Prophet Muhammad. In Libya, elements of al-Qaeda were part of a violent protest at the U.S. embassy that resulted in the death of the U.S. ambassador and three other embassy employees.

The United States in the Region

The U.S. government, over the years, has periodically tried to broker peace treaties and support more moderate governments on both sides of the issue. However, its support for Israel has been unwavering, even when more extreme factions have been in power. This support lowers our overall stature in the region, and our military and other aid to the Arab countries has not created a lot of leverage for us with Arab leaders

While trying to broker peace, the United States has also given and sold arms to both sides of the conflict. Military aid through arms transfers goes mostly to Israel and Egypt, but we also sell billions of dollars of arms to wealthy cash customers in the Middle East like the United Arab Emirates, Kuwait, and Saudi Arabia.[52] The Saudi government is the principal funder of schools promoting Wahhabism, the virulently anti-Semitic branch of Islamist teaching that influenced Osama bin Laden and others who joined al-Qaeda. (Almost all of the terrorists who attacked the United States on 9/11 were Saudis.)

THE ROLE OF FOREIGN POLICY IN GOVERNING

Unlike the economy, foreign policy is unlikely to have critics charging that it is not rightly the responsibility of the federal government. That does not mean that people agree on how much of government's time and resources should be devoted to it. In times of war or palpable threat to national security, the public is more accepting of a concentration on foreign policy. After 9/11, for example, there was no need to convince the public that a threat existed, and the public gave the president unprecedented support for military action against al-Qaeda. As long as the public believed in a connection between Iraq and the 9/11 attacks, there was substantial backing for President Bush's pre-emptive war policy. But when evidence for such a connection failed to materialize and the war turned into an occupation characterized by urban warfare and sectarian conflict, public support waned.

President Obama came to office determined to end the war in Iraq and to undertake more pragmatic policies in the Middle East, with China, and elsewhere. His successes in ending the Iraq War and the death of Osama bin Laden were viewed as positives in most of the world as well as at home. With the economic struggles faced here and abroad, foreign policy moved to the back burner of public attention.

SUMMARY

- As with any nation, America's foreign policy goals include protecting our own physical security and that of our allies, protecting our economic security, and extending our spheres of influence. As a rich and powerful nation, we have many tools at our disposal to achieve these goals, including some tools known as "soft power." At the same time, we are not all-powerful, and to achieve our goals we must work with our allies and other nations.

- The president and his inner circle have the most influence in foreign policy making. In the modern world of instant communication, however, Congress, interest groups, and the public know more than they did before and can play a larger role. Even so, their roles are smaller than in domestic policy.

- Different foreign policy ideas define U.S. policy at different times. Until World War I, the dominant idea was isolationism, but with some exceptions in Latin America and through entrance into World War I. After World War II, containment policy mobilized our soft and hard power alike to prevent the spread of communism. As the communist threat declined, American foreign policy makers entered into agreements with Soviet leaders in a policy called détente.

- Mikhail Gorbachev, the last leader of Soviet Russia, realized that the Soviet Union could not sustain its military efforts and sought agreements with the United States. During the latter part of his administration, Ronald Reagan also realized that the Cold War could no longer be sustained and became a partner in peace efforts.

- Bill Clinton put considerable efforts into America's trade and other economic relationships. He also believed that American power would be used most effectively in partnership with our allies, a policy called multilateralism. When George W. Bush took office, he spurned multilateralism, but the attacks of 9/11 led him to work with our NATO allies to attack Afghanistan and later Iraq.
- Among the many foreign policy challenges the United States faces, the chapter describes four: the challenges posed by nonstate actors, such as guerillas and revolutionary movements; the problem of being at war or ready for war over a sustained period of time; our relationship with China; and the political situation in the Middle East.

DISCUSSION QUESTIONS

1. What are American foreign policy goals in broad terms? Give examples of one use of hard power and one use of soft power in promoting each goal.
2. Discuss the role of Congress and the public in making foreign policy. Compare the influence of each of them to the influence of the president. Why does the public have a lesser role in foreign than domestic policy?
3. Describe isolationism, containment, and détente. How did each policy fit the nature of the times and the power of the United States at that time? Which policy does the war in Vietnam illustrate? Give some reasons why the war failed. Did this lead to a change in overall policy?
4. Why was Ronald Reagan eager to negotiate with Mikhail Gorbachev? Why was Gorbachev eager to negotiate with Reagan? What were the consequences of their negotiations?
5. How did George W. Bush's foreign policy goals and tactics change after 9/11? Were his actions after 9/11 an example of multilateralism or unilateralism or both? Explain. Contrast Bush's foreign policy views with those of Bill Clinton.
6. (a) What are nonstate actors, and why are they important to the United States?
    (b) What implications does being at war most of the time have? Are there ways of mitigating the negative consequences? Describe the military-industrial-political complex.
    (c) How does China's economic power have political consequences? What are some of the current features of U.S. policy toward China?
    (d) How have U.S. presidents sought to mediate conflicts in the Middle East? What are some of the key interests, and why does the United States have a stake in the Middle East?

Appendix A

THE DECLARATION OF INDEPENDENCE*

In Congress, July 4, 1776.

A Declaration by the Representatives of the United States of America, in General Congress assembled.

When in the Course of human Events, it becomes necessary for one People to dissolve the Political Bonds which have connected them with another, and to assume among the Powers of the Earth, the separate and equal Station to which the Laws of Nature and of Nature's God entitle them, a decent Respect to the Opinions of Mankind requires that they should declare the causes which impel them to the Separation.

We hold these Truths to be self-evident, that all Men are created equal, that they are endowed by their Creator with certain unalienable Rights, that among these are Life, Liberty, and the Pursuit of Happiness—That to secure these Rights, Governments are instituted among Men, deriving their just Powers from the Consent of the Governed, that whenever any Form of Government becomes destructive of these Ends, it is the Right of the People to alter or to abolish it, and to institute new Government, laying its Foundation on such Principles, and organizing its Powers in such Forms, as to them shall seem most likely to effect their Safety and Happiness. Prudence, indeed, will dictate that Governments long established should not be changed for light and transient Causes; and accordingly all Experience hath shewn, that Mankind are more disposed to suffer, while Evils are sufferable, than to right themselves by abolishing the Forms to which they are accustomed. But when a long Train of Abuses and Usurpations, pursuing invariably the same Object, evinces a Design to reduce them under absolute Despotism, it is their Right, it is their Duty, to throw off such Government, and to provide new Guards for their future Security. Such has been the patient Sufferance of these Colonies; and such is now the Necessity which constrains them to alter their former Systems of Government. The History of the present King of Great Britain is a History of repeated Injuries and Usurpations, all having in direct Object the Establishment of an absolute Tyranny over these States. To prove this, let facts be submitted to a candid World.

He has refused his Assent to Laws, the most wholesome and necessary for the public Good.

He has forbidden his Governors to pass Laws of immediate and pressing Importance, unless suspended in their Operation till his Assent should be obtained; and when so suspended, he has utterly neglected to attend to them.

He has refused to pass other Laws for the Accommodation of large Districts of People, unless those People would relinquish the Right of Representation in the Legislature, a Right inestimable to them, and formidable to Tyrants only.

He has called together Legislative Bodies at Places unusual, uncomfortable, and distant from the Depository of their Public Records, for the sole Purpose of fatiguing them into Compliance with his Measures.

He has dissolved Representative Houses repeatedly, for opposing with manly Firmness his Invasions on the Rights of the People.

He has refused for a long Time, after such Dissolutions, to cause others to be elected; whereby the Legislative Powers, incapable of Annihilation, have returned to the People at large for their exercise; the State remaining in the mean time exposed to all the Dangers of Invasion from without, and Convulsions within.

He has endeavoured to prevent the Population of these States; for that Purpose obstructing the Laws for Naturalization of Foreigners; refusing to pass others to encourage their Migration hither, and raising the Conditions of new Appropriations of Lands.

He has obstructed the Administration of Justice, by refusing his Assent to Laws for establishing Judiciary Powers.

He has made Judges dependent on his Will alone, for the Tenure of their offices, and the Amount and payments of their Salaries.

He has erected a Multitude of new Offices, and sent hither Swarms of Officers to harass our People, and eat out their Substance.

He has kept among us, in times of Peace, Standing Armies, without the consent of our Legislatures.

He has affected to render the Military independent of, and superior to the Civil Power.

He has combined with others to subject us to a Jurisdiction foreign to our Constitution, and unacknowledged by our Laws; giving his Assent to their Acts of pretended Legislation:

For quartering large Bodies of Armed Troops among us:

For protecting them, by a mock Trial, from Punishment for any Murders which they should commit on the Inhabitants of these States:

For cutting off our Trade with all Parts of the World:

For imposing Taxes on us without our Consent:

---

*The spelling, capitalization, and punctuation of the original have been retained here.

For depriving us, in many cases, of the Benefits of Trial by Jury:

For transporting us beyond Seas to be tried for pretended Offences:

For abolishing the free System of English Laws in a neighbouring Province, establishing therein an arbitrary Government, and enlarging its Boundaries, so as to render it at once an Example and fit Instrument for introducing the same absolute Rule into these Colonies:

For taking away our Charters, abolishing our most valuable Laws, and altering fundamentally the Forms of our Governments:

For suspending our own Legislatures, and declaring themselves invested with Power to legislate for us in all Cases whatsoever.

He has abdicated Government here, by declaring us out of his Protection and waging War against us.

He has plundered our Seas, ravaged our Coasts, burnt our towns, and destroyed the Lives of our People.

He is, at this Time, transporting large Armies of foreign Mercenaries to compleat the works of Death, Desolation, and Tyranny, already begun with circumstances of Cruelty and Perfidy, scarcely paralleled in the most barbarous Ages, and totally unworthy the Head of a civilized Nation.

He has constrained our fellow Citizens taken Captive on the high Seas to bear Arms against their Country, to become the Executioners of their Friends and Brethren, or to fall themselves by their Hands.

He has excited domestic Insurrections amongst us, and has endeavoured to bring on the Inhabitants of our Frontiers, the merciless Indian Savages, whose known Rule of Warfare is an undistinguished Destruction, of all Ages, Sexes and Conditions.

In every state of these Oppressions we have Petitioned for Redress in the most humble Terms: Our repeated Petitions have been answered only by repeated Injury. A Prince, whose Character is thus marked by every act which may define a Tyrant, is unfit to be the Ruler of a free People.

Nor have we been wanting in Attentions to our British Brethren. We have warned them from Time to Time of Attempts by their Legislature to extend an unwarrantable Jurisdiction over us. We have reminded them of the Circumstances of our Emigration and Settlement here. We have appealed to their native Justice and Magnanimity, and we have conjured them by the Ties of our common Kindred to disavow these Usurpations, which would inevitably interrupt our Connections and Correspondence. They too have been deaf to the Voice of Justice and of Consanguinity. We must, therefore, acquiesce in the Necessity, which denounces our Separation, and hold them, as we hold the rest of Mankind, Enemies in War, in Peace Friends.

We, therefore, the Representatives of the UNITED STATES OF AMERICA, in General Congress Assembled, appealing to the Supreme Judge of the World for the Rectitude of our Intentions, do, in the Name, and by Authority of the good People of these Colonies, solemnly Publish and Declare, That these United Colonies are, and of Right ought to be, Free and Independent States; that they are absolved from all Allegiance to the British Crown, and that all political Connection between them and the State of Great Britain, is and ought to be totally dissolved; and that as Free and Independent States, they have full Power to levy War, conclude Peace, contract Alliances, establish Commerce, and to do all other Acts and Things which Independent States may of right do. And for the support of this declaration, with a firm Reliance on the Protection of divine Providence, we mutually pledge to each other our Lives, our Fortunes, and our sacred Honor.

Appendix B

CONSTITUTION OF THE UNITED STATES OF AMERICA*

We the people of the United States, in Order to form a more perfect Union, establish Justice, insure domestic Tranquility, provide for the common defence, promote the general Welfare, and secure the Blessings of Liberty to ourselves and our posterity, do ordain and establish this Constitution for the United States of America.

ARTICLE I

Section 1.   All legislative Powers herein granted shall be vested in a Congress of the United States, which shall consist of a Senate and House of Representatives.

Section 2.   The House of Representatives shall be composed of Members chosen every second Year by the People of the several States, and the Electors in each State shall have the Qualifications requisite for Electors of the most numerous Branch of the State Legislature.

No person shall be a Representative who shall not have attained to the Age of twenty-five Years, and been seven Years a Citizen of the United States, and who shall not, when elected, be an Inhabitant of that State in which he shall be chosen.

Representatives and direct [Taxes][1] shall be apportioned among the several States which may be included within this Union, according to their respective Numbers [which shall be determined by adding to the whole Number of free Persons, including those bound to Service for a Term of Years, and excluding Indians not taxed, three fifths of all other Persons].[2] The actual Enumeration shall be made within three Years after the first Meeting of the Congress of the United States, and within every subsequent Term of ten Years, in such Manner as they shall by Law direct. The Number of Representatives shall not exceed one for every thirty Thousand, but each State shall have at Least one Representative; and until such enumeration shall be made, the State of New Hampshire shall be entitled to chuse three, Massachusetts eight, Rhode Island and Providence Plantations one, Connecticut five, New-York six, New Jersey four, Pennsylvania eight, Delaware one, Maryland six, Virginia ten, North Carolina five, South Carolina five, and Georgia three.

When vacancies happen in the Representation from any State, the Executive Authority thereof shall issue Writs of Election to fill such Vacancies.

The House of Representatives shall chuse their Speaker and other Officers; and shall have the sole Power of Impeachment.

Section 3.   The Senate of the United States shall be composed of two Senators from each State [chosen by the Legislature thereof],[3] for six Years; and each Senator shall have one Vote.

Immediately after they shall be assembled in Consequence of the first Election, they shall be divided as equally as may be into three Classes. The Seats of the Senators of the first Class shall be vacated at the Expiration of the second year, of the second Class at the Expiration of the fourth Year, and of the third Class at the Expiration of the sixth Year, so that one third may be chosen every second Year [and if Vacancies happen by Resignation, or otherwise, during the Recess of the Legislature of any State, the Executive thereof may make temporary Appointments until the next Meeting of the Legislature, which shall then fill such Vacancies.][4]

No Person shall be a Senator who shall not have attained to the Age of thirty Years, and been nine Years a Citizen of the United States, and who shall not, when elected, be an Inhabitant of that State for which he shall be chosen.

The Vice President of the United States shall be President of the Senate, but shall have no Vote, unless they be equally divided.

The Senate shall chuse their other Officers, and also a President pro tempore, in the Absence of the Vice President, or when he shall exercise the Office of President of the United States.

The Senate shall have the sole Power to try all Impeachments. When sitting for that Purpose, they shall be on Oath or Affirmation. When the President of the United States is tried, the Chief Justice shall preside: And no Person shall be convicted without the Concurrence of two thirds of the Members present.

Judgment in Cases of Impeachment shall not extend further than to removal from Office, and disqualification to hold and enjoy any Office of honor, Trust or Profit under the United States; but the Party convicted shall nevertheless be liable and

---

*The spelling, capitalization, and punctuation of the original have been retained here. Brackets indicate passages that have been altered by amendments to the Constitution.

[1] Modified by the Sixteenth Amendment.

[2] Modified by the Fourteenth Amendment.

[3] Repealed by the Seventeenth Amendment.

[4] Modified by the Seventeenth Amendment.

subject to Indictment, Trial, Judgment and Punishment, according to Law.

Section 4. The Times, Places and Manner of holding Elections for Senators and Representatives, shall be prescribed in each State by the Legislature thereof; but the Congress may at any time by Law make or alter such Regulations, except as to the Places of chusing Senators.

[The Congress shall assemble at least once in every Year, and such Meeting shall be on the first Monday in December, unless they shall by Law appoint a different Day.][5]

Section 5. Each House shall be the Judge of the Elections, Returns and Qualifications of its own Members, and a Majority of each shall constitute a Quorum to do Business; but a smaller Number may adjourn from day to day, and may be authorized to compel the Attendance of absent Members, in such Manner, and under such Penalties as each House may provide.

Each House may determine the Rules of its Proceedings, punish its Members for disorderly Behaviour, and, with the Concurrence of two thirds, expel a Member.

Each House shall keep a Journal of its Proceedings, and from time to time publish the same, excepting such Parts as may in their Judgment require Secrecy; and the Yeas and Nays of the Members of either House on any question shall, at the Desire of one fifth of those present, be entered on the Journal.

Neither House, during the Session of Congress, shall, without the Consent of the other, adjourn for more than three days, nor to any other Place than that in which the two Houses shall be sitting.

Section 6. The Senators and Representatives shall receive a Compensation for their Services, to be ascertained by Law, and paid out of the Treasury of the United States. They shall in all Cases, except Treason, Felony and Breach of the Peace, be privileged from Arrest during their Attendance at the Session of their respective Houses, and in going to and returning from the same; and for any Speech or Debate in either House, they shall not be questioned in any other Place.

No Senator or Representative shall, during the Time for which he was elected, be appointed to any civil Office under the Authority of the United States, which shall have been created, or the Emoluments whereof shall have been encreased during such time; and no Person holding any Office under the United States, shall be a Member of either House during his Continuance in Office.

Section 7. All Bills for raising Revenue shall originate in the House of Representatives; but the Senate may propose or concur with Amendments as on other Bills.

Every Bill which shall have passed the House of Representatives and the Senate, shall, before it become a Law, be presented to the President of the United States; If he approves he shall sign it, but if not he shall return it, with his objections to that House in which it shall have originated, who shall enter the Objections at large on their Journal, and proceed to reconsider it. If after such Reconsideration two

thirds of that House shall agree to pass the Bill, it shall be sent, together with the Objections, to the other House, by which it shall likewise be reconsidered, and if approved by two thirds of that House, it shall become a Law. But in all such Cases the Votes of both Houses shall be determined by yeas and Nays, and the Names of the Persons voting for and against the Bill shall be entered on the Journal of each House respectively. If any Bill shall not be returned by the President within ten Days (Sundays excepted) after it shall have been presented to him, the Same shall be a Law, in like Manner as if he had signed it, unless the Congress by their Adjournment prevent its Return, in which Case it shall not be a Law.

Every Order, Resolution, or Vote to which the Concurrence of the Senate and House of Representatives may be necessary (except on a question of Adjournment) shall be presented to the President of the United States; and before the Same shall take Effect, shall be approved by him, or being disapproved by him, shall be repassed by two thirds of the Senate and House of Representatives, according to the Rules and Limitations prescribed in the Case of a Bill.

Section 8. The Congress shall have Power To lay and collect Taxes, Duties, Imposts and Excises, to pay the Debts and provide for the common Defence and general Welfare of the United States; but all Duties, Imposts and Excises shall be uniform throughout the United States;

To borrow Money on the credit of the United States;

To regulate Commerce with foreign Nations, and among the several States, and with the Indian Tribes;

To establish a uniform Rule of Naturalization, and uniform Laws on the subject of Bankruptcies throughout the United States;

To coin Money, regulate the Value thereof, and of foreign Coin, and fix the Standard of Weights and Measures;

To provide for the Punishment of counterfeiting the Securities and current Coin of the United States;

To establish Post Offices and post Roads;

To promote the Progress of Science and useful Arts, by securing for limited Times to Authors and Inventors the exclusive Right to their respective Writings and Discoveries;

To constitute Tribunals inferior to the supreme Court;

To define and punish Piracies and Felonies committed on the high Seas, and Offences against the Law of Nations;

To declare War, grant Letters of Marque and Reprisal, and make Rules concerning Captures on Land and Water;

To raise and support Armies, but no Appropriation of Money to that Use shall be for a longer Term than two Years;

To provide and maintain a Navy;

To make Rules for the Government and Regulation of the land and naval Forces;

To provide for calling forth the Militia to execute the Laws of the Union, suppress Insurrections and repel Invasions;

To provide for organizing, arming, and disciplining the Militia, and for governing such Part of them as may be employed in the Service of the United States, reserving to the States respectively, the Appointment of the Officers, and the Authority of training the Militia according to the discipline prescribed by Congress;

[5.] Changed by the Twentieth Amendment.

To exercise exclusive Legislation in all Cases whatsoever, over such District (not exceeding ten Miles square) as may, by Cession of particular States, and the Acceptance of Congress, become the Seat of the Government of the United States, and to exercise like Authority over all Places purchased by the Consent of the Legislature of the State in which the Same shall be, for the Erection of forts, Magazines, Arsenals, dockYards, and other needful Buildings;—And

To make all Laws which shall be necessary and proper for carrying into Execution the foregoing Powers, and all other Powers vested by this Constitution in the Government of the United States, or in any Department or Officer thereof.

Section 9.   The Migration or Importation of such Persons as any of the States now existing shall think proper to admit, shall not be prohibited by the Congress prior to the Year one thousand eight hundred and eight, but a Tax or duty may be imposed on such Importation, not exceeding ten dollars for each Person.

The Privilege of the Writ of Habeas Corpus shall not be suspended, unless when in Cases of Rebellion or Invasion the public Safety may require it.

No Bill of Attainder or ex post facto Law shall be passed.

[No Capitation, or other direct, Tax shall be laid, unless in Proportion to the Census or Enumeration herein before directed to be taken.][6]

No Tax or Duty shall be laid on Articles exported from any State.

No Preference shall be given by any Regulation of Commerce or Revenue to the Ports of one State over those of another; nor shall Vessels bound to, or from, one State, be obliged to enter, clear, or pay Duties in another.

No Money shall be drawn from the Treasury, but in Consequence of Appropriations made by Law; and a regular Statement and Account of the Receipts and Expenditures of all public Money shall be published from time to time.

No Title of Nobility shall be granted by the United States; and no Person holding any Office or Profit or Trust under them, shall, without the Consent of the Congress, accept of any present, Emolument, Office, or Title, of any kind whatever, from any King, Prince, or foreign State.

Section 10.   No state shall enter into any Treaty, Alliance, or Confederation; grant Letters of Marque and Reprisal; coin Money; emit Bills of Credit; make any Thing but gold and silver Coin a Tender in Payment of Debts; pass any Bill of Attainder, ex post facto Law, or Law impairing the Obligation of Contracts, or grant any Title of Nobility.

No State shall, without the Consent of the Congress, lay any Imposts or Duties on Imports or Exports, except what may be absolutely necessary for executing its inspection Laws; and the net Produce of all Duties and Imposts, laid by any State on Imports or Exports, shall be for the Use of the Treasury of the United States; and all such Laws shall be subject to the Revision and Controul of the Congress.

No State shall, without the Consent of Congress, lay any duty of Tonnage, keep Troops, or Ships of War in time of Peace, enter into any Agreement or Compact with another State, or with a foreign Power or engage in War, unless actually invaded, or in such imminent Danger as will not admit of delay.

ARTICLE II

Section 1.   The executive Power shall be vested in a President of the United States of America. He shall hold his Office during the Term of four Years, and, together with the Vice President, chosen for the Same Term, be elected, as follows.

Each State shall appoint, in such Manner as the Legislature thereof may direct, a Number of Electors, equal to the whole Number of Senators and Representatives to which the State may be entitled in the Congress; but no Senator or Representative, or Person holding an Office of Trust or Profit under the United States, shall be appointed an Elector.

[The Electors shall meet in their respective States, and vote by Ballot for two Persons of whom one at least shall not be an Inhabitant of the same State with themselves. And they shall make a List of all the Persons voted for, and of the Number of Votes for each; which List they shall sign and certify, and transmit sealed to the Seat of the Government of the United States, directed to the President of the Senate. The President of the Senate shall, in the Presence of the Senate and House of Representatives, open all the Certificates, and the Votes shall then be counted. The Person having the greatest Number of Votes shall be the President, if such Number be a Majority of the whole Number of Electors appointed; and if there be more than one who have such Majority, and have an equal Number of Votes, then the House of Representatives shall immediately chuse by Ballot one of them for President; and if no Person have a Majority, then from the five highest on the List the said House shall in like Manner chuse the President. But in chusing the President, the Votes shall be taken by States, the Representation from each State having one Vote; A quorum for this Purpose shall consist of a Member or Members from two thirds of the States, and a Majority of all the states shall be necessary to a Choice. In every Case, after the Choice of the President, the Person having the greatest Number of Votes of the Electors shall be the Vice President. But if there should remain two or more who have equal Votes, the Senate shall chuse from them by Ballot the Vice President.][7]

The Congress may determine the Time of chusing the Electors, and the Day on which they shall give their Votes; which Day shall be the same throughout the United States.

No person except a natural born Citizen, or a Citizen of the United States, at the time of the Adoption of this Constitution, shall be eligible to the Office of President; neither shall any Person be eligible to that Office who shall not have attained to the Age of thirty five Years, and been fourteen Years a Resident within the United States.

[In Case of the Removal of the President from Office, or of his Death, Resignation, or Inability to discharge the Powers

---

[6.] Modified by the Sixteenth Amendment.

[7.] Changed by the Twelfth Amendment.

and Duties of the said Office, the same shall devolve on the Vice President, and the Congress may by Law provide for the Case of Removal, Death, Resignation or Inability, both of the President and Vice President, declaring what Officer shall then act as President, and such Officer shall act accordingly, until the Disability be removed, or a President shall be elected.][8]

The President shall, at stated Times, receive for his Services, a Compensation, which shall neither be increased nor diminished during the Period for which he shall have been elected, and he shall not receive within that Period any other Emolument from the United States, or any of them.

Before he enter on the Execution of his Office, he shall take the following Oath or Affirmation:—"I do solemnly swear (or affirm) that I will faithfully execute the Office of President of the United States, and will to the best of my Ability, preserve, protect and defend the constitution of the United States."

Section 2. The President shall be Commander in Chief of the Army and Navy of the United States, and of the Militia of the several States, when called into the actual Service of the United States; he may require the Opinion, in writing, of the principal Officer in each of the executive Departments, upon any Subject relating to the Duties of their respective Offices, and he shall have Power to grant Reprieves and Pardons for Offences against the United States, except in Cases of Impeachment.

He shall have Power, by and with the Advice and Consent of the Senate, to make Treaties, provided two thirds of the Senators present concur; and he shall nominate, and by and with the Advice and Consent of the Senate, shall appoint Ambassadors, other public Ministers and Consuls, Judges of the supreme Court, and all other Officers of the United States, whose Appointments are not herein otherwise provided for, and which shall be established by Law; but the Congress may by Law vest the Appointment of such inferior Officers, as they think proper, in the President alone, in the Courts of Law, or in the Heads of Departments.

The President shall have Power to fill up all Vacancies that may happen during the Recess of the Senate, by granting Commissions which shall expire at the end of their next Session.

Section 3. He shall from time to time give to the Congress Information of the State of the Union, and recommend to their Consideration such Measures as he shall judge necessary and expedient; he may, on extraordinary Occasions, convene both Houses, or either of them, and in Case of Disagreement between them, with Respect to the Time of Adjournment, he may adjourn them to such Time as he shall think proper; he shall receive Ambassadors and other public Ministers; he shall take Care that the Laws be faithfully executed, and shall Commission all the Officers of the United States.

Section 4. The President, Vice President and all civil Officers of the United States, shall be removed from Office on Impeachment for, and Conviction of, Treason, Bribery, or other high Crimes and Misdemeanors.

ARTICLE III

Section 1. The judicial Power of the United States, shall be vested in one supreme Court, and in such inferior Courts as the Congress may from time to time ordain and establish. The Judges, both of the supreme and inferior Courts, shall hold their Offices during good Behaviour, and shall, at stated Times, receive for their Services, a Compensation, which shall not be diminished during their Continuance in Office.

Section 2. The judicial Power shall extend to all Cases, in Law and Equity, arising under this Constitution, the Laws of the United States, and Treaties made, or which shall be made, under their Authority;—to all Cases affecting Ambassadors, other public Ministers and Consuls;—to all Cases of admiralty and maritime Jurisdiction;—to Controversies to which the United States shall be a Party;—to Controversies between two or more States;—[between a State and Citizens of another State;][9]—between Citizens of different States,—between Citizens of the same State claiming Lands under Grants of different States, [and between a state, or the Citizens thereof, and foreign States, Citizens or Subjects.][10]

In all cases affecting Ambassadors, other public Ministers and Consuls, and those in which a State shall be Party, the supreme Court shall have original Jurisdiction. In all the other Cases before mentioned, the supreme Court shall have appellate Jurisdiction, both as to Law and Fact, with such Exceptions, and under such Regulations as the Congress shall make.

The Trial of all Crimes, except in Cases of Impeachment, shall be by Jury; and such Trial shall be held in the State where the said Crimes shall have been committed; but when not committed within any State, the Trial shall be at such Place or Places as the Congress may by Law have directed.

Section 3. Treason against the United States, shall consist only in levying War against them, or in adhering to their Enemies, giving them Aid and Comfort. No Person shall be convicted of Treason unless on the Testimony of two Witnesses to the same overt Act, or on Confession in open Court.

The Congress shall have Power to declare the Punishment of Treason, but no Attainder of Treason shall work Corruption of Blood, or Forfeiture except during the Life of the Person attainted.

ARTICLE IV

Section 1. Full Faith and Credit shall be given in each State to the public Acts, Records, and judicial Proceedings of every other State. And the Congress may by general Laws prescribe the Manner in which such Acts, Records and Proceedings shall be proved, and the Effect thereof.

[8.] Modified by the Twenty-fifth Amendment.

[9.] Modified by the Eleventh Amendment.

[10.] Modified by the Eleventh Amendment.

Section 2. The Citizens of each State shall be entitled to all Privileges and Immunities of Citizens in the several States.

A Person charged in any State with Treason, Felony, or other Crime, who shall flee from Justice, and be found in another State, shall on Demand of the executive Authority of the State from which he fled, be delivered up, to be removed to the State having Jurisdiction of the Crime.

[No Person held to Service or Labour in one State under the Laws thereof, escaping into another, shall, in Consequence of any Law or Regulation therein, be discharged from such Service or Labour, but shall be delivered up on Claim of the Party to whom such Service or Labour may be due.][11]

Section 3. New States may be admitted by the Congress into this Union; but no new State shall be formed or erected within the Jurisdiction of any other State; nor any State be formed by the Junction of two or more States, or Parts of States, without the Consent of the Legislatures of the States concerned as well as of the Congress.

The Congress shall have Power to dispose of and make all needful Rules and Regulations respecting the Territory or other Property belonging to the United States; and nothing in this Constitution shall be so construed as to Prejudice any Claims of the United States, or of any particular State.

Section 4. The United States shall guarantee to every State in this Union a Republican Form of Government, and shall protect each of them against Invasion, and on Application of the Legislature, or of the Executive (when the Legislature cannot be convened) against domestic Violence.

ARTICLE V

The Congress, whenever two thirds of both Houses shall deem it necessary, shall propose Amendments to this Constitution, or on the Application of the Legislatures of two thirds of the several States, shall call a Convention for proposing Amendments, which, in either Case, shall be valid to all Intents and Purposes, as Part of this Constitution, when ratified by the Legislatures of three fourths of the several States, or by Conventions in three fourths thereof, as the one or the other Mode of Ratification may be proposed by the Congress; Provided that no Amendment which may be made prior to the Year One thousand eight hundred and eight shall in any Manner affect the first and fourth Clauses in the Ninth Section of the first Article; and that no State, without its Consent, shall be deprived of its equal Suffrage in the Senate.

ARTICLE VI

All Debts contracted and Engagements entered into, before the Adoption of this Constitution, shall be as valid against the United States under this Constitution, as under the Confederation.

This Constitution, and the laws of the United States which shall be made in Pursuance thereof; and all Treaties made, or which shall be made, under the Authority of the United States, shall be the supreme Law of the Land; and the Judges in every State shall be bound thereby, any Thing in the Constitution or Laws of any State to the Contrary notwithstanding.

The Senators and Representatives before mentioned, and the Members of the several State Legislatures, and all executive and judicial Officers, both of the United States and of the several States, shall be bound by Oath or Affirmation, to support this Constitution; but no religious Test shall ever be required as a Qualification to any Office or public Trust under the United States.

ARTICLE VII

The Ratification of the Conventions of nine States, shall be sufficient for the Establishment of this constitution between the States so ratifying the Same.

Done in Convention by the Unanimous Consent of the States present the Seventeenth Day of September in the Year of our Lord one thousand seven hundred and Eighty seven and of the Independence of the United States of America the Twelfth. In Witness whereof we have hereunto subscribed our Names.

Go. WASHINGTON
Presid't. and deputy from Virginia
Attest
William Jackson
Secretary

Delaware

Geo. Read	*Gunning Bedford jun*
John Dickinson	*Richard Basset*
Jaco. Broon	

Massachusetts

Nathaniel Gorham	*Rufus King*

Connecticut

Wm. Saml. Johnson	*Roger Sherman*

New York

Alexander Hamilton	

New Jersey

Wh. Livingston	*David Brearley*
Wm. Paterson	*Jona. Dayton*

Pennsylvania

B. Franklin	*Thomas Mifflin*
Robt. Morris	*Geo. Clymer*
Thos. FitzSimons	*Jared Ingersoll*
James Wilson	*Gouv Morris*

Virginia

John Blair	*James Madison Jr.*

North Carolina

Wm. Blount	*Richd. Dobbs Spaight*
Hu Williamson	

South Carolina

J. Rutledge	*Charles Cotesworth*
Pinckney	*Charles Pinckney*
Pierce Butler	

Georgia

William Few	*Abr. Baldwin*

[11.] Repealed by the Thirteenth Amendment.

New Hampshire

John Langdon   *Nicholas Gilman*

Maryland

James McHenry   *Dan of St Thos. Jenifer*

Danl. Carroll

AMENDMENT I[12]

Congress shall make no law respecting an establishment of religion, or prohibiting the free exercise thereof; or abridging the freedom of speech, or of the press; or the right of the people peaceably to assemble, and to petition the Government for a redress of grievances.

AMENDMENT II

A well regulated militia, being necessary to the security of a free State, the right of the people to keep and bear arms, shall not be infringed.

AMENDMENT III

No Soldier shall, in time of peace be quartered in any house, without the consent of the owner, nor in time of war, but in a manner to be prescribed by law.

AMENDMENT IV

The right of the people to be secure in their persons, houses, papers, and effects, against unreasonable searches and seizures, shall not be violated, and no warrants shall issue, but upon probable cause, supported by oath or affirmation, and particularly describing the place to be searched, and the persons or things to be seized.

AMENDMENT V

No person shall be held to answer for a capital, or otherwise infamous crime, unless on a presentment or indictment of a Grand Jury, except in cases arising in the land or naval forces, or in the militia, when in actual service in time of war or public danger; nor shall any person be subject for the same offence to be twice put in jeopardy of life or limb; nor shall be compelled in any criminal case to be a witness against himself, nor be deprived of life, liberty, or property, without due process of law; nor shall private property be taken for public use, without just compensation.

AMENDMENT VI

In all criminal prosecutions, the accused shall enjoy the right to a speedy and public trial, by an impartial jury of the State and district wherein the crime shall have been committed, which district shall have been previously ascertained by law,

and to be informed of the nature and cause of the accusation; to be confronted with the witnesses against him; to have compulsory process for obtaining witnesses in his favor, and to have the assistance of counsel for his defence.

AMENDMENT VII

In Suits at common law, where the value in controversy shall exceed twenty dollars, the right of trial by jury shall be preserved, and no fact tried by a jury, shall be otherwise reexamined in any Court of the United States, than according to the rules of the common law.

AMENDMENT VIII

Excessive bail shall not be required, nor excessive fines imposed, nor cruel and unusual punishments inflicted.

AMENDMENT IX

The enumeration in the Constitution, of certain rights, shall not be construed to deny or disparage others retained by the people.

AMENDMENT X

The powers not delegated to the United States by the Constitution, nor prohibited by it to the States, are reserved to the States respectively, or to the people.

AMENDMENT XI (RATIFIED FEBRUARY 7, 1795)

The Judicial power of the United States shall not be construed to extend to any suit in law or equity, commenced or prosecuted against one of the United States by Citizens of another State, or by Citizens or Subjects of any Foreign State.

AMENDMENT XII (RATIFIED JUNE 15, 1804)

The Electors shall meet in their respective states, and vote by ballot for President and Vice-President, one of whom, at least, shall not be an inhabitant of the same state with themselves; they shall name in their ballots the person voted for as President, and in distinct ballots the person voted for as Vice President, and they shall make distinct lists of all persons voted for as President, and of all persons voted for as Vice-President, and of the number of votes for each, which lists they shall sign and certify, and transmit sealed to the seat of the government of the United States, directed to the President of the Senate;—The President of the Senate shall, in the presence of the Senate and House of Representatives, open all the certificates and the votes shall then be counted;—The person having the greatest number of votes for President, shall be the President, if such number be a majority of the whole

---

[12] The first ten amendments were passed by Congress on September 25, 1789, and were ratified on December 15, 1791.

number of Electors appointed; and if no person have such majority, then from the persons having the highest numbers not exceeding three on the list of those voted for as President, the House of Representatives shall choose immediately, by ballot, the President. But in choosing the President, the votes shall be taken by states, the representation from each state having one vote; a quorum for this purpose shall consist of a member or members from two-thirds of the states, and a majority of all the states shall be necessary to a choice. [And if the House of Representatives shall not choose a President whenever the right of choice shall devolve upon them, before the fourth day of March next following, then the Vice-President shall act as President, as in the case of the death or other constitutional disability of the President.][13]—The person having the greatest number of votes as Vice-President, shall be the Vice-President, if such number be a majority of the whole number of Electors appointed, and if no person have a majority, then from the two highest numbers on the list, the Senate shall choose the Vice-President; a quorum for the purpose shall consist of two-thirds of the whole number of Senators, and a majority of the whole number shall be necessary to a choice. But no person constitutionally ineligible to the office of President shall be eligible to that of Vice-President of the United States.

AMENDMENT XIII (RATIFIED ON DECEMBER 6, 1865)

Section 1.   Neither slavery nor involuntary servitude, except as a punishment for crime whereof the party shall have been duly convicted, shall exist within the United States, or any place subject to their jurisdiction.

Section 2.   Congress shall have power to enforce this article by appropriate legislation.

AMENDMENT XIV (RATIFIED ON JULY 9, 1868)

Section 1.   All persons born or naturalized in the United States, and subject to the jurisdiction thereof, are citizens of the United States and of the State wherein they reside. No State shall make or enforce any law which shall abridge the privileges or immunities of citizens of the United States; nor shall any State deprive any person of life, liberty, or property, without due process of law; nor deny to any person within its jurisdiction the equal protection of the laws.

Section 2.   Representatives shall be apportioned among the several States according to their respective numbers, counting the whole number of persons in each State, excluding Indians not taxed. But when the right to vote at any election for the choice of electors for President and Vice President of the United States, Representatives in Congress, the Executive and Judicial officers of a State, or the members of the Legislature thereof, is denied to any of the male inhabitants

of such State, being [twenty-one][14] years of age, and citizens of the United States, or in any way abridged, except for participation in rebellion, or other crime, the basis of representation therein shall be reduced in the proportion which the number of such male citizens shall bear to the whole number of male citizens twenty-one years of age in such State.

Section 3.   No person shall be a Senator or Representative in Congress, or elector of President and Vice President, or hold any office, civil or military, under the United States, or under any State, who having previously taken an oath, as a member of Congress, or as an officer of the United States, or as a member of any State legislature, or as an executive or judicial officer of any State, to support the Constitution of the United States, shall have engaged in insurrection or rebellion against the same, or given aid or comfort to the enemies thereof. But Congress may by a vote of two-thirds of each House, remove such disability.

Section 4.   The validity of the public debt of the United States, authorized by law, including debts incurred for payment of pensions and bounties for services in suppressing insurrection or rebellion, shall not be questioned. But neither the United States nor any State shall assume or pay any debt or obligation incurred in aid of insurrection or rebellion against the United States, or any claim for the loss or emancipation of any slave, but all such debts, obligations and claims shall be held illegal and void.

Section 5.   The Congress shall have power to enforce, by appropriate legislation, the provisions of this article.

AMENDMENT XV (RATIFIED ON FEBRUARY 3, 1870)

Section 1.   The right of citizens of the United States to vote shall not be denied or abridged by the United States or by any State on account of race, color, or previous condition of servitude.

Section 2.   The Congress shall have power to enforce this article by appropriate legislation.

AMENDMENT XVI (RATIFIED ON FEBRUARY 3, 1913)

The Congress shall have power to lay and collect taxes on incomes, from whatever source derived, without apportionment among the several States, and without regard to any census or enumeration.

AMENDMENT XVII (RATIFIED ON APRIL 8, 1913)

The Senate of the United States shall be composed of two Senators from each State, elected by the people thereof, for six years; and each Senator shall have one vote. The electors in

---

[13.] Changed by the Twentieth Amendment.

[14.] Changed by the Twenty-sixth Amendment.

each State shall have the qualifications requisite for electors of the most numerous branch of the State legislatures.

When vacancies happen in the representation of any State in the Senate, the executive authority of such State shall issue writs of election to fill such vacancies: *Provided,* That the legislature of any State may empower the executive thereof to make temporary appointments until the people fill the vacancies by election as the legislature may direct.

This amendment shall not be so construed as to affect the election or term of any Senator chosen before it becomes valid as part of the Constitution.

AMENDMENT XVIII (RATIFIED ON JANUARY 16, 1919)

Section 1.   After one year from the ratification of this article the manufacture, sale, or transportation of intoxicating liquors within, the importation thereof into, or the exportation thereof from the United States and all territory subject to the jurisdiction thereof for beverage purposes is hereby prohibited.

Section 2.   The Congress and the several States shall have concurrent power to enforce this article by appropriate legislation.

Section 3.   This article shall be inoperative unless it shall have been ratified as an amendment to the Constitution by the legislatures of the several States, as provided in the Constitution, within seven years from the date of the submission hereof to the States by the Congress.[15]

AMENDMENT XIX (RATIFIED ON AUGUST 18, 1920)

The right of citizens of the United States to vote shall not be denied or abridged by the United States or by any State on account of sex.

Congress shall have power to enforce this article by appropriate legislation.

AMENDMENT XX (RATIFIED ON JANUARY 23, 1933)

Section 1.   The terms of the President and Vice President shall end at noon on the 20th day of January, and the terms of Senators and Representatives at noon on the 3rd day of January, of the years in which such terms would have ended if this article had not been ratified, and the terms of their successors shall then begin.

Section 2.   The Congress shall assemble at least once in every year, and such meeting shall begin at noon on the 3rd day of January, unless they shall by law appoint a different day.

Section 3.   If, at the time fixed for the beginning of the term of the President, the President elect shall have died, the Vice President elect shall become President. If a President shall not have been chosen before the time fixed for the beginning of his term, or if the President elect shall have failed to qualify, then the Vice President elect shall act as President until a President shall have qualified; and the Congress may by law provide for the case wherein neither a President elect nor a Vice President elect shall have qualified, declaring who shall then act as President, or the manner in which one who is to act shall be selected, and such person shall act accordingly until a President or Vice President shall have qualified.

Section 4.   The Congress may by law provide for the case of the death of any of the persons from whom the House of Representatives may choose a President whenever the rights of choice shall have devolved upon them, and for the case of the death of any of the persons from whom the Senate may choose a Vice President whenever the right of choice shall have devolved upon them.

Section 5.   Sections 1 and 2 shall take effect on the 15th day of October following the ratification of this article.

Section 6.   This article shall be inoperative unless it shall have been ratified as an amendment to the Constitution by the legislatures of three-fourths of the several States within seven years from the date of its submission.

AMENDMENT XXI (RATIFIED ON DECEMBER 5, 1933)

Section 1.   The eighteenth article of amendment to the Constitution of the United States is hereby repealed.

Section 2.   The transportation or importation into any State, Territory, or possession of the United States for delivery or use therein of intoxicating liquors, in violation of the laws thereof, is hereby prohibited.

Section 3.   This article shall be inoperative unless it shall have been ratified as an amendment to the Constitution by conventions in the several States, as provided in the Constitution, within seven years from the date of the submission hereof to the States by the Congress.

AMENDMENT XXII (RATIFIED ON FEBRUARY 27, 1951)

No person shall be elected to the office of the President more than twice, and no person who has held the office of President, or acted as President, for more than two years of a term to which some other person was elected President shall be elected to the office of the President more than once. But this Article shall not apply to any person holding the office of President when this Article was proposed by the Congress, and shall not prevent any person who may be holding the office of President, or acting as President, during the term within which this Article becomes operative from holding the

---

[15.] The Eighteenth Amendment was repealed by the Twenty-first Amendment.

office of President or acting as President during the remainder of such term.

AMENDMENT XXIII (RATIFIED ON MARCH 29, 1961)

Section 1. The District constituting the seat of Government of the United States shall appoint in such manner as the Congress may direct:

A number of electors of President and Vice President equal to the whole number of Senators and Representatives in Congress to which the District would be entitled if it were a State, but in no event more than the least populous State; they shall be in addition to those appointed by the States, but they shall be considered, for the purposes of the election of President and Vice President, to be electors appointed by a State; and they shall meet in the District and perform such duties as provided by the twelfth article of amendment.

Section 2. The Congress shall have power to enforce this article by appropriate legislation.

AMENDMENT XXIV (RATIFIED ON JANUARY 23, 1964)

Section 1. The right of citizens of the United States to vote in any primary or other election for President or Vice President, for electors for President or Vice President, or for Senator or Representative in Congress, shall not be denied or abridged by the United States or any State by reason of failure to pay any poll tax or other tax.

Section 2. The Congress shall have power to enforce this article by appropriate legislation.

AMENDMENT XXV (RATIFIED ON FEBRUARY 10, 1967)

Section 1. In case of the removal of the President from office or of his death or resignation, the Vice President shall become President.

Section 2. Whenever there is a vacancy in the office of the Vice President, the President shall nominate a Vice President who shall take office upon confirmation by a majority vote of both Houses of Congress.

Section 3. Whenever the President transmits to the President pro tempore of the Senate and the Speaker of the House of Representatives his written declaration that he is unable to discharge the powers and duties of his office, and until he transmits to them a written declaration to the

contrary, such powers and duties shall be discharged by the Vice President as Acting President.

Section 4. Whenever the Vice President and a majority of either the principal officers of the executive departments or of such other body as Congress may by law provide, transmit to the President pro tempore of the Senate and the Speaker of the House of Representatives their written declaration that the President is unable to discharge the powers and duties of his office, the Vice President shall immediately assume the powers and duties of the offices as Acting President.

Thereafter, when the President transmits to the President pro tempore of the Senate and the Speaker of Representatives his written declaration that no inability exists, he shall resume the powers and duties of his office unless the Vice President and a majority of either the principal officers of the executive department or of such other body as Congress may by law provide, transmit within four days to the President pro tempore of the Senate and the Speaker of the House of Representatives their written declaration that the President is unable to discharge the powers and duties of his office. Thereupon Congress shall decide the issue, assembling within forty-eight hours for that purpose if not in session. If the Congress, within twenty-one days after receipt of the latter written declaration, or, if Congress is not in session, within twenty-one days after Congress is required to assemble, determines by two-thirds vote of both Houses that the President is unable to discharge the powers and duties of his office, the Vice President shall continue to discharge the same as Acting President; otherwise, the President shall resume the powers and duties of his office.

AMENDMENT XXVI (RATIFIED ON JULY 1, 1971)

Section 1. The right of citizens of the United States, who are eighteen years of age or older, to vote shall not be denied or abridged by the United States or by any State on account of age.

Section 2. The Congress shall have the power to enforce this article by appropriate legislation.

AMENDMENT XXVII (RATIFIED ON MAY 7, 1992)

No law, varying the compensation for the services of the Senators and Representatives, shall take effect, until an election of Representatives shall have intervened.

FEDERALIST PAPER 10

Among the numerous advantages promised by a well-constructed Union, none deserves to be more accurately developed than its tendency to break and control the violence of faction. The friend of popular governments never finds himself so much alarmed for their character and fate as when he contemplates their propensity to this dangerous vice. He will not fail, therefore, to set a due value on any plan which, without violating the principles to which he is attached, provides a proper cure for it. The instability, injustice, and confusion introduced into the public councils have, in truth, been the mortal diseases under which popular governments have everywhere perished, as they continue to be the favorite and fruitful topics from which the adversaries to liberty derive their most specious declamations. The valuable improvements made by the American constitutions on the popular models, both ancient and modern, cannot certainly be too much admired; but it would be an unwarrantable partiality to contend that they have as effectually obviated the danger on this side, as was wished and expected. Complaints are everywhere heard from our most considerate and virtuous citizens, equally the friends of public and private faith and of public and personal liberty, that our governments are too unstable, that the public good is disregarded in the conflicts of rival parties, and that measures are too often decided, not according to the rules of justice and the rights of the minor party, but by the superior force of an interested and overbearing majority. However anxiously we may wish that these complaints had no foundation, the evidence of known facts will not permit us to deny that they are in some degree true. It will be found, indeed, on a candid review of our situation, that some of the distresses under which we labor have been erroneously charged on the operation of our governments; but it will be found, at the same time, that other causes will not alone account for many of our heaviest misfortunes; and, particularly, for that prevailing and increasing distrust of public engagements and alarm for private rights which are echoed from one end of the continent to the other. These must be chiefly, if not wholly, effects of the unsteadiness and injustice with which a factious spirit has tainted our public administration.

By a faction I understand a number of citizens, whether amounting to a majority or minority of the whole, who are united and actuated by some common impulse of passion, or of interest, adverse to the rights of other citizens, or the permanent and aggregate interests of the community.

There are two methods of curing the mischiefs of faction: the one, by removing its causes; the other, by controlling its effects.

There are again two methods of removing the causes of faction: the one, by destroying the liberty which is essential to its existence; the other, by giving to every citizen the same opinions, the same passions, and the same interests.

It could never be more truly said than of the first remedy that it was worse than the disease. Liberty is to faction what air is to fire, an aliment without which it instantly expires. But it could not be a less folly to abolish liberty, which is essential to political life, because it nourishes faction than it would be to wish the annihilation of air, which is essential to animal life, because it imparts to fire its destructive agency.

The second expedient is as impracticable as the first would be unwise. As long as the reason of man continues fallible, and his is at liberty to exercise it, different opinions will be formed. As long as the connection subsists between his reason and his self-love, his opinions and his passions will have a reciprocal influence on each other; and the former will be objects to which the latter will attach themselves. The diversity in the faculties of men, from which the rights of property originate, is not less an insuperable obstacle to a uniformity of interests. The protection of these faculties is the first object of government. From the protection of different and unequal faculties of acquiring property, the possession of different degrees and kinds of property immediately results; and from the influence of these on the sentiments and views of the respective proprietors ensues a division of the society into different interests and parties.

The latent causes of faction are thus sown in the nature of man; and we see them everywhere brought into different degrees of activity, according to the different circumstances of civil society. A zeal for different opinions concerning religion, concerning government, and many other points, as well of speculation as of practice; an attachment to different leaders ambitiously contending for pre-eminence and power; or to persons of other descriptions whose fortunes have been interesting to the human passions, have, in turn, divided mankind into parties, inflamed them with mutual animosity, and rendered them much more disposed to vex and oppress each other than to cooperate for their common good. So strong is this propensity of mankind to fall into mutual animosities that where no substantial occasion presents itself the most frivolous and fanciful distinctions have been sufficient to kindle their unfriendly passions and excite their most violent conflicts. But the most common and durable source of factions has been the various and unequal distribution of property. Those who hold and those who are without property have ever formed distinct interests in society. Those who are creditors, and those who are debtors, fall under a like discrimination. A landed interest, a manufacturing interest, a mercantile interest, a moneyed interest, with many lesser interests, grow up of necessity in civilized nations, and divide them into different classes, actuated by different sentiments and views. The regulation of these various and interfering interests forms the principal task of modern legislation and involves the spirit of party and faction in the necessary and ordinary operations of government.

No man is allowed to be a judge in his own cause, because his interest would certainly bias his judgment, and, not improbably, corrupt his integrity. With equal, nay with greater reason, a body of men are unfit to be both judges and parties at the same time; yet what are many of the most important acts of legislation but so many judicial determinations, not indeed concerning the rights of single persons, but concerning the rights of large bodies of citizens? And what are the different classes of legislators but advocates and parties to the causes which they determine? Is a law proposed concerning private debts? It is a question to which the creditors are parties on one side and the debtors on the other. Justice ought to hold the balance between them. Yet the parties are, and must be, themselves the judges; and the most numerous party, or in other words, the most powerful faction must be expected to prevail. Shall domestic manufacturers be encouraged, and in what degree, by restrictions on foreign manufacturers? are questions which would be differently decided by the landed and the manufacturing classes, and probably by neither with a sole regard to justice and the public good. The apportionment of taxes on the various descriptions of property is an act which seems to require the most exact impartiality; yet there is, perhaps, no legislative act in which greater opportunity and temptation are given to a predominant party to trample on the rules of justice. Every shilling with which they overburden the inferior number is a shilling saved to their own pockets. It is in vain to say that enlightened statesmen will be able to adjust these clashing interests and render them all subservient to the public good. Enlightened statesmen will not always be at the helm. Nor, in many cases, can such an adjustment be made at all without taking into view indirect and remote considerations, which will rarely prevail over the immediate interest which one party may find in disregarding the rights of another or the good of the whole.

The inference to which we are brought is that the *causes* of faction cannot be removed and that relief is only to be sought in the means of controlling its *effects*.

If a faction consists of less than a majority, relief is supplied by the republican principle, which enables the majority to defeat its sinister views by regular vote. It may clog the administration, it may convulse the society; but it will be unable to execute and mask its violence under the forms of the Constitution. When a majority is included in a faction, the form of popular government, on the other hand, enables it to sacrifice to its ruling passion or interest both the public good and the rights of other citizens. To secure the public good and private rights against the danger of such a faction, and at the same time to preserve the spirit and the form of popular government, is then the great object to which our inquiries are directed. Let me add that it is the great desideratum by which alone this form of government can be rescued from the opprobrium under which it has so long labored and be recommended to the esteem and adoption of mankind.

By what means is this object attainable? Evidently by one of two only. Either the existence of the same passion or interest in a majority at the same time must be prevented, or the majority, having such coexistent passion or interest, must be rendered, by their number and local situation, unable to concert and carry into effect schemes of oppression. If the impulse and the opportunity be suffered to coincide, we well know that neither moral nor religious motives can be relied on as an adequate control. They are not found to be such on the injustice and violence of individuals, and lose their efficacy in proportion to the number combined together, that is, in proportion as their efficacy becomes needful.

From this view of the subject it may be concluded that a pure democracy, by which I mean a society consisting of a small number of citizens, who assemble and administer the government in person, can admit of no cure for the mischiefs of faction. A common passion or interest will, in almost every case, be felt by a majority of the whole; a communication and concert results from the form of government itself; and there is nothing to check the inducements to sacrifice the weaker party or an obnoxious individual. Hence it is that such democracies have ever been spectacles of turbulence and contention; have ever been found incompatible with personal security or the rights of property; and have in general been as short in their lives as they have been violent in their deaths. Theoretic politicians, who have patronized this species of government, have erroneously supposed that by reducing mankind to a perfect equality in their political rights, they would at the same time be perfectly equalized and assimilated in their possessions, their opinions, and their passions.

A republic, by which I mean a government in which the scheme of representation takes place, opens a different prospect and promises the cure for which we are seeking. Let us examine the points in which it varies from pure democracy, and we shall comprehend both the nature of the cure and the efficacy which it must derive from the Union.

The two great points of difference between a democracy and a republic are: first, the delegation of the government, in the latter, to a small number of citizens elected by the rest; secondly, the greater number of citizens and greater sphere of country over which the latter may be extended.

The effect of the first difference is, on the one hand, to refine and enlarge the public views by passing them through the medium of a chosen body of citizens, whose wisdom may best discern the true interest of their country and whose patriotism and love of justice will be least likely to sacrifice it to temporary or partial considerations. Under such a regulation it may well happen that the public voice, pronounced by the representatives of the people, will be more consonant to the public good than if pronounced by the people themselves, convened for the purpose. On the other hand, the effect may be inverted. Men of factious tempers, of local prejudices, or of sinister designs, may, by intrigue, by corruption, or by other means, first obtain the suffrages, and then betray the interests of the people. The question resulting is, whether small or extensive republics are most favorable to the election of proper guardians of the public weal; and it is clearly decided in favor of the latter by two obvious considerations.

In the first place it is to be remarked that however small the republic may be the representatives must be raised to a certain number in order to guard against the cabals of a few; and that however large it may be they must be limited to a certain number in order to guard against the confusion of a multitude. Hence, the number of representatives in the two cases not being in proportion to that of the constituents, and being proportionally greatest in the small republic, it follows that if the proportion of fit characters be not less in the large than in the small republic, the former will present a greater option, and consequently a greater probability of a fit choice.

In the next place, as each representative will be chosen by a greater number of citizens in the large than in the small republic, it will be more difficult for unworthy candidates to practice with success the vicious arts by which elections are too often carried; and the suffrages of the people being more free, will be more likely to center on men who possess the most attractive merit and the most diffusive and established characters.

It must be confessed that in this, as in most other cases, there is a mean, on both sides of which inconveniencies will be found to lie. By enlarging too much the number of electors, you render the representative too little acquainted with all their local circumstances and lesser interests; as by reducing it too much, you render him unduly attached to these, and too little fit to comprehend and pursue great and national objects. The federal Constitution forms a happy combination in this respect; the great and aggregate interests being referred to the national, the local and particular to the State legislatures.

The other point of difference is the greater number of citizens and extent of territory which may be brought within the compass of republican than of democratic government; and it is this circumstance principally which renders factious combinations less to be dreaded in the former than in the latter. The smaller the society, the fewer probably will be the distinct parties and interests composing it; the fewer the distinct parties and interests, the more frequently will a majority be found of the same party; and the smaller the number of individuals composing a majority, and the smaller the compass within which they are placed, the more easily will they concert and execute their plans of oppression. Extend the sphere and you take in a greater variety of parties and interests; you make it less probable that a majority of the whole will have a common motive to invade the rights of other citizens; or if such a common motive exists, it will be more difficult for all who feel it to discover their own strength and to act in unison with each other. Besides other impediments, it may be remarked that, where there is a consciousness of unjust or dishonorable purposes, communication is always checked by distrust in proportion to the number whose concurrence is necessary.

Hence, it clearly appears that the same advantage which a republic has over a democracy in controlling the effects of faction is enjoyed by a large over a small republic—is enjoyed by the Union over the States composing it. Does this advantage consist in the substitution of representatives whose enlightened views and virtuous sentiments render them superior to local prejudices and to schemes of injustice? It will not be denied that the representation of the Union will be most likely to possess these requisite endowments. Does it consist in the greater security afforded by a greater variety of parties, against the event of any one party being able to outnumber and oppress the rest? In an equal degree does the increased variety of parties comprised within the Union increase this security. Does it, in fine, consist in the greater obstacles opposed to the concert and accomplishment of the secret wishes of an unjust and interested majority? Here again the extent of the Union gives it the most palpable advantage.

The influence of factious leaders may kindle a flame within their particular States but will be unable to spread a general conflagration through the other States. A religious sect may degenerate into a political faction in a part of the Confederacy; but the variety of sects dispersed over the entire face of it must secure the national councils against any danger from that source. A rage for paper money, for an abolition of debts, for an equal division of property, or for any other improper or wicked project, will be less apt to pervade the whole body of the Union than a particular member of it, in the same proportion as such a malady is more likely to taint a particular county or district than an entire State.

In the extent and proper structure of the Union, therefore, we behold a republican remedy for the diseases most incident to republican government. And according to the degree of pleasure and pride we feel in being republicans ought to be our zeal in cherishing the spirit and supporting the character of federalists.

FEDERALIST PAPER 51

To what expedient, then, shall we finally resort, for maintaining in practice the necessary partition of power among the several departments as laid down in the Constitution? The only answer that can be given is that as all these exterior provisions are found to be inadequate the defect must be supplied, by so contriving the interior structure of the government as that its several constituent parts may, by their mutual relations, be the means of keeping each other in their proper places. Without presuming to undertake a full development of this important idea I will hazard a few general observations which may perhaps place it in a clearer light, and enable us to form a more correct judgment of the principles and structure of the government planned by the convention.

In order to lay a due foundation for that separate and distinct exercise of the different powers of government, which to a certain extent is admitted on all hands to be essential to the preservation of liberty, it is evident that each department should have a will of its own; and consequently should be so constituted that the members of each should have as little agency as possible in the appointment of the members of the others. Were this principle rigorously adhered to, it would require that all the appointments for the supreme executive, legislative, and judiciary magistracies should be drawn from the same fountain of authority, the people, through channels having no communication whatever with one another. Perhaps such a plan of constructing the several departments would be less difficult in practice than it may in contemplation appear. Some difficulties, however, and some additional expense would attend the execution of it. Some deviations, therefore, from the principle must be admitted. In the constitution of the judiciary department in particular, it might be inexpedient to insist rigorously on the principle: first, because peculiar qualifications being essential in the members, the primary consideration ought to be to select that mode of choice which best secures these qualifications; second, because the permanent tenure by which the appointments are held in that department must soon destroy all sense of dependence on the authority conferring them.

It is equally evident that the members of each department should be as little dependent as possible on those of the others for the emoluments annexed to their offices. Were the executive magistrate, or the judges, not independent of the legislature in this particular, their independence in every other would be merely nominal.

But the great security against a gradual concentration of the several powers in the same department consists in giving to those who administer each department the necessary constitutional means and personal motives to resist encroachments of the others. The provision for defense must in this, as in all other cases, be made commensurate to the danger of attack. Ambition must be made to counteract ambition. The interest of the man must be connected with the constitutional rights of the place. It may be a reflection on human nature that such devices should be necessary to control the abuses of government. But what is government itself but the greatest of all reflections on human nature? If men were angels, no government would be necessary. If angels were to govern men, neither external nor internal controls on government would be necessary. In framing a government which is to be administered by men over men, the great difficulty lies in this: you must first enable the government to control the governed; and in the next place oblige it to control itself. A dependence on the people is, no doubt, the primary control on the government; but experience has taught mankind the necessity of auxiliary precautions.

This policy of supplying, by opposite and rival interests, the defect of better motives, might be traced through the whole system of human affairs, private as well as public. We see it particularly displayed in all the subordinate distributions of power, where the constant aim is to divide and arrange the several offices in such a manner as that each may be a check on the other—that the private interest of every individual may be a sentinel over the public rights. These inventions of prudence cannot be less requisite in the distribution of the supreme powers of the State.

But it is not possible to give to each department an equal power of self-defense. In republican government, the legislative authority necessarily predominates. The remedy for this inconveniency is to divide the legislature into different branches; and to render them, by different modes of election and different principles of action, as little connected with each other as the nature of their common functions and their common dependence on the society will admit. It may even be necessary to guard against dangerous encroachments by still further precautions. As the weight of the legislative authority requires that it should be thus divided, the weakness of the executive may require, on the other hand, that it should be fortified. An absolute negative on the legislature appears, at first view, to be the natural defense with which the executive magistrate should be armed. But perhaps it would be neither altogether safe nor alone sufficient. On ordinary occasions it might not be exerted with the requisite firmness, and on extraordinary occasions it might be perfidiously abused. May not this defect of an absolute negative be supplied by some qualified connection between this weaker department and the weaker branch of the stronger department, by which the latter may be led to support the constitutional rights of the former, without being too much detached from the rights of its own department?

If the principles on which these observations are found be just, as I persuade myself they are, and they be applied as a criterion to the several State constitutions, and the federal Constitution, it will be found that if the latter does not perfectly correspond with them, the former are infinitely less able to bear such a test.

There are, moreover, two considerations particularly applicable to the federal system of America, which place that system in a very interesting point of view.

First. In a single republic, all the power surrendered by the people is submitted to the administration of a single government; and the usurpations are guarded against by a division of the government into distinct and separate departments. In the compound republic of America, the power surrendered by the people is first divided between two distinct governments, and then the portion allotted to each subdivided among distinct and separate departments. Hence a double security arises to the rights of the people. The different governments will control each other, at the same time that each will be controlled by itself.

Second. It is of great importance in a republic not only to guard the society against the oppression of its rulers, but to guard one part of the society against the injustice of the other part. Different interests necessarily exist in different classes of citizens. If a majority be united by a common interest, the rights of the minority will be insecure. There are but two methods of providing against this evil: the one by creating a will in the community independent of the majority—that is, of the society itself; the other, by comprehending in the society so many separate descriptions of citizens as will render an unjust combination of a majority of the whole very improbable, if not impracticable. The first method prevails in all governments possessing an hereditary or self-appointed authority. This, at best, is but a precarious security; because a power independent of the society may as well espouse the unjust views of the major as the rightful interests of the minor party, and may possibly be turned against both parties. The second method will be exemplified in the federal republic of the United States. Whilst all authority in it will be derived from and dependent on the society, the society itself will be broken into so many parts, interests and classes of citizens, that the rights of individuals, or of the minority, will be in little danger from interested combinations of the majority. In a free government the security for civil rights must be

the same as that for religious rights. It consists in the one case in the multiplicity of interests, and in the other in the multiplicity of sects. The degree of security in both cases will depend on the number of interests and sects; and this may be presumed to depend on the extent of country and number of people comprehended under the same government. This view of the subject must particularly recommend a proper federal system to all the sincere and considerate friends of republican government, since it shows that in exact proportion as the territory of the Union may be formed into more circumscribed Confederacies, or States, oppressive combinations of a majority will be facilitated; the best security, under the republican forms, for the rights of every class of citizen, will be diminished; and consequently the stability and independence of some member of the government, the only other security, must be proportionally increased. Justice is the end of government. It is the end of civil society. It ever has been and ever will be pursued until it be obtained, or until liberty be lost in the pursuit. In a society under the forms of which the stronger faction can readily unite and oppress the weaker, anarchy may as truly be said to reign as in a state of nature, where the weaker individual is not secured against the violence of the stronger; and as, in the latter state, even the stronger individuals are prompted, by the uncertainty of their condition, to submit to a government which may protect the weak as well as themselves; so, in the former state, will the more powerful factions or parties be gradually induced, by a like motive, to wish for a government which will protect all parties, the weaker as well as the more powerful. It can be little doubted that if the State of Rhode Island was separated from the Confederacy and left to itself, the insecurity of rights under the popular form of government within such narrow limits would be displayed by such reiterated oppressions of factious majorities that some power altogether independent of the people would soon be called for by the voice of the very factions whose misrule had proved the necessity of it. In the extended republic of the United States, and among the great variety of interests, parties, and sects which it embraces, a coalition of a majority of the whole society could seldom take place on any other principles than those of justice and the general good; whilst there being thus less danger to a minor from the will of a major party, there must be less pretext, also, to provide for the security of the former, by introducing into the government a will not dependent on the latter, or, in other words, a will independent of the society itself. It is no less certain than it is important, notwithstanding the contrary opinions which have been entertained, that the larger the society, provided it lie within a practicable sphere, the more duly capable it will be of self-government. And happily for the *republican cause,* the practicable sphere may be carried to a very great extent by a judicious modification and mixture of the *federal principle.*

Appendix E

ABRAHAM LINCOLN'S GETTYSBURG ADDRESS

President Abraham Lincoln gave this speech on November 19, 1863 as he dedicated the Soldier's National Cemetery in Gettysburg, Pennsylvania. Earlier that year, in July, Union troops had defeated the Confederate Army at the Battle of Gettysburg, with a loss of 6000 lives and 38,000 wounded or missing of the estimated 160,000 troops fighting this three-day battle.

Four score and seven years ago our fathers brought forth on this continent a new nation, conceived in liberty and dedicated to the proposition that all men are created equal. Now we are engaged in a great Civil War, testing whether that nation or any nation so conceived and so dedicated can long endure. We are met on a great battle-field of that war. We have come to dedicate a portion of that field as a final resting place for those who here gave their lives that that nation might live. It is altogether fitting and proper that we should do this. But in a larger sense, we cannot dedicate—we cannot consecrate—we cannot hallow this ground. The brave men, living and dead, who struggled here have consecrated it far above our poor power to add or detract. The world will little note nor long remember what we say here, but it can never forget what they did here. It is for us the living, rather, to be dedicated here to the unfinished work which they who fought here have thus far so nobly advanced. It is rather for us to be here dedicated to the great task remaining before us—that from these honored dead we take increased devotion to that cause for which they gave the last full measure of devotion—that we here highly resolve that these dead shall not have died in vain, that this nation, under God, shall have a new birth of freedom, and that government of the people, by the people, for the people shall not perish from the earth.

Endnotes

Introduction

[1] Garry Wills, *A Necessary Evil: A History of American Distrust of Government* (New York: Simon & Schuster, 1999), 320.

[2] Ibid.

[3] Thomas Hobbes (1588–1679), an English philosopher whose work was known and cited by the Founders.

[4] Although the Pilgrims had been persecuted in England, when they moved to Holland they were tolerated. In fact, they feared that their children would adopt Dutch ways and stray from their own religion, so they fled Holland for America. Richard Shenkman, "*I Love Paul Revere, Whether He Rode or Not*" (New York: HarperPerennial, 1991), 20–21.

[5] Seymour Martin Lipset, "Why No Socialism in the United States?" in *Sources of Contemporary Radicalism,* eds. Seweryn Bialer and Sophis Sluzar (Boulder, Colo.: Westview Press, 1977), 86.

[6] Robert Calhoon, *The Loyalists in Revolutionary America, 1766–1781* (New York: Harcourt Brace Jovanovich, 1973).

[7] For elaboration of this process and an explanation of the theory of path dependence, see John W. Kingdon, *America the Unusual* (Boston: Bedford/St. Martin's, 1999). There is also a hypothesis among scientists that the early settlers, as well as later immigrants, had a different genetic makeup than the people they left behind. That is, along with their views they brought their DNA, which predisposed them to restless curiosity, novelty seeking, and risk taking. The scientists are looking for genetic markers that would confirm this hypothesis. Thus immigrants may be a self-selected group in more than the obvious ways. Emily Bazelon, "The Hypomanic American," *New York Times Magazine,* December 12, 2006, 76.

[8] James Madison, *Federalist Paper* 51.

[9] There are earlier instances of government involvement in health care. The Pilgrims promised pensions to those who were disabled in their fight against Indians. The Continental Congress encouraged enlistment in the Revolutionary Army by promising pensions to disabled soldiers. (See United States Department of Veterans Affairs, http://www.va.gov/about_va/vahistory.asp.) George Washington signed a law in 1792 requiring ship owners to buy medical insurance for their sailors that covered doctors and medicines. In 1798, under President Adams, the government imposed a tax on private seamen to cover their hospital care, which was then handled at government hospitals for sailors.

[10] Adam Cohen, *Nothing to Fear: FDR's Inner Circle and the Hundred Days That Created Modern America* (New York: Penguin, 2009), 14–15.

[11] Ibid., 16.

[12] James L. Sundquist, *Dynamics of the Party System* (Washington, D.C.: Brookings Institution Press, 1973), 191.

[13] The mother of a coauthor of this text has vivid memories of these requests night after night as a child in Davenport, Iowa.

[14] Cohen, *Nothing to Fear,* 1.

[15] Ibid., 15–16.

[16] Otto Friedrich, "F.D.R.'s Disputed Legacy," *Time,* February 1, 1982, 25.

[17] Karl Vick, "A President Who Woke Up Washington," *Washington Post National Weekly Edition,* April 28, 1997, 8.

[18] Theodore J. Lowi, *The Personal President* (Ithaca, N.Y.: Cornell University Press, 1985), 44.

[19] Ibid., xi.

[20] Daniel J. Elazar, *The American Partnership* (Chicago: University of Chicago Press, 1962).

[21] For examination of this growth spurt, see Garry Wills, *Bomb Power: The Modern Presidency and the National Security State* (New York: Penguin, 2010).

[22] Timothy Conlan, *From Federalism to Devolution: Twenty-five Years of Intergovernmental Reform* (Washington, D.C.: Brookings Institution Press, 1998), 6.

[23] President Clinton and congressional Democrats were able to reduce military spending somewhat during the 1990s because the Cold War had ended and fears of terrorism had not yet taken hold among the public.

[24] Adam Sheingate, "Why Can't Americans See the State?" *The Forum* 7, no. 4 (2009), http://www.bepress.com/forum/vol7/iss4/art1.

[25] *Statistical Abstract of the United States, 2010,* tab. 449.

[26] Margit Tavits, "The Size of Government in Majoritarian and Consensus Democracies," *Comparative Political Studies* 37 (2004), 340, cps.sagepub.com/cgi/content/abstract/37/3/340. DOI: 10.1177/0010414003262068; Heinz Handler, Bertrand Koebel, Philipp Reiss, and Margit Schratzenstaller, "The Size and Performance of Public Sector Activities in Europe," *Public Economics,* no. 0507011, http://ideas.repec.org/p/wpa/wuwppe/0507011.html.

[27] There are some exceptions. The United States has a much larger military and defense establishment, a more extensive criminal justice system, a more extensive public education system, and more pervasive civil rights regulations. Kingdon, *America the Unusual.*

[28] Richard Neustadt, *The American Presidency,* episode 5, PBS, April 2000.

[29] Quoted Wills, *A Necessary Evil,* **15.**

[30] Richard Stengel, "So, What Would Warren Do?" *Time,* January 23, 2012, 3.

[31] The health spending data are from 2006, the most recent date that form of the question was asked on this national survey. An alternative question, asked most years since 1983, found that, over time, 54 percent thought government should help the sick and another 30 percent thought that both government and families themselves should help the sick. The 2006 percentages were almost identical.

[32] His son, Rand Paul, who won a Senate seat from Kentucky, might not be quite as Libertarian.

[33] Frederick Rudolph, "The American Liberty League, 1934–1940," *American Historical Review* 56 (October 1950), 19–33.

[34] Frank Luntz, "What Americans Really Want," *Los Angeles Times,* September 27, 2009, latimes.com/news/opinion/la-oe-luntz27-2009sep27,0,4242608.story.

[35] Andy Serwer, "The Decade from Hell," *Time,* December 7, 2009, 30–38.

[36] Pollster Bill McInturff, quoted in Nina Easton, "The End of Audacity," *Time,* December 14, 2009, 33.

[37] Sam Tanenhaus, "North Star: Populism, Politics, and the Power of Sarah Palin," *New Yorker,* December 7, 2009, 88.

[38] Robin Abcarian, Kate Linthicum, and Richard Fausett, "Conservatives Say It's Their Turn for Empowerment," *Los Angeles Times,* September 17, 2009, latimes.com/news/nationworld/nation/la-na-white-victimhood17-2009sep17,0,2618101.story.

[39] Tim Rutten, "America the Delusional," *Los Angeles Times,* August 19, 2009, http://articles.latimes.com/2009/aug/19/opinion/oe-rutten19.

40 After chastising the Republican representative who hosted the meeting for "ignoring" Obama's birth certificate. Jim Nelson, "What We Talk about When We Talk about Birth Certificates," *GQ,* September 2009, 108.

41 Frank Rich, "The Obama Haters' Silent Enablers," *New York Times,* June 14, 2009, WK8.

42 John Jeremiah Sullivan, "American Rage," *GQ,* January 2010, 69.

43 Kathleen Hennessey, "'Tea Party' Convention a Forum for Woes, Worries," *Los Angeles Times,* February 6, 2010, latimes.com/news/nationworld/nation/la-na-tea-party6-2010feb06,0,568141.story.

44 See, in general, Ben McGrath, "The Movement," *New Yorker,* February 1, 2010, 40–19; see also Theda Skocpol and Vanessa Williamson, "Whose Tea Party Is It?" *New York Times,* December 26, 2011, http://campaignstops.blogs.nytimes.com/2011/12/26/whose-tea-party-is-it/; and their book, *The Tea Party and the Remaking of Republican Conservatism* (New York: Oxford University Press, 2011).

45 Matt Bai, "The New Old Guard," *New York Times Magazine,* August 30, 2009, 11–12.

46 Skocpol and Williamson, "Whose Tea Party Is It."

47 Pew Research Center, reported in Charles Babington, "GOP Contenders for 2012 Drift to the Right," *Lincoln Journal Star,* May 31, 2011, A6.

48 Frank Bruni, "Pizzas and Pessimism," *New York Times,* October 30, 2011, SR3.

49 Brian Montopoli, "43% Agree with Occupy Wall Street," *New York Times,* October 25, 2011, http://www.cbsnews.com/8301-503544_162-20125515-503544/poll-43-percent-agree-with-views-of-occupy-wall-street/.

50 John Dean, *Conservatives without Conscience* (New York: Penguin, 2006), xxxiv–xxxv.

51 Thomas Mann and Norman Ornstein, It's Even Worse Than It Looks, (New York: Perseus Press, 2012), quoted in "Extremism in Congress Is Even Worse Than It Looks," http://www.npr.org/2012/04/30/151522725/even-worse-than-it-looks-extremism-in-congress.

52 Quoted in http://www.washingtonpost.com/blogs/plum-line/post/richard-mourdock-and-the-gops-idea-of-bipartisanship/2012/05/09/gIQAoaQ8CU_blog.html.

53 E. E. Schattschneider, *Two Hundred Million Americans in Search of a Government* (New York: Holt, Rinehart, and Winston, 1969), 53.

54 Sheri Berman, "Keeping Them Down," *New York Times Book Review,* October 9, 2011, 24.

55 Joe Klein, "The War of Ideas," *Time,* February 4, 2008, 25.

56 Survey of Tea Party supporters and others, reported in http://www.nytimes.com/interactive/2010/04/14/us/politics/20100414-tea-party-poll-graphic.html?ref=politics#tab=0. This was a *New York Times*/CBS News poll done in April 2010 with 1580 adults, including an oversample of Tea Party supporters.

57 John Hibbing and Elizabeth Theiss-Morse, *Congress as Public Enemy* (New York: Cambridge University Press, 1995).

58 "Fewer Are Angry at Government, but Discontent Remains High," Pew Research Center for the People and the Press, http://www.people-press.org/2011/03/03/fewer-are-angry-at-government-but-discontent-remains-high/.

59 Frank Rich, "No One Listened to Gabrielle Giffords," *New York Times,* January 16, 2011, WK10.

60 "Open-carry laws" allow people to carry loaded weapons in public places. At one appearance in Arizona, at least a dozen people displayed weapons, including assault rifles. Rutten, "America the Delusional."

61 Sharron Angle, sponsored by the Tea Party and nominated by the Republican Party for the U.S. Senate. Quoted in Frank Rich, "The Rage Won't End on Election Day," *New York Times,* October 17, 2010, WK10.

62 "Candidate: Overthrow Is 'On the Table,'" *Lincoln Journal Star,* October 23, 2010, A4.

63 Esther J. Cepeda, "It's No Laughing Matter," *Lincoln Journal Star,* March 2, 2011, B7.

64 Ariel Edwards-Levy, "'Kill the Claire Bear' Comment about Claire McCaskill Applauded by GOP Opponent's Son," *Huffington Post,* http://www.huffingtonpost.com/2012/05/09/kill-claire-mccaskill-applauded-son_n_1503243.html.

65 Rich, "No One Listened to Gabrielle Giffords."

66 Virginia A. Chanley, "Trust in Government in the Aftermath of 9/11," *Political Psychology* 23, no. 3 (December 2002), 469–483; Timothy E. Cook and Paul Gronke, "The Skeptical American: Revisiting the Meanings of Trust in Government," *Journal of Politics* 67, no. 3 (August 2005), 784–803; Jack Citrin and Donald Philip Green, "Presidential Leadership and the Resurgence of Trust in Government," *British Journal of Political Science* 16, no. 4 (October 1986), 431–453.

67 Elaine C. Karmack, "The Evolving American State: The Trust Challenge," *The Forum* 7, no. 4 (2009), 2, 10, http://www.bepress.com/forum/vol7/iss4/art9.

68 CBS/*New York Times* poll, February 2010, http://document.nytimes.com/new-york-times-cbs-news-poll.

69 In the Gallup poll. Christopher Hayes, "The Twilight of the Elites," *Time,* March 22, 2010, 56.

70 http://www.gallup.com/poll/116599/Economy-Republicans-Trust-Business-Dems-Trust-Gov.aspx.

71 Views on major institutions drawn from Harris poll, February 16–21, 2010, from a national survey of about 1000 adults. PollingReport.com.

72 Wills, *A Necessary Evil,* 320 and 16.

73 Karmack, "The Evolving American State," 1.

Chapter 1

1 John Sugden, *Tecumseh: A Life* (New York: Holt, 1998).

2 Kenneth C. Davis, "The Founding Immigrants," *New York Times,* July 3, 2007, A17.

3 Rich Morin, "The Public Assesses Social Divisions," Pew Research Center, September 24, 2009, 1, pewsocialtrends.org.

4 "Summary of Key Findings: U.S. Religious Landscape Survey," Pew Forum on Religion and Public Life, February 26, 2008, 1. The findings are the results of two 2007 surveys for which more than 35,000 adults were interviewed. religions.pewforum.org/affiliations.

5 James Q. Wilson, "The History and Future of Democracy," lecture delivered at the Ronald Reagan Presidential Library, November 15, 1999.

6 If you would like to check the religious affiliations of people in your community or state, the Association of Religion Data Archives contains a user-friendly set of data to allow you to do just that. http://www.thearda.com/.

7 Morin, "The Public Assesses Social Divisions," 1.

8 See, for example, the discussion in Larry M. Bartels, *Unequal Democracy: The Political Economy of the New Gilded Age* (Princeton, N.J.: Princeton University Press, 2008).

9 Rich Morin, "Rising Share of Americans See Conflict between Rich and Poor," *Pew Social and Demographic Trends,* January 12, 2012.

10 David Armitage, *The Declaration of Independence: A Global History* (Cambridge, Mass.: Harvard University Press, 2007), 77.

11 Thurgood Marshall, "Remarks at the Annual Seminar of the San Francisco Patent and Trademark Law Association," May 6, 1987, www.thurgoodmarshall.com/speeches/constitutional_speech.htm.

12 President Johnson quoted in Tim Funk, "Civil Rights Act of 1964 Paved Way for Prosperity," *Champaign-Urbana News-Gazette,* July 11, 2004, B1.

13 John W. Kingdon, *America the Unusual* (Boston: Wadsworth Cengage Learning, 1999), 32–38.

14 For all crimes, except minor crimes that don't result in any incarceration or probation.

15 Princeton professor and chair of the Obama Council of Economic Advisors, Alan Krueger, argues that the question is, instead, "At what point is there too much inequality? What, then, is the role of government?" Ezra Klein, "Q&A: CEA Chair Alan Krueger on Inequality," January 13, 2012, http://www.washingtonpost.com/blogs/ezra-klein/post/qanda-cea-chair-alan-krueger-on-inequality/2011/08/25/gIQAEcaVwP_blog.htm.

16 Thomas Hobbes, *The Leviathan,* Chapter 13, "Of the Natural Condition of Mankind, as Concerning Their Felicity and Misery."

17 Hobbes, *The Leviathan,* Chapter 17, "Of the Causes, Generation, and Definition of a Common-Wealth."

18 John Locke, *The Second Treatise on Government,* Chapter 2, "Of the State of Nature," and Chapter 9, "Of the Ends of Political Society and Government."

19 Locke, *The Second Treatise on Government,* Chapter 7, "Of the Beginning of Political Societies," and Chapter 9, "Of the Ends of Political Society and Government."

20 Franklin D. Roosevelt, "State of the Union Message to Congress," January 11, 1944, http://docs.fdrlibrary.marist.edu/011144.html.

21 Alan Wolfe, "Couch Potato Politics," *New York Times,* March 15, 1998, sec. 4, 17.

22 John R. Hibbing and Beth Theiss-Morse, *Congress as Public Enemy: Public Attitude toward American Political Institutions* (Cambridge: Cambridge University Press, 1995); John R. Hibbing and Beth Theiss-Morse, "Civics Is Not Enough: Teaching Barbarics in K–12," *PS,* March 1996, 57–62.

23 For a historical survey of this tension, see E. J. Dionne Jr., *Our Divided Political Heart: The Battle for the American Idea in an Age of Discontent* (New York: Bloomsbury, 2012), esp. 155–188.

24 Originally spoken by Theodore Parker, nineteenth-century abolitionist and Unitarian minister, and later revised and quoted by Martin Luther King in a 1967 speech to the Southern Christian Leadership Conference.

25 The origins of governmental systems are discussed by John Jay in *Federalist Paper 2.*

26 Garry Wills, *Lincoln at Gettysburg: The Words That Remade America* (New York: Simon & Schuster, 1992), 145.

27 Carl F. Kaestle, "Introduction," in *School: The Story of American Public Education,* eds. Sarah Mondale and Sarah B. Patton (Boston: Beacon Press, 2001), 13.

28 Ibid., 16.

29 "The Educated Citizen," in *School,* eds. Mondale and Patton, 22.

30 Ibid.

31 Adam Cohen, "According to Webster: One Man's Attempt to Define 'America,'" *New York Times,* February 12, 2006, sec. 4, 13.

32 Noah Webster quoted in Jack Lynch, "Dr. Johnson's Revolution," *New York Times,* July 2, 2005, sec. 4, A15.

33 For many years, the flag was not flown in battle or over government buildings or public schools.

34 The Spanish-American War and World War I also gave a boost to efforts to use the flag as a symbol.

35 Daniel Elazar, *American Federalism: A View from the States,* 3rd ed. (New York: Harper & Row, 1984).

36 Pew Research Center, "Who Moves Where," 12 (pewresearch.org), http://www.usatoday.com/news/nation/2007-11-29-Mobility_N.htm; Haya El Nasser and Paul Overberg, "Millions More Americans Move to Another State," USA Today, November 29, 2007.

Chapter 2

1 Jeffrey Rosen, "Radical Constitutionalism," *New York Times Magazine,* November 26, 2010, 34; Ruth Marcus, "Perry, by the Book, Scary," *Lincoln Journal Star,* August 31, 2011, B7. Additional information in the paragraphs below was drawn from these articles.

2 Ben Evans, "A Hot-and-Cold Take on the Constitution," *Lincoln Journal Star,* August 26, 2010, A5.

3 Rosen, "Radical Constitutionalism."

4 For a history of this doctrine, see Garry Wills, *A Necessary Evil: A History of American Distrust of Government* (New York: Simon & Schuster, 1999), 123–178.

5 The Indians, of course, had their own governments, and the Spanish may have established Saint Augustine, Florida, and Santa Fe, New Mexico, before the English established Jamestown. The Spanish settlements were extensions of Spanish colonization of Mexico and were governed by Spanish officials in Mexico City.

6 This is not to suggest that the Pilgrims believed in democracy. Apparently, they were motivated to draft the compact by threats from some on the *Mayflower* that when the ship landed they would "use their owne libertie; for none had power to command them." Thus the compact was designed to bind them to the laws of the colony. Richard Shenkman, *"I Love Paul Revere, Whether He Rode or Not"* (New York: HarperCollins, 1991), 141–142.

7 David Hawke, *A Transaction of Free Men* (New York: Scribner, 1964), 209.

8 For an account of the foreign affairs problems under the Articles of Confederation, see Frederick W. Marks III, *Independence on Trial: Foreign Affairs and the Making of the Constitution* (Baton Rouge: Louisiana State University Press, 1973).

9 Max M. Edling, *A Revolution in Favor of Government* (New York: Oxford University Press, 2003), 149–162.

10 Louis Fisher, *President and Congress* (New York: Free Press, 1972), 14.

11 The government under the Articles, however, could boast one major accomplishment: the Northwest Ordinance, adopted in 1787, provided for the government and future statehood of the land west of Pennsylvania (land that would become most of the Great Lakes states). The law also banned slavery in this territory.

12 Gordon S. Wood, "The Origins of the Constitution," *This Constitution: A Bicentennial Chronicle,* Summer 1987, 10–11.

13 Eric Black, *Our Constitution* (Boulder, Colo.: Westview Press, 1988), 6.

14 For development of this idea, see Kenneth M. Dolbeare and Linda J. Medcalf, "The Political Economy of the Constitution," *This Constitution: A Bicentennial Chronicle,* Spring 1987, 4–10.

15 Black, *Our Constitution,* 59.

16 The Constitution would, however, retain numerous positive aspects of the Articles. See Donald S. Lutz, "The Articles of Confederation as the Background to the Federal Republic," *Publius* 20 (Winter 1990), 55–70.

17 Robert McCloskey, *The American Supreme Court* (Chicago: University of Chicago Press, 1960), 29.

18 Robert A. Dahl, *A Preface to Democratic Theory* (Chicago: University of Chicago Press, 1956), 5.

19 Yet according to a poll in 1987, the bicentennial of the Constitution, only 1 percent of the public identified Madison as the one who played the biggest role in creating the Constitution. Most—31 percent—said Thomas Jefferson, who was a diplomat in France during the convention. Black, *Our Constitution,* 15.

Some argue that Hamilton, rather than Madison, was the driving force behind the Constitution, especially if his efforts after ratification—as an influential member of Washington's cabinet and later—are taken into account. Kenneth M. Dolbeare and Linda Medcalf, "The Dark Side of the Constitution," in *The Case against the Constitution: From the Antifederalists to the Present,* eds. Kenneth M. Dolbeare and John F. Manley (Armonk, N.Y.: Sharpe, 1987), 120–141.

20 Only Hamilton suggested a monarchy, and only one delegate—Gouverneur Morris of Pennsylvania—suggested an aristocracy.

21 Robert A. Dahl, *How Democratic Is the American Constitution?* (New Haven, Conn.: Yale University Press, 2001), 11–12.

22 Ibid., 14.

23 The large states did extract a concession that all taxing and spending bills must originate in the house in which representation is based on population. This provision would allow the large states to take the initiative on these important measures.

24 For further examination of the compromises at the convention, see Richard Beeman, *The Making of the American Constitution* (New York: Random House, 2009).

25 Paul Finkelman, "Slavery at the Philadelphia Convention," *This Constitution: A Bicentennial Chronicle* (1987), 25–30.

26 Ibid., 29.

27 Ibid., 18.

28 Quoted in Thomas G. West, *Vindicating the Founders: Race, Sex, Class, and Justice in the Origins of America* (Lanham, Md.: Rowman & Littlefield, 1997), 15.

29 Theodore J. Lowi, *American Government* (Hinsdale, Ill.: Dryden, 1976), 97.

30 Quoted in Richard Hofstadter, *The American Political Tradition* (New York: Vintage, 1948), 6–7.

31 Under some state constitutions.

32 Wills, *A Necessary Evil,* 72.

33 Ibid., 77, 83. Creating a separate executive branch and making the selection of president independent of Congress also strengthened the national government, because it gave the president a political base from which to exercise national leadership.

34 Edling, *A Revolution in Favor of Government,* 73–88.

35 *Federalist Paper* 51.

36 Although we use this term today, neither it nor the word *federal* appears in the Constitution.

37 In the United States, each state government is unitary with respect to its local governments. The state government can alter or eliminate cities, counties, townships, or school districts.

38 James Madison, *Federalist Paper 10.*

39 Madison also saw our vast territory as a way to limit factions, because it would be difficult for a group to extend its influence throughout the entire country.

40 Max Farrand, *The Framing of the Constitution of the United States* (New Haven, Conn.: Yale University Press, 1913).

41 Charles O. Jones, *The Presidency in a Separated System* (Washington, D.C.: Brookings Institution, 1994), 14.

42 Charles O. Jones, *Separate but Equal Branches* (Chatham, N.J.: Chatham House, 1995), 12.

43 *Federalist Paper* 51.

44 Jones, *Presidency in a Separated System,* 16, thus modifying Neustadt's classic definition of "a government of separated institutions sharing powers." Richard E. Neustadt, *Presidential Power and the Modern Presidents* (New York: Macmillan, 1990), 29.

45 Juan J. Linz and Alfred Stepan, "Comparative Perspectives on Inequality and the Quality of Democracy in the United States," *Perspectives on Politics* 9 (December 2011), 841–856. These researchers didn't count the courts as a veto point, but at least American courts, with frequent use of judicial review, are.

46 In particular, the more veto points, the less likely the government will adopt policies promoting equality among its citizens. Ibid.

47 Jones, *Presidency in a Separated System,* xiii.

48 Dahl, *How Democratic Is the American Constitution?* 115.

49 This configuration has also provided the opportunity for one branch to pick up the slack when the others became sluggish. The overlapping of powers ensured by checks and balances allows every branch to act on virtually every issue it wants to. In the 1950s, President Eisenhower and Congress were reluctant to push for civil rights, but the Supreme Court did so by declaring segregation unconstitutional.

50 Jones, *Presidency in a Separated System,* 3.

51 Richard Morin, "Happy Days Are Here Again," *Washington Post National Weekly Edition,* August 25, 1997, 35.

52 About 25 percent split their ticket between candidates for president and representative. In addition, others split their vote between candidates for president and senator or between candidates for representative and senator. For an examination of the research about divided government, see Morris Fiorina, *Divided Government,* 2nd ed. (Boston: Allyn & Bacon, 1996), 153.

53 For elaboration, see Dahl, *How Democratic Is the American Constitution?* 24–25.

54 Ibid.

55 Locke called for majority rule but never resolved the conflict between majority rule and natural rights—in particular, the rights of the minority.

56 Donald S. Lutz, "The Relative Influence of European Writers on Later Eighteenth-Century American Political Thought," *American Political Science Review* 78 (1984), 139–197.

57 Alpheus T. Mason and Richard H. Leach, *In Quest of Freedom: American Political Thought and Practice,* 2nd ed. (Englewood Cliffs, N.J.: Prentice Hall, 1973), 51.

58 For development of this idea, see Martin Landau, "A Self-Correcting System: The Constitution of the United States," *This Constitution: A Bicentennial Chronicle,* Summer 1986, 4–10.

59 John P. Roche, "The Founding Fathers: A Reform Caucus in Action," *American Political Science Review* 55 (1961), 799–816.

60 Benjamin F. Wright Jr., "The Origins of the Separation of Powers in America," in *Origins of American Political Thought,* ed. John P. Roche (New York: Harper & Row, 1967), 139–162.

61 Roche, "Founding Fathers," 805.

62 James MacGregor Burns, *The Vineyard of Liberty* (New York: Knopf, 1982), 33.

63 Bernard Bailyn, *Voyagers to the West* (New York: Knopf, 1982), 20.

64 The Boston Tea Party, contrary to myth, was not prompted by higher taxes on British tea. Parliament lowered the taxes to give the British East India Company, facing bankruptcy, an advantage in the colonial market. This threatened American shippers who smuggled tea from Holland and controlled about three-fourths of the market. The shippers resented Parliament's attempt to manipulate the economy from thousands of miles away. Shenkman, *"I Love Paul Revere,"* 155.

65 *Federalist Paper* 10.

66 Of the fifty-five delegates, forty were owners of government bonds that had depreciated under the Articles, and twenty-four were moneylenders. Black, *Our Constitution,* 21.

67 For elaboration, see Dolbeare and Medcalf, "Dark Side of the Constitution."

68 Calvin C. Jillson and Cecil L. Eubanks, "The Political Structure of Constitution Making," *American Journal of Political Science* 29 (1984), 435–458.

69 For a detailed history, see Pauline Maier, *Ratification* (New York: Simon & Schuster, 2010).

70 Wills, *A Necessary Evil,* 208.

71 Jonathan Elliot, *The Debates in the Several State Conventions on the Adoption of the Federal Constitution as Recommended by the General Convention at Philadelphia, in 1787,* 2nd ed., 5 vols. (Philadelphia, 1896), 2: 102.

72 Wills, *A Necessary Evil,* 91–111.

73 Edling, *A Revolution in Favor of Government,* 42, 89, 107–108.

74 Ibid., 42.

75 Ibid., 184.

76 Ibid., 45.

77 Ibid., 179.

78 Wills, *A Necessary Evil,* 16–17, and generally throughout the book.

79 On Antifederalist thinking, see William B. Allen and Gordon Lloyd, eds., *The Essential Antifederalist,* 2nd ed. (Lanham, Md.: University Press of America, 2002); John F. Manley and Kenneth M. Dolbeare, *The Case against the Constitution* (Armonk, N.Y.: Sharpe, 1987).

80 Richard S. Randall, *American Constitutional Development,* vol. 1, *The Powers of Government* (New York: Longman, 2002), 54.

81 "A Fundamental Contentment," *This Constitution: A Bicentennial Chronicle,* Fall 1984, 44.

82 Quoted in Charles Warren, *The Making of the Constitution* (Boston: Little, Brown, 1928), xiv. Jefferson made this observation from afar, as he was serving as ambassador to France at the time of the Constitutional Convention.

83 Keith Perine, "Congress Shows Little Enthusiasm for Bush's Marriage Amendment," *CQ Weekly,* February 28, 2004, 533.

84 Alan P. Grimes, *Democracy and the Amendments to the Constitution* (Lexington, Mass.: Lexington Books, 1978). Grimes also shows how the adoption of new amendments reflects the rise of new power blocs in society.

85 4 Wheaton 316 (1819).

86 Historian James McPherson, quoted in George P. Fletcher, *Our Secret Constitution: How Lincoln Redefined American Democracy* (New York: Oxford University Press, 2001), 57. For a similar view, see Bruce Ackerman, *We the People,* vol. 2, *Transformations* (Cambridge, Mass.: Belknap Press, 1998), 10. This discussion borrows heavily from Fletcher and Ackerman and also from Garry Wills, *Lincoln at Gettysburg* (New York: Simon & Schuster, 1992). For complementary views, see Charles Black, *A New Birth of Freedom: Human Rights, Named and Unnamed* (New York: Grosset/Putnam, 1997); Marc Landy and Sidney M. Milkis, "The Presidency in the Eye of the Storm," in *The Presidency and the Political System,* ed. Michael Nelson, 9th ed. (Washington, D.C.: Sage, 2010), 68–107.

87 Many of Lincoln's prejudicial comments came in response to more blatant racist remarks by his opponents. Lincoln abandoned his support for black emigration before he was elected to a second term as president. For a critical perspective on Lincoln's racial views, see Lerone Bennett Jr., *Forced into Glory: Abraham Lincoln's White Dream* (Chicago: Johnson, 2000). For positive perspectives, see William Lee Miller, *Lincoln's Virtues: An Ethical Biography* (New York: Knopf, 2002); and Michael Burlingame, *Abraham Lincoln: A Life* (Baltimore: Johns Hopkins, 2008). For a Pulitzer Prize–winning examination of Lincoln's racial attitudes, see Eric Foner, *The Fiery Trial: Abraham Lincoln and American Slavery* (New York: Norton, 2010). Historian Henry Louis Gates aptly calls Lincoln "a recovering racist." "Ten Questions," *Time,* February 16, 2009, 6.

88 Fletcher, *Our Secret Constitution,* 24.

89 For the role of abolitionist sentiment in Lincoln's decisions, see James Oakes, *The Radical and the Republican: Frederick Douglass, Abraham Lincoln, and the Triumph of Antislavery Politics* (New York: W. W. Norton, 2007).

90 Thomas Mallon, "Set in Stone," *New Yorker,* October 13, 2008, 136.

91 These paragraphs rely on the interpretations of Wills, *Lincoln at Gettysburg,* and Fletcher, *Our Secret Constitution.*

92 Fletcher, *Our Secret Constitution,* 53.

93 A precursor of this view was the era of Jacksonian democracy in the 1830s.

94 A contemporaneous celebration of the nation as an entity can be seen in the poetry of Walt Whitman.

95 Wills, *Lincoln at Gettysburg,* 38. Wills insists that this was not a coincidence, and he debunks the notion that Lincoln hastily dashed off his remarks while on his way to the town or to the speech itself (27–31).

96 Fletcher, *Our Secret Constitution,* 35, 4. Others might nominate Lincoln's second inaugural address, in which he offered reconciliation to the South, or Martin Luther King Jr.'s "I Have a Dream" speech.

97 The *Dred Scott* case is explained in Chapter 15.

98 The equal protection clause is covered fully in Chapter 14, and the due process clause is covered fully in Chapter 13.

99 Fletcher, *Our Secret Constitution,* 25.

100 In this vein, Congress first experimented with an income tax during the war. It would return to this tax in the decades after the war.

101 For example, the abolitionist movement and the Fifteenth Amendment would fuel the drive for women's suffrage, as explained in Chapter 14.

102 E. J. Dionne Jr., "Culture Wars," *Washington Post National Weekly Edition,* March 17–23, 2008, 25.

103 Adam Cohen, *Nothing to Fear: FDR's Inner Circle and the Hundred Days That Created Modern America* (New York: Penguin, 2010), 32.

104 Ibid., 34.

105 This section borrows heavily from Ackerman, *We the People,* and Theodore J. Lowi, *The Personal President* (Ithaca, N.Y.: Cornell University Press, 1985). For a different view about the impact of the New Deal, see G. Edward White, *The Constitution and the New Deal* (Cambridge, Mass.: Harvard University Press, 2001).

106 We never had a pure laissez-faire approach—there always was some governmental regulation—but this is the term most associated with the attitudes of the time.

107 At least one legal scholar dismisses the notion that the Court's "old men" were reactionaries or fools. Although today people consider them mistaken, at the time they were following established doctrine. Ackerman, *We the People.*

108 Lowi, *Personal President,* 49. Writers during the Depression and in the decades after it also recognized this as a revolution. Ernest K. Lindley, *The Roosevelt Revolution, First Phase* (New York: Viking, 1933); Mario Einaudi, *The Roosevelt Revolution* (New York: Harcourt, Brace & World, 1959).

109 Karl Vick, "A President Who Woke Up Washington," *Washington Post National Weekly Edition,* April 28, 1997, 8.

110 Lowi, *Personal President,* 44.

111 Ibid., xi; Ackerman, *We the People.*

112 Of course, the process was evolutionary; the changes did not spring solely from these two crises. Moreover, some might maintain that the Supreme Court under the leadership of Chief Justice Earl Warren in the 1950s and 1960s also remade the Constitution because of its rulings expanding the Bill of Rights. Yet the changes brought about by the Warren Court probably had less impact overall than those wrought by Reconstruction or the New Deal.

113 John W. Kingdon, *America the Unusual* (Boston: Bedford/St. Martin's, 1999), 7–22. Exceptions include education and regulation of civil rights and the environment. They also include a massive national defense establishment and an extensive criminal justice system. In these aspects, our government is bigger than those in many other advanced industrialized countries.

114 For a discussion of the role played by the philosophy of pragmatism in resolving these conflicts, see Fletcher, *Our Secret Constitution,* ch. 11.

115 Henry Steele Commager, *Living Ideas in America* (New York: Harper & Row, 1951), 109.

116 West, *Vindicating the Founders,* xi.

117 Parts of the Constitution have been copied by some Latin American countries, Liberia (founded by Americans), and the Philippines (formerly an American territory).

118 "South Africa Looks at U.S. Constitution," *Lincoln Journal Star,* October 7, 1990; David Remnick, "'We, the People,' from the Russian," *Washington Post National Weekly Edition,* September 10, 1990, 11.

119 European countries, Australia, Canada, Costa Rica, Israel, Japan, and New Zealand.

120 Dahl, *How Democratic Is the American Constitution?* tabs. 1 and 2, 164–165. Dahl counts only countries that have "strong" federalism, bicameralism, and judicial review.

Chapter 3

1 Kirk Johnson, "States' Rights Is Rallying Cry of Resistance for Lawmakers," *New York Times,* March 16, 2010, A1.

2 Ralph Blumenthal, "Citing Violence, 2 Border States Declare a Crisis," *New York Times,* August 17, 2005, A14; John M. Broder, "Governors of Border States Have Hope, and Questions," *New York Times,* May 17, 2006, 1.

3 "Vigilantes or Civilian Border Patrol? A Debate on the Minuteman Project," April 5, 2005, www.democracynow.org/2005/4/5/vigilantes_or_civilian_border_patrol_a. The Minuteman Project has continued its initiatives in subsequent years, but there have been a number of organizational changes due to leadership controversies.

4 http://abcnews.go.com/Politics/john-mccain-baffled-controversy-wildfire-illegal-immigrants-comments/story?id=13892534.

5 Paul Davenport, "Napolitano Calls Summit on Immigration Law," June 8, 2005, www.azcentral.com.

6 Pew Research Center Publications, "Public Supports Arizona Immigration Law," May 12, 2010, 1, pewresearch.org/.

7 National Conference of State Legislatures, "2010 Immigration-Related Bills and Resolutions in the States," January–March 2010, 1, www.ncsl.org/default.aspx?TabId=20244.

8 William H. Riker, *The Development of American Federalism* (Boston: Kluwer Academic, 1987), 6.

9 See Madison's discussion of this in *Federalist Paper* 39.

10 See, for example, Michael Freeman, "A Law Enforcement Collaboration with ICE Melts the Gang Problem in Haines City," April 24, 2012, freelinemediaorlando.com; Farid Zakaria, "Berkeley Challenges Law Enforcement Collaboration in Order to Restore Civil Liberties," People's Blog for the Constitution, January 3, 2012, www.constitutioncampaign.org/blog; Daniel M. Stewart, "Collaboration between Federal and Local Law Enforcement: An Examination of Texas Police Chiefs' Perceptions," *Police Quarterly* 14, no. 4 (December 2011), 407–430.

11 Larry N. Gerston, *American Federalism: A Concise Introduction* (Armonk, N.Y.: M.E. Sharpe, 2007).

12 Ibid.

13 For a listing of unfunded mandates whose costs exceed the threshold set by the reform legislation, see Standing Committee on Budgets and Review, National Conference on State Legislatures, "Mandate Monitor: Intergovernmental Mandates under UMRA That Exceed the Threshold," 2012, www.ncsl.org/state-federal-committees/scbudg/mandate-monitor-overview.aspx.

14 For a review of the politics surrounding the law, its provisions, and limitations, see Timothy J. Conlon, *From New Federalism to Devolution: Twenty-five Years of Intergovernmental Reform* (Washington, D.C.: Brookings Institution Press, 1998), ch. 13. See also Gerston, *American Federalism.*

15 Alice Rivlin, *Reviving the American Dream: The Economy, the States, and the Federal Government* (Washington, D.C.: Brookings Institution Press, 1992).

16 See, for example, William J. Clinton, "Federalism," Executive Order 13132, *Federal Register* 54, no. 163 (August 10, 1999), 43255–43259. Clinton discussed his views on state activism and federalism in general with the historian Gary Wills in "The War between the States and Washington," *New York Times Magazine,* July 5, 1998, 26.

17 James W. Brosnan, "Not Taxing Internet Sales Hurts," *Champaign-Urbana News-Gazette,* February 21, 2000, A6. "With Congress Stalled, States Work Their Own 'Amazon Tax' Deals," *StateNet Capitol Journal* 20, no. 14 (May 7, 2012).

18 Rep. Barney Frank (D-Mass.), quoted in Michael Grunwald, "Everybody Talks about States' Rights," *Washington Post National Weekly Edition,* November 1, 1999, 29. Frank was referring to Republicans only, but the quote fits Democrats as well.

19 Alfred Kelly and Winfred Harbeson, *The American Constitution: Its Origins and Development* (New York: Norton, 1976).

20 Linda Greenhouse, "In Roberts Hearing, Specter Assails Court," *New York Times,* September 15, 2005, 1.

21 Dan Carney, "Latest Supreme Court Rulings Reinforce the Federalist Trend," *Congressional Quarterly,* June 26, 1999, 1528; Linda Greenhouse, "High Court Faces Moment of Truth in Federalism Cases," *New York Times,* March 28, 1999, 20.

22 National Conference of State Legislatures, "Looking Back: Total Measures on the Ballot, 1998–2010," www.ncsl.org/legislatures-elections/elections/ballot-measures-2010-an-overview.aspx.

23 John Tierney, "New York Wants Its Money Back, or at Least Some of It," *New York Times,* June 27, 2004, sec. 4, 4.

24 Robert Pear, "U.S. Report Criticizes States' Use of Medicaid Consultants," *New York Times,* June 28, 2005, A20.

25 Monica Davey, "States Barter Fish and Bullets to Save Money," *New York Times,* May 23, 2009.

26 John M. Broder, "Geography Is Dividing Democrats over Energy," *New York Times,* January 27, 2009.

Chapter 4

1 Pew Research Center for the People and the Press, "Political Knowledge Update: Well Known: Twitter; Little Known: TARP," July 15, 2010, http://pewresearch.org/pubs/1668/political-news-iq-update-7-2010-twitter-tarp-roberts.

2 Center for Information and Research on Civic Learning and Engagement, Tufts University, Jonathan M. Tisch College of Citizenship and Public Service, "Massachusetts Senate Election: Youth Turnout Was Just 15%, Compared to 57% for Older Citizens; Young Voters Favored Coakley," *Quick Facts,* http://www.civicyouth.org/ (accessed February 4, 2010).

3 Jon Henke, "Ideologically Conservative, Operationally Liberal," June 27, 2006, http://www.qando.net/details.aspx?Entry=4137 (accessed February 28, 2012).

4 Rasmussen Reports, *Obama Approval Index Month-by-Month,* June 2, 2010, http://www.rasmussenreports.com/public_content/politics/obama_administration/obama_approval_index_month_by_month (accessed July 28, 2010).

5 Timothy E. Cook, "The Bear Market in Political Socialization and the Costs of Misunderstood Psychological Theories," *American Political Science Review* 79 (1985), 1079–1093.

6 S. W. Moore et al., "The Civic Awareness of Five- and Six-Year-Olds," *Western Political Quarterly* 29 (1976), 418.

7 R. W. Connell, *The Child's Construction of Politics* (Carlton, Australia: Melbourne University Press, 1971).

8 Fred I. Greenstein, *Children and Politics* (New Haven, Conn.: Yale University Press, 1965), 122; see also Fred I. Greenstein, "The Benevolent Leader Re-visited: Children's Images of Political Leaders in Three Democracies," *American Political Science Review* 69 (1975), 1317–1398; Robert D. Hess and Judith V. Torney, *The Development of Political Attitudes in Children* (Chicago: Aldine, 1967).

9 Amy Carter and Ryan Teten, "Assessing Changing Views of the President: Ravishing Greenstein's Children and Politics," *Presidential Studies Quarterly* 32 (2002), 453–462.

10 Greenstein, *Children and Politics.*

11 Hess and Torney, *The Development of Political Attitudes in Children;* Connell, *The Child's Construction of Politics.*

12 F. Christopher Arterton, "The Impact of Watergate on Children's Attitudes toward the President," *Political Science Quarterly* 89 (1974), 269–288; see also P. Frederick Hartwig and Charles Tidmarch, "Children and Political Reality: Changing Images of the President," paper presented at the 1974 Annual Meeting of the Southern Political Science Association; J. Dennis and C. Webster, "Children's Images of the President and Government in 1962 and 1974," *American Politics Quarterly* 4 (1975), 386–405; Robert Hawkins, Suzanne Pingree, and D. Roberts, "Watergate and Political Socialization," *American Politics Quarterly* 4 (1975), 406–436.

13 Michael Delli Carpini, *Stability and Change in American Politics: The Coming of Age of the Generation of the 1960s* (New York: New York University Press, 1986), 86–89.

14 Richard M. Merelman, *Political Socialization and Educational Climates* (New York: Holt, Rinehart and Winston, 1971), 54; more recently, the percentage of liberals among college freshmen and the public is about the same.

15 Roberta Sigel and Marilyn Hoskin, *The Political Involvement of Adolescents* (New Brunswick, N.J.: Rutgers University Press, 1981).

16 John R. Hibbing and Elizabeth Theiss-Morse, *Congress as Public Enemy: Public Attitudes toward American Political Institutions* (Cambridge, England: Cambridge University Press, 1995). It is plausible to assume that the content of early political socialization influences what is learned later, but the assumption has not been adequately tested. Thus, we might expect the positive opinions toward government and politics developed early in childhood to condition the impact of traumatic events later in life; David Easton and Jack Dennis, *Children in the Political System: Origins of Regime Legitimacy* (New York: McGraw-Hill, 1969); Robert Weissberg, *Political Learning, Political Choice, and Democratic Citizenship* (Englewood Cliffs, N.J.: Prentice Hall, 1974). See also Donald Searing, Joel Schwartz, and Alden Line, "The Structuring Principle: Political Socialization and Belief System," *American Political Science Review* 67 (1973), 414–432.

17 John Alford, Carolyn Funk, and John Hibbing, "Are Political Orientations Genetically Transmitted?" *American Political Science Review* 99 (May 2005), 153–168; Kevin Smith, John R. Alford, Peter K. Hatemi, Carolyn Funk, and John R. Hibbing, "How Do We Know Political Attitudes Are Inherited and Why Should We Care?" *American Journal of Political Science* 56 (January 2012), 17–33; How do scientists determine hereditary traits from those environmentally determined? Much of this research looks at identical twins, who share the exact same genetic traits, and compares them with nonidentical twins, who do not.

18 Christopher Achen, "Parental Socialization and Rational Party Identification," *Political Behavior* 24 (June 2002), 151–170.

19 Kent Tedin, "The Influence of Parents on the Political Attitudes of Adolescents," *American Political Science Review* 68 (1974), 1579–1592.

20 Dean Jaros, Herbert Hirsch, and Frederic J. Fleron Jr., "The Malevolent Leader: Political Socialization in an American Subculture," *American Political Science Review* 62 (1968), 564–575.

21 M. Kent Jennings, *Generations and Politics* (Princeton, N.J.: Princeton University Press, 1981).

22 Kathleen Dolan, "Attitudes, Behaviors, and the Influence of the Family: A Re-examination of the Role of Family Structure," *Political Behavior* 17 (1995), 251–264.

23 On the impact of the public schools and teachers on political socialization, particularly with respect to loyalty and patriotism, see Hess and Torney, *The Development of Political Attitudes in Children.*

24 Gabriel A. Almond and Sidney Verba, *The Civic Culture: Political Attitudes and Democracy in Five Nations, an Analytic Study* (Boston: Little, Brown, 1965); John R. Hibbing and Elizabeth Theiss-Morse, "Civics Is Not Enough: Teaching Barbarics in K–12," *PS: Political Science and Politics* (1996), 12; Norman H. Nie, Jane Junn, and Kenneth Stehlik-Barry, *Education and Democratic Citizenship in America* (Chicago: University of Chicago Press, 1996).

25 Nie et al., *Education and Democratic Citizenship in America.*

26 Richard G. Niemi and Jane Junn, *Civil Education: What Makes Students Learn* (New Haven, Conn.: Yale University Press, 1998). See also Richard G. Niemi and Julia Smith, "Enrollments in High School Government Classes: Are We Shortchanging Both Citizenship and Political Science Training?" *PS: Political Science and Politics* 34 (2001), 281–288. Honors and advanced placement (AP) programs, along with active learning, can improve student understanding and achievement in American history.

27 Stephen Bennett, Staci Rhine, and Richard Flickinger, "Reading's Impact on Democratic Citizenship in America," *Political Behavior* 22 (2000), 167–195.

28 Nie et al., *Education and Democratic Citizenship in America.*

29 Alfonso Damico, M. Margaret Conway, and Sandra Bowman Damico, "Patterns of Political Trust and Mistrust: Three Moments in the

Lives of Democratic Citizens," *Polity* 32 (2000), 377–400.

[30] Joel Westheimer and Joseph Kahne, "Educating the 'Good' Citizen: Political Choices and Pedagogical Goals," *PS: Political Science and Politics* 2 (2004), 241–247.

[31] J. H. Pryor, L. DeAngelo, L. Palucki Blake, S. Hurtado, and S. Tran, *The American Freshman: National Norms for Fall 2011* (Los Angeles: Higher Education Research Institute, UCLA, 2012).

[32] http://www.nytimes.com/2010/01/18/arts/ 18liberal.html.

[33] Ibid.

[34] Rebecca Trounson, "Poll Says College Freshmen Lean Left," www.commondreams.org/headlines02/ 0128-01.htm.

[35] Alexander W. Astin, William S. Korn, and Linda Sax, *The American Freshman: Thirty Year Trends* (Los Angeles: Higher Education Research Institute, Graduate School of Education and Information, 1997).

[36] Maxwell McCombs and Donald Shaw, "The Agenda Setting Function of the Media," *Public Opinion Quarterly* 36 (1972), 176–187.

[37] Benjamin I. Page, Robert Y. Shapiro, and Glenn R. Dempsey, "What Moves Public Opinion?" *American Political Science Review* 81 (1987), 23–44.

[38] Herbert F. Weisberg, "Marital Differences in American Voting," *Public Opinion Quarterly* 51 (1987), 335–343.

[39] Michael A. Fletcher, "On Campus, a Patriotic Surge," *Washington Post National Weekly Edition,* December 10, 2001, 31.

[40] Philip E. Converse, Aage R. Clausen, and Warren E. Miller, "Electoral Myth and Reality: The 1964 Election," *American Political Science Review* 59 (1965), 321–326.

[41] For a review of the history of polling, see Bernard Hennessy, *Public Opinion*, 4th ed. (Monterey, Calif.: Brooks/Cole, 1983), 42–44, 46–50. See also Charles W. Roll and Albert H. Cantril, *Polls: Their Use and Misuse in Politics* (New York: Basic Books, 1972), 3–6.

[42] Peverill Squire, "Why the 1936 Literary Digest Poll Failed," *Public Opinion Quarterly* 52 (1988), 125–133; see also Don Cahalan, "The Digest Poll Rides Again," *Public Opinion Quarterly* 53 (1989), 107–113.

[43] Jack Rosenthal, "Precisely False vs. Approximately Right: A Reader's Guide to Polls," *New York Times*, August 27, 2006, Week in Review, 10.

[44] Hennessy, *Public Opinion,* 46.

[45] Joshua Green, "The Other War Room," *Washington Monthly,* April 2002, 11–16.

[46] Joe Klein, *The Natural* (New York: Doubleday, 2002), 7.

[47] Green, "The Other War Room."

[48] John F. Harris, "Presidency by Poll," *Washington Post National Weekly Edition,* January 8-14, 2001, 9-10.

[49] Steven Mufson and John E. Harris, "Clinton's Global Growth," *Washington Post National Weekly Edition,* January 22, 2001, 11.

[50] Lawrence R. Jacobs and Robert Y. Shapiro, *Politicians Don't Pander: Political Manipulation and the Loss of Democratic Responsiveness* (Chicago: University of Chicago Press, 2000).

[51] Ibid., 12.

[52] David Broder, "Push Polls Plunge Politics to a New Low," *Lincoln Journal Star,* October 9, 1994, 5E.

[53] Richard Morin, "Surveying the Surveyors," *Washington Post National Weekly Edition,* March 2, 1992, 37.

[54] Bill Kovack and Tom Rosensteil, "Campaign Lite," *Washington Monthly,* January–February 2001, 31–38.

[55] *All Things Considered*, National Public Radio, October 30, 1992.

[56] Richard Morin, "Voters Are Hung Up on Polling," *Washington Post National Weekly Edition*, November 1–7, 2004, 12.

[57] Scott Keeter, Leah Christian, and Michael Dimock, Pew Research Center, "The Growing Gap between Landline and Dual Frame Election Polls: Republican Vote Share Bigger in Landline-Only Surveys," November 22, 2010, http:// pewresearch.org/pubs/1806/growing-gap-between-landline-and-dual-frame-election-polls.

[58] Morin, "Voters Are Hung Up on Polling," 12.

[59] Ibid.

[60] "Real Clear Politics," www.realclearpolitics.com/ polls.html; see also Pew Research Center for the People and the Press, "Pre-Election Polls Largely Accurate," November 23, 2004, www.peoplepress. org/commentary/display.php3?AnalysisID5102.

[61] http://www.cbsnews.com/stories/2008/11/07/ politics/main4581355.shtml. Fivethirtyeight.com's analyst, Nate Silver, examining pre-election polls, correctly predicted 49 of 50 state votes.

[62] Scott Keeter, Jocelyn Kiley, Leah Christian, and Michael Dimock, "Perils of Polling in Election '08," Pew Research Center for the People and the Press, June 25, 2009, http://pewresearch.org/ pubs/1266/polling-challenges-election-08-suc- cess-in-dealing-with.

[63] Michael Lewis-Beck, Charles Tien, and Richard Nadeau, "Obama's Missed Landslide: A Racial Cost?" *PS: Political Science and Politics* 43, no. 1 (January 2010), 69–76.

[64] Richard Morin and Claudia Deane, "Why the Florida Exit Polls Were Wrong," *Washington Post,* November 8, 2000.

[65] *New Yorker,* March 20, 1999, 18.

[66] A study by the Pew Foundation, http://peoplepress .org/reports/display.php3?ReportID5319.

[67] Richard Morin, "Tuned Out, Turned Off," *Washington Post National Weekly Edition,* February 5, 1996, 6–8.

[68] Pew Research Center for the People and the Press, "Political Knowledge Update," March 31, 2011, http://pewresearch.org/pubs/1944/political-news-quiz-iq-congress-control-obesity-energy-facebook.

[69] Pew Foundation study, "Political Knowledge Update: Most of the Public Is Familiar with Key Political and Iraq Facts," September 24, 2007, people-press.org/ reports/display.php3?Report ID5319.

[70] Ibid.

[71] Center for Political Studies, 1986 National Election Study, University of Michigan, "Wapner Top Judge in Recognition Poll," *Lincoln Journal Star,* June 23, 1989, 1.

[72] Richard Morin, "They Know Only What They Don't Like," *Washington Post National Weekly Edition,* 35.

[73] Ibid.

[74] Richard Morin, "Foreign Aid: Mired in Misunderstanding," *Washington Post National Weekly Edition,* March 20, 1995, 37.

[75] Richard Morin, "What Informed Public Opinion?" *Washington Post National Weekly Edition,* April 10, 1995, 36.

[76] Richard Morin, "We Love It—What We Know of It," *Washington Post National Weekly Edition,* September 22, 1997, 35.

[77] Michael Delli Carpini and Scott Keeter, "Stability and Change in the U.S. Public's Knowledge of Politics," *Public Opinion Quarterly* (1991), 583–612.

[78] Pew Research Center for the People and the Press, "Many Voters Unaware of Basic Facts about GOP Candidates," January 12, 2012, http:// pewresearch.org/pubs/2169/republican-candidates-voter-knowledge-mitt-romney-newt-gingrich-ron-paul.

[79] Vladimer Orlando Key, *The Responsible Electorate* (Cambridge, Mass.: Harvard University Press, 1966); Norman H. Nie, Sidney Verba, and John R. Petrocik, *The Changing American Voter* (Cambridge, Mass.: Harvard University Press, 1976), ch. 18; Samuel L. Popkin, *The Reasoning Voter: Communication and Persuasion in Presidential Campaigns* (Chicago: University of Chicago Press, 1994).

[80] Popkin, *The Reasoning Voter.*

[81] Morin, "Tuned Out, Turned Off," 8.

[82] Harold Meyerson, "Fact-Free News," *Washington Post National Weekly,* October 10–26, 2003, 26.

[83] Lloyd Free and Hadley Cantril, *The Political Beliefs of Americans* (New Brunswick, N.J.: Rutgers University Press, 1967).

[84] Lydia Saad, "Conservatives Remain the Largest Ideological Group in U.S.," January 12, 2012, http://www.gallup.com/poll/152021/ Conservatives-Remain-Largest-Ideological-Group.aspx.

[85] Jonathan Rauch, "Bipolar Disorder," *Atlantic Monthly,* January–February 2005, 102.

[86] http://www.washingtonpost.com/wp-dyn/ content/article/2008/04/11/AR200804 1103965_2 .html?sid=ST2008041200232.

[87] Naomi Cahn and June Carbone, *Red Families v. Blue Families: Legal Polarization and the Creation of Culture* (New York: Oxford University Press, 2010).

[88] Jeremy White , Robert Gebeloff, Ford Fessenden, Archie Tse, and Alan McLean, "The Geography of Government Benefits," *New York Times*, February 11, 2012, http://www.nytimes.com/interactive/2012/02/12/us/entitlement-map.html?ref=us (accessed February 21, 2012).

[89] Andrew Gelman, *Red State, Blue State, Rich State, Poor State: Why Americans Vote the Way They Do* (Princeton, N.J.: Princeton University Press, 2009).

[90] Various studies are summarized in Rauch, "Bipolar Disorder," 102–110.

[91] "A Polarized Nation?" (editorial), *Washington Post,* November 14, 2004, 6. Several of these ideas were summarized nicely in this article.

[92] This section draws heavily on Howard Schuman, Charlotte Steeh, and Lawrence Bobo, *Racial Attitudes in America* (Cambridge, Mass.: Harvard University Press, 1985); Howard Schuman, Charlotte Steeh, Lawrence Bobo, and Maria Krysan, *Racial Attitudes in America,* rev. ed. (1997); data summaries are drawn from the General Social Surveys of the National Opinion Research Center, University of Chicago, and National Elections Studies of CPS, University of Michigan; see also Lee Sigelman and Susan Welch, *Black Americans' Views of Racial Inequality* (Cambridge, Mass.: Cambridge University Press, 1991).

[93] General Social Survey, National Opinion Research Center, University of Chicago, 1996; Richard Morin, "Polling in Black and White: Sometimes the Answers Depend on Who's Asking the Questions," *Washington Post National Weekly Edition,* October 30, 1989, 37.

[94] General Social Survey, 1996; "Whites Retain Negative Views of Minorities, a Survey Finds," *New York Times,* January 10, 1991, C19; Mary R. Jackman, "General and Applied Tolerance: Does Education Increase Commitment to Racial Inequality?" *American Journal of Political Science* 25 (1981), 256–269; Donald Kinder and David Sears, "Prejudice and Politics: Symbolic Racism versus Racial Threats to the Good Life," *Journal of Personality and Social Psychology* 40 (1981), 414–431.

[95] "Whites Retain Negative Views of Minorities, a Survey Finds," C19.

[96] General Social Survey, 1998; see also Donald Kinder and Lynn Saunders, *Divided by Color: Racial Politics and Democratic Ideals* (Chicago: University of Chicago Press, 1996); Howard Schuman and Lawrence Bobo, "Survey-Based Experiments on White Attitudes toward Residential Integration," *American Journal of Sociology* 94 (1988), 519–526; see also Schuman et al., *Racial Attitudes in America,* rev. ed.

[97] General Social Survey, 1998.

[98] Richard Morin, "It's Not as It Seems," *Washington Post National Weekly Edition*, July 16, 2001, 34.

[99] Ibid.

[100] Ibid.; ABC/*Washington Post* poll, 1981 and 1986.

[101] Steven A. Holmes and Richard Morin, "Poll Reveals Shades of Promise and Doubt," *Washington Post National Weekly Edition,* June 12–18, 2000, 9–11.

[102] "Survey Reports: Blacks Upbeat about Black Progress, Prospects A Year After Obama's Election," January 12, 2010, http://people-press.org/report/576/.

[103] Susan Page and Carly Mallenbaum, "Poll: MLK's Dream Realized, but a Gulf between Races Remains," *USA Today,* http://www.usatoday.com/news/nation/2011-08-17-race-equality-poll-mlk_n.htm.

Chapter 5

[1] Information for this vignette is drawn from Ashley Parker, "At Pundit School, Learning How to Smile and Interrupt," *New York Times,* October 26, 2008, ST1.

[2] James David Barber, *The Pulse of Politics* (New York: Norton, 1980), 9.

[3] Kevin Phillips, "A Matter of Privilege," *Harper's,* January 1977, 95.

[4] Shanto Iyengar, *Is Anyone Responsible? How Television Frames Political Issues* (Chicago: University of Chicago Press, 1991), 1.

[5] Media time overlaps with work time per day, because many people listen to music, watch TV, or surf the Web while working. Richard Harwood, "So Many Media, So Little Time," *Washington Post National Weekly Edition,* September 7, 1992, 28.

[6] Harold W. Stanley and Richard G. Niemi, *Vital Statistics on American Politics* (Washington, D.C.: Congressional Quarterly Press, 1998), 47; Edwin Diamond, *The Tin Kazoo* (Cambridge, Mass.: MIT Press, 1975), 13.

[7] Study by Kaiser Family Foundation, cited in Lauran Neergaard, "Parents Encouraging TV Use among Young Kids, Study Says," *Lincoln Journal Star,* May 25, 2006, 4A, and in Ruth Marcus, "Is Decency Going down the Tubes?" *Washington Post National Weekly Edition,* June 26–July 9, 2006, 26.

[8] Lindsey Tanner, "Studies Suggest Watching TV Harms Children Academically," *Lincoln Journal Star,* July 5, 2005, 6A.

[9] Doris A. Graber, *Mass Media and American Politics* (Washington, D.C.: Congressional Quarterly Press, 1980), 2.

[10] William Lutz, *Doublespeak* (New York: Harper & Row, 1989), 73–74.

[11] According to the Kaiser Family Foundation. Dalton Conley, "Wired for Distraction," *Time,* February 21, 2011, 55; Claudia Wallis, "The Multitasking Generation," *Time,* March 27, 2006, 50–51.

[12] Rob McGann, "Internet Edges Out Family Time More than TV Time," *ClickZ,* January 5, 2005, www.clickz.com/stats/sectors/demographics/article.php/3455061.

[13] "The New News Landscape: Rise of the Internet," Pew Research Center Publications, March 1, 2010, pewresearch.org/pubs/1508/internet-cell-phone-users-news-social-experience.

[14] Charles Peters, *How Washington Really Works* (Reading, Mass.: Addison-Wesley, 1980), 32.

[15] Mark Bowden, "Mr. Murdoch Goes to War," *The Atlantic,* July–August 2008, 110.

[16] Ibid.

[17] Elizabeth Gleick, "Read All about It," *Time,* October 21, 1998, 66; Dana Millbank, "A Bias for Mainstream News," *Washington Post National Weekly Edition,* March 28–April 3, 2005, 23. See also Tom Rosenstiel, *The State of the News Media, 2004* (Washington, D.C.: Project for Excellence in Journalism, 2004).

[18] Eric Alterman, "Out of Print," *New Yorker,* March 31, 2008, 49.

[19] Since 1960. James Rainey, "More News Outlets, Fewer Stories: New Media 'Paradox,'" *Los Angeles Times,* March 13, 2006, www.latimes.com/news/nationworld/nation/la-nanews13mar13,0,2018145.story?

[20] Belinda Luscombe, "Killing the News to Save It," *Time,* August 17, 2009, 49.

[21] Project for Excellence in Journalism, "The Changing Newsroom," July 21, 2008, http://journalism.org/node/11963.

[22] Bill Keller, quoted in "Verbatim," *Time,* August 14, 2009, 14.

[23] Millbank, "A Bias for Mainstream News."

[24] Michael J. Wolf and Geoffrey Sands, "Fearless Predictions," *Brill's Content,* July–August 1999, 110. For a discussion of the future impact of the Internet on media concentration and diversity, see Robert W. McChesney, *The Problem of the Media* (New York: Monthly Review Press, 2004), 211–217.

[25] Ibid.

[26] "Media Use and Evaluation," Gallup poll, December 2008, gallup.com/poll/1663/Media-Use-Evaluation.aspx.

[27] Pew Research Center Project for Excellence in Journalism, cited in Michael Liedtke, "Study: Newspapers Still a Step Ahead," *Lincoln Journal Star,* January 11, 2010, A7.

[28] Scarborough Research, cited in "Study: 74 Percent of U.S. Adults Read Papers at Least Weekly," *Lincoln Journal Star,* November 20, 2009, D1.

[29] "Media Use and Evaluation."

[30] Ibid.

[31] Ibid.

[32] Ibid. The exact percentage in 2008 was 31, but given the rate of increase shown in these polls since 1995, the actual percentage today would be higher.

[33] "The New News Landscape."

[34] Brian Stelter, "Finding Political News Online, the Young Pass It On," *New York Times,* March 27, 2008, www.nytimes.com/2008/03/27/us/politics/27voters.html?ref5todayspaper&pagewant.

[35] Eve Gerber, "Divided We Watch," *Brill's Content,* February 2001, 110–111.

[36] Donald Kaul, "Effects of Merger between AOL, Time Warner Will Be Inescapable," *Lincoln*

Journal Star, January 18, 2000; Ken Auletta, "Leviathan," *New Yorker,* October 29, 2001, 50.

[37] McChesney, *Problem of the Media,* 235–240; Robert W. McChesney and John Nichols, "It's the Media, Stupid," in *Voices of Dissent,* eds. William F. Grover and Joseph G. Peschek (New York: Longman, 2004), 120.

[38] For examination of this development, see Lawrence Lessing, *The Future of Ideas* (New York: Random House, 2001). For an alternative view, see McChesney, *Problem of the Media,* 205–209.

[39] Benjamin M. Compaine, *Who Owns the Media?* (White Plains, N.Y.: Knowledge Industry Publications, 1979), 11, 76–77; Michael Parenti, *Inventing Reality* (New York: St. Martin's Press, 1986), 27; Paul Farhi, "You Can't Tell a Book by Its Cover," *Washington Post National Weekly Edition,* December 5, 1988, 21; Edmund L. Andrews, "A New Tune for Radio: Hard Times," *New York Times,* March 1992.

[40] Robert McChesney, "AOL–Time Warner Merger Is Dangerous and Undemocratic," *Lincoln Journal Star,* January 17, 2000.

[41] Rosenstiel, *State of the News Media,* 9.

[42] Daren Fonda, "National Prosperous Radio," *Time,* March 24, 2003, 50; Marc Fisher, "Sounds All Too Familiar," *Washington Post National Weekly Edition,* May 26, 2003, 23.

[43] McChesney, *Problem of the Media,* 178.

[44] Mary Lynn F. Jones, "No News Is Good News," *American Prospect,* May 2003, 39. For a history of the development of Clear Channel, see Alec Foege, *Right of the Dial: The Rise of Clear Channel and the Fall of Commercial Radio* (New York: Faber & Faber, 2008).

[45] "Broadcaster: *Nightline* Won't Air on Its Stations," *Lincoln Journal Star,* April 30, 2004. Sinclair was the largest television chain, as measured by number of stations, at the time.

[46] "Clear Channel Growth the Result of 1996 Deregulation," *Lincoln Journal Star,* October 5, 2003.

[47] Elizabeth Lesly Stevens, "Mouse.Ke.Fear," *Brill's Content,* December 1998–January 1999, 95. For other examples, see Jane Mayer, "Bad News," *New Yorker,* August 14, 2000, 30–36.

[48] Jim Hightower, *There's Nothing in the Middle of the Road but Yellow Stripes and Dead Armadillos* (New York: HarperCollins, 1997), 121.

[49] The Project for Excellence in Journalism, affiliated with Columbia University's Graduate School of Journalism, concluded after a five-year study that newscasts by stations owned by smaller companies were significantly higher in quality than newscasts by stations owned by larger companies. "Does Ownership Matter in Local Television News?" February 17, 2003, www.journalism.org.

[50] Neil Hickey, "Money Lust," *Columbia Journalism Review,* July–August 1998, 28.

[51] David Simon, "Does Anyone Care?" *Washington Post National Weekly Edition,* January 28–February 3, 2008, 27.

[52] *Now, with Bill Moyers,* PBS, April 11, 2003. Clear Channel uses "voice tracking" to give the illusion that the programming is originating locally. The company's disc jockey tapes short segments with local references and integrates these into the program feed to the local station.

[53] Ted Turner, "Break Up This Band!" *Washington Monthly,* July–August 2004, 35.

[54] After an effort to lure conservatives from Fox by unleashing Lou Dobbs to bash immigrants and give the "birthers" a microphone.

[55] In response, ABC made all of its prime-time programming available in Spanish in 2005.

[56] Ken Auletta, "War of Choice," *New Yorker,* January 9, 2012, 32. Also see Laura M. Colarusso, "The Anchor," *Washington Monthly,* May/June, 2012, 13–19.

[57] Scott Shane, "For Liberal Bloggers, Libby Trial Is Fun and Fodder," *New York Times,* February 15, 2007, www.nytimes.com/2007/02/15/washington/15bloggers.html? hp&ex=1171602000&en=5afe9e7498071C7f&ei=50948partner=homepage.

[58] Howard Kurtz, "Welcome to Spin City," *Washington Post National Weekly Edition,* March 16, 1998, 6. See also Roger Parloff, "If This Ain't Libel . . . ," *Brill's Content,* Fall 2001, 95–113.

[59] Matt Bai, "Can Bloggers Get Real?" *New York Times Magazine,* May 28, 2006, 13.

[60] Daniel Lyons, "Arianna's Answer," *Newsweek,* August 2, 2010, 45.

[61] Bill Keller, "Let Me Take Off My Tinfoil Hat for a Moment," *New York Times Magazine,* June 5, 2011, 12.

[62] Charles Peters, "Tilting at Windmills," *Washington Monthly,* September 2007, 8.

[63] Bill Keller, quoted in Eric Alterman, "Out of Print," *New Yorker,* March 31, 2008, 56.

[64] Eric Lawrence, John Sides, and Henry Farrell, "Self-Segregation or Deliberation? Blog Readership, Participation, and Polarization in American Politics," *Perspectives on Politics* 8 (March 2010), 141–157. However, a minority of liberals do read blogs across the ideological spectrum.

[65] Virginia Heffernan, "Clicking and Choosing," *New York Times Magazine,* November 16, 2008, 22.

[66] Times Mirror Center for the People and the Press, *The Vocal Minority in American Politics* (Washington, D.C.: Times Mirror Center for the People and the Press, 1993).

[67] In addition, she received $50,000 for a book elaborating on her story, $250,000 for posing nude for *Penthouse* magazine, and about $20,000 for appearing on German and Spanish television shows. "Flowers Says She Made Half Million from Story," *Lincoln Journal Star,* March 21, 1998.

[68] McChesney, *Problem of the Media,* 96; Paul Taylor, "The New Political Theater," *Mother Jones,* November–December 2000, 30–33. Research suggests that they may actually get substantive information about political issues from these shows. Michael Parkin, "Taking Late Night Comedy Seriously," *Political Research Quarterly* 63 (March 2010), 3–15.

[69] Quoted in Richard Corliss, "Look Who's Talking," *Time,* January 23, 1995, 25.

[70] Ibid.

[71] Anne Barnard and Alan Feuer, "Outraged, and Outrageous," *New York Times,* October 10, 2010, Y27.

[72] Richard A. Posner, "Bad News," *New York Times Book Review,* July 31, 2005, 10–11.

[73] Herb Jackson, "Hoax E-mails Report Senators' Deaths," *Lincoln Journal Star,* July 8, 2010, A2.

[74] Garance Franke-Ruta, "Blog Rolled," *American Prospect,* April 2005, 40. Also see Rebecca Mead, "Rage Machine," *New Yorker,* May 24, 2010, 26, for a profile of Andrew Breitbart.

[75] Eli Saslow, "In Findlay, Ohio, False Rumors Fly," *Washington Post National Weekly Edition,* July 7–13, 2008, 16.

[76] Paul Farhi, "The E-mail Rumor Mill Is Run by Conservatives," *Washington Post,* November 20, 2011, washingtonpost.com/opinions/when-it-comes-to-e-mailed-political-rumors-co.

[77] Mickey Kaus, quoted in James Poniewozik, "The 24-Minute News Cycle," *Time,* November 10, 2008, 50.

[78] The primary blogger was conservative Andrew Sullivan. Nick Gillespie, "A Politically Charged Lightning Rod," *Washington Post National Weekly Edition,* November 16–22, 2009, 39.

[79] Louis Menand, "Comment: Chin Music," *New Yorker,* November 2, 2009, 40.

[80] Mark Carl Rom, "President Obama's Health Care Reform," in Andrew J. Dowdle, Dirk C. Van Raemdonck, and Robert Maranto, eds., *The Obama Presidency: Change and Continuity* (New York: Routledge, 2012), 157.

[81] Report by the Anti-Defamation League, cited in Tim Rutten, "In Beck, Fox Has a Familiar Demagogue," *Lincoln Journal Star,* November 11, 2009, B7.

[82] David Von Drehle, "The Agitator," *Time,* September 28, 2009, 33.

[83] *All Things Considered,* NPR, September 18, 2009.

[84] Leonard Pitts Jr., "The Other 'N' Word Roars Back in a Sick World," *Lincoln Journal Star,* August 20, 2009, B5.

[85] *Fresh Air,* NPR, September 10, 2009; Rick Perlstein, "Crazy Is a Preexisting Condition," *Washington Post National Weekly Edition,* August 24–30, 2009, 25.

[86] Theda Skocpol and Lawrence Jacobs, "Reaching for a New Deal: Ambitious Governance, Economic Meltdown, and Polarized Politics in Obama's First Two Years," paper prepared for the Working Group on *Obama's Agenda and the Dynamics of U.S. Politics* (New York: Russell Sage Foundation, 2010), 46.

[87] Leonard Pitts, Jr., "The Daily Newspaper's Value," *Seattle Times,* June 24, 2012, A!4.

[88] Clay Shirky, quoted in ibid.

[89] Dom Bonafede, "Press Paying More Heed to Substance in Covering 1984 Presidential Election," *National Journal,* October 13, 1984, 19–23.

[90] Seth Mnookin, "Advice to Ari," *Brill's Content,* March 2001, 97.

91 Ken Auletta, "Non-Stop News," *New Yorker*, January 25, 2010, 41.

92 According to historian Michael Beschloss, quoted in ibid., 38 and 43.

93 Auletta, "Non-Stop News," 42.

94 Diane J. Heith, "Obama and the Public Presidency: What Got You Here Won't Get You There," in Bert A. Rockman, Andrew Rudalevige, and Colin Campbell, eds., *The Obama Presidency: Appraisals and Prospects* (Washington, D.C.: CQ, 2012), 144.

95 Hal C. Wingo, "The Mail," *New Yorker*, April 23, 2012, 3.

96 Peters, *How Washington Really Works*, 18.

97 William Greider, "Reporters and Their Sources," *Washington Monthly*, October 1982, 13–15.

98 See, for example, Jeffrey Toobin, *A Vast Conspiracy: The Real Story of the Sex Scandal That Nearly Brought Down a President* (New York: Simon & Schuster, 1999), 310.

99 The initial leak came from the vice president's office. Barton Gellman, *Angler: The Cheney Vice Presidency* (New York: Penguin, 2008), 362–363. For another examination of this incident and the practice of leaking, see Max Frankel, "The Washington Back Channel," *New York Times Magazine*, March 25, 2007, 40.

100 When a spy's identity becomes public, foreign governments try to retrace the spy's movements and determine his or her contacts to see how the CIA operated in their country.

101 Ann Devroy, "The Republicans, It Turns Out, Are a Veritable Fount of Leaks," *Washington Post National Weekly Edition*, November 18, 1991, 23.

102 Daniel Schorr, "A Fact of Political Life," *Washington Post National Weekly Edition*, October 28, 1991, 32.

103 Howard Kurtz, "How Sources and Reporters Play the Game of Leaks," *Washington Post National Weekly Edition*, March 15, 1993, 25.

104 And the Justice Department threatened media organizations with prosecution, under a 1917 statute, for revealing secret information. Dan Eggen, "Bush's Plumbers," *Washington Post National Weekly Edition*, March 13–19, 2006, 11.

105 Nancy Franklin, "Rather Knot," *New Yorker*, October 4, 2004, 108–109.

106 The majority opinion rejected one constitutional basis for the mandate before accepting another.

107 Samuel Kernell, *Going Public: New Strategies of Presidential Leadership* (Washington, D.C.: Congressional Quarterly Press, 1986), 59. Woodrow Wilson also tried to cultivate correspondents and host frequent sessions, but he did not have the knack for this activity and so scaled back the sessions. Kernell, *Going Public*, 60–61. He did perceive that "some men of brilliant ability were in the group, but I soon discovered that the interest of the majority was in the personal and the trivial rather than in principles and policies." James Bennet, "The Flack Pack," *Washington Monthly*, November 1991, 27.

108 Dwight Eisenhower was actually the first president to let the networks televise his press conferences, but he did not do so to reach the public. When he wanted to reach the public, he made a formal speech. The networks found his conferences so untelegenic that they stopped covering the entire session each time. Kernell, *Going Public*, 68.

109 Bennet, "The Flack Pack," 19.

110 Frank Rich, "The Armstrong Williams NewsHour," *New York Times*, June 26, 2005, WK13.

111 Dom Bonafede, "'Mr. President,'" *National Journal*, October 29, 1988, 2756.

112 Charles Hagen, "The Photo Op: Making Icons or Playing Politics?" *New York Times*, February 9, 1992, H28.

113 "The Man behind the Curtain Award," *Mother Jones*, September–October 2002, 67.

114 Kiku Adatto, cited in Howard Kurtz, "Networks Adapt to Changed Campaign Role," *Washington Post*, June 21, 1992, A-19. See also Diana Owen, "Media Mayhem: Performance of the Press in Election 2000," in *Overtime! The Election 2000 Thriller*, ed. Larry J. Sabato (New York: Longman, 2002), 123–156.

115 Lance Morrow, "The Decline and Fall of Oratory," *Time*, August 18, 1980, 78.

116 Hedrick Smith, *The Power Game* (New York: Random House, 1988), 420.

117 Jill Lepore, "Back Issues," *New Yorker*, January 26, 2009, 73.

118 George E. Reedy, *The Twilight of the Presidency* (New York: New American Library, 1970), 112.

119 Larry J. Sabato, *Feeding Frenzy: How Attack Journalism Has Transformed American Politics* (New York: Free Press, 1991).

120 Deborah Tannen, *The Argument Culture* (New York: Ballantine, 1998), 81.

121 Ibid.

122 Orville Schell, "Preface" to Michael Massing, *Now They Tell Us: The American Press and Iraq* (New York: New York Review of Books, 2004), xiv.

123 See Sabato, *Feeding Frenzy*, for additional reasons for this increase.

124 Jonathan Alter, *The Promise: President Obama, Year One* (New York: Simon & Schuster, 2010), 216.

125 Jim Rutenberg, "Behind the War between White House and Fox," *New York Times*, October 23, 2009, A16.

126 An examination of 224 incidents of criminal or unethical behavior by Reagan administration appointees found that only 13 percent were uncovered by reporters. Most were discovered through investigations by executive agencies or congressional committees, which then released the information to the press. Only incidents reflecting personal peccadilloes of government officials, such as sexual offenses, were exposed first by reporters. John David Rausch Jr., "The Pathology of Politics: Government, Press, and Scandal," *Extensions* (University of Oklahoma), Fall 1990, 11–12. For the Whitewater scandal, reporters got most of their tips from a Republican Party operation run by officials from Republican presidential campaigns. Regarding sexual matters, reporters got most of their tips from prosecutors for the independent counsel, lawyers for Paula Jones, or a book agent for Linda Tripp. See Steven Brill, "Pressgate," *Brill's Content*, July–August 1998, 134.

127 Except for a reporter at a small paper in North Carolina. Charles Peters, "Tilting at Windmills," *Washington Monthly*, October–November 2005, 15.

128 Howard Kurtz, "Was the Watchdog Asleep?" *Washington Post National Weekly Edition*, October 13–19, 2008, 35.

129 Edward Jay Epstein, *News from Nowhere* (New York: Random House, 1973), 13.

130 Graber, *Mass Media and American Politics*, 62.

131 Milton Coleman, "When the Candidate Is Black like Me," *Washington Post National Weekly Edition*, April 23, 1984, 9.

132 Roper Organization, "A Big Concern about the Media: Intruding on Grieving Families," *Washington Post National Weekly Edition*, June 6, 1984. See also Joseph N. Cappella and Kathleen Hall Jamieson, *Spiral of Cynicism* (New York: Oxford University Press, 1997), 210.

133 Herbert J. Gans, *Democracy and the News* (New York: Oxford University Press, 2003), 87.

134 According to conservative journalist David Frum. David Frum, "When Did the GOP Lose Touch with Reality?" *New York Magazine*, November 20, 2011, nymag.com/news/politics/conservatives-david-frum-2011.

135 David Brock, *The Republican Noise Machine* (New York: Crown Publishers, 2004), 50 and 130. Brock himself used to attend these meetings.

136 Frum, "When Did the GOP Lose Touch with Reality?"

137 For further examination of this phenomenon, see Neal Gabler, "Cannibal Liberals," *Los Angeles Times*, June 29, 2008, www.latimes.com/news/opinion/la-op-gabler29-2008jun29,0,2574530,print.story.

138 In 1987 Reagan appointees to the Federal Communications Commission (FCC) abandoned the Fairness Doctrine, which had required broadcasters to maintain editorial balance. When Congress reinstated the doctrine, President Reagan vetoed the bill, thus allowing broadcasters to cater to any audience.

139 "Media Use and Evaluation."

140 Karen Tumulty, "I Want My Al TV," *Time*, June 30, 2003, 59. A new liberal network, Air America Radio, began in 2004 but went off the air five years later. Even the Sunday talk shows of the major television networks lean right. Significantly more guests are conservative or Republican than liberal or Democrat, and the journalists who question them are more conservative than liberal, according to a study of the shows from 1997 through 2005. Paul Waldman, "John Fund Again? It's Not Your Imagination—the Sunday Shows Really Do Lean Right," *Washington Monthly*, March 2006, 9–13.

141 Liddy, who was convicted in the Watergate scandal, instructed listeners where to aim when

shooting to kill agents of the Bureau of Alcohol, Tobacco, and Firearms.

[142] For examination, see Kathleen Hall Jamieson and Joseph N. Cappella, *Echo Chamber: Rush Limbaugh and the Conservative Media Establishment* (New York: Oxford University Press, 2010).

[143] McChesney, *Problem of the Media,* 117.

[144] "The Structural Imbalance of Political Talk Radio," Center for American Progress and Free Press, June 22, 2007. Report available from www.themonkeycage.org/2008/02/post_54.html.

[145] For a history of the origins of Fox News, see David Carr, *Crazy like a Fox* (New York: Portfolio, 2004).

[146] For analysis, see Ken Auletta, "Vox Fox," *New Yorker,* May 26, 2003, 58.

[147] For a comparison of Fox's coverage of national issues with mainstream media (AP and UPI) coverage, see T. Groeling and M. A. Baum, "Barbarians inside the Gates: Partisan News Media and the Polarization of American Political Discourse," paper presented at the annual meeting of the American Political Science Association, Chicago (August 2007). For a more pointed examination of Fox's coverage, see David Brock, Ari Rabin-Havt, and Media Matters for America, *The Fox Effect: How Roger Ailes Turned a Network into a Propaganda Machine* (New York: Anchor Books, 2012).

[148] Geneva Overholser, "It's Time for News Networks to Take Sides," *Lincoln Journal Star,* August 26, 2001; David Plotz, "Fox News Channel," *Slate,* November 22, 2000, slate.msn.com. In sales pitches to potential advertisers, the network acknowledges its bias but claims that this bias makes its audience more faithful. The head of ad sales said that "people who watch Fox News believe it's the home team." Brian Stelter, "Fox's Volley with Obama Intensifying," *New York Times,* October 12, 2009, B1.

[149] Joe Klein, "Above the Fray," *Time,* April 28, 2008, 27. For analysis of coverage by Fox News's "Special Report with Brit Hume," see "Election Watch: Campaign 2008 Final: How TV News Covered the General Election Campaign," *Media Monitor,* Winter 2009, cmpa.com. This analysis doesn't include the other newscasts and commentaries on Fox News.

[150] "Obama's Media Image—Compared to What?" Center for Media and Public Affairs, January 25, 2010, cmpa.com/media_room_press_1_25_10.html.

[151] For a summary of its actions, see James Rainey, "Fox News, MSNBC Prejudge 'Tea Parties,'" *Los Angeles Times,* April 16, 2009, latimes.com/entertainment/news/la-et-onthemedia15-2009apr15,0,14235416.column. Also see Theda Skocpol and Vanessa Williamson, *The Tea Party and the Remaking of Republican Conservatism* (New York: Oxford University Press, 2011), 120-138; 201-202.

[152] Auletta, "Vox Fox," 63–64.

[153] Matt Gross, quoted in Brock, *The Republican Noise Machine,* 320.

[154] Bill Sammon, quoted on *All Things Considered,* NPR, March 29, 2011.

[155] Jeff Cohen and Jonah Goldberg, "Face-Off: Beyond Belief," *Brill's Content,* December 1999–January 2000, 54.

[156] For examination, see Tommy Nguyen, "The Reel Liberal Majority," *Washington Post National Weekly Edition,* August 2–8, 2004, 14.

[157] Edith Efron, *The News Twisters* (Los Angeles: Nash, 1971); L. B. Bozell and B. H. Baker, "And That's the Way It Isn't," *Journalism Quarterly* 67 (1990), 1139; Bernard Goldberg, *Bias* (New York: Regnery, 2002); Eric Alterman, *What Liberal Media?* (New York: Basic Books, 2003).

[158] S. Robert Lichter, Stanley Rothman, and Linda S. Lichter, *The Media Elite* (Bethesda, Md.: Adler & Adler, 1986), 21–25. See also Stephen Hess, *Live from Capitol Hill!* (Washington, D.C.: Brookings Institution Press, 1991), app. A, 110–130.

[159] Alterman, "Out of Print," 49.

[160] Stephen Hess, *The Washington Reporters* (Washington, D.C.: Brookings Institution Press, 1981), 89; see also Lichter et al., *Media Elite,* 127–128.

[161] James Fallows, "The Stoning of Donald Regan," *Washington Monthly,* June 1984, 57.

[162] Sometimes media executives or editors pressure reporters because they have contrary views. Kimberly Conniff, "All the Views Fit to Print," *Brill's Content,* March 2001, 105.

[163] Howard Kurtz, *Media Circus* (New York: Random House, 1994), 48.

[164] Russell J. Dalton, Paul A. Beck, and Robert Huckfeldt, "Partisan Cues and the Media Information Flows in the 1992 Presidential Election," *American Political Science Review* 92 (March 1998), 118.

[165] C. Richard Hofstetter, *Bias in the News* (Columbus: Ohio State University Press, 1976); Graber, *Mass Media and Politics,* 167–168; Michael J. Robinson, "Just How Liberal Is the News?" *Public Opinion,* February–March 1983, 55–60; Maura Clancy and Michael J. Robinson, "General Election Coverage: Part I," *Public Opinion,* December 1984–January 1985, 49–54, 59; Michael J. Robinson, "The Media Campaign, '84: Part II," *Public Opinion,* February–March 1985, 43–48.

[166] Dave D'Alessio and Mike Allen, "Media Bias in Presidential Elections: A Meta-Analysis," *Journal of Communication* 50 (2000), 133–156. Some studies did find some bias against incumbents, front-runners, and emerging challengers. For these candidates, the media apparently took their watchdog role seriously. Clancy and Robinson, "General Election Coverage"; Robinson, "Media Campaign, '84"; Michael J. Robinson, "Where's the Beef? Media and Media Elites in 1984," in *The American Elections of 1984,* ed. Austin Ranney (Durham, N.C.: Duke University Press, 1985), 184; Michael J. Robinson, "News Media Myths and Realities: What Network News Did and Didn't Do in the 1984 General Campaign," in *Elections in America,* ed. Kay Lehman Schlozman (Boston: Allen & Unwin, 1987), 143–170; Kim

Fridkin Kahn and Patrick J. Kenney, *The Spectacle of U.S. Senate Campaigns* (Princeton, N.J.: Princeton University Press, 1999), 126–129.

[167] "Election Watch '08: The Primaries: How TV News Covered the GOP and Democratic Primaries," *Media Monitor,* March–April 2008, Center for the Media and Public Affairs, cmpa.com. According to an analysis by the "Public Editor" of the *New York Times,* however, coverage of Obama and Clinton was balanced in that paper. Clark Hoyt, "Playing Favorites? Don't Be So Sure," *New York Times,* March 9, 2008, WK12.

[168] "Election Watch: Campaign 2008 Final."

[169] Auletta, "Non-Stop News," 41.

[170] Robert Shogan, *Bad News: Where the Press Goes Wrong in the Making of the President* (Chicago: Dee, 2001), 231.

[171] It helped the Democrat Carter in 1976 but hurt him in 1980. It helped the Republican Bush in 1988 but hurt him in 1992. Thomas E. Patterson, *Out of Order* (New York: Vintage, 1994), 131. It helped the Democrat Clinton in 1996, and at different stages of the campaign, it helped the Republican Bush or the Democrat Gore in 2000.

[172] Shogan, *Bad News,* 204–245.

[173] Fewer than one in ten stories on the 2000 debates focused on policy differences; seven in ten focused on candidates' performance or strategy. Bill Kovach and Tom Rosenstiel, "Campaign Lite," *Washington Monthly,* January–February 2001, 31–32.

[174] The media, however, did pay a lot of attention to Ross Perot's presidential bid in 1992 because he said he would spend $100 million on his campaign and because polls showed he could compete with Bush and Clinton.

[175] "Clinton Gains More Support from Big Papers," *Lincoln Journal Star,* October 25, 1992. Newspapers insist that there is little relationship between their editorial endorsements and their news coverage or even their political columns. An endorsement for one candidate does not mean more positive coverage or columns for that candidate because American media have established a tradition of autonomy in the newsroom. Dalton et al., "Partisan Cues," 118. However, some research shows that when papers endorse candidates, the papers show a small bias toward the candidates in their news stories (if the candidates are incumbents). Kim Fridkin Kahn and Patrick J. Kenney, "The Slant of the News: How Editorial Endorsements Influence Campaign Coverage and Citizens' Views of Candidates," *American Political Science Review* 96 (June 2002), 381–394.

[176] By Media Matters for America, cited in David Bauder, "Study Finds Conservatives Dominate Editorial Pages," *Lincoln Journal Star,* September 16, 2007, F5.

[177] Hofstetter, *Bias in the News;* Hess, *Live from Capitol Hill!* 12–13.

[178] Robinson, "Just How Liberal Is the News?" 58; Arthur H. Miller, Edie N. Goldenberg, and Lutz Erbring, "Type-Set Politics," *American Political Science Review* 73 (January 1979), 69; Patterson, *Out of Order,* 6; Charles M. Tidmarch and John J.

Pitney Jr., "Covering Congress," *Polity* 17 (Spring 1985), 463–483.

[179] Patterson, *Out of Order,* 25, 245.

[180] Lichter et al., *Media Elite,* ch. 7; Sabato, *Feeding Frenzy,* 87, and sources cited therein; Goldberg, *Bias,* ch. 5; Alterman, *What Liberal Media?* ch. 7. But a study examining twenty years' coverage of governors and their states' unemployment and murder rates shows no bias toward Democratic or Republican governors. David Niven, "Partisan Bias in the Media?" *Social Science Quarterly* 80 (December 1999), 847–857.

[181] Alterman, *What Liberal Media?* 104–117.

[182] For examination of "24," see Jane Mayer, "Whatever It Takes," *New Yorker,* February 19 and 26, 2007, 66.

[183] Mireya Navarro, "On Abortion, Hollywood Is No Choice," *New York Times,* June 10, 2007, ST1.

[184] Ibid., 118–138. Bruce Nussbaum, "The Myth of the Liberal Media," *Business Week,* November 11, 1996; James Fallows, *Breaking the News: How the Media Undermine American Democracy* (New York: Pantheon, 1996), 49.

[185] For an analysis of the coverage of the economy in the booming 1990s, see John Cassidy, "Striking It Rich: The Rise and Fall of Popular Capitalism," *New Yorker,* January 14, 2002, 63–73. Further, the media give scant attention to labor matters, except when strikes inconvenience commuters. Mark Crispin Miller, "The Media and the Bush Dyslexicon," in Grover and Peschek, *Voices of Dissent,* 137–146. In 2001, the three main television networks used representatives of corporations as sources thirty times more often than representatives of unions. McChesney, *Problem of the Media,* 70–71.

[186] McChesney, *Problem of the Media,* 106.

[187] Hightower, *There's Nothing in the Middle of the Road,* 137.

[188] This tendency is reflected even in the nature of the reporters' questions at presidential press conferences. For foreign issues, their questions are less aggressive than for domestic issues. Steven E. Claymans, John Heritage, Marc N. Elliott, and Laurie L. McDonald, "When Does the Watchdog Bark? Conditions of Aggressive Questioning in Presidential Press Conferences," *American Sociological Review* 72 (February 2007), 23–41. The researchers examined the period from 1953 to 2000.

[189] Robinson, "Just How Liberal Is the News?" 59. During the Cold War, this meant harsh attacks on not only the Soviet Union but also on leftist Latin American regimes. Parenti, *Inventing Reality,* ch. 7–11; Charles E. Lindblom, *Politics and Markets* (New York: Basic Books, 1977); J. Fred MacDonald, *One Nation under Television: The Rise and Decline of Network TV* (New York: Pantheon Books, 1990); Dan Nimmo and James E. Combs, *Mediated Political Realities* (White Plains, N.Y.: Longman, 1983), 135; Benjamin I. Page and R. Y. Shapiro, *The Rational Public* (Chicago: University of Chicago Press, 1992); John R. Zaller and Dennis Chiu, "Government's Little Helper: U.S. Press Coverage

of Foreign Policy Crises, 1945–1991," *Political Communication* 13 (1996), 385–405. During the Persian Gulf War, this meant jingoistic coverage and unquestioning acceptance of administration claims. John R. MacArthur, *Second Front: Censorship and Propaganda in the Gulf War* (New York: Hill & Wang, 1992); James Bennet, "How They Missed That Story," *Washington Monthly,* December 1990, 8–16; Christopher Dickey, "Not Their Finest Hour," *Newsweek,* June 8, 1992, 66. Even for the Vietnam War, which is often cited as an example of harsh criticism of governmental policies, the media in fact offered blindly positive coverage for many years and then relatively restrained criticism toward the end of the war. In the 1950s and early 1960s, newspapers, magazines, and television networks sent few correspondents to Vietnam, so most accepted the government's account of the conflict. Susan Welch, "The American Press and Indochina, 1950–1956," in *Communication in International Politics,* ed. Richard L. Merritt (Urbana: University of Illinois Press, 1972), 207–231; Edward J. Epstein, "The Selection of Reality," in *What's News?* ed. Elie Abel (San Francisco: Institute for Contemporary Studies, 1981), 124. When they did dispatch correspondents, many filed pessimistic reports, but their editors believed the government rather than the correspondents and refused to print these reports. Instead, they ran articles quoting optimistic statements by government officials. See David Halberstam, *The Powers That Be* (New York: Dell, 1980), 642–647. In 1968, the media did turn against the war, but rather than sharply criticize it, they conveyed the impression that it was futile. Daniel C. Hallin, *The "Uncensored War": The Media and Vietnam* (New York: Oxford University Press, 1986).

[190] David Domke, *God Willing? Political Fundamentalism in the White House, the "War on Terror," and the Echoing Press* (London: Pluto, 2004).

[191] "Return of Talk Show Is Healthy Sign," *Lincoln Journal Star,* October 6, 2001; Brock, *The Republican Noise Machine,* 256–258.

[192] Alterman, *What Liberal Media?* 202.

[193] Anthony Collings, "The BBC: How to Be Impartial in Wartime," *Chronicle of Higher Education,* December 21, 2001, B14.

[194] *Weapons of Mass Deception,* a documentary film by Danny Schechter (Cinema Libre Distribution, 2005).

[195] Alterman, *What Liberal Media?* 29; Todd Gitlin, "Showtime Iraq," *American Prospect,* November 4, 2002, 34–35.

[196] Frank Rich, *The Greatest Story Ever Sold* (New York: Penguin Press, 2006), 87.

[197] *Weapons of Mass Deception.* And for good measure, MSNBC removed Phil Donohue from his afternoon show out of fear that his liberal sensibilities would offend conservative viewers during wartime.

[198] For an example involving the *New York Times,* see Jane Mayer, *The Dark Side* (New York: Doubleday, 2008), 226.

[199] "Buying the War," PBS, April 25, 2007.

[200] James Poniewozik, "What You See vs. What They See," *Time,* April 7, 2003, 68–69. For example, that U.S. searches caused considerable damage to Iraqi homes and that these raids swept up many innocent family members, *Morning Edition,* National Public Radio, May 4, 2004. Also, that in the runup to the war, U.S. agents had bugged the homes and offices of United Nations Security Council members who had not proclaimed support for the war: Camille T. Taiara, "Spoon-Feeding the Press," *San Francisco Bay Guardian,* March 12, 2003, www .sfbg.com/37/24/x _mediabeat.html.

[201] Frank Rich, "The Spoils of War," *New York Times,* April 13, 2003, AR1; Paul Janensch, "Whether to Show Images of War Dead Is Media Dilemma," *Lincoln Journal Star,* March 31, 2003.

[202] Rich, *The Greatest Story Ever Sold,* 155.

[203] Todd Gitlin, "Embed or in Bed?" *American Prospect,* June 2003, 43.

[204] "The *Times* and Iraq," *New York Times,* May 26, 2004, A10; Daniel Okrent, "Weapons of Mass Destruction? Or Mass Distraction?" *New York Times,* May 30, 2004, WK1; Howard Kurtz, quoted in Todd Gitlin, "The Great Media Breakdown," *Mother Jones,* November–December, 2004, 58.

[205] Three times as many people believe the media are "too liberal" than believe they are "too conservative" (45 percent to 15 percent). McChesney, *Problem of the Media,* 114.

[206] M. D. Watts, D. Domke, D. V. Shah, and D. P. Fan, "Elite Cues and Media Bias in Presidential Campaigns: Explaining Public Perceptions of a Liberal Press," *Communication Research* 26 (1999), 144–175.

[207] One influential conservative downplayed liberal bias in an interview but at the same time was claiming liberal bias in subscription pitches for his magazine. William Kristol, quoted in Alterman, *What Liberal Media?* 2–3. Karl Rove, top aide to President George W. Bush, also dismissed the idea of liberal bias. Elizabeth Wilner, "On the Road Again," *Washington Post National Weekly Edition,* June 6–12, 2005, 22.

[208] Lymari Morales, "Majority in U.S. Continues to Distrust the Media, Perceive Bias," Gallup poll, September 22, 2011, gallup.com/poll/149624/ Majority-Continue-Distrust-Media. . . .

[209] Robert Vallone, Lee Ross, and Mark R. Lepper, "The Hostile Media Phenomenon," *Journal of Personality and Social Psychology* 49 (1985), 577–585; Roger Giner-Sorolla and Shelly Chaiken, "The Causes of Hostile Media Judgments," *Journal of Experimental Social Psychology* 30 (1994), 165–180.

[210] Dalton et al., "Partisan Cues."

[211] And although these partisans say that biased coverage will not affect them, they fear it will affect others who are less aware or astute. W. Phillips Davison, "The Third-Person Effect in Communication," *Public Opinion Quarterly* 47 (1983), 1–15.

[212] Dave D'Alessio, "An Experimental Examination of Readers' Perceptions of Media

Bias," unpublished manuscript, University of Connecticut, n.d.; Mark Peffley, James M. Avery, and Jason E. Glass, "Public Perceptions of Bias in the News Media," paper presented at the annual meeting of the Midwest Political Science Association, Chicago, April 19–22, 2001.

[213] According to experimental studies. Shanto Iyengar and Kyu S. Hahn, "Red Media, Blue Media: Evidence of Ideological Selectivity in Media Use," *Journal of Communication* 59 (2009), 19–39; Joel Turner, "The Messenger Overwhelming the Message: Ideological Cues and Perceptions of Bias in Television News," *Political Behavior* 29 (2007), 441–464.

[214] According to a statement by a CNN producer in the documentary *Outfoxed*.

[215] Rather was anchor when the network displayed the letter about George W. Bush's National Guard service, but the producer of the piece was the one responsible.

[216] Ted Koppel, "And Now, a Word for Our Demographic," *New York Times*, January 29, 2006, WK16. Also see Auletta, "Non-Stop News."

[217] Bill Kovach and Tom Rosenstiel, *Warp Speed: America in the Age of Mixed Media* (New York: Century Foundation Press, 1999), 64.

[218] Hess, *Live from Capitol Hill!* 34; Rosenstiel, *State of the News Media,* 21.

[219] Molly Ivins, "Media Conglomerates Profit at Expense of News, Public," *Lincoln Journal Star,* October 26, 2001.

[220] James Fallows, "On That Chart," *Nation,* June 3, 1996, 15.

[221] Maureen Dowd, "Flintstone Futurama," *New York Times,* August 19, 2001, WK13.

[222] A poll of reporters and executives found that a third admitted to avoiding stories that would embarrass an advertiser or harm the financial interests of their own organization. "Poll: Reporters Avoid, Soften Stories," *Lincoln Journal Star,* May 1, 2000; David Owen, "The Cigarette Companies: How They Get Away with Murder, Part II," *Washington Monthly,* March 1985, 48–54. See also Daniel Hellinger and Dennis R. Judd, *The Democratic Facade,* 2nd ed. (Belmont, Calif.: Wadsworth, 1994), 59. Through the 1920s, newspapers refrained from pointing out that popular "patent medicines" were usually useless and occasionally dangerous because the purveyors bought more advertising than any other business. Mark Crispin Miller, "Free the Media," *Nation,* June 3, 1996, 10.

[223] Roger Mudd, quoted in *Television and the Presidential Elections,* ed. Martin A. Linsky (Lexington, Mass.: Heath, 1983), 48.

[224] "Q&A: Dan Rather on Fear, Money, and the News," *Brill's Content,* October 1998, 117.

[225] Barry Sussman, "News on TV: Mixed Reviews," *Washington Post National Weekly Edition,* September 3, 1984, 37.

[226] Bill Carter, "Networks Fight Public's Shrinking Attention Span," *Lincoln Journal Star,* September 30, 1990.

[227] Epstein, *News from Nowhere,* 4.

[228] William A. Henry III, "Requiem for TV's Gender Gap," *Time,* August 22, 1983, 57.

[229] Richard Morin, "The Nation's Mood? Calm," *Washington Post National Weekly Edition,* November 5, 2001, 35.

[230] According to the Tyndall Report, cited in Nicholas Kristof, "Please, Readers, Help Bill O'Reilly!" *New York Times,* February 7, 2006, A21.

[231] Charles Peters, "Tilting at Windmills," *Washington Monthly,* September 2006, 7.

[232] John Mecklin, "Over the Horizon," *Miller-McCune,* June–July 2008, 6.

[233] For an examination of how the media exaggerated the Whitewater scandal, see Gene Lyons, *Fools for Scandal* (New York: Franklin Square Press, 1996).

[234] The third and final special prosecutor concluded that there might be some evidence of wrongdoing in the law firm records of Hillary Clinton but that there was not enough evidence to justify prosecution.

[235] The pope was making a historic visit to Cuba. The networks had considered this so important that they had sent their anchors to Havana. At the same time, renewed violence in Northern Ireland threatened to scuttle the peace talks between Catholics and Protestants, and continued refusal from Iraq to cooperate with United Nations biological and chemical weapons inspectors threatened to escalate to military conflict.

[236] Eric Pooley, "Monica's World," *Time,* March 2, 1998, 40.

[237] Quoted in Fallows, *Breaking the News,* 201.

[238] Lawrie Mifflin, "Crime Falls, but Not on TV," *New York Times,* July 6, 1997, E3. According to one researcher, crime coverage is also "the easiest, cheapest, laziest news to cover" because stations just listen to the police radio and then send a camera crew to shoot the story.

[239] Heather Maher, "Eleven O'Clock Blues," *Brill's Content,* February 2001, 99.

[240] Molly Ivins, "Don't Moan about the Media, Do Something," *Lincoln Journal Star,* November 1999.

[241] David S. Broder, "Can We Govern?" *Washington Post National Weekly Edition,* January 31, 1994, 23.

[242] Leonard Pitts Jr., "Can We All Get Along?" *Lincoln Journal Star,* November 4, 2010, B7.

[243] Epstein, *News from Nowhere,* 179, 195.

[244] Rosenstiel, *State of the News Media,* 18.

[245] John Horn, "Campaign Coverage Avoids Issues," *Lincoln Journal Star,* September 25, 1988. Another survey found that 28 percent of women and 40 percent of men change channels every time during commercial breaks. "Ticker," *Brill's Content,* September 1999, 128.

[246] John Eisendrath, "An Eyewitness Account of Local TV News," *Washington Monthly,* September 1986, 21.

[247] Interview with Larry King, *Larry King Live,* CNN, October 4, 2000, quoted in Jacob S. Hacker and Paul Pierson, *Winner-Take-All Politics* (New York: Simon & Schuster, 2010), 105.

[248] Lee Sigelman and David Bullock, "Candidates, Issues, Horse Races, and Hoopla: Presidential Campaign Coverage, 1888–1988," *American Politics Quarterly* 19 (January 1991), 5–32. So was emphasis on human interest. In 1846, the *New York Tribune* described the culinary habits of Rep. William "Sausage" Sawyer (D-Ohio), who ate a sausage on the floor of the House every afternoon: "What little grease is left on his hands he wipes on his almost bald head which saves any outlay for Pomatum. His mouth sometimes serves as a finger glass, his shirt-sleeves and pantaloons being called into requisition as a napkin. He uses a jackknife for a toothpick, and then he goes on the floor again to abuse the Whigs as the British party." Timothy E. Cook, *Making Laws and Making News: Media Strategies in the U.S. House of Representatives* (Washington, D.C.: Brookings Institution Press, 1989), 18–19.

[249] Patterson, *Out of Order,* 74; Marion R. Just, Ann N. Crigler, Dean E. Alger, Timothy E. Cook, Montague Kern, and Darrell M. West, *Crosstalk: Citizens, Candidates, and the Media in a Presidential Campaign* (Chicago: University of Chicago Press, 1996); Mathew Robert Kerbel, *Remote and Controlled* (Boulder, Colo.: Westview Press, 1995); Bruce Buchanan, *Electing a President* (Austin: University of Texas Press, 1991).

[250] Including the candidates' strategies and tactics.

[251] The remaining time was devoted to campaign conduct, vice-presidential choices, presidential and vice-presidential debates, and candidates' backgrounds and family and friends. Some of these stories also reflected the horse race and the candidates' strategy and tactics. "Election Watch: Campaign 2008 Final."

[252] Richard Morin, "Toward the Millennium, by the Numbers," *Washington Post National Weekly Edition,* July 7, 1997, 35.

[253] Patterson, *Out of Order,* 81–82.

[254] Jacob S. Hacker and Paul Pierson, *Off Center: The Republican Revolution and the Erosion of American Democracy* (New Haven, Conn.: Yale University Press, 2005), 177.

[255] Thomas E. Patterson, *The Vanishing Voter* (New York: Knopf, 2002), 92.

[256] Lara Logan, quoted in Brian Stelter, "Reporters Say Networks Put Wars on Back Burner," *New York Times,* June 23, 2008, nytimes.com/2008/06/23/business/media/23logan.html?dpc.

Chapter 6

[1] This total also includes a small amount of sugared iced tea, fruit punch, and other beverages with added sugar.

[2] See Tom Hamburger and Kim Geiger, "Beverage Industry Douses Tax on Soft Drinks," *Los Angeles Times,* February 7, 2010, www.latimes.com/news/la-na-soda-tax7-2010feb07,0,3020424,print.story; Mark Bittman, "A Sin We Sip Instead of Smoke," *New York Times,* February 14, 2010, 1.

[3] Jim Toedtman, "Tax Attack," *AARP Bulletin*, June, 2012, 3. At some point, of course, a product could be taxed so heavily that its sales and the revenue from its tax would dry up, but as experience with cigarettes shows, the tax would have to be extremely high before it would be counterproductive economically.

[4] Ibid.

[5] http://www.mayoclinic.com/health/tanning/HQ01487.

[6] Jeffrey H. Birnbaum, *The Lobbyists: How Influence Peddlers Get Their Way in Washington* (New York: Times Books, 1993), 32.

[7] Mark A. Peterson and Jack L. Walker Jr., "Interest Group Responses to Partisan Change: The Impact of the Reagan Administration upon the National Interest Group System," in *Interest Group Politics*, 2nd ed., eds. Allan J. Cigler and Burdett A. Loomis (Washington, D.C.: CQ Press, 1987), 162.

[8] Alexis de Tocqueville, *Democracy in America* (New York: Knopf, 1945), 191. (Originally published 1835.)

[9] Gabriel Almond and Sidney Verba, *Civil Culture* (Boston: Little, Brown, 1965), 266–306.

[10] David Truman, *The Governmental Process* (New York: Knopf, 1964), 25–26.

[11] Ibid., 59.

[12] James Q. Wilson, *Political Organizations* (New York: Basic Books, 1973), 198.

[13] Graham K. Wilson, *Interest Groups in America* (Oxford: Oxford University Press, 1981), ch. 5; see also Graham K. Wilson, "American Business and Politics," in *Interest Group Politics*, 2nd ed., eds. Cigler and Loomis, 221–235.

[14] Kay Lehman Schlozman and John T. Tierney, "More of the State: Washington Pressure Group Activity in a Decade of Change," *Journal of Politics* 45 (1983), 335–356.

[15] Christopher H. Foreman Jr., "Grassroots Victim Organizations: Mobilizing for Personal and Public Health," in *Interest Group Politics*, 4th ed., eds. Allan J. Cigler and Burdett A. Loomis (Washington, D.C.: CQ Press, 1994), 33–53.

[16] Beth Leech, Frank Baumgartner, Timothy LaPira, and Nicholas Semanko, "Drawing Lobbyists to Washington: Government Activity and the Demand for Advocacy," *Political Research Quarterly* 58 (March 2005), 19–30.

[17] William Brown, "Exchange Theory and the Institutional Impetus for Interest Group Formation," in *Interest Group Politics*, 6th ed., eds. Allan J. Cigler and Burdett A. Loomis (Washington, D.C.: CQ Press, 2002), 313–329; William Brown, "Benefits and Membership: A Reappraisal of Interest Group Activity," *Western Political Quarterly* 29 (1976), 258–273; Terry M. Moe, *The Organization of Interests: Incentives and the Internal Dynamics of Political Interest Groups* (Chicago: University of Chicago Press, 1980).

[18] This applies to public, or collective, goods rather than to private goods available only to the members.

[19] Mancur Olson, *The Logic of Collective Action* (Cambridge, Mass.: Harvard University Press, 1971).

[20] Lawrence R. Jacobs, "The Privileges of Access: Interest Groups and the White House," in *The Obama Presidency: Appraisals and Prospects*, eds. Bert A. Rockman, Andrew Rudalevige, and Colin Campbell (Washington, D.C.: CQ Press, 2012), 160. See also Suzanne Mettler, *The Submerged State* (Chicago: University of Chicago Press, 2011).

[21] E. E. Schattschneider, *Semi-Sovereign People* (New York: Holt, Rinehart and Winston, 1960), 35.

[22] Robert D. Putnam, *Bowling Alone* (New York: Simon & Schuster, 2000).

[23] Richard Stengel, "Bowling Together," *Time*, July 22, 1996, 35.

[24] Theda Skocpol, "Associations without Members," *American Prospect*, July–August 1999, 66–73.

[25] Mark T. Hayes, "The New Group Universe," in *Interest Group Politics*, 2nd ed., eds. Cigler and Loomis, 133–145.

[26] Jack L. Walker, "The Origins and Maintenance of Interest Groups," *American Political Science Review* 77 (June 1983), 390–406; Schattschneider, *Semi-Sovereign People*, 118.

[27] David S. Broder and Michael Weisskopf, "Finding New Friends on the Hill," *Washington Post National Weekly Edition*, October 3, 1994, 11.

[28] Charles E. Lindblom, "The Market as Prison," *Journal of Politics* 44 (1982), 324–336; Michael Genovese, *The Presidential Dilemma: Leadership in the American System* (New York: HarperCollins, 1995).

[29] According to a former Chamber economist. James Verini, "Show Him the Money," *Washington Monthly*, July–August 2010, 12.

[30] Verini, "Show Him the Money," 12; Jacob S. Hacker and Paul Pierson, *Winner-Take-All Politics* (New York: Simon & Schuster, 2010), 276.

[31] Hacker and Pierson, *Winner-Take-All Politics*, 277.

[32] Verini, "Show Him the Money," 11.

[33] "Guess What the U.S. Chamber of Commerce Will Spend?" http://guesswhattheuschamberwillspend.org/us-chamber/; "Business Group Blows $29 Million on Election Losers," *CNN Money*, November 9, 2012, http://money.cnn.com/2012/11/09/news/economy/chamber-election/; Seven Pearlstein, "How Business Can Recover from 2012 Election Debacle," *Washington Post*, November 11, 2012, http://bangordailynews.com/2012/11/11/opinion/how-business-can-recover-from-2012-election-debacle/.

[34] Ibid., 11.

[35] Hacker and Pierson, *Winner-Take-All Politics*, 276.

[36] Verini, "Show Him the Money," 13.

[37] "Insurers Paid Chamber $86M Opposing Health Law," *Lincoln Journal Star*, November 18, 2010, A7. See also Hacker and Pierson, *Winner-Take-All Politics*, 275.

[38] Michael Crowley, "Battlefield SOPA," *Time*, January 30, 2012, 12.

[39] Richard D. Kahlenberg, "Inequality and Solidarity," *Washington Monthly*, April 2008, 41; Paulo Frymer, "Labor and American Politics," *Perspectives on Politics* 8 (June 2010), 609–616.

[40] Sam Hananel, "Unions See Sharp Declines," *Lincoln Journal Star*, January 22, 2011, A4.

[41] Dorian T. Warren, "The American Labor Movement in the Age of Obama: The Challenges and Opportunities of a Racialized Political Economy," *Perspectives on Politics* 8 (September 2010), 851.

[42] Ibid.; Harold Meyerson, "Wal-Mart Comes North," *American Prospect*, April 2007, 28–29.

[43] Jeffrey Goldberg, "Selling Wal-Mart," *New Yorker*, April 2, 2007, 33.

[44] Warren, "The American Labor Movement in the Age of Obama," 849. In 2011, Republican senators tried to block three appointments to the NLRB so it wouldn't have a quorum to operate. Eventually, President Obama made controversial recess appointments, which did not require Senate confirmation.

[45] Hacker and Pierson, *Winner-Take-All Politics*, 128.

[46] Hananel, "Unions See Sharp Declines."

[47] Steven Brill, "The Teachers' Unions' Last Stand," *New York Times Magazine*, May 23, 2010, 35.

[48] William Finnegan, "The Storm," *New Yorker*, March 5, 2012, 28–34; David Firestone, "In Ohio, a Hint about 2012," *New York Times*, November 6, 2011, SR10.

[49] Theda Skocpol and Vanessa Williamson, *The Tea Party and the Remaking of Republican Conservatism* (New York: Oxford University Press, 2012), 168.

[50] Steven Greenhouse, "Union Membership Rose in '98, but Unions' Percentage of Workforce Fell," *New York Times*, January 20, 1999, A22; Paul E. Johnson, "Organized Labor in an Era of Blue-Collar Decline," in *Interest Group Politics*, 3rd ed., eds. Allan J. Cigler and Burdett A. Loomis (Washington, D.C.: CQ Press, 1991), 33–62.

[51] Thomas B. Edsall, "Working with the Union You Have," *Washington Post National Weekly Edition*, March 14–20, 2005, 15.

[52] Hacker and Pierson, *Winner-Take-All Politics*, 139.

[53] "Continuing Assault on Unions," *New York Times*, January 8, 2012, SR10.

[54] Except to forestall layoffs of state government workers and teachers.

[55] Catherine Rampell, "Somehow, the Unemployed Became Invisible," *New York Times*, July 10, 2011, BU1.

[56] Hacker and Pierson, *Winner-Take-All Politics*, 140–142.

[57] Bars to perch on and nesting boxes to lay eggs in. The accommodations would add one cent to the cost of one egg.

[58] *All Things Considered*, NPR, January 26, 2012.

[59] Information on annual expenditures is found in U.S. Census Bureau, *Statistical Abstract of*

the United States, 2003 (Washington, D.C.: Government Printing Office, 2003), tab. 812.

60 Andrew S. McFarland, *Common Cause: Lobbying in the Public Interest* (Chatham, N.J.: Chatham House, 1984); see also Andrew S. McFarland, *Public Interest Lobbies: Decision Making on Energy* (Washington, D.C.: American Enterprise Institute, 1976).

61 Ronald G. Shaiko, "More Bang for the Buck: The New Era of Full-Service Public Interest Groups," in *Interest Group Politics*, 3rd ed., eds. Cigler and Loomis, 109.

62 For a discussion of the evolution of NOW and its success in lobbying Congress, see Anne N. Costain and W. Douglas Costain, "The Women's Lobby: Impact of a Movement on Congress," in *Interest Group Politics*, 3rd ed., eds. Cigler and Loomis.

63 Richard Morin and Claudia Deane, "The Administration's Right-Hand Women," *Washington Post National Weekly Edition,* May 7, 2001, 12.

64 Barbara Burrell, "Political Parties and Women's Organizations: Bringing Women into the Electoral Arena," in *Gender and Elections: Shaping the Future of American Politics,* eds. Susan J. Carroll and Richard Fox (Cambridge: Cambridge University Press, 2006), 143–168; Rebecca Hannagan, Jamie Pimlott, and Levente Littvay, "Does an EMILY's List Endorsement Predict Electoral Success, or Does EMILY Pick the Winners?" *PS* 43 (July 2010), 503–508.

65 Eric M. Uslaner, "A Tower of Babel on Foreign Policy," in *Interest Group Politics,* 3rd ed., eds. Cigler and Loomis, 309.

66 Kenneth D. Wald, *Religion and Politics* (New York: St. Martin's Press, 1985), 182–212.

67 Hacker and Pierson, *Winner-Take-All Politics,* 202. Also see Randall Balmer, *God and the White House* (New York: Harper One, 2008), 95–96.

68 Sidney Blumenthal, "Christian Soldiers," *New Yorker,* July 18, 1994, 36.

69 "Citing 'Moral Crisis,' a Call to Oust Clinton," *New York Times,* October 23, 1998, A1, A8.

70 Richard Parker, "On God and Democrats," *American Prospect,* March 2004, 40. For example, the resistance was especially evident in 2005 after the strident attempts to use Terri Schiavo's case as a rallying cry. Schiavo, who was forty-one years old, had been kept alive by a feeding tube in a persistent vegetative state for fifteen years. Her husband petitioned to remove the tube, but her parents resisted. After nineteen Florida courts heard the case, and all three levels of the federal courts, including the Supreme Court, refused to intervene, the result was a court order to disconnect the tube. Conservative Christian groups, seeing a connection to their pro-life movement, made the case a cause célèbre, pressuring Florida officials and then Congress to intervene and overturn the court rulings. Congress urged federal courts to hear the case, and President Bush interrupted a break at his ranch to return to the capital to sign the bill. The courts, however, rejected the plea. So did 70 percent of the public. In an effort to rally the movement, religious and Republican leaders alienated moderate Americans.

71 Thomas Edsall, "The Renegade Republicans," *New York Times,* March 26, 2012, quoting the Faith and Freedom Coalition, http://campaignstops.blogs.nytimes.com/2012/03/26/the-renegade-republicans/?n=Top%2fOpinion%2fEditorials%20and%20Op%2dEd%2fOp%2dEd%2fContributors%2fThomas%20B%2e%20Edsall.

72 David Kuo, *Tempting Faith: An Inside Story of Political Seduction* (New York: Free Press, 2006).

73 Ibid.

74 Christopher J. Bosso, "Adaptation and Change in the Environmental Movement," in *Interest Group Politics,* 3rd ed., eds. Cigler and Loomis, 155–156.

75 Ibid., 162.

76 Hacker and Pierson, *Winner-Take-All Politics*, 209.

77 Michael Powell, "Funding Isn't Part of the Plan," *Washington Post National Weekly Edition*, May 12–18, 2003, 21.

78 Ibid.

79 Matt Bai, "Profiting from the Pummeling," *New York Times,* September 23, 2007, nytimes.com/gst/fullpage.html?res=9E07E4D71F3AF930A1575ACOA9619C8B63&pagewanted=all.

80 Brent Kendall, "License to Kill," *Washington Monthly,* January–February 2003, 11–14.

81 John Mintz, "Would Bush Be the NRA's Point Man in the White House?" *Washington Post National Weekly Edition,* May 8, 2000, 14; Mike Doming, "NRA Promises an All-Out Assault on Al Gore's Presidential Campaign," *Lincoln Journal Star,* May 21, 2000, 2A; Thomas B. Edsall, "Targeting Al Gore with $10 Million," *Washington Post National Weekly Edition,* May 29, 2000, 11.

82 Linda Greenhouse, "U.S., in a Shift, Tells Justices Citizens Have a Right to Guns," *New York Times,* May 8, 2002, A1.

83 Linda Greenhouse, "Justices Rule for Individual Gun Rights," *New York Times,* June 27, 2008, http://www.nytimes.com/2008/06/27/washington/27scotuscnd.html?_r=1&scp=2&sq=supreme%20courts%20gun%20rights%20decision&st=cse&oref=slogin.

84 Blaine Harden, "The NRA Moves Away from Bush," *Washington Post National Weekly Edition,* January 15–21, 2007, 12.

85 Robin Toner, "Abortion's Opponents Claim the Middle Ground," *New York Times,* April 25, 2004, sec. 4, 1.

86 The pro-life side claims that women have a choice to engage in sex and another choice to protect themselves from becoming pregnant. The pro-choice side claims that people who oppose abortion also oppose policies that would support children who are born to poor women. The pro-choice side also points to polls showing that conservatives who oppose abortion nonetheless favor the death penalty and aggressive foreign policies, such as the Iraq War, that lead to innocent civilians' deaths.

87 David S. Broder, "Let 100 Single-Issue Groups Bloom," *Washington Post,* January 7, 1979, C1–C2; see also David S. Broder, *The Party's Over: The Failure of Politics in America* (New York: Harper & Row, 1972).

88 Opensecrets.org, a website sponsored by the Center for Responsive Politics. The data were extracted on April 2, 2012.

89 "Winning Our Future," Fact.Check.org, January 10, 2012, factcheck, org/2012/01/winning-our-future/.

90 *Citizens United* v. *Federal Election Commission,* 558 U.S. 08-205 (2010).

91 Richard M. Skinner, Seth E. Masket, and David A. Dulio, "527 Committees and the Political Party Network," *American Politics Research* 40 (January 2012), 60–84, doi:10.1177/1532673X11420420.

92 Michael Crowley, "Elizabethan Drama," *Time,* July 11, 2011, 35.

93 Charles Peters, "Tilting at Windmills," *Washington Monthly,* July–August 2004, 4.

94 Amy McKay, "Negative Lobbying and Policy Outcomes," *American Politics Research* 40 (January 2012), 116–146.

95 "Some Funny Facts about D.C.," *Parade Magazine,* March 19, 2006, 25; an estimate of 90,000 lobbyists was made by political scientist James Thurbur on *Fresh Air,* National Public Radio, August 26, 2008.

96 Todd S. Purdum, "Go Ahead, Try to Stop K Street," *New York Times,* January 8, 2006, WK4.

97 According to a tabulation by LegiStorm. Charles Peters, "Tilting at Windmills," *Washington Monthly*, November–December, 2011, 7.

98 Alex Wayne and Bruce Armstrong, "Tauzin's $11.6 million Made Him the Highest Paid Health Law Lobbyist," *Bloomberg News,* November 11, 2011. http://www.bloomberg.com/news/2011-11-29/tauzin-s-11-6-million-made-him-highest-paid-health-law-lobbyist.htmlo.

99 "Cutting Out the Middleman," *New York Times,* April 3, 2011, WK9. Ethics laws limit officials from moving to lobbying firms immediately, but the laws don't limit lobbyists from moving to Congress immediately.

100 These data were drawn from Dan Eggen and Kimberly Kindy, "Three of Every Four Oil and Gas Lobbyists Worked for Federal Government," *Washington Post,* July 22, 2010, www.washingtonpost.com/wp-dyn/content/article/2010/07/21/AR20100721060468.htm.

101 For an examination of Enron's influence in this process, see Lowell Bergman and Jeff Gerth, "Power Trader Tied to Bush Finds Washington All Ears," *New York Times,* May 25, 2001, A1.

102 Quote attributed to Lord Acton, a nineteenth-century historian.

103 Jeffrey H. Birnbaum, "Seeking Influence," *Washington Post National Weekly Edition,* April 30–May 6, 2007, 17.

104 Diana M. Evans, "Lobbying the Committee: Interest Groups and the House Public Works and Transportation Committee in the Post-Webster Era," in *Interest Group Politics,* 3rd ed., eds. Cigler and Loomis, 257–276.

105 Birnbaum, *Lobbyists,* 40.

106 Dan Kaufman, "Land of Cheese and Rancor," *New York Times Magazine,* May 27, 2012, 32. Georgia has adopted this proposal.

107 Elizabeth Drew, *Politics and Money: The New Road to Corruption* (New York: Macmillan, 1983), 78.

108 Ibid.

109 See Kevin Grier and Michael Mangy, "Comparing Interest Group PAC Contributions to House and Senate Incumbents," *Journal of Politics* 55 (1993), 615–643.

110 J. David Gopoian, "Change and Continuity in Defense PAC Behavior," *American Politics Quarterly* 13 (1985), 297–322; Richard Morin and Charles Babcock, "Off Year, Schmoff Year," *Washington Post National Weekly Edition,* May 14, 1990, 15.

111 Tina Daunt, "Hollywood Leans Right, Too," *Los Angeles Times,* November 3, 2006, www.calendarlive.com/printedition/calendar/cl-et-cause3nov03,0,498316,print.story. However, individual contributions, rather than company contributions, went mostly to Democratic candidates.

112 Samuel Kernell, *Going Public: New Strategies of Presidential Leadership* (Washington, D.C.: CQ Press, 1986), 34.

113 William P. Browne, *Groups, Interests, and U.S. Public Policy* (Washington, D.C.: Georgetown University Press, 1998), 23.

114 Richard Harris, "If You Love Your Grass," *New Yorker,* April 20, 1968, 57.

115 Bai, "Profiting from Pummeling."

116 Hacker and Pierson, *Winner-Take-All Politics,* 144.

117 Alex Kaplun, "'Energy Citizens' Take Aim at Climate Legislation," *New York Times,* August 12, 2009, nytimes.com/gwire/2009/08/12/12greenwire-energy-citizens-take-aim-at-climate-legislatio-54732.html.

118 Stephanie Mencimer, *Blocking the Courthouse Door* (New York: Free Press, 2007).

119 Birnbaum, *Lobbyists,* 40.

120 The Union of Concerned Scientists. Britain's leading scientific academy drew similar conclusions. "Scientists: ExxonMobil Misleads the Public," *Lincoln Journal Star,* January 4, 2007, 3A.

121 There have also been charges that ExxonMobil funded scientists who aren't experts in climatology and whose research wasn't reviewed by scholars in the field. Greenpeace, *Denial and Deception: A Chronicle of ExxonMobil's Efforts to Corrupt the Debate on Global Warming* (Washington, D.C.: Greenpeace, 2002).

122 The term was attributed to Paul Collier by Thomas Friedman, in *Hot, Flat, and Crowded* (New York: Picador/Farrer, Strauss and Giroux, 2009), 292.

123 Matt Grossman, *The Not-So Special Interests: Interest Groups, Public Representation, and American Governance* (Palo Alto, Calif.: Stanford University Press, 2012); Matt Grossman, "Why Jews Are Better Represented than Catholics," *The Monkey Cage,* April 2, 2012, http://themonkeycage.org/blog/2012/04/02/why-jews-are-better-represented-than-catholics/.

124 For many examples, see David Cay Johnston, *Perfectly Legal* (New York: Portfolio/Penguin, 2003).

125 Dan Clawson, Alan Neustadt, and Denise Scott, *Money Talks* (New York: Basic Books, 1992), 91.

126 John Christensen (R-Nebr.), from Omaha. "It Takes Only One Cook to Spoil the Batter," *Time,* July 7, 1997, 18.

127 "Reckless Driver" (comment), *New Yorker Magazine,* March 8, 2004, 25. Nader was also one person uniquely responsible for the election of George W. Bush to the presidency, but that's another story.

128 Hacker and Pierson, *Winner-Take-All Politics,* 118.

129 Ibid., 121.

130 For the evolution and many examples of these changes, see Johnston, *Perfectly Legal.*

131 According to the Center for Responsive Politics, cited in Hacker and Pierson, *Winner-Take-All Politics,* 227.

132 Travis Plunkett, quoted in Steven Brill, "On Sale: Your Government. Why Lobbying Is Washington's Best Bargain," *Time,* July 1, 2010, 33.

Chapter 7

1 Frank Bruni, "Snowe's Sad Retreat," *New York Times,* March 4, 2012, SR3.

2 Abby Goodnough, "Retirement Throws Maine's Senate Race into 'Chaos,'" *New York Times,* nytimes.com/2012/03/01/us/politics/maines-senate-race-in. . . .

3 The five others: Jeff Bingaman (D-N.M.), Kent Conrad (D-N.D.), Joe Lieberman (independent-Conn.), Ben Nelson (D-Nebr.), and Jim Webb (D-Va.).

4 Kathleen Parker, "A Vote in Favor of Moderation," *Lincoln Journal Star,* March 27, 2012, A5.

5 Mark Leibovich, "The Tea-Party Primary," *New York Times Magazine,* January 10, 2010, 30.

6 E. E. Schattschneider, *Party Government* (New York: Holt, Rinehart and Winston, 1960), 1.

7 Frank J. Sorauf, *Political Parties in the American System,* 4th ed. (Boston: Little, Brown, 1980).

8 Maurice Duverger, *Political Parties* (New York: Wiley, 1963). See also Edward R. Tufte, "The Relationship between Seats and Votes in Two-Party Systems," *American Political Science Review* 67 (1973), 540–554.

9 In a few PR systems, citizens vote for multiple candidates rather than for a party slate.

10 Robert G. Kaiser, "Hindsight Is 20/20," *Washington Post National Weekly Edition,* February 19, 2001.

11 Ralph Nader, "My Untold Story," *Brill's Content,* February 2001.

12 In addition, some political scientists believe that American parties, compared with European parties, tend to be moderate because the United States lacks a history of feudalism with peasants and aristocrats pitted against each other. In Europe such a history seems to have produced more class-based divisions manifested in more ideologically based parties. For the classic explanations, see Louis Hartz, *The Liberal Tradition in America* (New York: Harcourt Brace, 1955); and Seymour Martin Lipset, "Radicalism or Reformism: The Sources of Working Class Politics," *American Political Science Review* 77 (1983), 1–18.

13 William A. Galston, "Barack Obama's First Two Years," in *The Obama Presidency: Change and Continuity,* eds. Andrew J. Dowdle, Dirk C. Van Raemdonck, and Robert Maranto (New York: Taylor and Francis, 2012), 190.

14 Jacob Hacker and Paul Pierson, *Off Center* (New Haven, Conn.: Yale University Press, 2005), 110; Jacob Hacker and Paul Pierson, *Winner-Take-All Politics* (New York: Simon & Schuster, 2010), 264, 293–294.

15 "GOP Hopefuls Face Pledge Proliferation," *Lincoln Journal Star,* July 19, 2011, A8.

16 Kathleen Parker, "Tea Fragging Party," *Lincoln Journal Star,* July 31, 2011, D9.

17 Rosalind S. Helderman, "GOP's Anti-Tax Pledge Loses Steam," *Lincoln Journal Star,* May 26, 2012, A3. Yet some Republicans running for election in 2012 have refused to sign the anti-tax pledge, and a few who had signed it had rejected it.

18 For examples, consider the pressure faced by conservative Republicans: Sen. Lindsey Graham (R-S.C.) over climate change, Sen. Charles Grassley (R-Iowa) over health care reform, and Sen. John McCain (R-Ariz.) over immigration reform. After the pressure, each gave up efforts to negotiate with Democrats over the issue.

19 Geoffrey Kabaservice, *Rule and Ruin: The Downfall of Moderation and the Destruction of the Republican Party, from Eisenhower to the Tea Party* (New York: Oxford University Press, 2012), xvi.

20 Ibid.

21 Duncan Hunter (R-Calif.), quoted in Dana Milbank, "The New Old Party of Reagan," *Lincoln Journal Star,* July 21, 2011, B5.

22 *CQ Weekly,* January 12, 2002, 136; *CQ Weekly,* January 2, 2004, 53.

23 Frank J. Sorauf, *Money in American Elections* (Glenview, Ill.: Scott, Foresman, 1988), 121–153; Paul Herrnson, *Party Campaigning in the 1980s* (Cambridge, Mass.: Harvard University Press, 1988).

24 Janet Hook, "Meet the Powers behind the Democrats' Strategy," *Los Angeles Times,* July 5, 2006, www.latimes.com/news/nationworld/nation/la-na-dems5jul05,0,1314589,print.story?c.

25 Ibid.

26 Richard Hofstadter, *The Idea of the Party System: The Rise of Legitimate Opposition in the United States, 1780–1840* (Berkeley: University of California Press, 1969).

27 Theodore Lowi, *The Personal President* (Ithaca, N.Y.: Cornell University Press, 1985), 35.

28 James MacGregor Burns, *The Vineyard of Liberty* (New York: Knopf, 1982).

29 Property requirements continued to exist in a few places until the 1850s.

30 Instead of the party's members in Congress.

31 In 1820, there had been about 1.2 million free white men over twenty-five years of age; by 1840, there were 3.2 million white men of over the age of twenty.

32 When Harvard students established a charity for poor people in the city, they got few takers because the machine was already providing welfare for these people, so they shut down the charity.

33 William L. Riordon, *Plunkitt of Tammany Hall* (New York: E. P. Dutton, 1963), 28.

34 They also were allowed to dispense jobs with private companies, such as streetcar, gas, electric, and phone companies, that wanted to curry favor with local officials.

35 Milton L. Rakove, *Don't Make No Waves, Don't Back No Losers* (Bloomington: Indiana University Press, 1975), 112.

36 Benjamin Ginsberg and Martin Shefter, *Politics by Other Means* (New York: Viking, 1999), 19.

37 When independent newspapers emerged as profit-making businesses, the party papers declined. But the independent papers tended to favor one side or the other for many years as a way to attract and retain readers used to the advocacy of party papers.

38 Ibid.

39 This was a gradual process, lasting about a century. First, independently owned newspapers replaced party-owned newspapers. Then more broad-based and objective-striving independently owned newspapers replaced narrower, biased, independently owned newspapers.

40 Walter Dean Burnham, *Critical Elections and the Mainstream of American Politics* (New York: Norton, 1970); Helmut Norpoth and Jerrold Rusk, "Partisan Dealignment in the American Electorate," *American Political Science Review* 76 (1982), 522–537; David W. Rhode, "The Fall Elections: Realignment and Dealignment," *Chronicle of Higher Education,* December 14, 1994, 131–132.

41 A fuller discussion here would encompass the "culture wars"; cable television, talk radio, and narrowcasting; interest group pervasiveness and aggressiveness; Republican congressional efforts in the 1990s and Republican presidential and congressional efforts in the 2000s to create a disciplined and ideological party; Democratic responses to these efforts; and the decreasing number of competitive congressional races.

42 For a discussion of party influence on voting in Congress, see William R. Shaffer, *Party and Ideology in the United States Congress* (Lanham, Md.: University Press of America, 1980).

43 On issues in which the parties opposed each other.

44 Bruce I. Oppenheimer, "The Importance of Elections in a Strong Congressional Era," in *Do Elections Matter?* eds. Benjamin Ginsberg and Alan Stone (Armonk, N.Y.: M.E. Sharpe, 1996), 120–138.

45 John W. Kingdon, *America the Unusual* (Boston: Bedford/St. Martin's, 1999), 11.

46 For years, discussion of party realignment and of realigning elections was standard in political science, but the concept of realigning elections has been challenged by David R. Mayhew, *Electoral Realignment: A Critique of an American Genre* (New Haven, Conn.: Yale University Press, 2002). In particular, Mayhew questions some specific criteria that previous researchers have put forth as markers for realigning elections. Mayhew also questions the overemphasis on realigning elections and the deemphasis on other significant elections that results from this focus. Mayhew's critique may be appropriate for the discipline's researchers, but general *party realignment,* as opposed to specific *realigning elections,* remains a useful concept, especially for introductory texts. And, as Mayhew notes, the realignment of the 1930s, which our chapter addresses, is the most clear-cut.

47 In this realignment, the Republicans went from a bare majority to an overwhelming majority, so they remained the dominant party. However, this realignment is the least clear-cut. Mayhew asserts that it shouldn't be considered a realignment. *Electoral Realignments.*

48 James L. Sundquist, *Dynamics of the Party System: Alignment and Realignment of Political Parties in the United States* (Washington, D.C.: Brookings Institution Press, 1973).

49 Carter in 1976 and Clinton in 1992 and 1996. For a prediction and an analysis of this change, see Kevin Phillips, *The Emerging Republican Majority* (New York: Doubleday, 1969).

50 If we take the 1960s, rather than 1948, as the starting point for southern whites, and the 1990s as the end point for white-collar professionals and regular churchgoers. If the movement of young voters to the Democratic Party, which became pronounced in the 2000s, continues or merely proves durable, this group and decade will also have to be featured.

51 Patrick Reddy, "Why It's Got to Be All or Nothing," *Washington Post National Weekly Edition,* October 18, 1999, 23.

52 Tali Mendelberg, *The Race Card* (Princeton, N.J.: Princeton University Press, 2001).

53 John Erlichman, *Witness to Power: The Nixon Years* (New York: Simon & Schuster, 1970), 233.

54 Ibid.

55 Mendelberg, *The Race Card,* 97.

56 Michelle Alexander, *The New Jim Crow: Mass Incarceration in the Age of Color Blindness* (New York: New Press, 2010), 44.

57 Ibid., 3.

58 The comment "We'll go after the racists" was included in a Nixon aide's memoirs. Otherwise, such comments weren't made to the public, at least until an unguarded moment celebrating the one-hundredth birthday in 2002 of Strom Thurmond, a segregationist who formed the Dixiecrats, ran for the presidency under their label, and later joined fellow southerners switching to the Republican Party. At Thurmond's birthday party, Sen. Trent Lott (R-Miss.) expressed pride that his state voted for Thurmond in 1948 and added, "And if the rest of the country had followed our lead, we wouldn't have had all these problems over the years either." Lott later apologized, but public condemnation and a rebuke from President Bush prompted him to resign his position as majority leader.

59 Despite its dubious political history, the phrase "states' rights" continues to elicit positive connotations among most Americans. In 2010, 77 percent of respondents considered it to be a positive rather than a negative phrase. (This was 1 percent more than said "civil liberties" is a positive phrase.) No doubt this positive connotation explains its frequent and enduring use. "'Socialism' Not So Negative, 'Capitalism' Not So Positive," Pew Research Center for the People and the Press, survey conducted April 21–26, 2010, http://pewresearch.org/pubs/1583/political-rhetoric-capitalism-socialism-militia-family-values-states-rights.

60 Thomas F. Shaller, "Forget the South," *Washington Post National Weekly Edition,* November 24, 2003, 21.

61 Thomas B. Edsall, "The Fissure Running through the Democratic Party," *Washington Post National Weekly Edition,* June 6, 1994, 11.

62 John R. Petrocik and Frederick T. Steeper, "The Political Landscape in 1988," *Public Opinion,* September–October 1987, 41–44; Helmut Norpoth, "Party Realignment in the 1980s," *Public Opinion Quarterly* 51 (1987), 376–390.

63 The shift of blue-collar workers from the Democrats to the Republicans occurred mostly in the 1970s and 1980s. Since then, there has been little movement. Lane Kenworthy, Sondra Barringer, Daniel Duerr, and Garrett Andrew Schneider, "The Democrats and Working-Class Whites," June 10, 2007, u.arizona.edu/~/lkenwor/thedemocratsandworkingclasswhites.pdf.

64 Edsall, "Fissure," 11.

65 Thomas B. Edsall, "The Shifting Sands of America's Political Parties," *Washington Post National Weekly Edition,* April 9, 2001, 11.

66 Ibid.

67 According to Pew Research Center surveys. Ross Douthat, "Crises of Faith," *The Atlantic,* July–August 2007, 38.

68 Quoted in Robert B. Reich, "Deepening the Religious Divide," *American Prospect,* May 2005, 40.

69 Tax cuts were doled out mostly to the wealthy; energy, environmental, and consumer regulations were rolled back for big business; and heated rhetoric about gay marriage and abortion was offered for religious conservatives.

70 Morley Winograd and Michael D. Hais, "'Millennial' Voters Avoid the Republican Party," *Lincoln Journal Star,* May 14, 2009, B7.

71 Kevin Phillips, "All Eyes on Dixie," *American Prospect,* February 2004, 24.

72 Ibid.

73 John Alford, Carolyn Funk, and John Hibbing, "Are Political Attitudes Genetically Transmitted?" *American Political Science Review* 99 (May 2005), 153–167.

74 Gebe Martinez and Mary Agnes Carey, "Erasing the Gender Gap Tops Republican Playbook," *CQ Weekly,* March 6, 2004, 565.

75 Mary Agnes Carey, "Democrats Want Women: Party Targets Single Female Voters," *CQ Weekly,* March 6, 2004, 567.

76 Mike Murphy, "The Ice Age Cometh," *Time,* June 22, 2009, 43.

77 In 2008, three in five Asian Americans backed Obama. Steven V. Roberts, "Lost in America, Found on a Field," *Washington Post National Weekly Edition,* May 4–10, 2009, 39.

78 Frank Rich, "'The Rage Is Not about Health Care," *New York Times,* March 28, 2010, WK10.

Chapter 8

1 Eileen Shields West, "Give 'Em Hell These Days Is a Figure of Speech," *Smithsonian,* October 1988, 149–151. The editorial was from the *Connecticut Courant.*

2 Larry Sabato, "Negative Campaigning—What's New?" *Los Angeles Times,* November 4, 2008, www.latimes.com/news/opinion/la-oe-sabato4-w008nov04,0,825765,print.story.

3 "Campaign Vitriol," http://main.gvsu.edu/hauenstein/?id=CC1039DF-07E1-A466-487D0921E38984B7.

4 Charles Paul Freund, "But Then, Truth Has Never Been Important," *Washington Post National Weekly Edition,* November 7, 1988, 29.

5 Robert McNamara, "The Election of 1828 Was Marked by Dirty Tactics," http://history1800s.about.com/od/leaders/a/electionof1828.htm.

6 Ibid., 29.

7 William H. Flanigan, *Political Behavior of the American Electorate,* 2nd ed. (Boston: Allyn & Bacon, 1972), 13. See also Chilton Williamson, *American Suffrage from Property to Democracy 1760–1860* (Princeton, N.J.: Princeton University Press, 1960).

8 Jill Lepore, "Rock, Paper, Scissors," *New Yorker,* October 13, 2008, 92.

9 James MacGregor Burns, *Vineyard of Liberty* (New York: Knopf, 1982), 363.

10 August Meier and Elliot M. Rudwick, *From Plantation to Ghetto: An Interpretive History of American Negroes* (New York: Hill & Wang, 1966), 69.

11 Robert Darcy, Susan Welch, and Janet Clark, *Women, Elections, and Representation* (Lincoln: University of Nebraska Press, 1994).

12 David S. Reynolds, "Sons of the South," *New York Times Book Review,* September 28, 2008, 20.

13 Conference on Research in Income and Wealth, *Trends in the American Economy in the Nineteenth Century,* National Bureau of Economic Research, 1960, Table 2, Daily Wage Trends, United States, Selected Years, 1800–1899, http://www.nber.org/chapters/c2486.pdf.

14 Ralph G. Neas, "The Long Shadow of Jim Crow: Voter Intimidation and Suppression in America Today," *People for the American Way Foundation,* August 2004, www.naacp.org/inc/pdf/jimcrow.pdf.

15 Grandfather clause: *Guinn v. United States,* 238 U.S. 347 (1915); white primary: *Smith v. Allwright,* 321 U.S. 649 (1944).

16 Data on black and white voter registration in the southern states are from the *Statistical Abstract of the United States* (Washington, D.C.: U.S. Bureau of the Census, various years).

17 California, Florida, Michigan, New Hampshire, New York, and South Dakota.

18 Richard J. Timpone, "Mass Mobilization or Government Intervention? The Growth of Black Registration in the South," *Journal of Politics* 57 (1995), 425–442.

19 Bob Benenson, "Arduous Ritual of Redistricting Ensures More Racial Diversity," *Congressional Quarterly Weekly Report,* October 24, 1992, 3385. For a thorough review of the legal and behavioral impact of the Voting Rights Act, see Joseph Viteritti, "Unapportioned Justice: Local Elections, Social Science, and the Evolution of the Voting Rights Act," *Cornell Journal of Law and Public Policy* (1994), 210–270.

20 *Shaw v. Reno,* 125 L.Ed.2d 511, 113 S. Ct. 2816 (1993); *Miller v. Johnson,* 132 L.Ed.2d 762, 115 S. Ct. 2475 (1995); *Bush v. Vera,* 135 L.Ed.2d 248, 116 S. Ct. 1941 (1996).

21 Darcy et al., *Women, Elections, and Representation.*

22 Speech in 1867 by George Williams, cited in Peter Pappas's "Re-defining the Role of Women in Industrial America," www.peterpappas.com/journals/industry/women3.pdf.

23 The discussion in this paragraph is drawn largely from Lois W. Banner, *Women in Modern America: A Brief History* (New York: Harcourt Brace Jovanovich, 1974), 88–90; Glenn Firebaugh and Kevin Chen, "Vote Turnout of Nineteenth Amendment Women," *American Journal of Sociology* 100 (1995), 972–996.

24 See Pamela Paxton, *Women, Politics, and Power* (Los Angeles: Pine Forge Press, 2007), especially 38–43.

25 Justin Levitt, *The Truth about Voter Fraud,* Bennan Center for Justice, New York University Law School.

26 http://thinkprogress.org/justice/2012/07/24/572971/glenn-grothman-voter-id/.

27 Jamelle Bouie, "Pennsylvania Admits It: No Voter Fraud Problem," http://www.washingtonpost.com/blogs/plum-line/post/pennsylvania-admits-it-no-voter-fraud-problem/2012/07/24/gJQAHNVt6W_blog.html?hpid=z3.

28 Sasha Abramsky, *Conned: How Millions Went to Prison, Lost the Vote, and Helped Send George W. Bush to the White House* (New York: New Press, 2006). This book is partly anecdotal but does point out the huge numbers of people disfranchised by both laws and intimidation.

29 Robert Pierre, "Botched Name Purge Denied Some the Right to Vote," *Washington Post,* May 31, 2001, A1, http://www.washingtonpost.com/ac2/wp-dyn/A99749-2001May30; Tom Fiedler, "The Perfect Storm," in *Overtime! The Election 2000 Thriller,* ed. Larry J. Sabato (New York: Longman, 2002), 11.

30 Lizette Alvarez, "Search for Illegal Voters May Violate Federal Safeguards, U.S. Tells Florida," *New York Times,* June 1, 2012, http://www.nytimes.com/2012/06/02/us/justice-dept-asks-florida-to-end-voter-purge.html.

31 Martha Irvine, "Could Tougher Voting Laws Squelch the 2012 Youth Vote?" *Lincoln Journal Star,* August 5, 2012, A3.

32 Alabama, Florida, Virginia, and Kentucky.

33 Nicholas Thompson, "Locking Up the Vote: Disenfranchisement of Former Felons Was the Real Crime in Florida," *Washington Monthly,* January–February 2001, 18.

34 "Groups Report Progress against Laws Banning Felons from Voting," *Lincoln Journal Star,* June 22, 2005, 4a.

35 Thompson, "Locking Up the Vote," 20.

36 Richard Jensen, "American Election Campaigns: A Theoretical and Historical Typology," paper delivered at the 1968 Midwest Political Science Association Meeting, quoted in Walter Dean Burnham, *Critical Elections and the Mainsprings of American Politics* (New York: Norton, 1970), 73.

37 Frances Fox Piven and Richard A. Cloward, *Why Americans Don't Vote* (New York: Pantheon Books, 1988), 30.

38 These examples are from the editorial "Barriers to Student Voting," *New York Times,* September 28, 2004, 26.

39 Part of the explanation for declining voting rates is that the number of citizens who are ineligible to vote has increased, which depresses voter turnout statistics. Immigrants, other noncitizens, and, in some states, convicted felons are not eligible to vote. When those individuals are removed from the calculation of proportion voting, the proportion voting is increased by about 5 points; and most of the turnout decline occurred in the 1960s. See Michael P. McDonald and Samuel Popkin, "The Myth of the Vanishing Voter," *American Political Science Review* 95 (2001), 963–974.

40 Alan Wolfe, "The Race's Real Winner: Democracy," *Washington Post National Weekly Edition,* May 19–25, 2008, 25.

41 Michael McDonald, http://elections.gmu.edu/voter_turnout.htm.

42 United States Election Project, "2012 Presidential Nomination Contest Turnout Rates," http://elections.gmu.edu/Turnout_2012P.html.

43 Ibid.

44 Daniel J. Elazar, *American Federalism: A View from the States* (New York: Crowell, 1972); *Statistical Abstract of the United States 2006*, tab. 406.

45 Norman H. Nie, Sidney Verba, Henry Brady, Kay Lehman Schlozman, and Jane Junn, "Participation in America: Continuity and Change," paper presented at the Midwest Political Science Association, April 1988. The standard work on American political participation, though now dated, is Sidney Verba and Norman H. Nie, *Participation in America: Political Democracy and Social Equality* (New York: Harper & Row, 1972).

46 Piven and Cloward, *Why Americans Don't Vote*, 162; *Statistical Abstract of the United States 2001*, tab. 401; Frances Fox Piven and Richard A. Cloward, *Why Americans Still Don't Vote: And Why Politicians Want It That Way* (Boston: Beacon Press, 2001).

47 G. Bingham Powell, "American Voter Turnout in Comparative Perspective," *American Political Science Review* 80 (1986), 30; Piven and Cloward, *Why Americans Don't Vote*, 119; Arend Lijphart, "Unequal Participation: Democracy's Unresolved Dilemma," *American Political Science Review* 91 (1997), 1–14.

48 Henry Brady, Sidney Verba, and Kay Lehman Schlozman, "Beyond SES: A Resource Model of Political Participation," *American Political Science Review* 89 (June 1995), 271–294.

49 Nie et al., "Participation in America: Continuity and Change"; Verba and Nie, *Participation in America: Political Democracy and Social Equality*.

50 Steven Hill and Rashad Robinson, "Demography vs. Democracy: Young People Feel Left Out of the Political Process," *Los Angeles Times*, November 5, 2002, 2. Posted by the Youth Vote Coalition, www.youthvote.org/news/newsdetail.cfm?newsid56. The survey cited was conducted by Harvard University.

51 Eric Plutzer, "Becoming a Habitual Voter: Inertia, Resources, and Growth in Young Adulthood," *American Political Science Review* 96 (2002), 41–56.

52 Anna Greenberg, "New Generation, New Politics," *American Prospect*, October 1, 2003, A3.

53 *Time Magazine*, February 11, 2008, 36.

54 Paul Allen Beck and M. Kent Jennings, "Political Periods and Political Participation," *American Political Science Review* 73 (1979), 737–750; Nie et al., "Participation in America: Continuity and Change."

55 George F. Will, "In Defense of Nonvoting," *Newsweek*, October 10, 1983, 96.

56 Richard Morin, "The Dog Ate My Forms, and, Well, I Couldn't Find a Pen," *Washington Post National Weekly Edition*, November 5, 1990, 38.

57 Lawrence R. Jacobs and Robert Y. Shapiro, *Politicians Don't Pander: Political Manipulation and the Loss of Democratic Responsiveness* (Chicago: University of Chicago Press, 2000).

58 Emmett H. Buell Jr. and Lee Sigelman, *Attack Politics: Negativity in Presidential Campaigns since 1960* (Lawrence: University Press of Kansas,

2008), especially 246ff. But see John Geer, *In Defense of Negativity: Attack Ads in Presidential Campaigns* (Chicago: University of Chicago Press, 2006), who found increased negativity in television ads.

59 Richard Lau, Lee Sigelman, Caroline Heldman, and Paul Babbitt, "The Effects of Negative Political Advertisements," *American Political Science Review* 93 (1999), 851–875; Steven E. Finkel and John Geer, "A Spot Check: Casting Doubt on the Demobilizing Effect of Attack Advertising," *American Journal of Political Science* 42 (1998), 573–595. Research on turnout is found in Stephen Ansolabehere and Shanto Iyengar, *Going Negative* (New York: Free Press, 1996). In her book *Packaging the Presidency: A History and Criticism of Presidential Campaign Advertising* (New York: Oxford University Press, 1984), Kathleen Jamieson also argues that there are checks on misleading advertising, but later ("Is the Truth Now Irrelevant in Presidential Campaigns?"), she notes that these checks do not always work well. See Jamieson, *Dirty Politics: Deception, Distraction, and Democracy* (New York: Oxford University Press, 1992).

60 Thomas E. Patterson, *The Vanishing Voter* (New York: Knopf, 2002); Curtis B. Gans, "The Empty Ballot Box," *Public Opinion* 1 (September–October 1978), 54–57; Curtis Gans, quoted in Jack Germond and Jules Witcover, "Listen to the Voters—and Nonvoters," *Minneapolis Star Tribune*, November 26, 1988. This effect was foreshadowed by Michael J. Robinson, "American Political Legitimacy in an Era of Electronic Journalism," in *Television as a Social Force: New Approaches to TV Criticism*, eds. Douglass Cater and Richard Adler (New York: Praeger, 1975). See also Austin Ranney, *Channels of Power: The Impact of Television on American Politics* (New York: Basic Books, 1983); and Richard Boyd, "The Effect of Election Calendars on Voter Turnout," paper presented at the annual meeting of the Midwest Political Science Association, April 1987, Chicago.

61 Boyd, "The Effect of Election Calendars on Voter Turnout," 43. See Piven and Cloward, *Why Americans Don't Vote*, 196–197, for illustrations of these kinds of informal barriers, and Piven and Cloward, *Why Americans Still Don't Vote: And Why Politicians Want It That Way*, for further examples.

62 "Numbers," *Time*, May 15, 2006, 17.

63 Anthony Downs, *An Economic Theory of Democracy* (New York: Harper, 1957).

64 U.S. Census, reported at http://www.census.gov/population/socdemo/voting/p20-542/tab12.pdf.

65 Kay Lehman Schlozman, Sidney Verba, and Henry Brady, "Participation's Not a Paradox: The View from American Activists," *British Journal of Political Science* 25 (1995), 1–36.

66 James Warren, "Want to Increase Voting? Discounts Seem to Work," *New York Times*, April 3, 2011, 25B, Chicago Edition.

67 Sasha Issenberg, "Nudge the Vote," *New York Times Magazine*, October 31, 2010, 28.

68 Henry E. Brady and John McNulty, "Turning Out to Vote: The Costs of Finding and Getting to the Polling Place," *American Political Science Review* 105 (February 2011), 115–134.

69 Ruy Teixeira, *Why Americans Don't Vote: Turnout Decline in the United States 1960–1984* (Boulder, Colo.: Greenwood, 1987); Ruy Teixeira, *The Disappearing American Voter* (Washington, D.C.: Brookings Institution, 1992); and Peverill Squire, Raymond Wolfinger, and David Glass, "Residential Mobility and Voter Turnout," *American Political Science Review* 81 (1987), 45–66.

70 More recent studies of turnout include Richard J. Timpone, "Structure, Behavior and Voter Turnout in the United States," *American Political Science Review* 92 (1998), 145–158; Brady et al., "Beyond SES."

71 Bill Winders, "The Roller Coaster of Class Conflict: Class Segments, Mass Mobilization, and Voter Turnout in the United States, 1840–1996," *Social Forces*, March 1999, 833–862. For a review of this literature, see John Petrocik, "Voter Turnout and Electoral Preference," in *Elections in America*, ed. Kay Lehman Schlozman (Boston: Allen & Unwin, 1987). See also Bernard Grofman, Guillermo Owen, and Christian Collet, "Rethinking the Partisan Effects of Higher Turnout," *Public Choice* 99 (1999), 357–376.

72 Tom Hamburger and Peter Wallsten, "Parties Are Tracking Your Habits," *Los Angeles Times*, July 24, 2005, www.latimes.com/news/nationworld/nation/lanarncdnc24jul24,0,535024,full.story.

73 Kim Quaile Hill, Jan Leighley, and Angela Hinton-Anderson, "Lower-Class Mobilization and Policy Linkage in the U.S. States," *American Journal of Political Science* 39 (1995), 75–86.

74 Mark Gray and Miki Caul, "Declining Voter Turnout in Advanced Industrial Democracies, 1950 to 1997," *Comparative Political Studies* 33 (November 2000), 1091–1122.

75 Piven and Cloward, *Why Americans Don't Vote*, 17.

76 Ibid.

77 Raymond E. Wolfinger and Steven J. Rosenstone, *Who Votes?* (New Haven, Conn.: Yale University Press, 1980), tab. 6–1.

78 Steven J. Rosenstone and Raymond E. Wolfinger, "The Effect of Registration Laws on Voter Turnout," *American Political Science Review* 72 (1978), 22–45; Glenn Mitchell and Christopher Wlezien, "Voter Registration Laws and Turnout, 1972–1982," paper presented at the annual meeting of the Midwest Political Science Association, April 1989, Chicago; Mark J. Fenster, "The Impact of Allowing Day of Registration Voting on Turnout in U.S. Elections from 1960 to 1992," *American Politics Quarterly* 22 (1994), 74–87.

79 Jacob Neiheisel and Barry C Burdon, "The Impact of Election Day Registration on Voter Turnout and Election Outcomes," *American Politics Research* 40 (4), 636–664.

80 Kim Quaile Hill and Jan E. Leighley, "Racial Diversity, Voter Turnout, and Mobilizing

Institutions in the United States," *American Politics Quarterly* 27 (1999), 275–295.

[81] "Block the Vote" (editorial), *New York Times,* May 30, 2006; *League of Women Voters of Florida v. Browning,* http://www.brennancenter.org/content/ resource/league_of_women_voters_of_florida_v_ cobb.

[82] Charles Peters, "Tilting at Windmills," *Washington Monthly* (May–June 2012), 10.

[83] Piven and Cloward, *Why Americans Don't Vote,* 230–231.

[84] Stephen Knack, "Does 'Motor Voter' Work?" *Journal of Politics* 57 (1995), 796–811.

[85] Jo Becker, "Voters May Have Their Say before Election Day," *Washington Post,* August 26, 2004, A01.

[86] Michael McDonald, "(Nearly) Final 2008 Early Voting Statistics," http://elections.gmu.edu/Early_ Voting_2008_Final.html.

[87] Ibid.

[88] These examples are drawn from Raymond Wolfinger, Benjamin Highton, and Megan Mullin, "How Postregistration Laws Affect the Turnout of Blacks and Latinos," paper presented at the 2003 annual meeting of the American Political Science Association, Philadelphia, Pennsylvania, August 28–31.

[89] David S. Broder, "Voting's Neglected Scandal," *Washington Post,* June 26, 2008, A19.

[90] Jill Lepore, "Bound for Glory," *New Yorker,* October 20, 2008, 80.

[91] The following discussion draws heavily from John H. Aldrich, *Before the Convention: Strategies and Choices in Presidential Nomination Campaigns* (Chicago: University of Chicago Press, 1980).

[92] Ibid. See also David W. Rohde, "Risk Bearing and Progressive Ambition: The Case of Members of the United States House of Representatives," *American Journal of Political Science* 23 (1979), 1–26.

[93] Quoted in Audrey A. Haynes, Paul-Henri Gurian, and Stephen M. Nichols, "The Role of Candidate Spending in Presidential Nomination Campaigns," *Journal of Politics* 59 (February 1997), 213–225.

[94] Ryan Lizza, "Life of the Party," *New Yorker,* March 12, 2012, 24.

[95] Robert Stacy McCain, "Perry's Slide Continues," *American Spectator,* September 23, 2011, http://spectator.org/archives/2011/09/23/perrys-slide-continues.

[96] Audrey Haynes, Paul-Henri Gurian, and Stephen Nichols, "Role of Candidate Spending in Presidential Nominating Campaigns," *Journal of Politics* 57 (February 1997), 223.

[97] Diana C. Mutz, "Effects of Horse-Race Coverage on Campaign Coffers: Strategic Contributing in Presidential Primaries," *Journal of Politics* 57 (1995), 1015–1042.

[98] Michael Luo, J. Becker, and Patrick Healy, "Donors Worried by Clinton Spending,"

New York Times, February 22, 2008, www.nytimes.com/2008/02/22/us/politics/22clinton.html?ref-opinion.

[99] "The Fall Campaign," *Newsweek Election Extra,* November–December 1984, 88.

[100] Hendrik Hertzberg, "This Must Be the Place," *New Yorker,* January 31, 2000, 36–39.

[101] Data in this paragraph from T. W. Farnam, "Negative Campaign Ads Much More Frequent, Vicious Than in Primaries Past," *Washington Post,* February 20, 2012, http://www.washingtonpost.com/politics/study-negative-campaign-ads-much-more-frequent-vicious-than-in-primaries-past/2012/02/14/gIQAR7ifPR_story_1.html.

[102] Andrew Rudalevige, "The Mittens Come Off," February 1, 2012, www.themonkeycage.org; John Sides, "Did Romney's Ad Advantage Help in Florida?" *FiveThirtyEight,* February 1, 2012.

[103] Although election commentary usually refers to "Super PACs," the organizations that can spend unlimited money on political ads and keep their donors secret are "501(c)4 organizations." They can keep their donors secret because they are classified as "social welfare" groups.

[104] These debates are listed and video recordings available at http://www.2012presidentialelectionnews.com/2012-debate-schedule/2011-2012-primary-debate-schedule/.

[105] These debates are listed and summarized at http://en.wikipedia.org/wiki/Democratic_Party_presidential_debates,_2008.

[106] Hendrik Hertzberg, "The Debate Debate," *New Yorker,* February 13 & 20, 2012, 31–32.

[107] B. Drummond Ayres Jr., "It's Taking Care of Political Business," *New York Times,* July 18, 1999, 22.

[108] Katharine Q. Seelye and Marjorie Connelly, "Republican Delegates Leaning to Right of G.O.P. and the Nation," *New York Times,* August 29, 2004, 13.

[109] Gerald M. Pomper and Susan S. Lederman, *Elections in America: Control and Influence in Democratic Politics* (New York: Longman, 1980), ch. 7. For an analysis of the polarization in state party platforms, see Daniel Coffey, "More than a Dime's Worth: Using State Party Platforms to Assess the Degree of American Party Polarization," *PS* (April 2011), 331–337.

[110] Joseph Cera and Aaron C. Weinschenk, "The Individual-Level Effects of Presidential Conventions on Candidate Evaluations," *American Politics Research* 40 (1), 3–28.

[111] Quote from Gerald M. Pomper in Adam Nagourney, "What Boston Can Do for Kerry," *New York Times,* July 18, 2004, 5.

[112] David Carr, "Whose Convention Is It? Reporters Outnumber Delegates 6 to 1," *New York Times,* July 27, 2004, E1.

[113] As told by Gail Collins, "Vice Is Nice," *New York Times,* June 21, 2008.

[114] Lee Sigelman and Paul Wahlbeck, "The 'Veep-stakes': Strategic Choice in Presidential Running

Mate Selection," *American Political Science Review* 94 (1997), 855–864.

[115] Philip Rucker and Rosalind S. Helderman, "Paul Ryan is Romney's VP Pic, Setting Up Stark Choice on Budget Issues," *Washington Post,* August 11, 2012, http://www.washingtonpost.com/politics/paul-ryan-is-romneys-pick-for-vice-presidential-nominee/2012/08/11/dc2f5070-e0f1-11e1-8fc5-a7dcf1fc161d_story.html.

[116] Ibid.

[117] Robert L. Dudley and Ronald B. Rapaport, "Vice-Presidential Candidates and the Home State Advantage: Playing Second Banana at Home and on the Road," *American Journal of Political Science* 33 (1989), 537–540.

[118] *New York Times,* July 11, 2004, 16.

[119] Collins, "Vice Is Nice."

[120] Daron Shaw, "A Study of Presidential Campaign Event Effects from 1952 to 1992," *Journal of Politics* 61 (1999), 387–422.

[121] See *Congressional Quarterly,* July 23, 1988, 2015; Thomas M. Holbrook, "Campaigns, National Conditions and U.S. Presidential Elections," *American Journal of Political Science* 38 (1994), 973–998.

[122] Total election and telephone expenses from Robert J. Samuelson, "The Super PAC Confusion," *Washington Post,* February 19, 2012, http://www.washingtonpost.com/opinions/the-super-pac-confusion/2012/02/17/gIQApb1FOR_story.html; entertainment expenses were calculated from Bureau of Labor Statistics, "Consumer Expenditures—2010," http://www.bls.gov/news.release/cesan.nr0.htm.

[123] *Buckley v. Valeo,* 424 U.S. 1 (1976).

[124] *Citizens United v. Federal Election Commission,* 558 U.S. 50 (2010).

[125] 558 U.S. 50 (2010). See Jill Abramson, "The Return of the Secret Donors," *New York Times,* October 17, 2010.

[126] Mike Allen, "Does an Embassy Trump the Lincoln Bedroom?" *Washington Post National Weekly Edition,* May 7, 2001, 14.

[127] Ibid.

[128] Quoted in *New York Times,* June 13, 1998, A7.

[129] Alan Abramson, "Setting the Record Straight: Correcting Myths about Independent Voters," *Sabato's Crystal Ball,* http://www.centerforpolitics.org/crystalball/articles/aia2011070702/.

[130] "Election Tracker: Candidate Visits," www.cnn.com/ELECTION/2008/map/candidate.visits/.

[131] Paul West, "President Obama Hits Battleground State of Ohio Hard," Los Angeles Times, August 31, 2012: http://articles.latimes.com/2012/aug/02/nation/la-na-ohio-obama-20120801.

[132] George F. Will, "Premature Triumphalism," *Time,* February 22, 2010, 24.

[133] Lanhee J. Chen and Andrew Reeves, "Turning Out the Base or Appealing to the Periphery? An Analysis of County-Level Candidate Appearances in the 2008 Presidential Campaign," *American Politics Research* 39 (3), 534–556.

134 See, for example, Adam Nagourney and Jeff Zeleny, "Already, Obama and McCain Map Fall Strategies," *New York Times,* May 11, 2008, 1ff.

135 The discussion of the functions of the media relies heavily on the excellent summary found in Stephen Ansolabehere, Roy Behr, and Shanto Iyengar, "Mass Media and Elections," *American Politics Quarterly* 19 (1991), 109–139.

136 Kate Kenski, Bruce Hardy, and Kathleen Hall Jamieson, *The Obama Victory* (New York: Oxford University Press), 266.

137 Ibid., 309.

138 L. Marvin Overby and Jay Barth, "Radio Advertising in American Political Campaigns," *American Politics Research* 34 (July 2006), 451–478.

139 Robert MacNeil, *People Machine: The Influence of Television on American Politics* (New York: Harper & Row, 1968), 182.

140 Elisabeth Bumiller, "Selling Soup, Wine and Reagan," *Washington Post National Weekly Edition,* November 5, 1984, 6–8.

141 Preferences listed in this paragraph were described in Lisa de Moraes, "Research Firm Breaks Down Politics of TV," *Washington Post,* December 6, 2011, http://www.washingtonpost.com/lifestyle/style/research-firm-breaks-down-politics-of-tv-this-old-house-vs-the-daily-show/2011/12/06/gIQAQPSkaO_story.html.

142 Ashley Parker, "Where Parties Look for an Audience," *New York Times,* October 31, 2010, 25.

143 Ibid.

144 Daron Shaw, "The Methods behind the Madness: Presidential Electoral College Strategies, 1988–1996," *Journal of Politics* 61 (1999), 893–913, shows the evolution of advertising focus during these three elections.

145 Through early summer, about three-fourths of Bush's were negative, whereas only one-fourth of Kerry's were. As election day drew nearer, the proportion of negative ads increased. Dana Milbank and Jim VandeHei, "The Mean Season Is in Full Bloom," *Washington Post National Weekly Edition,* June 7, 2004, 13. Both campaigns agreed that the figures were accurate.

146 Greg Sargent, "McCain's Campaign Spending Now Nearly 100 Percent Devoted to Negative Ads," tpmelectioncentral.talkingpointsmemo.com/2008/10/mccain_campaigns_ad_spending_n.php.

147 The study of negative advertising research was done by Richard Lau, Lee Sigelman, Caroline Heldman, and Paul Babbitt, "The Effects of Negative Political Advertisements," *American Political Science Review* 93 (1999), 851–875.

148 Independent reexaminations of the record found nothing to substantiate the Swift Boat Veterans' ad claims.

149 Democratic consultants are more likely to find negative advertising distasteful than Republican consultants. However, this does not necessarily translate into partisan differences in use.

150 Paul Taylor, "Pigsty Politics," *Washington Post National Weekly Edition,* February 13, 1989, 6.

151 Quoted in Frank Bruni, "Of Bile and Billionaires," *New York Times,* May 20, 2012, 3.

152 Yanna Krupnikov, "When Does Negativity Demobilize? Tracing the Conditional Effect of Negative Campaigning on Voter Turnout," *American Journal of Political Science* 55 (October), 797–813; see also Stephen Ansolabehere and Shanto Iyengar, *Going Negative: How Political Advertisements Shrink and Polarize the Electorate* (New York: Free Press, 1996).

153 Matthew Dowd, quoted in Jeff Zeleny, "Obama's Team Taking Gamble Going Negative," *New York Times,* July 28, 2012, nytimes.com/2012/07/29/us/politics/obama-campaign-takes….

154 Ansolabehere and Iyengar, *Going Negative.*

155 Jamieson, *Packaging the Presidency.*

156 Kenski et al., *The Obama Victory,* 305.

157 Ibid., 307.

158 These data on Internet use are from the Pew Foundation's Internet and American Life Project, "The Internet and the 2008 Election," June 15, 2008, www.pewinternet.org.

159 Kenski et al., *The Obama Victory,* 306.

160 David Perlmutter, "Political Blogs: The New Iowa?" *Chronicle of Higher Education,* May 26, 2006, B6.

161 Kenski et al., *The Obama Victory,* 307.

162 Thomas E. Patterson, *The Mass Media Election: How Americans Choose Their President* (New York: Praeger, 1980), 3.

163 Martin Schram, *The Great American Video Game: Presidential Politics in the Television Age* (New York: Morrow, 1987).

164 Daron Shaw, "A Study of Presidential Campaign Event Effects from 1952 to 1992," *Journal of Politics* 61 (May 1999), 387–422, reports on a systematic study of campaign events and their impact on the elections.

165 Kenski et al., *The Obama Victory,* 196–202.

166 John Heilemann and Mark Hallperin, *Game Change* (New York: Harper, 2010), 391.

167 Ibid., 392.

168 Margaret Hartmann, "Obama Has Some Time on His Hands, Visits the Hoover Dam," *New York Magazine,* October 3, 2012, http://nymag.com/daily/intel/2012/10/obama-avoids-debate-prep-visits-the-hoover-dam.html.

169 Waldman, "Majority Rule at Last," 18.

170 Ibid.

171 Robert Dahl, *How Democratic Is the American Constitution?* (New Haven, Conn.: Yale University Press, 2001).

172 Waldman, "Majority Rule at Last."

173 Akhil Reed Amar, *America's Constitution: A Biography* (New York: Random House, 2005).

174 Ibid.

175 Quoted in Alan M. Dershowitz, *Supreme Injustice: How the High Court Hijacked Election 2000* (New York: Oxford University Press, 2001), 25.

176 Hendrik Hertzberg, "Up for the Count," *New Yorker,* December 18, 2000, 41. At least 680 were flawed, including nearly 200 with U.S. postmarks, indicating that they had been mailed from within the country rather than from overseas; 344 were late, illegible, or missing postmarks; and even 38 reflected double voting by 19 voters.

177 Kosuke Imai and Gary King, "Did Illegally Counted Overseas Absentee Ballots Decide the 2000 U.S. Presidential Election?" gking.Harvard.edu.

178 David Barstow and Don Van Natta Jr., "How Bush Took Florida: Mining the Overseas Absentee Vote," *New York Times,* July 15, 2001, www.nytimes.com/2001/07/15/; www.national/15ball.

179 Ibid.

180 Jonathan Wand, Kenneth Shotts, Jasjeet Sekhon, Walter R. Mebane Jr., Michael Herron, and Henry Brady, "The Butterfly Did It: The Aberrant Vote for Buchanan in Palm Beach," *American Political Science Review* 95 (2001), 793–809. They examined the Palm Beach Buchanan vote in relation to all other counties in the United States compared to the absentee ballots (which did not use the butterfly format) in Palm Beach County, precinct-level data, and individual ballots.

181 Fiedler, "The Perfect Storm," 8.

182 Imai and King, "Did Illegally Counted Overseas Absentee Ballots Decide the 2000 U.S. Presidential Election?" 3.

183 Jimmy Carter, quoted from National Public Radio in Kellia Ramares's special report "House Strikes Truth from the Record," *Online Journal,* July 23, 2004. The full Ramares article is at www.onlinejournal.com/Special_Reports/072304Ramares/072304ramares.html.

184 Paul Abramson, John H. Aldrich, and David Rohde, *Change and Continuity in the 2000 Elections* (Washington, D.C.: CQ Press, 2003); Paul Abramson, John H. Aldrich, and David Rohde, *Change and Continuity in the 2004 and 2006 Elections* (Washington, D.C.: CQ Press, 2007).

185 Ibid.

186 In recent elections, the percentages able to correctly identify general differences between the major party candidates varied between 26 and 55 percent.

187 Paul Abramson, John Aldrich, and David Rohde, *Change and Continuity in the 2008 Election* (Washington, D.C.: CQ Press, 2009), 157–159; Abramson, Aldrich, and Rohde, *Change and Continuity in the 2004 and 2006 Elections.*

188 Abramson et al., *Change and Continuity in the 2008 Election,* 161.

189 Ibid.

190 Ibid., 166.

191 Morris Fiorina, *Retrospective Voting in American National Elections* (New Haven, Conn.: Yale University Press, 1981).

192 Edward R. Tufte, *Political Control of the Economy* (Princeton, N.J.: Princeton University

Press, 1978); Douglas Hibbs, "The Mass Public and Macroeconomic Performance," *American Journal of Political Science* 23 (1979), 705–731; John Hibbing and John Alford, "The Electoral Impact of Economic Conditions: Who Is Held Responsible," *American Journal of Political Science* 25 (1981), 423–439.

193 Abramson et al., *Change and Continuity in the 2008 Election*, 182.

194 Data from *New York Times* exit polling: "President Exit Polls," http://elections.nytimes.com /2012/results/president/exit-polls.

195 http://www.newstatesman.com/blogs/world -affairs/2012/08/todd-akin-legitimate-rape-quote -day; http://www.politico.com/news/stories/1012 /82795.html.

195a "Mapping Racist Tweets in Response to President Obama's Re-election," http://www.floatingsheep.org /2012/11/mapping-racist-tweets-in-response-to .html.

196 Morley Winograd and Michael D. Hais, "Millennial Voters Avoid the Republican Party," *Los Angeles Times*, May 14, 2009, B7.

197 Thomas Byrne Edsall, *The Age of Austerity* (New York: Doubleday, 2012), 97. Data from University of Virginia Center for Politics, Alan I. Abramowitz, "Beyond 2012: Demographic Change and the Future of the Republican Party," March 2010.

198 For example, see Norman J. Ornstein and Thomas E. Mann, eds., *The Permanent Campaign and Its Future* (Washington, D.C.: American Enterprise Institute and the Brookings Institution, 2000).

199 Paul Abramson, John H. Aldrich, and David Rohde, *Change and Continuity in the 2010 Election* (Washington, D.C.: CQ Press, 2010), ch. 6.

200 Ibid.

201 Benjamin I. Page and Robert Y. Shapiro, "Effects of Public Opinion on Policy," *American Political Science Review* 77 (1983), 175–190.

202 Joshua Tucker, "If Same-Sex Marriage Is So Popular, Why Does It Always Lose at the Ballot Box?" *American Prospect*, May 15, 2012, http:// prospect.org/article/if-same-sex-marriage -so-popular-why-does-it-always-lose-ballot -box-includes-state-level-data.

203 Arthur Schlesinger Jr., *Wall Street Journal*, December 5, 1986. But see also Jacobs and Shapiro, *Politicians Don't Pander*.

204 See, for example, Patrick Flavin, "Income Inequality and Policy Representation in the American States," *American Politics Research* 40 (1), 29–59.

Chapter 9

1 Brian Flynn, "What's Wrong with Congress? It's Not Big Enough," March 9, 2012, http://www.cnn .com/2012/03/09/opinion/flynn-expand -congress/index.html.

2 Hanna F. Pitkin, *The Concept of Representation* (Berkeley: University of California Press, 1967), 60.

3 Ibid., 60–61.

4 Roger H. Davidson, Walter J. Oleszek, and Frances E. Lee, *Congress and Its Members*, 11th ed. (Washington, D.C.: CQ Press, 2008), 191–194; Richard Fenno, *Home Style: House Members in Their Districts*, 2nd ed. (New York: Longman, 2003), 232–247.

5 Patricia Murphy, "Rep. Gwen Moore on Her Own Sexual Assault, Violence against Women Act," *The Daily Beast*, March 29, 2012, http:// www.thedailybeast.com/articles/2012/03/29/ rep-gwen-moore-on-her-own-sexual-assault- violence-against-women-act.html.

6 James R. Chiles, "Congress Couldn't Have Been This Bad, or Could It?" *Smithsonian*, November 1995, 70–80.

7 Susan Webb Hammond, "Life and Work on the Hill: Careers, Norms, Staff, and Informal Caucuses," in *Congress Responds to the Twentieth Century*, eds. Sunil Ahuja and Robert Dewhirst (Columbus: Ohio State University Press, 2003), 74.

8 David S. Broder, "Dumbing Down Democracy," *Lincoln Journal Star*, April 5, 1995, 18.

9 Quoted in Kenneth J. Cooper and Helen Dewar, "No Limits on the Term Limits Crusade," *Washington Post National Weekly Edition*, May 29, 1995, 14.

10 David Nather, "Term Limits Now Have Limited Interest," *CQ Weekly*, January 19, 2009, 102.

11 A list of cities and states that have term limits can be found at www.termlimits.org.

12 "Congress of Relative Newcomers Poses Challenge to Bush, Leadership," *Congressional Quarterly Weekly Review*, January 20, 2001, 179–181.

13 R. Eric Petersen, "Representatives and Senators: Trends in Member Characteristics since 1945," *Federal Publications*, Paper 887, 2012, http:// digitalcommons.ilr.cornell.edu/key_workplace/ 887.

14 See Thomas E. Mann, "Elections and Change in Congress," in *The New Congress*, eds. Thomas E. Mann and Norman J. Ornstein (Washington, D.C.: American Enterprise Institute for Public Policy Research, 1981); David R. Mayhew, *Congress: The Electoral Connection* (New Haven, Conn.: Yale University Press, 1974).

15 Christopher Buckley, "Hangin' with the Houseboyz," *Washington Monthly*, June 1992, 44.

16 Linda L. Fowler and Robert D. McClure, *Political Ambition: Who Decides to Run for Congress?* (New Haven, Conn.: Yale University Press, 1989), 47; John Hibbing and Sara Brandes, "State Population and the Electoral Success of U.S. Senators," *American Journal of Political Science* 27 (1983), 808–819. See also Glenn R. Parker, "Stylistic Change in the U.S. Senate, 1959–1980," *Journal of Politics* 47 (1985), 1190–1202.

17 *Budget of the United States, Fiscal 2011: Appendix* (Washington, D.C.: Government Printing Office, 2010).

18 Brad Fitch and Kathy Goldschmidt, *Communicating with Congress: How Capitol Hill Is Coping with the Surge in Citizen Advocacy* (Washington, D.C.: Congressional Management Foundation, 2005).

19 "Money Wins Presidency and 9 out of 10 Congressional Races in Priciest Election Ever," *Open Secrets*, http://www.opensecrets.org/news/ 2008/11/money-wins-white-house-and.html.

20 Larry Makinson and Joshua Goldstein, *Open Secrets: The Cash Constituents of Congress*, 2nd ed. (Washington, D.C.: CQ Press, 1994), 23.

21 Amy Dockser, "Nice PAC You've Got There … A Pity If Anything Should Happen to It," *Washington Monthly*, January 1984, 21.

22 Edward Walsh, "Wanted: Candidates for Congress," *Washington Post National Weekly Edition*, November 25, 1985, 9.

23 Christian R. Gross, *Congress in Black and White: Race and Representation in Washington and at Home* (New York: Cambridge University Press, 2011).

24 Quoted in Kenneth Shepsle, "The Failures of Congressional Budgeting," *Social Science and Modern Society* 20 (1983), 4–10. See also Howard Kurtz, "Pork Barrel Politics," *Washington Post*, January 25, 1982.

25 The official count of 541 members includes the nonvoting delegates from U.S. territories and the District of Columbia.

26 Congressional Quarterly, *The Origins and Development of Congress* (Washington, D.C.: CQ Press, 1976).

27 Historian David S. Reynolds, quoting a news-paper reporter of the time in Sheryl Gay Stolberg, "What Happened to Compromise," *New York Times*, May 29, 2005, sec. 4, 4.

28 Neil McNeil, *Forge of Democracy* (New York: McKay, 1963), 306–309.

29 Willie Brown, longtime speaker of the California state house, quoted in Edward Epstein, "Her Key to the House," *CQ Weekly*, October 29, 2007, 3161.

30 Epstein, "Her Key to the House," quoting Rep. Alan Boyd (D-Fla.), 3159.

31 Karen Tumulty, "#4 Nancy Pelosi," *Time*, December 28, 2009, 112.

32 Edward Epstein, "Struggle in the Best of Scenarios," *CQ Weekly*, January 4, 2010, 12. Ronald Peters, quoted in Edward Epstein, "A Place in the House Pantheon?" *CQ Weekly*, May 10, 2010, 1128.

33 Ibid.

34 Quoted by Carl Hulse, "Breakdown in Relations in the Senate Hobbles Its Ability to Get Things Done," *New York Times*, July 20, 2007.

35 Historian Robert Dallek, quoted in John M. Broder, "Let Them Persuade You," *New York Times*, November 19, 2006, WK2.

36 Kathleen Hunter, "Safe Seat Is No Job Perk for Today's Senate Leaders," *CQ Weekly*, May 5, 2008, 1157–1158.

37 For a review of all congressional committees and subcommittees in the 110th Congress, see the special report "CQ Guide to the Committees," *CQ Weekly*, April 16, 2007, 1084–1117.

38 Davidson and Oleszek, *Congress and Its Members*, 9th ed., 198.

39 See Roger Davidson, "Subcommittee Government," in Mann and Ornstein, *The New Congress*, 110–111. Some of this occurs because members of Congress tend to be wealthy, and the wealthy make investments in corporations. It also occurs because members' financial interests are often similar to the interests in their districts (for example, representatives from farm districts are likely to be involved in farming or agribusiness).

40 Robert O'Harrow Jr. and Dan Keating, "Lawmakers' Committee Assignments and Industry Investments Overlap," *Washington Post*, June 14, 2010, http://www.washingtonpost.com/wp-dyn/content/article/2010/06/13/AR2010061304881_2.html?sid=ST2010061304930.

41 Ronald Utt, "Federal Farm Subsidy Programs," June 7, 2007, http://www.heritage.org/Research/Reports/2007/06/Federal-Farm-Subsidy-Programs-How-to-Discourage-Congressional-Conflicts-of-Interest.

42 "Guides through the Swamp: A Big Shake-up for America's Tax-Preparation Industry," *The Economist*, March 24, 2012, http://www.economist.com/node/21551052.

43 For a review of how the task force has been used, see Walter J. Oleszek, "The Use of Task Forces in the House," Congressional Research Service, Report 96-8, 3-GOV, 1996, www.house.gov/rules/96-843.htm.

44 Ida A. Brudnick, "The Congressional Research Service and the American Legislative Process," Congressional Research Service, Report RL33471, March 19, 2008, 2.

45 *Budget of the United States, Fiscal 2011* (Washington, D.C.: Government Printing Office, 2010), 19–21.

46 www.willrogerstoday.com/will_rogers_quotes/quotes.cfm?w_ID=4.

47 Gail Collins, "The Age of Nancy," *New York Times*, June 26, 2010, A19.

48 Sarah A. Binder, "The History of the Filibuster," testimony before the U.S. Senate Committee on Rules and Administration, April 22, 2010, www.brookings.edu/testimony/2010/0422_filibuster_binder.aspx?p=1.

49 Ibid.

50 Joseph J. Schatz, "Looking for Room to Maneuver," *CQ Weekly*, April 19, 2010, 954.

51 Kathleen Hennessey, "Little Work Done in D.C.: 112th Congress One of the Least Productive," *Wichita Eagle*, July 5, 2011, http://www.kansas.com/2011/07/05/1921073/congress-among-least-productive.html.

52 Quoted in Carl Hulse, "In New Histories on Two Powerbrokers, Hints of the Future," *New York Times*, July 19, 2009, 22.

53 Thomas E. Mann, "The Negative Impact of the Use of Filibusters and Holds," testimony before the Senate Committee on Rules and Administration, June 23, 2010, www.brookings.edu/testimony/2010/0623_filibuster_mann.aspx?p=1.

54 Jim Abrams, "No Holds Barred as Senators Block Confirmation Votes," *Champaign-Urbana News-Gazette*, May 9, 2010, A5.

55 George Packer, "The Empty Chamber," *New Yorker*, August 8, 2010, 47.

56 Gail Collins, "No Holds Barred," *New York Times*, February 6, 2010, A19.

57 Sen. Sheldon Whitehouse (D-R.I.), quoted in Abrams, "No Holds Barred."

58 Ibid., 49.

59 Rep. George Miller, quoted in Schatz, "Looking for Room to Maneuver," 954.

60 Bert A. Rockman, Eric N. Waltenburg, and Colin Campbell, "Presidential Style and the Obama Presidency," in Bert A. Rockman, Andrew Rudalevige, and Colin Campbell, eds., *The Obama Presidency: Appraisals and Prospects* (Washington, D.C.: CQ, 2012), 348.

61 Paul C. Light, "Filibusters Are Only Half the Problem," *New York Times*, June 3, 2005.

62 David J. Vogler, *The Third House: Conference Committees in the United States Congress* (Evanston, Ill.: Northwestern University Press, 1971); see also Lawrence D. Longley and Walter J. Oleszek, *Bicameral Politics* (New Haven, Conn.: Yale University Press, 1989).

63 Edward Epstein, "Dusting Off Deliberation," *CQ Weekly*, June 14, 2010, 1441.

64 Morris Ogul, "Congressional Oversight: Structures and Incentives," in *Congress Reconsidered*, eds. Lawrence C. Dodd and Bruce I. Oppenheimer, 2d ed. (Washington, DC: *Congressional Quarterly Press*, 1981); see also Loch Johnson, "The U.S. Congress and the CIA: Monitoring the Dark Side of Government," *Legislative Studies Quarterly* 5 (1980), 477–501.

65 Joseph Califano, "Imperial Congress," *New York Times Magazine*, January 23, 1994, 41.

66 Lucy Madison, "Former GSA Chief Apologizes for 'Extravagant' Las Vegas Conference at House Hearing," *CBS News*, April 16, 2012, http://www.cbsnews.com/8301-503544_162-57414787-503544/former-gsa-chief-apologizes-for-extravagant-las-vegas-conference-at-house-hearing/.

67 Richard E Cohen, Kirk Victor, and David Baumann, "The State of Congress," *National Journal*, January 10, 2004, 96.

68 In 2010, earmarks were estimated to cost $16 billion; since 2001, the direct cost of the Iraq and Afghanistan wars is estimated at over $1.3 trillion, or more than $118 billion each year. Full estimates of the cost of war are very difficult to make because part of the cost includes providing for veterans' medical and other needs for decades after and the costs of economic disruption.

69 Kerry Young, "The Price of a Sluggish Purse," *CQ Weekly*, May 24, 2010, 1262–1268.

70 Herbert Asher, "Learning of Legislative Norms," *American Political Science Review* 67 (1973), 499–513. Michael Berkman points out that freshmen who have had state legislative experience adapt to the job faster than other members. See "Former State Legislators in the U.S. House of Representatives: Institutional and Policy Mastery," *Legislative Studies Quarterly* 18 (1993), 77–104.

71 Peter Orzag, "To Increase U.S. Productivity, Elect a New Congress," *Lincoln Journal Star*, March 16, 2012, B5.

72 Richard Rubin, "Party Unity: An Ever Thicker Dividing Line," *CQ Weekly*, January 11, 2010, 122.

73 Thomas Mann of the Brookings Institution, quoted in Cohen, Victor, and Baumann, "The State of Congress," 85.

74 Rep. Jim DeMint (R-S.C.), quoted in Davidson and Oleszek, *Congress and Its Members*, 9th ed., 264.

75 Gordon S. Wood, *Empire of Liberty: A History of the Early Republic, 1789–1815* (New York: Oxford University Press, 2009), 329–330.

76 *Minot* (N.D.) *Daily News*, June 17, 1976, quoted in Randall Ripley, *Congress: Process and Policy*, 3rd ed. (New York: Norton, 1983).

77 Roger H. Davidson, Walter H. Oleszek, and Frances E. Lee, *Congress and Its Members*, 11th ed. (Washington, D.C.: CQ Press, 2008), 299.

78 Peter Baker, "100 Ways to Become a Senator," *New York Times*, January 4, 2009, WK1.

79 A complete listing of House and Senate caucuses can be found in the *Congressional Directory*, which is issued twice each year.

80 Congressional Black Caucus, Press Release, n.d., http://thecongressionalblackcaucus.com/2012/03/29/chairman-cleaver-opposes-republican-budget/.

81 Baker, "100 Ways to Become a Senator," WK1.

82 Samuel Kernell, *Going Public* (Washington, D.C.: CQ Press, 1986).

83 Edward Epstein, "Weaving a Modern GOP Web," *CQ Weekly*, May 31, 2010, 1323; Faye Fiore, "Lawmakers Tweet Up a Storm," *Los Angeles Times*, February 22, 2010, 1.

84 "C-Span Milestones," www.c-span.org,about/company/index.asp?code=MILESTONES.

85 George Packer, "The Empty Chamber: Just How Broken Is the Senate?" *New Yorker*, August 9, 2010, 42, http://www.newyorker.com/reporting/2010/08/09/100809fa_fact_packer.

86 Carl Hulse, "3 Right-Hand Men Take a Turn at Center Stage," *New York Times*, November 13, 2009.

87 Molly Hooper and Alan K. Ota, "House Votes for Outside Ethics Review," *CQ Weekly*, March 17, 2008, 726.

88 A list of members under investigation and of members who hire family members, have close relatives who lobby Congress, or have used their positions to financially benefit members of their families can be found at the website of Citizens for Responsibility and Ethics in Washington, www.citizensforethics.org.

89 Michael Wines, "Washington Really Is in Touch. We're the Problem," *New York Times*, October 16, 1994, sec. 4, 2.

90 Davidson, Oleszek, and Lee, *Congress and Its Members*, 11th ed., 150.

91 Felicia Sonmez, "Gallup Poll Shows Anti-Incumbent Sentiment at All-Time High,"

December 9, 2011, http://www.washingtonpost .com/blogs/2chambers/post/gallup-poll-shows-anti-incumbent-sentiment-at-all-time-high/2011/ 12/09/gIQAGzb9hO_blog.html?wpisrc=nl_ pmpolitics.

[92] Thomas E. Mann and Norman J. Ornstein, *It's Even Worse Than It Looks: How the American Constitutional System Collided with the New Politics of Extremism* (New York: Basic Books, 2012).

Chapter 10

[1] Doris Kearns Goodwin, *Lyndon Johnson and the American Dream* (New York: Harper and Row, 1976), 283.

[2] Lyndon Johnson quoted by Bob Herbert, *New York Times*, March 3, 2009.

[3] Presidential historian Alan Brinkley in "The Making of a War President," *New York Times Book Review*, August 20, 2006, 10.

[4] Woodrow Wilson, *Congressional Government: A Study in American Politics* (New Brunswick, N.J.: Transaction, 2002). Originally published in 1885.

[5] Bob Dole, a Republican who ran in 1996, was the exception. David Leonhardt, "Who's in the Corner Office?" *New York Times*, November 27, 2005, BU1.

[6] Richard Norton Smith, "The Rich, the Poor, and the Oval Office," *Time*, February 20, 2012.

[7] Georgia Duerst-Lahti, "Presidential Elections, Gender Space and the Case of 2008," in *Gender and Elections, Shaping the Future of American Politics*, eds. Susan J. Carroll and Richard L. Fox (New York: Cambridge University Press, 2010).

[8] As quoted in Regina G. Lawrence and Melody Rose, *Hillary Clinton's Race for the White House: Gender Politics and the Media on the Campaign Trail* (Boulder, Colo.: Lynne Rienner Publishers, 2010), 139. Lawrence and Rose also provide a comprehensive analysis of public opinion and media responses to major themes throughout the Clinton campaign.

[9] Quoted in David von Drehle, "Does Experience Matter in a President?" *Time*, March 10, 2008, 30.

[10] James Garfield was shot in July 1881. He did not die until mid-September, and during this period he was unable to fulfill any of his duties. In 1919, Woodrow Wilson had a nervous collapse in the summer and a stroke in the fall and was partially incapacitated for seven months. No one was sure about his condition, however, because his wife restricted access to him.

[11] Information on all three impeachment proceedings can be found at www.historyplace.com.

[12] Francis Wilkinson, "Song of Myself," *New York Times*, January 31, 2006.

[13] For an engaging analysis of this speech in the context of space policy and presidential speech-making, see Mary E. Stuckey, *Slipping the Surly Bonds: Reagan's Challenger Address* (College Station: Texas A&M University Press, 2006).

[14] Alexander Hamilton, *Federalist Paper* 69.

[15] Richard Wolf, "Obama Uses Executive Powers to Get Past Congress," *USA Today*, October 27, 2011.

[16] Thomas E. Mann, "The Negative Impact of the Use of Filibusters and Holds," testimony before the Senate Committee on Rules and Administration, June 23, 2010, www.brookings.edu/testi-mony/2010/0623_filibuster_mann.aspx?p=1.

[17] For discussion of the president's removal powers in light of a 1988 Supreme Court decision regarding independent counsels, see John A. Rohr, "Public Administration, Executive Power, and Constitutional Confusion," and Rosemary O'Leary, "Response to John Rohr," *Public Administrative Review* 49 (1989), 108–115.

[18] Mark J. Rozell, "Executive Privilege Revived? Secrecy and Conflict during the Bush Presidency," *Duke Law Journal* 52 (2002), 403–421.

[19] Goodwin, *Lyndon Johnson and the American Dream*, 226.

[20] Mark Arsenault, "Nomination Delaying Tactic Irks Senators," *Washington Post*, June 22, 2010.

[21] Anne Joseph O'Connell, *Waiting for Leadership: President Obama's Record in Staffing Key Agency Positions and How to Improve the Appointments Process*. (Washington, D.C.: Center for American Progress, 2010), 5.

[22] Carl M. Cannon, "Veto This!" *National Journal*, October 13, 2007, 32.

[23] A complete list of vetoes cast since 1789 can be found at www.infoplease.com/ipa/A0801767.html.

[24] Andrew Sullivan, "We Don't Need a New King George," *Time*, January 23, 2006, 74.

[25] Charlie Savage, "Obama Looks to Limit Impact of Tactic Bush Used to Sidestep New Laws," *New York Times*, March 10, 2009.

[26] Charlie Savage, "Bush Challenges Hundreds of Laws: President Cites Powers of His Office," *Boston Globe*, April 30, 2006, A1.

[27] Eli Lake, "Obama Embraces Signing Statements after Knocking Bush for Using Them," *The Daily Beast*, January 4, 2012.

[28] Charlie Savage, "Obama's Embrace of a Bush Tactic Riles Congress," *New York Times*, August 9, 2009; U.S. Department of Justice, Office of Legal Counsel, "The Legal Significance of Presidential Signing Statements, Memorandum for Bernard N. Nussbaum, Counsel to the President," November 3, 1993.

[29] Louis Fisher, *Presidential War Power*, 2nd ed. (Lawrence: University Press of Kansas, 2004), 197–199. Fisher provides a thoughtful yet concise treatment of the legislative-executive contests, which subsequently also involved the judicial branch. Like Congress, the judiciary also failed to check the presidential exercise of war powers in this war.

[30] "What Is a Treaty?" Library of Congress, September 29, 2011, www.loc.gov/rr/main/gov-docsguide/TreatyDefinition.html.

[31] Rather than expressly authorizing the president to abrogate a treaty by himself, the majority ruled that the dispute was a "political question," which avoided a ruling on the merits of Carter's claim. Thus the Court allowed, but didn't authorize, the president to take this action. *Goldwater v. Carter*, 444 U.S. 996 (1979).

[32] President George W. Bush also refused to recognize the treaty creating the International Criminal Court, which President Clinton had signed but never submitted for Senate approval. Because Clinton had signed it, the United States was a participant in discussions of rules for the court even while not being an official party to the treaty. Bush's "unsigning" pulled the United States from these talks.

[33] See the discussion in Alexander Hamilton's *Federalist Paper* 69.

[34] Quoted in "Notes and Comment," *New Yorker*, June 1, 1987, 23.

[35] *Youngstown Sheet and Tube Co.* v. *Sawyer*, 343 U.S. 579 (1952).

[36] 2002 Congressional Resolution On The Use of Force in Iraq, Section 3.

[37] Ron Suskind, *The One Percent Doctrine: Deep inside America's Pursuit of Its Enemies since 9/11* (New York: Simon & Schuster, 2006), 65.

[38] The two principal lawyers were longtime Cheney aide David Addington, who became Cheney's chief of staff when Lewis Libby was indicted on obstruction of justice charges in 2006, and Deputy Assistant Attorney General John Yoo, later a law professor at the University of California–Berkeley. Yoo elaborated on his ideas in *The Powers of War and Peace: The Constitution and Foreign Affairs after 9/11* (Chicago: University of Chicago Press, 2005). For others involved, see Keith Perine, "Imbalance of Power," *Congressional Quarterly Weekly Report*, February 27, 2006, 545; and Charlie Savage, *Takeover: The Return of the Imperial Presidency and the Subversion of American Democracy* (New York: Little, Brown & Co., 2007). Savage's book won the Pulitzer Prize.

[39] Quoted in George Lardner Jr., "A High Price for Freedom," *New York Times*, March 26, 2007.

[40] Scott Shane and Neil A. Lewis, "Bush Commutes Libby Sentence, Saying 30 Months 'Is Excessive,'" *New York Times*, July 3, 2007.

[41] http://www.washingtonpost.com/blogs/the-fix/ post/obama-the-most-polarizing-president-ever/2012/01/29/gIQAmmkBbQ_blog .html?wpisrc=nl_pol_full.

[42] *Congressional Quarterly Weekly Report*, November 8, 2010, 2524; Roger H. Davidson, Walter J. Oleszek, and Frances E. Lee, *Congress and Its Members*, 11th ed. (Washington, D.C.: CQ Press, 2007), 107.

[43] Martha Joynt Kumar, "The White House World: Start Up, Organization, and the Pressures of Work Life," Report Number 6, White House Interview Project, The White House 2001 Project, December 2000.

[44] Office of Management and Budget, Table 4.1, Outlays by Agency, 1962–2017. http://www .whitehouse.gov/omb/budget/Historicals.

45 John Rogers, as quoted in Peri Arnold, Charles E. Walcott, and Bradley H. Patterson Jr., "The White House Office of Management and Administration," The White House 2001 Project, December 2000.

46 Karen M. Hult and Charles E. Walcott, *Empowering the White House: Governance under Nixon, Ford, and Carter* (Lawrence: University Press of Kansas, 2004); Lyn Ragsdale and John J. Theis III, "The Institutionalization of the American Presidency, 1924–1992," *American Journal of Political Science* 41, no. 4 (October 1997), 1280–1318.

47 Charles E. Walcott, Stephen J. Wayne, and Shirley Anne Warshaw, "The Chief of Staff," The White House 2001 Project, December 2000, 14.

48 MaryAnne Borrelli, *The Politics of the President's Wife* (College Station: Texas A&M University Press, 2011).

49 Michael Nelson, ed., *The Presidency A to Z* (Washington, D.C.: CQ Press, 1998), 487–488.

50 Karine Premont, "The Contemporary American Vice Presidency: A School for the Presidency?" *World Political Science Review* 5, no. 1 (2009), 7–8, www.bepress.com/wpsr/vol5/iss1/art13.

51 For a review of the backgrounds of men who have served in the vice presidency and the roles they have played, see L. Edward Purcell, *Vice Presidents* (New York: Facts on File, 2001); Michael Nelson, *A Heartbeat Away* (New York: Priority, 1988); Paul C. Light, *Vice-Presidential Power: Advice and Influence in the White House* (Baltimore: Johns Hopkins University Press, 1984); and George Sirgiovanni, "The 'Van Buren Jinx': Vice Presidents Need Not Beware," *Presidential Studies Quarterly* 18 (1988), 61–76.

52 Jane Mayer, "The Hidden Power," *New Yorker,* July 3, 2006, 50.

53 James Traub, "After Cheney," *New York Times Magazine,* November 29, 2009, 36.

54 "Hell from the Chief: Hot Tempers and Presidential Timber," *New York Times,* November 7, 1999, sec. 4, 7.

55 Quoted in Richard Pious, *The American Presidency* (New York: Basic Books, 1979), 244.

56 Walcott, Wayne, and Warshaw, "The Chief of Staff," 1.

57 Hillary Rodham Clinton, quoted in Carol Gelderman, *All the Presidents' Words: The Bully Pulpit and the Creation of the Virtual Presidency* (New York: Walker, 1997), 160.

58 A good description of Clinton's relationship to his White House staff can be found in Joe Klein, *The Natural: The Misunderstood Presidency of Bill Clinton* (New York: Doubleday, 2002).

59 For more on Bush's management style, see the several articles in the special section, "C.E.O. U.S.A.," *New York Times Magazine,* January 14, 2001, 24–58.

60 Mike Allen, "Living Too Much in the Bubble," *Time,* September 19, 2005, 44.

61 Ron Suskind, *The Price of Loyalty: George W. Bush, the White House, and the Education of Paul O'Neill* (New York: Simon & Schuster, 2004).

62 James P. Pfiffner, "Organizing the Obama White House," in *Obama in Office,* ed. James A. Thurber (Boulder, Colo.: Paradigm Publishers, 2011).

63 Wilson, *Congressional Government.*

64 Harold M. Barger, *The Impossible Presidency* (Glenview, Ill.: Scott, Foresman Publishers, 1984).

65 Jeffrey K. Tulis, *The Rhetorical Presidency* (Princeton, N.J.: Princeton University Press, 1987).

66 Quoted in Garry Wills, *Lincoln at Gettysburg* (New York: Simon & Schuster, 1992), 31.

67 Richard E. Neustadt, *Presidential Power* (New York: Wiley, 1960), 5–6.

68 George C. Edwards III argues that a president's actual ability to effect change is limited. See *The Strategic President: Persuasion and Opportunity in Presidential Leadership* (Princeton, N.J.: Princeton University Press, 2009).

69 Theodore Lowi, *The Personal President: Power Invested, Promise Unfulfilled* (Ithaca, N.Y.: Cornell University Press, 1985), x.

70 Scott McClellan, *What Happened: Inside the Bush White House and Washington's Culture of Deception* (New York: Public Affairs, 2008).

71 Reagan got his start in show business as a radio sportscaster in Des Moines, Iowa, announcing major league baseball games "live." He was not actually at the games: he got the barest details—who was at bat, whether the pitch was a strike or a ball or a hit—from the wireless and made up the rest to create a commentary that engaged listeners.

72 Timothy J. Russert, "For '92, the Networks Have to Do Better," *New York Times,* March 4, 1990, E23.

73 Steven K. Weisman, "The President and the Press," *New York Times Magazine,* October 14, 1984, 71–72; Dick Kirschten, "Communications Reshuffling Intended to Help Reagan Do What He Does Best," *National Journal,* January 28, 1984, 154.

74 Ari Fleischer, quoted in *Congressional Quarterly Today News,* May 19, 2003, www.cq.com.

75 Samuel Kernell, *Going Public: New Strategies of Presidential Leadership* (Washington, D.C.: CQ Press, 1986), 15.

76 George C. Edwards III, *On Deaf Ears: The Limits of the Bully Pulpit* (New Haven, Conn.: Yale University Press, 2003); Mary E. Stuckey, *Defining Americans: The Presidency and National Identity* (Lawrence: University Press of Kansas, 2004); Mary E. Stuckey, *Jimmy Carter, Human Rights, and the National Agenda* (College Station: Texas A&M University Press, 2008).

77 James David Barber, *The Presidential Character,* 2nd ed. (Englewood Cliffs, N.J.: Prentice Hall, 1977), 157.

78 Bruce Miroff, "The Presidency and the Public: Leadership and Spectacle," in *The Presidency and the Political System,* 5th ed., ed. Michael Nelson (Washington, D.C.: CQ Press, 1998), 320.

79 Barger, *The Impossible Presidency.*

80 Klein, *The Natural,* 208.

81 See, for example, the comments of Arthur M. Schlesinger Jr. in Carl M. Cannon, "Judging Clinton," *National Journal,* January 1, 2000, 22; Steven A. Holmes, "Losers in Clinton-Starr Bouts May Be Future U.S. Presidents," *New York Times,* August 23, 1998, 18; and Adam Clymer, "The Presidency Is Still There, Not Quite the Same," *New York Times,* February 14, 1999, sec. 4, 1.

82 Bruce Fein, former associate deputy attorney general in the Reagan administration, quoted in Mayer, "The Hidden Power," 46.

83 Charles O. Jones and Kathryn Dunn, "Shaping the 44th Presidency," Issues in Governance Studies, Paper 9, Brookings Institution, August 2007, 5.

84 Ibid.

Chapter 11

1 http://www.huffingtonpost.com/2011/01/28/dennis-kucinich-olive-pit-lawsuit_n_815687.html.

2 Francis Lam, "How Many Bugs Are Allowed in Your Pasta?" *Salon.com,* January 27, 2011, www.salon.com/2011/01/27/fda_food_defect_action_levels/print.

3 E. J. Levy, "The Maggots in Your Mushrooms," *New York Times,* February 13, 2009, http://www.nytimes.com/2009/02/13/opinion/13levy.html.

4 Bruce Adams, "The Frustrations of Government Service," *Public Administration Review* 44 (1984), 5.

5 James Q. Wilson, *Bureaucracy, What Government Agencies Do and Why They Do It* (New York: Basic Books, 1989).

6 Organisation for Economic Co-ordination and Development, *Policy Brief: Ten Steps to Equity in Education,* January 2008, 2.

7 Anne Marie Kelly, "Has Toyota's Image Recovered from the Brand's Recall Crisis?" *Forbes,* March 5, 2012. Angus MacKenzie and Scott Evans, "The Toyota Recall Crisis," *Motor Trend,* January 2010.

8 George Packer, "The Empty Chamber," *New Yorker,* August 8, 2010, 51.

9 Joyce Appleby, "That's General Washington to You," *New York Times Book Review,* February 14, 1993, 11, a review of Richard Norton Smith, *Patriarch* (Boston: Houghton Mifflin, 1993). See also James Q. Wilson, "The Rise of the Bureaucratic State," *Public Interest* 41 (1975), 77–103.

10 Wilson, "Rise of the Bureaucratic State."

11 Leonard D. White, *Introduction to the Study of Public Administration,* 4th ed. (New York: Macmillan, 1955), 4.

12 Paul C. Light, "Fact Sheet on the Continued Thickening of Government," Brookings Institution, July 23, 2004, http://www.brookings.edu/research/papers/2004/07/23governance-light.

13 Johanna Neuman, "FAA's 'Culture of Coziness' Targeted in Airline Safety Hearing," *Los Angeles Times,* April 4, 2008.

14 Holger Cahill, "American Resources for the Arts," in *Art for the Millions, Essays from the 1930s*

by Artists and Administrators of the WPA Federal Art Project, ed. Francis V. O'Connor (Boston: New York Graphic Society, 1973), 41.

15 Claudia Dreifus, "A Conversation with Sherwood Boehlert: A Science Advocate and 'An Endangered Species,' He Bids Farewell," New York Times, May 9, 2006, F2.

16 The Hatch Act and subsequent revisions can be found at the Office of Personnel Management's website by linking to its Office of Special Counsel (www.opm.gov).

17 John Solomon, Alec MacGillis, and Sarah Cohen, "How Rove Harnessed Government for GOP Gains," Washington Post, August 19, 2007, 1, A6. The Hatch Act violation came in a briefing to the General Services Administration, where it was recommended that GSA contracts be awarded with an eye to helping Republican candidates. The head of the GAO was later forced to resign.

18 Josh Gerstein, "Report: Bush Staff Violated Hatch Act," Politico, January 24, 2011.

19 Charlie Savage, "For White House, Hiring Is Political," New York Times, July 31, 2008, 17.

20 The lengthy report is available at the Department of Justice website. See also Alan Cooperman, "Bush Loyalist Rose Quickly at Justice," Washington Post, March 30, 2007. Eric Lichtblau, "Report Faults Aides in Hiring at Justice Dept.," New York Times, July 29, 2008.

21 Philip Shenon, "F.B.I. Raids Office of Special Counsel," New York Times, May 7, 2008, 18.

22 Fred Alford, quoted in Barbara Ehrenreich, "All Together Now," New York Times, July 15, 2004, A23.

23 Terry More, "Regulators' Performance and Presidential Administrations," American Journal of Political Science 26 (1982), 197–224; Terry More, "Control and Feedback in Economic Regulation," American Political Science Review 79 (1985), 1094–1116.

24 See, for example, "Fiscal Conservatives with a Taste for Pork, The Dirty Dozen," The Daily Beast/ Newsweek, October 30, 2011.

25 Roger H. Davidson, Walter J. Oleszek, and Frances E. Lee, Congress and Its Members, 13th ed. (Washington, D.C.: CQ Press, 2012), 338.

26 More, "Control and Feedback."

27 Harold C. Relyea and Michael W. Kolakowski, "Access to Government Information in the United States," Congressional Research Service, Report 9771 GOV, December 5, 2007, 2–3.

28 Clinton administration policy on compliance with FOIA can be found in Federation of American Scientists, Project on Government Secrecy, "Clinton Administration Documents on Classification Policy," 2003, www.fas.org/sgp/clinton/index.html.

29 "President Declassifies Old Papers," Omaha World-Herald, April 18, 1995, 1.

30 Ellen Nakashima, "Frustration on the Left—and the Right," Washington Post National Weekly Edition, March 11, 2002, 29; Scott Shane, "Increase in the Number of Documents Classified by the Government," New York Times, July 3, 2005, 12.

31 Ibid.

32 Shane, "Increase in the Number of Documents," 12; David Nather, "Classified: A Rise in State Secrets," CQ Weekly, July 18, 2005, 1960.

33 Alan Feuer, "When Media Giants Face Off against Financial Heavyweights," New York Times, February 14, 2010, 27. Noah Feldman, "In Defense of Secrecy," New York Times Magazine, February 15, 2009, 12.

34 Charlie Savage, "Loosening of F.B.I. Rules Stirs Privacy Concerns," New York Times, October 29, 2009.

35 Eric Schmitt, "Is This Any Way to Run a Nation?" New York Times, April 14, 2002, WK4.

Chapter 12

1 Law professor Orrin Kerr, a former clerk to conservative justice Anthony Kennedy, thought there was "a less than 1 percent chance" that the courts would invalidate the mandate. David G. Savage, "States Fighting Healthcare Law Don't Have Precedent on Their Side," Los Angeles Times, March 27, 2010, latimes.com/news/la-na-constitutionality27-2010mar27,0,6530779.story.

2 National Federation of Independent Business v. Sebelius, 183 L.Ed.2d 450 (2012).

3 It had dropped from 80 percent holding a favorable impression of the Court in 1994 to just 52 percent before the health care case. Chris Cillizza, "John Roberts, Umpire," Washington Post, June 28, 2012, washingtonpost.com/blogs/the-fix/post/john-roberts-umpire/2012/06/28/gJQAx....

4 Noah Feldman, "Roberts Chooses Restraint Over History on Obamacare," Bloomberg View, June 28, 2012, bloomberg.com/news/2012-06-28/roberts-chooses-restraint-over-history-on-obamacare.html.

5 Cillizza, "John Roberts, Umpire."

6 Charles M. Blow, "Obama, for the Win!" New York Times, June 30, 2012, A21.

7 John Hibbing and Elizabeth Theiss-Morse, Congress as Public Enemy: Public Attitudes toward American Political Institutions (New York: Cambridge University Press, 1995), chs. 2 and 3.

8 John R. Schmidhauser, Justices and Judges (Boston: Little, Brown, 1979), 11.

9 However, federalism doesn't require this exact arrangement. Most federal countries have one national court over a system of regional courts.

10 In addition, there is the Court of Appeals for the Federal Circuit, which handles customs and patents cases.

11 Occasionally, for important cases, the entire group of judges in one circuit will sit together, "en banc." (In the large Ninth Circuit, eleven judges will sit.)

12 If at least $75,000 is at stake, according to congressional law.

13 Quoted in Henry J. Abraham, "A Bench Happily Filled," Judicature 66 (1983), 284.

14 For elaboration on the Senate's role, see Stephen B. Burbank, "Politics, Privilege, and Power: The Senate's Role in the Appointment of Federal Judges," Judicature 86 (2002), 24.

15 Victor Navasky, Kennedy Justice (New York: Atheneum, 1971), 245–246.

16 Harry P. Stumpf, American Judicial Politics, 2nd ed. (Upper Saddle River, N.J.: Prentice Hall, 1998), 175. After Taft nominated a Catholic to be chief justice, the Speaker of the House cracked, "If Taft were Pope, he'd want to appoint some Protestants to the College of Cardinals." Henry J. Abraham, Justices and Presidents: A Political History of Appointments to the Supreme Court, 2nd ed. (New York: Oxford University Press, 1985), 168.

17 The Nixon administration was the first to recognize that it could accomplish some policy goals by selecting lower court judges on the basis of ideology. Elliot E. Slotnick, "A Historical Perspective on Federal Judicial Selection," Judicature 86 (2002), 13.

18 For an analysis of internal documents that established this process in the Reagan administration, see Dawn Johnsen, "Tipping the Scale," Washington Monthly, July–August 2002, 1–18.

19 Jo Becker and Barton Gellman, "The Veep Steered While Vetting Conservatives for the Court," Washington Post National Weekly Edition, July 16–22, 2007, 9.

20 Ibid.

21 Ginsburg, Kagan, Scalia, and Sotomayor.

22 The Jews are Breyer, Ginsburg, and Kagan.

23 347 U.S. 483 (1954).

24 Marilyn Nejelski, Women in the Judiciary: A Status Report (Washington, D.C.: National Women's Political Caucus, 1984).

25 Sheldon Goldman, "Reagan's Second-Term Judicial Appointments," Judicature 70 (1987), 324–339.

26 Sheldon Goldman, Elliott E. Slotnick, Gerard Gryski, Gary Zuk, and Sara Schiavoni, "W. Bush Remaking the Judiciary: Like Father like Son?" Judicature 86 (2003), 304, 308. For further examination, see Rorie L. Spill and Kathleen A. Bratton, "Clinton and Diversification of the Federal Judiciary," Judicature, March–April 2001, 256.

27 John Schwartz, "For Obama, a Record on Diversity but Delays on Judicial Confirmations," New York Times, August 7, 2011, Y17.

28 J. Paul Oetken (S.D., N.Y.).

29 Especially congressional power under the commerce clause.

30 Lauren Collins, "Number Nine," New Yorker, January 11, 2010, 52.

31 Tom Korologos, "Roberts Rx: Speak Up, but Shut Up," New York Times, September 4, 2005, www.nytimes.com/2005/09/04/weekinreview/04stol.html.

32 Scott v. Sandford, 60 U.S. 393 (1857).

33 Korematsu v. U.S., 323 U.S. 214 (1944).

34 "Judging Samuel Alito," New York Times, January 8, 2006, WK13.

35 Janet Malcolm, "The Art of Testifying," New Yorker, March 13, 2006, 74.

[36] See, for example, Erwin Chemerinsky, "Conservative Justice," *Los Angeles Times,* June 29, 2007, www.latimes.com/news/opinion/la-oe -chemerinsky29jun29,0,504056,print.story?col.

[37] Arlen Specter (R-Pa.), quoted in Jeffrey Toobin, "Comment: Unanswered Questions," *New Yorker,* January 23 and 30, 2006, 30.

[38] David Greenberg, "Actually, It Is Political," *Washington Post National Weekly Edition,* July 26–August 1, 2004, 23.

[39] One of President Reagan's nominees, Douglas Ginsburg, withdrew his nomination due to widespread opposition in the Senate, so officially his nomination was not denied.

[40] Nixon's nomination of G. Harold Carswell was a notable exception. At his confirmation hearing, a parade of legal scholars called him undistinguished. Even his supporters acknowledged that he was mediocre. Nixon's floor manager for the nomination, Sen. Roman Hruska (R-Neb.), blurted out in exasperation, "Even if he is mediocre, there are a lot of mediocre judges and people and lawyers. They are entitled to a little representation, aren't they, and a little chance? We can't have all Brandeises, Cardozos, and Frankfurters, and stuff like that there." Abraham, *Justices and Presidents,* 6–7.

[41] For an examination of the relationship between ethical lapses and ideological reasons, see Charles M. Cameron, Albert D. Cover, and Jeffrey A. Segal, "Senate Voting on Supreme Court Nominees: A Neoinstitutional Model," *American Political Science Review* 84 (1990), 525–534.

[42] For some time, the Senate confirmed fewer nominees to the lower courts in the fourth year of a president's term when the Senate's majority was from the other party. The senators hoped their candidate would capture the White House in the next election. They delayed confirmation so there would be numerous vacancies for their president and, through senatorial courtesy, for themselves to fill as well. Jeffrey A. Segal and Harold Spaeth, "If a Supreme Court Vacancy Occurs, Will the Senate Confirm a Reagan Nominee?" *Judicature* 69 (1986), 188–189.

[43] Quoted in Savage, "Clinton Losing Fight for Black Judge," *Los Angeles Times,* July 7, 2000, A1.

[44] Nancy Scherer, "The Judicial Confirmation Process: Mobilizing Elites, Mobilizing Masses." *Judicature* 86 (March-April 2003): 240–250.

[45] Instead, he became a justice on the California Supreme Court.

[46] Nancy Maveety, "A Transformative Politics of Judicial Selection?" in *Transforming America: Barack Obama in the White House,* ed. Steven E. Schier (Lanham, Md.: Rowman and Littlefield, 2011), 178.

[47] Charlie Savage, "Conservatives Map Strategies on Court Fight," *New York Times,* May 17, 2009, Y1.

[48] Collins, "Number Nine," 52.

[49] By, among others, Rush Limbaugh, Newt Gingrich, and Rep. Tom Tancredo (R-Colo.), who accused her of being in the "Latino KKK."

[50] Some other schools and groups of faculty filed lawsuits against the federal policy, seeking a ruling that would allow the schools to bar military recruiters from campus. Kagan followed the federal law until a federal court of appeals invalidated it; then she followed that court's ruling. When the Supreme Court reversed the court of appeals, Kagan followed the Supreme Court's ruling. For further explanation, see Amy Goldstein, "Foes May Target Kagan's Stance on Military Recruitment at Harvard," April 18, 2010, www.washingtonpost.com/wp-dyn/ content/article/2010/04/17/AR2010041701296. html?sid=ST20100417.

[51] James Oliphant, "GOP Looks beyond Court Pick," *Los Angeles Times,* April 13, 2010, latimes. com/news/nationworld/nation/la-na-gop- courts13-2010apr13,0,3941526.story. Savage, "Conservatives Map Strategies."

[52] Schmidhauser, *Justice and Judges,* 55–57.

[53] David Leonhardt, "Who Has a Corner Office?" *New York Times,* November 27, 2005, BU4.

[54] All except Kennedy, Sotomayor, and possibly Alito and Kagan.

[55] Bernie Becker, "Justices List Their Assets; Wide Range of Wealth," *New York Times,* June 7, 2008, query.nytimes.com/gst/fullpage.html?res=9B05E5 DF1F3CF934A35755COA96E9C8B63.

[56] Goldman et al., "W. Bush Remaking the Judiciary," 304, 308.

[57] As an alternative, Congress in 1980 established other procedures to discipline lower court judges. Councils made up of district and appellate court judges can ask their fellow judges to resign or can prevent them from hearing cases, but they cannot actually remove them. The procedures have been used infrequently, although their existence has prompted some judges to resign before being disciplined.

[58] Merle Miller, *Plain Speaking* (New York: Berkeley Putnam, 1974), 121.

[59] Harold W. Chase, *Federal Judges* (Minneapolis: University of Minnesota Press, 1972), 189.

[60] John Gruhl, "The Impact of Term Limits for Supreme Court Justices," *Judicature* 81 (1997), 66–72.

[61] The fourth, Rehnquist, disqualified himself because he had worked on the administration's policy toward executive privilege.

[62] *Jones v. Clinton,* 137 L.Ed.2d 945, 117 S. Ct. 1636 (1997).

[63] Martin Shapiro, "The Supreme Court: From Warren to Burger," in *The New American Political System,* ed. Anthony King (Washington, D.C.: American Enterprise Institute, 1978), 180–181.

[64] Robert Scigliano, *The Supreme Court and the Presidency* (New York: Free Press, 1971), 147–148.

[65] Quoted in Abraham, *Justices and Presidents,* 62.

[66] Earl Warren, *The Memoirs of Earl Warren* (Garden City, N.Y.: Doubleday, 1977), 5.

[67] Quoted in Abraham, *Justices and Presidents,* 63.

[68] Linda Greenhouse, "In the Confirmation Dance, the Past but Rarely the Prologue," *New York Times,* July 24, 2005, WK5.

[69] For elaboration, see Lee Epstein and Jeffrey A. Segal, *Advice and Consent* (New York: Oxford University Press, 2005), ch. 5. Choosing judges with extensive records on lower courts especially limits surprises. Adam Liptak, "Why Newer Appointees Offer Fewer Surprises from Bench," *New York Times,* April 18, 2010, Y1.

[70] "How Much Do Lawyers Charge?" *Parade,* March 23, 1997, 14.

[71] Lois G. Forer, *Money and Justice* (New York: Norton, 1984), 9, 15, 102.

[72] Jonathan Casper, "Lawyers before the Supreme Court: Civil Liberties and Civil Rights, 1957–1966," *Stanford Law Review,* February 1970, 509.

[73] Peter Slevin, "Courting Christianity," *Washington Post National Weekly Edition,* July 17–23, 2006, 29.

[74] Karen O'Connor and Lee Epstein, "The Rise of Conservative Interest Group Litigation," *Journal of Politics* 45 (1983), 481. See also Richard C. Cortner, *The Supreme Court and the Second Bill of Rights* (Madison: University of Wisconsin Press, 1981), 282.

[75] Rick Perlstein, "Christian Empire," *New York Times Book Review,* January 7, 2007, 15.

[76] Jeffrey Rosen, "Supreme Court Inc.," *New York Times Magazine,* March 16, 2008, 44. The Court also takes about this many to decide summarily— without oral arguments and full written opinions. Dahlia Lithwick, "Realignment?" *Washington Post National Weekly Edition,* June 23–July 6, 2008, 25.

[77] The dentist agreed to fill the cavity only in a hospital, where the procedure would be far more expensive. *Bragdon* v. *Abbott,* 141 L.Ed.2d 540 (1998).

[78] *Toyota Motor Manufacturing* v. *Williams,* 151 L.Ed.2d 615 (2001).

[79] *U.S.* v. *Jones,* 181 L.Ed.2d 911 (2012).

[80] Henry J. Abraham, *The Judicial Process,* 3rd ed. (New York: Oxford University Press, 1975), 324.

[81] *United States* v. *Butler,* 297 U.S. 1, at 94.

[82] Walter F. Murphy and C. Herman Pritchett, *Courts, Judges, and Politics,* 3rd ed. (New York: Random House, 1979), 586.

[83] Anthony Peccarelli, "The Meaning of Justice?" *DCBA Brief Online* (Journal of the DuPage County Bar Association), no date, http://www. dcba.org/brief/marissue/2000/art10300.htm.

[84] *Furman* v. *Georgia,* 408 U.S. 238 (1972). Blackmun did vote against the death penalty later in his career.

[85] Quoted in Alexander Bickel, *The Morality of Consent* (New Haven, Conn.: Yale University Press, 1975), 120.

[86] "Judicial Authority Moves Growing Issue," *Lincoln Journal,* April 24, 1977.

[87] Jeffrey A. Segal and Albert D. Cover, "Ideological Values and the Votes of U.S. Supreme Court Justices," *American Political Science Review* 83 (1989), 557–564. For different findings for state supreme court justices, see John M. Scheb II, Terry Bowen, and Gary Anderson, "Ideology, Role Orientations, and Behavior in the

State Courts of Last Resort," *American Politics Quarterly* 19 (1991), 324–335.

88 Harold Spaeth and Stuart Teger, "Activism and Restraint: A Cloak for the Justices' Policy Preferences," in *Supreme Court Activism and Restraint,* eds. Stephen P. Halpern and Clark M. Lamb (Lexington, Mass.: Lexington Books, 1982), 277.

89 *Burnet* v. *Coronado Oil and Gas,* 285 U.S. 293 (1932), at 406.

90 *Engel* v. *Vitale,* 370 U.S. 421 (1962).

91 *Abington School District* v. *Schempp,* 374 U.S. 203 (1963).

92 *Stone* v. *Graham,* 449 U.S. 39 (1980).

93 *Lee* v. *Weisman,* 120 L.Ed.2d 467 (1992).

94 *Santa Fe Independent School District* v. *Doe,* 147 L.Ed.2d 295 (2000).

95 *Roe* v. *Wade,* 410 U.S. 113 (1973).

96 *Planned Parenthood of Southeastern Pennsylvania* v. *Casey,* 120 L.Ed.2d 674 (1992).

97 *United States* v. *Butler,* 297 U.S. 1 (1936), at 79.

98 Some might say that judges, rather than make law, mediate among various ideas that rise to the surface, killing off some and allowing others to survive. Robert Cover, "Nomos and Narrative," *Harvard Law Review* 97 (1983), 4.

99 Quoted in Murphy and Pritchett, *Courts, Judges, and Politics,* 25.

100 Eric Lichtblau, "Groups Blanket Supreme Court on Health Care," *New York Times,* March 24, 2012, Y1.

101 Adam Liptak, "Reviewing the Health Care Arguments, Laugh Count Included," *New York Times,* June 26, 2012, A14.

102 Quoted in David J. Garrow, "The Rehnquist Reins," *New York Times Magazine,* October 6, 1996, 70.

103 Jeffrey Toobin, *The Nine: Inside the Secret World of the Supreme Court* (New York: Doubleday, 2007), 129, 195.

104 Adam Liptak, "Are Oral Arguments Worth Arguing About?" *New York Times,* May 6, 2012, SR5.

105 Collins, "Number Nine," 44.

106 Ibid., 263.

107 Quoted in Robert Wernick, "Chief Justice Marshall Takes the Law in Hand," *Smithsonian,* November 1998, 162.

108 Joan Biskupic, "Here Comes the Judge? Maybe Not," *Washington Post National Weekly Edition,* February 14, 2000, 30.

109 Jeffrey A. Segal and Harold J. Spaeth, *The Supreme Court and the Attitudinal Model* (New York: Cambridge University Press, 1993), 262–264.

110 Justice Breyer, quoted by Jeffrey Toobin, "Breyer's Big Idea," *New Yorker,* October 31, 2005, 43.

111 *Morning Edition,* National Public Radio, March 5, 2004.

112 Michael S. Serrill, "The Power of William Brennan," *Time,* July 22, 1985, 62.

113 Dahlia Lithwick, "Getting to Five," *New York Times Book Review,* October 10, 2010, 20.

114 Ibid.

115 David J. Garrow, "One Angry Man," *New York Times Magazine,* October 6, 1996, 68–69.

116 *Webster* v. *Reproductive Health Services,* 492 U.S. 490 (1989).

117 *United States* v. *Virginia,* 135 L.Ed.2d 735, 787–789 (1996).

118 Charles Evans Hughes, *The Supreme Court of the United States* (New York: Columbia University Press, 1928), 68.

119 Interview with Justice Ruth Bader Ginsburg, *Morning Edition,* National Public Radio, May 2, 2002. Ginsburg said that foreign jurists admit they disagree with each other but do not make it public.

120 Craig R. Ducat, *2005 Supplement for Constitutional Interpretation,* 8th ed. (Belmont, Calif.: Wadsworth, 2006), 3.

121 Linda Greenhouse, "The High Court and the Triumph of Discord," *New York Times,* July 15, 2001, sec. 4, 1. Perhaps this calls into question Rehnquist's reputation as an effective leader.

122 *Federalist Paper* 78.

123 Henry J. Abraham, *Justices and Presidents* (New York: Oxford University Press, 1974), 74.

124 Abraham, *Judicial Process,* 309.

125 Drew Pearson and Robert S. Allen, *The Nine Old Men* (New York: Doubleday/Doren, 1937), 7; Barbara A. Perry, *The Priestly Tribe: The Supreme Court's Image in the American Mind* (Westport, Conn.: Praeger, 1999), 8–9.

126 There's evidence that many Founders expected the federal courts to use judicial review eventually. Some state courts already used judicial review, and in *Federalist Paper* 78 Hamilton said that the federal courts would have authority to void laws contrary to the Constitution.

127 5 U.S. 137 (1803). Technically, *Marbury* was not the first use of judicial review, but it was the first clear articulation of judicial review by the Court.

128 Jefferson was also angry at the nature of the appointees. One had led troops loyal to England during the Revolutionary War. Eric Black, *Our Constitution: The Myth That Binds Us* (Boulder, Colo.: Westview Press, 1988), 66.

129 Debate arose over whether the four should be considered appointed. Their commissions had been signed by the president, and the seal of the United States had been affixed by Marshall, as secretary of state. Yet it was customary to require commissions to be delivered, perhaps because of less reliable record keeping by government or less reliable communications at the time.

130 Marbury had petitioned the Court for a writ of *mandamus* under the authority of a provision of the Judiciary Act of 1789 that permitted the Court to issue such a writ. Marshall maintained that this provision broadened the Court's original jurisdiction and thus violated the Constitution. (The Constitution allows the Court to hear cases that have not been heard by any other court before—if they involve a state or a foreign ambassador.

Marbury's involved neither.) Yet it was quite clear that the provision did not broaden the Court's original jurisdiction—so clear, in fact, that Marshall did not even quote the language he was declaring unconstitutional. Furthermore, even if the provision did broaden the Court's original jurisdiction, it is not certain that the provision would violate the Constitution. (The Constitution does not say that the Court shall have original jurisdiction only in cases involving a state or a foreign ambassador.) Many members of Congress who had drafted and voted for the Judiciary Act had been delegates to the Constitutional Convention, and it is unlikely that they would have initiated a law that contradicted the Constitution. And Oliver Ellsworth, who had been a coauthor of the bill, then served as chief justice of the Supreme Court before Marshall. But these interpretations allowed Marshall a way out of the dilemma.

131 Quoted in Walter F. Murphy and C. Herman Pritchett, *Courts, Judges, and Politics,* 3rd ed. (New York: Random House, 1979), 4.

132 John A. Garraty, "The Case of the Missing Commissions," in *Quarrels That Have Shaped the Constitution,* ed. John A. Garraty (New York: Harper & Row, 1962), 13.

133 *Fletcher* v. *Peck,* 10 U.S. 87 (1810); *Martin* v. *Hunter's Lessee,* 14 U.S. 304 (1816); *Cohens* v. *Virginia,* 19 U.S. 264 (1821).

134 In other cases, the Court narrowly construed state power, especially to regulate commerce. *Gibbons* v. *Ogden,* 22 U.S. 1 (1824).

135 For a development of this idea and a critique of judicial review, see James MacGregor Burns, *Packing the Court: The Rise of Judicial Power and the Coming Crisis of the Supreme Court* (New York: Penguin, 2009).

136 However, the Warren Court may not have been as out of step with the political branches as is often believed. See Lucas A. Powe, *The Warren Court and American Politics* (Cambridge, Mass.: Harvard University Press, 2000), 160–178.

137 Particularly regarding criminal defendants' rights.

138 One legal scholar says the most striking feature about Supreme Court decision making in the 1990s was the effort by five justices to resolve most issues as narrowly as possible, shunning sweeping pronouncements for case-by-case examination. Cass R. Sunstein, *One Case at a Time: Judicial Minimalism on the Supreme Court* (Cambridge, Mass.: Harvard University Press, 2001).

139 The Rehnquist Court reduced the scope of criminal defendants' rights, racial minorities' rights, and affirmative action. It also tightened access to the courts for individuals and groups trying to challenge government policies, and it limited efforts by Congress to impose new regulations on the states. However, the Court did take the first step toward homosexuals' legal rights.

140 Thomas M. Keck, *The Most Activist Supreme Court in History* (Chicago: University of Chicago Press, 2004).

141 531 U.S. 98 (2000).

142 The classic definitions of judicial activism don't include choosing the president because that hadn't occurred before. But legal scholars consider *Bush* v. *Gore* an example of judicial activism because the Court thrust itself into the political process even though the Constitution prescribes other means to resolve electoral deadlocks.

143 Scalia and Kennedy were appointed by Reagan; Thomas, Roberts, and Alito worked in the administration.

144 The possible exception is Justice Ginsburg, who replaced Justice Byron White. Jeffrey Rosen, "The Dissenter," *New York Times Magazine,* September 23, 2007, 52.

145 Adam Liptak, "The Most Conservative Court in Decades," *New York Times,* July 25, 2010, Y1.

146 Alito, Roberts, Scalia, and Thomas. William M. Landes and Richard A. Posner, "Rational Judicial Behavior: A Statistical Analysis," *Journal of Legal Analysis* 1 (2009), 775–831.

147 Adam Liptak, "Justices Offer Receptive Ear to Business Interests," *New York Times,* December 19, 2010, Y1.

148 *Citizens United* v. *Federal Election Commission,* 175 L.Ed.2d 753 (2010).

149 Lawrence Baum, *The Supreme Court,* 10th ed. (Washington, D.C.: CQ Press, 2010), 165.

150 Craig R. Ducat and Robert L. Dudley, "Federal Appellate Judges and Presidential Power," paper presented at the Midwest Political Science Association meeting, April 1987. The Court's rulings on the George W. Bush administration's detention policies are an exception.

151 Sheldon Goldman, "How Long the Legacy?" *Judicature* 76 (1993), 295.

152 The Eleventh Amendment overturned *Chisholm* v. *Georgia* (1793), which had permitted the federal courts to hear suits against a state by citizens of another state. The Fourteenth overturned the Dred Scott case, *Scott* v. *Sandford* (1857), which had held that blacks were not citizens. The Sixteenth overturned *Pollock* v. *Farmers' Loan and Trust* (1895), which had negated a congressional law authorizing a federal income tax. The Twenty-sixth overturned *Oregon* v. *Mitchell* (1970), which had negated a congressional law allowing eighteen-year-olds to vote in state elections.

153 *Goldman* v. *Weinberger,* 475 U.S. 503 (1986).

154 Richard Morin, "A Nation of Stooges," *Washington Post,* October 8, 1995, C5. See also "The Invisible Court," PEW Research Center Publications, August 3, 2010, pewresearch. org/pubs/1688/supreme-court-lack-of-public-knowledge-favorability.

155 Gregory A. Caldeira, "Neither the Purse nor the Sword," paper presented at the American Political Science Association meeting, August 1987.

156 Thomas R. Marshall, "Public Opinion and the Rehnquist Court," in *Readings in American Government and Politics,* 3rd ed. (Boston: Allyn & Bacon, 1999), 115–121. Also see Barry Friedman, *The Will of the People: How Public Opinion Has Influenced the Supreme Court and Shaped the Meaning of the Constitution* (New York: Farrar, Straus & Giroux, 2009).

157 Robert G. McCloskey, *The American Supreme Court* (Chicago: University of Chicago Press, 1960), 225. Also see Friedman, *The Will of the People.*

Chapter 13

1 In addition to the reference to a militia, the phrase "bear arms" at the time referred to military service, according to law professor Michael Dorf. Cited in Adam Liptak, "A Militia of One (Well Regulated)," *New York Times,* January 13, 2008, WK4.

2 The Supreme Court had not ruled directly on this issue; the last Supreme Court decision, in *U.S.* v. *Miller,* 307 U.S. 174 (1939), held that there was no right to have sawed-off shotguns. Lower courts had ruled overwhelmingly that the Second Amendment was only a collective right. By 2007, nine U.S. courts of appeals had reached this conclusion. (Two had reached the opposite conclusion.) Adam Liptak, "A Liberal Case for Gun Rights Helps Sway Federal Judiciary," *New York Times,* May 6, 2007, YT1.

3 Ibid., YT25.

4 A few law professors may have contributed by concluding that the amendment provides an individual right, because the militias at the Founding included all individuals who had political rights, such as the rights to vote and to serve on juries—that is, all white males who owned property. Today the individuals who have political rights would encompass all adult citizens (except felons in most states). For examination of the conflicting views, see David C. Williams, *The Mythic Meanings of the Second Amendment* (New Haven, Conn.: Yale University Press, 2003).

5 171 L.Ed.2d 637 (2008).

6 The majority cited these exceptions while acknowledging that future cases may test the limits.

7 Richard Morin, "The High Price of Free Speech," *Washington Post National Weekly Edition,* January 8, 2001, 34.

8 After 9/11, support for civil liberties dropped, reflecting people's fears. By 2005, however, support returned to pre-9/11 levels. First Amendment Center, in cooperation with the *American Journalism Review.* Survey conducted May 13–23, 2005 ($N = 1003$; sampling error = 3%).

9 The states didn't ratify a proposed amendment that would have required at least one representative in Congress for every fifty thousand people. That amendment would have put about five thousand members in today's Congress. The states also didn't ratify, until 1992, another proposed amendment that would have prohibited a salary raise for members of Congress from taking effect until after the next election to Congress.

10 *Reid* v. *Covert,* 354 U.S. 1 (1957).

11 *Barron* v. *Baltimore,* 32 U.S. 243 (1833).

12 Also, many states had their own bill of rights at the time, and other states were expected to follow.

13 *Gitlow* v. *New York,* 268 U.S. 652 (1925). *Gitlow* is usually cited as the first because it initiated the twentieth-century trend. However, *Chicago,*

Burlington and Quincy R. Co. v. *Chicago,* 166 U.S. 266 (1897), was actually the first. It applied the Fifth Amendment's just compensation clause, requiring government to pay owners "just compensation" for taking their property.

14 *Argersinger* v. *Hamlin,* 407 U.S. 25 (1972).

15 It hasn't applied the Fifth Amendment's guarantee of a grand jury in criminal cases or the Seventh Amendment's guarantee of a jury trial in civil cases. The grand jury no longer serves as a protective shield for potential criminal defendants; rather, it's become a prosecutorial tool. The Seventh Amendment guarantees a jury trial in civil cases when $20 or more is at stake, so that would require a commitment of scarce resources even for trivial cases.

16 The amendment also includes a right "to petition the government for a redress of grievances," which is incorporated in freedom of speech and assembly.

The language doesn't explicitly include freedom of association, but the Court has interpreted the amendment to encompass this right.

17 Anna Johnson, "Know Your First Amendment Rights? Poll Shows Many Don't," *Lincoln Journal Star,* March 1, 2006, 10A.

18 Even Justice Black, who claimed that he interpreted it literally. To do so, he had to define some speech as "action" so that it wouldn't be protected.

19 *Milk Wagon Drivers Union* v. *Meadowmoor Dairies,* 312 U.S. 287 (1941).

20 Thomas I. Emerson, *The System of Freedom of Expression* (New York: Random House/Vintage, 1971), 6–8.

21 Quoted in Deborah Tannen, *The Argument Culture* (New York: Ballantine, 1998), 25.

22 For a history of speech cases between the Civil War and World War I, see David M. Rabban, *Free Speech in Its Forgotten Years* (New York: Cambridge University Press, 1997).

23 Novelist Philip Roth observes, "McCarthy understood better than any American politician before him that people whose job was to legislate could do far better for themselves by performing; McCarthy understood the entertainment value of disgrace and how to feed the pleasures of paranoia. He took us back to our origins, back to the seventeenth century and the stocks. That's how the country began: moral disgrace as public entertainment." *I Married a Communist* (New York: Vintage, 1999), 284.

24 The Smith Act (1940). This act wasn't as broad as the World War I acts because it didn't forbid criticizing the government.

25 *Dennis* v. *United States,* 341 U.S. 494 (1951).

26 For the role of the Senate's Internal Security Committee, see Michael J. Ybarra, *Washington Gone Crazy: Senator Pat McCarran and the Great American Communist Hunt* (Hanover, N.H.: Steerforth, 2004).

27 Charles Peters, "Tilting at Windmills," *Washington Monthly,* May 2006, 8. See also Ted Morgan, *Reds: McCarthyism in Twentieth-Century America* (New York: Random House, 2003). For a review of other

books about Soviet spies in America, see Nicholas Lemann, "Spy Wars," *New Yorker*, June 27, 2009, 70.

28 In the cases of *Yates* v. *United States*, 354 U.S. 298 (1957), and *Scales* v. *United States*, 367 U.S. 203 (1961), among others.

29 The doctrine was created in a case in which a Ku Klux Klan leader said at a rally that the Klan might take "revengeance" against the president, Congress, and the Supreme Court if they continued "to suppress the white, Caucasian race." *Brandenburg* v. *Ohio*, 395 U.S. 444 (1969).

30 *Brandenburg* v. *Ohio*.

31 Attorney General Tom Clark quoted in *Esquire*, November 1974.

32 David Cole, "The Course of Least Resistance: Repeating History in the War on Terrorism," in *Lost Liberties*, ed. Cynthia Brown (New York: New Press, 2003), 1.

33 Jean E. Jackson, "ACTA Report Criticizes Professors," *Anthropology News*, March 2002, 7. Negative reaction prompted the organization to remove the names from its website.

34 Gia Fenoglio, "Is It 'Blacklisting' or Mere Criticism?" *National Journal*, January 19, 2002, 188.

35 For some examples, see Michael Tomasky, "Dissent in America," *American Prospect*, April 2003, 22. See also Ann Coulter, *Treason: Liberal Treachery from the Cold War to the War on Terrorism* (New York: Crown Forum, 2003), and Sean Hannity, *Deliver Us from Evil* (New York: Regan Books/HarperCollins, 2004).

36 C. Herman Pritchett, *The American Constitution*, 2nd ed. (New York: McGraw-Hill, 1968), 476, n. 2. However, police in some places continue to arrest for swearing. Judy Lin, "ACLU Fights Police on Profanity Arrests in Pittsburgh Area," *Lincoln Journal Star*, July 11, 2002.

37 *Gooding* v. *Wilson*, 405 U.S. 518 (1972); *Lewis* v. *New Orleans*, 408 U.S. 913 (1972).

38 *Cohen* v. *California*, 403 U.S. 15 (1971).

39 However, businesses can restrict the speech of their employees at work because they're private entities.

40 *Collin* v. *Smith*, 447 F.Supp. 676 (N.D. Ill., 1978); *Collin* v. *Smith*, 578 F.2d 1197 (7th Cir, 1978).

41 *United States* v. *Schwimmer*, 279 U.S. 644 (1929).

42 *Virginia* v. *Black*, 155 L.Ed.2d 535 (2003). Previously, the Court invalidated a St. Paul, Minnesota, ordinance prohibiting the display of a Nazi swastika or a cross-burning on public or private land, *R.A.V.* v. *St. Paul*, 120 L.Ed.2d 305 (1992).

43 For a legal analysis supporting these codes, see Richard Delgado and David H. Yun, "Pressure Valves and Bloodied Chickens: An Analysis of Paternalistic Objections to Hate Speech Regulation," *University of California Law Review* 82 (1994), 716.

44 Mary Jordan, "Free Speech Starts to Have Its Say," *Washington Post National Weekly Edition*, September 21–27, 1992, 31.

45 Michael D. Shear, "A Tangled World Wide Web," *Washington Post National Weekly Edition*, October 30–November 5, 1995, 36.

46 Stephanie Simon, "Christians Sue for Right Not to Tolerate Policies," *Los Angeles Times*, April 10, 2006, www.latimes.com/news/nationworld/nation/la-nachristians10apr10,0,6204444,story?

47 *All Things Considered*, National Public Radio, January 4, 2010.

48 *Barnes* v. *Glenn Theater*, 501 U.S. 560 (1991).

49 *Young* v. *American Mini Theatres*, 427 U.S. 50 (1976); *Renton* v. *Playtime Theatres*, 475 U.S. 41 (1986).

50 *FCC* v. *Pacifica Foundation*, 438 U.S. 726 (1968).

51 *FCC* v. *Fox Television Stations*, 173 L.Ed.2d 738 (2009). After the ruling, the FCC wrote a policy banning fleeting profanities, but the Supreme Court decided that the policy was too vague. *FCC* v. *Fox Television Stations*, 183 L.Ed.2d 234 (2012). As this edition went to press, it wasn't clear whether the FCC would rewrite the policy.

52 Jonathan D. Salant, "FCC Wants to Up Fine for Cursing," *Lincoln Journal Star*, January 15, 2004.

53 *Wilkinson* v. *Jones*, 480 U.S. 926 (1987).

54 *Southeastern Promotions* v. *Conrad*, 420 U.S. 546 (1975).

55 *Jeannette Rankin Brigade* v. *Chief of Capital Police*, 409 U.S. 972 (1972); *Edwards* v. *South Carolina*, 372 U.S. 229 (1963); *United States* v. *Grace*, 75 L.Ed.2d 736 (1983). The grounds around jails and military bases are off-limits due to the need for security. *Adderley* v. *Florida*, 385 U.S. 39 (1966); *Greer* v. *Spock*, 424 U.S. 828 (1976).

56 According to the Burger Court, which emphasized property rights over First Amendment rights. *Lloyd* v. *Tanner*, 407 U.S. 551 (1972); *Hudgens* v. *NLRB*, 424 U.S. 507 (1976).

57 Leonard Pitts Jr., "Intolerance Meets Its Nemesis at an Albany Mall," *Lincoln Journal Star*, March 10, 2003.

58 *Cox* v. *Louisiana*, 379 U.S. 536 (1965).

59 *Schenk* v. *Pro-Choice Network*, 137 L.Ed.2d 1 (1997).

60 *Frisby* v. *Schultz*, 101 L.Ed.2d 420 (1988).

61 The Court, however, did rule that the parents of a soldier whose funeral was picketed can't sue the picketers for intentional infliction of emotional distress when the picketers followed the law and remained 1000 feet away. *Snyder* v. *Phelps*, 179 L.Ed.2d 172 (2011).

62 *United States* v. *O'Brien*, 391 U.S. 367 (1968).

63 *Tinker* v. *Des Moines School District*, 393 U.S. 503 (1969).

64 *Smith* v. *Goguen*, 415 U.S. 566 (1974); *Spence* v. *Washington*, 418 U.S. 405 (1974).

65 *Texas* v. *Johnson*, 105 L.Ed.2d 342 (1989).

66 *United States* v. *Eichman*, 110 L.Ed.2d 287 (1990).

67 In some places, though not in Switzerland, Muslims are called to prayer from these minarets. The four existing minarets in Switzerland aren't affected by the provision.

68 *Tinker* v. *Des Moines School District*, 393 U.S. 503 (1969).

69 *Bethel School District* v. *Fraser*, 478 U.S. 675 (1986).

70 School officials persuaded the justices that the students were watching as part of an official school event. Hence the officials had authority over the students. If the students had been "out" of school and off of school property, the officials would have had no authority over them for this incident.

71 *Morse* v. *Frederick*, 168 L.Ed.2d 290 (2007).

72 *Hazelwood School District* v. *Kuhlmeier*, 98 L.Ed.2d 592 (1988).

73 *Hurley* v. *Irish-American Gay, Lesbian and Bisexual Group of Boston*, 515 U.S. 557 (1995).

74 *Boy Scouts of America* v. *Dale*, 147 L.Ed.2d 554 (2000).

75 The Court invalidated racial discrimination in labor unions and private schools and sexual discrimination in law firms, despite claims of freedom of association. *Railway Mail Association* v. *Corsi*, 326 U.S. 88 (1945); *Runyon* v. *McCrary*, 427 U.S. 160 (1976); *Hison* v. *King & Spalding*, 467 U.S. 69 (1984).

76 *Roberts* v. *U.S. Jaycees*, 468 U.S. 609 (1984); *Board of Directors of Rotary International* v. *Rotary Club of Duarte*, 481 U.S. 537 (1987).

77 Quoted in David Halberstam, *The Best and the Brightest* (Greenwich, Conn.: Fawcett, 1969), 769.

78 Bill Moyers, "Our Democracy Is in Danger of Being Paralyzed," *Keynote Address to the National Conference on Media Reform*, November 8, 2003, www.truthout.org/docs_03/printer_111403E.shtml.

79 *New York Times* v. *United States*, 403 U.S. 713 (1971). In addition to seeking injunctions, the Nixon administration sent a telegram to the *New York Times* demanding that it cease publication of the excerpts, but the FBI had the wrong telex number for the newspaper, so the telegram went first to a fish company in Brooklyn. R. W. Apple, "Lessons from the Pentagon Papers," *New York Times*, June 23, 1996, E5.

80 Actually, the Pentagon Papers did include some current information regarding ongoing negotiations and the names of CIA agents in Vietnam, but Ellsberg had not passed this information to the newspapers. However, the government and the Court were unaware of this, so the government argued that publication could affect national security, and the Court decided the case with this prospect in mind. Thus the Court's ruling was stronger than legal analysts realized at the time. Erwin N. Griswold, "No Harm Was Done," *New York Times*, June 30, 1991, E15.

81 *United States* v. *Progressive*, 467 F.Supp. 990 (W.D. Wisc., 1979).

82 Then radio and television stations used actors with Irish accents to dub the comments made by IRA members. In 1994, the government lifted the ban.

83 *Branzburg* v. *Hayes*, 408 U.S. 665 (1972).

84 Jeffrey Toobin, "Name That Source," *New Yorker*, January 16, 2006, 30.

85 *Cox Broadcasting* v. *Cohn,* 420 U.S. 469 (1975).

86 This was not a Supreme Court case.

87 *Time* v. *Hill,* 385 U.S. 374 (1967).

88 *Wilson* v. *Layne,* 143 L.Ed.2d 818 (1999); *Hanlon* v. *Berger,* 143 L.Ed.2d 978 (1999).

89 Adam Liptak, "When Free Worlds Collide," *New York Times,* February 28, 2010, WK1.

90 *New York Times* v. *Sullivan,* 376 U.S. 254 (1964).

91 Harry Kalven, "The New York Times Case: A Note on 'the Central Meaning of the First Amendment,'" *Supreme Court Review* (1964), 221.

92 *Monitor Patriot* v. *Roy,* 401 U.S. 265 (1971).

93 *Associated Press* v. *Walker,* 388 U.S. 130 (1967); *Greenbelt Cooperative* v. *Bresler,* 398 U.S. 6 (1970). This set of rulings began with *Curtis Publishing* v. *Butts,* 388 U.S. 130 (1967).

94 *Gertz* v. *Robert Welch,* 418 U.S. 323 (1974), and *Time* v. *Firestone,* 424 U.S. 448 (1976).

95 Eric Press, "Westmoreland Takes on CBS," *Newsweek,* October 22, 1984, 62.

96 The Pilgrims, who had experienced religious toleration in Holland (after persecution in England), left because they wanted a place of their own, not because they could not worship as they pleased. The Dutch were so tolerant that the Pilgrims' children had begun to adopt Dutch manners and ideas. Richard Shenkman, *"I Love Paul Revere, Whether He Rode or Not"* (New York: HarperCollins, 1991), 20–21.

97 The only religious reference in the Constitution occurs in the date when the document was written: "year of our Lord one thousand seven hundred and eighty-seven." And that may have been mere convention; "year of our Lord" is the English equivalent of A.D.

98 Apparently Roger Williams, a clergyman and the founder of Rhode Island, was the first to use this metaphor. Lloyd Burton, "The Church in America," *New Yorker,* September 29, 2003, 10. James Madison was another of the Founders who pioneered our religious freedom. For an analysis of his views, see Vincent Phillip Munoz, "James Madison's Principle of Religious Liberty," *American Political Science Review* 97 (2003), 17–32.

99 Gary Wills, quoted on *Thomas Jefferson,* PBS, February 18, 1997.

100 According to Mark Pachter, Curator of the National Portrait Gallery, *Morning Edition,* National Public Radio, June 25, 2006.

101 See, for example, Forrest Church, *So Help Me God: The Founding Fathers and the First Great Battle over Church and State* (Orlando, Fla.: Harcourt, 2007); David L. Holmes, *The Faiths of the Founders* (New York: Oxford University Press, 2006); Martha Nussbaum, *Liberty of Conscience: In Defense of America's Tradition of Religious Equality* (New York: Basic Books, 2008); Steven Waldman, *Founding Faith: Providence, Politics, and the Birth of Religious Freedom in America* (New York: Random House, 2008); and Garry Wills, *Head and Heart: American Christianities* (New York: Penguin, 2007).

102 *Torcaso* v. *Watkins,* 367 U.S. 488 (1961).

103 *Pierce* v. *Society of Sisters,* 268 U.S. 510 (1925).

104 *Cooper* v. *Pate,* 378 U.S. 546 (1963); *Cruz* v. *Beto,* 405 U.S. 319 (1972).

105 *Church of the Lukumi Babalu Aye* v. *Hialeah,* 124 L.Ed.2d 472 (1993).

106 *Reynolds* v. *United States,* 98 U.S. 145 (1879). Most Mormons, however, didn't approve of polygamy. Even when polygamy was most popular, perhaps only 10 percent of Mormons practiced it. Shenkman, *"I Love Paul Revere,"* 31. Yet today reports indicate that polygamy is still flourishing among Mormons, perhaps more than ever. Lawrence Wright, "Lives of the Saints," *New Yorker,* January 21, 2002, 43.

107 *Sherbert* v. *Verner,* 374 U.S. 398 (1963).

108 Although a congressional statute mandates "reasonable accommodation," the Court interpreted it so narrowly that it essentially requires only minimal accommodation. *Trans World Airlines* v. *Hardison,* 432 U.S. 63 (1977). For analysis, see Gloria T. Beckley and Paul Burstein, "Religious Pluralism, Equal Opportunity, and the State," *Western Political Quarterly* 44 (1991), 185–208. For a related case, see *Thornton* v. *Caldor,* 86 L.Ed.2d 557 (1985).

109 *United States* v. *Lee,* 455 U.S. 252 (1982).

110 *United States* v. *American Friends Service Committee,* 419 U.S. 7 (1974).

111 *Goldman* v. *Weinberger,* 475 U.S. 503 (1986); *O'Lone* v. *Shabazz,* 482 U.S. 342 (1986).

112 *Employment Division* v. *Smith,* 108 L.Ed.2d 876 (1990).

113 Congress did pass the American Indian Religious Freedom Act of 1994 to allow Indians to use peyote, but this law did not address the broader implications of the ruling. Ruth Marcus, "One Nation, under Court Rulings," *Washington Post National Weekly Edition,* March 18, 1991, 33.

114 *Boerne* v. *Flores,* 138 L.Ed.2d 624 (1997). Congress then passed another law that addressed just two kinds of government action—zoning and the rights of inmates at public correctional and mental institutions. The law required state and local governments to consider exceptions for religious practices. Although this was another attempt to override the Court's ruling, the Court upheld the law. *Cutter* v. *Wilkinson,* 125 S.Ct. 2113 (2005).

115 See page 21 of the twelfth edition of this text for a succinct summary and numerous sources.

116 William Lee Miller, "The Ghost of Freedoms Past," *Washington Post National Weekly Edition,* October 13, 1986, 23–24.

117 Richard Brookhiser, "Religious Intent," *New York Times Book Review,* April 13, 2008, 22.

118 Steven Waldman, "The Framers and the Faithful," *Washington Monthly,* April 2006, 33–38.

119 *Church of Holy Trinity* v. *United States,* 143 U.S. 457 (1892).

120 *Engel* v. *Vitale,* 370 U.S. 421 (1962); *Abington School District* v. *Schempp,* 374 U.S. 203 (1963).

121 *Stone* v. *Graham,* 449 U.S. 39 (1980). The Ten Commandments themselves have been divisive. In 1844, six people were killed in a riot in Philadelphia over which version of the Ten Commandments to post in the public schools. E. J. Dionne Jr., "Bridging the Church-State Divide," *Washington Post National Weekly Edition,* October 11, 1999, 21.

122 George W. Andrews (D-Ala.), quoted in C. Herman Pritchett, *The American Constitution,* 3rd ed. (New York: McGraw-Hill, 1977), 406.

123 Kenneth M. Dolbeare and Phillip E. Hammond, *The School Prayer Decisions* (Chicago: University of Chicago Press, 1971).

124 Robert H. Birkby, "The Supreme Court and the Bible Belt," *Midwest Journal of Political Science* 10 (1966), 304–315.

125 Julia Lieblich and Richard N. Ostling, "Despite Rulings, Prayer in School Still Sparks Debate, Still Practiced," *Lincoln Journal Star,* January 16, 2000.

126 "Five Schools Get Ten Commandments," *Lincoln Journal Star,* August 12, 1999.

127 J. Gordon Melton, quoted in Jon D. Hull, "The State of the Union," *Time,* January 30, 1995, 55.

128 Peter Cushnie, "Letters," *Time,* October 15, 1984, 21.

129 The Supreme Court invalidated Alabama's law that authorized a moment of silence "for meditation or voluntary prayer" because the wording of the law endorsed and promoted prayer. But most justices signaled approval of a moment of silence without such wording. *Wallace* v. *Jaffree,* 86 L.Ed.2d 29 (1985).

130 *Lee* v. *Weisman,* 120 L.Ed.2d 467 (1992).

131 *Jones* v. *Clear Creek,* 977 F.2d 965 (5th Cir., 1992).

132 *Moore* v. *Ingebretsen,* 88 F.3d 274 (1996).

133 *Santa Fe Independent School District* v. *Doe,* 530 U.S. 290 (2000).

134 Anna Quindlen, "School Prayer: Substitutes for Substance," *Lincoln Journal Star,* December 8, 1994.

135 A current guide for public school teachers, addressing practices that are permissible and those that are advisable in various situations, is Charles C. Haynes and Oliver Thomas, *Finding Common Ground* (Nashville, Tenn.: First Amendment Center, 2002).

136 *Widmar* v. *Vincent,* 454 U.S. 263 (1981). The law requires high schools that receive federal funds to allow meetings of students' religious, philosophical, or political groups if the schools permit meetings of any "noncurriculum" groups. Schools could prohibit meetings of all noncurriculum groups. A Salt Lake City high school banned all nonacademic clubs rather than let students form an organization for homosexuals in 1996. Interviews with teachers and students two years later indicated that, as a result of the ban on clubs, school spirit declined and class and racial rifts expanded. Clubs no longer brought students together, and clubs such as Polynesian Pride and the Aztec Club, for Latinos, no longer provided a link between these students and their school. "Club Ban Aimed at Gays Backfires," *Lincoln Journal Star,* December 6, 1998.

137 *Board of Education of the Westside Community Schools* v. *Mergens,* 496 U.S. 226 (1990).

138 Harriet Barovick, "Fear of a Gay School," *Time*, February 21, 2000, 52.

139 *Rosenberger* v. *University of Virginia*, 132 L.Ed.2d 700 (1995). Yet the Rehnquist Court later ruled that states that provide scholarships for students at colleges and universities don't have to provide them for students preparing for the ministry. *Locke* v. *Davey*, 158 L.Ed.2d 21 (2004).

140 *Christian Legal Society* v. *Martinez*, 177 L.Ed.2d 838 (2010).

141 For the nation's first celebration of Columbus Day in 1892, Francis Bellamy wrote, "I pledge allegiance to my flag and the republic for which it stands, one nation indivisible, with liberty and justice for all." For Bellamy, the key words were "indivisible," which referred to the Civil War and emphasized the Union over the states, and "liberty and justice for all," which emphasized a balance between freedom for individuals and equality between them. During the Cold War in the 1950s, Americans feared "godless communism." Some objected to communism as much because of the Soviet Union's official policy of atheism as because of its totalitarianism. A religious revival swept the United States as preachers such as Billy Graham warned that Americans would perish in a nuclear holocaust unless they opened their arms to Jesus Christ. Congress replaced the traditional national motto—"E Pluribus Unum" ("Out of Many, One")—with "In God We Trust," and it added this new motto to our paper money. Fraternal organizations, especially the Catholic Knights of Columbus, and religious leaders campaigned to add "under God" to the Pledge of Allegiance. The Presbyterian pastor of President Eisenhower's church in Washington urged the addition in a sermon as the president sat in a pew. With little dissent, Congress passed and the president signed a bill to do so in 1954. The legislative history of the act stated that the intent was to "acknowledge the dependence of our people and our government upon . . . the Creator . . . [and] deny the atheistic and materialistic concept of communism." The president stated that "millions of our school children will daily proclaim in every city and town . . . the dedication of our nation and our people to the Almighty." Thus the phrase was adopted expressly to endorse religion. David Greenberg, "The Pledge of Allegiance: Why We're Not One Nation 'under God,'" *Slate*, June 28, 2002, slate.com/articles/news_and_politics/history_lesson/2002/06/the_pledge_of_allegiance.html

142 *Elk Grove Unified School District* v. *Newdow*, 159 L.Ed.2d 98 (2004).

143 *Lynch* v. *Donnelly*, 79 L.Ed.2d 604 (1984).

144 *Allegheny County* v. *ACLU*, 106 L.Ed.2d 472 (1989). *Allegheny County* v. *ACLU*, 106 L.Ed.2d 472 (1989).

145 *Van Orden* v. *Perry*, 162 L.Ed.2d 607 (2005).

146 Initially they stood alone. As the cases proceeded through the lower courts, officials added other historical documents but never made a sincere effort to integrate them.

147 *McCreary County* v. *ACLU*, 162 L.Ed.2d 729 (2005).

148 *Epperson* v. *Arkansas*, 393 U.S. 97 (1968).

149 Some groups use the more sophisticated-sounding term *creation science*. Although these groups do address the science of evolution, courts consider creationism and creation science as interchangeable.

150 *Edwards* v. *Aguillard*, 482 U.S. 578 (1987).

151 They do acknowledge that some, limited evolution has occurred.

152 However, to avoid court rulings similar to those against creationism—that it reflects a religious view—they try to avoid mention of God.

153 Michael B. Berkman and Eric Plutzer, "Science Education: Defeating Creationism in the Courtroom, but Not in the Classroom," *Science* 28 (January 2011), 404–405, sciencemag.org/content/331/6016/404.full?sid=79219c8f-fcf9-45fd-9916-ab2a.

154 Wendy Kaminer, "The God Bullies," *American Prospect*, November 18, 2002, 9.

155 For further examination, see E.J. Dionne Jr., "Bridging the Church-State Divide," *Washington Post National Weekly Edition*, October 11, 1999, 21.

156 John Schwartz, "Name That Freedom," *New York Times*, October 24, 2010, WK3.

157 *McCreary County* v. *ACLU*, 162 L.Ed.2d 729 (2005).

158 *Rochin* v. *California*, 342 U.S. 165 (1952).

159 Seymour Wishman, *Confessions of a Criminal Lawyer* (New York: Penguin, 1981), 16.

160 *Stein* v. *New York*, 346 U.S. 156 (1953).

161 Wendy Kaminer, *It's All the Rage* (Reading, Mass.: Addison-Wesley, 1995), 78.

162 *Weeks* v. *United States*, 232 U.S. 383 (1914).

163 *Mapp* v. *Ohio*, 367 U.S. 643 (1961).

164 The Burger Court allowed use of evidence when police execute a search warrant that they did not know was invalid. *United States* v. *Leon*, 82 L.Ed.2d 677 (1984); *Massachusetts* v. *Sheppard*, 82 L.Ed.2d 737 (1984). The Roberts Court allowed use of evidence when police fail to knock and identify themselves before entering a residence, in situations in which they are required by law to do so. *Hudson* v. *Michigan*, 165 L.Ed.2d 56 (2006).

165 *Olmstead* v. *United States*, 277 U.S. 438 (1928).

166 *Katz* v. *United States*, 389 U.S. 347 (1967).

167 *U.S.* v. *Jones*, 181 L.Ed.2d 911 (2012).

168 Even phones without a GPS device can be tracked by the cellphone companies as users make calls.

169 Eric Lichtblau, "Police Are Using Phone Tracking as Routine Tool," *New York Times*, April 1, 2012, Y1.

170 An administration official, quoted in Zev Borow, "Very Bad People," *New Yorker*, February 6, 2006, 44.

171 See, for example, Jane Mayer, "The Secret Sharer," *New Yorker*, May 23, 2011, 47.

172 And perhaps the contents of the calls, too, though that is difficult to ascertain because the government has divulged little information about this program.

173 The Foreign Intelligence Surveillance Act required authorization for such eavesdropping from the Foreign Intelligence Surveillance Court. Charlie Savage, *Takeover* (New York: Back Bay Books, 2007), 131–132.

174 The Protect America Act of 2007 amended the Foreign Intelligence Surveillance Act, which had required judicial authorization. Now, under the act, judicial authorization is required only if the government targets specific American citizens.

175 Seymour M. Hersh, "National Security Dept.: Listening In," *New Yorker*, May 29, 2006, 25.

176 The USA PATRIOT Act, which expanded surveillance within the United States since 9/11, also has numerous implications for civil liberties, but the act is quite technical and beyond the scope of this text.

177 *Brown* v. *Mississippi*, 297 U.S. 278 (1936).

178 *McNabb* v. *United States*, 318 U.S. 332 (1943); *Mallory* v. *United States*, 354 U.S. 449 (1957); *Spano* v. *New York*, 360 U.S. 315 (1959).

179 *Ashcraft* v. *Tennessee*, 322 U.S. 143 (1944).

180 *Miranda* v. *Arizona*, 384 U.S. 436 (1966).

181 *Dickerson* v. *United States*, 530 U.S. 428 (2000).

182 Jan Hoffman, "Police Tactics Chipping Away at Suspects' Rights," *New York Times*, March 29, 1998, 35.

183 *Johnson* v. *Zerbst*, 304 U.S. 458 (1938).

184 The Court did require state courts to furnish an attorney when there were "special circumstances" involved. *Powell* v. *Alabama*, 287 U.S. 45 (1932).

185 *Gideon* v. *Wainwright*, 372 U.S. 335 (1963).

186 *Argersinger* v. *Hamlin*, 407 U.S. 25 (1972); *Scott* v. *Illinois*, 440 U.S. 367 (1974); *Alabama* v. *Shelton*, 152 L.Ed.2d 888(2002).

187 *Douglas* v. *California*, 372 U.S. 353 (1953).

188 Wendy Cole, "Death Takes a Holiday," *Time*, February 14, 2000, 68.

189 Jill Smolowe, "Race and the Death Penalty," *Time*, April 29, 1991, 69.

190 Peter Applebome, "Indigent Defendants, Overworked Lawyers," *New York Times*, May 17, 1992, E18.

191 Alan Berlow, "Texas, Take Heed," *Washington Post National Weekly Edition*, February 21, 2000, 22.

192 Richard Carelli, "Death Rows Grow, Legal Help Shrinks," *Lincoln Journal Star*, October 7, 1995.

193 The Innocence Project alone freed 254 inmates through DNA evidence from 1992 through spring 2010. Nathan Thornburgh, "Resumed Innocent," *Time*, May 31, 2010, 26. Texas holds the dubious record for the most exonerated, with 38. "Lining Up for Justice in Texas," *Newsweek*, February 22, 2010, 8.

194 The Burger Court did rule that the right to counsel entails the right to "effective" counsel, but the Court set such stringent standards for establishing the existence of ineffective counsel that few defendants can take advantage of this right. See *Strickland* v. *Washington*, 466 U.S. 668 (1984), and *United States* v. *Cronic*, 466 U.S. 640 (1984).

195 *Baldwin v. New York,* 339 U.S. 66 (1970); *Blanton v. North Las Vegas,* 489 U.S. 538 (1989).

196 *Duncan v. Louisiana,* 391 U.S. 145 (1968).

197 *Taylor v. Louisiana,* 419 U.S. 522 (1975).

198 *Swain v. Alabama,* 380 U.S. 202 (1965).

199 *Graham v. Florida,* 176 L.Ed.2d 825 (2010).

200 The Court implicitly upheld the death penalty in *Wilkerson v. Utah,* 99 U.S. 130 (1878), and *In re: Kemmler,* 136 U.S. 436 (1890).

201 *Furman v. Georgia,* 408 U.S. 238 (1972).

202 *Gregg v. Georgia,* 428 U.S. 153 (1976).

203 *Woodson v. North Carolina,* 428 U.S. 289 (1976).

204 *Coker v. Georgia,* 433 U.S. 584 (1977); *Kennedy v. Louisiana,* 171 L.Ed.2d 525 (2008).

205 And in the process, rejected the role of social science evidence of systematic racial discrimination. *McCleskey v. Kemp,* 95 L.Ed.2d 262 (1987). Studies of Florida, Illinois, Mississippi, and North Carolina have found similar results. Fox Butterfield, "Blacks More Likely to Get Death Penalty, Study Says," *New York Times,* June 7, 1998, 16.

206 Kevin Boyle, "Strange Justice," *New York Times Book Review,* March 18, 2012, 18.

207 As of October 2007.

208 David Grann, "Trial by Fire," *New Yorker,* September 7, 2009, 42–62.

209 The American Law Institute, which numbers about four thousand judges, lawyers, and law professors and which created the current framework for the death penalty, pronounced the framework and the penalty a failure in 2010. Adam Liptak, "Group Gives Up Death Penalty Work," *New York Times,* January 5, 2010, A11.

210 Frank R. Baumgartner, Suzanna De Boef, and Amber E. Boydstun, *The Decline of the Death Penalty and the Discovery of Innocence* (Cambridge, England: Cambridge University Press, 2008).

211 Adam Liptak, "Juries Reject Death Penalty in Nearly All Federal Trials," *New York Times,* June 15, 2003, 12; Alex Kotlowitz, "In the Face of Death," *New York Times Magazine,* June 6, 2003, 34.

212 *Atkins v. Virginia,* 153 L.Ed. 2d 335 (2002).

213 *Penry v. Lynaugh,* 106 L.Ed.2d 256 (1989).

214 *Roper v. Simmons,* 161 L.Ed.2d 1 (2005).

215 Some Asian countries (notably China) and many Middle Eastern countries also retain it.

216 *Brady v. United States,* 397 U.S. 742 (1970).

217 *Griswold v. Connecticut,* 38 U.S. 479 (1965).

218 For a rare exception, see *Time v. Hill,* 385 U.S. 374 (1967).

219 *Griswold v. Connecticut.*

220 *Eisenstadt v. Baird,* 405 U.S. 438 (1972); *Carey v. Population Services International,* 431 U.S. 678 (1977).

221 *Eisenstadt v. Baird.*

222 Lloyd Shearer, "This Woman and This Man Made History," *Parade,* 1983.

223 *Roe v. Wade,* 410 U.S. 113 (1973).

224 Bob Woodward, "The Abortion Papers," *Washington Post National Weekly Edition,* January 30, 1989, 24–25.

225 According to the Guttmacher Institute, cited in Rob Stein, "Another Look at Late-Term Abortions," *Washington Post National Weekly Edition,* June 15–21, 2009, 33.

226 All but New York's. Three other states allowed abortion on demand, though not quite as extensively as *Roe,* so the ruling also invalidated their laws. Jeffrey A. Segal and Harold J. Spaeth, *The Supreme Court and the Attitudinal Model* (New York: Cambridge University Press, 1993), 333.

227 Ironically, a Gallup poll a year before *Roe* found that more Republicans than Democrats were in favor of leaving the decision to the woman and her doctor. Linda Greenhouse, "One Man, Two Courts," *New York Times,* April 11, 2010, WK11.

228 For example, Alan Dershowitz, *Supreme Injustice* (New York: Oxford University Press, 2001), 191–196. For a contrast with same-sex marriage, see Jonathan Rauch, "A Separate Peace," *Atlantic Monthly,* April 2007, 21.

229 *Akron v. Akron Center for Reproductive Health,* 76 L.Ed.2d 687 (1983).

230 "The Supreme Court Ignites a Fiery Abortion Debate," *Time,* July 4, 1977, 6–8.

231 *Beal v. Doe,* 432 U.S. 438 (1977); *Maher v. Roe,* 432 U.S. 464 (1977); *Poelker v. Doe,* 432 U.S. 519 (1977); *Harris v. McRae,* 448 U.S. 297 (1980).

232 "The Abortion Dilemma Come to Life," *Washington Post National Weekly Edition,* December 25, 1989, 10–11.

233 Alan Guttmacher Institute, *Facts in Brief: Abortion in the United States* (New York: Alan Guttmacher Institute, 1992); Stephanie Mencimer, "Ending Illegitimacy as We Know It," *Washington Post National Weekly Edition,* January 17, 1994, 24.

234 *Webster v. Reproductive Health Services,* 106 L.Ed.2d 410 (1989).

235 *Planned Parenthood of Southeastern Pennsylvania v. Casey,* 120 L.Ed.2d 674 (1992). Justice Anthony Kennedy changed his mind after the justices' conference, from essentially overturning *Roe* to reaffirming it. His was the fifth vote to reaffirm, as it would have been to overturn.

236 Kathleen Sullivan, cited in Robin Toner and Adam Liptak, "In New Court, Roe May Stand, So Foes Look to Limit Its Scope," *New York Times,* July 10, 2005, YT16.

237 William Booth, "The Difference a Day Makes," *Washington Post National Weekly Edition,* November 23, 1992, 31.

238 *Planned Parenthood of Southeastern Pennsylvania v. Casey,* 120 L.Ed.2d 674 (1992).

239 *Hodgson v. Minnesota,* 111 L.Ed.2d 344 (1990); *Ohio v. Akron Center for Reproductive Health,* 111 L.Ed.2d 405 (1990); *Planned Parenthood Association of Kansas City v. Ashcroft,* 462 U.S. 476 (1983). Number of states from Holly Ramer, "Never-Enforced Abortion Law to Go before Supreme Court," *Lincoln Journal Star,* November 27, 2005, A4.

240 Margaret Carlson, "Abortion's Hardest Cases," *Time,* July 9, 1990, 24.

241 Research shows that this procedure has not had the anticipated impact in British Columbia, and anecdotal evidence suggests that it has not in Alabama either. Kevin Sack, "In Ultrasound, Abortion Fight Has New Front," *New York Times,* May 27, 2010, A1.

242 Erik Eckholm, "Ultrasound: A Pawn in the Abortion Wars," *New York Times,* February 26, 2012, SR4.

243 Peter Slevin, "Abortion in the States' Hands," *Washington Post National Weekly Edition,* June 15–21, 2009, 34. Although some pro-life groups insist that there is a link, the website operated by the U.S. National Library and the National Institutes of Health, with links to the American Cancer Society and the Mayo Clinic, concludes that there is no link. www.nlm.nih.gov/medlineplus/abortion.html.

244 Charlie Savage, "Appeals Courts Pushed to Right by Bush Choices," *New York Times,* October 29, 2008, A1. The second part of the quoted language was upheld by the appellate court in 2011.

245 Before this procedure was adopted for late-term abortions, doctors removed the fetus in pieces. Jeffrey Toobin, *The Nine: Inside the Secret World of the Supreme Court* (New York: Doubleday, 2007), 132.

246 *Stenberg v. Carhart,* 530 U.S. 914 (2000).

247 *Gonzales v. Carhart,* 167 L.Ed.2d 480 (2007). The Court didn't overrule the 2000 decision, because that Nebraska law, unlike this congressional law, was too broad.

248 A review of the research concluded that it is "unlikely" that the fetus can feel pain before twenty-eight weeks. Sarah Kliff, "A New Way to Talk about Abortion in Nebraska," *Newsweek,* March 19, 2010, 3.

249 Barry Yeoman, "The Quiet War on Abortion," *Mother Jones,* September–October 2001, 46–51.

250 "Committed to Availability, Conflicted about Morality," Public Religion Research Institute, June 9, 2011, publicreligion.org/research/?id=615.

251 For an analysis of the political dynamics that produced this moderate result, see William Saleton, *Bearing Right: How Conservatives Won the Abortion War* (Berkeley: University of California Press, 2003). The title is an exaggeration.

252 Alissa Rubin, "The Abortion Wars Are Far from Over," *Washington Post National Weekly Edition,* December 21, 1992, 25.

253 Richard Lacayo, "One Doctor Down, How Many More?" *Time,* March 22, 1993, 47.

254 Rebecca Mead, "Return to Sender the Usual Hate Mail," *New Yorker,* October 29, 2001, 34.

255 Douglas Frantz, "The Rhetoric of Terror," *Time,* March 27, 1995, 48–51.

256 Dan Sewell, "Abortion War Requires Guns, Bulletproof Vests," *Lincoln Journal Star,* January 8, 1995. Plus Dr. George Tiller in 2009.

257 "Blasts Reawaken Fear of Domestic Terrorism," *Lincoln Journal Star,* January 17, 1997.

258 Richard Lacayo, "Abortion: The Future Is Already Here," *Time,* May 4, 1992, 29; Jack Hitt, "Who Will Do Abortions Here?" *New York Times Magazine,* January 18, 1998, 20.

259 Jodi Enda, "The Women's View," *American Prospect,* April 2005, 26. However, a counter-movement to train more doctors is emerging. Emily Bazelon, "The New Abortion Providers," *New York Times Magazine,* July 18, 2010, 30.

260 Randall Terry, quoted in Anthony Lewis, "Pro-Life Zealots 'Outside the Bargain,'" *Lincoln Journal Star,* March 14, 1993.

261 Joseph Scheidler, quoted in Sandra G. Boodman, "Bringing Abortion Home," *Washington Post National Weekly Edition,* April 15, 1993, 6.

262 Stanley K. Henshaw, "Abortion Incidence and Services in the United States, 1995–1996," *Family Planning Perspectives,* November–December 1998; Stephanie Simon, "Abortions Down 25% from Peak," *Los Angeles Times,* January 17, 2008, www.latimes.com/news/nationworld/nation/la-na-abort17jan17,0,1592814.

263 Bazelon, "The New Abortion Providers."

264 Dorothy Samuels, "Where Abortion Rates Are Disappearing," *New York Times,* September 25, 2011, SR14.

265 Rob Stein, "As Clinical Abortions Decline, an Alternative Rises," *Washington Post National Weekly Edition,* January 28–February 3, 2008, 33. However, this method is used less in the United States, where the first pill must be administered in the doctor's office, than in other countries, where the pill may be taken at home. Nicholas D. Kristof, "Another Pill That Could Cause a Revolution," *New York Times,* August 1, 2010, WK8.

266 Much of this section is taken from Russell Shorto, "Contra-Contraception," *New York Times Magazine,* May 7, 2006, 48–55, 68.

267 Harris poll, ibid., 54.

268 Judie Brown, quoted in ibid., 50.

269 Jane Mayer, "Bully Pulpit," *New Yorker,* June 18, 2012, 61.

270 Judie Brown, quoted in ibid.

271 As the author concludes from the leaders' statements. Ibid., 54.

272 R. Albert Mohler Jr., quoted in ibid., 50.

273 "All Things Considered," NPR, June 20, 2012.

274 To mute the controversy slightly, the administration revised the protocol so religious institutions won't have to pay for any contraception or tell their employees that the institutions offer it or even tell their employees where to obtain it. (Because pregnancies and babies cost insurers far more than contraceptives, it is assumed that nobody will have to pay for the contraceptives, as the federal government found when Congress required coverage of contraceptives for federal workers in 1998. Ruth Marcus, "Way Out, Wrapped in Fig Leaf," *Lincoln Journal Star,* February 12, 2012, D9.)

275 Laurie Kellman and Larry Margasak, "Senate GOP Fails to Reverse Birth Control Rule," *Lincoln Journal Star,* March 2, 2012, A3.

276 For a representative explanation of this position, see Alysse Michelle Elhage, "Special Rights for Homosexuals," North Carolina Family Policy Council, ncfpc.org/PolicyPapers/Findings%209907%20Special%. For a critical analysis of this position, see Michael Nava and Robert Dawidoff, *Created Equal: Why Gay Rights Matter to America* (New York: St. Martin's, 1994).

277 For an elaboration of this history, see "In Changing the Law of the Land, Six Justices Turned to Its History," *New York Times,* July 20, 2003, WK7.

278 Four states at this time revised their statutes to bar sodomy only between homosexuals: Kansas, Missouri, Oklahoma, and Texas.

279 *Bowers v. Hardwick,* 92 L.Ed.2d 140 (1986); see also *Doe v. Commonwealth's Attorney,* 425 U.S. 901 (1976).

280 Dahlia Lithwick, "Extreme Makeover," *New Yorker,* March 12, 2012, 78.

281 *Lawrence and Garner* v. *Texas,* 539 U.S. 558 (2003). For a fascinating account of this case, see Dale Carpenter, *Flagrant Conduct* (New York: W.W. Norton, 2012).

282 "Gays Getting More Acceptance as They're More Open, Poll Says," *Lincoln Journal Star,* April 11, 2004.

283 Paul Gewirtz, quoted in Joe Klein, "How the Supremes Redeemed Bush," *Time,* July 7, 2003, 27.

284 The House sponsor of the act, Robert Barr (R-Ga.), said the act was necessary because "the flames of hedonism, the flames of narcissism, the flames of self-centered morality are licking at the very foundation of our society, the family unit." At the time he was protecting the family unit, he was in his third marriage. Margaret Carlson, "The Marrying Kind," *Time,* September 16, 1996, 26.

285 Jonathan Rauch, "Families Forged by Illness," *New York Times,* June 11, 2006, WK15.

286 For elaboration, see David Von Drehle, "Same-Sex Unions Take Center Stage," *Washington Post National Weekly Edition,* December 1, 2003, 29.

287 John Cloud, "1,138 Reasons Marriage Is Cool," *Time,* March 8, 2004, 32. A few go in the opposite direction, such as eligibility for Medicaid, which takes into account a spouse's income.

288 Frank Rich, summarizing attorney David Boies's arguments, "Two Weddings, a Divorce, and 'Glee,'" *New York Times,* June 13, 2010, WK10.

289 Advisory Opinion on Senate No. 2175, Supreme Judicial Court of Massachusetts, February 3, 2004.

290 David J. Garrow, "Toward a More Perfect Union," *New York Times Magazine,* May 9, 2004, 54.

291 Senator Wayne Allard (R-Colo.); Senator Rick Santorum (R-Pa.); James Dobson. Andrew Sullivan, "If at First You Don't Succeed . . . ," *Time,* July 26, 2004, 78.

292 Alan Cooperman, "Anger without Action," *Washington Post National Weekly Edition,* June 28, 2004, 30.

293 Lisa Leff and David Sharp, "Gay Marriage Foes Use Winning Argument," *Lincoln Journal Star,* November 7, 2009, A9.

294 Garrow, "Toward a More Perfect Union," 57.

295 Gallup poll, reported in Dorothy Samuels, "A Long, Winding Road to Marriage Equality," *New York Times,* November 13, 2011, SR10.

296 Especially by Republicans, conservatives, white evangelicals, weekly churchgoers, and African Americans, the last-mentioned of which had turned out in record numbers to vote for Obama for president. However, according to exit polls, the ballot measure would have passed (barely) even without African American opposition. Hendrik Hertzberg, "Comment: Eight Is Enough," *New Yorker,* December 1, 2008, 27.

297 California (which retains its civil union law after voters struck down its same-sex marriage law), Colorado, Delaware, Hawaii, Illinois, Maine, Maryland, Nevada, New Jersey, Oregon, Washington, and Wisconsin.

298 Geoff Mulvihill, "Transgender Protection Law Begins in New Jersey," *Lincoln Journal Star,* June 13, 2007, 7A.

299 *Roemer v. Evans,* 134 L.Ed.2d 855 (1996).

300 Israel does take homosexuality into account in the assignment of military jobs. Gays who admit their orientation to their superiors confidentially are restricted from security-sensitive jobs for fear that they could be subject to blackmail. But gays who acknowledge their orientation openly are treated the same as straights. Randy Shilts, "What's Fair in Love and War," *Newsweek,* February 1, 1993, 58–59. See also Randy Shilts, *Conduct Unbecoming: Gays and Lesbians in the U.S. Military* (New York: St. Martin's, 1993).

301 Nathaniel Frank, *Unfriendly Fire: How the Gay Ban Undermines the Military and Weakens America* (New York: St. Martin's, 2009), 35 and ch. 2 in general.

302 Joseph Rocha, "I Didn't Tell. It Didn't Matter," *Washington Post National Weekly Edition,* October 19–25, 2009, 27.

303 Dana Priest, "The Impact of the 'Don't Ask, Don't Tell' Policy," *Washington Post National Weekly Edition,* February 1, 1999, 35.

304 Charles McLean and P.W. Singer, "Don't Ask. Tell," *Newsweek,* June 14, 2010, 33; Michael O'Donnell, "Straight Away," *Washington Monthly,* March–April 2009, 45.

305 Rep. Duncan Hunter (R-Calif.), in interview on National Public Radio, February 2, 2010.

306 *Washington Post*/ABC News poll, cited in "U.S. Majority Supports Open Gays in Military," *Lincoln Journal Star,* February 13, 2010, A3.

307 David Mixner, quoted in Adam Nagourney, "Political Shifts in Gay Rights Are Lagging behind Culture," *New York Times,* June 28, 2009, Y18.

308 James C. McKinley Jr., "Gay Candidates Get Support That Causes May Not," *New York Times,* December 28, 2009, A17.

309 Charles M. Blow, "Gay? Whatever, Dude," *New York Times,* June 4, 2010, A25.

310 Al Kamen, "When Exactly Does Life End?" *Washington Post National Weekly Edition,* September 18, 1989, 31; Alain L. Sanders, "Whose Right to Die?" *Time,* December 11, 1989, 80.

311 *Cruzan* v. *Missouri Health Department,* 111 L.Ed.2d 224 (1990).

312 Otto Friedrich, "A Limited Right to Die," *Time,* July 9, 1990, 59.

313 Tamar Lewin, "Ignoring 'Right to Die' Directives, Medical Community Is Being Sued," *New York Times,* June 2, 1996, 1.

314 *Washington* v. *Glucksberg,* 138 L.Ed.2d 772 (1997); *Vacco* v. *Quill,* 138 L.Ed.2d 834 (1997).

315 *Gonzales* v. *Oregon,* 163 L.Ed.2d 748 (2006).

316 Kathy Barks Hoffman, "On Eve of Kevorkian Release from Prison, Little Has Changed," *Lincoln Journal Star,* May 29, 2007, 6A.

317 David E. Rosenbaum, "Americans Want a Right to Die—or So They Think," *New York Times,* June 8, 1997, E3.

318 Ibid.

319 Anemona Hartocollis, "Hard Choice for a Comfortable Death: Drug-Induced Sleep," *New York Times,* December 27, 2009, Y1.

Chapter 14

1 Information and quotations in Talking Points were drawn from Isabel Wilkerson, "A First Time for Everything," *New York Times Magazine,* December 25, 2011, 40.

2 The Spanish colony, and slavery, in Florida grew slowly. When Spain lost Florida to Britain in 1763, Spanish subjects, including 350 slaves, fled to Cuba. Jean M. West, "Slavery and Sanctuary in Colonial Florida," slaveryinamerica.org/history/hs_es_florida_slavery_short.htm.

3 Some historians believe that indentured servants—whites as well as blacks—were essentially slaves. Many servants were people whom the English upper classes were anxious to get rid of—street children, beggars, Gypsies, prostitutes, dissidents, and convicts. Some owners refused to free their servants when their indenture was supposed to end, and some courts refused to force the owners to fulfill their promises. Don Jordan and Michael Walsh, *White Cargo: The Forgotten History of Britain's White Slaves in America* (New York: New York University Press, 2008).

4 Exhibition "Slavery in New York," New York Historical Society, November 2005. For more details, see Ira Berlin and Leslie M. Harris, eds., *Slavery in New York* (New York: New York Historical Society/New Press, 2006). Also see Anne Farrow, Joel Lang, and Jenifer Frank, *Complicity: How the North Promoted, Prolonged, and Profited from Slavery* (New York: Ballantine, 2006).

5 Gary B. Nash, *The Forgotten Fifth* (Cambridge, Mass.: Harvard University Press, 2006). See also

Simon Schama, *Rough Crossings: Britain, the Slaves, and the American Revolution* (New York: Ecco, 2006).

6 In most of the North, slavery would be officially abolished shortly after ratification of the Constitution.

7 Adam Goodheart, "Setting Them Free," *New York Times Book Review,* August 7, 2005, 1.

8 Russell Nye, *Fettered Freedom* (Lansing: Michigan State University Press, 1963), 187, 227–229.

9 Annette Gordon Reed, "The Persuader," *New Yorker,* June 13 and 20, 2011, 120.

10 Michelle Alexander, *The New Jim Crow* (New York: New Press, 2010), 26.

11 *Scott* v. *Sandford,* 60 U.S. 393 (1857).

12 Taney considered slavery "a blot on our national character." Richard Shenkman, *"I Love Paul Revere, Whether He Rode or Not"* (New York: HarperCollins, 1991), 168.

13 David Von Drehle, "The Way We Weren't," *Time,* April 18, 2011, 42.

14 For an interesting account of this development, see Adam Goodheart, "The Shrug That Made History," *New York Times Magazine,* April 3, 2011, 40.

15 Bruce Ackerman, *We the People: Transformations* (Cambridge, Mass.: Harvard University Press, 1998); George Fletcher, "Unsound Constitution: Oklahoma City and the Founding Fathers," *New Republic,* June 23, 1997, 14–18. These conclusions make dubious the arguments that judges should be guided only by the intentions of the original Founders as they resolve contemporary cases. Ignoring the transformation that occurred as a result of the Civil War and these amendments amounts to using a highly selective and self-serving version of history.

16 Civil Rights Act of 1866; Civil Rights Act of 1871; Civil Rights Act of 1875. These acts reversed the "Black Codes" that southern states passed to deny rights to former slaves.

17 See Nicholas Lemann, *Redemption: The Last Battle of the Civil War* (New York: Farrar, Straus and Giroux, 2006).

18 See Eric Foner, *Reconstruction: America's Unfinished Revolution* (New York: Harper & Row, 1988).

19 Employers included this provision in the contract with their workers, so their workers could be charged with a crime if they quit their job.

20 This and the following paragraphs are drawn from Douglas A. Blackmon, *Slavery by Another Name: The Re-Enslavement of Black Americans from the Civil War to World War II* (New York: Doubleday, 2008).

21 The name *Jim Crow* came from a white performer in the 1820s who had a vaudeville routine in which he blackened his face with burnt cork and mimicked black men. He sang "Wheel About and Turn About and Jump, Jim Crow." This routine led to minstrel shows in high schools and

colleges, with students portraying and satirizing blacks. The shows were popular into the 1960s.

22 Kenneth Karst, "Equality, Law, and Belonging: An Introduction," in *Before the Law,* 5th ed., eds. John J. Bonsignore et al. (Boston: Houghton Mifflin, 1994), 429.

23 Alexander, *The New Jim Crow,* 34. And see pages 25–27 for the application of this strategy to slavery.

24 C. Vann Woodward, *The Strange Career of Jim Crow,* 2nd ed. (London: Oxford University Press, 1966), 44. Their subordination continued for many years. In a 1955 case that gained national attention, fourteen-year-old Chicagoan Emmett Till, visiting relatives in Mississippi, was tortured and murdered for allegedly whistling at a white woman. http://www.emmetttillmurder.com/Emerge%201995.htm.

25 *Civil Rights Cases,* 109 U.S. 3 (1883).

26 *Plessy* v. *Ferguson,* 163 U.S. 537 (1896). The Court's ruling prompted states to expand their Jim Crow laws. Before *Plessy,* states segregated only trains and schools.

27 *Cumming* v. *Richmond County Board of Education,* 175 U.S. 528 (1899). Then the Court enforced segregation in colleges. It upheld a criminal conviction against a private college for teaching blacks together with whites. *Berea College* v. *Kentucky,* 211 U.S. 45 (1908).

28 For an examination of the impact of racist attitudes on black residents in the North, see Thomas J. Shugrue, *Sweet Land of Liberty: The Forgotten Struggle for Civil Rights in the North* (New York: Random House, 2009).

29 See, generally, James W. Loewen, *Sundown Towns: A Hidden Dimension of American Racism* (New York: New Press, 2005).

30 Woodward, *The Strange Career of Jim Crow,* 113. Before the Civil War, northern states had passed some Jim Crow laws, which foreshadowed the more pervasive laws in southern states after the war. Leon F. Litwack, *Trouble in Mind: Black Southerners in the Age of Jim Crow* (New York: Knopf, 1998).

31 Jacqueline Jones, *The Dispossessed: America's Underclasses from the Civil War to the Present* (New York: Basic Books, 1992), 83. And they were still being cheated. One sharecropper went to the landowner at the end of the season to settle up but was told he would not receive any money that year because the landowner needed it to send his son to college. The sharecropper moved to the North. Interview with the sharecropper's son on *The Best of Discovery,* Discovery television channel, June 11, 1995.

32 For an examination of the Great Migration, see Isabel Wilkerson, *The Warmth of Other Suns: The Epic Story of America's Great Migration* (New York: Random House, 2010).

33 Richard Kluger, *Simple Justice* (New York: Knopf, 1976), 89–90.

34 Philip Dray, *At the Hands of Persons Unknown* (New York: Random House, 2002).

35 Ibid.

36 Woodward, *The Strange Career of Jim Crow,* 114.

37 Yet talk of the riot was banished from newspapers, textbooks, and everyday conversations. After some years, most Oklahomans were unaware of it, except those who lived through it. In the 1990s, newspaper articles prompted the state to establish a commission to investigate the riot, leading to more awareness. Jonathan Z. Larsen, "Tulsa Burning," *Civilization,* February–March 1997, 46–55; Brent Staples, "Unearthing a Riot," *New York Times Magazine,* December 19, 1999, 64–69. For an examination, see James S. Hirsch, *Riot and Remembrance: The Tulsa Race War and Its Legacy* (New York: Houghton Mifflin, 2002).

38 For histories, see Thomas R. Pegram, *One Hundred Percent American* (Chicago: Ivan R. Dee, 2011); and Kelly J. Baker, *Gospel According to the Klan: The KKK's Appeal to Protestant America, 1915–1930* (Lawrence: University Press of Kansas, 2011).

39 "Torn from the Land," Associated Press, wire. ap.org. The website offers an investigative report with numerous stories. Also see an examination of mass expulsions in Elliot Jaspin, *Buried in the Bitter Waters: The Hidden History of Racial Cleansing* (New York: Basic Books, 2007).

40 Wilson apparently opposed segregation in government but still allowed it to appease southerners, who were a major portion of his Democratic Party and whose support was essential for his economic reforms.

41 *Guinn v. United States,* 238 U.S. 347 (1915). This clause had been written into election laws to make it more difficult for freed blacks and their children to qualify to vote (their grandfathers having been illiterate slaves) while effectively exempting whites from having to submit to literacy testing.

42 *Buchanan v. Warley,* 245 U.S. 60 (1917).

43 In 1939, the NAACP established the NAACP Legal Defense and Educational Fund as its litigation arm. In 1957, the Internal Revenue Service, pressured by southern members of Congress, ordered the two branches of the NAACP to break their connection or lose their tax-exempt status. Since then, they have been separate organizations, and further references in this chapter to the NAACP are in fact to the NAACP Legal Defense and Educational Fund.

44 Juan Williams, "The Case for Thurgood Marshall," *Washington Post,* February 14, 1999, W16.

45 Kluger, *Simple Justice,* 134.

46 *Missouri ex rel. Gaines v. Canada,* 305 U.S. 337 (1938).

47 *Sweatt v. Painter,* 339 U.S. 629 (1950); *McLaurin v. Oklahoma State Regents,* 339 U.S. 637 (1950).

48 Esther Brown, a white woman from a Kansas City suburb, had a black maid who lived in nearby South Park. In 1948, when Brown saw the decrepit school for black students in South Park, she complained to the board of education in the town. At a meeting, she said, "Look, I don't represent these people. One of them works for me, and I've seen the conditions of their school. I know none of you would want your children educated under such circumstances. They're not asking for integration, just a fair shake." From the audience, Brown received catcalls and demands to go back where she came from. A woman behind her tried to hit her. The school board responded by gerrymandering the black neighborhood out of the South Park school district. Kluger, *Simple Justice,* 388–389.

49 Earl Warren, *The Memoirs of Earl Warren* (Garden City, N.Y.: Doubleday, 1977), 291. However, Eisenhower later advocated the Civil Rights Act of 1957, which created a civil rights commission to investigate voting irregularities and a civil rights division in the Justice Department to prosecute law violations, and he persuaded reluctant Republicans to drop their opposition to civil rights. David A. Nichols, "Ike Liked Civil Rights," *New York Times,* September 12, 2007.

50 Kluger, *Simple Justice,* 656.

51 *Brown v. Board of Education of Topeka,* 347 U.S. 483 (1954).

52 *Holmes v. Atlanta,* 350 U.S. 879 (1955); *Baltimore v. Dawson,* 350 U.S. 877 (1955); *Schiro v. Bynum,* 375 U.S. 395 (1964); *Johnson v. Virginia,* 373 U.S. 61 (1963); *Lee v. Washington,* 390 U.S. 333 (1968).

53 *Brown v. Board of Education II,* 349 U.S. 294 (1955).

54 Justice Tom Clark later told a political science conference that one justice had proposed desegregating one grade a year, beginning with kindergarten or first grade, but this concrete standard was rejected because the other justices felt it would take too long. In retrospect, it might have been quicker, and easier, than the vague standard used.

55 *Griffin v. Prince Edward County School Board,* 377 U.S. 218 (1964); *Norwood v. Harrison,* 413 U.S. 455 (1973); *Gilmore v. Montgomery,* 417 U.S. 556 (1974); *Green v. New Kent County School Board,* 391 U.S. 430 (1968).

56 Quoted in James F. Simon, *In His Own Image* (New York: McKay, 1974), 70.

57 *All Things Considered,* National Public Radio, December 10, 2003.

58 William Cohen and John Kaplan, *Bill of Rights* (Mineola, N.Y.: Foundation Press, 1976), 622.

59 *Swann v. Charlotte-Mecklenburg Board of Education,* 402 U.S. 1 (1971); *Columbus Board of Education v. Penick,* 443 U.S. 449 (1979); *Dayton Board of Education v. Brinkman,* 443 U.S. 526 (1979); *Keyes v. School District 1, Denver,* 413 U.S. 921 (1973).

60 Lee A. Daniels, "In Defense of Busing," *New York Times Magazine,* April 17, 1983, 36–37.

61 Some black parents opposed busing because it disrupted their children's lives and because it implied that their children could learn only by sitting beside white children. But other black parents favored busing because it offered their children an opportunity to go to better schools.

62 White flight began after World War II as affluent families moved to the suburbs. Although it continued for economic reasons, it increased because of busing as well.

63 *Milliken v. Bradley,* 418 U.S. 717 (1974).

64 For example, some suburbs of Kansas City, Missouri, didn't allow black students to attend high schools. Some black families, then, moved back to the city, aggravating both school segregation and residential segregation. James S. Kunen, "The End of Integration," *Time,* April 29, 1996, 41.

65 *Board of Education of Oklahoma City v. Dowell,* 112 L.Ed.2d 715 (1991). The Court said that school districts could stop busing when "the vestiges of past discrimination had been eliminated to the extent practicable." See also *Freeman v. Pitts,* 118 L.Ed.2d 108 (1992).

66 *Missouri v. Jenkins,* 132 L.Ed.2d 63 (1995).

67 Almost all white parents got their first or second choice. Julie Rawe, "When Public Schools Aren't Colorblind," *Time,* December 4, 2006, 54–56.

68 *Parents Involved in Community Schools v. Seattle School District,* 551 U.S. 701 (2007).

69 These districts use race in some way, although most don't use it as extensively as Louisville did. David G. Savage, "Justices Reject School Integration Efforts," *Los Angeles Times,* June 29, 2007, www.latimes.com/news/la-nascotus29jun29,0,2236400,print.story?coll5la-tot-topst. Unlike most justices in the majority, Justice Kennedy indicated that he may be willing to allow some efforts to promote desegregation.

70 Anjetta McQueen, "Desegregation Waning," *Lincoln Journal Star,* May 16, 1999.

71 Alan Finder, "Integrating Schools by Income Is Cited as a Success in Raleigh," *New York Times,* September 25, 2005, YT1. Also see Emily Bazelon, "The Next Kind of Integration," *New York Times Magazine,* July 20, 2008, 37.

72 FBI director J. Edgar Hoover ordered wiretaps that he hoped would link King with communists. When the taps failed to reveal any connection, Hoover had agents bug a hotel room, where they heard King having extramarital sex. Taylor Branch, *Pillar of Fire: America in the King Years, 1963–65* (New York: Simon & Schuster, 1998).

73 Although this sit-in usually is cited as the first, a sit-in at a lunch counter in a drugstore in Wichita, Kansas, actually was the first—in 1958. But the Greensboro sit-in prompted the wave of sit-ins through the South.

74 Woodward, *The Strange Career of Jim Crow,* 186.

75 This incident occurred in 1961. Nicholas Lemann, "The Long March," *New Yorker,* February 10, 2003, 88.

76 The Supreme Court had struck down discrimination in choosing juries, but discrimination continued through informal means. *Norris v. Alabama,* 294 U.S. 587 (1935); *Smith v. Texas,* 311 U.S. 128 (1940); *Avery v. Georgia,* 345 U.S. 559 (1952).

77 An excellent collection of articles is presented in *Reporting Civil Rights: American Journalism, 1941–1973* (New York: Library of America, 2003).

78 Henry Louis Gates Jr., "After the Revolution," *New Yorker,* April 29 and May 6, 1996.

79 Robert A. Caro, "The Compassion of Lyndon Johnson," *New Yorker,* April 1, 2002, 56.

80 Louis Menand, "He Knew He Was Right," *New Yorker,* March 26, 2001, 95.

81 Lemann, "Long March," 86.

82 Goldwater, syndicated columnist David Lawrence, and segregationist senator Richard Russell (D-Ga.), respectively. Frank Rich, "The Rage Is Not about Health Care," *New York Times,* March 28, 2010, WK10.

83 Patrick Reddy, "Why It's Got to Be All or Nothing," *Washington Post National Weekly Edition,* October 18, 1999, 23.

84 This was true for national elections. The transformation took longer for state and local elections.

85 Joseph A. Califano Jr., *The Triumph and Tragedy of Lyndon Johnson* (New York: Simon & Schuster, 1991), 177–178.

86 The Supreme Court unanimously upheld the law. *Heart of Atlanta Motel* v. *United States,* 379 U.S. 421 (1964).

87 For discussion of organized labor's ambivalence toward enactment and enforcement of the employment provisions of the act, see Herbert Hill, "Black Workers, Organized Labor, and Title VII of the 1964 Civil Rights Act: Legislative History and Litigation Record," in *Race in America,* eds. Herbert Hill and James E. Jones (Madison: University of Wisconsin Press, 1993), 263–341.

88 *Griggs* v. *Duke Power,* 401 U.S. 424 (1971). However, standards that hinder blacks more than whites aren't necessarily unlawful. Washington, D.C., required police applicants to pass an exam. Although a higher percentage of blacks failed to pass, the Court said the exam related to the job. *Washington* v. *Davis,* 426 U.S. 229 (1976). The Roberts Court, however, has signaled that it might not require the standards to *closely* relate to the job. *Ricci* v. *DeStefano,* 174 L.Ed.2d 490 (2009). For analysis, see Lani Guinier and Susan Sturm, "Trial by Firefighters," *New York Times,* July 11, 2009, A19.

89 *Shelley* v. *Kraemer,* 334 U.S. 1 (1948).

90 Less directly, the numerous national and state policies that encouraged urban sprawl—such as road building—provided the opportunity for middle-class whites to flock to the suburbs, leaving the cities disproportionately black.

91 For more extensive examination, see Andrew Hacker, *Two Nations: Black and White, Separate, Hostile, Unequal* (New York: Scribner, 1992).

92 Gary Orfield, *Reviewing the Goal of an Integrated Society: A 21st Century Challenge* (Los Angeles: The Civil Rights Project/Proyecto Derechos Civiles at University of California, Los Angeles, January 2010), 17.

93 Gary Orfield, quoted in Mary Jordan, "Separating the Country from the *Brown* Decision," *Washington Post National Weekly Edition,* December 20, 1993, 33. See also Maia

Davis, "Harvard Study Finds New Segregation," *Lincoln Journal Star,* January 20, 2003.

94 Jonathan Kozol, *The Shame of the Nation: The Restoration of Apartheid Schooling in America* (New York: Crown, 2005), 19.

95 Orfield, *Reviewing the Goal of an Integrated Society,* 26.

96 Kozol, *The Shame of the Nation,* 226–227.

97 Orfield, *Reviewing the Goal of an Integrated Society,* 17.

98 Consequently, magnet schools in minority neighborhoods often don't attract many white students. Sandy Banks, "Mixed Results for L.A.'s Magnet Schools," *Los Angeles Times,* January 20, 2006, www.latimes.com/news/local/la-me-magnet20jan20,0,6132919,fullstory?coll=la-home-headlines.

99 Thomas M. Shapiro, *The Hidden Cost of Being African American* (New York: Oxford University Press, 2004), 170–179.

100 Orfield, *Reviewing the Goal of an Integrated Society,* 4.

101 Jordan, "Separating the Country from the *Brown* Decision."

102 Orfield, *Reviewing the Goal of an Integrated Society,* 4–7.

103 Ibid., 7.

104 Kunen, "End of Integration," 39.

105 Jonathan Kozol, *Savage Inequalities: Children in America's Schools* (New York: HarperPerennial, 1992), 4.

106 Ibid., 3.

107 Ibid., 35. However, only three public schools in Alabama are named after King, a native of the state. "Numbers," *Time,* January 24, 2000, 23.

108 Kozol, *The Shame of the Nation,* 24–25.

109 David L. Kirp, "Making Schools Work," *New York Times,* May 20, 2012, SR1.

110 "That's Quite a Range," *Lincoln Journal,* January 21, 1993.

111 Shapiro, *Hidden Cost,* 144–145.

112 In addition, cities have numerous nonprofit institutions—colleges, museums, hospitals—that benefit the entire urban area but don't pay property taxes. According to one estimate, 30 percent of the cities' potential tax base is tax-exempt, compared with 3 percent of the suburbs'. There are a few exceptions.

113 Kozol, *The Shame of the Nation,* 245.

114 Ibid., 60.

115 For an examination of just what it would take, see Paul Tough, "Can Teaching Poor Children to Act More like Middle-Class Children Help Close the Education Gap?" *New York Times Magazine,* November 26, 2006, 44.

116 Charles Peters, "Tilting at Windmills," *Washington Monthly,* March 2006, 6.

117 Kozol, *The Shame of the Nation,* 172.

118 Ibid., 171.

119 Ibid., 53, 84.

120 Tough, "Can Teaching Poor Children to Act More like Middle-Class Children Help Close the Education Gap?" 71.

121 See discussion in Steven Brill, "The Teachers' Unions' Last Stand," *New York Times Magazine,* May 23, 2010, 38.

122 *All Things Considered,* National Public Radio, November 9, 2010.

123 Ben Feller, "Minorities See School as Rougher, Tougher Place," *Lincoln Journal Star,* May 31, 2006, 10A.

124 Paul Tough, "24/7 School Reform," *New York Times Magazine,* September 7, 2008, 17.

125 Steve Lopez, "Money for Stadiums but Not for Schools," *Time,* June 14, 1999, 54.

126 Howard Blume, "Charter Schools' Growth Promoting Segregation, Studies Say," *Los Angeles Times,* February 5, 2010, www.latimes.com/news/local/la-me-charters5-2010feb05,0,3300930.story.

127 Orfield, *Reviewing the Goal of an Integrated Society,* 3.

128 Earl G. Graves, *How to Succeed in Business without Being White* (New York: Harper Business, 1997).

129 Reed Abelson, "Anti-Bias Agency Is Short of Will and Cash," *New York Times,* July 1, 2001, BU1.

130 John Iceland and Daniel Weinberg with Erika Steinmetz, *Racial and Ethnic Residential Segregation in the United States, 1980–2000* (Washington, D.C.: United States Census, 2002), ch. 5. Available at census.gov/hhes/www/housing/housing_patterns/pdf/censr-3.pdf.

131 "Report of the National Commission on Fair Housing and Equal Opportunity," National Commission on Fair Housing and Equal Opportunity, 2008.

132 Iceland and Weinberg with Steinmetz, *Racial and Ethnic Residential Segregation,* ch. 5.

133 Hacker, *Two Nations,* 35–38. For information on why blacks do not want to live in white neighborhoods, see Maria Krysan and Reynolds Farley, "The Residential Preferences of Blacks: Do They Explain Persistent Segregation?" *Social Forces* 80 (2002), 937–980.

134 Ellis Cose, *The End of Anger* (New York: HarperCollins, 2011), 185–201.

135 The banks didn't care about the risk of foreclosure, because they intended to sell the loans to other investors after collecting their fees. Charlie Savage, "Justice Department Fights Bias in Lending," *New York Times,* January 14, 2010, A18; Michael Powell, "Suit Accuses Wells Fargo of Steering Blacks to Subprime Mortgages in Baltimore," *New York Times,* June 7, 2009, A16; Jacob S. Rugh and Douglas S. Massey, "Racial Segregation and the American Foreclosure Crisis," *American Sociological Review* 75, no. 5 (2010), 629–651.

136 According to the Supreme Court's interpretation of Fourth Amendment search and seizure law, police can stop and frisk individuals who officers have a "reasonable suspicion" to believe are committing a crime. But officers must have more

than a hunch to meet the standard of "reasonable suspicion" (though less than the "probable cause" required to obtain a search warrant). A person's race is not a valid criterion, except when the person's race and physical description match those of a particular suspect being sought.

137 Eugene Robinson, "Pulling Over for Prejudice," *Washington Post National Weekly Edition,* May 5–13, 2007, 31.

138 Sandy Banks, "Growing Up on a Tightrope," *Los Angeles Times,* March 3, 2006, www.latimes.com/news/local/la-me boys3mar03,0,2282338.full.story.

139 Richard Fausset and P. J. Huffstutter, "Black Males' Fear of Racial Profiling Very Real, Regardless of Class," *Los Angeles Times,* July 25, 2009, www.latimes.com/news/nationworld/nation/la-na-racial-profiling25-2009jul25,0,5049851,print.story.

140 Jake Tapper, "And Then There Were None," *Washington Post National Weekly Edition,* January 13, 2003, 9.

141 From the Mollen Commission study of police corruption and brutality in New York City in 1994. Cited in Joe Sexton, "Testilying," *New York Times,* May 7, 1994, B1.

142 Alexander, *The New Jim Crow,* 132.

143 Tammerlin Drummond, "Coping with Cops," *Time,* April 3, 2000, 72–73.

144 Alexander, *The New Jim Crow,* 194.

145 David Cole and John Lamberth, "The Fallacy of Racial Profiling," *New York Times,* May 13, 2001, sec. 4, 13.

146 Alexander, *The New Jim Crow,* 67.

147 Thurgood Marshall, quoted in Alexander, *The New Jim Crow,* 60.

148 Jeffrey Goldberg, "The Color of Suspicion," *New York Times Magazine,* June 20, 1999, 53; Alexander, *The New Jim Crow,* 204.

149 Alexander, *The New Jim Crow,* 97.

150 Ibid., 96–97.

151 Ibid., 59.

152 Brent Staples, "The Human Cost of 'Zero Tolerance,'" *New York Times,* April 29, 2012, SR10.

153 Alexander, *The New Jim Crow,* 96.

154 Ibid.

155 Ibid., 184–185.

156 Ibid., 175.

157 Persons caught with small amounts of marijuana may be charged with a misdemeanor and may be sentenced to a state jail or federal prison. Most drug offenses, however, result in a felony.

158 The Equal Employment Opportunity Commission ruled that it is illegal under the Civil Rights Act of 1964 for companies to exclude people based on arrest or conviction records, unless there is a compelling business reason. But companies routinely ignore this ruling and refuse to consider applicants with conviction records, even for entry-level jobs. Brent Staples, "A Fair Shot at a Job," *New York Times,* April 22, 2012, SR10.

159 Alexander, *The New Jim Crow.*

160 Kozol, *Savage Inequalities,* 179–180.

161 Leonard Pitts Jr., "Kramer's Meltdown: If Not Racism, Then What Was It?" *Lincoln Journal Star,* November 26, 2006, 9D.

162 Public Religion Research Center, "Old Alignments, Emerging Fault Lines: Religion in the 2010 Election and Beyond: Findings from the 2010 Post-election American Values Survey," November 2010, 15, publicreligion.org/research/published/?id=428.

163 Richard Thompson Ford, *The Race Card: How Bluffing about Bias Makes Race Relations Worse* (New York: Farrar, Straus and Giroux, 2008), 26.

164 Ibid., 27.

165 Stephan Thernstrom and Abigail Thernstrom, *America in Black and White: One Nation, Indivisible* (New York: Simon & Schuster, 1997), especially part 3. Some improvement began before the civil rights movement, when southern blacks migrated to northern cities in the 1940s.

166 Andrew Tobias, "Now the Good News about Your Money," *Parade,* April 4, 1993, 5.

167 James Smith and Finis Welch, "Race and Poverty: A 40-Year Record," *American Economic Review* 77 (1987), 152–158.

168 However, their rate of home ownership—48 percent—is the same as the national rate was in the 1940s. Whites' rate is 74 percent now. Deborah Kong, "Strides Made, but Still Much Disparity between Blacks, Whites," *Lincoln Journal Star,* July 22, 2002.

169 Joel Garreau, "Candidates Take Note: It's a Mall World after All," *Washington Post National Weekly Edition,* August 10, 1992, 25.

170 For a history of U.S. miscegenation laws, see Peggy Pascoe, *What Comes Naturally* (New York: Oxford University Press, 2009).

171 *Loving* v. *Virginia,* 388 U.S. 1 (1967).

172 Margaret Talbot, "Comment: Wedding Bells," *New Yorker,* May 21, 2012, 19.

173 Paul Taylor, of the Pew Research Center, quoted in Carol Morello, "Study: Intermarriage Rates Soar," *Lincoln Journal Star,* February 16, 2012, A5.

174 This percentage includes Latinos, although they aren't a race, as the chapter will explain. "The New Marriage Boom," *Time,* March 15, 2012, 10.

175 The rates for Asians and Latinos, despite their high levels, have not been expanding, because the increasing populations of these two groups provide more opportunities to date and marry within their group. Asian and Latino youths also report parental pressure to do so. *Weekend Edition,* National Public Radio, May 31, 2009.

176 Morello, "Study: Intermarriage Rates Soar."

177 Ford, *The Race Card,* 30.

178 This is not to say that opposition to affirmative action or welfare spending is necessarily racist. For a review of this research, and also for a creative and sophisticated example of such research, see Charles S. Taber, "Principles of Color: Race, Ideology, and Political Cognition" (Working Draft, 2008, Stony Brook University).

179 Susan Welch and Lee Sigelman, "The 'Obama Effect' and White Racial Attitudes," *Annals of the American Academy of Political and Social Science,* March 2011, 207–220.

180 Leonard Pitts Jr., "For These GOPers, There's Only One Problem: Obama," *Lincoln Journal Star,* August 7, 2011, D10; Clarence Page, "Recent Low Blows Signal Decay in the Art of Political Insults," *Lincoln Journal Star,* August 29, 2011, B5.

181 Maureen Dowd, "Boy, Oh, Boy," *New York Times,* September 13, 2009, WK17.

182 To a significant degree, racial attitudes are intertwined with age differences; older Americans are more racist but also more opposed to Obama's policies, making it difficult to ascertain the role of racial attitudes in their opposition. Matt Bai, "Beneath Divides Seemingly about Race Are Generational Fault Lines," *New York Times,* July 18, 2010, Y15. For other commentary, see Frank Rich, "Small Beer, Big Hangover," *New York Times,* August 2, 2009, WK8; Adam Bradley, "Can We Get Past Race?" *Washington Post National Weekly Edition,* April 13–19, 39. For an examination of the racial dimension of Obama's early presidency, see David Remnick, *The Bridge: The Life and Rise of Barack Obama* (New York: Knopf, 2010).

183 Ellis Cose, *The Rage of a Privileged Class* (New York: HarperCollins, 1993).

184 Ellis Cose, *The End of Anger* (New York: HarperCollins, 2011).

185 Orlando Patterson, quoted in Jervis Anderson, "Black and Blue," *New Yorker,* April 29 and May 6, 1996, 62.

186 From 1967 to 1987, according to calculations by William Julius Wilson. David Remnick, "Dr. Wilson's Neighborhood," *New Yorker,* April 29 and May 6, 1996.

187 Sociologist William Julius Wilson develops this idea extensively in *The Truly Disadvantaged* (Chicago: University of Chicago Press, 1987).

188 U.S. Census Bureau, *Statistical Abstract of the United States, 2001* (Washington, D.C.: Government Printing Office, 2001), tab. 38.

189 Wilson, *The Truly Disadvantaged.*

190 Remnick, "Dr. Wilson's Neighborhood," 98.

191 Richard Thompson Ford, "Why the Poor Stay Poor," *New York Times Book Review,* March 8, 2009, 8.

192 For an examination and analysis, see William Julius Wilson, *More than Just Race* (New York: W. W. Norton, 2009).

193 Rosa A. Smith, "Saving Black Boys," *American Prospect,* February 2004, 49.

194 "Doctor: Harlem's Death Rate Worse than Bangladesh's," *Lincoln Journal,* January 18, 1990.

195 Donald Kaul, "Only Surprise Is That Riots Didn't Happen Sooner," *Lincoln Journal,* May 19, 1992.

196 Kevin Boyle, "The Fire This Time," *Washington Post National Weekly Edition,* August 6–12, 2007, 25.

197 Drummond Ayres Jr., "Decade of Black Struggle: Gains and Unmet Goals," *New York Times,* April 2, 1978, sec. 1, 1.

198 See Veronica Chambers, *Having It All?* (New York: Doubleday, 2003).

199 "Inside America's Largest Minority," *Time,* August 22, 2005, 56.

200 Harold Meyerson, "A Tale of Two Cities," *American Prospect,* June 2004, A8.

201 Except for some immigrant farmworkers, whose situation will be addressed.

202 And among immigrants, skin color makes a difference. Those with lighter skin earn an average of 8 to 15 percent more than similar immigrants with darker skin. Each shade lighter has the same effect as one year more education. Study by Joni Hersch, cited in "Study Finds Higher Income for Lighter-Skinned Immigrants," *New York Times,* January 28, 2007, YT14.

203 Cubans have experienced less discrimination because they were admitted to this country under preferential treatment, and with financial support, due to the Cold War.

204 According to the most recent research, in 2002, Latinos might face somewhat more discrimination in housing than blacks. Latinos who tried to buy a house faced discrimination 20 percent of the time, and those who tried to rent an apartment did so 25 percent of the time. "Hispanics Face More Bias in Housing," *Lincoln Journal Star,* November 8, 2002.

205 Fifty-nine percent of voters in counties in which immigrants are less than 5 percent of the population say that all illegals should be deported. Joe Klein, "Bush Is Smart on the Border—and the G.O.P. Isn't," *Time,* May 29, 2006, 25.

206 Tammerlin Drummond, "It's Not Just in New Jersey," *Time,* June 14, 1999, 61.

207 Lawrence Downs, "When States Put Out the Unwelcome Mat," *New York Times,* March 11, 2012, SR10.

208 In search and seizure law, "reasonable suspicion" means more than a hunch but less than "probable cause." The phrase is vague and frequently the subject of court cases.

209 The state's instructional video for troopers and officers says that they cannot use a person's race to conclude that the person is in the country illegally but can use the person's dress and ability to speak English and can consider whether the person is in an area where illegal immigrants congregate.

210 "Perspectives," *Newsweek,* May 3, 2010, 14.

211 *Arizona v. United States,* 183 L.Ed.2d 351 (2012).

212 The Development, Relief, and Education for Alien Minors Act.

213 In the year ending September 30, 2011.

214 Alex Kotlowitz, "Our Town," *New York Times Magazine,* August 5, 2007, 31.

215 Kelefa Sanneh, "Raging Arizona," *New Yorker,* May 28, 2012, 34.

216 Ibid., 37.

217 Karin Brulliard, "At Odds over Assimilation," *Washington Post National Weekly Edition,* August 20–26, 2007, 35.

218 Kotlowitz, "Our Town," 52.

219 Jacob L. Vigdor, quoted in N. C. Aizenman, "Newcomers to the U.S. Assimilate Rapidly," *Washington Post National Weekly Edition,* May 19–25, 2008, 33. However, for reasons cited earlier in the paragraph, immigrants from Mexico, while following the historical pattern, are assimilating at a slower rate than those from other countries (though in some ways faster than those from India and China).

220 Thomas Boswell and James Curtis, *The Cuban American Experience* (Totowa, N.J.: Rowman & Allanheld, 1983), 191.

221 Kevin F. McCarthy and R. Burciaga Valdez, *Current and Future Effects of Mexican Immigration in California—Executive Summary* (Santa Monica, Calif.: RAND Corp., 1985), 27; Nancy Landale and R. S. Oropesa, "Schooling, Work, and Idleness among Mexican and Non-Latino White Adolescents," working paper, Pennsylvania State University, Population Research Institute, 1997; Pew Hispanic Center, cited in Frank Greve, "English Grows Each Generation," *Lincoln Journal Star,* November 30, 2007, A1.

222 Ruben Navarrette Jr., "Hispanics See Themselves as Part of United States," *Lincoln Journal Star,* December 23, 2002.

223 Ibid.

224 National Public Radio, September 11, 2007.

225 Guadalupe San Miguel, "Mexican American Organizations and the Changing Politics of School Desegregation in Texas, 1945–1980," *Social Science Quarterly* 63 (1982), 701–715.

226 Ibid., 710.

227 Even children of illegal aliens have been given the right to attend public schools by the Supreme Court. The majority assumed that most of these children, although subject to deportation, would remain in the United States, given the large number of illegal aliens who do remain here. Denying them an education would deprive them of the opportunity to fulfill their potential and would deprive society of the benefit of their contribution. *Plyler v. Doe,* 457 U.S. 202 (1982).

228 Luis Ricardo Fraga, Kenneth J. Meier, and Robert E. England, "Hispanic Americans and Educational Policy: Structural Limits to Equal Access and Opportunities for Upward Mobility," unpublished paper, University of Oklahoma, 1985, 6.

229 *San Antonio Independent School District v. Rodriguez,* 411 U.S. 1 (1973).

230 Anjetta McQueen, "Dual-Language Schools Sought," *Lincoln Journal Star,* March 16, 2000.

231 In 1968 Congress encouraged bilingual education by providing funding, and in 1974 the Supreme Court, in a case brought by Chinese parents, held that schools must teach students in a language they can understand. *Lau v. Nichols,* 414 U.S. 563 (1974). This can be their native language, or it can be English if they have been taught

English. These federal actions prompted states to establish bilingual education programs.

232 McQueen, "Dual-Language Schools Sought."

233 "Bilingualism's End Means a Different Kind of Change," *Champaign-Urbana News-Gazette,* June 7, 1998.

234 Margot Hornblower, "No Habla Espanol," *Time,* January 26, 1998, 63.

235 James Traub, "The Bilingual Barrier," *New York Times Magazine,* January 31, 1999, 34–35.

236 John Bowe, "Nobodies," *New Yorker,* April 21, 2003, 106.

237 "Survey: Hispanics Reject Cohesive Group Identity," *Lincoln Journal,* December 15, 1992.

238 Gregory Rodriguez, "Finding a Political Voice," *Washington Post National Weekly Edition,* February 1, 1999, 22–23.

239 A 1995 Census Bureau Survey indicated that 49 percent of native people preferred being called *American Indian,* 37 percent preferred *Native American,* 3.6 percent preferred "some other term," and 5 percent had no preference. Bureau of Labor Statistics, U.S. Census Bureau Survey, May 1995, www.census.gov/prod/2/gen/96arc/ivatuck.pdf.

240 *Cherokee Nation v. Georgia,* 30 U.S. 1 (1831); *Worcester v. Georgia,* 31 U.S. 515 (1832).

241 As the U.S. government got stronger, economically and militarily, in the nineteenth century, its treaty terms toward the Indian tribes got harsher. Arthur Spirling, "U.S. Treaty Making with American Indians: Institutional Change and Relative Power, 1784–1911," *American Journal of Political Science* 56 (January 2012), 84–97.

242 Treaties made exceptions for those who married whites and those who left their tribes and abandoned tribal customs.

243 Vine Deloria Jr. and Clifford M. Lytle, *American Indians, American Justice* (Austin: University of Texas Press, 1983), 221.

244 Ibid., 222–225.

245 Indian Self-Determination Act (1975).

246 Ellen Nakashima and Neely Tucker, "A Fight over Lost Lands, Money Owed," *Washington Post National Weekly Edition,* April 29, 2002, 30. The lawsuit was finally settled in 2009.

247 According to the Indian Gaming Regulatory Act (1988), tribes can establish casinos if their reservation lies in a state that allows virtually any gambling, including charitable "Las Vegas nights."

248 Kathleen Schmidt, "Gambling a Bonanza for Indians," *Lincoln Journal Star,* March 23, 1998.

249 Donald L. Bartlett and James B. Steele, "Wheel of Misfortune," *Time,* December 16, 2002, 44–48.

250 Ibid., 47.

251 W. John Moore, "Tribal Imperatives," *National Journal,* June 9, 1990, 1396.

252 Jack Hitt, "The Newest Indian," *New York Times Magazine,* August 21, 2005, 40–41.

253 Quoted in Ruth B. Ginsburg, *Constitutional Aspects of Sex-Based Discrimination* (Saint Paul, Minn.: West, 1974), 2.

254 Karen De Crow, *Sexist Justice* (New York: Vintage, 1975), 72.

255 Nadine Taub and Elizabeth M. Schneider, "Women's Subordination and the Role of Law," in *The Politics of Law: A Progressive Critique,* rev. ed., ed. David Kairys (New York: Pantheon, 1990), 160–162.

256 *Bradwell* v. *Illinois,* 83 U.S. 130 (1873).

257 From an *amicus curiae* ("friend of the court") brief by 281 historians filed in the Supreme Court case *Webster* v. *Reproductive Health Services,* 106 L.Ed.2d 410 (1989).

258 Donna M. Moore, "Editor's Introduction" in *Battered Women,* ed. Donna M. Moore (Beverly Hills, Calif.: Sage, 1979), 8.

259 Jill Lepore, "Vast Designs," *New Yorker,* October 29, 2007, 92.

260 For a recent biography of Stanton, see Lori D. Ginzberg, *Elizabeth Cady Stanton* (New York: Hill & Wang, 2009). Ginzberg also explores Stanton's racism and elitism.

261 Barbara Sinclair Deckard, *The Women's Movement,* 2nd ed. (New York: Harper & Row, 1979), 303.

262 For an examination of the book's impact, see Stephanie Coontz, *A Strange Stirring: The Feminine Mystique and American Women at the Dawn of the 1960s* (New York: Basic, 2011). In the early 1960s, a board game for girls—*What Shall I Be?*—offered these options: teacher, nurse, stewardess, actress, ballerina, and beauty queen. David Owen, "The Sultan of Stuff," *New Yorker,* July 19, 1999, 60.

263 Reprinted in "Regrets, We Have a Few," *Time Special Issue: 75 Years of* Time, 1998, 192.

264 For an examination of Betty Friedan's role in the movement and the political dynamics among the various factions in the movement, see Judith Hennessee, *Betty Friedan: Her Life* (New York: Random House, 1999). For an examination of women's views toward feminism, see Elinor Burkett, *The Right Women* (New York: Scribner, 1998).

265 Robert Alan Goldberg, *Enemies Within* (New Haven, Conn.: Yale University Press, 2002).

266 De Crow, *Sexist Justice,* 119.

267 This is why Betty Friedan later felt compelled to write a book espousing the concept of motherhood: *The Second Stage* (New York: Summit, 1981).

268 For a discussion of these points, see Jane Mansbridge, *Why We Lost the ERA* (Chicago: University of Chicago Press, 1986); Mary Frances Berry, *Why ERA Failed* (Bloomington: Indiana University Press, 1986); Janet Boles, "Building Support for the ERA: A Case of 'Too Much, Too Late,'" *PS: Political Science and Politics* 15 (1982), 575–592.

269 Shenkman, *"I Love Paul Revere,"* 136–137.

270 *Reed* v. *Reed,* 404 U.S. 71 (1971).

271 *Hoyt* v. *Florida,* 368 U.S. 57 (1961).

272 *Taylor* v. *Louisiana,* 419 U.S. 522 (1975).

273 *Stanton* v. *Stanton,* 421 U.S. 7 (1975).

274 Cases were from 2002. They were compiled by the WAGE Project (www.wageproject.org) and examined and reported in Evelyn F. Murphy, with E. J. Graff, *Getting Even: Why Women Don't Get Paid like Men—and What to Do about It* (New York: Simon & Schuster, 2005), 40–48. This total also includes sexual harassment suits, which, of course, reflect a type of sexual discrimination.

275 Ibid., 56.

276 Ibid., 157.

277 Ibid., 153

278 Ibid., 60–61.

279 Ibid., 84–85.

280 Ibid., 200.

281 Ibid., 199.

282 Ibid., 4.

283 Frank Bass, "Shining Shoes Surest Way Women Earn More," *Lincoln Journal Star,* March 18, 2012, B8. Also see Mika Brzezinski, *Knowing Your Value: Women, Money, and Getting What You're Worth* (New York: Weinstein Books, 2010).

284 *All Things Considered,* National Public Radio, September 1, 2010.

285 Murphy, *Getting Even,* 185.

286 The phrase itself is not new. It was used by workers in the nineteenth century and as the title of a book by a Catholic priest in 1906. Jon Gertner, "What Is a Living Wage?" *New York Times Magazine,* January 15, 2006, 42.

287 For discussion, see ibid., 38.

288 Lisa McLaughlin, "In Brief," *Time,* October 9, 2000, G12.

289 For discussion, see Murphy, *Getting Even,* 194–213.

290 See ibid. for numerous examples.

291 According to a *Time* poll. Nancy Gibbs, "What Women Want Now," *Time,* October 26, 2009, 30.

292 David Crary, "U.S. among Worst in Family vs. Work Policies," *Lincoln Journal Star,* February 1, 2007, 5A. And unlike 145 other countries, the United States doesn't require employers to provide paid sick days. Most employers do provide paid sick days for salaried employees but not for hourly employees.

293 The Family and Medical Leave Act. The act also requires employers to continue health insurance coverage during the leave and to give the employee the same job or a comparable one upon her or his return.

294 Lisa Genasci, "Many Workers Resist Family Benefit Offers," *Lincoln Journal Star,* June 28, 1995.

295 Tara Parker-Pope, "Now, Dad Feels as Stressed as Mom," *New York Times,* June 20, 2010, WK1.

296 Jodie Levin-Epstein, "Responsive Workplaces," *American Prospect,* March 2007, A16.

297 Joan C. Williams, "The Opt-Out Revolution Revisited," *American Prospect,* March 2007, A14.

298 Ruth Davis Konigsberg, "Chore Wars," *Time,* August 8, 2011, 46–47.

299 Heather Boushey, "Values Begin at Home, but Who's Home?" *American Prospect,* March 2007, A2.

300 Ann Crittenden, "Parents Fighting Back," *American Prospect,* June, 2003, 22.

301 *Mentor Savings Bank* v. *Vinson,* 91 L.Ed.2d 49 (1986).

302 *Oncale* v. *Sundowner Offshore Services,* 140 L.Ed.2d 201 (1998).

303 Ibid.

304 Joyce Gelb and Marian Lief Palley, *Women and Public Policies* (Princeton, N.J.: Princeton University Press, 1982), 102. The author of Title IX, Rep. Patsy Mink (D.-Hawaii), had applied to medical schools but was not considered because she was a woman. Mink intended Title IX to open the doors. She said it was "never intended to mean equal numbers or equal money" in athletics. Susan Reimer, "Title IX Has Unintended Consequences," *Lincoln Journal Star,* April 9, 2000.

305 R. Vivian Acosta and Linda Jean Carpenter, *Women in Intercollegiate Sport: A Longitudinal, National Study. A Thirty-Three-Year Update,* 2010, http://webpages.charter.net/womeninsport/; www.womenssportsfoundation.org/cgi-bin/iowa/issues/part/article.html?record=1107.

306 Welch Suggs, "Uneven Progress for Women's Sports," *Chronicle of Higher Education,* April 7, 2000, A52–A56; Bill Pennington, "More Men's Teams Benched as Colleges Level the Field," *New York Times,* May 9, 2002, A1; Susan Welch and Lee Sigelman, "Who's Calling the Shots: Women Coaches in Women's Division I Athletics," *Social Science Quarterly* 88 (December 2007), 1415–1434.

307 Suggs, "Uneven Progress for Women's Sports," A52.

308 Michele Orecklin, "Now She's Got Game," *Time,* March 3, 2003, 57.

309 "Title IX Facts Everyone Should Know," www.womenssportsfoundation.org/cgibin/iowa/issues/geena/record,html?record=862.

310 Mary Duffy, quoted in E. J. Dionne Jr., "Nothing Wacky about Title IX," *Washington Post National Weekly Edition,* May 19, 1997, 26.

311 *Mississippi University for Women* v. *Hogan,* 458 U.S. 718 (1982).

312 *Orr* v. *Orr,* 440 U.S. 268 (1979).

313 *Michael M.* v. *Sonoma County,* 450 U.S. 464 (1981).

314 *Rostker* v. *Goldberg,* 453 U.S. 57 (1981).

315 *Planned Parenthood of Southeastern Pennsylvania* v. *Casey,* 120 L.Ed.2d 674 (1992).

316 Early decisions include *University of California Regents* v. *Bakke,* 438 U.S. 265 (1978); *United Steelworkers* v. *Weber,* 443 U.S. 193 (1979); and *Fullilove* v. *Klutznick,* 448 U.S. 448 (1980).

317 Two critics include Thomas Sowell, *Preferential Policies: An International Perspective* (New York: Morrow, 1990), and Dinesh D'Souza, *Illiberal Education* (New York: Free Press, 1991).

318 *United Steelworkers* v. *Weber; Sheet Metal Workers* v. *EEOC,* 92 L.Ed.2d 344 (1986); *Firefighters* v. *Cleveland,* 92 L.Ed.2d 405 (1986); *United States* v. *Paradise Local Union,* 94 L.Ed.2d 203 (1987).

319 *Firefighters* v. *Stotts,* 467 U.S. 561 (1985); *Wygant* v. *Jackson Board of Education,* 90 L.Ed.2d 260 (1986).

320 *Richmond* v. *Croson,* 102 L.Ed.2d 854 (1989); *Adarand Constructors* v. *Pena,* 132 L.Ed.2d 158 (1995).

321 Quoted in Robert J. Samuelson, "End Affirmative Action," *Washington Post National Weekly Edition,* March 6, 1995, 5.

322 Private companies that have government contracts, and therefore are subject to affirmative action, have shown more improvement in hiring minorities and women than other companies have. State and local governments, also subject to affirmative action, have shown more improvement in hiring than private companies have.

323 James E. Jones, "The Genesis and Present Status of Affirmative Action in Employment," paper presented at the annual meeting of the American Political Science Association, Washington, D.C., September 1984; Nelson C. Dometrius and Lee Sigelman, "Assessing Progress toward Affirmative Action Goals in State and Local Government," *Public Administration Review* 44 (1984), 241–247; Peter Eisinger, *Black Employment in City Government* (Washington, D.C.: Joint Center for Political Studies, 1983); Milton Coleman, "Uncle Sam Has Stopped Running Interference for Blacks," *Washington Post National Weekly Edition,* December 19, 1983.

324 This "is one of the better kept secrets of the debate." Alan Wolfe, "Affirmative Action, Inc.," *New Yorker,* November 25, 1996, 107. See also the numerous sources cited there.

325 Joe Klein, "There's More than One Way to Diversity," *Time,* December 18, 2006, 29.

326 Gertrude Ezorsky, *Racism and Justice: The Case for Affirmative Action* (Ithaca, N.Y.: Cornell University Press, 1991), 48–49, 63–65.

327 Wilson, *The Truly Disadvantaged.*

328 Donald Kaul, "Privilege in Workplace Invisible to White Men Who Enjoy It," *Lincoln Journal Star,* April 9, 1995; Richard Morin and Lynne Duke, "A Look at the Bigger Picture," *Washington Post National Weekly Edition,* March 16, 1992, 9.

329 Eisinger, *Black Employment in City Government.*

330 Thomas J. Kane, "Racial and Ethnic Preference in College Admissions," paper presented at the Ohio State University College of Law Conference, "Twenty Years after *Bakke,*" Columbus, April 1998.

331 *Gratz* v. *Bollinger,* 156 L.Ed.2d 257 (2003); *Grutter* v. *Bollinger,* 156 L.Ed.2d 304 (2003).

332 These manifestations of affirmative action weren't at issue in the case, but the companies and the officers assumed that they could be affected, at least indirectly, by the ruling. Jeffrey Toobin, *The Nine: Inside the Secret World of the Supreme Court* (New York: Doubleday, 2007), 212–214.

333 Chief Justice Roberts and Justices Alito, Scalia, and Thomas. The question mark is Justice Kennedy.

334 James Traub, "The Class of Prop. 209," *New York Times Magazine,* May 2, 1999, 51.

335 John Larew, "Why Are Droves of Unqualified, Unprepared Kids Getting into Our Top Colleges?" *Washington Monthly,* June 1991, 10–14; Theodore Cross, "Suppose There Was No Affirmative Action at the Most Prestigious Colleges and Graduate Schools," *Journal of Blacks in Higher Education,* March 31, 1994, 47, 50; Klein, "There's More than One Way to Diversify," 29.

336 For an examination of the *Bakke* ruling and its impact on graduate schools, see Susan Welch and John Gruhl, *Affirmative Action and Minority Enrollments in Medical and Law Schools* (Ann Arbor: University of Michigan Press, 1998).

337 Richard H. Sander, "House of Cards for Black Law Students," *Los Angeles Times,* December 20, 2004, www.latimes.com/news/opinion/la-oe-sander20dec20,0,436015,print.story; Adam Liptak, "For Blacks in Law School, Can Less Be More?" *New York Times,* February 13, 2005, WK3.

338 Shelby Steele, "Affirmative Action Is Just a Distraction," *Washington Post National Weekly Edition,* August 3–9, 2009, 27.

339 Stephen Carter, quoted in David Owen, "From Race to Chase," *New Yorker,* June 3, 2002, 54.

Focus On...Spending and Taxing

1 As quoted in Michael Lind, *Land of Promise, An Economic History of the United States* (New York: HarperCollins, 2012), 21.

2 E. J. Dione Jr., *Our Divided Political Heart: The Battle for the American Idea in an Age of Discontent* (New York: Bloomsbury, 2012), 155–188.

3 Paul Krugman, "What a Real External Bank Bailout Looks Like," *New York Times,* June 17, 2012, http://krugman.blogs.nytimes.com/2012/06/17/what-a-real-external-bank-bailout-looks-like/. Another $50 billion bailed out savings and loans in the rest of the nation.

4 James Surowiecki, "The Financial Page: No End In Sight," *The New Yorker,* April 30, 2012, p. 23.

5 Ylan Q. Mu, "Decades of Wealth Gone," *Lincoln Journal Star,* June 12, 2012, A1.

6 "Recession Doubles Number of States with High Child Poverty Rates," *Capitol Journal,* January 9, 2012.

7 Alan Simpson echoing Erskine Bowles, cochairs of the president's deficit reduction commission, in "Ten Questions," *Time,* August 8, 2011, 64.

8 "The Great Prosperity," *New York Times,* September 4, 2011, SR6.

9 James K. Galbraith, *Balancing Acts: Technology, Finance, and the American Future* (New York: Basic Books, 1989); Robert L. Heilbroner and Lester C. Thurow, *Five Economic Challenges* (Englewood Cliffs, N.J.: Prentice Hall, 1981), 62.

10 For an accessible but brief analysis of deflation, see Paul Krugman, "Why Is Deflation Bad?" *New York Times,* August 2, 2010, krugman.blogs.nytimes.com/2010/08/02/why-is-deflation-bad/. For a more extended discussion by the same author, see "Can Deflation Be Prevented?" http://web.mit.edu/krugman/www/deflator.html.

11 Office of Management and Budget, *Historical Tables,* Table 15.3, http://www.whitehouse.gov/omb/budget/Historicals.

12 Congressional Budget Office, "Deficits or Surpluses Projected in CBO's March 2012 Baseline," supplement to *Updated Budget Projections: Fiscal Years 2012 to 2022,* March 2012.

13 Anna Stolley Persky, "Fiscally Unfit: Writing America's Future in Red," *Washington Lawyer,* April 2011.

14 It also borrows money from itself—the parts of government that have surplus funds.

15 Kimberly Amadeo, "U.S. Federal Budget Deficit," The *New York Times About.com,* based on Congressional Budget Office and Office of Management and Budget, 2012, http://useconomy.about.com/od/fiscalpolicy/p/deficit.htm.

16 CBO figures, provided by Ron Haskins in "Addressing the Budget Deficit: The Next President Must Solve the U.S. Deficit Crisis," policy brief, January 19, 2012, in Brookings Institution, Campaign 2012, www.brookings.edu. For an excellent debate regarding the need to cut the deficit, see the commentaries that accompany this paper.

17 After the first year with a budget surplus, the Clinton administration used Social Security and other funds to generate a larger "budget surplus" for the next two years. Previous administrations had not used these funds in this way, but subsequent administrations have followed Clinton's practice, so the official budget numbers reflect these funds now. The deficits would be larger without these funds.

18 Victor Allred, "PAYGO Goes by the Wayside," *Congressional Quarterly Weekly Report,* January 13, 2001, 96.

19 John Maggs, "Winners and Losers in the Bush Economy," *National Journal,* May 15, 2004, 1495.

20 These CBO numbers were reported by Bruce Bartlett, "The Fiscal Legacy of George W. Bush," June 12, 2012, http://economix.blogs.nytimes.com/2012/06/12/the-fiscal-legacy-of-george-w-bush/pagemode=print.

21 "Adding to the Deficit, Bush vs. Obama," *Washington Post,* January 31, 2012. Ezra Klein, "Doing the Math on Obama's Deficits," *Washington Post,* January 31, 2012, www.washingtonpost.com/business/economy/ezra-klein-doing-the-math-on-obamas-deficits/2012/01/31/gIQAnRs7fQ_print.html.

22 James K. Galbraith, "No Return to Normal," *Washington Monthly,* March/April 2009, pp. 21-22.

23 Tim Dickinson, "The Party of the Rich," *Rolling Stone* (24 November 2011): 46-57.

24 Ronald M. Peters, Jr., "Debt, Deficit, and Dysfunction," *extensions* (Summer 2012): 2-5.

25 Michael Grunwald, "One Nation, Subsidized," *Time,* September 17, 2012, p. 37

26 "Problems Cited at IRS Help Centers," *Champaign-Urbana News-Gazette,* September 4, 2003, 1.

27 Center on Budget and Policy Priorities, "Top Ten Tax Charts," April 14, 2011, www.offthechartsblog.org/top-ten-tax-charts/.

28 Alan Krueger, speech on inequality at the Center for American Progress, January 12, 2012. Transcript posted by Ezra Klein, *Washington Post,* January 12, 2012.

29 Kevin McCormally, "The Most-Overlooked Tax Deductions," *Kiplinger,* November 27, 2011, www.kiplinger.com/printstory.php?pid=18946.

30 Former chair of the Senate Finance Committee, Bob Packwood (R-Ore.), quoted in ibid., 323.

31 For a discussion of these multiple motivations in taxation and in budget politics, see Isabel Sawhill's commentary on Rep. Paul Ryan's budget proposal, "In Defense of Paul Ryan's Budget Plan," March 30, 2012, www.brookings.edu/opinions/2012/0320_republican_budget_sawhill.aspx?p=1.

32 Joseph L. Schatz, "The Power of the Status Quo," *CQ Weekly,* February 6, 2006, 322.

33 Alex Brill, "Framework for Evaluating Tax Extenders," testimony before the House Ways and Means Committee, June 8, 2012, www.aei.org/print/framework-for-evaluating-tax-extenders.

34 John Crawford, "Code Words: Tax Neutrality," *CQ Weekly,* February 7, 2005, 289. The economist quoted is Alice Rivlin, former director of the CBO and the OMB and former vice chair of the Fed.

35 As quoted in Lind, *Land of Promise,* 169.

36 As quoted in ibid., 363.

37 http://economistsview.typepad.com/economistsview/2010/08/cbo-estimated-impact-of-the-stimulus-package.html. See also "Did the Stimulus Work? A Review of Nine Best Studies," http://www.washingtonpost.com/blogs/ezra-klein/post/did-the-stimulus-work-a-review-of-the-nine-best-studies-on-the-subject/2011/08/16/gIQAThbibJ_blog.html.

38 See, for example, the speeches delivered by President Obama and Mitt Romney in Ohio on June 14, 2012. For the text of Obama's speech, see www.washingtonpost.com/politics/full-transcript-of-obamas-speech-on-the-economy-in-cleveland-ohio/2012/06/14/gJQAdY10cV_print.html.

39 Edward R. Tufte, *Political Control of the Economy* (Princeton, N.J.: Princeton University Press, 1978).

40 Andrew Dugan, "Special Briefing: The Top Five Challenges Obama Faces," The Gallup Poll, November 7, 2012.

41 The study was done by Irwin Kellner, senior economist for MarketWatch, cited in Marshall Loeb, "Where Will the Economy Go from Here?" *Lincoln Journal Star,* July 6, 2008, H1.

42 Larry M. Bartels, *Unequal Democracy: The Political Economy of the New Gilded Age* (Princeton, N.J.: Princeton University Press, 2008).

Focus On...Health Care Reform

1 Central Intelligence Agency, "Life Expectancy at Birth," *The World Factbook.* https://www.cia.gov/library/publications/the-world-factbook//fields/2102.html#xx.

2 Robert H. Frank, "Giving Health Care a Chance to Evolve," *New York Times,* July 1, 2012.

3 Ezekiel J. Emanuel, "How Much Does Health Cost?" *New York Times,* October 30, 2011, 5.

4 A history of the Public Health Service and its current mission is at www.usphs.gov/AboutUs/mission.aspx.

5 www.usphs.gov/AboutUs/mission.aspx.

6 Robert Fitch, "Big Labor's Big Secret," *New York Times,* December 28, 2005, A19.

7 Kevin Sack, "The Short End of the Longer Life," *New York Times,* April 27, 2008, WK1. David Morgan, "More Uninsured Americans Die Each Year," Reuters, June 20, 2012. For Gallup poll findings, see "Number of Uninsured in U.S. Rises as Workers Lose Jobs and Health Insurance," *Huffington Post,* February 14, 2012.

8 Ezra Klein, "How Big Is 50.7 Million Unemployed?" *Washington Post,* July 12, 2012; http://www.washingtonpost.com/blogs/ezra-klein/wp/2012/07/12/how-big-is-50-7-million-uninsured/.

9 "Who are the Uninsured?" *New York Times,* August 23, 2009, http://prescriptions.blogs.nytimes.com/2009/08/23/who-are-the-uninsured/.

10 The findings of a study on this subject appear in "Trends in Quality of Care and Racial Disparities in Medicare Managed Care," *New England Journal of Medicine,* August 18, 2005, 692–700.

11 Neal Boortz, quoted on *Real Clear Politics,* http://www.realclearpolitics.com/video/2010/10/14/neal_boortz_on_the_moocher_class.html. "The Moocher Class," *TheRightRant,* http://therightrant.blogspot.com/2011/06/moocher-class.html

12 The average recipient of Social Security and Medicare receives significantly more in benefits than he or she ever paid in Social Security and Medicare taxes (even if interest on the taxes over one's lifetime is factored in).

13 Clarke E. Cochran et al., *American Public Policy,* 6th ed. (New York: St. Martin's/Worth, 1999), 282.

14 Medicare does not cover most nursing home care, however.

15 Centers for Medicaid and Medicare, Medicaid Program—General Information, www.cms.hhs.gov; Robert Pear, "Nursing Home Inspections Miss Violations, Report Says," *New York Times,* January 16, 2006, A9.

16 Before the recession, the federal government paid, on average, 57 percent of the costs; after the recession, it paid 66 percent. Kaiser Family Foundation estimates.

17 Erin Heath, "Medicaid: The Pendulum Swings," *National Journal,* August 9, 2003, 2546.

18 Ricardo Alonso-Zaldivar, "Study: Medicaid Expansion May Be Lifesaver," *Lincoln Journal Star,* July 26, 2012, A3.

19 Kevin Sack, "Recession Drove Many to Medicaid Last Year," *New York Times,* September 30, 2010. The Kaiser Family Foundation, "Medicaid & CHIP," statehealthfacts.org.

20 Robert Pear, "New Medicaid Rules Allow States to Set Premiums and Higher Co-payments," *New York Times,* November 27, 2011.

21 Kaiser Family Foundation estimates.

22 Lou Cannon, "Cascading Medicaid Cuts Hurt the Poor and Burden the States," *StateNet Capitol Journal,* February 21, 2011.

23 Those interested in variations in health care across the United States and by hospital can find data at the Dartmouth Atlas of Health Care. Their studies are based on analyses of millions of Medicare records.

24 "All Over the Map: Elective Procedure Rates in California Vary Widely," *California Health Care Foundation,* September 2011, http://www.chcf.org/publications/2011/09/medical-variation-rates-california#procedure=hipr&region=hsa&c=6/37.41928/-123.39017.

25 "Europe Mulls Private Medical Care," *Champaign-Urbana News-Gazette,* November 29, 2003, A3.

26 Paul Krugman, "Our Sick Society," *New York Times,* May 5, 2006, A23; the study he quotes was published in the *Journal of the American Medical Association.* See also Anna Bernasek, "Health Care Problem? Check the American Psyche," *New York Times,* December 3, 2006, BU3.

27 Karen David, Cathy Schoen, and Kristof Stremitis, *Mirror, Mirror, on the Wall: How the Performance of U.S. Health Care Compares Internationally: 2010 Update,* http://www.commonwealthfund.org/~/media/Files/Publications/Fund%20Report/2010/Jun/1400_Davis_Mirror_Mirror_on_the_wall_2010.pdf.

28 Ibid.

29 Hillary Rodham Clinton, "Now Can We Talk about Health Care?" *New York Times Magazine,* April 18, 2004, 30; Price Waterhouse Cooper,, "The Price of Excess," http://www.pwc.com/us/en/healthcare/publications/the-price-of-excess.jhtml.

30 Robert Kelley, "Where Can $700 Billion in Waste Be Cut from Our Healthcare System?" Thompson-Reuters, 2009, http://www.factsforhealthcare.com/whitepaper/HealthcareWaste.pdf.

31 Katherine Q. Seelye, "Looking Abroad for Health Savings," *New York Times,* November 8, 2009, 25.

32 Jonathan Gruber, *Health Care Reform* (New York: Hill and Wang, 2011).

33 Paul Krugman, "After Reform Passes," *New York Times,* October 26, 2009.

34 U.S. Health and Human Services Department, "Massachusetts Health Care Reform: Six Years Later," *Focus on Health Reform,* May 2012. Gruber, *Health Care Reform.*

35 Mark Sherman, "Doctors Call for National Coverage," *Lincoln Journal Star,* August 13, 2003, 1.

36 Robin Toner and Janet Elder, "Most Support U.S. Guarantee of Health Care," *New York Times,* March 2, 2007, 1.

37 For insurance industry lobbying, see "Insurance," *Open Secrets,* http://www.opensecrets .org/industries/indus.php?ind=F09.

38 "Health Background," *Open Secrets,* http:// www.opensecrets.org/industries/background. php?cycle=2012&ind=H.

39 It can be debated whether forcing individuals to buy insurance stimulates individual responsibility, but that was the premise.

40 Dana Milbank, "An Ugly Finale for Health Care Reform," *Washington Post,* December 21, 2009. Kristina Wong, "Byrd Overcomes Health, Weather to Cast Vote for Final Senate Health Care Bill," *ABC News,* December 24, 2009, abcnews.go.com/ blogs/2009/12/byrd-overcomes-health-weather-to-cast-vote-for-final-senate-health-care-bill/.

41 It also reduces the tax break for health care costs, via "flex" (reimbursement) accounts, used by some middle-class people.

42 Fareed Zakaria, "Curbing the Cost of Health Care," *Washington Post,* July 4, 2012, http://www. washingtonpost.com/opinions/fareed-zakaria-curbing-the-cost-of-health-care/2012/07/04/ gJQAxkr7NW_story.html.

43 Although the law is an attempt to provide universal coverage, the government acknowl-edges that some people, especially those who don't qualify for Medicaid and who can't afford to buy insurance even with a subsidy, will be left uncovered.

44 Mark Meckler and Jenny Beth Martin, *Tea Party Patriots, The Second American Revolution* (New York: Henry Holt and Company, 2011), 42.

45 Theda Skocpol and Vanessa Williamson, *The Tea Party and the Remaking of Republican Conservativism* (New York: Oxford University Press, 2012), 169–171.

Focus On...
Environmental Policy

1 Albert Gore Jr., "Earth Days Have Become Earth Years," *New York Times,* April 23, 1995, E16.

2 Environmental Protection Agency, *Our Nation's Air: Status and Trends through 2008,* http://www. epa.gov/airtrends/2010/ (accessed May 13, 2010).

3 U.S. Centers for Disease Control, *The Fourth National Report on Human Exposure to Environmental Chemicals,* 2009, http://www.cdc .gov/exposurereport/ (accessed May 14, 2010).

4 Norman J. Vig and Michael E. Kraft, eds., *Environmental Policy: New Directions for the Twenty-first Century,* 7th ed. (Washington, D.C.: CQ Press, 2009), 16.

5 BBC News: *Science and Environment,* "Global Carbon Emissions Reach Record, Says IEA," May 30, 2011, http://www.bbc.co.uk/news/ science-environment-13595174.

6 Lynn White Jr., "The Historical Roots of Our Ecological Crisis," *Science* 155 (March 10, 1967).

7 See Robert Nisbet, *The History of the Idea of Progress* (New York: Basic Books, 1980), for an interesting examination of the idea of progress from antiquity to the present.

8 See Kenneth J. Meier, *Regulation* (New York: St. Martin's Press, 1985), ch. 6, for an overview of early attempts by the federal government to protect the environment.

9 Souder, William, *On a Farther Shore: The Life and Legacy of Rachel Carson* (New York: Crown Publishing, 2012).

10 James Anderson, David Brady, and Charles Bullock, *Public Policy and Politics in America* (North Scituate, Mass.: Duxbury, 1977), 74.

11 National Environmental Policy Act.

12 Meier, *Regulation,* 145; Norman Vig and Michael Kraft, "Environmental Policy from the Seventies to the Eighties," in *Environmental Policy in the 1980s,* eds. Vig and Kraft (Washington, D.C.: CQ Press, 1984), 16.

13 Information about the founding of the EPA is drawn from Steven A. Cohen, "EPA: A Qualified Success," in *Controversies in Environmental Policy,* eds. Sheldon Kamieniecki, Robert O'Brien, and Michael Clarke (Albany: State University of New York Press, 1986), 174–199; Meier, *Regulation,* 142–146.

14 Clean Air Act.

15 Juliet Eilperin, "Toxic Releases Rose 16 Percent in 2010, EPA Says," *Washington Post,* January 5, 2012, http://www.washingtonpost.com/national/ health-science/toxic-releases-rose-16-percent-in-2010-epa-says/2012/01/05/gIQAhbTpdP_story. html?wpisrc=nl_politics.

16 Meier, *Regulation,* 147.

17 Charles Duhigg, "Millions in U.S. Drink Dirty Water, Records Show," *New York Times,* December 8, 2009, http://www.nytimes.com/2009/12/08/ business/energy-environment/08water.html?_r=1 &scp=1&sq=December+8+2009&st=nyt (accessed December 9, 2009).

18 "Cold War Testing Could Have Killed 11,000," *Champaign-Urbana News-Gazette,* March 2, 2002, A5.

19 "They Lied to Us," *Time,* October 31, 1988, 64.

20 Edward Flattau, *Green Morality: Mankind's Role in Environmental Responsibility* (Los Angeles: The Way Things Are Publications, 2011).

21 See Walter A. Rosenbaum, *Environmental Politics and Policy,* 7th ed. (Washington, D.C.: CQ Press, 126–127; David Bollier and Joan Claybrook, *Freedom from Harm* (Washington, D.C.: Public Citizen and Democracy Project, 1986), 116.

22 *Statistical Abstract of the United States, 1999,* 119th ed., tab. 415 (Washington, D.C.: Bureau of the Census, Economics and Statistics Administration, 1999).

23 Quoted in Bollier and Claybrook, *Freedom from Harm,* 95.

24 "Geoengineering: We All Want to Change the World," *The Economist,* March 31, 2010, http:// www.economist.com/science-technology/ displaystory.cfm?story_id=15814427 (accessed April 28, 2010).

25 Pew Research Center for the People and the Press, *The Public's Political Agenda,* January 25, 2010, http://pewresearch.org/pubs/1472/public-priorities-president-congress-2010 (accessed May 15, 2010).

26 Josh Dorfman, "It's a Communication Challenge, not a Scientific Challenge," *Huffington Post,* August 25, 2010, http://www.huffingtonpost. com/josh-dorfman/its-a-communication-chall_b_694464.html.

27 Ibid.

28 Ker Than, "Americans Least Green—And Feel Least Guilt, Survey Suggests: Global survey reveals differing attitudes on green living," *National Geographic News,* July 12, 2012, http://news.nationalgeographic.com/ news/2012/07/120712-greendex-environment-green-sustainable-science-consumers-world/ (accessed September 17, 2012).

29 *New York Times*/CBS News poll on the Gulf of Mexico oil spill, June 16–20, 2010, http:// documents.nytimes.com/new-york-timescbs-news-poll-on-the-gulf-of-mexico-oil-spill (accessed July 10, 2010).

30 Daniel J. Weiss, "Excuses: Ten Industry Arguments against Action on Global Warming...and Why They Are Wrong," Center for American Progress, May 30, 2008, http://www.americanprogress.org /issues/2008/05/boxer_myths.html (accessed May 15, 2010).

31 Keith Schneider, "For the Environment, Com-passion Fatigue," *New York Times,* November 6, 1994, E3.

32 National Audubon Society fundraising letter, cited by Keith Schneider, "Big Environment Hits a Recession," *New York Times,* January 1, 1995, F4. Other critical assessments of the environmental movement's pessimistic outlook can be found in Martin W. Lewis, *Green Delusions* (Durham, N.C.: Duke University Press, 1992); Bill McKibben, "An Explosion of Green," *Atlantic Monthly,* April 1995, 61–83; and Evan J. Ringquist, "Is 'Effective Regulation' Always Oxymoronic? The States and Ambient Air Quality," *Social Science Quarterly* 76, no. 1 (March 1995), 69–87.

33 Daniel B. Smith, "Is There an Ecological Unconscious?" *New York Times,* January 31, 2010, http://www.nytimes.com/2010/01/31/ magazine/31ecopsych-t.html (accessed May 15, 2010).

34 David Osborne and Ted Gaebler, *Reinventing Government: How the Entrepreneurial Spirit Is Transforming the Public Sector* (New York: Penguin [Plume], 1992), 299–305.

35 Philip Shabecoff, "Tax Proposed on Products and Activities That Harm Environment," *New York Times,* February 10, 1991, 1.

36 This view was expressed in Philip Howard's best-selling book on regulatory law, *The Death of Common Sense* (New York: Warner Books, 1994).

37 Chuck Tremper, *As the Oceans Rise: Meeting the Challenges of Global Warming* (Bethesda, Md.: Sustainable Planet Publishing, 2008).

38 Doyle Rice and Chuck Raasch, "Little Relief from the Heat after Hottest July Ever," *USA Today*, August 8, 2012, http://www.usatoday.com/weather/climate/story/2012-08-08/hottest-july-us-history/56873854/1?csp=34news (accessed September 18, 2012).

39 Audrey, "The Health Costs of Climate Change: $14 Billion," *Public Health Newswire*, November 8, 2011, http://www.publichealthnewswire.org/?p=1826.

40 Justin Gillis, "Carbon Emissions Show Biggest Jump Ever Recorded," *New York Times*, December 4, 2011, http://www.nytimes.com/2011/12/05/science/earth/record-jump-in-emissions-in-2010-study-finds.html?_r=1.

41 Wynne Parry, "Greenhouse Gas Emissions Continue to Climb in 2011." CBS News. http://www.cbsnews.com/8301-205_162-57476887/greenhouse-gas-emissions-continue-to-climb-in-2011/. July 20, 2012 (accessed September 18, 2012).

42 S. Philander and Ed George, *Encyclopedia of Global Warming and Climate Change: An Introduction.* (Thousand Oaks, CA: Sage Publications, 2008).

43 Naomi Klein, "Capitalism vs. The Climate." *The Nation*, November 28, 2011, 11; Larry Bell, *Climate of Corruption: Politics and Power Behind The Global Warming Hoax* (Austin, Texas: Greenleaf Book Group, 2011).

44 Audrey, "New Report Outlines Anti-environment Votes in U.S. House," *Public Health Newswire*, December 16, 2011, http://www.publichealthnewswire.org/?p=2058.

45 Ibid., 11.

46 Paul Farhi, "Liberal Media Watchdog: Fox News E-mail Shows Network's Slant on Climate Change," *Washington Post*, December 15, 2010, http://www.washingtonpost.com/wp-dyn/content/article/2010/12/15/AR2010121503181.html?wpisrc=nl_pmpolitics.

47 "Most-Cited Climate Skeptics Linked to Big Oil," *SustainableBusiness.com News*, May 10, 2011, http://www.sustainablebusiness.com/index.cfm/go/news.display/id/22378.

48 Lydia Saad, "In U.S., Global Warming Views Steady despite Warm Winter," *Gallup Politics*, March 30, 2012, http://www.gallup.com/poll/153608/Global-Warming-Views-Steady-Despite-Warm-Winter.aspx (accessed May 22, 2012).

49 Andrew Kohut, Paul Taylor, Scott Keeter, and Carroll Doherty, *Angry Silents, Disengaged Millennials: The Generation Gap and the 2012 Election*, Pew Research Center, November 3, 2011, http://www.people-press.org/files/legacy-pdf/11-3-11%20Generations%20Release.pdf (accessed May 22, 2012).

50 J. M. Twenge, W. K. Campbell, and E. C. Freeman, "Generational Differences in Young Adults' Life Goals, Concern for Others, and Civic Orientation, 1966–2009," *Journal of Personality and Social Psychology*, May 102 (5), 2012.

51 Jane Mayer, "Covert Operations: The Billionaire Brothers Who Are Waging a War against Obama," *New Yorker*, August 30, 2010, 51.

52 Barry Rabe and Christopher P. Burick, *The Climate of Belief: American Public Opinion and Climate Change*, Issues in Governance Studies No. 31, Brookings Institution, January 2010, http://www.brookings.edu/papers/2010/01_climate_rabe_borick.aspx (accessed May 15, 2010).

53 Ibid.

54 Spencer Weart, *The Discovery of Global Warming: Revised and Expanded Edition* (Cambridge, Mass.: Harvard University Press, 2008).

55 Bob Deans, "Big Coal, Cold Cash, and the GOP," *On Earth* (NRDC), Spring 2012, 12.

56 Associated Press, "Gore, Criticizing Fellow Democrat, Says Obama Has Failed to Fight for Global Warming Cause," *Washington Post*, June 22, 2011, http://www.washingtonpost.com/politics/in-rolling-stone-essay-gore-says-obama-failed-to-fight-for-global-warming-cause/2011/06/22/AGHuJVfH_story.html?wpisrc=nl_pmpolitics.

57 Lauren Feldman with Matthew C. Nisbet, Anthony Leiserowitz, and Edward Maibach, "The Climate Change Generation? Survey Analysis of the Perceptions and Beliefs of Young Americans," Yale Project on Climate Change and the George Mason University Center for Climate Change Communication, http://environment.yale.edu/uploads/YouthJan2010.pdf (accessed May 15, 2010).

58 Vivian E. Thomson, *Garbage In, Garbage Out: Solving the Problems with Long-Distance Trash Transport* (Charlottesville: University of Virginia Press, 2009).

59 Thomas Friedman, *Hot, Flat, and Crowded: Why We Need a Green Revolution—and How It Can Renew America*, Release 2, updated and expanded (New York: Picador, 2009), 466.

Focus On...Foreign Policy

1 Mark Thompson, "How to Save a Trillion Dollars," *Time*, April 25, 2011, 24–29.

2 "Diplomacy's New Hit Man: The Free-Market Dollar," *New York Times*, May 24, 1998, sec. 4, 5.

3 Roger Lowenstein, citing work of Harvard economist Dani Rodrik in "Tariff to Nowhere," *New York Times Magazine*, June 15, 2008, 16.

4 Walter LaFeber, "Making Revolution, Opposing Revolution," *New York Times*, July 3, 1983, sec. 4, 13.

5 Jesse Lichtenstein, "Digital Diplomacy," *New York Times Magazine*, July 18, 2010, 25–29.

6 The group was known as the Project for the New Century (PNAC); it circulated its call for the overthrow of Saddam Hussein in 1995.

7 This was Michael Scheurer. For a discussion of his differences with the Bush administration, see *Imperial Hubris* (Washington, D.C.: Brassey's, 2004), originally published anonymously because of Scheurer's position in the intelligence community.

8 Philip Bobbitt, "Why We Listen," *New York Times*, January 30, 2006, A23.

9 *The 9/11 Commission Report: Final Report of the National Commission on Terrorist Attacks upon the United States* (New York: W. W. Norton, 2004).

10 James Madison, *Notes of Debates in the Federal Convention of 1787* (Athens: Ohio University Press, 1966), 389, 475–477; Madison's notes from *Documents Illustrative of the Formation of the Union of the American States*, quoted in Joan Biskupic, "Constitution's Conflicting Clauses Underscored by Iraqi Crisis," *Congressional Quarterly Weekly Report*, January 5, 1991, 34.

11 Ronald D. Elving, "America's Most Frequent Fight Has Been the Undeclared War," *Congressional Quarterly Weekly Report*, January 5, 1991, 37.

12 Representative Toby Roth (R-Wisc.), quoted in Katharine Q. Seelye, "House Defeats Bid to Repeal 'War Powers,'" *New York Times*, June 11, 1995, A7.

13 A principal author of this legal opinion was Deputy Assistant Attorney General John Yoo, later a law professor at the University of California-Berkeley. He elaborated on his ideas in *The Powers of War and Peace: The Constitution and Foreign Affairs after 9/11* (Chicago: University of Chicago Press, 2005).

14 For a discussion of the foreign policy establishment, see Walter Isaacson and Evan Thomas, *The Wise Men: Six Friends and the World They Made* (New York: Simon & Schuster, 1986).

15 On Mia Farrow's skillful use of the Beijing Olympics to pressure the Chinese government to change its policy toward the Sudan and Darfur, see Ilan Greenberg, "Changing the Rules of the Game," *New York Times Magazine*, March 30, 2008, 52–57.

16 Tom Zeller, "The Iraq-al-Qaeda Link: A Short History," *New York Times*, June 20, 2004, WK4.

17 Andrew Kohut, "Speak Softly and Carry a Smaller Stick," *New York Times*, March 24, 2006, A19. Kohut is a pollster for the Pew Foundation.

18 See, for example, icasualties.org.

19 Robert Wright, "Private Eyes," *New York Times Magazine*, September 5, 1999, 50–54; William J. Broad, "North Korea's Nuclear Intentions, Out There for All to See," *New York Times*, October 8, 2006, WK5; and www.earth.google.com.

20 Historian Michael Hogan, quoted in John M. Broder, "Gentler Look at the U.S. World Role," *New York Times*, October 31, 1999, 14.

21 Paul Johnson, "The Myth of American Isolationism," *Foreign Affairs*, May–June 1995, 162.

22 Quoted in Robert Dallek, *Lyndon B. Johnson, Portrait of a President* (New York: Oxford University Press, 2004), 179.

23 For one view of the impact of Vietnam on the thinking of today's high-ranking officers, see H. R. McMaster, *Dereliction of Duty* (New York: HarperCollins, 1997).

24 Robert S. McNamara, *In Retrospect: The Tragedy and Lessons of Vietnam* (New York: Times Books, 1995).

25 Michael Beschloss, *Reaching for Glory: Lyndon Johnson's Secret White House Tapes, 1964–1965* (New York: Simon & Schuster, 2001), 166.

26 Robert Weissberg, *Public Opinion and Popular Government* (Englewood Cliffs, N.J.: Prentice Hall, 1976), 144–148.

27 Ole Holsti, "The Three-Headed Eagle," *International Studies Quarterly* 23 (1979), 339–359; Michael Mandelbaum and William Schneider, "The New Internationalisms," in *The Eagle Entangled: U.S. Foreign Policy in a Complex World,* eds. Kenneth Oye, Donald Rothchild, and Robert J. Lieber (New York: Longman, 1979), 34–88.

28 For an analysis of U.S.-Soviet relations in the Reagan era, see Alexander Dallin and Gail Lapidus, "Reagan and the Russians," and Kenneth Oye, "Constrained Confidence and the Evolution of Reagan Foreign Policy," in *Eagle Resurgent?* eds. Kenneth Oye, Robert Lieber, and Donald Rothchild (Boston: Little, Brown, 1987); and John Newhouse, "The Abolitionist" (pts. 1 and 2), *New Yorker,* January 2 and 9, 1989.

29 See George F. Kennan, "After the Cold War," *New York Times Magazine,* February 5, 1989, 32ff.

30 Bill Clinton, "A Democrat Lays Out His Plan," *Harvard International Review,* Summer 1992, 26.

31 Thomas Friedman, "What Big Stick? Just Sell," *New York Times,* October 2, 1995, E3.

32 "National Security Strategy of the United States," September 2002. This is an annual report the president makes to Congress and during Bush's time in office was posted at www.whitehouse.gov.

33 "Bush Plans 'Strike First' Military Policy," *Champaign-Urbana News-Gazette,* June 10, 2002, A-3.

34 Fred Kaplan, "JFK's First-Strike Plan," *Atlantic Monthly,* October 2001, 81–86.

35 This and the following Eisenhower quotes are from Jonathan Rauch, "Learning from Ike," *National Journal,* April 14, 2007, 14–19.

36 Quoted in Robert W. Merry, "The Obama Doctrine," *New York Times Book Review,* July 15, 2012, 11. See also David E. Sanger, *Confront and Conceal* (New York: Crown Publishers, 2012).

37 See Joseph S. Nye, "Ten Years after the Mouse Roared," *Project Syndicate*, September 1, 2011, www.project-syndicate.org/print/ten-years-after-the-mouse-roared.

38 Interview for the documentary *Why We Fight,* 2005. President Eisenhower's military-industrial speech can also be heard in *Why We Fight.*

39 David Unger, *The Emergency State* (New York: Penguin Press, 2012).

40 Thom Shanker and Christopher Drew, "Pentagon Faces Growing Pressures to Trim Budget," *New York Times,* July 22, 2010, A1.

41 William D. Nordhaus, "The Economic Consequences of a War with Iraq" in *War with Iraq: Costs, Consequences, and Alternatives,* eds. Carl Kaysen et al., Report #52 issued by American Academy of Arts and Sciences, 2002, www.amacad.org.

42 Ibid.

43 Direct war costs for Iraq and Afghanistan are updated by the second at www.costofwar.com.

44 Joseph E. Stiglitz and Linda J. Bilmes, *Three Trillion Was the True Cost of the Iraq War* (New York: W. W. Norton, 2008).

45 Joseph Stiglitz and Linda Bilmes, testimony before the House Veteran's Affairs Committee hearing on the true cost of war, September 30, 2010, veterans.house.gov/news/PRArticle.aspx?NewsID=642; Miles A. Pomper with Niels C. Sorrels, "War: Deficit-Maker Supreme," *CQ Weekly,* January 11, 2003, 71.

46 John Snowe, quoted in David E. Rosenbaum, "Tax Cuts and War Have Seldom Mixed," *New York Times,* March 9, 2003, 13. On the relationship between tax policy and war, see W. Elliot Brownlee, *Federal Taxation in America: A Short History,* 2nd ed. (Washington, D.C.: Woodrow Wilson Center Press, 2004), 1–9; 58–133, 110.

47 See, for example, Jane Mayer, "The Secret Sharer," *New Yorker*, May 23, 2011, 47.

48 The Protect America Act of 2007 amended the Foreign Intelligence Surveillance Act, which had required judicial authorization. Now, under the act, judicial authorization is required only if the government targets specific American citizens.

49 Keith Bradsher, "China Moves to Retaliate against U.S. Tire Tariff," *New York Times,* September 14, 2009.

50 Keith Bradsher, "China Leans Less on U.S. Trade," *New York Times,* April 18, 2007, C1. The trade figures are from Goldman-Sachs.

51 James Fallows, "The $1.4 Trillion Question," *Atlantic Monthly,* January–February 2008, 46–48.

52 Thom Shanker and David E. Sanger, "Obama Is Said to Be Preparing to Seek Approval on Saudi Arms Sale," *New York Times,* September 17, 2010, A4.

Glossary

24-hour news cycle The system that provides nonstop news.

Activist judges Judges who are not reluctant to overrule the other branches of government by declaring laws or actions of government officials unconstitutional.

Administrative Procedure Act (APA) Legislation passed in 1946 that provides for public participation in the rule-making process. All federal agencies must disclose their rule-making procedures and publish all regulations at least thirty days in advance of their effective date to allow time for public comment.

Adversarial relationship A relationship in which two parties or groups are often in opposition, such as public officials and the media.

Affirmative action A policy in job hiring or university admissions that gives special consideration to members of historically disadvantaged groups.

Agents of political socialization Sources of information about politics; include parents, peers, schools, the media, political leaders, and the community.

American Civil Liberties Union (ACLU) A nonpartisan organization that seeks to protect the civil liberties of all Americans.

Americans with Disabilities Act Legislation passed to protect those with disabilities from discrimination in employment and public accommodations, such as stores, restaurants, hotels, and health care facilities.

Antifederalists Those who opposed the ratification of the U.S. Constitution.

Appointment power The president's power to appoint or nominate senior executive officials and judges.

Appropriations Budget legislation that specifies the amount of authorized funds that will actually be allocated for agencies and departments to spend.

Articles of Confederation The first constitution of the United States; in effect from 1781 to 1789.

Astroturf groups Groups that pretend to be broad-based groups but are run by industry lobbyists. They try to mobilize people through efforts similar to grassroots groups and often have misleading names.

Authorizations Budget legislation that provides agencies and departments with the legal authority to operate; may specify funding levels but does not actually provide the funding (the funding is provided by **appropriations**).

Ballot initiative An **initiative**.

Battleground states Also known as "swing states." During a presidential election, these are states whose Electoral College votes are not safely in one candidate's pocket; candidates will spend time and more money there to try to win the state.

Bible belt A term used to describe portions of the South and Midwest that were strongly influenced by Protestant fundamentalists.

Big Sort A term coined to describe how Americans tend to live among others of similar economic statuses and cultural beliefs.

Big tent The idea, usually accepted by the major political parties, that they should welcome diverse people holding diverse views as the way to gain supporters and win elections.

Bill of Rights The first ten amendments to the U.S. Constitution.

Biofuels Renewable resources produced from biomass, which is composed of recently living elements such as animals, plants, or wood. One popular biofuel is biodiesel, which is used to run automobiles.

Black budget The part of the U.S. budget, unknown to the public and to much of Congress, that funds certain intelligence activities.

Blockbusting The practice in which realtors would frighten whites in a neighborhood where a black family had moved by telling the whites that their houses would decline in value. The whites in panic would then sell their houses to the realtors at low prices, and the realtors would resell the houses to blacks, thereby resegregating the area from white to black.

Blog Common term for a web log, an independent website created by an individual or group to disseminate opinions or information.

Blue states The states that voted Democratic in 2000 and 2004 and are generally more liberal in outlook. They include New England, Middle Atlantic, upper Midwest, and Pacific Coast states.

Broadcasting An attempt by a network to appeal to most of the television or radio audience.

Brown v. *Board of Education* The 1954 case in which the U.S. Supreme Court overturned the **separate-but-equal doctrine** and ruled unanimously that segregated schools violated the Fourteenth Amendment.

Bubble concept A pollution-control system that permits reductions in overall pollutants within a given area rather than requiring reductions for every individual point of pollution within that area.

Budget deficit Occurs when federal spending exceeds federal revenues.

Bureaucracy A **hierarchical** organization that relies upon a **division of labor** and **formal rules**.

Burger Court The U.S. Supreme Court under Chief Justice Warren Burger (1969–1986). Though not as activist as the **Warren Court**, the Burger Court maintained most of the rights expanded by its predecessor and issued important rulings on abortion and sexual discrimination.

Bush v. *Gore* U.S. Supreme Court case in 2000 where the Supreme Court set aside the Florida Supreme Court's order for a manual recount of the presidential votes cast in the state. The Court's decision meant that Bush got Florida's electoral votes, giving him a majority of all electoral votes and, thus, the election.

Cabinet The president's advisory body, composed of the top executives of the executive branch departments, the vice president, and those designated by the president as having **cabinet rank**.

Cabinet rank The level of importance sufficient to serve in the president's **cabinet**; refers to those individuals who are viewed as having responsibilities of similar importance to department heads, such as the director of the Office of Management and Budget (OMB).

Cap-and-trade An approach to emissions trading used to control pollution by providing economic incentives to reduce emissions of pollutants. A governmental body usually sets a limit on permissible emissions levels in a geographical area. The limit (or cap) is allocated among entities, such as firms or industries, or other groupings as permits. Then entities within the geographical area that need to exceed their emissions can buy or "trade" permits from those who need fewer of them.

Capitalist economy An economic system in which the means of production are privately owned and prices, wages, working conditions, and profits are determined solely by the market.

Carbon dioxide (CO$_2$) One of the greenhouse gas chemical compounds. It is heavy, colorless, and formed by animal respiration and the decay or combustion of animal and vegetable matter. It is then absorbed by plants in photosynthesis.

Casework The assistance members of Congress provide to their constituents; includes answering questions and doing personal favors for those who ask for help. Also called **constituency service**.

Centers for Disease Control and Prevention (CDC) A federal agency founded in 1946 as the Communicable Disease Center, a successor to the agency that fought malaria in combat areas during World War II. The CDC was originally devoted to preventing the spread of mosquito-borne diseases but is now involved in all public health efforts directed at preventing and controlling infectious and chronic disease, injuries, workplace hazards, disabilities, and environmental health threats.

Chamber of Commerce A large organization that lobbies for business against regulation by government.

Checkbook members People who "join" interest groups by donating money.

Checks and balances The principle of government that holds that the powers of the various branches should overlap to avoid power becoming overly concentrated in one branch.

Chernobyl The 1986 nuclear accident in the former Soviet Union that is considered to be the worst nuclear power plant disaster in history.

Chief executive In the U.S. government, the president of the United States.

Chief of staff The person with responsibility for advising the president and managing the **White House Office**.

Christian right Evangelical Protestant denominations that came together as a political movement to forward their conservative agenda, usually through the Republican Party.

Civil case A case in which individuals sue others for denying their rights and causing them harm.

Civil disobedience Peaceful but illegal protest activity in which those involved allow themselves to be arrested and charged.

Civil liberties Individual rights outlined in the Constitution and the Bill of Rights.

Civil rights The principle of equal rights for persons regardless of their race, sex, or ethnic background.

Civil Rights Act of 1964 Major civil rights legislation that prohibits discrimination on the basis of race, color, religion, or national origin in public accommodations.

Civil Rights Act of 1968 Civil rights legislation that prohibits discrimination in the sale or rental of housing on the basis of race, color, religion, or national origin; also prohibits **blockbusting**, **steering**, and **redlining**.

Civil Service Commission An agency established by the Pendleton Act of 1883 to curb **patronage** in the federal bureaucracy and replace it with a merit system.

Clean coal An umbrella term for technologies to reduce emissions of carbon dioxide and other greenhouse gases that come from burning coal for electrical power; often involves carbon capture and sequestration, which pumps and stores CO$_2$ emissions underground.

Climate change A change in global temperatures and precipitation due to natural variability or to human activity.

Climate skeptics (deniers) Those who disagree with scientific conclusions about global warming.

Cloture A method of stopping a **filibuster** by limiting debate to only twenty more hours; requires a vote of three-fifths of the members of the Senate.

Coalition A network of **interest groups** with similar concerns that combine forces to pursue a common goal; may be short-lived or permanent.

Cold War The era of hostility between the United States and the Soviet Union that existed between the end of World War II and the collapse of the Soviet Union.

Commander in Chief The president's constitutional role as head of the armed forces with power to direct their use.

Commercial bias A slant in news coverage to please or avoid offending advertisers.

Comparable worth The principle that comparable jobs should pay comparable wages.

Concurring opinion The opinion by one or more judges in a court case who agree with the decision but not with the reasons given by the majority for it. The concurring opinion offers an alternate legal argument for the ruling.

Confederal system A system in which the central government has only the powers given to it by the subnational governments.

Conference committee A committee composed of members of both houses of Congress that is formed to try to resolve the differences when the two houses pass different versions of the same bill.

Conservatism The worldview that individuals and communities are better off without government assistance and that economic activity should be free from government interference.

Constituency Both the geographic area and the people a member of Congress represents: for a senator, the state and all its residents; for a member of the House, a congressional district and all its residents.

Constituency service The assistance members of Congress provide to residents in their districts (states, if senators); includes answering questions and doing personal favors for those who ask for help. Also called **casework**.

Constitutional Convention The gathering in Philadelphia in 1787 that wrote the U.S. Constitution; met initially to revise the **Articles of Confederation** but produced a new national constitution instead.

Containment A policy formulated by the Truman administration to limit the spread of communism by meeting any action taken by the Soviet Union with a countermove; led U.S. decision makers to see most conflicts in terms of U.S.-Soviet rivalry.

Cooperative federalism The day-to-day cooperation among federal, state, and local officials in carrying out the business of government.

Cracking, stacking, and packing Methods of drawing district boundaries that minimize black representation. With cracking, a large concentrated black population is divided among two or more districts so that blacks will not have a majority anywhere; with stacking, a large black population is combined with an even larger white population; with packing, a large black population is put into one district rather than two so that blacks will have a majority in only one district.

Crafted talk A way of packaging policies that caters to a specific base while appearing to remain mainstream.

Criminal case A case in which a government (national or state) prosecutes a person for violating its laws.

Cruel and unusual punishment Torture or any punishment that is grossly disproportionate to the offense; prohibited by the Eighth Amendment.

Cyberterrorism A form of asymmetrical warfare that attempts to disrupt an economy, its communication system, or its military defenses by hacking into the computer systems that control them and immobilizing them. It is one of the most urgent threats to U.S. national security.

De facto segregation Segregation that is based on residential patterns and is not imposed by law; because it cannot be eliminated by striking down a law, it is more intractable than **de jure segregation**.

De jure segregation Segregation imposed by law; outlawed by *Brown* v. *Board of Education* and subsequent court cases.

Dealignment Term used to refer to the diminished relevance of political parties.

Declaration of Independence A founding document that proclaimed "all men are created equal" and outlined the unalienable rights given to the American people.

Deepwater Horizon A deepwater offshore oil-drilling rig in the Gulf of Mexico that had drilled the deepest oil well in history. On April 20, 2010, it exploded and killed eleven crew members. On April 22, the rig sank, causing the largest offshore oil spill in U.S. history.

Deflation A condition in which prices fall so low that there is a disincentive to buy because consumers keep waiting for prices to fall lower.

Democratic Party   One of two major political parties in the United States; it grew out of the party established by Andrew Jackson in the early nineteenth century. In contrast to Republicans, Democrats are more likely to believe that government can help people improve their economic well-being and less likely to believe that government should regulate some forms of personal moral behavior, such as same-sex marriages and abortion.

Departments   The largest **bureaucracies** within the executive branch. There are fifteen executive departments, each of which is responsible for an issue area of national significance.

Depression   A period of prolonged high unemployment.

Deregulation   The reduction or elimination of government regulation in a specific industry. The U.S. government began deregulating the utility industry in the late 1990s. The goal was to create more competition and, therefore, lower the costs to consumers.

Détente   A policy designed to deescalate **Cold War** rhetoric and promote the notion that relations with the Soviet Union could be conducted in ways other than confrontation; developed by President Richard M. Nixon and Secretary of State Henry Kissinger.

Devolution   The delegation of authority by the national government to lower units of government (such as at the state and local level) to make and implement policy.

Direct democracy   A system of government in which citizens govern themselves directly and vote on most issues; e.g., a New England town meeting.

Discretionary spending   Spending levels set by the federal government in annual **appropriations** bills passed by Congress; includes government operating expenses and the salaries of many federal employees.

Dissenting opinion   The opinion by one or more judges in a court case who do not agree with the decision of the majority. The dissenting opinion urges a different outcome.

Divided government   The situation in which one political party controls the presidency and the other party controls one or both houses of Congress.

Division of labor   The allocation of work among personnel so that each worker or set of workers performs specific tasks; used by **bureaucracies** to focus and coordinate their workers.

Dred Scott case   An 1857 case in which the U.S. Supreme Court held that blacks, whether slave or free, were not citizens and that Congress had no power to restrict slavery in the territories; contributed to the polarization between North and South and ultimately to the Civil War.

Dual federalism   The idea that the Constitution created a system in which the national government and the states have separate grants of power with each supreme in its own sphere.

Due process   The Fourteenth Amendment guarantees that the government will follow fair and just procedures when prosecuting a criminal defendant.

Earth Summit   A 1992 conference held in Rio de Janeiro to address environmental protection in the context of global economic development. It was also the largest group meeting of world leaders in history, with representatives from 178 countries. The topics were biodiversity, global warming, sustainable development, and preservation of tropical rain forests. Five international agreements were signed.

Electoral College   A group of electors selected by the voters in each state and the District of Columbia; the electors officially elect the president and vice president.

Emancipation Proclamation   Abraham Lincoln's 1863 proclamation that the slaves "shall be . . . forever free." At the time, it applied only in the Confederate states and so had little practical impact because the Union did not control them. However, it had an immense political impact, making clear that the Civil War was not just to preserve the Union but also to abolish slavery.

Environmental impact statement   A report of the potential environmental effects of planned land use.

Environmental Protection Agency (EPA)   The U.S. government agency that sets and enforces national pollution-control standards, established in 1970 by President Nixon. EPA action has led to substantial improvements in air-pollution emissions, water quality, and waste disposal in the United States. The EPA also oversees the cleanup of Superfund sites.

Equal Pay Act   A statute enacted by Congress in 1963 that mandates that women and men should receive equal pay for equal work.

Equal protection clause   The Fourteenth Amendment clause that is the Constitution's primary guarantee that everyone is equal before the law.

Equal Rights Amendment (ERA)   A proposed amendment to the Constitution that would prohibit government from denying equal rights on the basis of sex; was passed by Congress in 1972 but failed to be ratified by a sufficient number of states.

Equality of opportunity   The idea that every person should have the chance to realize her or his potential economically, intellectually, and socially.

Equality of result   The idea that all individuals should be guaranteed a certain minimal standard or quality of life. If necessary, the government should help all persons get access to the same services or benefits.

Establishment clause   The First Amendment clause that prohibits the establishment of a state religion.

Exclusionary rule   A rule that prevents evidence obtained in violation of the Fourth Amendment from being used in court against the defendant.

Executive agreements   International agreements other than **treaties** that are binding on the United States under international law. They may be authorized by treaties, by Congress through statutes, or by the president acting unilaterally.

Executive Office of the President (EOP)   The president's personal bureaucracy that monitors the work done in cabinet departments and agencies.

Executive orders   Rules or regulations issued by the president that have the force of law; issued to implement constitutional provisions or statutes.

Executive privilege   The authority of the president to withhold specific types of information from the courts and Congress.

Exit polls   Election-day polls of voters leaving the polling places, conducted mainly by television networks and major newspapers.

Faithless elector   A member of the **Electoral College** who votes on the basis of personal preference rather than the way the majority of voters in his or her state voted.

Federal courts of appeals   Intermediate appellate courts that hear appeals from cases that have been decided by the district courts. There are twelve, based on regions of the country.

Federal district courts   The courts that try cases based on federal law. There are ninety-four in the United States.

Federalism (federal system)   A system in which power is constitutionally divided between a central government and subnational or local governments.

Federalists   Originally, those who supported the U.S. Constitution and favored its ratification; in the early years of the Republic, those who advocated a strong national government.

Filibuster   A mechanism for delay in the Senate in which one or more members engage in a continuous speech to prevent the Senate from voting on a bill.

First Amendment   The first amendment to the United States Constitution, guaranteeing freedom of expression, which includes freedom of speech, religion, assembly, and association, and freedom of the press.

Fiscal federalism   The allocation of government funds among the national, state, and local governments, which is routinely controversial.

527 organizations   A 527 organization is designed to influence elections. These organizations are named this because of the U.S. tax code that authorizes them. They are of interest because they are unregulated by the Federal Election Commission, and thus they can receive money and spend it freely to influence elections.

Formal rules   Written job descriptions and guidelines for good performance, for promotion, and for grievances; essential to **bureaucracies**.

Free exercise clause   The First Amendment clause that guarantees individuals the right to practice their religion without government intervention.

Free-rider problem   The problem created when individuals benefit from actions of groups they are not a part of, such as workers whose raises are influenced by union pressure but who are not members of unions.

Freedom from   Freedom from government interference.

Freedom of association The right of an individual to join with others to speak, assemble, and petition the government for a redress of grievances. This right allows a minority to pursue interests without being prevented from doing so by the majority.

Freedom of Information Act (FOIA) Law passed in 1966 that allows any person (corporate or individual) to apply to an agency, through a formal procedure, for access to unclassified documents in its archives. Updated in 1996 to provide access to electronic records. A "deliberative process" exemption allows the withholding of records describing behind-the-scenes decision making.

Freedom of speech The First Amendment guarantee of a right of free expression.

Freedom of the press Freedom from censorship, so the press can disseminate the news, information, and opinion that it deems appropriate.

Friend of the court briefs Legal arguments filed in court cases by individuals or groups who aren't litigants in the cases. These briefs often provide new information to the court and usually urge the judges to rule one way.

Freedom to Freedom to maximize one's potential.

Gaining access The ability of lobbyists to reach policy makers to make their case.

Gender gap An observable pattern of modest but consistent differences in opinion between men and women on various public policy issues.

Gerrymander A congressional district whose boundaries are drawn so as to maximize the political advantage of a party or racial group; often such a district has a bizarre shape.

Gettysburg Address Famous 1863 speech by President Lincoln to dedicate the battlefield where many had fallen during the Civil War. Lincoln used the occasion to advance his ideal of equality and to promote the Union.

Global warming The term used to describe an increase in the temperature of the earth. Most often, it is used to refer to the warming predicted as a result of increased emissions of greenhouse gases.

Going public The process in which Congress or its members carry an issue debate to the public via the media, such as through televised floor debates or media appearances by individual members.

Government contracts Agreements to provide goods or services to government.

Government corporations Corporations in the federal **bureaucracy** that are expected to be politically independent; include those run by the government and those run by private stockholders.

Grandfather clause A device used in the South to prevent blacks from voting; such clauses exempted those whose grandfathers had the right to vote before 1867 from having to fulfill various requirements that some people could not meet. Since no blacks could vote before 1867, they could not qualify for the exemption.

Grants-in-aid Federal money provided to state and, occasionally, local governments for community development and to establish programs to help people such as the aged poor or the unemployed; began during the New Deal.

Grassroots lobbying The mass mobilization of members of an **interest group** to apply pressure to public officials, usually in the form of a mass mailing.

Great Compromise The decision of the **Constitutional Convention** to have a bicameral legislature in which representation in one house would be by population and in the other house, by states; also called the Connecticut Compromise.

Great Depression The devastating economic depression beginning in 1929 and lasting until World War II. Many banks collapsed, ordinary people lost their savings, business activity declined, and one-quarter to one-third of all workers were unemployed. As a response, government intervened to provide unemployment assistance, assistance to businesses and farmers, and Social Security.

Great Migration The period during World War I and until World War II when more than a million southern blacks headed north to look for better jobs and housing.

Great Recession Term sometimes used by economists to refer to the period of 2008 to 2012 in the United States because of the severity and long duration of the **recession** during those years.

Green economy An economic model based on renewable energy such as solar energy that is predicted to create new green jobs, ensure sustainable economic development, and prevent increases in pollution, global warming, and resource depletion. The green economic model is contrasted to a "black" economic model based on fossil fuels (oil, coal, natural gas).

Greenhouse gases Any of the atmospheric gases that contribute to the greenhouse effect, such as carbon dioxide, water vapor, and methane.

Habeas corpus Latin for "Bring the body!" A writ of *habeas corpus* is a means for criminal defendants who have exhausted appeals in state courts to appeal to a federal district court.

Hate speech Racial, ethnic, sexual, or religious slurs that demean people for characteristics that are innate or beliefs that are deeply held.

Head of government The president's partisan, policy-making role as head of the executive branch and as head of his party in government, in contrast to his nonpartisan duties as **head of state** and representative of the country.

Head of state The president's role as a symbolic leader of the nation and representative of all the people.

Hierarchy/Hierarchical The allocation of power among different people, stipulating who can issue commands about what, to whom.

Horse race coverage The way in which the media report on the candidates' polling status and strategies, rather than covering their positions on relevant issues.

House of Representatives One house of Congress, where states are represented in proportion to their population size.

Ideology A highly organized and coherent set of opinions.

Impeachment The process provided for in the Constitution by which the House of Representatives can indict (impeach) a president for "Treason, Bribery, or other High Crimes and Misdemeanors." If the House votes to lodge formal charges against the president, he is impeached. But a president cannot be removed from office unless two-thirds of the Senate finds him guilty of the charges.

Imperial presidency A term that came into use at the end of the 1960s to describe the growing power of the presidency.

Implied powers clause The clause in the U.S. Constitution that gives Congress the power to make all laws "necessary and proper" for carrying out its specific powers.

Independent agencies Government bureaus that are not parts of departments. Their heads are appointed by and responsible to the president.

Independent regulatory agency(ies) A board- or commission-led independent agency, which enforces the laws that govern specific industries or financial relationships (e.g., the Securities and Exchange Commission regulates the stock market).

Independent spending Money spent on elections by groups that are not formally affiliated with the parties or candidates. Any interest group, business, or union can spend unlimited amounts, secretly, in this way.

Indirect democracy A system of government in which citizens elect representatives to make decisions for them.

Individualistic political subculture In the twentieth century, the subculture said to be typical of the industrial Midwest, the West, and the East, where the objective of politics was to get benefits for oneself and one's group.

Inflation The situation in which prices increase but wages and salaries fail to keep pace with the prices of goods.

Informal norms Unwritten rules designed to help keep Congress running smoothly by attempting to diminish friction and competition among the members.

Infotainment A word for television newscasts that attempt to entertain as they provide information.

Initiative A process that allows citizens and interest groups to collect signatures on petitions and place a proposal on the ballot.

Interest groups Organizations that try to achieve at least some of their goals with government assistance.

Intergovernmental Panel on Climate Change (IPCC) A scientific body set up by the United Nations in 1988 to evaluate the risks of climate change caused by human activity. It has over 2,500 scientists from more than 130 countries who are charged with determining how much the climate has changed over time and why. In response to its 2007 report on the climate, the IPCC shared the 2007 Nobel Peace Prize with former Vice President Al Gore.

Isolationism   A policy of noninvolvement with other nations outside the Americas; generally followed by the United States during the nineteenth and early twentieth centuries.

Issue vote   A vote for a candidate whose stands on specific issues are consistent with the voter's own.

Jacksonian democracy   Democracy in which participation is open to common people. Named for Andrew Jackson, who first mobilized common people to participate in government.

Jeffersonians (Jeffersonian Republicans)   Opponents of a strong national government. They challenged the **Federalists** in the early years of the Republic.

Jim Crow laws   Laws enacted in southern states that segregated schools, public accommodations, and almost all other aspects of life.

Judicial independence   The ability of federal judges to decide cases as they think the law requires without bending to political pressure.

Judicial review   The authority of the courts to declare laws or actions of government officials unconstitutional.

Jurisdiction   The authority of a court to hear and decide cases.

Keynesian economics   The argument by John Maynard Keynes that government should stimulate the economy during periods of high unemployment by increasing spending even if it must run **deficits** to do so.

Ku Klux Klan   A white supremacy group aimed at inflaming prejudice and terrorizing blacks during and after **Reconstruction**.

Labor unions   Groups that seek agreements with business and policies from the government that protect workers' jobs, wages, and benefits and ensure the safety of workplaces.

Leaks   Disclosures of information that some government officials want kept secret.

Libel   Printed or broadcast statements that are false and meant to tarnish someone's reputation.

Liberalism   Used in the American political context, the worldview that government can be a positive and constructive force in society and can assist individuals, businesses, and communities with social and economic problems.

Limited government   A government that is strong enough to protect the people's rights but not so strong as to threaten those rights; in the view of John Locke, such a government was established through a **social contract**.

Literacy tests   Examinations ostensibly carried out to ensure that voters could read and write but actually a device used in the South to disqualify blacks from voting.

Living wage   A wage that is high enough to allow full-time workers to meet the basic cost of living, something the minimum wage does not do.

Lobbying   The efforts of **interest groups** to influence government.

Lobbyist   A representative of a group or interest who attempts to influence government decisions, generally through personal contact.

Love Canal   The neighborhood in Niagara Falls, New York, that is the site of the worst chemical waste disaster in U.S. history. Love Canal became a dumping ground for chemical waste in the 1940s and 1950s. It was later filled in and housing was built on it. Leakage of toxic chemicals was detected in the 1970s, and residents were evacuated from their homes. Many received a monetary settlement from the chemical company responsible for the dumping, and the federal government worked to clean up the site. Later, the government declared parts of the neighborhood safe for residences.

Majority leader   The title of both the leader of the Senate, who is chosen by the majority party, and the head of the majority party in the House of Representatives, who is second in command to the **Speaker**.

Majority opinion   The joint opinion by a majority of the judges in a federal court case that explains why the judges ruled as they did.

Majority-minority district   A congressional district whose boundaries are drawn to give a minority group a majority in the district.

Mandate   A term used in the media to refer to a president having clear directions from the voters to take a certain course of action; in practice, it is not always clear that a president, even one elected by a large majority, has a mandate or, if so, for what.

Mandatory spending   Spending by the federal government that is required by permanent laws; e.g., payments for **Medicare**.

Marbury v. Madison   The 1803 case in which the U.S. Supreme Court enunciated the doctrine of **judicial review**.

Marshall Court   Supreme Court under Chief Justice John Marshall (1801–1835). This Court was responsible for articulating **judicial review** and confirming the supremacy of federal law over state law.

Marshall Plan   A plan that provided economic relief to the nations of western Europe in 1947, following World War II.

McCarthyism   Methods of combating communism characterized by irresponsible accusations made on the basis of little or no evidence; named after Senator Joseph McCarthy of Wisconsin, who used such tactics in the 1950s.

McCulloch v. Maryland   An 1819 U.S. Supreme Court decision that broadly interpreted Congress's powers under the **implied powers clause**.

Medicaid   A federal-state medical assistance program for the poor.

Medicare   A public health insurance program that pays many medical expenses of the elderly and the disabled; funded through **Social Security** taxes, general revenues, and premiums paid by recipients.

Merit system   A system of filling bureaucratic jobs on the basis of competence instead of **patronage**.

Message   Political groups, such as the president and his administration, or congressional Republicans, for example, want to communicate a consistent set of information. That is the message. The idea is that every spokesperson for the group should be consistent with the overall message and not introduce extraneous bits of information that might overshadow the message. The message might last for a few days or an entire campaign season.

Microtargeting   Directing campaigns to specifically defined demographic groups.

Minority leader   The leader of the minority party in either the House of Representatives or the Senate.

Minority rights   The individual rights of those not in the political or religious majority.

Miranda **rights**   A means of protecting a criminal suspect's rights against self-incrimination during police interrogation. Before interrogation, suspects must be told that they have a right to remain silent; that anything they say can be used against them; that they have a right to an attorney; and that if they cannot afford an attorney, one will be provided for them. The rights are named after the case *Miranda* v. *Arizona*.

"Mischiefs of factions"   A phrase used by James Madison in the *Federalist Papers* to refer to the threat to the nation's stability that factions could pose.

Misery index   The sum of the unemployment rate and the inflation percentage. An unofficial measure constructed around election time by those wanting to evaluate economic progress or lack of it during a president's term.

Mixed economies   Countries that incorporate elements of both capitalist and socialist practices in the workings of their economies.

Moderates   Also referred to as "middle of the roaders," these are persons with centrist positions on issues that distinguish them from liberals and conservatives.

Monroe Doctrine   A doctrine articulated by President James Monroe in 1823 that warned European powers not already involved in Latin America to stay out of that region.

Moralistic political subculture   In the twentieth century, a subculture in New England and the upper Midwest, where people tended to believe that politics was a way of improving life and that they had an obligation to participate politically.

Motor voter law   A statute that allows people to register to vote at public offices such as welfare offices and drivers' license bureaus.

Multiparty system   A type of political party system where more than two groups have a chance at winning an election.

Mutual assured destruction (MAD)   The capability of one country to absorb a nuclear attack and retaliate against the attacker with such force that it would also suffer enormous damage; believed to deter nuclear war during the **Cold War** because both sides would be so devastated that neither would risk striking first.

NAACP (National Association for the Advancement of Colored People)   An organization founded in 1909 to fight for black rights; its attorneys challenged segregation in the courts and won many important court cases, most notably *Brown* v. *Board of Education*.

Narrowcasting   An attempt by a network to appeal to a small segment of the television or radio audience rather than to most of the audience. The opposite of broadcasting, narrowcasting is targeted to specific groups, such as sports lovers and males.

Nation   Word used by Lincoln in the **Gettysburg Address** to describe the country as a whole rather than an aggregation of separate states.

National debt   The total amount of money owed by the federal government; the sum of all **budget deficits** over the years.

National Organization for Women (NOW)   A group formed in 1966 to fight primarily for political and economic rights for women.

Nation-centered federalism   The view that the Constitution was written by representatives of the people and ratified by the people. Nation-centered Federalists believe that the national government is the supreme power in the federal relationship. (Hamilton articulated this view in the *Federalist Papers*.) Nation-centered federalism was the view used by northerners to justify a war to prevent the southern states from seceding in 1861. The alternative view, **state-centered federalism**, holds that the Constitution is a creation of the states.

Natural rights   Inalienable and inherent rights such as the right to own property (in the view of John Locke).

Necessary and proper clause   A phrase in the **implied powers clause** of the U.S. Constitution that gives Congress the power to make all laws needed to carry out its specific powers.

Negative externalities   The bad effects of an action taken by one set of actors on others who had no input or choice about the action. In the case of the environment, a business may generate pollution or toxicity in a community that may cause its residents to suffer ill health.

Neoslavery   After slavery was declared unconstitutional, the practice of depriving southern blacks of their rights, casting them back to subordinate positions.

Neutral competence   The concept that bureaucrats should make decisions in a politically neutral manner in policy making and should be chosen only for their expertise, not their political affiliation.

New Deal   A program of President Franklin D. Roosevelt's administration in the 1930s aimed at stimulating economic recovery and aiding victims of the Great Depression; led to expansion of the national government's role.

New Deal coalition   The broadly based coalition of southern conservatives, northern liberals, and ethnic and religious minorities that sustained the Democratic Party for some forty years.

North Atlantic Treaty Organization (NATO)   An alliance formed by treaty in 1949, joining the United States, Canada, and their western European World War II allies in a mutual defense pact against Soviet aggression in Europe. Since the end of the Cold War, the alliance has expanded to twenty-eight members, including most of the countries formerly aligned with the Soviet Union.

Nullification   A doctrine that allows states to nullify—ignore—any federal law that they think violates the Constitution. This doctrine was championed by the southern states before the Civil War.

Originalism   The opinion of some judges and legal commentators that all judges should interpret the general provisions in the Constitution according to the Founders' intentions at the time the document was written.

Oversight   Congress's responsibility to make sure the bureaucracy is administering federal programs in accordance with congressional intent.

Ozone hole   A hole or gap in the protective layer of ozone in the atmosphere of the earth that exposes people to increased levels of ultraviolet radiation. Chemical pollution from chlorofluorocarbons (CFCs), which are used as refrigerants, as propellants in aerosol cans, and in plastic foam products, can reduce this protective layer. An international protocol was signed in 1987 to phase out CFCs in order to protect the ozone layer.

Pardon power   Authority given to the president to erase the guilt and restore the rights of anyone convicted of a federal crime, except an impeached president.

Partisan   Affiliated with, believing in, or acting on behalf of a political party.

Party caucus   Meetings of members of political parties, often designed to select party nominees for office, or of all members of a party in the House or Senate to set policy and select their leaders.

Party identification   A psychological link between individuals and a political party that leads those persons to regard themselves as members of that party.

Patronage system   A system in which elected officials appoint their supporters to administrative jobs; used by **political machines** to maintain themselves in power.

Pay-as-you-go (paygo)   Budgetary rules adopted by Congress that set caps on spending and bar legislation to increase spending without offsetting cuts in spending or increases in revenue.

Pentagon Papers   A top-secret study, eventually made public, of how and why the United States became embroiled in the Vietnam War; the study was commissioned by Secretary of Defense Robert McNamara during the Johnson administration.

Permanent campaign   The situation in which elected officials are constantly engaged in a campaign; fundraising for the next election begins as soon as one election is concluded.

Phony polls   Polls that pump thousands of calls into a district or state under the guise of conducting a poll but with the intent of spreading false information about a candidate. See also push polls.

Photo opportunity (photo op)   A situation in which the politician is framed against a backdrop that symbolizes the points the politician is trying to make.

Plea bargain   An agreement between the prosecutor, defense attorney, and defendant in which the prosecutor agrees to reduce the charge or sentence in exchange for the defendant's guilty plea.

Plessy* v. *Ferguson   The 1896 case in which the U.S. Supreme Court upheld segregation by enunciating the **separate-but-equal doctrine**.

Pocket veto   A legislative bill dies by pocket veto if a president refuses to sign it and Congress adjourns within ten working days.

Political action committees (PACs)   Groups that are developed to disperse money to political candidates and campaigns. PACs can be related to one business, to a group of businesses (e.g., poultry producers) or trades (e.g., chicken pluckers), or to interest groups of various sorts (e.g., civil liberties or right to life). Donations by PACs are regulated by federal law.

Political bias   A preference for candidates of particular parties or for certain stands on issues that affects a journalist's reporting.

Political culture   A shared body of values and beliefs that shapes perceptions and attitudes toward politics and government and, in turn, influences political behavior.

Political efficacy   The belief that a person can make a difference in government.

Political machines   Political organizations based on **patronage** that flourished in big cities in the late nineteenth and early twentieth centuries. The machine relied on the votes of the lower classes and, in exchange, provided jobs and other services.

Political parties   Groups that seek to gain and maintain political power though elections.

Political socialization   The process of learning about politics by being exposed to information from parents, peers, schools, the media, political leaders, and the community.

Poll tax   A tax that must be paid before a person can vote; used in the South to prevent blacks from voting. The Twenty-fourth Amendment prohibits poll taxes in federal elections.

Polychlorinated biphenyls (PCBs)   A group of industrial compounds produced by chlorination of biphenyl, a pollutant that accumulates in animal tissue and has damaging effects on human health.

Popular sovereignty   Rule by the people.

Pork barrel projects   Special projects, buildings, and other public works in the district or state of a member of Congress that he or she supports because they provide jobs for constituents and enhance the member's reelection chances, rather than because the projects are necessarily wise.

Practice of objectivity   The practice followed when newspapers and other mainstream media try to present the facts in their news stories, not opinions.

Pre-emptive war   The strategy of striking a country first without knowing whether it is going to attack the United States.

Pregnancy Discrimination Act   A congressional act from 1978 that forbids firing or demoting employees for becoming pregnant.

Presidential preference primary   A direct primary in which voters select delegates to presidential nominating conventions; voters indicate a preference for a presidential candidate, delegates committed to a candidate, or both.

Presidential press conference   A meeting at which the president answers questions from reporters.

Presumption of innocence   A fundamental principle of the U.S. criminal justice system in which the government is required to prove the defendant's guilt. The defendant is not required to establish his innocence.

Primary elections   Elections held several weeks or months before the general election that allow voters to select the nominees of their political party.

Private bureaucracy   A form of **bureaucracy** that measures success or failure by its profits, prioritizes efficiency, and uses market standards to value its workers, its performance, and its products.

Private interest groups   Interest groups that chiefly pursue economic interests that benefit their members; e.g., business organizations and labor unions.

Privatization   Outsourcing of the work of government to private industry; these are jobs that would otherwise be done by civil servants or military personnel.

Pro-choice groups   Groups that work to maintain women's right to choose abortion.

Progressive movement   Reform movement designed to wrest control from **political machines** and the lower-class immigrants they served. These reforms reduced corruption in politics, but they also seriously weakened the power of political parties.

Progressive reforms   Election reforms introduced in the early twentieth century as part of the **Progressive movement**; included the secret ballot, primary elections, and voter registration laws.

Progressive tax   A tax structured so that those with higher incomes pay a higher percentage of their income in taxes than do those with lower incomes.

Pro-life groups   Groups that work to outlaw abortion.

Proportional representation   An election system based on election from multimember districts. The number of seats awarded to each party in each district is equal to the percentage of the total the party receives in the district. Proportional representation favors the multiparty system.

Public bureaucracy   A form of **bureaucracy** that is not evaluated according to whether it makes a profit but whether it serves the "public interest"; therefore, success or failure is measured by elected officials and by the public.

Public forum   A public place such as a street, sidewalk, or park where people have a First Amendment right to express their views on public issues.

Public Health Service (PHS)   An agency founded in the early nineteenth century as a quasi-military organization to diagnose and treat illnesses (such as venereal disease) in sailors and merchant marines returning from foreign ports. Its mission expanded into public health and sanitation and disease prevention for the population as whole, and today it provides rapid response to public health emergencies. Renamed the Public Health Service Commissioned Corps, its 6,000 uniformed members serve under the U.S. surgeon general and the Department of Health and Human Services' assistant secretary of health.

Public interest groups   **Interest groups** that chiefly pursue benefits that cannot be limited or restricted to their members.

Public opinion   The collection of individual opinions toward issues or objects of general interest.

Pure democracy   A **direct democracy**.

Push poll   A public opinion poll presenting the respondent with biased information favoring or opposing a particular candidate. The idea is to see whether certain "information" can "push" voters away from a candidate or a neutral opinion toward the candidate favored by those doing the poll. Push polls seek to manipulate opinion.

Racial profiling   Practice that targets a particular group for attention from law enforcement based on racial stereotypes. A common occurrence is black drivers being stopped by police disproportionately.

Realignment   The transition from one stable party system to another, as occurred when the **New Deal coalition** was formed.

Reapportionment   The process of redistributing the 435 seats in the House of Representatives among the states based on population changes; occurs every ten years based on the most recent census.

Recall elections   A process that enables voters to remove officials from office before their terms expire.

Recession   Two or more consecutive three-month quarters of falling production.

Recognition power   The power of the president to receive or not receive the credentials of foreign ambassadors and thus officially recognize the nations that the ambassadors are representing.

Reconstruction   The period after the Civil War when black rights were ensured by a northern military presence in the South and by close monitoring of southern politics; ended in 1877.

Reconstruction Amendments   Three amendments (13th, 14th, and 15th), adopted after the Civil War from 1865 through 1870, that eliminated slavery (13), gave blacks the right to vote (15), and guaranteed due process rights for all (14).

Red states   The states that voted for George Bush in 2000 and 2004 and in general are more conservative in outlook. They include the states of the South, Great Plains, and Rocky Mountain West.

Redistricting   The process of redrawing the boundaries of congressional districts within a state after a census to take account of population shifts.

Redlining   The practice in which bankers and other lenders refused to lend money to persons who wanted to buy a house in a racially changing neighborhood.

Referendum   A process that allows the legislature to place a proposal on the ballot.

Re-Generation   A term coined by the journalist Thomas Friedman about college-age people, who he hopes will join with their parents and grandparents to ensure that sustainability is central to all activities.

Regressive tax   A tax structured so that those with lower incomes pay a larger percentage of their income in tax than do those with higher incomes.

Rehnquist Court   The U.S. Supreme Court under Chief Justice William Rehnquist (1986–2005); a conservative Court, but one that did not overturn most previous rulings.

Republic   A system of government in which citizens elect representatives to make decisions for them; an **indirect democracy**.

Republican Party   One of the major political parties in the United States since the era of the Civil War. Republicans tend to be more conservative than Democrats.

Resegregation   Increasing racial segregation in public schools since the 1980s, when desegregation efforts peaked.

Residual power   The power of state and local governments to exercise whatever power the national government does not explicitly claim or the Constitution does not explicitly allocate.

Responsible party government   A governing system in which political parties have real issue differences, voters align according to those issue differences, and elected officials are expected to vote with their party leadership or lose their chance to run for office.

Restrained judges   Judges who are reluctant to overrule the other branches of government by declaring laws or actions of government officials unconstitutional.

Restrictive covenants   Agreements among neighbors in white residential areas not to sell their houses to blacks.

Retrospective voting   Voting for or against incumbents on the basis of their past performance.

Revolving door Tradition in which high-ranking officials move into high-paying lobbying jobs when they leave public service.

Right to a jury trial The Sixth Amendment's guarantee of a trial by jury in any **criminal case** that could result in more than six months' incarceration.

Right to abortion U.S. Supreme Court ruling in *Roe* v. *Wade* (1973) establishing that women have a right to terminate a pregnancy during the first six months. States can prohibit an abortion during the last three months because at that time the fetus becomes viable—it can live outside the womb.

Right to counsel The Sixth Amendment's guarantee of the right of a criminal defendant to have an attorney in any felony or misdemeanor case that might result in incarceration; if defendants are indigent, the court must appoint an attorney for them.

Right to die The Rehnquist Court ruling that individuals can refuse medical treatment, including food and water, even if this means they will die. Individuals must make their decision while competent and alert. They can also act in advance, preparing a "living will" or designating another person as a proxy to make the decision if they are unable to do so.

Right to privacy A right to autonomy—to be left alone; is not specifically mentioned in the U.S. Constitution but has been found by the U.S. Supreme Court to be implied through several amendments.

Roberts Court The current Supreme Court under the leadership of Chief Justice John Roberts (2005–).

Sample A group of people who are surveyed. If the selection of the sample is random and large enough, their opinions should reflect those of the larger group from which they are drawn.

S-CHIP (State Children's Health Insurance Program) A federal program, adopted in 1997 after the Clinton health reform failed to pass, that allocated money to the states to expand their existing programs of health coverage for children whose parents cannot afford to purchase health insurance but who earn too much to qualify for Medicaid.

Scoops Leaks in information that enable reporters to break their stories before their competitors can report them.

Second Amendment "The right of the people to keep and bear arms." Some interpret this as an absolute right to own and use guns, others as only an indication that guns can be owned if one is part of a state militia.

Secret ballot A system of voting that protects the privacy of an individual's vote choice.

Seditious speech Speech that encourages rebellion against the government.

Senate One house of Congress, where each state is represented by two members.

Senate Judiciary Committee A Senate committee charged, among other things, with recommending for or against presidential appointees to the federal courts.

Senatorial courtesy The custom of giving senators of the president's party a virtual veto over appointments to jobs, including judicial appointments, in their states.

Separate-but-equal doctrine The principle, enunciated by the U.S. Supreme Court in *Plessy* v. *Ferguson* in 1896, that allowed separate facilities for blacks and whites as long as the facilities were equal.

Separation of church and state Constitutional principle that is supposed to keep church and state from interfering with each other. In practice it restricts government from major efforts either to inhibit or advance religion.

Separation of powers The principle of government under which the power to make, administer, and judge the laws is split among three branches—legislative, executive, and judicial.

Sexual harassment A form of job discrimination prohibited by the Civil Rights Act of 1964. Sexual harassment can consist of either (1) a supervisor's demands for sexual favors in exchange for a raise or promotion or in exchange for not imposing negative consequences; or (2) the creation of a hostile environment that prevents workers from doing their job.

Sharecropping System in which tenant farmers lease land and equipment from landowners and turn over a share of their crops in lieu of rent.

Shays's Rebellion A revolt of farmers in western Massachusetts in 1786 and 1787 to protest the state legislature's refusal to grant them relief from debt; helped lead to calls for a new national constitution.

Sierra Club An interest group whose goal is to protect the natural environment. It was created in 1890 to preserve the new Yosemite National Park from cattle ranchers who wanted the land.

Signing statements Written comments a president may attach to a law after signing it and sending it to the *Federal Register* for publication. Historically they have been used to indicate provisions in a law the president believes the federal courts may find unconstitutional. George W. Bush used them frequently to indicate sections of laws he would refuse to implement, thus setting up a conflict between the executive and legislative branches.

Single-issue groups **Interest groups** that pursue a single public interest goal and are characteristically reluctant to compromise.

Single-member districts Electoral districts in which only one individual is elected.

Social contract An implied agreement between the people and their government in which the people give up part of their liberty to the government in exchange for the government protecting the remainder of their liberty.

Social issue An important, noneconomic issue affecting significant numbers of the populace, such as crime, racial conflict, or changing values.

Soft power The ability of a country to get what it wants through the attractiveness of its culture, political ideals, and policies rather than military or economic coercion.

Sound bite A few key words or phrase included in a speech with the intent that television editors will use the phrase in a brief clip on the news.

Southern strategy The strategy followed by the Republicans in the latter part of the twentieth century to capture the votes of southern whites.

Speaker of the House The leader and presiding officer of the House of Representatives; chosen by the majority party.

Spin What politicians do to portray themselves and their programs in the most favorable light, regardless of the facts, often shading the truth.

Split-ticket voting Voting for a member of one party for one office and for a member of another party for a different office, such as for a Republican presidential candidate but a Democratic House candidate.

Spoils system "To the victor belong the spoils," a candidate rewards supporters with government employment following her/his electoral win, even if they are not qualified for the post (see also **patronage system**).

Standing committees Permanent congressional committees.

Stare decisis Latin for "stand by what has been decided." The rule that judges should follow precedents established in previous cases by their court or higher courts.

State-centered federalism The view that our constitutional system should give precedence to state sovereignty over that of the national government. State-centered Federalists argue that the states created the national government and the states are superior to the federal government.

States' rights The belief that the power of the federal government should not be increased at the expense of the states' power.

Statutes Laws passed by the legislative body of a representative government.

Steering The practice in which realtors promoted segregation by showing blacks houses in black neighborhoods and whites houses in white neighborhoods.

Straw polls Unscientific polls.

Succession Act Act passed in 1947 that establishes the order of succession among legislative leaders and cabinet secretaries if the president and vice president are both unable to hold office.

Suffrage The right to vote.

Sundown laws   During the Jim Crow period in the South, laws adopted to require blacks to be off the streets by 10 p.m. as a way to maintain white supremacy.

Sunshine Act   Adopted in 1976, this act requires that most government meetings be conducted in public and that notice of such meetings be posted in advance. Regulatory agencies, for example, must give notice of the date, time, place, and agenda of their meetings and follow certain rules to prevent unwarranted secrecy. Federal and state sunshine laws have made it difficult for any public body, such as a city council, to meet in secret to conduct official business.

Super PAC   A form of **political action committee (PAC)** that raises and spends money on political advertising.

Superfund   The popular name of a governmental program established to clean up abandoned hazardous waste sites. The "Superfund" law passed by Congress is 1980 was enacted as a result of discovery of toxic waste dumps such as **Love Canal**. The law allows the EPA to either clean up these sites or to require responsible parties to clean them up.

Supermajority   The 60-vote margin needed in the Senate to block a filibuster and bring a bill to the floor for an up or down vote.

Supply-side economics   The argument that tax revenues will increase if tax rates are reduced; based on the assumption that more money would be available for business expansion and modernization, which in turn would stimulate employment and economic growth and result in higher tax revenues.

Supremacy clause   A clause in the U.S. Constitution stating that treaties and laws made by the national government take precedence over state laws in cases of conflict.

Swing states   Also called **battleground states**.

Symbiotic relationship   A relationship in which the parties use each other for mutual advantage.

Symbolic speech   The use of symbols, rather than words, to convey ideas; e.g., wearing black armbands or burning the U.S. flag to protest government policy.

Tax neutrality   A tax policy that does not favor certain kinds of economic activity over others.

Tenth Amendment   Constitutional amendment stating that powers not delegated to the federal government or prohibited to the states are reserved to the states and to the people. This amendment has generally not had much impact, though a few recent Supreme Court cases have referred to it.

The commons   A term relating to communities as a whole; used to refer to the common good.

Three-fifths Compromise   The decision of the **Constitutional Convention** that each slave would count as three-fifths of a person in apportioning seats in the House of Representatives.

Title IX   Equal Opportunity in Education Act, which forbids discrimination on the basis of sex in schools and colleges that receive federal aid. The amendment was prompted by discrimination against women by colleges, especially in admissions, sports programs, and financial aid.

Tracking polls   Polls in which a small number of people are polled on successive evenings throughout a campaign to assess changes in the level of voter support.

Traditionalistic political subculture   During the twentieth century, the subculture associated with the states of the Deep South, where politics was seen as a way to maintain the status quo and little value was placed on participation.

Treaties   Agreements with foreign powers that are negotiated by the president but must be ratified by a two-thirds vote in the Senate, as opposed to **executive agreements**, which do not require Senate approval.

Turf wars   Within the federal **bureaucracy**, the jealous guarding of positions and projects from budget cutters and from other agencies with similar programs.

Twenty-fifth Amendment   Ratified in 1967, this amendment (1) provides for the presidential selection and congressional approval (by majorities in both houses) of a vice president in the event that the elected vice president leaves office and (2) outlines a procedure to determine whether a president is mentally or physically incapable of exercising power.

Twenty-second Amendment   Limits a president to two terms (or ten years if he or she completes the term of an incumbent who dies or resigns).

Two-party system   A political system like that in the United States in which only two parties have a realistic chance of winning most government offices. This system is rare among the world's other democracies.

Undernews   Political stories circulating in the fringe media, such as blogs or tabloids, but not covered by the mainstream media.

Unfunded mandates   Federal laws that require the states to do something without providing full funding for the required activity.

Unilateral actions   Actions taken by the president without consulting Congress; examples are **executive orders** and White House appointments.

Unitary system   A system in which the national government is supreme; subnational governments are created by the national government and have only the power it allocates to them.

Unreasonable searches and seizures   Searches and arrests that are conducted without a warrant or that do not fall into one of the exceptions to the warrant requirement; prohibited by the Fourth Amendment.

Veto points   Points in the political process where one official or group of officials can block proposals moving through the process.

Veto power   The president's constitutional authority to refuse to sign a law passed by Congress. Vetoes may be overridden by a two-thirds vote in each house of Congress.

Vice president   The president's second in command; has few formal duties but a budget for office and staff (housed adjacent to the White House), an official airplane (*Air Force Two*), and a white mansion (the former home of the chief of naval operations).

Voter registration   A process that requires voters to register their name and address before an election.

Voting Rights Act (VRA)   A law passed by Congress in 1965 that made it illegal to interfere with anyone's right to vote. The act and its subsequent amendments have been the main vehicles for expanding and protecting minority voting rights.

Warren Court   The U.S. Supreme Court under Chief Justice Earl Warren (1953–1969); an activist Court that expanded the rights of criminal defendants and racial and religious minorities.

Wedge issue   An issue that can split a party; abortion is an example.

Whips   Members of the House of Representatives who work to maintain party unity by keeping in contact with party members and trying to ensure they vote for party-backed bills. Both the majority and the minority party have a whip and several assistant whips.

Whistleblower   An individual employee who exposes mismanagement and abuse of office by government officials.

White House Office   The unit within the **Executive Office of the President** that "extends the president's reach" by gathering and analyzing information and that "magnifies the president's voice" by repeating the president's **message**.

White primary   A device for preventing blacks from voting in the South. Under the pretense that political parties were private clubs, blacks were barred from voting in Democratic primaries, which were the real elections because Democrats always won the general elections.

Winner-take-all provision   The rule that only one individual is elected from a district or state, the individual who receives the most votes. It contrasts with multimember systems in which more than one person wins seats in an election.

Writ of *certiorari*   An order issued by a higher court to a lower court to send up the record of a case for review; granting the writ is the usual means by which the U.S. Supreme Court agrees to hear a case.

Index

Note: Page references in **boldface** refer to photographs, figures, or tables.

Presidents, Elections, and Congresses, 1789–2012 (cont.)

Year	President	Vice President	Party of President	Election Year	Election Opponent with Most Votes*
1889–1893	Benjamin Harrison	Levi P. Morton	Rep	(1888)	Grover Cleveland
1893–1897	Grover Cleveland	Adlai E. Stevenson	Dem	(1892)	Benjamin Harrison
1897–1901	William McKinley	Garret A. Hobart (to 1901)	Rep	(1896)	William Jennings Bryan
		Theodore Roosevelt (1901)		(1900)	William Jennings Bryan
1901–1909	Theodore Roosevelt	(No VP, 1901–1905)	Rep		Took office upon death of McKinley
		Charles W. Fairbanks (1905–1909)		(1904)	Alton B. Parker
1909–1913	William Howard Taft	James S. Sherman	Rep	(1908)	William Jennings Bryan
1913–1921	Woodrow Wilson	Thomas R. Marshall	Dem	(1912)	Theodore Roosevelt
				(1916)	Charles Evans Hughes
1921–1923	Warren G. Harding	Calvin Coolidge	Rep	(1920)	James Cox
1923–1929	Calvin Coolidge	(No VP, 1923–1925)	Rep		Took office upon death of Harding
		Charles G. Dawes (1925–1929)		(1924)	John Davis
1929–1933	Herbert Hoover	Charles Curtis	Rep	(1928)	Alfred E. Smith
1933–1945	Franklin D. Roosevelt	John N. Garner (1933–1941)	Dem	(1932)	Herbert Hoover
		Henry A. Wallace (1941–1945)		(1936)	Alfred Landon
		Harry S. Truman (1945)		(1940)	Wendell Willkie
				(1944)	Thomas Dewey
1945–1953	Harry S. Truman	(No VP, 1945–1949) Alban W. Barkley	Dem		Took office upon death of Roosevelt
				(1948)	Thomas Dewey
1953–1961	Dwight D. Eisenhower	Richard M. Nixon	Rep	(1952)	Adlai Stevenson
				(1956)	Adlai Stevenson
1961–1963	John F. Kennedy	Lyndon B. Johnson	Dem	(1960)	Richard M. Nixon
1963–1969	Lyndon B. Johnson	(No VP, 1963–1965)	Dem		Took office upon death of Kennedy
		Hubert H. Humphrey (1965–1969)		(1964)	Barry Goldwater
1969–1974	Richard M. Nixon	Spiro T. Agnew	Rep	(1968)	Hubert H. Humphrey
		Gerald R. Ford (appointed)		(1972)	George McGovern
1974–1977	Gerald R. Ford	Nelson A. Rockefeller (appointed)	Rep		Took office upon Nixon's resignation
1977–1981	Jimmy Carter	Walter Mondale	Dem	(1976)	Gerald R. Ford
1981–1989	Ronald Reagan	George Bush	Rep	(1980)	Jimmy Carter
				(1984)	Walter F. Mondale
1989–1993	George Bush	J. Danforth Quayle	Rep	(1988)	Michael Dukakis
3–2001	William J. Clinton	Albert Gore	Dem	(1992)	George Bush
				(1996)	Robert Dole
	George W. Bush	Richard Cheney	Rep	(2000)	Albert Gore
				(2004)	John Kerry
	Barack Obama	Joseph Biden	Dem	(2008)	John McCain
				(2012)	Mitt Romney